COMPUTER NETWORKS

COMPUTER NETWORKS

Principles, Technologies and Protocols
for Network Design

Natalia Olifer

formerly of Moscow State Technical University (MSTU)

and

Victor Olifer

UK Education and Research Networking Association (UKERNA)

Translated from Russian into English by A-List Publishing, LLC

John Wiley & Sons, Ltd

Other Wiley Editorial Offices

John Wiley & Sons Inc., 111 River Street, Hoboken, NJ 07030, USA

Jossey-Bass, 989 Market Street, San Francisco, CA 94103-1741, USA

Wiley-VCH Verlag GmbH, Boschstr. 12, D-69469 Weinheim, Germany

John Wiley & Sons Australia Ltd, 33 Park Road, Milton, Queensland 4064, Australia

John Wiley & Sons (Asia) Pte Ltd, 2 Clementi Loop #02-01, Jin Xing Distripark, Singapore 129809

John Wiley & Sons Canada Ltd, 22 Worcester Road, Etobicoke, Ontario, Canada M9W 1L1

Wiley also publishes its books in a variety of electronic formats. Some content that appears in print may not be available in electronic books.

Library of Congress Cataloging-in-Publication Data

Olifer, Natalia.
   Computer networks : principles, technologies, and protocols for network design / Natalia Olifer and Victor Olifer ; translated from Russian into English by A-List Publishing, LLC.
     p. cm.
   Includes bibliographical references and index.
   ISBN-10: 0-470-86982-8 (cloth : alk. paper)
   ISBN-13: 978-0-470-86982-6 (cloth : alk. paper)
   1. Computer networks—Textbooks. 2. Computer networks—Design and construction. 3. Computer network protocols—Textbooks. I. Title: Principles, technologies, and protocols for network design. II. Olifer, Victor. III. Title.
   TK5105.5.O45 2005
   004.6—dc22

                                               2005017401

British Library Cataloguing in Publication Data

A catalogue record for this book is available from the British Library

ISBN 13   978-0-470-86982-6 (HB)
ISBN 10   0-470-86982-8 (HB)

Translated and typeset in 11/13 pt Minion by A-LIST Publishing, Wayne, PA, USA
Printed and bound in Great Britain by Antony Rowe Ltd, Chippenham, Wiltshire
This book is printed on acid-free paper responsibly manufactured from sustainable forestry in which at least two trees are planted for each one used for paper production.

CONTENTS

To Klavdia Korytchenko

and

Daniel Ekaette

PREFACE

APPROACH

This book is a fundamental course on computer networks, which combines coverage of the main topics, problems, and technologies of this rapidly developing knowledge area with comprehensive consideration of the details of each technology and the specific features of the equipment used. This book is the result of years of experience accumulated by the authors in the course of teaching students in various universities, commercial training centers, and training centers of various large corporations.

The following features are characteristic for this book:

- **Focusing on the network transport functions.** The transport functions are the ones that ensure data transmission among computers, thus organizing a computer network. Attention will be primarily focused on studying the network architecture, the main principles of the operation of telecommunications equipment, and the main protocols, including Internet protocol (IP), Ethernet, Bluetooth, IEEE 802.11 (Wi-Fi), Asynchronous Transfer Mode (ATM), frame relay, that the network uses to transport the data. Considering network services, we also concentrate on those directed mainly toward supporting network transport functions (such as domain name system, dynamic host configuration protocol, VPN, and IPSec) rather than on providing services for computer users (such as Web services).

- **Not only IP.** The success of the Internet has made IP the main means of building internetworks. Nevertheless, this book covers in detail not only IP technologies that allow several dissimilar networks to be joined into a unified supernetwork (such as the Internet) but also technologies for building constituent networks, such as Ethernet or ATM, on the basis of which the unified network is built. Both types of technologies are equally important for creating an efficient contemporary network, and this book restores the balance, which recently was often violated in favor of IP — an obvious bandwagon effect.

- **Combining computer science and computer engineering approaches.** In this book you'll find descriptions of the principles of operation of telecommunications networks and algorithms of the operation of communications protocols. This information is usually classified as computer science, and it is necessary for successful research work. We also provide a large number of technical details of communications devices and practical examples of designing networks of various types. This will be useful as you prepare for engineering work, which plays a significant role for any telecommunications professional.

- **Convergence of all types of telecommunications networks.** Convergence plays an increasingly significant role and has a constantly growing influence on computer, TV, and radio networks. From the opening chapters of this book, we reflect this contemporary trend and demonstrate the main mechanisms of computer networks, such as multiplexing, switching, and routing, from the most general positions true for communications networks of all types.

THE INTENDED AUDIENCE OF THIS BOOK

Materials of this book have been successfully tested on an audience with uncompromising attitude. This audience consisted of students with considerably different levels of experience and different professional interests. Among them were undergraduate and postgraduate students of the universities, heads of IT departments, and network administrators and integrators. The courses of lectures were built to provide a sound foundation for further study for beginners and, at the same time, to allow specialists to organize and improve their knowledge.

This book is mainly intended for undergraduate and postgraduate students, who would like to gain organized theoretical and practical knowledge about computer networks.

We also hope that the book will be useful for specialists starting out in IT technologies with only a general idea about network operation based on practical work with PCs connected to the Internet. Those willing to gain fundamental knowledge can use this book to continue theoretical study of network operation on their own.

The book will also be helpful to experienced network professionals who need to become acquainted with newer technologies, which they have not previously encountered in the course of their practical activities, and to organize their existing knowledge. The book can also be used as a practical reference in which it is possible to find the description of a specific protocol, frame format, etc. In addition, this book provides the required theoretical basis for preparing for Cisco certifications, such as CCNA, CCNP, CCDP, and CCIP.

THE BOOK'S STRUCTURE

This book comprises 24 chapters arranged in five parts.

- The first part, *Networking Basics,* covers the "first turn" of the spiral when studying computer networks. The process of cognition always has a spiral nature. It is not possible to immediately obtain a full understanding of a complex phenomenon. On the contrary, any such phenomenon must be studied from different points of view, in general and in particular, returning occasionally to materials that might already seem to be understood, and with each new turn of the cognition spiral accumulating information. In the first part consisting of seven chapters, the main and the most important principles and architectural solutions are described, which are a foundation for all contemporary network technologies considered in further parts of the book. According to the network convergence process, we consider the principles of switching, multiplexing, routing, and addressing and the architecture of computer networks from the most general positions, comparing them with the similar principles of other telecommunications networks — telephone, communications carrier, radio, and TV networks. This part is concluded by the chapter covering the quality of service (QoS) problems in packet-switched networks. Thus, the concepts of QoS that were long considered a nontrivial branch of the network technologies became one of the basic principles for building computer networks.

- The second part, *Physical Layer Technologies,* includes four chapters: *Chapter 8: Transmission Links, Chapter 9: Data Encoding and Multiplexing, Chapter 10: Wireless Transmission,* and *Chapter 11: Transmission Networks.* The first two chapters describe various types of transmission links and provide detailed information about the contemporary method of transmitting discrete information in networks. The presence of these materials in the book allows you to learn the required minimum of information without spending lots of time for reviewing a large number of specialized publications. The list of these knowledge areas includes information theory, spectral analysis, physical and logical data encoding, and error detection and correction. *Chapter 10* is dedicated to wireless data transmission, which is becoming increasingly popular. The high level of noise and complex paths of the wave propagation require special methods of signal encoding and transmission in wireless communications links. *Chapter 11* covers such technologies as plesiochronous digital hierarchy (PDH), SDH/SONET, and dense wave division multiplexing, which create the infrastructure of physical links for global telecommunications networks. Overlay computer or telephone networks operate on the basis of the channels created by transmission networks.

- In the third part, *Local Area Networks,* detailed descriptions of practically all main LAN technologies are provided, including Ethernet, Token Ring, and fiber distributed data interface (FDDI), as well as newer high-speed technologies. Contemporary LANs exist when one of the technologies, or, to be more precise, the family of technologies — Ethernet — is dominating. Naturally, we cover this technology in more detail than all the other ones. *Chapter 12* covers the classical 10 Mbps Ethernet technology, and

Chapter 13 describes high-speed versions of the Ethernet on the basis of the shared medium, namely, Fast Ethernet and Gigabit Ethernet. *Chapter 14* describes other LAN technologies that also use the shared medium, — Token Ring, FDDI, and two wireless technologies — the IEEE 802.11 LAN and the Bluetooth personal area network. The last two chapters of this part, *Chapters 15* and *16,* are dedicated to switched LANs. The first of them considers the main principles of the operation of such networks: the algorithm of the LAN switch operation, duplex versions of LAN protocols, and specific features of implementation of LAN switches. *Chapter 16* studies the extended capabilities of networks of this type, including backup links on the spanning tree algorithm, and the virtual LAN technique.

■ According to the logic dictated by the open systems interconnection model, the parts dedicated to the technologies of physical and data-link layers must be followed by *Part IV,* concentrating on the network-layer technologies that ensure the possibility of combining lots of different constituent networks into a unified internetwork. Because IP is the indisputable leader among the network-layer protocols, we give it the most attention in this book. *Chapter 17* describes various aspects of IP addressing: methods of mapping local, network, and symbolic addresses; methods of using network masks; contemporary methods of aggregating IP addresses; and methods of automatic configuration of IP nodes. *Chapter 18* covers in detail the operation of IP related to packet forwarding and fragmentation, describes the general format of the routing table, and offers examples of its particular implementation in software and hardware routers of different types. When describing specific features of the new IP version — IPv6 — we cover the method of addressing modernization in detail, as well as the main changes introduced into the format of the IP header. *Chapter 19* starts with a study of the transmission control protocol (TCP) and user datagram protocol (UDP) that play an intermediary role between the applications and the transport infrastructure of the network. Further on, routing information protocol (RIP), open shortest path first (OSPF), and border gateway protocol (BGP) are covered. The provided materials analyze the application areas of these protocols and the possibilities of their combined use. We conclude the chapter by considering the Internet control message protocol, which is the means of informing the sender why his packets were not delivered to the target node. *Chapter 20* describes the types and main characteristics of routers, variants of their internal organization, and methods of combining the functions of switching and routing within the same device — the Layer 3 switch. Thorough investigation of the TCP/IP stack in *Part IV* makes it valuable as standalone introduction to IP networks.

■ *Part V: Wide Area Networks,* comprises four chapters. The IP technology considered in the previous part of this book allows the building of internetworks of different types, both local and global. In addition, there are other technologies based on the virtual circuit technique that were developed especially for WANs. These technologies, implemented in frame relay and ATM networks, are covered in *Chapter 21.* The virtual circuit technique represents an alternative to the datagram method of packet forwarding, which is the basis for Ethernet and IP networks. The competition between these two main principles of data transmission has existed for a long time, practically from beginning the packet-switched network development. Various aspects of using the IP technology for building WANs are considered in *Chapter 22*. The multiprotocol label switching (MPLS) technology is the innovation in the field of integration between IP and virtual circuit technologies. This technology takes an intermediary position between the IP level and the level of such technologies as ATM, frame relay, or Ethernet, thus joining them into the unified and efficient transport system. The chapter concludes with a description of network management systems based on the simple network management protocol, which is widely used for controlling not only IP routers (for which this protocol was designed) but also telecommunications devices of various types. *Chapter 23* studies different approaches for organizing high-speed access to the network backbone for the network's users. The most efficient are technologies using the existing cabling infrastructure (for example, asymmetric digital subscriber lines operating on local loops of the telephone networks) or cabling modems using the systems of cable TV. An alternative solution consists of wireless access, either mobile or fixed. This part, as well as the entire book, is concluded by *Chapter 24,* which is dedicated to the issues of security of the network transport system. Here we cover various types of virtual private networks (VPNs), particularly the ones based on the secure version of the IP (IPSec) and one of the most popular contemporary VPN technologies, namely, MPLS VPN.

We have made every effort to allow your work with this book to be as efficient as possible. The detailed index will allow you to quickly find material of interest, using any of the multiple terms used in contemporary network industry. Every chapter features a summary section, which allows you to concentrate on the main ideas, topics, and results of the chapter. This will help you avoid missing the main principles because of the abundance of useful facts and details. Finally, each chapter concludes with review questions and problems intended for checking the level of knowledge obtained as the result of reading that chapter. In some cases, these problems have special meaning because they allow you to better comprehend certain ideas.

A SUPPORTING WEB SITE

Interested readers can find additional information on our Web site at the following address: http://www.olifer.co.uk. We intend to make this site a useful complement to this book for both students and professors, as well as for network professionals. Naturally, this site will constantly change. Initially, we plan to provide there the following materials:

- All illustrations from this book.
- Presentations in PowerPoint and HTML formats, offered sequentially for all chapters that make up this book.
- Answers to the questions placed at the end of each chapter of the book.

- A book road map, which is intended to help trainers create courses on the basis of this book: "Wireless Networks," "Introduction to IP," "Quality of Service," and "Remote Access" and so on. These road maps would briefly describe the sequence of chapters that contain appropriate material and even provide some tips about methods of teaching.
- Case studies, which you can use as topics for term papers.
- Internet links related to the topics covered in this book.
- Readers' comments, opinions, questions, and criticism about misprints or errors.

We will be grateful for all of your comments, which you can send to the following addresses: victor@olifer.co.uk or natalia@olifer.co.uk (Victor Olifer, Ph.D., CCIP, and Natalia Olifer, Ph.D., professor).

ACKNOWLEDGMENTS

We deeply appreciate the employees of John Wiley and Sons: Gaynor Redvers-Mutton, former senior commissioning editor for the computer science book program; Jonathan Shipley, associate commissioning editor for the computer science book program; Sarah Corney, executive project editor, higher education group; and David Barnard, project editor. We also appreciate the work of the employees of the A-List and BHV publishing houses, particularly Vadim Sergeev, Natalia Tarkova, Olga Kokoreva, and Julie Laing. With their help, our book, which has run through three editions in Russia, has now become available in English; they also helped to considerably improve the initial version of the book. Our special thanks to Alexey Jdanov, copyeditor of the Russian edition, whose remarks were valuable to the quality of this book.

Victor and Natalia Olifer

PART I

NETWORKING BASICS

The process of cognition always has a spiral-helix nature. It is impossible to immediately understand and appreciate an intricate phenomenon. To perceive it properly, we need to consider such a phenomenon from different viewpoints, both on the whole and in parts, separately and in relation to other phenomena, gradually accumulating our knowledge. Furthermore, from time to time it is necessary to return to the concepts that seemed to have already been understood, getting, with each turn of that spiral, a better insight into the nature of that phenomenon. Quite a good approach is initially studying the most general principles of specific knowledge area, followed by careful investigation of how these principles are implemented in specific methods, technologies or structures.

The opening part of this book is the first spiral turn in studying computer networks. It describes the main principles and architectural solutions that form the basis for all contemporary networking technologies that will be covered in further parts of this book. According to the concept of network convergence, we will try to explain the principles of switching, multiplexing, routing, addressing, and network architecture from the most basic and general point of view. We do this by comparing the underlying principles of computer networks with similar principles of other communication networks, such as telephone networks, transmission networks, radio and TV networks.

The last chapter of this part covers the Quality of Service (QoS) problems in packet-switched networks. The new role of computer networks as a foundation for the development of the Next-Generation Public Networks, capable of providing all kinds of informational services and transmitting data, voice and video traffic has resulted in the adoption of the QoS evaluation methods in practically all communication technologies. Thus, QoS concepts, which for quite a long time were considered a specialized and advanced area of network technologies, became one of the fundamental concepts used when building computer networks.

After detailed study of specific technologies it would be useful (and, the authors hope, interesting) to return to the first part of the book. This new iteration of the learning process will allow the reader to get a better understanding of the basic operating principles of computer networks and the implementation of these principles in various technologies.

Part I comprises the following chapters:

- Chapter 1: Evolution of Computer Networks
- Chapter 2: General Principles of Network Design
- Chapter 3: Packet and Circuit Switching
- Chapter 4: Network Architecture and Standardization
- Chapter 5: Examples of Networks
- Chapter 6: Network Characteristics
- Chapter 7: Methods of Ensuring Quality of Service

1

EVOLUTION OF COMPUTER NETWORKS

1.1 INTRODUCTION

Studying the evolution of any area of science or technology will not only stimulate your natural curiosity, it will also give you a deeper understanding of the main achievements in this area, make you aware of the existing trends, and help you to evaluate the prospects of specific developments. Computer networks emerged relatively recently, in the late 1960s. They have inherited many useful properties from their predecessors, namely, older and more widely adopted telephone networks. This is not surprising, since both computers and telephones are universal instruments of communications.

However, computer networks have brought something new into the world of communications — namely, the practically inexhaustible store of information accumulated by human civilization during the several thousand years of its existence. This information store is continuing to grow at a steadily increasing rate. This became especially noticeable in the mid-1990s, when the rapid growth of the Internet clearly demonstrated that free and anonymous access to information and instant, written communications were highly valued by most individuals.

The influence of computer networks on other types of telecommunications networks resulted in network convergence, a process that started long before the Internet. Digital voice transmission in telephone networks was one of the first signs of that convergence. More recent indications of convergence are the active development of new services in computer networks that previously were the prerogatives of telephone, radio, and TV networks, such as Voice over IP (VoIP), radio broadcasts, and TV services. The process of convergence is continuing, though without offering clear signs of its future. However, knowing the evolution of computer networks, which is described in this chapter, makes it easier to understand the main problems that developers of computer networks must face.

1.2 ROOTS OF COMPUTER NETWORKS

KEY WORDS: mainframe, batch-processing systems, time-sharing systems, multi-terminal systems, computer network, datacom network or data-transmission network, Grosch's Law, Local Area Networks (LANs), standard LAN technologies: Ethernet, Arcnet, Token Ring, FDDI

1.2.1 Computer Networks as a Result of the Computing and Communications Technologies Evolution

The **computer networks** covered in this book are obviously not the only type of networks created throughout human civilization. Possibly the oldest example of a network covering large territories and serving multiple clients is the water-supply sys-

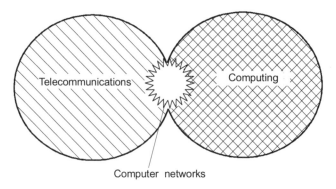

Figure 1.1 Evolution of computer networks at the interfaces of the computing and communications technologies

tem of ancient Rome. But no matter how remote and distinct by their nature different networks can seem, they all have something in common. For example, it is possible to draw a clear analogy between the components of electric networks and those of any large-scale computer network. That is, the information resources found in computer networks correspond to power stations; communications links of computer networks are analogous to high-voltage transmission lines, and access networks are similar to transforming stations. Finally, both in computer networks and in electric networks, one can find client terminals — end-user workstations in computer networks and household electric appliances in electric networks.

> Computer networks, also known as **datacom** or **data-transmission networks**, represent a logical result of the evolution of two of the most important scientific and technical branches of modern civilization — computing and telecommunications technologies.

On one hand (Figure 1.1), computer networks represent a particular case of distributed computing systems in which a group of computers operate in a coordinated manner to perform a set of interrelated tasks by exchanging data in an automated mode. Computer networks can also be considered a means for transmitting information over long distances. To do so, computer networks implement various methods of data encoding and multiplexing that are widely adopted in telecommunications systems.

1.2.2 Batch-Processing Systems

First, consider the origins of computer networks. The computers of the 1950s — large, bulky, and expensive — were intended for a small number of privileged users. Quite often, these monstrous constructions occupied entire buildings. Such computers were not able to serve users interactively. Instead, they batched jobs and delivered results later.

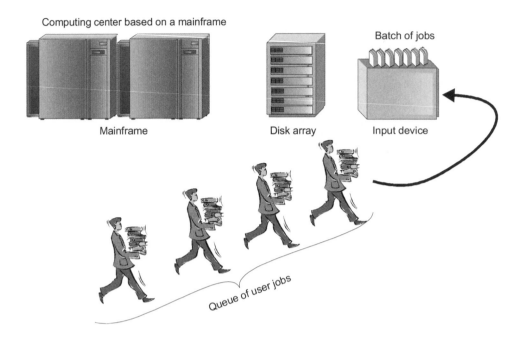

Figure 1.2   Centralized system based on a mainframe

Batch-processing systems were usually based on mainframes and were powerful and reliable universal computers. Users would prepare punched cards containing data and program code and then would transfer these cards to the computing center. Operators would enter these cards into the computer, and users would receive the results a day later in the form of a printout (Figure 1.2). Thus, a single punch card containing an error would mean a delay of at least 24 hours.

Obviously, from the end users' point of view, an interactive mode of operating that allows them to manage the processing of their data on the fly from the terminal is more convenient. The interests of end users were substantially neglected at the earliest stages of the evolution of computing systems. The efficiency of the operation of the most expensive component of a computer — the processor — was regarded as of paramount importance, even at the expense of the user productivity.

1.2.3   Multiterminal Systems: Prototype of the Computer Network

As processors became cheaper in the early 1960s, new methods of organizing computer processing appeared. These methods provided the possibility of taking end-user convenience into account. Thus, multiterminal systems evolved (Figure 1.3). In such time-sharing systems, the computer was at the disposal of several users. Users had their own terminals from which they could communicate with the computer. The response time of the computing system was short enough to mask that the computer served multiple users in parallel.

Terminals moved out of computing centers and onto desktops over entire organizations. Although processing power remained fully centralized, some functions, such as data input and output, became distributed. Such centralized, multiterminal systems looked similar to Local Area Networks (LANs). End users perceived working at the terminal practically the same way that most people now view working at a PC connected to a network. The user could access shared files and peripheral devices and maintain the illusion of using the computer in an exclusive mode, since the user could start any required program at any moment and receive the results almost immediately. (Some users were even convinced that all calculations were made somewhere inside the computer display.)

> Multiterminal systems, working in time-sharing mode, became the first step toward the development of LANs.

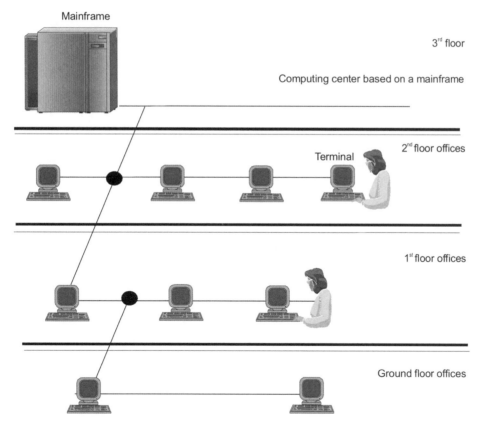

Figure 1.3 Multiterminal system as a prototype of a computer network

However, the evolution still had a long way to go before LANs appeared, because multi-terminal systems retained the essential features of centralized data processing despite superficial resemblance to distributed systems.

Organizations didn't feel a pressing need for LANs. Within a single building, there was nothing to connect to using a network. Most companies could not afford the luxury of purchasing more than one computer. During this period, the so-called *Grosch's Law* (named after Herbert Grosch) was universally true. It represented empirically the technological level of that time. According to this law, the cost of a computer system increases as a square root of the computational power of the system. Hence, it was more profitable to purchase one powerful machine rather than two less powerful ones because their total computational power proved to be significantly lower than that of the expensive machine.

1.3 FIRST COMPUTER NETWORKS

KEY WORDS: packet switching, bursty traffic, Wide Area Network (WAN), telephone network technology, backbone, transmission networks, packet, Internet, network operation system, standard LAN technologis: Ethernet, Arcnet, Token Ring, FDDI

1.3.1 First Wide Area Networks (WANs)

By contrast, the need for connecting computers located a long distance from one another was already imminent. It all started with the solution of a simpler task, i.e., providing access to a computer from remote terminals located hundreds and sometimes thousands of miles apart. Modems were used to connect terminals to computers through telephone lines. Such networks allowed multiple remote users to access the shared resources of several powerful super-computers. By the time distributed systems appeared, not only were there connections between *terminals and computers*, connections between *computers* were also implemented.

Computers became able to exchange data in automatic mode, which, essentially, is the basic mechanism of any computer network. Developers of the first networks implemented services for file exchange, database synchronization, e-mail, and other network services that have become commonplace.

Chronologically, **Wide Area Networks (WANs)** were the first to appear. WANs joined geographically distributed computers, even those located in different cities or countries.

It was in the course of the development of WANs that many ideas fundamental to modern computer networks were introduced and developed, such as:

- Multilayer architecture of communications protocols
- Packet-switching technology
- Packet routing in heterogeneous networks

Although WANs inherited many features from older and more widespread long-haul networks, such as **telephone networks**, the most innovative feature was to depart from the circuit-switching principle, which had been successfully used in telephone networks for decades.

A circuit with a constant speed allocated for the entire session could not be used efficiently by the **bursty traffic**[1] of computer data (bursty means periods of intense data exchange need to alternate with long pauses). Experiments and mathematical modeling have shown that networks based on the packet-switching principle can more efficiently transmit bursty traffic.

According to principle of **packet switching** data are divided into small fragments, known as **packets**. The target host address is embedded into a packet header, allowing each packet to travel over the network on its own.

Since the construction of high-quality communications lines connecting distant locations is very expensive, the first WANs often used available communications links, initially intended for quite different purposes. For example, WANs for a long time were constructed on the basis of the telephone lines. Because the transmission rate of discrete computer data using such links was rather low, hundreds of Kilobits per second (Kbps), the set of services provided by such networks was limited to file transfer, mainly in background mode, and to e-mail. In addition to the low transmission rate, such channels had another drawback — they introduced significant distortions into the transmitted signals. Therefore, network protocols in WANs using low-quality communications lines were characterized by complicated procedures for data control and data restoration. A typical example of such a network is the X.25 network developed in the early 1970s, when low-rate, analog channels leased from telephone companies were prevalent for connecting the computers and switches of WANs.

In 1969, the U.S. Department of Defense initiated research into joining the computers of defense and research centers into a network. This network, which became known as **ARPANET**, served as a starting point for the construction of the first and most widely known WAN, nowadays known as the **Internet**.

ARPANET joined computers of different types, running various operating systems with different add-on modules by implementing communications protocols common for all computers participating in the network. Such operating systems can be considered the first true **network operating systems**.

True network operating systems, in contrast to multiterminal ones, allowed the system not only to distribute users but also to organize data storage. They also allowed for processing to be distributed among several computers connected by electric links. Any network operating system is capable of performing all functions of a local operating system

---

[1] *Burst* and *bursty traffic* are recognized and commonly adopted data communications terms. According to technical definitions provided by Cisco Systems, burst is a sequence of signals counted as one unit in accordance with some specific criterion or measure, and bursty traffic refers to an uneven pattern of data transmission.

and of providing additional functionality, allowing the system to communicate with other operating systems via the network. Software modules, implementing networking functions, were introduced into operating systems gradually, with advances in network technologies and computer hardware, as new tasks requiring network processing appeared.

The progress of WANs depended mainly on the progress of telephone networks.

From the late 1960s, voice transmission in a digital format became increasingly common in telephone networks.

This resulted in the arrival of high-speed digital channels that connected automatic telephone exchange stations and allowed simultaneous transmission of tens or even hundreds of conversations. Special technology was developed for the construction of **transmission networks**, or **backbones**. Such networks do not serve end users; rather, they represent the foundation upon which high-speed "point-to-point" digital channels are based. These channels connect the equipment of another network (the *overlay network*) that serves end users.

Initially, transmission networks represented exclusively internal technology used only by telephone companies. Gradually, however, these companies started to lease part of their digital channels, connected into transmission networks, to companies that used them for creating their own telephone networks and WANs. Nowadays, transmission networks have raised data transmission speeds to hundreds of Gigabits per second (Gbps) and, in some cases, to several Terabits per second; these networks cover the territories of all main industrial states.

Both variety and quality of services have helped WANs catch up with LANs, which had been the leaders despite their relatively late arrival.

1.3.2 First Local Area Networks (LANs)

In the early 1970s, an event took place that has had the greatest influence on the evolution of computer networks. As a result of technological advances in the field of computer-components manufacturing, large-scale integrated circuits (LSI devices) appeared. LSI devices were characterized by relatively low cost and advanced functional capabilities. This led to the development of minicomputers, which became the real competitors for mainframes. Grosch's Law ceased to represent reality, since a dozen minicomputers, having the same cost as one mainframe, were capable of accomplishing some tasks (especially ones that could be executed in parallel) much faster.

From that moment, even small companies could enjoy the possibility of having their own computers. Minicomputers could carry out tasks such as controlling technical equipment or managing stocks. This was the origin of the distributed computing concept, with computing resources becoming distributed over the entire enterprise. All computers within the same organization, however, continued to operate independently (Figure 1.4).

With time, the needs of computer users evolved. End users were no longer satisfied with isolated work on a standalone computer. For instance, they needed to exchange com-

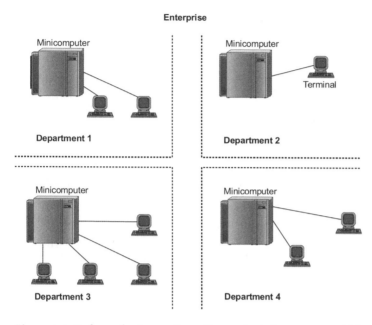

Figure 1.4 Independent operation of several minicomputers within the same enterprise

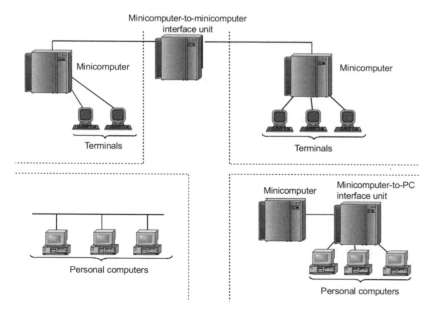

Figure 1.5 Types of links in the first LANs

puter data (often automatically) with users in other branches and offices. To satisfy these requirements, the first LANs appeared (Figure 1.5).

> LANs represent groups of computers concentrated in a relatively small region — usually within a radius not exceeding 1.5 miles, although LANs can be extended to cover larger areas (dozens of miles). In general, LANs represent a communications system belonging to a single organization.

At first, *nonstandard networking technologies* were used to connect computers to the network.

> **Network technology** is a coordinated set of software and hardware (for example, drivers, network adapters, cables and connectors) and mechanisms of data transmission across the communications links, sufficient for building a computer network.

Various proprietary interface units using proprietary methods for data representation on communications links, proprietary types of cables, etc., could connect only specific types and models of computers, namely, the ones for which they were designed. Some examples are the interfaces for connecting PDP-11 minicomputers to IBM 360 mainframes or Hewlett-Packard minicomputers to LSI-11 microcomputers.

> From the mid-1980s, the situation began to change radically. **Standard technologies** for connecting computers to the network, such as Ethernet, Arcnet, Token Ring, and, somewhat later, FDDI, became firmly established.

The adoption of personal computers was a powerful incentive for the development of these technologies. PCs became ideal elements for building networks. On the one hand, they were powerful enough to support networking software; on the other hand, they obviously needed to connect their processing powers to solve complex tasks and share expensive peripheral devices and disk arrays. Because of this, PCs became prevalent in LANs, not only playing the roles of clients but also performing data storage and processing center functions (i.e., becoming network servers). As PCs became more popular, they forced minicomputers and mainframes out of these roles.

All standard LAN technologies were based on the same switching principle that turned out to be so successful when transmitting traffic in WANs, i.e., the packet-switching principle.

The process of building LANs then turned from handcrafting to a standard procedure using standard networking technologies. To build a network, it was enough to purchase a standard cable and network adapters according to the required specification (Ethernet, for example), connect adapters to the cable using standard connectors, and install on the computer one of the network operating systems popular at that time (Novell NetWare, for example).

LAN developers introduced many innovations affecting the organization of end-user work. Tasks such as accessing shared network resources became significantly simpler. In contrast to WAN users, people using LANs were released from the necessity of memorizing complicated identifiers of shared resources. For this purpose, the system would provide the list of available resources in a user-friendly format (for example, in a hierarchical, tree-like structure). Another advantage of working in LANs was that after establishing the connection to the remote resource, people could access the resource using the same commands that were used when working with local resources. The arrival of a large number of end users freed from studying specialized (and rather complicated) networking commands became the consequence, as well as the driving force, of such progress.

So the question arises: Why did all these conveniences become available to end users only with the arrival of LANs? Mainly, because LANs use high-quality cable lines. Even first-generation network adapters ensured a data transfer rate up to 10 Mbps. Since LANs are characterized by limited expansion, the cost of such lines was manageable. For this reason, economizing on the bandwidth, an important matter with the early WAN technologies, was not a primary concern in the development of LAN protocols. Under these conditions, periodic server broadcasts of resources and services became the main mechanism of organizing transparent access to LAN resources. Based on these broadcasts, client computers composed lists of available network resources and presented them to users.

In the late 1990s, the Ethernet family became the indisputable leader among LAN technologies. Besides classic Ethernet (10 Mbps) technology, this family included Fast Ethernet (100 Mbps) and Gigabit Ethernet (1,000 Mbps).

Simple algorithms ensured the low cost of Ethernet equipment. The range of the data transmission speeds enabled network architects to use a rational approach when building LANs, choosing specific Ethernet technology that best satisfied the requirements of the enterprise. All Ethernet technologies closely resembled one another by operating principles, simplifying maintenance and integration of such networks.

The chronological sequence of milestones in the history of computer network evolution is shown in Table 1.1.

Table 1.1 Chronology of the most significant events
in the history of computer networks

First global connections between computers. First experiments with batch-processing networks.	Late 1960s
Start of digital voice transmission through telephone networks.	Late 1960s
Arrival of large-scale integrated circuits. First minicomputers. First proprietary LANs.	Early 1970s
Development of the IBM systems network architecture.	1974
Standardization of the X.25 technology.	1974
Arrival of the first personal computers.	Early 1980s
Creation of the Internet in its current form. Installation of the TCP/IP stack on all nodes.	Early 1980s
Arrival of the first standard LAN technologies.	Ethernet — 1980
	Token Ring — 1985
	FDDI — 1985
Start of commercial use of the Internet.	Late 1980s
Invention of the World Wide Web.	1991

1.4 CONVERGENCE OF NETWORKS

KEY WORDS: convergence, intranet; internet, Internet, Metropolitan Area Network (MAN), multiservice networks, Telecommunications networks, Data network, standard networking technologies, FDDI, Ethernet, Token Ring, ATM, Integrated Services Digital Network (ISDN); Internetwork, QoS

1.4.1 Convergence of LANs and WANs

By the late 1980s, the following differences between LANs and WANs were evident:

- *Length and quality of communications links.* LANs are distinguished from WANs by the small distances between network nodes. Principally, this factor enabled network developers to use communications lines of higher quality than those for WANs.
- *Complexity of data transmission methods.* Because of the low reliability of physical communications channels, WANs required more sophisticated methods of data transmission and more complex equipment than LANs.
- *Data exchange rate.* In LANs, the rates (10, 16, and 100 Mbps) were significantly higher than those in WANs (from 2.4 Kbps to 2 Mbps).
- *Variety of services.* High speeds of data exchange allowed network developers to implement a range of services in LANs. These services included broad capabilities of accessing and using files stored on the hard disks of other networked computers; sharing printing devices, modems, and faxes; accessing centralized databases; and e-mail. The range of services provided by WANs was mainly limited to mail and file services in their simplest forms (not the most convenient for end users).

Gradually, the differences between LANs and WANs began to diminish. Network developers started to join isolated LANs, using WANs as connecting media. Close integration between LANs and WANs resulted in significant interpenetration of appropriate technologies.

Convergence in data transmission methods is based on the platform of digital data transmission along fiber-optic communications lines. This transmission medium is used by practically all LAN technologies intended for high-speed data exchange at distances exceeding 110 yards. The same transmission medium is used as a basis for all contemporary backbones of transmission networks, providing digital channels for connecting WAN equipment.

The high quality of digital channels has changed the requirements of WAN protocols. Instead of procedures ensuring reliability, factors such as average speed of information delivery and priority processing of packets highly sensitive to traffic delays (such as voice traffic) were brought to the forefront. These changes were reflected in new WAN technologies such as Frame Relay and Asynchronous Transfer Mode (ATM). In such networks, it is assumed that bit corruption is such a rare event that it is much more profitable to simply discard erroneous packets. All problems related to packet loss are delegated to specific software modules of higher levels, which are not directly integrated into Frame Relay and ATM networks.

The dominance of the Internet protocol (IP) has contributed to the convergence of LANs and WANs. Nowadays, this protocol is used over any LAN or WAN technology, including Ethernet, Token Ring, ATM, and Frame Relay, to create a unified internetwork[2] on the basis of various subnets.

From the 1990s, WANs operating on the basis of fast digital channels have significantly widened the range of services, earlier developed in LANs. It became possible to create services whose operation is related to the delivery of large amounts of multimedia information in real time, including images, video, and voice. The World Wide Web (WWW), a hypertext information service that became the main information service on the Internet, is the most impressive example. Interactive capabilities of this service long ago exceeded the capabilities of similar services provided by LANs. Therefore, LAN architects have simply borrowed this service from WANs. The process of porting Internet technologies into LANs became so widespread that quite soon, the specialized term **intranet** appeared.

Nowadays, in LANs, users have to pay the same attention to the mechanisms of protecting information from unauthorized access that they do in WANs. This is because LANs are no longer isolated. Frequently, LANs have access to the "outside world" through WAN links.

Finally, it is necessary to mention that newer technologies continue to emerge. They were initially intended for both kinds of networks. The brightest specimen of the new-generation technologies is ATM,[3] which can serve as a basis for both LANs and WANs because it efficiently combines all kinds of traffic within a single transmission network. The Ethernet family of technologies, which originated from LANs, serves as another example. The new Ethernet 10G standard allows data transmission at 10 Gbps and is intended for the backbones of both WANs and large LANs.

> Other evidence of the LAN–WAN convergence is the arrival of **Metropolitan Area Networks (MANs)**, which take an intermediate position between LANs and WANs. These networks are intended for serving large cities.

---

[2] Internetwork is a common technical term referring to a collection of networks interconnected by routers and other devices. Generally, an internetwork functions as a single network. Sometimes it is called an internet. However, it is not to be confused with the Internet, the largest internetwork connecting tens of thousands of networks worldwide.

[3] Asynchronous Transfer Mode is a network technology that dynamically allocates bandwidth. ATM uses fixed-size data packets and a fixed channel between two points for data transfer. ATM was designed to support multiple services such as voice, graphics, data, and full-motion video. It allows telephone and cable TV companies to assign bandwidth to individual customers.

These MANs use digital communications channels, frequently fiber-optic, and are characterized by backbone speeds of 155 Mbps or higher. They provide an efficient way of interconnecting LANs as well as of connecting LANs to WANs. Initially, these networks were developed only for data transmission. Nowadays, the range of their services has been widened. For example, MANs support video conferences and integrated voice and text transmission. Contemporary MANs are distinguished by a variety of services, which enable their clients to connect communications equipment of various types, including Private Branch Exchange (PBX).

1.4.2 Convergence of Computer and Telecommunications Networks

The trend toward convergence of various computer and telecommunications networks of different types grows stronger every year. Attempts are made to create universal, so-called **multiservice networks,** capable of providing services for computer and communications networks.

Telecommunications networks include telephone, radio, and TV networks. The main feature that makes them similar to computer networks is that information is the main resource provided to clients. However, these networks, as a rule, provide information in a different form. For example, computer networks were initially intended for transmitting alphanumeric information, simply known as data. As a result, computer networks have another name — **data networks**. Telephone and radio networks were developed for transmitting voice information only; TV networks are capable of transmitting both voice and video.

Despite this, the convergence of computer and telecommunications networks is in progress.

First, *convergence of service types* provided to the clients is to be noticed. The first attempt to create a multiservice network capable of providing various services including telephony and data transmission, has resulted in the development of the Integrated Services Digital Network (ISDN) technology. In practice, however, ISDN now provides mainly telephone services.

For now, the Internet is the main candidate for the role of a global multiservice network of the new generation. Especially attractive are new types of integrated services combining several types of traditional services, such as Unified Messaging that combines e-mail, telephony, fax service, and paging. In practice, IP telephony, which is currently used, directly or indirectly, by millions of users all over the world, has proved to be the most successful. However, the Internet has a long evolutionary way to go before it becomes a true new-generation network.

Technological convergence of today's networks is based on the digital transmission of various kinds of information, packet switching, and service programming. Telephony long ago took several steps toward integration with computer networks. This is achieved because of voice presentation in digital format, allowing the possibility of transmitting telephone and computer traffic using the same digital channels. Currently, TV is also capable of transmitting information in digital format. Telephone networks routinely use a combination of circuit and packet switching. Thus, for transmitting service messages (known as signal messages) packet-switching methods are used that are similar to the protocols employed in computer networks; for voice transmission, traditional circuit switching is used.

Supplementary services provided by telephone networks, such as call transfer, conferencing, and telepolling, can be ensured by using the **Intelligent Network (IN)**, which represents a computer network with servers in which the service logic is programmed.

Today, packet-switching methods are gradually gaining on circuit-switching methods, traditionally used in telephone networks, even in the field of voice transmission. This trend has an obvious reason: packet switching allows more efficient bandwidth usage of both communications channels and switching equipment. For example, pauses in a telephone conversation can take up to 40% of the total connection time. However, only packet switching has the ability to "cut off" the pauses and use the released channel bandwidth for transmitting the traffic of other telephone subscribers. The popularity of the Internet, which is based on packet switching, is another argument in favor of migrating to packet switching.

The use of packet switching for the simultaneous transmission of heterogeneous traffic (including voice, video, and text) has increased the importance of developing new methods to ensure **Quality of Service (QoS)**. Methods to ensure QoS are intended to minimize the delay level for real-time traffic, such as voice traffic, and to ensure an average information rate and dynamic data traffic.

However, it should not be assumed that circuit-switching methods have become obsolete and, therefore, have no future. At this new stage of technological evolution, they also find their application, but in newer technologies.

Computer networks, in turn, have borrowed quite a lot from telephone and TV networks. In particular, although the Internet and corporate networks lack the high reliability typical for telephone networks, computer networks have started to add to their armory the reliability tools normally used in telephone networks.

It is becoming increasingly obvious that multiservice networks of the next generation cannot be created as a result of the victory of a single technology or approach. It can be created only as a result of a convergence process, which takes all the best features and characteristics from each technology and joins them into some new combination that provides the required quality for supporting the existing services and for creating new ones. To designate this approach, a new term was introduced — **infocommunications networks** — that explicitly specifies two components of contemporary networks. These are informational (computer-based) and telecommunications. Since this new term has not gained sufficient popularity yet, we will use the standard and generally accepted one — telecommunications network — in its extended meaning, i.e., including computer networks.

SUMMARY

▶ Computer networks are the logical result of the evolution of computer and communications technologies. They represent a particular case of distributed computer systems and can be considered a medium for transmitting information over long distances. For the latter purpose, they implement data encoding and multiplexing methods developed and adopted in various communications systems.

▶ All networks can be classified, based on geographical location, in the following categories: wide area networks (WANs), local area networks (LANs) and metropolitan area networks (MANs).

▶ Chronologically, WANs were the first networks to appear. They connect computers distributed over hundreds of miles. They are often based upon existing, low-quality communications links, resulting in low data-transmission speeds. Compared to LANs, WANs provide a limited set of services, mainly file transfer and e-mail, in background rather than in real time.

▶ LANs usually cover regions within a radius of no more than 1.5 miles. They are based on expensive, high-quality connection links that allow simple methods of data transmission at higher speeds of data exchange (about 100 Mbps) than allowed by WANs. Usually, LANs provide a range of services implemented online.

▶ MANs are intended for serving large cities. Being characterized by rather long distances between network nodes (sometimes tens of miles) they also provide high-quality communications links and support high speeds of data exchange. MANs ensure economic and efficient connection of LANs, providing them access to WANs.

▶ The most important stage in the evolution of computer networks was the arrival of standard networking technologies. These include Ethernet, FDDI, and Token Ring. These technologies allow different types computers to connect quickly and efficiently.

▶ During the late 1980s, LANs and WANs were characterized by significant differences between the length and the quality of communications links, the complexity of the data transmission methods, data exchange rates, the range of provided services, and scalability. Later, as a result of the close integration of LAN, WAN, and MAN, the convergence of these technologies took place.

▶ The trend of convergence of the different types of networks is characteristic not only for LANs and WANs but also for other types of telecommunications networks, including telephone, radio, and TV networks. For now, research is aimed at creating universal multiservice networks, capable of efficiently transmitting information of any kind, including data, voice, and video.

REVIEW QUESTIONS

1. Which characteristics of a multiterminal system make it different from a computer network?
2. When were the first important results achieved in the field of joining computers using long-haul links?
3. What is ARPANET?
   A. A network of supercomputers belonging to military organizations and research institutes in the United States
   B. An international scientific research network
   C. The technology of creating WANs
4. When did the first network operating systems appear?
5. In what order did the events listed here take place?
   A. The invention of the Web
   B. The development of standard LAN technologies
   C. The start of voice transmission in digital form through telephone networks
6. Which of the events stimulated LAN development?
7. Specify when the following technologies were standardized: Ethernet, Token Ring, and FDDI.
8. List the main directions in which the convergence of computer and telecommunications networks proceeds.
9. Explain the meaning of the following terms: multiservice network, info-communications network, and Intelligent Network.

PROBLEMS

1. Explain why WANs appeared earlier than LANs.
2. Using various sources on the Internet, find historical relationships between the X.25 technology and the ARPANET network.
3. Do you think that the history of computer networks can be interpreted as the history of the Internet evolution? Substantiate your opinion.

2

GENERAL PRINCIPLES OF NETWORK DESIGN

2.1 INTRODUCTION

When you start studying specific LAN, WAN, or MAN technologies, such as Ethernet, IP, or ATM, you soon realize that they have much in common. However, these technologies are not identical. On the contrary, each technology or protocol has its own specific features, preventing users from mechanically extending their knowledge of one technological area to another. The best approach to improving the efficiency of the learning process is to start with an investigation of the general principles of network design. These principles form the basis that determines the choice of network topology, as well as methods used for routing, switching, and multiplexing information flows. Thus, a well-known principle stating that "knowledge of several basic principles relieves the student of memorizing lots of facts" must not be interpreted too literally. Qualified experts must know lots of details. However, a sound understanding of the underlying principles helps. Using individual facts and details efficiently and then relating these facts to one another allows experts to form a harmonious system.

The system of principles for building data networks appeared as the solutions to several key problems, most of which are common for telecommunications networks of all types.

Switching is one of the fundamental problems you will face when building networks. Each network node engaged in the transmission of transit traffic must be capable of switching this traffic (i.e., of ensuring communication among network users).

The principle of choosing the route for transmitting information flows using the network directly influences the switching technology. The **route** (i.e., the sequence of network nodes that the data must pass to be delivered to the destination node) must be chosen to achieve two goals simultaneously. First, each user's data must be transmitted as quickly as possible, with minimum delay en route. Second, network resources must be used with maximum efficiency to ensure that the network transmits the maximum amount of data from all network users at any moment. The main problem is combining these goals (the egocentric goal of an individual user and the collective goal of the entire network as a unified system). Traditionally, computer networks solved this problem inefficiently, favoring individual data flows; they only recently began employing more advanced routing methods.

In this chapter, we cover the principles of multiplexing information flows and sharing a transmission medium, the problems of addressing and choosing network topology, as well as logical and physical structuring.

2.2 PROBLEMS OF SHARING COMPUTER RESOURCES

KEY WORDS: physical and logical interfaces, port, network interface cards, controller, driver, peripheral devices, printer, messages, client, server, redirector, operating system, distributed program, network services, applications, network applications, synchronization

The possibility of accessing and using peripheral devices (disks, printers, plotters, etc.) connected to other computers is one of the most obvious advantages of networked computers. Similar to standalone computers, networked computers can directly manage only those devices that are physically connected to them. To enable the users of different computers to share peripheral devices, it is necessary to equip the network with some additional tools. Consider these tools in the example of the simplest network, comprising only two computers (Figure 2.1). To begin with, consider interaction between one computer and a peripheral device.

2.2.1 Interaction between Computers and Peripheral Devices

To organize interaction between a computer and a peripheral device, both are equipped with external physical interfaces.

In a broader sense, the interface is a formally defined logical or physical boundary between communicating objects that are independent of each other. The interface defines parameters, procedures and characteristics of the interaction between objects.

The physical interface (also known as **port**) is defined by the set of electric connections and characteristics of the signals. As a rule, it represents a connector with a set of contacts, each assigned for a specific purpose. There must be a group of contacts for data transmission, a contact for data synchronization, and so on. The pair of sockets is connected by a cable made of a set of wires connecting respective contacts (Figure 2.2).

The logical interface is a set of information messages of a predefined format that two devices (in this case, a computer and a peripheral device) or programs use to exchange data, as well as a set of rules determining the logic of this exchange.

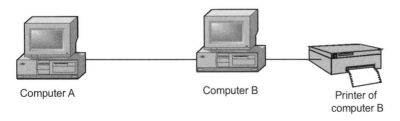

Computer A   Computer B   Printer of
                                        computer B

Figure 2.1 Printer sharing

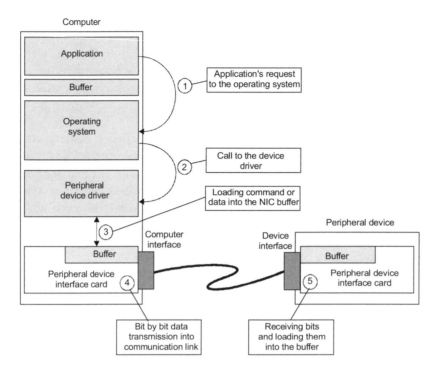

Figure 2.2 Connection between a computer and a peripheral device

The parallel (transmitting data by bytes) Centronics interface, which, as a rule, is intended for connecting printers, and the serial (transmitting data by bits) RS-232C interface (also known as the COM port) are illustrative examples of standard interfaces used in computers. The latter interface is used more universally, since besides printers, there are lots of other devices supporting it, including plotters and mice. There are also specialized interfaces meant for connecting unique peripherals, such as sophisticated facilities for physical experiments.

Interface operations in computers are implemented by a combination of hardware and software. The interface card (a hardware device, also known as a controller or adapter), and special programs manage physical devices. Such software is often called the peripheral device driver.

In peripheral devices, this interface is most frequently implemented as hardware device — **controller**,[1] although software-managed controllers equipped with a built-in processor can also be encountered. This is the case with peripherals whose operating logic is sophisticated. Contemporary printers are good examples.

---

[1] The terms interface card, adapter, and controller are most frequently used as synonyms. However, to distinguish the controller installed inside the computer from the controller built into the printer, we will use the term interface card for the former and controller for the latter.

Peripheral devices can receive from the computer both data (such as bytes of information that needs to be printed) and instructions, in response to which the peripheral device controller must accomplish specific actions. For example, printer controller can support a set of simple commands, such as *Print Character, Line Feed, Carriage Return,* and *Eject paper from the printer,* which it receives from the computer via the interface and completes by managing the electromechanical components of the printer.

As a rule, data exchange via the interface is bidirectional. For example, even printers that, by their nature, represent output devices return status information to the computer. Consider the sequence of operations that the application uses to output data to a printer.

■ An application that needs to output its data to a printer requests the operating system to perform an input–output operation. The following data must be specified in this request: the data address in RAM, the identifier of the required peripheral device, and the operation that needs to be accomplished.

■ Having received such a request, the operating system invokes the printer driver specified by the calling application. All further actions required to accomplish the input–output operation on the part of computer are implemented by the interface card under the control of the driver.

■ As for the printer driver, it operates with the commands understood by the printer controller: *Print Character, Line Feed, Carriage Return,* and *Eject paper from the printer.* The driver forms the sequence of command codes and places them into the buffer of the interface card, which then transfers them, byte by byte, to the printer controller. It is possible to develop different drivers for the same controller, which use the same set of available commands, but implement different algorithms for peripheral device management.

■ For coordinated operation of the driver and interface adapter, the latter implements low-level operations that allow it to interpret the data and commands transmitted to it by the driver as a uniform flow of bytes without requiring it to understand their meaning. After receiving the next byte from the driver, the interface adapter starts to sequentially transmit bits into the interface cable, representing each bit as an electric signal. To inform the peripheral device controller that the transmission of the next byte is about to start, the interface card issues a specific start signal before transmitting the first bit of information. After transmitting the last bit of information, the interface card issues the stop signal. These start and stop signals are used to synchronize the byte transmission. Having recognized the start bit, the controller begins to receive information bits, forming a byte in its reception buffer.

■ Besides information bits, the adapter transmits the parity control bit to ensure data exchange reliability. Provided that data are transmitted correctly, controller interprets the received byte and starts the requested printer operation.

■ Having completed printing of all characters of the document, the printer driver informs the operating system that it has accomplished the request. The operating system, in turn, informs the application about this event.

2.2.2 Simplest Interaction between Two Computers

Return to the initial problem: How can the user who works with some application running on computer A print some text on the printer connected to computer B (Figure 2.3)?

Applications running on computer A cannot directly access the resources of computer B, such as disks, files, or printers. To access these resources, the application can only call another program running on the computer whose resources it needs to use. Such requests are implemented in the form of **messages**, transmitted through communications links connecting computers that participate in the network. In general, such messages contain both instructions (for example, to open a file) and the information to be processed (the contents of a specific file, for example).

Interaction mechanisms used for communication between computers connected to a network have borrowed a lot from the interaction method used in communication between a computer and peripherals. In the simplest case, the communication between computers can be implemented using the tools that organize interaction between a computer and peripheral devices. For example, this can be achieved using the serial interface — COM port. COM ports on *both sides* operate under the control of their drivers. In cooperation, they ensure the transmission of one byte of information via the cable connecting two computers.

NOTE   *In true LANs, such functions are accomplished by network interface cards (NICs), often called network adapters, and their drivers. From the computer's viewpoint, the network adapter is a normal peripheral device, no different from the printer controller.*

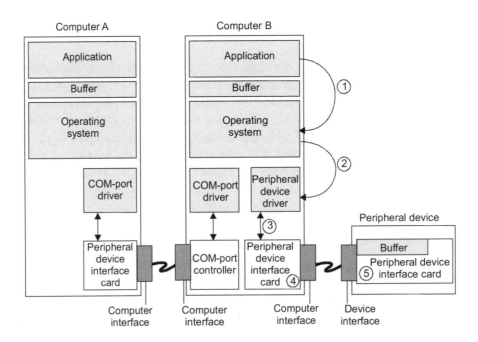

Figure 2.3 Printer sharing

Thus, the mechanism of exchanging bytes between two computers has been defined. However, this simplest tool is not sufficient for solving the problem, namely, printing text on the printer connected to another computer. It is necessary to ensure that computer B understands which operation it has to complete for the data transmitted to it, on which of available devices it must print, how the text to be printed must appear, and so on. Applications A and B must settle all these conditions by exchanging messages.

Furthermore, applications must know how to interpret the information that they receive from each other. For this purpose, the developers of applications A and B must agree on the message format and semantics. They can agree that the execution of any remote print operation must start with the transmission of a message inquiring if application B is ready, that the next message must contain identifiers of the computer and the user that has made the request, that specific code serves signals abnormal completion, etc. As will be shown later, these rules define the protocol of interaction between applications.

Consider interactions between all elements of this small network, which would allow application running on computer A to print a document on the printer connected to computer B.

■ Application A must generate a message for application B, requesting it to print a text. This message goes to a RAM buffer. To transmit this request to remote computer B, application A calls the local operating system. The local OS calls the COM-port driver and passes to it the address of the RAM buffer, where the required message can be found. According to the method just described, the COM-port controller and its driver of computer A interact with the COM-port driver and controller of computer B to pass the message, byte by byte, to computer B.

■ The COM-port driver of computer B permanently waits for incoming information from the outside world. In some cases, the driver is called asynchronously by interrupts from the controller. Having received the next byte and checked it for correctness, the driver loads it into the buffer of application B.

■ Application B receives the message, interprets it, and depending on its contents, generates the request to the local operating system for accomplishing specific actions with the printer. The operating system on computer B passes this request to the printer driver.

■ In the course of printing, situations might arise that need to be reported to application A. In this case, a symmetric design is used. The request for message transmission goes from application B to the local OS running on computer B. The COM-port controllers and drivers on both computers organize byte-by-byte transmission of the message, which then is loaded into the buffer of application A.

The users of many other applications (text or graphics editors, database management systems, etc.) may need to access remote files. Obviously, it isn't reasonable to build the previously described functions of application A into all standard applications that might be used in a network environment, although there are applications that have built-in networking functions. Usually, such applications have rather stringent requirements for the rate of data exchange. The most efficient solution, however, is the development of specialized software modules, designed exclusively for generating requests to remote machines and receiving the results intended for all applications. Such software modules are generally known as clients and servers.

> *Client* is the module intended for forming request messages to a remote machine from different applications, receiving the results and passing them to appropriate applications.
> *Server* is the module, which must permanently *listen* for client requests from the network to specific devices, connected to that computer. The server, having received the client request, tries to process and accomplish it, sometimes with participation of the local OS. One server can complete the requests from several clients sequentially or in parallel.

The most convenient and useful feature of a client component is the capability of distinguishing between requests to local and requests to remote resources. If a client program is capable of doing this, then it does not matter whether applications are dealing with local or remote resources, because the client program recognizes remote requests and *redirects* them to the remote machine. Hence, the client module of a network application is also widely known as the redirector. Sometimes, the functions responsible for recognizing local and remote requests are implemented in a separate software module; in this case, only this module, not the entire client component, is called the redirector.

Client and server software execute system functions related to serving requests from all applications running on computer A for remote access to the resources of computer B (printer, files, fax, etc.). To enable applications running on computer B to access the resources of computer A, this design must be symmetrically complemented by client software for computer B and a server module for computer A.

The method of client and server interaction with applications and local operating system is shown in Figure 2.4. Although we have considered the simplest method of interaction between two computers, program functions ensuring access to a remote printer have much in common with an operating system running in a network comprising a large number of computers connected in more sophisticated ways.

NOTE   *The terms* client *and* server *are used to designate both* software modules *and* computers *as a whole. If a computer provides its resources to other computers participating in the network, it is known as a server. A computer that uses resources provided by a server is known as a client. Sometimes the same computer can simultaneously play both roles.*

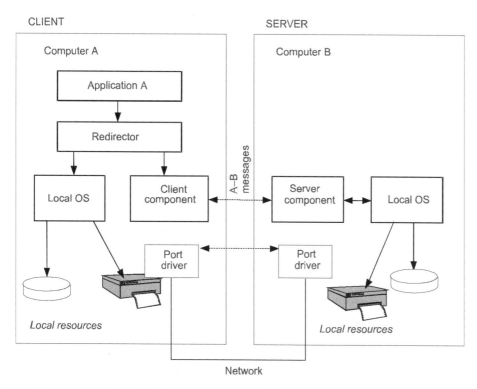

Figure 2.4 Interaction of software components when connecting two computers

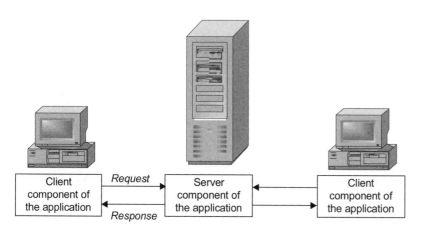

Figure 2.5 Interaction of the modules of a distributed application

2.2.3 Network Applications

Providing the users with shared access to specific type of resources, such as files, is also known as providing the service (file service, in this case). Usually network operating system supports several types of network services for its users — file service, print service, e-mail service, remote access service (RAS), etc. Programs that implement network services are classified as distributed programs.

> A *distributed program* comprises several interacting components (in the example shown in Figure 2.5, there are two such software modules). As a rule, each component can run on different network computers, which is usually the case.
>
> Network services are distributed *system* programs, quite often integral parts of the operating system.

However, there are also distributed *user* programs — **applications**. A **distributed** application also comprises several components, each performing certain operations to complete specific user tasks. For example, one part of such an application, running on an end-user's workstation, can support a specialized graphic user interface (GUI). Another module might run on a powerful, dedicated computer and perform statistical processing of the user-supplied data; the third part might load the results into the database residing on a computer where a standard DataBase Management System (DBMS) is installed. Distributed applications fully employ the potential of distributed processing provided by data networks. Therefore, they are often called **network applications**.

NOTE   *It is necessary to point out that not every application that runs in a network environment can be classified as a "true network application." There is a wide range of popular applications that, although they are capable of running in a network environment, do not represent distributed programs, since their components cannot be distributed over different computers. Nevertheless, even such applications can benefit from the advantages provided by networks, thanks to the presence of network services built into the operating system. A significant part of the history of LANs is bound to the usage of such applications. Consider how users worked with the dBase DBMS, which was quite popular in its time. Actually, dBase was one of the first DBMSs for PCs. Usually, database files accessed by all network users resided on the file server. The DBMS was installed on each client computer as a monolithic software module. Initially, dBase was intended for processing local data only (i.e., the data residing on the same computer as the DBMS software). Users started dBase on the local computer, and the program searched the data on local hard disks without taking into account the existence of a computer network. To process remote data using dBase, the user had to access file services, which delivered data from the server to the client computer and created for the DBMS an illusion of this data being stored locally.*

Most applications used in LANs in the mid-1980s were not truly distributed. This is understandable, since initially these programs were written for standalone computers. As networks became more popular, such applications were installed in the network environment. Although the development of truly distributed applications promised to provide lots of advantages (such as a reduction in the network traffic and specialization according to the roles of computers), in practice it proved to be a difficult task. It was necessary to solve many additional problems. Developers had to decide how many modules the application should comprise, how these modules should interact to ensure that after failures or malfunctions the remaining modules terminated correctly, and so on. Even now, only a small part of all existing applications are truly distributed. Nevertheless, it is obvious that the future belongs to these kinds of applications, since they can fully implement network potential in the field of parallel data processing.

2.3 PROBLEMS OF PHYSICAL DATA TRANSMISSION USING COMMUNICATIONS LINKS

KEY WORDS: encoding, pulse and potential methods, communications links, synchronization, checksum, acknowledgment, offered load, information rate (throughput), capacity, bandwidth, duplex, half-duplex and simplex links

Even when considering the simplest network comprising only two computers, many problems characteristic for any computer network can be seen. In the first place, these are problems related to the physical transmission of signals using communications links.

2.3.1 Encoding

In computing, information is represented using the binary code. Inside a computer, discrete electric signals correspond to ones and zeros.

Data representation in the form of electric or optical signals is known as encoding.

There are various approaches to encoding binary digits. For example, when using the so-called potential method, the specific voltage level corresponds to 1, and another voltage level corresponds to 0. Another possible method is the pulse method, in which pulses of different polarity are used to represent binary digits.

Similar data encoding approaches can be used for data transmission from computer to computer using communications links. However, these communications links have characteristics different from the ones existing inside a computer. The main difference between external communications links and internal ones is that external links are significantly longer. Furthermore, they lie outside the shielded computer case, running through spaces often exposed to intense electromagnetic noise. All these factors result in distortions of rectangular pulses (for example, distortions of the pulse fronts) that are more significant than the distortions that take place inside a computer case. Consequently, when ensuring reliable pulse recognition at the receiving end of the communications link, it is not always possible to use the same transmission rates and encoding methods within and outside the computer. For example, because of the high capacitive load of the communications link, the pulse front rises slowly. Thus, to avoid overlapping of the leading and trailing fronts of adjacent pulses while ensuring that the pulse has sufficient time to grow to the required level, it is necessary to reduce the transmission rate.

In computer networks, both potential and pulse encoding of discrete data are used as well as **modulation** — a specific method of data representation that is never used within computers (Figure 2.6). When using modulation, discrete information is represented by a sinusoidal signal of the frequency reliably transmitted by the available connection link.

Potential or pulse encoding is used *in high-quality communications links*; modulation based on sinusoidal signals is preferred when the link introduces significant distortions into the signals being transmitted. For example, modulation is used in WANs when transmitting data through analog telephone lines, which were developed for voice transmission in analog form and therefore are hardly suitable for direct transmission of pulses.

The number of wires in communications links connecting computers also influences the signal transmission method. To reduce the cost of network communications links, the common solution is to reduce the number of wires. To achieve this, sequential, bit-by-bit data transmission is usually employed, which requires a single pair of wires; the data transmission method used inside a computer transmits all bits that constitute a byte, or even several bytes, in parallel.

Synchronization of the transmitter of one computer and the receiver of another computer is another problem faced when transmitting signals from computer to computer. When organizing the interaction of hardware modules within a single computer, this problem is easily solved, since all modules are synchronized according to the common clock pulse generator. Synchronization problems that arise when organizing communication among computers can be solved both by exchanging special synchronizing clock pulses using separate lines and by a periodic synchronization using predefined codes or pulses of a form different from that of the data pulses.

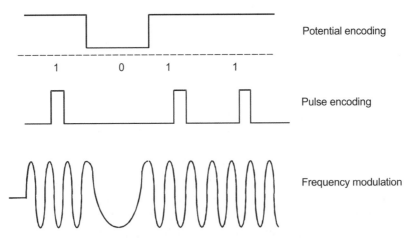

Figure 2.6 Examples of methods of representing discrete information

Even after choosing appropriate data exchange rates, using communications links with required characteristics, and selecting the method of synchronizing the transmitter and receiver, the probability of distortion of some bits of transmitted data persists. To ensure the reliability of data transmission between computers, a standard approach is generally used — calculating the **checksum** and transmitting it using communications links after each byte or block of bytes. Quite often, the acknowledge receipt is included in the data exchange protocol as a mandatory component. This **acknowledgment** is sent from the receiver to the sender and is intended to confirm the correctness of the data reception.

2.3.2 Characteristics of Physical Links

There are lots of important characteristics related to the transmission of the traffic using physical links. The ones that are required by you even now will be covered here, and some other characteristics will be covered in *Chapter 6.*

- **Offered load** is the data flow from the user to the network input. The offered load can be characterized by the rate of data input into the network. Normally, the transmission rate is measured in bits, kilobits, megabits, and so on, per second, denoted as bps, Kbps, Mbps, and so on.

- **Information rate** or throughput (the terms are synonymous and can be interchanged) is the actual rate of the data flow through the network. It can be lower than the offered load since the network, like any other real system, can behave in a way not desired by the user. For example, the data might get corrupted or lost, and as a result, the actual information rate might be decreased.

- **Capacity** is defined as the maximum possible transmission rate using a specific type of link. Specific feature of this characteristic is that its value depends on both physical characteristics of the medium and the chosen method of transmitting discrete information using this medium. For example, the link capacity in the fiber-optic Ethernet is 10 Mbps. This value specifies the rate limit for the combination of specific medium (the fiber-optic, in this case) and the chosen technology (Ethernet). This rate limit depends on the method of data encoding, the clock rate of the information signal, and other parameters. It is possible to develop another data transmission technology for the same medium, characterized by another capacity value. For example, the Fast Ethernet technology allows the transmission of data using the same fiber-optic connection at the maximum rate of 100 Mbps; the Gigabit Ethernet technology raises the maximum transmission rate to 1,000 Mbps. Transmitter of a communication device must operate at the rate equal to the link capacity. This rate is sometimes called bit rate of transmitter.

- **Bandwidth**. The usage of this term is confusing, because it can have two different meanings. First, it can be used to designate a physical characteristic of the transmission medium. In this case, the term refers to the width of a frequency band, which a communications line transmits without significant distortions. The origin of this term is evident from this definition. On the other hand, the same term can be used as a synonym for capacity. In the first case, bandwidth is measured in hertz (Hz), whereas in the second case, it is measured in bits per second. The meanings of this term are distinguished based on the context, although sometimes this can be difficult. Certainly, it would be better if different terms were used for different characteristics. However, some traditions are difficult to change. This dual usage of the term bandwidth has already become common and can be encountered in many standards and books. Therefore, we also will use this approach. Besides this, it is necessary to take into account that the second meaning of this term is more common. Therefore, this term is preferred except when it deviates from the actual meaning.

The next group of characteristics of a communications link is related to the possibility of transmitting information through this link in *one or both directions.*

In the course of interaction between two computers, it is usually necessary to transmit information in both directions, from computer A to computer B and vice versa. Even when it seems to users that they only receive information (downloading music files from the Internet) or only transmit information (sending an e-mail message), information exchange is bidirectional. There are two data flows — the main flow that is of practical interest to the user and the auxiliary flow transmitted in the reverse direction. This auxiliary data flow is formed by acknowledgments of receipt of the main data flow.

Physical links are classified based on their capability of transmitting information in both directions.

■ **Duplex link** ensures simultaneous transmission of information in both directions. Duplex links can comprise two physical media, each being used for transmitting information in a single direction. It is also possible to use the same medium for simultaneous transmission of data flows in both directions. However, in this case, it is necessary to use additional methods of isolating each flow.

■ **Half-duplex** links also ensure information transmission in both directions. This transmission is not simultaneous; rather, it is in turns. This means that during specific time intervals, information is transmitted in one direction, and during the next period, it travels in the reverse direction.

■ **Simplex link** allows the transmission of information in one direction only. Quite often, duplex links are composed of two simplex ones.

Various aspects of physical data transmission will be covered in more detail in Part II of this book — *Technologies of a Physical Layer.*

2.4 PROBLEMS OF INTERACTION AMONG SEVERAL COMPUTERS

KEY WORDS: topology, configuration, graph, fully connected topology, mesh, ring, star, common bus, tree, hierarchical star, mixed topology, concentrator, addressing, broadcast, unicast, anycast, numeric, symbolic, hardware, address space, flat (linear) or hierarchical address space, logical addresses, MAC address, address resolution protocols, port numbers, switching, routing

Until now, we have been describing the simplest network comprising only two machines. When more computers participate in a network, new problems arise.

2.4.1 Topology of Physical Links

As soon as the problem of interconnecting more than two computers arises, it becomes necessary to decide, how to interconnect them. In other words, you must choose the configuration of physical links, also known as the *topology*.

> **Network topology** refers to the configuration of a graph, whose vertices correspond to the network nodes (such as computers) and communications equipment (such as routers) and whose edges represent the physical or information connections between them.

The number of possible configurations rises sharply with an increase in the number of devices to be connected. For example, it is possible to connect three computers using two methods (Figure 2.7, *a*); for a configuration with four computers, there are six topologi-

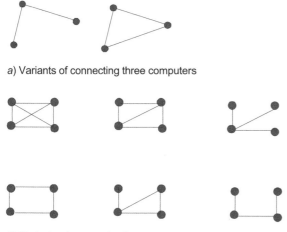

a) Variants of connecting three computers

b) Variants of connecting four computers

Figure 2.7 Possible variants of connecting multiple computers into a computer network

cally different configurations (provided that the computers cannot be distinguished from on another), as illustrated in Figure 2.7, *b*.

Each computer can be connected to each computer, or the computers can be connected sequentially. In the latter case, assume that they will communicate by transmitting "transit" messages. **Transit nodes** in this case must be equipped with special tools enabling them to carry out this specific intermediary operation. Both a universal computer and a specialized device can act as a transit node.

Most network characteristics depend on the choice of topology. For example, the availability of several routes between the nodes increases network reliability and ensures the possibility of load balancing for transmission links. Ease of connecting new nodes, typical of some topologies, makes the network extensible. Economic considerations often result in a choice of topologies for which a minimal total length of communications links is characteristic.

Among the large variety of possible configurations, it is possible to distinguish between fully connected and partially connected topologies.

A fully connected topology (Figure 2.8, *a*) corresponds to a network in which each computer is directly connected to all the other ones. Despite its logical simplicity, this topology is rather bulky and inefficient. Each computer must have a large number of communications ports sufficient for connecting to all other networked computers. For each pair of computers, there must be a physical connection link. (There must be two of them if a single line is insufficient for bidirectional transmission.) Fully connected topologies are rarely employed in large networks, since for connecting N nodes, it is necessary to have $N(N - 1)/2$ physical duplex connection links (i.e., the number of links is related to the number of nodes by a squared dependence). Most frequently, this kind of topology is used in multimachine complexes or in small networks connecting a rather limited number of computers.

All the other types of networks are based on **partially connected topologies**, when the transit transmission of data using other network nodes might be required for data exchange between two computers.

Mesh topology[2] is obtained from fully connected topology by deleting some of its links (Figure 2.8, *b*). Mesh topology allows a large number of computers to be connected and is typical for large networks.

In networks with **ring topology** (Figure 2.8, *f*), data are transmitted around the ring, from computer to computer. The main advantage of the ring is its property of providing redundant links. Each pair of nodes is connected by two routes — clockwise and counter-clockwise. The ring is a very convenient configuration for providing feedback, since the data, having completed the entire ring, return to the source node. Because of this, the source is able to control the process of data delivery to the destination node. Quite often, this property of the ring is used for testing network connectivity and for searching for those nodes that are operating incorrectly. On the other hand, in networks with ring

---

[2] Sometimes, the term **mesh** is used for designating fully connected topologies or topologies that are very close to it.

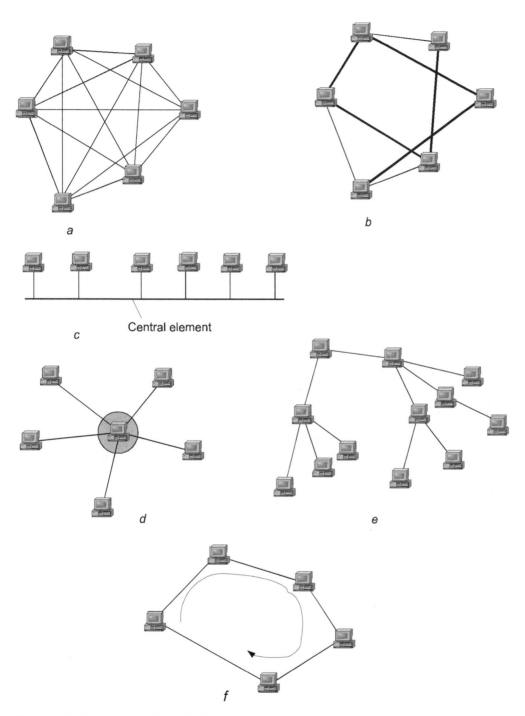

Figure 2.8 Typical network topologies

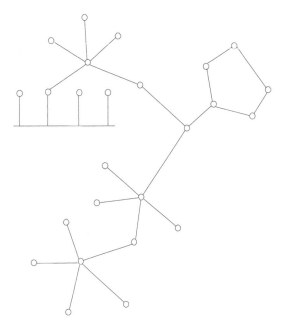

Figure 2.9 Mixed topology network

topology, it is necessary to take special measures to ensure that when one computer fails or temporarily goes down, the communications circuit for all other network nodes does not break down.

The **star topology** (Figure 2.8, *d*) assumes that each computer is directly connected to a central device known as the **concentrator**.[3] The concentrator functions include the redirection of information from one computer to a specific computer or to all computers that form the network. As a concentrator, it is possible to use either universal computers or specialized network devices. This network topology has drawbacks, such as the high price of network equipment because of the necessity of purchasing specialized central devices. Besides this, the possibilities of increasing the number of network nodes are limited by the number of available concentrator ports. Sometimes, it makes sense to build the network using several concentrators, hierarchically connected to one another by the links of the star type (Figure 2.8, *e*). The resulting structure is also known as **hierarchical star**, or **tree**. Currently, the tree structure is the most common and widely used in both LANs and WANs.

The **common bus** configuration is a special version of the star topology (Figure 2.8, *c*). Here, the role of the central element is delegated to the passive cable to which several computers are connected according to the *wired OR* design. Most wireless networks have the same topology. However, in this case, the common radio transmission medium

---

[3] In this case, the term concentrator is used in a broad sense, meaning any device with multiple inputs capable of serving as a central element (for example, it is possible to use a switch or a router).

plays the role of the common bus. Information is transmitted via the cable and is simultaneously available to all computers connected to this cable. Low price and the simplicity of connecting new nodes to the network are the main advantages of this design. The most serious drawback of the common bus is its low reliability, since any defect in the cable or in any of the numerous connectors paralyzes the entire network. Another drawback of the common bus is its low performance, since this method of connection means that only one computer can transmit data through the network at a time. Therefore, the communications link bandwidth is always divided among all network nodes. Until recently, the common bus was one of the most popular topologies for LANs.

Whereas small networks usually have one of the typical topologies — star, ring, or common bus — large networks are characterized by the presence of arbitrary connections among computers. In such networks, one can distinguish arbitrarily connected fragments (subnets) that have a typical topology. Therefore, such networks are known as **mixed topology** networks (Figure 2.9).

2.4.2 Addressing of Network Nodes

The problem of addressing needs to be taken into account when connecting three or more computers. To be precise, this is really a problem of addressing their network interfaces.[4] One computer can have several network interfaces. For example, to form physical rings, each computer must be equipped with at least two network interfaces to ensure connections to its two neighbors. To create a fully connective structure comprising N computers, it is necessary to equip each computer with $N - 1$ network interfaces.

By the number of addressed interfaces network addresses can be classified as follows:

- **Unicast addresses** are used for identifying individual interfaces
- **Multicast addresses** identify groups of several interfaces. Data labeled by a multicast address will be delivered to every node belonging to that group.
- Many network technologies support so-called **broadcast addresses**. The data directed to such addresses must be delivered to all network nodes.
- The new version of the Internet protocol — IPv6 — defines a new type of address, the **anycast address**. Similar to multicast addresses, anycast addresses define specific groups of addresses. However, the data sent to addresses of this type must be delivered to any address in the group rather than to all addresses belonging to this group.

Addresses can be **numeric** (129.26.255.255) or **symbolic** (site.domain.com).

---

[4] Sometimes, instead of the precise term network interface address, we will use the simplified term network node address.

Symbolic addresses (names) are intended for identifying network nodes in a human-friendly format; therefore, they usually have semantic associations. Symbolic addresses are easy to memorize. Network names used in large networks can have a hierarchical structure, such as **ftp-arch1.ucl.ac.uk**. This meaningful name specifies that the computer that has been assigned this address supports the ftp-archive in the network of one of the London University colleges (University College London, or ucl). Also, this network relates to the academic Internet branch (ac) of the United Kingdom (uk). When working within the limits of the London University network, such a long symbolic name is redundant. The shorthand name (ftp-arch1) is more convenient than this fully qualified name.

Symbolic names are convenient for humans. However, because of their variable format and their potentially significant length, their transmission through networks is not efficient.

> The entire set of all addresses valid within a specific addressing method is known as an **address space**.

Address spaces can have **flat** (linear; see Figure 2.10) or **hierarchical** (Figure 2.11) organization.

In the first case, the address space is not structured. A typical example of a flat numeric address is the so-called **MAC address**, intended for unique, unambiguous identification of network interfaces in LANs. Such addresses are normally used by hardware. Therefore, they are made as short as possible. As a rule, a MAC address is written in binary or hex format (e.g., 0081005e24a8). No manual work is required for specifying MAC addresses, because they are usually hard encoded by hardware manufacturers. For this reason, MAC addresses are also known as **hardware addresses**. The usage of flat addresses is not a flexible solution, since after replacement of network hardware (the network adapter, for example), the address of the network interface also changes.

When a **hierarchical addressing** method is used (Figure 2.11), address space is organized as nested subgroups, which define the specific network interface by sequentially narrowing the address range.

In the three-level structure of address space shown in Figure 2.11, the end node address is defined by the following three components: **the group identifier** (K), which specifies the group to which specific node belongs; the **subgroup identifier** (L); and the **node identifier** (n), which uniquely identifies the node within its subgroup. In most cases, hierarchical addressing is much more efficient than flat organization. In large networks comprising thousands of nodes, using flat addresses results in significant overhead, because end nodes and communications equipment have to operate with address tables comprising thousands of records. In contrast, the hierarchical addressing method in data transmission allows only the most significant (leftmost) part of address (e.g., K) to be used until a certain moment. Then, to further narrow the address range, the next part (L) can be used; finally the least significant part (n) can be used.

IP and IPX addresses are typical representatives of hierarchical numeric addresses. They support a two-level hierarchy, where an address is divided into the most significant part — the network number — and the least significant part — node number. Such division allows the transmission of messages among networks to be based on the network

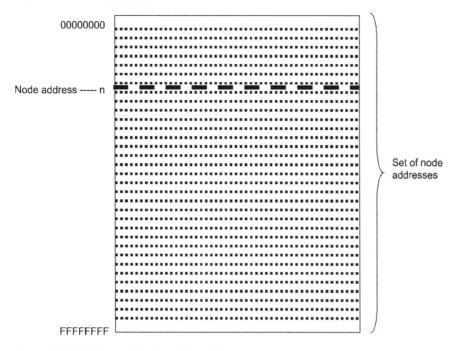

Figure 2.10 Flat organization of the address space

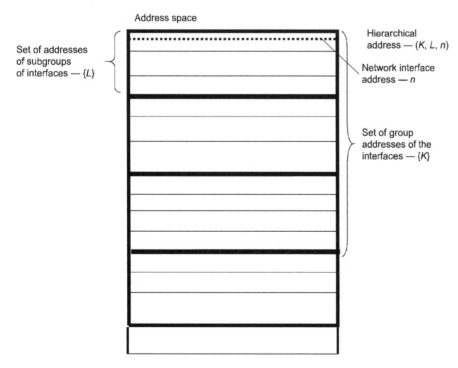

Figure 2.11 Hierarchical structure of the address space

number; the node number is used only after the delivery of the message into the required network. This method is similar to the one used for mail delivery using a street address. The street name is used only after the letter has been delivered to the destination town.

In practice, several addressing methods are used simultaneously. Therefore, network interfaces of the computer can have more than one address (or name). Each address is used when it is convenient. For translating addresses from one form to another, special protocols, known as **address resolution protocols**, are used.

Users address computers by hierarchical symbolic names. In messages transmitted using the network, these symbolic names are automatically replaced by hierarchical numeric addresses. Using these numeric addresses, messages are passed from network to network, and after delivery of the message to the destination network, the flat hardware address of the computer is used instead of the hierarchical numeric address.

Either centralized or distributed tools can be used to solve the problem of establishing correspondence between addresses of different types.

In the centralized approach, there are dedicated computers in the network, known as name servers, storing the table that maps different types of names (e.g., symbolic names and numeric addresses). All other computers request name servers to determine the numeric identifier of a specific computer using its symbolic name.

When using the distributed approach, each computer stores its own copy of the different types of addresses assigned to it. The computer that needs to determine the flat hardware address corresponding to the known hierarchical address sends a broadcast request to the network. All network computers compare the hierarchical address specified in this broadcast message to their own addresses. The computer that has the matching address sends a reply message containing the required flat hardware address. This method is used by the Address Resolution Protocol (ARP) of the TCP/IP stack.

The advantage of the distributed approach is that it does not require a dedicated computer, which, additionally, often requires manual configuration of the address-mapping table. However, the distributed approach also has disadvantages, the main one being the necessity of sending broadcast messages that overload the network because they are redirected to all nodes. Therefore, the distributed approach is used only in small LANs. For large networks, the centralized approach is more typical.

Until now, we have been focusing on the addresses of network interfaces of network nodes (i.e., computers or specialized communications devices). However, it is not the computer or router that represents the destination point of the data sent using the network. Rather, it is the software that runs on these devices. For this reason, the destination address, besides the information identifying the interface of the destination device, must also specify the address of the process for which the data sent using the network are intended. When the data reach the network interface specified in the destination address, the software running on that computer must redirect the data to the required program. Obviously, the program address does not have to be unique within the entire network. It is sufficient to ensure its uniqueness within a computer. TCP and UDP **port numbers** used in the TCP/IP stack represent examples of program addresses.

2.4.3 Switching

Assume that computers are physically connected to one another according to a specific topology and that a specific addressing method has been selected. Now the most important problem must be solved: Which method should be used in the network for transmitting data between nodes? This problem becomes very complicated when using partially connected network topologies. In this situation, data exchange between an arbitrarily selected pair of nodes (users) generally must take place via transit nodes.

> The process of connecting end nodes via the network of transit nodes is known as **switching**. The sequence of nodes on the path from the source to the destination nodes is known as the route.

For example, in the network shown in Figure 2.12, nodes 2 and 4, which are not connected directly, must pass the data via transit nodes (e.g., nodes 1 and 5). Node 1 must transmit data from interface A to interface B; node 5 needs to carry out the same operation by transmitting data from interface F to interface B. In this example, the route can be described as follows: 2–1–5–4, where 2 is the source node, 1 and 5 are transit nodes, and 4 is the destination node.

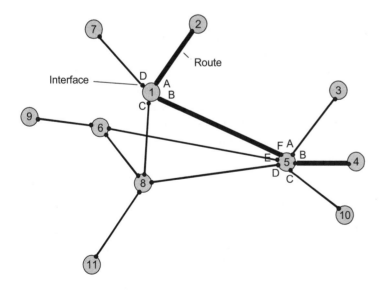

Figure 2.12 Switching via the network of transit nodes

2.5 GENERALIZED SWITCHING PROBLEM

KEY WORDS: switching, information flow or data flow, flow label, routing metric, Time Division Multiplexing (TDM) and Frequency Division Multiplexing (FDM), multiplexer, demultiplexer, daisy-chain connection, arbitrator, shared link, shared medium, circuit switching, packet switching, data forwarding, switching network

In the most general form, the task of switching can be represented as a set of the following interrelated tasks:

■ Determining the information flows for which it is necessary to define routes
■ Routing of information flows
■ Flow forwarding (i.e., flow recognition and local switching on each transit node)
■ Flow multiplexing and demultiplexing

2.5.1 Flow Definition

Obviously, it is possible to establish several routes through a single transit node. For example, all data directed by node 4 (Figure 2.12) must pass through node 5, as well as all incoming data to nodes 3, 4, and 10. Transit nodes must be capable of recognizing incoming data flows to redirect each of them to the interface that leads to the required destination node.

Information flow or data flow is the continuous sequence of data joined by a set of common attributes that distinguishes it from the total network traffic.

For instance, all data arriving from a specific computer can be determined to be a single flow for which the source address serves as a unifying attribute. The same data can be represented as a set of several smaller subflows, each of which uses the destination address as a differentiation attribute. Finally, each of these subflows can be further subdivided into data flows generated by different network applications, such as e-mail, file-copying programs, or Web servers.

Data forming a flow can be represented by data units — packets, frames, or cells.

NOTE   *Along with data flow, there are also concepts such as* data stream. *Usually, a data flow has an* uneven rate, *and a data stream has a* constant rate. *For instance, when passing a Web page through the Internet, the offered load represents data flow; during Internet music broadcasting, it is a data stream. For data networks, uneven rates are more typical; therefore, in most cases, we will use the term flow. The term stream will be used only when it is necessary to emphasize the isochronous character of this process.*

In the course of switching the data, the destination address is a mandatory attribute. Based on this attribute, the entire flow of data to the transit node is divided into subflows, each of which is directed to the interface corresponding to the data-forwarding route.

Source and destination addresses determine a single flow for each pair of end nodes. Quite often, it is useful to represent the data flow between two end nodes as a set of several subflows, each passing along its specific route. The same pair of end nodes can execute several applications interacting using the network. At the same time, each of these applications might have its own requirements for the network. In this case, the route selection must be accomplished within the application requirements. For example, for a file server, it is important that the large amounts of transmitted data be directed using a communications link, which has a high bandwidth. For a management system sending short messages that must be processed immediately, the reliability of the connection links and the minimal level of delays on the chosen route are of primary importance. Besides this, even for data that have similar requirements for the network, it might be necessary to establish several routes to speed up data processing with parallel usage of different communications links.

Flow attributes can be either *global* or *local*. In the first case, they unambiguously identify the flow within the limits of entire network. In the second case, they do so only within the limits of the specific transit node. A pair of unique addresses of the end nodes represents an example of the global attribute for flow identification. The ID of the interface of the specific transit node to which the data have been delivered can serve as an attribute locally defining the flow within a specific device. To illustrate these definitions, return to the network configuration shown in Figure 2.9. In this example, node 1 can be configured to transmit all data arriving from interface A to interface B and to redirect all data arriving from interface D to interface C. Specifying such a rule allows the data flow arriving from node 2 to be separated from the data flow arriving from node 7; it also allows them to be redirected for transit transmission via different network nodes. In this case, the data from node 2 will travel via node 5, and the data from node 7 will be transmitted via node 8.

There also is a specific type of flow attribute called *flow label*. Flow label represents a specific number borne by all data of the flow. The label can have a global value uniquely identifying the flow within the limits of the network. In this case, it is assigned to the flow data units and never changes on the entire route from the source node to the destination node. In some cases, local flow labels are used that dynamically change their values when passing from node to node.

> Thus, flow recognition during switching is based on attributes that, besides the mandatory *destination address*, can contain information such as the identifier of a specific application.

2.5.2 Routing

The problem of routing includes two other tasks:

❑ Determining routes
❑ Informing the network about the chosen route

Solving the problem of choosing the route for data transmission involves determining the sequence of transit nodes and their interfaces, through which it is necessary to pass the data to deliver them to the destination address. Determining the route is a complicated task, especially when network configurations allow several routes between a pair of interacting network interfaces. Most frequently, it is necessary to select only one route, *optimal*,[5] according to specific criteria. Several criteria can be used as the optimum criteria, such as a nominal bandwidth and load of the communications links, delays introduced by specific links, the number of transit nodes, and the reliability of communications links or transit nodes.

Even when there is only *one* possible route between end nodes, finding this route can be a daunting task in a complicated network topology.

The route can be determined empirically ("manually") by the network administrator, who frequently uses various considerations that cannot be formalized. The reasons for choosing specific routes might include the following: special requirements for the network implied by specific types of applications, the decision to transmit traffic using the network of a specific service provider, assumptions related to the peak loads on specific network links, and, last but not least, security considerations.

However, an empiric approach to determining routes is hardly suitable for large networks with complicated topology. In such networks, one uses automatic methods of determining routes.

To achieve this goal, end nodes and other network devices are equipped with specialized software tools that organize the exchange with service messages, allowing each network node to compose its own representation of the network. Then, based on the collected data and using various specialized software, rational routes are automatically determined.

Various kinds of network information can be used for choosing an optimal route. However, when solving this problem, most often only information on the network topology is taken into account. This approach is illustrated in Figure 2.13. There are two routes for transmitting the traffic between end nodes A and C: A–1–2–3–C and A–1–3–C. If no information about the network was taken into account except the links between its nodes, then it would be logical to choose the A–1–3–C route.

This solution was found by means of minimizing a chosen criterion.

The route parameter used to make this choice is known as the **route metric**.

---

[5] In practice, to reduce the amount of calculations, one usually chooses a rational route very close to optimal one rather than truly optimal one in mathematical sense.

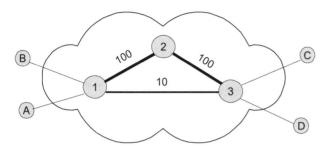

Figure 2.13 Route selection

In this case, the length of the route measured as the number of transit node was used as the minimization criterion. Minimization of the route metric is the main method of choosing the route.

However, it is possible that the choice may be far from rational. The design presented in Figure 2.13 shows that links 1–2 and 2–3 are characterized by a bandwidth of 100 Mbps, and link 1–3 has a bandwidth of 10 Mbps. Therefore, if one wanted the information to travel at the maximum speed, it is better to choose the A–1–2–3–C route, despite its three transit nodes.

Because of this reason, various metrics can be chosen for measuring the route length, including the number of transit nodes (as in the case just considered above), linear length of the route, and even its cost in terms of money. To build the metric in the case, when the information must travel at maximum speed, each link is characterized by a value inversely proportional to its bandwidth. To operate over integer numbers, one usually chooses some constant larger than the bandwidth values of the network links. For example, if the value of 100 Mbps was chosen as such a constant, then the metric of 1–2 and 2–3 links will be equal to 1, and the metric of the 1–3 link will be equal to 10. The route metric is equal to the sum of the metrics of the links that form it; therefore, the 1–2–3 part of the route has the metric value 2, and the 1–3 part of the route has the metric value 10. The rational route is the route with the smaller metric value, that is, A–1–2–3–C.

These approaches for choosing routes consider only the network topology, without taking into account the traffic workload of the communications links[6]. Using the analogy of automobile traffic, it is possible to say that we have chosen the route using a map, taking into account the number of transit towns and the road width (analogous to the link bandwidth) when establishing the preference of highways. However, we did not pay any attention to the radio or TV programs informing travelers about current traffic jams. Therefore, it is possible that our solution will be far from the best, especially if a large

---

[6] Methods that use information about the current workload of communications links allow for finding more efficient routes. However, they also cause network nodes to exchange auxiliary information more intensely.

number of flows is already being transmitted by the A–1–2–3–C route and the A–1–3–C route is practically empty.

After the route has been chosen (either manually or automatically), it is necessary to inform all network devices about the choice that has been made. Messages informing network devices about the chosen route must deliver a variation of the following information to each transit device: "Anytime the device receives data related to flow N, it is necessary to pass them for further forwarding to interface F." Each routing message of this type is processed by the device. As a result, the new record is placed into the switching table, where the local or global attributes of the flow (such as the label, the number of the input interface, or the destination address) are mapped to the number of the interface to which the device must redirect data related to this flow.

Table 2.1 is a fragment of the switching table containing the records instructing the node to redirect flow M to interface G, flow N to interface F, and flow P to interface H.

Table 2.1 A Fragment of the Switching Table

Flow attributes	Data redirection (interface number or next node address)
M	G
N	F
P	H

Naturally, detailed descriptions of the routing message structure and the contents of the switching table depend on specific network technology. However, these specific features do not change the essence of the processes under consideration.

Transmission of the routing information to transit devices, like route selection, can be performed manually or automatically. Network administrators can fix specific routes by manually configuring the device — for example, by hard-connecting specific pairs of input and output interfaces for a long time. This is similar to telephone operators working with the first switches. Besides this, network administrators can manually edit the switching table by entering the required record into it.

However, the network topology and information flows are subject to changes. These changes, for instance, might be caused by such factors as the failure of some nodes or the advent of new transit nodes. Moreover, network addresses might change, or new flows might be defined. Consequently, a flexible approach to solving the problems of determining and specifying routes implies the continuous analysis of the network state and the updating of routes and switching tables as needed. In such cases, the task of route determination cannot be solved without sophisticated software and hardware.

2.5.3 Data Forwarding

When the routes have been determined and recorded in the switching tables of all transit nodes, everything is ready for accomplishing the main operation — the actual data transmission between end nodes, or end node switching.

For each pair of end nodes, this operation can represent a combination of several *local* switching operations (their number corresponds to the number of transit nodes). That is, the sender must provide data to the specific interface from which the chosen route is originated, and all transit nodes must accordingly redirect the data from one interface to another. In other words, transit nodes must perform *local interface switching*.

The device intended for performing switching is known as the **switch** (Figure 2.14).

However, before performing switching, the switch has to recognize the flow. To do this, it must analyze the delivered data to find attributes of certain data flows specified in the switching table. If a match is found, these data are redirected to the interface defined for them in the route.

IMPORTANT *Terms such as* switching, switching table, *and* switch *can be ambiguously interpreted in telecommunications networks. We have already defined* switching *as the process of connecting network nodes via transit nodes. The same term is used for designating the connection of interfaces within a specific transit node. The* switch *in a broad sense is any device capable of accomplishing the operation of switching the data flow between*

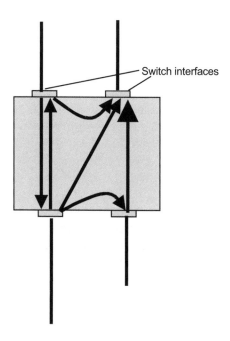

Switch interfaces

Figure 2.14 Switch

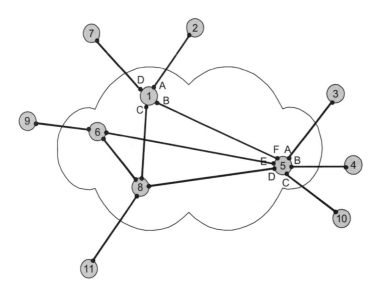

Figure 2.15 Switching network

interfaces. The switching operation can be accomplished according to different rules and algorithms. Some methods of switching and their corresponding switching tables and devices have special names. For example, in network-level technologies such as IP and IPX, different terms are used for designating similar concepts — routing, routing table, and router. *In Ethernet, the switching table is usually called the* forwarding table. *Other special types of switching and their appropriate devices have been assigned the same names — switching, switching table, and* switch used in the narrow sense, *for example, for LAN switch and LAN switching. For telephone networks, which appeared much earlier than computer networks, similar terminology is characteristic. Here, switch is synonymous with telephone exchange. Because of the age and prevalence of telephone networks, the term switch in telecommunications most frequently means telephone exchange.*

Both specialized devices and universal computers with built-in switching software can play the role of a switch. The computer can combine the switching functions with normal end-node functionality. In most cases, however, it is much more practical to dedicate specific network nodes to performing switching functions. These nodes form the switching network to which all other nodes are connected. Figure 2.15 shows the switching network formed by nodes 1, 5, 6, and 8 to which end nodes 2, 3, 4, 7, 9, and 10 are connected.

2.5.4 Multiplexing and Demultiplexing

To determine which interface to redirect the incoming data to, the switch must determine which flow they relate to. This task must be solved independently of whether a single "pure" or "mixed" flow is delivered to the switch input. The "mixed" flow is the result of aggregating several data flows. In this case, the task of flow recognition is complemented by the task of demultiplexing, or the separation of the resulting aggregate flow into several component flows.

As a rule, the switching operation is accompanied by a reverse multiplexing operation, during which a common aggregate flow is created from separate data flows. This aggregate flow can be transmitted using a single physical communications link.

Multiplexing and demultiplexing operations are of the same importance as switching. Without these operations, it would be necessary to provide a separate link for each flow. This, in turn, would result in a large number of parallel links within a network, which would neutralize all the advantages of the partially connected network.

Figure 2.16 depicts a network fragment composed of three switches. Switch 1 has five network interfaces. Consider what happens on the **int.1** interface. It receives the incom-

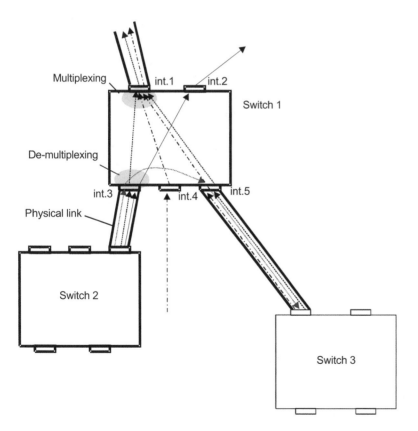

Figure 2.16 Multiplexing and demultiplexing operations during flow switching

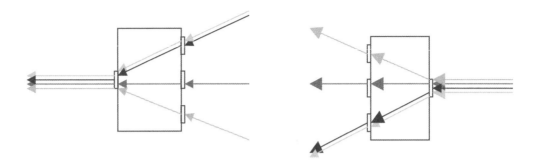

Figure 2.17 Multiplexer and demultiplexer

ing data from three interfaces — **int.3**, **int.4**, and **int.5**. It is necessary to pass all these data through a common link (i.e., to perform the multiplexing operation). Multiplexing ensures the availability of existing physical links for several network sessions between network end nodes.

There are several methods of flow multiplexing in a single physical link, the most important of which are **Time Division Multiplexing (*TDM*)** and **Frequency Division Multiplexing (*FDM*)**. When using TDM, each flow has the link at its disposal at fixed or arbitrary time intervals and transmits its data using this link. When using FDM, each flow transmits its data within a frequency range assigned to it.

Multiplexing technology must allow the receiver of such aggregate flows to perform a reverse operation — demultiplexing the data into separate flows. For example, on the int.3 interface, the switch demultiplexes the aggregate flow into three component flows. One is then forwarded to the int.1 interface, the second is sent to **int.2**, and the third component flow goes to **int.5**. As for the **int.2** interface, there is no need to perform multiplexing or demultiplexing, since this interface is for exclusive use by a single flow. In practice, both multiplexing and demultiplexing can be executed simultaneously on each interface that supports a duplex mode.

> When all incoming information flows are switched to a single output interface, where they are multiplexed into a single aggregate flow and forwarded to the common link, the switch is known as the *multiplexer*. A switch of this type is shown in Figure 2.17, *a*. A switch that has a single input interface and several output interfaces is known as a *demultiplexer* (Figure 2.17, *b*).

2.5.5 Shared Medium

The **number of network nodes connected to a physical link** represents another parameter of a link. In the examples provided previously, only two interacting nodes (to be more precise, two interfaces) were connected to a communications link (Figure 2.18, *a* and *b*).

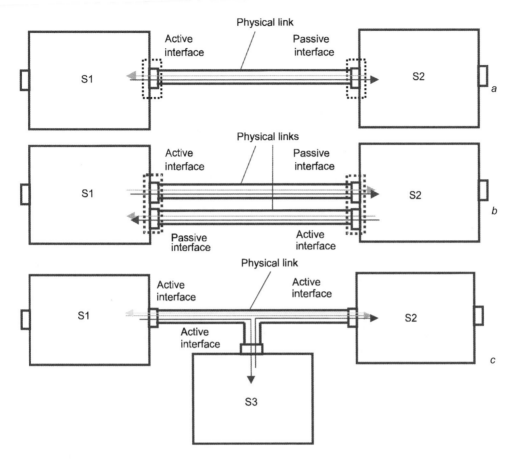

Figure 2.18 Shared use of the communications link

In telecommunications networks, another type of connection is used, in which several interfaces are connected to a single link (Figure 2.18, *c*). Such multiple connections of several interfaces result in the previously considered common bus technology, sometimes called a *daisy-chain connection*. In all such cases, one has to solve the problem of sharing the link among multiple interfaces.

Figure 2.18 shows various methods of sharing the link among multiple interfaces. In Figure 2.18, *a*, switches S1 and S2 are connected by two unidirectional physical links (i.e., each link is capable of transmitting information in a single direction). In this case, the transmitting interface is active, and the medium is under full control of this interface. The passive interface only receives the data. *In this case, there is no problem of sharing the link between the two interfaces.* Notice, however, that it is still necessary to solve the data-multiplexing problem in such a link. In practice, two unidirectional links implementing fully duplex connection between two devices are considered a single duplex link, and the two interfaces of a single device are interpreted as the receiving and transmitting parts of the same interface.

In Figure 2.18, *b*, switches S1 and S2 are connected by a link capable of transmitting data in both directions, though only alternately. *It becomes necessary to implement the mechanism of synchronizing access* of the S1 and S2 interfaces to such a link. The configuration shown in Figure 2.18, *c*, in which more than two interfaces are connected to the communications link, forming a common bus, represents a generalization of this case.

The physical link provided for simultaneous use by several interfaces is known as a **shared link**.[7] Quite often, another term is used: the **shared medium**. Shared communications links are used not only for switch–switch links but also for computer–switch and computer–computer links.

There are several methods of solving the task of organizing multiple access to shared communications links. Some of them use a centralized approach in which a special device known as the **arbitrator** controls access; other methods are based on a decentralized approach. The problems of sharing connection lines among different modules also exist within a computer. Access to the system bus, which is controlled by either the processor or a special bus arbitrator, is a good example. Organizing shared access to communications links in networks has some specific features because of the significantly longer time required for signal propagation. Because of this, the procedures of coordinating access to a communications link require very long time intervals and result in significant loss of network performance. Therefore, medium sharing is practically never used in WANs.

In LANs, medium sharing is used more often because of the simplicity and efficiency of its implementation. This approach is used in the Ethernet, currently the prevalent LAN technology, as well as in the Token Ring and FDDI technologies that were popular in the past.

In recent years, however, another trend became prevalent — namely, abandoning the shared medium, even in LANs. The price reduction that is the main advantage of this approach results in loss of network performance.

IMPORTANT *Networks with a shared medium composed of a large number of nodes will always operate slower than similar networks with individual point-to-point connection links, since the bandwidth of a shared communications link is divided among several computers participating in the network.*

Nevertheless, shared access to communications lines is preserved not only in classical network technologies but also in some new technologies developed for LANs. For example, developers of the Gigabit Ethernet technology, which was accepted as a new standard in 1998, have included the medium sharing mode in their specifications, as well as the mode for individual connection links.

---

[7] It is necessary to emphasize that the term shared medium is traditionally related to link sharing among interfaces and is practically never used to describe link sharing among flows (i.e., multiplexing–demultiplexing).

2.5.6 Switching Types

The complex of technical solutions to the generalized switching problem forms the foundation of any network technology. In general, the solution to **each** particular switching task depends on the solutions chosen for the **other** tasks of this set. The list of switching tasks includes:

■ Determining flows and appropriate routes
■ Forming switching tables
■ Recognizing flows
■ Transferring data among different interfaces of the same device
■ Flow multiplexing/demultiplexing
■ Medium sharing

> Among the possible methods of solving the switching problem, the following two fundamental approaches can be distinguished:
> ■ *Circuit switching*
> ■ *Packet switching*

Circuit-switched networks have a long history, since they originated from the first telephone networks. Packet-switched networks are relatively young. They appeared in the late 1960s as a result of experiments with the first WANs. Each of these networks has its advantages and drawbacks, but, according to the long-range forecasts of leading specialists, the future lies with the packet-switching technology, since it is more universal and flexible.

EXAMPLE   *Let us simplify the abstract description of the generalized switching model using the example of the postal service operation.*
1. The postal service operates with flows. In this case, flows are formed by mail items. As a rule, the recipient address serves as the main flow attribute. For the sake of simplicity, consider the destination country as the only address attribute: India, Norway, Brazil, Russia, and so on. Sometimes a specific requirement related to the reliability or speed of delivery serves as an additional flow attribute. For instance, if a mail item intended to be delivered to Brazil is labeled "AIRMAIL/PAR AVION," then a subflow that must be delivered by airmail will be separated from the common flow of mail intended for delivery to Brazil.
2. For each flow, the postal service has to define a route that will pass through a sequence of post offices, analogous to network switches. The long history of the postal service operation has resulted in predefined routes for most destination addresses. New routes may appear. This may be the result of the appearance of new transportation or political or economical changes and upheavals. After choosing a new route, it is necessary to inform the entire network of post offices about it. Obviously, these actions are similar to the ones carried out in a telecommunications network operation.
3. Information about the chosen routes for mail delivery is presented in each post office in the form of a table that specifies the mapping between the destination country and

the next post office in the sequence of delivery. For instance, in the central post office of Brussels, all mail items to be delivered to India may be directed to the post office in Rome; mail to be delivered to Tokyo may be sent to the central Moscow post office. Such a table of postal routing is analogous to the switching table of a communications network.

4. *Each post office operation is similar to the switch operation. All mail items from customers or other post offices are sorted, which means that flow recognition takes place. After that, mail items belonging to the same flow are packed into the common package for which the next post office is defined according to the switching table.*

SUMMARY

▶ To enable network users to access the resources of other computers, such as disks, printers, plotters, it is necessary to complement all network computers with special tools. The functions of transmitting data into a communications link on each computer are accomplished in coordination by special hardware — the Network Interface Card (NIC) and the NIC driver, the software module controlling it. Higher-level tasks such as generating requests to resources and completing these requests are performed by client and server modules of the OS, respectively.

▶ Even in the simplest network comprising just two computers, there are problems with physically transmitting data using communications links, such as encoding and modulation, synchronization of transmitting and receiving devices, and error control for transmitted data.

▶ Important characteristics related to the transmission of traffic through physical channels are the offered load, the information rate or throughput, the capacity and the bandwidth.

▶ When connecting more than two computers into the network, the problems of choosing the topology *have to be solved. These topologies are fully connected, star, ring, common bus, hierarchical tree, and hybrid.* The addressing method can be flat or hierarchical, numeric or symbolic. You also have to choose the switching mechanism and the mechanism of sharing communications links.

▶ In networks with partial connectivity, the connections between users are established by switching (i.e., by connecting through a network of transit nodes). In this case, it is necessary to solve the following problems: data flow and route definition, data forwarding on each transit node, and flow multiplexing and demultiplexing.

▶ Among the different approaches to the switching problem, one distinguishes the following two fundamental methods: *circuit switching* and *packet switching*.

REVIEW QUESTIONS

1. What information is transmitted using the link connecting the external interfaces of the computer and the peripheral device?
2. What components does the device interface include?
3. What tasks does the operating system perform when exchanging data with peripheral devices?
4. Which actions are typically accomplished by the peripheral device driver?
5. Define topology.
6. To which type of topology is it possible to attribute the structure formed by nodes connected to one another in a triangle?
7. To which type of topology is it possible to attribute the structure formed by nodes connected to one another in a square?
8. To which type of topology is it possible to attribute the structure formed by three sequentially connected nodes (the last node is not connected to the first one)?
9. The common bus topology is a particular case of:
   A. Fully connected
   B. Ring
   C. Star
10. Which topology is characterized by increased reliability?
11. Which topology is the most widely used in today's LANs?
12. What are the requirements for the system of addressing?
13. To what type can the addresses listed below be attributed?
    www.olifer.net
    20-34-a2-00-c2-27
    128.145.23.170
14. What are the differences between a flow and a stream?
15. Which attributes can be used as a flow characteristic?
16. Describe the main approaches and criteria used when choosing a route.
17. Which of the statements listed below can be true in some cases?
    A. Routes are fixed on switches by connecting pairs of interfaces.
    B. Routes are defined by the network administrator and manually entered into a special table.
    C. The routing table is entered into the switch at the manufacturing plant.
    D. The routing table is created automatically by the network hardware and software.
    E. Each switch has a special routing table stored on it.

18. Which of these devices — automatic telephone exchange, router, bridge, or multiplexer — can be called a switch?

19. Which methods are used for multiplexing?

20. Describe the difference between medium sharing and multiplexing.

PROBLEMS

1. Describe the main problems that need to be solved to ensure information exchange between any two subscribers in any type of communications network.

2. Explain how the division of common traffic into several different flows allows the optimization of control over an urban transportation system.

3. Suppose that there are several routes in the network between end nodes A and B. Consider the advantages and drawbacks of variants of data transmission between these nodes:

   • Is using all existing routes for parallel data transmission better than transmitting all data along a single route optimal according to a specific criterion?

   • Use several of the possible routes and share data transmission among them. What rule can be used to define the route needed to forward the next packet?

3

PACKET AND CIRCUIT SWITCHING

3.1 INTRODUCTION

In this chapter, we will continue our investigation into the general switching principles in telecommunications networks. Let us first concentrate on a detailed description and comparison of the two main principles of switching, circuit switching and packet switching.

Circuit switching appeared long before packet switching. This principle originates from the first telephone networks. The impossibility of the dynamic redistribution of the physical link bandwidth is the principal limitation of the circuit-switching principle.

The packet-switching principle was invented by developers of computer networks. It takes into account features of computer data traffic such as bursts and represents the switching method, which is most efficient for computer networks, rather than the traditional methods of circuit switching used in telephone networks.

However, the advantages and drawbacks of any network technology are relative. The use of buffer memory in the switches of packet-switched networks allows the efficient use of link bandwidth when transmitting bursty traffic. However, it results in arbitrary delays in packet delivery. These delays represent a drawback for real-time traffic. Such traffic is traditionally transmitted using a circuit-switching technique.

This chapter covers three methods of packet forwarding used in packet-switched networks: datagram transmission, connection-oriented transmission, and virtual circuit technique.

Finally, this chapter is concluded with a study of the media-sharing principle widely used in LANs.

3.2 CIRCUIT SWITCHING

KEY WORDS: Circuit switching, connection setup, setup request blocking, real-time traffic, guaranteed bandwidth, multiplexing, aggregate channel, subchannel, subscriber, frequency division multiplexing, time division multiplexing, bursty traffic, traffic pulsation coefficient

First, consider circuit switching in its most simplified form, which will explain the fundamental idea of this method. As shown in Figure 3.1, a switched network comprises switches connected to one another by communications links. Each link is characterized by the same bandwidth.

Each end node (user) is connected to the network using the terminal device that sends data to the network at a constant rate equal to the link bandwidth. If the offered load for some period is lower than the link bandwidth, the terminal device continues to *feed* the network with a constant data flow by supplementing useful user information with *blank* insignificant data (Figure 3.2). The terminal device *knows* that part of the bit flow contains useful information and part is simply padding. The receiving terminal device must discard insignificant information and supply to the user only the data sent to the network by the sender.

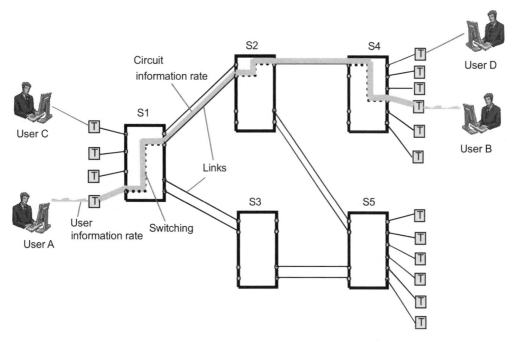

Figure 3.1 Circuit switching without multiplexing

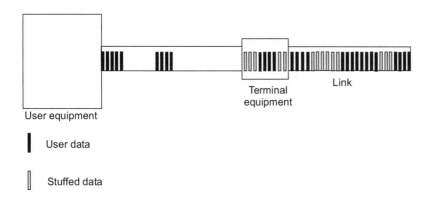

Figure 3.2 Supplementing the flow to the link bandwidth

Since most people are accustomed to telephone networks, the best-known representatives of the circuit-switched networks, our explanation will be accompanied by references to specific features characteristic for the telephony.

3.2.1 Connection Setup

Data exchange begins after a **connection setup**.

Suppose that two telephone subscribers (A and B) want to exchange some data. Before sending the data to the network (i.e., starting a conversation), subscriber A sends the *request* to the switching network. In this request, it is necessary to specify the address (i.e., the phone number) of subscriber B. The goal of sending this request is to establish the connection between subscribers A and B with an information channel, the properties of which are similar to that of a continuous communications link. It transmits data along the entire length of this link at the same rate. This means that *transit switches do not need to buffer the user data.*

To create such a link, the request must pass through a sequence of switches from A to B, making sure that all required route sections (communications links) are available. Besides this, for successful setup of the connection, the end node B must be free (i.e., not busy in another established connection). To fix the connection, each of the participating switches along the path from A to B stores the information that the appropriate section of the route is reserved for the A–B connection. In each switch, internal connection of the interfaces corresponding to the data route takes place.

3.2.2 Setup Request Blocking

The possibility of **setup request blocking** is an important feature of circuit-switching technology. If any other couple of subscribers should request the network to establish a connection that requires reserving at least one of the route sections reserved for the connection between A and B, the network will deny such a request. For example, if end node C sends a request for establishing a connection to end node D, the network will block this setup request, since the only link connecting switches S2 and S4 is reserved for connecting subscribers A and B.

The setup request blocking can also take place at the end section of the route. For instance, this will happen if the subscriber being called is already connected to another end node. When this happens, the network informs the calling subscriber about this unfavorable event. This is analogous to telephone networks, which respond with short beeps (or the **line busy** signal). Some telephone networks are able to distinguish different events, such as **network busy** or **subscriber busy**, and to inform the calling subscriber about the event by using beeps of different frequencies or by using different tones.

3.2.3 Guaranteed Bandwidth

Suppose that the connection between subscribers A and B has been established. Now, only these subscribers have the circuit characterized by a fixed bandwidth at their disposal. This means that during the entire connection time, they must send the data to the network at a fixed rate; the network will ensure delivery of this data to the called subscriber without loss and at the same rate. This is independent of whether other connections exist in the network during that time. The subscriber cannot transmit data into the network at a rate exceeding the line bandwidth. The network cannot decrease the transmission rate of the user data.

> Network load will influence only the probability of setup request blocking. The more connections established in the network, the higher the probability of setup request blocking.

It is good that the network will deliver the data with a small and fixed delay. Low and constant levels of data transmission delays characteristic of circuit-switched networks ensure high quality of transmission for data sensitive to delays. This is also known as **real-time traffic**, examples of which are voice or video.

3.2.4 Multiplexing

The simplified network being described, *in which each physical link always transmits data at the same rate,* operates inefficiently.

First, the users of such networks often do not get the service they require. They must be universal, standard users who always transmit information at only the available fixed rate. Today, it is hard to imagine such a user, especially with the wide availability of various kinds of terminal devices, such as fixed and mobile phones and computers. Therefore, in general, the rate of user traffic is different from the fixed bandwidth of physical circuit. The bandwidth can either significantly exceed or be below the user requirements. In the first case, the user is not getting the most out of the circuit possibilities; in the second case, the user must either limit requirements or use several physical links.

Second, the network is inefficiently using its resources. Obviously, the network shown in Figure 3.1 has an insufficient number of links between switches. Such a network structure was chosen to illustrate the reasons for setup request blocking. To reduce the probability of blocking to acceptable levels, it is necessary to lay a large number of parallel physical links between the switches. This is the *hang-the-expense* approach.

To improve the efficiency of circuit-switched networks, multiplexing can be used, which enables the simultaneous transmission of traffic from several logical connections using a single physical link. Multiplexing in circuit-switched networks has specific features. For example, the bandwidth of each link is divided into **equal parts**, thus providing an equal number of so-called **subchannels**. Note that for the sake of simplicity, subchannels are often simply called channels. Usually, the communications links connecting users to networks support a smaller number of channels than the links connecting the switches. In this case, the probability of blocking gets reduced. For example, the user link can comprise 2, 24, or 30 channels; the link between switches can comprise 480 or 1,920 channels. For the moment, the most common speed of a digital subchannel is 64 Kbps. This speed ensures quality voice transmission in a digital format.

After the circuit-switched network was complemented by the multiplexing mechanism, its operating scheme changed. User requests for establishing logical connections now reserve only one or several subchannels of the link rather than the entire link. Thus, connections are established at the subchannel level rather than at the link level. Several subchannels might be reserved in case the bandwidth of a single channel is insufficient. This enables the user to reserve the subchannel (or subchannels) with the data transmission rate closest to the one required. Furthermore, multiplexing allows for the construction of more efficient links between switches. To decrease the probability of blocking, a single physical link can be used, with a large number of logical subchannels, instead of several physical links.

Figure 3.3 shows the circuit-switched network with multiplexing. Two connections, A–B and C–D, are established in this network, first using one subchannel in each communications link, and the second — two subchannels in each link. Thus, although the physical structure the network shown in Figure 3.1, the second call, C–D, is not blocked, because switches support multiplexing.

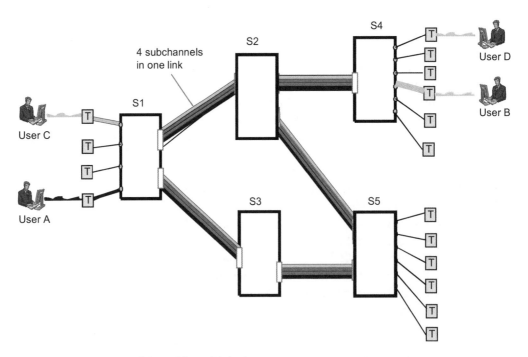

Figure 3.3 Circuit switching with multiplexing

NOTE   *When using multiplexing, the fundamental property of the circuit-switched networks is preserved, namely, the* **aggregate channel**, *or circuit, that comprises several route sections with the bandwidth used previously. The only difference now is that the subchannel is playing the role of link.*

Obviously, the usage of multiplexing complicates the procedure of traffic processing at the switches. Instead of simple and straightforward procedures of switching appropriate interfaces, it is now necessary to transmit data into the required channel. When using Time Division Multiplexing, a high level of synchronization between two information flows is required. When using Frequency Division Multiplexing, it is necessary to use frequency transformation.

3.2.5 Inefficiency of Transmitting Bursty Traffic

There is another reason that circuit-switched networks often operate inefficiently. *This lies in the fundamental operating principle of such networks, namely, in reserving a fixed bandwidth of the circuit for the entire connection time.*

We have already mentioned that multiplexing increases the efficiency of the circuit-switched network because users are now able to select the connection rate in better accordance with requirements. However, this relates only to those users who generate information flows at a constant rate. What about the users whose information flows are quite bursty (i.e., come in intervals of activity), such as sending data into the network followed by periods of idleness?

If you consider user traffic more carefully, you will discover that practically all users of telecommunications networks fall into this category. Recall that the users of telephone networks transmit information at a constant rate. This seeming constancy is achieved, because uneven flows of user data are processed by the terminal devices of the telephone network: the phones themselves. For example, a digital phone transmits information at a constant rate of 64 Kbps, whether the user is speaking or is quiet. Naturally, the phone will operate more efficiently if it could *cut out* pauses from the conversation and transmit only useful information to the network.

Finally, there is another category of users, whose requirements for information transmission at a variable rate are more obvious. These are computer users.

The activity of the user who surfs the Web generates bursty traffic. When downloading Web pages to the user PC, the traffic speed grows sharply and after the downloading process is complete, the traffic rate drops practically to zero. This process is repeated time and again.

The **traffic pulsation coefficient** for individual network users is equal to the ratio of the average intensity of data exchange to the maximum possible intensity. This coefficient can reach the value of 1:100. If circuit switching between the user PC and the server is implemented, the circuit will thrash during the main part of this session. On the other hand, some part of the network performance will be dedicated to this pair of network end nodes. Thus, it will be unavailable to other network users. Network operation during such times can be compared to an empty escalator in the subway station, which continues moving but doesn't accomplish any useful job.

> Circuit-switched networks transmit user traffic most efficiently when the traffic has constant intensity during the entire session and corresponds to the bandwidth of the network's physical channels.

The advantages and drawbacks of each network technology are relative. In some situations, advantages come to the forefront, and drawbacks become inconsequential. Thus, the circuit-switching technique is efficient when it is necessary to transmit only telephone traffic, since the impossibility of **cutting off** pauses from conversations can be tolerated. However, when transmitting computer traffic, which is bursty by nature, this inefficiency becomes a matter of importance.

3.3 PACKET SWITCHING

> **KEY WORDS:** packet, packet switching input buffer, store-and-forward technique, switching fabric, output queue, congestion, packet-forwarding methods, connectionless, datagram transmission, datagram, connection-oriented transmission, virtual circuit, switching table, the routing table, the forwarding table, load balancing, best effort service, signal propagation time

The technique of **packet switching** was designed specially for the efficient transmission of computer traffic.

When using packet switching, all data transmitted by the network user are divided into relatively small fragments known as **packets**. These are also known as frames or cells, though in this context the choice of term is of little importance. This operation is accomplished at the transmitting node (Figure 3.4). Each packet is provided with a header containing an address, which is necessary to deliver the packet to the destination node. *The presence of address in each packet* represents one of the most fundamental properties of the packet-switching technique, since each packet *may*[1] be processed by the switch independently of other packets of the information flow. Besides the header, the packet has another auxiliary field, which is usually located at the end of the packet and therefore is generally known as a trailer. The trailer contains the checksum, which allows you to check if the information was corrupted during transmission.

Packets are supplied to the network *without previously reserving communication links*, and at the rate at which the source generates them. This rate cannot exceed the band-

---

[1] The word "may" in this context is of special importance, since in some variants of the packet-switching technology, complete independence of packet processing is not ensured (see, for example, the virtual circuit technology).

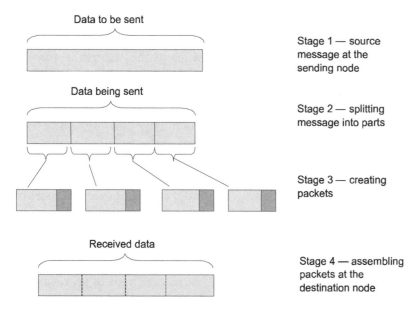

Figure 3.4 Division of the data flow into packets

width of the access link. It is assumed that the packet-switched network, in contrast to the circuit-switched network, is always ready to receive the packet from any of its end nodes.

NOTE   *The procedure of reserving the bandwidth can also be used in a packet-switched network. However, the main idea of such a reservation is different from the bandwidth reservation idea in circuit-switched networks. The difference is that the channel bandwidth in the packet-switched network can be dynamically redistributed among information flows, depending on the current requirements of each flow. This possibility cannot be provided in circuit-switched networks. The details of this bandwidth reservation technique will be covered in more detail in* Chapter 7.

3.3.1 Buffers and Queues

The packet-switched network, like the circuit-switched network, comprises switches connected by physical data links. However, switches operate differently in these networks.

The main difference is that *packet switches have internal buffers* for temporarily storing packets.

First, this is because the switch needs *all parts of the packet* to make a decision on its forwarding. These parts include the header, which should contain the destination address, the data field, and the trailer containing the checksum. The switch checks the checksum and, only when it is evident that the packet data are not corrupted, starts packet processing. That is, the switch determines the next switch by the destination address. Therefore, *each* packet is placed into the **input buffer** (i.e., it is sequentially, placed bit by bit into the memory allocated to the packet). Taking this circumstance into account, it is possible to say that packet-switched networks use the **store-and-forward technique.** Note that to achieve this, it is sufficient to have a buffer equal to the size of a single packet.

Second, buffering is required for coordinating the speed of the arrival of packets and the speed of their switching. If the unit performing packet switching (switching fabric) cannot keep pace with the processing of the packets, then input queues are created at the interfaces of the switch. To store the input queue, the buffer size must exceed the size of a single packet. There are different approaches to creating a switching fabric. The traditional approach is based on a single central processor that serves all the input queues of the switch. This method might result in long queues, since the processor performance is shared among several queues. Contemporary methods of building switching fabrics use multiprocessor approach, in which each interface has its own built-in processor for packet processing. Apart from this, there is also a central processor, which coordinates the operation of interface processors. Using interface processors improves the switch performance and reduces the queues at the input interfaces. However, such queues can still appear, since the central processor can become a bottleneck, as it had been earlier. Various aspects of the switch internal structure will be covered in more detail in *Chapter 15.*

Finally, buffers are needed for coordinating the speed of the links connected to a specific packet switch. If the speed at which the packets are supplied to the switch from one link exceeds the bandwidth of the link to which these packets need to be forwarded and this situation takes place for a certain interval, then to avoid packet loss, it is necessary to organize the **output queue** at the target interface (Figure 3.5).

Thus, the packet for some time resides in the buffer memory of the switch, after which it is forwarded to the next switch using the output interface. This method of data transmission smoothes over traffic bursts at the backbone links between the switches. This lets the channels be used in the most efficient way, allowing the increase of the overall network performance (Figure 3.6).

In the packet-switched network, traffic bursts of individual users, according to the law of large numbers, are distributed in time in such a way that their peaks, in most cases, do not coincide. Therefore, the switches are constantly and rather evenly loaded only if the number of served users is large. Figure 3.6 demonstrates that the traffic arriving from each of the end nodes to the switches has very uneven time distribution. However, the switches of the higher hierarchical level (those that serve connections between switches of lower level) are loaded more evenly, and the backbone links, connecting switches of higher level, have utilization close to maximum. Buffering smoothes the traffic bursts; therefore, the pulsation coefficient at the backbone links is significantly lower than at the user access links.

Since the buffer size in switches is limited, packets sometimes get lost. Temporary overloading of some network segments is known as **congestion**. Usually, this takes place when

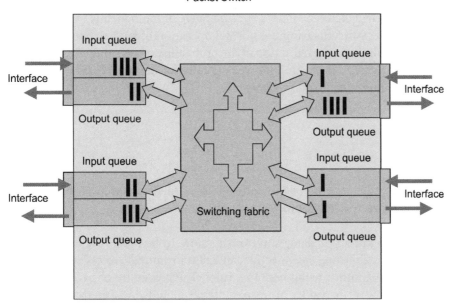

Figure 3.5 Queues in the packet switch

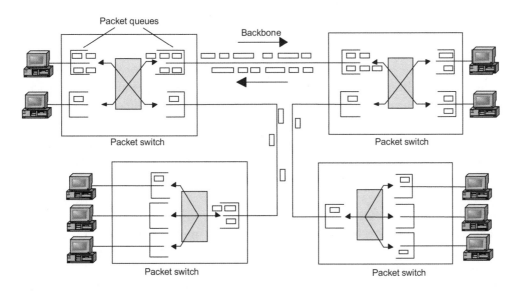

Figure 3.6 Smoothing the traffic pulsation in packet-switched networks

pulsation periods of several information flows coincide. Since packet losses are an inherent property of packet-switched networks, a specific range of mechanisms compensating for this undesirable effect and ensuring the normal operation of such networks was developed. The methods allowing the reduction of the probability of such undesirable events are being actively developed. These are known as **Quality of Service (QoS)** and **Traffic Engineering**; they will be considered in *Chapter 7*.

3.3.2 Packet-Forwarding Methods

The interface to which the arriving packet must be forwarded is chosen on the basis of one of the following three **packet-forwarding methods**:

- Connectionless, also known as datagram transmission. In this case, the transmission takes place without establishing a connection, and all transmitted packets are *forwarded independently* of one another, using the same rules. The procedure of packet processing is determined only by the values of the parameters included within the packet and by the current state of the network. For instance, depending on the current load, the packet might stay in the queue for a shorter or a longer time. However, the network does not store any information on packets that have already been transmitted, and this information is not taken into account when processing the next packet. This means that each packet is considered by the network to be an independent unit of data transmission, known as a datagram.
- **Connection-oriented transmission**. In this case, the connection-oriented process of data transmission is divided into so-called sessions or logical connections. The network registers the start and the end of each logical connection. Now the processing procedure is determined *for the entire set of the packets transmitted as part of the session rather than for an individual packet*. The process of serving each newly delivered packet directly depends on the session prehistory. For example, if several preceding packets were lost, the rate of sending all subsequent packets may be reduced.
- **Virtual circuit**. If the list of connection parameters includes the route, then all packets transmitted as part of a specific connection must take a specific route. This single, fixed, and predefined route, connecting end nodes in the packet-switched network, is known as a virtual circuit or **virtual channel**.

Classification of the existing switching methods is outlined in Figure 3.7.

The same network technology can use different methods of data transmission. For example, the IP datagram protocol is used for data transmission among different networks that make up the entire Internet. The reliable delivery of data between the end nodes of the Internet is delegated to the connection-oriented TCP protocol that establishes logical connections without fixing the route. Finally, the Internet represents

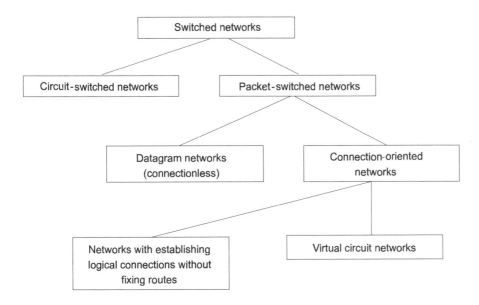

Figure 3.7 Taxonomy of switched networks

an example of a network using the virtual circuit technique, since it includes numerous ATM and Frame Relay networks that support virtual circuits.

3.3.3 Datagram Transmission

As was already mentioned, the datagram transmission method is based on the fact that all transmitted packets are processed independently. The selection of the interface to which it is necessary to forward the arriving packet is made on the basis of the **destination address** specified in the packet header. That a specific packet belongs to a specific information flow is not taken into account.

The solution of packet forwarding is based on a **switching table** containing the set of destination addresses and address information unambiguously determining the next network node on the route (either the transit or the end node). Recall that in different network technologies, other terms might be used for designating the switching table. These are the **routing table**, the **forwarding table**, and so on. Going forward, for the sake of simplicity, we will use the term switching table for tables of this type, which are used for datagram transmission based only on the destination node address.

Switching tables of the datagram network must contain entries for all addresses to which it is possible to forward the packets arriving at the switch interfaces. In general, the incoming packets can be addressed to any network node. In practice, approaches are usually implemented that help to reduce the number of entries in the switching table. One such approach is hierarchical addressing, according to which the switching table may contain only the most significant (leftmost) parts of addresses that correspond to a group of nodes (subnet) rather than to individual nodes. Therefore, it is possible to use the analogy of mail addresses, where the names of countries and cities correspond to the *most significant* parts of addresses. Naturally, the names of countries and cities are significantly less numerous than the street names, home numbers, and names of individuals. They are incommensurably fewer in number.

Despite using hierarchical addressing, in some large networks (e.g., the Internet), switches can still have switching tables containing thousands of entries. Figure 3.8 shows how the switching table of the S1 switch might look in a datagram network.

The switching table can contain several entries for the same destination address, specifying different addresses of the next switch. This approach is known as **load balancing** and is used for improving the performance and reliability of the network. In the example

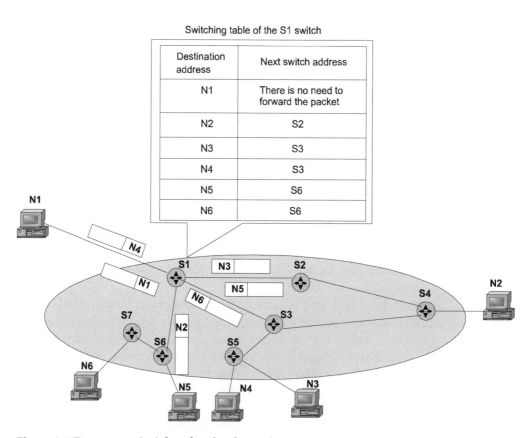

Switching table of the S1 switch

Destination address	Next switch address
N1	There is no need to forward the packet
N2	S2
N3	S3
N4	S3
N5	S6
N6	S6

Figure 3.8 Datagram principles of packet forwarding

shown in Figure 3.8, the packets arriving to the S1 switch, bound for the N2 destination node, are distributed between S2 and S3 next switches to balance the load. This reduces the workload of the S2 and S3 switches and, consequently, reduces queues while speeding up the delivery. Some **fuzziness** of the routes for the packets with the same destination address is a direct consequence of the principle of independent packet processing, which is inherent in the datagram method. Packets intended for the same destination address can be delivered to that address via different routes because of the change in the network state, such as the failure of some transit switches.

The datagram delivery method is fast, since no preparative actions are required before the actual transmission of data. However, when using this method, it is hard to track the packet delivery to the destination node. Thus, this method does not guarantee the packet delivery, although a network makes its best effort to get it to the desired destination. Such a service is known as **a best effort service**.

3.3.4 Logical Connection

Connection-oriented transmission is based on the knowledge of the packet exchange pre-history (i.e., current values of connection). It allows a more rational approach to be used when processing each newly arrived packet. Connection parameters can be used for different purposes. For example, packet numbering and tracking the numbers of sent and received packets can be used for improving the transmission reliability. This allows for discarding duplicate packets, ordering the received packets, and repeating transmissions of the lost packets within the context of the specific connection. A secure connection's parameters might contain, for example, information on the encryption method.

Connection parameters might be either constant during the entire connection time (e.g., the maximum packet size), or variable, dynamically reflecting the current connection state (e.g., the previously mentioned sequential packet numbers). When the sender and receiver establish a new connection, they first negotiate on the initial parameters of the exchange procedure and only after that start data transmission.

Connection-oriented protocols ensure more reliable transmission. However, they require more time for data transmission and impose higher computing loads on the end nodes (Figure 3.9).

When using connection-oriented transmission, the source node sends to the destination node a service packet of a special format containing a request for establishing a connection (Figure 3.9, *b*). If the destination node agrees to establish the connection, it responds to the source node with another service packet, confirming connection setup and suggesting some parameters to be used within this logical connection. These parameters might include a connection identifier, the maximum value of the packet data field length, and the maximum number of packets that can be sent without receiving acknowledgment. The node initiating the connection can complete the process of establishing the connection by sending the third service packet with information that the suggested

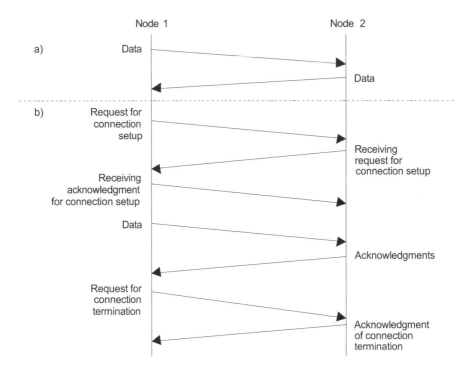

Figure 3.9 Transmission without establishing a connection (*a*) and establishing connection (*b*)

parameters are acceptable. After that, a logical connection is considered established. Logical connections can be intended both for unidirectional data transmission (from the connection initiator) and for bidirectional data exchange. Having transmitted some logically complete set of data (e.g., specific file), the sending node initiates the connection termination procedure by sending an appropriate service packet.

Note that in contrast to datagram transmission that supports only one type of packet, the information packet, connection-oriented transmission must support at least two types of packets. These are service packets used for establishing (or terminating) connections and information packets used for transmitting user data.

3.3.5 Virtual Circuit

The mechanism of **virtual circuits (virtual channels)** creates fixed stable routes for transmitting traffic in packet-switched networks. All packets related to the same logical connection follow the same route — virtual circuit. Networks based on the X.25, frame relay, and ATM technologies use this mechanism.

Virtual circuits account for the existence of data flows in the network. To identify a data flow in the aggregate traffic, each packet of such a flow is specially marked. In networks of this type, data transmission implies the preliminary procedure of establishing a logical connection, known as the virtual circuit. Similar to the procedure of establishing logical connections, the creation of virtual circuits starts with a request for establishing a connection sent by the source node. Connection requests represent service packets of a special format, also known as **set-up packets**. The set-up packet must contain the destination address and label of the flow for which this virtual circuit is created. The set-up packet passes via the network and registers control information on all switches located along the route from sender to recipient. Based on this information, the entry of the switching table is formed, specifying how the switch must serve the packet that has this label. A virtual circuit created in such a way is identified by the same label.[2]

After the creation of the virtual circuit, the network can start transmitting the appropriate data flow through it. In all packets that carry user data, the destination address is not specified. Instead of the destination address, the information packets contain only the virtual circuit label. When the packet arrives at the input interface of the switch, the switch reads the label value from the header of the arrived packet and consults its switching table. It then finds the entry specifying the output port to which this packet must be forwarded.

Switching tables in networks using the virtual circuit mechanism are different from the switching tables in datagram networks. In contrast to networks using the datagram-forwarding algorithm, in which switching tables contain information on all possible destination addresses, switching tables in virtual circuit networks contain entries only on virtual circuits passing through this switch. Usually, in a large network the number of virtual circuits passing through a specific node is significantly smaller than the total number of nodes. Therefore, the size of the switching table is significantly smaller. Consequently, looking up this table for the required entry takes less time and does not require significant processing power from the switch. Because of this, the label is significantly shorter than the destination node address, which decreases the packet overhead since it now contains a short data flow ID instead of a long destination address.

NOTE   *It is necessary to point out that using virtual circuit techniques in a network does not make it a circuit-switched network. Although they use the procedure of establishing the circuit, this circuit is* virtual. *It transmits individual packets rather than information flows travelling at a constant rate, like circuit-switched networks.*

Figure 3.10 shows a fragment of the network in which two virtual circuits are created. The first one starts from the end node with the N1 address and ends at the node with

---

[2] In different technologies, this label has different names: Logical Circuit Number (LCN) in X.25, Data Link Connection Identifier (DLCI) in frame relay, and Virtual Circuit Identifier (VCI) in ATM.

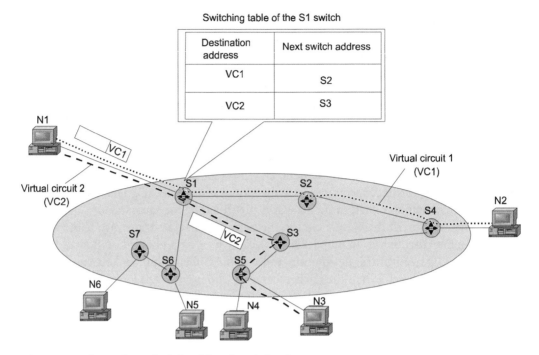

Figure 3.10 Operating principle of the virtual circuit

the N2 address, passing through the S1, S3, and S4 transit switches. The second circuit ensures data forwarding by the route N3–S5–S7–S4–N2. Thus, between two end nodes, there may be several virtual circuits.

3.3.6 Circuit-Switched Networks vs. Packet-Switched Networks

Before carrying out technical comparison of packet-switched and circuit-switched networks, it is useful to consider their informal comparison based on a helpful analogy with motor traffic.

Transport Analogy for Circuit-Switched and Packet-Switched Networks

When using this analogy, cars correspond to data packets, and roads and highways correspond to communications links. Similar to data packets, cars move independently. They share the road space and create obstacles for one another. If the traffic is too intense and does not correspond to the road space, congestion might occur. As a result, cars are delayed in traffic jams, which correspond to packet queues in switches.

The switching of car flows takes place on crossroads and street intersections, where each car's driver chooses an appropriate direction to get to the destination. Naturally, the role of a crossroad as compared to the packet switch is passive. Its active participation in traffic processing is only noticeable on signal-controlled crossroads, where the traffic light defines the turn for each car flow to cross the intersection. Naturally, if a police officer carries out this task, his role is even more active, because he can choose an individual car from the entire flow and allow its driver to carry out a maneuver.

The same analogy can be used with city transport for comparing packet-switched networks and circuit-switched networks.

Sometimes it becomes necessary to ensure specific conditions for the moving column of cars. For instance, assume that a long column of buses brings children to a summer camp. This column moves along the highway using multiple lanes. To ensure the movement without obstacles, it is necessary to choose its route beforehand. Then, along the entire predefined route that crosses several intersections, a separate lane is allocated to this column. The police officer reserves this lane for the buses with children, ensuring that no other cars use it. This reservation is cancelled only after the column reaches its destination.

In the course of travel, all buses move with the same speed at approximately equal intervals to avoid creating obstacles for one another. Obviously, privileged conditions are created for such a column. However, in this case, the cars cease to move independently. On the contrary, they turn into the flow, from which it is impossible to turn aside. The road under these conditions is used inefficiently because the lane is not used for a long time, similar to the inefficient use of bandwidth in circuit-switched networks.

Quantitative Comparison of Delays

Now, from the transport analogy, let us return to the network traffic. Imagine that a user needs to transmit bursty traffic, comprising periods of activity as well as pauses. Also assume that the user can choose whether to transmit this traffic through a circuit-switched network or through a packet-switched network. In both cases, the bandwidth of the communications link is the same. A circuit-switched network would be the most efficient for this user, as relates to time requirement; in a circuit-switched network, the user has a reserved communications circuit at his monopolistic disposal. Using this method, all data would be delivered to the destination without delay. During significant portions of the connection time, the reserved communications circuit would be used inefficiently (during the pauses), but is of little or no importance for the user, since the user's main goal is to solve problems as soon as possible.

When the user decides to use the packet-switched network, the data transmission process would be slower, since the packets sent by the user to the destination are likelier to be delayed in the queues more than once as they travel the route. Packet-switched networks slow data transmission for individual users, since the user's packets share all network resources with packets sent by other users.

Consider the origins of delays in data transmission in both types of networks in detail. Suppose that the N1 end node sends a message to the N2 end node. Along the route of data transmission, there are two switches.

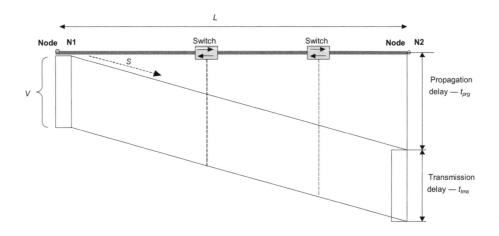

Figure 3.11 Time diagram of the message transmission in a circuit-switched network

In a circuit-switched network, the data transmission starts at the standard rate for the circuit, after an initial delay caused by the necessity of establishing the circuit (Figure 3.11). The time (T) required to deliver the data to the destination node is equal to the sum of the signal propagation time (t_{prg}) and the message transmission time (t_{trns}). Note that the presence of switches has no influence on the total time required for data transmission.

NOTE   *Note that the* message transmission time *exactly matches the time required to receive the message from the channel into the buffer of the destination node. In this case it is called* buffering time.

- **Signal propagation time** depends on the distance between the source and destination (L) and on the speed of the electromagnetic waves propagation in the physical medium (S), which varies within the range from $0.6v_{light}$ to $0.9v_{light}$, where v_{light} is the speed of light propagation in vacuum. Thus, $t_{prg} = L/S$.
- **Message transmission time** is equal to the ratio of the message volume (V) in bits to the circuit bandwidth (C) in bits per second: $t_{trns} = V/C$.

In packet-switched networks the procedure of data transmission doesn't require mandatory connection setup.

Assume that the packet-switched network (Figure 3.12) transmits a message of the same size (V) as the message in the previous example (see Figure 3.11). However, in this case, the message is split into packets, and each packet is supplied with the header. Packets are transmitted from the N1 node to the N2 node, between which there are two switches. The packets on each switch are shown twice: once when the packet arrives at the input

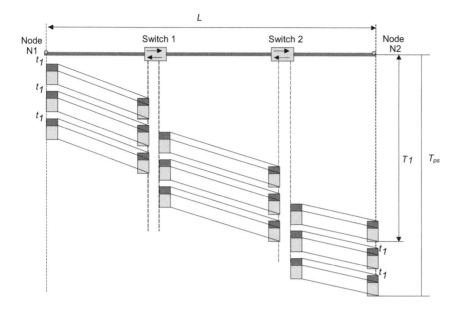

Figure 3.12 Time diagram for transmission of the message divided into packets in packet-switched network

interface and then as the packet is transmitted to the network from the output interface. It is clear that each switch delays packet transmission for some time. The time designated as T_{ps} stands for the time required to deliver the data to the destination in the packet-switched network, while T_1 is the time required to transmit a single (the very first) packet through the network.

When comparing the time diagrams, note the following two facts:

- The signal propagation time t_{prg} has the **same value** in both networks, provided that the transmission distance and physical medium are the same.
- Taking into account that the link bandwidth values of both networks are the same, it is possible to draw the conclusion that the message transmission time — t_{trns} — will also have the **same value**.

However, the process of splitting the message being transmitted into packets and the transmission of these packets through the packet-switched network significantly influences the time required to deliver the message to the destination. Delivery time increases as a result of additional delays.

Trace the route of a single packet, numbered 1, take note of the components that comprise the total time required to transmit it to the destination node, then determine which components are specific to packet-switched networks (Figure 3.13).

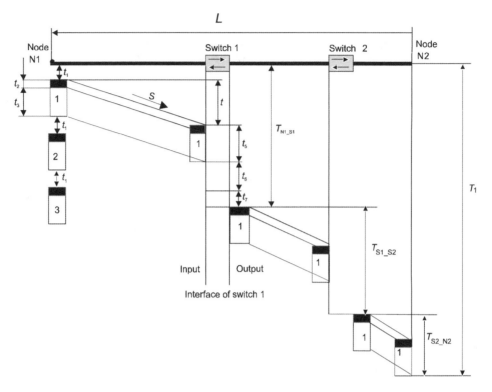

Figure 3.13 Time diagram for transmitting a single packet in the packet-switched network

The time required for transmitting a single packet from Node N1 to *Switch 1* can be represented as a sum of the following components:

■ In the source node, the time delay comprises the following components:
  ● t_1 — time required to form the packet. This time is also known as the packetizing time. The value of this delay depends on various parameters of the software and hardware of the sender node, and does not depend on the network parameters.
  ● t_2 — time required for sending the packet header into the channel.
  ● t_3 — time required for sending the packet data field into the channel.

■ Secondly, additional time is required for propagation of the signals through communications links. The time required for the signal representing one bit of information to propagate from node N1 to Switch 1 is denoted as t_4.

■ Third, some additional time is spent on the transit switch. It can be represented as a sum of the following components:
  ● t_5 — time required for receiving the packet with its header into the input buffer of the switch. As was already mentioned earlier, this time is equal to $(t_2 + t_3)$ — the time required for passing the packet with its header into the link from the source node.

- t_6 — time that the packet spends in the queue. This value can vary widely and is not known beforehand, since it depends on the current network load.
- t_7 — time required to switch the packet to the output port. This value is fixed for particular model of the switch and usually is rather small. It can range from several microseconds to several milliseconds.

The time required for passing the packet from node *N1* to the output interface of switch 1 is designated as T_{N1-S1}. This time is the sum of the following components:

$$T_{N1-S1} = t_1 + t_4 + t_5 + t_6 + t_7.$$

Note that t_2 and t_3 are missing from the list of the components. From Figure 3.13 it is obvious that bit transmission from the transmitter into the link coincides in time with bit transmission through the communication link.

The times required to transmit the packet through the remaining two route sections are designated accordingly — T_{S1-S2} and T_{S2-N2}. They have the same structure as T_{N1-S1}, except that they do not include the t_1 time component required to form the packet and, additionally, T_{S2-N2} does not include the switching time, because the section terminates with the end node. Thus, the total time required for transmitting a single packet through the network can be expressed as follows: $T_1 = T_{N1-S1} + T_{S1-S2} + T_{S2-N2}$.

How long, then, would it take us to transmit several packets? The sum of the times required for transmitting each packet? No! Recall that the packet-switched network operates as a pipeline (Figure 3.12). Packet processing happens in several stages, and all network devices accomplish these operations in parallel. Therefore, the time required to transmit such a message will be considerably shorter than the time required to transmit each packet individually. It is hard to compute this time precisely because of the uncertainty of the network state at any individual time instance. Consequently, the time that the packets will have to wait in the queues on the switches also is uncertain. However, based on the assumption that the packets wait in queues during approximately equal time intervals, it is possible to evaluate the total time T_{PS} required to transmit the message consisting from n packets as follows:

$$T_{PS} = T_1 + (n-1)(t_1 + t_5).$$

EXAMPLE   *Use the example shown in Figure 3.13 to perform a rough evaluation of the data transmission delay in packet-switched networks in comparison to circuit-switched networks. Assume that the text message that needs to be transmitted in both types of networks is about 200,000 bytes. The distance between sender and receiver is 5,000 km. The bandwidth of the communications links is 2 Mbps.*

The data transmission time in the circuit-switched network is made up of the following components:

■ *Signal propagation time that for the distance of 5,000 km can be roughly evaluated to be approximately 25 msec*
■ *Message transmission time, which for the given conditions (bandwidth equal to 2 Mbps and message size equal to 200,000 bytes) is approximately 800 msec*

This means that the total time required for transmitting this message is 825 msec. Now evaluate the extra time that will be needed to transmit the same message through the packet-switched network. Suppose that the route from the sender to the receiver includes ten switches. Furthermore, assume that the network does not operate under full load; therefore, there are no queues in the switches. The source message is split into 200 packets, 1,000 bytes each.

If we assume that the interval between each packet sending is equal to 1 msec, then additional delays caused by these intervals will come to about 200 msec. Thus, an additional delay for splitting the message into packets equal to 280 msec will arise in the source node. Suppose that the overhead information contained in the packet headers makes up approximately 10% of the total size of the message. Consequently, the additional delay related to the transmission of the packet headers makes up 10% of the total message transmission time (i.e., 80 msec). As messages pass through every switch, a buffering delay is introduced. For a packet length equal to 1,000 bytes and a communications link bandwidth equal to 2 Mbps, this value will be 4.4 msec for every switch. Furthermore, there is the switching delay. In this example, assume that switching takes approximately 2 msec. As a result, the packet that has passed 10 switches arrives with total delay equal to 64 msec due to buffering and switching. As a result, additional delay created by the packet-switched network will be 344 msec.

With the data transmission in the circuit-switched network at 825 msec, this additional delay can be considered significant. Although the calculation provided here is rather rough, it helps to clarify the reasons why, for individual users, the process of data transmission in packet-switched networks is often significantly slower than the same process in circuit-switched networks.

What conclusion can be drawn on the basis of this calculation? Are circuit-switched networks more efficient than the packet-switched networks?

When considering networks in general, it is not expedient to use the speed of transmission of an individual user's traffic as an efficiency criterion. Rather, it makes sense to use more integral criteria, such as *the total amount of data transmitted by the network per time unit*. According to this criterion, the efficiency of the packet-switched network will prove to be significantly higher than the efficiency of the circuit-switched network with the same bandwidth of communications links. This result was demonstrated in the 1960s both experimentally and analytically (based on the queuing theory).

EXAMPLE   *Compare the efficiency of circuit-switched and packet-switched networks using the simple example shown in Figure 3.14. Two switches are connected by the link with the bandwidth of 100 Mbps. Users are connected to the network through the access links characterized by the bandwidth of 10 Mbps. To simplify this argument, assume that all users create the same bursty traffic with the average rate of 1 Mbps. At the same time, for quite short time periods, the rate of this offered load increases to the maximum bandwidth of the access link (i.e., to 10 Mbps). Such periods never last for more than one second. To further simplify the comparison, suppose that all users connected to the S1 switch constantly need to transmit information to the users connected to the S2 switch.*

Assume that the network presented in Figure 3.14 is a circuit-switched network. Since peaks of the user traffic reach 10 Mbps, every user needs to establish a connection characterized by the bandwidth of 10 Mbps.

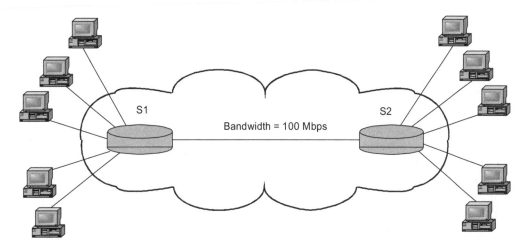

Figure 3.14 Comparison of the packet-switched and circuit-switched networks

Thus, only ten users will be able to simultaneously transmit data through the network. The total average rate of information transmission through this network will be equal to 10 Mbps. That is, ten users transmit the data at an average rate of 1 Mbps. Consequently, although the communications link between the switches has the bandwidth equal to 100 Mbps, only 10% of this bandwidth is actually used.

Now consider a situation in which the same network operates on the basis of packet switching. For the average data rate of the user traffic equal to 1 Mbps, the network is capable of simultaneously transmitting up to 100/1 = 100 information flows of user data, fully utilizing the bandwidth of the link connecting the two switches. However, this is true only for the cases when the switch buffer sizes is enough for storing the packets during the time of congestion, when the total rate of the data flow exceeds 100 Mbps. Try to roughly evaluate the required buffer size of the S1 switch. We know that each flow transmits the data at the maximum possible rate of 10 Mbps (limited by the access link bandwidth) for no longer than 1-second intervals. During this time, the flow will transmit 10 Mbit of user data, and in the worst-case scenario of network congestion, 100 such flows will arrive at the input interfaces of the S1 switch. The total amount of data supplied to the S1 switch during this time will be 1,000 Mbit. During the same period, the S1 switch will be able to transmit only 100 Mbit into the output link. Consequently, to ensure that no packet gets lost during network congestion, it is necessary to ensure that the S1 switch has input buffers no smaller than 1,000 − 100 = 900 Mbit, or approximately 100 MB. This memory size is quite large for the contemporary electronics industry. Most frequently, switches have smaller buffer sizes, between 1 and 10 MB. However, do not forget that the probability that the peak load periods will coincide for all flows is rather small. Therefore, even if the switch has smaller amount of buffer memory than the one required for the most difficult situation, in most cases, it will handle the offered load ensuring a higher quality of service for each flow.

Here, one can draw an analogy with multitasking operating systems. In such systems, each specific program or task runs longer than it does in a single-tasking system, where all processor time is allocated to the program until it terminates execution. However, the total number of programs executed per time unit in a multitasking system is significantly larger. Similar to a single-tasking operating system, in which either the processor or the peripheral devices are running idle from time to time, circuit-switched networks often do not use a significant part of the reserved channel bandwidth when transmitting bursty traffic.

The indeterminate throughput of the packet-switched network is the payment for its overall efficiency. Of course, the interests of individual users are somewhat infringed upon. Similarly, in multitasking operating systems, it is impossible to predict the application execution time, since it depends on the number of other applications with which this application must share the processor.

To conclude this section, look at a table summarizing the properties of both types of networks. Based on this information, one can make a well-grounded decision as to when it is more efficient to use circuit-switched networks and when packet-switched networks should be preferred.

Table 3.1 Properties of Circuit-Switched and Packet-Switched Networks

Circuit switching	Packet switching
Before starting the data transmission, it is necessary to establish connection.	Necessity of establishing a connection is not mandatory (datagram method).
Address is used only when establishing the connection (connection setup).	Address, along with other overhead information, is transmitted with each packet.
Network can deny the user request to establish a connection.	Network is always ready to receive user data.
Bandwidth is guaranteed for interacting users.	Information rate is not known for the individual user. Transmission delays are random.
Real-time traffic is transmitted without delays.	Network resources are efficiently used when transmitting bursty traffic.
High reliability of transmission.	Data loss because of buffer overflow is possible.
Inefficient use of the circuit bandwidth reduces overall network efficiency.	Possibility of automatic dynamical redistribution of the physical links bandwidth among all users according to the requirements of their traffic.

3.4 PACKET SWITCHING IN SHARED MEDIUM NETWORKS

KEY WORDS: shared medium, random access method, home PNA, Ethernet, FDDI, Token Ring, network adapters, network interface cards, monopolizing, determinate access method access token, marker, collision repeater, hub, concentrator, bridge, switch, physical network structure, logical network links, logical network structure, bottleneck, logical segment

Earlier in this chapter, we mentioned the principles of sharing a link between several interfaces, or, in other words, the principles of sharing medium. Now, let us explain how these principles work in packet-switched LANs.

Medium sharing has been the most popular LAN concept for a while: this principle is the basis of such popular technologies as Ethernet, FDDI, and Token Ring. However, it can be agreed that networks based on shared medium have already outlasted the peak of their popularity. Currently, switched Ethernet is prevalent in LANs. On the other hand, the networking world changes so rapidly that the evidence of reviving interest in shared medium technologies becomes increasingly noticeable.

Examples of new areas of shared medium application are home wired networks, as well as personal and local wireless networks. The Home PNA technology has emerged, developed specially for home users. This technology represents a modification of the standard Ethernet technology, where the home telephone or electric wiring is used as a shared medium. Personal radio networks based on Bluetooth technology, intended for interconnecting all high-tech personal devices (besides desktop computers, this list includes PDAs, mobile phones, high-tech TVs, and even refrigerators), also use the shared medium principle.

Furthermore, RadioEthernet LANs have emerged and are quickly gaining popularity. These networks are used for connecting users to the Internet in airports, railway stations, and other places where mobile users congregate in numbers. However, since nothing is ever truly new, recall that classical Ethernet originated from the ALOHA radio network developed at the University of Hawaii, in which a shared medium was tested for the first time. Simply, air did not appear as a possible medium in the Ethernet standards for a long time, although there always were some exotic products of specific companies available on the market. With the arrival of Radio Ethernet in the late 1990s, historical justice was restored.

3.4.1 Principles of Medium Sharing

A **shared medium** is a physical medium used for data transmission to which multiple end nodes of the network are connected directly, which they can use only by turns. This means that at any time, only one of the end nodes gets access to the shared medium and uses it for transmitting packets to another node connected to the same medium.

The list of possible types of shared media includes coaxial cable, twisted pair, optical fiber, and radio waves.

One of the possible approaches to medium sharing is the principle that serves as a basis for Ethernet technology, **random access method**. In this case, control over access to the communications line is decentralized: all network interfaces participate in this process. Particularly, in computers, access to a shared medium is provided by special controllers called **network adapters** or **network interface cards**.

Here is the idea of the random access method:

- Computers in such a network can transmit data through the network only if the medium is available, i.e., if no data exchange operations between computers are currently in progress, and there are no electric (or optical) signals on the medium.
- After making sure that the medium is available, the computer starts data transmission, thus **monopolizing** the medium. The time of exclusive access to the shared medium provided to a single node is limited by the time required for transmitting a single frame.
- When the frame is supplied to the shared medium, all network adapters simultaneously start receiving this frame. Each adapter inspects the destination address placed into one of the starting fields of the frame.
- If this address matches with adapter's own address, the frame is placed into the internal buffer of the network adapter. Thus, the destination computer receives the data intended for it.

When using random access method, situations are possible when two or more computers simultaneously decide that the network is free and start transmitting information. This situation, known as **collision**, represents an obstacle to correct data transmission through the network. Signals from several transmitters overlap, distorting the resulting signal. All network technologies based on a shared medium provide for an algorithm of detecting and correctly handling collisions. The probability of collisions depends on the traffic intensity.

After detecting a collision, the network adapters that tried to pass their frames stop transmission, pause for a random duration, then once again try to access the medium and retransmit the frame that caused the collision.

The **determinate access method** represents another way of accessing the shared medium. This method is based on using a frame of a special type, usually known as a **marker** or **access token**. The computer has the right to access the shared medium only when it owns the token. The time during which the computer can own the token is limited; therefore, after this interval elapses, the computer is obliged to pass the token to another computer.

The rule defining the order of token passing should ensure for each computer access to the shared medium during some fixed interval.

The determinate access method can be implemented using both centralized and decentralized approaches. In the first approach, the network does not contain any special node that defines the queue for accessing the shared medium; in the second case, there is such a node, known as an access arbitrator.

3.4.2 Reasons for LAN Structuring

The first LANs were made up of a small number of computers (usually, 10–30) and used a single shared medium common for all devices participating in the network. At the same time, because of technological limitations, networks had typical topologies — common bus (star) for Ethernet or ring for FDDI and Token Ring. These topologies are characterized by the property of homogeneity (i.e., computers in such a network are indistinguishable at the level of physical links). Such homogeneity of structure simplifies the procedure of increasing the number of computers. It also simplifies network operation and maintenance.

However, when building large-scale networks, a homogeneous structure of links becomes a drawback. In such networks, using typical structures becomes the source of limitations, the most important of which are the following:

■ Limitations on the length of the link between network nodes
■ Limitations on the number of network nodes
■ Limitations on the intensity of the traffic generated by network nodes

For example, Ethernet technology, based on thin coaxial cable, allowed the use of cable no longer than 185 meters to which it was possible to connect no more than 30 computers. However, when computers started intense information exchange, their number had to be reduced to 20 or even to 10. This was necessary to ensure that each computer received an acceptable share of the total channel bandwidth.

To remove these limitations, networks were structured on the basis of specialized structuring communications equipment:

■ Repeaters
■ Hubs
■ Bridges
■ Switches

3.4.3 Physical Structuring of LANs

It is necessary to distinguish between the topology of physical network links (**physical network structure**) and the topology of logical network links (**logical network structure**).

The configuration of physical links is defined by electric (or optic) connections between computers and can be represented in the form of a graph, whose nodes are computers and communications equipment, and whose ribs correspond to sections of cable connecting pairs of nodes. Logical links correspond to routes, along which information flows pass through the networks. They create the appropriate configuration of communications equipment.

In some cases, physical and logical network topologies coincide. For example, the network shown in Figure 3.15, a, has the ring physical topology. Assume that computers participating in this network are using a token access method. The token is always passed sequentially from computer to computer in the order corresponding to the one computers use to form a physical ring. This means that computer A passes the token to computer B, computer B passes it to computer C, and so on. In this case, the logical network topology represents the ring topology.

The network shown in Figure 3.15, b, illustrates the case in which physical and logical network topologies do not match. Physically computers are connected according to the common bus (star) topology. However, access to the bus does not follow the random access algorithm used in Ethernet technology. On the contrary, it takes place by passing the token in a ring order: from computer A to computer B, from computer B to computer C, and so on. Here, the order of passing the token does not reflect the order of the physical links; rather, it is determined by the logical configuring of the drivers of the network adapters. Nothing prevents us from configuring network adapters and their drivers in such a way as to make computers form the ring in another order, for example: B, A, C. However, for all that, the physical network structure does not change.

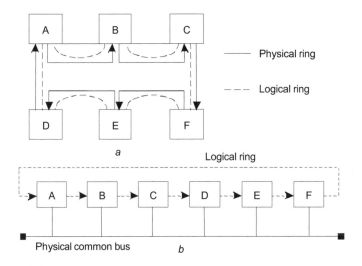

Figure 3.15 Logical and physical topologies of the network

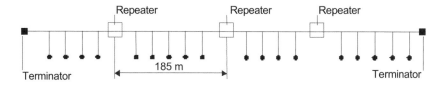

Figure 3.16 Repeaters allow the length of the Ethernet network to increase

Physical structuring of the common shared medium represented the first step toward building LANs of higher quality. The aim of physical structuring is to ensure the possibility of building the network from several physical sections of cable, rather than on the basis of a single section of cable. With all this going on, these physically different sections had to continue operating as a common shared medium (i.e., logically, they had to remain indistinguishable).

The main means of the physical structuring of LANs are repeaters and concentrators, or hubs.

A **repeater** is the simplest communications device used for physically connecting different segments of LAN cable to increase the total network length. Repeaters retransmit the signals coming from one network segment into other network segments (Figure 3.16), simultaneously improving their physical characteristics. For instance, a repeater amplifies the signal and improves its form and synchronism. The latter is done by correcting the unevenness of the intervals between pulses. In that way, the repeater overcomes the limitations for the length of communications links. Since the flow of signals transmitted by the node into the network propagates along all network segments, such a network retains the properties of the shared medium network.

A repeater that has several ports and connects several physical segments is often called a **concentrator** or **hub**. These names reflect that all links between network segments are concentrated in this device.

IMPORTANT   *Adding concentrators into the network always changes its physical topology but leaves its logical topology without changes.*

Concentrators are mandatory devices in practically all basic LAN technologies — Ethernet, Arcnet, Token Ring, FDDI, Fast Ethernet, Gigabit Ethernet, and 100VG-AnyLAN.[3]

---

[3] Not all of the listed technologies have retained their importance. For example, Arcnet and 100VG-AnyLAN can be considered only examples of original technical solutions.

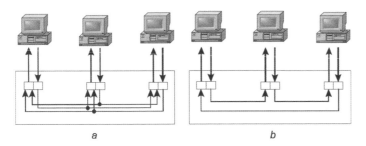

Figure 3.17 Concentrators of different technologies

It is necessary to emphasize that the operation of the concentrators of any technology have much in common. They repeat signals coming from one of their ports to their other ports. In fact, these ports repeat the incoming signals that make the difference. Thus, the Ethernet concentrator repeats input signals on all of its ports except the one from which the signals arrive (Figure 3.17, *a*). On the other hand, the Token Ring concentrator (Figure 3.17, *b*) repeats input signals arriving from some port on only one of its ports — namely, on the one to which the next computer in the ring is connected.

3.4.4 Logical Structuring of the Shared Medium Network

The physical structuring of a network is unable to overcome such important problems as the shortage of bandwidth and the impossibility of using communications links of different bandwidths in different network segments. In such a case, a logical structuring of a network could help.

A typical physical network topology (bus, ring, or star), which limits all network devices by providing them with a single shared medium for data exchange, proves to be inadequate for the structure of the information flows in a large-scale network. For example, in the common bus network, any couple of interacting computers monopolizes it for the entire time of data exchange. Therefore, as the number of computers in the network increases, the bus becomes a bottleneck.

EXAMPLE   *Suppose that an enterprise had an extremely simple Ethernet network, with just a single segment (Figure 3.18). All computers of the enterprise were connected to a coaxial cable. With time, the number of users increased, and the network became busy frequently. Therefore, users had to wait longer for network applications to respond. Besides this, limitations on the length of connection links between computers became increasingly noticeable, since it proved to be impossible to place all computers within the premises allocated to a new workgroup. A decision was made to use concentrators. The rebuilt network obtained as a result of this physical restructuring is shown in the top part of Figure 3.18. Now it became possible to place computers at larger distances, and the physical network structure was brought into accordance with the administrative structure of the enterprise. However, the problems related to performance remained unsolved. For example, any time the user of computer A sent the data to neighbor user B, the entire network was blocked. This is not surprising, since according to the logic of the concentrator operation, the frame sent by computer A to computer B was repeated on all interfaces of all network nodes. This meant that until computer B received the frame addressed to it, no other computer of this network was able to access the shared medium. This situation arose because the use of concentrators changed only the physical structure of the network, without changing its logical structure (lower part of Fig. 3.18), according to which the information continued to propagate the entire network, where all computers had equal rights to access the medium, independently of their location.*

The solution to this problem consists in abandoning the idea of using the shared medium common for all nodes. Thus, in the example considered in Figure 3.18, it would be desirable to ensure that frames transmitted by computers belonging to Department 1 never leave the limits of this part of the network, except when they are addressed to any computer belonging to another department. On the other hand, only those frames addressed to the nodes of the particular department must be passed to its network. Thus, within the limits of each department, a separate shared medium is used, "owned" by that department.

IMPORTANT *Propagation of the traffic intended for a specific network segment only within the limits of that segment is known as* traffic localization. *Logical structuring of the network is the process of dividing the network into the segments with localized traffic.*

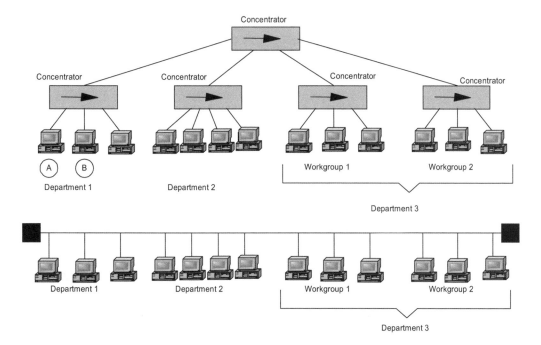

Figure 3.18 Physical structuring of the network did not improve network performance

Such an approach to network organization will significantly improve the performance of the network, since computers of one department will not have to wait while computers from other departments are exchanging data. Besides this, logical structuring allows the available bandwidth to be differentiated in different parts of the network.

Logical structuring of the network is achieved by using bridges, switches, routers, and gateways.

A **bridge** divides the shared medium into parts (often called **logical segments**) by transmitting information from segment to segment only when such a transmission is necessary, i.e., when the address of the destination computer belongs to another segment (Figure 3.19). By doing so, the bridge isolates the traffic of one segment from the traffic of another segment, thus improving overall performance of the network. Traffic localization not only uses the bandwidth more sparingly but also reduces the possibility of unauthorized access to the data. Since frames do not leave the limits of their segment, it becomes harder for intruders to intercept them.

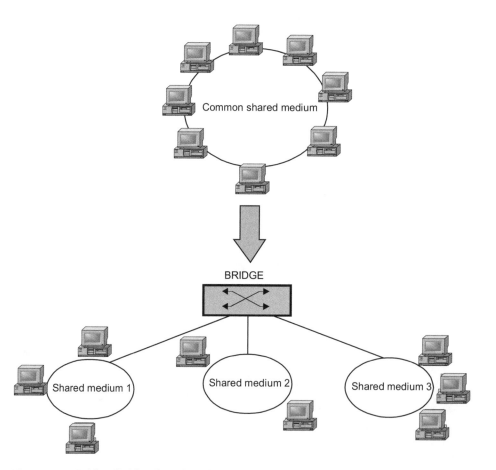

Figure 3.19 Bridge divides shared media

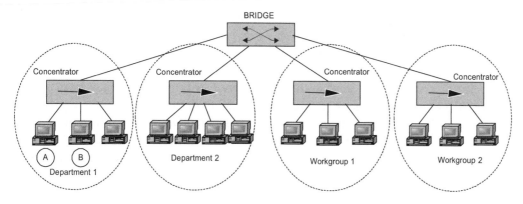

Figure 3.20 Logical structuring of the network: using the bridge, a common shared medium was separated into four separate shared media

Figure 3.20 shows the network obtained from the network with a central concentrator (see Fig. 3.19) by replacing the central concentrator with the bridge. The networks of Departments 1 and 2 comprise one logical segment each; the network of Department 3 has two logical segments. Each logical segment is based on the concentrator and has the simplest physical structure formed by cable sections connecting computers to the concentrator ports. If the user working on computer A sends the data to the user of computer B located within the same segment, this data will be repeated only on the network interfaces marked with circles.

For traffic localization, bridges use the hardware addresses of the computers. The question can be asked: How can the bridge know which interface it should forward the frame to? After all, hardware addresses do not contain any information about the segment to which the computer with the specific address might belong. Certainly, network administrator can specify this information to the bridge by manually configuring it. However, this method is not suitable for large-scale networks. The bridge solves this task automatically by implementing a simple learning algorithm.

All frames coming to a specific interface are generated by computers belonging to the segment connected to that interface. The bridge retrieves the sender addresses from the incoming frames and places them into a special table, which also specifies the interface to which the specific frame has arrived. Thus, the bridge determines which computers are connected to each of its interfaces. Later, the bridge uses this information for forwarding the frame exactly to that interface through which the route to the destination computer passes. Since the bridge does not know the exact topology of the links between the logical segments of the network, it can correctly operate only in those networks where intersegment links do not form loops.

The *LAN switch* is functionally similar to the bridge. (In this context, the term "switch" is used in a narrow sense, denoting a LAN switch.) Its main difference from the bridge lies in its higher performance. Each interface of the switch is equipped with a specialized processor that processes frames using the same algorithm as the one used in the bridge, independently of the processors of other ports. Because of this feature, the overall performance of the switch is usually significantly higher than that of the traditional bridge, which has a single processing unit. It is possible to say that switches are advanced bridges, processing frames in parallel mode. When the usage of specialized processors on each port of a communications device became economically justified, switches replaced bridges.

3.4.5 Ethernet as an Example of Standard Technology

Consider how the general approaches to solving the important problems encountered while building networks are implemented in one of the first standard network technologies: Ethernet based on a shared medium. In this section, we will consider only general principles, which form the foundation of one of the Ethernet variants. Detailed descriptions of all types of Ethernet, including switched Ethernet, will be provided in *Part III*.

Topology. The Ethernet standard strictly defines the topology of physical links — the *common bus* (Figure 3.21). This illustration shows the simplest implementation of this topology, comprising a single segment in which all network computers are connected to the common shared medium.

Switching method. The Ethernet uses datagram packet switching. In Ethernet, the data unit used in data exchange is denoted as a frame. Functionally, a frame is identical to a packet. A frame has a fixed format and, besides a data field, contains various overhead information.

And where is the switching network in the single-segment Ethernet? Is there at least one switch that, as was already mentioned, represents the main element of any packet-switched network? Perhaps Ethernet represents a special type of switching?

Actually, there is a switch in a single-segment Ethernet, though it is rather hard to detect since its functions are distributed over the entire network. This Ethernet "switch" comprises network adapters and a shared medium. Network adapters are the interfaces

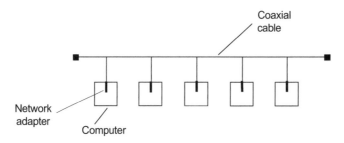

Figure 3.21 Ethernet network

of such a virtual switch; the shared medium plays the role of the switching unit that transmits frames between interfaces. Adapters also perform the functions of the switching unit, since they decide which frame is addressed to the local computer and which is not.

Addressing. Each computer — or, to be more precise, each network adapter — has a unique hardware address. This is the so-called MAC-address, mentioned earlier. An Ethernet address is a flat numeric address, since no hierarchy is used here. The following types of addresses are supported: unicast, broadcast, and multicast.

Medium sharing and multiplexing. End nodes use a single shared medium for data exchange, using the random access method.

Information flows coming from end nodes of the Ethernet are multiplexed in a single transmission link on the basis of time-sharing. This means that frames belonging to different flows get access to the link by turns. To emphasize the difference between the concepts of multiplexing and medium sharing, which is not always obvious, consider the situation in which only one of computers connected to the Ethernet needs to transmit data, which generally are produced by several applications. In this case, the problem of sharing the medium between network interfaces does not arise; the problem of transmitting several information flows through a common link (i.e., the multiplexing problem) remains.

Encoding. Ethernet adapters operate at a clock frequency of 20 MHz, transmitting into the medium rectangular pulses corresponding to binary ones and zeros. When frame transmission starts, all its bits are transmitted into the network at a constant rate equal to 10 Mbps. The transmission of each bit takes two clocks. This rate is the link bandwidth in the Ethernet.

Reliability. To improve the reliability of data transmission, Ethernet uses standard techniques. These include calculating the checksum and transmitting it in the frame trailer. If the receiving adapter detects an error in the frame data by recalculating the checksum, then such a frame is discarded. Ethernet protocol does not retransmit the frame; this task is delegated to other technologies (e.g., to the TCP protocol in TCP/IP networks).

Half-duplex transmission method. The Ethernet shared medium represents a half-duplex communications channel. Actually, the network adapter cannot use this channel simultaneously for both transmitting and receiving data. These tasks have to be accomplished in turn.

Queues. At first, it might seem that in the Ethernet based on a shared medium there are no queues characteristic for packet-switched networks. However, the lack of a switch with buffer memory in such networks does not mean that there are no queues. Simply, in this case, the queues have been moved into the buffer memory of the network adapters. When the medium is busy transmitting frames of other network adapters, the data (offered load) continue to arrive at the network adapter. Since at that time the data cannot be transmitted into the network, they start to accumulate in the internal buffer of the Ethernet adapter, thus forming a queue. Therefore, similar to all other packet-switched networks, variable delays in frame delivery exist in the Ethernet.

However, the Ethernet also has its specific feature. Shared medium is a kind of regulator of the rate of frame transmission, and when it is busy, it does not receive other frames. Thus, the network implements back pressure when it gets heavily overloaded, thereby forcing the end nodes to decrease the rate of transmitting data into the network.

SUMMARY

▶ In circuit-switched networks, continuous information channels known as circuits are created on the requests of users. The circuit is formed, reserving a chain of communications links connecting users during the time of data transmission. Along its entire length, the circuit transmits data at a constant rate. This means that a circuit-switched network can ensure the high-quality transmission of delay-sensitive data (voice and video) known as real-time traffic. However, the impossibility of dynamically redistributing the bandwidth of the physical link represents a limitation of the circuit-switched network. This limitation makes such networks inefficient when transmitting bursty traffic typical for computer networks.

▶ When using packet switching, the source node divides the data to be transmitted into small fragments known as packets. The packet is supplied with the header specifying the destination address. Therefore, it can be processed by the switch independently of other data. The packet-switching method improves network performance when transmitting bursty traffic, because when serving a large number of independent flows, their activity periods do not always match. Packets are transmitted into the network without having previously reserved resources at the rate at which they are generated by the source. However, this switching method has its dark side: transmission delays are random in nature; therefore, the problems arise in the course of transmission of real-time traffic.

▶ Packet-switched networks can use one of three forwarding algorithms: without establishing a connection (connectionless), also known as datagram transmission; connection oriented; and virtual circuit.

▶ A shared medium is a physical medium for data transmission (coaxial cable, twisted pair, optic fiber, or radio waves) to which a specific number of the end nodes of the network is connected directly, which they can use only in turn. The shared medium principle forms a basis for such well-known technologies as Ethernet, FDDI, and Token Ring. Although it might seem that networks based on a shared medium have outlasted the peak of their popularity, there are obvious signs of reviving interest in this technology. For example, such newer technologies as home wired networks and personal and local wireless networks use the shared medium principle.

REVIEW QUESTIONS

1. What types of multiplexing and switching are used in telephone networks?
2. Which properties of circuit-switched networks can be considered drawbacks?
3. Which properties of packet-switched networks negatively affect the transmission of multimedia information?
4. Is buffering used in circuit-switched networks?
5. Which element of the circuit-switched network can deny the node requesting to establish circuit?
   A. None, the network is always ready to receive data from a user
   B. Any transit node
   C. The destination node
6. Which concepts are characteristic for the Ethernet technology?
7. Do datagram networks take into account the existing flows?
8. Give a definition of a logical connection.
9. Is it possible to provide a reliable data transfer without a logical connection between end nodes?
10. Which logical connections could be named as a virtual circuit?
11. Which networks use the virtual circuit technology?
12. Specify which of the devices listed here are functionally similar:
    A. Hub
    B. Switch
    C. Concentrator
    D. Repeater
    E. Router
    F. Bridge
13. List the differences of a bridge and a switch.
14. Is the following statement true? Ethernet built according to the star topology with the hub in the center is more reliable than the same network built on coaxial cable with the common bus topology.
15. How could you increase the bandwidth available to each end-user computer in a network built on hubs?

PROBLEMS

1. Determine how the data transmission time will increase in the packet-switched network as compared to the circuit-switched network given the following data:
   - Total size of transmitted data — 200 KB
   - Total length of the connection link — 5,000 km
   - Assumed signal propagation speed — 0.66 light speed
   - Link bandwidth — 2 Mbps
   - Packet size (without header size) — 4 KB
   - Header size — 40 bytes
   - Interpacket interval — 1 msec
   - Number of transit switches — 10
   - Switching time in each switch — 2 msec

   Assume that the network operates in the underloaded mode. Therefore, there are no queues in the switches.

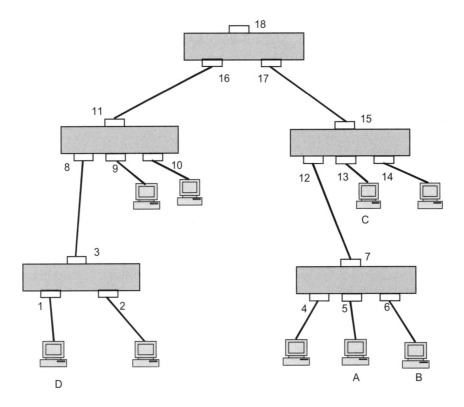

Figure 3.22 Fragment of the network

2. If all communications devices in the network fragment shown in Figure 3.22 are concentrators, on which ports will the frame sent from computer A to computer B appear?

    1. 5 and 6
    2. 4, 5, and 6
    3. 4, 5, 6, and 7
    4. 4, 5, 6, 7, and 12
    5. On all ports

3. Provided that all communications devices in the network fragment in Figure 3.22 represent switches, on which port will the frame sent from computer A to computer B appear?

4. If all communications devices in the network fragment in Figure 3.22 are switches, except one concentrator to which computers A and B are connected, on which ports will the frame sent from computer A to computer D appear?

5. In a datagram network, between nodes A and B there are three flows and three alternate routes. Is it possible to forward each flow via a different route?

6. In a virtual circuit network, between nodes A and B there are three flows and three alternate routes. Is it possible to forward each flow via a different route?

7. A network is based on a shared medium with the bandwidth of 10 Mbps and comprises 100 nodes. What will be the maximum exchange rate between two computers in such a network?

8. A network can transmit data in two modes: datagram and virtual circuit. What would you take into account when choosing a specific mode for transmitting your data, if the main criteria are the speed and reliability of data delivery?

9. Do you think circuit-switched networks will soon be replaced by packet-switched networks? Or the contrary, that packet-switched networks will be replaced by circuit-switched networks? Or that the technologies will coexist? Provide arguments that support your opinion. Consider various areas of application for these technologies.

4

NETWORK ARCHITECTURE AND STANDARDIZATION

CHAPTER OUTLINE

4.1 INTRODUCTION

Network architecture is a representation of the network as a system composed of various elements, each of which performs a specific function. All network elements coordinate their operations to solve the common task of interaction among computers. In other words, network architecture decomposes a common problem into a set of subproblems that need to be solved by individual network components. One of the most important elements of the network architecture is the **communications protocol**. This can be defined as a formalized set of rules of interaction among network nodes.

The development of the Open Systems Interconnection (OSI) was a breakthrough in the standardization of the computer network architecture. This model, developed in the early 1980s, summarized all the accumulated experience of that time. The OSI model represents an international standard, defining the method of *vertically* decomposing the problem of computer interaction by delegating this task to communications protocols, which were divided into seven layers. Communications protocol layers form a hierarchy, known as a **protocol stack**, in which each layer uses the underlying layer as a convenient instrument for solving its tasks.

Currently used protocol stacks (or the ones popular until recently) generally reflect the OSI model architecture. However, each protocol stack has specific features and differences from the OSI architecture. Thus, the most popular TCP/IP stack comprises four layers rather than seven.

Standard architecture of computer networks also determines the distribution of protocols among network elements, such as end nodes (computers) and transit nodes (switches and routers). Transit nodes support only a limited subset of the protocol stack functions; they carry out transport functions by transmitting network traffic between end nodes. End nodes support the entire protocol stack, since they have to provide information services such as the Web service. Such distribution of functions moves intellectual network functions to the network periphery.

4.2 DECOMPOSITION OF NETWORK NODE INTERACTION

> **KEY WORDS**: decomposition, module, protocol, multilayer approach, service interface, interlayer interface, peer-to-peer interface, protocol stack, protocol set, protocol suite

Organizing interaction between network devices is a complicated task. The most common, well-known, and universal approach to solving any complicated task consists of its **decomposition** (i.e., dividing a single complicated problem into several simpler tasks or modules). Decomposition implies the strict definition of the functions of each module, as well as of the way they interact. This is known as an intermodule interface. When using

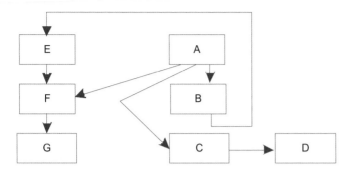

Figure 4.1 Example of the problem of decomposition

this approach, each module can be considered a *black box* by abstracting it from its internal mechanisms and concentrating all attention on the way they interact. By logically simplifying this problem, it becomes possible to develop, modify, and test each module independently. Thus, each of the modules shown in Figure 4.1 can be rewritten without modifying other modules. Consider module A. Provided that the developers leave intermodule interfaces without changes (in this case, these will be the A–B and A–C interfaces), no changes to other modules will be required.

4.2.1 Multilayer Approach

The **multilayer approach** is an even more efficient concept. After representing the initial task as a set of modules, these modules are grouped and ordered by layers, forming a hierarchy. Using the hierarchical principle for each intermediate layer, it is possible to specify directly the adjoining layers above and below it (Figure 4.2).

The group of modules forming each layer must request services only from the modules of the underlying layer when carrying out their tasks. They must pass the results of their operation only to the modules belonging to the layer directly above them. Such a hierarchical decomposition assumes clear definitions of functions and interfaces not only for specific modules but also for each layer.

The **interlayer interface**, also known as a **service interface**, defines the set of functions that the underlying layer provides to the layer directly above it (Figure 4.3).

This approach allows the development, testing, and modification of specific layers independent of other layers. By moving from lower layers to higher ones, hierarchical decomposition allows the creation of more abstract and, consequently, simpler representations of the initial problems.

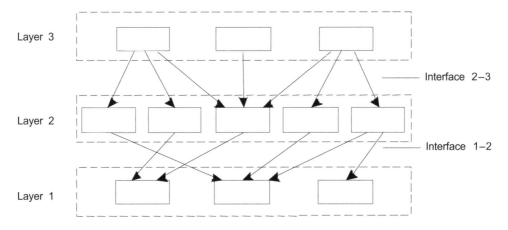

Figure 4.2 Multilayer approach — creating a hierarchy of tasks

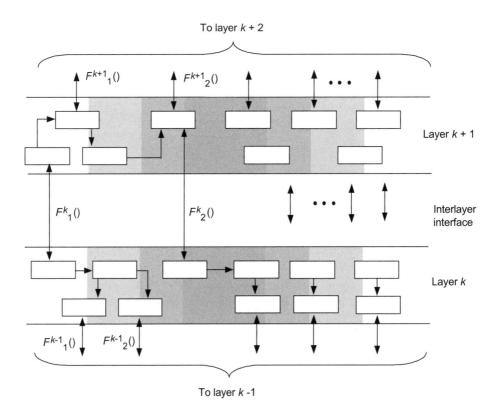

Figure 4.3 Concept of multilayer interaction

EXAMPLE *Consider the simplified description of the task consisting of reading a logical record from the file stored on the hard disk. This task can be represented as a hierarchy of the following particular tasks:*

1. *Using a symbolic file name, search for the file characteristics required for accessing the data. These can be the physical location of the file, its size, etc. Since functions of this layer relate only to directory lookup, the representation of file systems at this layer is rather abstract. A file system is represented as a tree whose nodes are directories (folders) and whose leaves represent files. No other details of physical or logical data organization on the hard disk are of any interest to this layer.*

2. *Next, it is necessary to determine the specific part of the file that needs to be read. To accomplish this task, go to the lower abstraction layer of the file system. The functions of this layer interpret files as sets of physical disk blocks related to one another in specific ways.*

3. *Finally, read the required data from the disk. After determining the physical block number, the file system requests the input/output system to accomplish the read operation. At this level, it is already necessary to deal with such file system details as the numbers of cylinders, tracks, and sectors.*

For example, among the functions that applications might call when requesting the highest layer of the file system, there might be one like this: READ THE 22ND LOGICAL RECORD FROM THE FILE NAMED DIR1/MY/FILE.TXT.

The upper layer of abstraction is incapable of performing this request on its own. Having defined the physical address of the file by its symbolic name (DIR1/MY/FILE.TXT), it sends the following request to the underlying layer: READ THE 22ND LOGICAL RECORD FROM THE FILE LOCATED BY THE FOLLOWING PHYSICAL ADDRESS: 174 AND HAVING THE SIZE EQUAL TO 235.

In response to this request, the second layer determines that the file with address 174 takes up five nonadjacent areas on the disk, and that the required record is located in the fourth file fragment located in physical block 345. Then it sends the request to the disk driver to read the required logical record.

According to our simplified method, the interaction between file system layers was unidirectional, from top to bottom. However, the real situation is much more complicated. To determine file characteristics, the top layer must decode the symbolic file name (i.e., sequentially read the entire path of directories specified in the fully qualified file name). This means that the top layer must send a request to the underlying layer more than once. The underlying layer must ask the disk driver several times to read the directory structure data from the physical disk. Each time, the results of the accomplished operations will be passed from bottom to top.

The problem of organizing the interaction between computers using the network also can be represented as a set of hierarchically organized modules. For example, the tasks of ensuring reliable data transmission between neighboring nodes can be delegated to the modules of the lower layer. Modules at higher levels can undertake message transportation within the entire network. Obviously, the latter task — organizing the interaction between any two network nodes, not necessarily adjacent ones — is more general. Therefore, this issue can be accomplished using multiple requests to the underlying layer. Thus, the organization of the interaction between nodes A and B (Figure 4.4) can be reduced to sequentially connecting the pair of transit nodes.

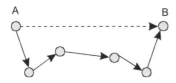

Figure 4.4 Connecting any pair of network nodes

4.2.2 Protocol and Protocol Stack

Multilayer representation of network tools has specific features, since at least *two parties* are involved in the process of message exchange. This means that in this particular case, it is necessary to organize coordinated operation of two hierarchies of network tools running on two computers. Both participants of the network exchange must accept several agreements. For example, they must agree about the levels and forms of electric signals, the method of determining message size, and the methods of error detection. In other words, agreements have to be made at all layers, from the lowest one — the bit transmission layer — to the highest layer implementing services for network users.

Figure 4.5 illustrates the model of interaction between two nodes. On each part, the interconnection tools are represented by four layers. Each layer supports two types of interfaces. First, there are service interfaces to upper and lower layers of the local hierarchy of network tools. Second, there must be an interface to the interaction tools of the other party, located at the same hierarchical level. This type of interface is known as a **protocol**. Thus, the protocol always represents a **peer-to-peer interface**.

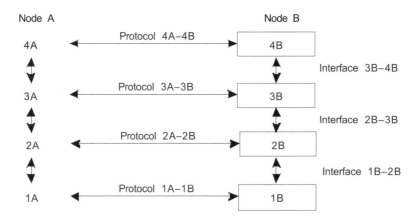

Figure 4.5 Interaction between two nodes

NOTE   *Principally, the terms protocol and interface mean the same thing, namely, formalized descriptions of the procedure of interaction between two objects. However, in networks, they traditionally have different fields of application: protocols define the rules of interaction between the same-layer modules running on different nodes, and interfaces define the rules of interaction between the modules of adjacent layers within the same node.*

A hierarchically organized set of protocols sufficient for implementing network node interaction is known as a **protocol stack** (or a **protocol set** or **protocol suite**).

Lower-layer protocols often are implemented as a combination of hardware and software; higher-level protocols have software-only implementation.

A software module implementing a specific protocol is known as **protocol entity** or simply a protocol. The same protocol can be implemented more or less efficiently. This is why it is necessary to account for both the protocol operation logic and the quality of implementation when comparing different protocols. Furthermore, *the efficiency of interaction among network devices depends on the quality of the entire set of protocols that form the protocol stack.* In particular, it is necessary to evaluate how efficiently the functions are distributed among protocols of different layers and how clearly the interfaces between protocol layers are defined.

Same-layer protocol entities of two interacting parties exchange messages according to the protocol rules. Usually, messages comprise the header and the data field (sometimes, it can be left blank). Message exchange is a kind of language the parties use to *explain* to each other what should be done at each stage of the interaction. The operation of each protocol module consists of interpreting the headers of incoming messages and accomplishing the related actions. Message headers of different protocols have different structures that correspond to the differences in their functionality. The more complicated the structure of the message header, the more sophisticated the functions delegated to the corresponding protocol.

4.3 OSI MODEL

KEY WORDS: Organization for Standardization (ISO), ITU Telecommunication Standardization Sector (ITU-T), Open Systems Interconnection (OSI), reference model, application programming interface (API), header, trailer, frame, packet, datagram, frame, segment, message, Protocol Data Unit (PDU), physical layer, data link layer, network layer, transport layer, session layer, presentation layer, application layer, point-to-point protocols, Frame Check Sequence (FCS), Medium Access Control (MAC), internet, internetwork, internetworking, network or global addresses, router, routing, routing tables, routed and routing protocols

The protocol represents an agreement accepted by two interacting network nodes, but this does not necessarily serve as evidence that this protocol is a standard one. However, in practice, network architects make every effort to use standard protocols when implementing networks. These protocols might be of proprietary, national, or international standards.

In the early 1980s, several international standards organizations, including the **International Organization for Standardization (ISO)** and **ITU Telecommunication Standardization Sector (ITU-T)**, developed the **Open Systems Interconnection (OSI)**. This model plays an extraordinary role in the further development of computer networks.

4.3.1 General Characteristics of the OSI Model

By the end of the 1970s, there existed a large number of proprietary stacks of communications protocols, examples of which are DECnet and System Network Architecture (SNA). This variety of internetworking tools made clear the incompatibility of devices using different protocols. By that time, one of the possible ways of overcoming this problem seemed to lie in migration to the usage of unified, common protocol stacks created to account for the drawbacks of the existing protocol stacks. Such an academic approach to the development of the new protocol stack originated from the development of the OSI model. The OSI model does not contain descriptions of any specific protocol stack since its aim is different — to provide a generalized description of internetworking tools. The OSI model was developed as a kind of universal language for networking specialists. Because of this, it is often called a **reference model**. The development of the OSI model took seven years (from 1977 to 1984).

The OSI model defines the following:

■ Intercommunication layers of the systems in packet-switched networks
■ Standard names for these layers
■ Functions that have to be accomplished by each layer

In the OSI model (Figure 4.6), intercommunication tools are divided into seven layers: the application layer, presentation layer, session layer, transport layer, network layer, data link layer, and physical layer. Each layer deals with a strictly defined aspect of internetworking.

IMPORTANT *The OSI model describes only* system *tools implemented by the operating system, system utilities, and system hardware. This model does not include the tools for interaction among user applications. It is important to distinguish between the level of interaction among applications and the application layer of the OSI model.*

Applications can implement their own interaction protocols using the seven-layer set of system tools. Especially for this purpose, a special **application programming interface (API***)* is provided to programmers. According to the canonic design of the OSI model, the application can send its requests to the topmost level of the hierarchy — the application layer. In practice, however, most stacks of communications protocols provide programmers with the possibility of directly calling upon the lower-layer services.

For example, some DBMSs have built-in tools for remote file access. In this case, the application does not use the system file service when accessing the remote resource. Instead, it bypasses the upper layers of the OSI model and directly requests the system tools responsible for message transportation, which reside at the lower layers of the OSI model.

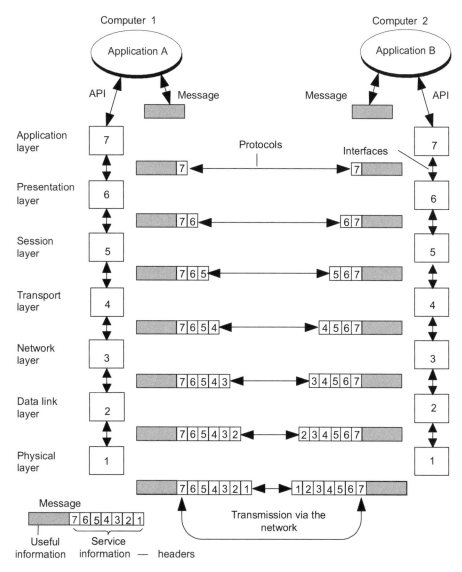

Figure 4.6 ISO/OSI model

Suppose that the application A running on computer 1 needs to communicate with the application B running on computer 2. To achieve this, application A requests an application-layer service, for example, the file service. Based on this request, the application-layer software forms a message in the standard format. However, to deliver this information to the destination, it is necessary to accomplish several other tasks, the responsibility for which is delegated to the underlying layers.

After forming a message, the application layer directs it down the stack to the presentation layer. The presentation-layer protocol, based on the information received from the **header** of the application-layer message, accomplishes the required actions and adds its own information to the message — the presentation-layer header. The presentation-layer header contains instructions for the presentation-layer protocol of the target machine. The resulting message is then passed to the underlying session layer, which, in turn, adds its header, and so on. Some protocol implementations place their own information not only into the beginning of the message, in the form of a header, but also at the end of the message, into the so-called **trailer**. Finally, the message reaches the lowest physical layer, the one that actually sends it to the target machine using connection links. By this time, the message carries the headers of all layers (Figure 4.7).

The physical layer places the message to the output interface of computer 1, from where it starts its travel through the network. Note that until this moment, the message was passed from layer to layer within computer 1.

When the message is delivered to computer 2, it is received by its physical layer and is sequentially passed upward, layer by layer. Each layer inspects the header of its own layer, accomplishes the required functions, then deletes the header and passes the message to the next layer.

It becomes clear that protocol entities of the same layer never communicate directly. This interaction is always mediated by the tools of the underlying-layer protocols. Only physical layers of different nodes interact directly.

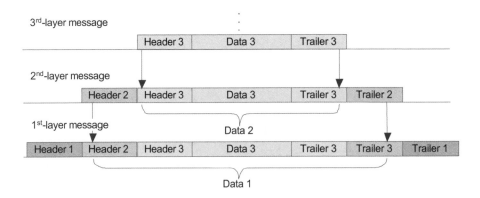

Figure 4.7 Nesting of the messages of different layers

Beside the term **message**, there are other terms used by networking professionals to denote the units of data exchange. In ISO standards, there exists a general name for data exchange units dealing with the protocols of different layers — **Protocol Data Unit (PDU)**. Specialized terms are often used for denoting data exchange units of different layers: **frame, packet, datagram**, and **segment**.

4.3.2 Physical Layer

The **physical layer** deals with transmission of the byte stream using physical links such as coaxial cable, twisted pair cable, fiber-optic cable, or a long-distance digital circuit. We already considered the basic properties of this layer in *Chapter 2* (see the section titled *"Problems of Physical Data Transmission using Communications Links"*).

The functions of the physical layer are implemented in all devices connected to the network. On the part of computer, the functions of the physical layer are accomplished either by network adapter or by serial port.

The 10Base-T specification of Ethernet technology can serve as an example of the physical layer protocol. This specification defines the unshielded twisted pair of Category 3 with the impedance of 100 ohm as a cable, an RJ-45 jack, a maximum segment length of 100 meters, the Manchester code for data representation in the wire, and other characteristics of the transmission medium and electric signals.

The physical layer does not go into the meaning of the information it transmits. From its point of view, this information represents a uniform stream of bits that need to be delivered to the destination point without distortions and according to the specified clock frequency (the predefined interval between adjacent bits).

4.3.3 Data Link Layer

The **data link layer** is the first layer (from bottom to top) that operates in packet-switching mode. At this layer, the PDU is usually called a **frame**.

For LANs and WANs, the data link-layer functions are defined differently. By the time the OSI model was under construction, LAN and WAN technologies were so dissimilar that it proved impossible to generalize their operations unconditionally. Thus, the data link-layer tools must provide the following functions:

■ **In LANs** — ensure frame delivery between *any* two network nodes. It is assumed that the network has a typical topology, such as the common bus, ring, star, or tree (hierarchical star). Examples of networks whose use is limited to standard topologies include Ethernet, FDDI, and Token Ring.

■ **In WANs** — ensure frame delivery only between two *neighboring* nodes connected by individual communications links. Examples of **point-to-point protocols** (as such protocols are often called) include such widely known protocols as PPP and HDLC. Based on the point-to-point links, it is possible to build networks of any topology.

For interconnecting LANs or for ensuring message delivery between any two nodes of a WAN, it is necessary to use networking tools of a higher layer.

One of the functions performed by the data link layer is *support for interfaces* to the underlying physical layer and to the next higher (network) layer. The network layer directs packets that need to be transmitted using the network to the data link layer and receives from it packets that have arrived from the network. The physical layer is used by the data link layer as a tool that either receives a sequence of bits from the network or transmits the sequence of bits into the network.

Consider the operation of the data link layer, starting from the moment the sender's network layer addresses the data link layer and sends it a packet with the destination node address. To accomplish this task, the data link layer creates a frame that contains the data field and the header. The data link layer encapsulates the packet into the frame data field and fills the frame header with the appropriate service information. The destination address that will be used by network switches for packet forwarding is the most important information in the frame header.

Error detection and correction is another task of the data link layer. To achieve this, the data link layer fixes the frame boundaries by placing a special sequence of bits into its beginning and into its end. After that, the data link layer adds a special checksum to the frame, also known as the **Frame Check Sequence (FCS)**. The checksum is calculated according to a certain algorithm as a function of all bytes making up the frame. Using the FCS value, the destination node will be able to determine whether or not the frame data was corrupted during transmission through the network.

However, before passing the frame to the physical layer for transmission through the network, the data link layer might need to solve another important problem. If the network uses a shared medium, then, before the physical layer starts data transmission, the data link layer has to *check medium availability* (when a shared medium is not used, such a check is omitted). The functions implementing the availability check for a shared medium are sometimes classified as a separate sublayer — **Medium Access Control (MAC)**.

If the shared medium has been released, the frame is passed into the network by the physical layer, travels using communications links, and arrives at the physical layer of the destination node in the form of a bit sequence. This layer, in turn, passes the received bits *upward* to the data link layer of the destination node. The latter layer groups bits into frames, recalculates the checksum of the received data, and compares the result to the frame checksum. If the checksum values match, the frame is considered correct. If the checksum values do not match, an error is reported. Data link-layer functions include both error detection and error correction by retransmitting corrupted frames. However, this function is not mandatory. Some data link-layer implementations, such as Ethernet, Token Ring, FDDI, and Frame Relay, lack this feature.

Data link-layer protocols are implemented by computers, bridges, switches, and routers. In computers, the data link-layer functions are implemented by the coordinated operation of network adapters and their drivers.

The data link-layer protocol usually operates within a network that represents a fragment of a larger network, joined by the protocols of a network layer. Data link-layer addresses are used for frame delivery only within a network; addresses of the higher (network) layer are used for packet forwarding between networks.

In LANs, the data link layer represents a rather powerful and complete set of functions for message forwarding between network nodes. In some cases, the LAN data link-layer protocols are self-sufficient transport tools and may allow application-layer protocols or applications to operate directly over them. In this case, there is no need to use the tools of the network layer or transport layer. Nevertheless, to ensure the high-quality transmission of messages in networks with arbitrary topology, the data link-layer functions are insufficient. This statement is even truer for WANs, where data link-layer protocols implement the simple function of data transmission between nearest-neighbor nodes. In the OSI model, these tasks are delegated to the next two higher layers — network and transport.

4.3.4 Network Layer

The network layer creates the unified transport system joining several networks, also known as the **internetwork**, or **internet** for short. Do not confuse the terms *internet* and *Internet*. The Internet is the best-known implementation of the internetwork built on the basis of the TCP/IP technology and spanning the entire world.

> The technology for the connection of a large number of networks, which in general are built on different technologies, into a single network is known as **internetworking**.

Figure 4.8 shows several networks, each using specific data link technology: Ethernet, FDDI, Token Ring, ATM, and Frame Relay. Based on these technologies, each of these networks can connect any two users within a local network, but one network is unable to ensure data transmission to another network. The reason for this is obvious: the significant differences of network technologies. Even the most similar LAN technologies — Ethernet, FDDI, and Token Ring — implementing the same addressing system (MAC sublayer addresses, known as MAC addresses) have different frame formats and logic of protocol operation. LAN and WAN technologies have even more differences. Most WAN technologies use the technique of previously establishing virtual circuits, the identifiers of which are used as addresses. All technologies use specific frame formats. The ATM frame even has a specific term to denote this — **cell**. Certainly, they all have their own protocol stacks.

To connect networks based on such dissimilar technologies, *additional tools are required*. It is the network layer of the OSI model that provides such tools.

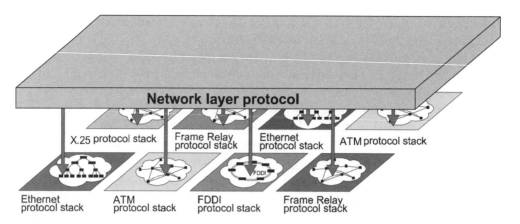

Figure 4.8 Necessity of the network layer

Network-layer functions are implemented by:

■ Group of protocols
■ Special devices known as *routers*

Ensuring the *physical connection of different networks* is one of the functions of the **router**. The router has several network interfaces similar to computer interfaces, each of which can be connected to one network. Thus, all router interfaces can be considered nodes of different networks. Routers can be implemented as a software module on the basis of a universal computer. For example, the typical configuration of UNIX or Windows includes a software router. However, most frequently, routers are implemented on the basis of specialized hardware platforms. Router software includes protocol entities of the network layer.

Thus, to interconnect the networks shown in Figure 4.8, it is necessary to connect all these networks using routers and to install network-layer protocol entities on all end-user computers that need to communicate using the internetwork (Figure 4.9).

Data that needs to be transmitted using the internetwork arrive to the network layer from the upper transport layer, after which they are complemented by the network-layer header. The data and the header form a *packet* — the common term for denoting the network-layer PDU. The header of the network-layer packet has a unified format. This format does not depend on the formats of the data link-layer frames, which are specific for the networks that might be part of the internet. Along with other information, this header contains the destination address of this packet.

To ensure that network-layer protocols are able to deliver packets to any node of the internetwork, it is necessary to ensure that each node has an address that is unique within the limits of this internetwork. Such addresses are called **network addresses** or **global addresses**. Each node of the internetwork that has to exchange data with other internet nodes must have a network address, along with the address assigned to it by the data link-layer

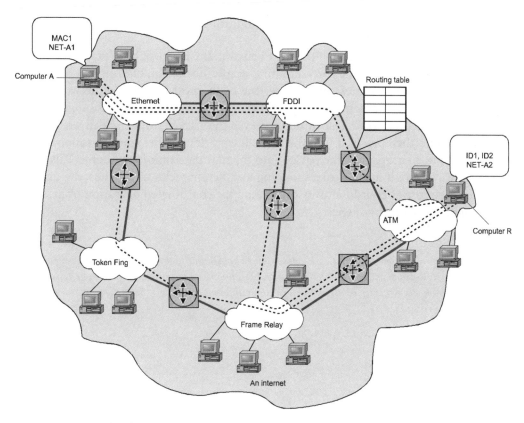

Figure 4.9 Example of internet

technology. For example, in Figure 4.9, a computer within the Ethernet within the inter-network has the *MAC1* data link-layer address and the *NET-A1* network-layer address. Similarly, the node in the ATM network addressed by the *ID1, ID2* virtual circuit identifiers has the *NET-A2* network address. The network-layer packet must specify the network-layer address as a destination address. The packet route will be determined on the basis of this address.

Routing is an important task of the network layer. The route is described by a sequence of networks (or routers) through which the packet must pass to be delivered to the destination node. Figure 4.9 shows three routes along which the data can be transmitted from computer A to computer B. The router collects information on the topology of the internetwork links and creates switching tables on the basis of this topology. Note that in this case, these switching tables have a special name — **routing tables**. The task of selecting a route was briefly explained in *Chapter 2* (see the "*Generalized Switching Problem*" section).

According to the multilayer approach, the network layer appeals to the underlying data link layer to accomplish its tasks. The entire path through the internet is divided into sections, each section corresponding to the path through the specific network, from router to router.

To transmit the packet through the next network, the network layer places the packet into the data field of the frame corresponding to specific data link technology and specifies the data link-layer address of the interface of the next router. The network, using appropriate data link-layer technology, delivers the frame with its encapsulated packet using the specified address. The router retrieves the packet from the delivered frame, processes it, and then passes it into the next network for further transportation. Before doing so, it must encapsulate the packet into the new data link-layer frame. This frame might have a different format corresponding to different technology. Thus, the network layer plays the role of coordinator by organizing the coordinated operation of networks based on dissimilar technologies.

EXAMPLE   *The operation of the network layer is somewhat similar to that of an international postal service, such as DHL or TNT (Figure 4.10). Suppose that some goods need to be delivered from city A to city B, which are located on different continents. For delivering the goods,*

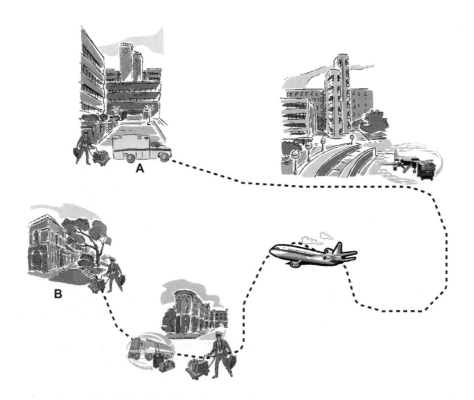

Figure 4.10 Operation of the international postal service

the international postal service might use the services provided by different regional service providers, including:

- *Railroad*
- *Sea transport*
- *Airline companies*
- *Motor transport*

These transport companies can be considered analogous to the data link-layer networks, each network being built on the basis of specific technology. The international postal service must organize the unified, well-coordinated network from these regional service providers. To achieve this, the international postal service must first plan the route for the transportation of goods and then coordinate the operation at the points where regional service providers are changed. This can be, for instance, the discharge of cargo from a goods car. The cargo is then placed into the freight compartment of an airplane. Each transport service provider is responsible for the transportation of goods through its part of the route and is not held responsible for the condition or the transportation of goods outside its part.

In general, the functions of the network layer are broader than simply ensuring data exchange within the internet. For example, the network layer solves the problem of creating reliable and flexible barriers for the paths of undesirable traffic between networks.

To conclude the description of the network layer, let us mention that at this layer, there are two types of protocols. **Routed protocols** *represent the first kind of protocols that implement packet forwarding through the network.* These protocols are the ones usually referred to when discussing network-layer protocols. However, there is another type of protocol — **routing protocols** *that are often classified as network-layer protocols.* Using routing protocols, routers collect information on the topology of internetwork links, on the basis of which the route for packet forwarding is chosen.

4.3.5 Transport Layer

Packets can be lost or corrupted on the way from sender to receiver. Although some applications have their own error-handling tools, there are other applications that initially prefer to deal with reliable connections.

The **transport layer** provides applications or the upper layers of the OSI model — the application, presentation, and session layers — with the service of data transmission with the required level of reliability. The OSI model defines five classes of the transport service, starting from class 0 (the lowest) to class 4 (the highest). These classes differ in the quality of the services they provide: urgency, the possibility of restoring broken connections, the availability of tools for multiplexing several connections among different application-layer protocols using a common transport protocol, and most importantly, the capability of detecting and correcting transmission errors, such as data distortion, packet loss, or duplication.

Selection of the service class of the transport layer depends, on the one hand, on the extent to which the problem of ensuring reliability is solved by applications and protocols of the layers higher than the transport layer. On the other hand, this choice depends on the reliability of the data transportation system of the network, which is ensured by the layers lower than transport layer — the network, data link, and physical layers. For example, if the quality of communications links is high and the probability of errors that cannot be detected by the underlying-layer protocols is low, it makes sense to use one of the lightweight transport-layer services, which are not overloaded by multiple checks, acknowledgments of receipt, and other techniques for improving reliability. If transport tools of the underlying layers are not reliable enough, it makes sense to use the more advanced services of the transport layer, which use the maximum possible number of error detection and correction tools, including the logical connection setup, message delivery control by checksums and cyclic packet numbering, and establishing delivery timeouts.

All protocols of the transport layer and higher are implemented by software tools installed on the network end nodes — components of their network operating systems. Examples of transport protocols are TCP and UDP of the TCP/IP stack and SPX protocol of the Novell protocol stack.

The four lower-layer protocols are known as the **network transport** or **transport subsystem**, since they solve the problem of message transportation with the specified level of quality in networks using arbitrary topology based on different technologies. Three higher layers solve the problems of providing application services using the underlying transport subsystem.

4.3.6 Session Layer

The **session layer** ensures control over interactions between parties. It registers the active party and provides the tools for session synchronization. These tools allow the insertion of checkpoints into long transmissions to ensure a smooth return to the latest checkpoint in case of failure, instead of starting everything from scratch. In practice, applications that use the session layer are not numerous. This layer is rarely implemented in the form of separate protocol entity. Quite often, functions of this layer are combined with the application-layer functions and implemented within a single protocol.

4.3.7 Presentation Layer

The **presentation layer** deals with the form in which information transmitted through the network is represented, without changing its contents. Thanks to this layer, information transmitted by the application layer of one system is always understandable to the application layer of another system. Using the tools of this layer, application-layer protocols can overcome syntax differences in data presentation or differences in character codes, such as differences between ASCII and EBCDIC. Data encryption and decryption, which ensure data exchange security for all application services, are also completed at this layer. An example of such a protocol is Secure Socket Layer (SSL), which ensures secure message exchange for application-layer protocols of the TCP/IP stack.

4.3.8 Application Layer

The **application layer** is really a set of several protocols that network users can use to access shared network resources, such as files, printers, or Web pages. They can also organize group work using, for example, e-mail protocols. The data unit with which the application layer operates is generally known as a **message**.

There are many application-layer services. Examples of the most widely known implementations of network file services include NFS and FTP in the TCP/IP stack, SMB in Microsoft Windows, and NCP in Novell NetWare.

4.3.9 OSI Model and Circuit-Switched Networks

As already mentioned, the OSI model describes the process of interaction between devices in a *packet-switched network*. And what about *circuit-switched networks*? Is there a reference model for such networks? Is it possible to compare the functions of circuit-switching technologies to the OSI model layers?

Certainly, internetworking tools for circuit-switched networks are also represented using a multilayer approach, according to which there are several layers of protocols that form a hierarchy. However, for circuit-switched networks, there is no common reference model similar to the OSI model. For example, different types of telephone networks use network-specific protocol stacks, differing by the number of layers and the distribution of functions between them. Transmission networks, such as Synchronous Digital Hierarchy (SDH) or Dense Wavelength Division Multiplexing (DWDM), also have their own protocol hierarchy. The situation is even more complicated, since most contemporary networks of this type use circuit-switched networks only for transmitting user data. For controlling the process of connection setup and general network management, the packet-switching technique is used. For example, SDH, DWDM and modern telephone networks use this approach.

Although circuit-switched networks have rather sophisticated organization and support their own protocol hierarchy, they provide physical-layer service for packet-switched networks.

As an example, consider several packet-switched LANs interconnected using a digital telephone network. Obviously, internetworking functions are delegated to network-layer protocols, making it necessary to install a router in each LAN. The router must be equipped with an interface capable of establishing connections to another LAN using a telephone network. When such a connection is established, a bit stream of a constant rate will be generated in the telephone network. This connection will provide physical-layer service for routers. To organize data transmission, routers use some point-to-point data link-layer protocol over this circuit.

4.4 NETWORK STANDARDIZATION

KEY WORDS: open system, specification, open specifications, proprietary standards, standards of special committees, national standards, international standards, Requests For Comments (RFCs), Internet Society (ISOC), Internet Architecture Board (IAB), Internet Research Task Force (IRTF), Internet Engineering Task Force (IETF), OSI model, OSI protocol stack, IPX/SPX stack, NetBIOS/SMB stack, TCP/IP stack, stream, segment, frame

A statement on the advantages of standardization, true for most technologies, has a special meaning in computer networks. The main idea behind networks lies in ensuring communication among various types of equipment. Consequently, compatibility is one of the most urgent and important problems. No progress in the field of networking would be possible without accepting some standards for equipment and protocols. Because of this, the entire evolution of computing is reflected in standards. Any new technology gets *legalized* status only when it is reflected by the appropriate standard or standards.

The previously considered OSI model represents an ideological basis for standardization in computer networks.

4.4.1 Concept of an Open System

What is an open system?

In a broad sense, an **open system** is any system (be it a standalone computer, computer network, operating system, application software, or any other hardware or software) built according to open specifications.

Remember that the term **specification** in computing means a formalized description of hardware or software components, the methods of their operation, their interaction with other components, operating conditions, and other special characteristics. Obviously, not every specification is a standard.

Open specifications are published, openly available ones, which comply with the agreed-upon standards after a thorough and manifold discussion among all interested parties.

The use of open specifications in the creation of a system allows third parties to develop various hardware or software extensions or modifications for that system. It also allows system integrators to combine hardware and software products supplied by different manufacturers.

The open nature of standards and specifications is important not only for communications protocols but also for all hardware devices and software products used when building networks. Most standards adopted nowadays are open. The time of proprietary systems, exact specifications for which were known only to their respective manufacturers, ended long ago. Everyone seems to have realized that the capability of smooth and easy interaction with competing products does not reduce the value of a product. On the contrary, the value is significantly improved, since such products can be employed in most heterogeneous networks built on the basis of products from different vendors. Therefore, even the companies that once manufactured proprietary systems, such as IBM, Novell, and Microsoft, now actively participate in the development of open standards, implementing them in their products.

Unfortunately, for real-world systems, complete openness remains an unattainable ideal. Usually, even in systems named open, only specific parts supporting external interfaces are truly open. For example, the open features of the UNIX family of operating systems include the availability of a standard software interface between the OS kernel and applications, which makes it possible to easily port applications from one UNIX version to the environment of another version.

The OSI model relates to a single aspect of openness, namely, to the openness of interaction among devices connected into a computer network. Here, the open system is interpreted as a network device ready to interact with other network devices using standard rules defining the format, contents, and meanings of sent and received messages.

If two networks are built according to the principles of open systems, the following advantages are provided:

■ Possibility of building a network based on hardware and software from different vendors supporting the same standard
■ Possibility of seamless replacement of specific network components by more advanced ones, which allows a network to be scaled with minimum expense
■ Possibility of easily interconnecting networks
■ Simplicity and ease of network maintenance

4.4.2 Types of Standards

All activities in the standardization of computer networks are conducted by several organizations. Depending on the status of the organization, the standards are classified as follows:

- **Proprietary standards** — *Some of these are the* SNA protocol stack, which is the property of IBM, and the OPEN LOOK graphical interface for UNIX systems, which is the property of Sun Microsystems.
- **Standards of special committees** — These are created by the cooperation of several companies, for example, the ATM technology standards developed by the specially created ATM Forum, which includes more than 100 companywide participants, or the Fast Ethernet Alliance standards for 100 Mbps Ethernet.
- **National standards** — *These include* FDDI, one of the numerous standards developed by the American National Standards Institute (ANSI), and the operating system security standards developed by the National Computer Security Center (NCSC) of the U.S. Department of Defense.
- **International standards** — Examples are the OSI model and stack of communications protocols developed by the ISO, numerous standards of the ITU, including standards for X.25, Frame Relay, ISDN networks, and modems.

Some standards can move from category to category in the course of their evolution. For example, proprietary standards for products that become popular and widely used usually become de facto international standards, since manufacturers all over the world are forced to follow these standards to ensure compatibility of their products. For example, because of the phenomenal success of the IBM PC, the proprietary standard for the IBM PC architecture became the de facto international standard.

Furthermore, because of their popularity, some widespread proprietary standards become the foundation for national and international standards *de jure*. For example, the Ethernet standard initially developed by Digital Equipment, Intel, and Xerox after some time was, in a slightly modified form, adopted as the IEEE 802.3 national standard. Later on, ISO approved it as the ISO 8802.3 international standard.

4.4.3 Internet Standardization

The Internet is the best example of an open system. This network evolved according to the requirements for open systems. Thousands of IT professionals — users of this network from various universities, scientific organizations, and manufacturers of hardware and software all over the world — participated in development of the standards of this network. The standards defining the operation of the Internet are known as **Requests For**

Comments (RFCs). This name emphasizes the public and open nature of the standards being adopted. As a result, the Internet has succeeded in joining various equipment and software of the vast number of networks scattered around the world.

Because of the large and steadily growing popularity of the Internet, RFCs become de facto international standards. Most RFCs later get the status of official international standards, usually as a result of approval by one of the previously listed organizations (as a rule, by ISO or ITU-T).

Several organizational departments are responsible for development, particularly, for the standardization of the Internet architecture and protocols. The most important role belongs to the **Internet Society (ISOC),** a scientific and administrative community of about 100,000 individuals. This community is engaged in common aspects of the Internet evolution and related social, political, and technical problems. The ISOC coordinates the work of the **Internet Architecture Board (IAB),** the organization whose jurisdiction covers the coordination of research and development for the TCP/IP stack. This organization is the highest authority when approving new Internet standards.

IAB comprises two main groups: the **Internet Research Task Force (IRTF)** and the **Internet Engineering Task Force (IETF).** The IRTF coordinates long-term research projects related to TCP/IP. The second group, the IETF, is the engineering group engaged in solving the current technical problems of the Internet. It is the IETF that defines specifications, which eventually become Internet standards. The process of the development and approval of an Internet standard comprises several mandatory states.

According to the openness principle of the Internet, all RFCs are available for free access. The list of all documents can be found at the RFC editor site: **http://www.rfc-editor.org**. Any RFC can be freely downloaded, in contrast to, for example, the ISO standards.

4.4.4 Standard Stacks of Communications Protocols

The most important direction of standardization in the field of computer networks is in the standardization of communications protocols. The best-known protocol stacks are OSI, TCP/IP, IPX/SPX, NetBIOS/SMB, DECnet, and SNA, though not all of them are in practical use nowadays.

OSI Stack

It is necessary to clearly distinguish between the **OSI model** and the **OSI protocol stack**. In contrast to the OSI model, a conceptual method of interaction between open systems, the OSI stack is a set of specifications for specific protocols.

Unlike other protocol stacks, the OSI stack (Figure 4.11) fully complies with the OSI model and includes specifications of protocols for all seven layers of interaction defined

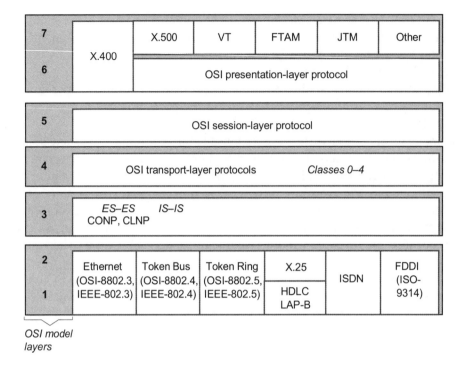

Figure 4.11 OSI protocol stack

by this model. This is not surprising; the developers of this stack used the OSI model as a reference and as a direct guide to action.

The protocols of the OSI stack are characterized by sophisticated and ambiguous specifications. Their properties represent a result of the common policy of the stack developers, who tried to take into account the variety of all the existing and emerging technologies.

At the physical and data link layers, the OSI stack supports such protocols as Ethernet, Token Ring, and FDDI as well as LLC, X.25, and ISDN. In other words, it uses lower-layer protocols developed outside the stack framework. In this, it is similar to most other protocol stacks.

Services of the network, transport, and session layers are also present in the OSI stack, though they are rarely used in practice. At the network layer, it is possible to use either Connection-Oriented Network Protocol (CONP) or Connectionless Network Protocol (CLNP). With these protocols, the following two routing protocols are used: End System–Intermediate System (ES–IS) and Intermediate System–Intermediate System (IS–IS).

The transport protocol of the OSI stack, according to the functions defined for it in the OSI model, hides the differences between connection-oriented and connectionless services so that the users receive the required quality of service independent of the underlying network layer. To ensure this, the transport layer requires the user to specify the quality of service needed.

The application layer includes file transfer, terminal emulation, directory services, and e-mail. The most popular services are directory service (X.500 standard); e-mail (X.400); Virtual Terminal Protocol (VTP); File Transmission, Access, and Management protocol (FTAM); and Job Transfer and Management protocol (JTM).

IPX/SPX Stack

The IPX/SPX stack is the original protocol stack developed by Novell in the early 1980s for its network operating system, NetWare. The structure of the IPX/SPX stack and its correspondence to the OSI model is illustrated in Figure 4.12. Protocols of the network and transport layers — Internetwork Packet Exchange (IPX) and Sequenced Packet Exchange (SPX) — gave their names to the entire protocol stack. To the network layer of this stack, one also relates routing protocols — RIP and NLSP. Representatives of the three upper layers are the protocol of remote access to NetWare files — NetWare Core Protocol (NCP) and Service Advertising Protocol (SAP).

NOTE   *Until 1996, this stack was the undisputed world leader by its number of installations. However, the situation changed abruptly, and the TCP/IP stack began to lead the other stacks by growth rate and by number of installations. By 1998, TCP/IP had become an absolute leader.*

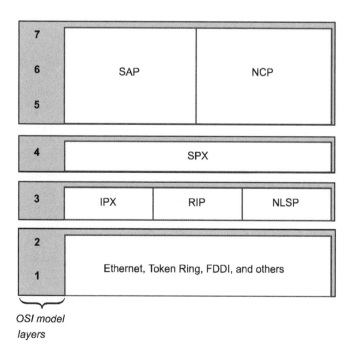

OSI model
layers

Figure 4.12 IPX/SPX protocol stack

Many specific features of the IPX/SPX stack can be attributed to the orientation of earlier NetWare versions toward small LANs comprising PCs characterized by limited resources. To achieve this goal, Novell required protocols whose implementation would need the minimum amount of RAM (rather limited on IBM-compatible PCs running MS-DOS — 640 KB only). Furthermore, these protocols had to ensure fast operation on such weak computers. As a result, protocols of the IPX/SPX stack until recently did a fine job in LANs. However, in large companywide networks, they heavily overloaded slow global links with the broadcast packets widely used by some protocols of this stack (for example, SAP). In addition, the IPX/SPX stack is the property of Novell, and to implement it, a license has to be purchased, which means that open specifications are not supported. These circumstances have long limited its use to only NetWare networks.

NetBIOS/SMB Stack

The **NetBIOS/SMB stack** was developed by IBM and Microsoft (Figure 4.13). At the physical and data link layers of this stack, most of the popular protocols are employed, including Ethernet, Token Ring, and FDDI. At the upper layers of this stack, the NetBEUI and SMB protocols are used.

The Network Basic Input/Output System (NetBIOS) protocol first appeared in 1984 as a network extension of the standard IBM PC BIOS functions for the IBM PC Network software. Later, this protocol was replaced by the NetBIOS Extended User Interface

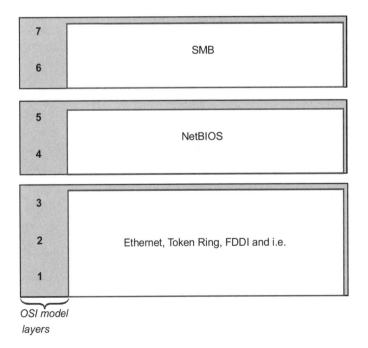

OSI model
layers

Figure 4.13 NetBIOS/SMB stack

(NetBEUI) protocol. To ensure application compatibility, the NetBIOS interface was retained as an interface to the NetBEUI protocol. NetBEUI was developed as an efficient protocol with low requirements of computer resources intended for small networks comprising no more than 200 workstations. This protocol implements a large number of useful network functions that fall into the transport and session layers of the OSI model. Unfortunately, this protocol doesn't allow packet routing. This limits the use of the NetBEUI protocol to small LANs not divided into subnets and makes impossible its usage in internets.

The Server Message Block (SMB) protocol performs the functions of session, presentation, and application layers of the OSI model. SMB serves as a basis for implementing file service as well as print and messaging services.

TCP/IP Stack

The **TCP/IP stack** was developed at the initiative of the U.S. Department of Defense more than 20 years ago to ensure connectivity between the experimental ARPANET network and other networks. TCP/IP was implemented as a protocol suite for a heterogeneous network environment. The University of California at Berkeley has brought the greatest contribution to development of the TCP/IP stack, named after its most popular protocols — IP and TCP — by implementing the protocols of this stack in its popular version of the UNIX operating system. The popularity of UNIX has resulted in the prevalence of TCP, IP, and other protocols of this stack. Nowadays, this stack is used for communications among computers connected to the Internet and in numerous companywide networks.

Since the TCP/IP stack was initially developed for the Internet, it has many advantages over other protocols, especially when it comes to building networks that include WAN links. In particular, the TCP/IP capability of fragmenting packets is very useful, making it possible to use this protocol stack in large-scale networks. A large internetwork often is built of different networks based on quite different principles. For each of these networks, there might be a network-specific value of the maximum transfer unit (frame size). In this case, when data are transferred from a network with a larger maximum frame length to a network with a smaller value of this parameter, it might be necessary to divide the frame being transferred into several fragments. The Internet protocol of the TCP/IP stack solves this problem efficiently.

The flexible addressing system is another advantage of the TCP/IP technology. This property also encourages the use of TCP/IP in building large-scale, heterogeneous networks.

The TCP/IP stack uses its broadcasting capabilities rather sparingly. This property is absolutely necessary when using slow links, which are still frequently used in long-distance networks.

However, as usual, advantages come at a price. In this case, the previously listed advantages are achieved at the expense of high requirements for resources and complications

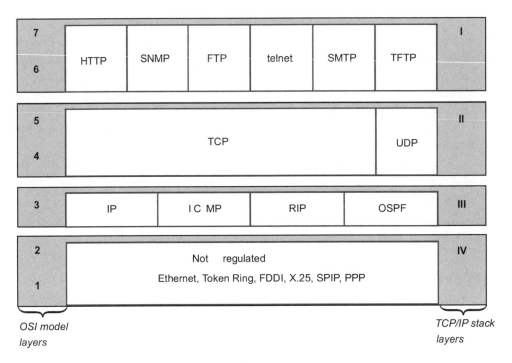

Figure 4.14 Architecture of the TCP/IP stack

of IP network administration. Powerful functional capabilities of the TCP/IP stack require quite significant resources for their implementation. Flexible addressing and broadcasts abandonment makes it necessary to have various centralized services in IP networks, such as Domain Name System (DNS) and DHCP. Each of these services is aimed at the facilitation of the network administration procedures. However, each service requires the close attention of network administrators.

It is possible to provide other pros and cons of the TCP/IP stack. Regardless, this protocol stack is the most popular and widely used today, both in WANs and LANs.

The architecture of the TCP/IP stack is shown in Figure 4.14. Similar to the OSI model, the TCP/IP stack has a multilayer structure. However, the TCP/IP stack was developed earlier than the ISO/OSI model. The correspondence of the TCP/IP stack layers to the OSI model layers is rather conditional.

The TCP/IP stack defines four layers:

The *application layer* of the TCP/IP stack corresponds to the three upper layers of the OSI model: the application, presentation, and session layers. It combines the services provided by the system to user applications. During its operation in various networks of different countries and organizations, the TCP/IP stack has accumulated a large number of protocols and services of the application layer. The list of such protocols and services is rather long and includes such widely used protocols as File Transfer Protocol (FTP), terminal emulation protocol (telnet), Simple Mail Transfer Protocol (SMTP), and Hypertext Transfer Protocol (HTTP).

Application-layer protocols are installed on the **hosts**.[1]

The *transport layer* of the TCP/IP stack can provide the following two types of services to the upper layer:

- Guaranteed delivery — the Transmission Control Protocol (TCP)
- Best effort delivery — User Datagram Protocol (UDP)

To ensure reliable data delivery, TCP makes provisions for establishing a logical connection, which allows it to number packets, acknowledge their receipt, and ensure retransmission of any lost packet. It can also detect and discard duplicate packets and deliver the packets to the application layer in the order in which they were sent. This protocol allows the objects on the source and destination computers to support data exchange in the duplex mode. TCP ensures error-free delivery of the byte stream formed on one computer to any other computer connected to the internetwork. TCP divides the byte stream into the fragments and passes them to the underlying layer, the internet. After these fragments are delivered by the internetworking tools to the destination computer, TCP reassembles them into a continuous byte stream.

The second protocol of this layer — UDP — is the simplest datagram protocol used when the problem of reliable data exchange either is not posed or is solved by the tools of a higher layer, the application layer, or user applications.

The functions of TCP and UDP include the role of a link between the application layer and the underlying internet layer. The transport layer takes the job of data transmission with the specified quality from the application layer and informs it after accomplishing this task. On the other hand, TCP and UDP use the underlying internet layer as a kind of tool, which is not characterized by high reliability but is capable of transmitting the packet through the internetwork. Similar to the application-layer protocols, TCP and UDP are installed on hosts.

The *network layer*, also called the *internet layer,* is at the core of the entire TCP/IP architecture. It is this layer whose functions correspond to the OSI model network layer and ensure packet forwarding within the internetwork, created by joining several networks. Network-layer protocols support interface to the upper transport layer and receive from it the requests for data transmission using internet, and to the underlying network interface layer, the functions of which will be covered later.

The Internet protocol (IP) is the main protocol of the internet layer. Its tasks include packet forwarding between networks — from one router to another, until the packet reaches the destination network. In contrast to the application-layer and transport-layer protocols, IP is installed not only on all hosts but also on all gateways. IP is a connectionless datagram protocol, operating according to the best effort principle.

---

[1] In the Internet terminology, the end node is traditionally named the **host**, and the router is called the **gateway**. *In this chapter, we use this terminology.*

Protocols that accomplish auxiliary functions in relation to IP are often classified as belonging to the TCP/IP network layer. The list of these protocols includes routing protocols such as Routing Information Protocol (RIP) and Open Shortest Path First (OSPF), involved in studying network topology, determining routes, and creating routing tables that help IP forward packets in the direction needed. For the same reason, two other protocols can also be classified as belonging to the network layer: the Internet Control Message Protocol (ICMP), intended for transmitting information about packet transmission errors from the router to the information source, and the Internet Group Management Protocol (IGMP), used for packet forwarding to several addresses simultaneously.

> Ideological differences of the TCP/IP stack architecture from multilayer organization of other stacks lies in the interpretation of the lowest-layer functions. These are the functions of the *network interface layer.*

Recall that the lowest layers of the OSI model (the data link and physical layers) implement many of the functions responsible for medium access: framing, coordination of the levels of electric signals, encoding, synchronization, etc. All these rather specific functions are the essence of such data exchange protocols as Ethernet, Token Ring, PPP, HDLC, and many others.

The lower layer of the TCP/IP stack solves a significantly simpler problem: It is responsible only for organizing an interaction to network technologies, used in the networks that form the internet. TCP/IP considers any network included into the internet a tool for transporting a packet to the next router within the route.

Hence, the task of providing interface between TCP/IP technology and any other technology of the intermediate network is reduced to the following tasks:

■ Defining the method of encapsulating an IP packet in the PDU of the intermediate network

■ Determining the method of translating network addresses into addresses adopted by the technology used by this intermediate network

Such an approach makes the TCP/IP internetwork open for the incorporation of any other network, independent of the internal data transmission technology used in that network. For each technology used in a network included in the internetwork, it is necessary to develop specific interfacing tools. Hence, the functions of this layer cannot be defined permanently.

The network interface layer in TCP/IP stack is not strictly regulated. It supports all popular network technologies. For LANs, these are Ethernet, Token Ring, FDDI, Fast Ethernet, and Gigabit Ethernet; for WANs, these are point-to-point protocols such as SLIP and PPP; for circuit-switched networks, these are the X.25, Frame Relay, and ATM technologies.

Usually, when any new LAN or WAN technology emerges, it is quickly included in the TCP/IP stack by developing the appropriate RFC that determines the method of encapsulating IP packets in its frames. For instance, RFC 1577, which defines the IP operation over ATM networks, appeared in 1994 soon after the adoption of the main standards of ATM.

NOTE *Note that the TCP/IP stack allows the inclusion of component networks into the internet regardless of the number of layers in those networks. Thus, for example, data forwarding in X.25 networks is ensured by the protocols of the physical, data link, and network layers (in OSI terminology). Nevertheless, the TCP/IP stack considers the X.25 network and other technologies only as tools for transporting IP packets between two boundary gateways. The network interface layer provides this technology method of encapsulating an IP packet in an X.25 packet as well as techniques of translating IP addresses into X.25 network layer addresses. If this network organization is in strict accordance with the OSI model, it is necessary to admit the presence of an explicit contradiction — one network-layer protocol (IP) operates over another network-layer protocol (X.25). However, this is quite normal for the TCP/IP stack.*

Each communications protocol manipulates a specific unit of transmitted data. Naming conventions for these units are sometimes specified in the standard; more frequently, they are determined by tradition. During the long existence of the TCP/IP stack, specific terminology has been commonly adopted (Figure 4.15).

Stream is the term used to designate the data arriving from applications to the input of the transport-layer protocols, TCP and UDP.

The TCP divides the stream into **segments**.

The protocol data unit of the UDP is frequently referred to as a **datagram**. Datagram is the common name for PDUs used by connectionless protocols. The list of such protocols includes IP; therefore, its PDU is also called a datagram. However, another term is often used: the IP packet.

According to TCP/IP stack terminology, **frames** are PDUs of any technology into which IP packets are encapsulated for subsequent transportation over networks that are part of the internet. In this case, it does not matter what name is used for this PDU in the technology of a specific network. Thus, Ethernet frame, ATM cell, and X.25 packet are all considered frames by the TCP/IP stack, since all these PDUs are interpreted as containers within which an IP packet travels through the internet.

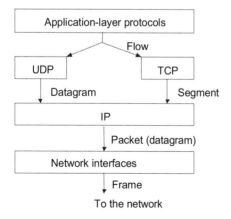

Figure 4.15 TCP/IP PDU names

4.4.5 Correspondence between Popular Protocol Stacks and the OSI Model

Figure 4.16 shows the correspondence between standard protocol stacks and the OSI reference model. As you can see, this correspondence is rather conventional. In most cases, stack developers sacrificed modular structure to speed of network operation. Only the OSI stack is divided into seven layers. Most frequently, stacks are divided into 3–4 layers: the network adapter layer, where physical and data link layers of the OSI model are implemented; the network layer; the transport layer; and the service layer, which combines functions of the session, presentation, and application layers of the OSI model.

Besides this, there are other reasons the structure of protocol stacks often isn't in accordance with OSI recommendations. Recall the characteristic features of ideal multilayer decomposition. First, it is necessary to observe the principle of hierarchy: each upper layer requests only it's nearest underlying layer, and each underlying layer provides services only to the nearest upper layer. In protocol stacks, this results in upper-layer PDU always being encapsulated within the lower-layer PDU.

Second, the ideal multilayer decomposition assumes that all modules of the same layer are responsible for accomplishing the common task. However, these requirements often contradict real-world construction of protocol stacks. For example, the main function of the network layer of the TCP/IP stack (similar to the network layer of the OSI stack) is ensuring packet transmission using the internet. The TCP/IP stack provides several protocols for solving this problem. Examples are IP, which is used for forwarding packets, as well as RIP and OSPF, which are routing protocols. If protocols solving the common

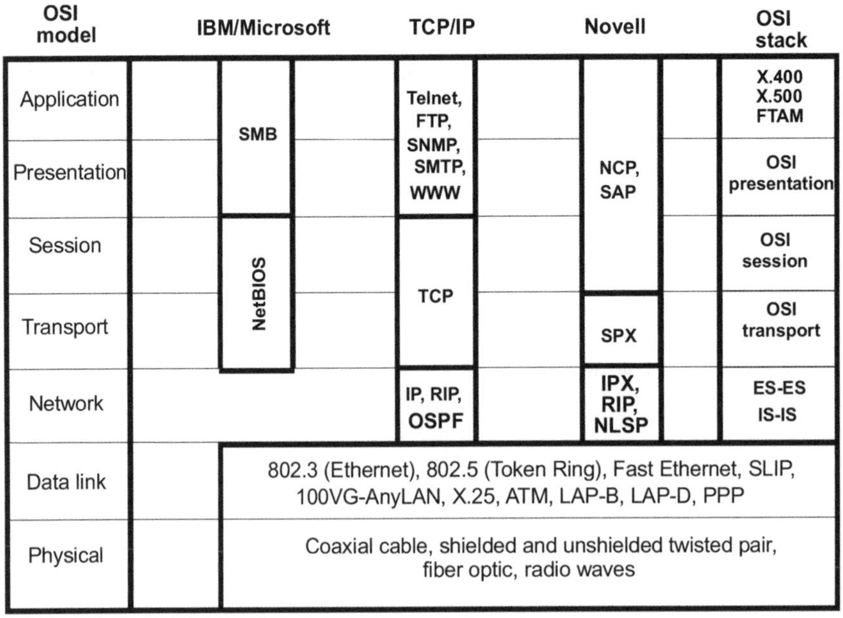

OSI model	IBM/Microsoft		TCP/IP	Novell		OSI stack
Application	SMB	NetBIOS	Telnet, FTP, SNMP, SMTP, WWW	NCP, SAP		X.400 X.500 FTAM
Presentation						OSI presentation
Session			TCP			OSI session
Transport				SPX		OSI transport
Network			IP, RIP, OSPF	IPX, RIP, NLSP		ES-ES IS-IS
Data link	802.3 (Ethernet), 802.5 (Token Ring), Fast Ethernet, SLIP, 100VG-AnyLAN, X.25, ATM, LAP-B, LAP-D, PPP					
Physical	Coaxial cable, shielded and unshielded twisted pair, fiber optic, radio waves					

Figure 4.16 Correspondence between popular protocol stacks and the OSI model layers

task is considered a sign that these protocols belong to the same layer, then the Internet and routing protocols must belong to the same layer. However, RIP messages are encapsulated into UDP datagrams, and OSPF messages are encapsulated into IP packets; therefore, formally following the hierarchical structure of the stack, the OSPF protocol should belong to the transport layer, and RIP should belong to application layer. In practice, however, routing protocols are usually considered protocols of the network layer.

4.5 INFORMATION AND TRANSPORT SERVICES

KEY WORDS: Transport services, Information services, infocommunications networks, RIP, OSPF, BGP, address translation, network management, User Plane, Control Plane, Management Plane, Simple Network Management Protocol (SNMP)

The services of a computer network can be classified in the following two categories:

- Transport services
- Information services

Transport services assume that data is transmitted among network users in an unchanged form. The network inputs user data at one of its interfaces, transmits it via transit switches, and outputs the data to another user through another interface. When providing transport services, the network does not change the information being transmitted. Rather, it transmits the data to the receiver in the same form as it was supplied to the network by the sender. An example of a transport service provided by WANs is the interconnecting of a client's LANs.

Information services include providing new information to the user. An information service is always related to the data processing operations: storing it in some ordered form (file system or database), searching for the required information, and presenting it in the required form. Information services existed long before the arrival of the first computer networks. The directory inquiry service provided by telephone networks is a typical example of an information service. With the arrival of computers, information services have survived a revolution, because the computer was invented for automatic information processing. Various information technologies, including programming, databases, file archives, WWW, and e-mail, are used for providing information services.

In telecommunications networks of the pre-computer era, transport services always prevailed. Transmission of voice traffic between subscribers always was the main service of telephone networks; inquiry services were supplementary. In computer networks, both kinds of services are equally important. This feature of computer networks is reflected in the name of the new generation of telecommunications networks that appear as a result of convergence of different types of networks. Nowadays, such networks are frequently called

infocommunications networks. This name is not commonly accepted yet, although it reflects new trends rather well, including both components of network services on equal terms.

The division of computer network services into two categories manifests itself in many ways. For example, there is currently a strict division among specialists in the field of computer networks. There are IT professionals and network professionals. The first category of specialists includes programmers, database developers, OS administrators, Web designers — that is, all specialists involved in computer software and hardware development and support. The second category includes specialists involved in solving network transport problems. These specialists deal with communications links and communications equipment such as switches, routers, or hubs. They solve the problems of choosing network topology, defining routes for traffic flows, defining the required bandwidth of the links and communications equipment performance, and other problems related exclusively to the transmission of traffic using networks.

Undoubtedly, each category of specialists must know the problems and methods of the adjoining area. Specialists involved in the development of distributed applications must understand which transport services they can get from the network to organize a coordinated operation of the distributed components of their applications. For example, network programmers must understand that the TCP/IP stack provides two different transport services — TCP and UDP. Therefore, it is up to the programmer to decide which of these services is better suited for a specific application. Similarly, a developer of network transport tools must understand the requirements of the applications for traffic transmission to take these requirements into account in network design. Still, specialization in the IT or networking areas exists, reflecting the dual purpose of computer networks.

The classification of network services into transport and information is also reflected in the organization of protocol stacks and in the distribution of the components of various protocol stacks by network elements.

4.5.1 Distribution of Protocols by Network Elements

Figure 4.17 shows the main components of computer networks: end nodes, or computers, and transit nodes, or switches and routers. Protocols of the TCP/IP stack are chosen for this example, since they are the most common.

From this illustration, it is obvious that the complete protocol stack is implemented only on the end nodes; transit nodes support the protocols of the three lower layers. This can be explained by the functional capabilities of the three lower layers, since they are sufficient for packet-forwarding communications devices. Furthermore, a communications device can support only protocols of the two lower layers or even only that of the physical layer — this depends on the type of device.

■ *Concentrator* — It operates with stream of bits and, therefore, is limited to supporting a physical-layer protocol.

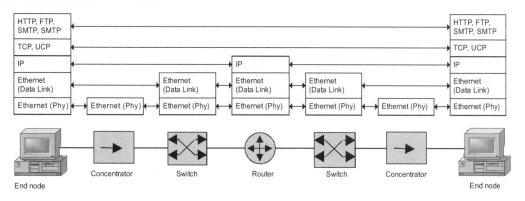

Figure 4.17 Correspondence of the functions of network devices to the OSI model layers

■ *LAN switches* — They support protocols of the two lower layers, the physical and data link, thus allowing them to operate within the limits of standard topologies.

■ *Routers* — They must support protocols of all three lower layers, since they need the network layer for interconnecting networks based on different technologies. Protocols of the two lower layers are needed for interacting with component networks (for example, Ethernet or Frame Relay).

■ *WAN switches* — Switches of WANs, such as ATM, that operate on the basis of virtual circuits can support either two or three protocol layers. The network-layer protocol is required when they support the procedures of automatically establishing virtual circuits. Since the topology of a WAN is arbitrary, one cannot do without a network protocol. On the other hand, if virtual circuits are set manually by network administrators, it is sufficient for the WAN switch to support only the physical-layer and data link-layer protocols to transmit data through existing virtual circuits.

Computers running network applications must support protocols of all layers. Application-layer protocols, using services provided by the presentation- and session-layer protocols, provide applications with a set of network services in the form of the network API. The transport-layer protocol also operates on all end nodes. When it is necessary to organize data transmission using the network, two transport protocol entities operating at the sending and receiving nodes interact to ensure providing the required quality of the transport service. Network communications devices deliver the messages of the transport protocol transparently, without inquiring about their contents.

In computers, communications protocols of all layers (except for the physical layer and some functions of the data link layer) are implemented by system software.

The end nodes of the network (computers and computer-based high-tech devices, such as mobile phones) always provide information and transport services, and transit network nodes provide only transport services. If some network provides only transport services, it means that the end nodes are outside the network boundary. Usually, this is the case with commercial networks providing services to their clients. If we say that a network also provides information services, it means that computers providing these services are included in the network. A typical example of this situation is one in which the Internet service provider, besides providing Internet access, also supports its own Web servers.

4.5.2 Subsidiary Protocols of the Transport System

Obviously, Figure 4.17 illustrated a simplified version of protocol distribution over the network elements. In real-world networks some communication devices support not only protocols of the three lowest layers, but also higher-layer protocols. For example, routers implement routing protocols allowing for automatically building routing tables. Concentrators and switches often support SNMP and telnet protocols, which are not mandatory for carrying out main functions of these devices, but allow for remotely configuring and controlling them. All these protocols are application-layer protocols, which carry out some auxiliary functions of the transport system. Obviously, in order to support application-layer protocols, network equipment must also support intermediate-layer protocols, such as IP and TCP/UDP.

Subsidiary protocols can be divided into groups according to their functions.

The first group includes *routing protocols* such as RIP, OSPF, and BGP. Without these protocols, routers would be unable to route the packets, since the routing table would remain empty (unless, of course, the network administrator fills it manually — not a suitable solution for large-scale networks). If we consider not only the TCP/IP stack but also the protocol stacks of the networks supporting virtual circuits, this group would include protocols used for virtual circuit setup.

Another group of subsidiary protocols is involved in **address translation**. In particular, it includes the DNS protocol, which translates symbolic node names into IP addresses. Another protocol of this group, DHCP, allows IP addresses to be dynamically assigned to network hosts. This is in contrast to static IP addresses, which must be assigned manually by network administrators. Therefore, the job of network administrators also is simplified.

The third group includes protocols used for **network management**. For this purpose, the TCP/IP stack includes Simple Network Management Protocol (SNMP) protocol, which allows automatic collection of information on errors and device failures, as well as the telnet protocol, which network administrators can use to remotely configure switches or routers.

When considering subsidiary protocols, we have encountered situations when the hierarchical classification of the protocols by layers (i.e., vertical division) adopted in the

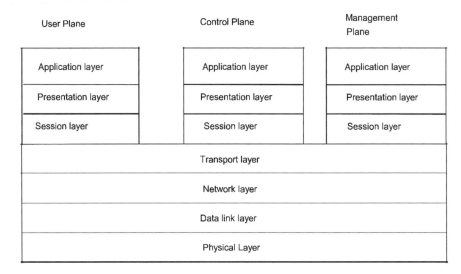

Figure 4.18 Three groups of protocols

OSI model proves insufficient. Besides hierarchical layers, it is also necessary to divide the horizontal classification of protocols into several groups.

Although the OSI model does not provide such a division, it does exist in practice. In fact, this approach was used in the standardization of ISDN networks, which, as we have already mentioned, use both packet-switching and circuit-switching techniques. ISDN standards classify all protocols in three groups, named User Plane, Control Plane, and Management Plane (Figure 4.18).

■ The **User Plane** group includes the protocols needed for transmitting user voice traffic.

■ The **Control Plane** group includes protocols required for establishing network connections.

■ The **Management Plane** group joins the protocols supporting network-management operations, such as error detection and analysis of device configuration.

It is clear from this description that there are direct analogies between the Planes functions and the groups of subsidiary functions of computer networks based on TCP/IP or other technologies. Although such horizontal division of protocols is not widely accepted in computer networks, it is still useful, since it helps to better understand the purpose of each protocol. Besides this, horizontal classification helps to explain the difficulties of correlating some protocols to the OSI model layers. For example, some authors place routing protocols to the network layer, and other authors classify them as belonging to the application layer. This is not because of the authors' negligence but is caused by the objective difficulties of classification. The OSI model is well suited for the standardization of protocols involved in transporting user traffic (i.e., the protocols that can be classified as User Plane). However, it is significantly less suited for the standardization of subsidiary protocols. Therefore, many authors place routing protocols in the network layer to reflect their functional resemblance to the transport services of the network implemented by IP.

SUMMARY

▶ The efficient model of network interaction between computers is the multilayer structure, in which the upper-layer modules use the tools of the underlying layer as instruments for accomplishing their tasks. Each layer supports two types of interfaces — service interfaces with upper and lower layers of the hierarchy of network tools of the node and the peer-to-peer interface to the tools of the same layer running on the remote node. The latter interface is known as a protocol.

▶ A protocol stack is a set of protocols for hierarchically organizing interaction between network nodes. Protocols of the lower layers are often implemented by combinations of software and hardware. Upper-layer protocols are usually implemented on the basis of software tools. Software modules implementing a specific protocol are called protocol entities.

▶ In the early 1980s, ISO, ITU-T, and other international organizations working in the field of standardization developed the standard OSI model. This model contains descriptions of the generalized representation of internetworking tools. It is used as a kind of universal language for network professionals; therefore, it is known as a reference model. The OSI model defines seven layers of interaction, gives them standard names, and specifies the functions that each layer needs to accomplish.

▶ *An open system is any system* (computer, computer network, software product, operating system, or any other software or hardware) built according to public specifications, corresponding to standards and adopted as a result of public discussion by all interested parties.

▶ Depending on the status of organizations, it is possible to classify their standards according to the following categories: proprietary standards of specific companies, standards developed by specialized committees, national standards, and international standards.

■ The most important advance of standardization in the field of computer networks is the standardization of communications protocols. The list of standardized protocol stacks includes TCP/IP, IPX/SPX, NetBIOS/SMB, OSI, DECnet, and SNA. The leading position belongs to the TCP/IP stack, which is used for communications between tens of millions of computers participating in the worldwide information network — the Internet. The TCP/IP stack has four layers: application, transport, internet, and network interfaces. Correspondence between the TCP/IP and OSI layers is conventional.

REVIEW QUESTIONS

1. What does the OSI model standardize?

2. Is it possible to present another variant of OSI containing a different number of layers, e.g., five or eight?

3. Is the protocol the software module that solves the problem of interaction between systems, or does it represent a formalized description of the interaction rules, including the sequence of message exchange and their formats?

4. Are the terms *interface* and *protocol* synonymous?

5. At which layer of the OSI model do application programs operate?

6. On which network elements are transport-layer protocols installed?

7. At which layer of the OSI model do network services operate?

8. Which of the devices listed below implement the physical-layer functions of the OSI model? Which implement the data link layer?
   A. Router
   B. Switch
   C. Bridge
   D. Repeater
   E. Network adapter

9. Which names are traditionally used for the protocol data unit at each layer? Fill in the table.

	Packet	Message	Frame	Flow	Segment
Data link layer					
Network layer					
Transport layer					
Session layer					
Presentation layer					
Application layer					

10. Give examples of open systems.

11. Suppose a small company, which is not widely known, offers a product that you need, characterized by parameters that exceed the parameters of similar products supplied by well-known companies. You could accept the offer after reviewing the manufacturer's documentation and ensuring that it does specify parameters that exceed the similar parameters of well-known products. Or you could accept the offer only after careful testing that confirms the technical parameters of the product under consideration are better than those of similar products available on the market. Or you could choose the product of a world-known company, since the latter is guaranteed to comply with the standards, and there is no risk of it going out of business and, consequently, no risk of experiencing problems with technical support. In which case will your action comply with the principle of open systems?

12. Which organization has developed the Ethernet standards?

13. Which of the administrative forces of the Internet is directly involved with standardization?

14. Are the terms standard, specification, and RFC synonyms?

15. Which type of standards do contemporary RFCs represent?

    A. Proprietary standards

    B. Governmental standards

    C. National standards

    D. International standards

16. Which organization originated the creation and standardization of the TCP/IP stack?

17. Specify the main properties of the TCP/IP stack.

18. Compare the functions of lowest layers of the TCP/IP and OSI reference models.

19. Define transport and information services.

20. Which protocols belong to Control Plane? Which belong to Management Plane?

21. Is it necessary for routers to support the transport-layer protocols?

PROBLEMS

1. Suppose that you have two computers connected to the network using Ethernet adapters. Adapter drivers installed on these computers support different interfaces to the IP network-layer protocol. Will these computers interact normally?

2. How can you organize interaction between two computers if they use different protocols of the following layers:
   - Physical and data link?
   - Network?
   - Application?

3. Describe the steps that you will need to take if you have to check the state of the process of standardizing the MPLS technology?

4. Find the area in which the IETF has concentrated its activities (for instance, by the number of workgroups).

5

EXAMPLES
OF NETWORKS

CHAPTER OUTLINE

5.1 INTRODUCTION

This chapter describes the organizational architecture of the most popular types of networks — networks of telecommunications carriers, enterprise-wide networks, and the Internet.

Despite the differences in these types of networks, they have much in common. First, their architectures are similar. For example, any telecommunications network consists of a backbone, access networks, information centers, and client equipment. Naturally, this generalized design has specific information content for each specific type of a network.

Telecommunications carrier networks are different in that they provide a public service. Traditionally, the list of services they provide includes telephony services and leased line services for organizations building their own networks. As computer networks become widespread, telecommunications carriers have significantly extended the range of their services. For instance, most now provide Internet access, Virtual Private Networks (VPNs), Web hosting, e-mail, IP telephony, audio, and video broadcasting.

In the mid-1980s, demonopolization of this area started all over the world. As a result, traditional telecommunications carriers were deprived of the monopoly on providing public services. This process led to the arrival of competitive carriers, which try to attract clients by using an extended set of services and a better price–quality relationship in their services. Knowledge of the administrative structure of the telecommunications world is useful for understanding of specific features of network technologies, which, in some cases, are especially designed for carriers of a specific type.

Enterprise-wide networks have a hierarchical structure similar to that of telecommunications carriers. However, they are different in that they usually provide services only to employees of the company that owns the network.

This chapter ends with a description of the Internet. This network is unique in many ways. It is the most powerful influence on the development of network technologies all over the world.

5.2 GENERALIZED STRUCTURE OF A TELECOMMUNICATIONS NETWORK

KEY WORDS: telecommunications network, structure, data terminal equipment, access network, backbone, core network, data centers, service control point, private branch exchange (PBX), user information, subsidiary information

Despite differences among computer, telephone, TV, radio, and transmission networks, there are several common features in their structures. In general, any telecommunications network comprises the following components (Figure 5.1):

■ Data terminal equipment (possibly connected to the network)
■ Access networks

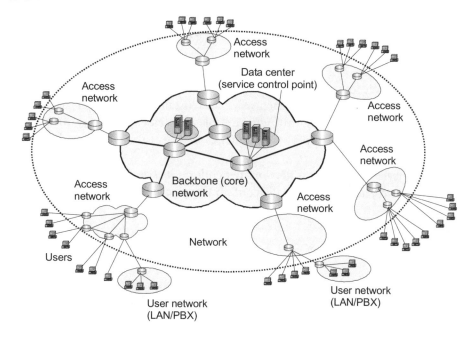

Figure 5.1 Generalized structure of a telecommunications network

- Backbone (or core) network
- Data centers or service control points

Both the access network and the backbone are built on the basis of switches. Each switch is equipped with several ports, which are connected to the ports of other switches by **communications links.**

5.2.1 Access Networks

> **Access networks** make up the lower hierarchical layer of the telecommunications network. The main purpose of the access network is the concentration of information flows, arriving through various types of links from the user equipment, within a relatively small number of nodes of the backbone.

When dealing with computer networks, end nodes are computers; with telephone networks, end nodes are phone sets; and with TV or radio networks, they are the appropriate TV and radio receivers. The terminal equipment of the end users can be joined into networks that are not included in the telecommunications network, since it represents the end user's property and is located at the user's territory. End user's computers are joined to form LANs; telephones can be connected to the **Private Branch Exchange (PBX).**

Access network is a regional network characterized by significant branching. Access networks, similar to telecommunications networks, can comprise several layers. The illustration in Figure 5.1 shows two of them. Switches installed in the lower-layer nodes multiplex the information arriving through multiple subscriber channels, often called local loops, and transmit it to upper-layer switches that, in turn, pass it to backbone switches.

The number of layers of the access network depends on its size. Small access networks can comprise one layer; larger ones usually contain two or even three.

5.2.2 Backbones

The **backbone** (**core**) network joins separate access networks and transmits transit traffic between them using fast links.

Backbone switches can operate not only with information connections between individual users but also with aggregate information flows transporting the data of a large number of user connections. As a result, information travelling via backbone arrives to the receivers' access network, where it is demultiplexed and switched so that each user's input port receives only the information addressed to that user.

EXAMPLE   *You can easily see that any national system of roads has the same hierarchical structure as a large telecommunications network. As a rule, villages and small towns are connected by an extensive, branched infrastructure of local roads. These roads are narrow; the intensity of traffic between these settlements is low, so there is no reason to make such roads multilane. Such roads join highways, which are wider and ensure higher speeds. Highways, in turn, connect to freeways. This reflects the intensity of traffic between individual settlements and regions of the country and makes motor traffic more efficient.*

5.2.3 Data Centers

Information (or **data**) **centers,** or **service control points** (**SCP**), provide the information services of the network. Such centers can store two types of information:

- User information, which directly interests the end users of the network
- Subsidiary information, which helps to provide services to end users

Examples of information resources are Web portals containing reference information, news, the data of Internet shops, etc. In telephone networks, such centers provide services such as emergency calls (e.g., calls to police or an ambulance service) and the inquiry services of organizations such as railway stations, airports, or shops.

Information centers, which store resources of the second type, include various systems for user authentication and authorization that the network owner uses to check user rights to specific services, billing systems that calculate the payment for services in commercial networks, user account databases storing user logins and passwords, and lists of services to which each user is subscribed. In telephone networks, there are centralized SCPs, where computers run programs for nonstandard handling of user phone calls, such as calls to the free inquiry services of commercial organizations (1-800 services) or calls made during telepolling.

Naturally, each type of network has many specific features; nevertheless, its structure generally corresponds to the previously described one. At the same time, depending on the network's aims and size, some components of the generalized structure might or might not be present. For example, in a small LAN, there are no pronounced access networks or backbone, since they are merged into a common and relatively simple structure. As a rule, in an enterprise-wide network, there is no billing system, since the company provides services to its employees on a noncommercial basis. Data centers might lack some telephone networks. In TV networks, the access network looks more like a distribution network, since information flows in such networks are unidirectional — from network to subscribers.

5.3 TELECOMMUNICATIONS CARRIER NETWORKS

KEY WORDS: telecommunications, carrier, services service provider, enterprise-wide network, telephony services, computer network services, transport services, information services, interactive services, broadcast services, mass individual clients, corporate clients, Infrastructure, RBOC, BOC, CLEC, ILEC, Interexchange Carriers (IXC), points of presence (POPs), traditional local carriers, regional, competitive, national, and international carriers

As already mentioned, one of the most important characteristics of network classification is the variety of users to which the network provides services. Networks belonging to telecommunications carriers (service providers) provide public services; enterprise-wide networks usually serve only the employees of the company that owns the network.

Telecommunications carrier is a traditional term denoting a specialized company that creates telecommunications networks for providing public services, owns this network, and maintains its operation.

Telecommunications carriers provide commercial services to their customers according to service agreements.

Telecommunications carriers differ from one another in the following ways:

- Set of provided services
- Territory within the limits of which the services are provided
- Type of clients toward which the services are oriented
- Infrastructure that the carrier owns — communications links, switching equipment, information servers, etc.
- Relation to the monopoly in the field

5.3.1 Services

Contemporary telecommunications carriers usually provide services of various types, for example, telephony services and Internet services. **Services** can be classified by several layers and groups. Figure 5.2 shows only some or the main layers and groups. However, even this incomplete pattern demonstrates the range of modern telecommunications services and the complexity of their interrelations. Services of higher layers are based on the services of the underlying layers. Groups of services are combined according to the type of networks that provide them — telephone or computer networks. For a more complete pattern, one could complement this illustration by including services provided by TV and radio networks.

Leased line services are the services of the lowest layer, since the customers who get this service have to build their own network infrastructure on the basis of these leased lines.

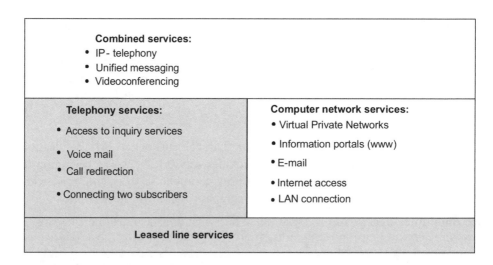

Figure 5.2 Classification of the services provided by telecommunications networks (the filled areas correspond to the traditional services of telecommunications carriers)

They need to install telephone switches or packet-switched network switches before they can benefit from this service. Usually, the customers that subscribe to this service are either telecommunications carriers that do not own communications links or large companies that build private, enterprise-wide networks based on these leased lines. Enterprise-wide networks will be covered in the next section.

The next layer comprises two large groups of services — **telephony services** and **computer network services**. Telephony and leased line services represented a traditional set of services for a long time.

Computer network services appeared much later than telephony services, and even now they are significantly behind traditional telephony services on the level of financial income. Nevertheless, most telecommunications carriers provide computer network services, since they have excellent prospects and are significantly ahead of traditional services in rate of growth. In absolute amounts, data traffic has already exceeded voice traffic. However, low rates for data transmission services still prevent them from keeping pace with traditional services in terms of income.

Each of the previously described layers of services can be divided into sublayers. For example, on the basis of the Internet access service (transport connection of a computer or LAN to the Internet), the carrier might provide the customer the ability to organize a VPN, secured against other Internet users, or to create the customer's Web portal, hosting it within the service provider network.

Currently, the top layer of service hierarchy is occupied by combined services implemented on the basis of the coordinated operation of computer and telephone networks. International IP telephony that has taken a significant proportion of customers from traditional international telephony is a striking example of such services.

> Combined services are a direct consequence of network convergence as well as the driving force behind this process.

Services can also be classified using the principles of **transport services** or **information services**. According to this classification, telephone conversations are a transport service, since telecommunications carriers deliver voice traffic from subscriber to subscriber. Inquiry services of the telephone network of Web sites are an example of information services.

This type of difference in services provided by telecommunications companies is reflected by the differences in their names. Traditional companies whose main field of business activity has always been telephony services and leased line services (i.e., transport services) are usually referred to as **carriers**. The term **service provider** (*SP*) became popular with the explosive growth of the Internet and its WWW service (i.e., an information service).

Services can be differentiated not only by the type of information they provide but also by the level of interactivity. Thus, telephone networks provide **interactive services**, since two subscribers participate in a conversation (or several subscribers, if it is a conference) and interact alternately. Similar services are provided by computer networks, where users can view the site contents while answering the questions of the registration form or, for example, playing interactive games.

On the other hand, radio networks and TV networks provide noninteractive **broadcast services**: information is transmitted only in one direction — from network to subscribers, according to the point-to-multipoint arrangement.

5.3.2 Clients

The audience consuming infocommunications services can be divided into two large groups: **mass individual clients** and **corporate clients**.

In the first group, the customer's premise usually is a private dwelling, and the clients are lodgers who need basic services like telephone communications, TV, radio, and Internet access. For such clients, the most important factor is the economy of the service: a low monthly rate; the possibility of using standard terminal devices such as telephones, TV sets, or PCs; and the possibility of using the existing wiring such as twisted pair or TV coaxial cables. Sophisticated, difficult to use, and expensive terminal devices such as computerized TV sets or IP telephones are not likely to become widespread until their cost becomes comparable to that of traditional TV sets or telephones.

Beside the price factor, such devices must support a simple user interface that does not require the user to attend special courses to master the device. The wiring that exists in most buildings also presents a limitation for Internet access and new services provided by computer networks, since initially it was not intended for data transmission. An installation of a new high-quality cable (fiber optic, for example) is expensive. Because of this, home users most often connect to the Internet using low-speed, dial-up modem connections. However, nowadays, new technologies such as Digital Subscriber Line (DSL) are becoming more popular, allowing the transmission of data through existing telephone lines at significantly faster speeds than traditional modems. Besides this, there are access technologies that use existing cable TV networks for data transmission.

Corporate clients are usually various organizations or corporations. Small businesses are not significantly different from individual clients, if you look at the set of required services. As a rule, these are the same basic telephony and TV services and standard dial-up access to Internet information resources. The only difference lies in the number of phone numbers needed (usually, two or more).

Large corporations, comprising several geographically distributed departments or affiliations and employing mobile users that often work at home (telecommuters), need an extended set of services. Such services must include *VPN*. The carrier that provides such a service creates for the company the illusion that all of its departments and affiliations are connected by the private network (i.e., that the network is entirely owned and managed by the customer). The carrier's network is used for these purposes. The carrier's network is a public one, simultaneously transmitting the data of a large number of clients.

Nowadays, corporate customers frequently require not only transport but also information services. For instance, they move their Web sites and databases to the premises of the service provider, which is delegated the responsibility of maintaining their operation and ensuring quick access to these information resources for employees of the corporation and, possibly, for other subscribers of the carrier's network.

5.3.3 Infrastructure

Infrastructure: Beside the subjective reasons influencing the formation of services supplied by the telecommunications carrier, technical factors play a significant role. Thus, to provide line-leasing services, the carrier must have transmission networks at his disposal. As an example, consider SDH or circuit-switched network such as ISDN. To provide information services, it is necessary to create Web sites connected to the Internet so that Internet users can access it.

If the carrier doesn't own the entire infrastructure required for providing a specific service, it is possible to use the services of another carrier. Such services, combined with some elements of the carrier's own infrastructure, make it is possible to construct the service required by the customer. For example, a telecommunications carrier hired to create a public e-commerce Web site might not have its own IP network connected to the Internet. To provide this service, it is sufficient to create the content and place it on the computer of another carrier whose network is connected to the Internet. The leasing of physical communications links for creating a telephone or computer network is another example of providing services when one of the elements of the hardware or software infrastructure is missing. The carrier that provides services to other telecommunications carriers is often called the carrier of carriers.

In most countries, telecommunications carriers must obtain licenses for providing specific kinds of services from governmental structures. The situation was not always like this. In practically all countries, carriers were monopolists in the telecommunications services market on a national scale. Nowadays the process of demonopolizing telecommunications services is proceeding rapidly.

DEMONOPOLIZATION OF THE TELECOMMUNICATIONS MARKET IN THE USA

As a result, monopolists lose their privileges. Sometimes they are forcibly broken into smaller companies. For example, in the United States, AT&T had a monopoly for providing both local telephony services and long-distance telecommunications until 1984. In 1984, according to a court decision, AT&T was broken into smaller parts, the most important of which were AT&T Long Lines, which was allowed only to provide long-distance service, and 23 Bell Operating Companies (BOCs), which have the right to provide telephony services only on a local scale. To provide services on a regional scale, the BOCs were joined into seven Regional BOCs (RBOCs).
National monopolists, deprived of their privileges and divided into smaller companies, have to compete for clients with new carriers that appear in the local services markets as well as in the regional markets and long-distance services market. Such carriers are

usually called competitive. In the United States, the competitive evolution of the telecommunications services market was sped up in 1996, when Congress approved the Telecommunications Act, removing telecommunications carrier limitations on providing services only in one market segment, either long-distance/regional or local services. Nowadays, competitive local exchange carriers (CLECs) in the United States are numerous, as are former local monopolists — incumbent local exchange carriers (ILECs). The competition is no less intense in the U.S. regional and long-distance market, where a lot of large carriers known as Interexchange Carriers (IXC) exist. This terminology is important because it is sometimes is used when describing project solutions and technologies. Therefore, the type of telecommunications carrier (IXC, CLEC, or ILEC) marks the carrier's position within the system of carriers and service providers as well as the specific services provided.

5.3.4 Coverage Territory

According to the territory covered by their services, carriers are divided into local, regional, national, and international.

Local carriers operate within a city or rural area. **Traditional local carriers** (ILECs, in U.S. terminology) are the operators of the city telephone networks that own all appropriate transport infrastructures: local loops connecting subscribers' premises (flats, buildings, and offices) with a central office. Telephony switches and communications links lie between them. Currently, besides traditional local carriers, there are **competitive** ones (CLEC), which often provide new types of services, mainly related to the Internet. Sometimes they compete with traditional carriers in the telephony sector as well.

Despite the demonopolization of telecommunications, traditional local carriers remain the owners of local loops.

Under such conditions of unequal rights, competitive local carriers often experience difficulties running their businesses. They have several options. First, they can specialize in providing additional services only related to data transmission and processing: arranging Internet access, hosting information resources of their clients, and so on. To organize subscriber access to these resources, such carriers have to sign contracts with the traditional carriers that direct the subscriber's traffic connected to its network to the network of the competitive carrier. In this case, the natural specialization of service providers is clearly noticeable, since each specializes in the area for which the available infrastructure of the company is most suitable. Under such conditions, cooperation encourages new services. Second, competitive carriers can lease local loops from traditional carriers. Usually, traditional carriers are reluctant to do so, although legislation in some countries encourages or even forces such action. The third option is to create one's own networks of local loops. Here, the competitive carrier has two options: wired or wireless local loops. Taking into account the number of private residences, the difficulties in laying cables, and the necessity of purchasing a license from local authorities, a wired version often proves to be economically inefficient. This circumstance has generated significant interest in wireless solutions, which are growing rapidly.

Regional and **national carriers** providing services for large territories have the appropriate transport infrastructures at their disposal. Traditional carriers of this scale transmit telephone traffic between the branch exchanges of local carriers. Usually, they own large transit branch exchanges connected to high-speed communications links. These companies usually are carriers of carriers. Among their clients are local carriers or large corporations with affiliations and departments in various cities of a specific region or even a country. Their own advanced transport infrastructure allows such carriers to provide long-distance services and transmit large volumes of information without processing.

The services of international carriers span several countries. The best-known among them are Cable & Wireless, Global One, and Infonet. They own backbones that sometimes cover several continents. Often, such carriers operate in close cooperation with national carriers, using their access networks for delivering information to clients.

5.3.5 Relationships among Different Types of Carriers

Figure 5.3 illustrates the relationships among different types of carriers and among their networks. This illustration also shows two types of clients — individual and corporate. Bear in mind that each client usually requires two kinds of services — telephony services and data services. As a rule, individual clients have telephones and computers in their homes. Corporate clients own appropriate networks — telephone networks supported by PBX and LAN for data transmission built on the basis of the company's switches.

For connecting client equipment, carriers organize **points of presence** (**POPs**) — buildings or premises where they place access equipment for connecting a large number of local loops from clients. Sometimes, these POPs are called central offices, a term used by telephone carriers. Subscribers connect to POPs of local carriers; local carriers or large-scale corporate clients, which need high-speed access and coverage to connect their offices and branches in different cities and countries, connect to the POPs of top-level carriers.

Since the process of convergence has not yet resulted in the creation of a unified network for serving all kinds of traffic, each carrier network in this illustration represents two networks — a telephone network and data network.

As can be seen from Figure 5.3, in today's competitive world of telecommunications, there is no strict hierarchy of carriers. Interrelations among carriers and their networks can be complicated. For instance, the CLEC2 network has a direct connection not only to Regional carrier3, as required by the hierarchy, but also to National carrier 3. This may be because the company provides less expensive services for transmitting international traffic than Regional carrier3. Furthermore, as Figure 5.3 shows, not all carriers own transport infrastructure (e.g., CLEC1). CLEC1 often only provides additional information services (e.g., it supplies video on demand to ILEC1 subscribers or develops and supports their home pages). Such carriers also place their equipment (such as video servers) in the POP of another carrier, as is shown.

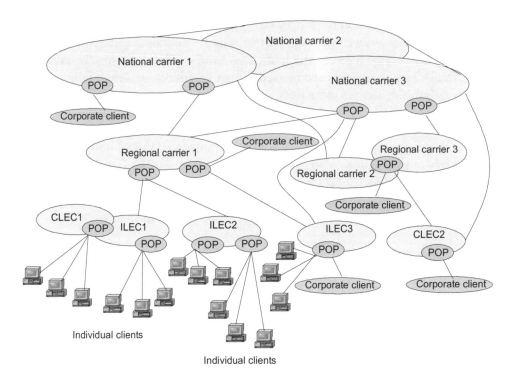

Figure 5.3 Interrelations among different types of communications carriers

5.4 CORPORATE NETWORKS

KEY WORDS: Department network, corporate network, building or campus network, workgroup network, enterprise-wide networks, subnetwork

A **corporate network** is the network whose main goal is to support the operation of the specific company that owns it. Users of an enterprise-wide network are the employees of that specific company. In contrast to telecommunications carrier networks, enterprise-wide networks do not provide services to third-party organizations or external users.

Although any network owned by a company of any size can formally be considered a enterprise-wide network, this term is generally used for the networks owned by large corporations that have departments or affiliations in different cities and, probably, in different countries. Therefore, an enterprise-wide network is usually an internet comprising LANs and WANs.

The structure of an enterprise-wide network generally corresponds to the structure of the telecommunications network considered previously. However, there are differences.

For example, LANs, connecting end users in this case, are integrated into the enterprise-wide network. Furthermore, the names of structural divisions of the enterprise-wide network usually reflect not only the coverage territory but also the organizational structure of the company. It is, therefore, common to divide enterprise-wide networks into subnetworks of departments or workgroups, building or campus networks, and a backbone.

5.4.1 Department Networks

Department networks are networks used by relatively small groups of employees working in the same department of the company. These employees solve common problems or accomplish common tasks, working in departments such as accounting or marketing. It is generally assumed that a single department might have 100–150 employees. Department networks consist of a LAN spanning all premises owned by the department. Depending on the situation, this might be several rooms or an entire floor of a building.

The main goal of the department network is to share local resources such as applications, data, laser printers, and modems. Usually, department networks have one or two file servers, some hubs and switches and, have no more than 30 users (Figure 5.4). Most company

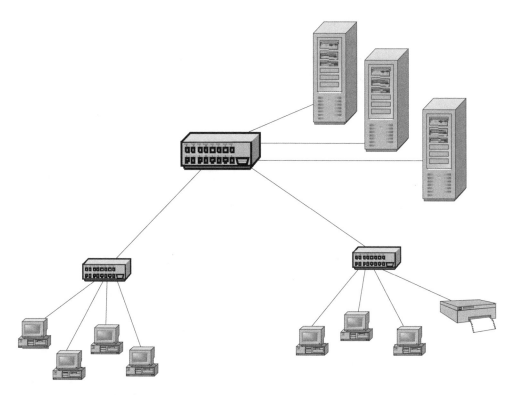

Figure 5.4 Example of a department-wide network

traffic is localized within these networks. Department networks are usually based on a single network technology — Ethernet (or several technologies of the Ethernet family — Ethernet, Fast Ethernet, or more rarely, Gigabit Ethernet), Token Ring, or FDDI. Typically, such networks use no more than two types of operating systems.

The tasks related to network maintenance at the department level are relatively simple: adding new users, eliminating the consequences of simple failures, and installing new nodes and new versions of software products. The tasks of managing and maintaining such networks can be delegated to an employee only dedicated to administrative tasks part-time. Most frequently, the administrator of the department-level network is not a specially trained expert. However, usually this individual is the one with a better understanding of computer hardware and software than other employees. His or her task is to accomplish administrative functions.

There is another type of network similar to a department-level network — the **workgroup network**. These are quite small networks of 10–20 computers. Workgroup networks are practically no different from the previously described department networks. Properties such as network simplicity and homogeneity are the most evident in workgroup networks.

Workgroup networks often use LAN technologies based on shared media. The higher the network hierarchical level, the less frequently shared media are used; instead, they are replaced by switched LANs.

Department networks can be situated within the building or campus network. They can also represent the network of a remote office. A department network is connected to the building or campus network using LAN technology. Nowadays, this probably will be one of the representatives of the Ethernet family. The remote office network connects directly to the backbone, using one of the WAN technologies (e.g., Frame Relay).

5.4.2 Building or Campus Networks

Building or campus networks connect a number of networks owned by several departments of the same company, located in a separate building or spanning several square miles (Figure 5.5). In building such networks, LAN technologies are used, since their functional capabilities are sufficient for ensuring this coverage area.

Normally, a building or campus network is built according to the hierarchical principle (i.e., it has its own backbone, usually based on the Gigabit Ethernet technology). Networks of workgroups and departments, connected to this backbone, are usually based on Fast Ethernet or Ethernet. The Gigabit Ethernet backbone is practically always switched, although there is a variant of this technology based on a shared medium.

Services provided by this network include internetworking among department networks and access to company databases, fax servers, fast modems, and printers. As a result, employees of each department get access to some files and other resources of the networks of other departments. Independent access to enterprise-wide databases is an important service provided by campus networks.

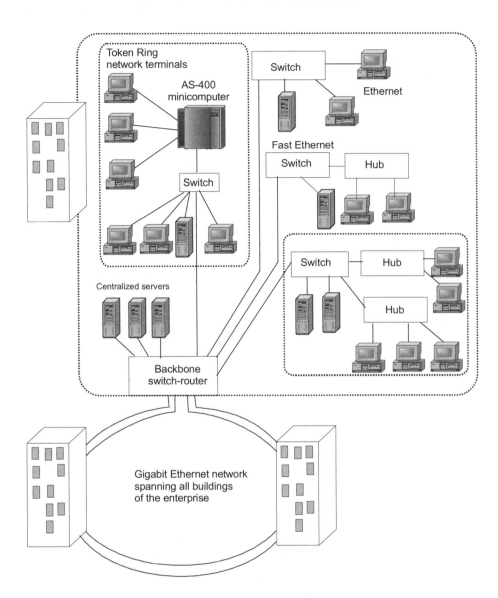

Figure 5.5 Example of a campus network

It is only at campus level that the problems of integrating heterogeneous hardware and software start to arise. The types of computers, network operating systems, and network equipment might be different in each department. Hence, campus networks become difficult to manage and control. Most frequently, networks of this scale are internetworks based on IP technology.

5.4.3 Enterprise-Wide Networks

Enterprise-wide networks are distinguished in that information services come into foreground. These networks cannot be limited to transport services only. In contrast to telecommunications carrier networks, which may or may not provide information services (since end-user computers are outside the limits of their responsibility), enterprise-wide networks cannot afford them. Both desktop computers of end users and servers are integral parts of any enterprise-wide network. Developers and support personnel involved in maintaining networks of this type must take this into account. It is possible to say that enterprise-wide networks are an example of infocommunications networks, where two types of services are on a par with each other. Enterprise-wide networks can be represented as LAN islands that flow in the telecommunications environment.

Another feature of the enterprise-wide network is its scale. Department-level or building-level networks are rarely called enterprise-wide, although this is formally true. Usually, the term enterprise-wide is used to designate a network comprising a large number of department-wide or building-wide networks located in different cities and connected by WAN links.

The structure of the enterprise-wide network is not principally different from the generalized one shown in Figure 5.1. WAN technologies are used for connecting company LANs, which may be workgroup, department, or building/campus networks. Such networks consist of the *backbone* and *access* network. Corporations use the same WAN technologies as telecommunications carriers: ATM or Frame Relay. IP technology is commonly used for connecting LANs and WANs into the enterprise-wide network.

The number of users and computers in a enterprise-wide network can reach thousands; the number of servers may be hundreds. The distances between networks spanning separate regions might be so vast that the use of WAN links becomes a must (Figure 5.6). For connecting distant LANs and standalone computers to enterprise-wide networks, various telecommunications tools can be used, including circuits of transmission networks, radio channels, and satellite communications.

The high level of heterogeneity is a required attribute of such complex and large-scale networks. It is impossible to satisfy the requirements of a large number of users using software and hardware of the same type. An enterprise-wide network uses various types of computers, ranging from mainframes to PCs; several types of operating systems; and a variety of applications. Heterogeneous parts of enterprise-wide networks must operate as one, providing users convenient and easy access to all the resources they might require.

The arrival of enterprise-wide networks is a good illustration of a well-known philosophical postulate on a transition from quantity to quality. When connecting separate networks of a large, geographically distributed company into a single network, most qualitative characteristics of the internetwork exceed the critical threshold, after which it gains new qualitative characteristics. Under these conditions, the existing methods and approaches to solving problems typical of smaller networks became inapplicable. Problems that were minor in workgroup, department, or even campus networks (or that did not

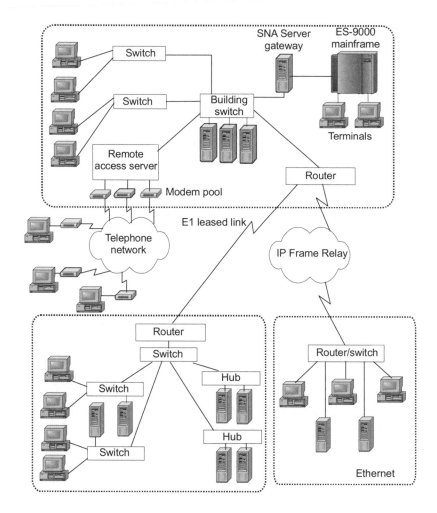

Figure 5.6 Example of an enterprise-wide network

even arise there) move to the foreground. This can be illustrated by a simple task, such as the supporting of user account information.

The simplest way of solving this problem is to store account data of all users in a local user account database on each computer. When any user attempts to gain access to these resources, the required data are retrieved from the local user account database. Based on this information, access may be granted or denied. This method works well for a small network of 5–10 computers. However, if the network has several thousand users, each of which might need access to tens of servers, this solution becomes extremely inefficient. Administrators must repeat the operation of creating user accounts as many times as there are servers in the network. Furthermore, the end user is forced to repeat the login procedure any time access to the resources of a new server is needed. A good solution to this problem in a large-scale network is the use of a centralized directory service, whose database can store accounts for all network users. The administrator completes the operation of creating user accounts only once, and, the user has to log in to the network only once (note that in this case, the user logs in to the entire network rather than to a single server).

When migrating from simple networks to more complicated ones, from department-wide networks to a enterprise-wide environment, geographical distances become wider, and it becomes increasingly difficult and expensive to support communications between computers. As the scale of the network grows, the requirements for its reliability, performance, and functional capabilities grow accordingly. Data volumes circulating within the network grow larger, and, besides the availability of these data, the network must ensure their security. All these factors result in the construction of enterprise-wide networks based on more powerful and versatile equipment and software.

5.5 INTERNET

KEY WORDS: the Internet, TCP/IP stack, WWW hypertext service, Internet service provider (ISP), Internet uniqueness, content, E-mail, FTP, VPN Tier 1, Tier 3, Tier 4, Backbone ISPs, regional ISPs, local ISPs, Internet Exchange (IX), Network Access Point (NAP), billing service provider, application service providers, content distribution providers, hosting provider

The Internet is not just a unique network; it is also a phenomenon of contemporary civilization. The changes that resulted from the arrival of the Internet are multifaceted. The WWW hypertext service has radically changed the method of presenting information by combining text, graphics, and sound within Web pages. Internet transport — inexpensive and available to practically all companies (and to most individuals through telephone networks) — has significantly simplified the task of building enterprise-wide networks. At the same time, it has brought to the foreground the important task of protecting enterprise-wide data during transmission using highly available public networks supporting millions of users. The TCP/IP stack, on which the entire Internet is based, has become the most popular protocol stack.

Internet steadily evolved to become the worldwide network for public communications. Its usage is gradually increasing, not only for publishing information (including promotions) but also for performing business transactions, such as purchasing goods and services and moving financial assets. For many companies, this means a radical change in their way of doing business. Furthermore, this changes client behavior, as more individuals begin to prefer electronic business operations.

5.5.1 Internet Uniqueness

Internet *uniqueness* manifests itself in many ways:

■ It is the *largest* network in the world by number of users, covered territory, total amount of transmitted traffic, and number of connected networks. Although the rate of the Internet growth has slightly decreased since the Internet revolution in the mid-1990s, it still remains quite rapid and has significantly exceeded the rate of growth in telephone networks.

■ Internet is a network that has *no single control center*. Nevertheless, it operates according to rules, providing all its users with the unified set of services. Internet is the network of networks, but any network connected to it is managed by an independent operator known as an **Internet service provider (ISP)**. Some central authorities exist, but they are responsible only for the unification of technical policy, a coordinated set of technical standards, and for the centralized assignment of parameters vitally important in such a giant network. This includes the names and addresses of computers and networks connected to the Internet. However, they are not responsible for day-to-day maintenance of the Internet or for supporting it in a usable state.

■ This high degree of decentralization has advantages and drawbacks. One advantage is the *ease of scaling*. For example, to start a business, it is sufficient for a new ISP to conclude an agreement with at least one of the existing ISPs, after which all users of the new ISP get access to all Internet resources. Negative consequences of decentralization include the complications related to the modernization of Internet technologies and services. Radical changes require coordinated efforts by all ISPs (note that if the network had a single owner, such modifications would be significantly easier). Because of these complications, many new, promising technologies are used only within the network of a single provider. A good example is the technology of group broadcasting, which is badly needed for efficient organization of audio and video broadcasting over the Internet. This technology still cannot overcome the boundaries separating ISPs. Another example is the relatively low reliability of Internet services. This is because no ISP is responsible for the final result, such as the access of client A to site B if they belong to the networks of different ISPs.

■ The Internet is an *inexpensive network*. For instance, the popularity of the new Internet service — Internet telephony — is in many respects the result of its significantly lower rates for international telephone communications compared to the rates of traditional telephone networks. More importantly, this low rate is not caused by a temporary price reduction used as a marketing trick by the companies hoping to conquer new territory. On the contrary, low prices are caused by objective reasons, such as the significantly lower cost of the Internet transport infrastructure characteristics for packet-switching networks in comparison to the infrastructure of traditional telephone networks. There are some anxieties, of course, that the Internet will grow more expensive over time as technologies and services become more advanced. Developers of Internet technologies and ISPs know about this danger and, therefore, examine each innovation from this aspect.

However, the Internet would never have become what it is if not for another unique feature — its vast information **content** and *the ease of access to this content* for all Internet users. The Internet stores terabytes of information available to end users as Web pages. Until 1991, the Internet was a popular network for a relatively narrow but worldwide audience of users. These were mainly employees and students of universities and research centers. All other clients, such as large corporations, banks, and governmental organizations, that required data networks services used other packet networks, namely X.25.

Neither X.25 networks nor the Frame Relay networks that replaced them in the mid-1990s had anything similar to the WWW service. With the arrival of the Web, users immediately understood that something convenient and useful had appeared. Before the invention of the Web, the Internet was mainly used as an information system, not as transport. E-mail and FTP archives existed from the first years of the Internet's existence. However, the tools providing access to text information stored in FTP archives, which mainly provided the results of scientific research, were rather primitive. Consequently, searching for required information by file name required hours or even days.

Convenient forms of presenting interrelations among different parts of information content, such as hyperlinks, and the standard graphical browser, which easily and efficiently runs in all popular operating systems, resulted in the Internet revolution. Internet was quickly filled with information presented as Web pages, gradually turning into encyclopedias, daily newspapers, promotion agencies, and a vast shop. Nowadays, many individuals can't imagine their life without regularly surfing the Web — for communicating with friends, for searching for urgently needed information, for hunting for a new job, or for paying the bills.

NOTE   *However, it would be incorrect to consider that Internet technology has forced or is forcing all other network technologies out of use. This is far from true and is unlikely to happen. TCP/IP is internetworking technology that leaves room for other technologies, namely, ones used within each separate network forming the Internet. Therefore, Internet success does not serve as a reason to study only TCP/IP technologies. In contemporary networks, TCP/IP closely interacts with many other technologies, such as Ethernet, ATM, Framer Relay, MPLS, and ADSL.*

5.5.2 Internet Structure

Rapid growth in the number of people attracted by the information contained in Web sites has significantly changed the attitude of corporate users and telecommunications carriers toward this network. Nowadays, Internet is supported by practically all traditional telecommunications carriers. Furthermore, many new companies have created businesses exclusively on the basis of providing Internet services. Therefore, the general structure

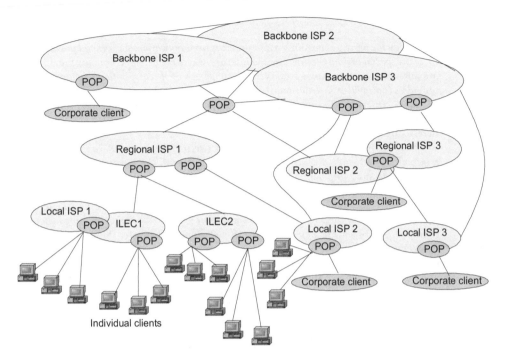

Figure 5.7 Internet structure

of the Internet shown in Figure 5.7 is in many respects a reflection of the general structure of the worldwide telecommunications network, a fragment of which was considered in Figure 5.3.

There are various approaches to the classification of ISPs. Figure 5.7 shows one of them, which is similar to the existing classification of telecommunications carriers. According to this classification, the main characteristics of an ISP are coverage, territory, and the set of provided services. **Backbone ISPs** are similar to international telecommunications carriers. They own backbones covering large territories (specific countries, continents, and the entire world). Examples of backbone ISPs are companies like Cable & Wireless, MCI, and Global One. Accordingly, **regional ISPs** provide Internet services within the limits of specific regions (state, county, and district — depending on the administrative division adopted in specific countries), and **local ISPs** usually work within the limits of a city.

Relations between ISPs are based on *peer-to-peer commercial agreements* for the mutual transmission of traffic. Backbone providers usually have such agreements with all other backbone providers (since they are not numerous), and regional providers usually make such arrangements with one of the backbone providers and several other regional providers. At the same time, providers configure their equipment to ensure that traffic passes from one network to another in both directions.

NETWORK ACCESS POINTS/INTERNET EXCHANGE

To simplify the process of organizing interprovider communications for regional providers, there are special exchange centers on the Internet, where the networks of many providers are connected. Such exchange centers can be supported by specific, sufficiently high level providers (national or international) for lower-level providers connected to the network. Exchange centers can be supported by companies dedicated to accomplishing this task. Such exchange centers have special names — usually Internet Exchange *(IX) or* Network Access Point *(NAP).*

The role played by NAP/IX in traffic exchange between networks of ISPs can vary. In the minimal variant, such a center simply provides ISPs with the premises for installing communications equipment. The ISPs establish all their own physical and logical connections. The situation in which the communications equipment of the NAP/IX takes part in the traffic exchange between ISPs is more common. In this case, NAP/IX only provides physical connections among the equipment of all ISPs, without creating logical connections between ISP networks for traffic exchange. Therefore, ISPs connected to NAP/IX using this method still have to make arrangements with one another. Finally, there are data exchange centers that combine traffic exchange functions with commercial functions. These centers, known as clearinghouses, act as a stock exchange for wholesale bandwidth trading. All ISPs connecting to such centers declare their cost for data transmission, and the center plays the role of mediator when making arrangements.

Another popular ISP classification divides them into four categories — **Tier 1, Tier 2, Tier 3**, and **Tier 4** (see **http://www.nwfusion.com**).

Definitions of the Tier 1, Tier 3, and Tier 4 ISPs coincide with the previously provided definitions of backbone, regional, and local ISPs. However, the Tier 2 category is defined for special types of ISPs.

A Tier 2 ISP provides Internet services to a large number of end users in a specific country or even on an entire continent. It provides a range of information and communications services. A Tier 2 ISP is similar to a local ISP in that it works directly with Internet users. However, the scale of the coverage area distinguishes it from local providers. Companies such as America Online are Tier 2 ISPs.

The arrival of Tier 2 ISPs is based on arrangements with multiple local telecommunications carriers that do not provide Internet services on their own. In Figure 5.7, the ILEC2 company is an example of such a carrier. ILEC2 owns local loops initially intended for telephone traffic. Nowadays, its subscribers can use the same physical channels for transmitting data using modems. Two types of modems are currently applicable for local loops — dial-up and Asymmetric Digital Subscriber Line (ADSL). Dial-up modems connect the end user's computer to the ISP network temporarily, similar to the way in which the telephone connects the user to the telephone network just for the period of a conversation. An ADSL modem ensures a persistent connection between a computer and an ISP network.

Since ILEC2 provides only telephone services, it separates telephone traffic from data traffic in its POP. Then, it processes telephone traffic in the usual manner, using telephone switches and directing data traffic to the ISP with which it has made an arrangement (Regional ISP1, in Figure 5.7). If the ISP has agreements with a larger number of local operators, it becomes a Tier 2 ISP that does not have its own infrastructure for client access.

As a rule, Tier 2 ISPs interact with other ISPs through a Tier 1 ISP, which transmits their traffic long distances and provides other useful services such as settling mutual payments.

The previously described interpretation of the Tier 1–Tier 4 terms is not the only one possible. For example, in some books you can find that the definitions of these terms take into account only the territory covered by services (i.e., they coincide with the definitions of international, backbone, regional, and local ISPs).

It is also possible to classify ISPs according to the types of the services they provide. In this case, the general term ISP is usually applied to companies that only provide transport services to end users. That is, they ensure the transmission of their traffic to the networks of other ISPs.

- If an ISP has its own Web sites and fills them with content, it is referred to as an **Internet content provider (ICP)**. Most ISPs are also ICPs because they support their own information sites.

- If the company provides premises, links, and servers for content created by other companies, it is called **a hosting provider**.

- There are also **content distribution providers (CDPs)**, which do not create content but are involved in hosting content in multiple locations closest to the users to increase the speed of user access to the information.

- **Application service providers (ASPs)** provide clients with access to large-scale, universal software products that are difficult to support. Generally, these are enterprise-wide users interested in company-management applications, such as SAP R3.

- Since the Internet became a phenomenon of social life, the number of providers offering appropriate services is steadily growing. For example, some companies provide a service for universal payment of the bills (**billing service provider**) in cooperation with municipal authorities and the suppliers of heat and electricity.

5.5.3 Internet Boundaries

Now, examine Internet boundaries. After reading this section, you'll probably ask a reasonable question: Is it possible to outline the Internet's boundaries if it is integrated into the common infrastructure of the telecommunications carriers?

To answer this question, consider a typical network of an ISP and its client in more detail (Figure 5.8).

The ISP considered in this example has two corporate clients and a large number of individual clients. Naturally, this ISP also has several connections to other ISPs through which it gets access to all the other ISPs making up the Internet. In the ISP network, there are several servers that host Web sites available to all Internet users. However, the CC1 client also has information resources containing confidential company information.

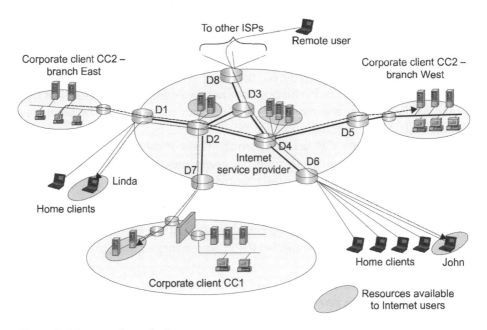

Figure 5.8 Internet boundaries

Such resources must be available only to the employees of the corporation. Therefore, corporate client CC1 has installed specialized communications devices in its networks, known as firewalls. A firewall protects the part of the network that contains servers intended for internal use, providing access to those servers only to clients located within that network. All requests to these servers from external clients are blocked by the firewall. A firewall allows access by internal clients to external information resources (i.e., Internet resources). It also passes the replies from external servers to the corporate employees. If corporate users do not need access to Internet resources, it would be easier to physically disconnect the internal network from the ISP network rather than to install a firewall.

The CC1 corporate client has its own network that includes several servers storing information and numerous computers used by company employees. The CC1 corporate client has a persistent high-speed connection to the ISP and uses the basic Internet access service that ensures data exchange between the enterprise-wide network and the ISP network. ISP networks also serve as transit networks for exchanging data with the networks of other ISPs. The CC1 client supports several Web sites of its own, which are available to all Internet users.

Most individual clients of the ISP in Figure 5.8 connect to its network using dial-up modems. Two individual clients — John and Linda — have persistent connections to the ISP network, installed using ADSL modems. John and Linda have created personal Web sites on their home computers, and each Internet user can connect to them and use the information contained in the sites.

The CC2 corporate client has two divisions located in different towns — West branch and East branch. Each of these divisions has its own LAN. These networks are based on the TCP/IP technology, the one used for the Internet. The CC2 client uses the ISP to connect the division networks into the enterprise-wide network rather than to get Internet access. Internet access is not needed for this client. On the contrary, this company needs to ensure a high level of data security. Because of this, in contrast to the CC1 client, the CC2 company uses the VPN service provided by its ISP rather than protecting its resources on its own. The VPN service ensures that the two networks of the CC2 clients will be isolated from Internet traffic. Therefore, all the information resources of these two networks — Web sites, databases, and so on — will be available to internal users only. Employees of the CC2 company cannot use Internet services, since their requests are not transmitted to the Internet.

Now answer our question. Is the ISP network a part of the Internet? On the one hand, you can answer *yes*, since it transmits client traffic into the Internet and contains public information resources. The remote Internet user shown in Figure 5.8 can request access to any Web site of the ISP.

On the other hand, part of the ISP's transport infrastructure does not relate to the Internet. The list of such network devices includes the D5 communications devices used exclusively for supporting the operation of the CC2 client and the link connecting D5 and D4. Besides this, the ISP network contains devices and links that only partially serve Internet clients. These are devices D1, D2, and D4, as well as the links connecting these devices.

Because of this, *yes* does not reflect the exact situation. The boundaries of the ISP network do not coincide with the Internet boundaries, even though the Internet is made up of ISP networks.

A similar situation exists for the CC1 client network. On the one hand, it is possible to state that its network is not a part of the Internet, because this company is not an ISP; rather, it is a client. Furthermore, the CC1 network contains resources protected by a firewall, which, consequently, are not part of the Internet. On the other hand, the CC1 network contains Web sites available to all Internet users, including the remote user. From the remote client's point of view, these Web sites are no different from the Web sites located within the ISP network. The CC1 network also contains resources protected by a firewall. Naturally, the resources protected by the firewall are not part of the Internet.

Home clients that connect to the Internet with dial-up connections usually do not place their Web sites on their home computers, because these sites would be unavailable to other Internet users most of the time. However, home users who have persistent Internet connections through ADSL modems are able to do so. In the network in Figure 5.8, John and Linda support their own Web sites, and remote users can use their content whenever desired.

From the point of view of its users, the Internet provides a set of information resources distributed over different networks — ISP networks, enterprise-wide networks, and the home networks and computers of individual users.

Transport tools of the Internet are also virtual. It is possible to consider them part of the resources (communications devices and links) of telecommunications carriers that ensure the transmission of Internet traffic — that is, the traffic between Internet clients and information resources (or between two Internet clients, in the case of e-mail or Internet telephony traffic).

In general, the network of an ISP is usually called a private IP network, since in using this network, the carrier usually provides both Internet services and other types of services such as VPN. If this is done using the technologies on which the Internet is based (i.e., the TCP/IP transport and the WWW information service), such services are called **intranet services**.

SUMMARY

▶ Computer networks provide services of two types: information and transport. Quite often, the term *network services* is interpreted as transport services, considering that information transmission is the main function of the network. Information services are provided by the end nodes of the network — servers; transport services are provided by the transit nodes — network switches and routers.

▶ Computer networks can be described using a generalized structure applicable to any telecommunications network. Such a generalized structure comprises the following components: *access network, backbone*, and *data centers*.

▶ Specialized companies that create telecommunications networks to provide public services, own these networks, and support their operation are called *telecommunications carriers*.

▶ Telecommunications carriers differ from one another by their set of supplied services, the territory within which these services are provided, the type of clients for which their services are intended, and the infrastructure owned by the carrier. These include links, communications equipment, and information servers. Telecommunications carriers specializing in providing computer network services are usually called service providers.

▶ A enterprise-wide network is a network whose main goal is to support the operation of the company that owns this network. Users of the enterprise-wide network are employees of that company.

▶ The Internet is a unique computer network providing various services all over the world. The Internet uses the TCP/IP stack for interconnecting networks based on various technologies. As a result of the Internet's popularity and its information services (e-mail, Web, and chat), the transport protocols of the TCP/IP stack became the ones used for building internetworks.

REVIEW QUESTIONS

1. Which term corresponds to the following definition: "Network intended for concentrating information flows arriving through multiple links from the equipment of the end users"?
   A. Backbone
   B. Access network
   C. Core network
   D. Operating network
2. Give examples of the data centers of different types of telecommunications networks.
3. List the main requirements for access and backbone networks.
4. List the types of clients that communications carriers may have.
5. When can a carrier network be named a corporate network?
6. What are the main characteristics of communications carrier networks?
7. Are leased line services traditional or a fairly new development for telecommunications carriers?
8. What additional services are offered by a competitive carrier just starting its business for attracting clients?
9. What is the difference between Tier 1 and Tier 2 ISPs?
10. What kind of service provides Internet access?
11. Is it possible for a communications carrier to provide Internet access without owning any communications links?
12. Establish the correlation between the descriptions of networks and their types (one network type is not described).

Network type	Enterprisewide network	Campus network	Department network	Telecommunications carrier network
Used by a group of employees (100–150 users). All network users are solving a particular business task. Based on a single technology.				

continues

Continued

Network type	Enter-prisewide network	Campus network	Depart-ment network	Telecommuni-cations carrier network
Thousands of computers, hundreds of servers. High heterogeneity level of computers, communications equipment, operating systems, and applications. WAN links are used.				
Connects smaller networks within the limits of a building. No WAN links. Services give all employees access to company databases.				

13. In what kind of networks (enterprise-wide or ISP) is the share of LANs greater?
14. What are hierarchical levels into which a enterprise-wide network can be divided?
15. List the kinds of ISP specializations.
16. If a corporate network has a persistent connection to the Internet, does this mean that it is a part of the Internet?

PROBLEMS

1. How can a competitive local carrier provide individual clients access to the resources of its network?
2. Which problems had to be solved to demonopolize the telecommunications industry?
3. Describe the Virtual Private Network service for telephone subscribers.
4. Describe the sequence of steps that company management has to take to make the company an ISP and to start providing services to its clients.
5. An ISP owns a backbone and access networks. To which kind of network is it expedient to connect a new data center?

6
NETWORK CHARACTERISTICS

6.1 INTRODUCTION

Computer networks are sophisticated and expensive systems that perform business-critical tasks and serve numerous users. Therefore, it is important to ensure not just the network operation but also the reliability and high quality of this operation.

The *quality of service* concept can be interpreted in a *broad* sense. This concept can include all possible properties of the network and of the service provider desirable for the end user. To enable both the user and the service provider to discuss service problems and establish relations on a formal basis, there are several commonly adopted characteristics of a network. In this chapter, we cover the characteristics related to the quality of network transport services. They are easier to formalize than characteristics of the quality of information services. The transport characteristics reflect such important network properties as performance, reliability, and security.

Some of these characteristics can be evaluated quantitatively and measured when serving users. The user and service provider can make the so-called *Service Level Agreement*, specifying requirements for quantitative values of some characteristics, for example, service availability.

The quality of service concept is often used in a narrow sense, as one of contemporary directions of network technologies and in this case the acronym QoS is used. This direction is aimed at the development of methods ensuring high-quality transmission of the traffic using the network. QoS characteristics have one common feature — they all reflect the negative effect of the queuing mechanism on traffic transmission, such as the temporary decrease of traffic delivery speed, variable delays in packet delivery, and packet loss because of overloading of the switch buffers. Methods of ensuring QoS will be covered in the next chapter.

6.2 TYPES OF CHARACTERISTICS

KEY WORDS: traffic, quality of service, QoS, performance, reliability, security, provider-only characteristic, queuing mechanism, requirements, Long-term characteristics, Medium-term characteristics, Short-term characteristics, congestion control, congestion avoidance, Service Level Agreement (SLA)

6.2.1 Subjective Quality Characteristics

If we polled several users to clarify what they mean when speaking about the quality of networking services, we might get a broad range of answers. The following opinions are the ones most likely to be encountered:

■ The network operates quickly and without delays.

■ Traffic is reliably transmitted.

- Service is provided continuously.

- Support and help desk services are working well, providing useful advice and really helping to solve the problems.

- Service is provided according to a flexible plan. I like that the speed of network access can be increased by a wide range at any desired time.

- The provider not only transmits my traffic but also protects my network from virus attacks and intrusions.

- I am always able to check how fast the provider transmits my traffic and whether data losses occur.

- Besides standard Internet access, the provider offers a wide range of supplementary services, such as hosting my personal Web site and IP telephony services.

These subjective evaluations reflect users' wishes related to the quality of network services. Clients (users) represent the most important part of every business, including data networks. However, there is another part — the service provider (commercial if the network is public, and noncommercial if the network is corporate). To enable both users and service providers to objectively assess the quality of network services, there are *formalized characteristics of the quality of network services* which allow for the quantitative evaluation of specific quality aspects.

6.2.2 Network Characteristics and Requirements

Using network **characteristics**, the subscriber can formulate specific **requirements** to the network. For example, the user can claim the following requirement: *average transmission rate of my information through the network must be no less than 2 Mbps.* In this case, the user applies the characteristic known as the average rate of data transmission through the network and defines the range of values for this characteristic that corresponds to good quality of service for the user (i.e., to efficient operation of the network).

All QoS characteristics for the transport services can be classified in one of the following groups:

- Performance
- Reliability
- Security
- Provider-only

The first three groups correspond to the transport service properties, which are most important for the user. The network must transmit information at the specified rate (*performance*), without losses or delays in service (*reliability*), and ensure protection against unauthorized access or forgery (*security*).

Naturally, service providers, aiming at client satisfaction, pay attention to *all* characteristics important for users. At the same time, there is the entire range of network characteristics, which are vital for service providers, but are of no importance for users.

Networks serve a large number of users, and service providers must organize their operations to simultaneously satisfy the requirements of *all* users. As a rule, this is a difficult problem, since the main network resources — links and switches/routers — are shared by user information flows. Providers must find a balance in resource distribution among concurrent flows that satisfies the requirements of all users. The solution to this problem includes planning resource utilization and controlling it when transmitting user traffic. Thus, the provider is interested in characteristics describing properties of resources used to serve network clients. For example, the provider is interested in switch performance, since providers must evaluate the number of flows that can be served using that switch. On the other hand, end users are not interested in the performance of a specific switch; rather, they are interested in the final result — whether or not their information flow is served with high quality.

The fourth group combines QoS characteristics that are of interest only to the service provider. One of the examples of such characteristics is network scalability (i.e., the possibility of increasing the number of users without changing network technologies).

6.2.3 Time Scale

Before covering the characteristics and methods of ensuring QoS, it would be useful to get acquainted with another classification — the time scale on which these characteristics are defined and on which QoS methods work.

Long-term characteristics are defined for periods ranging from several months to several years. These characteristics can be called project-solution characteristics, and appropriate methods of ensuring them are *network design and planning methods*. This group includes project solutions such as choosing the models and numbers of switches or selecting network topology and bandwidths of communications links. These parameters directly influence QoS characteristics. Some project solutions might prove to be successful and well balanced, ensuring that the network never gets congested. Other solutions might be less efficient, resulting in traffic bottlenecks, so delays and packet losses exceed the maximum limits.

Obviously, the total replacement of network equipment and full-scale network upgrades are labor-intensive operations, which usually require significant financial expense. Therefore, they do not occur frequently and continue to influence QoS for a long time.

Medium-term characteristics are defined by time intervals ranging from several seconds to several days. Examples of such characteristics are average rates of traffic flow or average delays in packet delivery, which are defined by quite long time intervals, during which large numbers of packets are processed. Methods of determining traffic routes are an example of methods working in this range. Traffic routes can remain unchanged for hours or days, provided that network topology and traffic parameters remain constant and data links and network switches do not fail.

Short-term characteristics are defined by intervals corresponding to the rate of processing individual packets (i.e., in milliseconds or microseconds). This group includes such characteristics as buffering time or the time spent by an individual packet in a queue of a switch or router. Methods developed specifically for analyzing and ensuring characteristics of this group are known as **congestion control** and **congestion avoidance** methods. They will be described further.

6.2.4 Service Level Agreement

The contract or agreement is a natural basis for normal cooperation between service providers and their clients (end users). Service providers for public data networks and their clients always make some form of agreement. However, such agreements do not always specify quantitative requirements for the efficiency of provided services. Quite often, such an agreement specifies the service to be provided too generally (e.g., Internet access). There exists another type of agreement, usually called a **Service Level Agreement (SLA)**. In such an agreement, the service provider and the client describe the quality of services to be provided in quantitative terms, using popular characteristics of network efficiency.

For instance, the SLA might state that provider is obliged to transmit the client's traffic without losses at the same average rate at which the client sends it to the network. The SLA also might stipulate that the present agreement remains in force provided that the average rate of the client traffic does not exceed a specific value (e.g., 3 Mbps). Otherwise, the provider has the right to discard excessive traffic. To make such agreements more definite and to enable each party to control its observance, it is necessary to specify the time period for which the average traffic rate is to be measured (day, hour, or second). The SLA becomes even more definite when both the tools and the methods used for measuring network characteristics are specified, so that both the service provider and the client understand the agreement unambiguously.

SLAs must not be concluded only between providers of commercial services and their clients but also within large companies. In the latter case, the SLA is made between different departments of the same company (e.g., the IT or telecom department) and the network service provider and between users and the functional departments of the company, such as the production department.

6.3 PERFORMANCE

KEY WORDS: Information rate, packet delays, corruption, distribution histogram, distribution density of the packet delay, statistical methods, average delay, jitter, coefficient of variation, maximum delay, maximum delay variation, network response time, round trip time, information rate, sustained information rate, commitment information rate, peak information rate, burst size, traffic burst coefficient, burstiness, bottlenecks

You already know of the main characteristics of network devices — link bandwidth and the performance of communications devices such as switches and routers. These are long-term characteristics of network resources of interest only to the service provider. Knowing these characteristics, providers can plan their business by determining the maximum number of users that they can serve.

Users, however, are interested in other performance characteristics, which would allow them to perform quantitative evaluations of the traffic rate and the quality of its transmission. To define these characteristics, begin by considering how the ideal network transmits traffic.

6.3.1 Ideal Network

Therefore, consider the network to be *ideal* if it transmits each bit of information with a constant delay equal to the delay of light propagation in a physical medium. Furthermore, no network link has an infinite bandwidth: Link bandwidth is finite; therefore, the information source transmits packets into the network within certain finite time intervals rather than instantly. This finite time interval, as you know already, is equal to the quotient obtained by dividing the packet size (measured in bits) by the bandwidth of the link.

The result of transmitting packets by such an ideal network is illustrated in Figure 6.1. The upper axis shows the times of packet transmission into the network from the source node; the lower axis shows the times of packet arrival to the destination node. In other words, the upper axis shows the offered load of the network, and the lower one demonstrates the results of transmitting this traffic through the network. Count the packet departure and arrival times from the instance of transmission of the first bit of the packet into the network and from the instance of arrival of the first bit to the destination node, respectively.

As can be seen from this illustration, the ideal network:

■ Delivers all packets to the destination node, losing or distorting none of them
■ Delivers all packets in the same order as they were sent
■ Delivers all packets with the minimum delay ($d_1 = d_2$, and so on)

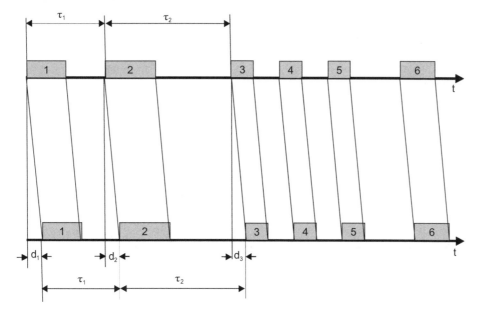

Figure 6.1 Packet transmission in an ideal network

It is important that all intervals between adjacent packets remain unchanged. For instance, the interval between the first packet and the second packet was equal to τ_1 when they were sent. This value remained the same when these packets arrived at the destination node.

> Reliable delivery of all packets with minimum delay and at a constant interpacket interval would satisfy any network user, no matter what kind of traffic is transmitted through the network — be it Web-service or IP-telephony traffic.

Now, let us investigate the deviations from the ideal model that can be encountered in a real network and the characteristics that can be used to describe these deviations (Figure 6.2).

■ Packets are delivered to the destination node *with variable delays.* As you already know, this is a generic property of the packet-switched networks. The random nature of the queuing process results in variable delays; at the same time, delays in the delivery of some packets might be considerable — tens of times more than the average delay value ($d_1 \neq d_2 \neq d_3$, and so on). Thus, the time correlation between adjacent packet changes, and this, in turn, may result in critical failures of some applications. For instance, during digital voice transmission, the unevenness of interpacket intervals results in significant voice distortions.

■ Packets can be delivered to the destination node *in an order different from the order in which they were sent.* For example, the diagram in Figure 6.2 shows that packet 4 has arrived at the destination node before packet 3. Such situations can be encountered in datagram networks, when different packets of the same flow are transmitted via

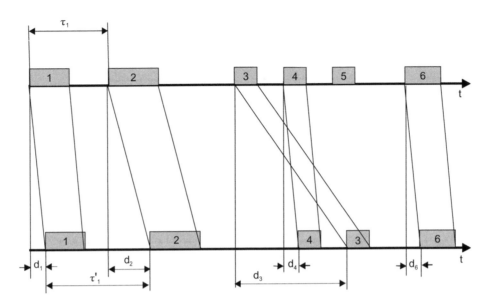

Figure 6.2 Packet transmission in a real network

different routes. Consequently, such packets wait in queues with different delay levels. Obviously, packet 3 passed a congested node or nodes. Therefore, its total delay proved to be so significant that packet 4 arrived before it.

■ Packets *can be lost or corrupted.* The latter situation is equivalent to packet loss, since most protocols cannot restore damaged data. In most cases, protocols are only able to detect that data corruption occurred, using the Frame Check Sequence (FCS).

■ The average rate of information flow at the input of the destination node can differ from the average rate of the information flow sent into the network by the source node. This is because of packet losses rather than packet delays. Thus, in the example shown in Figure 6.2, *the average rate of the outgoing flow decreases* because of the loss of packet 5. The more packets are lost or corrupted; the lower is the rate of information flow.

Obviously, the set of values of the transmission times of each individual packet provides a comprehensive characteristic of the traffic transmission quality. However, this characteristic of network performance is too bulky and redundant.

To represent QoS characteristics in compact form, it is necessary to use **statistical methods**. Statistical characteristics reveal such trends in the network behavior, which become stably apparent only during long periods. Trends in network behavior can be revealed only when tracing the transmission of millions of packets. In contemporary networks, the transmission time of a single packet is in the microsecond range of the time scale. For example, in Fast Ethernet, this transmission takes about 100 μsec; for Gigabit Ethernet, about 10 μsec; and for an ATM cell, from fractions of a microsecond to 3 μsec (depending on the transmission rate). Therefore, to obtain stable results, it is necessary to monitor the network for several minutes or, better still, several hours. Such time intervals are considered *long*.

There are two groups of statistical characteristics related to network performance:

- Characteristics of packet delays
- Characteristics of information rate

6.3.2 Characteristics of Packet Delays

The so-called **distribution histogram** of a random variable is the main tool of statistics. In our case, the random variable to be evaluated is the *delay of packet delivery*.

Assume that we have measured the delay of delivery for each packet and saved these results. To obtain the distribution histogram, we have to divide the entire range of possible delays into several intervals and calculate how many packets from the sequence fit within each interval. As a result, we obtain the histogram shown in Figure 6.3. In this example, all delay values fit within the range from 25 to 75 msec. The network introduces a fixed delay equal to 25 msec, related to the signal propagation and packet buffering. We have divided this range into six intervals. Consequently, we can use the following six numbers to characterize the network: $n1$, $n2$, $n3$, $n4$, $n5$, and $n6$. This form of representation is significantly more compact. The smaller the number of intervals into which we divide the entire range of values, the smaller the number of values used to characterize the measurements. However, it is necessary to observe a reasonable balance between our desire to reduce the number of intervals to a minimum and the information density of the characteristic.

The delay histogram provides quite a good representation of the network performance. Using it, we can evaluate which delays are probable and which are unlikely. The longer the time period during which we accumulate the data for creating the histogram, the more precisely the resulting chart will reflect the behavior trends of the network. This means that we will be able to predict the behavior of the network more precisely (with a higher level of probability). For example, using the bar chart shown in Figure 6.3, it is possible to state that the delay of packet delivery will not exceed 50 msec with the probability of 0.6. To obtain this assessment, we found the total number of packets for which delivery delays fell into all intervals smaller than 50 msec and divided this value by the total number of packets. In other words, we found the percentage of packets for which delays in delivery did not exceed 50 msec.

If we increase the number of intervals and the time of monitoring, at the limit we will get a continuous function known as the **distribution density of the packet delay** (in Figure 6.3, it is shown as a dashed line). From the probability theory it is known that to determine the probability of the random variable's taking one of the values from specific range, it is necessary to find an integral of this function within the lower and upper limits of the specified range. In other words, we need to find a superficial area of the figure limited by the distribution curve and X-axis within the specified range.

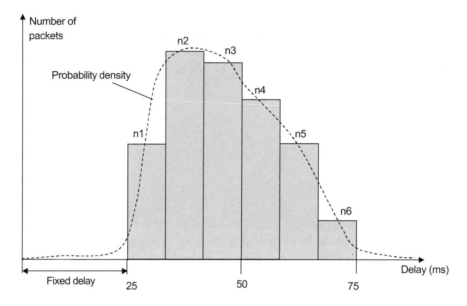

Figure 6.3 Histogram illustrating delay distribution

The most important feature of packet-switched networks is that many characteristics of such networks are of a *statistical* (probability) nature. We cannot guarantee that such characteristics at any given instance have any specific predefined values. We only can state that such events have specific probability, since data transmission processes in packet-switched networks are *random* by nature.

Consider several other delay characteristics frequently used in practice:

■ **Average delay (D)** is expressed as the sum of all delays (d_i), divided by the total number of all measurements (N):

$$D = \frac{\sum_{i=1}^{N} d_i}{N} \qquad (6.1)$$

■ **Jitter**[1] **(J)** represents the average deviation of delays from the average delay:

$$J = \sqrt{\frac{1}{N-1} \sum_{i=1}^{N} (d_i - D)^2} \qquad (6.2)$$

Both average delay and jitter are measured in seconds. Obviously, if all d_i delay values are equal, then $D = d_i$ and $J = 0$ (i.e., there is no jitter).

---

[1] The term *jitter* is the network jargon. The mathematical term for this value is standard deviation.

■ **Coefficient of variation** (C_v). This is a dimensionless value equal to the ratio of jitter to average delay:

$$C_v = \frac{J}{D} \tag{6.3}$$

Coefficient of variation characterizes the traffic without relating it to absolute values of the time scale. Ideal synchronous flow (i.e., a stream) will always have a standard deviation of 0. If the coefficient of variation is equal to 1, then the traffic is bursty.

■ **Maximum delay** is the value packet delays must not exceed with the predefined probability. Quite recently, we determined such values using the delay histogram. To obtain an assessment that definitely serves as evidence of the quality of the network operation, it makes sense to specify a high probability, for example, 0.95 or 0.99. If a company tells a user that the network ensures a delay level of 100 msec with a probability of 0.5, it is unlikely to satisfy him, since the user would not know anything about the delay level of half of the total packet number.

■ **Maximum delay variation** is the maximum value that the deviation of delay from its average value does not exceed with the predefined probability.

■ **Network response time** is an integral characteristic of the network from the user's viewpoint. It is this characteristic that users mean when they say that the network is operating slowly on any given day.

The response time is the time interval between the generation of the user request to some network service and the reception of a response to that request.

Network response time can be represented as a sum of several components (Figure 6.4). In general, it includes the time of request generation on the client computer $(t_{client1})$, the time required to transmit the request from client to server across the network $(t_{network1})$, the time required for processing requests at the server side (t_{server}), the time required for transmitting the responses from server to client across the network $(t_{network2})$,

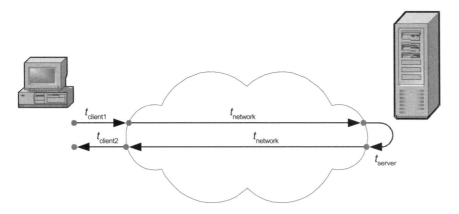

Figure 6.4 Network response time and Round Trip Time

and the time required for processing the server responses on the client computer ($t_{client2}$). Network response time characterizes the network as a whole. Among other factors, it depends on the quality of operation of the server hardware and software.

■ **Round Trip Time (RTT)** This is the *net* time required for data transportation from the source node to the destination node and back again, without accounting for the time required by the destination node for generating a response. This means that:

$$RTT = t_{network1} + t_{network2} \qquad (6.4)$$

In contrast to network response time, which characterizes the network as a whole, RTT allows for evaluating transport capabilities of the network individually and, consequently, allows us to improve them.

RTT is a useful characteristic, provided that transmission times in each direction are different. Similar to one-way delays, RTT can be evaluated by its average value and by its maximum value (with predefined probability).

Depending on the application type, it is possible to use a specific set of delay characteristics. Consider, for example, music broadcasting over the Internet. Since this service is not interactive, it tolerates significant delays for individual packets, sometimes of several minutes. However, delay variation must not exceed 100 to 150 ms; otherwise, the playback quality is significantly degraded. Consequently, in this case the requirements to the network must include limitations on the average delay variation or on the maximum value of the delay variation.

6.3.3 Characteristics of Information Rate

Information rate is always measured on some time interval as a result of dividing the volume of transmitted data by the interval duration. This means that information rate always represents an average value. However, depending on the duration of the measurement interval, this characteristic is known under different names.

Sustained Information Rate (SIR) is defined as relatively long time period, long enough to allow us to speak about stable behavior of the information rate. It is necessary to specify in SLA the monitoring period for this value (10 seconds, for instance). This means that every 10 seconds, the rate of information flow is measured and compared to the requirement. If such control measurements are not carried out, it would deprive the user of the possibility of presenting a claim to the provider in case of conflict. Suppose that during one day of the month the provider did not transmit user traffic, but on all other days allowed the user to exceed the predefined quota, so that the average rate per month was within the agreed limits. Under these conditions only regular control over the information rate would allow users to assert their rights. SIR is a medium-term characteristic. **Commitment Information Rate (CIR)** is a synonym of SIR.

Peak Information Rate (PIR) is the maximum rate the user traffic flow is allowed to reach during the agreed, short time period T.

This period is usually called the **burst period**. Obviously, when transmitting traffic it is possible to speak about this value only with a certain level of probability. For example, the requirement to this characteristic can be formulated as follows: The information rate must not exceed 2 Mbps during 10 ms, with the probability of 0.95. Quite often, the probability value is omitted, since it is assumed to be close to 1. PIR is a short-term characteristic.

PIR allows the evaluation of a network's ability to withstand loads characteristic of bursty traffic and resulting in network congestion. If SLA stipulates both SIR and PIR, bursty periods must be accompanied by the periods of relative *calm*, when the rate falls below the average value. If this is not the case, the average information rate would not correspond to the agreed value.

Burst size (usually designated *B*) is used for evaluating the switch buffer volume required for temporary data storage during congestion periods. Burst size is equal to the total volume of data that arrives at the switch during the allowed period of peak load.

$$B = \text{PIR} \times T \qquad (6.5)$$

In *Chapter 3*, we mentioned another parameter of the traffic rate — **traffic burst coefficient**, sometimes is called **burstiness**. We have defined this coefficient as a ratio between the traffic average rate measured on a long time interval and the maximum rate measured at some small time period. Uncertainty of time intervals makes the burst coefficient a *qualitative characteristic* of the traffic nature.

Data transmission rate can be measured between any two network interfaces: between the client computer and the server, between input and output ports of the router, etc. To analyze and tune the network, it is useful to know the bandwidths for specific network elements. It is important to note that because of the sequential character of data transmission by different network elements, a bandwidth of any composite network path will be equal to that of the path element that has the *minimum* bandwidth. Therefore, the maximum data transmission rate is always limited by the elements that have minimum bandwidth. To increase the bandwidth of the composite route, it is necessary to first pay attention to the slowest elements, known as **bottlenecks**.

6.4 RELIABILITY

KEY WORDS: reliability, availability loss packets ratio, mean time between failures, failure probability, failure rate, fault tolerance, redundancy, alternative routes, connection-oriented protocol, positive acknowledgment, negative acknowledgment, the idle-source method, the sliding window method, window size

For describing service reliability, the following two characteristics are often used:

- Percentage of the lost packet in the total packet flow
- Service availability

Both characteristics describe the reliability of the transport service from the user's viewpoint. The difference between them is that they characterize reliability at different time ranges. The first characteristic is short term; the second characteristic is medium term or long term.

6.4.1 Packet Loss Characteristics

This characteristic is defined as a ratio of the number of lost packets to the total number of transmitted packets:

$$\textbf{Loss packets ratio} = N_L/N \qquad\qquad (6.6)$$

Here, N equals the total number of packets transmitted during a specific time period, and N_L equals the number of packets lost during the same time period.

6.4.2 Availability and Fault Tolerance

For describing the reliability of individual devices, there are such reliability characteristics as *Mean Time Between Failures* (*MTBF*), *failure probability*, and *failure rate*. However, these parameters are suitable only for evaluating the reliability of simple elements and devices, which become unusable when any of their components fails. Complex systems comprising many components may remain usable when one of their components fails.

In this relationship, another set of characteristics is used for evaluating the reliability of complex systems.

Availability is the ratio between the time period during which the system or service retains usability and the overall time of system life. Availability is a long-term statistical characteristic. Typical intervals of measurements for it are day, month, or year. The communications equipment of telephone networks is an example of a high availability system, since the best specimens are characterized by the *five nines* availability. This means that the availability of this equipment is 99.999%, which corresponds to slightly more than 5 minutes of downtime per year. Equipment and services of data networks only strive to achieve such a high availability. However, the boundary of *three nines* has already been reached.

Service availability represents a universal characteristic used by both end users and service providers.

Another characteristic used to evaluate reliability of complex systems is **fault tolerance.** This is the system capability of hiding failures of individual system components from users.

For instance, if the switch is equipped with two switching fabrics operating in parallel, then failure of one such fabric would not result in total failure of the switch. However, the performance of this switch will decrease, since it will process packets two times slower. In fault-tolerant system, failure of one of its elements results in performance degradation rather than in total failure. Another example illustrating fault-tolerance implementation is the use of two physical links for connecting switches. In normal operating mode, the traffic is transmitted by two links at a rate of 2C Mbps. If one link fails, the fault tolerant system will continue to transmit traffic at a rate of C Mbps. However, since it is difficult to obtain a quantitative evaluation of system or service performance degradation, fault tolerance is most frequently used as a qualitative characteristic.

Further on, we will consider the most frequently used methods of ensuring high reliability of transport services.

6.4.3 Alternative Routes

Service availability can be improved using two methods:

■ The first method implies using *reliable network elements* that rarely fail. However, this method is always limited by the capabilities of technology used in the process of manufacturing electronic components (integral circuits, printed circuit boards, etc.).

■ The second method is also well known. It is based on the introduction of *redundancy* into the design of the system: key elements of the system must exist in several duplicating instances so that if one element fails, the duplicates will ensure system operation. Therefore, switches and routers operating in the network backbone are always equipped with redundant units — power supplies, processors, and interfaces.

To ensure the required level of availability for the transport service, a network should have redundancy. The main means of achievement of this purpose is alternative routes. Figure 6.5, *a* shows an example of a network with no alternative routes for traffic transmission between node A and node B. Therefore, this network design does not provide fault tolerance, and the service provider must rely on the fault tolerance of the network elements — data links and switches on the route from node A to node B.

Fig 6.5, *b* shows a network that can transmit traffic between node A and node B using two routes. In case of failure of the equipment along one of the routes, the second route remains usable, and network continues to provide service to its clients. Still, switching from route to route might require some time. During some transition periods, user traffic losses might occur. Therefore, the reduction of this period is one of the main goals of the techniques of ensuring network fault tolerance.

There are several methods of using alternative routes in the network:

■ *The network determines the alternative route only after the failure of the main route.* This means that only one route is specified in the forwarding tables of the network switches for each information flow. After the failure of a communications link or switch on the route of this flow, network switches use a special routing protocol to search for an alternative route. Usually, this takes tens of seconds or several minutes, depending on the network scale and the complexity of its topology. This is the slowest method of using alternative routes. During the transition period, losses of user data are inevitable.

■ *The network finds two routes beforehand and uses them both*, thus creating a redundant flow invisible to the user. At the network output, only one flow is chosen, and the data from it are passed to the user. Thus, one of the routes is considered a main route, and the other is the backup route. When the main route fails, the user receives the data via the backup route. This method is the fastest, since it ensures the highest QoS for user flow. However, it relates to high losses of network performance, since the network transmits two flows instead of one. Normally, this method is used for servicing a small number of crucially important data flows that require a high level of service availability.

■ *The network finds two routes beforehand, but uses only one of them*. When the main route fails, the transition to the alternative goes faster than when the first method is used, since the system must not spend time searching for an alternative route. This method is significantly more economical than the second approach. However, data losses are higher than when using the second method, since the data already sent by the failed route are lost. Some time is required for the first switch along the flow route to know that there was a failure in the network and that the main route is no longer valid.

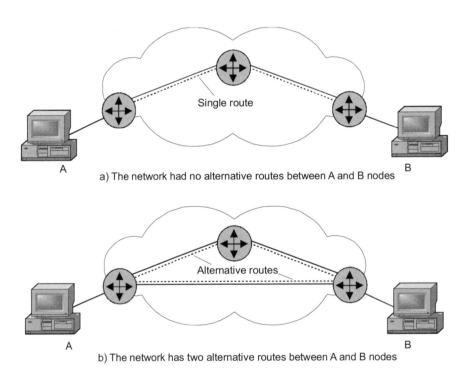

a) The network had no alternative routes between A and B nodes

b) The network has two alternative routes between A and B nodes

Figure 6.5 Alternative routes

Computer networks mainly use the first and the third methods alternate routing. Technologies based on the second principle (two active routes) are used only in computer networks that must ensure enhanced reliability. The second method is widely used in high-speed transmission networks, which create reliable link infrastructure for telephone and computer traffic.

6.4.4 Data Retransmission and the Sliding Window

Methods of packet retransmission are used when other methods of ensuring reliability have failed and the packet is lost. These methods require the use of connection-oriented protocols.

To make sure that it is necessary to retransmit data, the sender numbers the sent packets; for each packet, the sender expects **Positive Acknowledgment (ACK)** from the receiver. ACK is a special packet or a special field in a data packet informing the sender that the source packet was received and that its data proved to be correct. To organize such numbering, the procedure of establishing a logical connection is required, since it provides the reference point from which the numbering is started. The waiting period of the acknowledgment is limited — when sending each packet, the sender starts the timer, and if the acknowledgment is not received after the predefined period elapses, it considers the packet to be lost. If the destination receives the packet with corrupted data, it might send a **Negative Acknowledgment (NACK)**, specifying that the packet needs to be retransmitted.

There are two approaches to organizing the process of exchanging acknowledgments: idle source method and sliding window method.

The idle source method requires the source sending the packet to wait for acknowledgment (either positive or negative) from the receiver. The sender can send the next packet only after receiving positive acknowledgment[2]. If acknowledgment is not delivered after the timeout period has elapsed or a negative acknowledgment has been received, the packet is considered lost and has to be retransmitted. Figure 6.6, *a*, illustrates that this significantly degrades the performance of data exchange. In other words, link utilization is very low. Although the sender is capable of sending the next packet immediately after sending the previous one, the sender has to wait for an acknowledgment. Performance degradation with this method of error correction is especially noticeable on slow links (i.e., in WANs).

The second method of error correction is known as **the sliding window method**. To increase the data rate, this method allows the sender to transmit a specific number of packets in continuous mode, i.e., at the maximum possible rate, without receiving positive acknowledgments for these packets. The number of packets that can be transmitted in such a way is known as the **window size**. Figure 6.6, *b* illustrates this method for the window comprising *W* packets.

---

[2] For brevity, we will refer to positive acknowledgments simply as acknowledgments.

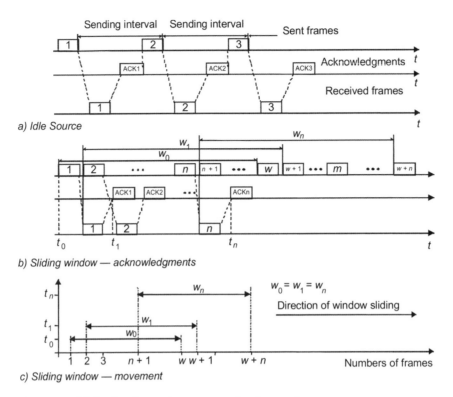

a) Idle Source

b) Sliding window — acknowledgments

c) Sliding window — movement

Figure 6.6 Methods of restoring corrupted or lost packets

At the starting moment, when no packets have been sent, the window defines the range of packets with numbers from 1 to W, inclusively. The source starts transmitting packets and receiving acknowledgments. For simplicity, suppose that acknowledgments arrive in the same order as the packets to which they correspond. At time instance t_1, after receiving the first acknowledgment (ACK1), the window is moved by one position, defining a new range: from 2 to $(W + 1)$.

The processes of sending packets and receiving acknowledgments are sufficiently independent. Consider an arbitrary time instance, t_n, when the source has received acknowledgment for all packets with numbers from 1 to n. The window has slid to the right and has defined a new range of packets allowed for transmission. These range from $(n + 1)$ to $(W + n)$. The entire set of packets from the source can be classified in the following groups (see Figure 6.6, b):

■ *Packets with numbers from 1 to n* have already been sent, and the appropriate acknowledgments for these packets have already been received, which means that they are located outside the left window boundary.

■ *Packets from number (n + 1) to the number (W + n)* are located within the limits of the window. Such packets can be sent without waiting for any acknowledgment. This range can be subdivided into the following intervals:

   ● Packets with the numbers from $(n + 1)$ to m, which have already been sent but for which acknowledgments have not been received yet

   ● Packets numbered from m to $(W + n)$, which can be sent but have not

■ *All packets with numbers greater than (W + n)* are located outside the right boundary of the window and, therefore, cannot be sent yet.

The process of sliding the window along the sequence of packet numbers is illustrated by Figure 6.6, *c*. Here, t_0 is the initial time instance, and t_1 and t_n are the times of acknowledgment arrivals for the first and nth packets, respectively. Each time an acknowledgment arrives, the window slides to the right, its size remaining unchanged and equal to W.

Thus, when sending a packet with the number equal to n, the time-out interval is set at the source node. If during this time the acknowledgment for packet n does not arrive, packet n is considered lost and has to be retransmitted.

If the flow of acknowledgments arrives regularly, so the source always has packets that it has the right to send, the exchange rate reaches the maximum value possible for a specific link and adopted protocol. From the description of the sliding window method, it is obvious that the idle source method represents a particular case of this algorithm for which the window size is equal to 1.

Some implementations of the sliding window algorithm do not require the receiver to send acknowledgments for each correctly received packet. If there are no gaps between the received packets, the receiver can send the acknowledgment only to the last received packet, and this acknowledgment will be considered by the sender as a sign that all previous packets also were delivered successfully.

Some methods use negative acknowledgments. Negative acknowledgments fall into two categories — group and selective. Group acknowledgment contains the number of the packet from which it is necessary to start retransmitting all the packets sent by the source. Selective negative acknowledgment requires retransmission of a single packet.

The sliding window method has two parameters that can significantly influence the efficiency of data exchange between sender and receiver. These are the window size and the value of the timeout during which the sender waits for acknowledgment. The choice of timeout value depends on the packet delays.

In reliable networks, where packets are rarely lost or corrupted, it is necessary to increase the window size to increase the data exchange rate. Using this approach, the sender will send packets with smaller pauses. In unreliable networks, the window size must be decreased, since under conditions of frequent losses, data corruption, or both, the volume of retransmitted packets increases sharply. When this happens, network bandwidth is used inefficiently, and effective network bandwidth drops.

Window size can be a *constant* parameter of this algorithm, which means that it is chosen at connection setup and does not change during the entire session.

There are also *adaptive* versions of this algorithm, when the window size changes during the session according to the reliability and load of the network. Under conditions of low network reliability and high load, the sender reduces the window size, attempting to find an optimal mode of data transmission. Network reliability in such algorithms is determined by such packet loss symptoms as timeout expiration for positive acknowledgment or arrival of acknowledgment duplicates for certain packets. Arrival of the acknowledgment duplicate serves as evidence that the timeout for the next packet on the destination node has expired, and it requests retransmission of that packet.

Destination nodes also can change the window size. This might happen if the destination node is overloaded and cannot process all arriving packets in due time. We will consider this problem later in the "Feedback" section of *Chapter 7*, when studying the problems of eliminating network congestion.

There are also implementations of the sliding window algorithm that use the number of bytes as the window size, rather than the number of packets. TCP protocol represents the best-known example of such an approach.

The sliding window method is more difficult to implement than the idle source method, since the sender must store in its buffer all the packets for which positive acknowledgments have not yet been received. Furthermore, it is necessary to track several parameters of this algorithm, including window size, numbers of the packets for which acknowledgments have been received, and numbers of the packets that can be transmitted before receiving a new acknowledgment.

6.5 SECURITY

KEY WORDS: computer security tools, network security tools, firewall, virtual private network (VPN), confidentiality, information availability, authentication, integrity, encryption, cryptographic system, digital signature, identification authorization, auditing, protected channel technology

Computer networks are outstanding means of accessing various information and are marvelous communications tools. However, computer networks also have a reverse side. The dark side of computer networks manifests itself in various potential threats to the integrity and confidentiality of the information that you entrust to the network. For instance, companies that have persistent connections to the Internet regularly suffer from attacks of intruders on their information resources. Individual Internet users who establish dial-up connections also are exposed to attacks. Information stored in their computers might suffer from mail worms or vulnerabilities typical of instant messaging systems such as ICQ.

SOME STATISTICS

In the edition of the annual report Issues and Trends: 2002 CSI/FBI Computer Crime and Security Survey *published in April 2002, a sharp growth in computer crime is tracked. About 90% of the respondents (mainly employees of large companies and governmental organizations) reported that during the preceding 12 months, security incidents took place in their organizations. Close to 80% of the respondents registered financial losses caused by these security violations. 44% evaluated the losses quantitatively. According to the data they reported, total financial loss exceeded $455 million.*

Intruders attempting to get unauthorized access to computer information or to destroy it can use the Internet and corporate networks. No one can guarantee that some disgruntled employee would not be willing to misuse privileges by attempting to access documents that he or she has no right to read. Attempts to destroy information (such as deleting files or causing computers to malfunction) are also possible.

Obviously, network users would like to protect their information from these kinds of incidents. The security level of the network user information is another important characteristic of the network. Security level is not a quantitative characteristic. On the contrary, it can be evaluated only qualitatively, for example, as high, medium, or low level. Normally, to adequately evaluate network security level, it is necessary to consult experts.

6.5.1 Computer and Network Security

The varieties of information protection tools can be divided into two classes:

- **Computer security tools** intended to protect internal information resources located within a LAN or on an individual end-user computer
- **Network security tools** intended to protect information being transmitted across the network

Security functions in these two classes differ significantly. In the first class, it is necessary to protect from unauthorized access all resources within the internal LAN, including hardware (servers, disk arrays, and routers), software (operating systems, DBMS, mail services, and so on), and data stored in files and processed in RAM. To achieve this, it is necessary to inspect all traffic incoming to the local network from a public network (for the moment, the Internet is the prevalent public network) and to try to deny external access to any information that might help intruders abuse confidential information resources.

The most frequently used protection tool of this sort is the **firewall** installed between all connections of internal network to the Internet. Firewalls represent internetwork filters that check messages exchanged by all levels of protocols and do not admit suspicious traffic into the protected network.

Firewalls can also be used within the network to protect subnetworks from one another. This configuration might be needed in large companies with independent departments. Such problems can also be solved using the built-in security tools of operating systems and applications (such as a database management system) as well as built-in security hardware.

In the second class, information that is outside the limits or out of reach needs to be protected. Usually, this information travels across provider networks in the form of IP packets. Currently, the Internet is used by most companies, not only as a powerful source of information distributed over numerous Web sites but also as a relatively inexpensive transport environment allowing the headquarters network to connect with networks of different departments. It also allows numerous mobile users and telecommuters to be connected. In most cases, it is vitally important to ensure that information transmitted using the Internet will not get corrupted, destroyed, or viewed by unauthorized third parties. For the moment, **Virtual Private Network (VPN)** tools are most frequently used for this purpose.

Standalone computers can be efficiently protected from external intrusions using various tools. For example, it is possible to simply lock the keyboard or remove the hard disk and place it into a safe. Computers participating in a network, by definition, cannot be totally isolated from the outside world, since they have to communicate with other computers, some of which are probably located a significant distance apart. Therefore, ensuring network security is a much more complicated task in comparison to securing a standalone machine. Situations when remote users establish logical connections to your computer are standard, provided that your computer is connected to the network. Ensuring security under this condition implies making these connections controllable — each network user must have strictly defined access rights to the information stored on each of the local computers, access rights to peripheral devices, and privileges for performing specific administrative actions on each of the networked computers.

Besides the problems caused by the possibility of remote login to network computers, networks are exposed to other threats: the sniffing and analyzing of messages transmitted across the network and the generation of the falsified traffic. Most network security tools are aimed at preventing these types of security incidents.

Network security aspects are especially important now, when most companies are migrating from leased lines to public networks (Internet, Frame Relay) when creating corporate networks.

6.5.2 Data Confidentiality, Integrity, and Availability

A secure information system is the system that, first, protects the data from unauthorized access; second, is always ready to provide the required data to authorized users; and third, reliably stores information and guarantees its invariability. Thus, a secure system is characterized by confidentiality, availability, and integrity.

- **Confidentiality** is a guarantee that the data will be available only to those users who have the right to access this information. They are known as authorized users.
- **Information availability** is a guarantee that authorized users will always get access to the required data.
- **Integrity** is a guarantee that the data will retain correct values. This is ensured by denying access to unauthorized users and preventing them from changing, modifying, deleting, or creating new data.

An intruder might aim at violating all components of the information security — availability, integrity, and confidentiality. Security requirements might change, depending on the system goals, the type of data used, and possible threats. It is hard to imagine a system for which the properties of integrity and availability would be unimportant. However, the confidentiality property is not always mandatory. For example, if you publish information on a Web site in the Internet and intend to make it available to the widest audience of users, confidentiality is not required. Nevertheless, requirements such as integrity and availability retain their importance.

If you do not take special measures to ensure data integrity, the intruder might change the data stored on your server and cause damage to your company. Malicious users might, for example, introduce such changes into the price list published on the Web server, which would reduce the competitive potential of your company. It is also possible to corrupt the codes of freeware supplied by your company, which would certainly cause damage to its business reputation.

Ensuring data availability in this example is of no less importance. After making significant financial investments into creating and supporting a Web site, a company has the right to expect the return of this investment in the form of increased number of clients, growth of sales, and so on. However, the intruder might undertake an attack that results in the data published on the server becoming unavailable to the users for whom this information was intended. Examples of such attacks include flooding the server with IP packets containing an incorrect return address. These packets, with the internal logic of this protocol, can cause timeouts and, finally, make the server unavailable for all user requests. This attack represents a particular case of a Denial of Service (DoS) attack.

NOTE   *The concepts of confidentiality, availability, and integrity can be defined not only in relation to information but also in relation to other resources of the data network, including peripheral devices and applications. For example, unrestricted access to a printer might enable an intruder to obtain copies of the documents being printed, change printer settings, or even cause the device to fail. The confidentiality property, with respect to printers, can be interpreted as follows: only those users authorized to use the device must have the right to access it. Furthermore, even authorized users must be able to perform only those operations that they are allowed to do. The availability property in this case means that the device must be ready for use at any time. As it relates to integrity, it can be defined as the invariability of the settings defined for a specific device.*

6.5.3 Network Security Services

Various software and hardware products intended for data protection often use similar approaches, techniques, and technical solutions. Consider the most important ones.

- **Encryption** is the basis of all information security services, be it authentication or authorization system, tools for creating protected channels, or methods of securing data storage. Any encryption procedure that turns information from its readable form (plain text) into encrypted data (ciphertext) must be complemented with a decryption procedure that, being applied to the ciphertext, turns it back into readable form. A pair of such procedures (encryption and decryption) is known as **cryptographic system.**

- **Authentication** prevents unauthorized access to the network and allows logon only for legal users. The term *authentication* has a Latin origin and means verification of originality. The list of objects that might require authentication, besides users, includes various devices, applications, and information. For example, users sending a request to a corporate server must prove their authenticity and make sure that they are communicating with the server belonging to the company. In other words, both client and server must undergo procedures of mutual authentication. This is application-level authentication. When establishing a communications session between two devices, authentication procedures at the lower, data link layer might be required. Data authentication means proving data integrity as well as that the data have been received from the individual who claimed to supply this information. For this purpose, the **digital signature** method is widely used. Authentication should not be confused with identification.

- **Identification** means that the user specifies a personal identifier to the system; authentication is the procedure of verifying that the user is actually who he or she claims to be. In particular, when the user logs on, he or she must supply the password to prove that this is the person to whom the specified identifier belongs. User identifiers are exploited in the same ways as identifiers of other objects, such as files, processes, and data structures. They are not directly related to security.

- **Authorization** is the procedure of controlling the access of authenticated users to the system resources. An authorization system provides each user with exactly those rights granted to them by the administrator. Besides providing users with access rights to files, directories, printers, etc., an authorization system might control user privileges (i.e., the possibility of carrying out specific actions), such as local access to the server, setting the system time, creating backup copies of the data, and server shutdown. An authenticated user who is granted specific access rights and privileges is known as an authorized user.

- **Auditing** is the process of registering all events related to access to the protected system resources in the system log. The auditing subsystem of contemporary operating systems allows us to differentiate events of interest to system administrators using a convenient graphical user interface. Auditing and monitoring tools provide the possibility of detecting and registering important security-related events as well as any attempts to create new system resources and to access, modify, or delete existing resources. Auditing is used to detect any attempts at intrusion, even failed ones.

■ **Protected channel technology** is intended to ensure the security of data transmission over public networks, such as the Internet. Protected channel implies the observance of the following three requirements:

- Mutual authentication of users when establishing a connection, which can, for example, be carried out by exchanging passwords
- Protection of messages transmitted using protected channel from unauthorized access, for example, by data encryption
- Guarantee of the integrity of the messages arriving through protected channel, which can be accomplished, for example, by simultaneous transmission of the digital signature

The protected channel technology is widely used when creating VPNs.

6.6 PROVIDER-ONLY CHARACTERISTICS

KEY WORDS: extensibility, scalability, network manageability, network management system compatibility, integration capabilities, heterogeneous network, integrated network

Consider the main characteristics service providers use when evaluating the efficiency of their networks. These characteristics are often qualitative.

6.6.1 Extensibility and Scalability

The terms extensibility and scalability are sometimes used as synonyms. This is incorrect, since each of these terms has strictly defined, independent meanings.

■ **Extensibility** is the possibility of relatively easily adding users, as well as new network components (e.g., computers, switches, routers, or services); increasing the length of network segment cables; and replacing the existing equipment with new devices, which are more advanced and powerful. The ease of extending the network can sometimes be ensured only within certain limits. For instance, Ethernet based on a single segment of the thick coaxial cable is characterized by good extensibility, since it provides the possibility of easily connecting new workstations. However, such networks are limited by the number of connected workstations, which must not exceed 40. Although this network allows the physical connection of a greater number of workstations to the segment (up to 100), network performance, in this case, drops significantly. The presence of such limitations is a sign of poor system scalability, although the extensibility of such a system is rather good.

■ **Scalability** means the possibility of greatly increasing the number of network nodes and link length without degrading network performance. To ensure network scalability, it is necessary to employ additional communications equipment and to observe special rules for structuring the network. Usually, a scalable solution has multilayer hierarchical structure, which allows the addition of new elements at each hierarchical layer without changing the main idea of the project. The Internet is an example of a scalable network, since its technology (TCP/IP) is capable of supporting the network on a worldwide scale. The organizational structure of the Internet, which was covered in *Chapter 5*, comprises several hierarchical layers: user networks, local ISP networks, and so on, up to the international ISP networks. TCP/IP technologies, upon which the entire Internet is based, also allow the construction of hierarchical networks. The main Internet protocol — IP — is based on a two-layer model. The lower layer is created by individual networks (most frequently, corporate networks), and the upper layer represents the internetwork that joins these networks together. In the TCP/IP stack, there is the concept of an autonomous system. The autonomous system includes all internetworks of a single ISP, so the autonomous system represents a higher hierarchical layer. The presence of autonomous systems on the Internet allows simplification of the solution to the rational route problem. It is sufficient to first find a rational route between autonomous systems and then for each autonomous system, to find a rational route within its boundaries.

To ensure a scalable solution, not only must the network itself be scalable, but so must backbone devices, since network growth must not result in the constant necessity of replacing equipment. Therefore, backbone switches and routers are usually built on the modular principle, which provides the possibility of easily increasing the number of interfaces and packet processing performance.

6.6.2 Manageability

Network manageability is a qualitative characteristic and assumes the possibility of centrally controlling the state of main network elements, detecting and solving network problems, analyzing performance, and planning network growth. Manageability implies the presence of automated management and control tools within the network. These automated tools interact with network hardware and software using communications protocols.

Ideally, a **Network Management System (NMS)** monitors, controls, and manages each network element — from the simplest devices to the most sophisticated ones. At the same time, such a system considers the network as a single whole rather than as a set of individual, standalone devices.

A good NMS monitors the network and, having detected a problem, activates a specific action, corrects the situation, and notifies the administrator about the event that has occurred and about the corrective actions. At the same time, the NMS must accumulate data, on the basis of which it is possible to plan further network development. Finally, the NMS should provide a convenient user interface, allowing all operations to be done from a single console.

The usefulness of the NMS becomes especially evident in large networks, such as corporate networks' public WANs. Without an NMS, such networks would require the constant presence of highly qualified maintenance and support professionals in each building of each city in which the network equipment is installed. Therefore, it becomes necessary to have a large number of support specialists on the staff.

There are lots of unsolved problems in the field of network management systems. Convenient, compact, and multiprotocol network management tools are needed. Most existing tools are not actually network management tools; they only carry out network monitoring and report important events, such as device failures.

6.6.3 Compatibility

Compatibility, or **integration capabilities**, means that the network is capable of including various software and hardware (i.e., dissimilar operating systems supporting different protocol stacks, as well as dissimilar hardware and software products from different vendors, can coexist within it). The network comprising such dissimilar elements is called a **heterogeneous network**. If a heterogeneous network operates smoothly, it is called an **integrated network**. The main approach to building integrated networks implies the use of network modules designed according to open standards and specifications.

SUMMARY

▶ The main requirement of computer networks is to ensure high quality of service (QoS). When using this term in a broad sense, the QoS concept includes all possible properties of the network and its services desirable to the user.

▶ Requirements for the quality of network services are expressed using the values of formalized characteristics.

▶ Quality of transport services is evaluated using the following groups of characteristics:

- Performance
- Reliability

- Security
- Provider-only characteristics, which include extensibility, scalability, manageability, and compatibility.

▶ Network performance is evaluated using the following two types of statistical characteristics: *information rate characteristics and transmission delays characteristics.* The first group includes the sustained rate and the maximum rate during burst periods, as well as the burst period length. The second group includes the average delay value, the average value of the delay variation (jitter), the coefficient of variation, and the maximum values of delay and delay variation.

▶ Various characteristics are used for evaluating network reliability, including the *percentage of packet losses*; the *availability coefficient,* which means the time during which the system is usable; and the *fault tolerance,* or the system's ability to operate when some of its components have failed.

▶ Reliability of transport services provided by the network is ensured by reliability of its components (communications links and communications equipment), availability of alternate routes, and retransmission of lost or damaged packets.

▶ Network security tools include:
- Computer security tools intended for protecting internal information resources located within the LAN or localized on an individual computer
- Network security tools intended for protecting information in the course of its transmission through the network.

▶ The main characteristics of information security are:
- Confidentiality — guarantees that data will be available only for authorized users who have the right to access this information.
- Availability — guarantees that authorized users will always be able to access the data
- Integrity — guarantees that the data retain correct values, which is ensured by preventing unauthorized users from accessing, modifying, deleting, or creating new data

▶ To protect network information, the mechanisms of encryption, authentication, authorization, and auditing are used. Data transmission through the network is accomplished using techniques of protected channels.

REVIEW QUESTIONS

1. What is the difference between a characteristic and a requirement?
2. What characteristics are included within the concept quality of service (QoS), in a broad sense?
3. What QoS characteristics are of interest only to end users? Only to providers? Both to service providers and to users?

4. What are QoS characteristics, in the narrow sense of this term?

5. What performance characteristics are of interest only to service providers?

6. What parties conclude Service Level Agreements?

7. Suggest a set of characteristics that you would like to include into a SLA, provided that you need to transmit the traffic of an IP telephony application through the network.

8. What type of information representation is used for the results of measuring packet delays?

9. What is the advantage of using characteristics such as coefficient of variation over jitter?

10. Which component is not taken into account when defining Round Trip Time?

11. Is it possible to transmit traffic with long delays but without jitter?

12. List the burst parameters. Are these parameters independent?

13. Does average flow rate depend on packet delays?

14. Which characteristic of the transport service reliability is used in the short-term range, and which is used in the medium-term range?

15. Describe two main approaches to ensuring network reliability.

16. How many methods of using alternate routes are available for improving the reliability of traffic transmission? What are their advantages and drawbacks?

17. What are two components of information security?

19. What is the difference between scalability and extensibility?

PROBLEMS

1. Two switches are connected by two physical links to improve reliability (Figure 6.7). Evaluate the volume of lost data in case of link failure for two variants of using these links as alternative routes, according to method 2, "Network finds two routes beforehand and uses them," and according to method 3, "Network finds two routes beforehand, but uses only one." The length of each link is 5,000 km, the data transmission rate is 155 Mbps, and the signal propagation speed in the link is 200,000 km/sec. In both cases, the S2 switch detects the link failure and switches to the backup link within 10 ms.

Figure 6.7 Alternative routes

2. Evaluate the link utilization coefficient if the data are transmitted in it using the protocol based on the idle source algorithm. The transmission rate is equal to 100 Mbps, the Round Trip Time (RTT) is 10 ms, and packets are not lost and do not get corrupted. Packet size is fixed and is equal to 1,500 bytes. Acknowledgment size can be neglected.

3. Determine the minimum size of the window that allows the transmission of packets using the link without the source running idle. The transmission rate is 100 Mbps, the RTT time is 10 ms, and packet are not lost and do not get corrupted. Packet size is fixed and equal to 1,500 bytes. Acknowledgment size can be neglected.

7

METHODS OF ENSURING QUALITY OF SERVICE

7.1 INTRODUCTION

Quality of service methods currently take one of the most important positions among technologies of packet-switched networks, since the operation of contemporary multimedia applications such as IP telephony, video and radio broadcasting, and interactive remote learning is impossible without their implementation. These methods operate with the network characteristics of the following three groups:

■ Information rate
■ Packet delays
■ Packet losses

The definitions of these characteristics were given in the previous chapter.

The QoS technique focuses on the influence of the queues of communications devices on traffic transmission. QoS methods use various algorithms of queue management, reservation, and feedback, which allow negative effects to be reduced to some minimum value acceptable for the user.

Queues are a generic attribute of packet-switched networks. The packet-switching principle itself assumes the presence of buffers at each input or output interface of the packet switch. Packet buffering during times of network congestion is the main mechanism of supporting bursty traffic, ensuring high performance of this type of network. On the other hand, queues mean indefinite and variable delays in packet transmission across the network, the main source of problems for delay-sensitive traffic. Since packet network carriers are highly interested in the transmission of such traffic, they require special tools intended to ensure the compromise between their intention to load their network to the maximum and their intention to comply with the QoS requirements for all types of network traffic.

All these characteristics describe the negative effects of queuing. Actually, if network congestion takes place, this usually decreases the flow rate during congestion periods, packet delays, and even packet losses. The losses happen when the queue fills the buffer entirely.

QoS methods use various mechanisms to decrease the negative effects of queues. The set of these mechanisms is rather wide, and they will be covered in sufficient detail. Most of them take into account the various types of traffic that exist in the network.

QoS methods can be supplemented by traffic engineering methods that manage traffic routes for load balancing and the elimination of queue overflow.

7.2 APPLICATIONS AND QOS

KEY WORDS: types of applications, QoS requirements, bit rate, packet delays, corruption or losses, asynchronous applications, interactive applications, isochronous applications, applications oversensitive to delays, application sensitivity to packet delays, ATM applications classification

7.2.1 QoS Requirements of Different Types of Applications

The current trend of convergence of different types of networks described in *Chapter 1* means a data network now has to carry all kinds of traffic, not just file access and e-mail traffic.

In the previous section, we listed various QoS characteristics used for evaluating the quality of traffic transmission across the network. These characteristics are especially important when the network simultaneously transmits different types of traffic, for example, traffic of Web applications and voice traffic. This is because different kinds of traffic have different requirements of QoS characteristics. The task of achieving simultaneous observance of *all* QoS requirements for *all* types of traffic is very difficult. Therefore, the following approach is usually chosen: all types of traffic existing in the network are categorized onto the several aggregated traffic classes, and then efforts are made to achieve simultaneous observance of QoS requirements for each of these classes of traffic.

Impressive research has been accomplished, aimed at the classifying of applications by the generated traffic. The following three application characteristics were taken as the main traffic criteria:

- Relative predictability of the information rate of traffic generated by an application
- Application sensitivity to packet delays
- Application sensitivity to packet corruption or losses

7.2.2 Predictability of the Information Rate

In relation to the predictability of the information rate, all applications are divided into the following two classes: applications that generate streaming traffic and applications that generate bursty traffic.

Streaming applications generate data at a **constant bit rate** (CBR). If packet switching is used, the traffic of such applications is a sequence of packets of the same size, equal to B bits, following one another after the same time interval, T (Figure 7.1).

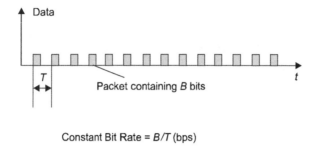

Constant Bit Rate = B/T (bps)

Figure 7.1 Streaming traffic

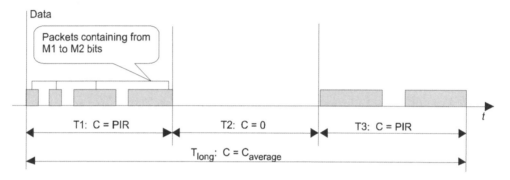

Figure 7.2 Bursty traffic

The constant rate of the streaming traffic (CBR) can be calculated by averaging a period of T:

$$CBR = B/T \text{ (bps)} \qquad (7.1)$$

The constant rate of the streaming traffic is lower than the nominal maximum bit rate of the data transmission protocol, since there are pauses between packets. As will be shown in *Chapter 12*, the maximum rate of data transmission using the Ethernet protocol is 9.76 Mbps (when the frame has the maximum length), smaller than the nominal rate of this protocol (10 Mbps).

Applications generating bursty traffic are characterized by low predictability levels, since periods of silence are followed by bursts during which the packets follow each other rather densely. As a result, the traffic has a **variable bit rate** *(VBR)*, as shown in Figure 7.2. Thus, when working with file service applications, the intensity of the traffic generated by such applications might drop to zero (provided that no files are being transmitted) or rise to the maximum (limited only by the functional capabilities of the network) when the file server transmits a file.

Figure 7.2 shows three measurement periods — T1, T2, and T3. To simplify the calculations, it is assumed that the peak rates during the first and the third periods are equal and have the PIR value and that both periods have the same duration T. Given the T value, it is possible to calculate the burst size, B, which is equal to the number of bits transmitted during the burst period:

$$B = PIR \times T \qquad (7.2)$$

Thus, the burst size for $T1$ and $T3$ periods is equal to B, and for the T2 period it is equal to zero.

For this example, it is possible to calculate the burst coefficient. Recall, that it is equal to the ration of the peak rate at some small time interval to the average traffic rate measured during a lengthy time period. The peak rate for $T1$ and $T3$ periods is equal to B/T, and the average rate during the entire measurement period $C_{average} = T1 + T2 + T3$ is equal to $2B/3T$. Hence, the burst coefficient $3/2 = 1.5$.

7.2.3 Application Sensitivity to Packet Delays

Another criterion of application classification by traffic type is application sensitivity to packet delays and their variations. The main types of applications, in the order of growing sensitivity to packet delays, are listed here:

- **Asynchronous applications.** With this type of application, there are practically no limitations to packet delay time. In this case, users are dealing with **elastic traffic**. E-mail is a typical example of such an application.
- **Interactive applications.** Users may notice delays, but they do not have a negative effect on the application functionality. A text editor used for accessing remote file is an example of such an application.
- **Isochronous applications**. These applications have a threshold of sensitivity to delay variations. If this threshold value is exceeded, application functionality degrades drastically. For example, when working with voice transmission applications, the quality of voice playback significantly degrades after exceeding the threshold value of delay variation (100–150 msec).
- **Applications oversensitive to delays.** Delays in data delivery practically reduce application functionality to zero. Applications that carry out real-time control over technical objects are an example of such applications. If the controlling signal is delayed, the object might be wrecked.

Generally, interactive functions of an application always increase its sensitivity to delays. For example, audio information broadcasting can tolerate significant delays in packet delivery (while remaining sensitive to delay variations), but interactive telephone or videoconferences do not tolerate them. This can be clearly noticed when the conversation is translated using a satellite. Long pauses in the conversation often confuse the participants. Consequently, they lose patience and start speaking simultaneously.

NOTE   *Along with the classification given previously, which provides subtle differentiation between application sensitivity to delays and their variations, another classification provides a rougher division of applications by the same criterion. According to this second classification, there are two classes of applications — asynchronous with elastic traffic and synchronous with delay-sensitive (or time-sensitive) traffic.* **Asynchronous applications** *are those that tolerate data delivery delays of up to several seconds. All other applications, whose functionality suffers from delays in data delivery, are classified as* **synchronous applications**. *Interactive applications can be classified both as asynchronous (for example, text editors) and as synchronous (such as videoconferencing software).*

7.2.4 Application Sensitivity to Packet Losses

The last criterion of application classification is their sensitivity to packet losses. As a rule, applications fall into two groups.

- **Applications sensitive to losses**. Practically all applications transmitting alphanumeric data (text documents, source code, numeric arrays, etc.) are highly sensitive to the loss of individual data fragments, however small they might be. Such losses often make all successfully received information practically unusable. For example, a single missing byte in the source code of a program can make it practically useless. All traditional network applications (file services, database management systems, e-mail service, etc.) belong to this group.

- **Applications tolerant to data losses**. This group includes many applications that transmit the traffic carrying information on inertial physical processes. Loss tolerance means a small amount of missing data can be restored on the basis of successfully received information. Thus, if a single packet carrying several sequential voice measurements was lost, during playback the missing data can be replaced by approximations based on adjacent values. This group of applications includes most applications working with multimedia traffic (audio and video applications). However, the level of loss tolerance has its limits, and the percentage of lost packets cannot be too significant (as a rule, no more than 1%).

Not all multimedia traffic is tolerant to data losses. For example, compressed voice or video are very sensitive to losses; therefore, they are classified as applications of the first type.

7.2.5 Application Classes

An application might belong to different groups depending on the classification criterion used — relative predictability of the data rate, traffic sensitivity to packet delays, and traffic sensitivity to packet losses or corruption. This means that streaming applications can be classified as synchronous or asynchronous. A synchronous application can be sensitive to packet losses, or it can tolerate them. However, practice has shown that among the combinations of application features, some combinations are characteristic of most applications used today.

For instance, an application characterized as "generated traffic — stream, isochronous, tolerant to data losses" corresponds to such popular applications as IP telephony, videoconference support, and audio broadcasting over the Internet. On the other hand, there are such combinations of these characteristics for which it is rather hard to provide an example of an existing application. One combination would be "generated traffic — stream, asynchronous, sensitive to losses."

Stable combinations of characteristics corresponding to specific classes of popular applications are not numerous. For example, during standardization of the ATM technology, which initially was developed for supporting various types of traffic, the four **application classes** were defined: A, B, C, and D. For each class of applications, it is recommended to use a specific set of QoS characteristics. Apart from this, for all applications that do not fit within these classes, a special class (class X) was defined for which the combination of application characteristics can be arbitrary.

ATM classification is, for the moment, the most detailed and generalized one. It does not depend on technology and does not require us to know it. This classification is briefly outlined in Table 7.1.

Table 7.1 Classes of Traffic

Traffic class	Characteristic
A	Constant bit rate (CBR)
	Sensitive to delays
	Connection oriented
	Examples: Voice traffic, TV traffic
	QoS characteristics: Peak information rate, delay, jitter
B	Variable bit rate (VBR)
	Sensitive to delays
	Connection-oriented
	Examples: Compressed voice, compressed video
	QoS parameters: Peak information rate, burst, sustained information rate, delay, jitter

Table 7.1 Classes of Traffic *(Continued)*

Traffic class	Characteristic
C	Variable bit rate (VBR)
	Elastic traffic
	Connection oriented
	Examples: Traffic of computer networks, where end nodes operate using connection-oriented protocols (Frame Relay, X.25, TCP)
	QoS parameters: Peak information rate, burst, sustained information rate
D	Variable bit rate (VBR)
	Elastic traffic
	Connectionless
	Examples: Traffic in computer networks, where end nodes operate using connectionless protocols (IP/UDP, Ethernet)
	QoS parameters: Not defined
X	User-defined traffic type and its parameters

This application classification serves as a basis for typical requirements for QoS parameters and mechanisms used in contemporary networks.

7.3 QUEUE ANALYSIS

KEY WORDS: queue, queuing theory, M/M/1 model, request flow, server, buffer, FIFO, queue length, waiting time, random process, utilization coefficient, variation coefficient

If you have defined the main QoS characteristics and have formulated the requirements to them, you have solved half of the problem. The user formulates requirements to QoS using a set of threshold values of QoS characteristics. For example, the user can specify that the packet delay variance must not exceed 50 msec with a probability of 0.99.

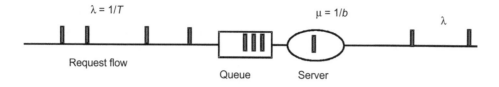

Figure 7.3 M/M/1 model

However, how can the user ensure that the network is capable of successfully accomplishing the formulated task? What steps should be taken to guarantee that delay variations do not exceed the specified value? How can the user guarantee that the average rate of outgoing user flow corresponds to the average rate of the incoming user flow?

These questions were not considered important for quite a long time. Packet-switched networks were initially developed for transmitting asynchronous traffic; therefore, delays could be tolerated. Nowadays, however, when data networks started to carry different kinds of traffic, including real-time traffic, the QoS aspects became urgent.

To understand QoS support mechanisms, it is necessary to first investigate the queuing process in network devices and understand the most important factors that influence the queue length.

7.3.1 M/M/1 Model

Queuing theory is a branch of applied mathematics that studies the queuing processes. We are not going to dive into the mathematical foundations of this theory. Rather, we will limit ourselves to examining some of its conclusions, essential for the QoS problem that we need to consider.

Figure 7.3 shows the simplest model of the queuing theory, known as the M/M/1 model[1].

The main elements of this model are listed here:

- Input flow of abstract requests for service
- Output flow of served requests
- Buffer
- Server

Requests arrive to the buffer input at random time instances. If the buffer is empty and the server is free when a new request arrives, the request is immediately passed to the server. Serving time is also random.

---

[1] Here, 1 means that the model has one server, the first M stands for the type of distribution function for request arrival intervals (Markovian), and the second M designates the type of distribution of servicing times (also Markovian).

If at request arrival the buffer is empty but the server is busy with the previous request, the arrived request must wait in the buffer until the server becomes available. As soon as the server completes the previous request, the request is passed to the output, and server retrieves the next request from the buffer. Requests leaving the server form the output flow. The buffer is infinite, which means that requests never get lost because of the buffer overflow.

If the newly arrived request finds that the buffer is not empty, it is placed into the queue and waits for servicing. Requests are retrieved from the queue according to the order in which they arrived — that is, according to the **First In, First Out** (**FIFO**) servicing order.

Queuing theory allows the evaluation of an average queue length and an average waiting time for this model, depending on the characteristics of the input flow and servicing time.

Suppose the average time between the arrivals of two requests is equal to T. This means that the rate of request arrivals, traditionally designated λ in queuing theory, is:

$$\lambda = 1/T \text{ requests per second} \qquad (7.3)$$

The random process of request arrivals in this model is described by the distribution function of the intervals between request arrivals. For simplicity and to obtain compact analytic results, it is usually assumed that these intervals are described by so-called **Markovian** (also known as **Poisson**) distribution, whose distribution density is shown in Figure 7.4. From this illustration, it is obvious that the input flow is significantly bursty, since there are nonzero probabilities of the interval between requests that are very small (close to zero) or rather long. Average deviation of the intervals is also equal to T. Thus, the standard deviation is $T/T = 1$.

Also assume that the average servicing time of a single request is equal to b. This means that the server is capable of forwarding requests to the output at the rate of $1/b = \mu$. Once again, to obtain compact results in analytic form, it is assumed that the servicing time is a random variable characterized by the Poisson distribution density.

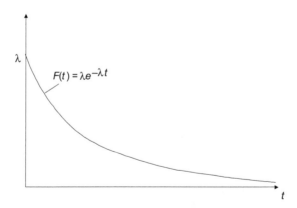

Figure 7.4 Distribution density of the input flow

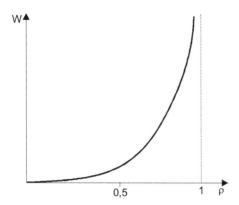

Figure 7.5 Dependence of the average request waiting time on ρ

Based on these assumptions, we can get a simple result for the average time that requests must wait in the queue:

$$W = \rho \times b / (1 - \rho) \qquad (7.4)$$

Here, ρ denotes the λ:μ ratio.

> The r parameter is the **utilization coefficient** of the server. For any time period this coefficient is equal to the ratio of the server's busy time to the length of the entire period.

The dependence of average waiting time W on ρ is shown in Figure 7.5. As can be clearly seen, the ρ parameter plays a key role in the queuing process. If ρ is close to zero, the average waiting time is also close to zero. This means that requests do not have to wait in the buffer (it is empty at request arrival); they can and do immediately go to the server. However, if ρ tends toward 1, then the waiting time increases rapidly, and the dependence has a nonlinear nature. Such behavior of the queue is intuitively clear, since ρ represents the ratio of average rate of the input flow to the average rate of its servicing. The closer the average values of interpacket intervals are to the average servicing time, the more difficult it is for the server to handle the load.

7.3.2 M/M/1 as a Packet-Processing Model

Figure 7.6 illustrates the correspondence between the elements of the previously described model and the elements of the packet-switched network.

■ The flow of the packets coming to the input of the switch interface corresponds to the input flow of service requests. Parameter l corresponds to the packet arrival rate.

■ The buffer of the input interface of the switch corresponds to the buffer of the M/M/1 model.

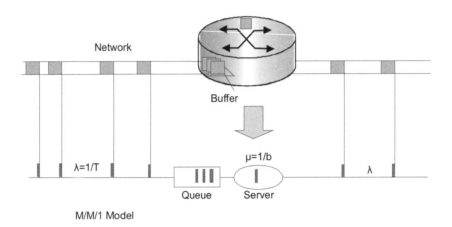

Figure 7.6 Correspondence of the M/M/1 model to network elements

■ The processor that processed packets and sends them to the output interface corresponds to the server. The average time of packet forwarding from the input buffer to the output channel corresponds to the average request-servicing time. The m parameter corresponds to the performance of the resource (the processor or the interface of a switch).

It is necessary to mention that the previously described model presents a rather simplified description of the processes that take place in the network. Many specific features typical for packet processing (the finite size of the switch buffer, the nonzero time required to load the packet into the buffer, etc.) are not taken into account by this model. However, its value is that it demonstrates the qualitative nature of the queue behavior. Therefore, it is useful for understanding the main factors that influence queue length.

Network engineers are well acquainted with the graph shown in Figure 7.5. They interpret this graph as the dependence of network delays on the network load. The ρ parameter of the previously described model corresponds to the utilization coefficient of the network resource participating in traffic transmission. Examples are switch interface, switch processor, channel, and shared medium.

Figure 7.5 also presents something unexpected. It is hard to imagine that the server or network resource practically ceases to handle the load when its utilization coefficient gets close to 1. After all, in this case, the load does not exceed its capabilities. On the contrary, it only tends toward this limit. Also, the reasons that would explain the existence of queues at the values of ρ around 0.5 are not intuitive. Traffic transmission capabilities exceed the load twice, but the queues exist, and on average, the queue contains several waiting requests (packets).

These somewhat paradoxical results are characteristic for systems in which random processes take place. Since λ and μ are average rates at long time intervals, nothing prevents the flows from deviating from these values for short time periods. The queue is generated when the packet arrival rate significantly exceeds the servicing rate.

> The main conclusion that this model allows us to draw is as follows: to ensure high QoS, it is necessary to prevent the utilization coefficient of network resources from rising any higher than 0.9.

Resource overloading can result in complete degradation of the network. If this happens, the effective data transmission rate might be zero, even despite that the network continues to transmit packets. This will be the case if the delays in delivery of all packets exceed a certain threshold value. As a result, the destination node discards all such packets because the time-out has been exceeded. If the protocols operating in the network use reliable data transmission procedures based on acknowledgments and packet retransmission, the congestion process will grow as an avalanche.

There is another important parameter that directly influences the queuing process in packet-switched networks. This is a variation of the interpacket intervals of the input packet flow (i.e., the burst of incoming traffic). We have analyzed the behavior of the M/M/1 model based on the assumption that the input flow is described by the Poisson distribution. This distribution has a rather significant standard deviation of the delay (recall that the average variation is equal to T, provided that the average interval is equal to T and the variance coefficient is 1). What will happen if the variation of the interpacket intervals of the input flow is smaller? Or what will the effect be if the input flow proves to be extra bursty (i.e., the standard deviation is 10 or even 100)?

Unfortunately, models of the queuing theory do not provide simple analytical dependencies similar to formula 7.4 for this case. Therefore to obtain the results, the user has to employ methods of network simulation or conduct measurements in a real-world network.

Figure 7.7 shows the family of curves produced by a simulation model and corresponding to the dependence of W on ρ, obtained for different values of the variation coefficient (CV) of the input flow. The simulation model took into account the existence of a fixed delay in a real-world network. One of the curves, with the CV parameter equal to 1, corresponds to the Poissonian input flow. From the illustration, it can be seen that the smaller the burst of input flow (CV tends toward 0), the smaller the effect of the avalanche-like process of queue generation when the utilization coefficient approaches the value of 1. On the other hand, the greater the CV value, the earlier (and at smaller values of ρ) this process will start to manifest itself.

Two conclusions can be drawn by analyzing the behavior of the graphs shown in Figure 7.7.

- Information on resource utilization alone (ρ) is not sufficient for determining the delays in queues of the network switches. To get a more precise evaluation, it is necessary to know the traffic burst parameters.
- To improve QoS (reduce the delay level), it is necessary to try to smooth the traffic (i.e., to reduce its bursts).

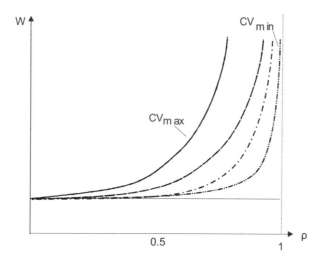

Figure 7.7 Influence of traffic burst on delays

7.4 QOS MECHANISMS

KEY WORDS: QoS requirements, QoS mechanism, utilization coefficient, underloaded mode, heavily loaded network, delay-sensitive traffic, real-time traffic, synchronous traffic, elastic traffic, asynchronous traffic

7.4.1 Operation in Underloaded Mode

Usually, a large number of information flows are carried across the network simultaneously. Each flow requires servicing according to specified QoS requirements. Each flow passes several network switches along its route from the source node to the destination node. On each switch, it passes two queues — to the switch processor and to the output interface of the switch. You have already found out that the most important factor that directly influences the delay values and, consequently, network QoS is the resource utilization coefficient. Therefore, to ensure the required QoS, it is important to ensure that the utilization coefficient of each resource (the processors and the interfaces of switches) serving the flow on its route does not exceed the predefined value.

The simplest method of guaranteeing the observation of QoS requirements for all flows is to run the network in underloaded mode, when all processors and interfaces of switches use only 20–30% of their maximum performance.

This, however, neutralizes the main advantage of the packet-switched network, namely, its high performance when transmitting bursty traffic.

7.4.2 Different Service Classes

Supporting QoS in a **heavily loaded** network is a difficult but important task. In this case, the existence of different classes of flows within the network is helpful. For simplicity, divide all flows into two classes:

- **Delay-sensitive traffic** (real-time or synchronous traffic)
- **Elastic traffic** that can tolerate significant delays but is still sensitive to data losses (asynchronous traffic)

We do not know the exact dependence of delays on the resource utilization coefficient, but we know its general dependence. If for delay-sensitive traffic we ensure a utilization coefficient of each resource no greater than 0.2, it is obvious that delays in each queue will be rather small. These delays probably will be acceptable for most types of applications in this class. For elastic traffic, it is possible to allow a higher utilization coefficient (though it still must not exceed 0.9). To make sure that packets of this class do not get lost, it is necessary to provide buffer memory volume sufficient to store all packets arriving during burst periods. The effect achieved by such load distribution is shown in Figure 7.8.

Delays of the delay-sensitive traffic are equal to w_s; delays of the elastic traffic are w_e.

For a long time, packet-switched networks transmitted only elastic traffic. Therefore, the main QoS requirements included the minimization of packet losses and provided a means for ensuring that the utilization coefficients of each network resource do not exceed 0.9. Methods of solving this task are known as congestion-control methods.

From the early 1990s, when it became necessary to transmit delay-sensitive traffic, the situation became more complicated, and it became necessary to search for new methods.

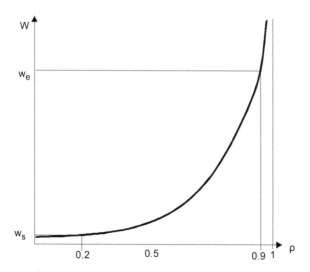

Figure 7.8 Servicing elastic traffic and real-time traffic

It was during this time that the term quality of service appeared. It reflected the more detailed and differentiated requirements of different kinds of traffic.

To achieve different values of the resource utilization coefficients for these two classes of traffic, it is necessary to support two queues in each switch for each resource. The algorithm of retrieving packets from queues must give preference to the queue of packets sensitive to delays. If all packets of this queue are served in a priority mode and the packets of another queue are served in this mode only when the first queue is empty, then the second queue would have no influence on the first one, as if it were nonexistent. Therefore, if the ratio of the average rate of priority traffic (λ_1) to the resource performance (μ) is 0.2, then the utilization coefficient for this traffic will also be 0.2.

For elastic traffic, the packets of which always wait until priority packets are served, the utilization coefficient must be calculated in another way. If the average rate of elastic traffic is equal to λ_2, then the utilization coefficient for this traffic will be equal to $(\lambda_1 + \lambda_2)/\mu$. Thus, if we want to ensure that the utilization coefficient for elastic traffic is 0.9, its intensity must be found from the following calculation: $\lambda_2/\mu = 0.7$.

> The general idea that serves as a basis for all QoS support methods is as follows: the total performance of each resource must be *nonuniformly* distributed among different classes of traffic.

It is possible to introduce more than two service classes and to try to ensure that each class is served according to its value of a utilization coefficient. When this task is solved, further improvement of QoS characteristics can be achieved using other methods (e.g., by lowering traffic burst).

Now, it is necessary to find out how it is possible to ensure such conditions for different classes of traffic in each network node.

Network developers have tried to solve this problem throughout the existence of packet-switched networks. Various mechanisms in different combinations are used for achieving this purpose.

7.5 QUEUE MANAGEMENT ALGORITHMS

> **KEY WORDS**: queue management, FIFO algorithm, priority, priority queuing algorithm, traffic classification, network management policy, buffer size, traffic classification points, granularity, traffic aggregate, weighted queuing algorithm, weighted fair queuing

Queue management is needed for operation during periods of congestion, when network devices cannot cope with the task of transmitting packets to the output interface at the same rate at which they arrive. If this overload is caused by insufficient performance of the processor unit of the network device, then the input queue of the respective input interface is used for temporary storage of unprocessed packets. When we differentiate the requests into several classes, there might be several input queues in the same interface. If the overload is caused by insufficient bandwidth of the output interface, then packets are temporarily stored in the output queue or queues of this interface.

7.5.1 FIFO Algorithm

The essence of traditional **FIFO algorithm** lies in that if overload occurs, all packets are placed into a single common queue and retrieved from it according to the order in which they arrived — that is, first in, first out. In all packet-switching devices, the FIFO algorithm is used by default. Its advantages include the ease of implementation and the lack of need to configure it. However, it has rather a serious drawback — *the impossibility of differentiated processing of the packets belonging to different flows.* All packets are placed into the common queue and have the same priority. This relates to packets of delay-sensitive voice traffic as well as to packets of backup traffic, which is insensitive to delays but rather intense and whose long bursts are capable of delaying voice traffic for quite a long time.

7.5.2 Priority Queuing

Priority queuing algorithms are popular in many areas of computing — for example, in multitasking operating systems, where certain applications must have priority over others. These algorithms are also used for priority queuing, when some classes of traffic must have priority over others.

The priority-queuing mechanism is based on dividing all network traffic into a small number of classes and assigning some numeric characteristic, known as **priority**, to each class.

Traffic classification is a separate task. Packets can be attributed to priority classes based on various characteristics: destination address, source address, identifier of the application that has generated this traffic, or any combination of other characteristics contained in packet headers. The rules of packet classification are part of the **network management policy**.

Traffic classification points can reside in each communications device. A more scalable solution implies delegating traffic classification functions to one or more dedicated devices located at the network edge. For instance, this function can be delegated to the corporate network switches, to which end-user workstations are connected, or to the edge routers of the service provider network. In this case, it is necessary to include a special field in the packet, which would store the assigned priority value, so that all other network devices processing the traffic after the classifying device can use this information. Packet headers of most protocols provide such fields. When the packet header has no special priority field, it is necessary to develop an additional protocol that would include a new header providing such a field. Such a solution was chosen for the Ethernet protocol.

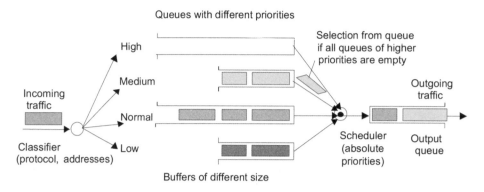

Figure 7.9 Priority queues

Priorities can be assigned not only by switches or routers but also by applications running on the source node. It is also necessary to bear in mind that if there is no centralized policy for assigning priorities in the network, then each network device might disagree with the priority assigned to the packet by another network node. In this case, the device will overwrite the priority value according to the local policy stored on that device.

Independent of the chosen method of traffic classification, there are *several* queues in the network device supporting priority queuing. The number of these queues corresponds to the number of priority classes.[2] The packet that arrived during the congestion period is placed into the queue corresponding to its priority class. Figure 7.9 provides an example illustrating the usage of four priority queues characterized by high, medium, normal, and low priorities. The device will not proceed with processing of the queue with lower priority while the queue with a higher priority contains packets. Therefore, packets with medium priority are always processed only if the queue of packets with a high priority is empty. Accordingly, packets with low priority are processed only when all queues of higher priorities (high, medium, and normal) are empty.

Usually, buffers of the same size are assigned to all priority queues by default. However, many devices allow administrators to individually configure the buffer size for each queue. Buffer size determines the maximum number of packets that can be stored in the queue of a specific priority. If the packet arrives when the buffer is full, it is discarded.

As a rule, *buffer size* is defined to be on the safe side when handling queues of average length. However, it is rather difficult to evaluate this value, since it depends on the network load. Because of this, to achieve this goal, it is necessary to continuously monitor network operation for long periods of time. In general, the higher the importance of the traffic for the user, the higher its rate and bursts, and the larger the buffer size

---

[2] Sometimes several queues are represented as a single queue containing requests of different classes. If requests are retrieved from the queue according to their priorities, it is just another representation of the same mechanism.

required for it. In the example presented in Figure 7.9, large buffers are assigned for traffic of high and normal priorities; for other two classes, smaller buffers were allocated. For high-priority traffic, the motives of this solution are obvious. As for traffic with normal priority, it is expected to be rather intense and bursty.

Priority queuing ensures high QoS for the packets from the queue with the highest priority. If the average rate at which these packets arrive to the device does not exceed the bandwidth of the output interface (and the processor performance of the device), then packets with the highest priority always get the bandwidth that they require. The delay level for such packets is also at a minimum. However, it is not 0 and depends mainly on characteristics of the flow of such packets. The higher the flow burst and information rate, the higher the probability of generation of the queue formed by packets of this high-priority traffic. Traffic of all other priority classes is nearly transparent for the packets with high priority. Notice that we say *nearly*, since such situations are possible in which the packet with higher priority has to wait until the device accomplishes processing of the packet with lower priority. This happens when the arrival of the packet with higher priority coincides with when the device started to process the packet of lower priority.

As relates to other priority classes, the QoS provided to them will be lower than for the packets with the highest priority. Note that the degree of this quality decrease is difficult to predict. This decrease can be very significant if the traffic of highest priority is intense. If the utilization coefficient of the device, determined only by the traffic of highest priority, rises close to 1 for specific time instances, then the traffic of all lower priority classes becomes practically frozen for such intervals.

Because of this, priority queuing is used when there is one class of real-time traffic in the network but its intensity is not high; consequently, serving this class does not impair serving all other traffic. For example, voice traffic is rather sensitive to delays, though its rate rarely exceeds 8–64 Kbps. Therefore, if this traffic is assigned the highest priority, service provided to all the other classes of traffic would not be significantly infringed upon. However, other situations are possible. For example, consider a network where it is necessary to transmit video traffic, which also requires priority serving but has a significantly higher rate. For such cases, special queuing algorithms are developed, providing some guarantees that low-priority traffic will also be served even when the rate of the higher-priority classes significantly rises. Such algorithms are covered in the next section.

Careful readers have certainly noticed that when describing priority queuing, we operated with traffic classes rather than with individual flows. This specific feature is rather important, and it relates not only to priority queuing algorithms but also to other mechanisms of ensuring QoS.

The network can serve traffic with different levels of **granularity**. An individual flow is the minimum service unit taken into account by QoS mechanisms.

If we ensure individual QoS parameters for each flow, we are dealing with QoS at the flow level.

If we combine several flows within a common aggregate flow and cease to distinguish individual flows when ensuring QoS parameters, then we are dealing with QoS at the traffic-class level. Such classes are also called **traffic aggregates**.

IMPORTANT *To combine several flows into an aggregate, it is necessary to ensure that they impose the same QoS requirements and have common input and output points to and from the network.*

7.5.3 Weighted Queuing

The **weighted queuing algorithm** is developed to provide a certain minimum of bandwidth to all classes of traffic, or at least to guarantee the observance of some requirements to delays. Class weight is the percentage of the total bandwidth of the resource (e.g., processor or output interface of a switch) that is guaranteed to this class of traffic.

Like priority queuing, weighted queuing requires the division of traffic into several classes. For each class, a separate packet queue is created. However, in weighted queuing, each queue is assigned the percentage of the resource bandwidth guaranteed to this class under conditions of resource overload rather than a specific priority. For input flow, the role of resource is played by the processor, and for the output flow (after accomplishing the switching), this role is played by the output interface.

EXAMPLE *Figure 7.10 illustrates an example in which the network device supports five queues to the output interface. Under conditions of congestion, these queues are allocated 10%, 10%, 30%, 20%, and 30% of the bandwidth of the output interface, respectively.*
The formulated goal is achieved by serving the queues in a round-robin manner. In each service cycle, a specific number of bytes is retrieved from each queue, corresponding to the weight of that queue. If the queue lookup cycle in the example under consideration is equal to 1 second and the rate of the output interface is 100 Mbps, then under conditions of congestion, the first queue will obtain 10% of time (i.e., 100 msec) and 10 Mbit of data will, therefore, be retrieved from this queue. The volume of data retrieved from the second queue will also be 10 Mbit. Accordingly, 30 Mbit of data will be retrieved from the third queue, 20 Mbit from the fourth queue, and 30 Mbit from the fifth queue.
As a result, each traffic class will get its guaranteed minimum bandwidth. In most cases, this result is more desirable than the suppressing of the low-priority traffic classes by classes of higher priorities.

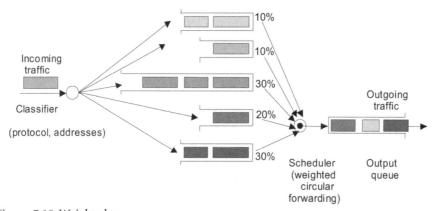

Figure 7.10 Weighted queues

Since data are retrieved from the queue in packets rather than in bits, the actual distribution of the bandwidth among traffic classes is always different from the planned one. For example, the first traffic class may receive 9% or 12% instead of 10% under conditions of network congestion.

The longer the cycle time, the more precisely the required proportions between the traffic classes are observed. This happens because large number of packets are selected from every queue, and, therefore, the influence of the size of each packet gets averaged.

On the other hand, a lengthy cycle results in significant packet transmission delays. For instance, if the cycle is equal to 1 second chosen in the above-provided example the delay may be more than one second, since the arbitrator returns to each queue no more than once per second. Besides this, each queue might contain more than one packet. Therefore, when choosing the cycle duration it is necessary to ensure the balance between the precision of the bandwidth proportions and natural desire to reduce the delay.

For the above-provided example, the work cycle duration of 1,000 μsec is ensuring such a balance. On one hand, it ensures the queue of each class is served once per 1,000 μs. On the other hand, this time is sufficient to retrieve several packets from each queue. In our example, the first queue will have 100 μs, sufficient for transmitting one Fast Ethernet frame or ten Gigabit Ethernet frames into the network.

When the weighted queuing algorithm is used, the utilization coefficient for the traffic of a specific class significantly influences the delay and the delay variation values for the packet of that class. In this case, the coefficient is calculated as the ratio of the input rate of a specific class of traffic to the bandwidth allocated to that class according to its weight. For instance, if we allocated 10% of the total bandwidth of the output interface to the first queue (i.e., 10 Mbps), and the average rate of the flow that falls into this queue is 3 Mbps, then the utilization coefficient for this flow will be $3/10 = 0.3$. The dependence shown in Figure 7.5 demonstrates that delays will be insignificant at such a value of the utilization coefficient. If the input flow rate for this queue were 9 Mbps, the queue would grow significantly. If the limit of 10 Mbps was exceeded, part of the flow packets would be constantly discarded because of queue overflow.

Qualitative behavior of the queue and, consequently, of delays looks approximately similar to the behavior of FIFO queue — that is, the smaller the utilization coefficient, the smaller the average queue length and the smaller the delays.

As with priority queuing, when using weighted queuing, the administrator can manually assign different buffer sizes for different queue classes. Reduction of the buffer size for the queues will result in the growth of the number of lost packets under conditions of congestion. However, waiting times for the packets that were not discarded will be reduced.

There exists another type of weighted queuing — **weighted fair queuing** *(WFQ). In this case, the resource bandwidth is divided between all flows equally (i.e., fairly).*

NOTE   *Weighted queuing ensures the required relations between the rates of traffic from different queues only during periods of congestion, when each queue is constantly filled. If any queue is empty (which means that for the traffic of this class, the current period is not the period of congestion), then this queue is omitted during the current round-robin lookup, and the time allocated for serving this queue is distributed between all other queues according to their weights. Thus, during specific time periods, traffic of a specific class may have a higher rate than the appropriate percentage of the output interface bandwidth.*

7.5.4 Hybrid Algorithms of Queuing

Each of the two approaches described previously has specific advantages and drawbacks. Priority queuing ensures minimum delay levels, at least for the traffic of the highest priority. This algorithm serves all traffic from the queue of the highest priority, no matter how high its rate might be, and does not provide any guarantees in relation to the average bandwidth for the traffic from queues of lower priorities.

Weighted queuing guarantees average traffic rate but does not provide any guarantee with regard to delays.

There are also hybrid algorithms of queuing that try to find a compromise between these methods. The most popular type of such an algorithm uses one priority queue and serves all other queues according to the weighted algorithm. Usually, priority queues are used for real-time traffic, and other queues are used for elastic traffic of several classes. Each class of elastic traffic gets some guaranteed minimum of the bandwidth during congestion periods. This minimum is calculated as a percentage of the bandwidth remaining after serving the priority traffic. Obviously, it is necessary to limit the priority traffic somehow to prevent it from consuming the entire bandwidth of the resource. As a rule, this is achieved using the **traffic profiling tools** that will be covered later in this chapter.

7.6 FEEDBACK

> **KEY WORDS:** congestion control mechanisms, network congestion, feedback mechanism, reserving, congestion indication, maximum transmission rate, credit, implicit information

7.6.1 Purpose

Queue management algorithms are mandatory tools for preventing network congestion. However, these tools are not sufficient. Such algorithms interpret the situation *as is* and do their best to improve the situation to achieve fair resource distribution under conditions of resource shortage. However, they are unable to eliminate bandwidth shortage. These mechanisms are classified as **congestion control mechanisms**, which are activated when the network is already operating under conditions of congestion.

There is another class of tools that try to predict and **prevent network congestion**. These tools are called congestion avoidance mechanisms. The main aim of such tools is to prevent congestion situations, because it is much better to transmit data at lower rate but without losses than at a high rate and losing packets during periods of congestion.

Prevention of network congestion is possible only when the total rate of all data flows transmitted using each interface of each network switch is smaller than the bandwidth of that interface. Two approaches can be implemented to achieve this goal: either increasing the interface bandwidth or decreasing the flow rates. The first approach relates to network design and planning tools and will not be considered here.

The second approach can be implemented using two principally different methods. One of them is based on exploiting the **feedback mechanism** that the congested network node uses to ask the previous nodes located along the traffic route (or the flows belonging to the same traffic class) to temporarily decrease the traffic rate. When congestion at this node is finished, it sends another message allowing the increase of the data transmission rate. This method does not require any previous knowledge of the traffic intensity. It simply reacts to congestion. This method also assumes that the protocols operating on all nodes would react to the message informing them of congestion and would decrease the traffic rate accordingly.

Another method is based on **reserving** the bandwidth for the flows carried across the network. This method requires preliminary information on the flow rates as well as updates to this information if flow rates change. The principles of resource reservation will be covered in more detail in the next section. For the moment, concentrate on the feedback mechanisms.

7.6.2 Feedback Participants

There are several types of feedback mechanisms. They differ in the information supplied by the feedback as well as in the type of the node that generates this information and the type of the node that reacts to it: end node (computer) or transit node (switch or router).

Figure 7.11 presents various methods that can be used for organizing feedback.

Feedback 1 is organized between two network end nodes. This is the most radical method for lowering network loads, since only end nodes (senders) can reduce the rate at which information is sent to the network. However, this type of feedback is not classified as a congestion control method, since its main goal is the reduction of loads on the destination node rather than on the network devices. Principally, this is the same problem, since it arises because the rate at which packets arrive to the network resource temporarily exceeds the rate at which this resource processes them. However, in this case, it is not the switch that plays the role of network resource but rather the end node. Traditionally, this type of feedback is called flow control. Network devices do not participate in the operation of this kind of feedback mechanism. They only pass appropriate messages between

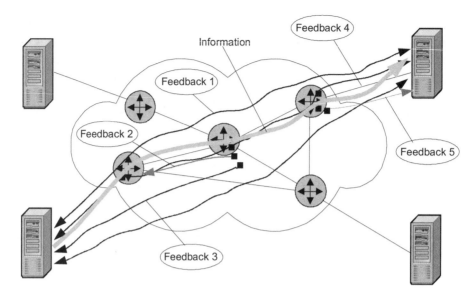

Figure 7.11 Feedback participants

end nodes. Despite different names, congestion control methods and flow control methods use common mechanisms.

When organizing feedback, it is necessary to account for the time required to transmit information across the network. In high-speed WANs, the source node might transmit thousands of packets during the time interval required to pass the message informing it that the destination node is overloaded. Therefore, the overload will not be eliminated in due time.

From the automatic control theory, it is known that delays in the feedback circuit might produce many undesirable effects opposite to the initial intentions. For example, oscillatory processes might start in the system, preventing it from coming to a state of equilibrium. At the early stages of the Internet evolution, such phenomena were not rare. For instance, because of the imperfection of the feedback and routing algorithms, overload zones appeared and periodically moved along the network. The reason for such a problem is clear: Delays in the feedback circuit supply obsolete information about the state of the controlled element to the controlling element.

In this case, the source node gets information on the queue state of the destination node with the delay. Therefore, a situation is possible in which the source node starts to reduce transmission speed but no reduction is needed because there is no queue on the destination node. Sometimes the source node, having received delayed information, starts to increase the information rate when the destination node starts to experience overload. To eliminate such effects, an integrating element is usually included in the feedback circuit. This integrating unit takes into account not only the current feedback message but also several previous messages to consider the dynamics of the changes in the situation and to react accordingly.

Feedback 2 is organized between two neighboring switches. The switch informs its upstream (regarding a given flow) neighbor that it is experiencing congestion and its buffer has been filled to the critical value. Having received such a message, the upstream neighbor must temporarily reduce the data transmission rate in the direction of the congested switch, thus eliminating the congestion problem. This solution is less efficient for the network as a whole, since the flow would continue to leave the source node at the same rate as before. For the switch that experiences congestion, this still is a good solution, since it has time to unload the overflowing queue. However, the problem is moved to the upstream switch, where the overload can appear, since it starts to transmit data from its buffer at a lower rate. The advantage of this method is its low feedback delay, since both nodes are neighbors, provided that they are not connected by a satellite channel.

Feedback 3 is organized between the transit switch and the source node. Although feedback messages are transmitted by several transit switches in the direction of the source node, these transit switches do not react to it.

Feedback 4 is the most general case (Figure 7.11). Here, the message on the overload is generated by the destination node and passed to the source node, similar to the first case. However, this case is different in that each transit switch reacts to this message. First, this method reduces the rate of data transmission in the direction of the destination node, and second, this method allows changing of the message contents along the feedback circuit. For example, if the destination node asks to reduce the rate to 30 Mbps, then the transit switch may reduce this value to 20 Mbps after evaluating the state of its buffer. The versatility of this approach lies in that not only the destination node but any of transit switches can generate the feedback message.

When describing different versions of organizing feedback, we have assumed that the overload message travels in the direction opposite of the direction of user information transmission. However, some communications protocols do not provide the possibility for transit nodes to generate such messages. Under these conditions, an artificial technique is used — that is, the transmission of the message about congestion to the destination node, which transforms it to the feedback message and sends it in the required direction (i.e., toward the source node). This variant is shown in our illustration as *feedback 5.*

7.6.3 Feedback Information

Feedback methods employed nowadays use the following types of information:

- Congestion indication
- Maximum transmission rate
- Maximum amount of data (credit)
- Implicit information

Congestion indication. This does not contain the level of network or node congestion. It simply reports the congestion. Reactions of the node that receives such a message might be different. In some protocols the node must stop transmitting information in a specific direction until it receives another feedback message, allowing it to continue transmission. In other protocols, the node behaves in an adaptive manner: it reduces the speed by a specific value and awaits network response. If feedback messages containing congestion indications continue to arrive, the node continues to decrease the transmission rate.

Maximum transmission rate. The second type of messages uses indications about the speed threshold that the source or transit node has to observe. This is a more precise method of congestion control than the previous one, since it explicitly informs its upstream neighbors as to what level they have to decrease the transmission rate. It is obliged to take into account the time of the message transmission by the network to eliminate oscillations in the network, thus ensuring the required response to congestion. Therefore, in WANs, this method is usually implemented as the feedback 4 provided in our example, employing all switches of the network.

Maximum data volume. The last type of messages is related to the sliding window algorithm widely used in packet-switched networks. The sliding window algorithm was covered earlier in this chapter. This algorithm not only allows reliable data transmission to be ensured but also provides the possibility of organizing feedback for flow control (if feedback is organized between end nodes) or congestion control (if feedback is organized between network switches).

The parameter that carries feedback information is the current window size (when describing the operating principles of this mechanism, we designated it W). Most protocols implementing the sliding window algorithm make provisions for indicating the current window size in acknowledgments, confirming receipt of the next portion of data. This information on the current window size corresponds to the current state of the receiving node.

This parameter is also called credit, provided by the receiving node to the sender node. The sender node can send a specified volume of information (or a specified number of packets, if the window size is measured in packets) corresponding to the credit. However, if the credit is exhausted, the sender node has no right to transmit any information until it receives the next credit. Under conditions of congestion, the receiving node decreases the window size, thus reducing the load. If congestion is eliminated, the receiving node increases the window size again.

The applicability of this algorithm is limited because it operates only when using connection-oriented protocols.

Implicit information. This method is based on the principle according to which the sender node decides that the receiving node or nodes are overloaded, basing the decision on some implicit indications without using direct feedback messages. For instance, packet loss can serve as implicit indications. To be capable of detecting packet losses, the protocol must be connection oriented. Provided that this is so, the time-out expiration or the arrival of the duplicate positive acknowledgment can be interpreted as implicit evidence of packet loss. However, packet loss is not always evidence of network congestion. In fact, network congestion is only one of the possible reasons for packet loss. The list of other reasons for packet loss includes such causes as unreliable operation of communications devices. These include hardware failures and data distortion because of noise. However, since the reaction to congestion and to unreliable network operation must be the same, namely, a decrease of the transmission rate, the ambiguity of the causes of packet losses does not present any problem.

An example of a protocol using implicit congestion information is the TCP protocol. This protocol uses explicit feedback information (window size) when controlling the flow and implicit information (packet losses, acknowledgment duplicates) when controlling congestion. In the first case, the source node sets the window size to the value specified by the destination node. In the second case, the source node itself decides to which level it is necessary to decrease the window to reduce the effect of network congestion or to react to low transmission reliability.

7.7 RESOURCE RESERVATION

KEY WORDS: QoS, traffic shaping, traffic policing, traffic classification, traffic-conditioning mechanisms, resource reservation protocol (RSVP), virtual circuit, traffic profile, queue-serving mechanisms

7.7.1 Resource Reservation and Packet Switching

Resource reservation is an alternative to the feedback mechanism. This mechanism is also classified as a congestion-avoidance tool. However, instead of trying to react on the fly to the congestion, the resource reservation mechanism tries to limit the congestion level by some acceptable value. This value must ensure that congestion control algorithms implemented in network switches are able to handle short-term overloads and provide the required values of QoS parameters without using the feedback mechanism.

Resource reservation in packet-switched networks is principally different from a similar procedure in circuit-switched networks. In circuit-switched networks, a fixed part of the bandwidth of the physical channel is reserved for each connection (circuit). The flow is transmitted across the network at a constant rate equal to the reserved bandwidth, and this rate is equal to the maximum flow rate. The circuit bandwidth is always reserved for this flow, and it cannot be dynamically redistributed to another flow. Without previously reserving resources, circuit-switched networks simply cannot operate, and this is their fundamental principle.

In packet-switched networks, resource reservation is not mandatory. However, when resource reservation is accomplished in packet-switched networks, this procedure is different from resource reservation in circuit-switched networks in at least two respects:

- Reservation is accomplished for the average flow rate
- Bandwidth can be dynamically redistributed between different flows

Reservation consists in requiring all resources along the flow route to check that the sustained rate of flow does not exceed the resource performance. If this condition is satisfied, then each resource remembers that it will pass this flow and that specific parts of resource performance are allocated to this flow.

EXAMPLE   *Consider the example of the resource reservation procedure (Figure 7.12). Suppose that in the initial state, the network resources were not reserved. Later, we decided to allocate some network resources to flow 1. To achieve this, we must know at least the required average rate of the flow. Assume that the sustained rate of flow 1 is 15 Mbps and that the bandwidth values of all communications links (and consequently, those of the switch interfaces) are 100 Mbps. For simplicity, consider that each input interface is equipped with a built-in processor and that its performance exceeds the bandwidth of its interface.*

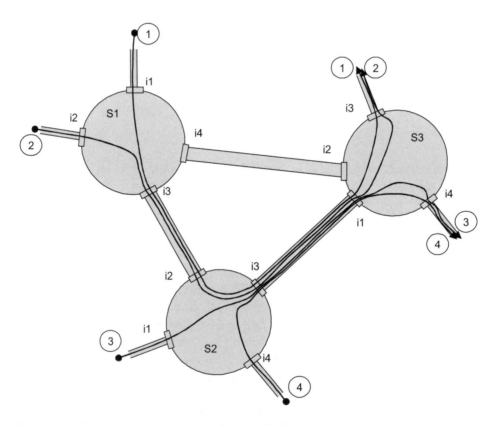

Figure 7.12 Resource reservation in packet-switched networks

Provided that these requirements have been met, the processor cannot become a bottleneck. Therefore, we will take into account the bandwidth of output interfaces only when making a decision related to resource allocation.

Flow 1 can be taken for serving, since all interfaces along its route have bandwidth sufficient for serving this flow (15 < 100). Therefore, the reservation is carried out, and each interface along the flow route remembers that it has allocated 15 Mbps of its bandwidth to flow 1.

Now assume that some time later it became necessary to make a reservation for flow 2, which is characterized by a sustained rate of 70 Mbps. Such a reservation can also be accomplished, since all interfaces along the route of flow 2 have available (not reserved for another flow) bandwidth of more than 70 Mbps. The interfaces through which both flow 1 and flow 2 pass (interfaces i3/S2 and i1/S3) had 85 Mbps free bandwidth, and all other interfaces had 100 Mbps. After the reservation, i3/S2 and i1/S3 interfaces will have 15 Mbps free bandwidth each.

The attempt to reserve the bandwidth for flow 3 will also prove to be successful. The sustained rate of this flow is 10 Mbps. However, an attempt at resource reservation for flow 4, having a sustained rate of 20 Mbps, will fail, since interfaces i3/S32 and i1/S3 will have only 5 Mbps free bandwidth each.

The example shows that the network refuses to take the flow for servicing if it cannot guarantee it the required QoS level. Of course, we have simplified the resource reservation scheme, since we concentrated on the main idea of this mechanism. In practice, the network is capable of ensuring not only the average flow rate, but also other QoS characteristics, such as maximum delay, maximum delay variation allowed level of data loss. However, to achieve this, the network must know some additional flow parameters, such as, for example, maximum burst level, in order to reserve the required buffer space.

Free bandwidth for delay-sensitive traffic and elastic traffic must be taken into account separately when accomplishing resource reservation. To ensure an acceptable level of delays and their variations for delay-sensitive traffic, the maximum total reserved bandwidth must not exceed 50% of the total bandwidth of each resource. As you may remember, in this case, under conditions of priority queuing, such traffic will encounter a small delay level. Let us illustrate this statement by the example under consideration. Assume that we have decided to reserve 30% of resource bandwidth for delay-sensitive traffic. Then, if flows 1 and 3 are sensitive to delays, the reservation is possible. On the other hand, if flows 1 and 2 are sensitive to delays, reservation is impossible, since the total average rate of these flows is 85 Mbps, which is more than 30% of 100 Mbps (30 Mbps).

If we assume that delay-sensitive traffic will be served in the priority queue, then when reserving the bandwidth for elastic traffic, it is necessary to account for the fact that only the part of the bandwidth, that remaining after delay-sensitive traffic, can be reserved for it. For example, if flows 1 and 3 are sensitive to delays, and we have allocated them the required bandwidth, then only 70 Mbps of unreserved bandwidth will be available to elastic flows.

What happens after resource reservation is accomplished for some flows in the network? Principally, nothing changes in the packet processing. The only difference between the networks with and the networks without resource reservation is that the network with resource reservation is rationally loaded. Such a network does not contain resources that certainly operate in congestion mode.

Queuing mechanisms continue to operate and ensure temporary packet buffering during burst periods. Since we planned resource loads based on average rates, flow rates during the burst periods may for some rather short time intervals exceed average rates. Thus, congestion control methods are still needed. For ensuring the required average flow rates during congestion periods, it is possible to serve such flows using weighted queues.

The main advantage of the packet-switching method is retained. If a certain flow does not fully use the bandwidth allocated to it, this bandwidth can be used for serving another flow. Reserving bandwidth only for parts of all flows is a normal practice. The remaining part of the flows will be served without reservation, obtaining the best-effort service. Temporarily, free bandwidth may be dynamically used for serving such flows without violating its obligations to serving flows with reservation.

> Circuit-switched networks cannot accomplish such resource redistribution, since they have no independently addressed information units such as packets.

EXAMPLE *Let us illustrate the principal difference between resource reservation in packet-switched networks and circuit-switched networks on the example of car traffic. Assume that in some town local authorities decided to ensure some privileges for ambulances. In the course of discussion of the project, two competing ideas were suggested. The first idea dedicated a separate lane for ambulances on all roads that all other cars have no right to use, even if there are no ambulances on the road.*
The second approach also suggested dedicating a separate lane for ambulances; however, other transport means had the right to use it provided that there were no ambulances at the moment. When an ambulance appeared, all cars driving in the privileged lane had to free it immediately. As can be easily noticed, the first variant corresponds to resource reservation in circuit-switched networks, since in such networks the dedicated lane is used exclusively by ambulances, whether they need it or not. The second approach is analogous to resource reservation in packet-switched networks. In this case, the road throughput is used more efficiently. However, such a variant is less favorable for ambulances, since nonprivileged cars create obstacles for them.

Returning from the analogy to packet-switched networks, it is necessary to point out that to ensure the guarantees of service for each flow, the previously described reservation scheme is insufficient.

We have assumed that we know exactly the average rate and burst parameters of the flows. In practice, however, such information is not always reliable. What will happen if the flow is supplied to the network at a rate that exceeds the one that was taken into account when carrying out the resource reservation? There is another question that remains without an answer in this respect — that is, how can automatic reservation of the bandwidth be ensured along the flow route?

To solve the problems that we have just formulated, it is necessary to have a system of QoS tools that would include mechanisms besides the queuing algorithms.

7.7.2 Reservation-Based QoS System

The QoS system has a distributed nature, since its elements must be present in all network devices that carry out packet forwarding: switches, routers, and access servers. On the other hand, the operation of individual network devices aimed at ensuring QoS support needs to be coordinated. This is necessary to ensure that QoS is the same along the entire route the flow packets are traveling. This is why the QoS system must also include elements of centralized management, enabling network administrators to coordinate the process of configuring QoS mechanisms in individual network devices.

The QoS system based on resource reservation comprises several types of mechanisms (Figure 7.13):

- Queue-serving mechanisms
- Resource reservation protocol
- Traffic-conditioning mechanisms

Queue-serving mechanisms are used for operation during periods of temporary congestion. Weighted queues are used for serving elastic traffic; for real-time traffic, priority queues are used. To reduce the load on switches and routers, traffic class service is used, since it is necessary to support significantly smaller number of queues and store less information on the status of flows.

Reservation protocol is needed for the automation of the resource reservation procedure along the entire route of some flow (i.e., on an end-to-end basis). Reservation pro-

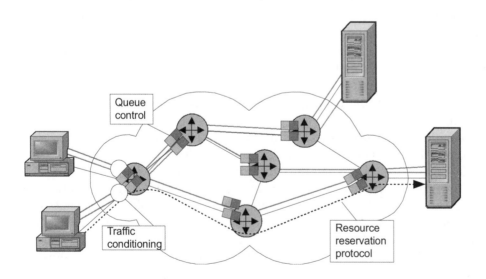

Figure 7.13 Architecture of the reservation-based QoS system

tocols are an analogue of the connection setup protocols in circuit-switched networks. Therefore, they are sometimes called signaling protocols, according to the terms used for this type of network.

Resource reservation protocol makes two passes through the network. First, it passes from the information sender to the information receiver. The message of the reservation protocol specifies the so-called **traffic profile**, which includes such characteristics as average rate, burst parameters, and requirements for the delay level. Based on this profile, each switch along the flow route decides whether or not it can carry out the reservation for this flow. If it agrees to carry out the reservation, the message is transmitted further, and the switch saves information on it. If all switches along the route agree with the requested reservation, then the last switch sends a new message about the resource reservation protocol. This new message travels in a reverse direction. As such messages pass by the switches, each of them registers the reservation state for this flow.

Not only the end node but also a transit device can initiate the operation of the resource reservation protocol. In this case, the guaranteed flow service will take place not along the entire route of the traffic but only within the boundaries of specific network region, which would certainly reduce the QoS provided to the traffic.

The reservation protocol can carry out a reservation both for individual flows and for traffic classes. The principles of its operation in each case remain the same. However, for the traffic class, the role of reservation initiator is not played by the end node, which is mainly interested in its own flow. Rather, this role is played by one of the network switches. As a rule, this is one of the edge switches of the service provider network, which receives flows from different users.

In networks with virtual circuits, the functions of resource reservation protocol are usually accomplished by the protocol of **establishing a virtual circuit**. It is necessary to mention that the connection setup protocol itself may not accomplish resource reservation, since this is an optional function of this protocol. In datagram networks, the reservation protocol is an independent one. An example of such a protocol is the **resource reservation protocol** (RSVP), which works in IP networks.

Reservations can be carried out even without the reservation protocol. To do so, network administrators must manually set reservation parameters for each flow in each network switch.

Traffic-conditioning mechanisms look after current flow parameters and ensure that they correspond to the values declared during reservation. They are a kind of checkpoint that checks the traffic before it enters the switch. Without such mechanisms, it would be impossible to guarantee the required QoS for the traffic, because if average flow rates or bursts exceed the level declared at the time of reservation, packet delays and losses will also exceed the level required for the flow. This may happen for various reasons. First, it is difficult to make precise evaluations of the traffic parameters. Preliminary measurements of average rates and bursts may produce inaccurate results because these characteristics may change with the time, so that a week later the measured results might not correspond to reality. Furthermore, purposeful distortions of the traffic parameters should not be neglected, especially when using commercial services.

The traffic-conditioning mechanism usually includes several functions:

- **Traffic classification**. This function selects packets of the same flow, having common requirements to QoS, from the common sequence of packets arriving to the device. In networks with virtual circuits, no additional classification is required, since the virtual circuit label indicates the specific flow. In datagram networks, as a rule, there are no such indications; therefore, classification is carried out on the basis of several formal packet characteristics: source and destination addresses, application identifiers, etc. Without packet classification, it is impossible to ensure QoS support in datagram networks.

- **Traffic policing**. For each input flow, in each switch there is an appropriate set of QoS parameters known as traffic profiles. Policing assumes the check of correspondence of each input flow to the parameters of its profile. There are algorithms that allow this check to be accomplished automatically at the same rate at which packets arrive to the input interface of the switch. Examples of policing algorithms include *leaky bucket* and *token bucket* algorithms. These algorithms will be covered in more detail when we describe individual technologies, such as IP, Frame Relay, and ATM.

  If profile parameters are violated (e.g., if the burst size or average rate are exceeded), the packets of such a flow are discarded or marked. Discarding some packets reduces the flow rate and conforms its parameters to the values specified in the traffic profile. Packet marking without discarding is needed to ensure that all packets are still served by the current node (or its downstream neighbors) — though with deteriorated QoS parameters different from the ones specified in the profile (e.g., with increased delays).

- **Traffic shaping**. This function is intended for time shaping of the traffic that has undergone policing. Mainly, this function is used to smooth the traffic burst to make the output flow more uniform than the flow at the device input. Burst smoothening helps to decrease queues in network devices that will process the traffic after the given device. It is also expedient to use it for restoring the time relationships of applications traffic working with streams, such as voice applications.

  Traffic-conditioning mechanisms may be supported by each network node or be implemented only in edge network devices. Service providers frequently use the latter variant, when conditioning the traffic of their clients.

There is a principal difference in the behavior of the above-described system for ensuring average flow rate on one hand, and for ensuring the required thresholds for delays and delay variations, on the other hand.

The required value of the average servicing rate is ensured by configuring the allocated percentage of the bandwidth when using the weighted queuing. Therefore, the network can carry out the request for any average flow rate, provided that it doesn't exceed the bandwidth available on the network along the route of specific flow.

However, the network cannot configure the priority queuing algorithm in such a way as to ensure that it strictly observes the requirement to some predefined threshold values of delay and delay variation. Directing the packets into the priority queue only allows to guarantee that the delays will be low enough, at least, considerably lower than for the packets served according to the weighted queuing algorithm. However, it is difficult to numerically evaluate the delays. How can the service provider observe the SLA?

As a rule, this problem is solved by means of measuring the network traffic. The service provider must organize the priority queuing for the traffic, using one or more priority queues, measuring the delays of real-world traffic and processing the results using statistical methods. To achieve this, the service provider must build the delay distribution histograms for various flow routes and determine average delays, delay variations and maximum delay variations for every class of the delay-sensitive traffic. Based on these characteristics, the service provider chooses some threshold QoS characteristics that it can guarantee to its clients. As a rule, these values are chosen with some reserve, so that the network would be able to observe the declared guarantees even when some number of new clients appear.

7.8 TRAFFIC ENGINEERING

KEY WORDS: QoS requirements, traffic engineering, traffic profile, traffic classes, traffic burst, resource reservation, suboptimal traffic routes, aggregate flows, transit switches, level of resource utilization, congestion control mechanism, packet-switched networks

When considering a reservation-based QoS system, we did not cover such aspects as routes along which the flows travel across the network. To be more precise, we considered these routes as predefined, a choice that was made without taking QoS requirements into account. Under the conditions of predefined routes, we tried to ensure that such a set of flows passes along this route for which it is possible to ensure conformity to QoS requirements.

The task of ensuring QoS support can be solved more efficiently if we assume that traffic routes are not fixed and can be chosen. This would allow the network to serve more flows and to ensure QoS requirements, provided that the characteristics of the network (i.e., link bandwidth and switch performance) remain unchanged.

Traffic engineering (TE) methods solve the problem of choosing routes for flows (or traffic classes) and accounting for QoS requirements. These methods simultaneously try to achieve another goal: to ensure balanced loading of all network resources as close to the maximum as possible. When this aim is achieved, the network will have maximum total performance and will ensure the specified QoS characteristics.

TE methods are also based on resource reservation. Besides selecting an optimal route for the flow, they reserve the bandwidth of network resources along this route for that flow.

TE methods are relatively new for packet-switched networks. Mainly, this is because the transmission of elastic traffic did not make strong demands on QoS parameters.

Furthermore, for a long time, the Internet was a noncommercial network; therefore, the maximum use of resources was not the problem of primary importance for IP technologies that serve as a foundation for the Internet.

The situation has changed. Packet-switched networks must transmit various types of traffic, provide the specified QoS, and ensure maximum use of their resources. However, to achieve this goal, it is necessary to change some traditional approaches to route selection.

7.8.1 Drawbacks of Traditional Routing Methods

Route selection based on network topology without taking into account the information on the current network load was the main operating principle of routing protocols in packet-switched networks.

For each source address–destination address pair, such protocols chose the only route without accounting for information flows traveling through the network. As a result, all flows between these pairs of end nodes passed along this route, the shortest route according to metric measurements. The chosen route may be either more rational (e.g., accounting for the nominal bandwidth of communications links or delays introduced by these links) or less rational (e.g., accounting for only the number of transit routers between the source and the destination nodes).

IMPORTANT *Traditional routing methods consider the best chosen route as the only possible one, even if there are other routes, although somewhat longer.*

The *fish*, the network with the topology shown in Figure 7.14, is a classic example illustrating the inefficiency of this approach. Despite the two routes between the A and E switches — the upper one via the B switch and the lower one via the C and D switches — the entire traffic from switch A to switch E will be forwarded along the upper route according to traditional routing principles. This happens for one reason, namely, that the lower path is longer by one transit node. Therefore, this route is ignored, although it could work in parallel with the upper one.

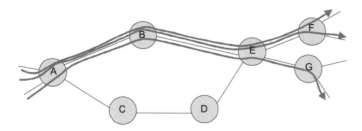

Figure 7.14 Inefficiency of the approach to choosing the shortest route

As a result, even the shortest route is congested, and the packets will be sent along this path anyway. For example, in the network shown in Figure 7.15, the upper path will continue to be used even when its resources prove to be insufficient for serving traffic from A to E. At the same time, the lower path will be ignored despite the resources of B and C switches that might be sufficient for high-quality transmission of this traffic.

> The inefficiency of the methods used for network resource distribution is evident. Some resources operate under conditions of overload; other resources are not used. The congestion control methods are unable to solve this problem, since they start to handle it under admittedly losing conditions when it is impossible to find a rational solution. Reservation methods also cannot solve this problem if they attempt to reserve resources along the routes chosen without accounting for the current load on network switches. Consequently, principally different mechanisms are needed.

7.8.2 Idea of Traffic Engineering

TE methods use the following initial data:

- Characteristics of the network — its topology, as well as the performance of its switches and the bandwidth of its communications links (Figure 7.15).

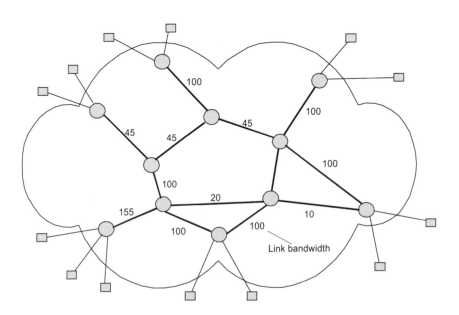

Figure 7.15 Network topology and the performance of its resources

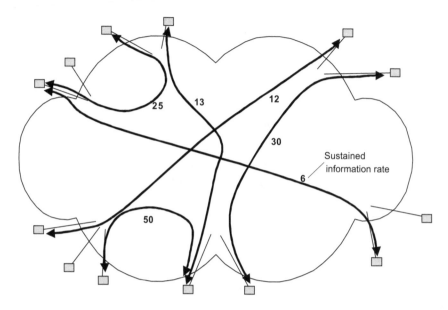

Figure 7.16 Offered load

■ Information on the offered load — that is, on the flows of traffic that the network must transmit between its edge switches (Figure 7.16).

Assume that the performance of the processor of each switch is sufficient for serving the traffic from all its input interfaces even if the traffic arrives to the interface at the maximum possible rate, equal to the interface bandwidth. Therefore, when carrying out resource reservation, consider as resources the bandwidth of the link-connecting switches, which determines the bandwidth of the two interfaces connected by the link.

Each flow is characterized by the point of entrance into the network, the point of exit from the network, and the traffic profile. To obtain optimal solutions, it is possible to use detailed descriptions of each flow. For example, take into account the value of possible traffic burst or variation of interpacket intervals. However, since it is difficult to quantitatively evaluate their influence on the network operation, and the influence of these parameters on the QoS characteristics is less important, to find the suboptimal distribution of traffic routes, one usually takes into account only the sustained information rates of flows, which are shown in Figure 7.17.

TE methods frequently operate with aggregate flows joining several flows rather than with individual flows. Since we are searching for a common route for several flows, only the flows that have common network entrance and exit points can be aggregated. Flow aggregation simplifies the problem of choosing routes, since when considering individual user flow, transit switches have to store excessive amounts of information because individual flows might be rather numerous. However, it is necessary to point out that the aggregation of several individual flows is possible only when the component flows make the same demands on the QoS. For brevity, later in this section we will use the term flow to designate both individual and aggregate flows, since this doesn't change the TE principles.

> The goal of TE is to determine the routes for passing flows across the network, which means that for each flow, it is necessary to find the exact sequence of transit switches and their interfaces. These routes must be chosen in such a way as to load all network resources to the maximum and to ensure that each flow gets the required QoS.

The maximum level of resource utilization is chosen in such a way as to enable the congestion control mechanism to ensure the required QoS. For simplicity, later on, we will assume that our network transmits only one class of traffic (e.g., delay-sensitive traffic) and then explain the ways of generalizing TE methods when the network has to transmit different kinds of traffic.

The solution to the TE problem is such a set of routes for the specified set of traffic flows for which all values of resource utilization coefficients along the route do not exceed some predefined threshold, K_{max}.

Figure 7.17 illustrates one possible solution to the problem shown in Figures 7.16 and 7.17. The chosen routes guarantee that the maximum utilization coefficient of any resource for any flow does not exceed 0.6 (i.e., K_{max} in this example is 0.6).

There are different approaches to solving the TE problem. First, it is possible to find a solution beforehand in the background mode. For this purpose, it is necessary to know the initial data: network topology and performance as well as network entry and exit points of the traffic flows and their average rates. After that, the problem of rationally

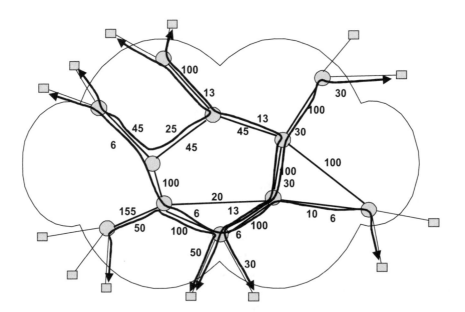

Figure 7.17 Distribution of the load over the network — choosing routes for the traffic

distributing routes among traffic flows with fixed exit and entry points and predefined levels of the maximum utilization coefficients can be delegated to some program. For example, such a program may find the solution by testing all possible variants. The result of its operation will be presented in the form of exact routes for each flow, specifying all transit switches.

The second approach assumes that the TE problem is solved by delegating it to the network switches. For this purpose, it is possible to use modified versions of the standard routing protocols. Modifications introduced into routing protocols mean that switches and routers not only inform one another about topological information but also exchange the current values of available bandwidth on each resource.

After finding the solution, it is necessary to implement it in the form of routing tables. At this stage, another problem might arise if you need to establish these routes in a datagram network. Routing tables in such networks only account for the destination addresses of the packets. Switches and routers of such networks (for example, IP networks) do not operate with flows, since individual flows do not exist in an explicit form. In such networks, each packet is an individual switching unit during forwarding. In other words, the forwarding tables of such networks reflect only the network topology (the forwarding directions to specific destination addresses).

Therefore, the infusion of reservation methods into datagram networks comes with significant difficulties. Reservation protocols similar to the already mentioned RSVP use some sets of characteristics besides the destination address to define the flow for datagram routers. In this case, the concept of flow is used only at the reservation stage, and during forwarding, the traditional scheme continues to work (i.e., the one that uses only the destination address).

Now imagine having several flows (still assume that all flows belong to the only traffic class) between two end nodes and needing to forward them along different routes. Such a need might arise when solving the TE problem for providing the network load balance. Datagram switches or routers cannot implement the solution, since for all these flows it has only one record in the forwarding table, the one corresponding to the common destination address of the packets belonging to these flows. Changing the logic of operation of switches and routers of datagram networks is inexpedient, since this requires fundamental changes.

Therefore, TE methods are currently used in networks with virtual circuits for which implementation of the solution obtained for a group or groups of flows does not present any problem. Each flow (or group of flows with the same route) receives allocated virtual circuits created according to the chosen route. TE methods are successfully employed in ATM and Frame Relay networks operating on the basis of virtual circuit technique. IP networks can also benefit from TE advantages when they are used in ATM or Frame Relay networks operating as part of an internet built on the basis of the IP protocol. A new technology, MPLS, was developed specifically as a tool for integrating the virtual circuit techniques with IP networks. MPLS can be used for solving TE problems in IP networks.

TE methods for each individual technology will be covered in detail, along with detailed descriptions of those technologies, in the next parts of this book.

7.8.3 Traffic Engineering for Different Traffic Classes

The problem of TE considered in the previous section was presented in a simplified form. All traffic flows belonged to the same traffic class and had the same QoS requirements. This allowed the same maximum value of the utilization coefficient K_{max} to be used for all flows.

There are situations in which for each network user, there are several classes of traffic. We already explained a similar problem when considering resource reservation.

This means that it is necessary to provide a value, K_{max}, for each traffic class.

TE methods taking into account the presence of traffic with different levels of QoS requirements solve this problem in the same way as the methods of resource reservation of individual nodes. If we have two classes of traffic, we must specify two maximum levels of resource utilization. For example, for elastic traffic, the maximum value of the utilization coefficient must not be greater than 0.9, and for delay-sensitive traffic, this value must not exceed 0.5. As a rule, reservation is not carried out for all flows, since part of the bandwidth must be available. For this reason, the maximum values provided previously are usually decreased to around 0.75 and 0.25, respectively.

To achieve such results, each resource must have two related counters of available bandwidth: one for delay-sensitive priority traffic and another for elastic traffic. When determining the possibility of laying the route using specific resources, the average rate of the new flow for priority traffic must be compared to the bandwidth available for priority traffic. If available bandwidth is sufficient, and the new flow will pass using this interface, then the rate of the new flow must be subtracted from the counter of bandwidth available to priority traffic, as well as from the counter of the bandwidth available to elastic traffic, because priority traffic will always be served before elastic traffic. Thus, priority traffic will also generate an additional load for elastic traffic. If the TE problem is being solved for elastic traffic, then its rate is compared to the counter of the bandwidth available for elastic traffic.

If a positive decision is made, the value of this rate must be subtracted only from the elastic traffic counter, because elastic traffic is transparent for priority traffic.

Modified routing protocols must distribute over the network information on two parameters of available bandwidth, separately for each traffic class. If this problem is generalized for transmitting several classes of traffic, then each resource must have the same number of associated counters according to the number of traffic classes existing in the network. Routing protocols must distribute the vector of free bandwidth values containing the appropriate number of elements.

SUMMARY

▶ Quality of service in a narrow sense focuses on the influence of the queues of communications devices on traffic transmission. Currently, QoS methods take one of the most important positions in the range of technologies used in packet-switched networks. Without implementation of these methods, operation of contemporary multimedia applications such as IP telephone, video and audio broadcasting, and interactive remote learning is impossible.

▶ Application traffic can be divided onto two broad classes in relation to its requirements to QoS characteristics: time-sensitive traffic and elastic traffic.

▶ QoS characteristics reflect the negative effects of the packets spending time in queues, which manifest themselves in a reduction of the transmission rate, packet corruption, and losses.

▶ Priority and weighted queues as well as resource reservation and feedback allow QoS to be guaranteed for both delay-sensitive and elastic traffic.

▶ The sliding window algorithm ensures reliable packet transmission and is an efficient feedback tool.

▶ The architecture of a reservation-based QoS system includes:

- Queuing mechanisms
- Reservation protocols allowing automatically reservation of the required resources for the flows
- Traffic-conditioning tools that carry out traffic classification, policing, and shaping

▶ Traffic engineering methods consist of choosing rational routes for transmitting flows using the network. Route selection maximizes use of network resources and ensures conformity with the QoS requirements.

REVIEW QUESTIONS

1. Give examples of applications that generate elastic traffic.
2. Which QoS characteristics are the most important for time-sensitive traffic?
3. What are the positive and negative effects of using queues in packet switches?
4. Which parameter has the greatest influence on queue size? Which parameter is the second most important?
5. What kinds of traffic does the packet-switched network transmit? What are their requirements for the network?

6. What are the advantages and drawbacks of priority queuing?

7. For what kind of traffic is weighted queuing most suitable?

8. Is it possible to combine priority and weighted queuing?

9. Can packets of the highest priority be delayed in queues?

10. List the methods of congestion control and congestion avoidance.

11. What are the differences of bandwidth reservation in packet-switched and circuit-switched networks?

12. What are the components of the reservation-based QoS system?

13. What problem is solved by traffic engineering methods?

14. What traffic parameter is changeable in traffic engineering?

PROBLEMS

1. Suppose that some data flow belongs to the CBR class. Data are transmitted in packets equal to 125 bytes through a 100 Mbps link. The traffic profile has the following parameters: PIR for burst periods is 25 Mbps, maximum deviation of the interpacket interval is 10 ms, and the burst period is 600 ms. If the traffic conforms to its profile, what is the maximum volume of the burst?

2. Which of the five flows will on average spend less time in the queue to the output interface 100 Mbps if these flows are served by weighted queues and are allocated 40%, 15%, 10%, 30%, and 5% of the interface bandwidth, respectively? Average flow rates are 35, 2, 8, 3, and 4 Mbps, respectively. Coefficient of variation of interpacket intervals is the same for all flows.

3. For which of the events listed here might the flow from the queue with the highest priority have to wait in a queue?

   A. Queues of lower priorities

   B. Its own burst

   C. Bursts of low-priority traffic

4. There are three queues to the output interface 10 Mbps, served according to the weighted queuing algorithm. There are three packets in the first queue, packet 1 is 1,500 bytes, packet 2 is 625 bytes, and packet 3 is 750 bytes. In the second queue are packet 4 (500 bytes), packet 5 (1,500 bytes), and packet 6 (1,500 bytes). In the third queue, there are packet 7 (100 bytes), packet 8 (275 bytes), packet 9 (1,500 bytes), and packet 10 (1,500 bytes). In the queues, the packets are in ascending order (i.e., the first packet in the first queue is packet 1; in the second queue, it's packet 4; and in the third queue, it's packet 7).

5. In what order will the packets appear at the output of the 2 Mbps interface, if the working cycle of the algorithm is 10 msec, and queues are allocated 50%, 30%, and 20% of the resource bandwidth, respectively? In each cycle, the algorithm always takes a packet from the queue (provided that it is not empty), even if the packet size guarantees that its transmission will exceed the time allocated for this queue.

6. How much time would it take to complete each of the two cycles of processing queues (see the previous question)? At what rate was each flow served at this interval comprising two cycles?

7. How is it necessary to change the cycle time of the algorithm described in question 4 to make flow rates closer to the planned ones? Increase or decrease?

8. At the network ingress, some flow is undergoing policing according to the 3 Mbps profile. This flow is allocated 30% of the 10 Mbps output interface bandwidth in the transit network switch. Which of the statements here are correct?

   A. The result of applying either of these mechanisms is the same; therefore, it is not necessary to implement reservation in the switch.

   B. The result of applying either of these mechanisms is the same, but the reservation in the switch is necessary because at the network ingress and within the switch, the flow competes for resources with other flows.

   C. The results of applying either of these mechanisms are different. At the network ingress, the flow rate is limited by 3 Mbps; in the switch for this flow, the rate of 3 Mbps is guaranteed even during periods of congestion.

9. Is it possible to have no queue in a system whose utilization coefficient is close to 1?

10. Which of the mechanisms listed here is necessary to use to ensure the high-quality transmission of voice traffic (64 Kbps stream) using the packet-switched network?

    A. Reserve 64 Kbps bandwidth on all switches along the route of the voice traffic.

    B. Serve this flow in the priority queue on all switches along the traffic route.

    C. Use the input packet buffer on the receiving network node.

    D. Smooth the traffic in the output queues of all switches along the route.

11. Is the following statement correct? Resource reservation in packet-switched network deprives the user of the possibility of dynamically redistributing the bandwidth between flows.

12. What mechanism must be applied to avoid the suppression of low priority traffic by traffic of high priority?

PART II

PHYSICAL LAYER TECHNOLOGIES

The physical basis of any computer (or telecommunications) network is transmission links. *Without these links, switches would be unable to exchange packets, and computers would remain isolated devices.*

After studying the principles of computer networks design, readers might imagine an easy pattern of a computer network — computers and switches connected to one another by lengths of cable. However, when considering a computer network in more detail, things prove to be significantly more complicated than they seem when studying the OSI model.

Dedicated cables are used for connecting network devices only for short distances (i.e., in LANs). When building WANs and MANs, this approach becomes too expensive and inefficient because of the high cost of long-distance transmission links. Moreover, to install such cables, it is necessary to get official permission. Therefore, using the existing regional circuit-switched networks — either telephone networks or transmission networks — is a more efficient solution for connecting WAN and MAN switches. Therefore, in the circuit-switched network, a circuit that carries out the same functions as the section of cable is created. That is, it ensures physical point-to-point connections. This circuit is a significantly more complicated technical system than the cable. However, these complications are transparent for computer networks. Transmission networks are built specifically for creating communications links infrastructure, making their links more efficient with respect to the price:capacity ratio. Currently, the designers of computer networks have a range of transmission links at their disposal, covering rates from 64 Kbps to 10 Gbps.

Despite the differences in the physical and technical natures of communications links, they can all be described using a unified set of characteristics. The most important technical parameters of any communications link transmitting discrete information are its bandwidth, measured in hertz, and its capacity, measured in bits per second (bps). The capacity is the maximum rate of the bit stream that can be achieved on a given communications link. The capacity depends on the bandwidth and on the method used for encoding discrete information.

Wireless links are becoming increasingly popular. They are the only type of links that ensure mobility for the users of a computer network. Furthermore, wireless communications are used when cable installation is impossible or too expensive. This can be seen in thinly populated regions, in buildings already included in the existing cable infrastructure of the competitors, etc. Wireless communications use electromagnetic waves of different frequencies — radio waves, microwaves, infrared waves, or visible light. High levels of noise and complex paths of propagation typical for wireless links require the use of special methods of signal encoding and transmission.

Part II comprises the following chapters:

■ Chapter 8: Transmission Links
■ Chapter 9: Data Encoding and Multiplexing
■ Chapter 10: Wireless Transmission
■ Chapter 11: Transmission Networks

8 TRANSMISSION LINKS

CHAPTER OUTLINE

8.1 INTRODUCTION

When building networks, it is possible to employ various communications links using different physical media: telephone and telegraph wires slung between poles, coaxial copper and fiber-optic cables laid underground, copper twisted pairs connecting all contemporary offices, and, finally, radio waves that penetrate everything.

In this chapter, we will cover the general characteristics of communications links, independent of their physical nature. Examples of these characteristics are bandwidth, capacity, error probability, and noise immunity. Bandwidth is a fundamental characteristic of a communications link, since it determines the maximum possible information rate of the link, known as link capacity. The **Nyquist formula** expresses this dependence for an ideal link; the **Shannon formula** takes into account the noise interference always present in real communications links. This chapter will conclude with a description of contemporary cable standards, which form the foundation for guided communications links.

8.2 TAXONOMY

> **KEY WORDS:** link, circuit, channel, line, transmission links, transmission network, telephone network, physical medium, Unshielded twisted pair (UTP), shielded twisted pair (STP), coaxial cable, fiber-optic cable, radio channels, satellite communications, amplifier, regenerator, data circuit-terminating equipment (DCE), data service unit/circuit service unit (DSU/CSU), data terminal equipment (DTE), multiplexer, demultiplexer, analog and digital links

8.2.1 Transmission Networks, Circuits, and Links

When describing a technical system that transmits information between two neighboring network nodes, four terms are encountered: **link**, **circuit**, **channel**, and **line**. These terms are often used as synonyms, and in many respects this does not cause any problems. At the same time, their usage has some specific features.

■ The term *link* is used to designate the segment between two neighboring nodes. This means that the link does not include transit switching and multiplexing devices.

■ The term *channel* is most frequently used for designating the part of the link bandwidth used independently of other channels. For example, a circuit within a transmission network might comprise 30 channels, each ensuring the bandwidth of 64 Kbps.

■ A *circuit* is a complex path between network end nodes. Thus, circuits comprise individual links and internal connections within switches.

■ Finally, the term *line* can be used as a synonym for the other three terms.

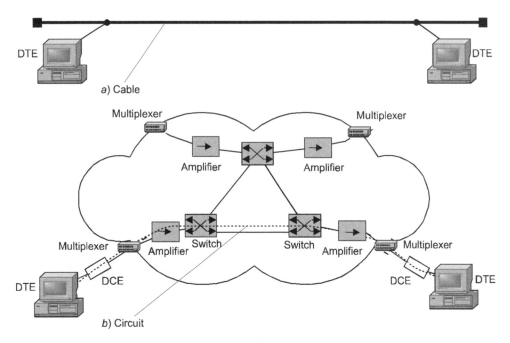

a) Cable

b) Circuit

Figure 8.1 Components of a communications link

However, it is necessary to understand that there are various traditions because of which confusion in the use of terms must not be judged too severely. This is especially true with respect to terminological differences between traditional telephony and a newer technological area — computer networks. The process of convergence has only intensified the problems of terminology. This happened because many mechanisms of these networks became common for both kinds of networks, but they retain two (or sometimes more) names from each technological area.

Besides this, there are objective reasons for the ambiguous interpretations of networking terms. Figure 8.1 shows two variants of a transmission line. In the first variant (Figure 8.1, *a*), the line consists of the cable tens of meters long. In the second variant (Figure 8.1, *b*), the transmission line is a circuit established in a circuit-switched network. This might be either a **transmission network** or a **telephone network**.

Consider the case in which two switches of computer networks are connected by a transmission link created within a transmission network. For computer networks, this connection is a link, since it connects two neighboring nodes, and all transit equipment is transparent for those nodes. However, for transmission networks this connection is a circuit — or, to be more precise, a channel — since it probably uses part of the bandwidth of each link connecting switches of the transmission network. Thus, the ground for mutual misunderstanding at the terminological level between specialists in the field of computer networks and transmission networks is obvious here. Note that a telephone network itself might be built on the basis of the links of a transmission network. Transmission networks are created to provide transport services to computer or telephone networks. In such cases, it can be said that computer or telephone networks operate **over** transmission networks.

8.2.2 Media

Transmission links also differ in the physical medium they use for transmitting information.

A **physical medium** used for data transmission may be a set of wires by which the signals are transmitted. Open wire and cable communications (underground or submerged) lines are built on the basis of these wires (Figure 8.2). Information signals can also propagate in other physical media, such as the Earth's atmosphere or space. The first case has a *wired (guided) medium*. The second case has a *wireless (unguided) medium*.

In contemporary telecommunications systems, information is transmitted using electric current or voltage, radio, or light signals. These physical processes are electromagnetic field oscillations of differing frequencies.

Open wire (aerial) communications lines are wires without insulation or shielding strung overhead between power poles. Such communications lines were the most common for transmitting telephone and telegraph signals until fairly recently. Nowadays, such wired aerial lines are quickly being moved out of use by cable lines. However, they can be used for transmitting computer data if more advanced communications lines are unavailable. The transmission rate and noise immunity of these lines are far from perfect.

Cable lines have a rather sophisticated design. The cable consists of wires enclosed within several layers of insulation coating: electric, electromagnetic, mechanical, and possibly,

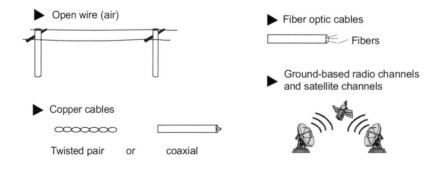

Figure 8.2 Types of transmission media

climatic. The cable might also be equipped with connectors that enable quick connections among various devices. The following three types of cable are used in computer (and telecommunications) networks:

■ **Unshielded twisted pair** (UTP) and shielded twisted pair (STP)
■ **Coaxial cables** with copper strand
■ **Fiber-optic cables**

The first two types of cables are also known as copper cables.

Radio channels of ground-based and satellite communications are formed by the transmitter and receiver of radio waves. There are numerous radio channels that differ in frequency and range. Broadcast radio ranges (long wave, medium wave, and shortwave, also known as amplitude modulation or AM ranges) ensure long-distance communications at rather low data transmission rates. The channels operating within a high frequency range, for which frequency modulation (FM) is used, provide higher data rates. Other frequency ranges, known as ultra-high frequency or microwaves (above 300 MHz), are also used in data transmission. The signals with frequencies above 30 MHz are not reflected by the Earth's ionosphere; therefore, to ensure stable communications, the transmitter and receiver must be located within line of sight. Such frequencies are used in satellite channels, radio-relay channels, and local area or mobile networks, where this condition is satisfied.

Nowadays practically all previously described types of physical media are used for data communications in computer networks. Many good capabilities are provided by fiber-optic cables because of their broad bandwidth and high noise immunity. Therefore, fiber-optic cables are used for building the backbones of large-scale regional networks and MANs as well as high-speed LANs. Twisted pair is another popular medium, since it is characterized by an excellent price/quality ratio as well as by ease of mounting. Wireless channels are most frequently used when it is impossible to use cable links. For example, if the channel passes through a sparsely populated region or it is necessary to communicate with mobile network users, wireless channels are used. Ensuring mobility has affected telephone networks. Computer networks cannot yet keep pace with them in this respect. Still, building computer networks on the basis of wireless technologies such as Radio Ethernet is considered one of the most promising technological areas of telecommunications. Wireless links are covered in more detail in *Chapter 10.*

8.2.3 Transmission Equipment

As shown in Figure 8.1, besides transmission media, transmission lines include certain equipment. Even when the transmission line does not pass through transmission networks but is created on the basis of a cable, the transmission line consists of **data circuit-terminating equipment (DCE).**

DCE in computer networks directly connects computers of switches to communications links, making it terminal equipment. Traditionally, DCE is included into communications link. The list of DCE devices includes **modems** (for telephone lines), **terminal adapters in ISDN networks**, and **devices for connecting to the digital links** of transmission networks data service unit/circuit service unit (DSU/CSU).

DCE operates at the physical layer of the OSI model and is responsible for transmitting and receiving the signals of the required shape, power, and frequency into or from physical media.

The equipment of the user who generates the data for transmission using communications links connected directly to DCE has a generalized name — **data terminal equipment** (*DTE*). Computers, switches, or routers are examples of DTE. This equipment is not included in the communications lines.

NOTE   *It is not always possible to strictly delimit DTE and DCE in LANs. For example, a LAN adapter can be considered both part of a computer (i.e., DTE) and part of a communications link (i.e., DCE). To be more precise, one part of the network adapter carries out DTE functions; another part of it (the one that directly receives and transmits signals to and from the line) is the DCE.*

There are several *standard interfaces* for connecting DCE devices to DTE devices (i.e., to computers, switches, or routers)[1]. They all operate at short distances, usually several meters.

Intermediate equipment is usually employed in long-distance communications links. It carries out the following tasks:

- Improvement of the signal quality
- Creating a persistent communications circuit between two subscribers of the network

In LANs there might be no intermediate equipment if the length of physical medium — cables or radio range — allows one adapter to receive signals directly from another adapter without amplification. If this is not the case, it is necessary to use intermediate devices such as *repeaters* or *concentrators* (hubs).

In WANs, it is necessary to ensure high-quality signal transmission over hundreds or even thousands of miles. Because of this, it is impossible to build long-distance communications lines without **amplifiers** (which increase signal power) and **regenerators** (which amplify and restore the shape of signals distorted during long-distance transmissions). Usually, such devices are installed at a specific predefined distance.

In transmission networks, apart from the previously considered equipment ensuring high-quality signal transmission, transit switching equipment is also required — **multiplexers**, **demultiplexers**, and **switches**. This equipment creates the continuous circuit built from sections of physical medium (cables with amplifiers) between two network subscribers.

Depending on the type of intermediate equipment, all communications links are divided into analog and digital links. In **analog links** (or **analog channels**) intermediate

---

[1] DTE-DCE interfaces are described by the standards of the V ITU-T series and by the EIA Recommended Standards (RS) series. These two lines of standards duplicate each other in many respects. The most popular standards are RS-232, RS-530, V.35, and HSSI.

equipment is intended for the amplification of analog signals (i.e., the signals with a continuous range of values). Such links were traditionally used in telephone networks for interconnecting telephone switches. For creating high-speed channels, which multiplex several low-speed local loops, the *frequency division multiplexing (FDM)* technique is usually implemented.

In **digital lines** the signals being transmitted have a finite number of states. As a rule, elementary signal — i.e., the signal transmitted per clock cycle of the transmitting device — has two, three, or four states. These states are transmitted through communications lines as rectangular pulses or as potentials. Both computer data and digitized voice and video are transmitted in the form of such signals. In fact, transmission networks became possible because of the unified discrete information representation in contemporary computer, telephone, and TV networks. In digital communications links, intermediate equipment is used. Regenerators improve the shape of pulses and ensure their resynchronization (i.e., restore the interpulse period). Intermediate multiplexing and switching equipment of transmission networks operates according to *the time division multiplexing* (TDM) principle.

8.3 TRANSMISSION LINK CHARACTERISTICS

KEY WORDS: harmonic, signal spectrum, spectrum width, external and internal noises, attenuation, linear attenuation, transparency windows, impedance, receiver sensitivity threshold, noise immunity, electric coupling, magnetic coupling, crosstalk signals, near end cross talk (NEXT), far end cross talk (FEXT), cable protection, attenuation to cross-talk ratio (ACR), data transmission reliability, bit error rate (BER), bandwidth, capacity, bauds, carrier signal, carrier frequency, modulation, Fourier formula, Claude Shannon, Harry Nyquist

8.3.1 Spectrum Analysis of the Signals in Communications Links

Spectral distribution of the signal transmitted through communications links plays an important role in determining parameters of that line. *From the theory of harmonic analysis, it is known that any periodic process can be represented as a sum of sinusoidal oscillations of different frequencies and amplitudes* (Figure 8.3).

Each component sine curve is known as **harmonic**, and entire set of harmonics is known as **signal spectrum**. The **spectrum width** is interpreted as the difference between the maximum and minimum frequencies of the set of harmonics the sum of which produces the source signal.

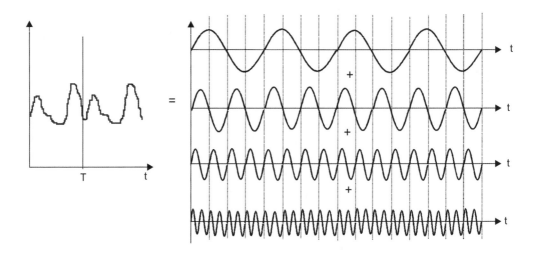

Figure 8.3 Representation of a periodic signal by the sum of sine curves

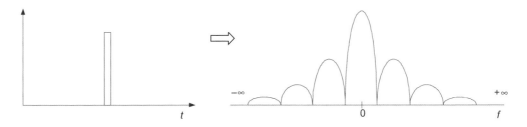

Figure 8.4 Spectrum of the ideal pulse

Nonperiodic signals can be represented by integral sine signals with a continuous frequency spectrum. Particularly, the spectrum of the ideal pulse (unit power and zero duration) contains the components of the entire frequency spectrum, from $-\infty$ to $+\infty$ (Figure 8.4).

The technique of finding the spectrum of any source signal is well known. For some signals that can be described analytically (e.g., for the sequence of rectangular pulses of the same duration and amplitude), the spectrum is easily calculated based on the **Fourier formula**.

For signals with an arbitrary shape, the spectrum can be found using special devices known as spectrum analyzers, which measure the spectrum of real signals and display the amplitudes of component harmonics on screen, print them, or transmit them for processing and storing in computers.

The distortion of any component sine curve at any frequency by the communications line distorts the amplitude and shape of any type of transmitted signal. Shape distortions appear when the sine curves of different frequencies are distorted differently. If this is an analog signal transmitting voice, then the voice timbre changes because of the distortion

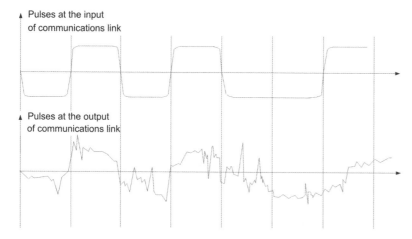

Figure 8.5 Pulse distortion in a communications link

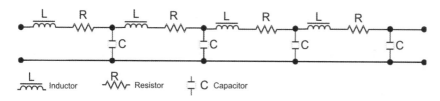

Figure 8.6 Representation of a communications link as a distributed inductance and capacitance load

of the overtones or side frequencies. When transmitting pulse signals characteristic of computer networks, low-frequency and high-frequency harmonics are distorted, and as a result, pulse fronts lose their rectangular shape (Figure 8.5). Consequently, there might be problems with signal recognition at the receiving end of the line.

Communications lines distort the signals being transmitted because their physical parameters differ from the ideal ones. An ideal transmission medium that doesn't introduce any distortions into the signal being transmitted must, at least, have zero resistance, capacitance and inductance. Copper wires, for example, are always some combination of active resistance, capacitance, and inductance loads (Figure 8.6). As a result, for sinusoids of different frequencies, the links will have different impedance values. Consequently, they will be transmitted differently.

Apart from signal distortions introduced by internal physical parameters of communications link, there are **external noises** that contribute distortions to the shape of the signal at the output of communications links. This noise is generated by various electric engines, electronic devices, atmospheric phenomena, etc. Despite protective measures taken by developers of cables and the presence of amplifying and regenerating equipment, it is impossible to completely compensate for the influence of external noise.

Besides external noise, there is **internal noise** in the cable known as cross talk. This is noise caused by one pair of wires to another pair. As a result, the signals at the link output usually have a complex shape (as shown in Figure 8.5).

8.3.2 Attenuation and Impedance

The degree of distortion of the sinusoidal signals by communications links is evaluated using characteristics such as attenuation and impedance.

Attenuation shows how the power of the reference sinusoidal signal decreases at the output of the communications link when compared to the power of the reference signal supplied to the input of this line. Attenuation (A) is usually measured in decibels and calculated according to the following formula:

$$A = 10 \lg P_{out} / P_{in} \tag{8.1}$$

Here, P_{out} is the power of the signal at the line output, and P_{in} is the power of the signal supplied to the line input. Since attenuation depends on the length of communications links, so-called **linear attenuation** is used as link characteristic (i.e., attenuation of communications links of specific lengths). For the cable of a LAN, a 100 m link is generally used. This value is the maximum cable length for most LAN technologies. For WAN links, the linear attenuation is 1 km.

Usually, attenuation characterizes the passive sections of the communications links, consisting of cables and cross connects without amplifiers and regenerators. Since the power of the output signal at the cable without intermediate amplifiers is always lower than the power of the input signal, cable attenuation is always a *negative value.*

The degree of power attenuation of a sinusoidal signal depends on the sinusoid frequency; this dependence is also used for characterizing communications links (Figure 8.7).

Usually, attenuation values *for only some frequencies* are provided when describing the parameters of communications links. The use of only some values and not all character-

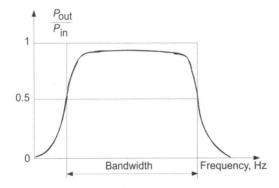

Figure 8.7 Dependence of attenuation on the frequency

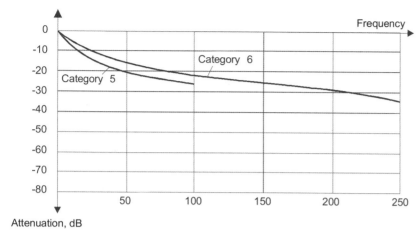

Figure 8.8 Attenuation of unshielded twisted pair cables

istics is related, on the one hand, to simplifying of measurements when testing the line quality and, on the other hand, to the main frequency of the transmitted signal, often known beforehand. This is the frequency whose harmonic has the largest amplitude and power. Therefore, it is often sufficient to know the attenuation at this frequency to roughly evaluate the distortions of signals transmitted using the line.

NOTE   *As was already mentioned above, cable attenuation is always a negative value. However, specialists often omit the "minus" sign when speaking about attenuation. They may say that the higher the quality of the line, the smaller its attenuation. This statement would be correct only if the absolute value of attenuation is meant. If the sign is taken into account, then, the greater is the attenuation, the higher is the quality of the communications link. Consider an example. For indoors wiring the Category 5 twisted pair cable is used. This cable is employed in practically all LAN technologies. It is characterized by attenuation no less than −23.6 dB for the frequency of 100 MHz, having the cable length of 100 m. The higher-quality Category 6 cable at 100 MHz is characterized by attenuation not lower than −20.6 dB. Naturally, −20.6 > −23.6, but, at the same time, 20.6 < 23.6.*

Typical dependencies of attenuation on the frequency for an unshielded twisted pair (categories 5 and 6) are shown in Figure 8.8.

Fiber-optic cable has significantly smaller (by absolute value) attenuation coefficients, usually from −0.2 to −3.0 dB for a 1,000 m cable. Consequently, its quality is significantly higher than that of the twisted pair cable. Practically all optical fibers have a rather complex dependence of attenuation on the wave length, which has three so-called **transparency windows**. Figure 8.9 shows a typical dependence of attenuation for optical fiber. From this illustration, it is clear that the area of efficient application of contemporary fibers is limited to wavelengths of 850 nm, 1,300 nm, and 1,550 nm (or frequencies of 35 THz, 23 THz, and 19.4 THz, respectively). The 1,550 nm window ensures the small-

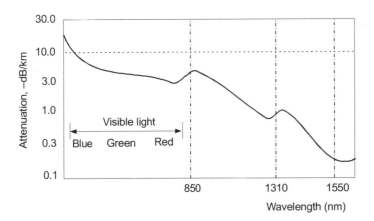

Figure 8.9 Transparency windows of optical fiber

est losses and, consequently, the longest transmission for the fixed power of transmitter and receiver sensitivity.

Absolute and relative power levels are used as characteristics of signal power. The **absolute power level** is measured in watts. *The **relative power level**, similar to attenuation, is measured in decibels.* At the same time, 1 mW is taken as the reference value in relation to which the signal power is measured. Thus, the relative power level *p* is calculated according to the following formula:

$$p = 10 \lg P/1mW \; [dBm] \qquad (8.2)$$

Here, *p* is the absolute signal power in milliwatts, and dBm is a measurement unit for relative power level (decibel per milliwatt).

Relative power values are convenient when calculating the power budget of transmission links.

EXAMPLE *Suppose that we need to determine the minimum relative power x (dBm) of the transmitter, it is enough to ensure that the relative power of the output signal is not lower than the threshold value y (dBm). Line attenuation is known and is equal to A. Assume X and Y are absolute values specified in mW of the signal power at the line input and output, respectively.*

By definition:

$$A = 10 \lg X/Y$$

Using the logarithm properties:

$$A = 10 \lg X - 10 \lg Y = 10 \lg X/1mW - 10 \lg Y/1 \; mW$$

Note that the last two terms of this equation are the relative powers of the signal at line input and output. This creates the following simple relationship:

$$A = x - y$$

From here, it follows that the minimum power of a transmitter can be defined as the sum of attenuation and the power of the output signal:

$$x = A + y$$

The calculation is easy because it uses the relative powers of the input and output signals as initial data.

The value y *is known as the* **receiver sensitivity threshold**. *It is the minimum signal power at the receiver input at which the receiver is capable of correctly recognizing discrete information contained in the signal. For accurate operation of the communications link, it is necessary to ensure that the minimum power of the transmitter signal, attenuated by the communications link fading, exceeds the sensitivity threshold of the receiver:* $x - A > y$. *The check of this condition is the main idea behind the calculation of power budget of transmission link.*

Another important parameter of the copper communications link is its **impedance**. This parameter is the full (complex) resistance to the propagation of electromagnetic waves of specific frequencies in the uniform circuit. Impedance is measured in ohms and depends on such line parameters as active resistance, linear inductance, and linear capacitance, as well as on signal frequency. Output resistance of the transmitter must be coordinated with the line impedance. Otherwise, signal attenuation will be excessive.

8.3.3 Noise Immunity and Transmission Reliability

Noise immunity of the line, *as is clear from its name, determines the capability of the line to withstand the influence of noise created in the ambient environment or in the internal conductors of the cable itself.* Noise immunity of the line depends on the type of the physical medium used and on the shielding and noise-suppressing properties of the line. Radio channels are the least resistant to noise. Copper cable lines are more immune to noise, and fiber-optic cables have the best noise immunity, being resistant to external electromagnetic radiation. Usually, to reduce the noise appearing as a result of external electromagnetic fields, it is necessary to use shielded or twisted conductors.

Electric and magnetic coupling also are parameters of the copper cable that characterize the noise influence. **Electric coupling** is determined by the ratio of the current induced in the affected circuit to the voltage in the affecting circuit. **Magnetic coupling** is the ratio of the electromotive force induced in the affected circuit to the current in the affecting circuit. The results of electric and magnetic coupling are **cross-talk signals** in the affected circuit. There are several parameters characterizing the cable stability against cross talk.

Near end cross talk (NEXT) determines cable stability in case cross talk is induced as a result of the influence of the signal generated by the transmitter connected to one of the neighboring pairs at the cable side on which the receiver connected to the affected pair operates (Figure 8.10). The NEXT parameter expressed in decibels is equal to $10 \lg P_{out}/P_{ind}$, where P_{out} is the power of the output signal, and P_{ind} is the power of the induced signal.

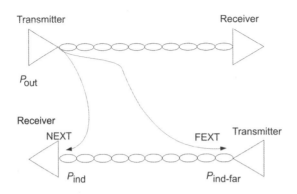

P_{out} — Power of the signal at the transmitter output
P_{ind} — Induced signal power at the near end of the cable
$P_{ind\text{-}far}$ — Induced signal at the far end of the cable

Figure 8.10 Transient attenuation

The smaller (taking into account the sign) the NEXT value, the better the cable. For example, for the category 5 twisted pair, the NEXT value must be less than −27 dB at 100 MHz.

Far end cross talk (FEXT) allows the evaluation of cable stability against cross talk when the transmitter and the receiver are connected to different sides of the cable (and to different pairs). This parameter of the line is usually better (smaller) than NEXT, since the signal arrives to the far end of the cable, being attenuated by the fading of each pair.

As a rule, NEXT and FEXT parameters are used with a cable comprising several twisted pairs because mutual cross talk might reach rather impressive values. For a single-wire coaxial cable (i.e., one comprising a single shielded strand), this parameter makes no sense. For a double-strand coaxial cable, this parameter is not used because of the high protection of each strand. Optical fibers also do not create any noticeable noise with each other.

Because some new network technologies implement simultaneous data transmission using several twisted pairs, cross-talk parameters have recently been introduced with the **PowerSUM** (PS) prefix, such as **PS-NEXT** and **PS-FEXT**. These parameters reflect the cable's stability against the total power of cross talk affecting a single cable pair and originating from all the remaining pairs that make up the cable (Figure 8.11).

Cable protection representing the **attenuation to cross-talk ratio (ACR)** is another important cable characteristic. Protection is defined as the difference between the level of the effective signal and that of the noise. The higher the ACR value, the higher the potential data rate at which this cable is capable of transmitting data according to the Shannon formula. Figure 8.12 shows a typical characteristic reflecting the dependence of the unshielded twisted pair cable ACR on the signal frequency.

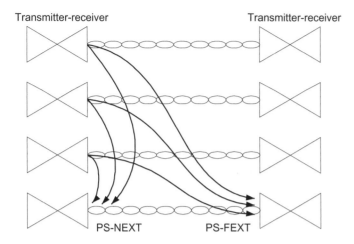

Figure 8.11 Total transient attenuation

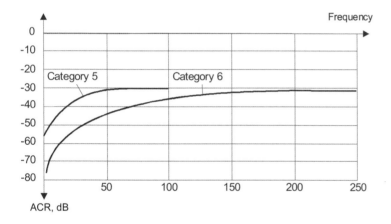

Figure 8.12 ACR of an unshielded twisted pair

Data transmission reliability characterizes the probability of distortion of any bit of transmitted data. Sometimes this parameter is called the **bit error rate (BER)**. As a rule, the BER value for communications links without additional error correction equipment (such as self-correcting codes or protocols supporting retransmission of distorted frames) is $10^{-4} — 10^{-6}$. In fiber-optic lines, this would be 10^{-9}. The value of the data transmission reliability of, say, 10^{-4} is evidence that on average, only 1 of 10,000 transmitted bits is distorted.

8.3.4 Bandwidth and Capacity

Bandwidth is a continuous frequency range for which line attention does not exceed some predefined limit. This means that bandwidth determines the frequency range of a sinusoidal signal within which this signal is transmitted through the line without significant distortions.

Often, frequency limits are taken as the frequencies at which the power of output signal decreases twice when compared to the input signal, which corresponds to an attenuation of −3 dB. As will be explained later, bandwidth has the greatest influence on the maximum possible rate of data transmission using communications links.

Bandwidth depends on the line type and its length. Figure 8.13 shows the bandwidths of the most popular types of communications links, as well as, the frequency ranges most widely used in technologies.

Link capacity characterizes the maximum possible information rate that can be achieved at this line. This characteristic depends on the parameters of the *physical medium*. It also

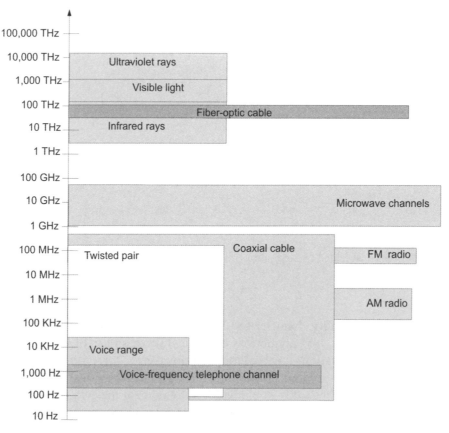

Figure 8.13 Bandwidth of the most widely used types of communications links and the most popular frequency ranges

is determined by the *data transmission method.* Consequently, it is impossible to speak about line capacity before defining a physical-layer protocol for it.

For instance, since the physical-layer protocol specifying the data bit rate for digital links is always defined, the digital links throughput is also always known beforehand — 64 Kbps, 2 Mbps, and so on.

When the existing protocol that can be used on a specific link must be determined, other link characteristics — such as bandwidth, cross-talk parameters, and noise immunity — become important.

Capacity, similar to information rate, is measured in bits per second as well as in derived units such as kilobits per second (Kbps).

NOTE   *The capacity and information rate (throughput) of links and communications equipment are traditionally measured in* bits per second *rather than in* bytes per second. *This is because the data in networks are transmitted sequentially, bit by bit, rather than in parallel (in bytes) as they are inside internal devices within computers. In network technologies, measurement units such as kilobit, megabit, and gigabit correspond to powers of 10 (which means that 1 Kb is 1,000 bits, and 1 Mb is 1,000,000 bits) rather than to powers of 2 like in programming, where 1 KB = 2^{10} = 1,024, and 1 MB = 2^{20} = 1,048,576.*

Link capacity depends not only on characteristics such as attenuation and bandwidth but also on the spectrum of the signals being transmitted. If significant harmonics of the

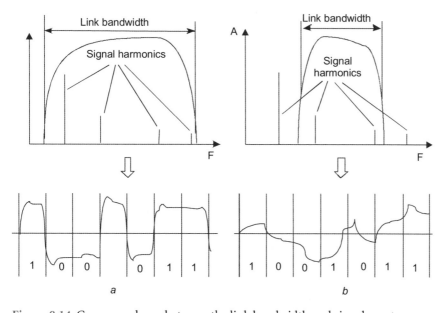

Figure 8.14 Correspondence between the link bandwidth and signal spectrum

signal (i.e., harmonics the amplitudes that make the main contributions to the resulting signal) fall within the link bandwidth, this link will transmit such high-quality signals, and receivers will be able to correctly recognize the information sent by the transmitter through the link (Figure 8.14, *a*). If significant harmonics fall outside the limits of the link bandwidth, the signal will be significantly distorted, and the receiver will make errors during information recognition (Figure 8.14, *b*).

8.3.5 Bits and Bauds

Choosing the method to represent discrete information as signals supplied to the communications link is known as *physical* or *line encoding*. The signal spectrum and, consequently, the link throughput depend on the chosen encoding method.

So, for different encoding methods, the capacity of the same link might be different. For example, the category 3 twisted pair can transmit data with a bandwidth of 10 Mbps when the 10Base-T physical-level encoding method is used. If the encoding method of the 100Base-T4 standard is used, the link capacity will be 33 Mbps.

ATTENTION *According to the main postulate of the information theory, any distinct and unpredictable change of the received signal carries certain information. Hence, the reception of the sinusoid with constant amplitude, phase and frequency, doesn't carry any information, since although the signal changes take place, they are predictable. Similarly, clock pulses on the clock line of the control bus, which is part of the computer's system bus, do not carry information, since their changes are predictable. The pulses at the data bus cannot be predicted beforehand. This is the feature that makes them informative, since these pulses carry information between computer units or devices.*

Most encoding methods change a specific parameter of the periodic signal — sinusoid frequency, amplitude or phase, or the potential sign of the pulse sequence. A changed periodic signal parameter is known as a **carrier signal** or **carrier frequency**, provided that the sinusoid is used as such a signal. The process of changing parameters of the carrier signal according to the information that needs to be transmitted is called **modulation**.

If the signal is changed in such a way that it is possible to distinguish only two states, then each change of such signal will correspond to 1 bit — the smallest unit of information. If the signal has more than two distinguishable states, then any of its changes will carry *several bits of information*.

Transmission of discrete information in telecommunications networks is clocked, which means that the signal changes after the fixed time interval called **clock**. This means that the information receiver considers that in the beginning of every clock new information is supplied to its input. With all this being so, the receiver gets new information from the transmitter, whether or not the signal repeats the state of the previous clock or has the state different from the previous one. For example, if the clock has the duration of 0.3 sec, and the signal has two states, 1 being encoded by potential of 5 V, the presence of the 5 V signal at the receiver input during 3 seconds is equivalent to the delivery of information represented by the following binary value: 1111111111.

The number of changes of the information parameter of the carrier signal per second is measured in *bauds*. One baud is equal to one change of the information parameter per second. The time between two changes of information signal is known as the transmitter clock.

IMPORTANT *The information rate generally is not equal to the baud rate. It could be higher than, lower than, or equal to the baud rate. This relationship depends on the chosen encoding method.*

If the signal has more than two distinguishable states, then the information rate in bits per second will be *higher* than the baud rate. Assume that we have chosen the phase and amplitude of the sinusoid as information parameters, that we have four discernible states of the phase — 0, 90, 180, and 270 degrees — and two discernible values of the signal amplitude. This means that the information signal can have eight discernible states. Consequently, each change of this signal carries 3 bits of information. In this case, a modem operating at a rate of 2,400 bauds (meaning that it is capable of changing the information signal 2,400 times per second), transmits information at a rate of 7,200 bps, since each change of the signal transmits 3 bits of information.

If the signal has only two states (which means that it carries 1 bit of information), then the information rate usually corresponds to the baud rate. However, the situation might be the opposite: The information rate can be lower than the baud rate. This happens when, to ensure reliable recognition of user information by the receiver, each bit in the sequence is encoded by several changes of the information parameter of the carrier signal. For example, when representing the value of one, by the pulse of positive polarity, and the zero value, by the pulse of negative polarity, the physical signal changes its value twice when transmitting each bit. When using such an encoding method, the bit rate is two times lower than the baud rate.

The higher the frequency of the carrier signal, the higher the modulation frequency may be. Consequently, a higher throughput of the transmission link might be achieved.

However, the spectrum width of the carrier signal increases with the increase of its frequency. The line transmits this spectrum with distortions defined by its bandwidth. The greater the discordance between the link bandwidth and the width of the spectrum of transmitted information signals, the more they are distorted and the higher the probability of errors on the receiving side. Consequently, the possible information rate proves to be lower.

8.3.6 Dependence between Bandwidth and Capacity

The relationship between the link bandwidth and its capacity, independent of the chosen method of physical encoding, was established by *Claude Shannon*:

$$C = F \log_2 \left(1 + P_c/P_{noise}\right) \tag{8.3}$$

Here, C is the link capacity in bits per second, F is the width of the link bandwidth in hertz, P_c is power of the signal, and P_{noise} is the power of the noise.

From this formula, it follows that there is no theoretical limit to the throughput for the line with fixed bandwidth. In practice, however, this limit exists. It is possible to increase the link capacity by increasing the transmitter power or by reducing the line noise. Both of these components are hard to change. Increasing transmitter power significantly increases its size and cost. Reduction in the noise level requires special cables with high-quality shielding, which is rather expensive, as well as reduction of the noise in transmitter and transit equipment, which is hard to achieve. Furthermore, the influence of the powers of the effective signal and noise on the capacity is limited by the logarithmic dependence, which grows slower than proportional dependence. This results in a typical initial value of the signal-to-noise ratio of 100. Duplication of the transmitter power increases the line capacity only 15%.

Another relation, derived by *Harry Nyquist* and close to the Shannon formula, determines the maximum throughput of the communications link (e.g., capacity). This, however, does not take into account the line noise:

$$C = 2F \log_2 M \tag{8.4}$$

Here, M is the number of distinguishable states of the information parameter.

If the signal has two distinguishable states, then the throughput is equal to the doubled value of the link bandwidth (Figure 8.15, *a*). If the transmitter uses more than two stable

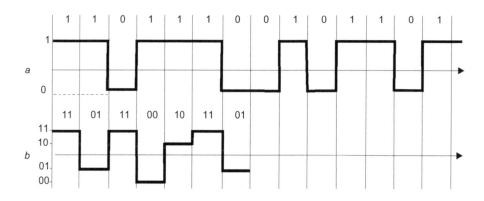

Figure 8.15 Increasing the information rate with additional signal states

states of the signal, available for data encoding, then the line throughput increases. This is because the transmitter sends several bits of data per clock — e.g., 2 bits, provided that four discernible signal states are available (Figure 8.15, *b*).

Although the Nyquist formula does not explicitly take noise into account, its influence is implicitly reflected by the number of choices of the information signal states. To increase the link capacity, it makes sense to increase the number of signal states. In practice, however, the line noise presents an obstacle to this approach. For example, the line capacity (Figure 8.15, *b*) can be doubled once more, provided that 16 signal levels are used for data encoding instead of 4. However, if the noise amplitude occasionally exceeds the difference between adjacent layers, the receivers would not be able to reliably recognize the transmitted data. Therefore, the number of possible signal states is limited by the ratio between the power of the effective signal and the power of the noise, and Nyquist formula determines the maximum transmission rate when the number of states has already been chosen, taking into account the possibility of stable signal recognition by the receiver.

8.4 CABLE TYPES

KEY WORDS: unshielded and shielded twisted pair, coaxial cable, fiber-optical cable, categories of cables, types of cables, "thick" coaxial cable, "thin" coaxial cable, TV cable, multimode fiber (MMF), MMF with smooth change of the refraction factor, single-mode fiber (SMF), ray mode, structured cabling system (SCS)

Nowadays, three classes of wired communication lines are used both for indoor and outdoor wiring:

- *Twisted pair*
- *Coaxial cables*
- *Fiber-optical cables*

8.4.1 Unshielded and Shielded Twisted Pair

A couple of wires twisted together are known as a **twisted pair**. This kind of transmission medium is rather popular and forms the foundation for most cables, both internal and external. A cable may contain several twisted pairs. External cables sometimes comprise tens of such pairs.

Wire twisting reduces the influence of external noise and of cross talk on the effective signals transmitted through the cable.

The main features of cable construction are briefly outlined in Figure 8.16.

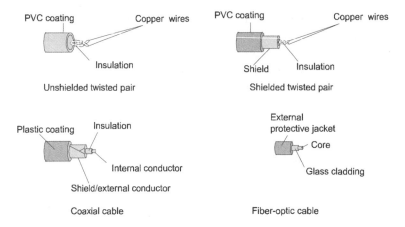

Figure 8.16 Cable design

Cables based on a twisted pair are *symmetric* cables, which are composed of two wires identical in construction. Symmetric cables might be shielded, based on STP, or unshielded, based on UTP.

It is necessary to distinguish the *electric insulation* of conducting strands, which is present in any cable, from the *electromagnetic shielding*. Electric insulation consists of insulating layers of paper or polymers, such as polyvinylchloride (PVC) or polystyrene. Besides electric insulation, the conductors are enclosed within electromagnetic shielding, which most frequently consists of copper sleeving.

Copper cable for indoor wiring on the basis of unshielded twisted pair falls into several **categories** according to international standards (category 1– category 7).

- Cables classified as **category 1** are used when requirements for transmission rates are minimal. Usually, this is the cable for digital and analog voice transmission, which is also suitable for low-speed (up to 20 Kbps) data transmission. Until 1983, this was the main type of cable used for telephone cabling.

- **Category 2** cables were first used by IBM when building their proprietary cabling system. The main requirement for the cables in this category lies in the capability of transmitting signals with a spectrum up to 1 MHz.

- **Category 3** cables were standardized in 1991, with the development of the *standard of telecommunications cabling systems for commercial buildings* (EIA-568), on the basis of which the current EIA-568A standard was developed. The EIA-568 standard has defined the electric characteristics of category 3 cables within a frequency range up to 16 MHz. Thus, category 3 cables are capable of supporting high-speed network applications.

- **Category 4** cables are an improved version of category 3 cables. Category 4 cables must withstand tests at signal transmission frequencies equal to 20 MHz and ensure improved noise immunity and low signal losses. They are rarely used in practice.

■ **Category 5** cables were specifically designed to support high-speed protocols. Therefore, their characteristics are determined up to 100 MHz. Most high-performance standards are oriented toward the use of category 5 twisted pair. This cable is used with high-speed protocols with data transmission rates of 100 Mbps, such as FDDI, Fast Ethernet, and faster protocols — ATM at a rate of 155 Mbps and Gigabit Ethernet at a rate of 1,000 Mbps. Category 5 cable has replaced category 3 cable, and currently this type of cable (with fiber-optic cable) is used for creating new cabling systems in large buildings.

■ The industry started to manufacture cables of **categories 6** and **7** fairly recently. For category 6 cable, characteristics are defined up to the frequency of 250 MHz. For category 7 cables, the frequency is up to 600 MHz. Category 7 cables must be shielded, applicable both to each pair and to the entire cable. A category 6 cable can be shielded or unshielded. These cables are mainly intended to support high-speed protocols at longer sections of cable than the ones supported by a category 5 UTP cable.

Independently on their category, all UTP cables are manufactured as 4-pair cables. Each pair has specific color and lay of strand. Usually, two pairs are used for data transmission, and two – for voice transmission.

Shielded twisted pair protects the transmitted signal from external noise rather well. Besides this, it is characterized by a lower emission of electromagnetic waves, thus protecting network users from harmful electromagnetic radiation. However, the presence of grounded shielding raises the price of the cable and makes the procedures of its installation more complicated, since it requires high-quality grounding.

The proprietary IBM standard is the main standard determining the parameter of shielded twisted pair intended for use inside buildings. According to this standard, cables are classified by types and not by categories: type 1, type 2, ..., type 9.

A *type 1* cable according to the IBM standard comprises two pairs of twisted wires shielded by conductive cable armoring, which is grounded. Electric parameters of the type 1 cable approximately correspond to that of the category 5 UTP cables. However, impedance of a type 1 cable, which is 150 ohms, is significantly higher than that of a category 5 UTP cable (100 ohms). Therefore, an improvement of the cable armoring by simply replacing unshielded UTP with STP type 1 is impossible. Transmitters intended for operation with the cable having impedance of 100 ohms will not operate satisfactorily with a cable that has impedance of 150 ohms.

8.4.2 Coaxial Cable

Coaxial cable consists of *asymmetric* pairs of conductors. Each pair is an internal copper strand and coaxial external strand, which may be a hollow copper tube or armoring separated from internal strands by dielectric insulation. The external strand plays a dual role.

First, it is used for transmitting information signals; second, it is a shield protecting the internal strand from external electromagnetic fields. There are several types of coaxial cable, differing in characteristics and in application areas, for LANs, WANs, telecommunications networks, cable TV, etc.

Contemporary standards do not consider coaxial cable a good choice for structured cabling systems of buildings. Provided here are the main types and characteristics of these cables according to U.S. classification:

■ **"Thick" coaxial cables** were developed for Ethernet 10Base-5 networks. They have impedance equal to 50 ohms and an external diameter of 0.5 inch (about 12 mm). These cables have a thick internal conductor (2.17 mm in diameter), which ensures good electric and mechanical characteristics (attenuation at 10 MHz – no worse than 18 dB/km). However, these cables are not flexible and therefore are hard to install.

■ **"Thin" coaxial cables** for Ethernet 10Base-2 networks. Thin coaxial cable has impedance equal to 50 ohms, but its mechanical and electric characteristics are significantly worse when compared to the thick coaxial cable. Thin internal conductors have diameters of 0.89 mm and are not strong, but they are flexible, convenient for cable installation. Attenuation in this type of cable is higher than in the thick coaxial cable, which results in the necessity of decreasing the cable length to get the same attenuation within a segment.

■ **The TV cable** with impedance equal to 75 ohms. It is widely used in cable TV. There are standards for LANs capable of using such cable for data transmission.

8.4.3 Optical Cable

Optical fiber cable consists of thin (5–60 μm) flexible glass fibers (optical waveguides) along which light signals propagate. This type of cable is the best quality, since it ensures data transmission at a very high rate (10 Gbps or higher). Besides this, it ensures better data protection against external noise than other transmission media. Because of specific features of light propagation, such signals can be easily shielded.

Each light waveguide consists of the central waveguide (core) — optical fiber — and a glass covering with a smaller refraction factor than the core. Light waves propagate via the core without leaving it, since they are reflected from the covering layer. Depending on the distribution of the refraction factor and on the diameter of the core, optical fiber cables are classified into the following categories:

■ Multimode fiber (MMF) with stepwise change of the refraction factor (Figure 8.17, *a*)
■ MMF with smooth change of the refraction factor (Figure 8.17, *b*)
■ Single-mode fiber (SMF) (Figure 8.17, c)

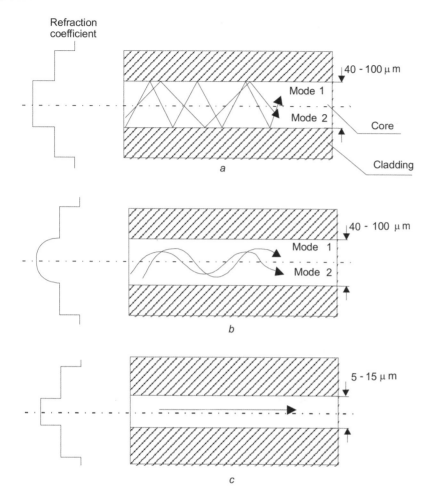

Figure 8.17 Types of optical fiber cables

The concept of mode describes the mode of propagation of the light rays within the internal core of the cable. In **SMF**, the central core has a very small diameter comparable to the light wave length, from 5 to 10 μm. Under these conditions, practically all light waves propagate along the optical axis of the waveguide without being reflected from the external coating. Manufacturing superthin, high-quality fibers for *SMF* cable is a complicated technological process. Consequently, *SMF* cable is expensive. Furthermore, it is difficult to direct a beam of light into the fiber with such a small diameter, without losing a significant part of its energy.

In **MMF** cables, wider internal cores are used, which are significantly easier to manufacture. In *MMF* cables, the core conducts several light rays simultaneously. These rays are reflected from the external coating at different angles. The reflection angle of the light ray is called **the ray mode**. In multimode cables with the smooth change of the refraction factor, the nature of each propagation mode is rather complex. Interference of rays of different modes degrades the quality of the signal being transmitted, which results in distortions of the transmitted pulses. *MMF* cables are easier to manufacture; therefore, they are significantly cheaper than single-mode cables. At the same time, their characteristics are significantly worse than those of the single-mode cables.

As a result, multimode cables are mainly used for transmitting data for small distances (300–2,000 m) at rates not exceeding 1 Gbps, and single-mode cables are intended for data transmission at the highest possible rates — tens of gigabits per second (when using DWDM technology this can even be several terabits per second), for distances ranging from several kilometers (LANs and MANs) to tens and even hundreds of kilometers (long-distance communications).

As light sources, fiber-optic cables use:

■ Light emitting diodes (LED)
■ Laser diodes

For single-mode cables, only laser diodes are used; having such a small diameter of the optical fiber, the light beam created by LED cannot be directed into the waveguide without significant losses because of its wide directional radiation pattern. Laser diode, in contrast to LED, has a narrow directional diagram. For this reason, less expensive LEDs are used only for MMF cables.

The cost of fiber-optic cables does not significantly exceed that of cables based on twisted pair. However, installation work when dealing with fiber-optic cables is difficult and expensive because of the labor intensiveness in all installation operations and high cost of installation facilities.

8.4.4 Structured Cabling System of Buildings

The **structured cabling system (SCS)** of a building is a set of switching elements (cables, connectors, sockets, switching boards, and closets) as well as methods of their shared usage, which enables the creation of regular, easily extensible communications structures in computer networks. The building is a regular structure in itself. It comprises floors, and each floor contains a specific number of rooms connected by passages. Building structure defines the structure of the cabling system.

The structured cabling system of a building is a kind of set of building blocks, which the network designer uses to build the required configuration from standard cables connected with standard connectors and switched with standard switchboards. When necessary, the configuration of connections can be easily changed. For instance, it is possible to add a computer, segment, and switch, to remove unnecessary equipment, and to change the connections between computers and hubs.

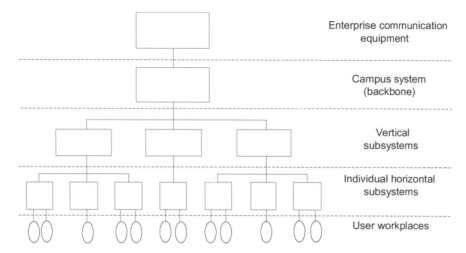

Figure 8.18 Hierarchy of the structured cabling system subsystems

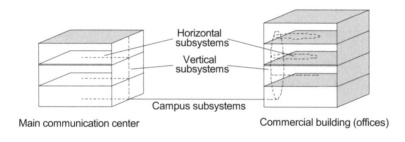

Figure 8.19 Structure of cabling subsystems

Nowadays, cabling systems for commercial buildings are well defined. A hierarchical approach to the process of creating such cabling system allows it to be called structured. On the basis of the SCS of commercial buildings, several LANs belonging to different organizations or several departments of a single organization may operate. The SCS is planned and built hierarchically on the basis of the main backbone and multiple taps (Figure 8.18).

The typical hierarchical structure of SCS (Figure 8.19) includes:

- **Horizontal subsystems** correspond to the building floors: they connect floor-switching closets with the sockets of end-users.
- **Vertical subsystems** connect switching closets of each floor to the central equipment room of the entire building.
- **Campus subsystem** connects several buildings to the central equipment room of the entire campus. This part of the cabling system is usually called the backbone.

In the use of structured cabling system, cables laid out in a random way provide lots of advantages to the enterprise. *If the* SCS structure has been carefully planned, it can provide a *universal medium* for transmitting computer data in LANs, organizing local telephone network, transmitting video information and even sending signals from the sensors of fire safety and security systems. This allows for the automation of most processes of controlling, monitoring, and managing various enterprise services, including household and life support systems.

Furthermore, the use of an SCS *makes the process of adding new users or changing their workspaces more efficient and economical.* It is well known that the cost of a cabling system is mainly defined by the cost of its installation rather than by the cost of the cable. Therefore, it is much more efficient to accomplish cable installation beforehand, probably with redundancies to be on the safe side. This is preferred to laying out the cable several times, by simply extending its length.

SUMMARY

▶ Depending on the type of intermediate equipment, all communications links are divided into analog and digital. In analog links (or analog channels) intermediate equipment is intended for amplification of analog signals. Analog links use frequency division multiplexing (FDM) or wavelength division multiplexing (WDM).

▶ In digital links, the signals being transmitted have a finite number of states. Digital channels use special intermediate equipment — regenerators, which improve the shape of pulses and ensure their resynchronization (i.e., they restore interpulse intervals). Intermediate multiplexing and switching equipment of transmission networks operates according to the time division multiplexing (TDM) principle, in which each slow link is allocated a specific time slot of the high-speed channel.

▶ The bandwidth describes the frequency ranges transmitted by the communications link with acceptable attenuation.

▶ Link capacity depends on internal parameters, particularly on its bandwidth, on external parameters such as noise level and the degree of noise suppression, and on the adopted method of discrete data encoding.

▶ The Shannon formula defines the capacity of the communications link at fixed values of the link bandwidth and the ratio of signal power to noise power.

▶ The Nyquist formula expresses the capacity of the link through its bandwidth and through the number of information signal states.

▶ Cables based on the twisted pair are divided into unshielded (UTP) and shielded (STP). UTP cables are easier to manufacture and install, but STP cables ensure a higher level of protection.

▶ Fiber-optic cables have excellent electromagnetic and mechanical characteristics. However, their main drawback lies in their difficult and expensive installation.

▶ A structured cabling system is a set of communications elements — cables, connectors, slots, switchboards, and switching closets — that satisfy standards and allow the creation of regular, easily extensible communications structures.

REVIEW QUESTIONS

1. What is the difference between a transmission link and a circuit?
2. Can circuits include links? Can links include circuits?
3. Can a digital channel transmit analog data?
4. What are the functions of DTE and DCE? To which type of devices do network adapters belong?
5. To what type of communications link characteristics do the following belong: noise level, bandwidth, and linear capacitance?
6. What measures can be taken to increase the information rate of the link?
7. Why is it not always possible to increase the channel capacity by increasing the number of information signal states?
8. What mechanism helps to suppress noise in UTP cables?
9. What cable ensures a higher quality of signal transmission: the one with a larger value for the NEXT parameter or the one with a smaller NEXT value?
10. What is the spectrum width of an ideal pulse?
11. List the types of fiber-optic cable.
12. What would happen if a UTP cable was replaced with a STP cable?
13. List the main advantages of the structured cabling system.
14. What types of cables are used for the horizontal subsystem of the SCS?
15. What are the problems related to using fiber-optic cables in horizontal subsystems?

PROBLEMS

1. The following values are given:
   - Minimum transmitter power P_{out} (dBm)
   - Cable attenuation A (dB/km)
   - Receiver sensitivity threshold P_{in} (dBm)

Find the maximum possible length of the communications link at which signals will be transmitted adequately.

2. What will be the theoretical limit of transmission rate (bps) using the channel with a bandwidth equal to 20 kHz if the power of transmitter is 0.01 mW and the noise level in the channel is 0.0001 mW?

3. Determine the capacity of the duplex communications link for each direction provided that its bandwidth equals 600 kHz and the encoding method uses 10 states of the information signal.

4. Calculate the signal propagation delay and data transmission delay for transmitting a 128 bytes packet (the signal propagation speed is considered to be light propagation speed in a vacuum — i.e., 300,000 km/sec):

   • Using a 100 m twisted pair cable at a transmission speed equal to 100 Mbps

   • Using a 2 km coaxial cable at a transmission rate equal to 10 Mbps

   • Using a 72,000 km satellite channel at a transmission rate equal to 128 Kbps

5. Calculate the rate of the channel, given that the transmitter clock frequency is 125 MHz and the signal has five states.

6. Transmitters and receivers of the network adapter are connected to adjacent pairs of the UTP cable. What is the power of induced noise at the receiver input, provided that the transmitter has the power of 30 dBm and the NEXT parameter of the cable is 20 dB?

7. Provided that a modem transmits data in duplex mode at a rate of 33.6 Kbps, calculate how many states the signal has if the channel bandwidth is 3.43 kHz.

9

DATA ENCODING AND MULTIPLEXING

9.1 INTRODUCTION

The guided media considered in the previous chapter provide only potential possibilities for transmitting discrete information. To enable the transmitter and receiver connected by a specific medium to exchange information, it is necessary to agree upon the signals that will correspond to binary ones and binary zeros when transmitting discrete information. Two types of signals are used for representing discrete information in the transmission medium: rectangular pulses and sinusoidal waves. In the first case, the method of representing discrete information is known as encoding, and in the second case this method is called modulation.

There are many encoding methods, which differ according to the width of the signal spectrum at the same information rate. For transmitting information with minimum errors, the link bandwidth must be wider than the signal spectrum. If not, the signals chosen to represent ones and zeros will be significantly distorted, and the receiver will be unable to correctly recognize the transmitted information. Therefore, the signal spectrum is one of the main criteria for the evaluation of the efficiency of the chosen encoding method. Besides this, an encoding method must help the receiver synchronize with the transmitter and must ensure an acceptable signal-to-noise ratio. These requirements are contradictory. Therefore, each encoding method used is a compromise between the main requirements.

Bit errors in communications links cannot be eliminated completely, even if the chosen code provides a good level of synchronization and high values of the signal-to-noise ratio. Therefore, when transmitting discrete information, special codes are used. These codes are capable of detecting bit errors, and some of them are even capable of correcting errors.

This chapter will end with a description of multiplexing methods, which provide the possibility of creating several channels within a single transmission link.

9.2 MODULATION

KEY WORDS: modulation, amplitude modulation, frequency modulation, phase modulation, analog signals, discrete signals, amplitude shift keying (ASK), frequency shift keying (FSK), phase shift keying (PSK), carrier frequency, modulator, demodulator, modem, potential code, binary FSK (BFSK), four-level FSK, multilevel FSK (MFSK), binary PSK (BPSK), quadrature PSK (QPSK), quadrature amplitude modulation (QAM), trellis codes, Fourier formula, fundamental frequency

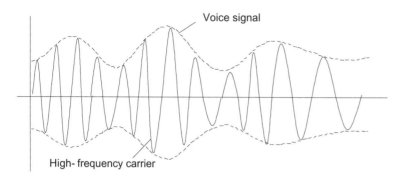

Figure 9.1 Modulation of the voice signal

9.2.1 Modulation When Transmitting Analog Signals

Historically, modulation was first used for the transmission of **analog** rather than **discrete** information.

The need in modulating analog information arises when it is necessary to transmit low-frequency analog signal through the channel that falls into the high-frequency range of the spectrum. Examples of such a situation include voice transmission by radio or TV. Human voice has the spectrum with the width of approximately 10 KHz, and radio ranges use considerably higher frequencies — from 30 KHz to 300 MHz. TV uses even higher frequencies. Obviously, direct voice transmission through such media is impossible.

Therefore, to solve this problem, it was decided to change (modulate) the amplitude of the high-frequency signal according to the changes of the low-frequency signal (Figure 9.1). In this case, the spectrum of the resulting signal fits within the required high-frequency range. This type of modulation is known as **amplitude modulation** (AM), since the amplitude of the high-frequency signal is the parameter carrying information.

Besides the carrier amplitude, frequency also can be used as an information parameter. In such cases we are dealing with **frequency modulation** (FM)[1].

The high-frequency component of the signal is also called the *carrier frequency*, since this signal plays the role of carrier in relation to the low-frequency information signal.

9.2.2 Modulation When Transmitting Discrete Signals

When transmitting discrete information using modulation, ones and zeros are encoded by the change of amplitude, frequency, or phase of the carrier sinusoidal signal. In cases

---

[1] Note that when analog information is modulated, phase is not used as information parameter.

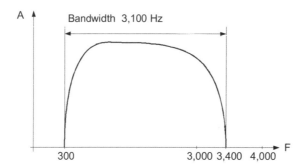

Figure 9.2 Amplitude–frequency characteristic of the tone frequency channel

where the modulated signals transmit discrete information, the following terminology is used:

- Amplitude shift keying (ASK)
- Frequency shift keying (FSK)
- Phase shift keying (PSK)

Perhaps, the best-known example of the use of modulation when transmitting discrete information is transmission of computer data through telephone lines. Typical amplitude-frequency characteristic of a standard subscriber line, also called the tone channel is presented in Figure 9.2. This circuit passes through transit switches of a telephone network and connects telephone sets of subscribers. Tone channel passes the frequencies ranging from 300 to 3,400 Hz, thus, its bandwidth is equal to 3,100 Hz. Such a narrow bandwidth is quite sufficient for high-quality voice transmission; however, it is not wide enough for transmitting computer data in the form of rectangular pulses. The solution to this problem was found using the Amplitude shift keying. The device that modulates the carrier sinusoid at the transmitting side and demodulates it at the receiving side is known as a **modem** (**mod**ulator–**dem**odulator).

The main methods of modulation used for transmitting discrete information are illustrated in Figure 9.3. The diagram (Figure 9.3, *a*) shows the sequence of bits of the source information, represented by high-level potentials for logical ones and zero-level potentials for logical zeros[2]. Such a method of encoding is known as *potential code* and is frequently used when transmitting data among various units within a computer.

When using ASK (Figure 9.3, *b*), different levels of the carrier amplitude are chosen for denoting logical ones and zeros. This method is rarely used because of its poor noise immunity. However, it is frequently used with PSK modulation.

---

[2] Generally, potential codes use two different values for logical ones and zeros — positive for one, and negative for zero.

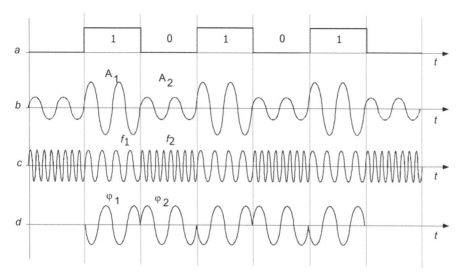

Figure 9.3 Different types of modulation

When using FSK (Figure 9.3, *c*), the values of 0 and 1 in the source data are transmitted by sinusoids having different frequencies — f_0 and f_1. This method of modulation does not require the implementation of sophisticated circuits in modems and, as a rule, is used in low-speed modems operating at rates of 300 or 1,200 bps. When using only two frequencies, 1 bit of information is transmitted per clock, therefore, this method is called *Binary FSK* (*BFSK*). It is also possible to use four frequencies for encoding 2 bits of information per clock. This method is known as *four-level FSK*. Another term, *Multilevel FSK* (*MFSK*) is also used.

When using PSK (Figure 9.3, *d*), signals of the same frequency but with different phases (for example, 0° and 180° or 0°, 90°, 180°, and 270°) correspond to the values 0 and 1. In the first case, such a modulation is called *Binary PSK* (*BPSK*); the second variant is known as *Quadrature PSK* (*QPSK*).

9.2.3 Combined Modulation Methods

To increase the data rate, combined modulation methods are used. The most common are **quadrature amplitude modulation** (QAM) *methods based on a combination of phase and amplitude modulation.*

Figure 9.4 shows the variant of 16-QAM modulation, in which eight different values of phase and four values of amplitude are used. However, only 16 of 32 signal combinations are used, since allowed values of amplitude differ for the neighboring phases. This improves noise immunity of the code but decreases the information rate twice. Another

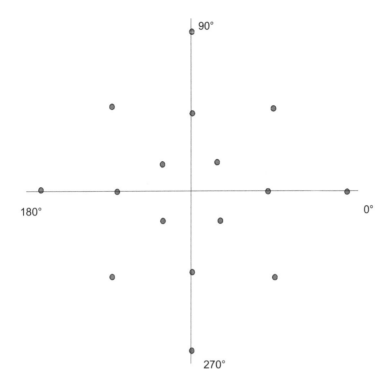

Figure 9.4 Quadrature amplitude modulation with 16 states of the signal

solution for improving the code reliability at the expense of introducing redundancy is *trellis codes. These codes add a fifth bit to each 4 bits of information. This additional bit allows you to determine with a high level of probability the correct set of 4 information bits, even when errors are present.*

The spectrum of the resulting modulated signal depends on the type and speed of modulation (i.e., on the desirable transmission rate of the source information).

First, consider the signal spectrum when using potential encoding. Assume that logical one is encoded by positive potential, and logical zero is encoded by the negative potential of the same value. For simplicity, assume that the information being transmitted consists of an infinite sequence of alternating ones and zeros, as shown in Figure 9.3, *a.*

The spectrum can be directly derived from the **Fourier formula**[3] for periodic function. If discrete information is transmitted at a bit rate equal to N bps, then the spectrum consists of the DC component of zero frequency and an infinite sequence of harmonics with frequencies equal to f_0, $3f_0$, $5f_0$, $7f_0$, and so on, where $f_0 = N/2$. The f_0 frequency of this spectrum is known as the **fundamental frequency**.

---

[3] See any textbook in the field of mathematics adopted for university education

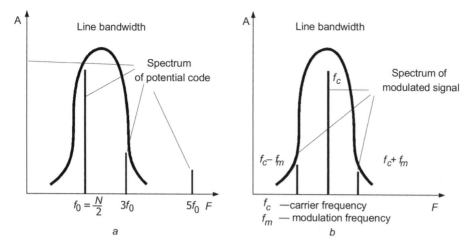

Figure 9.5 Signal spectrums when using potential encoding and amplitude modulation

Amplitudes of these harmonics decrease rather slowly — with factors of 1/3, 1/5, 1/7, and so on, of the amplitude of the f_0 harmonic (Figure 9.5, a). As a result, to ensure high-quality transmission, the spectrum of the potential code requires a wide bandwidth. Besides this, it is necessary to take into account that in reality the signal spectrum constantly changes depending on the data being transmitted through the line. For example, the transmission of a long sequence of zeros or ones shifts the spectrum toward low frequencies. In the extreme case, when the data being transmitted consists of ones only (or of zeros only), the spectrum consists of the harmonic of zero frequency. When transmitting alternating ones and zeros, there is no DC component. Therefore, the spectrum of the resulting signal of the potential code in the course of the transmission of arbitrary data takes the frequency band spanning the range from some value close to 0 Hz to a frequency approximately equal to $7f_0$. Harmonics with frequencies higher than $7f_0$ can be neglected, since their contribution into the resulting signal is rather small. For the channel of tone frequency, the upper limit for potential encoding is reached at a 971 bps transmission rate, and a lower limit is not acceptable for any rate, since the channel bandwidth starts at 300 Hz. As a result, potential codes are never used in tone channels.

When using AM, the signal spectrum comprises the sinusoid of the carrier frequency (f_c), two lateral harmonics $f_c + f_m$ and $f_c - f_m$, and the lateral harmonics $f_c + 3f_m$ and $f_c - 3f_m$. Here, f_m is the frequency, at which the information parameter of the sinusoid changes, which coincides with the data transmission rate when using two amplitude levels (Figure 9.5, b). The f_m frequency determines the link bandwidth for the chosen encoding method. At small modulation frequencies, the width of the signal spectrum also proves to be small. In fact, it is equal to $2f_m$, provided that $3f_m$ harmonics that have less power are neglected.

When using phase and frequency modulation, the signal spectrum becomes more complex, than when AM is used since in the latter case, there are more lateral harmonics. However, they are located symmetrically in relation to the main carrier frequency, and their amplitudes decrease rapidly.

9.3 DIGITIZING ANALOG SIGNALS

KEY WORDS: digitizing, pulse code modulation (PCM), analog-to-digital converter (ADC), digital-to-analog converter (DAC), Nyquist-Kotelnikov Signal Sampling Theory, digitizing voice, elementary digital channel

In this section, we concentrate on a solution to the inverse problem, namely, transmitting analog information in a discrete form.

In practice, this problem was solved in the 1960s, when telephone networks started transmitting voice as a sequence of ones and zeros. The main reason for this conversion is the impossibility of improving the quality of data transmitted in analog form if they were significantly distorted during transmission. The analog signal itself does not provide indications that distortions took place or instructions about correcting these distortions. This happens because the signal may have any waveform, including the one registered by the receiver. Improvement of the line quality (especially as it relates to regional carriers) requires a lot of efforts and financial investment. Therefore, analog equipment for voice recording and transmission was replaced by digital equipment. This technique uses **pulse modulation** of the source analog processes, continuous in time.

9.3.1 Pulse Code Modulation

Consider the principles of pulse modulation in the example of **pulse code modulation** *(PCM)*, which is widely used in digital telephony.

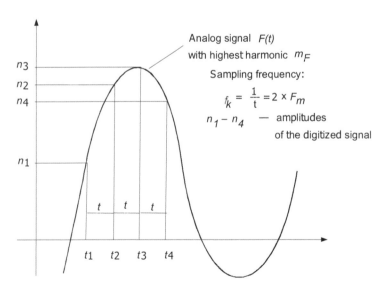

Analog signal $F(t)$
with highest harmonic m_F

Sampling frequency:

$$f_k = \frac{1}{t} = 2 \times F_m$$

$n_1 - n_4$ — amplitudes of the digitized signal

Figure 9.6 Discrete modulation of the continuous process

Methods of pulse modulation are based on the sampling of continuous processes, both by amplitude and by time (Figure 9.6):

■ The amplitude of the continuous source function is being measured with the predefined period. This allows the user to carry out time sampling.

■ Then, each measured value is represented as a binary number of a specific width, which in turn represents quantization of the function values — a continuous set of possible amplitude values is replaced by a discrete set of its values.

The device that carries out such a function is known as an **analog-to-digital converter** **(ADC)**. After that, the sampled values are transmitted using communications links in the form of a sequence of ones and zeros. At the same time, the same encoding methods are used, as in case of transmitting initially discrete information (e.g., methods based on B8ZS or 2B1Q codes), which will be considered later in this chapter.

At the receiving side of the line, the codes are transformed into the source bit sequence, and special equipment, known as a **digital-to-analog converter (DAC)**, accomplishes demodulation of the digitized amplitudes of a continuous signal, thus restoring the source continuous time function.

Pulse modulation is based on the **Nyquist-Kotelnikov Signal Sampling Theory**. According to this theory, the analog continuous function transmitted in the form of the sequence of its time-sampled values can be reconstructed without losses, provided that the sampling frequency was two or more times higher than the frequency of the highest harmonic of the spectrum of the source function.

If this condition has not been observed, the reconstructed function will be significantly different from the source one.

The advantage of digital methods of recording, reproducing, and transmitting information is the possibility of controlling the reliability of the data read from the medium or received using the communications line. For this purpose, it is possible to use the same methods as for computer data, such as calculating the checksum, retransmitting distorted frames, and using self-correcting codes.

9.3.2 Digitizing Voice

For high-quality voice transmission, the PCM method uses a sampling frequency of sound oscillation amplitude of 8,000 Hz. This is because in analog telephony, the range from 300 to 3,400 Hz was chosen for voice transmission. This range allows the transmission of all main harmonics of human speech with sufficient quality. According to the *Nyquist-Kotelnikov theorem,* for high-quality voice transmission, it is enough to choose the sampling frequency that exceeds the highest harmonic of the continuous signal by at least two (i.e., $2 \times 3,400 = 6,800$ Hz). The actual chosen sampling frequency (8,000 Hz) provides some quality reserve. As a rule, the PCM method uses 7 bits or 8 bits of code for representing each sample. These values correspond to the 127 grades or 256 grades of the sound signal, which proves to be sufficient for high-quality voice transmission.

When using the PCM method, each voice channel requires a bandwidth of 56 Kbps or 64 Kbps, depending on the number of bits used for representing each sample. If 7 bits are used for this purpose, then, having the sampling frequency of 8,000 Hz, the result will be:

$$8,000 \times 7 = 56,000 \text{ bps, or } 56 \text{ Kbps}$$

Accordingly, for 8 bits, the result will be:

$$8,000 \times 8 = 64,000 \text{ bps, or } 64 \text{ Kbps}$$

The 64 Kbps digital channel, also known as the **elementary digital channel**, is standard.

Transmission of a continuous signal in discrete form requires the network to strictly comply with the requirement that prescribes the interval between two adjacent samples to be 125 μsec. This interval corresponds to the sampling frequency of 8,000 Hz. This means that the network must synchronously transmit data between network nodes. If arriving samples are out of synch, the source signal will be restored incorrectly, which distorts voice, image, or other multimedia information transmitted using digital networks. Thus, synchronization distortion of 10 msec might result in an echo effect, and delays between samples of 200 msec or more will make the recognition of individual words impossible. At the same time, the loss of a single sample has practically no effect on the sound reproduction quality, provided that all other samples arrive synchronously. This is because of the smoothing devices in DACs, which are based on the inertial properties of any physical signal. In this case, the amplitude of sound oscillations cannot immediately change by a significant value.

The signal quality after DAC is influenced not only by the synchronization of samples arriving to its input but also by the quantization error of these samples. In the Nyquist-Kotelnikov theory, it is supposed that function amplitudes are measured precisely. However, the use of binary numbers of limited width distorts these amplitudes. Accordingly, the reconstructed continuous signal also becomes distorted. This phenomenon is known as quantization noise.

9.4 ENCODING METHODS

KEY WORDS: signal spectrum synchronization, encoding methods, self-synchronizing codes, detection and correction of distorted data, potential nonreturn to zero code (NRZ), bipolar alternate mark inversion (AMI), nonreturn to zero with ones inverted (NRZI), scrambler, descrambler, bipolar pulse code, Manchester code, 2B1Q potential code, redundant codes, 4B/5B code, B8ZS, HDB3, data compression, adaptive compression, decimal packing, relative encoding, symbol suppression, codes of variable length, Huffmann algorithm

9.4.1 Choosing Encoding Methods

When choosing the encoding method, several goals should be achieved simultaneously:

■ Minimizing the spectrum width of the signal obtained as the result of encoding
■ Ensuring synchronization between the transmitter and the receiver
■ Ensuring noise immunity
■ Ensuring bit error detection and, if possible, correction of such errors
■ Minimizing the transmitter power

The signal spectrum covered in *Chapter 8* is one of the most important characteristics of the encoding method. A narrower signal spectrum allows a higher data transmission rate of the same link (having the same bandwidth). In general case, the signal spectrum depends both on the encoding method and on the clock frequency of the transmitter. For example, assume that we have developed two encoding methods, each transmitting 1 bit of information during each clock (i.e., binary codes). Assume also that in the first method, the width of the signal spectrum F is equal to the clock rate of the signal f (e.g., $F = f$) and that the second method ensures the following dependence: $F = 0.8f$. Then, with the same bandwidth B, the first method allows the transmission of data at the rate of B bps, and the second ensures data transmission at a rate equal to $B/0.8 = 1.25B$ bps.

Synchronization of the transmitter and the receiver is needed to ensure that the receiver knows when it must read new information from the communications lines. When transmitting discrete information, time is always divided into clock cycles of the same duration, and the receiver tries to read each new signal in the middle of each clock (i.e., to synchronize its actions with the transmitter).

The problem of synchronization in networks is more complicated than in data exchange among devices located close to one another (e.g., among various units of a computer or between the computer and the local printer). For shorter distances, a setup based on a separate clocking communications line (Figure 9.7) works rather well. According to this method, information is read from the data line only when the clock pulse arrives.

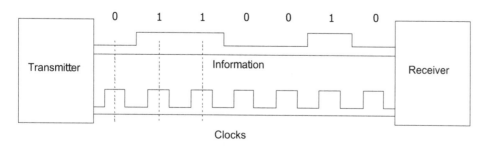

Figure 9.7 Synchronization of the transmitter and the receiver at small distances

In networks, the use of this method causes difficulties because of the nonuniformity of conductor characteristics in cables. At large distances, the nonuniformity of the signal propagation speed can result in situations in which the clock pulse arrives significantly earlier or later than the corresponding data signal, leading to the data bit being omitted or read twice. Another reason that clock pulses have been abandoned in networks is to economize on conductors in expensive cables.

In networks, to solve this problem, **self-synchronizing codes** are used. The signals of these codes carry directions for the receiver, specifying the time at which it is necessary to recognize the next bit (or several bits if the code is oriented toward more than two states of the signal). Any sharp drop of the signal level — the so-called **front** — is a good indicator for synchronization between the receiver and the transmitter.

When using sinusoids as carrier signals, the resulting code has the self-synchronization property. This is because the change of the amplitude of the carrier frequency allows the receiver to detect the starting moment of the next clock.

Detection and correction of distorted data are hard to carry out using the means provided by the physical layer. Therefore, this job is most often done using the protocols of higher layers: data link, network, transport, or application layer. On the other hand, error detection at the physical layer saves time, since the receiver does not wait until the entire frame is loaded into the buffer but discards it immediately when erroneous bits are detected within it.

Requirements for encoding methods are mutually contradictory. Therefore, each of the popular encoding methods considered in this chapter has advantages and drawbacks when compared to other methods.

9.4.2 Potential Nonreturn to Zero Code

Figure 9.8, *a*, illustrates the **potential encoding method** already considered, also known as **nonreturn to zero (NRZ) encoding.** The latter name reflects that when transmitting a sequence of ones, the signal does not return to zero during the clock cycle, in contrast to the other encoding methods.

The NRZ method is characterized by the following advantages:

- Ease of implementation
- Good error detection capabilities (because of two distinct potentials)
- Narrow spectrum (because the fundamental harmonic f_0 has low frequency equal to N/2 Hz, as was shown in the section entitled *"Combined Modulation Methods"*)

Unfortunately, this method is not free from drawbacks, the most important of which are:

- Lack of a self-synchronization property. Even if the receiver is equipped with a high-precision clock oscillator, errors in determining the instance of data read are still possible, since the frequencies of two oscillators are never identical. At the same time, recall, that when transmitting a long sequence of ones or zeros, the signal on the line does not change. Consequently, at a high data exchange rate, provided that long sequences of ones or zeros are transmitted, even a small discordance in the clock frequencies of the transmitter and the receiver can result in an error equal to the entire clock. As a result, the receiver will read an incorrect bit value.

■ The presence of a constant low-frequency component, which approaches zero when transmitting long sequences of ones or zeros. Because of this, many communications links that do not provide a direct galvanic connection between transmitter and receiver do not support this encoding method. As a result, NRZ code in its pure form is not used in networks. Nevertheless, networks employing some of its modifications are used. These modifications eliminate poor self-synchronization of the NRZ code and the problems caused by the constant low-frequency component.

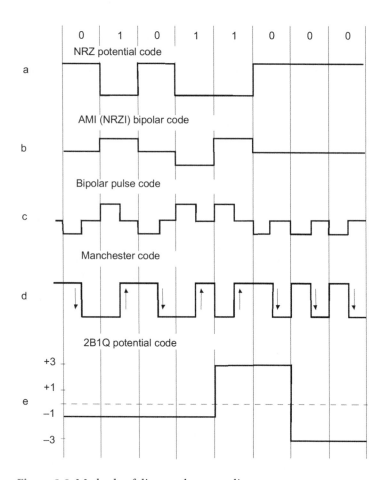

Figure 9.8 Methods of discrete data encoding

9.4.3 Bipolar Alternate Mark Inversion Encoding

Bipolar alternate mark inversion (AMI) encoding is one of the modifications of the NRZ method. This method (Figure 9.8, *b*) uses three levels of potential — negative, zero, and positive. Zero potential is used for encoding binary zero, and binary potentials are encoded by nonzero pulses of alternating polarity.

The AMI code partially eliminates the problems of DC component and the lack of self-synchronization characteristic of the NRZ code. This happens when transmitting long strings composed of ones. In such cases, the signal on line is a sequence of pulses of alternating polarity with the same spectrum as that of the NRZ code used for transmitting alternating ones and zeros (i.e., without a DC component) and with the main harmonic equal to $N/2$ Hz. As relates to long strings composed of zeros, they are no less dangerous for AMI code than for NRZ code, because in this case, the signal degenerates into the constant potential of zero amplitude.

On the whole, for different bit combinations, the use of AMI code results in narrower signal spectrums than those in the use of the NRZ code. Consequently, AMI code increases the line capacity. For example, when transmitting alternating ones and zeros, the main harmonic f_0 has a frequency equal to $N/4$ Hz. AMI code also provides some capabilities for error detection. For example, violation of the strict alternation of the signal polarity serves as evidence of false pulse or loss of correct pulse from the line.

AMI code uses three signal levels instead of two. The additional signal level requires an increase of the transmitter power by approximately 3 dB to ensure the same reliability of bit reception. This drawback is common for all codes with several signal states.

9.4.4 Nonreturn to Zero with Ones Inverted Code

There is a code similar to AMI with only two signal levels. When transmitting zeros, this code transmits the potential that was set in the previous clock cycle (i.e., it does not change it), and when transmitting one, the code inverts the potential. This code is known as **nonreturn to zero with ones inverted** (*NRZI*). It is convenient when the third signal level is undesirable, for example, in fiber-optic cables, where only two signal states are detected stably — light and dark.

Two methods are used for improving potential codes similar to AMI and NRZI. The first method is based on adding redundant bits containing logical ones to the source code. In this case, long strings of zeros are broken, and the code obtains self-synchronizing properties for any data being transmitted. The DC component is also eliminated, which means that the signal spectrum narrows. However, this method reduces the effective line bandwidth, since redundant ones do not carry any user information.

Another method is based on mixing the original information to make the probabilities of zeros and ones appearing approximately equal on the line. Devices or units that perform this operation are known as **scramblers**. In the course of scrambling, a well-known algorithm is used; therefore, the receiver, having received binary data, passes them to the **descrambler**, which restores the initial sequence of bits.

9.4.5 Bipolar Pulse Code

Besides potential codes, networks also use pulse codes in which the data are represented either by a complete pulse or by a part of it — the front. The **bipolar pulse code**, where one is represented by a pulse of one polarity and zero is represented by the pulse of inverse polarity (Figure 9.8, *c*), is the simplest case of the code implementing this approach. Each pulse lasts half of the clock cycle. Such a code is characterized by excellent self-synchronization properties. However, the DC component might be present, for example, when transmitting long strings composed of ones or zeros. Besides this, the spectrum of this code is wider than the spectrum of potential codes. For instance, when transmitting all zeros or all ones, the frequency of the main harmonic will always be equal to N Hz, which is twice as high as the frequency of the NRZ code main harmonic and four times higher than the frequency of the main harmonic of the AMI code when transmitting alternating ones and zeros. Because of the excessive width of the spectrum, a bipolar pulse code is rarely used.

9.4.6 Manchester Code

Until recently, the **Manchester code** was the most popular encoding method used in LANs (Figure 9.8, *d*). This code is used in such technologies as Ethernet and Token Ring.

In Manchester code, the potential transition (i.e., pulse front) is used for encoding ones and zeros. When using Manchester encoding, each clock cycle is divided into two parts. Information is encoded by potential transitions that occur at the midpoint of each clock cycle. One is encoded by the swing from the low signal level to the high level. Zero is represented by a drop. In the beginning of each clock cycle, a service signal transition might occur if it is necessary to transmit several ones and zeros one after another. Since transmission of a single data bit requires the signal to change as least once per clock, the Manchester code has rather good self-synchronization characteristics. The bandwidth for the Manchester code is narrower than for bipolar pulse code. Moreover, the Manchester code has no DC component, and the main harmonic in the worst case (i.e., when transmitting a long string composed of ones or zeros) has a frequency of N Hz. In the best case (when transmitting alternating ones and zeros), the frequency of the main harmonic is $N/2$ Hz, as it is for AMI or NRZ codes. On average, the bandwidth of the Manchester code is 1.5 times narrower than it is for bipolar pulse code, and the main harmonic frequency fluctuates around $3N/4$. The Manchester code has another advantage when compared to the bipolar pulse code, since the latter uses three signal levels, and the Manchester code uses only two levels.

9.4.7 2B1Q Potential Code

Figure 9.8, *e*, shows a potential code with four signal levels used for data encoding. This is the **2B1Q** code, whose name reflects its main idea — every 2 bits (2B, or two binary) are transmitted every one clock by a signal that has four states (1Q, or one quaternary). The pair of bits equal to 00 is encoded by the potential equal to –2.5 V, 01 by the potential equal to –0.833 V, 11 by the potential of +0.833 V, and 10 by the potential equal to +2.5 V.

When using this encoding method, it is necessary to take additional steps for eliminating long strings of identical pairs of bits, since in this case, the signal turns into DC component. When bits alternate randomly, the signal spectrum is twice as narrow as that of the NRZ code, since at the same bit rate, the clock duration is increased twice. Thus, using the 2B1Q code, it is possible to transmit data over the same line twice as fast as using AMI or NRZI codes. However, to implement this code, the transmitter power must be increased to ensure that four signal levels are clearly recognized by the receiver despite the background noise.

For improvement of potential codes such as AMI, NRZI, or 2Q1B, redundant codes and scrambling are used.

9.4.8 Redundant Codes

Redundant codes are based on breaking the source bit sequence into portions, often called *symbols*. Then, each source symbol is replaced by another symbol with a larger number of bits.

For instance, a logical code such as the **4B/5B** code used in FDDI and Fast Ethernet technologies replaces the source symbols that have a length of 4 bits with symbols that have a length of 5 bits. Since the resulting symbols contain redundant bits, the common number of bit combinations in them is larger than in the source characters. For example, in the 4B/5B code, the resulting characters can contain 32 bit combinations, and the initial ones have only 16 combinations (Table 9.1). Therefore, it is possible to choose 16 such combinations from the resulting code (the ones that do not contain a large number of zeros) and consider all the other combinations as *code violations*. Besides eliminating the DC component and ensuring the self-synchronization property of the code, redundant bits allow the receiver to detect distorted bits. If the receiver encounters the code violation, signal distortion took place on the line.

After dividing, the resulting 4B/5B code is transmitted through the line using one of the methods of potential encoding, which is sensitive only to long strings of zeros. Five bit symbols of the 4B/5B code ensure that no more than three successive zeros can be encountered on the line for any combination of the resulting code symbols.

NOTE *The letter B in the 4B/5B code name stands for Binary and means that the elementary signal has two states. There are also codes with three signal states. For example, the 8B/6T design encodes 8 data bits with six ternary symbols, which means that each such symbol has three states. The redundancy of the 8B/6T code is higher than that of the 4B/5B, since there are $3^6 = 729$ resulting characters for encoding $2^8 = 256$ source codes.*

Table 9.1 Correspondence of the source and resulting codes of the 4B/5B code

Source code	Resulting code	Source code	Resulting code
0000	11110	1000	10010
0001	01001	1001	10011
0010	10100	1010	10110
0011	10101	1011	10111
0100	01010	1100	11010
0101	01011	1101	11011
0110	01110	1110	11100
0111	01111	1111	11101

The use of the code conversion table is a simple operation. Therefore, this approach does not complicate the network adapters and interface units of switches and routers.

To ensure the specified line bandwidth, the transmitter using redundant code must operate at increased clock frequency. Thus, for transmitting 4B/5B codes at a rate of 100 Mbps, the transmitter must operate at a clock frequency of 125 MHz. At the same time, the signal spectrum on the line widens compared to when code without redundancy is transmitted through the line. Still, the spectrum of the redundant potential code proves to be narrower than the spectrum of the Manchester code. This fact justifies an additional stage of logical encoding as well as the operation of both transmitter and receiver at an increased clock frequency.

9.4.9 Scrambling

Scrambling methods consist of bit-by-bit computing of the resulting code based on the bits of the initial code and the bits of the resulting code obtained during preceding clock cycles. For example, a scrambler can implement the following relation:

$$B_i = A_i B_{i-3} B_{i-5} \qquad (9.1)$$

Here B_i is the binary digit of the resulting code obtained at the ith clock cycle of the scrambler operation; A_i is the binary digit of the source code arriving at the ith clock cycle to the scrambler input; and B_{i-3} and B_{i-5} are binary digits of the resulting code obtained at the preceding clock cycles of the scrambler operation (three and five clocks earlier than the current clock, respectively) and joined by the exclusive OR (XOR) operation (e.g., modulo-2 addition).

For example, if the source sequence is 110110000001, the scrambler will produce the following code (the first three digits of the resulting code will coincide with the source code, since the required preceding digits are not available yet):

$$B_1 = A_1 = 1$$
$$B_2 = A_2 = 1$$
$$B_3 = A_3 = 0$$
$$B_4 = A_4\,B_1 = 1\,1 = 0$$
$$B_5 = A_5\,B_2 = 1\,1 = 0$$
$$B_6 = A_6\,B_3\,B_1 = 0\,0\,1 = 1$$
$$B_7 = A_7\,B_4\,B_2 = 0\,0\,1 = 1$$
$$B_8 = A_8\,B_5\,B_3 = 0\,0\,0 = 0$$
$$B_9 = A_9\,B_6\,B_4 = 0\,1\,0 = 1$$
$$B_{10} = A_{10}\,B_7\,B_5 = 0\,1\,0 = 1$$
$$B_{11} = A_{11}\,B_8\,B_6 = 0\,0\,1 = 1$$
$$B_{12} = A_{12}\,B_9\,B_7 = 1\,1\,1 = 1$$

Thus, the following string will appear at the scrambler output: 110001101111, which does not contain the substring containing six successive zeros that was in the source code.

After receiving the resulting string, the receiver passes it to the descrambler, which restores the initial sequence based on the inverse relationship:

$$C_i = B_i\,B_{i-3}\,B_{i-5} = (A_i\,B_{i-3}\,B_{i-5})\,B_{i-3}\,B_{i-5} = A_i \qquad (9.2)$$

Scrambling algorithms differ in the number of operands that produce the digit of the resulting code and in the shift between them. For instance, in ISDN networks, the scrambling algorithm uses a transformation with shifts of 5 and 23 positions when transmitting data from the network to the subscriber; when transmitting data from the subscriber to the network, the scrambling conversion uses shifts of 18 and 23 positions.

There are simpler methods of eliminating the strings of successive ones, also classified as scrambling methods.

To improve the bipolar AMI code, two methods are used based on the artificial distortion of zero strings by invalid characters.

Figure 9.9 illustrates the use of the bipolar with eight zeros substitution (**B8ZS**) code and high-density bipolar three zeros (**HDB3**) code for correcting the AMI code. The source code consists of two long strings of zeros: in the first case, there are eight zeros, and in the second case, there are five.

The B8ZS code corrects only the strings consisting of eight consecutive zeros. To achieve this, the code inserts five digits after the first three zeros: $V–1^*–0–V–1^*$. Here, V stands for the one signal of polarity that is invalid for the current clock cycle (i.e., the signal that does not change the polarity of the previous "one"). 1^* stands for the "one" signal

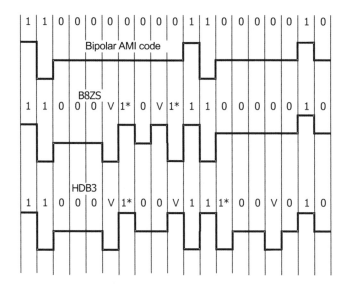

Figure 9.9 B8ZS and HDB3 codes

of correct polarity (the asterisk specifies that in the source, code there was a zero in this clock). As a result, during eight clocks, the receiver detects two distortions. It is extremely unlikely that this would have happened because of noise on the line or other transmission faults. Therefore, the receiver considers such violations as encoding of the string comprising eight consecutive zeros. After receiving this string, the receiver replaces it with the initial eight zeros. The B8ZS code is constructed in such a way that its DC component is equal to zero having any string of binary digits.

The HDB3 code corrects any four consecutive zeros in the initial sequence. The rules for forming the HDB3 code are more complicated than those for the B8ZS code. Each group of four zeros is replaced by four signals, where there is one *V* signal. To suppress the DC component, the polarity of the *V* signal alternates at consecutive replacements. Besides this, two patterns of four-clock codes are used for replacement. If before replacement the source code contained an odd number of ones, the *000V* pattern is used, and if the number of ones was even, the *1*00V* pattern is used for replacement.

Improved potential codes have a rather narrow bandwidth for any strings of ones and zeros that can be encountered in the transmitted data. Figure 9.10 illustrates signal spectrums for different codes obtained when transmitting arbitrary data, where any combination of ones and zeros is equally probable to be encountered in the source code. When building graphs, the spectrum was averaged by all possible sets of initial sequences. Naturally, the resulting codes can have different distributions of ones and zeros. From the illustration, it can be seen that the NRZ potential code has a good spectrum with only one drawback — it has a DC component. Codes obtained from the potential code by logical encoding have a narrower spectrum than the Manchester code. This is true even for

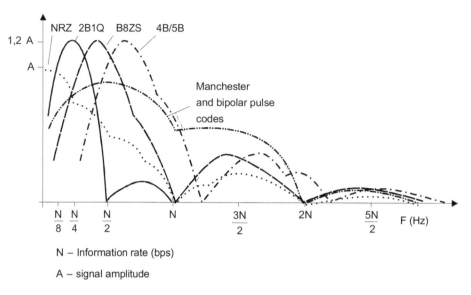

Figure 9.10 Spectrums of potential and pulse codes

increased clock frequency. (In Figure 9.10, the spectrum of the 4B/5B code would coin-cide approximately with the B8ZS code instead of being shifted to the zone of higher frequencies, since its clock frequency is increased by one-fourth from that of other codes.) This explains why potentially redundant and scrambled codes are used in contemporary technologies similar to FDDI, Fast Ethernet, Gigabit Ethernet, ISDN, and so on, instead of Manchester or bipolar pulse code.

9.4.10 Data Compression

Data compression is a technique that reduces a volume of original information without loss of its content. Data compression is used in networking to reduce the transmission time. Usually, the benefits resulting from reduction of transmission time because of data compression are noticeable only on slow links. This happens because the transmitting party spends additional time compressing the data, and the receiving party has to spend similar time for data decompression. This threshold of the transmission rate is approxi-mately 64 Kbps for contemporary equipment. Most network software and hardware tools are capable of accomplishing *dynamic data compression* in contrast to static compression, when data to be transmitted are compressed beforehand (e.g., using popular archiving utilities such as WinZip) and only then are sent to the network.

Several compression algorithms can be used in practice, each algorithm being applica-ble to a specific type of data. Some modems (known as intellectual) provide **adaptive**

compression. When adaptive compression is used, the modem chooses the specific compression algorithm depending on the data being transmitted. Consider several common compression algorithms.

Decimal packing means the data comprise only numbers and it is possible to achieve significant economy by decreasing the number of bits used for encoding a digit. Using simple binary encoding of decimal digits instead of the ASCII code will reduce the number of bits used for representing a digit from 7 to 4. Three of the most significant bits of all ASCII codes corresponding to decimal numbers contain the 011 combination. If all the data in the information frame contain decimal digits only, then it is possible to significantly reduce the frame length by placing an appropriate control character into the frame header.

Relative encoding is an alternative to the decimal packing when transmitting numeric data with small deviations between consecutive digits. In this case, it is possible to transmit only these deviations along with the known reference value. In particular, this method is used in the ADPCM digital voice-encoding method, where in each clock only the difference between two consecutive voice measurements is transmitted.

Symbol suppression can be explained thus: Quite often, the data being transmitted contain a large number of duplicated bytes. For instance, when transmitting black-and-white images, black surfaces will generate a large number of zero values, and maximally illuminated image regions will contain a large number of bytes containing only ones. The transmitter scans the sequence of bytes being transmitted and, if the string containing three or more identical bytes is detected, it is replaced by a special 3-byte sequence that specifies the byte value, notes the number of duplicates, and marks the starting point of the sequence with a special control character.

The **codes of variable length** encoding method is based on the fact that not all characters contained in the frame being transmitted are encountered with the same frequency. Because of this, many encoding methods replace the codes for the most frequently encountered characters with shorter codes. The codes of rarely encountered characters are replaced with longer codes. Such encoding is also known as statistic encoding. Because symbols have different lengths, only bit-oriented transmission is possible for transmitting frames.

When **statistic encoding** is used, the codes are selected to make it possible to unambiguously determine the correspondence of a certain portion of bits to a specific symbol or to an invalid bit combination when analyzing a bit sequence. If a specific bit combination represents a violation, it is necessary to add one more bit to this sequence and repeat the analysis. For example, if the code 1 is chosen for the most frequent character — E, which comprises 1 bit — then the value 0 of the single-bit code will be a violation. Otherwise, the user will be able to encode only two characters. For another frequent character — T — it is possible to use the 01 code and consider the 00 code violation. Then, for the A character, it is possible to choose the code 001, and 0001 can be chosen for the I character. Using variable-length codes is the most efficient when the irregularity of the frequency distribution of the transmitted symbols is significant. This is the case with long text strings. On the contrary, this approach is inefficient when transmitting binary data, such as program source code, since 8-bit codes are distributed nearly uniformly.

One of the most common algorithms on the basis of which variable-length codes are built is the **Huffmann algorithm**, allowing codes to be built automatically based on the known frequencies of character occurrences. There are adaptive modifications of the Huffmann method that allow the code tree to be built as the data from the source are received.

Many types of communications equipment, such as modems, bridges, switches, and routers, support dynamic compression protocols that allow a reduction in the volume of transmitted information by 4 or even 8 times. In such cases, the protocol ensures a compression ratio of 1:4 or 1:8. There are standard compression protocols, such as V.42bis, as well as a large number of proprietary protocols. The actual compression ratio depends on the type of data being transmitted. For example, graphic and text data are usually compressed rather well, but the compression of the program source code is less efficient.

9.5 ERROR DETECTION AND CORRECTION

KEY WORDS: self-correcting codes, checksum, frame check sequence (FCS), parity control, vertical and horizontal parity control, cyclic redundancy check (CRC), forward error correction (FEC), Hamming distance, Hamming codes

The reliable transmission of information can be ensured using various methods. In *Chapter 6*, we considered the operating principles of the protocols responsible for ensuring reliability by retransmitting lost or corrupted packets. Such protocols are based on the receiver's ability to detect the corruption of information in the received packet. Special methods of error detection are used for this purpose. There is one other method of ensuring reliability — the use of self-correcting codes. These codes, besides detecting errors in the received frame, are capable of correcting these errors. The latter method is significantly faster than frame retransmission.

9.5.1 Error Detection Technique

Methods of error detection are based on the transmission of redundant information within data blocks. Using this information, it is possible to state whether the received information is correct with a certain level of probability. In packet-switched networks, the PDU of any layer can serve as such an information unit: frames, packets, or segments. For distinctness, consider this as controlling frames.

The redundant service information is known as the **checksum** or **frame check sequence** (*FCS*). The checksum is calculated as a function of the main information, not necessarily by summing only. The receiving party recalculates the checksum of the frame according to the known algorithm and, in case it coincides with the checksum calculated by the transmitting party, draws a conclusion on the correctness of the data transmission through the network. The code that contains redundant bits, besides the source information, is often called a codeword.

There are several common algorithms for calculating the checksum, differing in their levels of sophistication in their ability to detect errors in the data.

Parity control is the simplest method of controlling data. This also is the least powerful error control algorithm, since its usage only allows the detection of isolated errors in the data being checked. This method consists of the modulo-2 summing of all bits that make up the information being controlled. For instance, if the byte is equal to 100101011, the checksum will be equal to 1. As can be easily noticed, for information containing an odd number of ones, the parity check always gives 1, and for an even number of ones, the result will be 0. The result of calculating the checksum is a redundant data bit sent with the information being controlled. If during transmission any bit of the source data (or checksum) becomes corrupted, the result of the checksum calculation will be different from the initially calculated checksum, which serves as evidence of the error. However, a double error such as 110101010 will remain unnoticed and will be erroneously considered the correct data. Therefore, parity control is usually applicable to small portions of data (1 byte, as a rule), which produces the redundancy coefficient of 1/8. This method is rarely used in computer networks because of significant redundancy and insufficient diagnostic capabilities. Parity control has two variations — control by even parity, when the number of ones is complemented to an even number (as in the preceding example), and control by odd parity, when the result of a calculation is inverted, complementing the number of ones to an odd number.

Vertical and horizontal parity control is a modification of the method just described. Its difference lies in that the initial data are considered a matrix, the rows of which make up data bytes. The control bit is calculated separately for each row and for each column. This method allows the detection of most of double errors. However, its redundancy is much more significant when compared to the previous method. In practice, this method is never used for transmitting information using the network.

Cyclic redundancy check (CRC) is currently the most popular error control method in computer networks. This method is not limited to networks; for example, it is actively used when writing data to hard and floppy disks. This method is based on considering the source data as one multibit binary number. For instance, the Ethernet frame comprising 1,024 bytes will be considered a single number comprising 8,192 bits. The remainder from the division of this number by a known divider, R, is considered control information. As a rule, either a 17-bit or 33-bit number is chosen as a divider to ensure that the remainder from division has a length of either 16 bits (2 bytes) or 32 bits (4 bytes). This involves taking into account that the remainder is always 1 bit shorter than divided number. When receiving data frame, the remainder from division by the same divider, R, is calculated once again. However, in this case, the checksum within the frame is added to the frame data. If the remainder by R is equal to zero, it is possible to conclude that there are no errors in the received frame. If not, the frame is considered distorted.

This method is much more complicated even though its diagnostic capabilities are much higher than that of the parity control methods. The CRC method detects all solitary errors, double errors, and errors in an uneven number of bits. The redundancy level of this method is not high. For example, for an Ethernet frame with a size of 1,024 bytes, the control information has a length of 4 bytes, which comes to only 0.4%.

9.5.2 Error Correction

The encoding technique that allows the receiver not only to detect errors in received data but also to correct them is known as **forward error correction** (FEC). The codes ensured by this FEC require a higher redundancy of the transmitted data than the codes that only detect errors.

When using any redundant code, not all code combinations are allowed. For instance, the parity control allows only half of all codes. If you control three information bits, then the following 4-bit codes that complement an odd number of ones will be allowed:

000 1, 001 0, 010 0, 011 1, 100 0, 101 1, 110 1, 111 0

This is only 8 codes out of 16.

To evaluate the number of auxiliary bits required for error correction, it is necessary to know the so-called Hamming distance between allowed code combinations. The **Hamming distance** is the minimum number of bits by which any pair of allowed codes differs. For parity control methods, the Hamming distance is 2 bits.

It is possible to prove that if you have constructed redundant code with Hamming distance equal to n, such a code will be able to detect $(n-1)$ errors and correct $(n-1)/2$ errors. Since parity control codes have a Hamming distance of 2 bits, they are only capable of detecting solitary errors and are unable to correct any errors.

Hamming codes efficiently detect and correct isolated errors (i.e., individual distorted bits separated by many correct bits). However, if a long sequence of distorted bits is encountered (also known as an error burst), Hamming codes become inadequate.

Situations in which error bursts are encountered are typical for wireless channels. In this case, *convolution coding methods* are used. Since for detecting the most probable correct code this method uses a trellis diagram, these codes are named *trellis codes*. These codes are used not only in wireless channels but also in modems.

9.6 MULTIPLEXING AND SWITCHING

KEY WORDS: frequency division multiplexing (FDM), wave division multiplexing (WDM), time division multiplexing (TDM), code division multiple access (CDMA), subband, Dense WDM (DWDM), asynchronous TDM mode, synchronous TDM mode, time slot, multiplexer, T1 standard fundamental frames, demultiplexer, switch synchronous transfer mode (STM), statistical TDM (STDM), asynchronous transfer mode (ATM), frequency division duplex (FDD), division duplex (TDD)

Encoding and error correction methods allow users to create the transmission link in transmission media, such as in copper wires of the cable. However, this is not sufficient for efficiently connecting network users. Within this link, it is necessary to create individual channels that would be used for switching the information flows of the users. For creating a user channel, switches of transmission networks must support some multiplexing and switching techniques. Switching methods are closely related to the multiplexing method used for creating channels; therefore, they will be covered together in this chapter.

For the moment, the following methods are used for multiplexing user channels:

- Frequency division multiplexing (FDM)
- Wave division multiplexing (WDM)
- Time division multiplexing (TDM)
- Code division multiple access (CDMA)

TDM is used both by circuit-switching and by packet-switching techniques. Methods such as FDM, WDM, and CDMA are applicable only for the circuit-switching technique. The CDMA method is used only when using the spread spectrum method and will be covered in more detail in the next chapter, which is dedicated to wireless transmission.

9.6.1 Circuit Switching Based on FDM and WDM

The **FDM technique** was developed for telephone networks, though it is applicable to other types of networks as well. Some examples are transmission networks (microwave channels) or cable TV networks.

The main idea behind this method consists of allocating each connection-specific frequency band in the common bandwidth of the link.

Based on this subband, the **channel** is created. The data transmitted through the channel are modulated using one of the methods described previously and using the carrier frequency belonging to the channel band. Multiplexing is carried out by using the frequency mixer, and demultiplexing is accomplished using a narrow-band filter with a width equal to the width of the channel band.

Consider some specific features of this type of multiplexing in telephone networks.

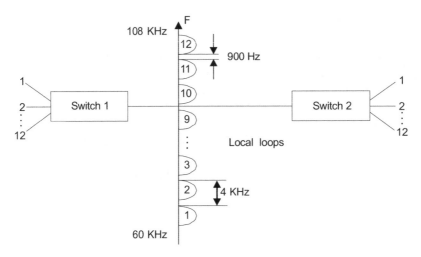

Figure 9.11 Switching based on FDM

Source signals from subscribers of the telephone network are supplied to the inputs of the FDM switch. The switch shifts the frequency of each channel to the band allocated to it by modulating the specific carrier frequency. To prevent mixing of the low-frequency components of different channels, the bands are allocated 4 KHz rather than 3.1 KHz, allowing for a special 900 Hz insurance interval between them (Figure 9.11). The link between two FDM switches simultaneously transmits signals of all subscriber channels, though each of them takes its own frequency band. Such a link is called a multiplexed link.

An output FDM switch allots modulated signals of each carrier frequency and passes them to the appropriate output channel to which the subscriber's phone set is directly connected.

FDM switches can carry out both dynamic and permanent switching. When dynamic switching is used, one subscriber initiates a connection to another subscriber by sending the phone number of the subscriber being called into the network. The switch dynamically allocates one of the available bands of the multiplexed channel to that subscriber. When permanent switching is used, the 4 KHz-wide band is allocated to the subscriber for a long time by appropriate tuning of the switch by a specific input unavailable to subscribers.

The principle of FDM switching does not change in other types of networks. Only band boundaries allocated to specific local loops, as well as several low-rate channels within a single high-rate channel, are changed.

The **WDM method** uses the same principle of FDM in another area of the electromagnetic spectrum. The information signal here is neither electric current nor radio waves; instead, it is light. For organizing WDM channels in fiber-optic cable, the waves from three transparency windows are used, which correspond to an infrared range having a wavelength from 850 nm to 1,565 nm or to frequencies ranging from 196 to 350 THz.

In the backbone link, several spectral channels are usually multiplexed —16, 32, 40, 80, or 160 (starting from 16 channels). This multiplexing technique is called **Dense WDM**

(**DWDM**). Within such spectral channels, the data can be encoded either by a discrete or by an analog method. WDM and DWDM are implementations of the idea of analog frequency multiplexing but in different form. The difference between WDM or DWDM networks and FDM networks is the maximum rate of information transmission. FDM networks usually ensure simultaneous transmission of up to 600 conversations using the backbone, which corresponds to a total rate of 36 Mbps. In comparison, in digital channels, the rate is recalculated on the basis of allocating 64 Kbps per conversation, and DWDM networks usually ensure total throughput of hundreds of gigabits or even terabits per second.

DWDM technology will be covered in more detail in *Chapter 11*.

9.6.2 Circuit Switching Based on TDM

The circuit-switching technique based on FDM was developed for a transmission of analog signals representing voice. When migrating to the digital form of voice representation, a new multiplexing technique was developed, oriented toward the discrete nature of data being transmitted.

This technique is known as *TDM*. The TDM principle consists of allocating a channel to each connection for a specific time period. Two types of TDM are used: asynchronous and synchronous. You are already acquainted with **asynchronous TDM mode**, since it is used in packet-switched networks. Each packet takes a channel for a specific time that is required to transmit it between channel end points. There is no synchronism among different information flows, and each user attempts to use the channel when there is a need to transmit information.

In this section, we consider the **synchronous TDM mode**[4], when all information flows synchronize access to the channel. As a result, each information flow periodically has the channel at its disposal for a fixed time period, a so-called **time slot**.

Figure 9.12 illustrates the principle of circuit switching based on the TDM method on the example of voice transmission.

The equipment of TDM networks — multiplexers, switches, and demultiplexers — operates in the time-sharing mode, serving all channels in turns during the operating cycle. The operating cycle of the TDM equipment is equal to 125 µsec, which corresponds to the period between consecutive voice measurements in the digital channel. This means that the multiplexer or switch has time to serve any channel and to transmit the consecutive measurement further using the network. Each connection is allocated one time quantum of the equipment operating cycle, known as a time slot, as previously mentioned. The length of the time slot depends on the number of channels served by the TDM multiplexer or switch.

---

[4] It is necessary to mention that when the TDM abbreviation is used without specifying the mode of operation, it always means synchronous TDM mode.

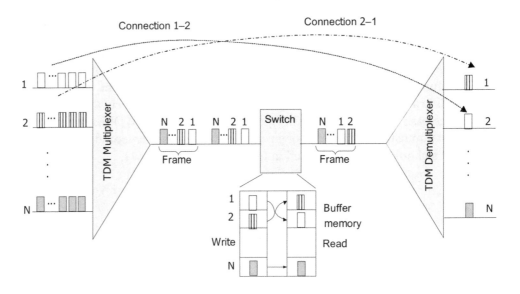

Figure 9.12 Circuit switching based on TDM

The multiplexer receives information through *N* input channels, each transmitting the data at a rate of 64 Kbps (i.e., 1 byte every 125 μsec). During each cycle, the multiplexer carries out the following operations:

■ Receives the next byte of data from each channel
■ Creates a frame from the received bytes
■ Transmits the multiplexed frame to the output channel at a bit rate equal to $N \times 64$ Kbps

The order of bytes in the multiplexed frame corresponds to the number of the input channel from which that byte was received. The number of channels served by the multiplexer depends on its operating speed. For example, the T1 multiplexer, the first industrial multiplexer operating on the basis of the TDM technology, supports 24 input channels and creates at the output *T1 standard fundamental frames*, transmitted at a bit rate of 1,544 Mbps.

Demultiplexer carries out an inverse task. It parses bytes that make up the frame and distributes them over its output channels, considering that the ordinal number of the bytes in the fundamental frame corresponds to the number of the output channel.

The switch receives the frame through a high-speed channel from the multiplexer and writes each byte from this frame into a separate cell of its buffer memory in the same order as these bytes were packed into the multiplexed frame. For switching, bytes are retrieved from the buffer memory in the order corresponding to the number of subscribers connected by the specific channel and not in the order of their arrival. For instance, if the first subscriber of the left-hand part of the network (Figure 9.12) connects to the second subscriber in the right-hand part of the network, the byte written to the first cell of buffer memory will be the second byte retrieved. By mixing the bytes within the frame in the required order, the switch ensures the establishment of connections between subscribers.

The allocated number of the time slot is at the disposal of the connection between the input channel and the output slot during the entire connection, even if the transmitted traffic is bursty and does not always require the allocated number of time slots. This means that the connection in the TDM network always has a known and fixed bandwidth, which is a multiple of 64 Kbps.

The operation of TDM equipment is similar to the operation of packet-switched networks, since each byte can be considered an elementary packet. However, in contrast to the packet in a computer network, the packet in a TDM network does not have an individual address. The role of its address is delegated to the ordinal number of bytes within the fundamental frame or the number of its allocated time slot in the multiplexer or switch. Networks using the TDM technique require synchronous operation of all equipment, because of which the second name of this technology is **Synchronous Transfer Mode, STM**.

Violation of the synchronism wrecks the requirement switching between subscribers, since the address information gets lost. Thus, the dynamic redistribution of time slots among different channels in TDM equipment is impossible even if, in a specific cycle of the multiplexer operation, the time slot in a specific channel proves to be redundant because there are no data for transmission at the input of that channel. An example is a telephone subscriber staying silent.

There is a modification of the TDM technique, known as **statistical TDM (STDM**). This technique was developed specifically to provide the possibility of increasing the bandwidth of other channels in case the time slots of some channels were temporarily available. To carry out this task, each data byte is complemented by the short address field (e.g., 4 or 5 bits), which allows the multiplexing of 16 or 32 channels. STDM is the packet-switching technique with simplified addressing and a narrow area of application. The STDM technique has not found wide application and is mainly used in nonstandard equipment for connecting terminals to mainframes. **Asynchronous transfer mode (ATM)** technology is a further development of the ideas of statistic multiplexing. ATM is a packet-switching technique.

TDM networks can support a dynamic switching mode, a permanent switching mode, or both. For instance, the main mode of digital telephone networks operating on the basis of TDM technology is dynamic switching. However, such networks also support permanent switching by providing their subscribers leased line services.

9.6.3 Duplex Mode of Channel Operation

The duplex mode is the most universal and efficient mode of channel operation. The simplest variant of ensuring duplex mode is using two independent physical links (e.g., two pairs of wires or two optical fibers) in the cable, each operating in the simplex mode (i.e., transmitting data in one direction). This idea served as a foundation for implementing many network technologies, among them Fast Ethernet and ATM.

Sometimes such simple solutions prove to be impossible or inefficient. Most frequently, this happens when only one physical link is available for duplex data exchange, and the organization of a second link requires significant expense. For instance, when exchanging data through telephone networks using modems, users have only one physical link connecting to the automatic exchange — a pair line. It is economically inefficient to purchase another one. In such cases, the duplex mode is organized on the basis of dividing the channel into two logical ones using either FDM or TDM techniques.

When using FDM for organizing a duplex channel, the frequency band is divided into two parts. This division can be symmetric or asymmetric. In the latter case, the rates of information transmission in each direction are different. A popular example of the implementation of this approach is ADSL technology used for broadband Internet access. When FDM ensures duplex operation mode, it is called **frequency division duplex** (**FDD**).

When using digital encoding, duplex mode on a two-wire line is organized using the TDM technique. Part of the time slot is used for transmitting data in one direction; another part is for data transmission in the other direction. Usually, time slots of opposite directions are interleaved; therefore, such a method is sometimes called "ping pong" transmission. Duplex TDM mode became known as **time division duplex** (**TDD**).

In fiber-optic cables with a single optical fiber, DWDM technology can be applied to implement a duplex operating mode. Data transmission in one direction is carried out using a light beam with one wavelength, and data transmission in the opposite direction is performed using a light beam of another wavelength. In fact, the solution to this particular problem, of organizing two independent spectral channels within a single transparency window resulted in the development of the WDM technology. This later became DWDM.

The arrival of powerful *digital signal processors (DSP)*, capable of implementing sophisticated algorithms of signal processing in real-time mode, provided the possibility of implementing another variant of the duplex mode. In this case, two transmitters operate simultaneously in opposite directions, creating the total additive signal in the channel. Since each transmitter knows the spectrum of its signal, it subtracts it from the total signal and receives the signal sent by another transmitter as a result.

SUMMARY

▶ For representing discrete information, two types of signals are used: rectangular pulses and sinusoidal waves. In the first case, the representation method is called encoding; in the second case, it is modulation.

▶ When transmitting discrete information, ones and zeros are encoded by changes of the amplitude, frequency, or phase of the sinusoidal signal.

▶ To increase the data rate, combined modulation methods are used. The most widely used are *quadrature amplitude modulation methods*. These methods are based on the combination of phase and amplitude modulation.

▶ When choosing the method of encoding, it is necessary to try to achieve several goals simultaneously:
  ● Minimize the possible width of the spectrum of the resulting signal
  ● Ensure synchronization between transmitter and receiver
  ● Ensure noise resistance
  ● Detect and, if possible, correct errors
  ● Minimize the transmitter power

▶ The signal spectrum is one of the most important characteristics of the encoding method. Narrow signal spectrum allows the achievement of a higher data transmission rate having the fixed bandwidth of the medium.

▶ The code must provide self-synchronization properties, which means that its signals must contain indications according to which the receiver can determine at what time instance it becomes necessary to carry out the recognition of the next bit.

▶ When using discrete encoding, binary information is represented by different levels of constant potential or by the pulse polarity.

▶ Nonreturn to zero (NRZ) code is the simplest potential code. However, it doesn't provide self-synchronization features.

▶ For improving the properties of the NRZ potential code, special methods are used that implement synchronization. These methods are based on the following:
  ● Introduction of redundant bits into the source data
  ● Scrambling of the source data

▶ Hamming codes and convolution codes allow not only the detection but also the correction of repeating errors. These codes are the most frequently used forward error correction tools.

▶ For improving effective data rates in networks, dynamic data compression based on different algorithms is used. The compression ratio depends on the data type and on the algorithm used and can vary within the range from 1:2 to 1:8.

▶ For organizing several channels within the transmission link, various methods of multiplexing are used: frequency division multiplexing, time division multiplexing (TDM), wave division multiplexing, and code division multiple access. Packet-switching techniques are compatible only with TDM, but circuit-switching techniques can use any type of multiplexing.

REVIEW QUESTIONS

1. What are the advantages and the drawbacks of the NRZ code?
2. What type of information is transmitted using ASK?
3. Why is ASK modulation not used in broadband channels?
4. What parameters of the sinusoid change when using the QAM method?
5. How many bits are transmitted by one character of a code that has seven states?
6. Explain the reasons the bandwidth of 64 Kbps has been chosen for an elementary channel of digital telephone networks.
7. Which method is used for improving self-synchronization properties of the B8ZS code?
8. What are the differences between logical encoding and physical encoding?
9. What principles serve as a basis for error detection and correction methods?
10. List the compression methods most suitable for text information. Why are they inefficient for the compression of binary data?
11. What is Hamming distance?
12. What value does the Hamming distance have for parity control methods?
13. Is it possible to use frequency division multiplexing in the Ethernet network?
14. Which TDM mode is used in packet-switching networks?
15. Is it possible to combine different multiplexing methods? If yes, provide appropriate examples.
16. What are common features of the FDM and WDM methods?
17. Based on which technique is the duplex mode implemented for the channel if both transmitters use the same frequency range simultaneously?

PROBLEMS

1. Find the first two harmonics of the spectrum of the NRZ signal when transmitting the sequence 110011001100... if the transmitter frequency is 100 MHz.
2. Which 16 codes would you choose for transmitting user information when using 3B/4B code?
3. Suggest redundant code with a Hamming distance of 3 bits.
4. Is it possible to reliably transmit the data through a channel with a bandwidth from 2.1 GHz to 2.101 GHz if the following transmission parameters are used: carrier frequency of 2.1005 GHz, ASK modulation with two amplitude values, and clock frequency of 5 MHz?
5. Suggest variable-length codes for each of the A, B, C, D, F, and O characters if it is necessary to transmit the following message: BDDACAAFOOOAOOOO. Is it possible to achieve compression as compared to the use of:
   - Traditional ASCII codes?
   - Fixed-length codes taking into account only the presence of the previously listed characters?
6. How many times would the spectrum width of the NRZ signal improve if the transmitter clock frequency is doubled?

10

WIRELESS TRANSMISSION

10.1 INTRODUCTION

Wireless transmission became popular as a means of communication just a few years after transmission using guided media. By the 1890s, the first experiments in the field of transmitting telegraph messages using radio signals had been conducted. In the 1920s, people began using radio for voice transmission.

Nowadays, there are several wireless communications systems that are not limited to broadcasting, like TV or radio. Wireless systems are widely used as transports for the transmission of discrete information. For the creation of long-distance communications links, radio relay and satellite systems are available. Wireless access systems also exist for accessing communications carrier networks and wireless LANs.

Wireless media mainly use the microwave range and are characterized by high levels of noise. This noise is generated by external radiation sources as well as by multiple reflections of signals from walls and other barriers. Therefore, wireless communications systems have to implement various noise suppression methods. The range of such tools includes forward error correction codes, which we already considered, as well as protocols with information delivery acknowledgment. The spread spectrum technique developed especially for wireless systems is an efficient tool of noise suppression.

In this chapter, we provide the basic information on the elements, operating principles, and encoding methods of wireless systems used for building point-to-point, point-to-multipoint, and multipoint-to-multipoint communications channels.

10.2 WIRELESS MEDIA

KEY WORDS: IEEE 802.11, mobile wireless communications, fixed wireless communications, mobile telephony, mobile network, wireless link, directional and omnidirectional waves propagation, parabolic antenna, isotropic antenna, electromagnetic spectrum, radio band, microwave band, infrared band, wireless local loops (WLL), reflection, diffraction, scattering, multipath propagation, intersymbol interference, multipath fading, licensing, comparative bidding, auction, industrial, scientific, medical ranges (ISM)

10.2.1 Advantages of Wireless Communications

The possibility of transmitting information without wires, thereby freeing subscribers from being limited to a specific location, has always been an attractive prospect. As long as technologies sufficient for ensuring that new wireless service gains two required components of success — convenience of use and low cost — are available, its success is practically guaranteed.

Figure 10.1 First car telephone
(Published with kind permission of the author — Anders Suneson)

Mobile telephony became the most recent proof of this. The first mobile telephone was invented by *Lars Magnus Ericsson* in 1910. This telephone was intended for use in a car but was wireless only en route. Under those conditions, it was impossible to use the device. To make a call, the driver had to stop the car. Then, a set of long sticks were used to connect the telephone to the roadside telephone wires (Figure 10.1). Naturally, inconvenience of use and limited mobility prevented this kind of telephony from becoming commercially successful.

A long time passed before radio access technologies became sufficiently mature to ensure the production of relatively compact and inexpensive radiotelephones. In the late 1970s, the boom of mobile telephony started that continues today.

Wireless communications do not necessarily mean only mobile wireless communications. There are also **fixed wireless communications** in which communicating nodes are constantly located within the boundaries of some small territory, for example, inside specific building, territory, or district.

Fixed wireless communications are used instead of guided media communications if for some reason the use of a cabling system is impossible or inefficient. These reasons might differ. Thinly populated areas or locations difficult to access, such as boggy regions, the jungles of Brazil, deserts, the Arctic, and Antarctic regions will have to wait a long time for their own cabling systems. Buildings that are historic monuments and whose walls cannot be compromised by cabling are another example. Another common situation is when it becomes necessary to provide access to subscribers whose homes are already connected to points of presence of incumbent carriers. Finally, it is sometimes necessary to organize temporary communications. Consider, for example, a conference that takes place in a building with no cable links capable of ensuring a communications rate sufficient for providing high-quality service to all participants.

Wireless communications have been employed for data transmission for a long time. Until recently, most of its applications in computer networks were bound to a fixed variant. Network users and even network architects are not always aware that at certain fragments of the network path, information is not being transmitted through wires. Instead, it is propagated through the Earth's atmosphere or space in the form of electromagnetic waves. This might happen when a computer network leases a channel from a communications carrier and the specific link of such a channel is a satellite or terrestrial microwave link.

In the mid-1990s, **mobile network technology** reached the required level of maturity. With the adoption of the IEEE 802.11 standard in 1997, it became possible to build mobile Ethernet networks, which ensured communication among users irrespective of their locations and of the manufacturer or vendor of the equipment used. For the moment, such networks play a rather modest role when compared to mobile telephone networks. However, most analysts predict rapid growth in this area in the near future.

Quite often, wireless networks are associated with *radio signals,* though this is not always correct. Wireless communications use a wide range of the electromagnetic spectrum. These range from low-frequency radio waves (several hertz) to visible light (about 8×10^{14} Hz).

10.2.2 Wireless Link

A *wireless link* is created according to rather simple method (Figure 10.2).

Each node is equipped with an antenna, which simultaneously functions as a transmitter and a receiver of electromagnetic waves. Electromagnetic waves propagate in the atmosphere or in a vacuum at a speed of 3×10^8 m/sec.

Electromagnetic waves can propagate in all directions (*omnidirectional*) or within a specific sector (*directional*). The type of propagation depends on the type of antenna. Figure 10.2 shows a **parabolic antenna**, which is a directional.

An **isotropic antenna** is quite common as well. It is a vertical conductor with a length equal to a quarter of the radiation wavelength. Such antennae are *omnidirectional.* They are widely used in cars and portable devices. Omnidirectional propagation of electromagnetic waves can also be ensured by several directional antennae.

In omnidirectional propagation, electromagnetic waves fill the entire space within the limits of a certain radius determined by attenuation of the signal power. This space becomes a shared medium. Medium sharing gives rise to the same problems as the ones existing in LANs. However, in wireless communications, the situation becomes worse

Figure 10.2 Wireless transmission link

because the surrounding space is open to public access. This is in contrast to cables, which belong to specific organizations.

A wireless medium is often called unguided in contrast to guided media, where the conductor (copper wire or optical fiber) strictly defines the direction of signal propagation. The sharing of the transmission medium generates the same problems as LANs.

For transmitting discrete information using a wireless channel, it is necessary to modulate electromagnetic oscillations of the transmitter using the flow of bits being transmitted. This function is carried out by the DCE device connecting the computer, the switch or router of the computer network, and the antenna.

10.2.3 Electromagnetic Spectrum

Characteristics of wireless communications links — the distance between nodes, covered territory, information transmission rate, and so on — in many respects depend on the frequency of the electromagnetic spectrum used. The frequency f and the wavelength λ are related by the following formula:

$$c = f \times \lambda \tag{10.1}$$

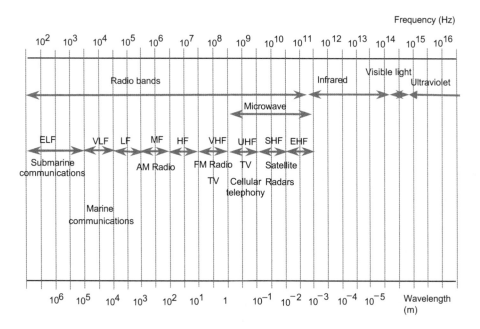

Figure 10.3 Frequency bands of electromagnetic spectrum

Figure 10.3 shows the frequency bands of electromagnetic spectrum. When considering the frequency bands of the electromagnetic spectrum, it is possible to say that wireless communications systems fall into one of the following four groups:

The band spanning from 20 GHz to 300 GHz is called the **radio band**. ITU has divided it into several subranges (the lower row of arrows in Figure 10.3), ranging from extremely low frequency (ELF) to *extra high frequency* (EHF). Radio stations to which we are accustomed and with which radio is usually associated operate in the 20 KHz to 300 MHz range. For these ranges, a special name is widely used even though it is not defined in the standards — *broadcast radio*. This group includes low-speed systems that use amplitude modulation (AM) and frequency modulation (FM) ranges for transmitting data at rates from tens to hundreds of kilobits per second. Examples of such devices are radio modems that connect two segments of the same LAN at rates of 2,400 Kbps, 9,600 Kbps, or 19,200 Kbps.

The range from 300 MHz to 3,000 GHz also has a nonstandard name — **microwave band**. This is the widest class of systems, comprising radio relay lines, satellite channels, wireless LANs, and fixed wireless access networks. They are also known as *wireless local loops* (WLL).

Directly above the microwave band is the **infrared band**. Microwave and infrared bands are also widely used for wireless information transmission. Since this kind of radiation cannot penetrate walls, systems of this type are used for creating small LAN segments within a single room.

Visible light band. During the past few years, visible light has also found application for information transmission using lasers. These systems are used as a high-speed alternative to point-to-point wireless channels for organizing short-distance access.

NOTE   *Visible light was probably the first medium of wireless communications, since it was used in ancient civilizations (e.g., in Greece) for relay-race transmission of signals along chains of observers standing on top of hills.*

10.2.4 Propagation of Electromagnetic Waves

There are some common patterns of electromagnetic wave propagation related to the radiation frequency:

The higher the carrier frequency, the higher the possible information rate.

The higher the frequency, the worse the characteristics of signal penetration through walls or other barriers. Low-frequency radio waves of AM bands easily penetrate homes, thus allowing home users to make do with a home antenna. TV signals, which have higher frequencies, usually require an external antenna. Finally, infrared radiation and visible light cannot penetrate walls, thus limiting the transmission by line of sight.

The higher the frequency, the faster the signal energy decreases with the growth of the distance from the transmitter. When electromagnetic waves propagate in open space (without reflections), the power attenuation of the signal is proportional to the product of the square of the distance from the source to the square of the signal frequency.

Signals of low frequencies, up to 2 MHz, propagate along the Earth's surface. For this reason, AM radio signals can propagate at distances of hundreds of kilometers.

Signals of frequencies from 2 MHz to 30 MHz are reflected by the Earth's ionosphere. Consequently, they can propagate at even larger distances — thousands of kilometers if the transmitter is powerful enough.

Signals from the range above 30 MHz propagate only along straight lines. This means that they are line-of-sight signals. At frequencies exceeding 4 GHz, some problems arise. For instance, signals can be absorbed by water, and this means that not just rain but also fog can significantly degrade the transmission quality for microwave systems. Therefore, not without reason, tests of laser data transmission systems are often conducted in Seattle, a city famous for its rain.

The need for fast data transmission is prevailing; therefore, all contemporary wireless communications systems operate in high-frequency bands, starting from 800 MHz, despite the advantages of signal propagation along the Earth's surface or its reflection from ionosphere, which are provided by low-frequency bands.

For successful use of the microwave range, it is also necessary to take into account additional problems encountered by signals propagating in line-of-sight mode and coming across obstacles on their way.

Figure 10.4 shows that a signal, having encountered a barrier, can propagate according to the following three mechanisms: reflection, diffraction, and scattering.

When the signal encounters the barrier, which is partially transparent for its wavelength and is of a size that significantly exceeds the signal wavelength, part of the signal energy is **reflected** off of the barrier. Waves of the microwave bands have wavelengths of several centimeters. Therefore, they are partially reflected from the walls of buildings when signal transmission takes place in a city.

If the signal encounters an impenetrable barrier (such as a plate of metal) whose size significantly exceeds the signal wavelength, then **diffraction** takes place. In this case,

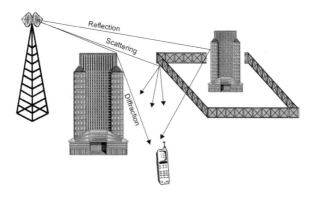

Figure 10.4 Propagation of electromagnetic waves

the signal goes around the obstacle in such a way that it is possible to receive the signal even though it is not within the line-of-sight zone.

Finally, when the signal encounters a barrier whose size is comparable to the wavelength, it becomes **scattered** and starts to propagate at different angles.

Because of these mechanisms, which are common for wireless communications within cities, the receiver can get several copies of the same signal. Such an effect is known as **multipath propagation**. The results of multipath propagation are often negative, since one of the copies might arrive out of phase, suppressing the main signal. Usually the propagation time along different paths is different; an effect known as **intersymbol interference** can also take place. This effect corresponds to situations in which delays cause the signals that encode adjacent data bits to arrive at the receiver simultaneously. Distortions caused by multipath propagation result in signal attenuation, an effect known as **multipath fading**. In towns, multipath fading results in signal attention becoming proportional to the third or even to the fourth power of the distance rather than to its square.

All these signal distortions combine with external electromagnetic noise, which are numerous and powerful in cities. It is enough to mention that microwave ovens also operate in the band of 2.4 GHz.

NOTE   *The mobility gained because of a lack of wires has a price. In this case, this price is the high level of noise in wireless communications channels. This is a problem common to all kinds of wireless communications. In promising high-frequency bands, this problem becomes quite serious. In contrast to the probability of bit errors in guided communications links (10^{-9} or 10^{-10}), in wireless communications links, it reaches the value of 10^{-3}!*

The problem of high noise levels in wireless links can be solved using various methods. Special encoding methods that distribute the signal energy in a wide frequency range play an important role. Besides this, it is common practice to place signal transmitters (and, if possible, receivers) on tall towers to avoid multiple reflections.

The use of connection-oriented protocols ensuring frame retransmission at the data link layer of the protocol stack is another popular method. This allows for faster error correction, since transport protocols, such as TCP, operate with large time-out values.

10.2.5 Licensing

Electromagnetic waves can propagate in all directions, can propagate over long distances, and are capable of penetrating barriers such as walls. Therefore, the problem of sharing bands of electromagnetic spectrum is urgent and requires centralized control. Each country has a specialized authority that, according to ITU recommendations, grants **licenses** to communications carriers, allowing them to use a specific band of the spectrum sufficient for transmitting information according to the chosen technology. The license is granted for a specific territory within which the carrier has exclusive rights to use the allocated frequency band.

When granting licenses, governmental authorities use various strategies. The most popular ones are listed here:

Comparative bidding. Communications carriers participating in comparative bidding develop detailed offers. In these documents, they describe their planned services, the technologies they will use for implementing these services, the price levels for potential clients, and so on. The committee then considers all offers and chooses the company that would best satisfy the community's needs and expectations. The complexity of criteria used to choose the winner often results in significant delays in the decision-making process and even in corruption among officials. For this reason, some countries, including the United States, abandoned this method. However, in some countries this method is still in use, most frequently when making decisions related to services vital for the country, such as the deployment of 3G systems.

Lottery. The lottery is the fastest and fairest method. However, it doesn't always produce the best results. This is especially when false carriers participate in the lottery (i.e., those who do not intend to provide carrier services themselves but plan to resell the license).

Auction. Auctions are rather popular nowadays. They cut off unfair competitors, and they also bring significant profits to a country's budget. For the first time, such an auction was held in New Zealand in 1989. Because of the buzz around 3G mobile systems, many countries have made significant augmentations to their budgets from such auctions.

There are also three frequency bands — 900 MHz, 2.4 GHz, and 5 GHz — recommended by the ITU for international use without licensing[1]. These bands are intended for general-purpose goods that use wireless communications (e.g., door-locking devices installed in cars). Besides this, some scientific or medical devices also operate in this range. The ranges were named as an allusion to these devices — **industrial**, **scientific**, **medical** (**ISM**). The 900 MHz band is the most common and, therefore, the most densely populated. This is understandable, since the higher the frequency used by a specific device, the more difficult the task of ensuring its low cost. High-frequency devices are always expensive. Nowadays, the 2.4 GHz band is actively being mastered. For instance, it is used by such new technologies as IEEE 802.11 and Bluetooth. The mastering of the 5 GHz band has just started. Nevertheless, this band seems very attractive because it ensures high speeds of data transmission.

The mandatory requirement for shared use of these bands is a limitation on the maximum power of transmitted signals, which cannot exceed 1 W. This condition limits the range of the device use, preventing signals from becoming interference for other users who might be using the same band within other districts of the city.

There are also special encoding methods that reduce the mutual interference of the devices operating in the ISM bands. These methods will be covered later in more detail.

---

[1] The problems related to using 900 MHz and 5 GHz frequency bands are that they are not free from licensing in all countries.

10.3 WIRELESS SYSTEMS

KEY WORDS: radio relay lines, indoor microwave communications, built-in infrared port, Point-to-Point System, Point-to-Multipoint System, Multipoint-to-Multipoint System, base station, access point, honeycomb, cell, handoff, diffuse transmitter, satellite communications, geostationary orbit (GEO), medium Earth orbit (MEO), low Earth orbit (LEO), very small aperture terminals (VSATs), global positioning system (GPS), intersatellite channel, Iridium Globalstar system, Orbcomm

10.3.1 Point-to-Point System

The typical design of the point-to-point wired channel is also popular for wireless communications. Various wireless links intended for different purposes and using different frequency bands can operate using the point-to-point design.

In transmission networks, this design is frequently used for creating **radio relay lines**. Such a line usually comprises several towers upon which parabolic, directed antennas are installed (Figure 10.5). Each link within such a line operates in the microwave range at frequencies of several gigahertz. Directed antennae concentrate energy in narrow beams, which allows the transmission of information at significant distances (usually up to 50 km). High towers ensure direct line of sight between antennae.

The channel bandwidth might be rather high. As a rule, it ranges from several megabits per second to hundreds of megabits per second. Such channels might represent both backbones and access links (in the latter case, they usually comprise only one link). Communications carriers most frequently use such channels when it is impossible to install fiber-optic cabling because of either natural conditions or economic inefficiency.

The same principle of communications can be used within a city for connecting two buildings. Since a high rate is not always required (e.g., it might be necessary to connect

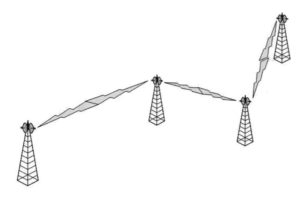

Figure 10.5 Radio relay channel

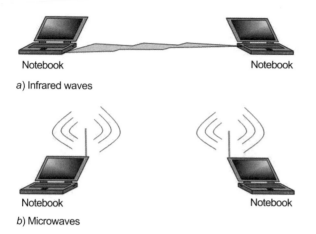

Figure 10.6 Wireless communications between two computers

a small LAN segment to the main LAN of the company); in this case, it might be possible to use radio modems operating in the AM frequency band. It is also possible to use lasers for connecting two buildings. This ensures a high information rate — up to 155 Mbps — provided that atmospheric conditions are favorable.

Another example of a wireless point-to-point channel is shown in Figure 10.6. In this instance, it is used for connecting two computers. Such channels makes up the simplest segment of a LAN; therefore, distances and signal power are principally different.

For communications within the same room, it is possible to use either an infrared band (Figure 10.6, *a*) or a microwave band (Figure 10.6, *b*). Most contemporary notebooks are equipped with built-in infrared ports, allowing such connections to be established automatically. This happens as long as infrared ports of two computers are within direct line of sight or along the line of reflected beam.

Indoor microwave communications operate within a range from tens to hundreds of meters. Exact distances cannot be predicted, since a microwave signal propagating within a room is subject to multiple instances of reflection, diffraction, and scattering. This is apart from the influence of environmental noises penetrating walls and ceiling panels.

10.3.2 Point-to-Multipoint System

This design of wireless channel is characteristic of organizing access when multiple user terminals connect to a **base station**.

Wireless point-to-multipoint channels are used both for fixed and for mobile access.

Figure 10.7 shows the variant of fixed access using microwave channels. The communications carrier uses a high tower (such as a TV tower) to ensure direct line of sight

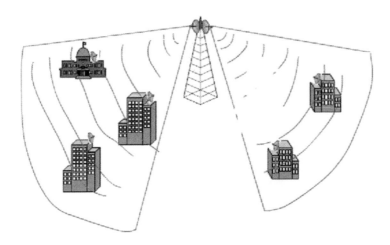

Figure 10.7 Fixed wireless access

between antennae installed on the roofs of client's buildings. In practice, such a variant might be a set of point-to-point channels — corresponding to the number of buildings that need to be connected to the base station. However, this approach is wasteful, since for each new client it is necessary to install a new antenna on a tower. For this reason, most frequently, antennae spanning specific sectors (for example, 45 degrees) are used. In this case, the carrier can ensure communications within the full sector (360 degrees) by installing several antennae at limited distances from one another.

Users of access channels can exchange information only with the base stations, which, in turn, serve as transit nodes to ensure communication between individual users.

A base station is usually connected to the guided part of the network, thus ensuring communication with users of other base stations or users of guided networks. Because of this, the base station is often called an **access point**. Often, an access point includes not only DCE equipment, which is required to create a channel (i.e., to be a physical layer device), but also a telephone or packet switch. This allows it to operate as a switch of the network to which it provides access.

Most systems of mobile access currently use the honeycomb principle, where each **honeycomb** (**cell**) represents a small territory serviced by a single *base station*. This idea was not used initially, and the first mobile phones were not based on it. Early cell phones accessed a single base station covering a large territory. The idea of small cells was first formulated in 1945. However, a long time elapsed until the first commercial cellular phone networks appeared. The first test segments appeared in the late 1960s, and wide commercial use started in the early 1980s.

The principle of dividing the entire covered territory into small cells is complemented by the idea of frequency reuse. Figure 10.8 shows a variant of the cellular network organization using only three frequencies, where neither adjacent cell pair uses the same frequency. Frequency reuse allows the carrier to sparingly use the licensed frequency range;

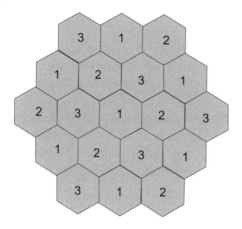

Figure 10.8 Frequency reuse in a cellular network

at the same time, subscribers and base stations of adjacent cells experience no related signal interference problems. Certainly, the base station must control the power of an emitted signal to avoid noise interference between two nonadjacent cells using the same frequency.

When the cells have a hexagonal shape, the number of reused frequencies can vary. In other words, it is not limited to three, as shown in Figure 10.8. The number of reused frequencies (N) can take the values 3, 4, 7, 9, 12, 13, and so on.

Given the minimum distance between the centers of two cells using the same frequency, N can be selected according to the following formula:

$$N = \frac{D^2}{3R^2} \qquad (10.2)$$

Here, R is the cell radius, and D is the reuse distance.

Small cells ensure small sizes and low power of the end-user terminal device. This circumstance as well as general technological progress has allowed the creation of compact cellular phones.

Mobile computer networks are not yet as common as mobile telephone networks. However, they are both based on the same principles of organizing wireless channels.

The transition of the terminal device from one cell to another is a problem of mobile channels. This procedure, known as a **handoff**, does not exist in fixed wireless access. However, this function relates to protocols of layers higher than the physical one.

10.3.3 Multipoint-to-Multipoint System

In this case, a wireless channel is a common electromagnetic medium shared by several nodes. Each node can use this medium for interacting with any other node without accessing the base station. Since there is no base station, it is necessary to use a decentralized algorithm for accessing the medium.

Most frequently, such methods of organizing wireless channels are used for connecting computers (Figure 10.9). For telephone traffic, the uncertainty of the bandwidth share obtained under conditions of medium sharing can significantly degrade the quality of voice transmission. Therefore, telephone networks always use a base station for bandwidth distribution (i.e., the previous method).

The first LAN, created in the 1970s in Hawaii, corresponded exactly to the design provided in Figure 10.9. It differed from contemporary wireless LANs because of its low speed of communications (9,600 bps). This, along with an ineffective medium access method, resulted in only 18% of the network bandwidth being used.

Nowadays, such networks operate at speeds of up to 52 Mbps in microwave or infrared bands. Omnidirectional antennae are used for multipoint-to-multipoint communications. To ensure omnidirectional propagation of infrared waves, **diffuse transmitters** are used, which dissipate the beams using systems of lenses.

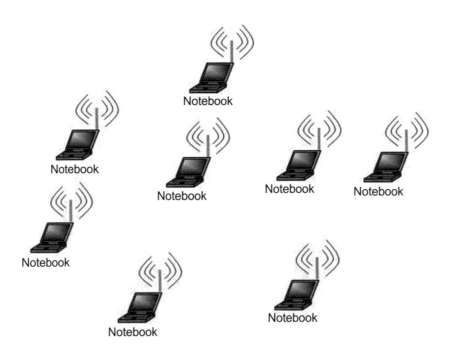

Figure 10.9 Wireless multipoint-to-multipoint channel

10.3.4 Satellite Systems

Satellite communications are used for organizing high-speed, long-distance microwave channels. Such channels require line-of-sight communications that cannot be ensured over large distances because of the Earth's surface curvature. The satellite provides a natural solution to this problem, playing the role of a signal reflector (Figure 10.10).

The idea of using artificial Earth satellites for creating communications channels appeared long before the U.S.S.R. launched the first such satellite in 1957. *Arthur C. Clarke* continued and further developed the lifework of *Jules Verne* and *H. G. Wells*, who described many technical inventions before they were implemented. In his paper titled "Extraterrestrial Relays" published in 1945, Clarke described a geostationary satellite suspended over a specific equatorial location, ensuring communications for most of Earth's territory.

The first satellite launched by the U.S.S.R. during the Cold War wasn't a geostationary one, and it provided very limited communications capabilities. In fact, it only transmitted the beep-beep radio signal to alert people all over the world of its presence in outer space. However, this success of the U.S.S.R. urged the United States to play catch up. In 1962, the first American telecommunications satellite, named Telstar-1 and supporting 600 voice channels, was launched.

More than 40 years have passed since the first telecommunications satellite was launched, and the functions of such satellites have naturally become more sophisticated. Nowadays, a satellite can play the role of transmission network node, telephone switch, or switch or

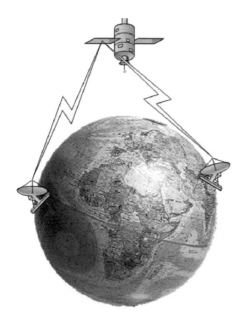

Figure 10.10 Satellite as a signal reflector

router of a computer network. Satellite equipment is now capable of interacting both with terrestrial stations and with equipment installed on other satellites, thus forming direct wireless channels in space. The techniques of transmitting microwave signals in space and on the Earth's surface have no principal differences. However, satellite channels have specific features — one of the nodes forming such a channel is constantly in flight at a significant distance from other nodes.

ITU has allocated several frequency bands for satellite communications (Table 10.1):

Table 10.1 Frequency bands allocated by ITU for satellite communications

Band	Downlink frequency (GHz)	Uplink frequency (GHz)
L	1.5	1.6
S	1.9	2.2
C	3.7–4.2	5.925–6.425
Ku	11.7–12.2	14.0–14.5
Ka	17.7–21.7	27.5–30.5

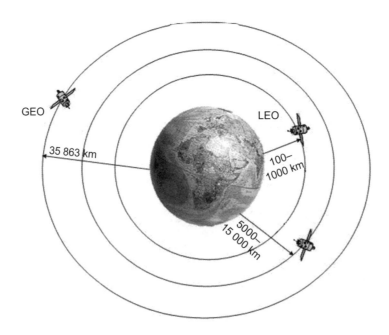

Figure 10.11 Types of satellite orbits

The **C** band was the first to be used. In this band, 500 MHz was allocated for each of the Earth-satellite (uplink frequency) and satellite-Earth (downlink frequency) duplex flows, which is enough to organize a large number of channels. The **L** and **S** bands are meant for organizing mobile services that use satellites. Quite often, they are also used by ground-based systems. The **Ku** and **Ka** bands are currently thinly populated on Earth — for a reason. The high cost of equipment prevents most companies from using this band. This is especially true for the Ka band.

Artificial satellites orbit Earth according to the laws put forward by *Johannes Kepler*. Generally, the satellite orbit is elliptic. However, to maintain a constant height above the Earth's surface, a circular orbit can be chosen.

Nowadays, the following three groups of circular orbits are in use, differing by their distance from the Earth's surface (Figure 10.11):

Geostationary orbit, or GEO (35,863 km)

Medium Earth orbit, or MEO (5,000–15,000 km)

Low Earth orbit, or LEO (100–1,000 km)

10.3.5 Geostationary Satellite

A **geostationary satellite** hangs above a specific location of the equator, precisely following the Earth's rotation. This position is convenient for the following reasons. First, a quarter of the Earth surface is within its line of sight at any given time. Thus, by using geostationary satellites, it is easy to organize *broadcasting within an entire country or even an entire continent.*

Second, the satellite is fixed for Earth-based antennae, which significantly simplifies the process of organizing communications. In fact, it eliminates the need for the automatic correction of the direction of the ground-based antenna (in contrast to MEO and LEO satellites). The situation changed with the arrival of small omnidirectional antennas in 1990s — now it is not necessary to constantly trace the position of LEO satellites; it is sufficient to ensure that the satellite is within line of sight.

Third, a geostationary satellite orbits above the Earth atmosphere and is, therefore, less worn than MEO and LEO satellites. LEO satellites, because of air resistance, are constantly losing height, which they have to correct by the periodic use of engines.

Geostationary satellites usually support many channels because of their several antennae.

As a rule, the use of GEO satellites relates to the use of large antennae with diameters of about 10 m. This complicates the use of GEO satellites by small organizations and individuals. However, the situation has changed with the development of directed antennae installed on satellites. Such antennae generate signals that can be received using relatively small ground-based antennae, known as very small aperture terminals (VSATs). VSAT diameter is about 1 m. Ground-based stations equipped with VSATs currently support a range of services, such as telephony, data transmission, and conferences.

However, geostationary satellites are not free from drawbacks. The most obvious one is their significant distance from the Earth's surface. This results in significant propagation delays, ranging from 230 to 280 msec. When using such satellites for transmitting a conversation or teleconference, inconvenient pauses occur that interfere with normal contact.

Besides this, at such distances, signal losses are high, which means that it is necessary to use powerful transmitters and antennae of large diameters. This doesn't relate VSATs, but when using VSATs, coverage territory is reduced.

The principal drawback of a geostationary satellite with its circular orbit is poor quality of communication for the regions close to the North and South Poles. The signals for such regions pass a longer distance than the signals intended for equatorial regions and low or moderate latitudes. Consequently, they have significantly stronger attenuation. A good solution to this problem is launching a satellite with a pronounced elliptic orbit, which comes close to the Earth in the regions of South or North Poles.

ITU also regulates the positions of geostationary satellites on their orbit. Nowadays, there is a clear shortage of such positions, since GEO satellites cannot be closer than 2 degrees to one another in orbit. This means that in each orbit, there may be no more than 180 similar satellites. Since not every country is capable of launching a GEO satellite, the situation resembles the competition for a specific frequency band. In this case, however, it is intensified by the political ambitions of competing countries.

10.3.6 Medium and Low Earth Orbit Satellites

The MEO class of satellites is not currently as popular as GEO and LEO. MEO satellites ensure a coverage diameter ranging from 10,000 to 15,000 km and a signal propagation delay of 50 msec. The best known and most popular service provided by MEO satellites is the **global positioning system** (GPS). *GPS* is a global system for determining the current coordinates of the user on the Earth's surface or within the space near earth. GPS comprises 24 satellites, a special ground-based network for tracing them, and an unlimited number of end-user devices (receivers). Using radio signals from satellites, GPS receivers constantly (and rather precisely) determine the current coordinates of the user location. As a rule, errors never exceed tens of meters. This is sufficient for solving navigation tasks for moving objects (airplanes, vessels, cars, etc.).

LEO satellites have different advantages and drawbacks than geostationary satellites. The main advantage of such satellites is their proximity to Earth. Consequently, they require reduced power to transmitters, small antennae, and short propagation time (from 20 to 25 msec) of the signal. Furthermore, they are easier to launch. The main drawback is their small coverage area (only about 8,000 km in diameter). Such a satellite revolves around the Earth in 1.5–2 hours and is visible to the ground-based station for a very short time — 20 minutes only. This means that continuous communications using LEO satellites can be ensured only if a sufficient number of such satellites has been launched into orbit. Besides this, atmospheric resistance reduces the working life of such satellites to 8–10 years.

In contrast to GEO satellites, which are mainly intended for broadcasting and long-distance fixed communications, LEO satellites are considered important means of supporting mobile communications.

In the early 1990s, Motorola executives evaluated the advantages of terminal devices for LEO satellites. In cooperation with some of their largest partners, this company started the *Iridium* project, whose main goal was rather ambitious — the creation of a worldwide satellite network ensuring mobile communications in any geographical location. By the end of the 1980s, the cellular system of mobile telephony was not as dense as it is now. Therefore, commercial success seemed to be guaranteed.

In 1997, the system of 66 satellites was launched, and commercial operation of the Iridium system started in 1998. Iridium satellites cover the Earth's entire surface, rotating on six orbits passing over the poles. In each orbit, there are 11 satellites equipped with transmitters with frequencies of 1.6 GHz and a bandwidth of 10 MHz. This bandwidth is used for organizing 240 channels of 41 KHz each. Thanks to frequency reuse, the Iridium system supports 253,440 channels, thus organizing the system of cells along the Earth's surface. The main services provided to the Iridium users are telephone communications (at $7 per minute) and data transmission at 2.4 Kbps.

Iridium satellites are characterized by their intellectual behavior. For instance, they can use special intersatellite channels for exchanging information at a rate of 25 Mbps. Therefore, a telephone call from the Iridium satellite telephone goes directly to the satellite currently in the line of sight. This satellite then forwards the call using the system of transit satellites to the satellite currently closest to the called subscriber. The Iridium system is a network with a functionally complete proprietary protocol stack that ensures worldwide roaming.

Unfortunately, the commercial success of Iridium was modest, and the company went into bankruptcy after two years of existence. Their banking on the viability of mobile telephone subscribers proved to be wrong. By the time their system began commercial operation, a ground-based network of cellular telephony had already covered the territory in the industrial countries. At the same time, the services ensuring data transmission at 2.4 Kbps did not meet the requirements of the users by the end of the 20th century.

Today, the Iridium system has again been brought into operation. However, it has a new owner and a new brand name — Iridium Satellite. For the moment, it has a rather modest plan related to the creation of local systems for mobile communications in those parts of the world that have practically no communications systems. Satellite software is being upgraded and modified practically spontaneously, which will allow the data transmission rate to be raised to 10 Kbps.

The Globalstar system is another well-known LEO satellite network. In contrast to Iridium, the 48 LEO satellites of the Globalstar system carry out traditional bent pipe functions. They receive telephone calls from mobile subscribers and transmit them to the nearest terrestrial base station. The base station carries out call routing by transferring the incoming call to the nearest satellite. The called subscriber is located in its line of sight. Intersatellite channels are not used. Besides telephone communications, Globalstar also transmits data at 4.8 Kbps.

Another LEO network is Orbcomm, which provides service oriented toward data transmission. Unfortunately, message delivery doesn't take place in the real-time mode. If the satellite is invisible, the Orbcomm terminal simply memorizes the packets until the satellite enters the line-of-sight zone again. As a result, data transfer is too bursty. Instead of delays lasting fractions of a second, which most Internet users are accustomed to, delays for this network can last several minutes.

Nowadays, when it is clear that mobile telephony will mainly be supported by ground-based cellular networks, most satellite systems are changing their orientation. Providing fast Internet access comes to the foreground. One such system is Teledesic, among whose founders is Microsoft creator Bill Gates. In this system, which began development in the early 1990s, the satellites are full-featured routers connected by intersatellite 64 Mbps channels.

Internet access systems based on GEO satellites — Spaceway, Astrolink, and Euro Skyway — are also under construction. These systems are oriented toward the use of VSAT terminals and promise to provide their users with 2–20 Mbps access channels.

10.4 SPREAD SPECTRUM TECHNOLOGY

KEY WORDS: spread spectrum technology, noise immunity, jamming of radio signals, orthogonal frequency division multiplexing (OFDM), frequency-hopping spread spectrum (FHSS), hopping sequence, slow FHSS, fast FHSS, IEEE 802.11, Bluetooth, direct sequence spread spectrum (DSSS), chip, chip period, a chipping rate, code division multiplexing access (CDMA)

The spread spectrum technology has been developed specially for wireless transmission. It allows improvement of the noise immunity of code for low-power signals, which is of prime importance for mobile applications. However, it is important to note that the spread spectrum technique is not the only encoding technique employed for wireless channels of the microwave band. All types of FSK and PSK, described in the previous chapter, are also used. ASK is not used because microwave channels have a broad bandwidth and the amplifiers that ensure the same amplification coefficient for a wide frequency band are rather expensive.

Broad bandwidth also provides the possibility of using multi-subcarrier modulation in which the bandwidth is divided into several subchannels, each using a specific carrier frequency. Accordingly, the bit stream is divided into several substreams with lower rates. Then each substream is modulated using a specific subcarrier, usually a multiple of the first subcarrier frequency (i.e., f_0, $2f_0$, $3f_0$, and so on). Modulation is carried out using standard FSK or PSK methods. This technique is called **orthogonal frequency division multiplexing (OFDM)**.

Before transmission, all subcarriers are mathematically convoluted into the common signal using fast Fourier transform. The spectrum of such a signal is approximately equal to the spectrum of the signal encoded using a single carrier. After transmission, the inverse Fourier transform is used to detect carrier subchannels. Then, a bit stream is received from each channel. The gain from dividing the source high-rate bit stream into several low-rate streams manifests itself in that the interval between individual symbols of the code is increased. This means that the effect of intersymbol interference because of multipath propagation of electromagnetic waves is reduced.

10.4.1 Frequency-Hopping Spread Spectrum

The idea of **a** spread spectrum appeared during World War II, when radio was widely used for secret negotiations as well as for controlling military objects, such as torpedoes. To prevent eavesdropping or jamming of radio signals with narrow-band noise, radio transmissions were done while constantly changing the carrier frequency within a wide frequency range. As a result, the signal power was distributed over the entire range, and the listening of a specific frequency produced only insignificant noise. The sequence of carrier frequencies was chosen to be pseudorandom, known only to the transmitter and the receiver. Attempts at suppressing the signal within a specific narrow band did not negatively affect the spread signal, since only a small share of information was suppressed.

The concept of this method, known as the **frequency-hopping spread spectrum (FHSS)**, is illustrated in Figure 10.12.

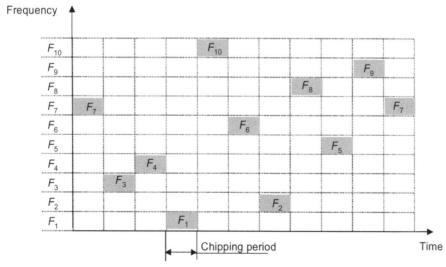

Hopping sequence: F_7-F_3-F_4-F_1-F_{10}-F_6-F_2-F_8-F_5-F_9

Figure 10.12 Frequency-hopping spread

Time intervals during which the transmission continues at the same carrier frequency are known as chip periods. On each carrier frequency, standard modulation methods, such as FSK or PSK, are used for the transmission of discrete information. To synchronize the receiver with the transmitter, at the beginning of each chip period, a specific time interval is allocated for transmitting several synchronization bits. Thus, the effective rate of this encoding method proves to be lower because of constant synchronization overhead.

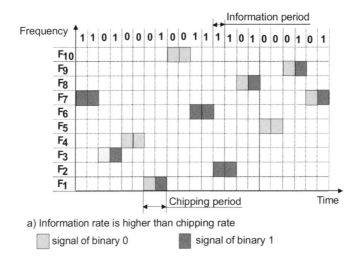

a) Information rate is higher than chipping rate

signal of binary 0   signal of binary 1

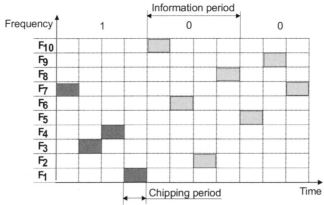

b) Information rate is lower than chipping rate

Figure 10.13 Relationship between the information rate and the chipping rate

The carrier frequency changes constantly according to the numbers of the frequency subchannels produced by the pseudorandom number generator. The pseudorandom sequence depends on a specific parameter known as a seed. Provided that both the transmitter and the receiver know the seed value, they change frequencies according to the same sequence. The sequence according to which carrier frequencies are changed is called a **hopping sequence**.

The frequency at which subchannel frequencies are changed is known as a **chipping rate**. If the chipping rate is lower than the information rate of the channel, this operation mode is called *slow FHSS* (Figure10.13, *a*). Otherwise, you will mostly encounter *fast FHSS* (Figure 10.13, *b*).

Fast FHSS ensures better noise immunity; narrow-band noise suppressing a signal in specific subchannel does not result in bit loss, since this bit value is repeated several times in different subchannels, and only one copy of this value is distorted. In this mode, the intersymbol interference does not occur because by the time a signal arrives, having been delayed along one of the routes, the system has had time to shift to another frequency.

Slow FHSS does not provide this property even though it is much easier to implement and is characterized by a lower overhead.

FHSS methods are employed in such wireless technologies as IEEE 802.11 and Bluetooth.

The FHSS approach to using the frequency band is different from approaches employed by other encoding methods. Instead of sparing use of a narrow frequency band, it tries to use the entire available range. At first, this method might seem to be far from efficient, since at any given time, only one channel is operating. However, this is not an accurate assumption, since spread spectrum codes can also be used for multiplexing several channels within a wide range. In particular, FHSS allows the organizing of the operation of several channels by choosing pseudorandom sequences for each channel to ensure that, at any moment, each channel operates at a different frequency. This can be achieved only if the number of channels does not exceed the number of available subchannels.

10.4.2 Direct Sequence Spread Spectrum

The **direct sequence spread spectrum (DSSS)** method also uses the entire frequency band allocated for a single wireless link. However, the technique it uses to achieve this is different from the one employed by FHSS. It uses the entire range allocated to it, but this is not done by constantly switching frequencies. In this case, each bit of information is replaced by N bits so that the signal transmission clock rate is increased N times. This, in turn, means that the signal spectrum also increases N times. Thus, it is sufficient to properly choose the information rate and the N value to make the signal spectrum span the entire range.

The goal of DSSS encoding is the same as for FHSS encoding — namely, to improve noise immunity. Narrow-band noise would distort only specific frequencies of the signal spectrum. Therefore, the receiver would correctly recognize the transmitted information with high probability.

The code used to replace a bit of the source information is known as a spreading sequence, and each bit of such a sequence is called a **chip**. Accordingly, the transmission rate of the resulting code is known as the chipping rate. Binary zero is encoded by the inverse value of the spreading sequence. The receivers must know the spreading sequence value used by the transmitters to correctly recognize the transmitted information.

The number of bits in a chipping sequence is the spreading factor, since it defines the expansion coefficient of the source code. As with FHSS, any kind of modulation (e.g., BFSK) can be used for encoding bits of the resulting code.

The larger the value of the spreading factor, the wider the spectrum of the resulting signal, and the higher the noise suppression level. The spectrum band taken up by the signal also grows. Usually, the spreading factor takes the values from 10 to 100.

An example of a spreading sequence is the so-called Barker sequence, which comprises 11 bits: 10110111000. If a transmitter uses this sequence, then the transmission of the three bits 110 will result in the transmission of the following bits:

10110111000 10110111000 01001000111

The Barker sequence allows the receiver to quickly achieve the symbol synchronism with the transmitter (i.e., to reliably detect the starting point of the sequence). The receiver detects such an event by comparing sequentially received bits with the sequence pattern. If the Barker sequence is compared with the same pattern shifted 1 bit to the right or left, less than half of the bits will match. This means that even if several bits are distorted, the receiver will correctly determine the starting point of the sequence with a high probability. Consequently, it will be able to correctly interpret the received information.

DSSS is less protected against noise than fast FHSS, since powerful narrow-band noise influences part of the spectrum and, consequently, the results of the recognition of ones or zeros.

10.4.3 Code Division Multiple Access

Like FHSS, DSSS encoding allows the multiplexing of several channels within the same band. The technique of such multiplexing is called **code division multiplexing access (CDMA)**. It is widely used in cellular networks. The CDMA multiplexing technique can be used with FHSS or DSSS encoding. In practice, it is used more frequently when the wireless networks use DSSS codes.

Each node of the network using CDMA sends data to the shared medium any time it needs to do so, which means that there is no synchronization among network nodes. The idea of the CDMA consists in that each network node uses its own value of the spreading sequence. The values of the sequence are chosen to ensure that the receiving node knows the spreading sequence of the transmitting node could pick the data of the transmitting node from the signal created as a result of the simultaneous transmission of information by several nodes.

To ensure that such a demultiplexing operation can be accomplished, the values of the spreading sequence are chosen in a special way. Let us explain CDMA by using an example.

Suppose that there are four nodes in the network: A, B, C, and D. Each node uses its own value of the spreading sequence:

A: 0 0 0 0
B: 0 1 0 1
C: 0 0 1 1
D: 0 1 1 0

Suppose also that when transmitting ones and zeros using a spreading sequence (transformed source code), additive and inverse signals are used. Inverse property means that binary one, for example, is encoded by a sinusoid having +A amplitude; binary zero is encoded by a sinusoid with the −A amplitude. From the additive property, it follows that if the phases of these sinusoids coincide, then the signal will be of level 0, when simultaneously transmitting binary one and binary zero. To simplify the writing of the spreading sequence, designate the sinusoid with positive amplitude as +1 and the sinusoid with negative amplitude as −1. For simplicity, suppose that all nodes of the CDMA network are synchronized.

Thus, when transmitting the one bit of the source code, the four nodes transmit the following sequences into the medium:

A: −1   −1   −1   −1
B: −1   +1   −1   +1
C: −1   −1   +1   +1
D: −1   +1   +1   −1

When transmitting a zero bit of the source code, the spreading sequence signals are inverted.

Now, suppose that each of the four nodes transmits 1 bit of the source information independently of the other nodes: the A node transmits a bit set to 1, the B node a bit set to 0, the C node a bit set to 0, and the D node a bit set to 1.

The following sequence of signals will be transmitted into the network medium (S):

A: −1   −1   −1   −1
B: +1   −1   +1   −1
C: +1   +1   −1   −1
D: −1   +1   +1   −1

According to the additive property:

S: 0   0   0 −4

Suppose that the E node needs to receive information from the A node. To do so, it has to use its CDMA demodulator by specifying to it the spreading sequence of the A node as a parameter.

The CDMA demodulator operates in the following way: It sequentially adds all four total signals (Si) received during each clock of operation. The Si received during the clock when the spreading code of the A node is +1 is taken into account with its sign, and the signal received during the clock when the spreading code of the A node is –1 is added to the sum with an inverted sign. In other words, the demodulator calculates the scalar product of the vector of the received signals and the vector of spreading sequence values of the required node:

$$S \times A = (0\ 0\ 0\ -4) \times (-1\ -1\ -1\ -1) = 4$$

To find out which bit was sent by node A, the result needs to be normalized, for example, by dividing it by the number of nodes in the network: 4/4 =1.

If the E node needs to receive information from the B node, it has to use the spreading code of the node for demodulation, or B $(-1\ +1\ -1\ +1)$:

$$S \times B = (0\ 0\ 0\ -4) \times (-1\ +1\ -1\ +1) = -4.$$

After normalization, we would receive the signal –1, which corresponds to the binary zero of the source information of the B node.

A feature of the spreading sequences used in CDMA is that they are mutually orthogonal. This means that if you consider them as vectors, they would produce 0 when multiplied in pairs. Vectors of the (1 0 0), (0 1 0), and (0 0 1) of three-dimensional space are another example of mutually orthogonal vectors. However, to use vectors in CDMA, it is necessary to ensure that they are not only mutually orthogonal but also orthogonal to the inverted members of the set of vectors. This is because inverted members are used for encoding the zeros of the source information.

Here, we have explained only the fundamental idea of the CDMA by means simplifying the situation as much as possible. In practice, CDMA is sophisticated technology that does not operate with conventional +1 and –1; rather, it operates with modulated signals, such as BPSK signals. Moreover, network nodes are not synchronized. Finally, the signals arriving from the nodes located different distances from the receiver have different powers. The problem of synchronization between the receiver and the transmitter is solved by sending a long sequence of predefined code known as a *pilot signal*. To make the powers of all transmitters seem approximately equal for the base station, CDMA uses special procedures for controlling the power.

SUMMARY

▶ Wireless communications are classified in the mobile wireless and the fixed wireless categories. For organizing mobile communications, there is no alternative to the wireless medium. Fixed wireless communications ensure access to network nodes located within the limits of a small territory (such as a building).

▶ Each node of the wireless communications channel is equipped with an antenna, which is the transmitter and the receiver of electromagnetic waves simultaneously.

▶ Electromagnetic waves can propagate in all directions (omnidirectional) or within a certain sector (directional). The type of propagation depends on the type of antenna.

▶ Wireless data transmission systems fit into the following four groups, depending on the range of electromagnetic spectrum used:
  - Radio (broadcast) systems
  - Microwave systems
  - Infrared wave systems
  - Visible light systems

▶ Because of the reflection, diffraction, and scattering of electromagnetic waves, the effects of multipath propagation of the same signal occur. This results in intersymbol interference and multipath fading.

▶ Data transmission in bands of 900 MHz, 2.4 GHz, and 5 GHz, called industrial, scientific, medical bands, does not require licensing, provided the transmitter power does not exceed 1 W.

▶ Wireless point-to-point channels are used for the creation of radio relay lines for communication between buildings and pairs of computers.

▶ Wireless point-to-multipoint channels are created on the basis of the base station. Such channels are used in mobile cellular networks and in systems of fixed access.

▶ The multipoint-to-multipoint topology is characteristic for wireless LANs.

▶ Satellite telecommunications systems use three groups of circular orbits, differing in their distance above the Earth's surface:
  - Geostationary orbit (35,863 km)
  - Medium Earth orbit (5,000–15,000 km)
  - Low Earth orbit (100–1,000 km)

▶ For encoding discrete information, wireless systems use the following types of modulation:
  - FSK and PSK
  - OFDM modulation using several carrier frequencies
  - Spread spectrum methods — frequency hopping spread spectrum (FHSS) and direct sequence spread spectrum (DSSS).

▶ Spread SPECTRUM methods use a range of frequencies for representing information. This decreases the influence of narrow-band noises on the signals.

▶ Based on FHSS and DSSS, it is possible to multiplex several channels within the same frequency band. This multiplexing technique is known as code division multiple access.

REVIEW QUESTIONS

1. List the main areas of application for wireless communications channels.

2. What are the advantages and drawbacks of wireless information transmission when compared to the transmission methods using guided media?

3. How is it possible to organize omnidirectional propagation of radio waves and microwaves?

4. What factors allow radio waves of frequencies ranging from 2 MHz to 30 MHz to propagate for hundreds of kilometers?

5. What spectrum is used for satellite communications?

6. Which atmospheric conditions impede the propagation of microwaves?

7. What devices are used for omnidirectional propagation of infrared waves?

8. What barriers cause diffraction of electromagnetic waves? What barriers cause scattering?

9. When is it necessary to use the elliptic orbits of telecommunications satellites?

10. What are the drawbacks of a geostationary satellite?

11. In your opinion, what are the reasons for the commercial failure of the Iridium project?

12. What condition must be observed for the FHSS technology to be fast?

13. Which property of the Barker sequence is the reason for its use in DSSS technology?

14. What is the main property of the spreading sequences used in CDMA?

PROBLEMS

1. Is it possible to use the values $1\,0\,0 \ldots 0, 0\,1\,0\,0 \ldots 0, 0\,0\,1\,0 \ldots 0, 0\,0\,0\,1\,0 \ldots 0$, and so on as spreading sequences of the nodes of a network supporting CDMA based on DSSS?

2. Suggest an 11-bit spreading sequence, different from the Barker sequence, and provide the possibility of reliably detecting the starting instance of transmission of the next bit of source information.

11

TRANSMISSION NETWORKS

CHAPTER OUTLINE

11.1 INTRODUCTION

Transmission networks are intended for creating a switched infrastructure, using which it is possible to quickly and flexibly organize a permanent "point-to-point" channel between two end-user devices. Transmission networks employ the circuit-switching technique. Overlay networks, such as computer or telephone networks, operate on the basis of circuits formed by transmission networks. The channels provided by transmission networks to their subscribers are distinguished by high bandwidth — usually ranging from 2 Mbps to 10 Gbps.

There are three generations of transmission networks:

■ Plesiochronous digital hierarchy (PDH)

■ Synchronous digital hierarchy (SDH) (in the United States, the SONET standard corresponds to the SDH technology)

■ Dense wave division multiplexing (DWDM)

The first two technologies — PDH and SDH — use time division multiplexing for sharing a broadband link and transmitting data in a digital form. Each of these technologies supports a transmission rate hierarchy, so the user can choose the desired rate for the channels on the basis of which the overlay network will be built.

The SDH technology ensures higher rates than PDH; therefore, when building a large transmission network, its backbone is usually based on the SDH technology and the access network employs the PDH technology.

DWDM networks are the latest achievement in the creation of fast communications channels. They are not digital, since they provide their users with a separate wave for information transmission. The users are free to use this wave as they like, implementing either modulation or encoding. Nowadays, the DWDM technology is forcing SDH out of long-distance backbones to the network periphery, turning SDH into access network technology.

Three technologies of switching and multiplexing allow the creation of a flexible and scalable transmission network, capable of serving a large number of computer and telephone networks.

11.2 PDH NETWORKS

KEY WORDS: transmission network, Plesiochronous digital hierarchy (PDH), Synchronous digital hierarchy (SDH), SONET, Dense wave division multiplexing (DWDM), Rate Hierarchy, T-carrier systems, E-carrier systems, T-1 multiplexer, signaling protocol, bit robbing, digital signal level n, fractional T-1/E-1 channel, multiplexing/demultiplexing operations, back hauling

The **plesiochronous digital hierarchy** (PDH) technology was developed in the late 1960s by AT&T to solve the problem of interconnecting the switches of large telephone networks. FDM channels, which were used previously for solving this problem, by that time had exhausted their possibilities of organizing high-speed multichannel communications through a single cable. In FDM, twisted pair was used for simultaneous transmission of the data from 12 local loops. To improve the communications rate, it was necessary to install cables with numerous pairs or to replace them with more expensive coaxial cables.

11.2.1 Rate Hierarchy

The starting point of the PDH technology evolution was the development of the T-1 multiplexer, which could multiplex, switch, and transmit in digital form (continuously) voice traffic from 24 subscribers. Since subscribers continued to use standard phone sets, which meant that voice transmission took place in an analog form, T-1 multiplexes automatically sampled voices at a rate of 8,000 Hz and encoded voices using pulse code modulation. As a result, each local loop formed a 64 Kbps digital data flow, and the entire T-1 line ensured bandwidth of 1,544 Mbps.

T-1 links were not sufficiently powerful and flexible multiplexing tools for connecting large, automatic exchanges. Therefore, the idea of forming communications links with a **rate hierarchy** was implemented. *Four* T-1 links were joined to form the links of the next level of digital hierarchy — T-2, transmitting data at a rate of 6,312 Mbps. The T-3 link created by joining seven T-2 links has a rate of 44,736 Mbps. The T-4 link joins six T-3 links; as a result, its rate is 274,176 Mbps. This technology became known as **T-carrier systems**.

In the mid-1970s, telephone companies started to provide dedicated links built on the basis of T-carrier systems for commercial leasing, and they ceased to be an internal technology of those companies. The T-1 — T-4 links allow the transmission not only of voice but also of any other data represented in digital form, including computer data, TV, and fax.

The T-carrier systems technology was standardized by the American National Standards Institute (ANSI) and later by CCITT, now known as the ITU-T. After standardization, it became known as PDH. As a result of modifications introduced by CCITT, American and international versions of the PDH standard became incompatible. In the international standard, the analogues of the T links are the E-1, E-2, E-3, and E-4 links differing by rates of 2,048 Mbps, 8,488 Mbps, 34,368 Mbps, and 139,264 Mbps, respectively. The American version of the standard was also adopted in Canada and Japan (with minor differences); in Europe, the international CCITT standard is in use.

Despite the differences in the American and international versions of the standard, technologies of digital hierarchy use the same notation for designating the hierarchy of speeds — **digital signal level n** (DS-n). Table 11.1 lists the values for all levels of data rates introduced by the standards of both technologies.

Table 11.1 Hierarchy of digital data rates

Rate designation	America				CCITT (Europe)		
	Number of voice channels	Number of channels of the previous hierarchical level	Rate, Mbps unless noted		Number of voice channels	Number of channels of the previous hierarchical level	Rate, Mbps unless noted
DS-0	1	1	64 Kbps		1	1	64 Kbps
DS-1	24	24	1,544		30	30	2,048
DS-2	96	4	6,312		120	4	8,488
DS-3	672	7	44,736		480	4	34,368
DS-4	4,032	6	274,176		1,920	4	139,264

In practice, the T-1/E-1 and T-3/E-3 links are most widely used.

11.2.2 Multiplexing Methods

The T-1 multiplexer ensures the transmission of data from 24 subscribers at 1,544 Mbps in a frame that has a simple format. In this frame, user data are transmitted sequentially, 1 byte from each subscriber at a time, and after 24 bytes, one *synchronization bit* is added. Initially, T-1 devices (which gave their name to the entire technology of data transmission at 1,544 Mbps) operated only on an internal clock, and each frame could be transmitted asynchronously using synchronization bits. T-1 devices, as well as faster T-2 and T-3 equipment, have undergone significant changes during the long years of their existence. Nowadays, multiplexes and switches of the transmission network operate using the centralized clock frequency distributed from a single network location. However, the principle of framing remained the same; therefore, synchronization bits are still present in the frame. The total rate of user channels is 24 subscribers × 64 Kbps = 1.536 Mbps, and 8 Kbps are added by synchronization bits, which in sum makes 1.544 Mbps.

Now, consider another feature of the T-1 frame format. In T-1 equipment, the eighth bit of *each byte* of the frame has a special meaning depending on the type of the data being transmitted and the generation of the equipment. When transmitting voice, this bit is used for service information, such as the number of the called subscriber and other information needed for establishing a connection between network subscribers. The protocol ensuring such a connection in telephony is known as the **signaling protocol**. Therefore, the actual rate of user voice transmission is 56 Kbps instead of 64 Kbps. The technique of using the eighth bit for service purposes was called **bit robbing**.

When transmitting computer data only, the T-1 line provides 23 channels for user data, and the 24th channel is dedicated to internal use, mainly for the restoration of corrupted frames. Computer data are transmitted at 64 Kbps, since the eighth bit is not "stolen."

During simultaneous transmission of voice and computer data, all 24 channels are used and both voice and computer data are transmitted at 56 Kbps.

When multiplexing four T-1 channels into a single T-2 channel, one synchronization bit is used between DS-1 frames as before, and DS-2 frames (which contain four sequential DS-1 frames) are separated by 12 service bits, which are intended not only for separating but also for synchronizing frames. Accordingly, DS-3 frames comprise seven DS-2 frames separated by service bits.

As already mentioned, the PDH technology version described in the G.700–G.706 CCITT international standards differs from the American T-carrier systems technology. In particular, it does not use the method of bit robbing. When going to the next level of the hierarchy, the rate multiplier has a constant value of 4. Instead of the 8th bit, the E-1 line allocates for service purposes 2 bytes out of 32, namely, the 0th (for synchronization between transmitter and receiver) and 16th (for transmitting signaling information). For voice or data transmission, there are 30 channels available, each having a rate of 64 Kbps.

The user can lease several 56/64 Kbps channels of the T-1/E-1 link. Such a compound channel is known as *fractional* T-1/E-1. In this case, the user is allocated several time slots of the multiplexer operation.

The physical layer of the PDH technology supports various types of cables: twisted pair, coaxial, and fiber-optic. The main variant of organizing subscriber access to T-1/E-1 links is a cable consisting of two twisted pairs with RJ-48 jacks. Two pairs are needed for organizing the duplex mode of data transmission at a rate of 1.544/2.048 Mbps. T-1 channels use B8ZS bipolar potential code for data representation, and E-1 channels use the HDB3 bipolar potential code for the same purpose. For signal amplification in T-1 lines, regenerators and line control equipment are installed after every 1,800 m (1 mile).

Coaxial cable, thanks to its broad bandwidth, supports one T-2/E-2 channel or four T-1/E-1 channels. For T-3/E-3 channels, coaxial cable, fiber-optic cable, or microwave channels are used.

The physical layer of the international variant of this technology is described by the G.703 standard, whose name designates the type of bridge or router interface connected to the E-1 channel. The American version of the standard has the name T-1.

11.2.3 PDH Technology Limitations

Both the American and the international version of the PDH technology standard have several drawbacks, the most important of which are complications and the *inefficiency of multiplexing/demultiplexing operations* over user data. The term itself — "plesiochronous" (i.e., nearly synchronous) — used for naming this technology is implicit evidence of the lack of full synchronization when multiplexing slow channels into faster ones. Initially, the asynchronous approach to frame transmission makes it necessary to insert synchronization bits between frames.

As a result, to retrieve user data from a multiplexed channel, it is necessary to **fully** demultiplex the frames from the aggregate channel. For example, to retrieve the data of a specific 64 Kbps subscriber channel from the frames of the T-3 channel, it is necessary to demultiplex these frames down to the level of T-2 frames, continue this operation down to the level of T-1 frames, and finally to demultiplex T-1 frames.

If the PDH network is used only as a backbone between two large nodes, the multiplexing/demultiplexing operations are carried out only on end nodes; consequently, no problems arise. However, when it is necessary to drop one or more subscriber channels on the transit node of the PDH network, then there is no simple solution. One possible approach to carrying out this task is to install two T3/E3 (or higher-level) multiplexes in each network node (Figure 11.1). The first multiplexer carries the full demultiplexing of

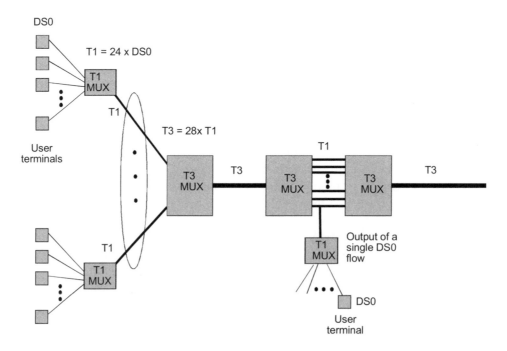

Figure 11.1 Separation of a low-speed channel using full demultiplexing

the flow and directs part of the slow channels to subscribers; the second device again multiplexes the high-speed output stream from the remaining channels. When implementing this approach, the number of devices in operation is doubled.

Another variant is **back hauling**. In the transit node, where it is necessary to separate and redirect the subscriber flow, only the high-speed demultiplexer is installed, which simply transfers the data further through the network without demultiplexing them. This operation is carried out only by the demultiplexer of the end node, after which the data intended for a specific subscriber are returned to the transit node through a separate physical link. Naturally, such sophisticated interoperation of the switches complicates the operation of the entire network and requires fine-tuning. This increases the required amount of manual configuration operations and results in errors.

Moreover, PDH technology did not provide built-in network management and fault tolerance tools.

Finally, PDH ensures data transmission rates that are too low according to contemporary requirements. Fiber-optic cables allow data transmission at the rates of several gigabits per second through a single fiber, which allows the multiplexing of tens of thousands of subscriber channels within a single cable. However, the PDH technology does not employ this capability, since its hierarchy of speeds is limited at 139 Mbps.

11.3 SONET/SDH NETWORKS

KEY WORDS: synchronous transport module level N (STM-N), synchronous transport signal level N (STS-N), optical carrier level N (OC-N), virtual container, connection table, cross-connection table, pointer, tributary unit, administrative unit, SDH multiplexer, terminal multiplexer, Add/Drop multiplexer, tributary port, add/drop ports, aggregate port, line port, regenerator, SDH protocol stack, regenerator section, regenerator section overhead, multiplex section, multiplex section overhead, positive alignment, negative alignment, SDH network topology, SDH ring, linear sequence of multiplexes, fault tolerance, automatic protection switching, self-healing network, equipment protection switching (EPS), card protection, multiplex section protection (MSP), subnetwork connection protection (SNC-P), multiplex section shared protection ring (MS-SPRing)

The previously mentioned drawbacks of the PDH technology were taken into account and eliminated by the developers of the **synchronous optical NET (SONET)** technology. The first version of this standard appeared in 1984. After that, this technology was standardized by the T-1 Committee of ANSI. International standardization of this technology took place under the coordination of the European Telecommunications Standards Institute (ETSI) and ITU-T in cooperation with ANSI and leading telecommunications companies of America, Europe, and Japan. The main goal of the developers of the international standard was to create technology capable of transmitting the traffic of all existing digital channels of the PDH level (both American T1–T3 and European E1–E4) using a high-speed backbone based on fiber-optic cables and to ensure a speed hierarchy that would continue the PDH hierarchy to the rates of several gigabits per second.

As a result of lengthy cooperation, ITU-T and ETSI developed the international standard known as **synchronous digital hierarchy (SDH)**. The SONET standard also was elaborated to ensure the compatibility of equipment. Thus, the SDH and SONET networks are compatible (but not identical) and can multiplex input streams of practically any PDH standard — European or American.

11.3.1 Rate Hierarchy and Multiplexing Methods

The rate hierarchy supported by SONET/SDH technologies is outlined in Table 11.2.

Table 11.2 SONET/SDH speed hierarchy

SDH	SONET	Rate
	STS-1, OC-1	51.84 Mbps
STM-1	STS-3, OC-3	155.520 Mbps
STM-3	OC-9	466.560 Mbps
STM-4	OC-12	622.080 Mbps
STM-6	OC-18	933.120 Mbps
STM-8	OC-24	1.244 Gbps
STM-12	OC-36	1.866 Gbps
STM-16	OC-48	2.488 Gbps
STM-64	OC-192	9.953 Gbps
STM-256	OC-768	39.81 Gbps

In the SDH standard, all rate levels (and, accordingly, the frame formats for these levels) have a common name: **synchronous transport module level N (STM-N)**. In the SONET technology, there are two designations for the speed levels: **synchronous transport signal level N (STS-N)**, used for data transmission by electric signals, and **optical carrier level N (OC-N)**, used when data are transmitted by fiber-optic cable. Further on, for simplicity, we concentrate on the SDH technology.

STM-N frames have a complicated structure allowing the aggregation of SDH and PDH streams of different rates into the common backbone stream and the performance of add/drop operations without full demultiplexing of the backbone stream.

Multiplexing and add/drop operations use **virtual containers** in which PDH data blocks can be transported through the SDH network. Besides PDH data blocks, auxiliary control information is placed into virtual containers, including the container's path overhead header. This header contains statistic information on the process of passing along the container its route from source to destination (error messages) as well as control data, such as an indicator of connection establishment between the end points. As a result, the size of virtual container is larger than the corresponding PDH payload that it carries. For example, VC-12, besides the 32 bytes of data of the E-1 flow, contains 3 bytes of control information.

In SDH technology, there are several types of virtual containers (Figure 11.2) for transporting the main types of PDH data blocks: VC-11 (1.5 Mbps), VC-12 (2 Mbps), VC-2 (6 Mbps), VC3 (34/45 Mbps), and VC-4 (140 Mbps).

Virtual containers are *switching units* of SDH multiplexes. In each multiplexer, there is a **connection table** (also called a **cross-connection table**) that specifies, for example, that VC-12 of the P1 port is connected to VC-12 of the P5 port and VC-3 of the P8 port is connected to VC-3 of the P9 port. The network administrator forms the connection table on each multiplexer, using either a management system or a control terminal. This operation must be done in such a way as to ensure the path connecting two network end nodes to which the user equipment is connected.

To combine the synchronous transmission of STM-N frames with the asynchronous nature of the PDH user data carried by these frames within the same network, SDH technology uses **pointers**. The concept of pointers is the key to the SDH technology; it replaces the rate equalization of asynchronous sources by redundant bits, which was adopted in PDH.

The pointer determines the current position of a virtual container in the higher-layer structure — a **tributary unit** or an **administrative unit**. The main difference of these units from virtual containers is the presence of an additional pointer field. Because of the use of pointers, a virtual container can "float" within certain limits inside its tributary or administrative unit, which, in contrast, has a fixed position within a frame. Because of the system of pointers, the multiplexer is able to find the position of user data in the synchronous byte stream of the STM-N frames and to retrieve them "on the fly." Note that the multiplexing mechanism implemented in PDH does not provide this capability.

Tributary units are joined into groups, which, in turn, are grouped into administrative units. The group of N administrative units makes up the payload of the STM-N frame. Besides this, the frame has a header containing control information common to all administrative units. At each step of user data transformation, several control bytes are added to the source data. These auxiliary bytes help to recognize the structure of the block or group of blocks and then, using pointers, determine the starting point of the user data.

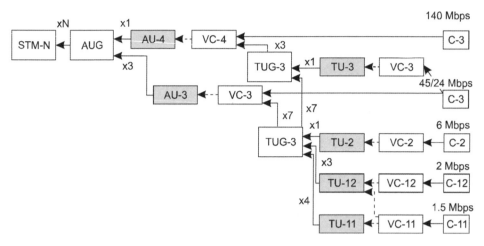

Figure 11.2 Method of data multiplexing in SDH

Figure 11.2 shows structure units of the SDH frame. The units containing pointers are hatched, and the relationship between containers and units, allowing a phase shift of the data, is shown by the dashed line.

The SDH multiplexing method provides different capabilities of aggregating PDH user flows. For example, for the STM-1 frame, it is possible to implement the following variants:

■ 1 E-4 stream

■ 63 E-1 streams

■ 1 E-3 stream and 42 E-1 streams

Certainly, you can suggest other variants.

11.3.2 Equipment Types

The main element of the SDH network is the **multiplexer** (Figure 11.3). Usually, it is equipped with a certain number of PDH and SDH ports, for example, 2 Mbps and 34/45 Mbps PDH ports and STM-1 ports intended for 155 Mbps and STM-4 ports intended for 622 Mbps. Ports of the SDH multiplexer are classified into aggregate and tributary. *Tributary ports* are often called *add/drop ports*, and *aggregate ports* are called *line ports*. This terminology reflects the typical topologies of SDH networks, where there is a pronounced backbone (line) in the form of the chain or ring along which data streams arriving from network users through add/drop ports are transmitted.

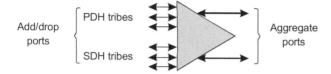

Figure 11.3 SDH multiplexer

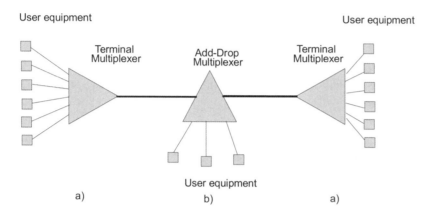

Figure 11.4 Types of SDH multiplexers

SDH multiplexers are usually divided into the following two types, the difference between which depends on the multiplexer position in the SDH network:

■ **Terminal multiplexers**. A terminal multiplexer terminates aggregate channels by multiplexing in them numerous tributary channels (Figure 11.4, *a*). Thus, the terminal multiplexer is equipped with one aggregate port and many tributary ports.

■ **Add/Drop multiplexers**. An add/drop multiplexer takes an intermediate position in the backbone (ring, chain, or hybrid topology). It has two aggregate ports for transmission of the aggregate data stream (Figure 11.4, *b*). Using a small number of tributary ports, such a multiplexer adds or drops the data of tributary channels to or from the aggregate stream.

Sometimes there are **digital cross-connects** — multiplexes that carry out switching operations over arbitrary virtual containers. In such multiplexes, there are no differences between aggregate and tributary ports, since such a multiplexer is intended for operation in the mesh topology, where it is impossible to single out aggregate streams.

Besides multiplexes, the SDH network can contain **regenerators** necessary to eliminate the limitations on the distance between multiplexes. These limitations depend on the power of optical transmitters, the sensitivity of receivers, and the attenuation of the fiber-optic cable (this problem was considered in an exercise on power budget in *Chapter 8*).

The regenerator transforms the optical signal into an electric one and then back to an optical signal. In the course of this operation, the signal shape and its time characteristics are restored. Currently, SDH regenerators are used rarely, since their cost is not significantly lower than that of the multiplexer and their functional capabilities are incommensurable to those of the multiplexes.

11.3.3 Protocol Stack

The **SDH protocol stack** comprises four layers of protocols. These layers are not related to the OSI model layers. For the OSI model, the entire SDH network is made of physical-layer equipment.

- In the SDH protocol stack, the **photonic layer** deals with encoding information bits using light modulation. For encoding of the optical signal, the NRZ potential code is used. This self-synchronization property of code is achieved by scrambling data before transmission.

- The **section layer** supports the physical integrity of the network. In SDH terms, a section is any continuous portion of fiber-optic cable that connects a pair of SONET/SDH devices (for example, it might connect a multiplexer and a regenerator or a regenerator to another regenerator). The section often is called a **regenerator section**, assuming that accomplishing functions of this layer doesn't require the terminating devices of the section to be multiplexes. The regenerator section protocol deals with a specific part of the frame header, known as the **regenerator section overhead**. On the basis of control information, this protocol can test the section and support administrative control functions.

- The **line layer** is responsible for data transmission between two network multiplexes. The protocol of this layer deals with STS-N layer frames for multiplexing and demultiplexing as well as adding or dropping user data. The line protocol is also responsible for line reconfiguration if one of its elements fails — be it optical fiber, a port, or an adjacent multiplexer. The line is often called a **multiplex section**. The control information of the multiplex section is placed within the frame header part called **multiplex section overhead** (MSOH).

- The **path layer** is responsible for data delivery between two users of the network. The path is a composite virtual connection between users. The path layer protocol must receive the data supplied in the user's format (e.g., in the T-1 format) and transform them into synchronous STM-N frames.

Figure 11.5 illustrates the distribution of SDH protocols by the types of SDH equipment.

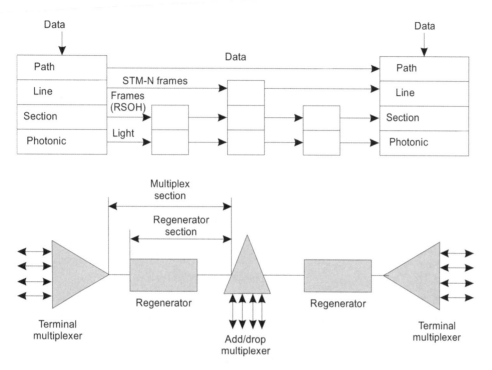

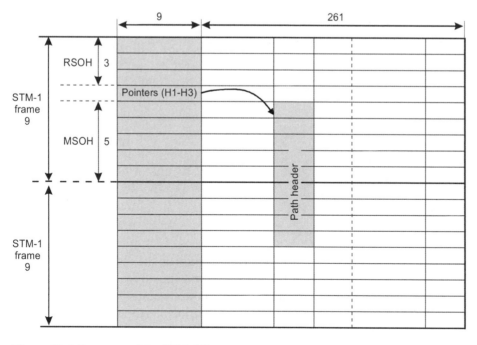

Figure 11.5 Protocol stack of the SDH technology

Figure 11.6 Structure of the STM-1 frame

11.3.4 STM-N Frames

The main elements of the STM-1 frame are shown in Figure 11.6, and Table 11.3 outlines the structure of the headers of regenerator and multiplex sections. Usually, the frame is represented as a matrix comprising 270 columns and 9 rows. The first 9 bytes of each row are allocated for the service data of the headers, and 260 bytes out of the subsequent 261 bytes are dedicated to the payload (e.g., data of structures such as administrative units, administrative unit groups, tributary units, tributary unit groups, and virtual containers). One byte of each row is allocated for the path header, which allows the connection from point to point to be controlled.

Table 11.3 Structure of regenerator and multiplex section headers

Regenerator section header	Multiplex section header
Synchronization bytes	Error control bytes for the multiplex section
Error control bytes for regenerator section	6 bytes of the DCC operating at a rate of 576 Kbps
One byte of the auxiliary radio channel (64 Kbps)	2 bytes of the automatic traffic protection protocol (the K1 and K2 bytes), ensuring network survivability
3 bytes of the data communication channel (DCC), operating at a rate of 192 Kbps	1 byte for status messages of the synchronization system
Bytes reserved for use at discretion of national communications carriers	All remaining bytes of the MSOH header are either reserved for use at discretion of national communications carriers or are not used.
The H1, H2, and H3 pointer fields specify the position of the starting point of VC-4 or three VC-3s in relation to the pointers field.	

Consider the mechanism of H1–H2–H3 pointer operation on the example of the STM-1 frame, which carries VC-4. The pointer takes 9 bytes of the fourth row of the frame, each of the H1, H2, and H3 fields being allocated 3 bytes. Allowed pointer values belong to the range from 0 to 782. The pointer marks the starting position of VC-4 in 3-byte units. For example, if the pointer is set to 27, then the first byte of VC-4 is located $27 \times 3 = 81$ bytes from the last byte of the pointer field, which means that it is the 90th byte (the numbering starts from 1) in the fourth row of the STM-1 frame. The fixed value of the pointer takes into account the phase shift among the data source (whose role can be played by the PDH multiplexer, end-user equipment with the PDH/SDH interface, or another SDH multiplexer), and the current multiplexer. As a result, the virtual container is transmitted in two sequential STM-1 frames, as shown in Figure 11.6.

The pointer can process not only fixed phase shift but also clock frequency mismatch between the multiplexer and the device from which user data are being received. To compensate for this effect, the pointer value is periodically increased or decreased by 1.

If the rate of data arrival of VC-4 is lower than the rate of STM-1 sending, the multiplexer periodically (this period depends on the value of the synchronization frequency mismatch) experiences a shortage of the user data needed to fill the appropriate fields of the virtual container. Therefore, the multiplexer inserts three "dummy" (insignificant) bytes into the virtual container data, after which it continues to fill VC-4 with the user data that arrived during the pause. The pointer is increased by one, which reflects the shift of the starting point of the next VC-4 by 3 bytes. This operation over the pointer is known as **positive alignment**. As a result, the average rate of user data transmission becomes equal to the rate of their arrival without inserting redundant bits in the PDH style.

If the rate of VC-4 data arrival is higher than the rate of STM-1 frame sending, the multiplexer periodically needs to insert "extra" bytes into the frame (extra means that there is no place in VC-4 field for these bytes). To place these bytes, the three least significant bytes of the pointer are used — that is, the H3 field (the pointer value itself fits within the bytes of the H1 and H2 fields). In this case, the pointer is decreased by one; therefore, such an operation became known as **negative alignment**.

The reason that alignment of VC-4 takes place in 3-byte units can be explained easily. The STM-1 frame can carry either one VC-4 or three VC-3s. Each VC-3, in general, has an independent phase value in relation to the starting point of the frame and has its own value of frequency mismatch. The VC-3 pointer, in contrast to the VC-4 pointer, comprises 3 bytes instead of 9 bytes: H1, H2, and H3 (each of these fields is 1 byte long). These three pointers are placed into the same bytes as the VC-4 pointer; however, the byte interleaving method is used, according to which the pointers are in the following order: H1-1, H1-2, H1-3, H2-1, H2-2, H2-3, H3-1, H3-2, and H3-3 (the second index identifies the specific VC-3). The values of VC-3 pointers are interpreted in bytes rather than in 3-byte units. When accomplishing negative alignment of VC-3, the extra byte is placed into the appropriate byte — H3-1, H3-2, or H3-3 — depending on the VC-3 over which this operation is carried out.

Thus, we must explain the choice of the offset size for VC-4s. It was chosen to unify these operations over containers of any type, placed directly into the administrative unit group of the STM-1 frame. Alignment of lower-layer containers always takes place with a step of 1 byte.

When joining tributary unit and administrative unit blocks into groups according the previously described method (see Figure 11.6), they are sequentially interleaved byte by byte so that the period of the user data arrival in the STM-N frame coincides with the period of their arrival in tributary ports. This excludes the need for their temporary buffering; therefore, it is correct to say that *SDH multiplexes transmit data in real-time mode.*

11.3.5 Typical Topologies

Various topologies of links are used in SDH networks. The most frequent are rings and linear chains of multiplexes. Mesh topology close to the fully connected one also has found a growing area of application.

An **SDH ring** is built on the basis of the add/drop multiplexes that have at least two aggregate ports (Figure 11.7, *a*). User data streams are added into the ring and dropped from the ring using tributary ports, making point-to-point connections (the illustration shows two such connections). The ring is a classic regular topology that has fault-tolerance potential — under conditions of a single cable break or the failure of one multiplexer, the connection will be preserved, provided that it is directed along the ring in the opposite

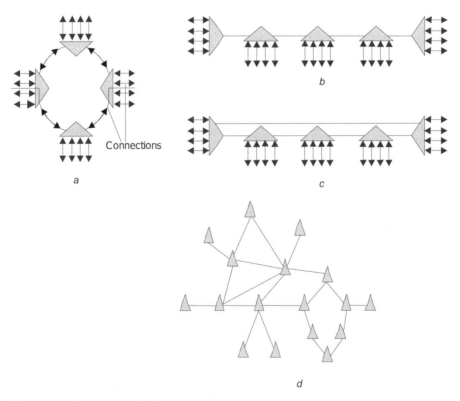

Figure 11.7 Typical topologies

direction. The ring is usually built on the basis of a cable with two optical fibers. Sometimes, however, cables with four fibers are used for improved reliability and bandwidth.

The chain (Figure 11.7, *b*) is a **linear sequence of multiplexes** in which the two multiplexes at the end points play the role of terminals and other multiplexes are add/drop multiplexes. Usually, the network with the chain topology is used when network nodes have a specific geographic location, for example, when they have to be located along a railroad or trunk pipeline. In such cases, however, it is also possible to use flat ring (Figure 11.7, *c*), which ensures a higher level of fault tolerance through the use of two additional fibers in the backbone cable and the presence of one additional aggregate port on each terminal multiplexer.

These base topologies can be combined to build a complex and extensive SDH network with lots of branches, creating sections with radial-ring topology, "ring-to-ring" connections, etc. The most general case is mesh topology (Figure 11.7, *d*), where multiplexes are connected to one another by many links that make it possible to achieve very high levels of performance and reliability.

11.3.6 Methods of Ensuring Network Survivability

One of the strongest points of SDH transmission networks is a reach set of various tools for ensuring fault tolerance. These tools allow the network to recover rather quickly (within tens of milliseconds) after the failure of some network elements — be it a communications link, a multiplexer port or card, or a multiplexer as a whole.

SDH fault tolerance mechanisms are known under a general term — **automatic protection switching**, which reflects the switching to a reserve path or a reserve multiplexer element in case of failure of the primary element. Networks supporting such mechanisms are called **self-healing networks** in SDH standards.

In SDH networks, the following three protection methods are used:

- *1+1 protection* means that a redundant element carries out the same tasks as the primary element. For example, when protecting the tributary card according to the 1+1 method, the traffic passes both through the primary card (the working one) and through the backup card (the redundant one).

- *1:1 protection* means that the redundant element does not carry out the functions of the primary element in the normal operation mode. Rather, it takes over in the case of the failure of the primary element.

- *1:N protection* allocates one redundant element for *N* working elements (i.e., the ones that need protection). In the case of failure of one of the primary elements, the redundant element takes over and starts carrying out the functions of the failed element. If this happens, other elements remain without any protection until the failed element is replaced.

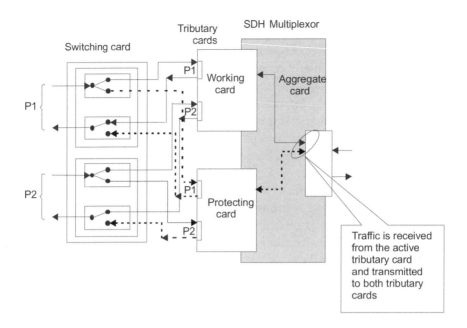

Figure 11.8 Card protection according to the 1+1 method

Depending on the type of element being protected by introducing redundant elements, five main types of automatic protection switching are used in SDH equipment and networks.

Equipment protection switching (EPS) protects units and elements of SDH equipment. It is used for such vitally important elements of the multiplexer as the processor unit, the switching unit (cross-connect), the power supply unit, and the synchronization signals input unit. As a rule, EPS operates according to 1+1 or 1:1 method.

Card protection protects aggregate and tributary cards of the multiplexer. It allows the multiplexer to automatically continue operation in case of failure of one of the aggregate or tributary cards. In card protection, all three methods — 1+1, 1:1, and 1:N — are used. Protection according to the 1+1 method ensures continuity of the transport service, since the traffic of the user connection is not discontinued in the case of the card failure. Figure 11.8 provides an example of a multiplexer supporting protection of tributary two-port cards according to the 1+1 method. One of the tributary cards is the primary (or working one), and the other is redundant (protection). The mode of operation of the pair of cards connected in such a way is set by a special command for multiplexer configuration. When both tributary cards are usable, the cards process the traffic in parallel.

For traffic switching between tributary cards, an auxiliary switch card is used. Incoming (add) traffic from each port is supplied to the input bridge of the switch card, which branches the traffic and supplies it to the inputs of the appropriate ports of the tributary cards. The aggregate card receives both STM-N signals from the tributary cards and chooses the signal from the active card. The outgoing (drop) traffic from the aggregate card is also processed by both tributary cards, but only the traffic from the active card is supplied by the switch card to its output.

When the main card fails (or any other event occurs that requires switching to the protection card, such as signal degradation, signal error, or card removal), the aggregate card, by a command from the multiplexer control unit, switches to receiving the signal from the protection tributary card. The switch card simultaneously starts transmitting the signals of the drop traffic from the protection card to its output.

This method ensures automatic protection of all connections passing via the protected card. When specifying card protection, configuration of the working card connections is duplicated for the protection card.

Multiplex section protection (MSP) ensures protection of the multiplex section (i.e., the network section between two adjacent SDH multiplexes). It acts more selectively in comparison to card protection. The protected object is the section between two multiplexes, including two ports and the communications link (which might include regenerators but no multiplexes). As a rule, the 1+1 protection method is used. When using this method, a protection link (the lower pair of ports) is configured for the working link (the upper pair of ports connected by a cable, as shown in Figure 11.9, *a*. When establishing MSP, it is necessary to configure each multiplexer by specifying the relationship between the working and the protection ports. In the initial state, all traffic is transmitted both through the working and through the protection links.

MSP can be unidirectional or bidirectional. When using unidirectional protection (shown in Figure 11.9) only one of the multiplexes — the receiver for the failed link — decides whether to switch to the protection link. After detecting the failure (port failure, signal error, signal degradation, etc.), this multiplexer switches to receiving the signal

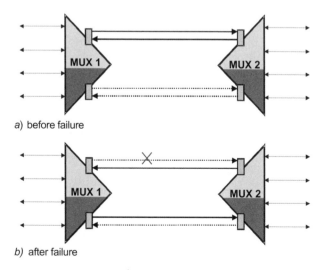

a) before failure

b) after failure

Figure 11.9 Multiplex section protection (MSP)

through the protection link. In this case, transmission and reception are done through different ports (Figure 11.9, *b*).

When using bidirectional MSP, in the case of failure of the working link in any direction, the multiplexes are fully switched to protection ports. To notify the transmitting multiplexer (which uses the working link) of the necessity of switching to the protection link, the receiving multiplexer uses a protocol known as K-byte. This protocol inserts the status of the working and protection links, with detailed information about the failure, into 2 bytes of the STM-N frame header (the K1 and K2 bytes in MSOH). The MSP mechanism ensures the protection of all connections passing through the protected multiplex section. According to the requirements of the standard, the time of switching must not exceed 50 msec.

Subnetwork connection protection (SNC-P) protects the path (connection) through the network for a specific virtual container. It ensures the switching of a specific user connection to an alternate path in the case of the main path failure. The object of SNC-P is to place the tributary traffic into a specific type of virtual container (for example, VC-12, VC-3, or VC-4). The 1+1 protection method is used.

SNC-P is configured in two multiplexes — the input multiplexer, where the tributary traffic placed into the virtual container are branched, and the output multiplexer, where two alternate paths of traffic meet. An example of the implementation of SNC-P is shown in Figure 11.10. In the ADM1 multiplexer, two connections are specified for the VC-4 of the T2 tributary port: to one of the four VC-4s of the A1 aggregate port and to one of the four VC-4s of the A2 aggregate port. One of these connections is configured as a working connection; another one becomes a protection connection. In the normal operating mode, the traffic is transmitted through both connections. Transit multiplexes (for these two

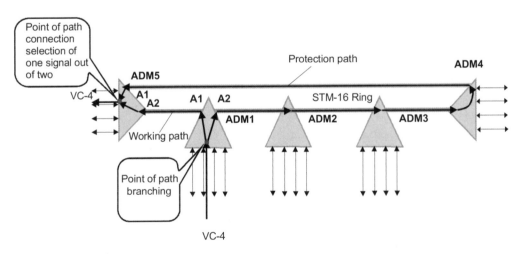

Figure 11.10 SNC-P

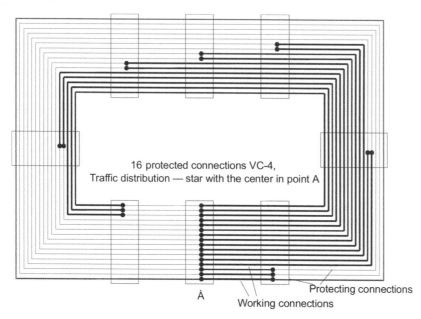

Figure 11.11 SNC-P in the ring

connections) are configured in the usual way. In the ADM5 output multiplexer, the VC-4 of the tributary T3 port is also connected to containers — that of the A1 aggregate port and that of the A2 aggregate port. The higher-quality flow is chosen from the two flows arriving to the T3 port. If the quality of both flows is normal and equal, the signal from the aggregate port configured as the working one is selected.

SNC-P works in SDH networks of any topology where there are alternate routes for traffic (i.e., in ring and mesh topologies).

Multiplex section shared protection ring (MS-SPRing) is the path protection in the ring topology shared among user connections. In some cases, it ensures more efficient protection of the traffic in the ring. Although SNC-P is suitable for the ring topology of the SDH network, in some cases, its implementation reduces the effective bandwidth of the ring, since each connection takes doubled bandwidth along the entire ring. For instance, in the STM-16 ring, it is possible to establish only 16 VC-4 connections protected according to the SNC-P method (Figure 11.11).

MS-SPRing allows the ring bandwidth to be used more efficiently, since the bandwidth is not reserved beforehand for each connection. Instead, half of the ring bandwidth is reserved, but this protection bandwidth is dynamically allocated to connections as needed (i.e., after detecting a link or multiplexer failure). The level of spare bandwidth when using MS-SPRing depends on the traffic distribution.

If all traffic comes to the same multiplexer (i.e., "star" distribution takes place), MS-SPRing does not provide any economy as compared to SNC-P. An example of such a situation is shown in Figure 11.12, *a.* In this illustration, the A multiplexer is the center

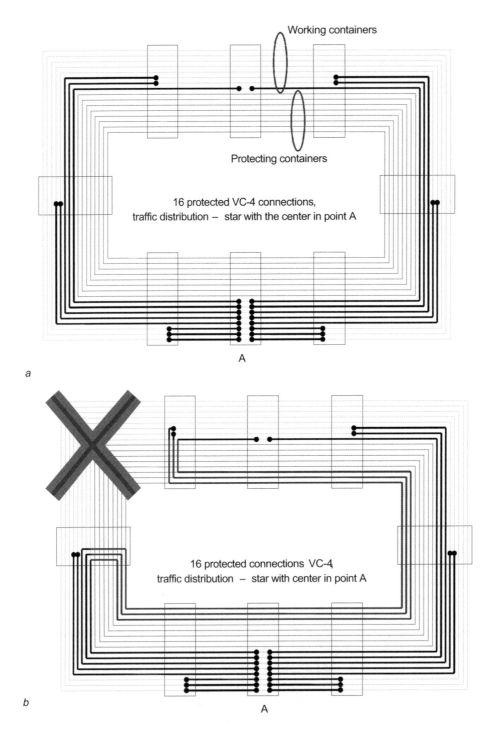

Figure 11.12 MS-SPRing — protection with ring sharing

in which all traffic is concentrated, and in the ring, the same 16 protection connections are established as in the example of SNC-P shown in Figure 11.11. For protection of the connections, 8 of 16 virtual containers of the STM-16 aggregate stream are reserved.

In the case of failure or malfunctions, such as link fault (Figure 11.12, b), the traffic in multiplexes whose connection is broken is reversed in the opposite direction. This is achieved using protection virtual containers of the aggregate ports to which the virtual containers of the affected connections are connected. All connections that are not affected by the failure continue to operate in the normal mode, without using the protection containers. The K-byte protocol is used for notifying multiplexes about the ring reconfiguration. The time of switching to the protection connections of the MS-SPRing method is about 50 msec. When using mixed traffic distribution, the bandwidth economy in the MS-SPRing may be even more significant.

11.4 DWDM NETWORKS

KEY WORDS: wave division multiplexing (WDM), dense wave division multiplexing (DWDM), high-dense WDM, separate spectral channel, fiber amplifier, all-optical network, terminal multiplexer, multiplexing/demultiplexing unit, input amplifier, booster, preamplifier, set of transponders, colored interface, network with intermediate connections, optical add/drop multiplexes, optical cross-connects, ring topology, mesh topology, thin-film filter, diffraction phase grating, arrayed waveguide gratings (AWG), photonic switches, wave routers, lambda routers, micro-electro mechanical systems (MEMS)

The **dense wave division multiplexing (DWDM)** technology is intended for creating optical backbones of the new generation, operating at multigigabit or -terabit rates. Such a revolutionary performance leap is ensured by the multiplexing method, principally different from the one used in SDH networks. In DWDM networks, information in optic fiber is transmitted simultaneously by numerous light waves — *lambdas* (from traditional designation of the wavelength adopted in physics — λ).

DWDM networks operate according to the circuit-switching principle, and each light wave is a separate spectral channel. Each wave carries its own information.

DWDM equipment is not directly engaged in solving the problems of data transmission on each wavelength — that is, in choosing the method of information encoding and the protocol of its transmission. Its main functions are *multiplexing* and *demultiplexing* operations, namely, combining different waves within the same signal beam and separating the function of each spectral channel from the aggregate signal. The most advanced DWDM devices can also switch waves.

NOTE   *DWDM technology is innovative not only because it raises the upper rate limit of data transmission through optical fiber tens of times; it also opens a new era in the techniques of multiplexing and switching, since it carries out these operations over light signals without transforming them into an electric form. All other types of technologies that use light signals for transmitting information through optic fibers, such as SDH or Gigabit Ethernet, need to transform optical signals to electric ones and only then are capable of performing multiplexing and switching operations.*

The first application of the DWDM technology was the long-distance backbones intended for connecting two SDH networks. With this simplest point-to-point topology, the capability of DWDM devices to accomplish wave switching is redundant. However, as technology evolves and topology of DWDM networks becomes more sophisticated, this function will become a necessary one.

11.4.1 Operating Principles

Nowadays the DWDM equipment allows transmission using one optical fiber of 32 or more waves of various lengths in the transparency window of 1,550 nm, each wave being capable of carrying information at a rate up to 10 Gbps (when using the protocols of STM or 10 Gigabit Ethernet for transmitting information at any wavelength). Research work in progress aims to increasing the information rate at each wavelength to between 40 Gbps and 80 Gbps.

The predecessor of DWDM was the **wave division multiplexing** (**WDM**) technology, which uses four spectral channels in transparency windows of 1,310 nm and 1,550 nm, with spacing between the 800 GHz and 400 GHz carriers. (Since there is no standard WDM classification, WDM systems with other characteristics can be encountered.)

DWDM multiplexing is called dense because it uses a significantly smaller distance between wavelengths than that used by WDM. Nowadays, the ITU-T G.692 recommendation defines two frequency (wavelength) grids (i.e., sets of frequencies separated from each other by some specific value):

■ Frequency grid with frequency spacing between adjacent channels of 100 GHz ($\Delta\lambda = 0.8$ nm), according to which 41 waves ranging from 1,528.77 nm (196.1 THz) to 1,560.61 nm (192.1 THz) are used

■ Frequency grid with a spacing of 50 GHz ($\Delta\lambda = 0.4$ nm), allowing transmission of 81 wavelengths in the same range

Some companies also manufacture equipment known as **high-dense WDM**, capable of operating with the frequency step of 25 GHz (for the moment, these are mainly experimental devices rather than batch productions).

The implementation of frequency grids with steps of 50 GHz and 25 GHz places stringent requirements to the DWDM equipment, especially when each wave transports

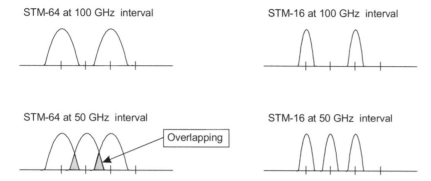

Figure 11.13 Spectrum overlapping of adjacent wavelengths for different frequency plans and data transmission rates

signals at a modulation rate of 10 Gbps or higher (STM-64, 10GE, or STM-256). Again, it is necessary to stress that DWDM technology (like WDM) is not directly involved in encoding of the information carried at each wavelength; this problem is solved by higher-layer technologies, which use the allocated wavelengths as needed for transmitting either analog or discrete information. These might be either SDH or 10 Gigabit Ethernet technologies.

Theoretically, the gaps of 50 GHz or even 25 GHz between adjacent wavelengths allow data to be transmitted at a rate of 10 Gbps. However, in this case, it is necessary to ensure a high precision of frequency and the minimum spectrum width. Furthermore, it is necessary to reduce the noise level to minimize the effect of spectrum overlapping (Figure 11.13).

11.4.2 Fiber Amplifiers

Practical success of the DWDM technology, whose equipment already operates as the backbones of most leading communications carriers, has in many respects determined the appearance of *fiber amplifiers*. These optical devices directly amplify the light signals in the range of 1,550 nm, thus eliminating the necessity of intermediate conversion of these signals into electric form, as is done by the regenerators used in SDH networks. Furthermore, the systems of electric signal regeneration are expensive and protocol dependent because they need to perceive a specific method of signal encoding. Optical amplifiers, which transmit the information "transparently," allow the backbone rate to be increased without upgrading the amplifying units.

The length of the section between two optical amplifying units can reach 150 km or more, which ensures the economic efficiency of the DWDM backbones, where the length of a multiplex section are 600–3,000 km provided that from one to seven intermediate optical amplifiers are used.

ITU-T G.692 defines three types of amplifying sections (i.e., sections between two neighboring DWDM multiplexes):

- **Long (L)** — The section comprises eight spans of fiber-optic communications links and seven optical amplifiers. The maximum distance between amplifiers is up to 80 km, having a total maximum length of the section of 640 km.

- **Very long (V)** — The section comprises no more than five spans of fiber-optic communications lines and four optical amplifiers. The maximum distance between amplifiers is up to 120 km, and the maximum section length is 600 km.

- **Ultralong (U)** — The section does not contain intermediate amplifiers and has a length of 160 km.

Limitations on the number of passive sections and their lengths are related to the degradation of optical signal in the course of optical amplification. Although the EDFA optical amplifier restores the signal power, it does not fully compensate the effect of chromatic dispersion[1] and other nonlinear effects. Because of this, for building long-distance backbones, it is necessary to install DWDM multiplexes between the amplification sections. These DWDM multiplexes regenerate the signal by transforming it to electric form and then back to optic. For a reduction of nonlinear effects, DWDM systems also imply a limitation on the signal power.

Optical amplifiers not only are used to increase the distance between multiplexes but also are used within multiplexes. Although multiplexing and cross-connections are carried out using exclusively optical tools, without transforming the signals into electric form, the signals lose power in the course of passive optical conversions, and they must be amplified before they are supplied into the line.

New research in the field of optical amplifiers has resulted in the appearance of amplifiers operating in the so-called L-range (the fourth transparency window) from 1,570 nm to 1,605 nm. The use of this range, as well as the reduction of the spacing between wavelengths to 50 GHz and 25 GHz, allows the number of simultaneously transmitted wavelengths to be increased to 80 or more. This means that it becomes possible to ensure traffic transmission at the rates of 800 Gbps — 1.6 Tbps in one direction through a single optical fiber.

DWDM success has resulted in the appearance of another promising technological area — **all-optical networks**. In such networks, all operations related to multiplexing/demultiplexing, add/drop, and cross-switching/routing user information are carried out without transforming the optical signal into electric form. The elimination of signal transformations into electric forms ensures the possibility of significantly reducing the network costs. Unfortunately, today's level of optical technologies is insufficient for creating large-scale, all-optical networks. Therefore, practical use of such networks is limited by all-optical segments between which the signal is electrically regenerated.

---

[1] Chromatic dispersion occurs due to the difference of propagation speeds of the lightwaves having different lengths. Because of this the signal at the receiving side of the fiber gets "smeared."

11.4.3 Typical Topologies

Chronologically, the first area of DWDM application (similar to SDH) became the creation of ultralong-distance, high-speed backbones having the **point-to-point chain** topology (Figure 11.14).

For organizing such a backbone, it is sufficient to install terminal DWDM multiplexes in its terminal points. In transit points, optical amplifiers must be installed if the distance between terminal points exceeds the distance limitations.

A terminal multiplexer includes:

- Multiplexing/demultiplexing unit
- Input amplifier, or booster (B)
- Preamplifier (P)
- Set of transponders (T)

Transponders convert the input signals from the sources whose wavelengths do not correspond to the frequency grid of the multiplexer as waves of the required length. When the device connected to the DWDM network is capable of producing the signal at one of the wavelengths supported by the DWDM multiplexer (according to the ITU-T G.692 frequency grid or to the frequency grid of a specific manufacturer), transponders are not used. In this case, the device connected to a DWDM network is said to have a *colored* interface.

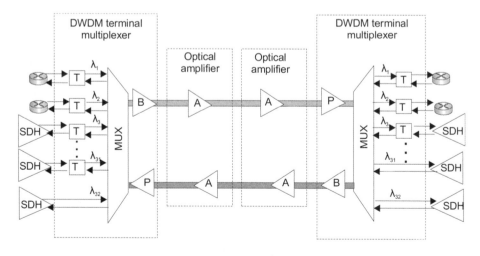

Computer network equipment (router, switch)

Figure 11.14 Ultralong-distance point-to-point backbone based on DWDM terminal multiplexers

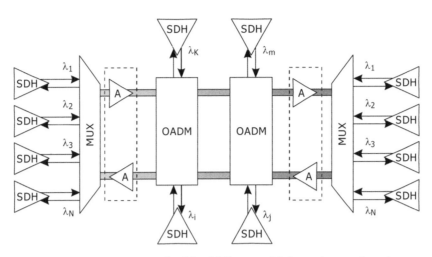

Figure 11.15 DWDM network with add/drop multiplexers in transit nodes

In the method provided previously, duplex exchange between network users takes place at the expense of unidirectional transmission of the entire set of waves through two fibers. There is another variant of DWDM network operation, when only one fiber is used for communications between nodes. Duplex mode in this case is ensured by bidirectional signal transmission using the fiber — half of the waves of the frequency plan transmit information in one direction, and the other half of the waves is used for data transmission in the opposite direction.

Network with intermediate connections. The network in which transit nodes carry out functions of add/drop multiplexers is a natural development of the previous topology (Figure 11.15).

Optical add/drop multiplexers. OADM can separate (drop) a wave of a specific length from the aggregate optical signal and add there a signal of the same wavelength, so the spectrum of transit signal won't change and the connection would be established to one of the subscribers connected to a transit multiplexer. OADM can add or drop either by optical methods or by converting the signal into an electric form. Usually, fully optical (passive) add/drop multiplexers can drop a small number of waves. This is because every drop operation requires the optical signal to pass through optical filter, which adds attenuation. If the multiplexer uses electric regeneration of the signal, then it is possible to drop any number of waves within the limits of available wavelength set, since the transit optic signal was fully demultiplexed previously.

Ring. The ring topology (Figure 11.16) ensures the survival of the DWDM network because of the presence of reserve paths. Methods of traffic protection used in DWDM are similar to SDH methods (although in DWDM they are not standardized yet). To protect a specific connection, two paths are established between its endpoints — the main one and protection one. The multiplexer of the endpoint compares two signals and chooses the signal of better quality (or the default signal).

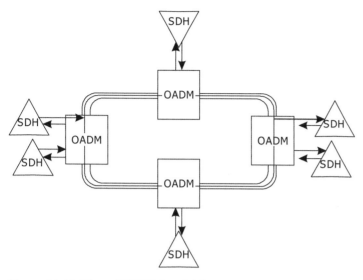

Figure 11.16 Ring of DWDM multiplexers

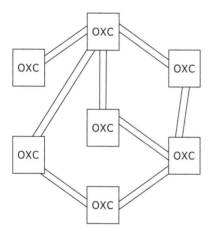

Figure 11.17 Mesh topology of the DWDM network

Mesh topology. With the evolution of DWDM networks, the mesh topology (Figure 11.17) will be used in their design more frequently, because it ensures higher flexibility, performance, and fault tolerance than other topologies. However, for implementing mesh topology, it is necessary to employ **optical cross-connects** (OXC). OXCs not only add and drop waves to and from the aggregate transit signal, as add/drop multiplexers do, but also support arbitrary switching between optical signals transmitted by the waves of different lengths.

11.4.4 Optical Add/Drop Multiplexers

An optical multiplexer multiplexes several wavelengths in a common aggregate signal and drops the waves of different lengths from the aggregate signal.

For wave dropping, the multiplexer can use various optical mechanisms. In optical multiplexers supporting relatively small number of wavelengths, usually from 16 to 32, **thin-film filters** are used. They comprise the plates with multilayer coating. In practice, the ends of optical fibers skewed at an angle between 30 and 45 degrees and covered with several layers of coating are used as thin-film filters. For systems with larger numbers of wavelengths, other filtering and multiplexing methods are required.

In DWDM multiplexes, integral **diffraction phase gratings**, or **Arrayed Waveguide Gratings (AWG)** are used. The functions of slabs are carried out by optical waveguides or fibers. The incoming multiplexed signal is supplied to the input port (Figure 11.18, *a*). Then, this signal passes through the slab waveguide and is distributed over a set of waveguides representing the diffraction AWG structure. The signal in each waveguide remains the multiplexed signal, and each channel (λ_1, λ_2, ..., λ_N) remains present in all waveguides. Further on, the signals are reflected from the mirror plate, and, finally, the light beams are again concentrated in the slab waveguide. Here, they are focused, and interference takes place. As a result, the interference maximums appear, which are distributed in space. These intensity maximums correspond to different channels. The geometry of the slab waveguide — in particular, the positions of output poles and the values of the lengths of the AWG waveguides — are calculated to make interference maximums coincide with the output poles. Multiplexing is accomplished in the inverse way.

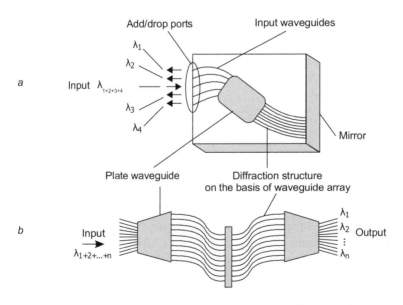

Figure 11.18 Full demultiplexing of the signal using diffraction phase grating

Another method of building the multiplexer is based on the pair of slab waveguides (Figure 11.18, *b*). The operating principle of such a device is similar to the previous case except for the additional plate used for focusing and interference.

Integral AWG gratings (also known as phasers) became one of the key elements of the DWDM multiplexes. Usually, they are employed for full demultiplexing of the light signal, since they can be successfully scaled and are potentially capable of successfully operating in the systems with hundreds of spectral channels.

11.4.5 Optical Cross-Connects

In networks with mesh topology, it is necessary to ensure flexible capabilities of changing the route of wave connections between network subscribers. Such capabilities are ensured by OXCs, allowing any of the waves of the input signal of any port to be directed to any of the output ports (provided that no other signal of this port uses this wave; otherwise, it will be necessary to translate the wavelength).

OXCs fall into the following two categories:

■ OXCs with intermediate conversion of the signal into electric form
■ Fully optical OXCs

Optoelectronic cross-connects were the first to appear, and they were commonly named OXCs. Therefore, the manufacturers of fully optical devices of this type try to use different names for their products, such as **photonic switches**, **wave routers**, or **lambda routers**. OXCs have a principal limitation — they do their job well when operating at rates up to 2.5 Gbps; however, starting from the rate of 10 Gbps, the sizes of such devices and their energy consumption exceed all limits. Photonic switches are free from such a limitation.

In photonic switches, various optical mechanisms are used, including diffraction phase gratings and **micro-electro mechanical systems (MEMS)**.

MEMS is the set of tiny moving mirrors, no more than 1 mm in diameter (Figure 11.19). The MEMS switch is used after the demultiplexer, when the source signal

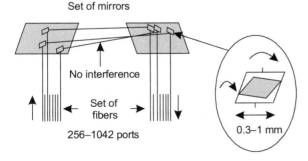

Figure 11.19 MEMS for cross-switching

is already divided into component waves. By turning the small mirror a specified angle, the source beam of the specific wavelength is directed to the corresponding output fiber. Then, all rays are multiplexed into the aggregate output signal.

In comparison to OXCs, photonic switches are approximately 30 times smaller and consume approximately 100 times less energy. However, this type of device has drawbacks, the most important ones being slow response and sensitivity to vibration. Nevertheless, MEMS are widely used in new models of photonic switches. Nowadays, such devices are capable of ensuring switching for 256×256 spectral channels, and the release of devices enabling switching 1024×1024 or higher is expected soon.

11.5 CASE STUDY

This case study describes the transmission network of a large energetic company, ABC-Power. Although this is an assumed name, as in all case studies provided in this book, these case studies are based on real-world projects and systems.

The ABC-Power company supplies electricity to a large region covering hundreds of square kilometers. The company includes several large power stations generating energy, as well as a distribution network used to supply energy to clients — large companies and individual customers.

ABC-Power objects, power stations and distribution stations, are dispersed over 50 cities and settlements of the region. The power circuit is controlled using a three-level hierarchical control system: the first level is the central management node, the second level holds the regional control nodes, and third level consists of power stations and distribution stations. ABC-Power uses various tools for managing the processes of producing and distributing energy, including:

■ Telemetry and automatic control systems for controlling various technological objects (power and distribution stations). These systems are made of sensors supplying online information about the state of power modules and actuating mechanisms that control them, performing operations such as power redistribution from one part of the distribution network to another. Telemetry data are transmitted among objects in the real-time mode. These data are also supplied to the central board used by the supervisors of the central and regional offices.

■ Specialized dispatches communications. This is a voice communications system similar to a telephone network, complemented with numerous supplementary functions that help dispatches to solve the arising problems in a coordinated manner.

■ Private telephone network based on PBX. This network supplements the capabilities of the dispatcher communications system and has a connection to the national telephone network.

■ Custom, automated computer system for managing company resources.

Each of the listed systems comprises subsystems located in all 50 points of presence of ABC-Power. Obviously, a high-quality telecommunications network is required to ensure stable operation of the control and management systems, which would connect all ABC-Power points of presence by reliable and high-speed links.

Over a long period, ABC-Power leased communications links of rates from 64 Kbps to 2 Mbps from the regional communications carrier. These links were used for connecting PBX and routers/switches of LANs. Telemetric and automatic control systems partially used the copper links owned by ABC-Power. These links were installed along power transmission lines to objects located beyond the zone serviced by the regional communications carrier.

Further development of the ABC-Power business required the use of the most advanced methods of management, including the installation of new digital PBXs capable of combining the functions of dispatcher communications and traditional telephony, the deployment of a powerful integrated SAP R/3 management system instead of isolated departmental management systems, and the improvement of the telemetry and automatic control systems.

Such modernization of management tools required upgrading of the communications links, including reliability improvement and bandwidth increase.

An analysis of possible variants of upgrading the infrastructure of communications links showed that leasing high-speed links ensuring rates from 34 Mbps to 155 Mbps was economically inefficient. As a result, ABC-Power decided to create its own transmission network using the advantages of the existing network of power transmission lines. This method was chosen by many railway, power, and oil and gas companies. Installation of optical fiber along the existing railways or gas pipeline does not require significant expense and usually is characterized by fast return on investment.

The transmission network of ABC-Power was built within two years. Fiber-optic cable connected SDH multiplexes in all 50 points of presence of the company (Figure 11.20).

This transmission network has mesh topology, which allows the company to apply the path protection methods of the SDH technology and ensure high reliability. Three types of multiplexes are used in the network: M4, M1, and MA. M4 multiplexes are add/drop multiplexes of the STM-4 level — that is, their aggregate ports operate at the STM-4 rate (622 Mbps). These multiplexes form the backbone ring that connects large regional control nodes as well as the central control node. M4 multiplexes tolerate the replacement of the STM-4 aggregate ports with STM-16 aggregate ports (2.5 Gbps), which operate at one of the waves of the DWDM frequency plan. This ensures the possibility of further increase of the network backbone rate without the need of replacing the equipment, including the possibility of connecting the SDH network to the DWDM backbone.

The transmission access network is based on M1 and MA multiplexes (STM-1 155 Mbps aggregate ports). It spans all power stations and smaller regional control nodes. The access network combines mesh topology with tree topology, ensuring redundancy only for the most critical routes. MA multiplexes are distinguished by numerous PDH ports for connecting the equipment of overlay networks, such as telephone, computer, and telemetric or control networks (Figure 11.21).

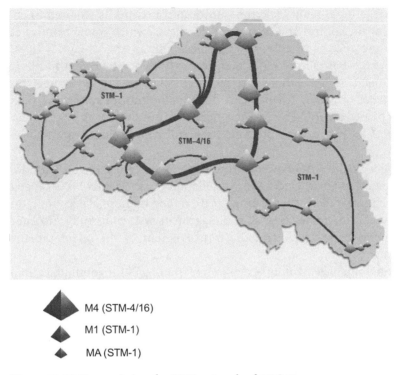

Figure 11.20 Transmission the SDH network of ABC-Power

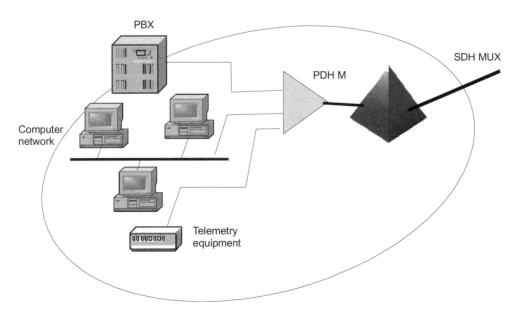

Figure 11.21 Connecting equipment to the SDH network

The creation of the private SDH network allowed ABC-Power to be on the safe side when ensuring the needs of the company in high-speed communications links. The company plans to use the spare links in commercial activity as an ISP.

SUMMARY

▶ Transmission networks are intended for creating switched infrastructure, using which it is possible to quickly and flexibly create persistent channels organizing an arbitrary topology.

▶ Transmission networks use various types of the circuit-switching technique, using frequency division multiplexing (FDM), time division multiplexing, or wave/dense wave division multiplexing (WDM/DWDM).

▶ In FDM networks, each local loop is allocated the frequency band with the width of 4 kHz. There is a hierarchy of FDM channels, where 12 local loops make up the first-level channels (the base group) with a frequency of 48 kHz. Five channels of the first level are joined into the second-level channel (the supergroup) with a frequency band of 240 kHz. Ten second-level channels make up the channel of the third hierarchical layer (the main group) with a frequency band of 2.4 MHz.

▶ Digital transmission networks (PDH) allow the creation of channels with a throughput ranging from 64 Kbps to 140 Mbps, providing their subscribers with four levels of rate hierarchy.

▶ The drawback of PDH networks is the impossibility of direct separation of the data of the low-rate channel from that the high-speed channel, as these channels operate at nonadjacent levels of rate hierarchy.

▶ The asynchronous mode of adding subscriber streams into the SDH frame is ensured by the concept of virtual containers and the system of floating pointers that mark the starting point of the user data in the virtual container.

▶ SDH multiplexes can operate in networks with different topologies, including chain, ring, and mesh topologies. There are several special types of multiplexers that take a specific place in the network: terminal multiplexers, add/drop multiplexers, and cross-connects (OXCs).

▶ In SDH networks, many supported fault-tolerance mechanisms protect data traffic at the level of specific blocks, ports, or connections: EPS, card protection, MSP, SNC-P, or MS-SPRing. The most efficient method of protection is chosen depending on the logical topology of connections in the network.

▶ The WDM/DWDM technique of multiplexing implements the principles of frequency multiplexing for the signals of another physical nature and at another level of the speed hierarchy. Each WDM/DWDM channel is a specific range of light waves, allowing it to carry data in analog or digital form. At the same time, the bandwidth of the channel is 25–50–100 GHz, ensuring rates of several gigabits per second (when transmitting discrete data).

▶ In early WDM systems, a small number of spectral channels was used, from 2 to 16. In DWDM systems, 32 to 160 channels are used on a single optic fiber, which ensures data rates up to several terabits per second for a single fiber.

▶ Contemporary fiber amplifiers allow the optical section of the connection link to be extended to 700–1,000 km without changing the signal into an electric form.

▶ To separate several channels from the aggregate light signal, relatively inexpensive devices are usually combined with optical amplifiers to organize add/drop multiplexers in long-distance networks.

▶ For interaction with traditional optical networks (SDH, Gigabit Ethernet, and 10 Gigabit Ethernet), DWDM networks use transponders and wavelength translators, which transform the wavelength of the input signal into one of the wavelengths of the standard frequency plan of DWDM.

▶ In fully optical networks, all multiplexing and switching operations are carried out over light signals without changing the signal into an electric form. This simplifies the network and reduces its price.

REVIEW QUESTIONS

1. Which drawbacks of FDM transmission networks have resulted in the creation of digital transmission networks?

2. The T-1 name means:
   A. Multiplexing equipment developed by AT&T
   B. Rate level of 1.544 Mbps
   C. International standard for a communications link
   D. Method of multiplexing 64 Kbps digital flows

3. What functions are delegated to the least significant bit of each byte in the T-1 channel when transmitting voice?

4. Is it possible to separate the DS-0 channel directly from the DS-3 channel in a PDH network?

5. What methods are used in practice for solving the previous problem?

6. What mechanisms are implemented in the E-1 channel to replace the bit robbing of the T-1 channel?

7. Why do transmission networks ensure high quality of service for all kinds of traffic?

8. What property of the PDH technology is reflected by the term "plesiochronous"?

9. How does the SDH technology compensate for the lack of synchronism in tributary streams?

10. What is the maximum number of E-1 channels that can be multiplexed by the STM-1 frame?

11. How many T-1 channels can be multiplexed by the STM-1 frame, provided that it already contains 15 E-1 channels?

12. Which layers of the SDH protocol stack are responsible for network reconfiguration in the case of equipment failure?

13. What is the maximum rate of the data communication channel between SDH regenerators?

14. Why does the STM-1 frame use three pointers?

15. What is the purpose of using an interleaving byte in PDH and SDH technologies?

16. What is the difference between 1+1 and 1:1 protection methods?

17. Under what conditions is MS-SPRing more efficient than SNC-P?

18. What are the common features between FDM and DWDM transmission networks?

19. What type of networks are DWDM networks — analog or digital?

20. What is the goal of using regenerators that transform an optical signal to an electric one in DWDM networks?

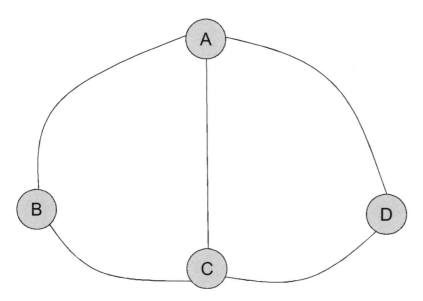

Figure 11.22 Traffic distribution

21. What are the reasons for optical signal deterioration when passing many passive DWDM sections?

22. What principles of switching of light signals are used in OXCs?

PROBLEMS

1. What will be the frequency of negative alignment of the pointer of VC-4 in the STM-1 frame if the relative difference between the clock frequencies of transmitting and those of receiving SDH multiplexers is 10^{-5}?

2. The SDH network comprises four STM-4 multiplexers: A, B, C, and D. Figure 11.22 shows the traffic distribution among multiplexers. All flows have a rate of STM-1. Multiplexers are joined into the STM-4 ring. Which protection method should be chosen to protect all connections?

PART III

LOCAL AREA NETWORKS

LANs are an integral part of any contemporary computer network. If you look at the structure of any WAN, such as the Internet or simply a large-scale, enterprise-wide network, you will notice that practically all of that network's information resources are concentrated within LANs; the WAN simply is the transport connecting numerous LANs.

One of the most important goals of a LAN is to connect computers within a building or group of buildings located short distances apart to provide network users with access to the information services of local servers. LANs also provide a convenient method of grouping computers to connect them to a WAN, since for a WAN, it is much easier to forward data among networks than among individual computers. Wireless LANs serving airports or railway stations are a good example: As a rule, such networks are not intended for ensuring information exchange among temporary users. On the contrary, their main aim is to provide users with Internet access. It should be emphasized that in these cases, Internet access is organized for the entire LAN rather than for individual users. LANs are also used in other telecommunications networks, such as telephone and transmission networks. For example, systems managing telephone switches or transmission networks are usually built on the basis of a LAN, which connects computers of network operators, thus guaranteeing them access to control devices built into the telecommunications network's equipment.

LAN technologies have come a long way in their evolution. Practically all technologies in the 1980s used *shared media* as a convenient and economical means of joining computers at the physical layer. Basic principles of media sharing were explained in *Chapter 2*. In this part of the book, we return to the problem to consider it in more detail at the level of standards and specific algorithms.

In the mid-1990s, LANs began to employ *switched versions* of technologies. Abandoning the use of shared media helped to improve the performance and scalability of LANs. Switched LANs use the same protocols as shared media LANs but in full duplex mode. Another advantage of switched LANs is their various methods of ensuring quality of service (QoS); this is especially important when a LAN transmits real-time traffic, such as IP telephony traffic.

Despite the popularity of switched LANs, shared media are still often used in both traditional and new technologies. They are efficient in small segments of wired LANs as well as in wireless LANs, where the medium is shared by nature.

LANs are not only seeing changes in media use: The maximum information transfer rate of LAN protocols is also increasing. With the adoption of the 10G Ethernet standard in 2002, LAN standards began to support a rate hierarchy that keeps pace with that of transmission networks: from 10 Mbps to 10 Gbps. This makes it possible to build MANs, as well as LANs, on the basis of these technologies.

The evolution of LANs is also tending toward miniaturization. A new type of network, the *personal area network* has appeared: A network of this type connects a single user's electronic devices inside a range of a few hundred meters.

Contemporary LANs exist under conditions dominated by one network technology, or to be more precise, by an entire family of network technologies: Ethernet. Naturally, this family of technologies receives significantly more attention in this book than other technologies. Part III comprises the following chapters:

- *Chapter 12 (Ethernet Technology)* covers the classic Ethernet 10 Mbps technology based on shared media.
- *Chapter 13 (High-Speed Ethernet)* considers high-speed Ethernet technologies based on shared media: Fast Ethernet and Gigabit Ethernet.
- *Chapter 14 (Shared Media LANs)* describes other LAN technologies based on shared media (Token Ring and FDDI) and two wireless technologies: IEEE 802.11 and Bluetooth.

The final two chapters concentrate on switched LANs.

- *Chapter 15 (Switched LANs)* covers the basics of switched LAN operation: the working algorithm of LAN switching, full-duplex versions of LAN protocols, and specific implementation features of LAN switches.
- *Chapter 16 (Advanced Features of Switched LANs)* covers advanced properties of LANs of this type, including redundant links on the basis of the spanning tree algorithm, link aggregation, and VLAN technique.

12

ETHERNET

12.1 INTRODUCTION

Ethernet is currently the most common LAN standard: The total number of networks using the Ethernet protocol is estimated at several millions.

The term Ethernet usually means a variant of the technology; variants include Fast Ethernet, Gigabit Ethernet, and 10G Ethernet.

In a narrower sense, *Ethernet* is a network standard for data transmission at the rate of 10 Mbps that appeared in the late 1970s as a proprietary standard of three companies: Digital Equipment Corp. (DEC), Intel, and Xerox. In the early 1980s, Ethernet was standardized by the IEEE 802.3 workgroup, and since then, it has become an international standard. Ethernet was the first technology to suggest the use of a shared medium for network access.

Being packet-switched networks, LANs employ the time division multiplexing principle, which means that they share the transmission medium in time. The medium-sharing algorithm, media access control (MAC), is one of the most important characteristics of any LAN technology, because it has significantly more influence on the type of technology than the method of signal encoding or frame format. Ethernet uses the random access method as the medium-sharing mechanism: Although it is far from perfect, since effective network bandwidth drops sharply as network load increases, the main reason for Ethernet's success was its simplicity.

The popularity of 10 Mbps Ethernet served as a powerful incentive for its development: The Fast Ethernet standard was adopted in 1995, the Gigabit Ethernet standard appeared in 1998, and 10G Ethernet arrived in 2002. Each of the newer standards was ten times faster than its predecessor, creating an impressive rate hierarchy:

10 Mbps – 100 Mbps – 1,000 Mbps – 10,000 Mbps.

In this chapter, we cover in detail the classical Ethernet 10 Mbps technology, most principles of which are employed at higher transmission rates.

12.2 GENERAL CHARACTERISTIC OF LAN PROTOCOLS

KEY WORDS: shared data transmission media, standard topologies of physical connections, LAN protocol stack, Logical Link Control (LLC), Media Access Control (MAC), random access, deterministic access, collision, polling algorithm, arbitrator, demultiplexing, multiplexing, destination service access point (DSAP), source service access point (SSAP), LLC1, LLC2, LLC3, IEEE 802.x standards, half-duplex datagram transmission mode

Ethernet belongs to the entire family of LAN technologies, which also includes Token Ring, FDDI, IEEE 802.11, and 100VG-AnyLAN.[1] Despite some specific features, all these technologies have the same goal: building LANs. Therefore, it makes sense to start with studying Ethernet and to look at the general principles used in the development of LAN technologies.

12.2.1 Standard Topology and Shared Media

The main goal that the developers of the first LANs had to achieve in the late 1970s was to find a simple and inexpensive solution to join hundreds of computers located within the same building into a computer network. The solution had to be inexpensive, since the network was meant to connect inexpensive minicomputers (as compared to mainframes), which had appeared and quickly become widespread (they cost $10,000–$20,000 each). The number of such computers in a single organization was small; therefore, an upper limit of a few hundred computers seemed enough for practically any LAN. The problem of joining LANs into WANs was not a priority at the time, so practically all LAN technologies ignored it.

> For simplicity and, consequently, the reduction of both hardware and software costs, the developers of the first LANs decided to use **shared data transmission media**.

This method of organizing intercomputer communications was first tested with the ALOHA radio network at the University of Hawaii under Norman Abramson in the early 1970s. A radio channel of a specific frequency band naturally is a shared medium for all transmitters that use frequencies from this band for data encoding. The ALOHA network used the random access method, according to which any node could start the transmission of a packet at any time. If the node did not receive acknowledgment before a certain time-out, it retransmitted the packet. The shared medium was a radio channel with a carrier frequency of 400 MHz and bandwidth of 40 KHz, ensuring a data transmission rate of 9,600 bps.

Some time later, *Robert Metcalfe* implemented the idea of a shared medium for wired LAN: A continuous segment of coaxial cable became the analog of the common radio medium. All computers were connected to this segment according to the wired OR design (Figure 12.1). For this reason, when one transmitter sent signals, all receivers received the same signal, as with the use of radio waves.

In Token Ring and FDDI, the fact that all computers use the shared medium is not as pronounced as with Ethernet. The networks are based on a physical ring topology in which each node is connected by the cable to the two neighboring nodes (Figure 12.2). Nevertheless, these sections of cable are also shared, since at any moment, only one computer can use the ring to transmit packets.

---

[1] The 100VG-AnyLAN technology is practically out of use nowadays. However, the original concept of medium sharing implemented in it is of theoretical interest.

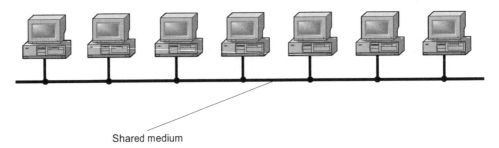

Figure 12.1 Shared medium on the basis of coaxial cable

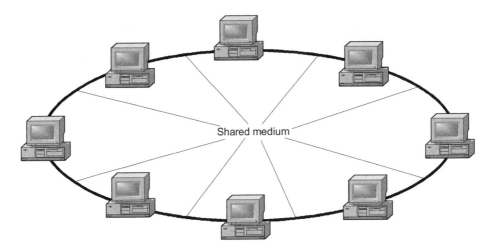

Figure 12.2 Shared medium in ring topologies

Simple **standard topologies of physical connections** (star in coaxial Ethernet and ring in Token Ring and FDDI) ensure the ease of using cable as a shared medium.

The use of shared media *simplifies* the operating logic of network nodes. Since only one operation of data transmission is in progress at a time, there is no need to buffer frames in transit nodes. Also, there are no transit nodes (this unusual variant of a packet-switched network was considered in *Chapter 2*). Consequently, the need for complicated flow management and congestion control procedures is also eliminated.

The main drawback of the shared medium is *poor scalability*. This drawback is important because the bandwidth of this medium is divided among all network nodes regardless of the method of medium access in use. In this case, the result obtained using the queuing theory described in *Chapter 7* is applicable: As soon as the utilization coefficient of the shared medium exceeds a certain threshold, the queues for accessing the medium start to grow nonlinearly. As a result, the network becomes practically unusable. The threshold value of the utilization coefficient depends on the access method used. For example, in ALOHA networks, this value was exceedingly low (about 18%). In Ethernet, this value is higher (about 30%), and in Token Ring and FDDI networks, it reaches 60% – 70%.

12.2.2 LAN Protocol Stack

As a rule, LAN technologies implement only the functions of the two lowest layers of the OSI model — that is, the *physical* and *data link* layers (Figure 12.3); this is because the functionality of these two layers is sufficient for frame delivery within the framework of standard LAN topologies: star (common bus), ring, and tree.

However, this does not mean that computers connected by a LAN do not support the protocols of layers higher than data link. These protocols are also installed and operate on LAN nodes. However, their functions *do not relate to specific LAN technologies.* Network and transport-layer protocols are needed for LAN nodes to communicate with computers connected to other LANs, the path to which might include WAN links. If it were necessary to ensure computer interoperations only within the limits of a single LAN, then application-layer protocols could operate directly over the data link layer. However, since such limited communications capabilities do not satisfy users, each computer connected to a LAN has to support the entire protocol stack. Therefore, one of the network-layer protocols (e.g., IP or IPX) operates over the logical link control (LLC) layer. Furthermore, the entire protocol stack, not just the physical and data link protocols, has to be installed on the LAN end-nodes to ensure application compatibility. Applications must run correctly in any network environment (or at least, their operation must not depend on the network size, be it a small single-segment LAN or a large-scale routed network).

The data link layer in LANs is divided into two sublayers, often also called layers:

■ Logical link control (LLC)
■ Media access control (MAC)

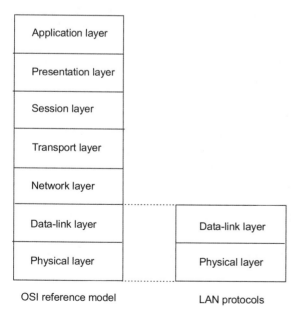

Figure 12.3 Correspondence of LAN protocols to the OSI model layers

LLC functions are usually implemented by an appropriate software module of the operating system, and MAC functions are implemented both by hardware (network adapter) and software (network adapter driver).

MAC Layer

Main functions of the MAC layer are:

■ Ensuring access to the shared medium

■ Transmitting frames between end nodes using functionality of the physical-layer devices

> **Random access** is one of the main algorithms used for accessing the shared medium. Its idea is that a node with a frame to transmit tries to send it without coordinating the use of the shared medium with other network nodes.

Random access methods are *decentralized*, since they do not require a special node playing the role of an arbitrator to be present in the network. Consequently, the random access method is characterized by the high probability of collisions. A **collision** is a simultaneous attempt at frame transmission by several stations[2]. As a result of a collision, signals from several transmitters overlap, and information in all frames transmitted during the collision period becomes distorted. Since LANs implement fairly simple methods of signal encoding, they do not allow the required signal to be distinguished from the aggregate one, in contrast to CDMA, for example, which is capable of doing so.

There are lots of random access algorithms that reduce the probability of collisions, thus improving network performance. For example, one class of algorithms allows a node to start frame transmission only at the starting of a specific time interval, usually called a slot. This improvement was first suggested for ALOHA, and the modified version of this algorithm became known as slotted ALOHA. *Synchronizing frame transmission* with the starting moments of the slots has halved the collision probability in slotted ALOHA, thus ensuring normal operation of the network at a medium utilization coefficient of up to 36%.

Introducing a *carrier sensing procedure* before starting transmission is another way to improve random access. Nodes are not allowed to transmit a frame if they detect that the medium is busy with transmission of another frame. This reduces the probability of collision, although it does not eliminate collisions entirely.

Random access algorithms do not guarantee that a specific node will gain access to the shared medium within a specific time interval. No matter how large the chosen time value, the probability that the real waiting interval will exceed it is always greater than zero. Also, random access algorithms do not provide any capabilities for differentiated quality of service (QoS) support for different kinds of traffic. In any case, all frames have equal levels of access to the medium.

---

[2] The terms *station* and *node* are used in this book as synonyms.

Deterministic access is another popular method of accessing shared media. It acquired its name because the maximum waiting time required for access to the medium is always known beforehand.

Deterministic access algorithms use two mechanisms: token passing and polling.

Token passing is usually implemented on the basis of a *decentralized* approach. Each computer receiving a token has the right to use the shared medium during a fixed period of time: a *token-holding interval*. The computer transmits its frames during this time, and after it elapses, the computer has to pass the token to another computer. Thus, if the number of computers in the network is known, the maximum waiting time is equal to the token-holding interval multiplied by the number of computers in the network. The actual waiting time may be shorter, because if the computer that gets the token has no frames for transmission, it passes the token without waiting for the holding interval to elapse.

The sequence of passing the token from computer to computer can be defined using different methods. In Token Ring and FDDI networks, it is defined by the links topology. A computer in a ring network has two neighbors: *upstream* and *downstream*. It receives the token from the upstream neighbor and passes it to the downstream neighbor. The algorithm for passing the token can be implemented in networks with nonring topologies. For example, the outdated *Arcnet*, which has fallen out of use, employed shared coaxial cable (like Ethernet) for physically connecting computers, and token passing was used to access the medium. The token was passed from computer to computer according to a predefined sequence that did not depend on the locations at which computers were connected to the cable.

Polling algorithms are most frequently based on the *centralized* method. In this case, there is a dedicated node in the network that plays the role of the *arbitrator* of the shared medium.

The arbitrator periodically polls other network nodes, asking if they have frames for transmission. Having collected the claims, the arbitrator then decides to which node it will grant access to the shared medium. After that, it informs the chosen node of this, and the node transmits its frame to the shared medium. After frame transmission is accomplished, the polling phase is repeated.

A polling algorithm can also be based on the *decentralized* method. In this case, all nodes must inform each other of their frame transmission needs beforehand, using the shared medium. Then, according to specific criteria, each node, independent of other nodes, determines its position in the queue for frame transmission. After that, the node transmits its frame when its turn comes.

Deterministic access algorithms differ from random access algorithms in that they operate more efficiently under conditions of high network load, when the utilization coefficient becomes close to one. On the other hand, random access algorithms are more efficient when network load is low. This is because they allow frames to be transmitted immediately, without spending time determining if the node has the right to access the medium.

The advantage of deterministic medium access methods is their capability to prioritize traffic. Because of this capability, such methods can ensure QoS support.

Frame delivery is carried out by the MAC layer. It comprises several stages, which, in general case, do not depend on the chosen access method.

■ *Frame formatting*. At this stage, frame fields are filled with the information obtained from the higher-layer protocol. This information includes source and destination addresses, user data, and the code of the higher-layer protocol that sends this data. When the frame has been created, MAC layer computes its checksum and places it into its corresponding field.

■ *Frame transmission into the medium*. After the frame has been created, and when the node gets access to the shared medium, MAC layer passes the frame to the physical layer, which transmits all its fields into the transmission medium, byte by byte. It is the transmitter of the network adapter that carries out the physical-layer functions. The transmitter converts all bytes of the frame into the sequence of bits, encodes them using appropriate electric or optical signals, and then transmits them into the medium. After the signals pass over the transmission medium, they arrive at the receivers of network adapters connected to the shared medium. Receivers then carry out an inverse procedure by converting the signals to the frame bytes.

■ *Frame reception*. MAC layer of every network node connected to the shared medium checks the destination address of the frame just delivered. If this address matches the address of the receiver, then MAC layer of the destination node continues its processing, otherwise the frame is discarded. Further processing consists in the check of the frame CRC. If the CRC of the received frame is correct, then MAC layer passes it to the higher layer of the protocol stack. If the frame CRC is invalid, this means that the information got corrupted in the course of transmission, and such a frame must be discarded.

On the basis of this description, it is clear that Ethernet implements **half-duplex datagram transmission** mode.

LLC Layer

The LLC layer carries out the following two functions:

■ Organizing an interface to the network layer, which is directly adjacent to it
■ Ensuring reliable frame delivery with the predefined reliability level.

The *LLC layer's interface functions* include the transmission of user and control data between the MAC layer and the network layer. When transmitting data *from top to bottom*, the LLC layer receives a packet (e.g., an IP or IPX packet) that contains user data. Besides the packet, the network layer also transmits the destination node address in the appropriate LAN format. This address will be used to deliver the packet within the LAN. In terms of the TCP/IP stack, this sort of address is known as a hardware address. The LLC layer transmits the data received from the network layer downward to the MAC layer for execution. Besides this, the LLC layer also carries out *multiplexing*, since the data

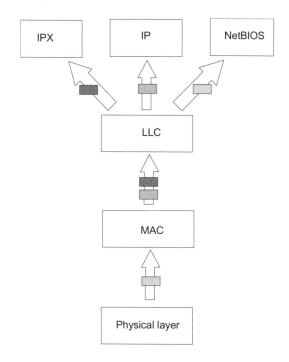

Figure 12.4 Demultiplexing of frames by the LLC protocol

Destination service access point (DSAP)	Source service access point (SSAP)	Control field	Data

Figure 12.5 LLC frame format

received from several network-layer protocols are transmitted to a single MAC-layer-protocol.

When transmitting data *from bottom to top*, the LLC layer receives user data (e.g., a network-layer packet received from the network) from the MAC layer. Then it has to accomplish an additional interface function, namely, to decide to which network protocol it should pass the data it has received. This is a *demultiplexing* task, since the aggregate data flow arriving from the MAC layer must be divided into several subflows, according to the number of network protocols supported by the computer (Figure 12.4).

Multiplexing and demultiplexing tasks are characteristic not only of the LLC protocol but also of any other protocol above which several higher-layer protocols can operate. The LLC protocol uses special fields in its header for data demultiplexing (Figure 12.5). The **destination service access point** (**DSAP**) field is used for storing the code of the protocol to which the data (e.g., the contents of the *Data* field) are sent. Accordingly, the **source service access point** (**SSAP**) field is used for specifying the code of the protocol, from which the data are sent. Using two fields for demultiplexing is not typical: Protocols can usually manage with a single field. For example, IP usually sends its packets to IP, and IPX to IPX. Two fields are useful when a higher-layer protocol supports several operating modes so that the protocol at the sending node can use different values of DSAP and SSAP for notifying the receiving node of the switch to another mode of operation. The NetBEUI protocol frequently makes use of this LLC property.

Consider the second function of the LLC layer: *ensuring reliable frame delivery.* The LLC protocol supports several modes of operation that differ in the availability or lack of frame recovery procedures in cases of frame loss or corruption. This means that these operating modes differ in the quality of the transport services that they provide. The LLC layer, directly adjacent to the network layer, receives requests from the network layer to carry out transport operations of the data link layer characterized by a specific quality.

NOTE   *Obviously, LLC functions for ensuring reliable data transmission in a LAN bear resemblance to the functions of the transport layer of the OSI model, although the LLC is not directly involved in frame delivery among network nodes (as defined for the transport protocol). The job of frame delivery is delegated to the MAC layer after it gains access to the shared medium. However, the MAC layer carries out delivery in the datagram mode, which means that it does not establish a logical connection and does not restore lost or corrupted frames. If upper-layer protocols require a reliable transport service, they have to request it from the LLC. In this case, the LLC establishes a connection to the destination node and organizes frame retransmission.*

The LLC layer provides three types of transport services to the higher layers:

■ *LLC1* — connectionless service without delivery acknowledgment. **LLC1** provides the user with data transmission tools characterized by minimum overheads. In this case, LLC supports the datagram operating mode, similar to the MAC, so that the entire LAN technology operates in the datagram mode. This procedure is used when data restoration after errors and data ordering are carried out by higher-layer protocols and therefore do not need to be duplicated at the LLC layer.

■ *LLC2* — connection-oriented service with restoration of damaged or lost frames. **LLC2** gives the user the ability to establish a *logical connection* before starting to transmit a data block. If necessary, it also allows the execution of procedures for *restoring corrupted or lost data blocks* and the ordering these blocks within the framework of the established connection. LLC2 uses the sliding window algorithm for this purpose.

■ *LLC3* — *connectionless service with delivery acknowledgment.* In some cases, a time over-head for establishing a logical connection is undesirable but delivery acknowledgment that the data have been received correctly is necessary. A good example of this is real-time management systems for controlling industrial equipment. The additional **LLC3** is provided for just such situations. This service is a compromise between LLC1 and LLC2, since it does not establish a connection but acknowledges data reception.

The choice of LLC operating mode depends on the requirements of the higher-layer protocol. Information on the required LLC transport service is passed through the inter-layer interface to the LLC layer with the hardware address and user data using the inter-layer service interface.

For example, in the TCP/IP stack, where the task of ensuring reliable data delivery is carried out by TCP, the LLC layer always operates in the LLC1 mode, performing simple operations of retrieving packets from frames and sending them to one of the stack's higher-layer protocols.

Of all protocols used, only the Microsoft/IBM stack, based on NetBIOS/NetBEUI, uses the LLC2 mode. This happens when the NetBIOS/NetBEUI protocol must itself operate in the mode to ensure the restoration of lost or corrupted data. In this case, all these operations are delegated to the LLC2 layer. If the NetBIOS/NetBEUI protocol operates in the datagram mode, it uses LLC1.

12.2.3 Structure of IEEE 802.x Standards

In 1980, the IEEE 802 Committee was organized in IEEE: Its goal was standardization of LAN technologies, and the IEEE 802.x family of standards is the result of its efforts. IEEE 802.x standards contain recommendations on the design and implementation of the lower layers of LAN technologies. These standards were developed on the basis of popular proprietary network standards, such as Ethernet, Arcnet, and Token Ring.

The results of the IEEE 802 Committee's work served as a basis for the set of international standards known as ISO 8802-1...x. The IEEE 802 Committee is currently the main international committee developing LAN technology standards.

Other organizations were also involved in standardizing LAN protocols. For instance, ANSI developed the FDDI standard for fiber-optic networks, ensuring a data transfer rate of 100 Mbps. It was the first LAN protocol to achieve such a rate, ten times higher than that of classical Ethernet.

The structure of IEEE 802 is illustrated in Figure 12.6.

Above the MAC layer of all technologies shown in Figure 12.6 is the LLC layer, which is common to all of them and independent of any specific LAN technology. The LLC standard is controlled by the **IEEE 802.2** working group (WG). Even technologies standardized outside the framework of the IEEE 802 Committee (such as ANSI's FDDI protocol), are oriented toward the use of the LLC protocol as defined by the 802.2 standard.

Description of each technology in the standard is divided into two parts: MAC layer and physical layer. As shown in Figure 12.6, in practically any technology there are several variants of the physical-layer protocol, each corresponding to a single MAC-layer protocol. For reasons of space, only Ethernet and Token Ring are illustrated in Figure 12.6. However, all of these statements are true for other technologies, such as Arcnet, FDDI, Fast Ethernet, Gigabit Ethernet, and 10G Ethernet.

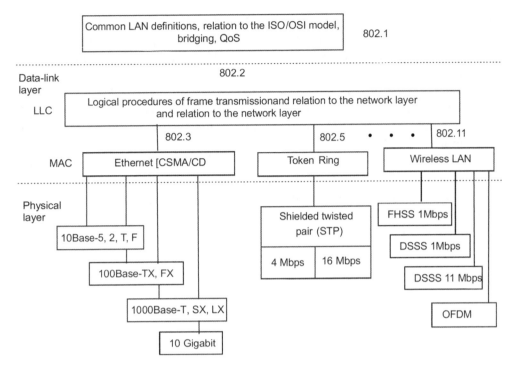

Figure 12.6 Structure of IEEE 802.x standards

The standards developed by the **IEEE 802.1** working group occupy a special position, as they are common to all technologies. For example, the 802.1 subcommittee has provided common definitions for LANs and their properties and for the relationship between the three layers of the IEEE 802 model and the OSI model. In practice, the most important 802.1 standards describe the interactions of different technologies as well as the standards providing a foundation for building more sophisticated networks on the basis of typical topologies. This group of standards is known under the common name of **internetworking standards**. It includes such important standards as 802.1D, which describes the operating logic of a transparent bridge or switch; the 802.1H standard, which describes the operation of a translating bridge capable of connecting Ethernet to FDDI or Token Ring networks without a router; etc. The list of standards developed by the IEEE 802.1 working group continues to grow. For example, it recently gained two important standards: 802.1Q, defining the method of building virtual LANs (VLANs) in switched networks, and 802.1p, describing the traffic prioritization method at the data link layer (e.g., ensuring support for QoS mechanisms).

Standards of the **802.3, 802.4, 802.5,** and **802.12** workgroups describe LAN standards; they are the result of improving proprietary technologies that served as a foundation for those standards. For example, the basis of the 802.3 standard was the experimental Ethernet Network developed and implemented by Xerox in 1975. In 1980, DEC, Intel, and Xerox (in an alliance known as DIX) jointly developed and published version 2 of the

Ethernet standard, intended for the network based on coaxial cable. This version of Ethernet is known as Ethernet DIX or Ethernet II. The Ethernet DIX standard, in turn, served as a basis for the development of the IEEE 802.3 standard, which in many respects is similar to its predecessor. The 802.4 standard appeared as a generalization of the Arcnet technology, developed by Datapoint, and the 802.5 standard is generally compliant with the Token Ring technology, designed by IBM.

The **802.11** workgroup is involved in the development of wireless LANs using medium access methods close to those used in Ethernet. Therefore, 802.11 standards are widely known as radio Ethernet standards (although Ethernet does not appear in the names of 802.11 standards).

The initial proprietary technologies and their modified versions — 802.x standards — have coexisted for a long time. For example, Arcnet was not made fully compliant with the 802.4 standard (and now it is too late to do so, as the production of Arcnet equipment was phased out in 1993). The only exception is Ethernet. The latest proprietary Ethernet standard is Ethernet DIX version II. Since then, no manufacturers have attempted to continue proprietary development of Ethernet. All innovations in the Ethernet family appear as the result of adoption of open standards by the IEEE 802.3 Committee.

Later standards were developed by groups of interested companies and then passed to appropriate IEEE 802 workgroup for approval. This was the case with technologies such as Fast Ethernet, 100VG-AnyLAN, and Gigabit Ethernet. First, a group of interested companies would form an alliance that could be joined by other companies in the course of standard development. Therefore, the process of standard development was open by nature.

12.3 CSMA/CD

> **KEY WORDS**: MAC address, unicast, multicast, broadcast, Organizationally Unique Identifiers (OUI), multiple access (MA), carrier frequency, carrier sense (CS), preamble, start of frame byte, interpacket gap (IPG), collision, collision detection (CD), jam sequence, slot time, truncated binary exponential backoff, Path Delay Value (PDV), maximum network diameter

Networks based on the Ethernet use a special method, known as **CSMA/CD**, to access the data transmission medium.

12.3.1 MAC Addresses

At the MAC layer, which ensures access to the medium and frame transmission, unique 6-byte addresses are used. These addresses are defined by the IEEE 802.3 standard and are known as **MAC addresses**. MAC addresses are usually written as six pairs of hex digits separated by dashes or colons, for example: 11-A0-17-3D-BC-01. Each network adapter has at least one MAC address.

Besides individual interfaces, a MAC address can define a group of interfaces or even all network interfaces. The first (least significant) bit of the most significant byte of the destination address indicates whether this is an individual or group address. If this bit is set to 0, it is a **unicast** (individual) address identifying a single network interface. If the bit is set to 1, it is a **multicast** (group) address. A multicast address pertains only to interfaces configured (either manually by an administrator or automatically by a request from a higher layer) as group members whose number is specified in the multicast address. If the network interface is included into a group, then as well as a unicast MAC address, it has another address associated with it, namely, a multicast address. If a multicast address comprises only ones (i.e., has a 0xFFFFFFFFFFFF hex representation), it identifies all network nodes. This is called a **broadcast address**.

The second bit of the most significant byte of the address identifies the method used to assign an address: **centralized** or **local**. If this bit is set to 0 (nearly always the case with standard Ethernet equipment), then the address has been assigned centrally using IEEE 802 rules.

NOTE   *In IEEE Ethernet standards, the least significant bit of the byte is in the leftmost position of the field, and the most significant bit occupies the rightmost position. This nonstandard order of bits in the byte corresponds to the order in which the Ethernet transmitter sends them into the communications line (the least significant bit is transmitted first). Standards of other organizations, such as RFC IETF, ITU-T, and ISO, use traditional byte representation in which the least significant bit takes the rightmost position and the most significant bit occupies the leftmost position. At the same time, traditional byte order is retained. Therefore, when reading standards published by these organizations and when interpreting data displayed on the screen by the operating system or protocol analyzer, the values of each byte must be reversed to get the correct notion of the values of its bits according to the IEEE documentation. For example, a multicast address represented in IEEE notation as 1000 0000 0000 0000 1010 0111 1111 0000 0000 0000 0000 0000 (or 80-00-A7-F0-00-00 in hex notation), most probably, will be displayed in a traditional form by a protocol analyzer (i.e., as 01-00-5E-0F-00-00).*

The IEEE Committee distributes **organizationally unique identifiers** (**OUI**) to equipment manufacturers. Each manufacturer places the allocated identifier in the three most significant bytes of the address (for example, 0x0020AF corresponds to 3COM, and 0x00000C denotes Cisco). Equipment manufacturers are responsible for ensuring the uniqueness of the three least significant bytes of the address. The 24 bits allocated to manufacturers for interface addressing in their products allow the production of approximately 16 million unique interfaces under a single organizational identifier. The uniqueness of centrally distributed addresses is in force for all main LAN technologies, including Ethernet, Token Ring, and FDDI. Local addresses are assigned by the network administrator, whose responsibilities include ensuring their uniqueness.

12.3.2 Medium Access and Data Transmission

For simplicity, when considering the CSMA/CD algorithm for accessing the shared medium, assume that each node (station) has only one network interface.

All computers in a shared medium network can immediately (with the account of the delay for the signal propagation through the physical medium) receive the data that any of the computers started to transmit into the shared medium. The medim to which all workstations operating in this mode is said to operate in the **multiple access (MA)** mode.

To obtain the possibility of transmitting a frame, the sending interface has to make sure that the shared medium is not busy. This can be achieved by listening for the main harmonic of the signal, also known as the **carrier frequency**. This approach, accordingly, is known as **carrier sense (CS).** The main indication of the medium availability is the lack of the carrier frequency in it. Provided that Manchester code is used, which is adopted for all variants of Ethernet 10 Mbps, the carrier frequency will be 5 MHz — 10 MHz depending on the sequence of ones and zeros being transmitted.

If the medium is free, the node has the right to start frame transmission. In the example shown in Figure 12.7, node 1 has detected that the medium is free and has started to transmit its frame. In classical Ethernet based on coaxial cable, the signals from the transmitter of node 1 propagate in both directions so that all network nodes receive them. The data frame is always accompanied by a **preamble**, which comprises 7 bytes, each with a value of 10101010, and an eighth byte of 10101011. The last byte is called the **start of frame byte.** The preamble is needed for bit and byte synchronization between the transmitter and the receiver. The presence of two ones, the second immediately following the first, informs the receiver that the preamble has finished, and the next bit is the starting bit of the frame.

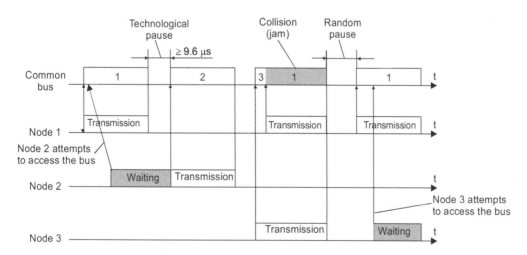

Figure 12.7 CSMA/CD random medium access method

All stations connected to the cable start to load the bytes of the frame being transmitted into their internal buffers. The first 6 bytes of the frame contain the destination address. The station that recognizes its own address in the frame header continues to load frame contents into its internal buffer, and the other stations stop receiving the frame at this stage. The destination node processes the received data, passes them upward along its protocol stack, and then sends the answering frame through the cable. The Ethernet frame contains both the destination and the source addresses; therefore, the receiver knows where to send an answer.

During frame transmission by node 1, node 2 also tried to start sending its frame. However, it noticed that the medium was busy because the carrier frequency was present. Therefore, node 2 has to wait until node 1 completes transmission of its frame.

After frame transmission is accomplished, all network nodes have to hold a technological pause: the **interpacket gap (IPG),** which lasts 9.6 μsec. This pause is needed to return network adapters to their initial states as well as to prevent a situation in which one station monopolizes the medium. When the IPG elapses, network nodes get the right to start transmission of their frames, since the medium is free. In the example provided in Figure 12.7, node 2 waits until node 1 had accomplished frame transmission, makes a 9.6 μsec pause, and starts transmission of its frame.

12.3.3 Collisions

Carrier sensing and inserting a pause between frames do not guarantee the elimination of situations in which two or more stations simultaneously decide that the medium is free and start transmission of their frames. Such a situation is known as a **collision**, since the contents of simultaneously transmitted frames collide in the common cable. As a result, the information of all frames gets corrupted, since encoding methods adopted in Ethernet do not allow each station's signals to be picked out from the common signal.

Collisions are normal in Ethernet operation. In the example shown in Figure 12.8, the collision originated from simultaneous transmission of data by nodes 3 and 1. For a collision to arise, it is not necessary for several stations to start transmission synchronously: On the contrary, this is rare. More probable is that one node starts frame transmission and later the second node, having monitored the medium and detected no carrier (since the signals from the first node have not reached it yet), starts transmission of its frame. Thus, collisions are caused by the distributed location of network nodes.

To handle collisions correctly, all stations simultaneously sense the signals in the cable. If the signals being transmitted and received are different, then **collision detection (CD)** is registered. To increase the probability of collision detection by all network nodes as soon as possible, the station that detects a collision stops transmitting its frame (at an arbitrary point, not necessarily a byte boundary) and escalates the collision by sending a sequence of 32 bits, known as a **jam sequence**, into the network.

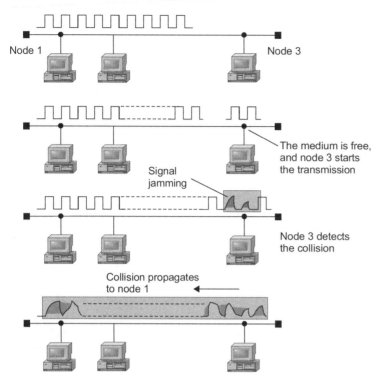

Figure 12.8 Collision origination and propagation

The station that detected the collision must then stop transmission and pause for a short, random interval. After that, it can repeat its attempt to capture the medium and transmit the frame. An arbitrary pause is chosen according to the following algorithm:

$$\text{Pause} = L \times (\text{slot time}) \tag{12.1}$$

In Ethernet, the **slot time** is chosen in 512 bit intervals (bt). The bit interval corresponds to the time between the appearance of two sequential bits of data in the cable. For 10 Mbps, the bit interval is 0.1 µsec, or 100 nsec.

L represents an integer number chosen with equal probability from the range $[0, 2^N]$, where N is the number of the repeated attempt of retransmitting this frame: 1, 2, ..., 10.

> After the 10th attempt, the interval from which the pause has to be chosen stays fixed and is not increased. Thus, a random pause in the Ethernet technology can last from 0 to 52.4 msec.

If 16 sequentially repeated attempts at frame transmission cause a collision, the transmitter must give up and discard this frame. The previously described algorithm is known as **truncated binary exponential backoff**.

Ethernet behavior under conditions of significant load (when the medium utilization coefficient grows and starts to approach 1) generally corresponds to the figures in *Chapter 7* when analyzing the M/M/1 model of the queuing theory. However, the waiting time before accessing the medium in Ethernet starts to grow earlier than in the M/M/1 model: This happens because the M/M/1 model is too simplistic and does not take into account important features of the Ethernet such as collisions.

Administrators of Ethernet networks based on a shared medium use a simple empiric rule, according to which the medium utilization coefficient must not exceed 30%. For supporting delay-sensitive traffic, Ethernet (and other networks based on a shared medium) can use only one QoS support method, namely, the *underloaded mode of operation.*

12.3.4 Path Delay Value and Collision Detection

Reliable detection of collisions by all network workstations is a necessary condition for correct Ethernet operation. If one transmitting station does not detect a collision and decides that its data frame is transmitted correctly, this frame will be lost. Because of signal overlap under collision conditions, frame information will become distorted. The distorted frame will be discarded by the receiving workstation because of checksum mismatch. The data that were not delivered to the receiver probably will be retransmitted by some of the connection-oriented higher-layer protocols (e.g., the transport or application-layer protocols or the LLC protocol, provided that the receiver operates in the LLC2 mode). However, message retransmission by higher-layer protocols will take place significantly later (sometimes several seconds) than retransmission by Ethernet, which operates with microsecond intervals. Therefore, if collisions are not reliably detected by Ethernet network nodes, this significantly reduces the effective bandwidth of the network.

To ensure reliable collision detection, the following condition must be satisfied:

$$T_{min} \geq \text{PDV} \qquad (12.2)$$

Here, T_{min} is the time required for transmitting a frame of minimum length, and PDV stands for *path delay value*, which represents the time during which the collision signal propagates to the most distant network node. In the worst case, the signal has to pass twice between the two network nodes separated by the longest distance. In this case, the undistorted signal passes in one direction, and the signal distorted by collision propagates in the reverse direction.

If the condition (Formula 12.2) is satisfied, the transmitting workstation must have time to detect a collision caused by the frame that it has transmitted before it completes transmission of the frame.

Observance of this condition depends on the minimum frame length, the protocol's information rate, the length of the network cable, and the propagation speed of the signal in the cable. This speed slightly differs for different types of cable.

> All parameters of the Ethernet protocol are chosen to ensure reliable collision detection under conditions of normal operation of network nodes.

Thus, the Ethernet standard defines the minimum data field length as 46 bytes, which with auxiliary fields, produces a minimum frame length of 64 bytes; this, with the preamble, makes 72 bytes, or 576 bits.

Hence, it is possible to calculate distance limitations between workstations. In the Ethernet 10 Mbps standard, the time required for transmitting a frame of minimum length is 575 bt. Consequently, the PDV must be less than 57.5 μsec. The distance that the signal can pass during this time depends on the cable type: For thick coaxial cable, it is approximately 13,280 meters. Taking into account that during this time the signal must pass along the communications link twice, the distance between two nodes must not exceed 6,635 m. The standard specifies a significantly shorter distance, taking into account other, more restrictive limitations.

One such limitation is related to the maximum permitted signal attenuation. To ensure the required signal power as it passes between the two nodes separated by the longest distance, the maximum length of the continuous segment of thick coaxial cable is chosen as 500 m, taking into account the attenuation that it introduces. Obviously, in a 500 m cable, the conditions for correct collision detection will be observed with a high level of reliability for the frames of any standard length, including 72 bytes. The PDV for the 500 m cable section is only 43.3 bt. Therefore, it is possible to make the minimum frame length even smaller. However, the developers of the technology did not reduce it, because they had more complex networks in mind, ones comprising several segments connected by repeaters.

Repeaters increase the power of signals transmitted from segment to segment. As a result, signal attenuation decreases, which allows network length to be increased significantly by using several segments. In coaxial implementations of the Ethernet, developers have limited the maximum number of network segments to *five*; this in turn limits the total network length to 2,500 m. Even in such a long multisegment network, the condition of collision detection is still observed with significant reserve. For example, compare the distance of 2,500 m, obtained on the basis of maximum allowable attenuation, with the maximum possible distance of 6,635 m, calculated on the basis of the signal propagation time. In practice, however, the time reserve is significantly smaller since in multisegment networks, repeaters themselves introduce an additional delay of several dozen bit intervals into signal propagation. Naturally, a small reserve was taken also into account to compensate for deviations of both cable and repeater parameters.

As a result of accounting for all these factors, the relationship between the minimum frame length and the maximum possible distance between network workstations was carefully chosen. This relationship ensures reliable collision detection. The maximum distance between two network nodes is also known as the **maximum network diameter**. For all types of Ethernet networks this distance must not exceed 2,500 m.

With the increased frame transmission rate characteristic of newer standards based on the same CSMA/CD medium access method, such as Fast Ethernet, the maximum distance between network stations decreased proportionally to growth in transmission rate: In Fast Ethernet, it is about 210 m; in Gigabit Ethernet, it would be limited to 25 m were it not for the developers' decision to increase minimum packet length.

Table 12.1 provides the values of the main parameters for frame transmission specified in IEEE 802.3. These parameters do not depend on the physical medium. It is important to note that each variant of the physical medium of the Ethernet technology introduces additional, often more restrictive, limitations. These limitations also must be observed; they will be considered later in this chapter.

Table 12.1 Ethernet MAC layer parameters

Parameter	Value
Bit rate	10 Mbps
Slot time	512 bt
Interpacket gap (IPG)	9.6 μsec
Maximum number of retransmission attempts	16
Maximum number of pause growth	10
Length of the jam sequence	32 bits
Maximum frame length (without preamble)	1,518 bytes
Minimum frame length (without preamble)	64 bytes (512 bits)
Preamble length	64 bits
Minimum length of random pause after collision	0 bt
Maximum length of the random pause after collision	524,000 bt
Maximum distance between workstations	2,500 m
Maximum number of workstations within the network	1,024

12.4 ETHERNET FRAME FORMATS

KEY WORDS: Ethernet DIX, Ethernet II, 802.3/LLC, 802.3/802.2, Novell 802.2, Raw 802.3, Novell 802.3, Ethernet SNAP, Start-of-frame delimiter, preamble, Frame check sequence (FCS)

The Ethernet standard defined in IEEE 802.3 provides the only possible format of the MAC-layer frame. Since the MAC-layer frame must include the LLC-layer frame described in IEEE 802.2, then according to IEEE standards, Ethernet networks can use only one variant of the data link layer frame, the header of which is a combination of the MAC and LLC sublayer headers.

Nevertheless, in practice, Ethernet networks use four frame formats. The same frame type can have different names, so here are some of the most popular names for each frame type:

- The first version of the Ethernet frame — **Ethernet DIX/Ethernet II** — appeared in 1980 as a result of the combined efforts of three companies: DEC, Intel, and Xerox. An alliance of these three companies presented its proprietary version of the Ethernet standard to the IEEE 802.3 Committee and positioned it as an international standard project.

- However, the standard approved by the 802.3 workgroup differed from the DIX proposal in some details; these differences also pertained to the frame format. Thus, the second variant of the Ethernet frame appeared: **802.3/LLC** (**802.3/802.2**, or **Novell 802.2**).

- The third variant of the Ethernet frame — **Raw 802.3/Novell 802.3** — appeared as a result of Novell's efforts to speed up the operation of its proprietary stack in Ethernet networks.

- Finally, there is a fourth version of the frame format: **Ethernet SNAP** (SNAP stands for subnetwork access protocol). This was the result of the activities of the IEEE 802.2 Committee aimed at ensuring compliance with a common standard and the flexibility required to add certain fields or change their aim in the future.

Frame format differences can result in incompatibility of network hardware or software intended for operation with only one Ethernet frame format. Today, however, practically all network adapters and their drivers, bridges, switches, or routers are capable of operating with all Ethernet frame formats used. Required recognition operations are carried out automatically.

The formats of all four types of Ethernet frames are shown in Figure 12.9.

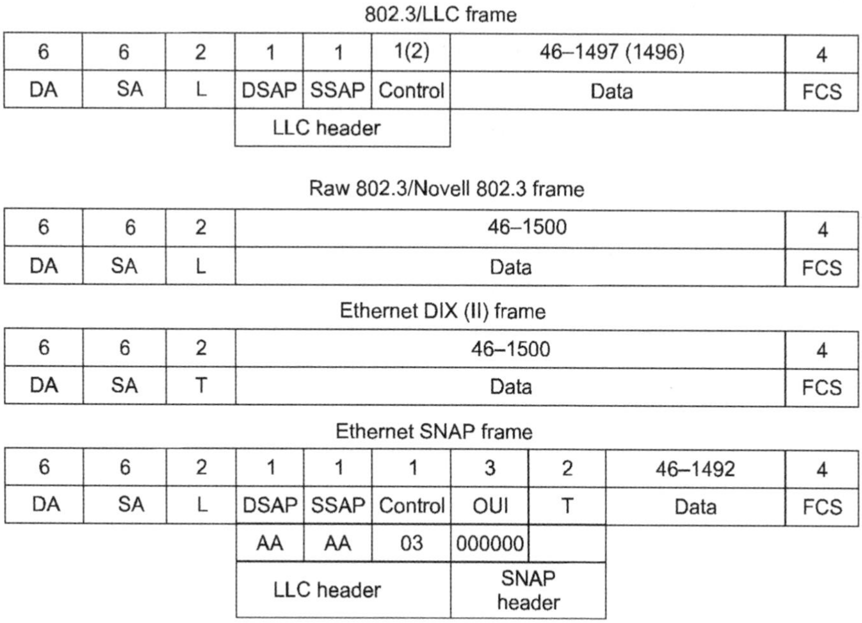

802.3/LLC frame

6	6	2	1	1	1(2)	46–1497 (1496)	4
DA	SA	L	DSAP	SSAP	Control	Data	FCS
			LLC header				

Raw 802.3/Novell 802.3 frame

6	6	2	46–1500	4
DA	SA	L	Data	FCS

Ethernet DIX (II) frame

6	6	2	46–1500	4
DA	SA	T	Data	FCS

Ethernet SNAP frame

6	6	2	1	1	1	3	2	46–1492	4
DA	SA	L	DSAP	SSAP	Control	OUI	T	Data	FCS
			AA	AA	03	000000			
			LLC header			SNAP header			

Figure 12.9 Ethernet frame formats

12.4.1 802.3/LLC

The header of the *802.3/LLC frame* is the result of joining the frame header fields defined in the IEEE 802.3 and 802.2 standards.

The 802.3 standard defines eight header fields (the preamble and start-of-frame delimiter are not shown in Figure 12.9):

- The *preamble* consists of 7 synchronization bytes with the following pattern: 10101010. When using Manchester code, this combination is represented by a periodic wave signal with a frequency of 5 MHz in the physical medium.
- *Start-of-frame delimiter* comprises a single byte with the following pattern: 10101011. The occurrence of this bit combination indicates that the next byte is the first byte of the frame header.
- *Destination address* (DA) can be 2 bytes or 6 bytes long. In practice, MAC addresses with 6 bytes are always used.
- *Source address* (SA) is a 2- or 6-byte field containing the sender's MAC address. The first bit of the address is always set to zero.
- *Length* (L) is a 2-byte field that determines the length of the frame's data field.
- The *data* field can contain from 0 to 1,500 bytes. However, if the field length is less than 46 bytes, the next field, padding, is used to complement the frame to the *minimum acceptable length of 46 bytes.*
- The *padding* field contains enough padding bytes to guarantee the minimum length of the data field: 46 bytes. This ensures correct operation of the collision detection mechanism. If the length of the data field is sufficient, there is no padding field in the frame.
- *Frame check sequence* (FCS) comprises 4 bytes containing the checksum. This value is calculated according to the CRC-32 mechanism.

The 802.3 frame represents the MAC sublayer frame; therefore, according to the 802.2 standard, its data field encapsulates the LLC sublayer frame with removed frame start and end flags. The LLC frame format was described previously. Since the LLC frame has a header length of 3 bytes (LLC1 mode) or 4 bytes (LLC2 mode), the maximum size of the data field is reduced to 1,497 bytes or 1,496 bytes.

12.4.2 Raw 802.3/Novell 802.3 Frame

Raw 802.3, also known as *Novell 802.3*, is also shown in Figure 12.9, from which it can be clearly seen that this is the MAC sublayer frame according to the 802.3 standard without the encapsulated frame of the LLC sublayer. Novell did not use the auxiliary fields of the LLC frame in its NetWare operating system for a long time. There was no need to identify the type of information encapsulated into the data field, since it always contained the IPX packet. IPX was for a long time the only network-layer protocol in Novell NetWare.

When the need to identify the higher-layer protocol appeared, Novell began to employ the possibility of encapsulating the LLC frame into the MAC-layer frame (i.e., it started using standard 802.3/LLC frames). The company now designates such frames as 802.2 frames in its operating systems, although they are actually a combination of 802.3 and 802.2 headers.

12.4.3 Ethernet DIX/Ethernet II Frame

Ethernet DIX, also known as *Ethernet II*, has a structure that coincides with the structure of the Raw 802.3 frame (see Figure 12.9). However, the 2-byte *L* field of the Raw 802.3 frame is used as a protocol type field in the *Ethernet DIX* frame. This field, called *Type* (T) or *EtherType*, is intended for the same purposes as the LLC frame's *DSAP* and *SSAP* fields, namely, for specifying the type of the higher-layer protocol whose packet is encapsulated into the data field of this frame.

In contrast to protocol codes in SAP fields, which are 1 byte long, the *T* field provides 2 bytes for the protocol code. Therefore, in general, the same protocol will be encoded by different numeric values in the SAP and *T* fields. For example, IP has the code 2048_{10} (0x0800) for the *EtherType* field, and in the SAP fields, the same protocol is encoded by the value 6. The values of the protocol codes for the *EtherType* field appeared before the SAP values, since the proprietary version of Ethernet DIX existed before the adoption of the 802.3 standard. Therefore, by the time 802.3-compliant equipment became widespread, these values were the de facto standard for most hardware and software products. Since the structures of Ethernet DIX and Raw 802.3 frames coincide, the *Length/Type* field is often designated as the *L/T* field in the documentation. The number in this field determines its usage: If this value is smaller than 1,500, then it is the *L* field; otherwise, it is the *T* field.

12.4.4 Ethernet SNAP Frame

To eliminate inconsistency in encoding types of protocols whose messages are encapsulated into the data field of the Ethernet frames, the IEEE 802.2 workgroup has made efforts for the further standardization of the Ethernet frames. As a result, a new Ethernet frame has appeared: Ethernet SNAP (see Figure 12.9), an extension of the 802.3/LLC frame. This extension was achieved by introducing an additional SNAP header comprising two fields: *OUI* and *Type* (T). The *T* field comprises 2 bytes and is a copy of the *T* field of the Ethernet II frame in both format and goal. This means that this field uses the same values of the protocol codes. The *OUI* field defines the identifier of organization that controls the protocol codes in the *T* field. Introducing the SNAP header allowed compatibility with the protocol codes in the Ethernet II frame to be achieved and a universal method of protocol encoding to be created. Protocol codes for 802 technologies are controlled by IEEE, which has the OUI value of 000000. If some new technologies that are likely to appear require other protocol codes, it will be sufficient to specify another OUI value for the organization assigning these codes; old code values will remain in force (with the appropriate OUI).

Since SNAP is a protocol encapsulated into the LLC protocol, the *DSAP* and *SSAP* fields contain the 0xAA code assigned to the SNAP protocol. The *Control* field of the LLC header is set to 0x03, which corresponds to the use of unnumbered frames.

The SNAP header is a supplement to the LLC header, so it is allowed not only in the Ethernet frames but also in frames of other 802 technologies. For example, IP always uses the structure of LLC/SNAP headers in the course of encapsulating its packets into the frames of all LAN protocols: FDDI, Token Ring, 100VG-AnyLAN, Ethernet, Fast Ethernet, and Gigabit Ethernet. Still, when transmitting IP packets using Ethernet, Fast Ethernet, and Gigabit Ethernet networks, IP uses Ethernet DIX frames.

12.4.5 Using Various Types of Ethernet Frames

Since there are four types of Ethernet frames, network-layer protocols must solve the problem of choosing specific frame type. They must take a decision — either always use the only frame type, use all four types, or give the preference only to specific frame types.

IP can use two types of frames: original Ethernet II or Ethernet SNAP, which has more sophisticated structure. Ethernet II is the preferred frame type for IP.

Contemporary network adapters automatically recognize Ethernet frame type based on the values of the frame fields. For example, Ethernet II frames can be easily distinguished from all other types of frames by the value of the *L/T* field. If this value exceeds 1,500, this means that this is the T field, since the values of the protocol codes are chosen so as to always exceed 1,500. The presence of the *T* field means that this is an Ethernet II frame, which is the only one that uses this field in the given frame position.

IPX is the maximalist in this respect, because it can work with all types of Ethernet frames. It recognizes Ethernet frames using the above-described method, and, if the frame under consideration has another type, in which case the *L/T* field has the value smaller than or equal to 1,500, then further checks are carried out. Further recognition of the frame type is enabled by the presence or lack of LLC fields. LLC fields can be missing only when the *L* field is directly followed by the starting point of the IPX packet, namely, by the 2-byte field. This field is always filled with ones, which produces a value of 0xFFFF, or two sequential bytes set to 255. First, an attempt is made to interpret these 2 bytes as *DSAP* and *SSAP* fields. However, it is impossible for the *DSAP* and *SSAP* fields to contain such values simultaneously, so the presence of 2 bytes set to 255 indicates that this is the Raw 802.3 frame.

In all other cases, further analysis is carried out depending on the values of the *DSAP* and *SSAP* fields. If they are set to 0xAA, then it is the Ethernet SNAP frame; otherwise, it is the 802.3/LLC frame.

12.5 MAXIMUM PERFORMANCE OF THE ETHERNET NETWORK

KEY WORDS: nominal protocol rate, effective protocol bandwidth, Ethernet segment network utilization coefficient

Network performance depends on the speed of frame transmission over communication links and on the rate at which communication devices process them. When processing frames, communication devices transmit them between their ports, to which communication links are connected. The rate of frame transmission via communication links depends on the physical and data-link layer protocols being used. For example, these might be Ethernet 10 Mbps, Ethernet 100 Mbps, Token Ring, or FDDI.

The rate at which the protocol transmits bits over communication link is called the **nominal protocol rate**.

The rate at which frames are processed by the communication device depends on the performance of the device's processors, internal architecture and other parameters. Obviously, the performance of the communication device must be in accordance to the link transmission rate. If it is lower than the link rate, frames will be delayed in queues and discarded in case of buffer overflow. On the other hand, using communication devices characterized by performance hundreds times higher than that of the communication link also doesn't make any sense.

To evaluate the required performance of communication devices equipped with Ethernet ports, it is necessary to evaluate the performance of the *Ethernet segment*. However, this evaluation must be carried out not in bps (as we know already, this value is equal to 10 Mbps), but, rather, in frames per second. This is because a bridge, router, or switch takes approximately the same time to process each frame, regardless of its length: the time required to look up the forwarding table, to form a new frame (with a router), etc. On the other hand, when frame length is at the minimum, the number of frames arriving to the device per time unit, naturally, reaches its maximum. Consequently, the most difficult operating mode for communications equipment involves **processing a flow of frames having a minimum length**.

Using the parameters provided in Table 12.1, calculate the maximum performance of the Ethernet segments in the number of frames (packets) of minimum length transmitted per second.

NOTE   *When specifying network performance, terms such as frame and packet are used as synonyms. Accordingly, measurement units such as frames per second (fps) and packets per second (pps) are also similar.*

Figure 12.10 Calculating Ethernet protocol throughput

Before starting to calculate the maximum number of frames of minimum length that can pass using an Ethernet segment, it should be noted that the size of a minimum-length frame plus preamble is 72 bytes; 46 bytes is the minimum size of the data field. Thus, the minimum frame length is 576 bits (Figure 12.10), and its transmission requires 57.5 μsec. Adding the IPG (9.6 μsec) produces the result: 67.1 μsec. *Hence, the maximum possible throughput of the Ethernet segment is 14,880 fps.* Naturally, the presence of several nodes within the segment reduces this value because of the time required for waiting until the node is allowed to access the medium and also because of the presence of collisions.

Frames of maximum length in Ethernet have a data field length of 1,500 bytes. Including auxiliary information, this is 1,518 bytes; with the preamble, the total size of such a frame is 1,526 bytes, or 12,208 bits. *The maximum throughput of an Ethernet segment when processing frames of maximum length is 813 fps.* When working with large frames, the load on bridges, switches, and routers is significantly reduced.

Now, calculate the maximum effective bandwidth of an Ethernet segment (measured in bits per second) when using frames of different sizes.

> The **effective protocol bandwidth** is the maximum transmission rate of *user* data carried by the data field of the frame.

This bandwidth is always smaller than the nominal bit rate of the Ethernet protocol because of the following factors:

- Presence of the control information in the frame
- IPGs
- Waiting time to access the medium.

For frames of minimum length, the effective bandwidth is:

$$B_e = 14{,}880 \times 46 \times 8 = 5.48 \text{ Mbps} \tag{12.3}$$

This is somewhat smaller than 10 Mbps, although it should be taken into account that frames of minimum length are mainly used for transmitting acknowledgments. Therefore, this rate bears only a faint relation to the transmission rate of file data.

For frames of maximum length, the effective bandwidth is:

$$B_e = 813 \times 1{,}500 \times 8 = 9.76 \text{ Mbps} \tag{12.4}$$

When using frames of medium size, with a data field of 512 bytes, the protocol bandwidth is 9.29 Mbps.

In the latter two cases, the protocol bandwidth proved to be close enough to the maximum bandwidth of 10 Mbps, although in carrying out this estimation, it was supposed that no other stations interfere with the interaction of two communicating workstations (i.e., that there are no collisions and no need to wait to access the medium).

Thus, when there are no collisions, the network utilization coefficient depends on the size of the frame data field and has a maximum value of 0.976 when transmitting frames of maximum length.

12.6 ETHERNET PHYSICAL MEDIUM SPECIFICATIONS

KEY WORDS: 10Base-5, 10Base-2, 10Base-T, 10Base-F, terminator, transceiver, attachment unit interface (AUI), jabber control, collision detector, decoupling element, the 5-4-3 rule, the 4 hubs rule, T-connector, concentrators, hubs synchronous Ethernet, collision domain, FOIRL, 10Base-FL, 10Base-FB

Historically, the first Ethernet networks were created on the basis of coaxial cable with a diameter of 0.5 inch. Later, other physical-layer specifications were defined for the Ethernet standard that allowed the use of various data transmission media. CSMA/CD and all time parameters remain the same for any specification of the physical medium of Ethernet 10 Mbps.

Physical specifications for Ethernet include the following data transmission media:

❏ **10Base-5** — coaxial cable 0.5 inch in diameter, also called thick coaxial cable. It has impedance of 50 ohms. The maximum length of a segment is 500 m (without repeaters).

❏ **10Base-2** — coaxial cable 0.25 inch in diameter, also known as thin coaxial cable. It has impedance of 50 ohms. The maximum segment length (without repeaters) is 185 m.

❏ **10Base-T** — cable based on unshielded twisted pair (UTP). It makes up star topology based on a central concentrator. The distance between the concentrator and the end node must not exceed 100 m.

❏ **10Base-F** — fiber-optic cable whose topology is similar to 10Base-T. There are several versions of this specification: *Fiber-Optic Interrepeater Link*, or FOIRL (distances up to 1,000 m); 10Base-FL (distances up to 2,000 m); and 10Base-FB (distances up to 2,000 m).

The number 10 in specification names stands for the bit rate of data transmission according to these standards: 10 Mbps. The base component refers to the encoding method (baseband) using a single base frequency of 10 MHz (in contrast to methods using several carrier frequencies, which are called broadband). The last character in the standard name designates the cable type.

12.6.1 10Base-5

The 10Base-5 standard generally corresponds to the experimental Ethernet network built by Xerox and can be considered as a classical Ethernet standard.

Different components of the network based on thick coaxial cable and comprising three segments connected by repeaters are shown in Figure 12.11.

The cable is used as monochannel for all stations. A cable segment of the maximum length of 500 m (without repeaters) must have 50-ohm **terminators** attached to both of its end nodes. The terminators are intended to absorb the signals propagating through the cable so that they do not reflect back down the line. If terminators are lacking, stationary waves arise in the cable; therefore, some nodes receive powerful signals, and the signals delivered to other nodes are so weak that it is impossible to receive them.

The workstation must be connected to the cable using a **transceiver** — the network adapter part that carries out transmission and reception functions (**trans**mitter + re**ceiver** = transceiver). The transceiver is connected directly to the cable and powered from a network adapter installed in the computer. The transceiver can be connected to the cable either by a tap that penetrates the cable and ensures direct physical contact (vampire tap) or by a noncontact method.

A transceiver is connected to the network adapter using the **attachment unit interface (AUI)** interface cable, which may be up to 50 m. The AUI comprises four twisted pairs (the network adapter must have an AUI connector). The presence of the standard interface between the transceiver and the remaining part of the network adapter is very useful when migrating from one type of the cable to another. For this purpose, it is sufficient to replace the transceiver; the remaining part of the network adapter does not need replacement, since it implements the MAC-layer protocol. In this case, it is only necessary to ensure that the new transceiver (for example, the transceiver for a twisted pair) supports the standard AUI.

No more than 100 transceivers can be connected to a single segment, and the distance between transceiver connection points must not be less than 2.5 m. The cable has marks every 2.5 m indicating the points for connecting transceivers. When computers are con-

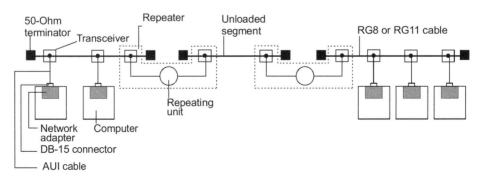

Figure 12.11 Components of the physical layer of a 10Base-5 network comprising three segments

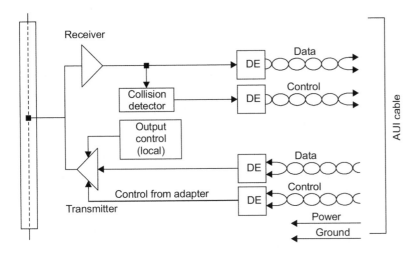

Figure 12.12 Structural design of a transceiver

nected according to these marks, the influence of stationary waves in the cable on network adapters is reduced to a minimum.

A simplified transceiver structure is shown in Figure 12.12. The transmitter and receiver are connected to the same point of the cable using a special circuit (e.g., transforming) that allows organization of simultaneous transmission and reception of signals to
and from the cable.

In case of adapter malfunction, the situation is possible when a sequence of arbitrary
signals is continuously passed into the cable. Because the cable is a shared medium for all
workstations, a single malfunctioning adapter will block network operation. To avoid
such situations, transceiver output is equipped by special scheme that checks frame transmission time. If the maximum possible time of the frame transmission is exceeded (providing some reserve), the scheme simply disconnects the transmitter output from the
cable. Maximum time of frame transmission (including the preamble) is 1,221 µs, and
frame transmission limit is 4,000 µs (4 ms). This transceiver function is sometimes called
jabber control.

A **collision detector** finds collisions in coaxial cable by the increased level of the signal's constant component. If the constant component exceeds a specific threshold value
(about 1.5 V), it means that at least two transmitters are transmitting signals to the cable
simultaneously.

Decoupling elements ensure galvanic decoupling of the transceiver from the remaining part of the network adapter, thus protecting the adapter and the computer from significant voltage drops arising in the damaged cable.

10Base-5 determines the possibility of using a special device known as a repeater.
A repeater joins several cable segments into a single network, thus increasing its total
length. The repeater receives signals from one cable segment and synchronously, bit by
bit, repeats them into the other segment, improving the signal shape, increasing its power,

and synchronizing pulses. A repeater comprises two (or more) transceivers, connected to cable segments, as well as a repeating unit with its own clock oscillator. For better synchronization, the repeater delays transmission of the first bits of the frame preamble, thus increasing the frame transmission delay from segment to segment and slightly reducing the IPG.

The standard allows no more than four repeaters in a network and, consequently, no more than five segments of cable. Given the maximum length of the cable segment (500 m), this gives a maximum length for a 10Base-5 network of 2,500 m. This exactly corresponds to the general limitation on the maximum network diameter for Ethernet.

Only three of the five segments can be loaded (i.e., have end nodes connected to them). Loaded segments must be separated by unloaded ones, so the maximum network configuration includes two loaded edge segments connected by unloaded segments to a central loaded segment. Earlier in this chapter, in Figure 12.11, an example of the Ethernet network was shown comprising three segments connected by two repeaters. Edge segments are loaded, and the intermediate is unloaded.

> The rule according to which repeaters are used in the Ethernet 10Base-5 network is known as the **5-4-3 rule**: five segments, four repeaters, three loaded segments.

The limited number of repeaters is explained by additional signal propagation delays introduced by repeaters. The use of repeaters increases the PDV, which for reliable collision detection must not exceed the time required for transmission of a maximum-length frame (i.e., one comprising 72 bytes, or 576 bits).

Each repeater is connected to the segment by its own transceiver, so no more than 99 nodes, not 100, can be connected to the loaded segment. Thus, the maximum number of end nodes in a 10Base-5 network is $99 \times 3 = 297$ nodes.

12.6.2 10Base-2

The 10Base-2 standard uses coaxial cable with central copper wire 0.89 mm in diameter and an external diameter about 5 mm (thin Ethernet) as the transmission medium. Cable impedance is 50 ohms. Maximum segment length without repeaters is 185 m; terminators with resistance of 50 ohms must be attached to the end nodes of the segment. Thin coaxial cable is cheaper than the thick cable, so 10Base-2 networks are sometimes called Cheapernet. However, the lower price has its downside, because thin coaxial cable is less protected against noise, has lower mechanical strength, and is characterized by narrower bandwidth.

Workstations are connected to the cable using a BNC **T-connector**, which is a T-joint, one tap of which is connected to the network adapter; two other taps are connected to the cable. The maximum number of workstations that can be connected to a single segment is 30. The minimum distance between workstations is 1 m. The thin coaxial cable has marking for connecting end nodes in steps of 1 m.

10Base-2 also provides for using repeaters according to the 5-4-3 rule.

In this case, the network will have a maximum length of $5 \times 185 = 925$ m. Obviously, this is more restricting than the common limitation of 2,500 m.

NOTE   *Many restrictions must be observed in building a correctly operating Ethernet network. Some of these restrictions relate to network parameters, such as maximum length of the network or maximum number of computers, which must simultaneously satisfy several conditions. A correct Ethernet network must satisfy all requirements. In practice, however, it is sufficient to observe only the most stringent ones. For example, the general limitation states that the Ethernet network must contain no more than 1,024 nodes, and the 10Base-2 standard limits the maximum number of workstations connected to a single segment to 30. Since the number of loaded segments is limited to three, the total number of nodes in a 10Base-2 network must not exceed $29 \times 3 = 87$.*

10Base-2 is similar to 10Base-5. However, in 10Base-2, transceivers are integrated into network adapters, since the more flexible thin coaxial cable can be routed directly to the BNC T-connector built into the rear of the network interface card installed inside a computer. The cable in this case hangs on the network adapter, which complicates physically moving computers.

A typical network based on 10Base-2 and comprising a single cable segment is shown in Figure 12.13.

Practical implementation of this standard results in the simplest solution for cable networks, since only network adapters, T-connectors, and 50-ohm terminators are needed to connect computers to the network. However, this type of cable connection is the most vulnerable to cable failures: Thin Ethernet cable is more sensitive to noise than thick coaxial cable, the monochannel has a large number of mechanical connections (each T-connector provides three mechanical connections, two of which are vitally important for the entire network), and users have access to connectors and can disturb the monochannel integrity. Furthermore, this solution is far from perfect in terms of aesthetics and ergonomics, since two rather noticeable pieces of cable are connected to each station using a T-connector. Under the table, they often form quite a mess, since it is necessary to provide some reserve just in case the workplace is shifted slightly.

A common drawback of the 10Base-5 and 10Base-2 standards is lack of online information about the state of the monochannel. Cable fault is detected immediately, since the network becomes inoperable, but a special device called a cable tester is needed to find the faulty cable section.

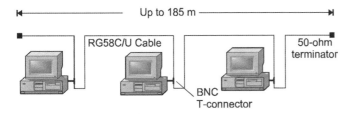

Figure 12.13 10Base-2 standard network

12.6.3 10Base-T

10Base-T networks use two UTPs as a transmission medium. Multipair cable based on Category 3 UTP has been used by telephone companies for quite a long time to connect telephone sets inside buildings. This cable also has a speaking name — Voice Grade — which means that it is mainly intended for voice transmission.

The idea of accommodating this popular cable for building LANs proved to be very fruitful, since most buildings were already equipped with the required cabling system. It only remained to develop a method of connecting network adapters and other communications equipment to the twisted pair in such a way as to minimize the changes in network adapters and communications software of network operating systems in comparison with Ethernet using coaxial cable. This problem was successfully solved: Switching to twisted pair requires only replacement of the transceiver of the network adapter or router port; the access method and all protocols of the data link layer remained the same as in coaxial Ethernet.

Two twisted pairs are used to connect end nodes to a special device called a multiport repeater according to the "point-to-point" topology. One twisted pair is needed for data transmission from the station to the repeater (the network adapter's T_x output), and another is required for data transmission from the repeater to the station (the network adapter's R_x input). Figure 12.14 shows an example of a three-port repeater. The repeater receives the signals from one of the end nodes and synchronously transmits them to all of its other ports except the one from which the signals were received.

Multiport repeaters in this case are usually called **concentrators**, or **hubs** in technical slang. The concentrator carries out the functions of a signal repeater on all sections of twisted pair connected to its ports, thus creating a common data transmission medium: a logical monochannel (or logical common bus). The concentrator detects collisions in the segment in case of simultaneous signal transmission through more than one of its

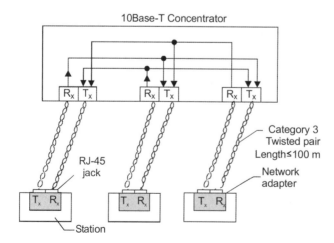

Figure 12.14 10Base-T standard network: T_x is the transmitter, and R_x is the receiver

R_x inputs. In this case, it sends the jam sequence to all its T_x outputs. The standard defines a data transmission rate of 10 Mbps and a maximum length of a twisted pair section between two directly connected nodes (stations and concentrators) of no more than 100 m, provided that twisted pair of Category 3 or better is used. This distance is defined by the twisted pair bandwidth, which allows data transmission at 10 Mbps over a distance of 100 m using Manchester code.

10Base-T concentrators can be connected to each other using the same ports as those intended for connecting end nodes. When doing so, it is necessary to make sure that transmitter and the receiver of one port are connected, respectively, to the receiver and the transmitter of another port.

> The 10Base-T standard sets the maximum number of concentrators between any two workstations of the network at four. This is known as the **4 hubs rule**.

The 4 hubs rule replaces the *5-4-3 rule* applicable to coaxial networks. It was introduced to ensure synchronization among workstations when implementing CSMA/CD access procedures and to guarantee reliable collision detection

When creating 10Base-T networks with a large number of workstations, concentrators can be interconnected using hierarchical method, thus forming a tree structure (Figure 12.15).

NOTE   *Loop connection of concentrators is not allowed by 10Base-T, since it results in incorrect network operation. This requirement means that parallel links between critically important concentrators are not allowed in 10Base-T networks. Parallel links are needed for link reservation in case of port, concentrator, or cable failure. Link reservation in a 10Base-T network is possible only by switching one of the parallel links into the blocked (inactive) state.*

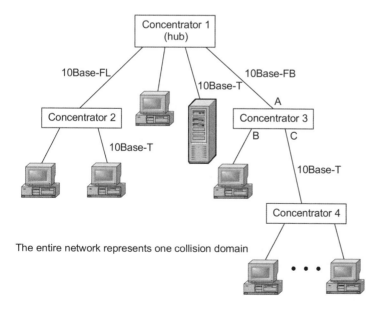

Figure 12.15 Hierarchical connection of Ethernet concentrators

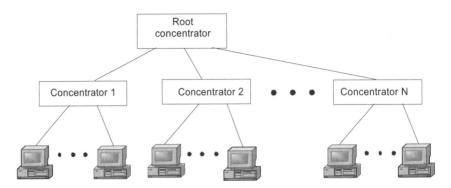

Figure 12.16 System with the maximum number of workstations

The total number of workstations in the 10Base-T network must not exceed the common limit of 1,024. For this type of physical layer, this limit is reachable: It is sufficient to create a two-tier hierarchy of concentrators, placing enough concentrators with 1,024 total ports at the lower level (Figure 12.16). End nodes must be connected to the ports of the lower-level concentrators. The four hubs rule in this case is satisfied, since between any two end nodes there will be three concentrators.

Since there must be no more than four repeaters between any two network nodes, it is obvious that *the maximum network diameter for 10Base-T networks is 5 × 100 = 500 m*. Note that this limitation is more stringent than the 2,500 m limitation general for Ethernet networks.

Networks built on the basis of 10Base-T have many advantages over coaxial Ethernet because of the division of the common physical cable into separate sections of cable connected to a central communications device. Although logically these sections continue to form a shared medium, their physical separation means that they can be controlled and disconnected individually if a network adapter breaks, short-circuits, or malfunctions. This circumstance significantly simplifies maintenance procedures for large Ethernet networks, since concentrators usually carry out such operations automatically and notify the network administrator of any existing problem.

10Base-T defines the procedure for testing the physical operability of two twisted pair sections connecting the end node's transceiver and the repeater's port. This procedure, known as a *link integrity test*, is based on transmitting special signals (J and K of Manchester code) between the transmitter and receiver of each twisted pair at 16 msec intervals. Information signals of Manchester code always change potential in the middle of a clock; J and K violate this rule by preserving potential in the middle of a clock. One of the two potential values corresponds to the J code, and another value corresponds to the K code. Since J and K are invalid during frame transmission, the test sequence has no influence on the operation of the medium access algorithm.

Introducing an active device between end nodes capable of controlling their operation and isolating incorrectly operating nodes from the network is the *main advantage* of the 10Base-T technology over coaxial networks, which are difficult to maintain. Because of concentrators, Ethernet has gained some basic fault-tolerance features.

12.6.4 Fiber-Optic Ethernet

The 10Base-F network uses fiber-optic cable as a shared medium. Fiber-optic standards recommend relatively inexpensive multimode optical fiber as the main type of the cable. This fiber has a bandwidth of 500 MHz–800 MHz over cable length of 1 km. More expensive single-mode optical fiber with a bandwidth of several gigahertz is also acceptable, although in this case, it is necessary to use a special type of transceiver.

Functionally, Ethernet based on optical cable comprises the same elements as 10Base-T, namely, network adapters, multiport repeaters, and cable sections connecting adapters to repeater ports. As in the case of twisted pair, two optical fibers are used for connecting adapters to repeaters: one fiber connects the adapter's T_X output to the repeater's R_X input, and another connects the adapter's R_X input to the repeater's T_X output.

FOIRL (Fiber Optic Inter-Repeater Link) was the IEEE 802.3 Committee's first standard for using optical fiber in Ethernet. It guarantees the length of the fiber-optic link between repeaters at 1 km, provided that the total network length does not exceed 2,500 m. The maximum number of repeaters between any two network nodes is four. In this case, the maximum diameter of 2,500 m can be achieved, although maximum lengths of cable sections between *all four* repeaters, as well as between repeaters and end nodes, are not allowed; otherwise, the resulting network would be 5,000 m.

The **10Base-FL** standard is a minor improvement on FOIRL. The power of transmitters was increased, so the maximum distance between the end node and the concentrator went up to 2,000 m. The maximum number of repeaters between nodes remained unchanged at 4, while maximum network length is 2,500 m.

The **10Base-FB** standard is intended only for connecting repeaters. End nodes cannot use this standard for connecting to concentrator ports. Up to five 10Base-FB repeaters can be installed between network nodes, with the maximum length of a single segment of 2,000 m and maximum network length of 2,740 m.

When repeaters connected according to 10Base-FB have no frames to transfer, they constantly exchange special signal sequences different from the data frame signals; this is done to support synchronism. Therefore, they introduce smaller delays when transferring data from segment to segment. This is the main reason that allowed the number of repeaters to rise to five. Manchester codes J and K are used as special signals in the following sequence: J-J-K-K-J-J-.... This sequence generates 2.5 MHz pulses, thus synchronizing the receiver of one concentrator and the transmitter of another one. Therefore, the 10Base-FB standard is also known as **synchronous Ethernet**.

As is the case with 10Base-T, fiber-optic Ethernet standards allow the connection of concentrators only into hierarchical tree structures. No loops between concentrator ports are allowed.

At the beginning of this chapter, the 10Base-F was used as generic term for all three 10 Mbps Ethernet fiber-optic standards. It is not the standard term, but network specialists sometimes use it as a common nickname.

12.6.5 Collision Domain

> The **collision domain** is part of the Ethernet network in which all the nodes detect a collision independent of the part of the network where the collision happens.

Ethernet built on repeaters always forms one collision domain. Bridges, switches, and routers divide the Ethernet network into several collision domains.

The network shown in Figure 12.15 is a single collision domain. For example, if a frame collision happened in concentrator 4, then according to the operating logic of 10Base-T concentrators, the collision signal will propagate to all ports of all concentrators.

On the other hand, if concentrator 3 is replaced by a bridge, then its port C, connected to concentrator 4, will receive the signal of collision but will not transmit it to all other ports, since this is beyond its responsibilities. The bridge will simply handle the collision situation using port C, which is connected to the shared medium where the collision happened. If the collision happened because the *bridge* attempted to transmit a frame via port C to concentrator 4, then having registered the collision signal, port C will stop frame transmission and will attempt to retransmit it after a random interval. If port C was receiving a frame at the moment of collision, it will simply discard the received fragment and wait until the node that has transmitted the frame via concentrator 4 reattempts frame transmission. After successfully receiving this frame into its buffer, the bridge will transmit it to another port, such as port A, as dictated by the forwarding table. All events related to collision handling by port C will remain unknown to all other network segments connected to other ports of the bridge.

12.6.6 Common Characteristics of 10 Mbps Ethernet Standards

Tables 12.2 and 12.3 summarize the main limitations and characteristics of the 10 Mbps Ethernet standards.

Table 12.2 Common limitations for all Ethernet standards

Characteristic	Value
Nominal bandwidth	10 Mbps
Maximum number of workstations within the network	1,024
Maximum distance between network nodes	2,500 m (2,750 m for 10Base-FB)
Maximum number of coaxial segments in the network	5

Table 12.3 Parameters of physical-layer Ethernet specifications

Parameter	10Base-5	10Base-2	10Base-T	10Base-F
Cable	Thick coaxial RG-8 or RG-11 cable	RG-58 thin coaxial cable	Category 3, 4, or 5 UTP	Multimode fiber-optic cable
Max. segment length (m)	500	185	100	2,000
Max. distance between network nodes (when using repeaters) (m)	2,500	925	500	2,500 (2,740 for 10Base-FB)
Max. number of workstations within a segment	100	30	1,024	1,024
Max. number of repeaters between two workstations	4	4	4	4 (5 for 10Base-BF)

12.7 CASE STUDY

In the early 1990s, the large engineering plant Transmash used 10 Mbps Ethernet with a shared medium to interconnect all its minicomputers and PCs (Figure 12.17). Computers were mainly used for carrying out autonomous tasks, and data exchange among them

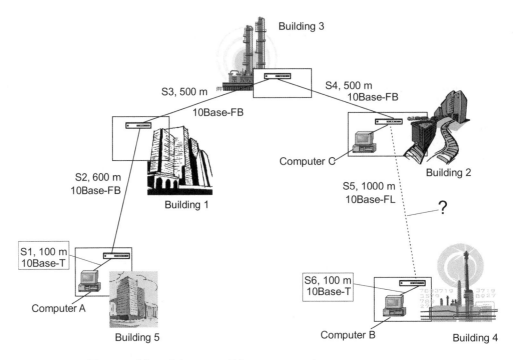

Figure 12.17 Transmash's multisegment Ethernet network

was relatively rare. The network transmitted small volumes of alphanumeric data, so a common shared medium was adequate to satisfy manufacturing needs. Fiber-optic networks on the 10Base-FB and 10Base-FL standards were used to connect the central segment of the network to segments of remote workshops. The network satisfied all requirements of multisegment Ethernet configuration: cable sections did not exceed the maximum allowed length, there were no more than four hubs between any two nodes, and the maximum distance between network nodes did not exceed 1,800 meters (computers A and C in Figure 12.17).

After a time, the need arose to connect another building, building 4, to the network. This building was located within the range for connecting it to the network using fiberoptic Ethernet standards (10Base-FB or 10Base-FL). However, such a connection would produce an incorrect configuration, because there would be five hubs between computers located in buildings 1 and 4. Moreover, the diameter of the network would reach 2,800 meters, which would be another violation of Ethernet limitations. However, at the time, Transmash's network architect did not want to radically change the network structure by installing bridge or router for connecting a new segment. He knew that Section 13 of the IEEE 802.3 standard, titled "System considerations for multisegment 10 Mbps baseband networks," provided a procedure for assessing network configuration correctness. This technique makes it possible to determine numerically if a specific network configuration will operate correctly. Calculations show that sometimes it is possible to violate the four hubs rule and limitations on the maximum network diameter but to preserve a correct configuration. These limitations were chosen in such a way as to ensure a significant re-serve for safety margins. For example, it is known that maximum PDV must not exceed 575 bt for reliable collision detection by any network node. The techniques provided in the standard for calculating the PDV for a 10Base-5 network comprising four 10Base-5 repeaters and five segments of maximum length (500 m) shows that this time interval is 537 bt. This means that the maximum configuration of the 10Base-5 network (four hubs and a network diameter of 2,500 m) has a reserve of 38 bt. At the same time, the proce-dure provided in Section 13 of the 802.3 standard specifies that even a reserve of 4 bt would allow the network to operate correctly.

Therefore, the network architect calculated the possible configuration of the Trans-mash engineering plant with a new segment. As it turned out, even with building 4 con-nected to the network, the network would have a reserve of 6.6 bt. After reviewing and checking the calculation, a fiber-optic cable was installed to connect building 4 to the plant network, and the new network configuration began to operate. Practice proved the calculation correct, as the entire network operated normally. Such a configuration was preserved for several years, until the growing requirements of new applications resulted in the need to divide the common shared medium into switched segments.

To check the calculation carried out by the Transmash network architect, it is necessary familiarize yourself with details of the procedure provided in Section 13 of the 802.3 standard.

This procedure states that the Ethernet network will operate correctly provided that the following conditions are satisfied:

■ The PDV between the two most distant workstations does not exceed 575 bt. Repeaters and the segment medium introduce additional delays into signal propagation. Data on the thresh-old levels of these delays are provided in tables of the Section 13 of the IEEE 802.3 standard.

■ Reduction of the IPG and path variability value (PVV) after passage of the frame se-quence through all repeaters does not exceed 49 bt. Each repeater reduces the IPG by specific value, which is provided in the tables of Section 13 of the standard.

The tables of the 802.3 standard provide the minimum and maximum values for pos-sible signal propagation delays and reductions of IPG, since their specific values depend on the repeater manufacturer. The Transmash network architect used more precise data for calculations that were provided by the manufacturer of the network equipment. These data are provided in Tables 12.4 and 12.5.

Consider how to evaluate the PDV using the data provided in Table 12.4.

The developers of the 802.3 standard tried to simplify the calculation as much as pos-sible, so the data provided in Table 12.5 include several stages of signal propagation. For example, delays introduced by the repeater consist of the delay introduced by the input transceiver, the delay introduced by the repeater unit, and the delay introduced by the output transceiver. Nevertheless, in the table all these delays are represented by a single value, called the *segment base.*

To avoid having to add the delays introduced by the cable twice, the table provides doubled delay values for each type of cable.

Table 12.4 Data for calculating PDV

Segment type	Left segment base (bt)	Intermediate segment base (bt)	Right segment base (bt)	Medium delay per 1 m (bt)	Maximum segment length (m)
10Base-5	11.8	46.5	169.5	0.0866	500
10Base-2	11.8	46.5	169.5	0.1026	185
10Base-T	15.3	42.0	165.0	0.113	100
10Base-FB	—	24.0	—	0.1	2,000
10Base-FL	12.3	33.5	156.5	0.1	2,000
FOIRL	7.8	29.0	152.0	0.1	1,000
AUI (>2 m)	0	0	0	0.1026	2,048

The table also operates with definitions such as *left segment, right segment,* and *intermediate segment*. Let's clarify these terms for the Transmash engineering plant (Figure 12.17). The aim is to calculate PDV for the worst-case situation, so let us choose nodes A and B, which are separated by five repeaters and have 2,800 m of network between them.

In 802.3 terminology, the left segment is where the signal path from the output of the end node transmitter starts. The term left is in no way related to the geographical location of segments (or their location on the chart): It simply is a conventional name for the segment from which the calculation starts. Choose the S1 segment, to which node A is connected, as the left network segment.

After that, the signal passes through intermediate segments S2–S5 and reaches the receiver (node B), connected to segment S6. This is the point at which, in the worst-case scenario, a collision happens, which is assumed in the table. The end segment, where the collision happens, is known as the right segment.

Each segment introduces a constant delay, known as the **base**, which depends only on the segment type and its position along the signal path (left, intermediate, or right). The base of the right segment, where the collision arises, significantly exceeds the bases of left and intermediate segments.

Besides this, each segment introduces a signal propagation delay, which depends on segment length and is calculated by multiplying the signal propagation time per 1 m of cable (in bit intervals) by the cable length (in meters).

The calculation involves evaluating delays introduced by each cable section (the length provided in the table for signal delay per 1 m of cable is multiplied by segment length). Then, all these delays are added to the bases of the left, intermediate, and right segments.

Since the left and the right segments have different values of base delay, the calculations must be carried out twice if there are different types of segments on the distant edges of the network. First, it is necessary to carry out an evaluation when considering one type of segment as the left segment and to repeat the calculation taking another type of segment as the left segment. The maximum PDV must be chosen as the final result. In this case, the edge segments are of the same type, namely, 10Base-T; therefore, duplicated calculation is not needed.

Now it is possible to calculate the PDV:

- Left segment S1:

  $15.3 \text{ (base)} + (100 \times 0.113) = 26.6$

- Intermediate segment S2:

  $24 + (600 \times 0.1) = 84.0$

- Intermediate segment S3:

  $24 + (500 \times 0.1) = 74.0$

- Intermediate segment S4:

  $24 + (500 \times 0.1) = 74.0$

- Intermediate segment S5:

  $33.5 + (1,000 \times 0.1) = 133.5$

- Right segment S6:

  $165 + (100 \times 0.113) = 176.3$

The sum of all these components gives a PDV of 568.4.

Since the PDV is smaller than the maximum 575 value allowed by 6.6 bt, the network configuration is correct, even though its total length exceeds 2,500 m and has more than four repeaters.

However, checking the PDV is not sufficient to make a positive conclusion: It is also necessary to evaluate the PVV.

The initial points for PVV calculation are provided in Table 12.5.

Table 12.5 Reduction of the IPG by repeaters		
Segment type	Transmitting segment (bt)	Intermediate segment (bt)
10Base-5 or 10Base-2	16	11
10Base-FB	–	2
10Base-FL	10.5	8
10Base-T	10.5	8

According to this information, calculate the PVV for the example:

- Left segment 1 10Base-T: 10.5 bt
- Intermediate segment 2 10Base-FL: 8
- Intermediate segment 3 10Base-FB: 2
- Intermediate segment 4 10Base-FB: 2
- Intermediate segment 5 10Base-FB: 2

The sum of these values gives a PVV of 24.5, which is smaller than the threshold of 49 bt. As a result, it is possible to conclude that the network in the example corresponds to Ethernet standards for all parameters, both segment length and number of repeaters.

SUMMARY

▶ Shared LANs are the most simple and inexpensive type of LAN implementation. The main drawback of LANs is their low level of scalability, since as the number of nodes increases, the part of the total bandwidth allocated to each node is reduced accordingly.

▶ The IEEE 802 Committee develops standards containing recommendations for designing the lower layers of LANs: physical and data link. Specific features of LANs are reflected by the division of the data link layer into two sublayers: LLC and MAC.

▶ The MAC sublayer is responsible for access to the shared medium and uses it for sending frames. IEEE 802 standards use various access methods divided into two categories: random and deterministic. Random access methods ensure minimum medium access delay under conditions of low medium load. However, as medium utilization approaches 100%, the use of random access methods results in large delay values. Deterministic methods are capable of operating at higher network loads.

▶ Standards of the 802.1 workgroup are common to all technologies. They define types of LANs, their properties, procedures of internetworking, and the operating logic of bridges and routers.

▶ The LLC protocol ensures the required quality of transport services for higher-layer protocols. It can transmit frames either using datagram transmission or using procedures of establishing connection and frame restoration.

▶ Today, Ethernet is the most common and widespread LAN technology. In a broad sense Ethernet is a family of technologies including the proprietary Ethernet DIX standard and open standards such as IEEE 802.3 Ethernet 10 Mbps, Fast Ethernet, Gigabit Ethernet, and 10G Ethernet. All types, except 10G Ethernet, use the same access method — CSMA/CD — which in many respects defines the technology features.

▶ Collision is an important event typical of Ethernet. It happens when two workstations simultaneously attempt to transmit data frame through the common medium. The presence of collisions is a natural property of Ethernet, representing the consequence of the adopted random access method. The possibility of reliable collision detection depends on the correct choice of network parameters, particularly by observing the relationship between minimum frame length and maximum network diameter.

▶ The maximum throughput of the Ethernet 10Mbps segment in frames per second is achieved when transmitting frames of minimum length: It is 14,880 fps. At the same time, effective network bandwidth is only 5.48 Mbps, slightly more than half the nominal bandwidth: 10 Mbps.

▶ Maximum possible Ethernet bandwidth is 9.75 Mbps, which corresponds to use of frames of a maximum length of 1,518 bytes transmitted at 513 fps.

▶ Ethernet supports four types of frames, which have a common format of node addresses. There are formal rules according to which network adapters automatically recognize the frame type.

▶ Depending on the type of physical medium, the IEEE 802.3 standard defines different specifications: 10Base-5, 10Base-2, 10Base-T, FOIRL, 10Base-FL, or 10Base-FB. For each specification, the following characteristics are defined: cable type, maximum length of continuous cable segments, and the rules of using repeaters for increasing network diameter, namely, the 5-4-3 rule for coaxial networks and the four hubs rule for twisted pair and optical fiber.

REVIEW QUESTIONS

1. Explain the difference between network extensibility and network scalability using the example of the Ethernet.
2. Compare random and deterministic methods of access to a shared medium.
3. Why are data link-layer protocols of WAN technologies not divided into MAC and LLC sublayers?
4. What functions are carried out by the LLC layer?
5. What is collision?
6. What are the functions of the preamble and the start-of-frame delimiter in the Ethernet standard?
7. Which network tools carry out jabber control?
8. Why was the interpacket gap introduced into the Ethernet?

9. What are the values of the following characteristics of the 10Base-5 standard?
    - Nominal bandwidth (bps)
    - Effective bandwidth (bps)
    - Throughput (fps)
    - Intrapacket transmission rate (bps)
    - Interbit gap (sec)

10. Why was minimum frame size in the 10Base-5 standard set at 64 bytes?

11. Why have 10Base-T and 10Base-FL/FB pushed coaxial Ethernet standards practically out of use?

12. Explain the meaning of each field of the Ethernet frame.

13. There are four standards for Ethernet frame format. From the list provided here, choose the names of these standards, taking into account that some standards have several names:
    A. Novell 802.2
    B. Ethernet II
    C. 802.3/802.2
    D. Novell 802.3
    E. Raw 802.3
    F. Ethernet DIX
    G. 802.3/LLC
    H. Ethernet SNAP

14. What may happen in a network in which Ethernet frames of different formats are transmitted?

15. How does a packet size value influence network operation? What problems are related to too long frames? Why are short frames inefficient?

16. How does the utilization coefficient influence Ethernet network performance?

17. How does the data transmission rate of a shared medium Ethernet network influence the maximum network diameter?

18. What considerations influence the choice of the maximum length of the physical segment in the Ethernet standards?

19. What allowed the maximum segment length to be increased during the switch from the FOIRL standard to 10Base-FL?

20. What is the reason that caused the limitation known as the four hubs rule?

21. Why is full-duplex Ethernet mode not supported in concentrators?

PROBLEMS

1. Do the network fragments shown in Figure 12.18 represent collision domains?
2. How long can the workstation wait until its frame will be discarded by the network adapter?
3. What will happen in a network built on concentrators if there are closed circuits (loops) in it, such as the ones shown in Figure 12.19?

   A. The network will operate normally.

   B. Frames will not reach the destination node.

   C. Collisions will happen when attempting to transmit any frame.

   D. Frames will get looped.

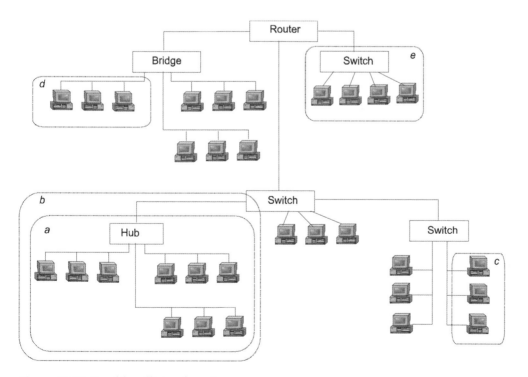

Figure 12.18 Possible collision domains

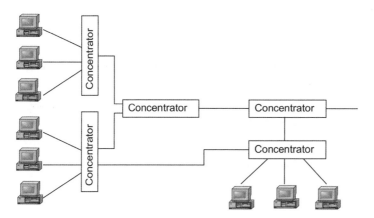

Figure 12.19 Loops in an Ethernet network built on concentrators

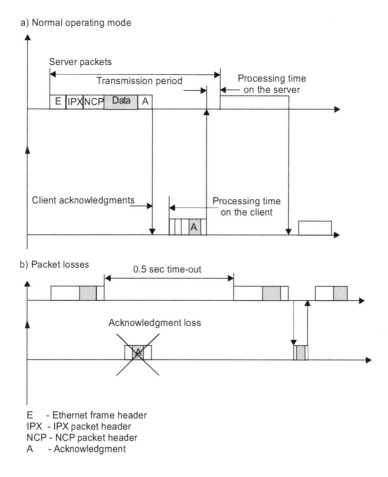

a) Normal operating mode

Server packets

Transmission period

Processing time
on the server

E │IPX│NCP│ Data │ A

Client acknowledgments

Processing time
on the client

A

b) Packet losses

0.5 sec time-out

Acknowledgment loss

A

E   - Ethernet frame header
IPX - IPX packet header
NCP - NCP packet header
A   - Acknowledgment

Figure 12.20 Ethernet network operation in the course of file transmission

4. Evaluate the performance drop of an Ethernet network when transmitting a file of 240,000 bytes if the level of lost or corrupted frames increases from 0% to 3%. Network operation is illustrated in Figure 12.20.

The file is being transmitted using the following protocols: Ethernet, IPX (network layer) and NCP (application layer of the file service). Header sizes of the protocol headers are as follows:

- Ethernet — 26 bytes (with a preamble and an *FCS* field)
- IPX — 30 bytes
- NCP — 20 bytes

The file is transmitted in 1,000 byte segments. Only NCP, operating according to the Idle Source method, restores lost or corrupted frames. Time-out for waiting for positive acknowledgments is fixed at 500 msec. (This is not the only mode of NCP operation: It can also operate using the Sliding Window algorithm, but in this case, this mode is not used). Acknowledgment size is 10 bytes. Processing time of a single packet on the client side is 650 μsec; on the server side, it is 50 μsec.

TIP

The problem comprises two parts. First, it is necessary to determine the actual rate of file transmission under conditions of ideal network operation, when the percentage of lost or corrupted Ethernet frames is zero. The second part of the problem requires determining the file transmission rate when frames begin to get lost or corrupted.

File transmission will require 240 packets in total. The size of an Ethernet frame carrying 1,000 bytes of the file being transmitted will be 1,000 + 20 + 30 + 26 = 1,076 bytes, or 8,608 bits.

The size of the Ethernet frame carrying the acknowledgment is 86 bytes (with the preamble), or 688 bits.

Under these conditions, the time of a single cycle of transmission of the next part of the file in ideal network will be 860.8 + 68.8 +650 + 50 = 1,629.6 msec.

Time required to transmit a file of 240,000 bytes will be 240 × 1,629.6 = 0.391 sec, and the information rate will be 240,000/0.391 = 613,810 bps.

Now, it remains to find the information rate when frames start to get lost or distorted.

13

HIGH-SPEED ETHERNET

13.1 INTRODUCTION

Classical 10 Mbps Ethernet was able to satisfy most users for about 15 years, but in the early 1990s its insufficient bandwidth started to become apparent. The 10 Mbps exchange rate became significantly smaller than internal computer bus rates, which by that time had exceeded the threshold of 1,000 Mbps (the PCI bus ensured data transmission at 133 MB/s). This resulted in slower network operation not only for servers but also for workstations, which began to use the PCI bus.

The need for a newer Ethernet technology became evident. This new technology had to be as efficient as the previous technology in terms of its price/quality ratio and to ensure performance at 100 Mbps. In the course of research and investigation, specialists divided into two groups, finally resulting in 1995 in the arrival of two new technologies: Fast Ethernet and 100VG-AnyLAN. However, in the long run, only Fast Ethernet — which retained more of the properties of classical Ethernet, including CSMA/CD — survived.

The success of Fast Ethernet further increased interest in high-speed Ethernet. The next variant, Gigabit Ethernet, was standardized three years later. Gigabit Ethernet is also distinguished by the high level of features retained from Ethernet 10 Mbps; it too has preserved the possibility of operating on the basis of a shared medium using CSMA/CD.

However, the latest version of Ethernet, 10G Ethernet, differs considerably from its ancestor. In particular, it operates only in the full-duplex mode, which means that it no longer supports a shared medium.

Therefore, this chapter will consider only Fast Ethernet and Gigabit Ethernet. 10G Ethernet will be covered in *Chapter 15*, with other technologies operating in the full-duplex mode that allow the construction of switched LANs.

13.2 FAST ETHERNET

KEY WORDS: *Fast Ethernet Alliance,* 100Base-TX, 100Base-T4, 100Base-FX, demand priority, Media independent interface (MII) Reconciliation sublayer, Physical layer device (PHY), Idle symbol, auto negotiation, 100Base-TX full duplex, fast link pulse (FLP) burst, Medium Dependent Interface (MDI) port, MDI-X port, Limitations on the Maximum Length, Class I and II repeaters, Fast Ethernet, one or two hubs rule, 100VG-AnyLAN

13.2.1 Historical Overview

In 1992, a group of network equipment manufacturers, including Ethernet leaders such as SynOptics and 3Com, created the noncommercial *Fast Ethernet Alliance*. The main goal of this Alliance was developing the standard for the new technology, which had to ensure considerable performance growth, but, at the same time, preserve as many Ethernet-specific features as possible.

By the same time, the IEEE 802 Committee had formed a research group to investigate the technological potential of new high-speed technologies. From the end of 1992 until the end of 1993, the IEEE group studied several 100 Mbit solutions suggested by various manufacturers. As well as the proposals of the Fast Ethernet Alliance, the group also considered high-speed technology suggested by Hewlett-Packard and AT&T.

The problem of preserving CSMA/CD was at the center of the discussion. The Fast Ethernet Alliance's suggestion preserved this method, thus providing compatibility and coordination between the 10 Mbps and the 100 Mbps technologies. The HP/AT&T coalition, which was supported by a significantly smaller number of network equipment manufacturers than the Fast Ethernet Alliance, suggested a newer and different access method, which became known as **demand priority**. This method significantly changed the pattern of network node behavior and therefore could not be blended with Ethernet and IEEE 802.3. A new IEEE workgroup (IEEE 802.12) was organized to standardize demand priority.

In autumn 1995, both technologies became IEEE standards. The IEEE 802.3 Committee adopted Fast Ethernet as the 802.3u standard. IEEE 802.3u is not a standalone standard, being a supplement to the existing 802.3 standard in the form of *Chapters 21–30*. The 802.12 Committee adopted 100VG-AnyLAN, which uses the new demand priority access method and supports frames of two formats: Ethernet and Token Ring.

13.2.2 Fast Ethernet Physical Layer

All the differences between Fast Ethernet and classical Ethernet technologies are concentrated at the physical layer (Figure 13.1). In Fast Ethernet, the MAC and LLC layers remained the same and are described in the same chapters of the 802.3 and 802.2 standards. Therefore, for Fast Ethernet, only a few versions of its physical layer will be considered here.

The more sophisticated structure of the Fast Ethernet physical layer is because of the use of three variants of cabling systems:

■ Fiber-optic multimode cable, two fibers
■ Category 5 twisted pair, two pairs
■ Category 3 twisted pair, four pairs

The coaxial cable that gave the world its first Ethernet network was not included in the list of allowed transmission media for Fast Ethernet. This trend is common for most new technologies, since Category 5 twisted pair allows data transmission at the same rate as coaxial cable. At the same time, the network becomes cheaper and more convenient to

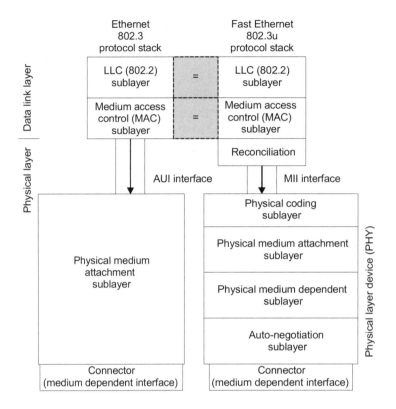

Figure 13.1 Differences between Fast Ethernet and classical Ethernet

support and maintain. Over larger distances, optical fiber provides significantly broader bandwidth than coaxial cable, and network cost is only slightly higher, especially taking into account the high cost of searching for malfunctions and troubleshooting in a large coaxial cabling system.

Because the use of coaxial cable was abandoned, Fast Ethernet networks on a shared medium always have a hierarchical tree structure based on concentrators similar to that of 10Base-T/10Base-F networks. The main difference in Fast Ethernet configurations is the reduction of the network diameter to approximately 200 m. This is explained by the tenfold reduction in the time required for transmitting a minimum-length frame because of a tenfold increase in data rate in comparison with classical Ethernet.

Nevertheless, this does not present a serious obstacle to building large networks based on Fast Ethernet. The mid-1990s were characterized not only by widespread use of inexpensive high-speed technologies but also by rapid development of *switched* LANs. When using switches, Fast Ethernet can operate in the full-duplex mode, which does not impose limitations on total network length. When using the full-duplex mode, the only limitations left are on the length of physical segments connecting neighboring devices (such as adapter–switch or switch–switch).

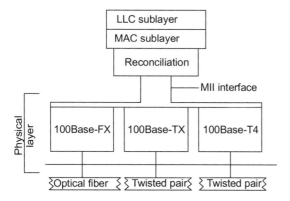

Figure 13.2 Structure of the Fast Ethernet physical layer

This section will concentrate on the classical, half-duplex variant of Fast Ethernet operation, which fully corresponds to the access method definition in the 802.3 standard. The specific features of the full-duplex mode of Fast Ethernet operation will be covered in *Chapter 15*.

In comparison with physical implementations of classical Ethernet (there are six), in Fast Ethernet, the differences among physical layer variants are more significant. This is because both the number of conductors and the method of encoding change from implementation to implementation. Moreover, physical implementations of Fast Ethernet were created simultaneously, rather than evolving, as was the case with classical Ethernet. Therefore, it was possible to define in detail sublayers of a physical layer that do not change with versions and sublayers specific for each variant of a physical medium.

The official 802.3 standard defines three specifications for the physical layer of Fast Ethernet (Figure 13.2):

- **100Base-TX** for two-pair cable based on Category 5 unshielded twisted pair (UTP) or Type 1 shielded twisted pair (STP)
- **100Base-T4** for four-pair cable based on UTP of Category 3, 4, or 5
- **100Base-FX** for multimode fiber-optic cable using two fibers

The following are true for all three specifications:

- Fast Ethernet frame formats do not differ from frame formats used in 10 Mbps Ethernet.
- The interpacket gap (IPG) is 0.96 μsec, and the bit interval (bt) is 10 nsec. All timing parameters of the access algorithm (slot time, time required to transmit the frame of

minimum length, etc.) are measured in bit intervals and remain the same, so no changes were introduced into the sections of the standard related to the MAC layer.

■ Transmission of the Idle symbol of appropriate redundant code using the medium indicates its availability (in contrast to 10 Mbps Ethernet standards, where lack of signals indicates that the medium is free).

The physical layer includes three elements:

■ **Media independent interface** (**MII**)

■ **Reconciliation sublayer**, which is needed to enable the MAC layer, intended for operating with the AUI, to communicate with the physical layer using MII

■ **Physical layer device** (**PHY**), which, in turn, comprises several sublayers (see Figure 13.1):

   • **Physical coding sublayer** (**PCS**), which transforms bytes arriving from the MAC layer into 4B/5B or 8B/6T symbols (both codes are used in Fast Ethernet).

   • **Physical medium attachment** (**PMA**) and **Physical medium dependent** (**PMD**) sublayers, which ensure formation of electrical or optical signals such as NRZI or MLT-3.

   • **Autonegotiation sublayer**, which allows two interacting ports to automatically select the most efficient operating mode, for example, half duplex or full duplex. This sublayer is optional.

MII supports a medium-independent method of data exchange between the MAC and PHY sublayers. By its goal, this interface is similar to the classical Ethernet's AUI, except that the AUI resided between the physical layer signaling (PLS) sublayer (with a different cable the same method of physical encoding, Manchester code, was used) and the PMA sublayer. MII, on the other hand, resides between the MAC layer's reconciliation sublayer and the PCS, which supports two encoding methods, as mentioned previously. PCS, PMA, and PMD form the PHY sublayer, of which there are three versions in Fast Ethernet: FX, TX, and T4 (Figure13.2).

13.2.3 100Base-FX/TX/T4 Specifications

The 100Base-FX, 100Base-TX, and 100Base-T4 specifications have much in common. Therefore, properties common for these specifications will be considered under generalized names, for example, 100Base-FX/TX or 100Base-TX/T4.

   The *100Base-FX* specification (multimode optical fiber, two fibers) defines Fast Ethernet protocol operation in the half-duplex and full-duplex modes.

Figure 13.3 Continuous data flow in 100Base-FX/TX

In contrast to 10 Mbps Ethernet, which uses Manchester code for data representation when transmitting data over the cable, Fast Ethernet defines another encoding method: 4B/5B. The details of 4B/5B encoding were considered in *Chapter 9*. Before Fast Ethernet was developed, this method had shown its efficiency in FDDI networks and therefore was introduced unchanged into 100Base-FX/TX. In this method, every 4 bits of MAC sublayer data (known as symbols) are represented by 5 bits. The redundant bit allows potential codes to be used when representing each of the 5 bits in the form of electric or optical pulses.

The existence of code violations because of 4B/5B and 8B/6T redundancy allows erroneous symbols to be discarded, improving the stability of 100Base-FX/TX networks. Thus, the indication of medium availability in Fast Ethernet is repeated transmission of the *Idle symbol (11111)*, a code violation when encoding user data. Such a method allows the receiver to always be synchronized with the transmitter.

To separate the Ethernet frame from the Idle symbols, the start delimiter combination is used. This consists of two symbols: *J (11000)* and *K (10001)* of 4B/5B code. When frame transmission is completed, the *T* symbol is inserted before the first Idle symbol (Figure 13.3).

After converting 4-bit chunks of MAC codes into 5-bit physical-layer chunks, they must be represented as optical or electric signals transmitted into the cable connecting network nodes. 100Base-FX and 100Base-TX use different methods of line encoding: NRZI and MLT-3, respectively.

The *100Base-TX* specification uses Category 5 UTP or Type 1 STP cable (two pairs) as a transmission medium.

Its main differences from the 100Base-FX specification are the use of the MLT-3 method for transmitting signals — 5-bit chunks of 4B/5B code — using twisted pair as well as the presence of the autonegotiation function for choosing the port operating mode.

The **autonegotiation** method allows two physically connected devices supporting different physical-layer standards in terms of bit rate and number of twisted pairs to choose the most efficient operating mode. Usually, the autonegotiation procedure takes place when connecting a network adapter capable of operating at 10 Mbps and 100 Mbps to the switch or router.

100Base-TX/T4 devices based on twisted pair support five operating modes:

■ 10Base-T

■ 10Base-T full duplex

- 100Base-TX
- 100Base-T4
- 100Base-TX full duplex

10Base-T has lowest priority in the course of negotiation, and full-duplex 100Base-TX mode has highest priority.

The negotiation process takes place when the device is powered up. It also can be initiated at any moment by the device's control unit.

The device that has started the process of autonegotiation sends its partner a sequence of special pulses, called a **fast link pulse** (**FLP**) **burst**, containing an 8-bit word encoding the proposed mode of interaction, starting from the highest-priority mode supported by the current node.

If the partner node supports the autonegotiation function and can also support the proposed mode, it replies with another FLP burst, confirming the proposed mode. The negotiation process at this point is completed. If the partner node can support only the lower-priority mode, it specifies this mode in its response, and this mode is chosen as the operating mode. Thus, the commonly supported mode with the highest priority is always chosen.

The *100Base-T4* specification (Category 3 UTP, four pairs) appeared later than other physical-layer specifications for Fast Ethernet. The main goal of developers of the earlier technologies, 100Base-TX/FX, was to create a physical-layer specification as close as possible to 10Base-T and 10Base-F that operated over two data transmission links: two twisted pairs or two optical fibers. To implement operation over two twisted pairs, it was necessary to change to Category 5 cable, which is characterized by higher quality.

At the same time, the developers of the competing 100VG-AnyLAN technology initially bet on operating using Category 3 twisted pair. The main advantage of this solution lay not so much in its lower price as in the required cabling already being installed in most buildings. Therefore, after 100Base-TX and 100Base-FX were released, Fast Ethernet developers also implemented their version of the physical layer for Category 3 twisted pair.

Instead of 4B/5B encoding, this method uses 8B/6T encoding, characterized by a narrower signal spectrum. At 33 Mbps, this method fits within the Category 3 twisted pair's 16 MHz band (when using 4B/5B encoding, the signal spectrum does not fit within this band). Each 8-bit chunk of MAC-layer information is encoded by six ternary symbols (i.e., by digits with three states). Transmission of each ternary digit lasts 40 nsec. The group of six ternary digits is then passed to one of the three transmitting twisted pairs, independently and sequentially.

The fourth pair is always used for sensing the carrier to detect collisions. The transmission rate over each of the three transmitting pairs is 33.3 Mbps, so the total rate of the 100Base-T4 protocol is 100 Mbps. At the same time, because of the adopted encoding method, the rate of signal change in each pair is only 25 Mbaud, so Category 3 twisted pair can be used.

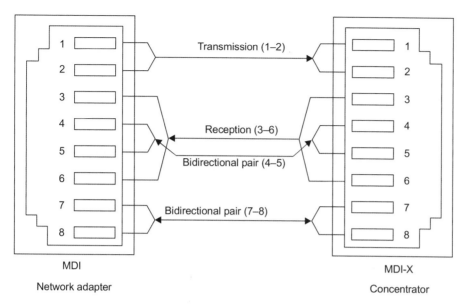

Figure 13.4 Node connection in 100Base-T4

Figure 13.4 shows the connection of a 100Base-T4 network adapter's **MDI** (Medium Dependent Interface) *port* to the concentrator's **MDI-X port**. (The X suffix indicates that in this port, the pins connecting the receiver and the transmitter are exchanged to route the transmit signals from one piece of equipment to the receive signals of another piece of equipment, and vice versa, which provides an easier way to join pairs in the cable without crossing them.) Pair 1–2 is required for transmitting data from the MDI port to the MDI-X port, pair 3–6 is for receiving data by the MDI port from the MDI-X port, and pairs 4–5 and 7–8 are bidirectional and used for both transmission and reception as needed.

13.2.4 Rules for Building Fast Ethernet Segments Using Repeaters

Fast Ethernet, like all Ethernet variants, is meant to use concentrators or repeaters for creating network links.

The rules for correctly building Fast Ethernet segments include:

- Limitations on the maximum length of segments connecting data terminal equipment (DTE) to DTE
- Limitations on the maximum length of segments connecting DTE to repeater port

- Limitations on the maximum network diameter
- Limitations on the maximum number of repeaters and the maximum length of the segment connecting repeaters

Limitations on the Maximum Length of DTE–DTE Segments

Any source of data frames for the network, including network adapters, bridge or router ports, network control modules, or other similar devices, can play the role of DTE. The distinguishing feature of a DTE device is that it generates a new frame for the shared segment. (Although bridges or routers transmit frames previously generated by network adapters using their output ports, these frames are new to the network segments to which specific output ports are connected.) The repeater port, however, is not a DTE device, since it repeats bit by bit the frames that have already appeared in the segment.

In a typical Fast Ethernet network configuration, several DTE devices are connected to repeater ports, thus forming a network with star topology. DTE–DTE connections are not encountered in shared segments (except for the exotic configuration in which network adapters of two computers are directly connected by cable). For bridges or routers, on the other hand, such connections are quite normal. In this situation, either a network adapter is directly connected to the port of one device, or these devices are directly connected to one another.

The maximum DTE–DTE segment lengths according to IEEE 802.3u are provided in Table 13.1.

Table 13.1 Maximum DTE–DTE segment lengths

Standard	Cable type	Maximum segment length
100Base-TX	Category 5 UTP	100 m
100Base-FX	Multimode optical fiber 62.5/125 μm	412 m (half duplex) to 2 km (full duplex)
100Base-T4	Category 3, 4, or 5 UTP	100 m

Limitations on Fast Ethernet Networks Based on Repeaters

Fast Ethernet repeaters are divided into two classes:

- **Class I repeaters** support all types of logical data encoding: 4B/5B and 8B/6T. This means that Class I repeaters allow translation of logical codes at 100 Mbps. For this reason, Class I repeaters can have ports of all three physical-layer types: 100Base-TX, 100Base-FX, and 100Base-T4.

■ **Class II repeaters** support either 4B/5B or 8B/6T. Class II repeaters have either all 100Base-T4 ports or 100Base-TX and 100Base-FX ports, since these physical-layer specifications both use 4B/5B coding.

In one collision domain there can be only one Class I repeater: It introduces a significant signal propagation delay because of the necessity of translating signals from one logical encoding to another. This delay is 70 bt.

Class II repeaters introduce a smaller signal propagation delay: 46 bt for TX/FX ports and 33.5 bt for T4 ports. Therefore, the greatest number of Class II repeaters in a single collision domain is two.

The limitation on the number of Fast Ethernet repeaters does not present a serious difficulty when building large networks, because the use of switches and routers divides the network into several collision domains, each of which can be based on one or two repeaters. Total network length in this case will have no limitations.

Table 13.2 lists the rules for building a network using Class I repeaters.

Table 13.2 Parameters of Fast Ethernet networks using Class I repeaters

Cable type	Maximum network diameter (m)	Maximum segment length (m)
Only twisted pair (TX)	200	100
Only optical fiber (FX)	272	136
Several segments based on twisted pair and one segment based on optical fiber	260	100 (TX) 160 (FX)
Several segments based on twisted pair and several segments based on optical fiber	272	100 (TX) 136 (FX)

These limitations are illustrated by the typical network configuration shown in Figure 13.5.

Thus, the four hubs rule turns into a *one* or *two hubs rule* for Fast Ethernet: The number of hubs depends on the hub class.

When determining the correctness of the network configuration, instead of using the one or two hubs rule, it is possible to calculate the path delay value (PDV), as shown in *Chapter 12* in the example for 10 Mbps Ethernet.

As with 10 Mbps Ethernet, the 802.3 standard provides reference data for calculating PDV in Fast Ethernet.

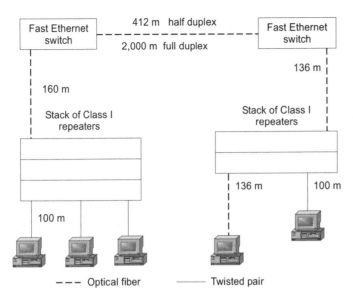

Figure 13.5 Examples of Fast Ethernet networks using Class I repeaters

13.2.5 Specific Features of 100VG-AnyLAN

Although **100VG-AnyLAN** implements many advanced technical solutions, it did not gain much support and fell out of use. It did not find its field of application, since in comparison with the traditional and more convenient Fast Ethernet, it proved to be too complicated. This is all the more true because Gigabit Ethernet supports applications that need high transmission rates; this ensures data transmission at 1,000 Mbps and preserves the historical link with Ethernet and Fast Ethernet.

Compared with Fast Ethernet, 100VG-AnyLAN differs from classical Ethernet in significantly more respects.

Access to the shared medium is carried out on the basis of the principally different method — the **demand priority**. This access method is based on delegating arbitrator functions to the concentrator, which solves the problem of access to the shared medium. A 100VG-AnyLAN network comprises a **central concentrator** (also referred to as the **root concentrator**) to which end nodes and other concentrators are connected (Figure 13.6).

Three levels of cascading are allowed in a 100VG-AnyLAN network. Each concentrator and 100VG-AnyLAN adapter must be configured for operation with either Ethernet or Token Ring frames. Simultaneous circulation of both types of frames is not allowed.

The concentrator performs round-robin polling of all ports. A station that needs to transmit a packet sends a special low-frequency signal to the concentrator, thus requesting permission to transmit a frame and specifying its priority. 100VG-AnyLAN net-

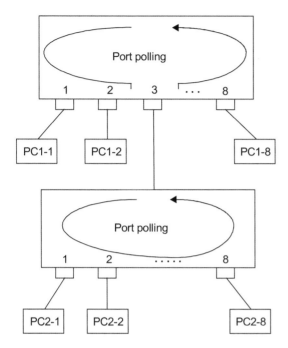

Figure 13.6 100VG-AnyLAN network

works use two priority levels: low and high. Low priority corresponds to normal data (file service, print service, etc.), and high priority corresponds to delay-sensitive data (such as multimedia). Request priorities have static and dynamic components, meaning that a low-priority station will be automatically assigned high priority if it does not obtain access to the network for a long time.

If the medium is available, the concentrator allows packet transmission. After analyzing the destination address of the received packet, the concentrator automatically sends it to the destination node. If the network is busy, the concentrator places the received request into the queue, which is processed according to the order of request arrivals, taking account of their priorities. If another concentrator is connected to the port, polling is deferred until the lower-level concentrator completes polling. Stations connected to concentrators of different hierarchical levels have no advantages related to accessing the shared medium, since the decision on providing access is made only when all concentrators complete polling of all their ports.

So how does the concentrator know to which port the destination station is connected? In all other technologies, the frame is transmitted to all other network stations, and the destination station, having recognized its address, copies that frame to its buffer. To solve this problem, the concentrator recognizes the station's MAC address when that station is physically connected to the network by the cable. In contrast to all other technologies, in which physical connection tests cable connectivity (the link integrity test in 10Base-T) and determines the port's operating rate (autonegotiation in Fast Ethernet), the 100VG-AnyLAN concentrator determines the MAC address of the station when establishing a physical connection and stores it in the table of MAC addresses (this table is similar to bridge or router tables). The difference between 100VG-Any-LAN concentrators and bridges or routers is that the concentrators have no internal buffer for storing frames: Therefore, they receive only one frame from networked workstations, send it to the destination port, and do not receive new frames until the frame is fully received by the destination station. This means that the effect of a shared medium is preserved. Thus, improvements pertain only to network security, since frames are not delivered to foreign ports, making them harder to detect.

100VG-AnyLAN supports several physical-layer specifications. The first version was intended to use four UTPs of Categories 3, 4, and 5. Some time later, other variants appeared, for two Category 5 UTPs, two Type 1 STPs, or two multimode optical fibers.

13.3 GIGABIT ETHERNET

> **KEY WORDS:** 802.3z and 802.3ab workgroups, Gigabit Ethernet, 8B/10B code, Category 5 twisted pair, Quality of service (QoS), Redundant links, CSMA/CD, fiber optic, STP, extension, burst mode, BurstLength, 1000Base-SX, 1000Base-LX, 1000Base-CX, 4B/5B code, AM5

13.3.1 Historical Overview

Not long after Fast Ethernet products appeared on the market, network integrators and administrators discovered certain limitations when building enterprise-wide networks. In many cases, servers connected using a 100 Mbps channel overloaded FDDI and Fast Ethernet backbones, which also operated at 100 Mbps. The need for the next layer of speed hierarchy became obvious. In 1995, higher rates could be provided only by ATM switches, which were rarely used in LANs because of their high cost and significant differences from classical LAN technologies.

Therefore, the IEEE's next step was quite logical. In summer 1996, the 802.3z workgroup was created: It aimed to develop a protocol as close to Ethernet as possible but providing a bit rate of 1,000 Mbps. As with Fast Ethernet, this news was enthusiastically received by Ethernet supporters.

The main reason for this enthusiasm was the prospect of a smooth transition of network backbones to Gigabit Ethernet, similarly to the transition from congested low-level Ethernet segments to Fast Ethernet. Additionally, by that time, some experience of data transmission at gigabit rates had already accumulated. In MANs and WANs, this was achieved on the basis of SDH, and in LANs, the same goal had been achieved on the basis of Fiber Channel. The latter is mainly used to connect high-speed periphery to powerful computers. It ensures data transmission over fiber-optic cable at rates close to 1 gigabit; this is achieved using redundant 8B/10B code.

The 8B/10B encoding method used in Fiber Channel was adopted as the first version of the physical layer of Gigabit Ethernet.

The 802.3z standard was approved on June 29, 1998. The task of implementing Gigabit Ethernet on the basis of Category 5 twisted pair was delegated to the 802.3ab task group. Mainly, this was because of complications of ensuring gigabit transmission rates using this type of cable, initially created to support rates of roughly 100 Mbps. The 802.3ab task group accomplished its task successfully, and Gigabit Ethernet for Category 5 twisted pair was soon adopted.

13.3.2 Problems

The main idea of the developers of Gigabit Ethernet was to preserve as much as possible from the ideas of classic Ethernet while achieving a bit rate of 1,000 Mbps.

Although it would be logical to expect the introduction of technical innovations reflecting common trends in technological evolution from any emerging new technology, these expectations were not satisfied in the case of Gigabit Ethernet. In particular, like its lower-speed predecessors, Gigabit Ethernet does *not* support the following features at the protocol layer:

- Quality of service (QoS)
- Redundant links
- Testing of network node and equipment usability (in the latter case, as with Ethernet 10Base-T, 10Base-F and Fast Ethernet, with the exception of port–port links)

All three functions are seen as promising and useful for contemporary networks and especially for networks in the near future. Why did the Gigabit Ethernet developers abandon them?

The answer is straightforward. In today's LANs, these useful features are ensured by switches, which support full-duplex versions of Ethernet family protocols. Therefore, the Gigabit Ethernet developers decided that the basic protocol must simply ensure fast data transmission, and more complicated functions that are not always necessary (such as QoS support) must be delegated to higher-layer protocols that operate with switches.

So what features does Gigabit Ethernet have in common with its predecessors, Ethernet and Fast Ethernet?

- All Ethernet frame formats are preserved.

> ■ The half-duplex version of the protocol supporting CSMA/CD is still present. Preserving an inexpensive solution on the basis of a shared medium allows Gigabit Ethernet to be applied in small workgroups with fast servers and workstations.
> ■ All the main types of cables used in Ethernet and Fast Ethernet are supported, including fiber optic, Category 5 twisted pair, and STP.

Although the Gigabit Ethernet developers decided to do without building in advanced new features, they encountered several complicated problems even when ensuring the basic functional capabilities of classical Ethernet:

■ *Ensuring an acceptable network diameter for operation on the basis of a shared medium.* Because of the limitations imposed by CSMA/CD on cable length, preserving frame size and all parameters of CSMA/CD would reduce the maximum segment length to 25 m for the shared-medium version of the Gigabit Ethernet. Since many fields of application require network diameter to be at least 200 m, it was necessary to find a solution to this problem without introducing major changes from Fast Ethernet.

■ *Achieving a 1,000 Mbps bit rate using fiber-optic cable.* Fiber Channel, the physical layer of which was taken as a basis for the fiber-optic version of Gigabit Ethernet, guarantees a data rate of only 800 Mbps.

■ *Providing support for the twisted pair cables.* At first, this problem seems to have no solution. Even 100 Mbit protocols require rather sophisticated encoding methods to ensure that the signal spectrum fits within the cable bandwidth.

To solve these tasks, the Gigabit Ethernet developers had to introduce changes not only to the physical layer, as was the case with Fast Ethernet, but also to the MAC layer.

13.3.3 Ensuring Network Diameter of 200 Meters

To extend the maximum diameter of the Gigabit Ethernet network to 200 m in half-duplex mode, the developers took natural steps. These solutions are based on the well-known ratio (described in the "Case Study" in *Chapter 12*) between the time required to transmit a frame of minimum length and the PDV.

Minimum frame size was increased (without taking the preamble into account) from 64 to 512 bytes, or 4,096 bt. Accordingly, the PDV can also be increased to 4,095 bt, which allows network diameter of about 200 m, provided that one repeater is used.

To increase the frame length to the required value, the network adapter has to fill the data field to 448 bytes with an **extension**, a field filled with zeros. Formally, the minimum frame size did not change, since it remains 64 bytes of 512 bits. However, this is because the *Extension* field is placed after the *FCS* field. Accordingly, the value of this field is not included into the checksum and is not taken into account when specifying the data field length in the *Length* field. The *Extension* field is simply padding for the carrier signal, which is necessary for correct collision detection.

To reduce the overhead when using too-long frames to transmit short acknowledgments, the standard developers allowed the end node to transmit several frames one after another, without passing the medium to other stations. This operating mode became known as **burst mode**. The station can transmit several frames one after another, provided that their total length does not exceed 65,536 bits, or 8,192 bytes. If the station needs to transmit several small frames, it is allowed to do so without filling the first frame to 512 bytes by adding the *Extension* field. In this case, the station can transmit several frames sequentially, until the limit of 8,192 bytes is reached (this limit includes all frame bytes, including preamble, header, data, and checksum). The limit of 8,192 bytes is referred to as **BurstLength**. If the station has started transmitting a frame, and the BurstLength limit has been reached in the course of frame transmission, the station is allowed to complete transmission of the frame.

Increasing the size of the "combined" frame to 8,192 bytes delays access to the medium for other stations; however, at 1,000 Mbps, this delay is not significant.

13.3.4 802.3z Physical Medium Specifications

The 802.3z standard defines the following types of physical medium:

- Single-mode fiber-optic cable
- Multimode 62.5/125 fiber-optic cable
- Multimode 50/125 fiber-optic cable
- Shielded balanced copper cable

To transmit data over traditional multimode fiber-optic cable, the standard defines the use of emitters working at two wavelengths: 1,300 nm and 850 nm. The use of LEDs with a 850 nm wavelength is explainable: They are significantly cheaper than LEDs operating at 1,300 nm. Nevertheless, the maximum cable length is decreased, since the attenuation of the multimode optical fiber at 850 nm wavelength is more than twice that at 1,300 nm. However, the lower price is very important for a generally expensive technology such as Gigabit Ethernet.

For multimode optical fiber, the 802.3z standard defines the following specifications: **1000Base-SX** and **1000Base-LX**.

In the first case, the wavelength is 850 nm (S stands for Short Wavelength); in the second case, it is 1,300 nm (L stands for Long Wavelength).

For 1000Base-LX, the light source is always a semiconductor LED with a 1,300 nm wavelength.

1000Base-LX allows the use of both multimode (maximum segment length up to 500 m) and single-mode cable (maximum segment length depends on the transmitter power and cable quality, and can reach several tens of kilometers).

The **1000Base-CX** specification uses shielded balanced copper cable as the transmission medium. This cable has impedance of 150 ohms. The maximum segment length is only 25 m, so this solution is suitable only for equipment within a single room.

13.3.5 Gigabit Ethernet Based on Category 5 Twisted Pair

Each Category 5 pair has guaranteed bandwidth of 100 MHz. To transmit data using such a cable at 1,000 Mbps, it was decided to organize parallel data transmission using all four cable pairs.

This reduced the data transmission rate over each pair to 250 Mbps. However, even at this rate, it was necessary to invent an encoding method that would ensure the spectrum did not exceed 100 MHz. For example, 4B/5B code cannot solve this problem, since at this rate, the frequency of 155 MHz makes the main contribution to the signal spectrum. It should also be remembered that each new technology must support not only the classical half-duplex mode considered in this chapter but also the full-duplex mode, which will be covered in detail in *Chapter 15*. At first, it might seem that simultaneous use of four pairs deprives the network of the possibility of operating in full-duplex mode, since no free pairs remain for simultaneous bidirectional data transmission from node to node.

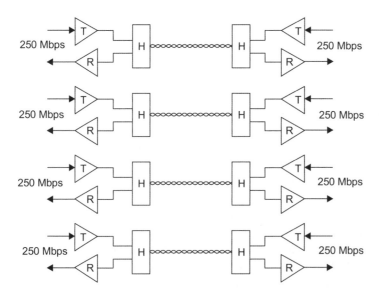

Figure 13.7 Bidirectional transmission using four Category 5 UTPs

However, the 802.3ab task group found answers to both of these questions.

For data encoding, the PAM5 code, using five levels of potential (−2, −1, 0, +1, and +2) was employed. Therefore, each pair transmits 2.322 bits of information ($\log_2 5$) per clock. Consequently, to achieve 250 Mbps, the clock frequency of 250 MHz can be decreased 2.322 times. The standard's developers decided to use a somewhat higher frequency: 125 MHz. At this clock frequency, PAM5 has a spectrum narrower than 100 MHz, which means that it can be transmitted without distortion over Category 5 cable.

During each clock, 8 bits of information are transmitted (rather than $2.322 \times 4 = 9.288$). This gives a total rate of 1,000 Mbps. Transmission of exactly 8 bits per each clock is achieved because only 256 ($2^8 = 256$) of the available 625 ($5^4 = 625$) combinations of PAM5 code are used. The receiver uses the remaining combinations for controlling the received information and distinguishing legitimate combinations from background noise.

To organize the full-duplex mode, the developers of the 802.3ab specification applied the technique of obtaining the received signal from the aggregate one. Two transmitters operate by transmitting information to each other in reverse directions using each of the four pairs in the same frequency range (Figure 13.7). The design of hybrid decoupling H allows the receiver and transmitter of the same node to use the twisted pair simultaneously for transmission and reception (similar to transceivers used in Ethernet based on coaxial cable).

To separate the received signal from the one that the node is currently transmitting, the receiver subtracts its own signal from the resulting one. Naturally, this is not an easy operation, and special digital signal processors (DSP) are required.

SUMMARY

▶ The need for high-speed but inexpensive technology to connect powerful workstations to a network in the early 1990s resulted in the creation of an initiative group that would develop a new technology as simple and efficient as the Ethernet but operating at 100 Mbps.

▶ Specialists divided into two groups, which finally developed two standards adopted in autumn 1995: The IEEE 802.3 Committee approved the Fast Ethernet standard, which almost duplicates Ethernet 10 Mbps, and the specially created 802.12 Committee adopted 100VG-AnyLAN, which preserves the Ethernet frame format but changes the access method significantly.

▶ Fast Ethernet preserved CSMA/CD, leaving unchanged its working algorithm and timing parameters in bit intervals (although the bit interval itself decreased 90%). All differences between Fast Ethernet and classical Ethernet manifest themselves at the physical layer.

▶ The Fast Ethernet standard defines three physical-layer specifications: 100Base-TX, 100Base-FX, and 100Base-T4.

▶ The maximum diameter of a Fast Ethernet network is approximately 200 m; more precise values depend on the physical medium specification. In the Fast Ethernet collision domain, there can be no more than one Class I repeater, or no more than two Class II repeaters.

▶ Fast Ethernet based on twisted pair allows two ports to choose the most efficient operating mode by implementing autonegotiation. The ports can choose either 10 Mbps or 100 Mbps as well as the half-duplex or the full-duplex mode.

▶ In 100VG-AnyLAN, a concentrator supporting demand priority plays the role of arbitrator and makes a decision on providing stations access to the shared medium.

▶ Gigabit Ethernet adds a new stage to the speed hierarchy of the Ethernet family: 1,000 Mbps. This level allows efficient construction of large LANs with servers and low-level backbones operating at 100 Mbps as the Gigabit Ethernet backbone connects them, ensuring significant reserves of bandwidth.

▶ The Gigabit Ethernet developers retained a large amount of continuity from Ethernet and Fast Ethernet. Gigabit Ethernet uses the same frame format as previous Ethernet versions and supports the full-duplex and half-duplex modes and CSMA/CD with minimum changes.

▶ The special 802.3ab task group developed Gigabit Ethernet for Category 5 UTP. Data transmission at 1,000 Mbps is ensured by the following:

- Simultaneous transmission of data through four UTPs
- PAM-5 encoding, ensuring data transmission at 250 Mbps using a single twisted pair
- Simultaneous bidirectional information transmission in the full-duplex mode, with separation of the received signal from the common signal using special DSPs.

REVIEW QUESTIONS

1. Which drawbacks of CSMA/CD are eliminated by demand priority?
2. Why did the developers of Fast Ethernet decide to preserve CSMA/CD?
3. Which topologies are supported by a Fast Ethernet network based on a shared medium?
4. What is the maximum diameter of a Fast Ethernet network?
5. How many pairs of cable are used for data transmission in 100Base-T4?

6. What are the differences between Class I and Class II Fast Ethernet repeaters?

7. Why is only one Class I repeater allowed in a Fast Ethernet network?

8. What is the minimum value of the interpacket gap in Gigabit Ethernet?

9. Because of bandwidth increase, the developers of Gigabit Ethernet had to increase the minimum frame size to 512 bytes. When the data being transmitted cannot fill the data field of the frame, it is complemented to the required length by padding, which does not carry any useful information. What steps have been taken in Gigabit Ethernet to reduce the overhead for short data transmission?

10. What steps have been taken in Gigabit Ethernet to ensure data transmission at 1,000 Mbps using twisted pair?

   A. Increased quality of twisted pair cable

   B. Use of four pairs of the cable instead of two

   C. Increased the number of states of the signal code

   D. Implemented Quadrature Amplitude Modulation

11. Why does Gigabit Ethernet use both multimode and single-mode optical fiber?

PROBLEMS

1. **Task:** Using Tables 13.3 and 13.4, determine what stability reserve a Fast Ethernet configuration with one Class I repeater has.

TIP

When determining the correctness of a Fast Ethernet network, instead of using the one or two hubs rule, it is possible to calculate the PDV, as was done in the "Case Study" in Chapter 12 for the Transmash network.

As for Ethernet 10 Mbps, the Fast Ethernet standard provides source data for calculating the signal PDV. However, the form of this data and the method of calculation have changed. Fast Ethernet provides data on doubled delays introduced by each network segment, without dividing network segments into left, intermediate, and right. In addition, delays introduced by network adapters take into account frame preambles. Therefore, PDV must be compared to 512 bt (i.e., to the time required to transmit a minimum-length frame without a preamble).

For Class I repeaters the RTT can be calculated as follows: Delays introduced during signal transmission using the cable are calculated based on the data provided in Table 13.3, which takes into account that the signal has to pass through the cable twice.

Delays introduced by two network adapters (or ports of the switches) interacting through a repeater are shown in Table 13.4.

Taking into account that the doubled delay introduced by a Class I repeater is 140 bt, it is possible to calculate RTT for any network configuration, (accounting for the maximum lengths of cable segments, provided in Table 13.2). If the resulting value is smaller than 512, then according to the collision detection criterion, this network configuration is correct. The 802.3 standard recommends ensuring a reserve of 4 bt for stable network operation. However, it allows choosing a value between 0 and 5 bt.

Table 13.3 Delays introduced by the cable

Cable type	Doubled delay (bit interval per 1 m)	Doubled delay on the cable of maximum length
UTP Cat 3	1.14 bt	114 bt (100 m)
UTP Cat 4	1.14 bt	114 bt (100 m)
UTP Cat 5	1.112 bt	111.2 bt (100 m)
STP	1.112 bt	111.2 bt (100 m)
Optical fiber	1.0 bt	412 bt (412 m)

Table 13.4 Delays introduced by network adapters

Network adapter type	Maximum delay for the round trip
Two TX/FX adapters	100 bt
Two T4 adapters	138 bt
One TX/FX adapter and one T4 adapter	127 bt

14

SHARED MEDIA LANS

14.1 INTRODUCTION

This chapter considers several shared media LAN technologies other than Ethernet. This list includes Token Ring and FDDI, which for a long time were successfully used in LANs that required superior performance and reliability as well as increased coverage area. Before the arrival of switched LANs, these technologies surpassed Ethernet in these terms. Because of this, they were given preference when building LAN backbones or creating networks for financial or governmental organizations — that is, where performance and reliability were of primary importance. Token Ring and FDDI employ a deterministic access method, allowing more efficient sharing of the transmission medium, and they even provide QoS support for real-time traffic.

Token Ring and FDDI use the ring topology of physical links, enabling them to control network operability automatically. FDDI networks additionally ensure automatic network recovery after failures. To provide this, they use a dual ring for connecting nodes; in this respect, they are similar to SDH networks.

Wireless communications media are shared by their physical nature. This chapter covers two wireless technologies, IEEE 802.11 and Bluetooth (IEEE 802.15.1). The first allows the creation of wireless LANs; the latter pertains to personal area networks (PANs). Each technology has its own medium access methods.

14.2 TOKEN RING

KEY WORDS: Token Ring, active monitor, token-holding time, early token release, priority, token-passing procedure, multistation access unit (MAU or MSAU), passive concentrator, active concentrator, STP Type 1, UTP Type 3, UTP Type 6, IBM cabling-system types, fiber-optic cable

The **Token Ring** technology was developed by IBM in 1984 and then passed to the IEEE 802 Committee as a proposed standard project. The IEEE 802 Committee used this technology as a basis for the 802.5 standard, which was adopted in 1985. For a long time, IBM used Token Ring as its main network technology for building LANs based on different classes of computers, from mainframes and powerful minicomputers to PCs. However, in recent years, the Ethernet family has dominated, even among IBM products.

Token Ring networks operate at two bit rates: 4 and 16 Mbps. Workstations operating at different rates within a single ring are not allowed. Token Ring networks operating at 16 Mbps include some improvements on the standard access algorithm used in 4 Mbps networks.

Token Ring is more sophisticated than Ethernet. It provides some basic fault-tolerance features. In a Token Ring network, special procedures for controlling network operation are defined. These procedures use the feedback property inherent to the ring topology: The sent frame always returns to the sender. In some cases, network errors are corrected automatically. For instance, a lost token can be restored. In other cases, the network only reports detected errors, and support personnel must eliminate them manually.

To control network operation, one of its workstations is delegated the role of **active monitor**. The active monitor is chosen during ring initialization. The maximum medium access control (MAC) address value is the criterion. If the active monitor fails, the ring initialization procedure is repeated, and a new active monitor is chosen. To enable the network to detect the failure of the active monitor, the latter generates a special frame notifying other workstations of its presence. This happens every 3 seconds (provided that the active monitor is running). If such a frame is not sent for more than 7 seconds, other workstations start the procedure of selecting a new active monitor.

14.2.1 Token-Passing Access

Token Ring networks use shared medium based on the token-passing access principle, described in *Chapter 12* when describing the MAC layer functions. We will describe in more detail some specific features of this method, which is characteristic of the **Token Ring 4 Mbps** technology described in the 802.5 standard.

In a Token Ring network, each station receives data directly from only one station: the one before it in the ring. Each station transmits the data to its nearest downstream neighbor.

Having received the token, the station analyzes it. If this station has no data to transmit, it passes the token to the next station. When the token is passed to a station that has data for transmission, it withdraws the token from the ring, which gives it the right to access the physical medium to transmit its data. After that, the station sequentially sends a special format frame into the ring. This frame contains source and destination addresses.

Data being transmitted always travel along the ring in one direction, from station to station. All stations in the ring retransmit the frame bit by bit, acting as repeaters. If the frame arrives to the destination node, this station recognizes its address, copies the frame into its internal buffer, and inserts the reception acknowledgment indicator into the frame. The station that sent the data frame into the ring, having received it again with the reception acknowledgment, withdraws the frame from the ring and passes a new token into the network, thus allowing other stations to transmit data.

Figure 14.1 provides a time diagram illustrating the medium access algorithm described here. It demonstrates passing packet A from station 1 to station 3 in a ring comprising six stations. After packet A passes the destination node, station 3, two flags are set in this packet: address recognition flag A and indicator C, specifying that the packet has been copied into the internal buffer. (In the illustration, this is denoted by an asterisk inside the packet.) When the packet returns to station 1, the sender recognizes its packet by the source address and withdraws the packet from the ring. The flags set by station 3 notify the sender that the packet was successfully delivered to its destination node and copied into its internal buffer.

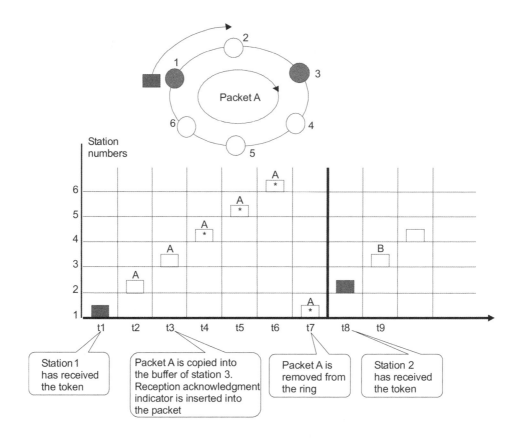

Figure 14.1 Token-passing access

The time during which the shared medium is monopolized in Token Ring networks is limited by a fixed value known as **token-holding time**. When this time elapses, the station must stop transmission of its data (transmission of the current frame is allowed to be completed) and pass the token along the ring. While holding the token, the station can transmit one or more frames, depending on the frame size and on the duration of the token-holding interval. By default, the token-holding time is usually set to 10 msec; the maximum frame size is not strictly defined in the 802.5 standard. As a rule, for 4 Mbps networks, it is 4 KB; for 16 Mbps networks, it is normally 16 KB. These values were chosen because during the token-holding time, the station must transmit at least one frame. At 4 Mbps, it is possible to transmit 5,000 bytes during 10 msec; at 16 Mbps, it is possible to transmit 20,000 bytes during the same time. Maximum frame sizes are chosen to have a certain reserve.

Token Ring 16 Mbps networks use a slightly different ring access algorithm, known as **early token release**. According to this algorithm, the station passes the access token to its nearest downstream *neighbor immediately after it completes the transmission of the last bit* *of the frame*, without waiting for the frame to return with set reception acknowledgment bits A and C. In this case, ring bandwidth is used more efficiently, since frames from several workstations are moving along the ring simultaneously. Nevertheless, at any moment, only one workstation can generate frames: the one that possesses the access token. All other workstations at that time only repeat the frames transmitted by other nodes, so that the time-sharing principle is retained. In this case, only the token-passing procedure is accelerated.

For different types of messages, the frames being transmitted can be assigned different *priorities*, from 0 (the lowest) to 7 (the highest). The transmitting workstation decides the priority of a specific frame. The Token Ring protocol receives this parameter using service interfaces from higher-layer protocols, such as application-layer protocols. The token always has some specific level of current priority. The station has the right to capture the token transmitted to it only if the priority of the frame that it has to transmit is equal to or higher than the token priority. Otherwise, the station has to pass the token to the next station along the ring.

The active monitor is responsible for the presence of a single copy of the token in the network. If the active monitor does not receive the token for a long time (for example, 2.6 sec), it generates a new token.

Priority access in Token Ring is intended to support QoS requirements for applications. However, developers of applications intended for LANs never used this capability.

14.2.2 Token Ring Physical Layer

The Token Ring standard developed by IBM initially made provision for building network links using **multistation access unit** (**MAU** or **MSAU**) concentrators (i.e., multistation access devices) (Figure 14.2). A Token Ring network can include 260 nodes. The use of concentrators gives Token Ring networks a physical "star" topology; their logical topology is a ring.

A Token Ring concentrator may be active or passive. A **passive concentrator** simply connects ports by internal links so that the stations connected to those ports can form a ring. A passive MSAU concentrator does not amplify or resynchronize signals. Such a device can be seen as a simple cross unit with one exception: MSAU ensures a specific port is bypassed if the computer connected to that port is powered down. This is required to ensure ring connectivity independent of the state of connected computers. Usually, port bypassing uses relay circuits supplied by a direct current from the network adapter. When the network adapter is powered down, the relay contacts, which are normally closed, connect the port input to its output.

An **active concentrator** carries out functions of signal regeneration. Therefore, it is sometimes called a repeater.

If the concentrator is a passive device, how can it ensure high-quality signal transmission over long distances, as with large-scale networks comprising hundreds of computers?

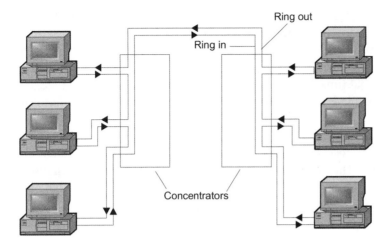

Figure 14.2 Physical configuration of a Token Ring network

The answer is simple. In this case, every network adapter takes on the role of signal amplifier; the role of the synchronizing unit is delegated to the network adapter of the ring's active monitor. Each Token Ring network adapter has a repeater unit capable of regenerating and synchronizing signals. However, the latter role is played only by the repeater unit of the active monitor.

In general, a Token Ring network has a combined star–ring configuration. End nodes are connected to MSAU according to the star topology, and MSAU concentrators are connected to one another using special ring in and ring out ports to form a physical backbone ring.

Token Ring allows the use of various types of cable for connecting end nodes and concentrators: STP Type 1, UTP Type 3, and UTP Type 6 (IBM cabling-system types) as well as fiber-optic cable.

When using STP Type 1 from the IBM cabling stable, it is possible to connect up to 260 workstations to the ring, with the maximum length of lobe cables at 100 m. If unshielded twisted pair is used, the maximum number of workstations is reduced to 72 and cable length to 45 m.

The distance between passive MSAU concentrators can reach 100 m when using STP Type 1 cable. When using UTP Type 3 cable, this distance is reduced to 45 m. The maximum distance between active MSAU concentrators is 730 m or 365 m, depending on the cable type.

The maximum ring length of a Token Ring network is 4,000 m.

NOTE   *Limitations on the maximum ring length and the number of workstations within the ring in Token Ring are not as restrictive as limitations in Ethernet. In Token Ring, restrictions are related to the time of the token turnaround along the ring, although there are additional considerations that define the choice of limitations. For example, suppose that the ring comprises 260 workstations. With a token-holding time of 10 msec, in the worst case, the token will return to the active monitor after 2.6 sec. This time equals the timeout for token turnaround. Principally, all timeout values for the network adapters of network nodes are adjustable in Token Ring networks. Therefore, it is possible to build a Token Ring network with a larger number of workstations and a longer ring.*

14.3 FDDI

KEY WORDS: FDDI (Fiber Distributed Data Interface), fiber-optic cable, NRZI, primary ring, thru mode, secondary ring, wrap mode, token-passing method, station management (SMT), fault tolerance, dual attachment (DA), dual attachment station (DAS), dual attachment concentrator (DAC), single attachment (SA), single attachment station (SAS), single attachment concentrator (SAC), optical bypass switches, dual homing

FDDI — Fiber Distributed Data Interface — was the first LAN technology to use fiber-optic cable as a transmission medium. Research into creating devices and technologies for LANs using fiber-optic links started in the 1980s soon after such links found application in WANs. From 1986 to 1988, ANSI's X3T9.5 research group developed the first versions of the FDDI standard ensuring frame transmission at 100 Mbps using a dual fiber-optic ring up to 100 km long.

14.3.1 Main FDDI Characteristics

FDDI is based in many respects on Token Ring, developing and improving its main ideas. FDDI developers had the following main goals:

■ Increase bit rate for data transmission to 100 Mbps
■ Improve network fault tolerance by introducing standard procedures for recovery after failures, such as cable faults, incorrect operation of a node, a concentrator malfunction, and a high level of noise in the line
■ Ensure maximum level of potential network bandwidth use for both asynchronous and synchronous (delay-sensitive) traffic

FDDI networks are built on the basis of two fiber-optic rings that form the main and the protection paths of data transmission between network nodes. The availability of two rings is the main method of improving fault tolerance in FDDI networks.

Critical nodes that need to benefit from this increased fault tolerance potential must be connected to both rings. For transmitting data using optical fibers, FDDI implements

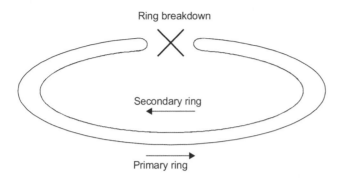

Figure 14.3 Reconfiguration of FDDI rings after a failure

4B/5B logical encoding with line nonreturn to zero with ones inverted (NRZI) encoding. This method transmits the signal using a communications link at a clock frequency of 125 MHz.

In normal operating mode, the transmitted data pass all nodes and all sections of only the **primary ring**. This mode is known as the **thru mode** (i.e., the transit mode). The **secondary ring** is not used in this mode.

If a failure occurs and part of the primary ring cannot transmit data (this can be caused by cable breakdown or node failure), the primary ring is joined to the secondary ring (Figure 14.3), once again forming a closed ring. This mode of network operation is known as the **wrap mode**. The wrapping operation is carried out by FDDI concentrators, network adapters, or both. To simplify this procedure, data transmission along the primary ring is always unidirectional (in diagrams, this is always counterclockwise). Data transmission along the secondary ring goes in the reverse direction (clockwise). Therefore, when forming a common ring out of the two rings, workstation transmitters remain connected to receivers of the neighboring workstations, allowing correct reception and transmission of information.

FDDI standards pay attention to the procedures that allow a failure of network equipment to be detected and the required reconfiguration to be carried out. FDDI complements the failure detection mechanisms of Token Ring by reconfiguring data transmission paths based on reserve links ensured by the secondary ring.

> FDDI networks can restore usability after the failure of individual elements. In the case of multiple failures, the network is decomposed into several standalone networks, which are not connected to one another.

Rings in FDDI are seen as a common shared medium for data transmission, so a special access method was developed. This method is close to the access method of Token Ring networks and is also called a **token-passing method**. FDDI workstations use the early token-release mechanism, similar to the mechanism used by Token Ring 16 Mbps networks.

The differences in Token Ring and FDDI access methods are as follows:

■ In contrast to Token Ring, the token-holding time is not a constant in FDDI networks. On the contrary, this time depends on the ring load. When this load is low, the token-holding time increases; during periods of congestion, it might drop to zero. These changes in the access method relate only to asynchronous traffic, which is not sensitive to small frame transmission delays. For synchronous traffic, the token-holding time remains fixed.

■ A frame priority mechanism similar to that in Token Ring is not implemented in FDDI. The developers decided that dividing traffic into eight priority levels is redundant and that it is enough to divide all traffic into two classes, asynchronous and synchronous. The latter served even when the ring is overloaded.

In all other respects, sending frames between ring workstations at the MAC layer corresponds to Token Ring.

Figure 14.4 illustrates the correspondence of the FDDI protocol stack to the seven-layer OSI model. FDDI defines the physical-layer protocol and MAC-sublayer protocol of the data link layer. As in many other LAN technologies, FDDI technology uses the logical link control (LLC) protocol defined in the IEEE 802.2 standard.

The distinguishing feature of the FDDI technology is the **station management** (**SMT**) layer. This layer carries out all functions related to managing and monitoring all other layers of the FDDI protocol stack. Each node of the FDDI network participates in controlling the ring. Therefore, all nodes exchange special SMT frames for controlling the network.

Protocols of other layers also participate in ensuring fault tolerance in FDDI networks. For example, the physical layer eliminates network failures for physical reasons, such as cable breakdown. On the other hand, the MAC layer helps to compensate for logical network failures, such as the loss of the required internal path for passing the token and frames between concentrator ports.

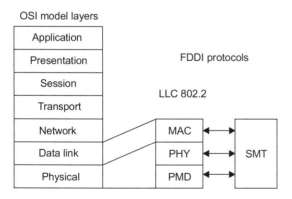

Figure 14.4 FDDI protocol stack

14.3.2 FDDI Fault Tolerance

To ensure fault tolerance, FDDI standard provides two fiber-optic rings: primary and secondary.

The FDDI standard defines two types of end nodes: **stations** and **concentrators**. To connect stations and concentrators to the network, one of the following methods can be used:

- **Dual attachment** (**DA**) — simultaneous attachment to both primary and secondary rings. Station or concentrator connected using this method are called **dual attachment station** (**DAS**) and **dual attachment concentrator** (**DAC**), respectively.

- **Single attachment** (**SA**) — connection to the primary ring only. Station or concentrator connected using this method are called **single attachment station** (**SAS**) and **single attachment concentrator** (**SAC**), respectively.

Usually, although not necessarily, concentrators are DA and stations are SA, as shown in Figure 14.5. To simplify connecting devices to the network, their connectors are marked. Connectors of types A and B must be in the devices with dual connection; the *master* (M) connector must be in concentrators for a single connection of the station, which must have a *slave* response connector of type S.

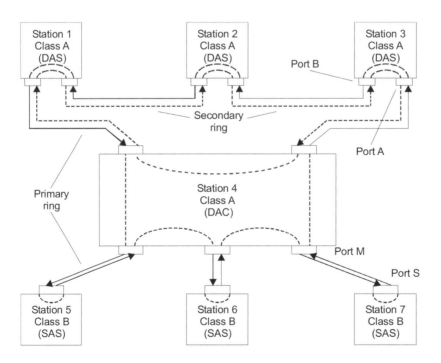

Figure 14.5 Connecting nodes to FDDI rings

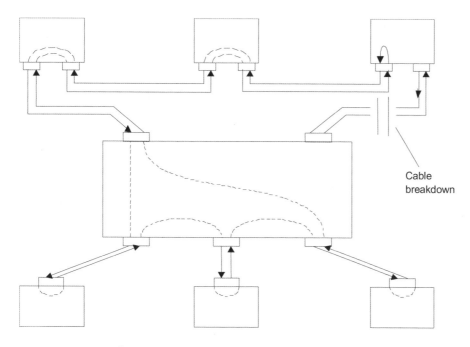

Cable
breakdown

Figure 14.6 Reconfiguration of an FDDI network after cable breakdown

In case of a single cable breakdown between devices with a dual connection, an FDDI network can continue normal operation through automatic reconfiguration of internal paths of frame transmission between the concentrator ports (Figure 14.6).

Double-cable breakdown will create two isolated FDDI networks. When a cable connecting a station with a single connection is broken, that station becomes isolated from the network but the ring continues to operate through reconfiguration of internal paths within the concentrator: Port M, to which that station was connected, will be excluded from the common path.

To preserve the network's ability to operate with dual-connection stations (i.e., DAS) that are powered down, such stations must be equipped with **optical bypass switches**, which create a bypass for light beams when power blackouts occur.

Finally, DAS or DAC can be connected to twoMports of one or two concentrators, thus creating a tree structure with main and reserve links. By default, port B supports the main link, and port A is intended for supporting a reserve link. This configuration is known as **dual homing**.

The SMT layer of workstations and concentrators supports fault tolerance by constantly tracing the time intervals of token and frame circulation and by checking the presence of physical connections between neighboring ports in the network. FDDI networks have no dedicated active monitor. All stations and concentrators have equal rights, and any of them can initiate network reinitialization and reconfiguration if deviations from normal behavior are detected.

Reconfiguration of internal paths in concentrators and network adapters is carried out by special optical switches, which redirect the light beam and have a rather complicated structure.

> The maximum total length of an FDDI ring is 100 km; the maximum number of dual-connection stations in a ring is 500.

FDDI was developed for use in critical network segments — backbone connections among large networks, such as building networks — as well as to connect high-performance servers to the network. Therefore, the list of its most important goals included ensuring high-speed data transmission, fault tolerance at the protocol level, and large distances between network nodes. All these goals were achieved. As a result, FDDI guarantees high quality but is rather expensive. Even the arrival of a cheaper version based on twisted-pair cabling has not significantly reduced the cost of connecting a single node to an FDDI network. Therefore, the main field of FDDI application is backbones of networks connecting several buildings, as well as MANs of large cities.

14.4 WIRELESS LANS

> **KEY WORDS**: external noise, spread spectrum, forward error correction (FEC), hidden terminal, collision avoidance and detection, polling, base station, residential and mobile access, 3G and 2G mobile cellular networks, IEEE 802.11, 802.11a, 802.11b, 802.11g, infrared waves, microwave range, complementary code keying (CCK), Basic Service Set (BSS), Extended Service Set (ESS), access point (AP), distribution system service (DSS), Distributed coordination function (DCF), Point coordination function (PCF), portal, contention window, point coordinator (PC), contention-free period, wired equivalent privacy (WEP)

14.4.1 Specific Features of Wireless LANs

Wireless LANs are now considered a complement to wired LANs rather than a competitive solution. However, wireless LANs were not always seen this way. In the mid-1990s, another view was popular: It was predicted that over time, more LANs would switch to wireless technologies. The advantage of wireless LANs is obvious: They are much easier to deploy and upgrade, since an entire bulky cable infrastructure is unnecessary. Ensured user mobility is another advantage. However, wireless LANs have many problems caused by the use of unstable and unpredictable wireless media. *Chapter 8* considered specific features of signal propagation in such a medium.

External noise from various home appliances, other telecommunications systems, atmospheric noise, and signal reflections create significant difficulties for reliable reception

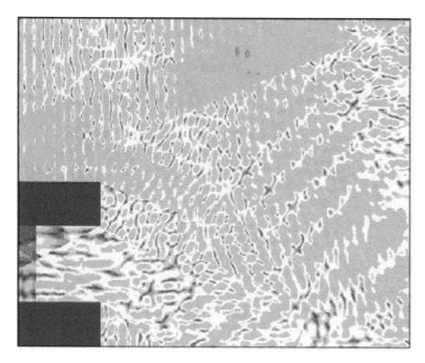

Figure 14.7 Distribution of the intensity of a radio signal

of information. LANs are mainly intended for connecting computers inside buildings, and the propagation of a radio signal inside a building is much more complicated than outdoors. The IEEE 802.11 standard provides a diagram of the distribution of signal intensity "for a simple square room with a standard metal desk and an open doorway" (Figure 14.7). The standard emphasizes that this distribution is static; in reality, the pattern changes dynamically. Thus, movement of various objects within a room can significantly change signal distribution.

Spread spectrum methods allow the noise that affects the useful signal to be reduced. Besides this, wireless networks widely use *forward error correction* (FEC) methods and protocols that ensure retransmission of lost frames. Nevertheless, practice has shown that when nothing prevents an organization from using a wired LAN, most of them prefer such a network even though it is impossible to do without a cabling system.

Uneven distribution of signal intensity results not only in bit errors in the information being transmitted but also in *uncertainty of the coverage zone of a wireless LAN*. In wired LANs there is no such problem, since all devices connected to the cabling system of a building or campus receive signals and participate in LAN operation. Wireless LANs have no precisely determined area of coverage: The commonly adopted notation depicting the area as a circle or a hexagon is nothing more than abstraction. In reality, in some parts of such a regular coverage zone, the signal might be so weak that devices located within those limits might be unable to receive or transmit information.

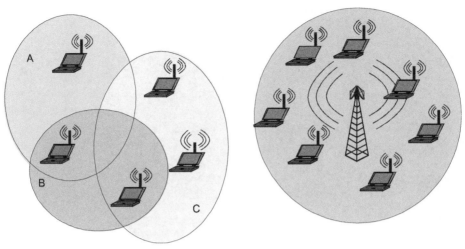

a) Ad-hoc wireless network

b) Wireless network with base station

Figure 14.8 Wireless LAN connectivity

The pattern shown in Figure 14.7 illustrates such a situation well. It is necessary to emphasize that over time, the signal distribution pattern might change rather significantly, in which case the LAN structure will change accordingly. Because of this, even fixed network nodes (ones not intended to be mobile) must take into account that the wireless LAN is not fully connected. Even supposing that the signal is ideally omnidirectional, radio signals fade proportionally to the square of the distance from their source, which may prevent the creation of a fully connected topology. Therefore, without a base station, some pairs of network nodes will be unable to communicate simply because they are located outside the coverage zone of their partner's transmitters.

The example shown in Figure 14.8 illustrates a fragmented LAN. The lack of full connectivity of a wireless network results in what is known as the **hidden terminal problem**. This arises when two nodes are located outside each other's limits (nodes A and C in the illustration), but a third node, B, is capable of receiving signals from both A and C. Suppose that the radio network uses a traditional access method based on carrier sense, such as CSMA/CD. In this case, collisions would be much more frequent than in traditional wired networks. For example, suppose that node B is exchanging information with node A. Node C will find it hard to detect that the medium is busy, and it will start transmitting its frame. As a result, the signals near node B would be distorted (i.e., collisions will occur). In a wired LAN, the probability of such collisions would be much lower.

Collision detection in a radio network is also complicated, since the signal of the node's own transmitter suppresses the signal of a remote transmitter. Consequently, it is difficult if not impossible to detect signal distortion.

Wireless networks' access methods abandon not only carrier sense but also collision detection. Instead, they implement various **collision avoidance** (**CA**) methods, including **polling**.

The use of a **base station** can improve network connectivity (Figure 14.8, *b*). The base station usually has higher power, and its antenna is usually established to cover the required territory more evenly and easily. As a result, all nodes of a wireless LAN are able to exchange information with the base station, which serves as a transit node for information exchange between the network end nodes.

Wireless LANs are considered promising for applications in which it is difficult or impossible to use wired LANs. The main areas of wireless LAN application are:

- *Residential access* of alternative providers, which have no wired access to clients living in apartment houses.

- *Mobile access* in airports, railway stations, etc.

- Organizing LANs in buildings where it is impossible to install a modern cabling system, such as historical buildings with original interiors.

- Temporary LANs, needed, for example, for a conference. Conference participants attending a session cannot use wired connections.

- *LAN extensions.* For example, one building of a company, such a workshop or test laboratory, might be isolated from other premises. The few working places in such a building make cable installation inefficient. Therefore, wireless communication proves to be more rational.

- *Mobile LANs.* If a user needs to access the LAN while moving from room to room or from building to building, wireless LANs have no competitors. A doctor visiting patients and using a notebook to connect to a hospital database is a typical example of such a user.

For the moment, mobile LANs do not pretend to cover large territories fully, like mobile cellular telephone networks do. However, they have good potential to do so. In the field of building mobile cellular networks for data transmission, wireless LAN technologies will have to compete with **third-generation** (**3G**) **mobile cellular networks. 2G mobile cellular networks** are not considered serious competitors, since they were developed mainly for voice transmission. Their capabilities in the field of data transmission are limited by rates of several kilobits per second; wireless LANs ensure rates of dozens of megabits per second. However, transmission rates in 3G systems are expected to be between 144 Kbps and 2 Mbps (the latter rate will be reached at small distances from the base station). Thus, competition may prove to be rather stiff.

Later in this chapter, the most popular wireless LANs standard — IEEE 802.11 — will be considered. Besides IEEE 802.11, there are other standards in this field: In particular, the European Telecommunications Standards Institute (ETSI) has developed the HIPER-LAN 1 standard. Nevertheless, most manufacturers produce equipment according to IEEE 802.11 specifications.

14.4.2 IEEE 802.11 Protocol Stack

Naturally, the protocol stack of this standard corresponds to the common structure of 802 Committee standards. This means that it comprises a physical layer and MAC layer over which the LLC layer operates. Like all technologies of the 802 family, **802.11** is defined by the two lowest layers: the physical layer and MAC sublayer. The LLC sublayer (LLC2) carries out its own functions, which are standard for all LAN technologies. Since frame distortions are more likely in wireless media than in guided media, LLC is most likely to be used in the LLC2 mode. This, however, does not depend on the 802.11 technology, since the LLC operating mode is selected by protocols of higher layers.

The structure of the IEEE 802.11 protocol stack is shown in Figure 14.9.

> At the *physical layer* there are several specifications that differ in terms of frequency range, encoding method, and consequently, information rate. All variants of the physical layer work with the same MAC-layer algorithm. However, some timing parameters of the MAC layer depend on the physical layer being used.

In 1997 the 802.11 Committee has adopted the standard, defining MAC functions with *three variants of the physical layer* ensuring data transmission rates of 1 Mbps and 2 Mbps.

- ■ The first variant uses **infrared waves** of 850 nm as a transmission medium. They are generated either by a semiconductor laser diode or by a light emitting diode (LED). Since infrared waves do not penetrate walls, coverage of such a LAN is limited by the unobstructed line of sight. The standard makes provision for three variants of wave propagation: omnidirectional antennas, reflection from the ceiling, and focused directional radiation. In the first case, a narrow beam is diffused using a system of lenses.

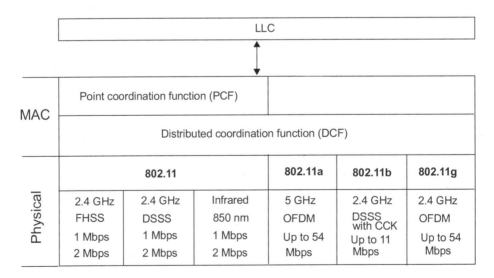

Figure 14.9 IEEE 802.11 protocol stack

The latter variant is intended for organizing "point-to-point" communications between, say, two buildings.

■ The second variant uses the **microwave range** of 2.4 GHz, which, based on ITU recommendations, is not licensed in most countries. One microwave variant of the physical layer uses FHSS, and the other employs DSSS.[1] When using FHSS, each narrow channel is 1 MHz wide. Using FSK modulation with two signal states (frequencies) gives a rate of 1 Mbps, and using four signal states produces a rate of 2 Mbps. When using FHSS, the network may consist of cells; to eliminate mutual interference, the neighboring cells can use orthogonal frequency sequences. The number of channels and the frequency of switching among channels are customizable parameters, so wireless LAN installers can take into account specific features of the frequency spectrum regulation of a specific country. For example, in the United States, up to 79 channels can be used within a 2.4 GHz-wide channel, and the maximum time spent on each channel must not exceed 400 msec.

■ The third variant, also using the same *microwave range* of 2.4 GHz, is based on the *DSSS encoding*. DSSS encoding uses the 11-bit code 10110111000 as a chipping sequence. Each bit is encoded using BPSK (1 Mbps) or QPSK (2 Mbps).

In 1999, two other variants of the physical layer were approved: **802.11a** and **802.11b**.

■ The *802.11a* specification achieves the increased information rate by using a higher range of frequencies: 5 GHz. For this purpose, this technology uses 300 MHz of this range, orthogonal frequency division multiplexing (OFDM) and FEC. The information rates that it achieves include 6, 9, 12, 18, 24, 36, 48, and 54 Mbps. The 5 GHz range, used by 802.11a, is currently sparsely populated and ensures high information rates. However, the use of this range causes two problems. First, equipment for operating at these frequencies is still too expensive. Second, in some countries, this range is licensed.

■ The second specification, *IEEE 802.11b*, continues to use 2.4 GHz, which allows the use of cheaper equipment. To increase the rate to 11 Mbps, comparable to that of classical Ethernet, this technology uses the more efficient DSSS method, employing **complementary code keying** (CCK) — an improved modulation scheme that in 1999 was adopted to replace the **Barker code** in wireless digital networks (see *Chapter 10*).

One of the latest 802.11 group standards for the physical layer, **IEEE 802.11g**, was approved in the summer of 2003.

■ *IEEE 802.11g* also operates at 2.4 GHz but ensures data transmission rates up to 54 Mbps. This specification also uses OFDM. Until recently, U.S. regulations allowed the use of only the spread spectrum technique at 2.4 GHz. The removal of this limitation offered incentive for new research and innovations, as a result of which a new high-speed wireless technology has appeared. To provide backward compatibility with 802.11b, CCK is also supported.

---

[1] More detailed information on these methods was provided in *Chapter 10*.

The diameter of an 802.11 network depends on many parameters, including the frequency range being used. Normally, the diameter of a wireless LAN is between 100 and 300 m.

The MAC layer carries out more functions in wireless LANs than in wired networks. MAC functions in the 802.11 standard include the following:

■ Providing access to the shared medium

■ Ensuring station mobility when several base stations are available

■ Ensuring security equal to that of wired LANs

14.4.3 Topologies of 802.11 LANs

The 802.11 standard supports two types of LAN topologies — Ad-hoc networks, also known as basic service set (BSS), and networks with infrastructure, called extended service set (ESS).

Ad-hoc networks, which, according to 802.11 terminology, are called **basic service set (BSS)**, are created by *individual stations.* They do not contain a base station, and nodes in such networks communicate directly with one another (Figure 14.10). To become a member of a BSS, the station must carry out the association procedure.

BSSs are not traditional cells in terms of coverage zones because they can be located large distances apart. They also can overlap either partially or fully. The 802.11 standard provides freedom for the network architect in this respect.

In networks with infrastructure, some stations are base stations. In 802.11 terminology, base stations are called **access points** (**APs**). A station performing AP functions is

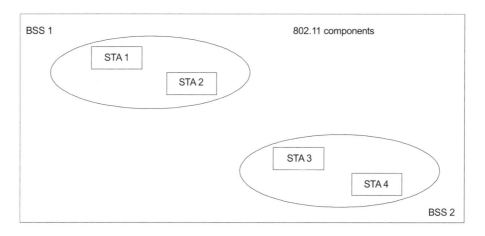

Figure 14.10 Basic service set

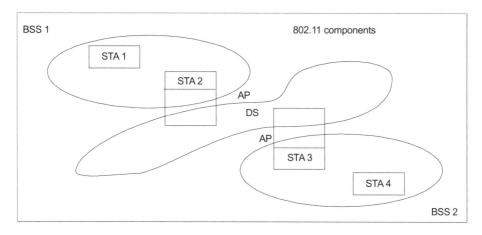

Figure 14.11 Extended service set and distribution system

a member of a BSS (Figure14.11). All network APs are connected to one another by the *distribution system* (DS). The role of the DS can be played either by the medium used for interconnecting stations (e.g., radio or infrared waves) or by a different medium, such as cabling. With the DS, APs carry out **distribution system service (DSS)**. The task of DSS is to transmit packets between stations that for some reason cannot (or do not want to) interact directly. The most obvious reason for using DSS is if stations belong to different BSSs. In this case, they transmit the frames to their APs, which use the DS to transmit such frames to the AP that serves the BSS to which the destination station belongs.

> **Extended Service Set (ESS)** networks are networks comprising several BSSs connected by a DS is an ESS in 802.11 terminology.

ESSs ensure mobility for the stations, because they can move from BSS to BSS. These movements are ensured by the MAC-layer functions of both stations and APs. Therefore, they are transparent for the LLC layer. An ESS can also communicate with a wired LAN. For this purpose, the DS must contain a **portal**[2].

14.4.4 Access to the Shared Medium

Stations can use the shared medium for the following purposes:

■ Directly transmitting data to one another within a single BSS
■ Transmitting data within a single BSS using an AP as a transit node

---

[2] The functions of a portal are not defined in detail: This role can be played by a switch or by a router.

- Transmitting data between BSSs using two APs and the DS
- Transmitting data between a BSS and a wired LAN using an AP, a DS, and a portal

In 802.11 networks, the MAC layer ensures two modes for accessing the shared medium:

- **Distributed coordination function (DCF)**
- **Point coordination function (PCF)**

Distributed Coordination Function Access Mode

First, consider the method of providing access using DCF. This method implements the well-known CSMA/CA algorithm. It belongs to the class of CA algorithms based on carrier sense. At the same time, it uses a "slotted algorithm." Instead of a direct procedure of collision detection based on the medium state, which is inefficient in wireless networks, this method uses indirect collision detection. For this purpose, each transmitted frame must be confirmed by an ACK frame sent by the destination station. If an ACK is not received during the predefined timeout period, the sender considers that a collision has occurred.

Using a slotted access algorithm requires stations to be synchronized. In 802.11 technologies, this problem has an elegant solution: Count off of the time intervals starts when transmission of the next frame is accomplished (Figure 14.12). This does not require transmission of special synchronization signals and does not limit packet size by slot size, because slots are taken into account only when making a decision on starting frame transmission.

A station that needs to transmit a frame must first sense the carrier. When it registers the end of frame transmission, it must wait for the time interval of the *interframe space* (IFS). If, after the IFS elapses, the medium is still free, then count off of the slots starts. Each slot has the duration *SlotTime*. It is possible to start frame transmission only when

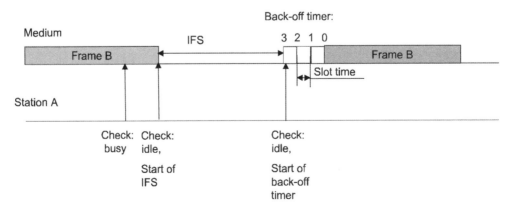

Figure 14.12 DCF algorithm

a slot starts, provided that the medium is free. The station chooses the slot based on the **truncated binary exponential back-off algorithm**, similar to the one used in CSMA/CD. The slot number is chosen as a random integer, evenly distributed within the [0, CW] interval (CW stands for **contention window**).

The method of choosing the slot size and the size of the contention window will be covered later in this chapter. For the moment, consider this sophisticated access method on a practical example (Figure 14.12). Assume that station A has chosen slot 3 for transmission based on the truncated binary exponential back-off algorithm. Having chosen the slot number, the station assigns the value 3 to the **back-off timer** (the purpose of which will be clear from the further discussion), and starts checking the medium state at the start of each slot. If the medium is available, the back-off timer value is decreased by 1. Frame transmission starts if the result is 0.

> Thus, the algorithm ensures that all slots, including the current one, are available. This condition is essential and must be observed for the transmission to start.

If the medium happens to be busy at the start of a specific slot, the counter is "frozen" (i.e., it is not decreased by one). If this happens, the station starts a new cycle of medium access, changing only the algorithm used for choosing the slot for transmission. As in the previous cycle, the station continues to sense the carrier. When the medium is free again, the station makes a pause the duration of which is equal to IFS. If the medium remains free after this interval elapses, the station uses the frozen value of the back-off timer as the slot number, and carries out the above-described procedure of checking free slots and decreasing the back-off timer starting from its frozen value.

The *slot size* depends on the method of signal encoding, since for FHSS method, slot size is 28 μsec, and for the DSSS method, it is 1 μsec. Slot size is chosen to exceed the value of signal propagation time between any two stations, plus the time required for the station to correctly recognize the medium availability. If this requirement has been met, then each station can correctly recognize the start of frame transmission when sensing the slots preceding the one it has chosen for transmission. This, in turn, means the following:

> A collision can occur only when several stations choose the same slot for transmission.

If a collision occurs, frames get distorted, and no ACK frames arrive from the destination stations. If stations do not receive an ACK from the destination station during a predefined period, they register a collision and try to retransmit their frames. After each failed attempt of frame transmission, the [0, CW] interval from which slot numbers are selected is doubled. For example, if initial window size was chosen to be 8 (i.e., CW = 7), then the window must be set to 16 (CW = 15) after the first collision. After the second collision, the window size must be set to 32, and so on. The 802.11 standard specifies that initial value of the CW must be chosen depending on the type of the physical layer used in the wireless LAN.

As in CSMA/CD, the number of failed attempts of retransmitting a frame is limited. However, the 802.11 standard does not provide an exact value for this upper limit. When the upper limit of *N* failed attempts is reached, the frame is discarded, and collision counter

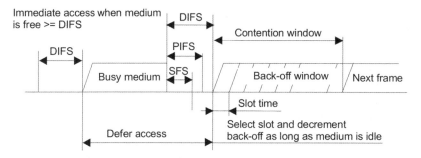

Figure 14.13 Coexistence of PCF and DCF

is set to 0. Naturally, if after a number of failed attempts the station manages to send a frame successfully, the counter is also set to 0.

DCF takes special measures to eliminate the **hidden terminal effect**. For this purpose, the station that needs to capture the medium and, according to the previously described algorithm, decides to start frame transmission in a specific slot must send a short *request-to-send (RTS) frame* instead of the data frame to the destination station. The destination station must reply with a *clear-to-send (CTS) frame*, after which the source station sends the data frame. The CTS frame must contain information on medium capturing intended for all the stations outside the reach of the sending station but within the coverage zone of the destination station (i.e., to the stations that are hidden terminals for the sender).

NOTE   *The maximum frame length according to the 802.11 standard is 2,346 bytes, the RTS length is 20 bytes, and the CTS frame takes 14 bytes. Since RTS and CTS frames are considerably shorter than the data frame, the losses caused by collisions of RTS or CTS frames are considerably smaller than losses caused by collisions of data frames. The procedure of exchanging RTS–CTS frames is optional: It can be abandoned when network load is low, since in this case collisions are rare, which means that there is no need to spend additional time carrying out the RTS–CTS procedure.*

Point Coordination Function Access Mode

If the BSS contains a station that carries out AP functions, the centralized access method implemented by the PCF algorithm can be used. This method ensures priority serving of traffic. In this case, the AP carries out the functions of **point coordinator** (PC)[3] (e.g., medium arbitrator).

PCF in 802.11 networks coexists with DCF. Their cooperation is coordinated using three types of IFS (Figure 14.13).

---

[3] In this section, PC stands for point coordinator.

After the medium is released, each station counts the medium idle time, comparing it with the values of three intervals:

- Short IFS (**SIFS**)
- PCF IFS (**PIFS**)
- DCF IFS (**DIFS**)

The medium-capturing procedure using the previously described DCF algorithm is possible only when the medium is free for a time greater than or equal to DIFS. This means that when describing DCF algorithm operation, DIFS (i.e., the longest of the three possible intervals) must be used as IFS. This gives the DCF method the lowest priority.

The smallest value, SIFS, is intended for highest-priority medium capturing by CTS or ACK frames, which continue or accomplish frame transmission that has already started.

PIFS is larger than SIFS but smaller than DIFS. The time interval equal to the difference between DIFS and PIFS is used by the medium arbitrator (i.e., the PC). During this interval, it can transmit a special beacon frame, informing all stations that the **contention-free period** has begun. Having received a beacon frame, stations that would like to use the DCF algorithm to capture the medium can no longer do so. To capture the medium, they must wait until the contention-free period elapses. The duration of this period is declared in the beacon frame, although it can elapse earlier if stations have no delay-sensitive traffic. In this case, the PC transmits the CF-End frame, after which the DCF access method starts to operate, provided that DIFS has elapsed.

During the contention-free interval, the PC uses the polling procedure to give each station participating in PCF the possibility of transmitting its frame. To achieve this, the PC in turns sends a special CF-POLL frame to each participating station, thus giving it the opportunity to use the medium. Having received this frame, the station can respond with the CF – ACK + DATA frame, which confirms the reception of the CF-POLL frame and simultaneously transmits data (either to the PC address for transit transmission or directly to the destination station).

To ensure that asynchronous traffic always gets some part of the bandwidth, the duration of the contention-free period is limited. When this period elapses, the PC transmits the CF-End frame and the contention period starts.

Any station can participate in PCF. For this purpose, it has to subscribe to this service when connecting to the network (i.e., when carrying out the association procedure).

14.4.5 Security

The developers of IEEE 802.11 set the goal of ensuring security of data transmission using a wireless LAN equivalent to the security of data transmission using a wired LAN, such as Ethernet.

The description of wired Ethernet included no special measures aimed at ensuring data security. Ethernet standards do not implement user authentication or data encryption. Nevertheless, wired networks are better protected against unauthorized access or confidentiality violations than wireless LANs, simply because they are wired: The intruder must physically connect to a wired network to access it. For this purpose the intruder must in some way penetrate premises equipped with sockets and connect the attacking computer to one of them. This action can be noticed and prevented, although it is still possible to gain unauthorized access to a wired LAN.

In a wireless LAN, it is much easier to carry out unauthorized access. It is enough to be within the range of such a LAN. To penetrate a wireless LAN successfully, it is not necessary to enter the building in which that LAN operates. Physical connection to the medium is also not needed, because the visitor can receive data without doing anything suspicious. It is sufficient simply to have a switched-on notebook in a bag.

The 802.11 standard provides security tools that raise the security level of a wireless LAN to that of a normal wired LAN. Therefore, the main data security protocol in 802.11 network has the name **wired equivalent privacy** (**WEP**). This allows encryption of data transmitted using a wireless medium, thus ensuring confidentiality. Another security mechanism in wireless networks is an authentication mechanism — *verification of originality that allows only authorized users to logon.* However, security tools of 802.11 networks are a popular target for criticism because they do not provide as reliable data protection as similar security tools of other standards. For example, by sniffing encrypted 802.11 traffic, a qualified intruder can decrypt the information within 24 hours. Therefore, the 802.11i workgroup is developing a more powerful standard for data protection in 802.11 networks.

14.5 PAN AND BLUETOOTH

KEY WORDS: PANs (Personal Area Networks), Bluetooth Special Interest Group (Bluetooth SIG), master, slaves, piconet, piconet shared medium, scatternet, synchronous connection-oriented (SCO) link, asynchronous connectionless (ACL) link, FHSS, BFSK modulation

14.5.1 Specific Features of PANs

PANs (**Personal Area Networks**) are intended for communications among devices belonging to a single owner over small distances, usually of 10 m. Examples of such devices are notebooks, mobile phones, printers, personal digital assistants (PDAs), television sets, and numerous hi-tech home appliances, such as refrigerators.

PANs must provide both fixed access (e.g., within a home) and mobile access (e.g., when the owner moves among rooms, buildings, or cities carrying the devices).

PANs are similar to LANs in many respects, but they also have specific features.

■ Many devices intended to participate in a PAN are *much simpler* than computers, the typical LAN nodes. Furthermore, such devices are usually small and inexpensive. There-fore, PAN standards must take into account that PAN implementation must result in inexpensive solutions with low energy consumption.

■ *A PAN coverage area is smaller than that of a LAN.* For interaction among PAN nodes, a distance of several meters is usually sufficient.

■ *Stringent requirements to security.* Personal devices that the owner carries often must work in different environments. Sometimes they need to communicate with devices of other PANs. This is the case when a user meets a colleague or friend somewhere and they decide to exchange addresses stored in the address books of their PDAs. In other cases, such interaction is extremely undesirable, because it can result in the leak of confidential information. Because of this, PAN protocols must ensure various meth-ods of device authentication and data encryption in the mobile environment.

■ When interconnecting small mobile devices, the need to get rid of cables becomes more evident than, say, when connecting a printer to a computer or concentrator. Because of this, *PANs tend to favor wireless solutions more than LANs do.*

■ If the user constantly carries the PAN device, it must not cause damage to the user's health. Therefore, the signals emitted by such a device must be *low powered*, preferably not exceeding 100 mW. (A normal cellular phone emits signals ranging from 600 mW to 3 W.)

> Nowadays, the most popular PAN technology is Bluetooth, which ensures interop-eration of up to eight devices using a shared medium at 2.4 MHz and at rates of up to 723 Kbps.

14.5.2 Bluetooth Architecture

The Bluetooth standard was developed by the **Bluetooth Special Interest Group (Blue-tooth SIG)** organized at the initiative of Ericsson. The Bluetooth standard also has been adopted by the IEEE 802.15.1 workgroup through the common structure of IEEE 802 standards.

The Bluetooth technology uses the **piconet** concept. The name of this concept empha-sizes the small coverage area of such networks, from 10 to 100 m depending on the power of the Bluetooth device transmitter.

A piconet can join up to 255 devices. However, only 8 of these devices can be active and carry out data exchange at any moment. One of the piconet devices is the **master**; all the other devices are **slaves** (Figure 14.14). The master is responsible for providing access to

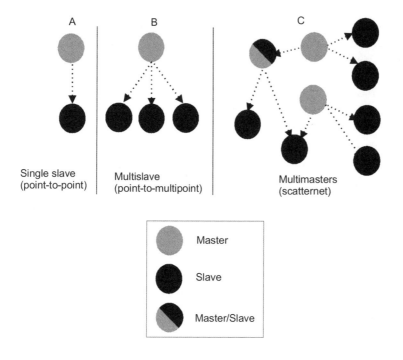

Figure 14.14 Piconet and scatternet

the piconet shared medium, which represents nonlicensed frequencies from the 2.4 GHz range. Such architecture allows simpler protocols to be used in slave devices (such as radio headsets) and more sophisticated network management functions to be delegated to the computer, the most likely to become the master of such a network.

Thus, each piconet has one master and up to seven active slaves. An active slave can exchange data only with its master. Direct data exchange among slaves is impossible. All slave devices of the current piconet except for the seven active ones must operate in PARK mode, characterized by low energy consumption. When operating in this mode, slaves periodically listen for the master's commands to switch to the active state.

Master is responsible for access to the **piconet shared medium**, which represents unlicensed frequencies of the 2.4 GHz range. The shared medium transmits data at 1 Mbps, although because of the packet header and frequency-hopping overhead, the effective information rate of the medium does not exceed 777 Kbps. The master divides the medium bandwidth among seven slave devices on the basis of the time division multiplexing (TDM) technique.

Such architecture allows for using simpler protocols in slave devices (such as earphones, for example), and delegates more sophisticated functions of network management to a computer, which, most probably, becomes the master of this piconet.

The procedure for connecting to a piconet is dynamic. The piconet master periodically collects information on the devices that fall into the zone of its piconet by polling them.

This procedure is known as inquiry. After detecting a new device, the master carries out the negotiation procedure with that device. If the intention of the slave device to connect to the piconet coincides with that of the master (which means that the device has carried out the authentication procedure and belongs to the list of allowed devices), then the master connects the new device to its network.

NOTE   *Security in Bluetooth networks is ensured by device authentication and encryption of traffic. Bluetooth protocols ensure a higher level of protection than the IEEE 802.11 standard's WEP protocol.*

Several piconets that fall within the same zone and carry out data exchange form a **scatternet**. Piconets that form a scatternet can interact, because the same node can simultaneously be part of several piconets. Such a device is usually called a *bridge*. The difference between scatternet and standard 802.11 ESS is that in the scatternet there are no analogues to the AP through which separate networks (more precisely, BSSs) interact. In the scatternet, the same node can play the role of master in one piconet and the role of a slave in another one.

To prevent interference of signals from different piconets, each master uses its *own* hopping sequence. Using different hopping sequences complicates the process of piconet interoperation. To achieve interoperation, the device playing the role of a bridge must, in turn, be part of each piconet that changes its frequency sequence.

Although collisions are unlikely, they can still take place when devices from different piconets choose the same frequency channel for their operation. However, the probability of this is small, since the number of piconets in the same area is likely to be small.

According to the standard description, a scatternet implements CDMA on the basis of FHSS.

To ensure reliable data transmission, Bluetooth uses FEC. When transmitting data, frame reception is confirmed using acknowledgments. FEC encoding is not a mandatory method.

Bluetooth networks use different methods for transmitting information of the following two kinds:

❏ For delay-sensitive traffic, the network supports **synchronous connection-oriented (SCO) links**. For the SCO channel, the bandwidth is reserved for the entire time of connection. SCO channels are normally used for transmitting voice traffic at 64 Kbps

❏ For elastic traffic there is the **asynchronous connectionless (ACL) link**. For the ACL channel, the bandwidth is allocated by a request from a slave or according to the needs of the master. ACL channels are intended for computer traffic at variable rates.

14.5.3 Bluetooth Protocol Stack

Bluetooth is an original and functionally complete technology intended for standalone usage in personal electronic devices. For this reason, it supports a complete protocol stack,

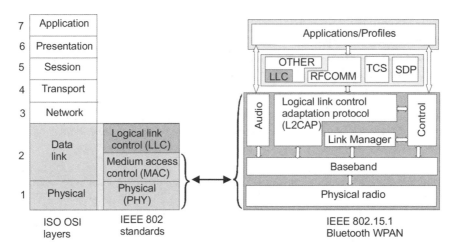

Figure 14.15 Correspondence of the Bluetooth protocol, OSI model, and IEEE 802 standards

including its own application protocols. This is its main difference from the technologies considered previously, such as Ethernet or IEEE 802.11, which carry out only the functions of the physical and data link layers.

The introduction of internal, built-in application protocols in Bluetooth is explained by the desire of its developers to implement the technology in various simple devices that are unable (and, in practice, that do not need to) support the TCP/IP stack.

Bluetooth appeared as a result of attempts to develop a standard for interaction between a mobile telephone and a wireless headset. Obviously, it makes no sense to use complicated protocols such as FTP or HTTP to solve this task.

As a result, a sophisticated protocol suite was developed, in addition to which a considerable number of profiles appeared.

> **Profiles** define the specific protocol set required to carry out a specific task. For example, there is a profile for interaction between a computer or mobile phone and a wireless headset (the Headset profile). There also is a File Transfer profile intended for devices that can transfer files (headsets probably will not use it, although it is difficult to predict the future) and a profile for emulating the RS-232 port.

When bringing Bluetooth standards into line with IEEE 802 standard architecture, the IEEE 802.15.1 workgroup limited itself only to *Bluetooth core protocols*, which correspond to the functions of the physical and MAC layers (Figure 14.15).

- The *Physical Radio* layer describes frequencies and powers of signals used for information transmission.

- The *Baseband* layer is responsible for organizing links in the radio medium. This layer's responsibilities include selecting the hopping sequence, synchronizing piconet devices, and forming and transmitting frames through established SCO and ACL links. The Bluetooth frame has a variable length: Its data field can comprise from 0 to 2,744 bits (343 bytes). For voice transmission, fixed-length frames are used with data fields of 240 bits (30 bytes).

- The *Link Manager* is responsible for device authentication and traffic encryption. Besides this, it controls the device state, such as changing from slave to master.

- The *Logical Link Control Adaptation Layer* (L2CAP) is the upper layer of the Bluetooth core protocols. This protocol is used only when the device transmits data. Voice traffic bypasses this protocol and addresses the Baseband layer directly. The L2CAP layer receives 64 KB data segments from the upper layers and segments them into small frames for the Baseband layer. When receiving frames, the L2CAP layer assembles frames into an initial segment and transfers it to the upper-layer protocol.

- The *Audio layer* ensures voice transmission through SCO channels. This layer applies pulse code modulation (PCM) encoding, which defines a voice channel rate of 64 Kbps.

- The *Control* layer transmits all information on the status of connection to the external unit and receives commands changing the device state and configuration from the external units.

14.5.4 Bluetooth Frames

The shared medium is a sequence of FHSS frequency channels in the 2.4 GHz range. Each channel is 1 MHz wide. The number of channels is 79 (in the United States, most of Europe, and most other countries) or 23 (in Spain, France, and Japan).

The chipping rate is 1,600 Hz, so the chip period is 625 μsec. The master divides the shared medium on the basis of the TDM technique, using the time spent by the system at each frequency channel (e.g., 625 μsec) as a time slot. Information is encoded at the clock frequency of 1 MHz using BFSK modulation. As a result, the bit rate is 1 Mbps.

During a single time slot, the Bluetooth piconet transmits 625 bits. However, not all of them are used for transmitting user information. When hopping to another frequency, network devices need some time for synchronization, so only 366 of 625 bits are used for transmitting information frames.

An information frame can take one, three, or five slots. When the frame takes more than one slot, the channel frequency remains unchanged during the entire time of frame transmission. In this case, the overhead for synchronization is smaller. Thus, the size of a frame comprising five sequential slots is 2,870 bits (the data field size can take up to 2,744 bits).

NOTE   *Only data frames (e.g., ACL channel frames) can comprise several slots; frames transmitting voice data (e.g., SCO channel frames) always comprise only one slot.*

Consider the format of a frame comprising a single slot — 366 bits (Figure 14.16).

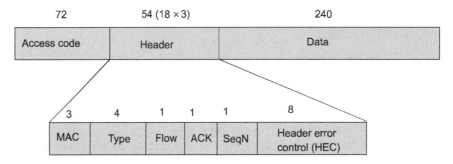

Figure 14.16 Format of a Bluetooth frame comprising a single slot

Of the 366 bits making up the frame:

■ 240 bits are allocated to the *data field*.

■ 72 bits are taken by the *access code*. An access code is used for identification of the piconet. Each Bluetooth device has a globally unique 6-byte address, so for piconet identification, the three least significant bytes of the master's unique address are used. When forming a frame, each device places these bytes into the access code field, complementing them with 1/3 FEC bits (the 1/3 abbreviation specifies that 1 bit of information is transformed into 3 bits of code). If a master or slave receives a frame containing an invalid access code, it discards the frame, since the frame probably has been received from another piconet.

■ 54 bits are needed for the *frame header*. The frame header contains the MAC address, a single-bit receive acknowledgment flag, the frame type, and some other flags. The MAC address consists of 3 bits; it is the temporary address of one of the seven slaves, with 000 as a broadcast address. The header information is also transmitted using the 1/3 FEC code.

The format of a frame comprising three or five slots differs only in the size of its data field. Information placed into the data field can be encoded using 1/3 FEC or 2/3 FEC, or it can be transmitted without using FEC.

14.5.5 How Bluetooth Operates

Consider an example of piconet operation. Suppose that this piconet contains a master and three active slaves. For simplicity, suppose that all devices use frames that take a single slot. Figure 14.17 shows how the master distributes slots among the members of the piconet.

To ensure the full-duplex mode of information exchange, the master always allocates two slots to each channel. The first slot is used for data transmission from master to slave, and the second is used to transmit data in the reverse direction.

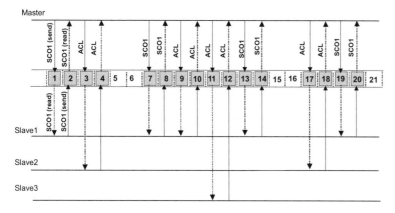

Figure 14.17 Sharing the medium

In the example shown in Figure 14.17, there is one SCO channel between the master and slave1. SCO channels are always allocated fixed bandwidth depending on the FEC method adopted for encoding voice information.

1. If FEC is not used, then every third pair of slots is allocated to the SCO channel, as shown in the illustration. This slot distribution ensures the transmission of 64 Kbps flows in each direction. You can verify this. The PCM codec samples voice data at 8 KHz (a 125 μsec period), representing each sample with 1 byte. Each frame carries 30 bytes (i.e., 240 bits, or 30 samples). Frames of SCO channels transmitted in one direction repeat every six slots, so the period between frames is $6 \times 625 = 3,750$ μsec. Accordingly, the information rate of the channel (in one direction) is $240/(3,750 \times 10^{-6}) = 64$ Kbps.

2. When 2/3 FEC encoding is used, the frame data field contains 20 samples instead of 30, so to ensure a rate of 64 Kbps, such an SCO channel must be allocated every second pair of slots.

3. Finally, 1/3 FEC encoding results in a frame transmitting only 10 voice samples, taking all the slots of the shared medium.

These calculations show that no more than three SCO channels can exist within a piconet (possibly, with different slave devices). However, this is only possible when the channel does not use FEC encoding to reduce bit errors. Employing FEC reduces the number of SCO channels to two or even one.

The bandwidth remaining after organizing SCO channels is used to transmit asynchronous data. For this purpose, the piconet uses the ACL channel. This is a point-to-multipoint channel connecting the master to all of the piconet's active slaves. There is no need to establish this channel, since it exists in any case.

The master periodically polls slave devices to find out whether they need to transmit asynchronous data. To do this, it uses a special POLL frame containing the MAC address of specific device. If the master has data for this device, it can combine data transmission and polling within a single frame.

Figure 14.17 shows that the master has used slots 3 and 4 for exchanging frames with slave2. Slots 9 and 10 were used for exchange with slave1, and slots 11 and 12 for exchange with slave3. The polling method eliminates collisions when accessing the ACL channel. However, the rate of access to this channel is not fixed: On the contrary, it depends on the number of devices that need to transmit asynchronous data.

> Thus, Bluetooth networks combine circuit switching (for SCO channels) and packet switching (for the ACL channel).

If SCO channels are not used in a Bluetooth network, the entire bandwidth is allocated to the ACL channel. When using frames consisting of five slots, the maximum data transmission rate is 432.6 Kbps in each direction (without using FEC). Asymmetric division of the ACL channel bandwidth is also possible. In this case, the maximum rate reaches 723.2 Kbps in one direction and 57.6 Kbps in the reverse direction. These are the rates of the ACL channel, not the data rates of the flow from a specific device. When several devices share the ACL channel, this rate is divided among all devices involved.

14.6 SHARED MEDIA LAN EQUIPMENT

> **KEY WORDS**: network interface card (NIC), concentrator, network adapter, cabling system, shared medium, LAN, switch, bridge, router, two-port repeater, multiport Ethernet repeater, RJ-45, reserve links, unauthorized network sniffing, data protection, multisegment concentrator, configuration switching, concentrators with a fixed number of ports, modular concentrator, stack concentrator, modular stack concentrator

Concentrators with network adapters and cabling system represent the required minimum of equipment using which it is possible to create a shared medium LAN. Obviously, such network cannot be too large, because the shared medium becomes a bottleneck provided that the number of network nodes grows significantly. Therefore, concentrators and network adapters allow for building a small basic fragments of networks, which are then joined together using switches, bridges and routers.

14.6.1 Main Functions of Network Adapters

Together with its driver, the **network interface card** (**NIC**) implements the second data link layer of the OSI model in the network end node (the computer). More precisely, in the network operating system, the adapter–driver pair carries out only physical- and MAC-layer functions; LLC-layer functions are usually implemented by the OS module common to all drivers and network adapters. For example, in Windows XP, the LLC layer is implemented in the network driver interface specification (NDIS) module common to all NIC drivers, independent of the technology supported by specific drivers.

The network adapter and its driver jointly carry out two operations: receiving and transmitting frames.

Frame transmission from the computer into the cable comprises the following stages:

■ Receiving the LLC frame through the service interface, with the MAC-layer address information. Within a computer, protocols usually interact using RAM buffers. Upper-layer protocols retrieve data to be transmitted through the network from a disk or from the file cache using the OS I/O subsystem and then load the data into RAM buffers.

■ Formatting the MAC-layer frame into which the LLC frame is encapsulated. This includes filling the source and destination addresses and calculating the checksum.

■ Forming code symbols, provided that redundant codes such as 4B/5B are used, and scrambling codes to obtain more even signal spectrum. Not every protocol implements this stage. For instance, 10 Mbps Ethernet does without it.

■ Transmitting the signal into the cable according to the line code adopted: Manchester, NRZI, MLT-3, etc.

Frame reception from the cable includes the following stages:

■ Receiving from the cable signals encoding the bit stream.

■ Separating signals from noise. This can be carried out by special circuits or digital signal processors. As a result, the adapter's receiver gets a sequence of bits that is highly likely to coincide with the sequence sent by the transmitter.

■ Passing the data through a descrambler if they were scrambled before being sent. After this operation, code symbols sent by the transmitter are restored in the adapter.

■ Checking the frame checksum. If the checksum is incorrect, the frame is discarded, and a specific error code is passed to the LLC protocol through the service interface. If the checksum is correct, the LLC frame is retrieved from the MAC frame and passed to the LLC protocol through the service interface.

Standards do not define the distribution of responsibilities between the adapter and its driver. Therefore, each manufacturer is free to solve this problem. As a rule, network adapters are classified into the two categories: adapters for client computers and adapters for servers.

In adapters for *client computers*, most work is delegated to the driver. Thus, the adapter becomes less sophisticated, and its price is significantly lower. The drawback of this approach is a high load on the CPU, which in this case must carry out routine operations such as frame transmission from RAM buffers into the network.

Adapters intended for *servers* are equipped with built-in processors that carry out most tasks related to frame transmission from RAM to the network and vice versa.

Based on the protocol implemented by the adapter, they are categorized as Ethernet adapters, Token Ring adapters, FDDI adapters, etc. Since Fast Ethernet allows the use of autonegotiation to choose the operating speed of the network adapter automatically, depending on the concentrator's capabilities, many Ethernet adapters now support two operating speeds and have the 10/100 prefix in their name.

Network adapters implement the pipelining method of frame processing. According to this method, the processes of frame reception from computer RAM and frame transmission into the network occur in parallel. Thus, having received several starting bytes of the frame, the adapter starts to transmit them. This considerably increases (by 25–55%) the performance of the *RAM – adapter – physical link – adapter – RAM* chain. This method is very sensitive to the threshold of transmission start (i.e., to the number of frame bytes that must be loaded into the adapter buffer before actual transmission starts). Network adapters carry out self-tuning of this parameter by analyzing the medium and computing the threshold value without network administrator involvement. Self-configuration ensures maximum performance for specific combinations of the internal computer bus and its IRQ and DMA settings.

Network adapters are based on application-specific integrated circuits (ASIC), which improves their performance and reliability while reducing their cost.

NOTE   *Improved operating speed of the channel between memory and adapter is important for an overall increase of network performance, since the frame transmission rate over a complex route, which might include, for example, concentrators, switches, routers, and WAN links always depends on the performance of its slowest element. Therefore, if the server's or client's network adapter operates slowly, even the fastest network communication devices will be unable to increase overall network operating speed.*

Network adapters manufactured today can be classified as 4G (Fourth Generation) adapters. They must include the application-specific integrated circuit (ASIC) chip, which carries out the functions of the MAC layer, as well as many high-level functions. The set of such functions can include support for a remote monitoring agent, frame-prioritization methods, and remote control functions. Network adapters intended for servers nearly always contain a powerful built-in processor, which reduces the load on the CPU.

14.6.2 Main Functions of Concentrators

Practically all contemporary LAN technologies define a device that has three names used interchangeably: *concentrator, hub,* or *repeater*. Depending on the area of application, its design and the set of its functions can vary considerably. Only its main function remains unchanged, namely, *repeating the frame* either on all of its ports (as defined in the Ethernet standard) or on only certain ports, according to the algorithm defined by the relevant standard.

Usually, the concentrator has several ports to which network end nodes and computers are connected using separate physical cable segments. The concentrator joins separate physical segments of the network into a common shared medium, access to which is carried out according to one of the previously considered LAN protocols: Ethernet, Token Ring, etc. Since access logic to the shared medium strongly depends on the technology, special concentrators are manufactured for all of the popular technologies.

Each concentrator performs a *main function* defined in the appropriate standard of the technology that it supports.

Besides the main function, the concentrator can perform several *add-on functions* that either are not defined in standards or are optional capabilities. For example, the Token Ring concentrator can disconnect the operating ports incorrectly and switch to the reserve ring, although the standard does not describe such functional capabilities. Concentrators proved to be convenient devices for carrying out auxiliary functions that simplify network maintenance and control.

Consider the specific implementation features of the concentrator's main function in an example of Ethernet concentrators.

In Ethernet, the devices joining several physical segments of coaxial cable into a single shared medium were used for a long time. Based on their main function — repeating on all output ports the signals received on one of their input ports — these devices became known as Ethernet repeaters. In networks based on coaxial cable, **two-port repeaters** were most common, connecting only two segments of cable. For this reason, the term concentrator is rarely applied to them.

With the adoption of 10Base-T for twisted pair, repeaters became an integral part of Ethernet networks, since without them communications could be organized only between two network nodes. **Multiport Ethernet repeaters** based on a twisted pair became known as concentrators or hubs, since a single device concentrated connections among a large number of network nodes. Figure 14.18 shows a typical Ethernet concentrator intended for creating small segments of a shared medium. It has 16 10Base-T ports with RJ-45 connectors and a single AUI port for connecting an external transceiver. As a rule, a transceiver using coaxial cable or optical fiber is connected to this port. Using this transceiver, the concentrator is connected to a backbone cable connecting several concentrators. Stations located 100 m or farther from the concentrator are connected in the same way.

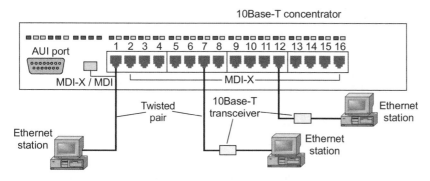

Figure 14.18 Ethernet concentrator

NOTE   *To connect 10Base-T concentrators into a hierarchical system, the same ports can be used as those connecting end-user workstations. However, there is a specific circumstance that needs to be taken into account in such a system: A normal RJ-45 port intended for connecting a network adapter and called* medium dependent interface with crossover *(MDI-X, where X stands for crossover) has the inverse arrangement of connector contacts to make it possible to connect a network adapter to the concentrator using a standard connection cable, which does not cross contacts (Figure 14.19). When concentrators are connected using a standard MDI-X port, it is necessary to use nonstandard cable with cross-connected pairs. Therefore, some manufacturers supply the concentrator with a dedicated MDI port, which does not use pair crossing. Thus, two concentrators can be connected as normal: straight through the cable using the MDI-X port of one concentrator and MDI port the other. Often, the same port of the concentrator can operate as both an MDI-X and an MDI port, depending on the position of the key switch, as shown in the lower part of Figure 14.19.*

A multiport Ethernet repeater–concentrator can be considered from different positions when applying the **four hubs rule**. In most models, all ports are connected to a single repeater unit; consequently, when the signal passes between two ports, the repeater unit introduces the delay only once. Therefore, such a concentrator must be con-

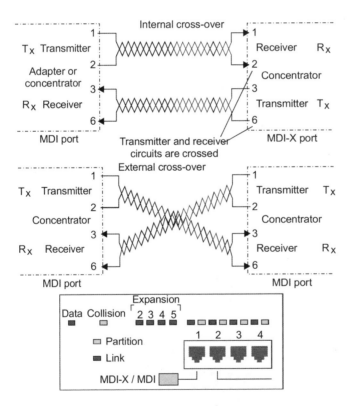

Figure 14.19 Station–concentrator and concentrator–concentrator connections based on twisted pair

sidered a single repeater imposing limitations according the four hubs rule. However, other models of repeaters have several ports with their own repeater units. In this case, each repeater unit must be considered a single repeater and must be taken into account separately when applying the four hubs rule.

However, in contrast to the differences in implementing the main concentrator functions, which are insignificant, the differences in implementing the auxiliary functions in concentrators are considerable.

14.6.3 Autopartitioning

Autopartitioning is a useful concentrator function allowing the concentrator to disconnect ports that are operating incorrectly. It helps to isolate all other parts of the network from problems arising in the incorrectly operating node[4]. The main reason for port disconnection in Ethernet and Fast Ethernet standards is lack of response to the sequence of link test pulses sent to all ports every 16 msec. In this case, the malfunctioning port is switched to the disconnected state. However, link test pulses will continue to be sent to the port so that when the device is restored, it will continue to operate automatically.

Consider situations in which Ethernet and Fast Ethernet concentrators disconnect ports:

- *Errors at the frame level.* If the intensity of erroneous frames passing via the port exceeds the predefined threshold, the port is disconnected. Then, provided that there are no errors during the predefined time intervals, the port is connected again. Such errors can include an incorrect checksum, invalid frame length (more than 1,518 bytes or less than 64 bytes), or incorrect frame header.
- *Multiple collisions.* If the concentrator registers that the same port was the source of collision more than 60 times, the port is disconnected. After some time, the port will be connected again.
- *Lengthy transmission (jabber).* Like a network adapter, the concentrator controls the time during which a single frame passes through the port. If this time exceeds the interval required to transmit a frame of the maximum length more than three times, the port is disconnected.

14.6.4 Support of Reserve Links

Since the use of reserve links in concentrators is defined only in FDDI, concentrator developers support this function in concentrators intended for other technologies only as an option. For example, Ethernet concentrators can form only hierarchical links without

---

[4] In FDDI concentrators, this function is the main one for most error situations, since it is defined in the protocol.

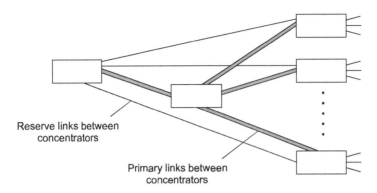

Figure 14.20 Reserve links between Ethernet concentrators

loops. Therefore, reserve links can exist only between disconnected ports to prevent violations of network operating logic. Usually, when configuring a concentrator, the network administrator must determine which are main ports and which are reserve ports (Figure 14.20). If the port is disconnected for any reason (i.e., the autopartitioning mechanism snaps into action), the concentrator activates its reserve port.

In some concentrator models, use of the port reservation mechanism is allowed only for the most important links, based on fiber-optic cable. In some other models, it is possible to reserve any port.

14.6.5 Protection against Unauthorized Access

Shared media make unauthorized network sniffing and accessing the data being transmitted easy. To achieve this, it is sufficient to connect a computer installed with a copy of the protocol analyzer to a free concentrator connector and save all traffic passing via the network into a file on the hard disk. After that, it is possible to retrieve all the required information.

Concentrator manufacturers provide some methods of data protection in shared media.

The simplest protection method is assigning allowed MAC addresses to the concentrator ports. In a standard Ethernet concentrator, ports have no MAC addresses. Data protection consists of manually assigning specific MAC address to each port of the concentrator. This MAC address is the address of the station allowed to connect to that port. For example, in Figure 14.21, the first port of the concentrator is assigned a specific MAC address (conventionally, 123). The computer with the equivalent MAC address can normally communicate with the network using that port. If an intruder disconnects that computer and connects another computer, the concentrator will notice that after the new computer starts up, the source address of frames incoming to the network from the new computer has changed (e.g., to 789). Since this address is invalid for the first port, these frames are filtered out, the port is disconnected, and a security incident can be registered.

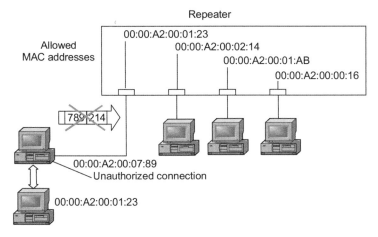

Figure 14.21 Port isolation: Frame transmission is allowed only from stations with predefined MAC addresses

To implement this method of concentrator data protection, the concentrator needs to be configured. For this purpose, the concentrator must be equipped with a control unit. Such concentrators are usually called intellectual concentrators. The control unit is a compact computing unit with built-in software. To ensure that the administrator can communicate with the control unit, the concentrator has a console port (most often, the RS-232 port) to which a terminal or PC installed with a terminal emulation program is connected. When the terminal connects to the console port, the control unit displays a dialog, using which the network administrator can enter MAC addresses. The control unit can support other configuration operations, such as manual connection or disconnection of ports. For this purpose, the control unit displays some form of menu on the terminal screen. Using this menu, the network administrator can choose the required action.

Another method of protecting data from unauthorized access is encryption in the concentrator. However, true encryption requires significant computing power. Therefore, for concentrators without frame buffering, it is rather problematic to encrypt data on the fly. Instead of true encryption, concentrators use random distortion of the data field in packets transmitted to ports with addresses different from the packet destination address. This method preserves the logic of random access to the medium, since all stations can notice that the medium is busy with the transmission of an information frame. However, only the destination station for which the frame being transmitted is intended can correctly interpret the contents of its data field (Figure 14.22). To implement this method, the concentrator must be supplied with the MAC addresses of all stations connected to its ports. Usually, data fields in frames sent to stations other than the destination nodes are filled with zeros.

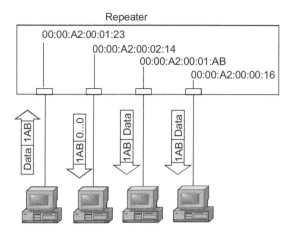

Figure 14.22 Distortion of the data field in frames not intended for reception by stations

14.6.7 Multisegment Concentrators

Why are some concentrators models equipped with such a large number of ports, say, 192 or 240? Is there any sense in dividing a medium of 10 or 16 Mbps among such a large number of stations? Ten or 15 years ago, the answer in some cases could have been yes. For example, this is true for networks whose computers used the medium only for sending small mail messages or copying small text files. Nowadays, there are not many such networks, and even five computers can fully load an Ethernet segment.

Why then is a concentrator with a large number of ports needed, especially if it is practically impossible to use all the ports because of the limitations on bandwidth per station?

The answer lies in such concentrators having several internal buses that are not interconnected. These buses are intended for creating several shared media. For example, the concentrator shown in Figure 14.23 has three internal Ethernet buses. If such a concen-

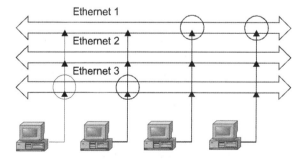

Figure 14.23 Multisegment concentrator

trator has 72 ports, each of these ports can be connected to any of the three internal buses. The configuration in Figure 14.23 shows that the first two computers are connected to the Ethernet 3 bus, and the third and the fourth stations are connected to the Ethernet 1 bus. The first two computers form one shared segment, and the third and fourth stations form another shared segment.

Computers connected to different segments cannot communicate using the concentrator, since its internal buses are not interconnected.

Multisegment concentrators are needed for connecting shared segments that can be easily changed. Most multisegment concentrators can carry out the connection of the port to one of its internal buses programmatically, for example, by local configuration using a console port. As a result, the network administrator can connect users' computers to any concentrator ports and then control the structure of each segment using the concentrator configuration program. For example, if segment 1 becomes congested, its computers can be distributed among the remaining segments of the concentrator.

> Programmatically changing connections among the ports and the concentrator's internal buses is known as **configuration switching**.

NOTE   *Configuration switching does not have anything in common with the packet switching carried out by bridges and switches.*

Multisegment concentrators form a programmable basis for large-scale networks. Interconnecting segments requires the use of other devices: bridges, switches, or routers. Such internetworking devices must be connected to several ports of a multisegment concentrator attached to different internal buses. The main goal of such a device is frame or packet forwarding among segments as if they were created using separate concentrators.

For a large-scale network, a multisegment concentrator plays the role of an intellectual rack, which creates a new connection programmatically by changing the internal device configuration instead of mechanically connecting the cable plug to another port.

14.6.8 Concentrator Design

The area of concentrator application has a considerable influence on its design. Workgroup concentrators are usually released as devices with a fixed number of ports, and corporate concentrators are modular devices based on a chassis. Department-level concentrators can have a stack structure. Such a division is not rigid, and modular concentrators can also be used as corporate-level devices.

Concentrators with a fixed number of ports have the simplest design. Such a device is a separate unit with all required elements (ports, indicators, controls, and a power supply unit). These elements cannot be replaced. Usually, all ports of such a concentrator support one transmission medium; the total number of ports varies from 4–48. One port can be dedicated to connecting the concentrator to the network backbone or to joining

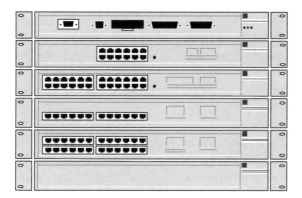

Figure 14.24 Ethernet stack concentrators

concentrators. (Most frequently, the AUI port is used for this purpose: In this case, the use of an appropriate transceiver allows the concentrator to be connected to practically any physical transmission medium.)

Modular concentrators are implemented as separate modules with a fixed number of ports installed on a common chassis. The chassis has an internal bus for joining separate modules into a common repeater. Often such repeaters are multisegment, in which case there are several noninterconnected repeaters within a single modular concentrator. Several types of modules can exist for a modular concentrator, differing in the number of ports and physical medium supported. Modular concentrators allow the concentrator configuration to be chosen more precisely. They also allow flexible, low-cost reactions to network-configuration changes.

Because corporate modular concentrators carry out crucial tasks, they are equipped with a control unit, a system of thermal control, redundant power supply units, and the possibility of replacing modules spontaneously.

High price is the most important drawback of chassis-based concentrators when a business needs to install only one or two modules at the initial stage of network deployment. The chassis is costly because it is supplied with all other devices, such as redundant power supply units. Therefore, **stack concentrators** have become the most popular for medium-sized networks.

Stack concentrators, like concentrators with a fixed number of ports, are supplied in the form of separate unit without the possibility of replacing individual modules. Typical examples of several Ethernet stack concentrators are shown in Figure 14.24.

Stack concentrators have special ports and cables for connecting several such units into a single repeater (Figure 14.25) that has a common repeater unit, ensures overall signal resynchronization, and therefore can be considered a single repeater in terms of the four hubs rule. If stack concentrators have several internal buses, these buses are joined and become common for all stack devices when joining these concentrators to the stack.

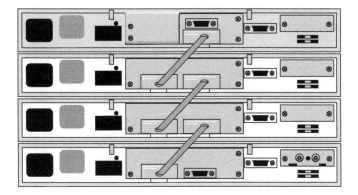

Figure 14.25 Connection of stack concentrators into a single device using special connectors at the rear panel

The number of devices joined to the stack can be quite large (normally up to eight, but sometimes even more). Stack concentrators can support various physical transmission media, which makes them almost as flexible as modular concentrators. However, the cost of stack concentrators per port is usually lower, since a business can start with a single device without a redundant chassis and then add similar devices to the stack as needed.

Stack concentrators from the same manufacturer usually have the same design, which makes it easy to install them on top of one another, thus forming a single desktop device, or to place them into a common chassis. When organizing a stack, it is also possible to economize on the control unit common to all devices of the stack; it can be inserted as an add-on module into the common chassis. Further savings potential is possible using a common redundant power supply unit.

Modular stack concentrators are modular concentrators joined into the stack using special links. As a rule, such concentrators' cases are intended for a small number of modules (1–3). These concentrators combine the advantages of both types of concentrators.

This classification of concentrator designs is applicable not only to concentrators but also to other types of communications devices: LAN bridges and routers and WAN switches and routers. Not all types of device imply such close interaction among stack elements as concentrators. Often, stack devices are joined only by common power supply units and control units; main functions are carried out autonomously by each stack device.

SUMMARY

▶ Token Ring networks use deterministic access implementing token passing. This method guarantees each station access to the shared ring during the time of token turnaround. The logical topology of a Token Ring is a ring, and the physical topology of such a network is star.

▶ Token Ring networks operate at two rates (4 or 16 Mbps) and can use shielded or unshielded twisted pair, as well as fiber-optic cable, as a transmission medium. The maximum number of stations in the ring is 260, and maximum length of the ring is 4 km. The use of the ring topology allows Token Ring networks to ensure basic fault-tolerance features.

▶ The succession from Token Ring to FDDI is quite significant: Both use the same network topology, and both use token passing as the access method. FDDI supports advanced fault-tolerance tools. In case of isolated failures of the cable system or one of the ring workstations, the network preserves operability by wrapping the dual ring into a single ring.

▶ Fiber distributed data interface (FDDI) was the first technology to employ fiber-optic cable in LANs and ensure data transmission at 100 Mbps.

▶ The maximum number of stations with a double connection in an FDDI ring is 500; the maximum diameter of a dual ring is 100 km. This makes FDDI suitable for use not only in LANs but also in MANs.

▶ Wireless LANs get rid of the bulky cabling system and ensure user mobility. However, they require network architects to solve a set of complicated problems related to the high level of noise characteristic of wireless media and an undefined network coverage zone.

▶ IEEE 802.11 standards are the most promising standards for wireless LANs. There are several variants of 802.11 physical-layer specifications, differing in terms of frequency range (2.4 or 5 GHz) and encoding method (FHSS, DSSS, or OFDM). The 802.11b physical layer ensures data transmission of up to 11 Mbps.

▶ The 802.11 access method is a combination of random access with collision avoidance and centralized deterministic access based on polling. The first mode is implemented by distributed coordination function (DCF) algorithms, and the second mode by point coordination function (PCF) algorithms.

▶ Flexible use of DCF and PCF allows QoS support for synchronous and asynchronous traffic.

▶ Personal area networks (PANs) are intended for organizing interaction among devices belonging to a single owner over small distances (usually, 10–100 m). PANs must ensure both fixed and mobile access, for example, within a building or when moving among rooms, buildings, or cities.

▶ Currently, Bluetooth is the most popular PAN technology. It uses the piconet concept. A piconet can include up to 255 devices, but only eight can be active and exchange data at any moment. One of the piconet devices is the master; the other devices are slaves.

▶ Several piconets located in the same area and exchanging data form a scatternet. Piconets forming a scatternet interact with each other by a single node (bridge) that is simultaneously part of several piconets.

▶ For delay-sensitive traffic, Bluetooth networks support synchronous connection-oriented (SCO) links; for elastic traffic, they use asynchronous connectionless (ACL) links. SCO links are normally used for transmitting voice traffic at 64 Kbps, and ACL channels are used for computer traffic at variable rates of up to 723 Kbps.

▶ Besides their main protocol function (bit-by-bit repeating of the frame to all ports or the next port), LAN concentrators always carry out several useful auxiliary functions, including:

- Autopartitioning one of the most important auxiliary functions, using which the concentrator can disconnect the port if it detects problems with the cable or end node connected to that port

- Network protection against unauthorized access by disallowing connection of computers with unknown MAC addresses to concentrator ports

REVIEW QUESTIONS

1. Describe the medium access algorithm used in Token Ring.

2. Which functions are carried out by the active monitor?

3. Why are Token Ring networks able to retain connectivity if one of the computers forming the ring is powered down?

4. Specify the maximum allowed data field sizes for:
   - Ethernet
   - Token Ring
   - FDDI
   - Bluetooth

5. On what basis is the maximum token turnaround time chosen for the Token Ring network?

6. Which element of the Token Ring network restores synchronization of the bit flow?

7. What are advantages of the early token-release mechanism?

8. What features do FDDI and Token Ring have in common, and how do they differ?

9. Which elements of FDDI networks ensure fault tolerance?

10. FDDI is fault tolerant. Does this mean that under conditions of any single cable breakdown the network can continue normal operation?

11. What are the consequences of duplicated cable breakdown in FDDI rings?

12. What will happen if a single attachment station (SAS) cable is damaged in an FDDI network?

13. Which methods of signal encoding are used in IEEE 802.11 networks?

14. What type of medium does the DS use for transmitting data among BSSs?

15. What is the influence of the hidden terminal effect?

16. How does the MAC layer in 802.11 networks detect collisions?

17. Is it possible for a station belonging to an 802.11 network to transmit a frame to another station belonging to the same BSS using AP?

18. What is the purpose of dividing the time period allowed for frame transmission into slots in DCF? What needs to be taken into account when choosing slot duration?

19. Why does PCF always have priority over DCF?

20. How are Bluetooth piconets joined into a scatternet?

21. Why are not all 625 bits of a Bluetooth time slot used for frame transmission?

22. In which cases can a single Bluetooth frame carry data of one, two, or three SCO channels?

23. What switching methods are used in Bluetooth?

24. Why was master–slave architecture chosen for Bluetooth?

25. How do network adapter bandwidth and concentrator port bandwidth influence network performance?

26. How do concentrators support reserve links?

27. According to their main function — repeating a signal — concentrators are classified as devices operating at the physical layer of the OSI model. Provide examples of auxiliary concentrator functions for which the concentrator needs information from higher-layer protocols.

28. What are the differences between modular and stack concentrators?

29. Why are special ports used for interconnecting concentrators?

PROBLEMS

1. Evaluate the maximum time of waiting for access to the medium in a Token Ring network with 160 stations and operating at 16 Mbps.

2. A Token Ring network includes 100 stations. The total length of the ring is 2,000 m. The transmission rate is 16 Mbps. The token-holding time is chosen to be 10 msec. Each station transmits frames of a fixed size of 4,000 bytes (with the header) and fully uses the token-holding time for transmitting all of its frames. Calculate the gain produced by using the early token-release mechanism in this network.

3. IEEE 802.11 and Bluetooth networks operate within the same territory. The 802.11 network uses the FHSS physical-layer specification for data transmission at 1 Mbps. The Bluetooth network operates with a standard chipping rate of 1,600 Hz, and the 802.11 network supports a chipping rate of 50 Hz. Both networks use 79 channels in the 2.4 GHz range.

   Determine the proportion of frames in each network that are corrupted because of the use of the same frequency channel by both networks. For precision, consider that all data in the Bluetooth network are transmitted in one-slot frames, and the 802.11 network uses frames of the maximum length.

15

SWITCHED LAN BASICS

15.1 INTRODUCTION

Shared media were used in LANs from the moment networks of this type first appeared. Such an approach to the use of communications links has several advantages, one of which is the simplicity of LAN communications equipment. However, the use of a shared medium is not free from drawbacks. The most obvious shortcoming of shared media LANs is low scalability, because an increase in the number of network nodes results in a proportional decrease in the bandwidth allocated to each node.

The natural solution to the problem of LAN scalability is dividing it into several segments, each representing a separate shared medium. Such logical partitioning is carried out using LAN bridges or switches. In *Chapter 3*, we considered the principles of logical network structuring. In this chapter, we cover the operating algorithms of bridges and switches in more detail.

LANs divided into logical segments are called **switched LANs**. A network segment comprising a single computer directly connected to the switch port is called a **microsegment**. In essence, a microsegment is no longer a shared medium. On the contrary, it is a duplex channel used by transmitters of the computer or switch port as needed without sharing it with other transmitters.

Although a switched LAN is always a more expensive solution than a shared-medium LAN, it ensures several advantages besides scalability. The main advantages of switched LANs are covered in this chapter.

15.2 LOGICAL NETWORK STRUCTURING USING BRIDGES AND SWITCHES

> **KEY WORDS**: switched LAN, microsegment, M/M/1 model, bridge, switch, transparent bridge algorinthm, MAC address, spanning free algorithm (STA)

15.2.1 Advantages and Drawbacks of Shared Media LANs

When building small networks comprising 10 to 30 nodes, the use of standard technologies based on a shared medium is an economical and efficient solution. This efficiency is the result of the following network properties:

- **Simple network topology**, which allows the number of network nodes to be easily increased within reasonable limits.
- **Elimination of frame losses** caused by buffer overflow on communications devices. This result is achieved because a new frame is not transmitted into the network until the previous one is received. The logic of medium sharing itself regulates the frame flow by forcing the stations that generate frames too often to defer their sending. Such stations must wait until they get access to the medium. Thus, procedures of flow control are carried out automatically.

■ **Simplicity of protocols**, which has ensured the low cost of network adapters, repeaters, and concentrators — and consequently, of the network as a whole.

However, the statement that large networks connecting hundreds or thousands of nodes cannot be created on the basis of a single shared medium is also true. This is true even for such high-speed technologies as Gigabit Ethernet. Practically all technologies limit both the maximum network length and the number of nodes in a shared medium. For example, for all technologies of the Ethernet family, this number is limited to 1,024 nodes; for Token Ring, this number is 260 nodes; and for FDDI, it is 500 nodes. However, this is not the only reason for such a limitation.

> The main problem with all networks based on a single shared medium is the bandwidth shortage.

A quantitative description of the processes that take place in a shared-medium LAN can be obtained using queuing models. One such model, namely, the M/M/1 model, was considered in *Chapter 7*. According to this model, the shared medium corresponds to the server, and frames generated by each networked computer correspond to service requests. The queue of service requests is distributed among all networked computers, where frames wait for their turn to use the medium.

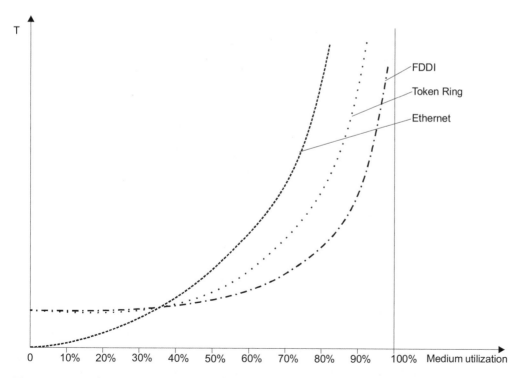

Figure 15.1 Medium access delays for Ethernet, Token Ring, and FDDI technologies

The M/M/1 model cannot adequately reflect many specific features of a shared-medium LAN, such as Ethernet collisions. Nevertheless, it is capable of demonstrating a qualitative pattern of the dependence between the medium access delays and the medium utilization coefficient.

Figure 15.1 shows dependence curves obtained for Ethernet, Token Ring, and FDDI using simulation techniques.

As can be seen from this illustration, all technologies have a qualitatively similar pattern of exponential growth of the delay versus load. In all cases, the medium access delays grow exponentially with the increase of shared medium usage. However, they differ in a threshold value at which sharp changes in network behavior occur, namely, when practically linear dependence turns to a sharply growing exponent. For all technologies of the Ethernet family, this value is 30–50% (because of the collision effect); for Token Ring, this value is about 60%; and for FDDI, it is 70–80%.

The number of nodes at which shared medium usage starts to get close to the dangerous limit depends on the type of applications running on the network nodes. For example, earlier it was considered that 30 nodes is an acceptable number of the Ethernet nodes in one shared segment. Nowadays, if network nodes run multimedia applications or exchange large data files, this number can be from five to ten nodes.

15.2.2 Advantages of the Logical Network Structuring

It is possible to overcome the limitations caused by the use of a single shared medium by dividing the network into several shared media and then connecting separate network segments using special communications devices, such as bridges, switches, or routers (Figure 15.2).

These devices transmit frames from port to port based on an analysis of the destination address contained in those frames. Bridges and switches carry out the operation of frame transmission based on flat data link-layer addresses (MAC addresses), and routers use hierarchical network-layer addresses for this purpose. Router operation will be covered in detail in *Part IV*. For the moment, concentrate on bridges and switches.

Logical network structuring was alredy briefly discussed in *Chapter 3*. In this section this problem will be covered in more details. Logical network structuring allows several tasks to be solved; the main tasks are improvement of the network performance, flexibility, security, and manageability.

Performance improvement. As an illustration of this effect, the main goal of logical structuring, consider Figure 15.3. This illustration shows two Ethernet segments connected by a bridge. Within those segments are several repeaters. Before the network was segmented, all traffic generated by the network nodes shared the same medium. For example, this would be the case if instead of an internetworking device (bridge), a repeater would be installed. This network was taken into account when determining the network utilization coefficient. If you designate the average intensity of the traffic traveling from node i to node j as C_{ij}, then the total traffic that the network would have to transmit before segmentation would be $C_\Sigma = \Sigma C_{ij}$ (considering that summation is carried out over all nodes).

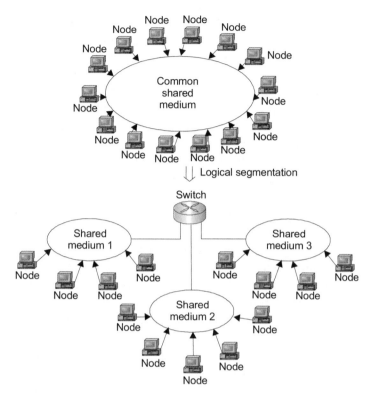

Figure 15.2 Logical network structuring

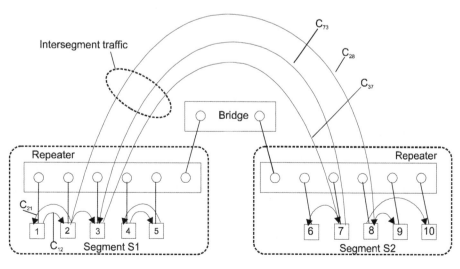

Figure 15.3 Changing the network load after segmentation

After segmentation, it became necessary to take into account the internal traffic of the segment — that is, the frames that circulate among the nodes within a single segment and intersegment traffic that is either directed from a node of this segment to the node of another segment or comes into the node of this segment from the node belonging to another segment.

Therefore, the segment load of, say, the S1 segment became equal to $C_{S1} + C_{S1-S2}$, where C_{S1} is the internal traffic of the S1 segment and C_{S1-S2} is the intersegment traffic. To see that the load on the S1 segment became lower than the load of the initial network, notice that the total network load before dividing it into segments could be written in the following form: $C_\Sigma = C_{S1} + C_{S1-S2} + C_{S2}$. Consequently, the load of the S1 after segmentation became equal to $C_\Sigma - C_{S2}$, which means that it has decreased by the value of the internal traffic of the S2 segment. Similar considerations can be repeated for the S2 segment. Thus, according to the graphs provided in Figure 15.1, delays in segments have decreased, and effective bandwidth per node has increased.

Earlier we mentioned that network segmentation practically always reduces the load in new segments. The word "practically" takes into account such a rare event as when a network is partitioned into segments so that the internal traffic of each segment is zero, which means that all traffic is intersegment traffic. For the example shown in Figure 15.3, this would mean that all computers of the S1 segment exchange data only with computers belonging to the S2 segment, and vice versa.

In practice, in any network, it is possible to select a group of computers that belong to employees that carry out some common tasks. These may be employees belonging to the same workgroup, department, or other structural unit of the company. In most cases, they need access to the network resources of their department and only rarely require access to remote resources.

In the 1980s, there was an empirical rule stating that it is possible to divide the network into segments to ensure that 80% of the entire traffic will be caused by attempts to access local resources and only 20% will be to access to remote resources. Such a rule is not always reflecting reality. On the contrary, it can be transformed into the 50-to-50% or even 20-to-80% rule. For instance, this is the case when most attempts to access resources are to access the Internet or the resources concentrated on the company servers. Nevertheless, there always is internal traffic of the segment. If there is no such traffic, the network is divided into segments incorrectly.

Subnets improve network flexibility. When building a network as a set of segments (subnets), each subnet can be adapted according to the specific requirements of a certain workgroup or department. For example, one subnet can use the Ethernet technology and UNIX operating system, and another subnet can be based on the Token Ring technology and run OS-400, according to requirements of a specific department or of existing applications. Users of both subnets can exchange data using bridges or switches. The process of dividing the network into logical segments can be considered from the opposite point of view, namely, as the process of creating a large network by interconnecting the existing subnets.

Subnets strengthen data security. By installing various logical filters on bridges or switches, it is possible to control user access to resources in other segments. Note that repeaters do not provide this capability.

Subnets simplify network management. The simplification of network management is a side effect of traffic reduction and data security improvement. Problems often are localized within a segment. Segments form logical domains of network management.

As already mentioned, a network can be divided into logical segments using two types of devices: bridges and/or switches. Soon after the arrival of switches in the early 1990s, marketing departments of the firms manufacturing these new devices tried to create a false impression that the bridge and the switch are different devices.

> Nevertheless, the bridge and the switch have so much in common that functionally they look like twins. The main difference between a bridge and a switch is that a bridge processes frames sequentially and a switch does the same operation in parallel.

Both devices forward frames based on the same algorithm, namely, the **transparent bridge algorithm** described in the IEEE 802.1D standard.

This standard, developed long before the first switch appeared, described the operation of a **bridge**. Therefore, it is natural that the term **bridge** was retained in its name. When the first models of switches appeared, some confusion arose because switches operated on the basis of the frame-forwarding algorithm described in the IEEE 802.1D standard. This algorithm has been worked through by bridges for about ten years. Although the bridges for which the algorithm was developed are practically out of use nowadays, being obsolete communications devices, the standards describing operation of the switch traditionally use the term **bridge**. We are not so conservative. When describing algorithms of the 802.1D standard in the next section, we use the term **switch** except when mentioning an official name of a standard or when it is necessary to emphasize the difference between the two types of devices.

15.2.3 Transparent Bridge Algorithm of the IEEE 802.1D Standard

The word *transparent* in the name of transparent bridge algorithm reflects the fact that bridges and switches in their operation do not take into account network adapters of end nodes, concentrators and repeaters. On the other hand, the above-listed devices also operate without noticing the presence of bridges and switches.

The algorithm of transparent bridge or switch does not depend on the LAN technology used in the LAN where the bridge is installed. Therefore, Ethernet transparent bridges or switches operate in the same way as FDDI or Token Ring transparent bridges or switches.

The switch creates its address table by passively tracing the traffic circulating in segments connected to its ports. The switch takes into account the source addresses of the data coming into the switch ports. The switch determines the network segment to which a specific source node belongs on the basis of the source address carried by a frame sent by that node.

*Each port of the switch operates as an end node of its segment with one exception —
namely, that switch port has no MAC address of its own. Switch ports do not need
addresses because they operate in the* promiscuous *mode of frame capturing. In this
mode, all frames coming into the port are loaded into the buffer memory, regardless of
their destination address. When operating in the promiscuous mode, the switch "sniffs"
all traffic circulating in the segments connected to it and uses frames that pass through
it to learn the network structure.*

Consider how the switch automatically generates and uses the address table in the example of a simple network shown in Figure 15.4.

The switch connects two network segments. Segment 1 is composed of computers connected by a single segment of coaxial cable to port 1 of the switch. Segment 2 is made up
of computers connected to port 2 of the switch using another section of coaxial cable.

Initially, the switch does not know the MAC addresses of the computers connected to
each of its ports. In this situation, the switch simply transmits any captured and buffered
frame to all of its ports except the port from which this frame was received. In this example, the switch has only two ports; therefore, it transmits frames from port 1 to port 2, and
vice versa. The difference between a switch operating in this mode and a repeater is that
the switch transmits the frame by buffering all frame data before frame forwarding instead of bit-by-bit transmission. The buffering breaks the logic of operation of all segments as a single shared medium. When the switch is going to transmit the frame from
segment to segment — for example, from segment 1 to segment 2 — it makes a new
attempt of accessing segment 2 similar to an end node using a specific medium access
algorithm (CSMA/CD, in this case).

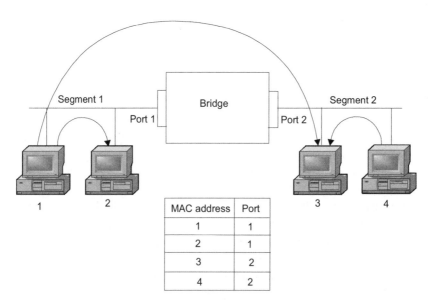

MAC address	Port
1	1
2	1
3	2
4	2

Figure 15.4 Operating principle of a transparent bridge or switch

During frame transmission to all ports, the switch learns the source address of the frame and enters the record that it belongs to specific segment into the switch *address table*, also known as a *filtering table* or *routing table*. For example, having received a frame from computer 1 to its port 1, the switch enters the first record into its address table:

MAC address1 — port 1

This record means that computer with **MAC address1** belongs to the segment connected to **port 1** of the switch. If all four computers of this network become active and exchange frames with one another, the switch soon builds a complete address table of this network comprising four records, one record per end node (Figure 15.4).

Any time when a frame arrives to the switch port, the switch tries to use it by comparing the destination addresses of all arriving frames to this address and checking if they match. Now continue discussing the switch operation on the example shown in Figure 15.4.

1. Having received a frame sent from computer 1 to computer 3, the switch would look up the address table to find the address that matches the destination address specified in the frame: **MAC address3**. There is such a record in the table.

2. The switch carries out the second stage of table analysis. At the second stage, the switch checks if computers with the source address (**MAC address1**) and the destination address (**MAC address3**) are located in the same segment — in other words, if they are connected to the same port. In this example, computers 1 and 3 are located in different segments; therefore, the switch carries out the operation known as frame forwarding — namely, it transmits the frame to another port, having previously gained access to another segment.

3. If the switch finds that the computers with the specified source and destination addresses belong to the same segment, the switch would simply delete the frame from its buffer. This operation is called *filtering*.

4. If the destination address is **unknown to (unlearned by) the switch**, which means that it is missing from address table, the switch transmits the frame to all its ports except the source port, similar to the initial stage of the learning process.

The learning process of the switch never stops, and it takes place in parallel with frame forwarding and filtering. The switch constantly traces the source addresses of the frames being buffered to be capable of automatically adapting to changes that might take place in the network, such as moving computers from segment to segment, removing computers, and introducing new computers.

Address table entries can be *dynamic*, created by the switch in the process of self-learning, and *static*, manually created by a network administrator. **Static entries** have no expiration time, which allows an administrator to influence the operation of a specific computer — for example, by limiting the transmission of frames having specific source addresses from segment to segment.

Dynamic entries have an expiration time — when an existing entry of the address table is updated or when a new entry is created, a time mark is associated with it. After the predefined timeout expires, the record is marked as invalid if during that time the switch has not received a single frame with that address in the source address field. This provides the possibility of automatically reacting to events when computers are moved from segment to segment. If a computer is disconnected from its previous segment, the address table entry specifying that this computer belongs to that segment will be removed from the address table after a time. After this computer gets connected to another segment, its frames will arrive to the switch buffer via another port, and a new record will be entered into address table corresponding to the new state of the network.

Frames with broadcast MAC addresses and frames with unlearned destination addresses are passed by the switch to all of its ports. This mode of frame propagation is known as a *flooding*. The presence of switches in the network does not prevent the propagation of broadcast frames by all network segments, thus preserving its transparency. However, this feature is an advantage only provided that broadcast address was created by the node that operates correctly.

However, situations often can arise in which, as a result of software or hardware failures or malfunctions, the upper-layer protocol or network adapter start to operate incorrectly, namely, by constantly generating broadcast frames during a long period. In this case, the switch transmits these frames to all segments, thus flooding the network with invalid traffic. Such a situation is known as a *broadcast storm*.

Unfortunately, switches are unable to protect networks against broadcast storms, at least by default — in contrast to routers (this property of routers will be covered in *Part IV*). The most an administrator can do to prevent a broadcast storm using a switch is to specify for each node the maximum intensity for generating frames with a broadcast address. In this case, it is necessary to know precisely what intensity is normal and what indicates an erroneous situation. When changing protocols, the situation in the network can change. In particular, the situation that yesterday was considered erroneous might today prove to be quite normal.

Figure 15.5 shows a typical structure of a switch. Medium access functions when receiving and transmitting frames are carried out by MAC circuits, which are similar to those of a network adapter.

The protocol that implements the switch algorithm resides between the MAC and the LLC layers (Figure 15.6).

Figure 15.7 shows a copy of the terminal screen with the address table of the local switch module. The terminal is connected to the console port, and information displayed on its screen is generated by the switch control unit.

From the address table (forwarding table) displayed on the screen, it can be seen that the network comprises two segments — LAN A and LAN B. In the LAN A segment, there are at least three stations; in the LAN B segment, there are two stations. The four addresses marked by asterisks are static addresses (i.e., they are manually assigned by a network administrator). The address marked by the plus sign is a dynamic address with the expired time to live.

The table has the column labeled as *Dispn* — disposition. The data in this column inform the switch what operation should be carried out over a frame that has the specified

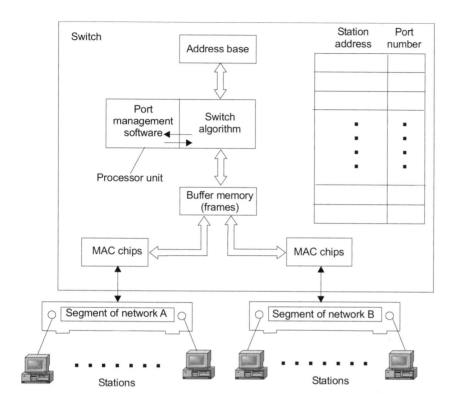

Figure 15.5 Switch structure

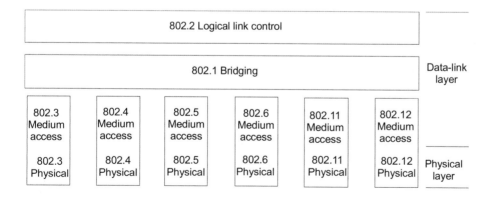

Figure 15.6 Location of the switch protocol in the protocol stack

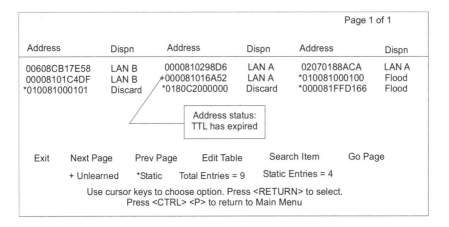

Address	Dispn	Address	Dispn	Address	Dispn
00608CB17E58	LAN B	0000810298D6	LAN A	02070188ACA	LAN A
00008101C4DF	LAN B	+000081016A52	LAN A	*010081000100	Flood
*010081000101	Discard	*0180C2000000	Discard	*000081FFD166	Flood

Address status:
TTL has expired

Exit   Next Page   Prev Page   Edit Table   Search Item   Go Page

+ Unlearned   *Static   Total Entries = 9   Static Entries = 4

Use cursor keys to choose option. Press <RETURN> to select.
Press <CTRL> <P> to return to Main Menu

Figure 15.7 Address table of a switch

destination address. When the table is created automatically, this field usually contains a conventional designation of the destination port. However, when the address is specified manually, it is possible to specify nonstandard operation of frame processing in this field. For example, the *Flood* operation makes the switch distribute the frame in broadcasting mode, even though its destination address is not a broadcast one. The *Discard* operation instructs the switch to discard the frame with such an address instead of delivering it to the destination port.

The operations specified in the *Dispn* column define specific conditions of frame filtering, complementing standard conditions of their propagation. Such conditions are usually called *user-defined filters*. They will be covered later in the "*Traffic Filtering*" section.

15.2.4 TOPOLOGICAL LIMITATIONS OF SWITCHED LAN

A serious limitation of functional capabilities of these communications devices is the impossibility of supporting loop configurations of the network.

Consider this limitation in the example of the network shown in Figure 15.8.

In this example, two Ethernet segments are connected in parallel by two switches so that an active loop is formed. Suppose that a new station having a MAC address of 123 is first connected to this network and starts operation. Usually, startup of any operating system is accompanied by transmission of broadcast frames in which the station informs other computers that it is in the network and simultaneously looks for network servers.

In the first stage, the station sends the first frame with the broadcast destination address and the source address 123 into the local segment. This frame arrives at switch 1 and at switch 2. In both switches, the new source address, 123, is entered into the address table with the mark specifying that it belongs to segment 1. This means that a new address table entry is created, which looks as follows:

MAC address	Port
123	1

Since the destination address is a broadcast address, each switch must transmit the frame to segment 2. This transmission goes in turns according to the random access method of the Ethernet technology. Assume that switch 1 was the first to get access to segment 2 (stage 2 in Figure 15.8). When the frame arrives at segment 2, switch 2 receives it, loads it into its buffer, and processes it. Switch 2 notices that address 123 is already in its address table; however, the just-arrived frame is newer, and it states that address 123 belongs to segment 2 rather than to segment 1. Therefore, switch 2 corrects the contents of its address table, creating a new entry specifying that address 123 belongs to segment 2:

MAC address	Port
123	2

Switch 1 proceeds in a similar way when switch 2 transmits its copy of the frame to segment 2.

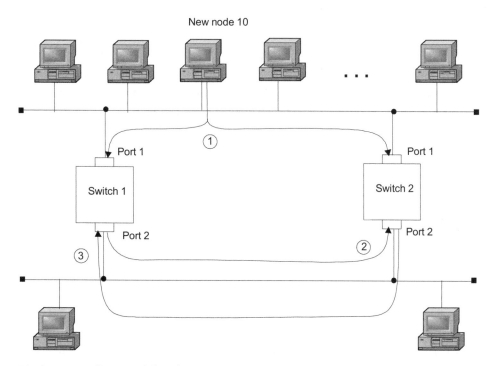

Figure 15.8 Influence of closed routes on the operation of a switch

Thus, the presence of the loop produces the following results:

- Frame "spawning" (e.g., appearance of several copies of the same frame). In this case, there are two copies; if the segments were connected by three switches, there would be three such copies, and so on.
- Endless circulation of both frame copies in inverse directions along the loop, which means flooding the network with useless traffic.
- Constant rebuilding of address tables of the switches, since the frame with the source address 123 will constantly appear on one port and then on another port.

To eliminate all these undesirable effects, switches must be used to eliminate loops between logical segments. This means that switches allow the construction only of tree-like structures that guarantee the presence of only one route between any two segments. The frames from each station would always arrive to the switch from the same port, and the switch would be able to correctly choose a rational route within the network. This is a tree network topology.

In small networks, it is comparatively easy to guarantee the existence of one possible path between two segments. However, as the number of connections grows, the probability of unintentionally creating loops also becomes high.

Furthermore, to improve network reliability, it is desirable to have reserve links between switches, which do not participate in frame transmission when main links operate normally but restore connectivity by creating a new working configuration without loops if one of the main links fails.

Therefore, in complex networks, redundant links are created between segments. These redundant links create loops. To eliminate active loops, some ports of the switches are locked. The simplest way of solving this problem is manual configuration. However, there are algorithms that allow this problem to be solved automatically. The best known among them is the **spanning tree algorithm** (**STA**), which will be covered in detail in *Chapter 16*.

15.3 SWITCHES

KEY WORDS: switch, bridge, spanning tree algorithm (STA), switching matrix, traffic filtering, Kalpana

15.3.1 Specific Features of Switches

With the radical changes in network evolution that took place in the late 1980s and early 1990s — which resulted in the arrival of fast protocols, high-performance PCs, and multimedia information as well as the division of networks into large numbers of segments — classical **bridges** ceased to carry out their tasks adequately. Serving flows of frames among several ports using a single processing unit required a significant increase in the processor operating speed, which was an expensive solution.

A more efficient solution was found, which resulted in the development of switches: For serving a flow arriving to each port, the device was equipped with a separate processor implementing the bridge algorithm. By its nature, switch is a multiprocessor bridge, capable of forwarding frames simultaneously between all pairs of its ports. However, in contrast to computers, which did not change their name after new processors were added but simply became "multiprocessor configurations," the situation with multiprocessor bridges was different; they became known as switches. This change of the device name was promoted by the method of organizing connections between individual processors within a switch — they were connected by a switching matrix, similar to the matrices of multiprocessor computers connecting processors to memory.

Gradually, switches have moved classical single-processor bridges out of LANs. The main reason for this was the high performance ensured by switches when transmitting frames between network segments. In contrast to bridges that could even slow network operation, switches are always equipped with port processors capable of transmitting frames at the maximum speed allowed by a protocol. Adding the capability of transmitting frames between ports in parallel has made switch performance tens of times higher than that of bridges. This factor has defined the perspectives of bridges and switches.

> Switches can transmit millions of frames per second; bridges usually processed from 3,000 to 5,000 frames per second.

During the time of their existence, without the competition of bridges, switches have adopted many additional functions that appeared as a natural result of the evolution of network technologies. The list of such functions includes support for virtual LANs (VLANs), traffic prioritization, and the use of the default backbone port.

The technology of switching Ethernet segments was first suggested by a quite small company, Kalpana, in 1990 in response to the growing requirements in increasing the bandwidth of links connecting high-performance servers with segments containing workstations.

If the output port is available at frame reception, the delay between the reception of the first byte and the arrival of the same byte to the output port is only 40 μsec for the Kalpana switch. This is a significantly lower value than the delay of frame being transmitted by a bridge.

The structural design of the EtherSwitch switch suggested by Kalpana is shown in Figure 15.9.

Each of the eight 10Base-T ports is served by a single **Ethernet packet processor** (EPP). Besides these, the switch has a system unit that coordinates the operation of all EPPs. The system unit supports the common address table of the switch. The switching matrix is used for transmitting frames between ports. It operates according to the circuit-switching principle and connects switch ports. For eight ports, such matrix can ensure 8 simultaneous internal channels when using half-duplex operating mode and 16 channels in full-duplex mode when the transmitter and receiver operate independently.

When a frame arrives to one of the ports, the EPP buffers the first several bytes of the frame to read the destination address. After receiving the destination address, the processor

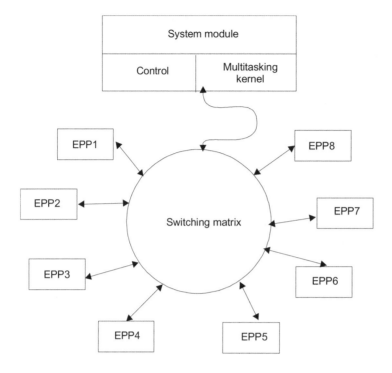

Figure 15.9 Structural design of the EtherSwitch switch suggested by Kalpana

immediately makes a decision about packet transmission without having to wait for the arrival of the remaining bytes of the frame. For this purpose, it views its own cache of the address table. If no match to the needed address is found there, the EPP addresses the system module that operates in the multitasking mode, serving requests from all EPPs in parallel. The system module reviews the common address table and returns the required entry to the processor. The EPP buffers this entry in its cache for future use.

■ If the destination address has been found in the address table, and the newly arrived frame must be filtered, the processor simply stops loading frame bytes into the buffer, clears the buffer, and waits for a new frame to arrive.

■ If the destination address has been found in the address table, and the newly arrived frame needs to be transmitted to another port, the processor addresses the switching matrix while continuing loading frame bytes into the buffer and attempts to establish the path connecting its port to the port through which the path to the destination address passes. The switching matrix can do this only when the port of the destination address is free, which means that it is not currently connected to another port.

■ If the port is busy, the matrix denies the request for connection, as is true for any device based on circuit switching. In this case, the frame gets fully buffered by the input port's processor, after which the processor waits until the output port is released and the switching matrix creates the required path.

■ After establishing the required path, buffered bytes of the frame are directed to it and the processor of the output port receives them. As soon as the processor of the output port gets access to the Ethernet segment connected to it (using the CSMA/CD algorithm), the frame bytes immediately start being transmitted into the network. The processor of the input port constantly stores several bytes of the frame being received in its buffer, which enables it to independently and asynchronously transmit and receive frame bytes (Figure 15.10).

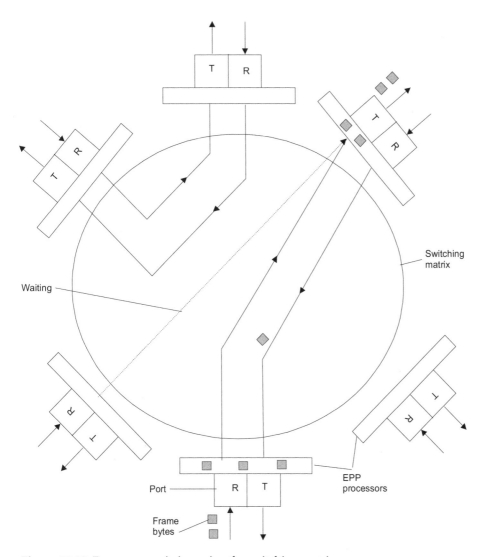

Figure 15.10 Frame transmission using the switching matrix

This method of frame transmission without accomplishing its full buffering became known as on-the-fly or cut-through switching. Principally, this method is pipelined frame processing in which several stages of its transmission are carried out in parallel. The stages are as follows:

1. Reception of the first bytes of the frame by the processor of the input port, including bytes containing the destination address

2. Search for the destination address in the address table of the switch, either in the EPP cache or in the common table of the system module

3. Switching of the matrix

4. Reception of the remaining bytes of the frame by the input port processor

5. Reception of the frame bytes (including the first ones) by the processor of the output port via the switching matrix

6. Access of the medium by the processor of the output port

7. Transmission of the frame bytes by the processor of the output port into the network

Figure 15.11 illustrates two modes of frame processing: pipelined frame processing in which several stages of its transmission are carried out in parallel, and normal processing with full buffering and sequential execution of all stages. (Note that stages 2 and 3 cannot be carried out in parallel, since without knowing the number of the output port, the operation of switching the matrix makes no sense).

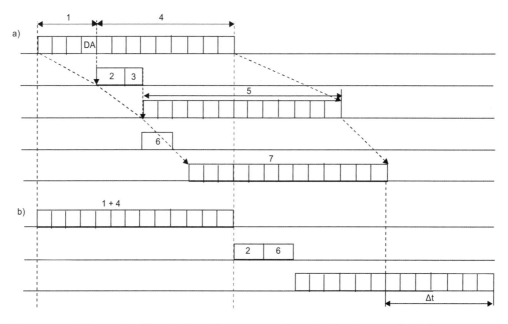

Figure 15.11 Time gained by pipelined frame processing: pipelined processing (*a*) and normal processing with full buffering (*b*)

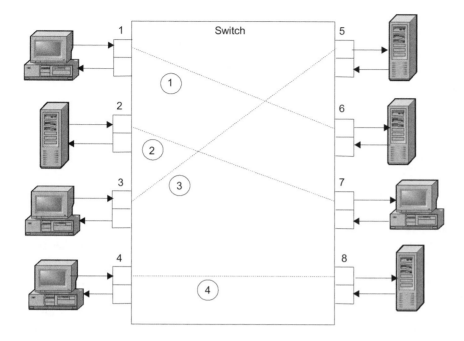

Figure 15.12 Parallel transmission of frames by a switch
(1–4 — frame flows between computers)

As can be seen from this illustration, in comparison to the full buffering mode, the gain in time ensured by pipelining looks rather impressive.

> However, the main element allowing an increase in the network performance when using switches is the parallel processing of several frames.

This effect is illustrated by Figure 15.12, showing ideal performance when four of eight ports are transmitting data at the maximum rate allowed by the Ethernet protocol — 10 Mbps — and these data are transmitted to the remaining four ports of the switch without conflicts. The absence of conflicts means that data flows between network nodes are distributed so that for each input port receiving frames there is an available output port. If the switch manages to process input traffic even at the maximum intensity of frame arrivals to the input port, the total performance of the switch in this example will be $4 \times 10 = 40$ Mbps. When generalizing this example for N ports, the total performance of the switch will be $(N/2) \times 10$ Mbps. **In this case, the switch provides each station or segment connected to its port the allocated bandwidth of the protocol.**

Naturally, this situation does not always take place in the network. For example, two stations (assume that these are the ones connected to ports 3 and 4) simultaneously need to write data to the same server, which is connected to port 8. In this case, the switch will not be able to allocate 10 Mbps data flow to each station because port 8 cannot transmit the data at the rate of 20 Mbps. Frames of both stations will wait in the internal queues of input ports 3 and 4 until output port 8 becomes available for transmitting the next frame. For such distribution of data flows, it would make sense to connect the server to the faster port such as Fast Ethernet.

15.3.2 Nonblocking Switches

> A *nonblocking* switch is a switch that can transmit frames through its ports at the rate at which they arrive to its ports.

As a rule, when speaking about stable nonblocking mode of the switch operation, it is assumed that the switch transmits frames at the same rate as they arrive during an arbitrary period. To ensure such a mode of operation, it is necessary to achieve a distribution of frame flows at which output ports can successfully handle the load. If this requirement has been observed, the switch always can transmit on average the same number of frames to its output ports as the number of frames that arrived to its input ports. If the incoming flow of frames (totaled for all ports) on average exceeds the output flow of frames (also totaled for all ports), the frames will accumulate in the buffer memory of the switch. If the amount of available buffer memory is exceeded (which is known as buffer overflow), the switch will start discarding frames.

> For ensuring nonblocking mode of switch operation, the following simple condition must be satisfied:
>
> $$C_k = (\Sigma C_{pi})/2 \qquad (15.1)$$
>
> Here, C_k is the performance of the swith, and C_{pi} is the maximum performance of the protocol supported by ith port of the switch.

Total performance of the ports takes account of each passing frame twice — first as an incoming frame and second as an outgoing frame. Since in the stable operating mode incoming traffic is equal to outgoing traffic, the minimum sufficient performance of the switch for supporting nonblocking mode of the operation is half of the total performance of its ports. If the port operates in half-duplex mode, for example, 10 Mbps Ethernet, then performance of the port (C_{pi}) is 10 Mbps; if it operates in the full-duplex mode, its performance is 20 Mbps.

Sometimes, statements declare that the switch ensures *instantaneous nonblocking mode*. This means that the switch can receive and process frames from all its ports at the maximum rate ensured by supported protocols whether or not the stable equilibrium between incoming and outgoing traffic is satisfied. To tell the truth, some frames might be processed incompletely — if the output port is busy, the frame is loaded into the switch buffer.

> To support a nonblocking, instantaneous mode of operation, the switch must provide higher total performance, which in this case must equal the total performance of all its ports:
>
> $$C_k = \Sigma C_{pi} \qquad (15.2)$$

It is not an accident that the first LAN switch was intended for Ethernet technology. Besides the high popularity of Ethernet, there was another, important reason: This technology is most vulnerable to an increase of the delay because of the need to wait for access to the medium when the segment is overloaded. Because of this, Ethernet segments in large networks were the first candidates that needed the elimination of network bottlenecks. Kalpana switches then switches from other manufacturers provided the means for solving this problem.

Some companies started to develop the switching technology aiming at improving performance of other LAN technologies, such as Token Ring and FDDI. Internal organization of switches from different manufacturers often had significant differences from the structure of the first EtherSwitch switch; however, the principle of parallel frame processing by each port did not undergo any changes.

Wide employment of switches was stimulated because the introduction of switching technologies did not require the replacement of equipment already installed in the networks, including network adapters, concentrators, and the cabling system. Switch ports operated in normal half-duplex mode; therefore, they allowed transparent connections of both the end node and the concentrator organizing the entire logical segment.

Since switches and bridges are transparent for network-layer protocols, their introduction into networks did not influence network routers if they were present in the network.

15.3.3 Overcoming Congestion

In classic half-duplex mode, the switch obtains the possibility of influencing the end node using the mechanisms of the medium access algorithm, which the neighboring node must carry out. Two main methods of controlling the frame flow are used: backpressure on the end node and aggressive medium capturing.

The *backpressure* method consists of creating artificial collisions in the segment that sends frames to the switch with too high intensity. For this purpose, the switch normally uses a jam sequence, sent to the output of the port to which the segment (or node) is connected, to suspend its activity.

The second method of slowing the frame flow is usually employed when the neighbor is an end node. This method is based on the *aggressive behavior of the port switch* when capturing the medium either after transmission of the next frame or after collision. These two cases are illustrated in Figure 15.13.

In the first case (Figure 15.13, *a*), the switch has completed transmission of the next frame. Instead of a technological pause, which lasts 9.6 μsec, it has made a pause lasting 9.1 μsec and started transmission of a new frame. The computer was unable to capture the medium, since it sustained a standard pause lasting 9.6 μsec then found that the medium was busy.

In the second case (Figure 15.13, *b*), the frames of the switch and the computer have collided, and the collision was registered. Since the computer after collision paused

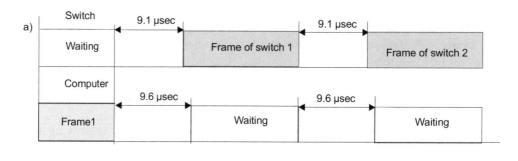

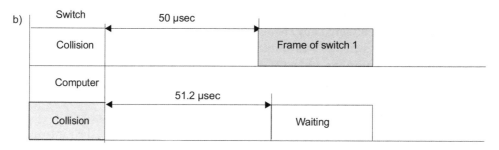

Figure 15.13 Aggressive behavior of the switch under conditions of buffer overflow

for 51.2 µsec, as required by the standard (the delay interval is 512 bit intervals), and the switch paused for 50 µsec, the computer again could not transmit its frame.

The switch can use this mechanism adaptively, increasing the level of its aggression as needed.

Many manufacturers implement rather sophisticated mechanisms of congestion control by combining these two methods. These methods use frame interleave algorithms based on alternating transmitted and received frames. A frame interleave algorithm must be flexible enough to allow the switch in critical situations to transmit several frames per received frame, thus unloading its internal frame buffer — not necessarily reducing the intensity of frame reception to zero, but simply reducing it to the required level.

15.3.4 Translation of the Data Link-Layer Protocols

Switches can translate one data link-layer protocol into another according to the IEEE 802.1H specifications and RFC 1042, for example, Ethernet into FDDI or Fast Ethernet into Token Ring.

Translation of LAN protocols is simplified because the most difficult task — namely, address translation, which is carried out by routers and gateways when connecting heterogeneous networks — is not necessary.

All end nodes of LANs have a unique address in the same format (MAC addresses) independent of the supported protocol.

Therefore, the address of the Ethernet network adapter is understood by the FDDI network adapter, and both nodes can use these addresses in the fields of their frames without considering that the node to which they are interacting belongs to a network that operates according to a different technology.

Therefore, when coordinating LAN protocols, switches do not build address translation tables; instead, they transfer frame source and destination addresses from the frame of one protocol to the frame of another protocol.

Besides changing the order of bits when transmitting address bytes, address translation of the Ethernet protocol (and the Fast Ethernet protocol, which uses the same frame format) to the FDDI and Token Ring protocols includes carrying out some or all of the following operations:

- Calculating the lengths of the frame data field and placing this value into the *Length* field when transmitting a frame from an FDDI or Token Ring network into an Ethernet 802.3 network. (FDDI and Token Ring frames do not contain the *Length* field.)

- Filling the frame status fields when transmitting frames from an FDDI or Token Ring network into an Ethernet network. FDDI and Token Ring frames have two bits that are set by the station for which the frame was intended: the address recognition bit (A) and frame copying bit (C). When the switch transmits a frame into another network, there are no standard rules for setting bits A and C in the frame returned by the ring to the source station. Therefore, switch manufacturers solve this problem at their discretion.

- Discarding frames with a data field longer that 1,500 bytes and transmitted from an FDDI or Token Ring network into an Ethernet network, because 1,500 bytes is the maximum length of the data field for Ethernet. Later on, having received no reply from the destination station in the Ethernet network, the upper-layer protocol of the source station in the FDDI or Token Ring network will, possibly, decrease the size of the data transmitted within a single frame. After that, the switch will be able to transmit frames between these stations. Another variant of solving this problem ensures that the switch supports IP fragmentation. However, this requires the switch to implement a network-layer protocol and to ensure that IP is supported by the interacting nodes of the translated networks.

- Filling the *Type* field (the protocol type in the data field) of an Ethernet II frame when transmitting a frame arriving from a network supporting FDDI or Token Ring frames, where there is no such field. Instead of the Type field, FDDI and Token Ring frames have *DSAP* and *SSAP* fields, which serve the same purpose but have other codes for designating protocols. For simplifying translation, the RFC 1042 specification suggests always using in FDDI and Token Ring network frames with LLC/SNAP headers, which have the same Type field with the same values as Ethernet II frames. When translating frames, the data from the Type field of the LLC/SNAP header is moved to the *Type* field of the Ethernet II frame, and vice versa. If there are frame formats different from those of Ethernet II in the Ethernet network, they also must have the LLC/SNAP header.

■ Recalculating the frame checksum according to the newly formed values of the frame service fields.

15.3.5 Traffic Filtering

Many switch models allow administrators to specify additional conditions of frame filtering that supplement the standard frame filtering conditions according to the information from the address table.

> **User-defined filters** are intended for creating additional barriers for frames, limiting access to specific network services for certain groups of users.

The simplest user-defined filters are the ones based on the MAC addresses of the stations. Since MAC addresses are the information with which the switch works, it allows the creation of such filters in a form convenient for the network administrator. For example, some conditions can be specified in an additional field of the address table, similar to the ones specified in the switch address table shown in Figure 15.7 (e.g., discard frames with specific address). In this case, the user working at the computer with the specified MAC address will be denied access to the resources of another network segment.

Quite often, the administrator needs to specify more sophisticated filtering conditions, for example, preventing some user from printing documents on a specific Windows print server from another segment while allowing that user to access all other resources of that segment. To implement such a filter, it is necessary to disallow the transmission of frames with a specific MAC address, containing encapsulated SMB packets, if the appropriate field of that packet contains the "print" service type. Switches do not analyze the upper-layer protocols, such as SMB; therefore, the administrator, to specify filtering conditions, must manually determine the field whose value it is necessary to filter. This filter is specified in the form of the "offset size" pair in relation to the starting position of the data field of the data link-layer frame, after which it is necessary to specify the hex value of this field corresponding to the print service.

Usually, filtering conditions are written as Boolean expressions, formed using AND and OR operators.

15.3.6 Switch Architecture and Design

Nowadays, to speed up the switching operations, all switches use specialized LICs: ASIC optimized for carrying out switching operations. Often, a single switch has several specialized LICs, each carrying out a functionally complete set of operations.

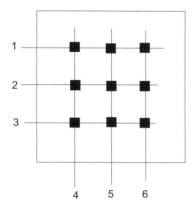

Figure 15.14 Switching matrix

Besides specialized processor chips, successful operation in nonblocking mode requires the switch to be equipped with a fast unit for transmitting frames among the processor chips of its ports.

Currently, switches use one of the three basic methods for building such an exchange unit:

■ Switching matrix

■ Common bus

■ Shared multiport memory

Quite often, these three methods are combined within the same switch.

The **switching matrix** ensures the simplest way of interaction between port processors. This method was implemented in the first production piece of a LAN switch. However, implementation of the switching matrix is possible only for a predefined and limited number of ports, and the complexity of the design grows proportional to the square of the number of the switch ports (Figure 15.14).

A more detailed representation of one variant of the switching matrix implementation intended for supporting eight ports is in Figure 15.15. The input units of the port processors, based on the lookup of the switch's address tables, determine the number of the output port by the destination address. They add this information to the bytes of the source frame in the form of a special tag. In this example, for simplicity, the tag is a 3-bit binary number corresponding to the output port number.

The matrix is made up of three levels of binary switches that connect its input to one of the two outputs depending on the tag's bit value. The switches of the first level are controlled by the first bit of the tag, the second-level switches are controlled by the second bit, and the third-layer switches are controlled by the third bit.

The matrix can be implemented in other ways based on other types of combinatory designs. Nevertheless, the technology of switching physical links remains its specific feature. The well-known drawback of this technology is the lack of data buffering inside the switching

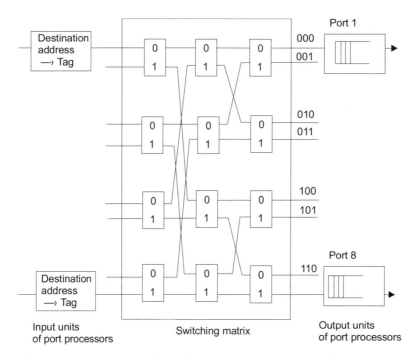

Figure 15.15 Implementation of the 8×8 switching matrix using binary switches

matrix. Thus, if the circuit cannot be formed because the output port of the intermediate switching element or elements is busy, the data must be accumulated within the data source, whose role in this case is played by the input unit of the port that received the frame. The main advantages of such matrices include the high speed of switching and the regular structure, which is convenient to implement in LICs. However, after implementing the N×N matrix as part of an LIC, another drawback becomes obvious, namely, the difficulty of increasing the number of switched ports.

In switches based on a **common bus**, port processors are connected by a high-speed common bus used in the time-sharing mode.

An example of such architecture is in Figure 15.16. To ensure that the bus does not block the switch operation, it is necessary to guarantee that its performance is at least the sum of the performance of all ports of the switch. For modular switches, some combinations of modules with low-speed ports may result in a nonblocking operation, and installing modules with high-speed ports might result in the mode in which the common bus becomes a bottleneck.

The frame must be transmitted via the bus in small parts, comprising several bytes, to make data transmission between ports part in a pseudoparallel mode without introducing delays into frame transmission as a whole. The size of such a data cell is determined by the switch manufacturer. Some manufacturers choose an ATM cell with its data field length of 48 bytes as the data portion transmitted via the bus per operation. Such an approach

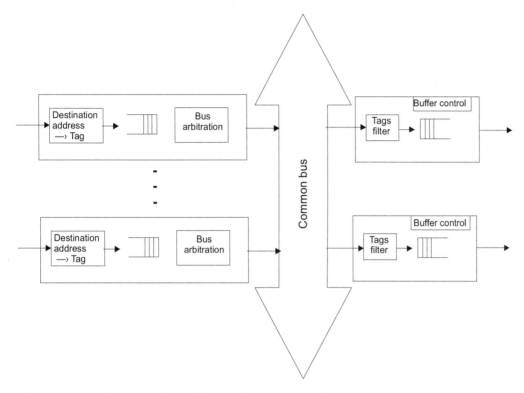

Figure 15.16 Architecture of a switch based on a common bus

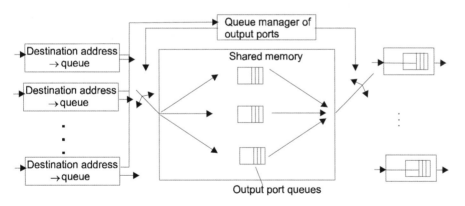

Figure 15.17 Architecture of a switch based on shared memory

simplifies the translation of LAN protocols into the ATM protocol if the switch supports these technologies.

The input unit of the processor complements the cell carried via the bus with a tag in which it specifies the destination port number. Each output unit of the port processor contains the tags filter that chooses tags intended for this port.

Like the switching matrix, the bus cannot carry out intermediate buffering; however, since frame data are split into small cells, this method is free from delays related to initially waiting for output port availability — the packet-switching method is implemented here instead of the circuit-switching method.

The third basic architecture of port interaction is a **shared memory**. An example of such architecture is provided in Figure 15.17.

The input units of processor ports are connected to the switched input of the shared memory, and the output units of the same processors are connected to the switched output of this memory. The queue manager of the output ports controls switching of the input and output of the shared memory. Within the shared memory, this manager organizes several data queues, one queue per output port. The input units of the processors pass to the manager requests for writing data into the queue of the port corresponding to the frame destination address. The queue manager in turns connects the memory input to one of the processor input units, and that unit writes part of the frame data into the queue of the specific output port. As the queues fill, the manager in turn connects the output of the shared memory to the output units of the processor ports, and data from the queues are written to the output buffers of the processors.

Using common buffer memory, flexibly distributed by the manager between individual ports, reduces the requirements for the buffer memory size of the port processor. However, the memory must be fast enough to support the speed of data transmission between *N* ports of the switch.

Combined Switches

Each of the previously described architectures has advantages and drawbacks; therefore, in sophisticated switches, these architectures are often used in combination. An example of such a combined architecture is shown in Figure 15.18.

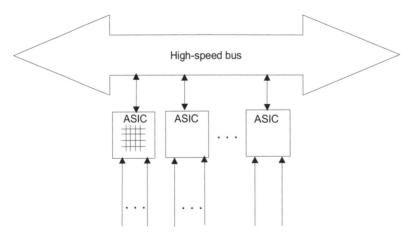

Figure 15.18 Architecture of a combined switch based on a switching matrix and a common bus

The switch is composed of modules with fixed number of ports (2–12), implemented on the basis of a specialized LIC implementing the architecture of a switching matrix. If the ports between which it is necessary to transmit a data frame belong to the same module, then frame transmission is carried out by the module processors on the basis of the switching matrix of the module. If the ports belong to different modules, then the processors communicate using the common bus. Having such architecture, data transmission within a module will take place faster than intermodule transmission, since the switching matrix provides the fastest method of interaction between ports, although this method is the least scalable. The rate of the internal bus of a switch can reach several gigabits per second, and some powerful models have the bus rate of tens of gigabits per second.

Other methods of combining architectures are also possible; for example, shared memory can be used for organizing interaction between modules.

15.3.7 Performance Characteristics of Switches

Filtering rate and forwarding rate are the two most important performance characteristics of a switch. These characteristics are integral parameters, since they do not depend on the technical implementation of a switch.

The *filtering rate* defines the rate at which the switch carries out the frame processing stages:

1. Loading the frame into the internal buffer
2. Looking up the address table to find the port for the frame destination address
3. Discarding the frames for which the source and destination ports belong to the same logical segment

The filtering rate for practically all switches is nonblocking, since the switch has time to discard frames at the same rate as they arrive.

The *forwarding rate* is the rate at which the switch carries out the following stages of the frame processing:

1. Loading the frame into internal buffer
2. Viewing the address table to find the port for the frame destination address
3. Passing the frame into the network using the port found in the address table

The filtering rate and the forwarding rate are usually measured in frames per second. If the switch characteristics are provided without specifying the protocol and frame size for which the values of filtering and forwarding rates are provided, by default, these parameters are specified for the Ethernet protocol and for frames of the minimum size — for example, 64 bytes. Frames of the minimum length always create the hardest operating mode for the switch in comparison to the frames of other format at the same rate of user data. Because of this, when testing the switch, the mode of transmitting data frames of the minimum length is used as the most complex test intended for additionally checking the switch's capability for operating under the worst combination of traffic parameters.

Frame transmission delay is measured as the time elapsed from the arrival of the first byte of the frame at the input port of the switch to the moment this byte appeared at the switch's output port. Frame transmission delay is made up of the time required for frame buffering and the time spent for frame processing by the switch, including viewing the address table, deciding whether to filter or forward the frame, and accessing the medium of the output port.

Switch performance is the number of user data transmitted per time unit via its ports (measured in megabits per second). Since the switch operates at the data link layer, from its point of view, user data are the data carried in the data field of the frames of the data link-layer protocols: Ethernet, Token Ring, FDDI, etc. The maximum value of switch performance is always achieved at the frames of maximum length, since the share of frame service information overhead is significantly lower than for the frames of minimum length. The switch is a multiport device; therefore, it is a common practice to provide its main performance characteristic as the total performance of the switch during simultaneous traffic transmission via all of its ports.

The method of frame transmission — on the fly or with full buffering — influences the switch performance. Switches that transmit frames on the fly introduce the smallest frame transmission delays per transit switch. Therefore, the total reduction of the data delivery delay can be rather significant, which is important for multimedia traffic. Moreover, the chosen switching method influences the possibilities of implementing several useful auxiliary functions, for instance, translation of the data link-layer protocols.

Table 15.1 provides a comparison of the two switching methods.

Table 15.1 Functional capabilities of switching on the fly and with full buffering

Function	On the fly	With full buffering
Protection against frame corruption	No	Yes
Support for heterogeneous networks (Ethernet, Token Ring, FDDI, and ATM)	No	Yes
Frame transmission delay	Low (5–40 μsec) at low load; medium at high load	Medium at any load
Support for reserved links	No	Yes
Traffic analysis function	No	Yes

The average delay of the switches that operate on the fly under a high load occurs because the output port often is busy receiving another frame; therefore, the newly arrived frame for the current port has to be buffered.

The switch that operates on the fly can check the frames being transmitted for correctness, but it is unable to discard the corrupted frame from the network, since part of its bytes (as a rule, most of them) are already transmitted into the network.

NOTE *Because each method has its advantages and drawbacks, switch models that must not translate protocols sometimes implement the mechanism of adaptively changing the switch operation mode. The main mode of such a switch is switching on the fly, but the switch constantly controls the traffic. When corrupted frames become frequent and their intensity exceeds a certain threshold, the switch changes the mode to full buffering. Later, the switch can return to the on-the-fly mode.*

Another important designed characteristic of any switch is the **maximum size of the address table**. It defines the maximum number of MAC addresses with which the switch can work simultaneously.

Most frequently switches use the dedicated processing unit for carrying out operations of each port, and each processing unit is equipped with the memory for storing its own copy of the address table. Every port stores only those data with which it worked most recently, therefore copies of the address tables of different processing units usually contain different address information.

The value of the maximum number of MAC addresses that can be stored in the processor port memory depends on the area of switch application. Workgroup switches usually support several addresses per port, since they are intended for creating microsegments. Department-level switches must support hundreds of addresses, and backbone switches must support thousands of addresses, usually 4,000–8,000.

The insufficient size of an address table can slow the switch operation and flood the network with unnecessary traffic. If the address table of the port processor is filled, and the port encounters a new address in the frame that has newly arrived, the processor must discard from the table some old address and replace it with the new one. This operation takes some processor time. However, the main performance losses will take place after the arrival of the frame containing the destination address that had to be deleted from the address table. Since the destination address of the frame is unlearned, the switch must transmit it to all other ports.

Some switch manufacturers solve this problem by changing the algorithm used to process frames with unlearned destination addresses. One of the ports is configured as a backbone port to which all frames with unknown addresses are passed by default[1].

A frame is transmitted to the backbone port if this port is connected to the port that holds a higher position in the hierarchy of a large-scale network and has sufficient volume of the address table, which allow it to know where each frame must be transmitted.

---

[1] In routers, such a technique has long been used, allowing the sizes of address tables to be reduced in a network organized according to the hierarchical principle.

15.4 FULL-DUPLEX LAN PROTOCOLS

KEY WORDS: microsegmentation, collision domain, 106Base-X, 106Base-R, 106Base-W, 106Base-LX4

15.4.1 Changes Introduced into the MAC Layer by Operation in Full-Duplex Mode

Switching technology is not directly related to the medium access method used by switch ports. When a segment representing a shared medium is connected to a switch port, that port must support half-duplex mode, as any other node of this segment.

However, when instead of the entire segment only one computer is connected to each port of the switch and this connection uses two physically separate channels, which is true for practically all Ethernet standards except coaxial Ethernet versions, the situation ceases to be so unambiguous. The port can operate in normal half-duplex mode as well as in full-duplex mode.

Connecting individual computers to switch ports instead of segments is known as *microsegmentation*.

In the half-duplex mode of operation, which is normal for Ethernet, the switch port continues to detect collisions. In this case, the collision domain is a network section that includes the switch transmitter, the switch receiver, the transmitter of the computer's network adapter, and two twisted pairs connecting transmitters to receivers (Figure 15.19).

Collision takes place when the transmitters of the switch port and network adapter start transmission of their frames practically simultaneously, assuming that the segment is free (see Figure 15.19). Although the probability of collision in such a segment is significantly smaller than in a segment comprising from 20 to 30 nodes, this probability is not zero. At the same time, the maximum performance of the Ethernet segment is 14,880 frames per second for the minimum frame length and is shared between the transmitter of the

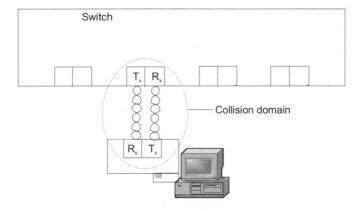

Figure 15.19 Collision domain created by a computer and a switch port

switch port and the transmitter of the network adapter. Assuming that it is divided in equal parts, each transmitter gets the possibility of transmitting approximately 7,440 frames per second.

In full-duplex mode, simultaneous transmission of data by the port switch and the network adapter is not considered collision. Principally, this mode of operation is natural for individual full-duplex communications channels. It is frequently used in WAN protocols. In case of full-duplex connection, 10-Mbps Ethernet ports can transmit data at the rate of 20 Mbps–10 Mbps in each direction.

Naturally, it is necessary to ensure that the MAC layers of the interacting devices support this special mode. When only the first node supports full-duplex mode, another node would constantly register collisions and suspend its operation, and the second node would continue transmitting the data, which nobody receives at that moment. Modifications that need to be introduced into the operation logic of MAC layer of the node to enable it to operate in full-duplex mode are minimal. It is merely necessary to cancel the registration and processing of collisions in Ethernet networks. In Token Ring and FDDI networks, network adapter and switch port must send their frames without waiting for the arrival of the access token — at any moment end node needs it. Actually, when operating in full-duplex mode, MAC layer of the node ignores the medium access method developed for a specific technology.

When developing new Fast Ethernet and Gigabit Ethernet technologies, full-duplex mode obtained full rights and became one of the standard modes of network node operation. Nowadays, network adapters can support both modes of operation, using the CSMA/CD access algorithm when connected to the concentrator port and operating in full-duplex mode when connected to the switch port.

15.4.2 Problems of Congestion Control in Full-Duplex Mode

Simply abandoning support of the shared medium access algorithm without protocol modification increases the probability of frame losses in switches since control over the flows of frames sent by end nodes into the network is lost. In half-duplex mode, typical for shared media networks, frame flow was regulated by the method of accessing the shared medium. After migration to the full-duplex mode, the node is allowed to send frames to the switch when it needs it; therefore, when operating in this mode, network switches might get congested and might have no means of slowing the frame flow.

Usually, congestion is not caused by the switch being a blocking one (i.e., by performance of its processors being insufficient for serving the frame flow). The true reason for congestion lies in the limited bandwidth of a specific output port, which is defined by parameters of the protocol.

Therefore, if incoming traffic is unevenly distributed among output ports, it is easy to imagine a situation in which traffic with total intensity exceeding the protocol maximum is directed to some of the switch's output ports. Such a situation is illustrated in Figure 15.20.

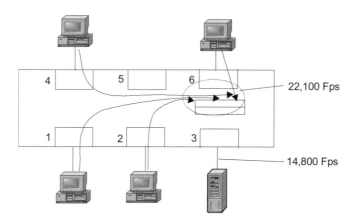

Figure 15.20 Overflow of the port buffer because of unbalanced traffic

Here, the flow of 64-byte frames from ports 1, 2, 4, and 6, having total intensity of 20,100 frames per second, is directed to port 3 of the Ethernet switch. Port 3 gets a 150% load. Naturally, when frames arrive to the port buffer at the rate of 20,100 frames per second and leave the port at the rate of 14,880 frames per second, the internal buffer of the output port will gradually fill with unprocessed frames.

It is not difficult to calculate that, in this example, a 100 KB buffer will be filled 0.22 seconds after it starts operation (a buffer of this size can store up to 1,600 frames of 64 bytes). Increasing the buffer size to 1 MB will increase the buffer filling time to 2.2 seconds, which also is not acceptable.

This problem can be solved using congestion control methods considered in *Chapter 7*.

As you know, there are different types of congestion control tools: queue management in switches, feedback, and bandwidth reservation. On the basis of these tools, it is possible to create an efficient system of QoS support for different classes of traffic.

In this section, we consider the feedback mechanism standardized for Ethernet in March 1997 as the IEEE 802.3x specification. The IEEE 802.3x feedback mechanism is used only in the duplex mode of the switch port operation. This mechanism is very important for LAN switches, since it allows frame losses to be reduced because of buffer overflow, whether the network ensures differentiated QoS support for different kinds of traffic or it provides only best-effort service. Other QoS mechanisms will be covered in the next chapter.

The 802.3x specification introduces a new sublayer into the Ethernet protocol stack: the MAC Control sublayer. This sublayer is located above the MAC layer and is optional (Figure 15.21).

Frames of this sublayer can be used for various purposes. For the moment, however, only one task is defined for them in Ethernet standards — namely, suspending frame transmission by all other nodes for a specified time.

The MAC Control frame is different from user data frames in that its *Type/Length* field always contains the 88-08 hex value. The MAC Control frame is intended for universal application; therefore, it has a rather complex format (Figure 15.22).

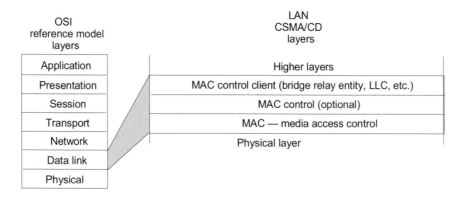

Figure 15.21 MAC Control sublayer

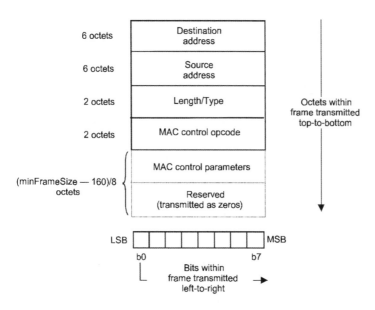

Figure 15.22 MAC Control frame format

The switch uses the MAC Control frame when it needs to temporarily suspend the arrival of frames from the neighboring node to unload its internal queues.

As a destination address, it is possible to use the multicast address reserved for this purpose: 01-80-C2-00-00-01. This approach is convenient when the neighboring node also is a switch (since switch ports have no unique MAC addresses). If the neighbor is an end node, it is also possible to use the unique MAC address.

The MAC Control OPCODE field specifies the code of the control operation. As already mentioned, only one operation has been defined; it is known as PAUSE and has the hex code 00-01.

The MAC Control Parameters field specifies the time for which the node that receives such a code must suspend frame transmission to the node that has sent the frame with the PAUSE operation. The time unit is 512 bit intervals of the particular Ethernet implementation; the possible suspension quantum ranges from 0 to 65,535.

As follows from this description, this feedback mechanism is related to the Feedback 2 type, according to the classification provided in *Chapter 7*. It also has its specific features, since in mechanisms of this type, two operations usually are used: suspend frame transmission and resume frame transmission. This is the mechanism implemented in one of the oldest protocols of packet-switched networks — namely, in the X.25 protocol, known as LAP-B.

15.4.3 10G Ethernet

> The 10G Ethernet standard defines only the full-duplex mode of operation; therefore, it can be used only in switched LANs.

Formally, this standard is designated IEEE 802.3ae and is a supplement to the main text of the 802.3 standard. This supplement to the Ethernet family describes seven new physical-layer specifications that interact with the MAC layer using a new variant of the Reconciliation sublayer (Figure 15.23). This sublayer provides all variants of the physical layer of 10G Ethernet with a unified interface known as the Extended Gigabit Medium Independent Interface (XGMII), which makes provision for parallel exchange by 4 bytes that form for data flows.

As can be seen from Figure 15.23, there are three groups of physical interfaces of the 10G Ethernet standard: 10GBase-X, 10GBase-R, and 10GBase-W. They differ in the data encoding method used: The 10Base-X method uses the 8B/10B code, and the other two groups employ the 64B/66B code. All variants use an optical medium for data transmission.

The 10GBase-X group comprises a single interface of the physical medium dependent (PMD) sublayer: 10GBase-LX4. The L character specifies that the information is transmitted using wavelengths of the second transparency range (i.e., 1,310 nm). Information is simultaneously transmitted in each direction using four waves (reflected by the digit 4 in the name of the interface), which are multiplexed on the basis of the wavelength division multiplexing (WDM) technique (Figure 15.24). Each of the four flows of XGMII is transmitted in the optical fiber at a rate of 2.5 Gbps.

The maximum distance between the transmitter and the receiver according to the 10GBase-LX4 standard on the basis of multimode fiber is 200–300 m (depending on the fiber bandwidth); for single-mode fiber, the maximum distance is 10 km.

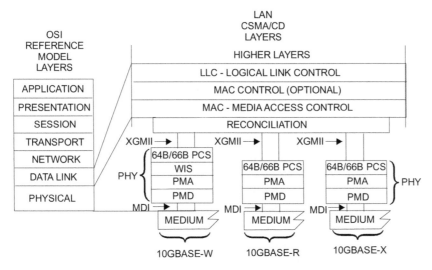

MDI = MEDIUM DEPENDENT INTERFACE
PCS = PHYSICAL CODING SUBLAYER
PHY = PHYSICAL LAYER DEVICE
PMA = PHYSICAL MEDIUM ATTACHMENT

PMD = PHYSICAL MEDIUM DEPENDENT
WIS = WAN INTERFACE SUBLAYER
XGMII = 10 GIGABIT MEDIUM INDEPENDENT INTERFACE

Figure 15.23 Three groups of 10G physical interfaces

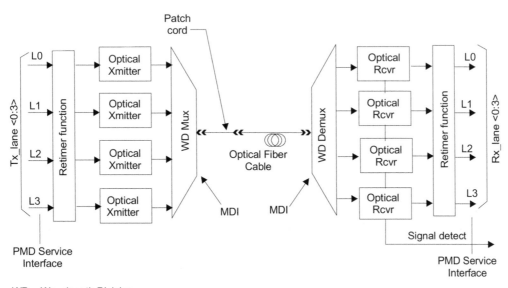

WD = Wavelength Division

Figure 15.24 10GBase-LX4 interface uses the WDM technique

Each of the 10GBase-W and 10GBase-R groups comprises three variants of the PMD sublayer (S, L, and E), depending on the wavelength used for information transmission (850 nm, 1,310 nm, and 1,550 nm, respectively). Thus, there are the following interfaces: 10GBase-WS, 10GBase-WL, 10GBase-WE, 10GBase-RS, 10GBase-RL, and 10GBase-RE. Each of them transmits information using a single wave of the appropriate range.

The difference between the 10GBase-W group and the 10GBase-R group lies in that physical interfaces of the W group ensure a data transmission rate and a data format compatible with the Sonet STS-192/SDH STM-64 interface. The bandwidth of the interfaces from the W group is 9.95328 Gbps, and the effective rate of data transmission is 9.58464 Gbps (part of the bandwidth is spent for STS/STM frame headers). Because the information rate for this group of interfaces is lower than 10 Gbps, the interfaces can interact only with one another, which means that the connection of interfaces such as 10GBase-RL and 10Base-WL is impossible.

Interfaces of the W group are not fully compatible by electric characteristics with SONET/SDH interfaces of respective speed. Therefore, to enable connection of 10G Ethernet networks using the SONET/SDH transmission network, multiplexers of the transmission network must be equipped with special 10G interfaces compatible with 10GBase-W specifications. Support of the 9.95328 Gbps rate by the 10GBase-W equipment ensures the possibility of transmitting the 10G Ethernet traffic using the SONET/SDH network in STS-192/STM-64 frames.

Physical interfaces operating in the E transparency window ensure data transmission over distances up to 40 km. This allows for the creation not only of LANs but also of MANs, reflected in corrections to the source text of the 802.3 standard.

SUMMARY

▶ Logical structuring of the network is necessary when building midsize and large networks. Using a common shared medium is acceptable only for a network comprising from five to ten computers.

▶ The division of a network into logical segments improves its performance, reliability, flexibility, and manageability.

▶ For the logical structuring of the network bridges and their successors, switches are used. This divides the network into logical segments using few tools only on the basis of the data link-layer protocols. Besides this, these devices do not require configuration.

▶ The passive method used by switches to build address tables traces the passing traffic. It makes operation impossible in a network containing closed loops. Another drawback of networks based on switches is the lack of protection against broadcast storms, which these devices must transmit because of their operating algorithm.

▶ The use of switches allows network adapters to use the full-duplex operating mode of the LAN protocols (Ethernet, Fast Ethernet, Gigabit Ethernet, Token Ring, and FDDI). In this mode, there is no stage of accessing the shared medium, and the data transmission rate is doubled.

▶ In full-duplex mode, switch overloads are prevented using the feedback method described in the 802.3x standard. It temporarily suspends frame transmission from the nearest neighbors of the overloaded switch.

▶ In the half-duplex mode of switch operation, switches use two methods for controlling frame flow: aggressive medium capturing and backpressure to the end node. The use of these methods allows sufficiently flexible flow control by interleaving several transmitted frames with one received frame.

▶ The main characteristics of switch performance are frame filtering rate, frame forwarding rate, performance by all ports in megabits per second, and frame transmission delay.

▶ Switch performance characteristics depend on the switching type — on the fly or with full buffering — on the size of the address table, and on the size of the frame buffer.

▶ Switches can filter the traffic being transmitted using various criteria, which take into account the source and destination addresses as well as the values of arbitrary fields. However, the method of specifying user-defined filters at the data link layer is rather complicated. To master this method, the administrator must have sound knowledge of the protocols and most carry out the difficult tasks of determining the location of the required attribute within the frame.

REVIEW QUESTIONS

1. List the main limitations of networks based on a shared medium.
2. Why in Ethernet networks does the sharp growth of delays start at lower values of the medium utilization coefficient than values in Token Ring and FDDI networks?
3. Which are advantages of LAN switches?
4. A switch forwarding table is created on the basis of:
   A. Source addresses
   B. Destination addresses
5. Is it possible to state that when dividing a shared medium into two segments, the load of each segment decreases twofold?
6. What are the negative consequences of the presence of closed loops in a network created on the basis of switches operating according to the transparent bridge algorithm?

7. What is the goal of limiting the time-to-live period of the entries of the forwarding table?

8. Compare the transparent bridge and SRB algorithms.

9. What are the purposes of user-defined filters in switches?

10. What parameters can be used when creating a user-defined filter of a switch?

11. Can the forwarding rate exceed the filtering rate?

12. What is a nonblocking switch?

13. Is it possible for a nonblocking switch to lose packets because of queue overflow?

14. What mechanisms are used by switches under conditions of internal queue overflow?
    - Traffic shaping
    - Feedback on the basis of the PAUSE frame
    - Back pressure (artificial collisions)
    - Prioritizing

15. Can the 10G Ethernet technology use a shared medium?

16. Which feature of the physical interface corresponds to the number 4 in the name of the 10GBase-LX4 specification?

17. Is it possible to directly connect a LAN switch with the 10GBase-WL interface to the STM-64 port of the SDH multiplexer?

18. Which property of LAN technologies simplifies the translation of Ethernet, Token Ring, and FDDI protocols?

19. In what cases can the FDDI frame not be translated into the Ethernet frame?

20. Specify the main types of switching matrix.

21. What is the main drawback of the switching matrix?

22. Which additional advantage is related to the use of shared memory as a switching matrix?

23. Why does switching on the fly have limited application in switches?

24. What happens if the number of LAN addresses exceeds the size of the switch address table?

PROBLEMS

1. The user-defined filter includes a logical condition and the action that must be carried out over the frame if this condition is satisfied. Formulate the filter conditions that discard frames arriving from computer A, which has the 06 DB 00 34 5E 27 MAC address, and from computer B, which has the CC 33 00 D5 43 4D MAC address, to server S, whose MAC address is CC 33 00 65 44 AA.

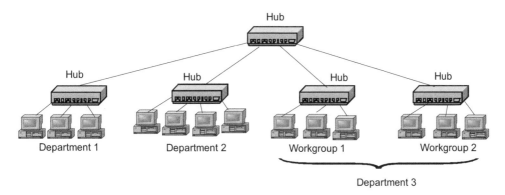

Figure 15.25 Network to be upgraded

2. It is necessary to improve the performance of a network based on a shared medium (Figure 15.25). Only one switch is at your disposal; it has two 1,000 Mbps ports and eight 100 Mbps ports. How would you transform the network if it is possible to continue using the hubs available in the initial variant?

16

ADVANCED FEATURES OF SWITCHED LANS

16.1 INTRODUCTION

Switches allow the building of significantly larger networks by dividing a shared medium into parts or abandoning the medium-sharing principle in favor of switched LANs. However, as the network scale grows, other problems arise that the switch based only on the transparent bridge algorithm, considered in the previous chapter, is unable to overcome. First, the reliability problem remains unsolved, since the tree-like topology of switched LANs is extremely vulnerable. For instance, failure of any switch or communications link results in loss of connectivity. If the segment switch fails, the network is split into two or more segments.

Limitations of the tree-like topology can be bypassed using additional switch mechanisms, which provide LANs with advanced features. For example, the spanning tree algorithm (STA) is widely used in switched LANs. This algorithm automatically finds a new variant of the tree-like topology in cases of switch or communications link failures, thus ensuring network fault tolerance. STA was developed simultaneously with the transparent bridge algorithm (i.e., in early 1980s), and since that time, it has been successfully used in LANs.

Another mechanism of using alternative routes was developed comparatively recently, with the beginning of widespread use of switched LANs. The link aggregation mechanism allows several physical links to be joined into one logical channel. This improves network performance and reliability.

New advanced capabilities of LAN switches allow to implement various common mechanisms of quality of service (QoS) support can be implemented, intended for different kinds of traffic: priority and weighted queues, feedback, and resource reservation.

Despite the progress achieved thanks to using new features added by STA and the link aggregation mechanism, LANs built only on the basis of switches, without using routers, are characterized by some limitations and experience certain problems. Part of these problems can be solved using an important advanced property of a switched LAN — the virtual LAN (VLAN) technique, which considerably simplifies the use of routers in such networks. The VLAN technique allows a LAN to be divided into several isolated logical segments. This is achieved using switch configuration (e.g., programmatically rather than by physically connecting or disconnecting cable plugs). These isolated segments can then be connected into the internetwork using the network-layer protocol. Programmatic division of a network into segments allows quick and easy changes to the composition of segments by moving computers from segment to segment as needed.

16.2 SPANNING TREE ALGORITHM

KEY WORDS: spanning tree algorithm (STA), spanning tree protocol (STP), segment, root switch, metric, switch identifier, root port, port identifier, designated port, designated switch, bridge protocol data unit (BPDU), hello interval

In those LANs where both technologies and equipment implement the functions of only the first and the second layers of the ISO/OSI model, the problem of using alternative routes has its own specific features: the base protocols support only *tree-like topologies* (i.e., the ones that do not contain any loops).

For automatic switching into a reserved state of all alternative links that do not fit within the framework of the tree topology, LANs use the **spanning tree algorithm** (**STA**). The protocol that implements this algorithm is called the **spanning tree protocol** (**STP**).

STA was developed quite a long time ago, in 1983. It was adopted by IEEE and included in the 802.1D specification describing the transparent bridge algorithm. Although bridges, for which this algorithm was initially intended, are already considered "dinosaur" communications devices, STA is widely used in the most widespread communications devices of contemporary LANs, namely, in switches. STA enabled network designers to build large-scale LANs on the basis of switches without using routers. Such LANs are characterized by high reliability because of the use of reserve links.

As a rule, manufacturers of network equipment implement STA in switches intended for network segments characterized by increased reliability requirements, such as backbone switches and switches of departments or large workgroups.

16.2.1 Required Definitions

STA represents the network in the form of a graph whose nodes are switches and network segments (Figure 16.1).

A **segment** is a connected part of a network that does not contain switches or routers. It can be shared (when STA was developed, this was the only type of segment) and can include physical-layer devices such as repeaters or concentrators, which are transparent for the switch. Nowadays, the segment often is a duplex point-to-point link between the adjacent ports of two switches.

STA ensures the building of a tree topology of links with only a path of minimum length from each switch and each segment to some dedicated **root switch**, the root of the tree. The *uniqueness* of the path ensures that it is loop free, and *minimality* of the distance allows an optimal path to be built for the traffic that travels from the network periphery to its backbone, whose role is played by the root switch.

As a measure of distance, STA uses the **metric** traditional for routing protocols, namely, the value inversely proportional to the segment bandwidth. In STA, the metric is also defined as the designated cost of the segment. It is calculated as the time required for

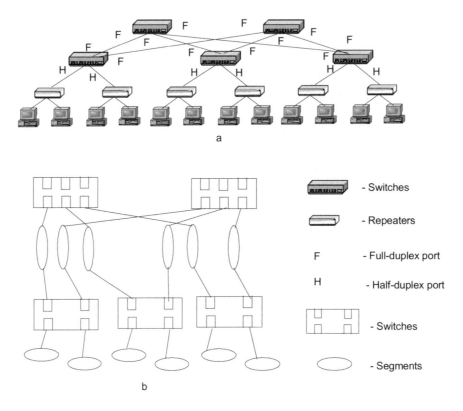

Figure 16.1 Formal representation of the network according to STA

transmitting 1 bit of information and is measured in 10 nsec units. Thus, for the 10 Mbps Ethernet segment, the designated cost is 10 conditional units; for 100 Mbps Ethernet, it is 1 unit; and for the Token Ring 16 Mbps segment, this value is 6.25. Taking into account that network speed is constantly growing, a modified and revised version of the conditional unit scale has appeared: 10 Mbps — 100, 100 Mbps — 19, 1 Gbps — 4, and 10 Gbps — 2.

The **switch identifier** is the 8-byte number whose six least significant bytes contain the MACaddress of the switch control unit implementing STA. Recall that ports of switches and bridges do not require MAC addresses to carry out their main function, so it is not a port MAC address. The two most significant bytes of the switch identifier are configured manually. As you'll see later, this allows a network administrator to influence the process of choosing the root switch.

The **root port** of the switch is the port that has the shortest distance from the root switch (more precisely, from any of the ports of the root switch).

The **port identifier** is a 2-byte number. The least significant byte contains the ordinal number of this port within a switch, and the most significant byte is set manually by the network administrator.

The **designated port** is the shortest distance from the root switch among all ports of all switches of this segment.

The **designated switch** of the segment is the switch to which the designated port of this segment belongs.

Bridge protocol data units (BPDUs) are special packets with which switches periodically exchange for automatic detection of the tree configuration. BPDUs carry data about switch and port identifiers and information on the path cost from the root switch. In STA, the interval at which BPDU packets are generated is called the *hello interval*. This interval is set by the administrator and usually is from 1 to 4 seconds.

16.2.2 Three-Stage Procedure of Building the Tree

Figure 16.2 provides the example network that we will use to illustrate the procedure of building a spanning tree.

STA determines the active configuration of the network in three stages.

Stage 1. The root switch is selected from which the tree will be built. According to STA, this role is delegated to the switch that has the *smallest identifier value.* If network administrator does not interfere with this process, the root switch will be chosen randomly. In fact, the device that has the minimum value of the MAC address of the control unit will be chosen for this role. Naturally, this choice might be far from optimal. For instance, if switch 5 is chosen to be the root switch (Figure 16.2), then most of the traffic will pass through many transit segments and switches. Therefore, the network administrator should not let this process take its course. It would be much better if administrator could influence this process and choose the root switch on the basis of reasonable considerations. This is achieved by setting an appropriate configuration of the most significant bytes of switch identifiers. Proceeding in such a way, it is possible to choose the switch that takes the central position in the intersegment connections. Suppose that switch identifiers correspond to the numbers shown in the illustration. In this case, switch 1 must be chosen for the role of root switch.

Stage 2. The root port is chosen for each switch. The distance from the root switch is determined by the BPDUs arriving from this switch. Based on the data of these packets, each switch can determine the minimum distances from the root switch for all of its ports. Each switch analyzes the received BPDU, increases the path cost from the root switch specified in that BPDU by the designated cost of the segment from which that packet was received, and then retransmits the BPDU. Thus, the distance from the root switch specified in a BPDU increases as it passes through switches. For instance, assuming that all segments in the example under consideration are 10 Mbps Ethernet segments, switch 2, having received a BPDU with the distance set to 0 from segment 1, will increase it by 10 conventional units.

When retranslating packets, each switch "memorizes" the minimum distance from the root encountered in all BPDUs received by each of its ports. Having accomplished the procedure of defining the configuration of the spanning tree, each switch finds its root port (i.e., the one that has the minimum distance from the root).

If the metric values are equal, the switch and port identifiers are used to eliminate ambiguity. Preference is given to ports and switches with minimum identifier values. For example, for segment 3, there are two paths to root switch 1, both having equal values of the metric. The first path goes via switch 3, and the second path goes via switch 4. The chosen path goes through the switch that has *smaller identifier value* (i.e., via switch 3). In this case, the port numbers within the switches match; however, when carrying out the comparison, the *switch identifier* is considered before the port number.

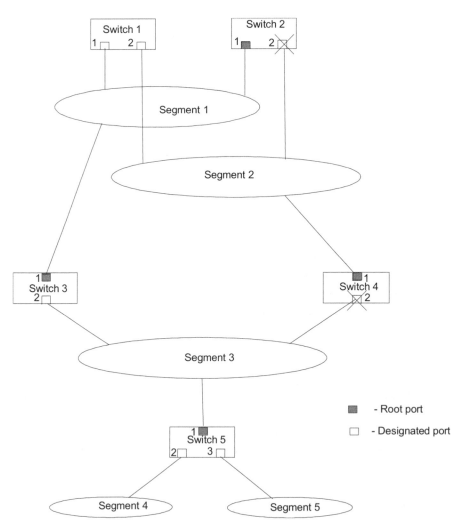

Figure 16.2 Example of the spanning tree built according to STA

In the example shown in Figure 16.2, switch 3 chooses port 1 as its root port, since for this port the minimum distance from the root is 10 units (a BPDU with such a distance was received from the root switch via segment 1). Port 2 of switch 3, on the basis of the received packets, has determined that the minimum distance from the root is 20 units. This corresponds to when the packet passes from port 2 of the root switch via segment 2 and then passes through switch 4 and segment 3. Switch 2, when choosing the root port, has encountered the situation in which its ports 1 and 2 are equidistant from the root, namely, 10 units. Port 1 receives packets from port 1 of the root switch via one transit segment, segment 1, and port 2 receives packets from port 2 of the root switch via segment 2. Since the numeric value of the port 1 identifier is smaller than that of port 2, port 1 will be chosen as the root port.

Stage 3. The designated port is elected from all ports of all switches within the limits of a network segment, and the switch corresponding to that port becomes the designated switch of that segment. Similar to the selection of the root port, the distributed procedure is used here. Each switch of the segment first excludes its root port from consideration because, for the segment to which that port is connected, there always is another switch closer to the root. For all remaining ports, their minimum distances from the root switch (before increasing it by the conventional time of the segment) are compared to the distance from the root obtained for the root port of this switch. If all distances received at this port are larger than the one determined for the root port of the switch, for the segment to which that port is connected, the shortest path to the root switch goes through this switch. Consequently, this switch becomes a designated one. The switch makes all its ports for which this condition is satisfied designated ports. When there are several ports with the same shortest distance from the root switch, the port with the smallest port identifier is chosen.

In the example under consideration, switch 2 has detected that packets with the shortest distance, 0 units, were received via port 2 (these were packets from port 2 of root switch 1). Since for the root port of switch 2 the distance from the root is 10, port 2 of this switch is not a designated port for segment 2.

By default, network switches have 15 seconds to complete all three stages. It is assumed that during this time each switch receives a sufficient number of BPDUs, allowing it to determine the state of all its ports.

All other ports, except root ports and designated ports, are switched to the blocking state (in the illustration, such ports are crossed out), and the procedure of building the spanning tree is accomplished. It has been mathematically proven that this method of choosing active ports eliminates loops in the network, and that remaining connections form a *spanning tree* (provided that it can be created with the existing network links).

NOTE   *In general, the tree topology chosen according to STA is not the optimal one for all possible paths of traffic transmission. For instance, in the provided example, the traffic goes along the following path when transmitting packets from segment 3 to segment 2: switch 3 — segment 1 — switch 1 — segment 2. The metric for this path is 30. If port 2 of switch 4 was not blocked, there would be a shorter path: the one going through switch 4. The metric of this path would be 20, which is better than the previous path.*

Such a variant is possible if the shortest path to the root switch for segment 4 is chosen through switch 4 instead of through switch 3. This can be achieved by appropriately assigning the values to the most significant parts of switch identifiers. However, if this variant is chosen, the shortest path from segment 4 to segment 1 would not be the optimal one.

Having built the spanning tree, the switch starts to receive (without forwarding) data packets and to build the forwarding table on the basis of their source addresses. This is a normal, transparent bridge-learning mode that could not be activated earlier, since the port was not sure if it remained a root or became a designated port that would transmit data packets. The "learning" stage also lasts for 15 seconds by default. At the same time, the port continues to participate in the STA operation, which means that the arrival of a BPDU with better parameters automatically switches it into the "blocking" state.

Only after a time interval twice as long as the predefined timeout value elapses does the port switch to the "forwarding" state and start processing packets according to the forwarding table that it has generated. Note that this table continues to be modified, reflecting the changes in the network structure.

In the course of normal operation, the switch continues to generate configuration BP-DUs at the hello interval; other switches receive them via their root ports and retranslate via designated ports. The switch might lack designated ports (e.g., switches 2 and 4); nevertheless, it participates in the STA protocol operation, because the root port continues receiving BPDU packets.

If the root port of any network switch does not receive a BPDU after the maximum **time to live** (TTL) of a message has elapsed (20 seconds by default), it initiates a new procedure of building the spanning tree. In this case, the switch generates a BPDU where it specifies itself as a root and translates this to all switches. All other network switches with the expired message TTL timer proceed in a similar way. As a result, a new active configuration is chosen.

16.2.3 STA Advantages and Drawbacks

One of the main advantages of STA is that in contrast to most other simplified algorithms, where the reserved connection takes over exclusively when the neighboring device fails, it carries out network reconfiguration not only with account of the links to its nearest neighbors but also with account of the state of links in distant network segments.

The drawbacks of this algorithm include that in networks with numerous switches, the time required to determine a new active configuration might be too long. If the network uses default timeout values, the transition to a new configuration might take more than 50 seconds. Twenty seconds are required to confirm the loss of connectivity with the root switch (timer expiration is the only way of getting information about this event in the standard variant of STA), and an additional 2×15 seconds will be needed to enter the "forwarding" state.

The existing nonstandard versions of STA, which are rather numerous, allow the reconfiguration time to be reduced by further complicating the algorithm. This can be achieved by adding new types of control messages. In 2001, a new version of the spanning tree was developed: the IEEE 802.1w specification, also intended to speed up the protocol operation, but in a standard way.

16.3 LINK AGGREGATION IN LANS

> **KEY WORDS:** link aggregation, trunk, eliminating frame spawning, port selection, logical port, physical ports, dynamic and static frame distribution, Link Control Aggregation Protocol (LCAP), IEEE 802.3ad

16.3.1 Trunks and Logical Channels

Link aggregation between two communications devices into a single logical channel is another form of using redundant alternative links in LANs.

> There is the principal difference between the link aggregation technique and the previously described STA.
>
> - STA switches redundant links into hot reserve, leaving in active state only the minimum set of channels required for ensuring connectivity of the network segments. In this case, network *reliability* is increased, but its performance remains the same.
> - When using link aggregation, all redundant links remain active, which improves both the network *reliability* and its *performance*.

In case of failure of one of the components of such an aggregate channel, often called a **trunk**, the traffic is distributed among the remaining links (Figure 16.3). In the illustration, the example of such a situation is trunk 2, in which one of the links (the central one) has failed so that all frames are transmitted using the remaining two links. This example illustrates the *reliability* improvement.

Now consider how link aggregation improves network *performance*. For example, in Figure 16.3, switches 1 and 3 are connected by three parallel links, which increases the performance of this section three times in comparison to the standard variant of tree topology, which does not allow parallel links. Performance improvement of the inter-switch connection achieved by link aggregation in some cases is more efficient than that achieved by replacement of a single physical link with a faster one. For example, despite the variety of physical link speeds provided by the Ethernet family — from 10 Mbps to 10 Gbps — a tenfold increase of the speed achieved by migration to a faster Ethernet standard is not always needed and economically justified. For example, if network switches

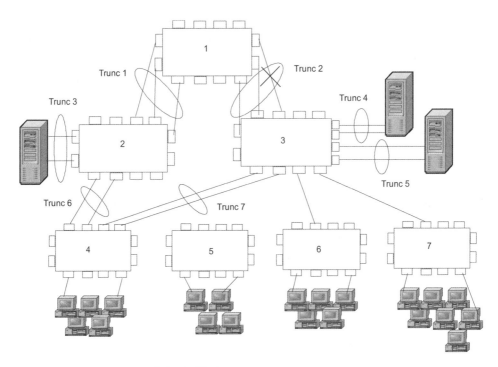

Figure 16.3 Aggregation of physical links

installed in the network do not provide the possibility of adding a module equipped with the Gigabit Ethernet port, increasing the speed to 1,000 Mbps on some links will require a total replacement of switches. On the other hand, the existing switches might have free Fast Ethernet ports. Therefore, it might be possible to increase the data rate to 600 Mbps by aggregating six Fast Ethernet links.

Link aggregation is a generalized form of the third method of using alternative routes described in *Chapter 6* ("The network finds two routes beforehand but uses only one of them")[1]. In this case, instead of two routes, N routes are found (where $N \geq 2$), and only one of them is used for each flow. When this route fails, the flow affected by this failure is switched to any of the $(N - 1)$ routes that remain in operation.

Link aggregation is used for links between the ports of two LAN switches, for links between computers and switches. Most frequently, this variant is implemented for fast or business-critical servers. In this case, all network adapters or switch ports that compose a trunk share the same network address. Because of this, trunk ports are indistinguishable for IP or any other network-layer protocol, which corresponds to the concept of a united logical channel, serving a basis for link aggregation.

Nearly all methods of link aggregation used nowadays have one significant limitation: They take into account only the links between two neighboring network switches,

---

[1] See the *"Alternative Routes"* section.

ignoring everything that takes place outside the limits of this network section. For example, the operation of trunk 1 is not coordinated with the operation of trunk 2, and the presence of a normal link between switches 2 and 3, which creates a loop with trunks 1 and 2, is not taken into account. Because of this, link aggregation must be used *with* STA if the network administrator wants to use all topological capabilities of connecting network nodes. For STA, the trunk must look like a single link; then, STA operating logic will remain in force.

There are lots of proprietary implementations of the link aggregation mechanism. Naturally, the most popular ones belong to the leaders in the field of LAN equipment industry. This list includes such popular implementations as Fast EtherChannel and Gigabit EtherChannel from Cisco, MultiLink Trunking from Nortel, and Adaptive Load Balancing from Intel. IEEE 802.3ad (link aggregation) summarizes and generalizes these approaches.

16.3.2 Eliminating Frame Spawning

Now, consider in more detail specific features of switch operation when its ports make up a trunk. In the network fragment shown in Figure 16.4, two switches, switch 1 and switch 2, are connected by four physical links. Note that a trunk can be either unidirectional or bidirectional. Each switch controls frame-sending only and makes a decision about the output port to which it must be transmitted. Therefore, if both switches consider the links that connect them as a trunk, this trunk will be bidirectional; otherwise, it will be a unidirectional trunk.

Figure 16.4 illustrates the behavior of switch 1 in relation to parallel links. If these links are not considered by a switch as an aggregate link, there will be problems with two types of frames:

- Frames carrying unique addresses that have *not been learned* by the switch
- Frames carrying a *broadcast* or a *multicast* address

The transparent bridge algorithm requires the switch to transmit a frame with an unlearned address (i.e., one missing from the forwarding table) to all ports except the one from which that frame was received. If there are parallel links, such a frame will be spawned, and the number of its copies will be equal to the number of parallel links. In the previously provided example, switch 2 would receive four copies of the original frame.

At the same time, frames would fall into an endless loop because they would constantly circulate between two switches. Note that such frames cannot be removed from the network, since data link-layer protocols often lack the *TTL* field, frequently used in upper-layer protocols such as IP or IPX.

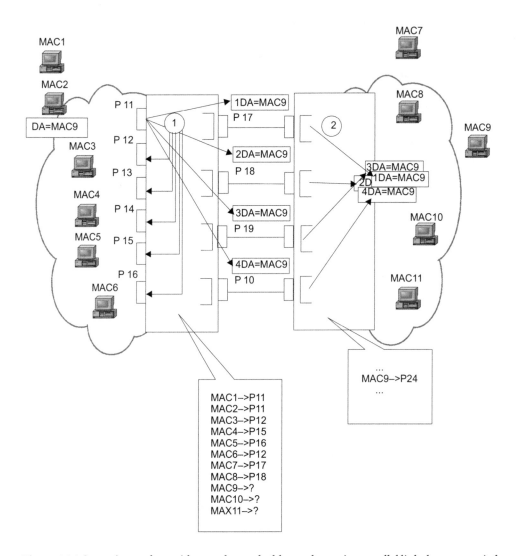

Figure 16.4 Spawning packets with an unlearned address when using parallel links between switches

In any case, the frame with the unlearned address would increase the network load by increasing the number of frames. This would likely result in jams, delays, and data losses. Besides growth of the network load, frame duplication also results in inefficient operation of many upper-layer protocols. Consider, for instance, the node running TCP, which uses ACK duplication as an indirect sign of network congestion.

Frames containing broadcast addresses create even more problems because they must be transmitted to all ports except for the source one. Thus, the network will become flooded with irrelevant traffic, this load will be rather significant, and the frames will fall into endless loops.

The problems with frames that have known and unique destination addresses do not arise. This is because the switch transmits such frames to a single port, namely, to the one through which the frame having that address in the source address field has arrived.

Developers of aggregation mechanisms have taken into account the problems that arise when processing frames with unlearned, broadcast, or multicast addresses. The solution to this problem is simple. It implies that all ports connected by parallel links are considered a single *logical port*, specified in the forwarding table, instead of several *physical ports*. In Figure 16.4, the forwarding table contains a single logical port, AL11, instead of the P17, P18, P19 and P10 ports. The addresses of all nodes, whose paths pass through switch 2, are mapped to this port. At the same time, learning a new address carried by the frame arriving from any of the physical ports included in the trunk inserts a new entry into the forwarding table. This new entry will contain the identifier of the logical port. The arriving frame, whose destination address is learned and mapped to the identifier of the logical port, is transmitted to only one output port of the switch, which is included in the trunk. The switch processes unlearned, broadcast, or multicast addresses the same way — namely, it uses only one of the links for frame transmission. This change in the frame processing logic is not applied to the switch ports that are not included in the trunk. For example, switch 1 always transmits frames with unlearned or broadcast addresses to ports P11 — P16.

Because of this decision, frames are not duplicated, and previously described problems do not arise.

NOTE   *In fact, this is correct only if both switches consider parallel links as a trunk. Thus, to make full use of the trunk properties, it is necessary to configure it on both sides.*

16.3.3 Port Selection

An open question remains: Which of the switch ports have to be used for frame forwarding via a trunk?

Several variants of answer can be suggested. Improvement of the total performance of the network section between two switches, or between a switch and a server, is one of the goals of link aggregation. Because of this, it is desirable to ensure **dynamic frame distribution** over the trunk ports, taking into account the current load of each port. This means that newly arrived frames are sent to the ports with lowest loads (e.g., with the shortest queues). It seems that the dynamic method of distributing frames, which takes into account the current load of each port and ensures load balancing over all links of the trunk, must result in the maximum performance of the entire trunk.

However, this statement is not always true, since it does not account for the behavior of the upper-layer protocols. There are some protocols whose performance can be significantly reduced if packets of the session established between two end nodes arrive in an order different from the one in which they were sent by the source node. Such a situation

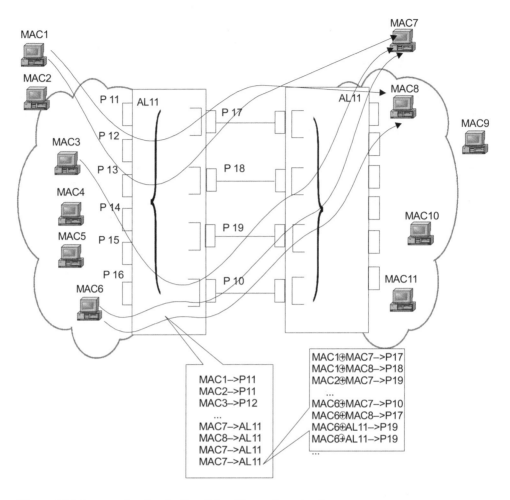

Figure 16.5 A network using the Fast EtherChannel mechanism

can arise if two or more sequential frames of the same session are transmitted via differ-ent ports of the trunk, because queues in buffers of these ports have different lengths. Consequently, frame transmission delays might also be different, so a frame transmitted later will arrive to the destination node before one transmitted earlier.

Therefore, most link aggregation mechanisms use methods of **static frame distribu-tion** among the ports instead of dynamic distribution methods. Static distribution as-sumes that a specific port of the trunk is allocated for the frame flow of a specific session established between two nodes. All frames of that session will pass through the same queue, which ensures that they will arrive to the destination node in the same order as they were sent.

Usually, when employing static distribution, the port for a specific session is selected on the basis of certain attributes in the arriving packets. Most often, source or destination MAC addresses, or even both, are used as such attributes. In the popular implementation of Cisco Fast EtherChannel switches belonging to the Catalyst 5000/6000 family, an exclusive OR (XOR) operation over the last two bits of the source and destination MAC addresses is used for choosing the trunk port number. The result of this operation can take one of four values: 00, 01, 10, or 11, which are the conventional numbers of the trunk ports. Figure 16.5 provides an example of a network in which the Fast EtherChannel mechanism is used. Distribution of flows for sessions between end nodes is, in this case, random. Since this distribution does not account for the actual load created by each session, total trunk bandwidth might be used inefficiently, especially if session intensities are significantly different. Furthermore, this algorithm does not guarantee even the quantitatively uniform distribution of sessions over the ports. Random set of MAC addresses in the network can result in one of the ports transmitting tens of sessions and another port transmitting only two or three sessions. When using this algorithm, load balancing for the ports can be achieved only if many networked computers and sessions are established among them.

Other methods of distributing sessions between ports can also be suggested. For example, this task can be carried out according to the IP addresses of the packets encapsulated into the data link-layer frames, or the types of application-layer protocols. For example, e-mail can be transmitted using one port, Web-traffic using another port, and so on. The practice in which sessions with MAC addresses learned via a specific port are assigned to the same port might be rather useful. In this case, the session traffic will go via the same port in both directions.

The standard method of creating aggregate channels described in the IEEE 802.3ad specification supposes the possibility of creating a logical port on the basis of physical ports distributed over several switches. To ensure that switches are automatically informed that some physical port belongs to a specific logical port, this specification suggests a special service protocol: **link control aggregation protocol (LCAP)**. Thus, it is possible to organize configurations of aggregate links that improve network fault tolerance not only in sections between two switches but also in more complicated topologies (Figure 16.6).

When one of the links aggregated within a trunk fails, all packets of the sessions assigned to its corresponding port will be directed to one of the remaining ports. Usually, such a procedure of restoring the connectivity takes from several to tens of milliseconds. This happens because in many trunk implementations, all MAC addresses mapped to the failed physical link are forcibly marked as unlearned. After that, the switch repeats the procedures of learning these addresses. After that, addresses are again marked as learned, and the procedure of session assignment is repeated. This time, only the available ports are taken into account. Since timeouts in LAN session-layer protocols are rarely large, the time required for restoring the lost connection is not too long.

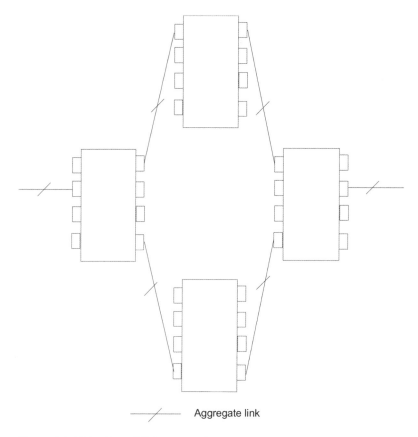

Figure 16.6 Distributed link aggregation

16.4 VIRTUAL LANS

KEY WORDS: Virtual LAN (VLAN), user-defined filter, broadcast domain, multisegment concentrator, layer 3 switch, IEEE 802.1Q, IEEE 802.1p, port grouping, grouping MAC addresses, Canonical Format Identifier (CFI), Tag Protocol Identifier (TPID), Tag Control Information (TCI)

The capability of controlling frame transmission between network segments is an important property of LAN switches. For various reasons, such as observing access rights and enforcing a security policy, it is not always necessary to transmit a frame to the specified destination address.

As shown in *Chapter 15*, this task can be carried out by *user-defined filters*. However, a user-defined filter can prevent frame transmission to specific destination addresses only. Broadcast traffic, on the contrary, will be transmitted to all network segments. This is required by the bridge algorithm implemented in switches. Therefore, networks created on the basis of bridges and switches are sometimes called *flat* because of the lack of barriers to the propagation of broadcast traffic.

The VLAN technology allows administrators to overcome this limitation.

> **Virtual LAN (VLAN)** is a group of network nodes whose traffic, including broadcasts, is isolated from other network nodes.

This means that frame transmission on the basis of data link-layer addresses between different virtual networks is impossible, no matter what kind of address is specified — unique, multicast, or broadcast. At the same time, frames within a VLAN are transmitted according to the switching technology (e.g., only to the port related to the frame destination address).

VLANs can *overlap* if one or more computers participate in more than one VLAN. In the example shown in Figure 16.7, the e-mail server participates in VLANs 3 and 4.

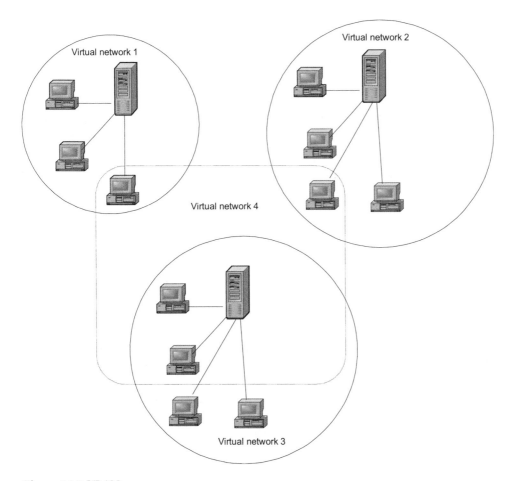

Figure 16.7 VLANs

This means that its frames are transmitted by switches to all computers that participate in those networks. If a specific computer participates only in VLAN 3, its frames will not reach network 4. However, it will be able to communicate with computers from network 4 via a common mail server. Such a method does not ensure full protection of VLANs from one another because, for instance, a broadcast storm originating at the mail server will flood both network 3 and network 4.

Thus, a virtual network makes up a *broadcast domain*, the name of which is chosen by analogy with a collision domain created by Ethernet repeaters.

16.4.1 VLAN Goal

The main goal of VLAN technology is the creation of isolated networks, which then must be connected by routers implementing some network-layer protocol, such as IP. Such network structure creates much more reliable barriers, preventing the propagation of undesirable traffic from network to network. Nowadays, it is commonly agreed that every large-scale network must include routers; otherwise, flows of erroneous frames, such as broadcasts to which switches are transparent, would periodically flood the entire network, thus disrupting its operation.

> The VLAN technology provides a flexible basis for building a large-scale network connected by routers, since switches allow administrators to create isolated segments by logical configuration without using physical switching.

Before the arrival of VLAN technology, separate networks were created using either physically isolated segments of coaxial cable or segments not connected to one another built on the repeaters and bridges. Later, these isolated networks were connected by routers into an entire internetwork (Figure 16.8).

When using this approach, the introduction of any changes into the segment structure, such as moving the user into another network or splitting large segments, implies physical switching of connectors at the front panels of repeaters or in cross panels. For large-scale networks, this approach is inconvenient, because it implies a large amount of manual operations and is characterized by a high probability of errors.

Partially this problem was solved by multisegment concentrators (they were considered in *Chapter 14*), which eliminated the need in physical switching of network nodes. This provided the possibility of programming the structure of the shared segment without physical reconnection.

However, the solution to the problem of changing segment structure with the use of concentrators was actually only partial, because it implies significant limitations on the network structure. The number of segments supported by such concentrators usually is not large. Therefore, it is unrealistic to hope that it would be possible to allocate a separate segment to each node using such a concentrator (in contrast to switches, which are capable of doing so). Furthermore, when using such an approach, the entire

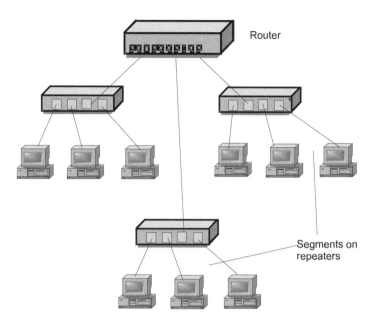

Figure 16.8 Internetwork comprising several networks built on the basis of repeaters

job of data transmission between segments is delegated to routers, and switches, with their high performance, remain "out of work." Consequently, networks built on the basis of repeaters with configuration switching are still based on the medium sharing among many nodes, and naturally, they have significantly lower performance than the networks built on the basis of switches.

For connecting VLANs into an internetwork, it is necessary to use the network-layer tools. Network-layer functions can be implemented in a separate router, or they can operate as part of the switch software. Note that the switch in this case becomes a combined device, a **layer 3 switch**. Layer 3 switches will be covered in *Chapter 20* of this book.

The technology of building switch-based VLANs and their operation was not standardized for a long time, although it was implemented in a wide range of switches from different manufacturers. This situation changed in 1998 after adoption of the IEEE 802.1Q standard, which defines the basic rules of building VLANs independent of the data link-layer protocols supported by a switch.

16.4.2 Creating VLANs Based on One Switch

When creating VLANs on the basis of one switch, the mechanism of a specific switch *port grouping* is often implemented (Figure 16.9). In this case, each port is assigned to a specific VLAN. The frame that arrived from the port belonging to another VLAN,

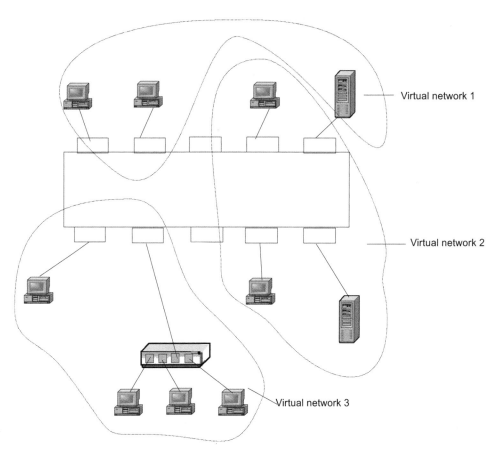

Figure 16.9 VLANs built on the basis of a single switch

for example, VLAN 1, will never be transmitted to the port that does not belong to this virtual network. The port can be assigned to several VLANs; however, in practice this is rare, since it eliminates the effect of full isolation of networks.

NOTE   *If a segment created on the basis of repeater is connected to one of the switch ports, it does not make sense to include the nodes of such a segment into different VLANs; the traffic of these nodes will be common in any case.*

Creating virtual networks on the basis of port grouping does not require a large amount of manual work from the administrator — it is sufficient to assign each port to one of the VLANs named beforehand. Usually, this operation is carried out using a special program supplied with the switch.

The second method of creating VLANs is based on *grouping MAC addresses*. Each MAC address learned by the switch is assigned to a specific VLAN. When the network comprises numerous nodes, this method requires the administrator to carry out lots of manual operations. However, this method provides more flexibility when building VLANs based on several switches than does the method of port grouping.

16.4.3 Creating VLANs Based on Several Switches

Figure 16.10 illustrates the problem that arises when building VLANs on the basis of several switches supporting the technique of **port grouping**.

If the nodes of some VLANs span several switches, then a special pair of ports must be assigned on switches to interconnect switches for each VLAN. Otherwise, when switches are connected by a single pair of ports, the information that a specific frame belongs to a specific VLAN will be lost when transmitting a frame from switch to switch. Thus, to get connected, switches with port grouping require the number of ports to correspond to the number of supported VLANs. Ports and cables are used wastefully when implementing this method. Besides this, when connecting VLANs using a router, a separate cable and a separate router port are assigned for each VLAN, which also results in considerable overhead.

Grouping MAC addresses into a VLAN on each switch eliminates the need to connect them using multiple ports, since in this case, the MAC address represents a VLAN label. However, this method requires numerous manual operations related to mapping MAC addresses to VLANs on each of the network switches.

The two approaches described here are based only on the addition of auxiliary information to the switch address tables. They lack the possibility of inserting directly into the frame information specifying that a frame belongs to a specific VLAN. The remaining approaches use the existing or auxiliary fields of the frame for storing information on the frame's VLAN in the course of sending it from switch to switch. In this case, there is no need to save information about the mapping MAC addresses to specific VLANs on each of the network switches.

An auxiliary field containing the mark of a specific VLAN is used only when the frame is passed from switch to switch. When transmitting the frame to the end node, it is

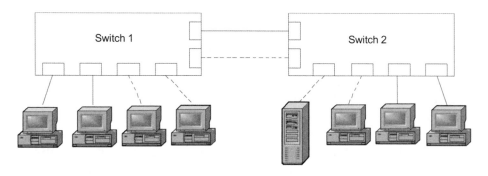

Figure 16.10 Building VLANs on the basis of several switches with port grouping

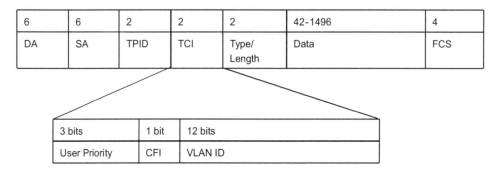

6	6	2	2	2	42-1496	4
DA	SA	TPID	TCI	Type/ Length	Data	FCS

3 bits	1 bit	12 bits
User Priority	CFI	VLAN ID

Figure 16.11 Structure of the tagged Ethernet frame

usually deleted. In this case, the "switch–switch" interaction protocol gets modified, and the hardware and software of the end nodes remain the same. Before the adoption of the IEEE 802.1Q standard, there were many proprietary protocols of this type. However, all these protocols have one common drawback — equipment from different manufacturers is incompatible when building VLANs.

For storing the number of a virtual network, the **IEEE 802.1Q** standard (also known as tag protocol, because it adds the tag to the header) provides an additional four-byte header (Figure 16.11). The first two bytes form the **Tag Protocol Identifier (TPID)**, and always carry the hex value 0x8100, by which network equipment must recognize that this frame is the tagged Ethernet frame. The next to bytes are called **Tag Control Information (TCI)**, and the **802.1Q** protocol shares them with the **802.1p** protocol, which will be covered in section 16.5 — "Quality of Service in LANs" section of this chapter. In this field 12 bits are used for storing the VLAN number (the VLAN ID field), and 3 bits are allocated for storing the frame priority as defined in the 802.1p standard (the User Priority field). One bit, known as **Canonical Format Identifier (CFI)** was introduced to provide the possibility of distinguishing Ethernet frames from Token Ring frames. For Ethernet frames this bit must be set to 0. The 12-bit VLAN ID field allows for creating up to 4,096 virtual networks. Since the data field of the Ethernet frame decreases by two bytes when adding the 802.1Q/p header, its maximum size also decreases. For example, for the Ethernet II frame these size become equal to 42–1,496 bytes in contrast to the standard 46–1,500 bytes values.

Adoption of the 802.1Q standard allowed equipment manufacturers to overcome the differences in proprietary VLAN implementations and to achieve compatibility when building VLANs. VLAN techniques are supported by manufacturers of switches as well as by manufacturers of network adapters. In the latter case, the adapter can generate and receive tagged Ethernet frames containing the VLAN TAG field. If the network adapter generates tagged frames, it maps them to a specific VLAN. Therefore, the switch must process such frames as appropriate (e.g., decide whether or not it has to transmit them to specific output port) depending on the port mapping to a certain VLAN. The network adapter driver gets the number of its VLAN or VLANs from the configuration

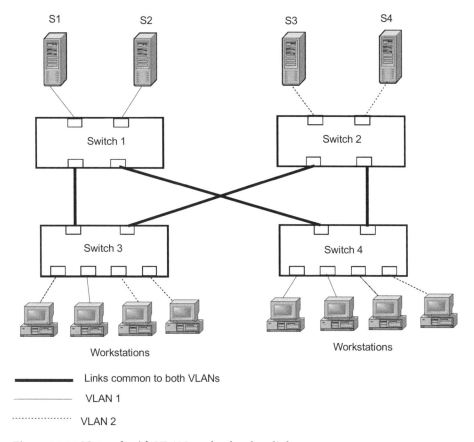

Figure 16.12 Network with VLANs and redundant links

data manually entered by the network administrator; alternatively, it can receive this information from some application running on the specific node. Such an application can also run on one of the centralized network servers and control the entire network structure.

The existence of VLANs in the network influences the choice of the active spanning tree topology. Consider the example shown in Figure 16.12.

There are two VLANs in this network: VLAN1 and VLAN2. These VLANs are built on the basis of the port grouping technique. The illustration shows connections between VLAN1 ports as continuous lines; connections between VLAN2 ports are shown as dashed lines.

Without considering the presence of VLANs in that network when building active STA topology, the result will be the spanning tree shown in Figure 16.13 (the Switch 1 switch was chosen as the root switch). This topology is inefficient for VLAN2 since, for instance, the path from computer W1 to server S3 goes through four transit switches. For comparison, the path from the computers of VLAN1 to server S1 goes through two transit switches. If Switch 2 switch is chosen as the transit switch, such topology would be inefficient for VLAN1.

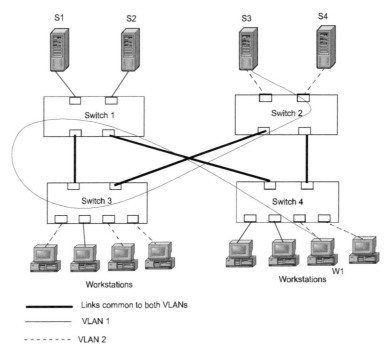

Figure 16.13 Spanning trees without taking into account VLANs

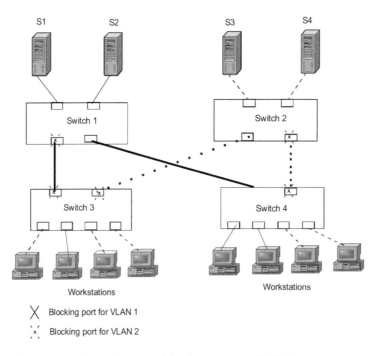

Figure 16.14 Spanning trees taking into account VLANs

Another solution is building active topology separately for each VLAN. In the example under consideration, such an approach would produce two trees, with the Switch1 root switch for VLAN1 and the Switch2 root switch for VLAN2 (Figure 16.14).

16.5 QUALITY OF SERVICE IN LANS

KEY WORDS: 802.1Q/p, traffic classification, traffic tagging, eight classes of LAN traffic, not real-time traffic, delay sensitive traffic, queue management, policing mechanism

LAN switches support practically all QoS mechanisms described in *Chapter 7*. This statement is true for LAN switches as a class of communications devices. On the other hand, each switch model might support only a certain set of QoS mechanisms or provide no support for such mechanisms. As a rule, workgroup switches do not support QoS, but for backbone switches this support is a must.

Traffic classification. LAN switches are Layer 2 devices that analyze only data link-layer headers. Therefore, switches normally classify the traffic using source and destination MAC addresses and number of the port to which the frame has arrived. It is also possible to use for classification any arbitrary subfield within the data field, specified by byte offset. These methods are not very convenient for administrator who needs, for example, to separate voice traffic from file transfer traffic. Therefore, some switch models carry out classification on the basis of the attributes contained in the headers of higher-layer protocols without fully supporting them (e.g., without using IP for packet forwarding). For instance, such classification can be carried out on the basis of IP addresses and application attributes contained in the packet headers.

Traffic tagging. Traffic tagging carries out its classification on the network edge only and then uses the classification results in all transit devices of the network. The Ethernet 802.3 frame does not contain any field that could store the traffic classification result. However, this drawback is corrected by the 802.1p specification, which uses 3 bits of the previously considered 802.1Q/p auxiliary header for storing the frame priority.

These 3 bits are used for storing one of the eight possible traffic classes. The 802.1D-1998 standard, which includes the 802.1p specification, interprets this field in this way. Appendix H of the 802.1D-1998 standard provides recommendations on dividing all LAN traffic into the eight classes listed in Table 16.1.

Background (BK) is the traffic least sensitive to delays, such as backup traffic. However, the source of this traffic may transmit considerable volumes of data. Therefore, it makes sense to assign it a separate class. This ensures that this traffic does not slow the processing of other types of traffic.

The Best Effort (BE), Excellent Effort (EE), and Controlled Load (CL) classes are not real-time classes, which means that they do not impose stringent requirements on the delay limits. However, for these classes, it is desirable to ensure some minimum level of bandwidth. It is expedient to serve these classes using the weighted queues mechanism.

The Video (VI), Voice (VO), and Network Control (NC) classes are delay sensitive. The recommended values of delay thresholds are provided in Table 16.1. It is expedient to serve these classes using the priority queues mechanism. The Network Control class has the highest priority, since all network characteristics depend on the timely decision-making and information delivery to the network devices.

Table 16.1 LAN traffic classes

User priority	Acronym	Traffic type
1	BK	Background
2	–	Space
0 (Default)	BE	Best Effort
3	EE	Excellent Effort
4	CL	Controlled Load
5	VI	"Video," < 100 ms latency and jitter
6	VO	"Voice," < 100 ms latency and jitter
7	NC	Network Control

Table 16.2 Traffic classes and number of queues

Number of queues	Defining traffic type						
1			BE				
2		BE			VO		
3		BE		CL		VO	
4	BK		BE	CL		VO	
5	BK		BE	CL	VI	VO	
6	BK	BE	EE	CL	VI	VO	
7	BK	BE	EE	CL	VI	VO	NC
8	BK	–	BE	EE	CL	VI	VO	NC

Queue management. The switch supporting QoS uses several queues for differentiated processing of traffic classes. The queues can be served according to the priority queuing or weighted queuing algorithms or on the basis of their combination.

Usually, the switch supports some maximum number of queues, which may be smaller than the required number of traffic classes. In this situation, several classes will be served by the same queue, which means they will be merged into the same class. The 802.1D-1998 standard gives the following recommendations in relation to the traffic classes that need to be implemented in the network under a limited number of switch queues (Table. 16.2).

When only one queue is available, then only one traffic class can exist in the network, namely, BE. It's QoS cannot be improved by queue management, although such capabilities as feedback and bandwidth reservation still remain available.

Two queues allow the traffic to be divided into two classes, BE and VO. Under such conditions, all delay-sensitive traffic should be classified as VO, not only voice but also video and network management traffic.

More queue numbers allow more differentiated traffic serving, increasing the number of classes to the recommended value of eight.

The suggested method is only a recommendation, and network administrators are free to classify traffic according to their needs.

Furthermore, serving individual traffic flows is also possible. However, in this case, every switch must independently separate individual flows from the aggregate traffic, since the Ethernet frame has no dedicated field for carrying a flow label across the network.

A VLAN number can also be used as an attribute of the traffic class. This attribute can be combined with the values of the frame priority field, which would allow the administrator to produce a large number of various traffic classes.

Reservation and policing. LAN switches support the methods of reserving the interface bandwidth for traffic classes or individual flows. Usually, the switch allows the administrator to assign the class or flow some minimum information rate, which is guaranteed for the periods of congestion, and the maximum information rate, which is controlled by the policing mechanisms.

For LAN switches, there is no standard resource reservation protocol. Therefore, to carry out such reservations, the network administrator has to individually configure each network switch.

16.6 LIMITATIONS OF BRIDGES AND SWITCHES

KEY WORDS: VLAN, repeater, bridge, switch, loop-free, traffic filtering, addressing, heterogeneous network, performance, reliability

The use of switches allows an administrator to overcome limitations typical for networks based on a shared medium. Switched networks can span significant territories, smoothly turning into MANs. They also can comprise segments with different bandwidths, thus forming networks of very high performance. Finally, they can use alternative routes for improving performance and reliability.

However, building complicated networks based only on repeaters, bridges, and switches (e.g., without using network-layer devices) has significant limitations and drawbacks.

- First, switched LAN topology still has rather considerable limitations. The use of the STA technique and link aggregation eliminate the limitations imposed by the requirement prescribing that the network must be only partially *loop-free*. STA does not allow all alternative routes to be used for transmitting user traffic, and link aggregation allows this only on the network sections between two neighboring switches. Such limitations do not allow many efficient topologies, which potentially could be used for traffic transmission.

- Second, logical segments of the network located between switches are *weakly isolated* from one another, which means that they lack protection against broadcast storms. Although most switches implement the VLAN mechanism allowing flexibility in creating isolated groups of workstations that do not share traffic, this solution is not free from drawbacks. The VLAN mechanism isolates individual VLANs so that nodes of one VLAN cannot talk to nodes from another VLAN.

- Third, the *problem of traffic filtering* on the basis of data values contained in the packet has no simple solution in networks created on the basis of bridges and switches. In such networks, this task can be accomplished only by implementing user-defined filters. To create user-defined filters, an administrator has to deal with binary representation of the packet contents.

- Fourth, implementation of the transport subsystem using only physical and data link-layer tools supported by switches results in an *insufficiently flexible flat addressing* system: A MAC address hard-encoded into the network adapter is used as the destination address.

- Finally, switches have *limited capabilities of protocol translation* when creating heterogeneous networks. For instance, switches cannot translate WAN protocols to LAN protocols because of the differences in the addressing systems of these networks and the different values of the maximum size of the data field.

The presence of serious limitations in the data link-layer protocols shows that building large, heterogeneous networks on the basis of the data link-layer tools is rather problematic. The natural solution for these cases is using the tools of the higher, network layer.

16.7 CASE STUDY

In *Chapter 12* we have considered the structure of the LAN built on the basis of 10 Mbps Ethernet repeaters built for internal needs of the Transmash engineering plant. That example corresponded to the situation that was typical for early 1990s, when a single 10 Mbps shared medium fully satisfied the enterprise needs, allowing traffic exchange between computers of the enterprise's departments, which were few in number. Here we will consider an upgraded version of the LAN of this engineering plant, which became typical for most large enterprise networks in late 1990s.

The main feature of this network is that the entire LAN is built on switches (Figure 16.15). Migration to a switched network design was due to the increased requirements to the LAN performance and reliability. By that time, computer data processing became vitally important for the production process. Consequently, the number of computers has sharply increased, and newer applications were introduced, which became able to exchange large volumes of multimedia information.

The foundation of the LAN of any of the five buildings is now formed by a powerful central switch on the basis of chassis, equipped with Fast Ethernet and Gigabit Ethernet ports (switches BS1 — BS5). Building switch connects floor switches, connected to it using trunks combining two or three Fast Ethernet ports. Every floor switch is used for connecting end-user equipment of two types: PCs and various technological equipment (in more details these connections are shown on the example of the building 2 LAN).

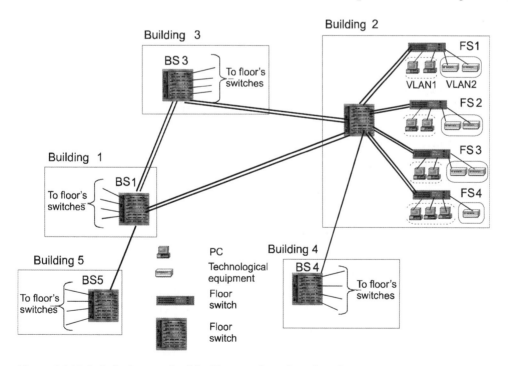

Figure 16.15 Switched network of the Transmash engineering plant

PC users work with applications that form the automated enterprise resource planning system (ERP), and technological equipment works with applications that form the automated computer-aided manufacturing (CAM) system.

Central switches of buildings 2, 3 and 4 form the backbone of the enterprise LAN. They are connected by two-port Gigabit Ethernet trunks, which ensures considerable performance reserve. Buildings 5 and 4 are connected to the backbone using normal Gigabit Ethernet connections (without using trunks). For connecting the switches of these buildings multimode optical fiber is used, which was installed for the repeater-based LAN, because its quality was satisfactory for ensuring stable operation of the 1000Base-SX ports.

Transmash network transmits two types of traffic: from ERP application and from CAM applications. These classes of traffic differ by their QoS requirements. For example, CAM traffic is the real-time traffic, while ERP traffic is not. Therefore, two VLANs are organized, in the Transmash network — VLAN1 for ERP traffic, and VLAN2 — for CAM traffic. This allows for reliable isolation of each traffic type, and additionally simplifies QoS support by switches, since VLAN number (in this case — 2) indicates that the traffic must be processed in priority queue.

Because LAN backbone has redundant links, switches use STA, individually for each VLAN. For VLAN1 the link between BS4 and BS2 switches is the reserve link, and VLAN2 this is the link between BS4 and BS3 switches. Data exchange between ERP and CAM is achieved, because several servers are members of both VLANs.

SUMMARY

▶ For automatic support of reserved links in complex networks, switches implement the spanning tree algorithm (STA). This algorithm is described in the IEEE 802.1D standard. STA is based on periodical exchange by special frames between switches. Using these frames, switches find and block closed loops that may exist in the network.

▶ The STA protocol finds the spanning tree configuration by accomplishing a three-stage procedure. At the first stage, the root switch is determined; at the second stage, root ports are found; and at the third stage, designated ports of the segments are chosen.

▶ The main drawback of the STA 802.1D protocol is the relatively long time required to establish a new active configuration — about 50 seconds. The newer 802.1w standard corrects this drawback.

▶ Aggregation of several physical links into a logical channel is one form of using several alternative routes in LANs built on the basis of switches.

▶ Link aggregation improves both reliability and performance of the network.

▶ An aggregate channel not only can be created between two neighboring switches but also can be distributed among the ports of several switches. For automatic notification that a specific physical port belongs to an aggregate port, a special protocol was developed, known as the link control aggregation protocol.

▶ The technology of virtual LANs (VLANs) allows the creation of isolated groups of end nodes within a network built on the basis of switches. No traffic, including broadcast traffic, exists among these isolated groups.

▶ VLAN configuration is usually carried out by port grouping. To build a VLAN based on several switches, it is desirable to label the transmitted frames with a special tag identifying the number of the network to which the sender of this frame belongs.

▶ A standard format of the VLAN tag is defined in the 802.1Q specification.

▶ LAN switches support all types of QoS mechanisms: traffic classification and policing, priority and weighted queues, and bandwidth reservation.

REVIEW QUESTIONS

1. What is the goal of STA?
2. Provide a definition of the spanning tree.
3. Which port of the switch is called the root port?
4. The designated port is the one defined as follows:
   A. The port that becomes the root port at discretion of the network administrator
   B. The port whose distance to the root switch has the minimum value for a specific segment
   C. The port switched to the blocked state
5. How is the distance between switches measured in STA?
6. List the three stages of the process of building an active spanning tree topology.
7. How is the root port chosen from several candidates for this role if their distances from the root switch are equal?
8. Is it possible for a network administrator to influence the choice of the root switch?
9. How do switches decide that selection of the active topology has been accomplished?
10. What triggers the switch to search for a new active topology?
11. What is the main drawback of STA?
12. Link aggregation:
    A. Improves network performance
    B. Improves network reliability
    C. Ensures both properties

13. In what cases is it more efficient to employ link aggregation rather than to migrate to the faster version of the Ethernet technology?

14. How do STA and link aggregation interact?

15. What are the limitations of the link aggregation techniques?

16. What is the difference between a unidirectional and a bidirectional trunk?

17. What considerations are taken into account when choosing the trunk port for frame transmission?

18. Why is it necessary to take into account that frames belong to the same session when using aggregate links?

19. Why can VLAN be called a broadcast domain?

20. How is it possible to join several VLANs?

21. List the main methods of creating VLANs.

22. Why is port grouping inefficient in networks based on several switches?

23. Which approach to solving the problem of building VLANs on the basis of several switches is chosen in the IEEE 802.1Q standard?

24. Is it possible to use port grouping and the IEEE 802.1Q standard together?

25. Is it necessary for STA to take into account VLAN presence within the network?

26. Which QoS mechanisms are supported by LAN switches?

27. What is the number of traffic classes recommended by the IEEE 802.1D-1998 standard?

28. What should you do if network switches support a smaller number of queues than the number of traffic classes?

29. List the limitations of networks built on the basis of switches.

PART IV

TCP/IP INTERNET-WORKING

Having studied most of materials presented in this book, recall what you have studied in the first three parts and consider what you will learn in the remaining three parts. In *Part I*, most problems described in this book were covered at the conceptual level. This is probably the most complicated and important part of the book. After all, quality of knowledge and level of professional skill strongly depend on the foundation upon which these are based. We have many times referred to the materials of *Part I* and will continue to do so.

Parts II and *III* are dedicated to specific technologies of transmitting data at physical and data link layers, respectively. Abstract network models in the form of a graph or a "cloud," in which computers "float," are rarely encountered in these parts. On the contrary, specific protocols, frame formats, and network equipment came into the foreground.

What topics will be covered in the next, fourth part of the book? According to the logic implied by the OSI model, the parts considering technologies of the physical and data link layers must be followed by a part considering the network-layer tools. These tools ensure the possibility of interconnecting a large number of networks into a larger internet. Since IP is an indisputable leader among all network-layer protocols, we consider all aspects of internetworking on the example of this protocol. However, because of the close relationships among IP and the other protocols of the TCP/IP stack, we try to provide a broad pattern of their interaction.

Note that in previous chapters, we mentioned and even explained various aspects directly related to the topic of TCP/IP internetworking. In *Chapter 2*, we considered the basic ideas and principles of routing. The concept of internetworking was introduced in *Chapter 4* with information about the network layer of the OSI model. According to the definition provided there, the network general is a combination of several networks and is called an *internetwork* or *internet*. Networks that make up an internetwork are called subnets, constituent networks, or simply networks. Subnets are interconnected by the routers. Components of the internet might be both LANs and WANs. All nodes within each constituent network communicate using some common technology, such as Ethernet, Token Ring, FDDI, Frame Relay, or X.25. However, none of these technologies are capable of creating an information link between two arbitrarily chosen nodes belonging to different networks. This task, namely, the organization of interaction between two arbitrary nodes in an internet, is solved by the protocols of the TCP/IP stack. In *Chapter 5*, we provided a description of the structure of the Internet, the largest network built on the basis of the TCP/IP technology. You are strongly recommended to review this material.

In the last part of the book, which covers various WAN technologies, we return to TCP/IP. We consider specific features of IP over ATM/FR, as well as the multiprotocol label-switching technology closely related to IP. Also covered are a simple network management protocol and a secure version of IP — IPSec.

Part IV comprises the following chapters:

- Chapter 17: Addressing in TCP/IP Networks
- Chapter 18: Internet Protocol
- Chapter 19: Core Protocols of the TCP/IP Stack
- Chapter 20: Advanced Features of IP Routers

17

ADDRESSING IN TCP/IP NETWORKS

17.1 INTRODUCTION

TCP/IP technology is aimed at solving the following addressing problems:

- *Coordinating the use of different types of addresses.* This includes mapping addresses of different types, for example, translating a network IP address into a local address or mapping a domain name to a specific IP address.
- *Ensuring address uniqueness.* Depending on the address type, it is necessary to ensure uniqueness of addressing within the limits of specific computer, subnet, internet, enterprise-wide network, or the Internet.
- *Configuring network interfaces and network applications.*

Each of these problems has quite a simple solution for networks with only tens of nodes. For example, to map a symbolic domain name to a specific IP address, it is sufficient to support on each host a table of all symbolic names used within the network and their mappings to IP addresses. Manual assignment of unique addresses to all interfaces within a small network also is not a difficult task. However, in large-scale networks, these tasks become so complicated that they require principally different solutions.

Scalability becomes a keyword that characterizes the approach to solving these problems.

Procedures provided by TCP/IP for assigning, mapping, and configuring addresses work equally well in networks of various scales. In this chapter, in addition to the options for IP addressing, we cover the most popular scalable tools for ensuring addressing support in TCP/IP networks: classless interdomain routing (CIDR), domain name system (DNS), and dynamic host configuration protocol (DHCP).

17.2 ADDRESS TYPES OF THE TCP/IP STACK

KEY WORDS: Local/hardware addresses, MAC addresses, network/IP addresses, symbolic addresses /domain names, network number, Address Resolution Protocol (ARP), Domain Name System (DNS)

For identifying network interfaces, the following three types of addresses are used in TCP/IP networks:

❏ Local (hardware) addresses
❏ Network (IP) addresses
❏ Symbolic addresses (domain names)

17.2.1 Local Addresses

Most LAN technologies, such as Ethernet, FDDI, and Token Ring, use **MAC addresses** for identifying interfaces. There are also lots of other technologies (for instance, X.25, ATM, and Frame Relay) that use different addressing systems. These systems also allow the unique identification of network interfaces within the limits of each network built on the basis of respective technology. Being autonomous, such a network uses the addressing system exclusively for an internal purpose — ensuring the connectivity of its own nodes. However, as soon as a specific network is connected to other networks, the functionality of these addresses is extended. They become a mandatory element of the higher-layer internetworking technology — in this case, the TCP/IP technology. The role played by these addresses in TCP/IP does not depend on the specific networking technology used in the constituent network. Therefore, these addresses have the common name of **local (hardware) addresses**.

ATTENTION *The definitions used here — local and hardware — can be interpreted ambiguously. The term local in the context of TCP/IP means that the address is in force within the constituent network but not within the limits of the entire internet. This is the sense in which it is necessary to interpret the following terms: local technology (the technology on the basis of which the constituent network is built) and local address (the address used by the local technology for node addressing within the constituent network). Recall that the constituent (local) network might be built on the basis of both a WAN technology (X.25, Frame Relay, etc.) and a LAN technology (Ethernet, FDDI, etc.). The word local is also used in LAN — local area network. However it has a different meaning there, characterizing specific features of the technology that limit the network to small distances.*

There also might be difficulties with interpreting the term hardware in the context of internetworking. In this case, the term emphasizes that developers of the TCP/IP stack interpreted a constituent network as an auxiliary hardware tool, the only goal of which is delivering IP packets using the constituent network to the nearest router. The underlying network technology might be complicated, but this is of little importance since TCP/IP technology is removed from these details.

For example, consider a situation in which a TCP/IP internet includes a constituent IPX/SPX network. The latter might be split into subnets. Similar to the IP network, it also identifies its nodes with hardware addresses and IPX network addresses. However, TCP/IP ignores the multilayer hierarchy of the IPX/SPX network and considers it, like the Ethernet network, a normal constituent network. Accordingly, the TCP/IP technology considers IPX the network addresses of the IPX/SPX network as local addresses. Similarly, if the constituent network is built on the X.25 technology, then X.25 addresses will be considered by the IP technology as local addresses.

17.2.2 IP Network Addresses

To carry out its task of interconnecting networks, the TCP/IP technology needs to have its own *global addressing system that does not depend on the methods of node addressing in constituent networks.* This addressing system must provide a universal method of uniquely identifying each interface of the internetwork.

A natural method of forming network addresses is uniquely identifying all constituent networks and numbering the nodes within the limits of each network. Thus, a **network address** is a pair of numbers: a **network number** and a **node number**.

As a node number, the following numbers might be used: the local address of that node (such a method is adopted in the IPX/SPX stack) or some number that uniquely identifies the node within the subnet but is not related to the local technology.

In the first case, the network address becomes dependent on local technologies, which limits its area of application. For instance, IPX/SPX network addresses are intended for use in the internets connecting networks that use only MAC addresses or addresses of a similar format. The second approach is more universal. It is characteristic for the TCP/IP stack.

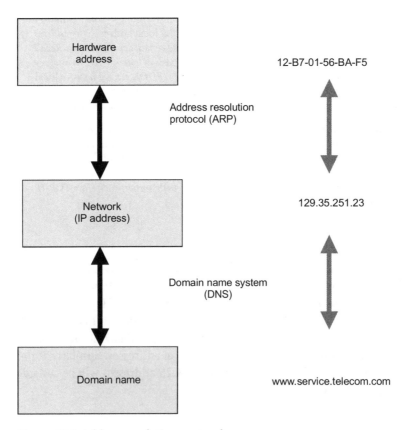

Figure 17.1 Address resolution protocol

In the TCP/IP technology, network address is called **IP address**.

ATTENTION *Consider an IP network. The router, by definition, participates in several networks. Therefore, each of its interfaces has its own IP address. End node also can participate in several IP networks. In this case, the computer must have enough IP addresses for the number of network links. Thus,* an IP address identifies a network link rather than a specific computer or router.

When the packet is sent to the receiver through the internet, its header must contain the IP address of the destination node. Each router finds the IP address of the next router by the number of the destination network. Before sending the packet to the next network, the router, based on the IP address of the next router, must determine its local address. For this purpose, IP uses the *address resolution protocol* (ARP), as shown in Figure 17.1.

17.2.3 Domain Names

The hardware and software of TCP/IP networks relies on IP addresses for identifying computers. For example, the **ftp://192.45.66.17** command will establish the session with the required ftp server, and the **http://203.23.106.33** command will open a home page on the corporate Web server. However, most users prefer to deal with the symbolic names of computers. Consequently, TCP/IP networks must implement symbolic names for hosts and a mechanism for mapping symbolic names to IP addresses.

Symbolic identifiers of network interfaces within the limits of the internet are built according to the hierarchical principle. The components of the fully qualified symbolic, or domain, name in IP networks are delimited by decimal points and listed in the following order: the name of the individual host, the name of the specific group of hosts (the organization name, for instance), the name of a larger group (domain), and so on, to the name of the highest-level domain, such as the one that groups organizations according to their geographical location: **us** — United States, **ru** — Russia, and **uk** — Great Britain (or United Kingdom). A domain name might look as follows: **server2.janet.ac.uk**.

There is no functional dependence between the domain name and the IP address of a host. Therefore, the only method of mapping symbolic names to IP addresses uses tables. TCP/IP networks use a special distributed service, Domain Name System (DNS), which establishes this mapping according to the mapping tables created by network administrators. Because of this, domain names are often called **DNS names**.

In general, a network interface can simultaneously have one or more local addresses, one or more network addresses, and one or more domain names.

17.3 IP ADDRESS FORMAT

KEY WORDS: IP Address format, mask, IP address classes, class A, class B, class C, class D, Class E, unicast, multicast, broadcast, limited broadcast, undefined address, loopback

The header of the IP packet has two fields for storing the sender and the receiver IP addresses. Each field has a fixed length of 4 bytes (32 bits). The IP address is a combination of two logical components — the network number and the host number within that network.

The most popular form of writing IP addresses is notation in the form of four numbers, representing the value of each byte in decimal notation and delimited by points. A typical IP address written in this dotted notation looks as follows:

```
128.10.2.30
```

The same address can be represented in the binary format:

```
10000000 00001010 00000010 00011110
```

It is also possible to show the IP address in the hexadecimal format:

```
80.0A.02.1D
```

Note that the address format does not provide special demarcation between network number and host number. However, when transmitting the packet through the network, it is often necessary to divide the address into these two parts. For instance, routing, as a rule, is carried out on the basis of the network number. Therefore, each router, having received the packet, must read an appropriate field of the packet header to find the destination host address and then locate the network number in this address. How can routers determine which part of the 32 bits allocated for storing IP address relates to the network number and which part of it relates to the host number?

Several solutions to this problem can be suggested.

■ The simplest one consists in using the **fixed boundary**. In this case, the entire 32-bit field of the address is divided into two parts beforehand. These parts must have fixed, but not necessarily equal, lengths. One part must always contain the network number the other part is allocated for storing the host number. This solution is very simple. However, is it good enough? Not quite. Since the field allocated for storing the host number has a fixed length, all networks will have the same maximum number of nodes. For instance, suppose that you have allocated only the first byte for storing the network number. In this case, the entire address space will be split into a relatively small number (2^8) of large networks (each containing up to 2^{24} hosts). If you move this boundary to the right, you will have more networks, but they all will be the same size. Obviously, such a rigid approach doesn't provide the means of differentiating the needs of individual organizations. For this reason, this method of address structuring did not find a wide application, although it was used at the initial stage of TCP/IP evolution as defined in RFC 760.

■ The second approach (RFC 950 and RFC 1518) is based on using a **mask**, which provides maximum flexibility when establishing the boundary between the network number and the host number. When using this approach, the entire address space can be represented as a set of networks of various sizes.

> The mask represents the number used with the IP address. Binary representation of the mask contains a sequence of binary ones in those positions of the IP address that must be interpreted as the network number. The boundary between the sequence of ones and the sequence of zeros in the mask corresponds to the boundary between the network number and the host number in the IP address.

■ Finally, the third approach, which was the most popular one until recently, uses **IP address classes** as defined in RFC 791. This method is a compromise between the two previously described approaches: Although network sizes are not arbitrary, as was the case when using masks, they also are not fixed, as was the case when establishing fixed boundaries. Five classes of addresses are defined, three of which are used for network addressing; the remaining two, as will be shown later, are reserved for special purposes.

17.3.1 Classes of IP Addresses

The values of several starting bits of the address serve as the criteria on the basis of which IP addresses are classified. Table 17.1 outlines the IP address structure for different address classes.

Table 17.1 Classes of IP addresses

Class	First bits	Smallest network number	Largest network number	Number of nodes
A	0	1.0.0.0 (0 – not used)	126.0.0.0 (127 – reserved)	2^{24} (3 bytes)
B	10	128.0.0.0	191.255.0.0	2^{16} (2 bytes)
C	110	192.0.0.0	223.255.255.0	2^8 (1 byte)
D	1110	224.0.0.0	239.255.255.255	Multicast addresses
E	11110	240.0.0.0	247.255.255.255	Reserved

- **Class A** includes addresses in which the most significant bit has the value **0**. In Class A networks, 1 byte is allocated for the network address, and the remaining 3 bytes are interpreted as the host number within the network. Networks in which all IP addresses have a value of the first byte ranging from 1 (**0**0000001) to 126 (**0**1111110) are known as Class A networks. Network 0 (**0**0000000) is not used, and network number 127 (**0**1111111) is reserved for special purposes, which will be covered in detail later in this chapter. Class A networks are not numerous. However, the number of hosts in such networks can reach 2^{24} (i.e., 16,777,216).

- **Class B** includes all addresses in which the two most significant bits are set to the value **10**. In Class B, addresses of 2 bytes are allocated for storing the network number and the host number. Networks in which the values of the first 2 bytes of addresses belong to the range from 128.0. (**10**000000 00000000) to 191.255 (**10**111111 11111111), are known as Class B networks. Naturally, Class B networks are more numerous than Class A networks, but their sizes are smaller. The maximum number of nodes in a Class B network is 2^{16} (i.e., 65,536).

- **Class C** includes all addresses in which the three most significant bits are set to **110**. In Class C networks, 3 bytes are allocated for the network number, and 1 byte is for the host number. Networks in which the three most significant bytes of an IP address belong to the range from 192.0.0 (**110**00000 00000000 00000000) to 223.255.255 (**110**11111 11111111 11111111) are known as Class C networks. Class C networks are the most widespread, but the number of hosts in such networks is limited to 2^8 (256).

- If an IP address starts with the sequence **1110**, it belongs to **Class D** and is a specific *group address.* In contrast to the addresses of Classes A, B, and C, which are used for identifying specific network interfaces (e.g., **unicast** addresses), a group address is known as a **multicast address**. Group addresses identify groups of network interfaces, which generally belong to different networks. The interface included in a group, besides the individual IP address, is assigned a group address. If a Class D address is specified as the destination address when sending a packet, such a packet must be delivered to all hosts included in that group.

- If an address starts with the **11110** sequence, it is a **Class E** address. Addresses of this class are reserved for future use.

NOTE   *To obtain the network number and the host number from the IP address, it is necessary to divide the address into two appropriate parts and then complement each part with zeros to the full 4 bytes. For instance, suppose that you have the following Class B address: 129.64.134.5. The first 2 bytes identify the network; the next 2 bytes specify the host number. Thus, you have a network number of 129.64.0.0 and a host number of 0.0.134.5.*

17.3.2 Special IP Addresses

TCP/IP has a limitation to assigning IP addresses, namely, that network numbers and host numbers *cannot consist only of binary ones or only of binary zeros*. Hence, the maximum number of hosts provided in Table 17.1 for networks of each class must be decreased by 2. For instance, in Class C addresses, 8 bits are allocated for storing the host number. This allows 256 numbers to be specified: from 0 to 255. In reality, the maximum number of hosts in Class C networks cannot exceed 254, since host numbers 0 and 255 are not allowed for assignment to network interfaces. Under the same considerations, an end node cannot have an IP address such as 98.255.255.255, because in this Class A address, the host number (0.255.255.255) comprises binary ones only.

Thus, some IP addresses placed into the header of an IP packet are interpreted in a specific way:

■ If the IP address entirely consists of binary zeros, it is called an **undefined address** and specifies the address of the host that generated this packet. In special cases, an address of this type is placed into the header of IP packet in the field of the source address.

■ If the network number field is entirely filled with zeros, by default the destination host belongs to the same network as the host that sent the packet. Such an address also can be used only as the source address.

■ If all positions of the IP address are filled with ones, the packet with such a destination address must be sent to all hosts located in the same network as the source of this packet. This type of delivery is known as **limited broadcast**. The limitation in this case means that the packet will never leave this network.

■ If all positions corresponding to the host number of the destination host are filled with ones, the packet with such an address is sent to **all** hosts of the network, the number of which is specified in the destination address. For instance, the packet containing the 192.190.21.255 address in the destination host field will be sent to all hosts belonging to the 192.190.21.0 network. This type of delivery is known as **broadcast**.

ATTENTION   *IP does not introduce the broadcast concept in the sense in which it is normally used in data link-layer LAN protocols, where the data must be delivered to all hosts without exceptions. Both IP limited broadcasts and IP broadcasts have propagation restrictions within internetworks. They are limited either by the boundaries of the network to which the source host belongs or by the network whose address is specified in the destination address. Therefore, network division using routers localizes broadcast storms within the limits of one of subnetwork simply because there is no method of addressing the packet to all hosts of the internetwork simultaneously.*

In IP addresses, the first octet of which is set to 127, have a special meaning. This address is an internal address of the computer or router protocol stack. It is used for testing programs and for organizing the operation of client and server components of the same application installed on the same computer. Both components of the client–server application are designed with the expectation that they will exchange messages using the network. However, when they are installed on the same computer, which IP address should they use for this purpose? It is possible to use the address of the network interface of the host where both components are installed. However, in this case, redundant packets will inevitably be transmitted into the network; therefore, this solution is inefficient. Using the 127.0.0.0 internal address is a more efficient and economic solution. As you may recall, IP addresses starting with 127 are not allowed to be assigned to network interfaces. When a program sends data to an IP address such as 127.x.x.x, this data will not be transmitted into the network. Instead of this, such packets are returned to the upper-layer protocol entities of the same computer as data just received from the network. The route of such data makes a loop; therefore, this address is called **loopback**.

Multicast addresses belonging to Class D are intended for economic distribution of audio and video programs to a large audience over the Internet or a enterprise-wide network. If a multicast address is placed in the destination address field of the IP packet, such a packet must be delivered to several nodes that form the group with the number specified in the address field. The same host can belong to several groups. Members of a specific multicast group must not necessarily belong to the same network. In general, they can be distributed over different networks located any distance from one another. Multicast addresses are not divided into network numbers and host numbers. Routers process such addresses in a specific way.

> The main goal of multicast addresses is the distribution of information in a "one-to-many" arrangement. For the moment, multicast addresses are used only within small, experimental segments within the Internet, comparable to islands in the ocean. Whether or not the Internet will become a serious competitor to radio and TV broadcasting companies depends on whether or not such multicast addresses become popular.

17.3.3 Using Masks in IP Addressing

Supplying each IP address with a mask allows abandoning the concept of address classes. This makes the addressing system more flexible.

As you recall, for standard network classes, network masks have the following values:

Class A	11111111. 00000000. 00000000. 00000000	(255.0.0.0)
Class B	11111111. 11111111. 00000000. 00000000	(255.255.0.0)
Class C	11111111. 11111111. 11111111. 00000000	(255.255.255.0)

The main idea of this approach is using masks, where the number of binary ones in the sequence determining the boundary of the network number must not necessarily be a multiple of eight (in which case, addresses are split into bytes), as was the case with standard network masks. For example, if you associate the 185.23.44.206 address with the 255.255.255.0 mask, then the network number will be set to 185.23.44.0 rather than to 185.23.0.0, as was defined by the system of classes.

Consider another example. Suppose that the 255.255.128.0 mask is specified for the IP address set to 129.64.134.5. In binary format, this would mean the following:

| IP address | 129.64.134.5 | 10000001. 01000000. 10000110. 00000101 |
| Mask | 255.255.128.0 | 11111111. 11111111. 10000000. 00000000 |

If you ignore the mask and interpret the address 129.64.134.5 on the basis of address classes, then 129.64.0.0 is the network number, and 0.0.134.5 is the host number, since this address belongs to Class B.

If you use the mask, then the sequence of 17 consecutive binary ones in the 255.255.128.0 mask, being "applied" to this IP address, would divide it into the following two parts:

		Network number	**Host number**
IP address	129.64.134.5	10000001. 01000000. 1	0000110. 00000101
Mask	255.255.128.0	11111111. 11111111. 1	0000000. 00000000

In decimal notation, the network number and host numbers supplemented by zeros to 32 bits will be 129.64.128.0 and 0.0.6.5, respectively.

Applying a mask can be interpreted as carrying out a logical AND operation.

For instance, in this example, the network number obtained from the 129.64.134.5 IP address is the result of a logical AND operation with the mask 255.255.128.0:

(10000001 01000000 10000110 00000101) AND (11111111. 11111111. 10000000. 00000000)

NOTE   *Other formats can be used for masks. For instance, it is convenient to interpret mask values in hex codes: FF.FF.00.00 is the mask for Class B networks. Another form of notation is encountered frequently: 185.23.44.206/16 means that the mask for this address contains 16 ones — that is, in this IP address, 16 bits are allocated for the network number.*

The mechanism of masks is widely used in IP routing. In routing, masks can be used for various purposes. For instance, a network administrator can use them to split a single network of a specific class, which was allocated to the company by its Internet service provider (ISP), into several subnets without additional network numbers from the ISP.

This operation is known as **subnetting**. Based on the same mechanism, ISPs can join the address spaces of several networks by introducing so-called prefixes to reduce the size of routing tables and improve the performance of network routing. This operation is called **supernetting**. We cover it in more detail later in this chapter, when describing the CIDR technology.

17.4 IP ADDRESS ASSIGNMENT ORDER

> **KEY WORDS:** private addresses, Internet Corporation for Assigned Names and Numbers (ICANN), prefix, address collisions, address space, address shortage, CIDR, NAT

According to its definition, the method of IP addressing must ensure the uniqueness of network numbering as well as the uniqueness of host numbering within the limits of each network. Consequently, the procedures of assigning numbers both to networks and to hosts must be **centralized**. The recommended order of assigning IP addresses is described in RFC 2050.

17.4.1 Address Assignment in an Autonomous Network

When it comes to a network that is part of the Internet, the uniqueness of numbering can be ensured only by the coordinated efforts of centralized authorities created specially for this purpose. As relates to a standalone, autonomous IP network, ensuring the uniqueness of network and host numbers can be achieved by the network administrator.

In this case, the network administrator has the entire address space at his disposal, because matching IP addresses in networks that are not connected would not produce negative effects. The administrator can choose addresses arbitrarily because it is sufficient to ensure that the assigned addresses have the correct syntax and to guarantee that they satisfy the previously listed limitations (network and host numbers cannot be composed only of zeros or only of ones). By the way, the host number in the TCP/IP technology is assigned independently of its local address.

However, if this approach is used, it would be impossible to connect such a network to the Internet in the future. Arbitrarily chosen addresses might match centrally assigned Internet addresses. To avoid address conflicts caused by such matches,

Internet standards have defined several **private addresses** recommended for autonomous use.

- In Class A — the network number 10.0.0.0
- In Class B — a range of 16 network numbers: 172.16.0.0 — 172.31.0.0
- In Class C — a range of 255 network numbers: 192.168.0.0 — 192.168.255.0

These addresses are excluded from the set of centrally distributed addresses. They make up a vast address space sufficient for numbering the hosts of networks of practically any size. Autonomous networks can use addresses from these ranges. Note that private addresses in different autonomous networks can coincide. At the same time, using private addresses for autonomous networks makes it possible to correctly connect them to the Internet. Special technologies[1] used for this purpose eliminate address collisions.

17.4.2 Centralized Address Assignment

In large networks similar to the Internet, the uniqueness of network addresses is ensured by a centralized, hierarchically organized system of address distribution. A network number can be assigned only on the recommendation of a specialized Internet authority. Since 1998, the main authority responsible for the registration of global Internet addresses is the **Internet Corporation for Assigned Names and Numbers (ICANN)**. This is a noncommercial nongovernmental, organization managed by a board of directors. This organization controls the operation of regional departments whose activities span vast geographical regions: ARIN (Americas), RIPE (Europe), and APNIC (Asia–Pacific). Regional departments allocate address blocks to large ISPs, which, in turn, assign them to their clients, among which there might be smaller ISPs.

A shortage of IP addresses is the main problem of their centralized distribution. For quite a long time, it became comparatively difficult to get a Class B address, and it is practically impossible to become an owner of a Class A address. This shortage is not only because of network growth but also because of inefficient use of the available address space. Quite often, the owners of Class C networks use only a small part of the 254 addresses available to them. For instance, consider an example in which it is necessary to connect two networks by a WAN link. In such cases, two routers connected according to the "point-to-point" design are used (Figure 17.2). For a degenerate network created by the link connecting the ports of two adjacent routers, it is necessary to allocate an individual network number, although there are only two nodes in such a network.

To mitigate the problem of address shortage, the developers of the TCP/IP stack suggest several approaches. The principally innovative and radical solution is migration to

---

[1] The network address translation technology considered in *Chapter 20* is an example of such a technology.

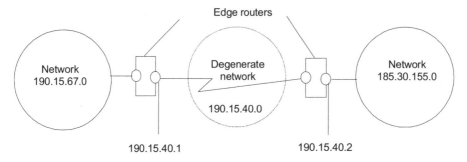

Figure 17.2 Inefficient use of the IP address space

a new IP version, IPv6, in which the available address space is sharply increased by using 16-byte addresses. Nevertheless, even the current IP version, IPv4, supports some technologies aimed at ensuring more efficient usage of IP addresses. Examples of such technologies are NAT and CIDR.

17.4.3 Addressing and CIDR

CIDR, officially introduced in 1993 and standardized in RFC 1517, RFC 1518, RFC 1519, and RFC 1520, allows address distribution centers to assign a certain number of addresses to their subscribers as needed.

In the CIDR technology, an IP address is divided into a network number and a host number on the basis of a variable-length mask rather than on the basis of one or more most significant bits, as it was before. This variable-length mask is assigned to the subscriber by the service provider. To apply CIDR, the organization managing the addresses must have continuous address ranges. Such addresses have the same **prefix** (i.e., the same values of the several most significant bits). Assume that some service provider has a continuous IP address space of 2^n (Figure 17.3). Hence, the prefix length is equal to $(32 - n)$ bits. The remaining n bits play the role of the counter of the sequential number.

When the client asks a service provider to allocate a specific range of addresses, the service provider "cuts out" the continuous range S1, S2, or S3, depending on the required number of addresses. At the same time, the following requirements must be satisfied:

■ The number of addresses in the allocated area must equal a power of two.
■ The initial boundary of the allocated address pool must be a multiple of the required number of hosts.

The prefix of each area shown in Figure 17.3 has its own length — the smaller the number of addresses in the given area, the longer its prefix.

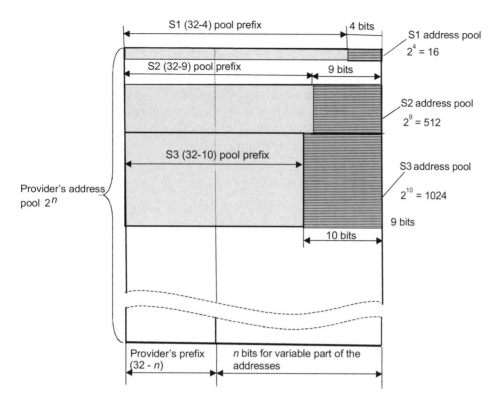

Figure 17.3 Address distribution on the basis of the CIDR technology

EXAMPLE   *Suppose that the ISP has a pool of addresses ranging from 193.20.0.0 to193.23.255.255 (1100 0001.0001 0100.0000 0000.0000 0000 — 1100 0001.0001 0111.1111 1111.1111 1111). This means that the number of addresses at the disposal of this ISP is 2^{18}. Accordingly, ISP's prefix has the length of 14 bits — 1100 0001.0001 01 or, in another form, 193.20/14.*

If a subscriber of this ISP needs a small number of addresses — say, 13 — then the ISP can offer this subscriber several variants: the 193.20.30.0/28 network, the 193.20.30.16/28 network, or the 193.21.204.48/28 network. In any case, the subscriber has the four least significant bits at his disposal for numbering network hosts. Thus, the number of nodes allocated to the subscriber is expressed by the minimum number satisfying the subscriber's requirements (13), which can be represented by a power of two ($2^4 = 16$). The prefix for each allocated pool in all these cases plays the role of the network number; it has a length of 32 − 4 = 28 bits.

Now, consider another variant in which a large corporate customer requested service from the ISP. This customer probably is planning to provide Internet access services itself. Suppose that this customer requires an address block for 4,000 hosts. For the numbering of such a large number of hosts, 12 bits will be required. This means that the size of the allocated address pool will be somewhat larger than required, namely, it will be 4,096. The boundary from which the allocated pool must start must be a multiple of the pool size; these might be any addresses such as 193.20.0.0, 193.20.16.0, 193.20.32.0, 193.20.48.0, or other numbers terminated by 12 zeros. Suppose that the ISP has offered this customer the 193.20.16.0 — 193.20.31.255 address range. For this range, the aggregate network number (prefix) has a length of 20 bits and is equal to 193.20.16.0/20.

Thanks to CIDR, the ISP has the possibility of "slicing" blocks out of the address space allocated to it according to the needs and requirements of each client.

In *Chapter 18*, we return to the CIDR technology to explain how it helps not only to sparingly use addresses but also to improve routing efficiency.

17.5 MAPPING IP ADDRESSES TO LOCAL ADDRESSES

KEY WORDS: broadcasting, IP address, local address, mapping addresses, ARP, ARP table, ARP reply, ARP requests, ARP cache, Reverse ARP, Proxy-ARP

One of the main problems that had to be solved when creating IP was ensuring coordinated operation of the internetwork composed of several constituent networks, which generally use different network technologies. Interoperation of TCP/IP with local technologies implemented in a constituent network takes place multiple times as the IP packet is forwarded across the internet. On each router, IP determines to which router of this network the packet should be forwarded. By solving this problem, the protocol determines the *IP address* of the network interface of the next router (or the end node if this network is the destination network). To enable local network technology to deliver the packet to the next router, it is necessary to carry out the following operations:

1. Encapsulate the packet into the frame that has the format corresponding to this network (Ethernet, for example)

2. Supply the frame with the *local address* of the next router.

As already mentioned,[2] all of these tasks are delegated to the network interface level of the TCP/IP stack.

17.5.1 ARP

Since there is no dependence between local addresses and IP addresses, the only method of establishing the mapping is using tables. As a result of network configuration, each interface knows its local address and IP address. This mapping can be considered as

---

[2] See the *"TCP/IP Stack"* section in *Chapter 4*.

a table distributed over individual network interfaces. The only problem here is organizing the exchange of this information between network hosts.

For defining the local address by the IP address, **Address Resolution Protocol (ARP)** is used. ARP is implemented differently depending on the data link-layer protocol operating in the local network. As you will recall, this might be one of the LAN protocols (Ethernet, Token Ring, or FDDI), with the possibility of broadcast access to all network nodes simultaneously, or one of the WAN protocols (X.25 or Frame Relay), which, as a rule, do not support broadcast access.

Consider ARP operation in LANs supporting **broadcasting**.

Figure17.4 shows the fragment of an IP network that includes two networks: Ethernet1 (comprising three end nodes, A, B, and C) and Ethernet2 (comprising the D and E end nodes). These networks are connected to router interfaces 1 and 2, respectively. Each network interface has an IP address and an MAC address. Suppose that at some instance, the IP module of host C sends a packet to host D. The protocol of node C has determined the IP address of the next router, IP_1. Before encapsulating the packet into the Ethernet frame and sending it to the router, it is necessary to determine its corresponding **MAC address**. To solve this problem, the IP requests ARP. ARP supports a separate **ARP table** on each interface of the network adapter or router. In the course of network operation, this table accumulates information on the correspondence between IP addresses and MAC addresses of other interfaces within this network. Initially, when the computer or router is connected to the network, all its ARP tables are empty.

- In Figure17.4, the stage (1) corresponds to the passing of the following message from IP to ARP: "What MAC address corresponds to the interface with the IP address IP_1?"
- ARP operation starts with the lookup of the ARP table of the appropriate network interface (stage (2) in Figure 17.4). Suppose that the requested IP address is not among the existing records.
- The outgoing IP packet for which it was impossible to determine the local address from the ARP table is stored in the buffer; ARP generates a request, encapsulates it into the Ethernet frame, and broadcasts it (stage (3) in Figure 17.4).
- All interfaces of the Ethernet1 network receive this **ARP request** and direct it to their "local" ARPs. ARP compares the IP_1 address specified in the packet to the IP address of the interface to which that request arrived. ARP detects a match (in this case, the ARP running on the router 1), formulates an **ARP reply** (stage (4) in Figure 17.4).

In the ARP reply, the router specifies its local address, MAC_1, and sends it to the requesting node (in this example, this will be node C) using its local address. In this case, the broadcast reply is not needed, since the format of the ARP request provides the fields for the local and network addresses of the sender. Note that the area within which the ARP requests can propagate is limited by Ethernet1, since the router is a barrier for broadcast frames.

Figure 17.5 shows the Ethernet frame with an encapsulated ARP message. ARP request and reply have the same format. Table 17.2 lists the values of the fields of a real ARP request passed using Ethernet.

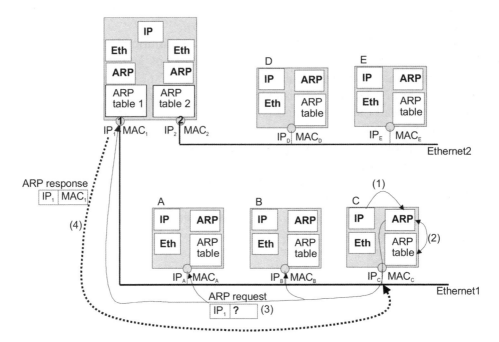

Figure 17.4 Method of ARP operation

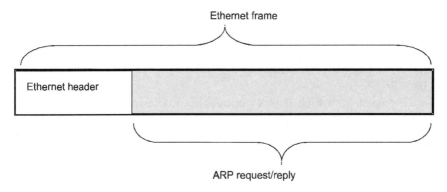

Figure 17.5 Encapsulation of an ARP message in the Ethernet frame

The *Network type* field contains 1 for Ethernet networks.

The *Protocol type* field allows the use of ARP not only for IP but also for other network protocols. For IP, this field contains the value of 0x0800.

The length of the local address for the Ethernet protocol is 6 bytes; the IP address length is 4 bytes. The *Operation* field for ARP requests contains 1 if this is a request and 2 if this is a reply.

Table 17.2 Example of ARP request

Network type	1 (0x1)
Protocol type	2048 (0x800)
Local address length	6 (0x6)
Network address length	4 (0x4)
Operation	1 (0x1)
Local address of the sender	008048EB7E60
Network address of the sender	194.85.135.75
Local address of the receiver (the requested one)	000000000000
Network address of the receiver	194.85.135.65

From this request, it follows that in the Ethernet network, the host with the 194.85.135.75 IP address attempts to determine the MAC address of another host from the same network, with the 194.85.135.65 IP address. *The field of the requested local address is filled with zeros.*

The host that has recognized its IP address sends a reply to the request. If there is no computer with the requested IP address in the network, then there will be no ARP reply. In this case, IP discards the IP packets sent to that address. Table 17.3 contains the values of the fields of ARP reply that could be sent to the previously provided ARP request.

Table 17.3 Example of ARP reply

Network type	1 (0x1)
Protocol type	2048 (0x800)
Local address length	6 (0x6)
Network address length	4 (0x4)
Option	1 (0x1)
Local address of the sender	00E0F77F1920
Network address of the sender	194.85.135.65
Local address of the receiver (the requested one)	008048EB7E60
Network address of the receiver	194.85.135.75

By exchanging these two ARP messages, the IP module that has sent the request from the interface with the address 194.85.135.75 has determined that the MAC address corresponding to the IP address 194.85.135.65 is 00E0F77F1920. This address will be placed in the header of the Ethernet frame encapsulating the IP packet waiting for sending.

To reduce the number of ARP messages in the network, the detected mapping between IP and MAC addresses is stored in the ARP table of the appropriate interface. In this case, this record will appear as follows:

194.85.135.65   00E0F77F1920

A new record is added to the table automatically several milliseconds after the ARP module completes its analysis of the ARP reply. Now, if a packet again needs to be sent to the address 194.85.135.65, IP will check if this address is already present in the ARP table before sending a broadcast request.

ARP table gets supplemented not only by ARP reply arriving to the interface for which it has been created, but also as a result of retrieving useful information from broadcast ARP requests. In fact, as can be seen from Tables 17.2 and 17.3, every request contains IP address and MAC address of the sender. All interfaces that have received this request can place information about local to network address mapping of the sender to their own ARP tables. In particular, all hosts that have received the ARP request shown in Table 17.2, can place the following record into their ARP tables:

194.85.135.75   008048EB7E60

Thus, an ARP table complemented by two above-mentioned records during network operation will appear as shown in Table 17.4.

Table 17.4 Example of ARP table

IP address	MAC address	Record type
194.85.135.65	00E0F77F1920	Dynamic
194.85.135.75	008048EB7E60	Dynamic
194.85.60.21	008048EB7567	Static

The *Record type* field can contain one of the following two values: *static* or *dynamic*. Static records are created manually using the ARP utility and have no expiration term. To be more precise, they exist until the computer or router is powered down.

Dynamic records are created by the ARP module using the broadcast capabilities of LAN technologies. The ARP table is complemented not only by analyzing ARP replies arriving to the current interface but also by retrieving useful information from broadcast ARP requests. As is obvious from Table 17.2, ARP requests, besides other data, contain the IP and MAC addresses of the sender. Even if there is no match with the requested address, the host places this valuable information into its own ARP table.

Dynamic records must be periodically refreshed. If the record was not updated during a predefined time interval (several minutes), it is discarded from the table. Thus, ARP tables store records on network hosts that actively participate in network operations rather than on all network hosts. Since such a method of storing information is known as caching, an ARP table is sometimes called an **ARP cache**.

NOTE   *Some implementations of IP and ARP do not place IP packets into the queue for the time required for waiting for ARP replies. Instead, they simply discard IP packets and delegate the task of its restoration to the TCP module or the application process operating through UDP. Such a restoration uses timeouts and a retransmission mechanism. Retransmission of the message will be accomplished successfully, since the first attempt had already updated the ARP table.*

The method of address resolution used in WANs is quite different. As you will recall, WANs do not support broadcast messages. In this case, the network administrator must manually create ARP tables and place them on one of the servers. These ARP tables specify, for instance, the mapping of IP addresses to X.25 addresses, which are interpreted as local addresses by IP. In WANs, there also is a trend toward ARP automation. For this purpose, a dedicated router is chosen from all routers connected to a WAN. This router supports the ARP table for all other hosts and routers of that network.

When using such a centralized approach, for all hosts and routers, it is only necessary to manually specify the IP addresses and the local address of the dedicated router. When powered up, each host and router register their addresses on the dedicated router. Any time it is necessary to determine the local address from an IP address, the ARP module requests the dedicated router and gets a reply automatically, without the administrator's participation. An ARP router operating in such a way is called an *ARP server*.

In some cases, an inverse problem has to be solved, namely, determining the IP address from the known local address. In this case, the *reverse address resolution protocol (Reverse ARP or RARP)* is used. This protocol is used, for instance, when starting diskless workstations that at startup do not know their IP addresses but know the MAC address of the network adapter.

17.5.2 Proxy-ARP

Proxy-ARP is one of the variants of the ARP allowing IP addresses to be mapped to hardware addresses in networks supporting broadcasting even when the requested host is located outside the boundaries of the current collision domain.

Figure 17.6 shows a network with one end node (computer D) that operates in the remote host mode. More details on this operating mode will be provided in *Chapter 23* of *Part V*. For the moment, it is sufficient to know that the end node operating in such a mode has all the possibilities available to computers located within the main part of the Ethernet. Among other features, it has the IP address, IP_D, belonging to the same network.

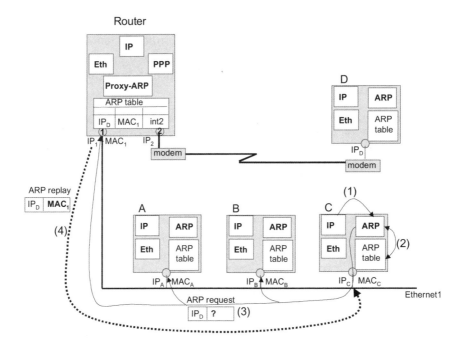

Figure 17.6 Method of Proxy-ARP operation

For all end nodes of the Ethernet, specific features of connecting a remote host (the presence of modems, dialup networking, and PPP) are absolutely transparent, and they interact with such a host in a normal way. To make such an operating mode possible, among other features, Proxy-ARP is required. Since the remote host is connected using PPP, it has no MAC address.

Suppose that the application running on computer C decides to send a packet to computer D. It knows the destination IP address, IP_D; however, as already mentioned, to transmit a packet using Ethernet, it is necessary to encapsulate that packet into the Ethernet frame and supply it with the MAC address. To determine the MAC address of computer D, the IP of computer C requests ARP, which sends a broadcast message containing an ARP request. Were it not for Proxy-ARP installed on a router, no host would reply to this request.

However, Proxy-ARP is installed and operates in the following way: When remote host D connects to the network, the following record is entered into the ARP table of the router:

$$IP_D - MAC_1 - int2$$

This record has the following meaning:

- When the ARP request in relation to the IP_D address arrives, the ARP reply must be supplied with the MAC_1 hardware address corresponding to the hardware address of the interface 1 of the router.
- The host with the IP_D address is connected to the second interface of the router.

Therefore, the router with Proxy-ARP installed will reply to the broadcast request sent by host C. The router places a "proxy" ARP reply in which it supplies its own hardware address MAC$_1$ instead of that of computer D.

Host C, without suspecting any "trick," sends the frame with the encapsulated IP packet to the MAC$_1$ address. Having received the frame, Proxy-ARP "understands" that this frame is not intended to it, since the packet contains the IP address of another host. Consequently, the destination address must be looked for in the ARP table. Table lookup shows that the frame must be sent to the host connected to the second interface.

This is the simplest method of Proxy-ARP usage; nevertheless, it reflects the operating logic with sufficient comprehension.

17.6 DNS

KEY WORDS: short names, relative names, fully qualified domain names (FQDN), flat symbolic names, hierarchical symbolic names, NetBIOS names, DNS servers, DNS clients, distributed database, recursive method, iterative method, reverse lookup zone

17.6.1 Flat Symbolic Names

In operating systems initially developed for operation in LANs, such as Novell NetWare, Microsoft Windows, or IBM OS/2, users always used the symbolic names of computers. Since LANs consisted of small numbers of computers, *flat names* were used, which represented text strings that were not divided into parts. Examples of such names are NW1_1, mail2, and LONDON_SALES_2. To establish mapping of symbolic names to MAC addresses, these operating systems used mechanisms of broadcast requests, similar to the one used by ARP. For instance, the broadcast name resolution mechanism is implemented in the NetBIOS protocol, which served as a basis for many LAN operating systems. So-called NetBIOS names have served as a main type of flat names in LANs for years.

For the TCP/IP stack, which generally is intended for operation in large, geographically distributed networks, such an approach proved to be inefficient.

17.6.2 Hierarchical Symbolic Names

The TCP/IP stack uses DNS, which has a hierarchical structure allowing the use of an arbitrary number of components in a name (Figure 17.7).

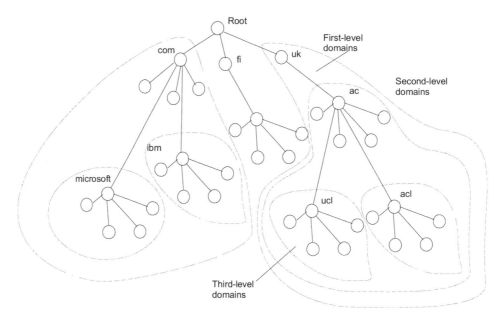

Figure 17.7 Domain name space

The hierarchy of domain names is similar to the hierarchy of file names adopted in most popular file systems. The name tree starts from the root, designated here by the point (.). The root is followed by the most significant symbolic part of the name, then the next most significant part of the name, and so on. The least significant part of the name corresponds to the network end node. In contrast to a file name, for which the most significant component goes first, followed by the component of the lower level, and so on, a domain name starts with the least significant components and is terminated by the highest-level component. The components of a domain name are delimited by points. For instance, in **partnering.microsoft.com**, the **partnering** component is the name of one of the computers in the **microsoft.com** domain.

Splitting names into parts splits administrative responsibilities for assigning unique names and divides them among several individuals or organizations within the specific limits of the hierarchy. Thus, for the example provided in Figure 17.7, it is possible to delegate the responsibilities for ensuring that all names terminating by the component "us" gave the unique part of the name of the lower hierarchical layer to an individual. If that individual is capable of holding that responsibility, then all names such as **www.us**, **mail.mmt.us**, or **m2.zil.mmt.us** will differ in their part second according to their significance.

Separation of administrative responsibilities solves the problem of generating unique names without the need of coordinating efforts among several organizations responsible for the names of the same hierarchical level. Obviously, there must be one organization responsible for assigning the names of the top hierarchical level.

The set of names with the same most significant parts comprising one or more components make up a domain. For instance, names like **www1.zil.mmt.ru**, **ftp.zil.mmt.ru**, **yandex.ru**, and **s1.mgu.ru** are part of the domain **ru**, since all these names have in common the most significant part of the name — **ru**. Another example is the **mgu.ru** domain. Among the names in Figure 17.8, the following names are part of this domain: **s1.mgu.ru**, **s2.mgu.ru**, and **m.mgu.ru**. This domain is made up of the names for which the two most significant parts are always **mgu.ru**. Administrator of the **mgu.ru** domain is responsible for the uniqueness of the names of the next level, which are part of the domain, e.g., names such as **s1**, **s2**, and **m**. The resulting subdomains **s1.mgu.ru**, **s2.mgu.ru**, and **m.mgu.ru** are subdomains of the **mgu.ru** domain, because they have the common most significant part of the name. For short, subdomains often are called by the least significant part of the name — **s1**, **s2**, and **m**.

NOTE   *The term "domain" has lots of meanings; therefore, it must always be interpreted within a specific context. Besides domain names of the TCP/IP stack, computing literature refers Windows NT domains, collision domains, and so on. The common feature of these domain concepts is that all describe some set of computers characterized by a specific common feature.*

If the uniqueness of names of the next level of the hierarchy is ensured in each domain or subdomain, the entire name system will consist of unique names.

By analogy with the file system, DNS provides *short names*, *relative names*, and *fully qualified domain names* (*FQDN*). A short name is the name of the network end node, such as the host or router port. The short name represents a leaf of the name tree. A relative name is the composite name starting from some hierarchical level (however, not from the top one). For instance, **www1.zil** is a relative name. An FQDN includes the name components of all levels of the hierarchy, starting from the short name and terminating with the root: **www1.zil.mmt.ru**.

A root domain is managed by centralized Internet authorities: IANA and InterNIC. Top-level domains are assigned for each country as well as on a centralized basis. The names of these domains must follow the ISO 3166 international standard. Two- or three-letter abbreviations are used for designating countries, for instance: us (United States), ru (Russia), uk (United Kingdom), and fi (Finland). For different kinds of organizations, the following abbreviations exist:

- **com** — commercial organizations (for example, **microsoft.com**)
- **edu** — educational organizations (for example, **mit.edu**)
- **gov** — governmental organizations (for example, **nsf.gov**)
- **org** — noncommercial organizations (for example, **fidonet.org**)
- **net** — organizations supporting networks (for example, **nsf.net**)

Each domain is administered by a separate organization that usually splits its domain into subdomains and delegates administrative functions for these subdomains to other organizations. To get a domain name, it is necessary to register with a specific organization to which InterNIC has delegated the rights of distributing domain names.

IMPORTANT *Computers are included in domains according to their fully qualified names. At the same time, they can have independent IP addresses that belong to different networks and subnets. For instance, the **mgu.ru** domain might include hosts with addresses such as 132.13.34.15, 201.22.100.33, and 14.0.0.6.*

DNS is implemented in the Internet; however, it also can operate as an autonomous name system in any enterprise-wide network that uses the TCP/IP stack but is not connected to the Internet.

17.6.3 DNS Operating Mode

The broadcast method of establishing the mapping of symbolic names and local addresses, similar to ARP, operates efficiently only in a small LAN that is not divided into subnets. In large-scale networks, where unlimited broadcasting is not supported, another method of symbolic name resolution is needed. The use of a centralized service supporting the mapping among addresses of different types for all computers of the network is a good alternative to broadcasting. For instance, Microsoft implemented the centralized WINS service for its corporate Windows NT operating system. WINS service supports the database of NetBIOS and IP addresses corresponding to them.

The mapping between domain names and IP addresses in TCP/IP networks can be established both by using the local host tools and by using the *centralized* service.

At the early stages of the Internet evolution, a text file named hosts.txt had to be manually created on each host. This file contained a certain number of networks, each containing one pair of "IP address — domain name," for instance, 102.54.94.97 — **rhino.acme.com**.

With the growth of the Internet, hosts files grew. Therefore, the development of a scalable solution for resolving names became a must. DNS became such a solution.

DNS is a centralized service based on the distributed database of mappings between domain names and IP addresses. In its operation, DNS uses the client–server protocol. This protocol defines DNS servers and DNS clients. DNS servers support distributed database of mappings, and DNS clients request servers to resolve domain names to IP addresses.

The DNS service uses text files having a format similar to that of the host file. These files are manually prepared by the network administrator. However, the DNS service relies on the domain hierarchy, and each server of the DNS service stores only part of the network names rather than all names, as was the case with the host files. As the number of hosts within the network grows, the problem of scaling is solved by creating new domains and subdomains and by adding new DNS servers.

For each domain of names, a DNS server must be created. There are two methods of name distribution on servers. In the first case, the server can store the "domain name — IP address" mapping for the entire domain, including all its subdomains. However, such a solution is poorly scalable, since as new subdomains are added, the load on this server might exceed its capabilities. Therefore, another approach is used more frequently. When using this approach, the name server stores only the names that terminate at the next lower level of hierarchy rather than the domain name. This approach is similar to the one used by file system directories, which contain records on files and the subdirectories within them. When using this method of organizing DNS service, the load is evenly distributed among all DNS servers of the network. For instance, in the first case, the DNS server of the **mmt.ru** domain will store the mappings for all names terminating with **mmt.ru**: **www1.zil.mmt.ru**, **ftp.zil.mmt.ru**, **mail.mmt.ru**, and so on. In the second case, this server will store the mappings only for names like **mail.mmt.ru**, **www.mmt.ru**, and so on; all other mappings must be stored on the DNS server of the **zil** subdomain.

Besides the mapping table, each DNS server contains the links to the DNS servers of its subdomains. These links connect separate SNS servers into the unified DNS service. The references are IP addresses of corresponding servers. For serving the root domain, several alternative DNS servers are dedicated, the IP addresses of which are well known (for instance, their list can be obtained from InterNIC).

The procedure of resolving a DNS name is in many respects similar to the procedure of searching for a file address in the file system, given its symbolic name. In both cases, the fully qualified name reflects the hierarchical structures of the organization of the appropriate reference tables — file directories and DNS tables, respectively. Here the domain and its DNS server are an analogue of the file system. Similar to symbolic file names, domain names are characterized by the independence of names from a physical location.

The procedure of searching for a file address by its symbolic name consists of sequential lookup of all directories, starting from root. In this case, the cache and the current directory are examined first. For defining the IP address by its domain name, it is also necessary to look up all DNS servers that form a chain of subdomains included into the host name, starting from the root domain. The most considerable difference between file system lookup and DNS lookup is that a file system is located on a single computer, and DNS is distributed.

There are two methods of resolving DNS names. In the first case, the DNS client coordinates the work related to searching for the IP address:

■ The DNS client requests the root DNS server and specifies the FQDN.

■ The DNS server replies by specifying the address of the next DNS server serving the upper-level domain specified in the most significant part of the requested name.

■ The DNS client requests the next DNS server, which redirects it to the DNS server of the required subdomain, and so on. This procedure continues until the required DNS server containing the mapping for the requested name to a specific address is found. This server sends the final reply to the client.

This method of interaction is known as a **nonrecursive** or **iterative method**. In this case, the client iteratively performs a sequence of requests to different name servers. This method is rarely used, since it loads the client with rather complicated tasks.

The second variant implements the **recursive procedure**:

■ DNS requests the local DNS server (e.g., the one that serves the subdomain to which the client name belongs).

■ If the local DNS server knows the answer, it immediately returns it to the client. This might happen when the requested name is part of the same subdomain as the client. This might also corresponds to a server that has already carried out this request for another client and stored it in its cache.

■ If the local server does not know the answer, it makes iterative requests to the root server as was done by the client in the first variant. Having received an answer, the DNS server sends it to the client, which during request execution simply waited for a reply from its local DNS server.

In this method, the client delegates the procedures to its server. Therefore, this method is known as indirect or recursive. Practically all DNS clients use a recursive procedure.

To speed up the procedure of searching for IP addresses, DNS servers widely use the caching procedure for all responses that pass through them. To enable the DNS service to process the changes that take place in the network in a timely manner, responses are cached for a relatively short time period, usually from several hours to several days.

17.6.4 Reverse Lookup Zone

DNS service is intended not only for finding IP addresses by host names but also for solving an **inverse problem**, namely, finding host names by known IP addresses.

Most programs and utilities using DNS try to find the host name by its address when the user has specified only the address or when that address is retrieved from the packet that the program received from the network. Reverse records do not necessarily exist, even for the addresses that have direct records. Administrators might simply forget to create them. Sometimes, the creation of such records requires extra payment, especially if the primary server of the reverse lookup zone is supported by an ISP. When there is no reverse lookup zone, such programs operate with significant delays, since they have to wait a long time for the reverse requests.

Therefore, an inverse problem is solved in the Internet by organizing the so-called *reverse lookup zones*.

> **A reverse lookup zone** is the set of tables that stores the mapping between the IP addresses of some network and the names of hosts belonging to the same network. For organizing a distributed service and using the same software to search for names and addresses, the composite IP address is considered in the same style as composite name.

For instance, an address such as 192.31.106.0 is considered as the one containing the most significant part corresponding to domain 194, followed by domain 31, which includes domain 106. For storing the mapping of all addresses starting with 192, the 194 zone with its own name servers — primary and secondary ones — is created. When writing an address, the most significant part of the address is the leftmost one; for names, the situation is opposite. Therefore, to achieve full correspondence in a reverse request, the address is specified in the reverse order (e.g., 106.31.192 for the previously provided example).

For records on the servers controlling the top-level reverse lookup zones, a special zone — in-addr.arpa — is created. Therefore, the complete record for the address used in this example looks as follows:

> 106.31.192.in-addr.arpa.

Primary servers for reverse lookup zones use the database files independent of the files of the main zones, where there are records on the direct mapping of the same names and addresses. Such organization can result in discordance, since the same mapping is introduced into the files twice.

17.7 DHCP

KEY WORDS: dynamic host configuration protocol (DHCP), DHCP server, DHCP client, static addresses, dynamic addresses, manual/automatic mode, assignment of addresses, lease duration, Dynamic DNS

For normal operation of the network, each network interface of a computer or router that will send or receive IP packets must be assigned an IP address.

Assignment of IP addresses can be carried out manually in the course of configuring the interface. For computers, this procedure consists of filling a series of dialogs displayed on screen. When proceeding this way, administrator must remember which addresses from the available set are already assigned to other interfaces and which ones are free. When carrying out the configuration procedure, the administrator must assign to the client a set of parameters that includes the IP address and other parameters of the TCP/IP stack required for efficient operation, such as the mask, the address of the default gateway, the IP address of the DNS server, and the domain name of the computer. Even with small networks, this is a routine and sometimes even tedious operation.

The **dynamic host configuration protocol (DHCP)** automates the process of configuring network interfaces, ensuring the elimination of address duplication through the use of the centrally managed address database. DHCP operation is described in RFC 2131 and RFC 2132.

17.7.1 DHCP Modes

DHCP operates according to the client–server model. At system startup, a DHCP client sends a broadcast request to the network, requesting that an IP address be assigned to it. The DHCP server responds to this request and sends a response message containing an IP address and several other configuration parameters.

The DHCP server can operate in various modes:

■ Manual assignment of static addresses

■ Automatic assignment of static addresses

■ Automatic distribution of dynamic addresses

In all operating modes, the administrator configures the DHCP server by specifying one or more ranges of IP addresses to it. All these addresses must relate to the same network (i.e., they must have the same value in the network number field).

In the *manual mode*, the administrator, besides providing the pool of available addresses, supplies the DHCP server with information that strictly defines the mapping of IP addresses to physical addresses or other identifiers of the client nodes. Using this information, the DHCP server always assigns the same predefined IP address to the DHCP client with a set of other configuration parameters.[3]

In the mode of *automatic assignment of static addresses*, the DHCP server arbitrarily chooses an IP address for the client without the participation of the administrator. This address is chosen from the pool of available IP addresses. An address from the pool is assigned to the client on a constant basis. This means that there is a constant mapping between the client's IP address and its identifying information, as was the case with manual assignment. This mapping was set when the DHCP server assigned the IP address to the client for the first time. All further client requests for assigning an IP address return the same IP address from the DHCP server.

When using *dynamic address distribution*, the DHCP server assigns IP addresses to its clients for a limited time, known as **lease duration**. If a computer that is a DHCP client is removed from the network, the IP address assigned to it is automatically released. When the computer connects to another subnet, it will be automatically assigned new address. Neither the end user nor the network administrator participates in this process.

Automatic address distribution provides the possibility of future reuse of the released IP address by assigning it to another computer. Thus, besides the main DHCP advantage of automation of the routine administrative work of configuring the TCP/IP stack on every computer, dynamic address assignment allows the building of IP networks in which the number of nodes exceeds the number of available IP addresses.

EXAMPLE   *Consider the advantages provided by dynamic distribution of the address pool on the example of a company whose employees spend most of their working time outside the*

---

[3] Sometimes we omit this specification for brevity.

office working from home or on business trips. Each employee has a notebook connected to the corporate IP network when working in the office. A question might be asked — how many IP addresses are necessary for such a company?

The first answer will be as follows: The number of addresses must equal the number of employees working in the network. *For instance, if there are 500 such employees, each of them must be assigned an IP address and allocated a working place. Thus, administration must request from the ISP the addresses of two Class C networks and equip the premises. However, recall that the employees of this company rarely visit the main office. Therefore, most of the time these resources will not be used if such a solution is chosen.*

Another approach is requesting a number of IP addresses that corresponds to the number of employees normally in the office *(with some reserve). For instance, if the normal number of employees in the office does not exceed 50, it will be sufficient to request a pool of 64 addresses and install a network with 64 connectors for connecting computers. However, another problem arises — who and how would configure computers constantly added to or removed from the network?*

There are two ways of solving this problem. First, the administrator (or a mobile user herself) can manually configure the computer when it becomes necessary to connect it to the office network. This approach requires a large number of routine operations; consequently, this is not a good solution. In such a situation, the possibilities of automatically assigning DHCP addresses look much more attractive. If this approach is used, the administrator can specify a range of 64 addresses once in the course of configuring the DHCP server. After that, each newly arriving mobile user will simply physically connect his or her computer to the network, and the DHCP client will start. The DHCP client requests the required configuration parameters and automatically receives them from the DHCP server. Thus, for supporting 500 mobile users, it is sufficient to have a pool of 64 IP addresses and 64 working places in the office network.

17.7.2 Algorithm of Dynamic Address Assignment

An administrator controls the process of network configuration by specifying the two main parameters of the DHCP server configuration: the pool of addresses available for distribution and the lease duration. Lease duration defines how long the computer can use the IP address assigned to it before it again requests an address from the DHCP server. The lease duration parameter depends on the working mode of network users. If this is a small network of an educational institution, where numerous students come with their notebooks for carrying out tests, labs, or workshops, lease duration might be the time required to do the work. If this is a corporate network, where employees work on a regular basis, lease time can be significantly longer — several days or weeks.

The DHCP server must be located within the same subnet as the clients, taking into account that clients send broadcast requests to it. To reduce the risk of network failure because of malfunction of the DHCP server, sometimes a redundant DHCP server is installed in the network. This variant corresponds to configuration of *network 1* shown in Figure 17.8.

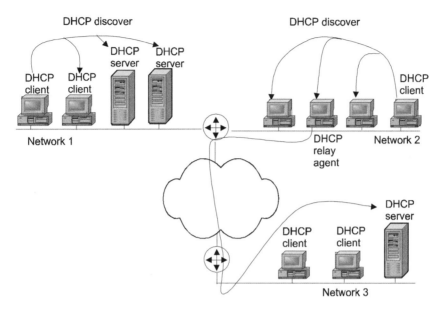

Figure 17.8 Methods of mutual disposition of DHCP clients and servers

Sometimes there is an opposite pattern: There are no DHCP servers in the network. In this case, the DHCP server is replaced by the DHCP relay agent — specialized software that carries out the role of mediator between DHCP clients and DHCP servers. An example of such a configuration is shown by the *network 2* in Figure 17.8. The agent redirects client requests from the local network to one of the DHCP servers located in another subnet (in this example, this is *network 3*). Thus, one DHCP server can serve DHCP clients from several subnets.

The next example is a simplified method of exchanging messages between a DHCP client and its server parts.

When a computer is powered on, the DHCP client sends a limited broadcast message known as *DHCPdiscover* (an IP packet with a destination address comprising only binary ones, which must be delivered to all hosts within this IP network).

DHCP servers located within a network receive this message. If the network does not contain DHCP servers, then the *DHCPdiscover* message is received by the DHCP relay agent. It sends this message into another, probably distant network — to the DHCP server whose IP address it knows beforehand.

All DHCP servers that have received the *DHCPdiscover* message send their offers to the DHCP client that has sent requests. The offers are sent in *DHCPoffer* messages. Each *DHCPoffer* messages contains an IP address and other configuration information (a DHCP server located in another network sends its response through the agent).

The DHCP client collects configuration offers from all DHCP servers. As a rule, it chooses the first offer from the *DHCPoffer* messages it receives and sends a *DHCPrequest* broadcast message containing information about the DHCP server whose offer it has accepted (with the values of configuration parameters).

All DHCP servers receive the *DHCPrequest* message, and the DHCP server chosen by the client sends the *DHCPacknowledgment* message (confirmation of the IP address and lease parameters). Other servers cancel their offers and return the offered addresses to their pools of available addresses.

The DHCP client receives the *DHCPacknowledgment* confirmation and enters the operating state.

From time to time, the computer attempts to renew lease parameters obtained from the DHCP server. It undertakes the first attempt long before the expiration of the lease term and requests the same server from which it has received the current parameters. If there is no response, or if the response is negative, it repeats its attempt to send the request after some time. If after several repeated attempts the client fails to receive parameters from the same server, it requests another server. Finally, if the attempt to obtain parameters from another server also fails, the client loses its configuration parameters and enters the autonomous operating mode.

The DHCP client can also release the parameters leased to it ahead of schedule by carrying out the *DHCP* release command.

In a network where IP addresses are assigned dynamically, it is not possible to tell which address is allocated to a specific host. This inconstancy of IP addresses results in some problems. First, *there might arise some difficulties when translating a symbolic domain name to an IP address.* Imagine the operation of DNS that must support mapping tables of domain names to IP addresses when the latter change every two hours! Taking this circumstance into account, it is recommended to assign static addresses to the servers that users frequently access by symbolic name and leave dynamic names for client computers only. However, in some networks, the number of servers is so large that their manual configuration becomes too labor intensive. This situation resulted in the development of an enhanced DNS version known as Dynamic DNS, which is based on the coordinated use of the address information database by DHCP and DNS services.

Second, *it is rather difficult to carry out remote control and automatic monitoring* (for instance, to accumulate statistics) for the interface if a dynamically assigned IP address is used as its identifier.

Finally, to ensure network security, most network devices can filter packets whose fields have predefined values. In other words, when using dynamically assigned IP addresses, *packet filtering by IP addresses gets complicated.*

The latter two problems are most easily solved by abandoning the use of dynamic addresses for the interfaces used in monitoring systems and security systems.

SUMMARY

▶ The TCP/IP stack uses three types of addresses: local addresses (also known as hardware addresses), IP addresses, and symbolic domain names. All these types of addresses are assigned independently to the hosts of the internetwork.

▶ An IP address is 4 bytes long and consists of the network number and the host number. For determining the boundary separating the network number from the host number, two approaches are used. The first approach is based on address classes, and the other method is based on the use of masks.

▶ An address class is defined by the values of several starting bits of the address. In Class A addresses, 1 byte stores a network number, and the remaining 3 bytes store the host number. Class A addresses are used in the largest networks. For smaller networks, Class C addresses are the most suitable. In Class C addresses, the network number takes 3 bytes, and for host numbering, 1 byte can be used. Class B networks take an intermediate position.

▶ To separate an IP address into a network number and a host number, the network mask associated with this address is used. Binary representation of the mask contains ones in those bits that must be interpreted as the network number in the current IP address.

▶ IP addresses uniquely identify the host within the limits of the internetwork; therefore, they must be assigned centrally.

▶ If the network is small and autonomous, then the uniqueness of the IP addresses within the limits of this network can be ensured by the network administrator. The administrator is free to choose any IP addresses for numbering networks and hosts. The only requirement is that the chosen addresses must have the correct syntax. However, it is preferable to use so-called private addresses intended for autonomous networks.

▶ If a network is very large, such as the Internet, the process of assigning IP addresses becomes too complicated and is split into two stages. At the first stage, network addresses are distributed. This stage is regulated by a special administrative authority, ensuring the uniqueness of network numbering. After the network receives the number, the second stage, assignment of addresses to its hosts, takes place.

▶ Assignment of IP addresses to network hosts can be carried out either manually or automatically. If IP addresses are assigned manually, the network administrator supports the lists of assigned and available network address and manually configures each network interface. When IP addresses are assigned automatically, DHCP is used. In this case, the administrator has previously assigned a range of available addresses to the DHCP server, and the server automatically assigns them to network hosts in response to their requests.

▶ Establishing mapping between an IP address and a hardware address of the network interface is carried out by ARP.

▶ In networks supporting broadcasting and in networks that do not support it, two different approaches to address resolutions are used. ARP operating in Ethernet,

Token Ring, and FDDI networks for translating an IP address into a MAC address carries out a broadcast ARP request. The ARP responses that arrive to the interface are saved in the tables created on each network interface. In networks that do not support broadcast addresses, ARP tables are stored centrally on the dedicated ARP server.

▶ The TCP/IP stack uses a domain system of symbolic names, which has a hierarchical tree structure allowing the use an arbitrary number of components in a name. The names for which the several most significant components coincide make up the name domain. Domain names are assigned centrally if the network is part of the Internet; otherwise, they are assigned locally.

▶ Correspondence between domain names and IP addresses can be set both using a local host file and using the centralized DNS service based on the distributed database of "domain name — IP address" mappings.

REVIEW QUESTIONS

1. What is the difference in the procedures for assigning hardware addresses and network addresses?

2. Which of the addresses listed here could be used as local addresses in the IP internetwork? Which addresses cannot be used this way?
   A. A 6-byte MAC address, such as 12-B3-3B-51-A2-10
   B. An X.25 address, such as 25012112654987
   C. A 12-byte IPX address, such as 13.34.B4.0A.C5.10.11.32.54.C5.3B.0
   D. A VPI/VCI address of an ATM network.

3. Which of these statements provided are always correct?
   A. Every interface of every bridge or switch has a MAC address.
   B. Each bridge or switch has a network address.
   C. Each interface of the bridge or switch has a network address.
   D. Each router has a network address.
   E. Each interface of the router always has a MAC address.
   F. Each interface of a router has a network address.

4. Which of the addresses provided here cannot be used as IP addresses of network interfaces for Internet hosts? For addresses that do not contain syntax error, determine the class: A, B, C, D, or E.

   (A) 127.0.0.1   (E) 10.234.17.25   (I) 193.256.1.16
   (B) 201.13.123.245   (F) 154.12.255.255   (J) 194.87.45.0
   (C) 226.4.37.105   (G) 13.13.13.13   (K) 195.34.116.255
   (D) 103.24.254.0   (H) 204.0.3.1   (L) 161.23.45.305

5. Suppose that an IP address of some host of a subnet of 198.65.12.67; the mask value for this subnet is 255.255.255.240. Determine the subnet number. How many hosts may this subnet contain?

6. Assume that you know the mapping between IP addresses and domain names for all computers in a network except one. For that computer, only the domain name is known. Provided with all this information, can you define its IP address with certainty?

7. How many ARP tables are there on a computer? How many are there on a router? And on a switch?

8. Functionally, ARP can be divided into the client part and the server part. Describe the functions of the client and server parts.

9. Which addresses does an administrator enter into an ARP table? For what purpose?

10. In what cases is it useful to use Proxy-ARP?

11. Is it possible to determine from the domain names of computers how close they are to one another geographically?

12. Some computer has the IP address 204.35.101.24 and the domain name new.firm.net. Determine which, if any, of the following domain names belongs to another computer that has the IP address 204.35.101.25: new1.firm.net, new.firm1.net, or new.1firm.net.

13. What are the common features of DNS and file system?

14. How many DHCP servers are sufficient for serving a network divided by two routers?

15. For reliability, there are two DHCP servers in the network. How should the administrator assign the pool of available addresses for each of them: allocate nonoverlapping parts of the pool to each one, or assign the common pool for both?

16. Why an inverse DNS problem, namely, finding host names by known IP addresses, is not solved using the same approach as the one used for solving the direct problem (i.e., using the same zone and domain files organized as a tree corresponding to the name hierarchy)?

PROBLEMS

1. Suppose that some ISP has a Class B network address at its disposal. For addressing hosts of its own network, this ISP uses 254 addresses. Determine the maximum number of customers that can be served by this ISP if the sizes of their networks correspond to Class C. What mask should be set on the ISP's router connecting its network to the networks of its clients?

2. What is the maximum theoretical number of subnets that you can organize if you have a Class C network at your disposal? What is the role of a network mask in this case? What is its value?

INTERNET PROTOCOL

18.1 INTRODUCTION

In this chapter, your attention will be drawn to the Internet Protocol (IP) defined in RFC 751. In each next network along the path of the IP packet, this protocol calls the transport tools adopted in the current network to use them for delivering the packet to the router connected to the next network or directly to the destination node. Thus, one of the most important of IP functions is supporting connection to the underlying technologies of the constituent networks. Functions of IP include supporting connection to the upper- and network-layer protocols and, in particular, to TCP, which in the TCP/IP stack carries out all tasks related to ensuring reliable data delivery using the Internet.

IP is a connectionless protocol. This means that it processes each IP packet as an independent data unit that has no relation to other IP packets. IP has no mechanisms that are usually implemented to ensure the authenticity of the delivered data. If any error has occurred in the course of packet forwarding, IP does not initiate any actions to correct this error. For example, if a packet was discarded on one of the transit routers because of the checksum error, the IP entity does not try to retransmit the lost packet. In other words, IP implements the best effort policy.

In this chapter, we cover in detail the main function of IP, namely, routing. We explain the structure of the routing tables, both with and without masks. We also provide examples using masks of fixed and variable lengths, overlapping address spaces, and applying subnetting and supernetting technologies. We then investigate the IP capability of packet fragmentation.

When describing specific features of IPv6, we concentrate on the modernization of the addressing method, which allowed better scalability. Also covered is the format of the IP header, which improved network bandwidth by reducing the amount of work delegated to routers.

18.2 IP PACKET FORMAT

> **KEY WORDS**: Internet Protocol, Version, IPv4, IPv6, IP packet, Type of service (ToS), differentiated services byte (DS-byte), route selection criterion Precedence, Flag, Fragment Offset, Time to live (TTL), Header Checksum, Source IP Address, Destination IP Address, IP Options, Padding

There is a direct relationship between the number of fields in the packet header and the functional complexity of the protocol working with this header. The simpler the header, the simpler the corresponding protocol. Most protocol operations relate to the processing of the control information carried in the packet header fields. By studying the value of each field in the IP packet header, you not only gain formal knowledge of the packet structure but also become acquainted with the main functions of **Internet Protocol**.

The IP packet includes the header and the data field. The header comprises the following fields (Figure 18.1):

Version. This field takes 4 bits and specifies the IP version. Currently, **IPv4** is used almost everywhere. However, the newer version, **IPv6**, is gradually becoming more common.

Header Length. The *Header Length* field of the IP packet also takes 4 bits. It specifies the header length, measured in 32-bit words. Usually, the header is 20 bytes long (five 32-bit words). However, if control information is added, this length can be increased using additional bytes in the IP Options field. The maximum header length is 60 bytes.

Type of service (ToS), also known by its newer name — **differentiated services byte (DS-byte)**. This field takes 1 byte. Two variants correspond to the names of this field: ToS (the former interpretation) and DS-byte (the newer meaning). In both cases, this field is used for storing parameters that reflect the packet's QoS requirements.

In ToS, this field is subdivided into two subfields. The starting 3 bits make up the Precedence subfield. The precedence (i.e., priority) can take values from 0 (a normal packet) to 7 (the control information packet). Routers and computers can take packet priority into account and process packets with the highest priority first. The *ToS* field also contains 3 bits determining the **route selection criterion**. There are three alternatives: short delay, high reliability, or high throughput. If the *delay* (D) bit is set to one, then the route should be chosen to minimize the delay in the delivery of this packet. The *throughput* (T) bit maximizes the throughput, and the *reliability* (R) bit maximizes reliability. The remaining 2 bits are reserved. They are always set to zero.

The differentiated services standards adopted by the end of the 1990s have given a new name to this field and redefined the values of its bits. DS-byte uses only the six most significant bits of this byte and reserves the two least significant ones. The aim of each bit of the *DS-byte* field will be covered in *Chapter 20* in the section describing methods of ensuring QoS in IP networks.

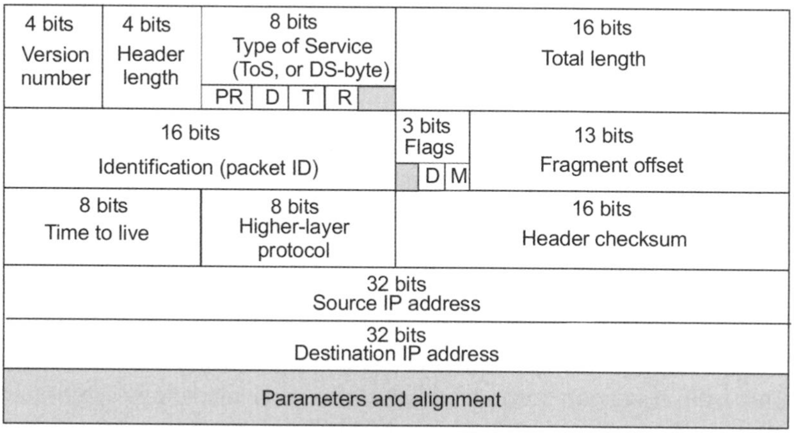

Figure 18.1 Structure of the IP packet header

Total Length. This field takes 2 bytes and characterizes the total length of the packet, taking account of the header and the data field. The maximum packet length is limited by the length of this field and makes 65,535 bytes. However, most networks do not use such long packets. When transmitting packets over a heterogeneous network, the packet length is chosen with the account of the maximum packet length of the lower-layer protocol, which carries IP packets. If these are Ethernet frames, the maximum packet length is 1,500 bytes, because such a packet will fit within the data field of the Ethernet frame. TCP/IP standards make provisions for ensuring that all hosts are capable of receiving packets 576 bytes long (whether or not they are fragmented).

Identification. This field takes 2 bytes and is used for identifying the packets created as a result of fragmenting the source packet. All fragments of the same packet must have the same value of this field.

Flags. The flags take 3 bits and contain attributes related to fragmentation. Setting the *do not fragment* (DF) bit to one instructs the router not to fragment this packet. If the *more fragments* (MF) bit is set to one, this means that this packet is fragmented, and this fragment is not the last one. The remaining bit is reserved.

Fragment Offset. This field takes 13 bits and specifies the offset (in bytes) of the data field of this packet from the starting point of the data field of the fragmented source packet. It is used when assembling or reassembling packets. The offset must be a multiple of eight.

Time to live (TTL). This field takes 1 byte and is used for specifying the maximum time interval during which the packet can travel across the network. The TTL is measured in seconds and is specified by the sender. The current TTL of the packet is decremented by one every second spent by the packet on each router through which the packet passes during its travel across the network. Even if a router processes the packet in less than a second, it still must decrement the TTL counter by one. Since contemporary routers rarely take more than a second to process a packet, the TTL can be interpreted as a maximum number of transit nodes through which the packet can pass. If the TTL value reaches zero before the packet is delivered to the destination host, the packet is discarded. Thus, the TTL parameter is a kind of "self-destruction" counter for the packet.

Protocol. This field takes 1 byte and contains the identifier specifying the higher-layer protocol for which the information in the data field is intended. Identifier values for various protocols are listed in the "Assigned Numbers" RFC. Until 1992 this was RFC 1340; later this RFC received the number 1700 (RFC 1700), and RFC 3232 was renewed on 2002. Currently, RFCs are available at **http://www.iana.org**, which is updated regularly. For instance, the number 6 means that the packet contains the TCP message, 17 stands for UDP, and 1 indicates ICMP.

Header Checksum. This field takes 2 bytes and is calculated for the header only. Since some header fields change values in the course of the packet transmission across the network (TTL, for instance), the checksum has to be checked and recalculated on each router and end node. The checksum — 16 bits — is calculated as a complement to the sum of all 16-bit words of the header. When calculating the checksum, the value of the *Header Checksum* field is set to zero. If the checksum value is incorrect, an error will be reported, and the packet will be discarded at the same instance as the error is detected.

Source IP Address and **Destination IP Address**. These fields have the same length — 32 bits.

IP Options. This field is optional. As a rule, it is used only when troubleshooting the network. This field contains several subfields, each having one of eight predefined types. In these subfields, it is possible to specify the exact route for passing the routers, to register routers passed by the packet, to store the security system data, or to save timestamps.

Padding. Since the number of subfields in the *IP Options* fields can be arbitrary, it is necessary to add several bytes to the end of the packet header to align the packet by the 32-bit boundary. The padding fields are filled with zeros.

Following is the listing of the header fields of a real IP packet captured from the Ethernet using the Microsoft Network Monitor (NM) protocol analyzer. In this listing, NM provides hex values of the fields (in parentheses). Furthermore, the program sometimes replaces the numeric codes of the fields with information in a more user-friendly format. For instance, the NM interface replaces the code in the *Protocol* field with a protocol name (in this case, it replaced the code 6 with the string TCP — see the line in bold).

```
IP: Version = 4 (0x4)

IP: Header Length = 20 (0x14)

IP: Service Type = 0 (0x0)

IP: Precedence = Routine

IP: ...0.... = Normal Delay

IP: ....0... = Normal Throughput

IP: .....0.. = Normal Reliability

IP: Total Length = 54 (0x36)

IP: Identification = 31746 (0x7C02)

IP: Flags Summary = 2 (0x2)

IP: .......0 = Last fragment in datagram

IP: ......1. = Cannot fragment datagram

IP: Fragment Offset = 0 (0x0) bytes

IP: Time to Live = 128 (0x80)

IP: Protocol = TCP — Transmission Control

IP: Checksum = 0xEB86

IP: Source Address = 194.85.135.75

IP: Destination Address = 194.85.135.66

IP: Data: Number of data bytes remaining = 34 (0x0022)
```

18.3 IP ROUTING METHOD

KEY WORDS: routing, route routing table, packet destination address, network address, interface, port, distance, service class, specific route, default route, gateway, next hop, minimum routing table, directly connected network, loopback address, routing protocol, DNS server/client, DNS response, DNS query, UDP datagram, FTP server/client

Consider the method of IP routing on the example of the internetwork shown in Figure 18.2. This network comprises 20 routers (designated by numbered squares) that join 18 networks into an internet: N1, N2, ..., N18 stand for network numbers. IP is installed on each router and on the A and B end nodes.

Routers have several interfaces (ports) to which networks are connected. Each router interface can be considered an individual network node: it has a separate network address

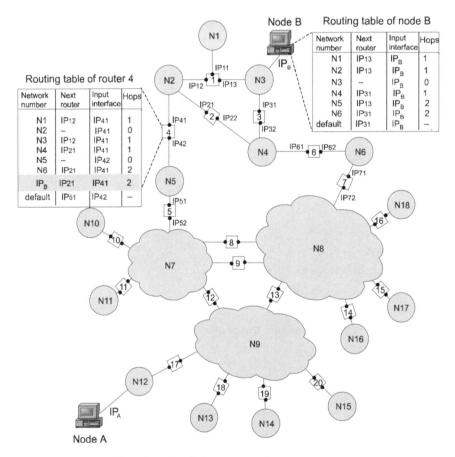

Figure 18.2 Principles of routing in internetworks

and the local address of the network connected to it. For instance, router 1 has three interfaces to which the N1, N2, and N3 networks are connected. In the illustration, network addresses of these ports are designated as IP_{11}, IP_{12}, and IP_{13}. Interface IP_{11} is the node of network N1; consequently, the network number field of the IP^{11} address contains the number N1. Similarly, the IP_{12} address is the node of network N2, and the IP_{13} address represents the node of network N3. Thus, a router can be considered a set of nodes, each of which is part of an individual network. As a unified device, the router has neither a network nor a local address.

NOTE   *If a router has a control unit (for instance, an SNMP control unit), it has its own local and network addresses by which it is accessed by the central control station.*

In complex internetworks, there always are several routes for packet transmission between two end nodes. For instance, the packet sent from node A to node B can pass via routers 17, 12, 5, 4, and 1 or via routers 17, 13, 7, 6, and 3. It is not difficult to find several other routes between nodes A and B.

The problem of choosing the router is solved by routers and end nodes. The router is chosen based on the information on the current network configuration provided to those devices and on the basis of the route selection criterion. Quite often, the delay of passing along the route by an individual packet, the average route bandwidth for the packet sequence, or even the simplest criterion taking into account only the number of transit routers passed along the route (hops) are route selection criteria. All information about routes obtained as the result of this analysis is placed into the **routing table**.

18.3.1 Simplified Structure of the Routing Table

We use conventional notation for designating the network addresses of routers and network numbers in the form shown in Figure 18.2. Using this notation, consider how routing table of, say, router 4, might look (Table 18.1).

NOTE   *Table 18.1 is considerably simplified as compared to real-world routing tables. For instance, this table does not provide fields containing mask values. It also lacks fields containing route state indicators and TTL values of the table records. The use of these attributes will be covered later. Instead of the destination network number, the fully qualified network address of a destination node can be specified. Besides this, as was already mentioned, this table provides network addresses in a conventional format. This means that in this example, network addresses do not correspond to any specific network protocol. Nevertheless, this table contains the main fields present in real-world routing tables.*

The first field of this table contains the **packet destination addresses**.

In each row of the table, the destination address is followed by the **network address of the next router**. To be more precise, this is the network address of the corresponding

Table 18.1 Routing table of router 4

Destination address	Network address of the next router	Network address of the output port	Distance from the destination network (hops)
N1	IP_{12} (R1)	IP_{41}	1
N2	–	IP_{41}	0 (connected)
N3	IP_{12} (R1)	IP_{41}	1
N4	IP_{21} (R2)	IP_{41}	1
N5	–	IP_{42}	0 (connected)
N6	IP_{21} (R2)	IP_{21}	2
IP_B	IP_{21} (R2)	IP_{41}	2
Default	IP_{51} (R5)	IP_{42}	–

interface of the next router to which the packet must be sent to be forwarded to the destination address along a rational route.

Before passing the packet to the next router, the current router must detect to which of its own ports (IP_{41} or IP_{42}) this packet must be sent. For this purpose, the third field of the routing table is used, which contains the **network addresses of the output interfaces**.

Some implementations of the network protocols tolerate the existence of several rows corresponding to the same destination address in the routing table. In this case, when choosing the route, the **distance from the destination network field** is taken into account. The distance is interpreted as any metric used according to the criterion specified in the network packet (this criterion is often called the **service class**). The distance can be measured as the number of hops, the time required for the packet to pass through communications links, or a specific link reliability characteristic on the chosen route. It can also be represented by any other value reflecting the quality of this route in relation to the specified criterion. In Table 18.1, the distance between networks was measured in hops. For networks directly connected to the router ports, the distance is assumed to be 0, although some implementations start counting distances from 1.

When the packet arrives at the router, the IP entity retrieves the destination network number from the header of the delivered frame and sequentially compares it to the network numbers from each row of the routing table. The row with the matching number specifies the nearest router to which it is necessary to forward the packet. For instance, if a packet intended for network N6 arrives at any port of router 4, the routing table shows that the address of the next router is IP_{21}. This means that at the next stage of the forwarding process, this packet will be sent to port 1 of router 2.

Most frequently, routing tables specify the destination network numbers instead of complete IP addresses. Thus, for all packets forwarded to the same network, IP will suggest the same route (for the moment, we are not taking into account possible changes in the network status, such as router failures or cable breakdowns). However, in some cases, it becomes necessary to choose a **specific route** for one of the network nodes. This specific route differs from the one specified for all other network nodes. To achieve this, it is necessary to enter a separate row for this host into the routing table. This row must contain the full IP address of the host along with appropriate route information. Such a record for host B is in Table 18.1. For instance, suppose that the administrator of router 4, with security considerations in mind, decided that all packets intended for host B (the full IP address is IP_B) must pass via router 2 (the IP_{21} interface) rather than via router 1 (the IP_{12} interface), through which packets are passed to all other hosts of network N3. If the table contains records specifying routes both to the entire network and to one of its hosts, the router will give preference to the specific route when the packet intended for that host arrives at the router.

Since the packet can be intended to any subnet of the internetwork, it might seem that each routing table must contain records on *all* networks included in the internet. However, in large networks this approach is inefficient because routing tables grow significantly. Searching a large routing table requires a long time. Furthermore, such a table requires more storage space. Therefore, in practice, it is wise to reduce the number of records in the routing table by using a special record known as the **default route.** If you consider the topology of the internet, you will discover that the routing tables of routers located at the internet periphery can record only the numbers of the networks directly connected to them or located nearby along dead-end routes. As relates to other networks, it is enough to enter the only record into the routing table, specifying the path to the router through which the path to all these networks passes. Such a router is called the **default router**. Instead of the network number, the appropriate row of the routing table must contain a specific record named **default**. In our example, router 4 specifies the paths only for packets traveling to networks N1–N6. For all other packets intended for networks N7–N18, this router suggests the same port, IP_{51}, of the same router, 5.

18.3.2 Routing Tables on End Nodes

The routing problem is solved not only by transit nodes (routers) but also by end nodes (computers). The process of solving this problem starts when IP installed on the end node detects if the packet is forwarded to another network or is addressed to a specific host within the limits of this network. If the number of the destination network coincides with the number of this network, then this packet does not need to be routed; otherwise, routing is necessary.

Structures of end node and transit node routing tables are similar. Once again, consider the network shown in Figure 18.2. The routing table of end node B belonging to network N3

Table 18.2 Routing table of computer B

Destination network number	Network address of the next router	Network address of the output port	Distance to the destination network
N1	IP_{13} (R1)	IP_B	1
N2	IP_{13} (R1)	IP_B	1
N3	–	IP_B	0
N4	IP_{31} (R3)	IP_B	1
N5	IP_{13} (R1)	IP_B	2
N6	IP_{31} (R3)	IP_B	2
Default	IP_{31} (R3)	IP_B	–

Table 18.3 Routing table of end node A

Destination network number	Network address of the next router	Network address of the output port	Distance to the destination network
N12	–	IP_A	0
Default	$IP_{17,1}$ (R17)	IP_A	–

might look as shown in Table 18.2. Here, IP_B is the network interface of computer B. Based on this table, computer B chooses to which of the two routers in the N3 local network (R1 or R3) it should send specific packets.

End nodes use the default routing technique to an even greater extent than routers. Although in general they also have routing tables at their disposal, the volume of such tables is usually small. This is because end nodes are located on the network periphery. Quite often, end nodes operate without routing tables. In such cases, they use only the information about the address of the default router. This variant is the only possible one for all end nodes if only one router is in the constituent network. However, even if several routers are in constituent network and end node has to choose the right one, the default route is often specified to improve the computer performance.

Table 18.3 shows the routing table of another end node of the internet, host A. The small size of this routing table reflects that all packets sent from node A must either pass via port 1 of router 17 or never leave the limits of network N12. This router is defined as the default router in this routing table.

Another difference between the behavior of a router and that of an end node is the method of building the routing table. As a rule, routers create routing tables automatically by exchanging control information. In contrast, routing tables for end nodes are often created manually by administrators. Manually created routing tables are then saved on hard disks as normal files.

18.3.3 Searching Routing Tables That Do Not Contain Masks

The routing table lookup algorithm used by IP installed on the router is described in this section. When describing this algorithm, we use Table 18.1 and Figure 18.2.

■ Suppose that a packet arrives to one of the router ports. IP retrieves the destination IP address from the newly arrived packet. For clarity, assume that this packet specifies IP_B in the destination address field.

■ The *first phase* of table lookup is carried out. It consists of *searching for a specific route to the destination host*. IP_B is compared sequentially, row by row, to the contents of the **destination address** field of the routing table. If a match is found (as in the example with Table 18.1), then the address of the next router (IP_{21}) is retrieved from the appropriate row along with the identifier of the output interface (IP_{41}). The table lookup procedure is accomplished at this stage.

■ Now suppose that the table does not contain a row with the IP_B destination address, which means that no match is found. In this case, IP proceeds with the *second phase* of table lookup. The second phase of this process consists of *searching for the route to the destination network*. The network number is retrieved from the IP address (in this example, network N3 will be retrieved from the IP_B address), and table lookup is repeated. This time, it is necessary to find a network number that matches the network number specified in the packet. If a match is found (this was the case in our example), the address of the next router (IP_{12}) and the identifier of the output interface (IP_{41}) are retrieved from the appropriate row of the table. When this operation is carried out, table lookup is accomplished.

■ Finally, suppose that neither the first nor the second phase of routing table lookup produced a match for the destination address in the received packet. In this case, IP either chooses the default route, in which case the packet goes to the IP51 address, or discards the packet if there is no default route. Table lookup is then accomplished.

IMPORTANT *The important point here is that the sequence of table lookup phases is strictly defined but the order of rows in the routing table, including the position of the record specifying the default route, has no affect on the result.*

18.3.4 Examples of Routing Tables of Different Formats

The structure of real-world routing tables of the TCP/IP stack generally corresponds to the simplified structure of the previously considered routing tables. However, the format of the specific IP routing table depends on the implementation of the TCP/IP stack. Consider several versions of routing tables with which the R1 router in the network shown in Figure 18.3 could operate.

Start with a somewhat artificial and simplistic variant of the routing table (Table 18.4). Here, there are three routes to networks (records 56.0.0.0, 116.0.0.0, and 129.13.0.0),

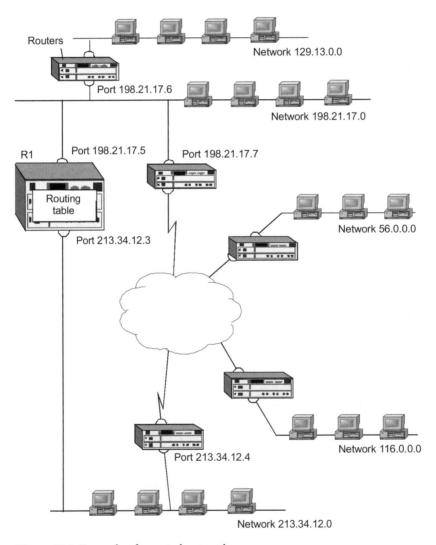

Figure 18.3 Example of a routed network

Table 18.4 Simplified routing table of the R1 router

Address of the destination network	Address of the next router	Address of the output interface	Distance to the destination network
56.0.0.0	213.34.12.4	213.34.12.3	15
116.0.0.0	213.34.12.4	213.34.12.3	13
129.13.0.0	198.21.17.6	198.21.17.5	2
129.13.0.0	198.21.17.5	198.21.17.5	1
213.34.12.0	213.34.12.3	213.34.12.3	1
Default	198.21.17.7	198.21.17.5	–

Table 18.5 Routing table of the built-in Windows 2000 router

Network address	Netmask	Gateway address	Interface	Metric
127.0.0.0	255.0.0.0	127.0.0.1	127.0.0.1	1
0.0.0.0	0.0.0.0	198.21.17.7	198.21.17.5	1
56.0.0.0	255.0.0.0	213.34.12.4	213.34.12.3	15
116.0.0.0	255.0.0.0	213.34.12.4	213.34.12.3	13
129.13.0.0	255.255.0.0	198.21.17.6	198.21.17.5	2
198.21.17.0	255.255.255.0	198.21.17.5	198.21.17.5	1
198.21.17.5	255.255.255.255	127.0.0.1	127.0.0.1	1
198.21.17.255	255.255.255.255	198.21.17.5	198.21.17.5	1
213.34.12.0	255.255.255.0	213.34.12.3	213.34.12.3	1
213.34.12.3	255.255.255.255	127.0.0.1	127.0.0.1	1
213.34.12.255	255.255.255.255	213.34.12.3	213.34.12.3	1
224.0.0.0	224.0.0.0	198.21.17.6	198.21.17.6	1
224.0.0.0	224.0.0.0	213.34.12.3	213.34.12.3	1
255.255.255.255	255.255.255.255	198.21.17.6	198.21.17.6	1

two records on the directly connected networks (129.13.0.0 and 213.34.12.0), and a record on the default route.

Routing tables generated in industrially manufactured network equipment have a more sophisticated format.

If you assume that the R1 router in the current network is the software router built into the Microsoft Windows 2000 operating system, its routing table might look as shown in Table 18.5.

If you replace the R1 router with one of the popular hardware routers, the routing table for the same network might look different—for example, as shown in Table 18.6.

Finally, Table 18.7 represents a routing table for the same R1 router implemented in the form of software routers of one of the operating systems of the UNIX family.

Table 18.6 Routing table of a hardware router

Destination	Mask	Gateway	Metric	Status	TTL	Source
198.21.17.0	255.255.255.0	198.21.17.5	0	Up	–	Connected
213.34.12.0	255.255.255.0	213.34.12.3	0	Up	–	Connected
56.0.0.0	255.0.0.0	213.34.12.4	14	Up	–	Static
116.0.0.0	255.0.0.0	213.34.12.4	12	Up	–	Static
129.13.0.0	255.255.0.0	198.21.17.6	1	Up	160	RIP

Table 18.7 Routing table of the UNIX router

Destination	Gateway	Flags	Refcnt	Use	Interface
127.0.0.0	127.0.0.1	UH	1	154	lo0
Default	198.21.17.7	UG	5	43270	le0
198.21.17.0	198.21.17.5	U	35	246876	le0
213.34.12.0	213.34.12.3	U	44	132435	le1
129.13.0.0	198.21.1.7.6	UG	6	16450	le0
56.0.0.0	213.34.12.4	UG	12	5764	le1
116.0.0.0	213.34.12.4	UG	21	23544	le1

NOTE   *Since there is no unambiguous correspondence between network structure and routing table, it is possible to suggest specific versions for each of the provided variants of the routing table. These versions may differ in the chosen route to specific network. In this case, attention is drawn to the significant differences in the form of representing routing information using different implementations of routers.*

Despite noticeable differences, all key data required by IP for packet routing are in all three real-world routing tables.

The list of such data includes **addresses of the destination network** (the *destination* fields in the hardware router and the UNIX router and the *network address* field in the Windows 2000 router). Another required field of the routing table is the address of the next router (the *gateway* fields in the hardware router and the UNIX router and the *gateway address* field in the Windows 2000 router).

The third key parameter is the **address of the port to which the packet should be forwarded**. In some routing tables it is specified directly (the *interface* field in the Windows 2000 router), and in other tables it is specified implicitly. For instance, the routing table of the UNIX router specifies conventional naming of the port instead of its address — *le0* for the port with the 198.21.17.5 address, *le1* for the port with the 213.34.12.3 address, and *lo0* for the internal port with the 127.0.0.1 address.

In the hardware router, the field specifying the output port in any form is missing. This is because the address of the output port can always be defined indirectly by the address of the next router. For instance, try to determine the address of the output port for the 56.0.0.0 network on the basis of Table 18.6. From this table, it follows that the next router for this network will be the router with the 213.34.12.4 address. The address of the next router must belong to one of the networks directly connected to this router. In this case, this is the 213.34.12.0 network. The router has the port connected to that network. The address of this port, 213.34.12.3, can be found in the *gateway* field of the second row of the routing table, which describes the directly connected 213.34.12.0 network. For directly connected networks, the address of the next router is always the address of the output port of the local router. Thus, for the 56.0.0.0 network, the address of the output port will be 213.34.12.3.

Currently, the use of the mask field in each record of the routing table is a standard solution. Consider, for example, the routing table of the Windows 2000 router (the *netmask* field) and that of the hardware router (the *mask* field). Mask processing on routers when deciding about packet routing will be considered later in this chapter. The lack of the mask field specifies either that the router is intended for operation only with the standard three address classes or that it uses the same mask for all records, which reduces routing flexibility.

Since every destination network is mentioned only once in the routing table of the UNIX router, there is no choice for route selection. Consequently, in this case, the metric is an optional parameter. In other tables, this field is present; however, it is used only as an indicator of the directly connected network. Therefore, the metric 0 for the hardware router or 1 for the Windows 2000 router simply informs the router that this network is directly connected to its port. Other values of the metric correspond to remote networks. The choice of metric value for directly connected network (1 or 0) is arbitrary. The main point here is that the metric of the remote network must be counted with this chosen initial value in mind.

> *The indicator of the directly connected network* informs the router that the packet has already reached its destination network. Therefore, the router does not pass it to the next router. Instead, it passes the packet directly to the destination host. Therefore, IP initiates an ARP request about IP address of the destination host instead of that of the next router.

However, there are situations in which the router must store the metric value for the record of each remote network. Such situations arise when records in the routing table are the result of operation of several routing protocols, such as RIP. In such protocols, the newly received information on any remote network is compared to the information in the table. If the new metric value is better than the current one, then a new record will replace the existing one. In the table of the UNIX router, the metric field is missing, which means that this router does not use RIP.

Flags are present only in the table of the UNIX router. They describe the following characteristics of the record:

- *U* — specifies that the route is active and usable. The *status* field of the routing table of the hardware router has a similar meaning.

- *H* — indicates the specific route to a certain host.

- *G* — specifies that the packet route passes through the transit router (gateway). If this flag is missing, then the network is connected locally.

- *D* — specifies that the route has been obtained from the *redirect* message of ICMP. This flag can be present only in the routing table of the end node. If it is set, this means that the end node in one of the previous attempts at transmitting the packet chose the next router, which was not the optimal one. This router, using ICMP, has reported that all future packets intended for this network must be sent through another router.

In the routing tables of UNIX routers, there are two other fields containing reference values. The *refcnt* field specifies how many times this route was referenced in the course of packet forwarding. The *use* field specifies the number of bytes sent along this route.

Routing tables of hardware routers also have two reference fields. In this case, the *time to live* (TTL) field has nothing to do with the packet's time to live. As in many other tables, this field prevents the use of records whose contents might become obsolete. The current value of the *TTL* field specifies record's TTL — that is, the time interval (in seconds) during which this record will remain valid. The *source* field specifies the source from which this record has appeared in the routing table. Although this field is not present in all routers, there are three main sources of records for practically all routers.

18.3.5 Sources and Types of Records in Routing Tables

For practically all routers, there are *three* main sources of records.

■ One of the sources of records in the routing table is *the software implementing the TCP/IP stack.* When a router is initialized, this software automatically inserts several records into the routing table. As a result, the **minimum routing table** is created.

The list of such records includes information on **directly connected networks** and **default routes** that is usually entered when manually configuring the interfaces of a computer or a router. In the examples provided previously, these are records on networks 213.34.12.0 and 198.21.17.0, the record on the default route in the UNIX router, and record 0.0.0.0 in the Windows 2000 router.

■ The TCP/IP software also automatically enters information on special addresses into the routing table. In the previously provided examples, the routing table of the Windows 2000 router contains the most comprehensive set of such records. Several records in this table are related to the **loopback address** (127.0.0.0) used for local testing of the TCP/IP stack. Records with the destination address 224.0.0.0 are required for processing multicast addresses. Besides this, the table might contain addresses intended for processing broadcasts (for instance, records 8 and 11 contain the broadcast message address in appropriate subnets, and the last record of this table contains the address of limited broadcast). Note that records for special addresses might be missing from some routing tables.

■ The second source of records in the routing table is *manual input.* A network administrator directly forms such records using some specialized network utility, such as the `route` program supplied with UNIX and Windows 2000. In hardware routers, there also is a special command for manually creating records in the routing table. Manually created records are always static. This means that they have no expiration term. These records might be persistent (i.e., preserved after rebooting the router) or temporary (i.e., stored in the routing table only until the device is powered down). Often administrators manually create the record on the default route. Records on specific routes to certain hosts can be created in the same way.

■ Finally, *routing protocols* such as RIP or OSPF can be the third source of records in the routing table. Such records are always dynamic. This means that they have limited TTL.

Software routers built into Windows 2000 and UNIX operating systems do not display the source from which the specific record has appeared in the routing table. A hardware router, on the contrary, uses the *source* field for this purpose. In the example provided in Table 18.6, the first two records were created by the TCP/IP stack software on the basis of port configuration data. This is shown by the *connected* attribute. The next two records are designated as *static*, which means that they were manually entered by the administrator. The last record appeared as a result of the RIP operation; therefore, its *TTL* field contains the value 160.

18.3.6 Example of IP Routing without Masks

Consider the process of packet forwarding over the internet on the example of the IP network shown in Figure 18.4. In this example, assume that all hosts of the network have class-based addresses. Special attention should be paid to the interaction of IP with ARP and DNS.

Assume that the user of the computer named **cit.mgu.com**, located in the Ethernet1 network, needs to establish a connection to the FTP server. The user knows the symbolic name of the server — **unix.mgu.com**. Therefore, that user issues the following command for accessing FTP server by name:

```
> ftp unix.mgu.com
```

Execution of this command can be represented as a three-stage process:

- Passing the DNS query from the client to determine the IP address of the destination host
- Passing the DNS response from the server
- Transmitting the packet from the FTP client to the FTP server

So, start from the first stage.

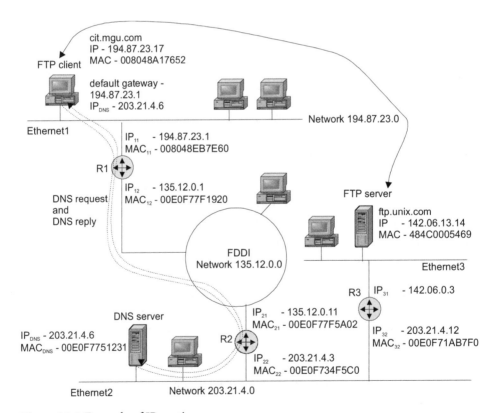

Figure 18.4 Example of IP routing

Passing a DNS Request

1. The FTP client passes the request to the client part of the DNS protocol running on the same computer. This module, in turn, formulates the request to the DNS server. In the most general form, this request sounds as follows: "Which IP address corresponds to the symbolic name **unix.mgu.com?**" The formulated request is encapsulated into the UDP datagram and then into the IP packet (Figure 18.5). The IP address of the DNS server — 203.21.4.6 — is specified as the destination address in the header of this packet. This address is known to the client software of the computer, since it was specified to it as a configuration parameter.

2. Before encapsulating this IP packet into the Ethernet frame, it is necessary to find out if this packet has to be routed through the internetwork or if it is intended for the host located in the same network as the sender. For this purpose, IP compares the network numbers in the source and destination addresses — for example, 194.87.23.17 and 203.21.4.6. As a result of this comparison, it becomes obvious that the packet is directed into another network; consequently, it must be passed to the nearest router. Since Ethernet1 contains only one router, R1, all end nodes of this network use the address of this router — 194.87.23.1 — as that of the default router. This address is also specified as a configuration parameter of the client computer.

3. To enable Ethernet1 network to deliver the packet to router R1, this packet must be placed into the data field of the Ethernet frame and supplied with a MAC address. This problem is solved using ARP, which searches the ARP table. If the required address is missing from the table, the client host sends a broadcast ARP request: "Which MAC address corresponds to IP address 194.87.23.1?" All nodes of the Ethernet1 network receive this request; however, only interface 1 of router R1 replies with the following response: "I have IP address 194.87.23.1, and my MAC address is 008048EB7E60." After receiving this information, the **cit.mgu.com** host sends the IP packet through local network. This packet is encapsulated into the Ethernet frame and has the fields shown in Figure 18.6.

IP header		UDP header	DNS query
IP address of the sender	IP address of the receiver		
194.87.23.17	203.21.4.6		

Figure 18.5 IP packet containing the DNS request

Ethernet header		IP header		UDP header	DNS query
MAC address of the sender	MAC address of the receiver	IP address of the sender	IP address of the receiver		
MAC_c- 008048A17652	MAC₁₁- 008048EB7E60	194.87.23.17	203.21.4.6		unix.mgu.com?

Figure 18.6 Ethernet frame containing the DNS request sent from the client computer

FDDI header		IP header		UDP header	DNS query
MAC address of the sender	MAC address of the receiver	IP address of the sender	IP address of the receiver		
MAC$_{12}$ 00E0F77F1920	MAC$_{21}$ 00E0F77F5A02	194.87.23.17	203.21.4.6		unix.mgu.com?

Figure 18.7 FDDI frame containing the DNS request sent from the R1 router to the R2 router

4. The frame is received by interface 1 of router R1. The Ethernet protocol retrieves the IP packet from this frame and passes it to IP. IP retrieves the destination address, 203.21.4.6, from this packet and searches its local routing table. Suppose that router R1 has the following record in its routing table:

    203.21.4.0   135.12.0.11   135.12.0.1

    This record specifies that packets directed to the 203.21.4.0 network must be passed to the router 135.12.0.11, located in the network connected to interface 135.12.0.1 of the R1 router. The R1 router looks up the parameters of the 135.12.0.1 interface and detects that an FDDI network is connected to it. Since the FDDI network has a larger MTU value than the Ethernet network, the IP packet does not need to be fragmented. (Recall that MTU is the maximum length of the datagram that can fit into the data field of the transmission unit of a specific network technology. The fragmentation will be covered in more detail later in this chapter.) Therefore, the R1 router forms a frame of the FDDI format.

5. At this stage, the IP entity of the R1 router must determine the MAC address of the next router by its known IP address — 135.12.0.11. To achieve this, it relies on ARP. Assume that this time the following record was present in the ARP table:

    135.12.0.11   —   00E0F77F5A02

    Now, knowing the MAC address of the R2 router (00E0F77F5A02), the R1 router sends the frame (Figure 18.7) into the FDDI network.

6. The IP entity running on the R2 router proceeds in a similar way. Having received the FDDI frame, it removes its header, and retrieves the destination IP address from the IP header. After that, it searches its own routing table. From this table, it finds out that the destination network is directly connected to its second interface. Therefore, it sends the following ARP request to the Ethernet2 network: "Which MAC address corresponds to the 203.21.4.6 IP address?" Having received the response on the MAC address of the DNS server — 00E0F7751231, the R2 router sends the frame shown in Figure 18.8 to the Ethernet2 network.

7. The network adapter of the DNS server captures the Ethernet frame, detects that the destination MAC address specified in the header matches its own MAC address, and

Ethernet header		IP header		UDP header	DNS query
MAC address of the sender	MAC address of the receiver	IP address of the sender	IP address of the receiver		
MAC₂₁- 00E0F734F5C0	MAC_DNS- 00E0F7751231	194.87.23.17	203.21.4.6		unix.mgu.com?

Figure 18.8 Ethernet frame containing the DNS request sent from the R2 router

sends it to its own IP entity. After analyzing the fields of the IP header, IP retrieves the data of upper-layer protocols from the packet. The DNS query is then passed to the software module of the DNS server. The DNS server searches its tables, possibly requesting other DNS servers. As a result of this operation, it formulates the response, which looks approximately as follows: "The unix.mgu.com symbolic name has the corresponding 142.06.13.14 IP address."

NOTE *During the entire time the packet spends traveling across the internet from the client computer to the DNS server, the source and destination addresses in the fields of the IP header never change. However, hardware addresses in the header fields of each new frame that carried the packet from router to router changed at every section of the path.*

Passing a DNS Response

1. The TCP/IP stack installed on the DNS server encapsulates the DNS response into the UDP datagram, which is then encapsulated into the IP packet. Note that the destination IP address is known from the DNS query. Then IP determines that the packet has to be routed.

2. IP searches the routing table and determines the IP address of the next router — IP22 — 203.21.4.3.

3. ARP determines the MAC address of the router interface — 00E0F734F5C0.

4. The IP packet is placed into the data field of the Ethernet frame and sent into the Ethernet2 network.

5. The R2 router receives the frame and carries out operations described in steps 2 and 3, after which it sends the FDDI frame to the R1 router.

6. The R1 router determines from the routing table that the arrived packet is intended for the network directly connected to its interface. Therefore, IP requests ARP to receive the MAC address of the destination node rather than that of the router.

7. The frame (Figure 18.9) intended for the FTP client is sent to the Ethernet1 network.

8. The FTP client receives the frame and retrieves the DNS response from there. Now it can continue execution of the command, since the symbolic name of the FTP server has been translated into the form of an IP address.

```
> ftp 142.06.13.14
```

Ethernet header		IP header		UDP header	DNS response
MAC address of the sender	MAC address of the receiver	IP address of the sender	IP address of the receiver		
MAC₁₁-008048EB7E60	MACс-008048A17652	203.21.4.6	194.87.23.17		*142.06.13.14*

Figure 18.9 Ethernet frame with the DNS response sent from the R2 router

Passing the Packet from an FTP Client to an FTP Server

This stage is similar to the previously described procedures of transmitting DNS queries and responses through the network. However, describing this process on your own will be a useful exercise. When doing this work, pay special attention to the values of the address fields of frames and encapsulated IP packets.

18.4 ROUTING USING MASKS

> **KEY WORDS**: subnet, router, distribution of the address space, mask, unstructured network, splitting a network, algorithm for searching the routing tables, retrieved destination addresses, demilitarized zones, prefix, address aggregation, subnetting, supernetting, classless interdomain routing (CIDR), address localization, overlapping address spaces

The routing algorithm becomes more complicated when additional elements, masks, are introduced into the node addressing system. Why was the addressing method based on classes abandoned after it had served as a tried-and-true technology for years? The main reason is the need for network structuring when there is a shortage of network numbers available for distribution.

Often, network administrators are inconvenienced because the quantity of network numbers centrally allocated to them is insufficient for proper structuring of the network. For instance, in a properly structured internet, computers that do not interact intensely and frequently must be placed into different networks. There are two possible ways of overcoming such a situation. The first method implies obtaining additional network numbers from some centralized authority. The second, more common method relates to using the mask technology, which allows one network to be split into several subnets.

18.4.1 Structuring a Network with Masks of the Same Length

For instance, assume that an administrator has obtained a Class B address: 129.44.0.0. He can organize a large network in which host numbers can be allocated from the following range: 0.0.0.1–0.0.255.254. The total number of addresses is 2^{16} ? 2, since addresses made up of only zeros or ones have special meanings and are not suitable for host addressing. However, that administrator does not need a single unstructured network. The needs of his company dictate another solution. According to this solution, the company network must be divided into three separate subnets, the traffic of each subnet being reliably localized. Such a solution will allow simplification of the network diagnostics and maintenance. It will also help to enforce the specific security policy for each subnet. Another important advantage of splitting a large network using masks is that it allows the internal structure of the company network to be hidden from outside observers, thus improving its security.

Figure 18.10 shows the division of the entire address space obtained by the network administrator into four equal parts, each containing 2^{14} addresses. Since the number of bits required for numbering hosts has decreased by 2 bits, the prefix of each of the four networks became 2 bits *longer*; consequently, each of the four address ranges can be written

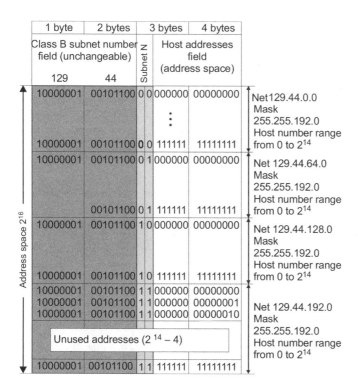

Figure 18.10 Dividing the address space of the Class B network (129.44.0.0) into four equal parts

in the form of an IP address with a mask comprising 18 binary ones or as 255.255.192.0 in decimal notation.

```
129.44.0.0/18      (10000001 00101100 00000000 00000000)
129.44.64.0/18     (10000001 00101100 01000000 00000000)
129.44.128.0/18    (10000001 00101100 10000000 00000000)
129.44.192.0/18    (10000001 00101100 11000000 00000000)
```

From the records provided previously, it is clear that the administrator has the possibility of using two additional bits for numbering subnets. This allows him to create four subnets out of the one large address space centrally allocated to him. In this example these are 129.44.0.0/18, 129.44.64.0/18, 129.44.128.0/18, and 129.44.192.0/18 subnets.

NOTE   *Some software and hardware routers, which follow obsolete recommendations of [RFC 950], do not support subnet numbers comprising only ones or only zeros. For this kind of equipment, the network number 129.44.0.0 with the mask 255.255.192.0, used in this example, will be invalid, since the bits in the subnet number have the value of 00. According to similar considerations, the network number 129.44.192.0 with the same mask will also be invalid. Here, the network number comprises only ones. However, contemporary routers supporting [RFC 1878] are free from these limitations.*

The example of a network created by dividing one large network into four subnets of equal size is shown in Figure 18.11. All traffic coming into the internal network 129.44.0.0 from the outside world is arriving through router R1. To further structure information flows, an additional router, R2, is installed in the internal network. All newly created networks,

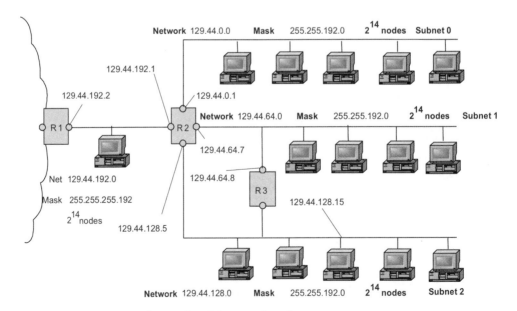

Figure 18.11 Routing using masks of the same length

129.44.0.0/18, 129.44.64.0/18, 129.44.128.0/18, and 129.44.192.0/18, were connected to appropriately configured ports of the internal router, R2.

NOTE   *In one of these networks, 129.44.192.0/18, dedicated for creating a connection between external and internal routers, only two addresses were used: 129.44.192.1 (port of the R2 router) and 129.44.192.2 (port of the R1 router). Two more addresses, 129.44.192.0 and 129.44.192.255, are special-purpose addresses. Many addresses in this network (2^{14} − 4) are not used. Of course, this example is chosen exclusively for demonstration purposes to illustrate inefficiency of dividing the network into subnets of equal size.*

From outside, this network still looks like a single Class B network. However, all traffic coming into this network is divided by the R2 local router among four subnets. When the class mechanism does not work, the router must have another mechanism allowing it to detect which part of the 32-bit number placed into the destination address field represents the network number. An additional mask field included into the routing table (Table 18.8) serves this purpose.

Table 18.8 Routing table of the R2 router in the network with masks of the same length

Destination address	Mask	Address of the next router	Port address	Distance
129.44.0.0	255.255.192.0	129.44.0.1	129.44.192.2	Connected
129.44.64.0	255.255.192.0	129.44.64.7	129.44.64.7	Connected
129.44.128.0	255.255.192.0	129.44.128.5	129.44.128.5	Connected
129.44.192.0	255.255.192.0	129.44.192.1	129.44.192.1	Connected
0.0.0.0	0.0.0.0	129.44.192.2	129.44.192.1	–
129.44.128.15	255.255.255.255	129.44.64.8	129.44.64.7	–

The first four records in this table correspond to internal subnets directly connected to the ports of router R2.

The record 0.0.0.0 with the mask 0.0.0.0 corresponds to the default route.

The latter record specifies a specific route to host 129.44.128.15. For the table records that specify the complete IP address of a host, the mask has the value 255.255.255.255. In contrast to all other nodes of the 129.44.128.0 network, to which the packets arrive from the interface 129.44.128.5 of router R2, to this host, the packets will arrive through the R3 router.

18.4.2 Algorithm of Table Lookup that Accounts for Masks

The algorithm for searching the routing tables containing masks has much in common with the previously described algorithm for the tables that do not contain masks. However, it also contains significant modifications:

1. IP starts searching of the next router for a newly arrived packet by *retrieving the packet's destination address.* For distinctness, designate it as IP_D. Then IP starts the procedure of routing table lookup. This procedure, similarly to the lookup procedure for the table that does not contain the mask field, also comprises two phases.

2. The *first phase consists of searching for a specific route for the IP_D address.* To achieve this, IP retrieves the destination address from each table record for which the mask value is set to 255.255.255.255. The retrieved destination addresses are compared to the destination address of the IP_D packet. If a match is found in any record, then the address of the next router is taken from this record.

3. The *second phase* is carried out if the entire table has been searched but no full match of addresses has been found. This phase consists in searching for a nonspecific route common for the group of hosts to which the packet with the IP_D address relates. To achieve this, IP searches the routing table once again.

4. The following actions are carried out for each *next record:*
   - The mask (M) contained in the current record is "applied" to the IP address of the destination node retrieved from the packet: IP_D AND M.
   - The result is compared to the value placed into the destination address field of the same record of the routing table.
   - If a match is found, IP *marks this record in an appropriate way.*
   - If not all records have been searched, IP processes the next record (return to step 4). If all records have been processed, including the one containing information on the default route, the protocol proceeds with step 5.

5. After viewing the entire routing table, the router carries out one of the following actions:
   - If no match has been found, and there is no default route, then the packet is discarded.
   - If one match has been found, the packet is forwarded along the route specified by the record containing the matching address.
   - If several matches have been found, then the protocol compares all marked records and chooses the route specified by the record with the maximum number of matching bits. In other words, when the destination address specified in the packet belongs to several subnets, *the router uses the most specific route.*

NOTE   *In many routing tables, the record with the address 0.0.0.0 and the mask 0.0.0.0 corresponds to the default route. Any address in the incoming packet, after applying the mask 0.0.0.0, will produce the network address 0.0.0.0, which corresponds to the address*

*specified in the record. Since the mask 0.0.0.0 has zero length, this route is consi-
dered the least specific and is used only if there are no matches to other records of
the routing table.*

Let us illustrate how router R2 (Figure 18.11) uses the previously described algorithm
for working with its routing table (Table 18.8). Suppose that a packet with the destination
address *129.44.78.200* arrives to the R2 router. The IP entity on that router will first compare this address with the address 129.44.128.15, for which a specific route has been defined. Since there is no match, IP will sequentially process all rows of the table, applying
the masks and comparing the results until it finds the match for the network number
both in the destination address and in the table row. Thus, the route for this packet has
been found: It must be forwarded to the output router port 129.44.64.7 and to the
129.44.64.0 network directly connected to this router.

18.4.3 Using Masks of Variable Length

In many cases, dividing the network into subnets of different sizes is more efficient. In
particular, for the subnet that connects two routers according to the "point-to-point"
method, even the number of addresses available in the Class C network is too large.

Figure 18.12 shows another example of distribution of the same address space used in
the previous example, namely, 129.44.0.0/16. Half of the available addresses (2^{15}) are allocated for creating a network with the address 129.44.0.0 and mask 255.255.128.0. The
next range of addresses, a quarter of the entire address space (2^{14}), was assigned to the
129.44.128.0 network with the mask 255.255.192.0.

After that, a small fragment was "cut out" of the address space, intended for creating a
network for connecting the internal R2 router to the external R1 router. For numbering
hosts in such a degenerate network, it is sufficient to allocate 2 bits. Of four possible
combinations of host numbers — 00, 01, 10 and 11 — two numbers have special meaning
and cannot be assigned to hosts. However, the remaining two numbers, 10 and 01, are
enough for addressing router ports. The host number field in this case has a length
of 2 bits, and the mask in decimal notation will appear as follows: 255.255.255.252.
The network number, as shown in Figure 18.12, is 129.44.192.0.

NOTE   *It is not necessary to assign IP addresses to point-to-point links between routers, since
no hosts can connect to such networks except two router ports. However, in most cases,
administrators choose to assign an IP address to such a network. For example, this is
done to hide the internal structure of the network. This is achieved by accessing this
network by the address of the input router port using the network address translation
(NAT) technique. In this example, this is the 129.44.192.1 address. Furthermore, this
address might be needed for tunneling the traffic using the IP network. For instance,
this approach can be used for tunneling IPX or encrypted IPSec traffic. Tunneling and
NAT will be covered in Chapter 20.*

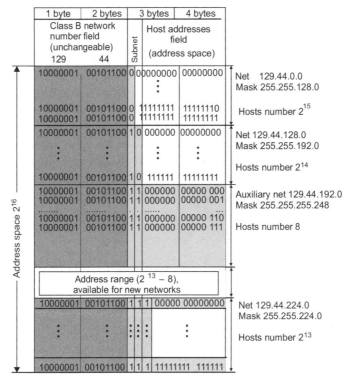

1 byte	2 bytes	Subnet	3 bytes	4 bytes	
Class B network number field (unchangeable) 129 44			Host addresses field (address space)		
10000001	00101100	0 0	00000000	00000000	Net 129.44.0.0 Mask 255.255.128.0
			:		
10000001	00101100	0	11111111	11111110	Hosts number 2^{15}
10000001	00101100	0	11111111	11111111	
10000001	00101100	1 0	000000	00000000	Net 129.44.128.0 Mask 255.255.192.0
:	:		:	:	
					Hosts number 2^{14}
10000001	00101100	1 0	111111	11111111	
10000001	00101100	1 1	000000	00000 000	Auxiliary net 129.44.192.0
10000001	00101100	1 1	000000	00000 001	Mask 255.255.255.248
....	....	. .	......	...	
10000001	00101100	1 1	000000	00000 110	Hosts number 8
10000001	00101100	1 1	000000	00000 111	
Address range (2^{13} – 8), available for new networks					
10000001	00101100	1 1 1	00000	00000000	Net 129.44.224.0 Mask 255.255.224.0
:	:	: : :	:	:	Hosts number 2^{13}
10000001	00101100	1 1 1	11111111	111111	

Address space 2^{16}

Figure 18.12 Dividing the address space of the Class B network (129.44.0.0) into networks of different sizes using masks of variable length

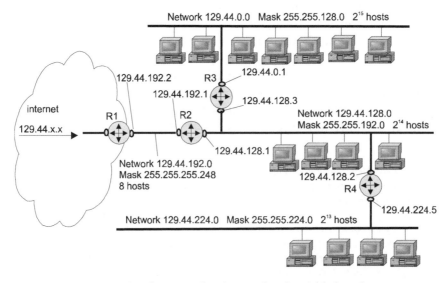

Figure 18.13 Structuring the network using masks of variable length

Table 18.9 Routing table of the R2 router
in the network with masks of variable length

Destination address	Mask	Address of the next router	Port address	Distance
129.44.0.0	255.255.128.0	129.44.128.3	129.44.128.1	1
129.44.128.0	255.255.192.0	129.44.128.1	129.44.128.1	Connected
129.44.192.0	255.255.255.248	129.44.192.1	129.44.192.1	Connected
129.44.224.0	255.255.224.0	129.44.128.2	129.44.128.1	1
0.0.0.0	0.0.0.0	129.44.192.2	129.44.192.1	–

The remaining address space can be "sliced" into any number of networks of any size, depending on the needs of the company. For instance, an administrator can create a sufficiently large network containing 2^{13} hosts from the remaining address pool $(2^{14}-4)$. Almost the same number $(2^{13} - 4)$ will remain available. These addresses, in turn, can be used for creating new networks. For example, this "remainder" can be used for creating 31 networks, each of which will be equal in size to a Class C network, and for creating several smaller networks. Clearly, another division might be chosen. However, it is clear that when using masks of variable lengths, an administrator has more capabilities of efficiently using all available addresses.

Figure 18.13 shows the example network structured using masks of variable length. Consider how router R2 processes the packets arriving to its interfaces (Table 18.9).

Assume that the packet coming into the R2 router has the destination address *129.44.192.5*. Since this table does not contain specific routes, the router proceeds with the second phase of table lookup, namely, with sequential analysis of all rows for a matching destination address:

(129.44.192.5) AND (255.255.128.0) = 129.44.128.0 — no matching destination addresses
(129.44.192.5) AND (255.255.192.0) = 129.44.192.0 — no matching destination addresses
(129.44.192.5) AND (255.255.255.248) = 129.44.192.0 — matching destination addresses
(129.44.192.5) AND (255.255.224.0) = 129.44.192.0 — no matching destination addresses

Thus, there was a match in one row. The packet will be sent to the network directly connected to the current router — to the 129.44.192.1 output interface.

Table 18.10 Fragment of the routing table of the R1 router

Destination address	Mask	Address of the next router	Port address	Distance
. . . .	. . . .	. . . .	. . . .	. . . .
129.44.0.0	255.255.0.0	129.44.192.1	129.44.192.2	2
129.44.192.0	255.255.255.252	129.44.192.2	129.44.192.2	Connected
. . . .	. . . .	. . . .	. . . .	. . . .

If the packet with the address *129.44.192.1* arrives from the external network and router R1 operates without using masks, then the packet will be passed to router R2 and returned to the transit network. Obviously, this is inefficient.

Routing will be more efficient if in the table of router R1 all routes are specified using masks of variable length. The fragment of such a table is in Table 18.10. The first of the two records provided in this table specifies that all packets that have destination addresses starting with 129.44 have to be passed to router R2. This record carries out **address aggregation** for all subnets created on the basis of the 129.44.0.0 network. The second record specifies that among all possible subnets of the 129.44.0.0 network, there is one network, 129.44.192.0/30, to which packets can be sent directly rather than through the R2 router.

NOTE   *When using the masks mechanism, only the destination IP address is passed in IP packets — without the mask of the destination network. Therefore, it is impossible to find which part of the IP address of the delivered packet relates to the network number and which part relates to the host number. If masks in all subnets have the same size, this does not create any problems. However, if masks of variable lengths are used for subnetting, then the router must have some mechanism allowing it to detect which masks correspond to which network addresses. For this purpose, routing protocols are used. Routing protocols carry information on network addresses along with information on network masks corresponding to these numbers among routers. The list of such protocols includes RIPv2 and OSPF. As relates to RIP, it does not carry network masks. Therefore, this protocol is not suitable for using masks of variable lengths.*

18.4.4 Overlapping Address Spaces

It is not when an administrator starts configuring network interfaces and creating routing tables when she encounters the complication of mask administration for the first time. This happens significantly earlier at the stage of network planning. Planning includes determining the number of networks that will be included into the companywide network, evaluating the required number of addresses for each network, obtaining an address pool from the provider, and distributing the available address space among networks. The latter task often proves to be a nontrivial one, especially under conditions of the address shortage.

Consider the example of mask usage for organizing **overlapping address spaces**.

Suppose that the management of some company has decided to request an address pool sufficient for creating a network, the structure of which is shown in Figure 18.14. The client network includes three subnets. Two of them are internal department-level networks: Ethernet intended for 600 users and a Token Ring network for 200 users. The company also makes a provision for the presence of a separate network including ten hosts, the main goal of which is providing information for potential clients in the public access mode. Such sections of a companywide network, in which Web servers, FTP servers, and other sources of public information are located, are generally known as **demilitarized zones (DMZs)**. Furthermore, an additional network containing only two hosts is required for connection to the service provider. Thus, the total number of addresses required for assigning network interfaces is 812. Besides this, it is necessary to ensure that the pool of available addresses includes broadcast addresses comprising only ones and addresses comprising only zeros. Because in any network addresses of all hosts must have the same prefixes, it becomes evident that the minimum number of addresses required for the client to build such a network might significantly differ from 812, which was obtained by simple summing.

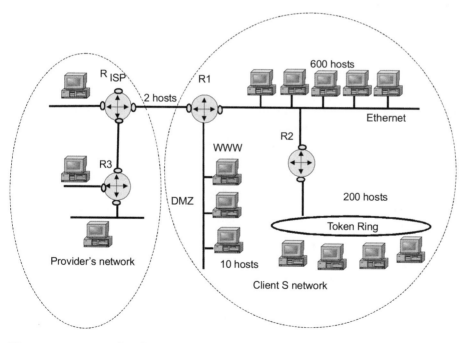

Figure 18.14 Networks of the provider and the client

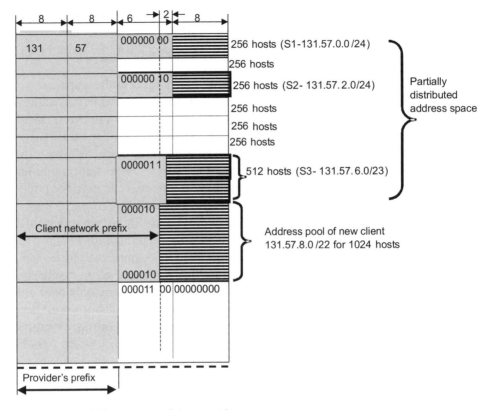

Figure 18.15 Address space of the provider

In this example, the provider decides to allocate the client a continuous address pool comprising 1024 addresses. The number 1024 was chosen because it is the power of two ($2^{10} = 1024$) the closest to the required number of addresses. The provider looks for the area of such a length in the address space available to it — 131.57.0.0/16. Note that usually part of this space is already allocated to other clients, as shown in Figure 18.15. Designate the address ranges allocated to customers as S1, S2, and S3. The provider finds a continuous range among available addresses that have not been distributed yet. The size of this range is 1024 addresses, and the starting address of the range is a multiple of the size of this range. Thus, the new client will obtain the address pool 131.57.8.0/22, designated as S in the illustration.

Then, the most difficult stage of network planning begins. It is necessary to distribute address pool S obtained from the provider among four networks of the company. First, the administrator decides to allocate the entire address pool 131.57.8.0/22 to the largest network, Ethernet, which contains 600 nodes (Figure 18.16). The network number assigned to this network matches the network number obtained from the provider. Well, what should the administrator do with the remaining three networks? Administrator bears in mind that Ethernet requires only 600 addresses. Of the remaining 424 addresses,

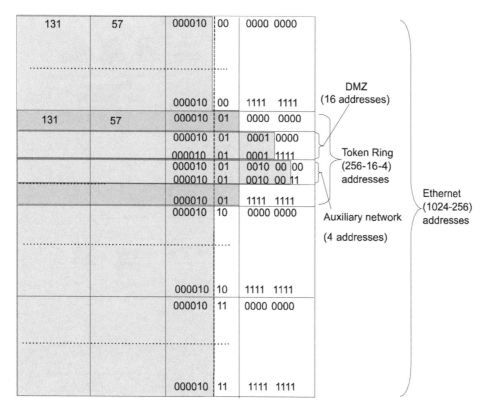

Figure 18.16 Planning address space for the customer's networks

the administrator "scrapes up" 256 addresses for the Token Ring network. Taking advantage of the fact that Token Ring requires only 200 addresses, the administrator "cuts out" two sections of it: 131.57.9.16/28 with 16 addresses for organizing a DMZ, and 131.57.9.32/30 with 4 addresses for the network that connects the company to the ISP network. As a result, all networks of this company have been allocated a sufficient (sometimes even a redundant) number of addresses.

The next stage is configuring network interfaces of the end nodes and routers. Each interface is configured with its IP address and appropriate mask. Figure 18.17 shows the configured network of the customer.

Having configured all network interfaces, it is necessary to create a routing table for customer's R1 and R2 routers. They can be generated automatically or manually by an administrator. Table 18.11 shows the routing table of the R2 router.

This table does not contain a default route, which means that all packets intended for the networks having addresses that are not explicitly specified in the table will be discarded by this router.

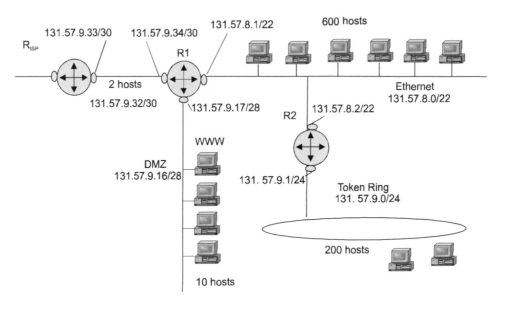

Figure 18.17 Configured the customer's network

Table 18.11 Routing table of the R2 router

Destination address	Mask	Next router address	Output interface address	Distance
131.57.8.0	255.255.252.0	131.57.8.2	131.57.8.2	Connected
131.57.9.0	255.255.255.0	131.57.9.1	131.57.9.1	Connected
131.57.9.16	255.255.255.240	131.57.8.1	131.57.8.2	1
131.57.9.32	255.255.255.252	131.57.8.1	131.57.8.2	1

For example, suppose that the packet with destination address 131.57.9.29 arrives to the R2 router. As a result of the table lookup, you will obtain the following results for each table row:

$$(131.57.9.29) \text{ AND } (255.255.252.0) = 131.57.8.0 — \text{match}$$
$$(131.57.9.29) \text{ AND } (255.255.255.0) = 131.57.9.0 — \text{match}$$
$$(131.57.9.29) \text{ AND } (255.255.255.240) = 131.57.9.16 — \text{match}$$
$$(131.57.9.29) \text{ AND } (255.255.255.252) = 131.57.9.28 — \text{no match}$$

According to the routing table lookup algorithm, if there are several matches, the route from that row in which the destination address from the packet that matches the destination address from the table has the maximum length will be chosen. Thus, it will be defined that the packet with the address 131.57.9.29 will be directed to the DMZ network.

18.4.5 Routing and CIDR

During the last few years, there were lots of changes in the Internet: The number of hosts and networks grew sharply, the traffic intensity increased, and the type of data being transmitted changed. Because of the imperfection of the routing protocols, the exchange of messages carrying information about routing table updates began to result in failures of backbone routers. This happened because of congestion caused by processing a large amount of control information. For example, routing tables of backbone Internet routers today can contain hundreds or even thousands of routes.

To overcome this problem, the **classless interdomain routing (CIDR)** technology was developed.

> The main idea of CIDR is as follows: Each ISP must be assigned a continuous range in the IP address space. When using such an approach, the addresses of all networks of each service provider will have a common most significant part — the **prefix**. Therefore, routing in the Internet backbones can be carried out on the basis of prefixes instead of fully qualified network addresses. This means that instead of several records, one record for each network, it will be sufficient to have a single record for the set of networks that have matching prefixes. Address aggregation will decrease the volume of routing tables in routers of all levels. Consequently, routers will operate faster, and the Internet bandwidth will be increased.

Earlier in this chapter, we offered examples in which administrators of companywide networks used masks for dividing a continuous address pool obtained from an ISP into several parts so as to use them for structuring their networks. Such a variant of using masks is known as **subnetting** (RFC 950).

At the same time, using masks for splitting a network into subnets also has an inverse effect – **network aggregation**. Simply speaking, in order to route all traffic incoming into the corporate network divided into subnets, it is sufficient to have only one record in all external routers. This record must specify the prefix common for all these networks as a destination address. The right boundary of the prefix is specified using an appropriate mask. This is **supernetting**, an operation inverse to subnetting. Supernetting means that masks are used for aggregating several networks into a single larger one.

Return to Figure 18.15, showing the address space of the ISP with the S1, S2, S3, and S address ranges allocated to four clients. This example is also illustrated by Figure 18.18. As a result of aggregating customer networks in Table 18.12 of the R_{ISP} router, one row will be allocated to each client independent of the number of subnets that they have organized in their networks. For instance, instead of providing four routes to seven networks of the customer S, the table contains only one route common for all these networks.

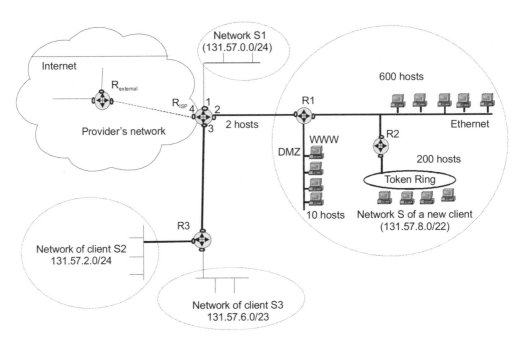

Figure 18.18 Supernetting

Table 18.12 Routing table of the R$_{ISP}$ router

Destination address	Mask	Next router	Number of the output interface	Distance
131.57.0.0 (S1)	255.255.255.0	–	1	Connected
131.57.2.0 (S2)	255.255.255.0	R3	3	1
131.57.6.0 (S3)	255.255.254.0	R3	3	1
131.57.8.0 (S)	255.255.252.0	–	2	1
Default	0.0.0.0	R$_{external}$	4	–

For a top-level provider supporting clients using the R$_{external}$ router, the efforts of the local provider for splitting its address space will not be noticeable. The record 131.57.0.0 with the mask 255.255.0.0 fully describes the networks of local provider in the R$_{external}$ router.

Thus, introduction of the CIDR technology provides the following solutions:

- More sparing use of the address space. With the CIDR technology, providers can "slice" the address space allocated to them according to the requirements of each client. At the same time, the clients will have some reserve for the future.
- Decreased number of records in routing tables because of the route aggregation. Thus, a single record in the routing table can represent a large number of networks. If all ISPs follow the CIDR strategy, the gain would be especially noticeable in backbone routers.

> Address localization is a mandatory requirement of efficient CIDR use. Address localization means that addresses with matching prefixes are assigned to networks located close to one another. Traffic aggregation is possible only when this condition has been observed.

Unfortunately, address distribution is in many respects random. Reassigning network numbers is a fundamental method of approaching this problem. However, this procedure requires both time and financial investments. Therefore, to carry it out, it is necessary to stimulate the users in some way. Such a stimulus can include billing for each row in the routing table or for the number of hosts in the network. The first requirement brings the customer to the idea of obtaining addresses from the provider that allow traffic routing into his network to be based on the network prefix. When this is achieved, the records with the company network numbers would no longer occur in backbone routers. The requirement for paying for each host address also can motivate the user to renumber and obtain a number of addresses that does not significantly exceed the required one.

The CIDR technology is successfully used in the current version of IP, IPv4. It is also supported by such routing protocols as OSPF, RIPv2, and BGP4 (mainly on the Internet backbone routers). Specific features of using CIDR in the new version of IP, IPv6, will be covered later in the section dedicated to IPv6.

18.5 FRAGMENTATION OF IP PACKETS

> **KEY WORDS:** fragmentation, fragment, MTU, heterogeneous networks, identifier; TTL, DF flag, MF flag, offset, best effort, assembling, IP packet, local technology frame, timer.

An important feature of IP, differing from all other network protocols (such as IPX), is its capability of carrying out **dynamic packet fragmentation** when transmitting packets from network to network. Fragmentation is needed if these networks have different maximum lengths of the frame data fields (maximum transmission unit, MTU). The capability of packet fragmentation characteristic to IP has in many respects improved the scalability of the TCP/IP technology.

18.5.1 MTU as a Technological Parameter

First, let us point out the difference between message fragmentation in the source node and dynamic fragmentation of messages in the transit nodes of the network — routers. In practically all protocol stacks, there are protocols responsible for dividing application-layer messages such fragments that fit into the data link-layer frames. For this purpose, they analyze the type of the underlying technology and define its MTU.

In the TCP/IP stack, this problem is solved by TCP, which splits the flow of bytes transmitted to it from the application layer into segments of the required size (for instance, 1460 bytes if Ethernet protocol is used as the underlying technology of the network). Therefore, the IP of the **sender** usually does not employ its fragmentation capabilities. However, the situation is different for routers, when it is necessary to pass the packet from the current network to another network that has a smaller MTU. In this case, IP fragmentation capabilities are used.

Table 18.13 Typical MTU values

Technology	MTU
DIX Ethernet	1,500 bytes
Ethernet 802.3	1,492 bytes
Token Ring (IBM, 16 Mbps)	17,914 bytes
Token Ring (802.5, 4 Mbps)	4,464 bytes
FDDI	4,352 bytes
X.25	576 bytes

From Table 18.13, it becomes clear that MTU values for most popular technologies are significantly different. This means that fragmentation is a common practice in contemporary heterogeneous networks.

18.5.2 Fragmentation Parameters

The main idea of fragmentation is splitting the packet arriving from the network with the larger MTU into shorter packets, **fragments**, if this packet has to be forwarded into the network with the smaller MTU. As fragments travel across the network, they are fragmented once again at some of the transit routers. Each fragment must be supplied by a full-value IP header.

Some of the header fields, such as the *identifier; TTL, DF,* and *MF flags;* and *offset,* are directly intended for the procedure of assembling fragments into the source message:

■ The receiver of a fragment uses the *identifier field for recognizing all fragments of the same packet.* The IP module that sends the packet fills the identifier field with the value that must be unique for the current "sender–receiver" pair. This condition must be observed during the entire time this packet (or any of its fragments) exists in the IP internetwork. To ensure the observance of these conditions, the IP entity that sends packets can trace the assigned identifiers. For example, this can be done by supporting the table in which each record is related to an individual destination host to which the connection has been established. Each record of such a table contains the last value of the packet's TTL in the IP network. However, because the identifier field allows 65,536 different values, some IP implementations randomly choose identifiers from this range, relying on the high probability that the identifier will be unique during the entire packet transmission.

■ The sender specifies the *TTL* during which the packet can exist in the network.

■ The *offset* field of a packet fragment informs the receiver about the position of this fragment in the source packet. Thus, the first fragment will always have zero offset. If the packet is not fragmented, the offset field will also have the zero value.

■ The *MF* flag set to 1 indicates that the just arrived fragment is not the last one. The IP entity that sends a nonfragmented packet sets the *MF* flag to zero.

■ The *DF* flag set to 1 indicates that the current packet must not be fragmented under any conditions. If the packet marked as the one that must not be fragmented cannot reach the destination node without fragmentation, the IP entity discards it and sends an appropriate ICMP message to the sender.

NOTE   *The possibility of blocking packet fragmentation can in some cases help to make applications run faster. To achieve this, it is first necessary to investigate the network and determine the maximum size of the packet that can travel along the entire path without fragmentation. After that, only packets that do not exceed this size should be used. This feature can also be used to prevent fragmentation when the resources of the destination host are not sufficient for assembling fragments.*

18.5.3 Procedures of Fragmenting and Assembling Packets

First consider the **fragmentation** procedure. Before splitting newly arrived packet into fragments, the IP installed on the router allocates several buffers for new fragments.

It then copies the contents of some fields of the IP header from the original packet into these buffers, thus creating IP "dummy" headers for all new fragmented packets. Some parameters of the IP header are copied into headers of all fragments; other ones remain only in the header of the first fragment. The fragmentation process can change the values of some fields of IP headers of the fragments from those of the IP header of the original packet. Thus, each fragment has its own value of the header checksum, fragment offset, and total packet length. In all packets except the last one, the *MF* flag is set to one; in the last fragment, it is set to zero.

The contents of the data field of each fragment are formed by splitting the contents of the data field of the original packet. With all this going on, the following two conditions must be met: First, the fragment size (IP header plus data field) must not exceed the MTU of the underlying technology. Second, the size of the data field of each fragment except the last one must be a multiple of 8 bytes. The size of the last part of the data is equal to the remainder.

Now consider how fragmented packets are reassembled. This procedure takes place at the destination host.

NOTE   *Note that IP routers do not assemble packet fragments into larger packets, even if along their path there are some networks allowing such aggregation. The reason for such behavior is straightforward. Different fragments of the same message may travel along different routes in the internet. Consequently, there is no guarantee that all fragments will go through the same router.*

Thus, for each fragmented packet, a special buffer is allocated at the destination host, into which the receiving IP entity places IP fragments that have matching source addresses, destination addresses, and values of the *identifier* and *protocol* fields. All these attributes specify that these packets are fragments of the same original packet. The assembling process consists of placing the data of each fragment into the position specified by the *offset* field of the packet header.

When the first fragment of the original packet arrives at the destination host, that host starts the reassembly timer that determines the maximum time during which it is allowed to wait for other fragments of this packet to arrive. In different implementations of IP, different rules of choosing this timeout period are applied. For example, the timer may be set to the fixed value (from 60 to 120 seconds) recommended by RFC. As a rule, this interval is sufficient for delivering the packet from sender to receiver. Other implementations can determine this interval using adaptive algorithms by measuring time in the network and statistically evaluating the expedited time of fragment arrivals. Finally, timeout may be chosen on the basis of TTL values carried in received fragments. The latter approach is based on the idea that there is no sense in waiting for other fragments to arrive if the TTL of one of the received fragments has expired.

NOTE   *If at least one fragment of the packet has not arrived in time to the destination host (in time means before the timer expires), then no actions are taken for duplication of the missing fragment, and all received fragments are discarded. The destination host sends an ICMP error message to the sender. This behavior of IP corresponds to its "best effort" plan (i.e., the protocol makes its best effort to deliver the packet but does not provide guarantees).*

The lack of blank intervals ("holes") in the data field and the arrival of the last fragment (*MF = 0*) indicate that the assembly process has been completed. After the data have been assembled, it is possible to transmit them to a higher-layer protocol, such as TCP.

18.5.4 Example of Fragmentation

Consider an example in which fragmentation is carried out on the router (Figure 18.19).

Assume that the sending host is connected to the network that has an MTU of 17,914 bytes. Let it be a Token Ring network. As a rule, the transport layer knows the MTU of the underlying technology and chooses the segment size in an appropriate way. Suppose that in this example, the message of 6,600 bytes is passed from the transport layer to the IP layer. IP forms the data field of the IP packet on the basis of this message and supplies it with the header. Pay special attention to the way in which the header fields related to packet fragmentation are filled. First, the packet is assigned a unique identifier, for instance, 12456. Second, since the packet has not been fragmented yet, the *offset* field is set to zero, and the *MF* flag is also set to zero to specify that there are no fragments to follow. Third, the *DF* flag is set to 1, which means that this packet can be fragmented. The total length of the IP packet is 6,600 + 20 (IP header size) — that is, 6,620 bytes. The length of this packet fits within the data field of the Token Ring frame. Then the IP entity of the sender host passes this frame to its network interface, which sends frames to the next router.

After the frame passes the network layer of the router's network interface and is stripped of the Token Ring header, the router's IP entity will retrieve the destination network address from the packet. By this address, it will determine that the newly arrived IP packet

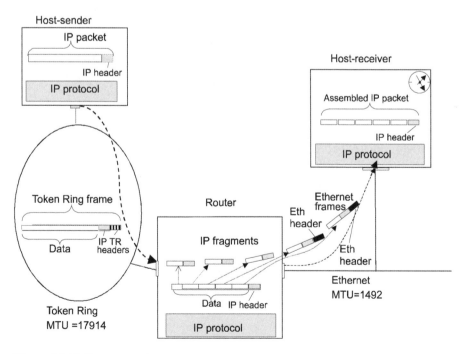

Figure 18.19 Fragmentation

must be passed to the Ethernet network, which has an MTU of 1,492. This value is significantly smaller than the size of the packet that arrived at the input interface. Consequently, the IP packet must be fragmented. The router retrieves the data field from the packet and divides it into parts of the following sizes: four fragments containing 1,400 bytes each and one fragment of 1,000 bytes. Note that each data fragment is a multiple of eight. Then, the IP entity forms new IP packets, four of which will have the length of $1,400 + 20 = 1,420$ bytes; the length of the last packet will be $1,000 + 20 = 1,020$. These values are smaller than 1,500 bytes; therefore, these packets will fit within the data fields of the Ethernet frames.

As a result, the destination host connected to Ethernet will receive five IP packets with the common identifier 12456. If these packets arrive within a time interval that does not exceed the time-out value, IP running on the destination host can assemble the original message. If these packets arrive in an order different from the order in which they were sent, then the *offset* field will specify the correct order for their assembling.

18.6 IPV6

KEY WORDS: IPv6, next generation Internet protocol (IPng), Internet, mass media, scalable addressing method, QoS, security, IPSec, address hexadecimal form, format prefix (FP), unicast, multicast, broadcast, anycast, private address, link-local address, site-local address, global aggregate unique address, top-level aggregation (TLA), next-level aggregation (NLA), site-level aggregation (SLA), IPv4-mapped IPv6 address, IPv4-compatible IPv6 addresses, Flexible Header Format

Since the early 1990s, the TCP/IP stack has encountered serious problems. By that time, the Internet was being used most actively for industrial purposes. For instance, most organizations began building their companywide networks using the Internet as the transport system. They also started using Web technologies for accessing corporate information. Besides this, e-commerce using the Internet became widespread, and the Internet was employed in mass media and entertainment industries, such as video and audio broadcasting and interactive gaming.

All these factors have resulted in explosive growth in the number of network hosts. In the early 1990s, new hosts were connected to the Internet every 30 seconds. Consequently, the traffic type changed, and QoS requirements became significantly more stringent.

18.6.1 Directions of TCP/IP Stack Modernization

The Internet community and then the entire telecommunications industry started to solve new problems by developing new protocols for the TCP/IP stack, such as RSVP, IPSec, and MPLS. However, even by that time it was clear to the leading experts that the TCP/IP technology cannot be improved only by adding new protocols. It was necessary to venture into modernization of the stack core, IP. The main justification for this approach was that some problems could not be solved without changing the IP packet format and re-working the processing logic of IP header fields. Among these problems, the most urgent one was the shortage of IP addresses available for distribution. This problem certainly could not be solved without extending the size of source and destination address fields.

Routing scalability became the most popular target for criticism. The point was that fast growth of the network congested routers, which even now must process routing tables containing information on tens of thousands of records. It is also necessary to bear in mind that routers also have to carry out several auxiliary tasks, such as fragmenting packets. Some solutions were suggested to this problem, but they also required changes to be introduced into IP.

Along with adding functions directly into IP, it was necessary to ensure its close interaction with the new protocols that became members of the TCP/IP stack. This also required adding fields to the IP header. The processing of these fields had to be carried out by these protocols. For instance, to ensure the operation of RSVP, it would be desirable to introduce the flow label field into the IP header, and for IPSec, special fields for data transmission are needed to support the functions ensuring its security.

As a result, the Internet community has decided to radically change IP, choosing the following goals as the main aims of this modernization:

- Create a scalable addressing method
- Reduce the operations carried out by routers
- Provide guarantees of transport service quality
- Ensure the protection of data transmitted through the network

Active research in the field of IP modernization and the development of new protocols associated with it started in 1992. At that time, several alternative versions of the new-generation IP were presented to the Internet community: IPv7 (developed by Ullman), TUBA (Callon), ENCAPS (Hinden), SIP (Deering), and PIP (Francis).

As a result of the development process, in 1993, such projects as ENCAPS, SIP, and PIP were combined within the framework of the common proposal that became known as SIPP. In June 1994, this proposal was adopted as the basis for development of IP of the next generation — the **next generation Internet protocol** (IPng). Nowadays, the **IPv6** abbreviation is commonly used for designating the new version of IP.

The document that registered the arrival of IPv6 is RFC 1752, "The Recommendation for the IP Next Generation Protocol." The basic set of protocols named IPv6 was adopted by the IETF in September 1995. In August 1998, the revised versions of the standards determining common IPv6 architecture (RFC 2460, *"Internet Protocol, Version 6 (IPv6) Specification"*) and its separate aspects such as the addressing system (RFC 2373) *"IP Version 6 Addressing Architecture"*) were adopted. The latest version of this standard describing the architecture of IPv6 addresses (RFC 3513) was adopted relatively recently, namely, in 2003.

18.6.2 Scalable Addressing System

The newer, sixth version of IP has introduced significant changes into the addressing system of IP networks. These changes relate foremost to the increase of the *address bit capacity*.

Address bit capacity. An IPv6 address comprises *128 bits* or *16 bytes*. This provides the possibility of numbering a vast number of hosts: 340,282,366,920,938,463,463,374,607, 431,762,211,456. The scale of this number is illustrated, for instance, by the following: if this theoretically possible number of IP addresses is divided among all inhabitants of the Earth (approximately 6 billion people), then each person would have a senselessly large number of IP addresses, namely, 5.7×10^{28}!

Obviously, such a significant increase in the address length was aimed not at eliminating the address shortage problem but at improving the overall efficiency of TCP/IP stack operation.

> The main goal of addressing modernization was not mechanical increase of the address space. On the contrary, this goal was extending its functionality at the expense of introducing new fields.

Instead of two hierarchical levels (network number and host number), IPv6 provides four levels of hierarchy, among which three levels are used for identifying networks and one level is dedicated to identifying hosts. Because of the increased number of address hierarchy levels, the new protocol efficiently supports the CIDR technology. This, as well as the improved system of group addressing and the introduction of the new type of addresses, the new IP version allows routing expenses to be decreased.

Address presentation. The changes also included purely cosmetic ones. For instance, the developers proposed to replace the decimal form of IP address representation by its *hexadecimal form*. Every four hex digits are separated by a colon. For instance, a typical IPv6 address now looks as follows: FEDC:0A98:0:0:0:0:7654:3210.

If the address includes a long sequence of zeros, this notation can be reduced. For example, the address provided previously can be written as follows: FEDC:0A98::7654:3210.

The "::" abbreviation can be used only once within an address. It is also possible to omit leading zeros at the beginning of each field of the address. For example, instead of FEDC:0A98::7654:3210 it is possible to write FEDC:A98::7654:3210.

Networks supporting both versions of IP — IPv4 and IPv6 — are allowed to use the decimal notation traditional for IPv4 for the 4 least significant bytes. For the 12 most significant bytes, the hex form is preferred: 0:0:0:0:0:FFFF:129.144.52.38 or ::FFFF:129.144.52.38.

Address types. The new version, IPv6, makes provision for the following three main types of addresses: *unicast, multicast,* and *anycast.* Address type is defined by the value of several most significant bits of the address, which are called the *format prefix* (FP).

■ Addresses of the **unicast** type define the unique identifier of an individual interface of the end node or router. The main goal of addresses of this type generally coincides with the goal of unique addresses in IPv4. Using such addresses, the protocol delivers packets to a specific network interface of the destination node. However, in contrast to IPv4, in IPv6 there are no concepts of network classes (A, B, C, and D) or of related fixed splitting of the address to the network number and the host number by 8-bit boundaries. Addresses of the unicast type are divided into several subtypes that reflect situations most common for contemporary networks.

■ Addresses of the **multicast** type form a group similar to the IPv4 group address in its main goal. It has the prefix of the 1111 1111 format and identifies the group of interfaces that usually relate to different hosts. The packet with such an address is delivered to *all* interfaces having that address. Addresses of the multicast type are also used in IPv6 for the replacement of **broadcast addresses**. For this purpose, a special group address is introduced, which joins all interfaces of the subnet.

■ Addresses of the **anycast** type are a new type of address that, similar to the multicast type, specifies a group of interfaces. However, the packet with such an address is delivered to only one of the interfaces that belong to the group. As a rule, this is the "nearest" interface according to the metric used by routing protocols. In syntax, an anycast address does not differ from a unicast address and is assigned from the same address range as unicast addresses. An address of the anycast type can be assigned only to the router interfaces. Router interfaces belonging to the same anycast group have individual unicast addresses and the common anycast address. Addresses of this type are oriented toward source routing, when the route for the packet is defined by the sender by specifying the IP addresses of all transit routers. For instance, the provider can assign the same anycast address to all its routers and specify that address to its subscribers. If the client desires that the packets from his network be transmitted through the network belonging to that ISP, it is sufficient to specify this anycast address in the chain of the source route addresses. The packet will then be passed through the nearest router of that provider.

■ In the sixth version of IP, similar to IPv4, there are **private addresses** intended for use in autonomous networks. In contrast to IPv4, in IPv6, these addresses have a special format. Addresses for local use have two variations in IPv6:

  • First, these are addresses for networks not split into subnets (and do not use routing). They are called **link-local addresses** and have a 10-bit prefix of the following format: 1111 1110 10. The link-local address contains only the 64-bit field of the interface identifier; all other bits except the FP must be set to zero, since in this case there is no need for a subnet number.

- Second, this group includes local addresses intended for use in networks split into subnets. Such addresses are called **site-local addresses**; they have a prefix of the following format: 1111 1110 11 and, in comparison to link-local addresses, contain an additional 2-byte field of the subnet number.

The main subtype of the unicast addresses is the global aggregate unique address. Such addresses can be aggregated to simplify routing. In contrast to a unique address of the IPv4 version, which comprise two fields — network number and host number — global aggregate unique addresses of IPv6 have more complicated structure that includes six fields (Figure 18.20).

■ The *FP* for addresses of this type comprises 3 bits and has the value of 001.

The following three fields — *top-level aggregation* (TLA), *next-level aggregation* (NLA), and *site-level aggregation* (SLA) — represent three levels of network identification.

■ *TLA* is intended for identifying networks of the largest providers. The specific value of this prefix represents the common part of addresses owned by that provider. The relatively small number of bits allocated for this field, 13, is chosen specially for limiting the size of routing tables in backbone routers of the top level of the Internet. This field allows 8,196 networks of the top-level providers. This means that the number of records describing routes between these networks also will be limited by the value 8196, which will speed up the operation of the backbone routers. The next 8 bits are reserved for future use, for extending the *TLA* field if necessary.

■ The prefix of the next level, *NLA*, is intended for numbering networks of medium and small providers. The size of the *NLA* field allows the creation of a multilevel address hierarchy through address aggregation. This hierarchy would reflect the multilevel hierarchy of ISPs.

■ *SLA* is intended for addressing networks of an individual subscriber, such as subnets representing parts of the same companywide network. It is assumed that the provider assigns for a specific company the number of its network comprising a fixed value of the *TLA* and *NLA* fields, which in combination represent an analogue of the network number in IPv4. The remaining part of address — the *SLA* and *interface ID* fields — are at the

3 bits	13 bits	8 bits	24 bits	16 bits	64 bits
Format prefix (FP)	Top-level aggregation (TLA)		Next-level aggregation (NLA)	Site-level aggregation (SLA)	Interface ID

Figure 18.20 Structure of a global aggregate unique address in an IPv6 packet

disposal of the administrator. The administrator of the companywide network controls the process of forming the address and must not agree on this process with the provider. At the same time, the *interface ID* field has a specific goal — it must store the physical address of the host. At this level, it is also possible to aggregate addresses of small subnets into larger subnets. The *SLA* field size provides sufficient flexibility for building a company-specific address hierarchy.

■ *Interface ID* is an analogue of the host number in IPv4. The difference in IPv6 is that generally, the interface identifier simply matches its local (hardware) address instead of representing a host number assigned arbitrarily by an administrator. The interface identifier has a length of 64 bits, which allows a MAC address (48 bits), an X.25 address (up to 60 bits), an ATM end node address (48 bits), or an ATM virtual connection number (up to 28 bits) to be placed there. In theory, it is expected to provide the possibility of using local addresses of technologies that will emerge. Such an IPX-style approach makes the use of ARP unnecessary, since the procedure of mapping an IP address to a local address becomes a trivial one — it is reduced to simply discarding the most significant part of the address. Furthermore, in most cases, the need to manually configure end nodes is eliminated. This is because the host gets the least significant part of address, the interface ID, from the hardware (network adapter, etc.), and the router informs the end node about the most significant part of address, the network number.

Obviously, having such an abundance of networks in IPv6, the operation of subnetting (i.e., using masks for dividing networks into subnets) becomes senseless. On the other hand, an inverse procedure — supernetting — gains special importance. Developers of IPv6 standards consider address aggregation as the main method of efficient use of the address space in the new version of IP.

EXAMPLE   *Suppose that the client has obtained from an ISP a pool of IPv6 addresses, defined by the following prefix: 20:0A:00:C9:74:05/48.*

Analyze this number. Since its first 3 bits are set to 001, this is a global aggregate unique address. Represent the prefix 20:0A:00:C9:74:05/48 using the standard format for this type of address (Figure 18.21).

This address belongs to the top-level provider, all networks of which have the prefix 20:0A/16. This provider can allocate some address range with the common prefix to the second-level provider. This common prefix will be created on the basis of the top-level provider's prefix and part of the NLA field. The length of the NLA field allocated for prefix is determined by the mask the top-level provider must specify for the client — the second-level provider. Assume that in this example the mask comprises 32 ones in the most significant bits and that the resulting prefix of the second-level provider looks as follows: 20:0A:00:C9/32.

Thus, the second-level provider has 16 bits of the NLA field for numbering networks of its clients. The list of clients of the second-level provider can include third-level and smaller providers as well as subscribers — companies and organizations. Suppose that the next byte of the NLA field (01110100) was used by the provider for passing to the third-level provider, which, in turn, has used the last byte of the NLA field for assigning an address pool for its client. Thus, the three-level hierarchy of providers has formed the prefix 20:0A:00:C9:74:05/48, which was assigned to the client.

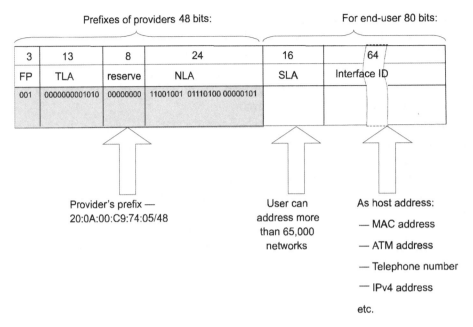

Figure 18.21 Example of a global aggregate unique address

IPv6 leaves at the client's disposal 2 bytes for numbering networks (the *SLA* field) and 8 bytes for numbering hosts (the *Interface ID* field).

Having such a large range of subnet numbers, the administrator can use it in different ways. For instance, she can choose flat addressing of the network by assigning a specific value from the available range of 65,535 addresses without using the remaining ones. In large networks, a hierarchical network structure based on address aggregation can become a more efficient method of organizing address space, since it reduces the size of routing tables on corporate routers. In this case, the traditional CIDR technology is used; however, it is implemented by the company network administrator rather than by ISP.

Besides the global aggregate unique address considered previously, there other types of unicast addresses.

■ The *loopback address* 0:0:0:0:0:0:0:1 in IPv6 plays the same role as the 127.0.0.1 address in IPv4.

■ The *undefined address* ::, comprising only zeros, is an analogue of the 0.0.0.0 address in IPv4. This value indicates that the host lacks an assigned IP address. This address must not appear in IP packets as a destination address. If it appears in the source address field, this means that the packet was sent before the host learned its IP address (for instance, before obtaining an address from the DHCP server).

It is assumed that Internet segments working on the basis of IPv6 will coexist with the other part of the Internet using IPv4 for a long time. To ensure that the host supporting

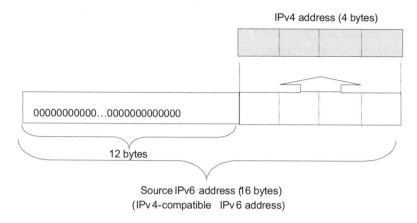

Figure 18.22 Conversion of IPv6 to IPv4

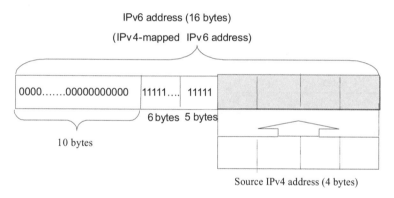

Figure 18.23 Conversion of IPv4 to IPv6

IPv6 can use the technique of passing IPv6 packets through the IPv4 network in automatic mode, a special subtype of addresses has been developed. Addresses of this subtype carry the IPv4 address in 4 least significant bytes of the IPv6 address; 12 most significant bytes of address are filled with zeros (Figure 18.22). This type of unicast address makes the procedure of converting IPv6 addresses to IPv4 addresses simple. They are known as **IPv4-compatible** IPv6 addresses.

There is one more variant of an IPv6 address carrying an IPv4 address — the IPv4-mapped IPv6 address. This type of address is intended for solving an inverse problem — passing IPv4 packets through Internet segments operating according to IPv6. Addresses of this type contain an IPv4 address in four least significant bytes, their ten most significant bytes are filled with zeros, and the fifth and sixth bytes contain ones, which indicates that the host supports IPv4 (Figure 18.23).

Research in the field of detailing subtypes of IPv6 is far from accomplished. Only 15% of the IPv6 address space has a clearly defined purpose; the remaining part of addresses waits for its turn to find application for solving some of the numerous Internet problems.

18.6.3 Flexible Header Format

One of the most important goals of changing the header format in IPv6 was the reduction of overhead — that is, the reduction of the amount of control information transmitted with each packet. For this purpose, the concepts of *main* and *additional* headers were introduced in new version of IP. The main header is always present, and **additional headers** are optional. For example, additional headers may contain information about fragmentation of the original packet, the complete route of the packet when using the source routing technique, and information required for protecting the data being transmitted.

The main header has the fixed length of 40 bytes. Its format is illustrated in Figure 18.24.

The *next header* field corresponds to the *protocol* field in IPv4 and defines the type of the header that follows the current one. Each next additional header also contains the *next header* field. If an IP packet does not contain additional headers, then this field would

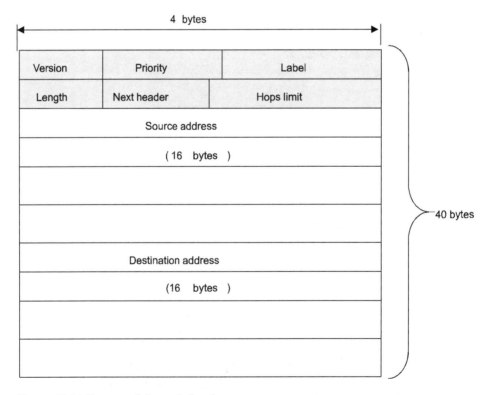

Figure 18.24 Format of the main header

contain the value assigned to such protocols as TCP, UDP, RIP, OSPF, or others defined in the IPv4 standard.

Currently, the following types of additional headers are mentioned in IPv6 standard proposals:

- **Routing** — used for specifying the complete route when using source routing.
- **Fragmentation** — contains information related to fragmentation of the IP packet. This field is processed on end nodes.
- **Authentication** — contains information required for authentication of the end node and ensuring the integrity of the contents of IP packets.
- **Encapsulation** — contains information required for ensuring confidentiality of the data being transmitted, using encryption and decryption.
- **Hop-by-Hop Option** — sets special parameters used when processing packets according to the Hop-by-Hop algorithm.
- **Destination Options** — contains auxiliary information for the destination node.

Thus, the IP packet format may look as shown in Figure 18.25.

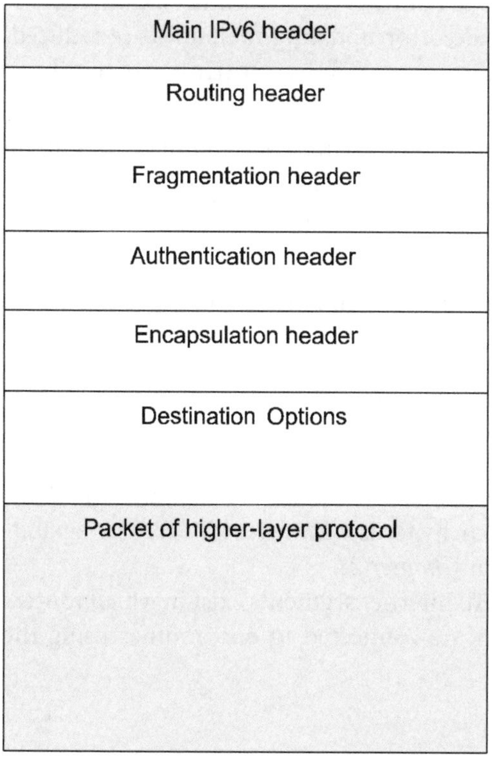

Main IPv6 header
Routing header
Fragmentation header
Authentication header
Encapsulation header
Destination Options
Packet of higher-layer protocol

Figure 18.25 Structure of the IPv6 packet

Since for packet routing only the main header is required (practically all additional headers are processed only by end nodes), this reduces the load on routers. On the other hand, the possibility of using a large number of additional parameters *extends the IP functionality and makes it open for introducing new mechanisms.*

18.6.4 Reducing the Load on Routers

To improve the performance of Internet routers related to their main function, packet forwarding, IPv6 makes provision for relieving routers from carrying out some subsidiary tasks:

■ Moving fragmentation functions from routers to end nodes. In IPv6, end nodes must detect the minimum size of the MTU along the entire route connecting the source host to the destination host (this technique, known as path MTU discovery, was used in IPv4). IPv6 routers do not carry out packet fragmentation. On the contrary, they only send the ICMP message **packet too long** to end nodes. Having received such a message, the host must reduce the packet size.

■ Address aggregation, which reduces the size of address tables on routers. Consequently, the table lookup time and the time required for updating the tables are reduced. With all this going on, auxiliary traffic created by routing protocols is also reduced.

■ Wide use of source routing in which the source node specifies the complete route along which the packet traverses the network. Such a technique relieves routers from the need to look up address tables when choosing the next router.

■ Abandoning processing of optional header parameters.

■ Using the MAC address of the node as its number, which relieves routers of the necessity of using ARP.

The new version of IP, a component of the IPv6 project, provides built-in data protection tools. Implementing protection tools at the network layer will make them invisible to applications, because between the IP layer and the application there will always be a transport-layer protocol. When this approach is used, there will be no need to redesign applications. The new version of IP with built-in security tools is known as IPSec. The capabilities of this protocol will be covered in detail in *Chapter 24*.

Transition from IPv4 to IPv6 has only started. Internet segments exist in which routers support both versions of IP. These fragments are connected to one another using the Internet, thus forming the **6Bone.**

SUMMARY

▶ IP solves the problem of data delivery between nodes of internets. Since it is a datagram protocol, it does not provide guarantees for the reliability of data delivery.

▶ A feature of IP, differing from other network protocols (such as IPX), is its capability of carrying out dynamic fragmentation of packets when transmitting them between networks that have different values of the maximum length of the data field (MTU).

▶ The maximum length of an IP packet is 65,535 bytes. The header usually has a length of 20 bytes and contains information on sender and receiver network addresses, fragmentation parameters, packet TTL, checksum, and some other data.

▶ The format of the IP routing table depends on the specific implementation of the router. Despite significant differences in the forms of tables displayed on screen, all of them include two mandatory fields without which it is impossible to carry out routing: *source address* and *destination address*.

▶ The records are supplied to the routing table from the three sources. First, the TCP/IP stack software, as a result of configuration, saves in this table records about directly connected networks and default routers as well as records about special-purpose addresses. Second, the administrator can manually enter records about specific routes or about the default router. Finally, routing protocols automatically record into this table dynamic records about the existing routes.

▶ Masks provide an efficient method of structuring IP networks. Masks divided a single network into several subnets (subnetting) or aggregate several networks into a larger one (supernetting).

▶ The classless interdomain routing (CIDR) technology plays an important role in the future of IP networks. This technology solves two main problems. The first problem is ensuring more efficient use of the available address space; the second is reducing the number of records in routing tables, since one record can represent multiple networks with a common prefix.

▶ From the early 1990s, the TCP/IP stack has encountered serious problems that could not be solved without changing the format of the IP packet and the logic of processing the fields of the IP header. As a result, the Internet community decided to develop a new version of IP, IPv6. This modernization had the following goals: create a scalable addressing system, improve the network bandwidth at the expense of reducing the number of operations carried out by routers, ensure the quality of transport services, and ensure security of the data being transmitted through the network.

REVIEW QUESTIONS

1. How does unreliability of IP manifest itself?

2. Compare the address table of a bridge or a switch to that of a router. Describe how these tables are created. What information do they contain? On what factors does the table size depend?

3. Consider a backbone Internet router. Which of the following records are in its routing table in the *destination address* field:

   A. Numbers of all Internet networks

   B. Numbers of some Internet networks (B)

   C. Numbers of some networks and full addresses of some Internet hosts for which specific routes are defined

   D. Special-purpose addresses like 127.0.0.0 or 255.255.255.255 (D)

4. How many records on default routes can be included into the routing table?

5. Provide examples illustrating situations in which the need for using specific routes might arise.

6. When routing is based on masks, does the IP packet contain the mask?

7. What are the advantages provided by the CIDR technology? What prevents its widespread use?

8. Is there any relation between the length of the prefix of a continuous pool of IP addresses and the number of addresses included in that pool?

9. Why does the record on the default route often contain 0.0.0.0 with the mask 0.0.0.0 as the address of the destination network?

10. Which of the following elements of the network can carry out fragmentation:

    A. Only computers

    B. Only routers

    C. Computers, routers, bridges, and switches

    D. Computers and routers

11. What will happen to the packet if it was fragmented in the course of being transmitted and one of the fragments did not arrive at the destination host after timeout expired?

    A. The IP entity of the sender host will retransmit the lost fragment.

    B. The IP entity of the sender host will retransmit the entire packet, which included the lost fragment.

    C. The IP entity of the destination host will discard all received fragments of the packet that contained the lost fragment. The IP entity of the sender host will not take any actions related to retransmission of this packet.

12. Figure 18.26 shows a computer with two network adapters to which two network segments are connected. This computer runs Windows 2000. Can computer A in one segment exchange data with computer B in another segment?

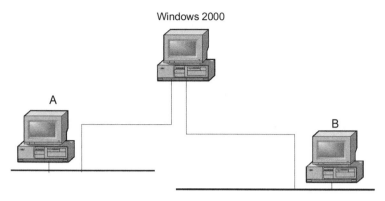

Figure 18.26 Two network segments connected by a computer

13. These segments use different data link-layer protocols, such as Ethernet and Token Ring. Can this influence the answer to the previous question?

14. How does an administrator of IPv6 use masks?

    A. Ignores them because they are not needed

    B. Uses supernetting

    C. Uses subnetting

    D. Uses both supernetting and subnetting

15. If someone states that a broadcast is a particular case of multicast, is this statement correct? Is it correct to state that a broadcast is a particular case of anycast?

16. Is it possible for the same network interface to have simultaneously several IPv6 addresses of different types: unicast, anycast, and multicast?

PROBLEM

1. The "Overlapping Address Spaces" section of this chapter contained the example of network planning. In this example, a network administrator has formulated the following requirements: 600 addresses for Ethernet, 200 addresses for the Token Ring network, 10 addresses for DMZ, and 4 addresses for connection network. Solve the same problem for the case in which 300 workplaces are planned for the Token Ring network.

   • What pool of addresses must be received from the ISP? In this example, the ISP will provide the customer with continuous address pool.

   • How should the administrator distribute these addresses among four networks?

   • How would the routing tables of the R1 and R2 routers look?

19

CORE PROTOCOLS OF THE TCP/IP STACK

19.1 INTRODUCTION

We start this chapter by studying TCP and UDP, protocols that play the role of intermediary between application programs and transport infrastructure of the network. Although the main goal of the Internet layer, to which the Internet protocol (IP) relates, is data transmission between network interfaces using the internet, the main task of the transport layer, carried out by such protocols as the transmission control protocol (TCP) and the user datagram protocol (UDP, consists of data transmission between *application processes* running on computers connected to the network.

Then, we consider routing protocols intended for automatic building of routing tables, used as the basis for forwarding of network-layer packets. In contrast to network protocols, such as IP or IPX, routing protocols are optional, because a routing table can be created manually by a network administrator. However, in large networks with complex topology and many alternative routes, routing protocols carry out the important job of automating the process of building routing tables. They also find new routes in case of network structure changes, including failures or cases in which new routers or communications links are introduced.

We also cover the Internet control message protocol (ICMP), the tool of informing the sender about the reasons his packets were not delivered to the destination. Besides diagnostics, ICMP is used for *network monitoring*. For example, ICMP messages are used as the basis for such popular IP network monitoring tools as `ping` and `traceroute`.

19.2 TCP AND UDP TRANSPORT-LAYER PROTOCOLS

KEY WORDS: transmission control protocol (TCP), user datagram protocol (UDP), port, socket, multiplexing, demultiplexing, standard port numbers, well-known port, Dynamic port, UDP port, TCP port, best effort, UDP packet, user datagram, Source Port, Destination Port, Sequence Number, Acknowledgment Number, Code Bits, Urgent Data, Window, Checksum, Urgent Pointer, Options, Padding, logical connections, segment, sliding window algorithm, round trip time (RTT)

As already mentioned, the main task of the transport layer is carried out by the transmission control protocol (*TCP*), defined in RFC 793, and user datagram protocol (*UDP*), defined in RFC 768. This task consists of data transmission between application processes running on computers connected to the network. Since TCP and UDP relate to the same layer, they have much in common. Both protocols ensure interface to the higher-layer, application protocols by transmitting the data coming into the host to the appropriate applications. At the same time, both protocols use the concepts of **port** and **socket**. Both also support interface to the underlying, network IP layer by encapsulating their PDUs into IP packets. Similar to application-layer protocols, the protocol entities of both

TCP and UDP are installed only on end nodes. However, as you will see later, the differences between TCP and UDP are more numerous than the similarities.

19.2.1 Ports

Each computer can execute several processes; furthermore, each application process can have several access points serving as destination addresses for data packets. Therefore, after the packet is delivered to the network interface of the destination host by IP, it is necessary to pass this data to the specific process for which this data is intended.

An inverse task also has to be carried out: The packets sent to the network by different applications running on the same end node are processed by the same IP. Consequently, the protocol stack must provide a means of "collecting" the packets from different applications and passing them to IP. Both TCP and UDP can accomplish this job.

The procedure carried out by TCP/UDP to receive the data arriving from several application services is called **multiplexing**. An inverse procedure, used by TCP/UDP to distribute the packets arriving from the network layer among the set of higher-layer services, is called **demultiplexing** (Figure 19.1).

For each application port, TCP and UDP support two queues: the queue of packets arriving to this application from the network and the queue of packets sent by the application to the network. Packets arriving to the transport layer are organized by the operating system as sets of queues to various access points of various application processes. In TCP/IP terminology, such system queues are called *ports*. (Do not confuse application ports with the hardware ports, i.e., network interfaces, of the network equipment.) Note

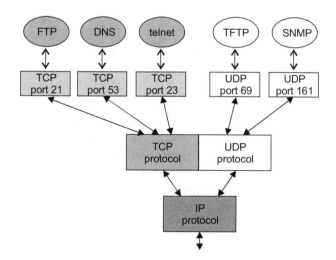

Figure 19.1 Multiplexing and demultiplexing at the transport layer

that both input and output queues of the same application are considered the same port. For unique and unambiguous identification of ports, they are assigned port numbers. Port numbers are used for addressing applications.

There are two methods of assigning port numbers to applications — *centralized* and *local*. Each of these methods has its own range of port numbers: For the centralized method, the port numbers from 0 to 1,023 are assigned, and the local method uses the port numbers from 1,023 to 65,535.

If the processes are popular public services, such as file transfer protocol (FTP), telnet, HTTP, TFTP, or DNS, they are assigned **standard port numbers**, also known as **well-known port numbers**. These numbers are listed Internet standards — RFC 1700 and RFC 3232. For instance, number 21 is assigned to the FTP service, and number 23 is assigned to the telnet service. Assigned addresses are unique, which means that they cannot be used by any other application.

For applications that are not so widely used and popular, numbers are assigned by application developers or the operating system in response to the request from the application. On each computer, the operating system supports the list of assigned and available port numbers. When a request arrives from some application running on a local computer, the operating system will allocate it the first available port number. Such numbers are called dynamic. Later, all network applications will have to access this application using the port number assigned to it. After the application terminates execution, the local port number assigned to it is returned to the list of available port numbers and can be assigned to another application. **Dynamic port** numbers are *unique within the limits of each computer*. However, the situation in which applications running on different computers have matching port numbers is quite common. As a rule, the client parts of well-known applications (DNS, WWW, FTP, telnet, and so on) receive dynamic port numbers from the operating system.

All this information that relates to ports is equally applicable to both transport-layer protocols. Principally, there is no dependence between assigning port numbers for applications using TCP and the same procedure for applications working with UDP. Applications that pass data to the IP layer using UDP get the numbers known as **UDP ports**. Similarly, applications using TCP are assigned **TCP ports**.

In both cases, these may be assigned and dynamic port numbers. The ranges from which TCP and UDP ports are allocated coincide: Numbers from 0 to 1,023 are for assigned port numbers, and numbers from 1,024 to 65,535 are for dynamic port numbers. However, there is no relation between assigned TCP and assigned UDP port numbers. Even if TCP and UDP port numbers coincide, they identify different applications. For instance, one application can be assigned TCP port 1750, and another application might use UDP port 1750. When an application can choose between TCP and UDP (an example of such application is DNS), it is assigned a coinciding TCP and UDP port number for convenience of memorizing. For example, DNS can use TCP port 53 or UDP port 53.

19.2.2 UDP

UDP is a datagram protocol (i.e., the protocol that operates according to the **best effort** principle without establishing a logical connection). Being a datagram protocol, UDP does not guarantee delivery of its messages and, consequently, does not compensate for insufficient reliability of IP, also a datagram protocol.

The data unit of UDP is known as a **UDP packet** or **user datagram**. Each UDP packet carries a *separate user message* (Figure 19.2). This results in a natural limitation: A UDP datagram cannot exceed the length of the IP data field, which, in turn, is limited by the frame size of the underlying network technology. Therefore, if the UDP buffer overflows, application data are discarded. The UDP header comprises four 2-byte fields, containing the port numbers of the sender and the receiver, the checksum, and the datagram length.

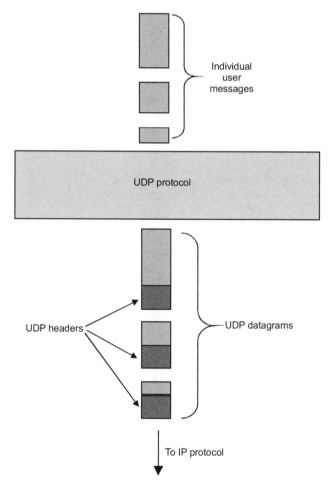

Figure 19.2 Forming the UDP datagram

Provided here is a fragment of the UDP header with filled fields:

```
Source Port = 0x0035
    Destination Port = 0x0411
    Total length = 132 (0x84) bytes
    Checksum = 0x5333
```

In this UDP datagram, the data field, as it follows from the header, has a length of 132 − 8 bytes. It contains the message from the DNS server. This can be detected by the port number of the source, `Source Port = 0x0035`, which corresponds to the standard port number of the DNS server, 53.

Judging from simplicity of the header, UDP is not a sophisticated protocol. Its functions are reduced to multiplexing and demultiplexing data between network and application layers. Consider how UDP solves the problem of demultiplexing. Using port numbers seems to be a natural way of carrying out this task. Frames carrying UDP datagrams arrive at the network interface of the host, where they are sequentially processed by the protocols of the stack and, finally, are passed to UDP. UDP retrieves the destination port number from the packet header and passes the data to the appropriate port of the corresponding application (i.e., carries out demultiplexing task).

This solution looks logical and simple. However, in practice, it will not work if *several copies of the same application* run on the same end node. Suppose that two DNS servers run on the same host, both using UDP for passing their messages (Figure 19.3). The DNS

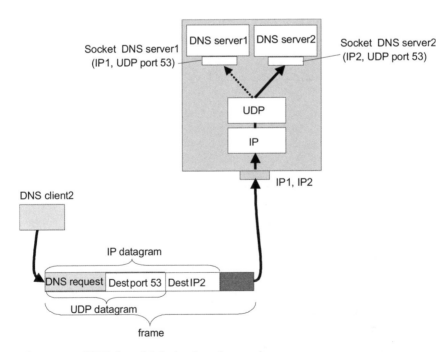

Figure 19.3 UDP demultiplexing based on sockets

server has been assigned a well-known UDP port, 53. At the same time, each DNS server might serve its own clients, have its own databases, and have individual custom settings. When a request from a DNS client arrives at the network interface of this computer, the UDP datagram will specify port number 53, which would equally relate to both DNS servers. To which of these servers must UDP pass the query? To eliminate this ambiguity, the following approach has been used: Different copies of the same applications installed on the same computer are assigned different IP addresses. In this example, DNS server1 has the IP1 address, and DNS server2 has been assigned the IP2 address.

> Thus, the address of the application process within a network (and, even more so, within a computer) is unambiguously defined by the pair of the *IP address* and the *UDP port* number. This pair is called the **UDP socket**. The use of sockets allows UDP to correctly demultiplex.

NOTE   *In this relationship, we must clarify the simplified pattern according to which the packet travels up the protocol stack. As mentioned in previous chapters, after the packet arriving from the network is processed by IP, the header of this packet is discarded and only the contents of the packet's data field are passed upward — for instance, this may be the UDP datagram. However, when explaining this mechanism, we omitted one important detail: With the contents of the data field,* the destination IP address retrieved from the packet header is passed to the transport layer. *UDP retrieves the port number from the UDP datagram header and, based on the* socket (destination IP address and destination port number) *carries out **demultiplexing**.*

19.2.3 TCP Segment Format

Information supplied to TCP from higher-layer protocols is considered by TCP as an **unstructured stream of bytes**. The arriving data are buffered by TCP. The protocol then "cuts out" some continuous data segment[1], supplies it with the header, and passes it to the network layer (Figure 19.4).

The header of the TCP segment contains significantly more fields than the UDP header. This is because of the more advanced capabilities of TCP:

- **Source Port** — this field takes 2 bytes and identifies the sender process.
- **Destination Port** — this field takes 2 bytes and identifies the destination process.
- **Sequence Number** — this field takes 4 bytes and specifies the number of the byte that defines the segment offset in relation to the flow of the data being sent (i.e., the number of the first byte in this segment).

---

[1] Note that the term *segment* is used both for designating the data transmission unit as a whole (the data field and the TCP header) and for designating just the data field.

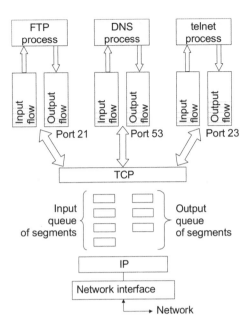

Figure 19.4 Forming TCP segments from an unstructured stream of bytes

- **Acknowledgment Number** — This field takes 4 bytes. It contains the maximum byte number in the received segment incremented by one. This value is the one used as acknowledgment. If the *ACK* check bit is set, this field contains the next number of queue that the sender of this datagram would like to receive in acknowledgment.

- **Header length (Hlen)** — This 4-byte field specifies the length of the header of the TCP segment, measured in 32-bit words. Header length is not fixed and can vary depending on the parameters set in the *Options* field.

- **Reserved** — This reserved field takes 6 bits. It is reserved for future use.

- **Code Bits** — This field takes 6 bits containing auxiliary information on the type of this segment. This information is specified by setting to one the following bits of this field:

  - **Urgent Data** — This is an urgent message.

  - **ACK** — This acknowledges the received segment.

  - **PSH** — This requests that the message be sent without waiting for the buffer to be filled. Note that TCP can wait until the buffer is filled before sending the segment. If immediate transmission is needed, the application must inform the protocol by using the push parameter.

  - **RST** — This requests connection restoration.

  - **SYN** — This message is used for synchronizing the counters of transmitted data when establishing a connection.

- ● **FIN** — This is the attribute specifying that the transmitting side has sent the last byte in the flow of data being transmitted.
- ■ **Window** — This 2-byte field specifies the number of data bytes, starting from the byte whose number is specified in the acknowledgment field, the arrival of which is awaited by the sender of the current segment.
- ■ **Checksum** — This 2-byte field contains the checksum.
- ■ **Urgent Pointer** — This field takes 2 bytes. It is used with the *URG* code bit and specifies the end of data that must be urgently received despite buffer overflow. Also, if some data need to be sent to the destination application out of turn, then the sender application must inform TCP by using the *URGENT DATA* parameter.
- ■ **Options** — This field has variable length and can be missing. Maximum length of this field is 3 bytes. The field is used for solving auxiliary tasks — for example, choosing the maximum segment length. Options may be located at the end of the TCP header, and their length must be a multiple of 8 bits.
- ■ **Padding** — This field can have variable length. It is a fictitious field used to complement the header so that its size equals an integer number of 32-bit words.

19.2.4 Logical Connections as a Basis of TCP Reliability

The main difference between TCP and UDP is that TCP has to carry out an additional task. This task consists of ensuring *reliable delivery* of messages through the internet, all nodes of which use the unreliable IP datagram protocol for message transmission.

Figure 19.5 shows networks connected by routers, where IP entities are installed. TCP entities installed on end nodes solve the problem of ensuring reliable data exchange by establishing **logical connections**[2] *to one another.* TCP makes sure that the segments being transmitted do not get lost, duplicated, or arrive at the receiver out of order.

- ■ When establishing a logical connection, TCP entities negotiate the parameters of the data exchange procedure. In TCP, each party sends the following parameters to its partner: *Maximum size of segments* it is ready to receive.
- ■ *Maximum volume of data* (possibly several segments) it allows another party to transmit in its direction, even if that party has not yet received an acknowledgment for the previous portion of data (this parameter is known as **window size**).
- ■ *Starting number of the byte* from which it starts counting the data flow within the framework of the current connection.

As a result of this negotiation process between TCP entities of both parties, the connection parameters are defined. Some parameters remain constant during the entire ses-

---

[2] See the *"Logical Connection"* section in *Chapter 3.*

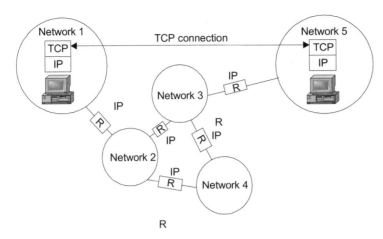

Figure 19.5 TCP connection creates a reliable communications channel between end nodes

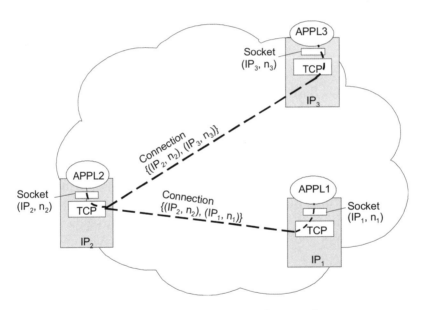

Figure 19.6 One socket can participate in several connections

sion; other parameters can be adaptively changed. For instance, the window size of the sending party changes dynamically depending on the buffer load of the receiving party and on the overall reliability of the network operation. Creation of the connection also means that the operating system on each computer allocates specific system resources for organizing buffers, timers, and counters. These resources will be allocated to the connection from the moment of its creation until the moment of connection termination.

Logical TCP connection is uniquely identified by a *pair of sockets.*

Each socket can simultaneously participate in several connections. For example, assume that there are three sockets of three applications: (IP_1, n_1), (IP_2, n_2), and (IP_3, n_3). IP_1, IP_2, and IP_3 are their IP addresses, and n_1, n_2, and n_3 are their TCP port numbers. In this case, it is possible to create the following connections:

Connection 1 — $\{(IP_2, n_2), (IP_1, n_1)\}$
Connection 2 — $\{(IP_1, n_1), (IP_3, n_3)\}$
Connection 3 — $\{(IP_2, n_2), (IP_3, n_3)\}$

Figure 19.6 shows connections 1 and 3 created by socket (IP_2, n_2).

Now, let us explain how TCP carries out the demultiplexing task. Consider the following example: Assume that some ISP provides Web hosting service, which means that clients can install their Web servers on the server belonging to this ISP. The Web server is based on the HTTP application-layer protocol, which, in turn, uses TCP. TCP waits for queries from Web clients (browsers) by listening to the well-known port 80.

Figure 19.7 shows the variant of hosting with two Web servers — **www1.model.com**, with the IP_1 IP address, and **www2.tour.com**, with the IP_2 address. Each server can

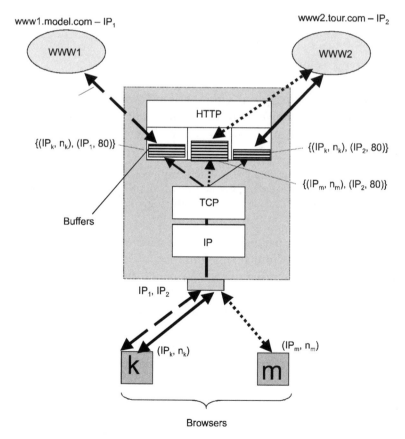

Figure 19.7 TCP connection-based demultiplexing

simultaneously serve many clients, and these clients may simultaneously work with WWW1 and WWW2. The work of each client requires the server to constantly save the numbers of read pages, the session parameters, and so on — that is, create an individual logical connection. Such a connection is created by TCP for each client–server pair. Each connection is uniquely identified by a pair of corresponding sockets.

Figure 19.7 shows two browsers with the sockets (IP_k, n_k) and (IP_m, n_m). The user of browser k simultaneously accesses WWW1 and WWW2 servers. The presence of individual connections for working with each of these two servers guarantees separation of information flows. The user will never have to ask which server has sent which page to her. Simultaneously with the user of browser k, the user of browser m accesses server WWW2. In this case, both users work within the framework of individual logical connections, which isolate the information flows of these users. Figure 19.7 shows several buffers, the number of which is defined by the number of logical connections rather than by the number of Web servers or the number of clients. Messages are sent to these buffers depending on the values of the sender and the receiver sockets.

Thus, *TCP carries out demultiplexing on the basis of logical connections.*

19.2.5 Sequence Number and Acknowledgment Number

In TCP, the correct transmission of each segment within the framework of the established connection must be acknowledged. *Acknowledgments* are one traditional method of ensuring reliable communications. TCP uses a particular acknowledgment mechanism, the **sliding window algorithm.**[3]

The sliding window algorithm implemented in TCP has one specific feature: Although the unit of data being transmitted is a *segment,* the window is defined as the set of the numbered *bytes* of unstructured data flow arriving from the higher layer and buffered by TCP.

When establishing a connection, both parties negotiate the starting number of the byte from which the counting will be carried out for the duration of the connection. Each party has its own initial number. The identifier of each segment is the number of its first byte. The bytes within the limits of a segment are numbered so that the first byte of data immediately following the header has the smallest number and the bytes that follow it have sequentially growing numbers (Figure 19.8).

When the sender sends a TCP segment, it places the number of its first byte into the *Sequence Number* field of the header. Thus, in Figure 19.9, the following numbers serve as segment identifiers: 32,600, 34,060, 35,520, etc. Based on these numbers, the TCP entity of the receiver distinguishes the specific segment from the other ones and positions the

---

[3] For more details, see the *"Data Retransmission and the Sliding Window"* section in *Chapter 6.*

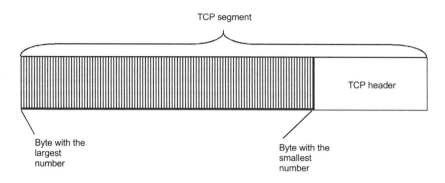

Figure 19.8 Numbering bytes within a TCP segment

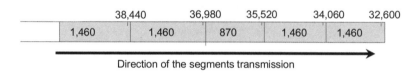

Figure 19.9 Sequence Number and Acknowledgment Number

received fragment within the common flow of bytes. Besides this, it is capable of determining if this segment is a duplicate or the previously received one, if some data are missing between two received segments, etc.

The receiver of the segment sends an acknowledgment in response. This acknowledgment is a segment into which the receiver places the number that exceeds the maximum byte number in the received segment by one. This number is called the *Acknowledgment Number*. For the segments shown in Figure 19.9, the number of the last byte of each segment incremented by one serves as a reception acknowledgment (an acknowledgment number). For the first sent segment, this will be the number 34,060; for the second segment, this will be the number 35,520; and so on.

The acknowledgment number is often interpreted as the number of the next expected data byte. In TCP, acknowledgment is sent only after correct data reception; negative acknowledgments are not sent. Thus, lack of acknowledgment means that the segment was lost, the receiver received a corrupted segment, or the acknowledgment was lost.

In the protocol, the same segment may contain both the data that the application sends to the other party and acknowledgment in which the TCP entity acknowledges data reception.

19.2.6 Receiver Window

TCP is a duplex protocol, which means that the procedure of bidirectional data exchange is regulated within the framework of a single connection. Each party simultaneously acts both as sender and receiver. Each party has a pair of buffers: One buffer is for storing received segments, and another is intended for segments waiting to be sent. Besides this, there is a buffer for storing copies of sent segments whose acknowledgments of reception have not arrived yet (Figure 19.10).

In the course of establishing a connection, and later in the course of bidirectional transmission, both parties, acting as receivers, send to each other so-called **Receiver Windows**. *Each of the parties, having received a receiver window, understands how many bytes it is*

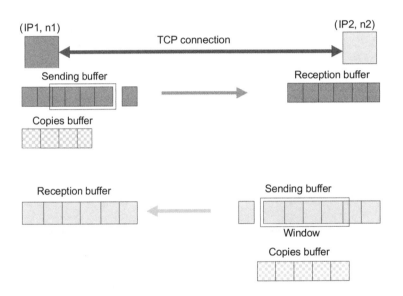

Figure 19.10 System of TCP connection buffers

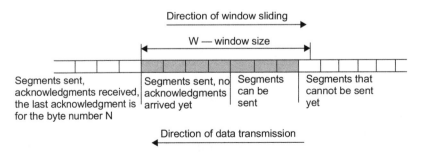

Figure 19.11 Implementation of the sliding window algorithm in TCP

allowed to send from the moment of reception of the last acknowledgment. In other words, by sending receiver windows, each party tries to regulate the byte flow in its direction, informing the other party of the number of bytes (starting from the number of the byte for which acknowledgment has been sent) it is ready to receive.

Figure 19.11 shows the flow of bytes arriving from the higher-level protocol to the output buffer of TCP. The TCP entity cuts the sequence of segments of this flow of bytes and prepares them for sending to another socket. In this illustration, the direction of data transmission is from right to left. In this flow, it is possible to specify several logical boundaries. The first boundary separates the segments that have been sent already and for which acknowledgments have arrived. On the other side of this boundary, there is the window with a size of W bytes. Some of the bytes that make up this window are segments that have been sent but whose acknowledgments have not arrived yet. The remaining part of the window is made up of segments that have not been sent yet but that can be sent because they fit within the limits of the window. Finally, the last boundary specifies the start of the sequence of segments that cannot be sent until the next acknowledgment arrives and the window is moved to the right.

If window size is equal to W and the last received acknowledgment contained the value N, the sender can send new segments until the byte with the number $N + W$ falls into the next segment. This segment goes beyond the limits of the window; therefore, it is necessary to defer transmission until the arrival of the next acknowledgment.

19.2.7 Cumulative Acknowledgment Principle

The receiver can send an acknowledgment that confirms the reception of several segments simultaneously, provided that these segments make up a continuous flow of bytes. For example (Figure 19.12, *a*), suppose that the buffer is densely, without gaps, filled with the flow of bytes up to byte 2,354. Segments (2,355–3,816), (3,817–5,275), and (5,276–8,400), where the numbers in parentheses designate the numbers of the first and the last bytes of each segment, sequentially arrive at that buffer. In this case, it is sufficient for the receiver to send only one acknowledgment for all three segments, specifying the number 8,401 as an acknowledgment number. Thus, the acknowledgment process is cumulative.

Consider another example (Figure 19.12, *b*). Segments may arrive at the receiver in an order different from the one in which they were sent. This means that in the reception buffer there may be a gap. For instance, suppose that after the previously mentioned three segments, segment (10,567–12,430) arrives instead of segment (8,401–10,566), which was expected to arrive next. It is not right to send the number 12,431 as the acknowledgment number, because this would mean that all bytes up to byte 12,430 have been received. Since a gap has appeared in the flow of bytes, the receiver can repeat acknowledgment 8,401, thus indicating that it still waits for the arrival of the byte flow starting from byte 8,401. From this example, it follows that in contrast to many other protocols,

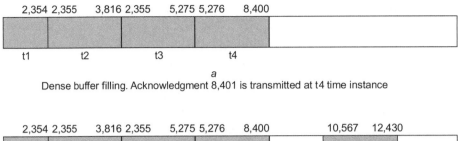

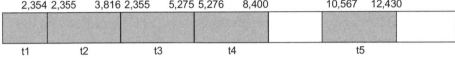

Figure 19.12 Cumulative principle of acknowledgment

TCP acknowledges the reception of a continuous sequence of bytes rather than that of separate data blocks.

19.2.8 Acknowledgment Timeout

Just to be on the safe side, when TCP sends a segment to the network, it places a copy of that segment into the resending queue and starts the timer. When an acknowledgment for this segment arrives, the copy is removed from the queue. If acknowledgment does not arrive before the timer expires, the segment is resent. It might happen that the resent segment arrives after the initial segment has been delivered. In this case, the duplicate will be discarded.

Selection of the acknowledgment timeout is an important problem, the solution to which influences the performance of TCP. Timeout must not be too short; it must exclude, whenever possible, redundant retransmission attempts that reduce the effective system performance. However, it also must not be too large; it must avoid long idle periods related to waiting for nonexistent or lost acknowledgments.

When choosing the timeout value, it is necessary to take into account the speed and reliability of the physical communications links, their lengths, and many other factors. In TCP, the timeout value is defined using a sophisticated adaptive algorithm, the main idea of which is as follows: During each transmission, the time elapsing from the moment of sending the segment until the arrival of acknowledgment of its reception is measured. This time is known as the **round trip time (RTT)**. The measured values of RTT are averaged using weight coefficients that grow with the sequential number of the measurements. This is done to increase the influence of the latest measurements. The timeout value is the average RTT value multiplied by some coefficient. Practice has shown that the value of this coefficient must exceed 2. In networks in which RTT varies significantly, RTT dispersion is also taken into account when choosing the timeout value.

19.2.9 Controlling the Receiver Window

The size of receiver window relates to the availability of data buffer space on the receiving party. Therefore, receiver windows generally have different sizes on different sides of a connection. For example, it is logical to expect that the server, which has a larger buffer, will send a larger receiver window to the client workstation than the one sent by the client to the server. Depending on the state of the network, the parties periodically can declare new values of the receiver window, dynamically increasing or decreasing them.

By varying the window size, it is possible to influence the network load. The larger the window, the larger the portion of unacknowledged data that can be sent to the network. However, if the amount of arrived data is larger than can be received by the TCP entity, the data will be discarded. This will result in excessive attempts to resend information and an unneeded increase in the load on the entire network in general and on the TCP software in particular.

On the other hand, specifying a small window might limit the data transmission to the rate determined by the time required for each segment being sent to travel across the network. To avoid the use of small windows, some TCP implementations propose that the data receiver defer changing the window size until available buffer space is 20% – 40% of the maximum amount of memory for this connection. However, the sender also must not hurry with sending the data until the receiver window of the receiving party becomes sufficiently large. Taking these considerations into account, the developers of TCP proposed a method according to which a large window is declared when establishing a connection but its size is significantly reduced later. There are other, different algorithms of window setup according to which a window of minimum size is chosen when establishing a connection and then its size is sharply increased if the network successfully handles the offered load.

Window size can be controlled not only by the party to which the data are sent within the framework of this window, but also by the sending party. If the sending party registers unreliable operation of a communications link (e.g., acknowledgments are delivered with delays regularly or retransmission is frequently required), it can reduce the window size through its own initiative. The following rule is applicable in such cases: The actual window size is chosen as the minimum of two values — the one suggested by the receiver and the value proposed by the sender.

The generation of queues in transit nodes (routers) and in end nodes (computers) indicates that the TCP connection is overloaded. In the case of buffer overflow on the end node, TCP, when sending an acknowledgment, places there a new, reduced size of the window. When it refuses reception altogether, a window of zero size is specified in the acknowledgment. However, even after this, the application can send a message to the port that refused to receive data. To achieve this, the message must be marked urgent. In such a situation, the port is obliged to receive the segment, even if it has to unload the data already in the buffer. After receiving the acknowledgment with the zero size of the window, the sender protocol sometimes makes test attempts at continuing data exchange. If the receiver protocol is ready to receive information, it sends an acknowledgment with a nonzero window size in response to such a query.

Although this description of TCP and UDP is far from comprehensive, it allows you to draw the conclusion that one of them, namely, TCP, is delegated the complicated and important task of ensuring the reliability of data transmission through a principally unreliable network.

On the other hand, the functional simplicity of UDP is the reason for the simplicity of its algorithm, its small size, and its high operating speed. Consequently, those applications that implement their own, sufficiently reliable mechanisms of connection-oriented messaging prefer to use less reliable but faster transport tools for data transmission through the network. UDP is exactly such a tool in comparison to TCP. UDP can also be used if the high quality of communications links ensures a sufficient level of reliability without the need of establishing logical connections and acknowledging the packets being transmitted. Finally, since TCP is connection oriented, *it cannot be used for broadcast or multicast data transmission,* in contrast to UDP.

19.3 ROUTING PROTOCOLS

KEY WORDS: Routing Protocol, convergence time, scalability, autonomous system, interior gateway protocol (IGPs), routing information protocol (RIP), open shortest path first (OSPF), intermediate system to intermediate system (IS-IS), exterior gateway protocol (EGPs), border gateway protocol (BGP), flood routing, event-dependent routing, source routing, static routing, adaptive routing, distributed approach, centralized approach, distance vector algorithm, link state algorithm, advertisement, next hop, BGPv4, triggered updates technique, hold down technique, router links advertisements, link state database, split horizon, metrics

19.3.1 Classification of Routing Protocols

Automatically created routing tables ensure the efficiency of packet routes across the network; because of that, the *criteria for choosing routes can be different.* Contemporary IP networks use routing protocols that choose the shortest route. In this case, the distance passed by a packet is interpreted as the number of transit nodes (routers), often called the number of hops. It is also possible to use some combined criterion that takes into account the nominal bandwidths of links connecting routers, link reliability, or link delays.

A routing protocol must create coordinated routing tables in routers. Coordinated routing tables ensure packet delivery from the source network to the destination network within a finite number of steps. It is also possible to imagine an uncoordinated pair of tables. In this situation, the routing table of router 1 may specify that the packet intended for network A must be passed to router 2, and the routing table of router 2 may send the same packet to router 1. Contemporary routing protocols ensure table coordination; however, this property is not absolute. For example, if changes take place in the network, such as failures of communications links or routers, there may exist periods of unstable network operation caused by a temporary lack of coordination among the routing tables of different routers. As a rule, a routing protocol usually requires some time, known as **convergence time**, during which all network routers, after several iterations of exchanging auxiliary information, enter the required changes into their routing tables. As a result of this operation, all routing tables become coordinated again. *Different routing protocols are characterized by different convergence time values.*

For successful operation on the Internet, network technologies must be **scalable**. This means that they must ensure hierarchical use in some form. Internet routing follows this principle and divides the Internet into **autonomous systems**. As a result, routing in the Internet has a pronounced hierarchical nature.

> Any of the existing routing protocols can be used within an autonomous system. However, between autonomous systems the same protocol must be used, as a kind of universal language, such as Esperanto, used by autonomous systems to communicate between one another.

In IP networks, the role of the **interior gateway protocols (IGPs)** used within autonomous systems is delegated to the following three protocols — **routing information protocol (RIP), open shortest path first (OSPF)**, and **intermediate system to intermediate system (IS-IS)**. Another class of protocols, known as **exterior gateway protocols (EGPs)**, includes routing protocols used for choosing routes between autonomous systems. Nowadays, this task is carried out by the **border gateway protocol (BGP)**.

Routing without Tables

Before we proceed with the classification of routing protocols, it is necessary to point out that in internets there also exist methods of packet forwarding that do not require the presence of routing tables in routers.

Flood routing is the simplest method of passing packets along the network. In this case, each router passes the packet to all its nearest neighbors except the one from which it received that packet. Naturally, this method is the least efficient, since network bandwidth is wasted. However, this method is workable, since bridges and switches do exactly this type of passing in relation to frames with unknown addresses.

Another variant of routing without routing tables is **event-dependent routing**, according to which the packet is sent to a specific destination network along the route that previously resulted in successful delivery (for the given destination address). This method of routing was used when the Internet was coming into being. According to this method, before a packet was sent, ICMP echo requests were sent to all or to several neighbors; then, on the basis of the time of arrived echo replies, the neighbor was chosen that had the minimum response time.

This method is suitable for use in networks operating on the basis of connection-oriented protocols. The request for establishing a connection can be sent simultaneously to several neighbors, and the acknowledgment must be sent to the first neighbor to send a reply.

Another type of routing that does not require routing tables is **source routing**. In this case, the sender places into the packet information about transit routers that must participate in packet delivery to the destination network. Based on this information, each router reads the address of the next router and, if it is the address of its nearest neighbor, passes the packet to it for further processing. The issue of determining the exact route along which the packet travels through the network remains open. This path can be either manually specified by an administrator or automatically determined by the sender node, which, in this case, must support some routing protocol. The routing protocol in this case must inform the sender about the network topology and state. Source routing was tested in early Internet experiments. It has been preserved as a practically unused option of IPv4. In IPv6, source routing is one of the standard modes of packet forwarding, and there is a special header for implementing this mode.

Adaptive Routing

When routing is carried out on the basis of tables, there is *static* and *adaptive* (dynamic) routing.

In case of **static routing**, routing tables are created and entered into each router *manually by the network administrator*. All records in the routing table have the static status, which means that they remain in effect infinitely. When the state of some network element changes, the administrator must manually enter the appropriate change into the routing tables of those routers influenced by it. For instance, it may be necessary to change a route or routes for packets. This must be done as soon as possible; otherwise, network will operate incorrectly.

Adaptive routing ensures *automatic updating of the routing tables* when network configuration changes. Updating of the routing tables is exactly the task for which routing protocols are needed. These protocols operate on the basis of algorithms allowing all routers to collect information on the link topology in the network and flexibly reflect all changes in link configuration on the fly. If adaptive routing is used, routing tables usually contain information on the interval during which each individual route remains valid. This interval is called the route's *time to live* (TTL). If the TTL period has expired and existence of the route has not been confirmed by the routing protocol, such a route is considered unworkable, and packets would not be sent along it.

Routing protocols are classified into distributed and centralized protocols.

- When using a **distributed approach**, the network does not contain any dedicated routers that would collect and summarize information on the network topology. On the contrary, this work is distributed among all routers of the network. Each router builds its own routing table based on the data received according to the routing protocol from other network routers.

- When a **centralized approach** is used, there is a dedicated router in the network. This router collects all information on the network topology and its state, supplied by other routers. Then this dedicated router, sometimes called a route server, can choose one of the possible variants of behavior. It can build routing tables for all remaining network routers and then distribute them over the network so that every router receives its own copy or routing table; later, it can make decisions about packet forwarding on its own..

> Routing protocols currently used in IP networks are classified as distributed adaptive protocols.

Adaptive routing algorithms must satisfy several important requirements. First, the routes chosen by these algorithms must be efficient if not optimal. Second, the algorithms must be sufficiently simple, because their implementation must not waste network resources. In particular, they must not require a vast amount of computations or generate intense control traffic. Finally, routing algorithms must be characterized by the property of convergence — that is, they must always coordinate the building of routing tables for assuring convergence of all network routers within a reasonable time.

Adaptive routing algorithms currently used in computer networks are divided into two groups, each of which implements one of the following types of algorithms:

- Distance vector algorithms
- Link state algorithms

Distance Vector Algorithms

In **distance vector algorithms (DVAs),** each router periodically broadcasts the vector, the components of which are the distances from this router to all networks known to it. Packets sent by routing protocols are usually called **advertisements**, because the router uses them to inform all other routers on the network structure known to it. As a rule, the distance in a DVA is interpreted as the number of hops. However, another metric is also possible, which takes into account not only the number of transit nodes (routers) but also the bandwidth of the link connecting two adjacent routers.

Having received a vector from its neighbor, the router increments the distances specified in this vector by a value equal to the distance from this neighbor and complements the vector with information about other networks known to it. Information about these networks might be obtained directly, when they are connected to ports of the current router, or from similar advertisements received from other routers. After that, the router broadcasts this new value of the vector to the network. Finally, each router will get from its neighbors information about all networks connected to the internet and the distances to them. After that, from several alternative routes to each network, it will choose the one that has the smallest metric value. The router that has passed information about this route is marked in the routing table as the **next hop**.

> DVAs operate efficiently only in small networks. In large networks, they overload communications links with intense periodic traffic. Furthermore, configuration changes may not be correctly processed according to this algorithm, since routers have no exact information on the topology of network links. On the contrary, they have only generalized information, the distance vector; moreover, this is mediated information, which was not received directly.

Among the protocols based on DVA, RIP is the most widely used. This protocol has two versions — RIP IP, intended for IP, and RIP IPX, which works with IPX.

Link State Algorithms

Link state algorithms (LSAs) provide each router with information sufficient for building an exact graph of the network links. All routers operate on the basis of the same graph, which makes the routing process more stable against configuration changes.

Each router uses the network graph for finding routes to each of the networks included into the internet. These routes are optimal ones according to some specific criterion.

To find the state of communications links connected to its ports, the router periodically exchanges short *HELLO* packets with its nearest neighbors.

> Advertisements on the link state are not repeated periodically, as was the case with DVA protocols. On the contrary, they are transmitted only if a change of state of a specific link was detected by exchanging *HELLO* messages. As a result, control traffic generated by LSA protocols is significantly less intense than that generated by DVA protocols.

Examples of LSA protocols are the IS-IS protocol of the OSI stack (this protocol is also used in the TCP/IP stack), the OSPF protocol of the TCP/IP stack, and the NetWare link-services protocol of the Novell stack.

Using Several Routing Protocols

Several routing protocols can simultaneously operate in the same network (Figure 19.13). This means that on some (but not necessarily on all) network routers, several routing protocols are installed and running. Naturally, only similarly named protocols interact using the network. This means that if router 1 supports the RIP and OSPF protocols, router 2 supports only RIP, and router 3 supports only OSPF, then router 1 will interact with router 2 according to RIP and with router 3 according to OSPF; routers 2 and 3 will be unable to communicate directly.

In a router that supports several protocols, each record in the routing table is the result of operation of one of these protocols. If information on a specific network is supplied by several protocols, then to ensure nonambiguity of the route selection, protocol priorities

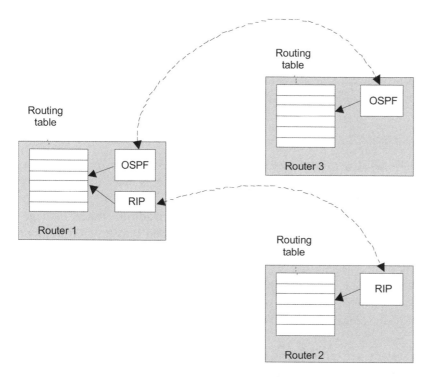

Figure 19.13 Operation of several routing protocols within the same network

are set; otherwise, data from different protocols may result in different efficient routes. As a rule, preference is given to LSA protocols because, in comparison to DVA protocols, they have more comprehensive information on the network DVA. In some operating systems, the forms for displaying or printing a routing table contain special marks specifying the routing protocol used to obtain each record. Even when this mark is not displayed, it is always in the internal representation of the routing table. By default, each routing protocol running on a specific router distributes only the information received by the router according to this protocol. Thus, if the router got information on some network from RIP, it will use the same protocol to distribute advertisements of this route over the network.

However, the following question might be asked: "How do routers that support different routing protocols used in the internet exchange routing information to make all constituent networks of the internet available?" To enable the router to use one routing protocol for distributing routing information received using another routing protocol, it is necessary to establish the specific internal mode of its operation, often called the *redistribute mode*. Such a mode ensures that a specific protocol can use not only its "native" records from the routing tables but also other records obtained using other routing protocols specified in the course of configuration.

As can be seen from the description, using several routing protocols within the limits of the same internet is not a trivial task. An administrator must carry out specific tasks related to configuring each router. Naturally, for large heterogeneous networks, a principally different solution is needed.

Such a solution was found for the Internet, the largest heterogeneous internet today.

Exterior and Interior Gateway Protocols

Besides the organizational structure of the Internet described in *Chapter 5* and determining Internet division into networks of various ISPs, the Internet is made up of autonomous systems.

An *autonomous system* is a set of networks joined by common administrative management, ensuring common routing policy for all routers included into the autonomous system. As a rule, an autonomous system is controlled by a single ISP. That ISP determines which routing protocols are used in a specific autonomous system and how routing information is distributed and redistributed among them. Top-level ISPs and large companies can represent their internets as sets of several autonomous systems. Autonomous system registration is centralized in a way similar to the registration of IP addresses and DNS names.

All autonomous systems are centrally numbered. The number of the autonomous system comprises 16 bits; it is not related to the IP prefixes of the networks making up the autonomous system.

According to this concept, the Internet looks like a set of interconnected autonomous system, each comprising interrelated networks (Figure 19.14).

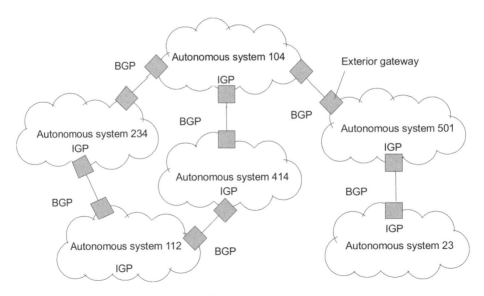

Figure 19.14 Autonomous systems of the Internet

The main goal of dividing the Internet into autonomous systems is ensuring a multi-level approach to routing. Before the introduction of autonomous systems, routing assumed a two-level approach — at the network layer the route was laid out between groups of nodes (networks), and routing between networks was ensured by lower-layer technologies. This means that the route defined the sequence of passing the networks.

With the arrival of autonomous systems, there appeared the third level of routing — the route is chosen first at the level of autonomous systems and then at the level of their constituent networks.

Autonomous systems are connected by **exterior gateways**[4]. What is important is that between exterior gateways only one routing protocol is allowed. Furthermore, this must not be an arbitrary protocol. On the contrary, this must be the protocol adopted by the Internet community as the standard protocol for exterior gateways. Such routing protocols are called **exterior gateway protocols (EGPs)**. For the moment, there is only one such routing protocol, BGPv4. All the other protocols (e.g., RIP, OSPF, and IS-IS) belong to the class of **interior gateway protocols (IGP)**.

The EGP is responsible for the choice of the route as a *sequence of autonomous systems*. As a result of the next router, the address of the access point into the next autonomous system is specified.

IGPs are responsible for the route *within an autonomous system*. In transit autonomous systems specify the exact sequence of routers from the access point to the point where the route leaves this autonomous system.

Autonomous systems form the Internet backbone. The concept of autonomous systems hides from Internet backbone administrators the problems of packet routing at the lower, network level. For the backbone administrator, the routing protocols used inside autonomous systems are of no importance. The only routing protocol that matters is **BGPv4.**

19.3.2 Routing Information Protocol

Building a Routing Table

The **routing information protocol (RIP)** is an IGP based on the DVA algorithm. It is one of the earliest routing protocols, which, thanks to the simplicity of its implementation, is widely used in computer networks.

For IP networks, there are two versions of RIP: RIPv1 and RIPv2. The first version, RIPv1, does not support masks. In contrast to RIPv1, RIPv2 also distributes information on network masks; therefore, it is better suited to today's requirements. However, since

---

[4] From now on, the terms router and gateway will be used as synonyms, to pay tribute to traditional Internet terminology without forgetting newer terminology.

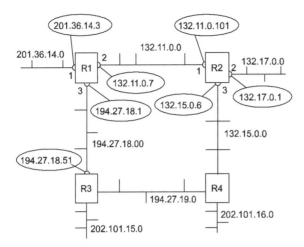

Figure 19.15 Network built on RIP gateways

the process of building a routing table used by RIPv2 is not principally different from that used by RIPv1, for simplicity, we describe this process on the example of the first version.

RIP versions allow using different types of metrics to define the distance to the network. For example, it is possible to use the simplest metric, hops, or more sophisticated types of metrics that take into account network bandwidths, introduced delays, and network reliability (i.e., corresponding to the flags *D*, *T*, and *R* in the *ToS* field of the IP packet) as well as any combination of these metrics. The metric must be characterized by the additivity property, namely, the metric of the combined route must be equal to the sum of metrics characterizing the components of this route. In most implementations of RIP, the simplest metric is used, namely, the number of hops (i.e., transit routers through which the packet has to pass to reach the destination network).

Consider the process of building a routing table using RIP on the example of the internet shown in Figure 19.15.

Stage 1. Creating Minimum Tables

The network under consideration consists of eight IP networks connected by four routers with the following identifiers: R1, R2, R3, and R4. The routers operating according to RIP must have identifiers. However, identifiers are not required for the operation of the protocol, because they are not passed in RIP messages.

In the initial state, the TCP/IP stack software automatically creates the **minimal routing table**, which takes into account only connected directly networks. In Figure 19.15, the addresses of the router ports are placed in ovals to contrast them from network addresses.

Table 19.1 allows you to evaluate how the minimal routing table of the R1 router might look.

The minimal routing table for other routers will look accordingly. For example, the routing table of the R2 router will contain three records (Table 19.2).

Table 19.1 Minimal routing table of the R1 router

Network number	Address of the next router	Port	Distance
201.36.14.0	201.36.14.3	1	1
132.11.0.0	132.11.0.7	2	1
194.27.18.0	194.27.18.1	3	1

Table 19.2 Minimal routing table of the R2 router

Network number	Address of the next router	Port	Distance
132.11.0.0	132.11.0.101	1	1
132.17.0.0	132.17.0.1	2	1
132.15.0.0	132.15.0.6	3	1

Stage 2. Sending Minimum Tables to Neighbors

After initialization, each router starts sending RIP messages containing its minimum table to its neighbors.

RIP messages are passed in UDP packets and include two parameters for each network: its IP address and the distance to this network from the router that transmits this message.

Neighbors are the routers to which the current router can pass the IP packet directly without using transit routers. For example, for the R1 router, the neighbors are R2 and R3, and for R4, these are R2 and R3.

Thus, the R1 router passes the following message to R2 and R3:

Network 201.36.14.0, distance 1
Network 132.11.0.0, distance 1
Network 194.27.18.0, distance 1

Stage 3. Receiving RIP Messages from Neighbors and Processing Routing Information

After receiving similar messages from routers R2 and R3, the R1 router increments each received metric value by one and "memorizes" through which port and from which router the new information was received. The address of this router will become the address of the next router if this record will be entered into the routing table. Then, the router starts to compare the new information with that stored in its routing table (Table 19.3).

Table 19.3 Adding records to the routing table of the R1 router

Network number	Address of the next router	Port	Distance
201.36.14.0	201.36.14.3	1	1
132.11.0.0	132.11.0.7	2	1
194.27.18.0	194.27.18.1	3	1
132.17.0.0	132.11.0.101	2	2
132.15.0.0	132.11.0.101	2	2
194.27.19.0	194.27.18.51	3	2
202.101.15.0	194.27.18.51	3	2
~~132.11.0.0~~	~~132.11.0.101~~	~~2~~	~~2~~
~~194.27.18.0~~	~~194.27.18.51~~	~~3~~	~~2~~

The records with numbers from 4 to 9 were received from the neighboring routers, and they are candidates for insertion into the table. However, only records 4–7 will be entered into the routing table; records 8 and 9 will not. This happens because these records contain data on networks already in the routing table of the R1 router, and the distance specified in these records is worse than the distance specified in the existing records of the routing table.

RIP replaces the record for a specific network only when the new information has a better metric (i.e., the distance in hops is smaller) than the existing one. As a result, only one record on each network remains in the routing table. Even if there are several paths to the same network characterized by equal distances, only one record will remain in the routing table, namely, the one that was the first to arrive at this router. There is an exception to this rule: If worse information about a specific network has arrived from the same router, based on whose message the current record was created, then the record with worse metric will replace the record with the better one. This happens because the situation in the network has changed to the worse, and the router that can be trusted reports about it.

Other network routers carry out similar operations for the new information they receive.

Stage 4. Sending a New Table to Neighbors

Each router sends its new RIP message to its neighbors. In this message, it places the data about all networks known to it, both directly connected ones and remote ones for which the router has received information in RIP messages from other routers.

Stage 5. Receiving New RIP Messages from Neighbors and Processing the Received Information

Stage 5 repeats stage 3 — all routers receive RIP messages and process the information contained there. Then, on the basis of this information, they correct their routing tables.

Consider how the R1 router carries out this operation (Table 19.4).

Table 19.4 Updating the routing table of the R1 router

Network number	Address of the next router	Port	Distance
201.36.14.0	201.36.14.3	1	1
132.11.0.0	132.11.0.7	2	1
194.27.18.0	194.27.18.1	3	1
132.17.0.0	132.11.0.101	2	2
132.15.0.0	132.11.0.101	2	2
~~132.15.0.0~~	~~194.27.18.51~~	~~3~~	~~3~~
194.27.19.0	194.27.18.51	3	2
~~194.27.19.0~~	~~132.11.0.101~~	~~2~~	~~3~~
~~202.101.15.0~~	~~194.27.18.51~~	~~3~~	~~2~~
202.101.16.0	132.11.0.101	2	3
~~202.101.16.0~~	~~194.27.18.51~~	~~3~~	~~3~~

At this stage, the R1 router has received from the R3 router information about the 132.15.0.0 network, which that router received at the previous stage from the R4 router. The R1 router already knows about the 132.15.0.0 network, and the earlier information has the better metric; therefore, the new information about this network is discarded.

Information about the 202.101.16.0 network was received by the R1 router for the first time. Information about this network arrived simultaneously from two neighbors, R3 and R4. Since metrics in both messages are equal, the record that arrived first will be entered into the routing table. In this example, the R2 router took the lead over the R3 router and was the first to send its RIP message to the R1 router.

If routers periodically repeat the stages of sending and processing RIP messages, then within a finite period, the correct routing mode will be established within the network. Here, under the correct routing mode, routing tables will be created in which all networks will be reachable from any network using some efficient route. The packets will reach their destination and not get lost in loop routes similar to the one formed by the R1–R2–R3–R4 routers (Figure 19.15).

If all network routers, all their interfaces, and all communications links connecting them are always operable, then it is possible to rarely send advertisements according to RIP, for instance, once per day. However, changes in network structure take place constantly. The usability of routers and communications links can change. New routers and communications links also may be added to or removed from the existing network.

To adapt to these changes in network structure, RIP uses several mechanisms.

Adapting RIP Routers to Network State Changes

RIP routers easily adapt to the new routes. They simply pass the new information in the next message sent to their neighbors. Thus, the new information gradually becomes known to all routers of the network. However, adaptation to the negative consequences related to the loss of some route is more difficult. This is because RIP messages do not contain a field that would specify that the path to this network no longer exists.

The following two notification mechanisms are used to inform routers that some route is no longer valid:

■ Expiration of the route TTL
■ Notification that a special distance (infinity) to the network has become unavailable

To implement the **Expiration of the route TTL** mechanism, each record of the routing table (as well as the records of the bridge/switch forwarding table) received according to RIP has a limited TTL. When another RIP message arrives, confirming the validity of a specific record, the TTL timer is reset to its initial state and then is decreased by one every second. If a new message on this route does not arrive within the timeout period, this route is marked as invalid.

The timeout period is related to the period of broadcasting vectors over the network. In RIP, this period is 30 seconds, and the timeout value is six times the length of this period (i.e., 180 seconds). The six fold time reserve is needed to make sure that a specific network has become unavailable and that the lack of connectivity is not caused by the loss of RIP messages. Note that the loss of RIP messages is possible, because RIP uses the UDP transport protocol, which does not ensure reliable message transmission.

If any router fails and ceases to send messages about the networks that can be reached via it, then after 180 seconds, all records generated by that router will be invalidated on its nearest neighbors. After that, this process will be repeated for the neighbors of the nearest neighbors. This time, invalid records will be discarded after 360 seconds, since during the first 180 seconds the nearest neighbors of the failed router still transmitted information about that router.

Information about the network that became unavailable because of router failure propagates through the network slowly. Because of this, the broadcasting period is chosen to be as small as 30 seconds.

The **timeout mechanism** works when the router cannot inform its neighbors about the failed route, either because it also has failed or because of failure of the communications link through which it would be possible to transmit the message.

When it is possible to send a message, RIP routers do not use any special attribute in the message. Instead, they specify an infinite distance to the network. Note that in RIP, this distance is 16 hops. If another metric is used instead of hops, it is necessary to specify a value of this metric that would be considered infinite by the router. Consider what happens when a router receives a message in which some network is characterized by an infinite distance (16 hops). Note that if that network is 15 hops away, the result will be the same, since the router increments the received value by 1. Having received such a message, the router must check whether this "negative" information came from the router that once sent the message on the basis of which the record on the network in question was entered into the routing table. If this is the case, then the information is considered reliable, and the route is marked as unavailable.

Such a small value of the "infinite" distance is chosen because in some cases link failures cause prolonged periods of incorrect operation of RIP routers. Incorrect behavior manifests itself as the infinite circulation of packets in network loops. The smaller the value used as "infinite," the shorter such periods of incorrect network operation.

EXAMPLE   *Consider a case of packet looping on the example network shown in Figure 19.15.*

Assume that router R1 has detected that its connectivity to the directly connected network 201.36.14.0 is lost. For example, this may happen because of the failure of the interface 201.36.14.3. The R1 router has marked the network 201.36.14.0 as unavailable in its routing table. In the worst case, the router detects this fact immediately after sending regularly scheduled RIP messages. In this case, nearly 30 seconds remain before the beginning of the new cycle of its advertisements in which it has to inform its neighbors that the distance to the network 201.36.14.0 became 16.

Each router operates on the basis of its internal timer, without synchronizing its advertisement sending operation to other routers. Therefore, it is highly probable that the R2 router would take the lead over R1 and pass its message to it before R1 will have time to pass information on the unavailability of the network 201.36.14.0. The message sent by the R2 router might contain data generated by the record from its routing table (Table 19.5).

Table 19.5 Record in the routing table of the R2 router

Network number	Address of the next router	Port	Distance
201.36.14.0	132.11.0.7	1	2

This record was received from the R1 router and was correct until the failure of the interface 201.36.14.3. This record became invalidated; however, the R2 router has not been informed about this yet.

Now, the R1 router will receive new information about the network 201.36.14.0. According to this information, this network can be reached through the R2 router with a metric of 2. Earlier, R1 also received the same information from the R2 router. However, the router ignored this information because its own metric for 201.36.14.0 was better. Now, R1 must receive the data about the 201.36.14.0 network from R2 and replace the record in the routing table, marking this network as unavailable (Table 19.6).

Table 19.6 Record in the routing table of the R1 router

Network number	Address of the next router	Port	Distance
201.36.14.0	132.11.0.101	2	3

As a result, a routing loop was generated in the network: packets sent to the modes of the 201.36.14.0 network will be passed by the R2 router to the R1 router, and the R1 router will return them to the R2 router. IP packets will circulate in this loop until the TTL for each packet expires.

The routing loop will exist in the network for a relatively long time. Consider periods that are multiples of the TTL of the routing table records:

- *0 to 180 seconds. After the failure of the interface, incorrect records will be preserved in routing tables of the R1 and R2 routers. The R2 router will continue to supply R1 router with its record about the 201.36.14.0 network with metric 2, because the TTL of this record has not expired yet. Consequently, the packets will fall into the loop.*

- *180 to 360 seconds. At the beginning of this period, the TTL of the record on the network 201.36.14.0 with metric 2 will expire on the R2 router. This will happen because R1, during the previous period, sent it advertisements on the 201.36.14.0 network with a worse metric, and they could not confirm this record. Now, R2 receives from the R1 router a record on the 201.36.14.0 network characterized by metric 3. It transforms this into the record with metric 4. On the other hand, R1 does not receive new messages from R2 concerning network 201.36.14.0 with metric 2; therefore, the TTL of its record starts to be decreased. The packets continue to circulate in the loop.*

- *360 to 540 seconds. The TTL of the record concerning network 201.36.14.0 with metric 3 on the R1 router expires. Routers R1 and R2 once again exchange their roles — now R2 supplies R1 with obsolete information about the path to the network 201.36.14.0; however, this time, the metric will be 4, and the R1 router would increment it by 1 and get 5. Packet circulation in the loop will continue.*

Were it not for the choice of the "infinite" distance of 16, this process would continue infinitely. To be more precise, it would continue until the length of the distance field is exceeded, which would overflow after the next attempt to increment the distance.

Finally, the R2 router at the next stage of the previously described process will return metric 15 from the R1 router, which, after incrementing, turns to 16. The R2 router then will register that the network is unreachable. The period of unstable network operation lasted 36 minutes!

The limitation of 15 hops reduces the area of RIP applicability to the networks in which the number of transit routers does not exceed 15. For larger networks, it is necessary to use other routing protocols, such as OSPF, or split the network into autonomous areas.

The previously described example illustrates the main reason for unstable operation of routers working according to RIP. This reason lies in the basic principle of the DVA protocols, namely, making use of information received through a third party. The R2 router has passed to R1 information about the availability of the 201.36.14.0 network without being able to confirm its reliability.

NOTE   *Routing loops are not generated when interfaces or routers fail. If the R1 router had time to pass the message about the unavailability of the 201.36.14.0 network before receiving obsolete information from R2, there would be no routing loop. It is necessary to mention that on average, routing loops arise in no more than 50% of all possible cases, even without taking special measures to prevent them. Methods of eliminating routing loops will be covered in the next section.*

Methods of Eliminating Invalid Routes in RIP

Although RIP cannot fully eliminate transient states in the network, when some routers use obsolete information about nonexistent routes, there are methods that in most cases help to solve such problems.

> The situation with a routing loop generated between two neighboring routers described in the previous section can be reliably solved using a method that became known as **split horizon.** This method implies that routing information about some network stored in the routing table of a specific router is never sent to the router from which it was received (this is the next router in the current route).

Practically all contemporary routers operating according to the RIP protocol, use the split horizon technique. If the R2 router in the previously described example supports the split horizon technique, it will never pass obsolete information about the 201.36.14.0 network to the R1 router because it received this information from the R1 router.

However, the split horizon technique cannot help when loops are created by more than two routers. Consider in more detail the situation that arises in the network shown in Figure 19.15 when router R1 loses connectivity to network 201.36.14.0. Suppose that all routers of this network support the split horizon technique. Routers R2 and R3 in this situation will not return data about the 201.36.14.0 network with the metric 2 to R1, since this router is the one from which they received this information. However, they would continue to pass information on the availability of the 201.36.14.0 with metric 4 between themselves, since they have received this information from combined route, not directly from the R1 router. For example, the R2 router received this information from the R4–R3–R1 chain. Therefore, the R1 router can potentially be deceived again until each of the routers in the R3–R4–R2 chain discards the record about availability of network 201.36.14.0.

To prevent packet circulation in complex loops after link failures, there are two other methods, known as *triggered updates* and *hold down.*

With the **triggered updates technique**, the router, having received data on the change of the metric to a specific network, does not wait for the expiration of the timeout period to update the routing table information. Instead of this, it transmits the data on the route change immediately. In many cases, this technique can prevent the transmission of obsolete information about the failed route. However, it overloads the network with control messages; therefore, trigger updates are carried out with a certain delay. Because of this, the situation is possible in which a regular update in some router will take place slightly earlier than the arrival of the trigger update from the previous router. Consequently, this router will still have time to transmit obsolete information about the nonexistent route into the network.

The **hold down technique** eliminates such situations. This method implies the introduction of the timeout for receiving new information on the network that recently became unavailable. This timeout prevents the reception of obsolete information on some route from those routers that are located at a certain distance from the failed link and that transmit obsolete data on its usability. It is assumed that during this hold-down period, these routers will discard this route from their routing tables, since they will not receive any new information concerning it. Consequently, they will not propagate obsolete information over the network.

19.3.3 Open Shortest Path First

The open shortest path first (OSPF) protocol is a contemporary implementation of the LSA algorithm. It was adopted in 1991 and is characterized by many capabilities oriented toward the use in large, heterogeneous networks.

Two Stages of Building the Routing Table

In OSPF, the process of building the routing table is divided into two large stages. At the first stage, each router builds the graph of the network links; the graph vertices are routers and IP networks, and the graph edges are router interfaces. To achieve this, all routers exchange information with their neighbors about the network graph that they had at their disposal until the current instance. This process is similar to the process of propagating the distance vectors in RIP. However, the information being propagated is principally different, since this time it is information about the network topology. The messages routers exchange are known as **router links advertisements**. Furthermore, when transmitting topological information, routers do not modify it, as was the case with RIP routers. As a result of distributing topological information, all routers will have identical information on the network graph. This information is stored in the **topological database** of the router, which is also called **link state database hold down technique**.

The second stage consists of determining optimal routes using the received graph. Each router considers itself to be the center of the network and looks for an optimal route to each of the known networks. The problem of finding the optimal path according to the network graph is rather sophisticated and resource consuming. To solve this problem, OSPF implements Dijkstra's iterative algorithm. In each of the routes found using this algorithm, only one step is memorized, namely, the hop to the next router according to the principle of single-step routing. The data on this step are entered into the routing table. If several routes have the same metric to the destination network, then the routing table will store the first steps of all these routes.

HELLO Route Advertisements

After building an original routing table, it is necessary to trace the state of network links and enter the corrections into the routing table. OSPF routers do not exchange the full information of routing table for controlling link states, as was the case with less efficient RIP routers. Instead, they transmit special, short *HELLO* messages. If the network state does not change, OSPF routers do not correct their routing tables and do not send link advertisements to their neighbors. If the link state changes, the router sends a new advertisement to its nearest neighbors, and this advertisement relates only to the link whose state has changed. Naturally, this approach allows for more sparing use of the network bandwidth. Having received a new advertisement on the change of the link state, the router rebuilds the network graph and repeats the procedure of searching for optimal routes. Note that the latter procedure does not relate to all routes: Only routes influenced by the change are recalculated. Having accomplished this, the router corrects its routing table. Simultaneously, the router retransmits the advertisement to its nearest neighbors except the one from which it received this advertisement.

When new links or new neighbors appear in the network, the router gets this information from new *HELLO* messages. Although the size of *HELLO* messages is relatively small, they still contain detailed information about the router that sent this message as well as data about its nearest neighbors, which allows unambiguous identification of the router. *HELLO* messages are sent every 10 seconds to increase the speed of adaptation of the router to all changes that take place in the network. The small size of these messages allows for a high frequency of testing network neighbors and links to them.

Metrics

As a rule, OSPF uses metrics that take into account network bandwidth. Besides this, it is possible to use two other metrics that take into account QoS requirements specified in IP packet, namely, packet transmission delay and reliability of packet delivery. For each of the metrics used, OSPF builds a separate routing table. Selection of the required routing table is carried out depending on the QoS requirement of the packet that arrived at the router (Figure 19.16).

The structure of such a network is reflected by the graph shown in Figure 19.17.

Routers are connected to LANs and directly to one another by "point-to-point" WAN links. In its advertisements, OSPF distributes information about the following two types of links: router–router and router–network. An example of the first type of link is the "R3–R4" link, and the connection "R4–195.46.17.0/24" is an example of the second type of link. Note that R3 and R4 also represent IP addresses; however, we use symbolic identifiers to distinguish these vertices of the graph from networks, for which we have preserved the standard notation of IP addresses. If point-to-point links are also assigned IP addresses, they will become additional vertices of the graph, like LANs. Information about the network mask is transmitted with the IP address.

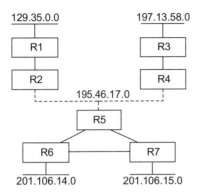

Figure 19.16 Network fragment

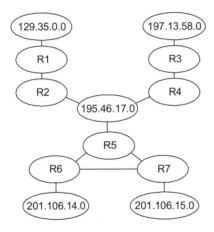

Figure 19.17 Graph of the network built using the OSPF protocol

Similarly to RIP routers, immediately after initialization, OSPF routers have information only about the links to directly connected networks. They start to distribute this information to their neighbors. In parallel with this process, they send *HELLO* messages through all their interfaces so that the router gets identifiers of its nearest neighbors practically instantly. This information complements its topology database information that it knew directly with new information. Later, the topological information starts to propagate through the network from neighbor to neighbor, and after some time, it reaches the most distant routers.

Each link is characterized by a metric. The OSPF protocol supports metrics that are standard for many protocols, such as STA. These values reflect actual network performance; for Ethernet, this value makes 10 units; for Fast Ethernet, it is 1 unit; for a T1 channel, it is 65 units; for a 56 Kbps channel, it is 1,785 units; and so on. When using high-speed links such as Gigabit Ethernet or STM-16/64, an administrator must specify another scale of speeds by specifying a conventional distance unit for the most high-speed link.

When choosing an optimal route on the graph, it is necessary to take into account the metric related to each edge of the graph. This metric is added to the path metric if a specific edge is included into that path. For instance, in the previously provided example, router R5 is connected to routers R6 and R7 by T1 links, and the R6 and R7 routers are connected to one another by the 56 Kbps link. In this case, R7 will determine an optimal route to the 201.106.14.0 network as a combined route, which first passes via the R5 router then goes via R6, because this router has the route metric 65 + 65 = 130 conventional units. The direct route via R6 would not be the optimal one, since the route metric would be 1,785. When using hops, the route going via R6 would be chosen as the optimal one even though it would not be optimal.

The OSPF protocol allows for the storage of several routes to the same network in the routing table, provided that these routes are characterized by the same metrics. If such records exist in the routing table, the router would implement the load-balancing mode by sending the packets through each route on alternating basis.

OSPF Stability

Each record in the topological database has its TTL, just like the routing records of RIP. Each record about the link state has its associated timer used for controlling the record's TTL. If any record of the topological database of the router, received from another router, becomes obsolete, the router can request another copy of that record using a special *link-state request* message of the OSPF protocol. For this message, the router has to receive the *link-state update* reply from the router directly testing the requested link.

When routers are initialized, and for more reliable synchronization of topological databases, they periodically exchange all records of the database. However, the period of exchange for all database records is significantly longer than the similar period of the RIP routers.

Because information on a specific link is generated only by those routers that have tested the state of that link by sending *HELLO* messages, and other routers simply retransmit this information without modifications, there is no possibility for obsolete information to appear in OSPF routers, in contrast to RIP routers. In OSPF routers, the information that becomes obsolete is quickly replaced by updated information, because after the link state changes, a new message is generated immediately.

In OSPF networks, there also might be periods of unstable operation. For instance, if the link fails, information on this fact does not reach all routers immediately. If this information has not reached a specific router, it continues to send the packets to the destination network, because it considers the specific link to be available and usable. However, these periods do not last long, and the packets do not fall into the route loops. On the contrary, if it is impossible to transmit the packet via an unavailable link, such a packet is simply discarded.

The main drawbacks of the OSPF protocol is its complexity, which requires considerable computing power that increases rapidly with the growth of the network scale (i.e., with an increase in the number of networks, routers, and links connecting them). To overcome this drawback, the concept of *area* was introduced into the OSPF protocol. This concept must not be confused with the autonomous system of the Internet. The routers belonging to specific area build the graph only for that area, which reduces the network size. Information about the links is not transferred between areas, and the boundary routers exchange only information about the addresses of the networks existing in each of the areas and information about the distance from the boundary router to each of those networks. When transmitting packets between areas, one of the boundary routers of a specific area is selected. As a rule, this router is the one from which the distance to the required network is the shortest.

19.3.4 Border Gateway Protocol

Nowadays, **border gateway protocol version 4 (BGPv4)** is the main protocol used to exchange routing information between Internet autonomous systems. BGP was developed to replace EGP,[5] used when the Internet had only one backbone. This backbone was a single autonomous system to which other autonomous systems were connected according to a tree-like topology. Since this structure eliminated any possibility of loops among autonomous systems, EGP did not take additional measures to eliminate the possibilities of route looping.

> BGPv4 successfully operates with any topology of links between autonomous systems, which corresponds to the current state of the Internet.

Let us explain the main principles of BGP operation using the example in Figure 19.18.

In any of the three autonomous systems (1021, 363, or 520) there are several routers that play the roles of exterior gateways. These routers run the BGPv4 protocol, which they use to communicate to one another. The router interacts with other routers according to BGP only when the network administrator has explicitly specified that these routers are its BGP neighbors in the course of configuration. For example, the EG1 router in the example under consideration will interact with the EG2 router according to BGP. This will be so because during configuration of the EG1 router, the administrator specified that the EG2 router that has 194.200.30.2 address, which was specified to it as a neighbor, not because these routers are connected point to point. Similarly, in the course of configuration of the EG2 router, the EG1 router with the address 194.200.30.1 was specified to it as a neighbor.

---

[5] EGP in this case is the name of the specific routing protocol. Recall that the EGP abbreviation also serves as the name of the entire protocol class used for routing between autonomous systems. This coincidence of names can become a source of confusion.

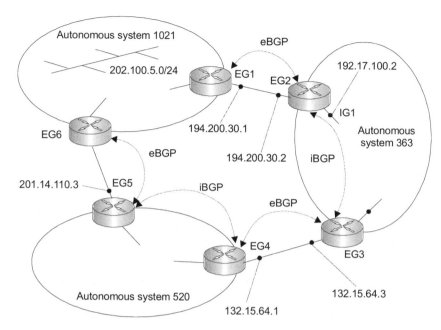

Figure 19.18 Searching for a route between autonomous systems using BGP

This method of interaction is convenient when routers exchanging route information belong to different ISPs. The administrator or administrators of a specific ISP may decide with which autonomous system this ISP will exchange traffic and with which systems such exchange must not be allowed. This task is carried out by configuring the list of neighbors for the ISP's exterior gateways. The RIP and OSPF protocols, designed for use within an autonomous system, exchange routing information with all routers located within their reach (using either a LAN or a point-to-point link). This means that information about all networks appears in the routing table of each router so that each network is reachable for any other network. For corporate networks, this situation is normal; for ISP networks, this is undesirable. Because of this, BGP plays a special role here.

For establishing a session with the specified neighbors, BGP routers use TCP (port 179). When establishing a BGP session, various methods of router authentication can be used for improving security of the autonomous system operation.

The main message of BGP is the *Update* advertisement, using which the router informs the router of the neighboring autonomous system about the reachability of the networks of its own autonomous system.

The name of this advertisement specifies that these are trigger updates sent to the neighbor only when some changes take place in the autonomous system. These changes might relate to the introduction of new networks or routes to the networks, or they might be the disappearance of networks or routes that existed earlier.

Within a single *Update* message, it is possible to advertise a single new route or revoke several routes that ceased to exist. BGP interprets a route as a sequence of autonomous systems that have to be passed to reach the network specified in the route. More formally, information about the BGP route to the network, specified as `Network/Mask_length`, looks as follows:

```
BGP Route = AS_Path; NextHop; Network/Mask_length;
```

AS_Path represents the set of autonomous system numbers, and NextHop is the IP address of the router through which it is necessary to pass the packets into the Network/Mask_length network. For example, if the EG1 router needs to inform the EG2 router that a new network, 202.100.5.0/24, has appeared in the AS1021 autonomous system, it forms the following message:

```
AS1021; 194.200.30.1; 202.100.5.0/24,
```

Then, the router passes it to the EG2 router of the AS363 autonomous system. Naturally, before doing so the EG1 router must establish a BGP session to the EG2 router.

The EG2 router, having received an *Update* message, saves information about the 202.100.5.0/24 network in its routing table with the `NextHop 194.200.30.1` and marks that this information was received from BGP. The EG2 router exchanges routing information with interior routers of AS363 using any protocol of the IGP group; for example, this may by OSPF. If the EG2 router is configured to operate in the mode of redistribution of the BGP routes to OSPF routes, then all interior routers of AS363 will know about the existence of the 202.100.5.0/24 network from the OSPF advertisement of the exterior type. Now, the EG2 router will specify the address of its own interior interface as the `NextHop`; for instance, this may be 192.17.100.2 (for IG1).

However, to propagate the advertisement related to the 202.100.5.0/24 network into other autonomous systems, such as AS520, the OSPF protocol cannot be used. The EG3 router connected to the EG4 router of the AS520 autonomous system must use BGP to generate *Update* messages of the required format. To carry out this task, it cannot use information on the 202.100.5.0/24 network received from OSPF via one of its internal interfaces, since it has different format and does not contain information on the number of the autonomous system where this network is located.

To solve the problem, EG2 and EG3 also must establish a session using BGP, although they belong to the same autonomous system. Such employment of BGP is known as interior BGP in contrast to the main use, exterior BGP. As a result, the EG3 router receives the required information from the EG2 router and passes it to its external neighbor, the EG4 router. When forming a new *Update* message, EG3 transforms the message received from the EG2 router by adding its own autonomous system, AS520, to the list of autonomous systems and replaces the received `NextHop` value with the address of its own interface:

```
AS363, AS1021; 132.15.64.3; 202.100.5.0/24.
```

Numbers of autonomous systems allow looping of *Update* messages to be eliminated. For example, when the EG5 router passes the message about the 202.100.5.0/24 network to the EG6 router, the latter will not use it, because this message will look as follows:

```
AS520, AS363, AS1021; 201.14.110.3; 202.100.5.0/24.
```

Since the list of autonomous systems already contains the number of the local autonomous system, it is clear that this message was looped.

Nowadays, BGP is used for more than exchanging routing information between autonomous systems.

19.4 INTERNET CONTROL MESSAGE PROTOCOL

KEY WORDS: Internet Control Message Protocol (ICMP), best effort, network monitoring, diagnostic (error) messages, information messages query/response, error message format, destination unreachable, ping utility, echo protocol, traceroute utility

ICMP plays an auxiliary role in the network. Specification of this protocol is described in RFC 792.

There are some situations in which IP cannot deliver the packet to the destination host. For instance, this happens if the packet's TTL has expired, if the route to the specified destination address is missing from the routing table, if the packet does not pass the check by the checksum, or if the gateway does not have sufficient buffer space for passing specific packet. As we already mentioned, IP operates according to the **best effort** principle, which means that it does not take any special measures to guarantee data delivery. This feature of IP is compensated by the higher-layer protocols such as TCP at the transport layer or, to some extent, by DNS at the application layer. These protocols assume the responsibilities of ensuring reliability. For this purpose, they use such well-known techniques as message numbering, delivery acknowledgment, and data retransmission.

ICMP serves as a supplement to IP; however, the nature of this supplement is different from the capabilities of ensuring reliable transmission by higher-layer protocols. ICMP is not intended for resolving the problems that may arise in the course of packet transmission: If the packet has been lost, ICMP cannot retransmit it. The goal of ICMP is simpler. This protocol is the means of informing the sender about any "accidents" that occur to its packets. Since IP sends the packet and "forgets" about its existence, ICMP "traces" the process of packet forwarding along the network; if the router discards it, ICMP sends the message to the source host informing it of this event. Thus, ICMP ensures constant feedback between the sent packets and the sender host.

For example, suppose that IP running on a specific router has detected that the packet needs to be fragmented for forwarding along the route but that the packet has the *Don't Fragment* (DF) flag set. The IP module, having detected that it cannot pass the packet further along the network, must send the ICMP *diagnostic* message to the source host and then discard the packet.

Besides diagnostics, ICMP is used for network monitoring. For instance, such popular diagnostic utilities intended for IP networks as `ping` and `tracert` work with ICMP messages. Using ICMP messages, an application can determine the route along which the data are forwarded, evaluate its usability, determine the time required for the data to pass to a specific host, request the mask value for a specific network interface, and so on.

Note that some packets can disappear from the network without acknowledgment. Particularly, ICMP does not make a provision for passing messages about the problems arising when processing IP packets that carry ICMP error messages. (However, this rule is not applicable to ICMP requests.) Developers of this protocol used such a solution to avoid the generation of "storms" in networks, when the number of error messages grows explosively. For the same reason, ICMP messages are not sent if an error occurs in the course of transmission of any fragment except the first one, if the lost packet had a broadcast IP address, or if the lost IP packet was encapsulated into the frame of underlying technology with a broadcast address.

Because an IP packet contains the sender address but does not contain any address information on transit routers, ICMP messages are sent only to end nodes. Here, these messages can be processed by the operating system kernel, by transport- or application-layer protocols, or by applications. On the other hand, such messages can be ignored. The most important point is that the processing of ICMP messages is not included on the list of responsibilities of IP and ICMP.

19.4.1 Types of ICMP Messages

All ICMP messages fall in the following two classes:

- Diagnostic (error) messages
- Information messages such as query and response

An ICMP message is encapsulated into the data field of an IP packet (Figure 19.19). An ICMP header is 8 bytes long and comprises the following fields:

Type (1 byte) — contains the code determining the message type. Table 19.7 lists the most common types of ICMP messages.

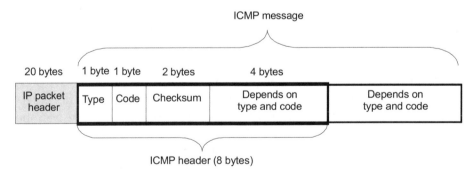

Figure 19.19 ICMP message format and encapsulation

Table 19.7 Possible values of the Type field

Value	Message type
0	Echo reply
3	Destination unreachable
4	Source quench
5	Redirect
8	Echo request
11	Time exceeded for a datagram
12	Parameter problem on a datagram
13	Timestamp request
14	Timestamp reply
17	Address mask request
18	Address mask reply

Code (1 byte) — contains the code that differentiates the error type more precisely.
Checksum (2 bytes) — the checksum field computed for the entire ICMP message.

The header also includes a field comprising 4 bytes. The contents of this field depend of the values of the *Type* and *Code* fields. In the query/reply messages, this field contains 2-byte *Identifier* and *Sequence number* subfields (Figure 19.20). The numbers contained in these subfields are duplicated from the query message to the response message. The *Identifier* field allows the destination host to determine for which application this response is intended, and the *Sequence number* field is used by the application to relate the response to a specific query (taking into account that the same application can produce several queries of the same type). In error messages, this field is not used and, consequently, is filled with zeros.

Errors of every type can be characterized more precisely by error codes. For example, Table 19.8 provides the codes for the message classified as type 3 — "destination unreachable." This table lists 15 reasons that can be specified in the message of this type. The impossibility of reaching the destination host may be caused, for instance, by temporary hardware malfunction, by an incorrect destination address, by the lack of an application-layer protocol, or by an open UDP/TCP port at the destination host.

Format of the ICMP data field also depends on the values of the *Type* and *Code* fields. To demonstrate the differences in the formats of the different message types, consider the following two examples:

■ Echo request/reply   ■ Destination unreachable

Table 19.8 Codes that detail the cause of the type 3 error — "destination unreachable"

Code	Cause
0	Network unreachable
1	Host unreachable
2	Protocol unreachable
3	Port unreachable
4	Fragmentation needed, but DF bit set
5	Source route failed
6	Destination network unknown
7	Destination host unknown
8	Source host isolated
9	Destination network administratively prohibited
10	Destination host administratively prohibited
11	Network unreachable for type of service (ToS)
12	Host unreachable for ToS
13	Communication administratively prohibited by filtering
14	Host precedence violation
15	Precedence cut off in effect

19.4.2 Format of the Echo Request/Reply Message: The Ping Utility

Figure 19.20 illustrates the format of the "echo request" and "echo reply" messages. They differ from one another only in the value of the *Type* field (0 for reply and 1 for request). In the request data field, the sender places information, which it then receives in the reply from the destination host.

Echo request and echo reply, which in aggregate are called the **echo protocol**, are the simplest tools for network monitoring. The computer or router sends an echo request via the internet, where the IP address of the host is specified, although it is necessary to check the possibility of reaching it. The host that receives the echo request, forms and sends an echo reply, and returns the message to the host that has sent the request. Since echo requests and echo replies are passed through the network in the form of IP packets, their successful delivery means that the entire transport system of the internet operates normally.

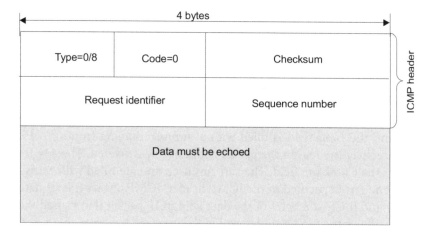

Figure 19.20 Format of the *echo request/echo reply* ICMP messages

Most operating systems use the built-in `ping` utility, intended for testing the possibility of reaching hosts. Usually, this utility sends a series of echo requests to the host being tested and provides the user with statistical information about the lost echo replies and the average time of network reaction to these requests. The ping utility displays messages informing the user of all received replies. Its output looks approximately as follows:

```
# ping server1.citmgu.ru
Pinging  server1.citmgu.ru [193.107.2.200] with 64 bytes of data:

Reply from 193.107.2.200: bytes=64 time=256ms   TTL= 123
Reply from 193.107.2.200: bytes=64 time=310ms   TTL= 123
Reply from 193.107.2.200: bytes=64 time=260ms   TTL= 123
Reply from 193.107.2.200: bytes=64 time=146ms   TTL= 123
```

From the listing provided here, it follows that four echo replies were received in response to the testing requests sent to the server1.mgu.ru host. The length of each message is 64 bytes. The next column contains the values of RTT, the intervals elapsing from the moment the request was sent to the moment the reply to this request arrives. As you can see, the network operation is unstable, because the RTT value in the last row is more than two times smaller than the RTT value of the second row. The remaining TTL for the arriving packets is displayed in the third column.

Depending on the specific implementation of the `ping` utility and its command-line options, the command output may differ from the one presented here. As a rule, the `ping` utility has several command-line options using which it is possible to specify the size of the message data field, the initial value for the *TTL* fields, the number of repeated attempts of packet transmission, and the setting for the *DF* flag.

If no replies arrive during the specified timeout interval or if ICMP replies with error messages, `ping` displays appropriate error messages on the screen.

19.4.3 Error Message Format: The Traceroute Utility

Figure 19.21 illustrates the format of the ICMP error message; in this example, this is the "destination unreachable" message. Other ICMP error messages have the same format and differ from one another only in the values of the *Type* and *Code* fields.

If the router cannot transmit or deliver an IP packet, it sends the "destination unreachable" error message to the host that has sent this packet. In this message, the *Type* field contains the value 3, and the *Code* field is filled with a number ranging from 0 to 15, which specifies more precisely the reason the packet could not be delivered. The 4 bytes that follow this field are the *Checksum* field. They are not used and are filled with zeros.

Besides the cause of the error specified in the ICMP header, ICMP always fills its data field with the IP header and the first 8 bytes of the data field of IP packet that caused the error. This information allows the sender to determine the cause of the error more precisely, since all protocols of the TCP/IP stack using IP packets for transmitting their messages contain the most important information in the first 8 bytes of their messages. Particularly, these might be the first 8 bytes of the TCP or UDP header, which contain the information identifying the application that has sent the lost packet. Consequently, application developers can provide built-in tools intended for reacting to ICMP messages on the packets that could not be delivered.

The destination host or destination network might be unreachable because of a temporary hardware malfunction, because of an incorrect destination address specified by the sender, or because the router has no information on the route to the destination net-

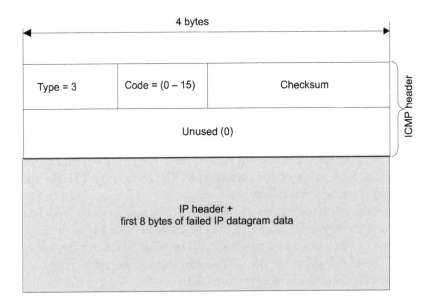

Figure 19.21 Format of the ICMP error message "destination unreachable"

work. The impossibility of reaching the protocol, the port, or both means that the destination host lacks the implementation of some application-layer protocol or lacks open UDP or TCP ports at the destination host.

As already illustrated in the example with the ping utility, ICMP messages are efficiently used for network monitoring. In particular, the error messages about another error, "time exceeded," serve as a basis of another popular utility — traceroute (UNIX) or tracert (Windows 2000). This utility allows tracing of the route to the remote host, defining the RTT, IP address, and domain name for every transit router (provided that this name is registered in the DNS reverse lookup zone). This information is useful for locating the router along which the packet's path to the destination host comes abruptly to an end.

Traceroute traces the route by sending normal IP packets with the destination address as the end point of the route being investigated. The idea of the tracing method lies in that the TTL of the first packet being sent is set to 1. When the IP of the first router receives this packet, it decreases the TTL by 1 according to its algorithm. The TTL gets a zero value, and the router discards the packet with the zero value of the TTL and returns the "time exceeded" message with the IP header and the first 8 bytes of the lost packet to the source host.

Having received the ICMP message informing the sender about the cause of packet nondelivery, the traceroute utility memorizes the address of the first router (retrieved from the IP header of the packet carrying that ICMP message). After that, it calculates the RTT value for the first router. Then, traceroute sends the next IP packet with the TTL value set to 2. This packet successfully passes the first router but is discarded on the second router, which immediately sends the same "time exceeded" ICMP message. The traceroute utility stores the IP address and the TTL for the second router, and so on. The same operation is carried out on each next router along the route to the destination host.

Naturally, we have considered the operation of the traceroute utility in a simplified form. However, even this information is sufficient to evaluate the elegance of the idea upon which it is based.

The listing provided here shows the typical output of the tracert utility (Windows) in the course of tracing the **ds.internic.net** [198.49.45.29] host:

```
 1   311 ms   290 ms   261 ms   144.206.192.100
 2   281 ms   300 ms   271 ms   194.85.73.5
 3   023 ms   290 ms   311 ms   moscow-m9-2-S5.relcom.eu.net [193.124.254.37]
 4   290 ms   261 ms   280 ms   MSK-M9-13.Relcom.EU.net [193.125.15.13]
 5   270 ms   281 ms   290 ms   MSK.RAIL-1-ATM0-155Mb.Relcom.EU.net [193.124.254.82]
 6   300 ms   311 ms   290 ms   SPB-RASCOM-1-E3-1-34Mb.Relcom.EU.net [193.124.254.78]
 7   311 ms   300 ms   300 ms   Hssi11-0.GW1.STK2.ALTER.NET [146.188.33.125]
 8   311 ms   330 ms   291 ms   421.ATM6-0-0.CR2.STK2.Alter.Net [146.188.5.73]
 9   360 ms   331 ms   330 ms   219.Hssi4-0.CR2.LND1.Alter.Net [146.188.2.213]
10   351 ms   330 ms   331 ms   412.Atm5-0.BR1.LND1.Alter.net [146.188.3.205]
11   420 ms   461 ms   420 ms   167.ATM8-0-0.CR1.ATL1.Alter.Net [137.39.69.182]
```

```
12   461 ms   441 ms   440 ms   311.ATM12-0-0.BR1.ATL1.Alter.Net [137.39.21.73]
13   451 ms   410 ms   431 ms   atlanta1-br1.bbnplanet.net [4.0.2.141]
14   420 ms   411 ms   410 ms   vienna1-br2.bbnplanet.net [4.0.3.154]
15   411 ms   430 ms   2514 ms  vienna1-nbr3.bbnplanet.net [4.0.3.150]
16   430 ms   421 ms   441 ms   vienna1-nbr2.bbnplanet.net [4.0.5.45]
17   431 ms   451 ms   420 ms   cambridge1-br1.bbnplanet.net [4.0.5.42]
18   450 ms   461 ms   441 ms   cambridge1-cr14.bbnplanet.net [4.0.3.94]
19   451 ms   461 ms   460 ms   attbcstoll.bbnplanet.net [206.34.99.38]
20   501 ms   460 ms   481 ms   shutdown.ds.internic.net [198.49.45.29]
Tracing complete.
```

The sequence of lines corresponds to the sequence of routers that form the route to the destination host. The first number in each line is the number of hops to the appropriate router. The traceroute utility tests each router three times; therefore, the next three numbers in each line are RTT values computed by sending three packets whose TTLs have expired on that router. If the reply from a specific router does not arrive during the time specified, then an asterisk (*) is displayed instead of the time.

Then, the IP address and domain name (if available) of the router are specified. From this listing, it is obvious that practically all router interfaces of ISPs are registered in the DNS service; the first ones, corresponding to local routers, lack this registration.

It is necessary to point out again that the time specified in each row is not the time required for the packet to pass between the two neighboring routers. Rather, this is the time during which the packet passes from the source to appropriate router and back again. Since the situation with the load of the Internet routers is constantly changing, the time required to pass to a specific router does not always grow steadily. Sometimes, it can change in an arbitrary way.

SUMMARY

▶ In contrast to IP, the main task of which is ensuring data transmission between network interfaces of the internet, the main goal of TCP and UDP is transmission of data between application processes running on different end nodes of the network.

▶ The main difference between TCP and UDP is that TCP carries out an additional task — ensuring reliable message delivery using the internet, all nodes of which use an unreliable IP datagram protocol for message transmission.

▶ UDP is a datagram protocol that operates according to the best effort principle, without establishing a logical connection. UDP does not guarantee delivery of its messages and, consequently, does not compensate for the unreliability of IP, which also is a datagram protocol.

▶ System queues to the access points of the application processes are called ports. Ports are identified by numbers and uniquely define applications within the limits of a computer. Applications that use UDP have numbers called UDP ports, and applications relying on TCP have TCP ports.

▶ If application processes are popular public services, such as FTP, telnet, HTTP, TFTP, or DNS, they have centrally assigned port numbers. Services that are not so widely used and are not assigned well-known port numbers have port numbers allocated by the local operating system. Such port numbers are called dynamic.

▶ The socket of an application process is the following pair of its parameters: *(IP address, port number)*.

▶ TCP solves the problem of ensuring reliable data exchange by establishing logical connections. A logical connection is uniquely identified by a pair of sockets.

▶ A TCP connection is a duplex connection; it is established as a result of negotiation over the maximum MTU size, the maximum volume of data that can be transmitted without receiving an acknowledgment, starting from the sequence number of the byte from which the data flow within a specific connection starts. When a connection is created, operating systems on both sides allocate a specific set of system resources to it. These resources are required for organizing buffers, timers, and counters.

▶ The procedure used by TCP/UDP when receiving data arriving from several application services is called multiplexing. The inverse procedure used by TCP/UDP for distributing the packets arriving from the network layer among the set of higher-layer services is called demultiplexing. UDP implements demultiplexing on the basis of sockets, and TCP carries out the same task on the basis of connections.

▶ For controlling the flow within the framework of the TCP connection, a specific variant of the sliding window algorithm is used. The receiving side transmits to the sender the window size in bytes. This decision is made on the basis of the speed at which it will be able to process the arriving data. However, the sender also can control the window size. If the sender notices that the operation of the communications link is unreliable, it can reduce the window size by its own initiative.

▶ Routing protocols generate for each router coordinated routing tables — that is, ones that would ensure packet delivery along a rational route from the source route to the destination network within a finite number of steps. For this purpose, the network routers exchange special information on the topology of the internetwork.

▶ Routing is classified into two classes: static and adaptive (dynamic).

  • During static routing, all routing tables are composed and entered into each router manually by the network administrator.

  • Adaptive routing ensures automatic updating of the routing table after changing the configuration of the network.

▶ Adaptive routing protocols are divided into two groups, each of which is related to a specific type of algorithm:

  ● In distance vector algorithms (DVAs), each router periodically sends broadcast messages over the network, with the components representing the distances from this router to all known networks.

  ● Link state algorithms (LSAs) *supply each router with information sufficient for building an exact graph of the network links.*

▶ Internet routing protocols are divided into external and internal ones. Exterior gateway protocols (EGPs) carry routing information between autonomous systems, and interior gateway protocols (IGPs) are used only within the limits of a specific autonomous system.

▶ RIP is the oldest routing protocol in the TCP/IP networks. Despite its simplicity, caused by the use of a DVA, RIP is successfully used in small networks with no more than 15 transit routers.

▶ RIP routers usually select the route on the basis of the simplest metric, the number of transit routers between networks, or hops.

▶ In networks using RIP and having loop routes, there may exist quite lengthy periods of unstable operation, when packets fall into loops and are not delivered to the destination. RIP routers provide several techniques that sometimes reduce instability periods. These techniques include split horizon, hold down, and triggered updates.

▶ The OSPF protocol was developed for efficient routing of IP packets in large networks with sophisticated topology that includes loops. This algorithm is based on LSA and is characterized by high stability against network topology changes.

▶ When choosing a route, OSPF routers use the metric that takes into account internet bandwidth.

▶ The OSPF protocol allows storage in the routing table of several routes to the same network if they have equal metrics. This allows the router to operate in the load-balancing state.

▶ OSPF is rather sophisticated and requires high computational power; therefore, it most frequently operates on powerful hardware routers.

▶ Nowadays, border gateway protocol (BGP) version 4 is the protocol for exchanging routing information between Internet autonomous systems. BGPv4 operates with high stability, having any topology of links between autonomous systems that corresponds to contemporary Internet structure.

▶ The internet control message protocol (ICMP) plays a subsidiary role in the network. It is used for diagnostic purposes and for network monitoring. Thus, ICMP messages form the basis for such popular utilities for monitoring IP networks as `ping` and `tracert`.

REVIEW QUESTIONS

1. When do software developers prefer to use UDP? When do they prefer to rely on TCP?

2. What volume of data (with a precision up to 1 byte) was received during the TCP session by the sender of the TCP segment whose header contained the value 1,845,685 in the ACK field, given that the first received byte had the number 50,046?

3. Is it possible to forward IP packets if the router lacks a routing table?
   A. No, this is impossible.
   B. Yes, it is possible provided that source routing is used.
   C. Yes, it is possible if the default route is specified in the router.

4. Is it possible to do without routing protocols in the network?

5. What are drawbacks of distance vector routing protocols?
   A. Intense extra traffic in a large network.
   B. Chosen routes are not always characterized by the minimal metric value.
   C. The process of coordinating routing tables takes a long time.

6. What is the main operating principle of routing protocols based on LSAs?

7. What is the difference between IGPs and EGPs?

8. Which metric is used in RIP?

9. Why does RIP consider the distance of 16 hops unreachable?
   A. The field allocated for storing the distance value has a length of 4 binary digits.
   B. Networks in which the RIP algorithm operates are rarely large.
   C. RIP tries to ensure an acceptable convergence time of the algorithm.

10. What methods are there for speeding up the convergence of RIP?

11. What are the main stages of building the routing table using OSPF?

12. What is the role of *HELLO* messages in the OSPF protocol?
    A. They establish a connection between two routers.
    B. They check the state of communications links and neighboring routers.
    C. They carry information that the OSPF protocol operates in the network.

13. What types of metrics does OSPF support?

14. For what purposes is the network of routers supporting OSPF divided into areas?

15. What are the main disadvantages of OSPF?

16. Why is EGP no longer used in the Internet?

17. What is the mechanism that allows BGP to operate in networks that have loops between autonomous systems?

18. What parameters are changed by the BGP router in the advertisement received from some autonomous system when it passes it to another autonomous system?

19. If a problem with an IP packet arises, in which cases is it impossible to send an ICMP error message?

20. What is the destination of an ICMP message? Which software module processes it?

21. How does an ICMP message improve the reliability of data transmission in an IP network?

PROBLEMS

1. Find a partner and model a TCP session. Negotiate the maximum segment size, the initial sizes of buffers, the initial values of the SEQUENCE NUMBER, and the window size. Then, start sending "segments" to each other asynchronously. The role of "segments" can be played by cards containing the values of the key fields — number of the first byte, the size of the segment being sent, the ACKNOWLEDGMENT NUMBER, and a new value of window size. You can pretend sometimes that you have lost the cards and act according to the TCP operating logic. Do not forget to mark the time on each "sent" copy of the segment to trace the arrivals of acknowledgments. This game will help you to better understand TCP. Feel free to ask questions.

2. What time, in the worst case, will elapse before the routing tables of the network shown in Figure 19.15 come to a coordinated state after the R1 router loses connection to the 201.36.14.0 network? Assume that all routers support the split horizon mechanism.

3. Suggest several variants of the metric that simultaneously takes into account the bandwidth, reliability, and latency of the communications link.

ADVANCED FEATURES OF IP ROUTERS

20.1 INTRODUCTION

The main functions of IP routers are creating routing tables and forwarding IP packets on the basis of these tables. To carry out these functions, the router must support the Internet protocol (IP) covered in *Chapter 18* as well as the routing protocols considered in *Chapter 19*. Besides these basic functions, contemporary IP routers support several advanced features, which make them powerful and flexible multifunctional traffic-processing devices. In this chapter, we consider the most important advanced capabilities of contemporary routers most frequently used by network administrators.

Routers are border devices that connect a computer network to the outside world. Therefore, it would be natural to delegate them several functions related to the *protection* of the internal network against attacks from the outside. IP routers carry out these functions based on user traffic filtering according to various attributes in IP packets, such as the source address, the type of protocol encapsulated in the IP packet, and the application that generated this traffic. Such functionality prevents undesirable traffic from penetrating the protected network. It also reduces the probability of attacks on the hosts located within that network. The *network address translation* (NAT) technology, which hides the actual addresses of hosts belonging to this network from outside users, plays an important role in the protection of these internal network resources.

QoS support is a relatively new property of IP networks. IP routers have long supported several congestion control and avoidance mechanisms. However, standards for ensuring QoS support for IP networks were developed only recently, in the late 1990s. There are two types of QoS architecture for IP networks: *integrated services* (*IntServ*) and *differentiated services* (*DiffServ*). The first architecture ensures QoS for individual flows from source to destination, and the second one was developed for aggregate flows, which represent a small number of traffic classes. Nowadays, the IntServ technology is mainly used on the network periphery, enterprise-wide networks, and in access networks. DiffServ has started to find application on network backbones. Such separation of the application areas is obvious, since ensuring QoS for individual flows creates an additional load on the router. This load is proportional to the number of flows being served. The backbone can transmit hundreds of thousands of user flows; therefore, IntServ implementation may place too-high requirements on the computing power and the amount of memory available to backbone routers.

This chapter ends by considering functional structure of contemporary routers.

20.2 FILTERING

KEY WORDS: data filtering, routing announcements filtering, router access lists, deny, permit, standard access list, source wildcards, access list, keywords, ICMP, ping, protection

IP routing protocols create routing tables. Based on these, any host of the internet can exchange information with any other host. This principle of datagram networks is often convenient. Because of it, every user of the Internet can access any public site.

Recall that in networks based on the virtual circuit technique, it is impossible to organize communications between any two hosts without previously establishing a virtual circuit between them.

However, such common availability of hosts and networks does not always correspond to the needs of their owners. Therefore, many routers support advanced features, such as user traffic filtering and routing protocol advertisements. These capabilities control host reachability with different levels of granularity.

20.2.1 User Traffic Filtering

Filtering is nonstandard processing of IP packets by routers, which results in discarding specific packets or changing their routes.

User traffic filtering implemented by routers is principally analogous to the similar function carried out by LAN switches (see *Chapter 15*).

The main goal of filtering lies in that not all IP packets that pass through the router must be processed according to the standard procedure described in *Chapter 18*. In the standard procedure, the type of packet processing is chosen on the basis of information contained only in the destination address field of an IP packet.[1] If this address is in the routing table, then the packet is transferred to the appropriate output interface.

Packet filtering conditions set on routers usually take into account a considerably larger number of attributes than similar filters implemented by LAN switches. For example, besides the destination IP address, the list of such attributes may include:

- Source and destination IP addresses
- Source and destination MAC addresses

---

[1] This description is simplified to emphasize the main feature of the standard procedure of the packet forwarding. In reality, even the standard procedure takes into account several other fields of the IP packet, such as *TTL*, the data field (namely, its size), *DF*, *IP precedence*, and *TOS*. If these fields do not require special processing of the packet (such as discarding the packet if TTL ≤ 1), then the router starts the procedure of the routing table lookup.

- Identifier of the interface from which the packet was received
- Type of protocol encapsulated in the IP packet (e.g., TCP, UDP, ICMP, or OSPF)
- TCP/UDP port number (e.g., type of application-layer protocol).

If the filter is set, the router first checks if the conditions specified in this filter are satisfied. If the result of this check is positive, the router carries out some nonstandard operations for this packet. For instance, the packet can be discarded (dropped), sent to the next router (which is different from the one specified in the routing table), or marked as a possible candidate for discarding if network congestion occurs. The normal procedure of passing the packet according to the routing table records might be one of such possible actions.

Consider some examples of filters written using the Cisco IOS command line interface language. These filters, also called **access lists**, are widely used for limiting user traffic in IP routers.

The **standard access list** is the simplest type of filter, which takes into account only the source IP address.

The general syntax of such a condition looks as follows:

```
access-list access-list-number {deny | permit}
          {source-address [source-wildcard] | any}
```

Standard access list defines two actions that can be carried out for the packet that satisfies the condition described by the filter: deny (i.e., discard the packet) and permit (i.e., pass the packet for standard processing according to the routing table). Specific action specified in the standard access list is chosen if the source IP address matches the source IP address specified in the list. The check is carried out in the same style as when checking a routing table. Here, source-wildcard is the analogue of a mask — however, in a slightly modified form. Binary zero in the source-wildcard means that this bit in the address of the arrived packet must match the address specified in the filter condition. Binary one means that the match in this position is not required. If you need to specify a condition for all addresses of a specific subnet, you must use the inverted value of the mask of this subnet. The any parameter means any value of the address; it is just a briefer and easily understandable form of writing the value 255.255.255.255 in the source-wildcard field.

An example of the standard access list is as follows:

```
access-list 1 deny   192.78.46.0   0.0.0.255
```

Here:

1 — access list number

deny — the action that must be carried out over the packet that satisfies the condition specified in this access list

192.78.46.0 — source address

0.0.0.255 — source wildcard

This filter blocks the transmission of packets, the three most significant bytes in addresses of which have the values 192, 78, and 46.

The access list can include several conditions. In this case, it comprises several lines starting with the `access-list` keyword, which has the same value of *access-list-number* that represents the list identifier. For example, if you need to allow the packets originating from host 192.78.46.12 to pass the router, disallowing transmission of the packets from all other hosts belonging to this subnet, then the access list will look as follows:

```
access-list 1 permit  192.78.46.12  0.0.0.0
access-list 1 deny    192.78.46.0   0.0.0.255
access-list 1 permit  any
```

Access list conditions are checked one by one. If any of them gives a match, then the `permit` or `deny` action is carried out as specified in this condition. After that, the other conditions specified in this list are not checked. By default, at the end of each list, there is the following implicit condition:

```
[access-list 1 deny any]
```

Therefore, to prevent this list from interfering with the normal processing of packets from other networks, the following condition is written in it:

```
access-list 1 permit any
```

The access list can be applied to any interface of the router and in any direction. If the list is applied with the `in` keyword, it is applied to the incoming packet; if the `out` keyword is used, the condition is applied to the outgoing packets. For example, `access-list 1` can be applied to some interface for the incoming traffic using the following command:

```
access-group 1 in
```

There are more powerful types of access lists for Cisco routers, such as extended access lists. The general format of these lists is as follows:

```
access-list access-list-number {deny|permit}
{protocol|protocol key word}
{source address [source-wildcard]] [source port] | any}
[destination address [destination-wildcard]]   [destination port]
```

Using an extended access list, it is possible to prevent ftp traffic that receives client requests using TCP with the well-known port number 21 from passing into the internal network of the company. To achieve this, it is necessary to include the following condition into the access list:

```
access-list 102 deny  TCP any 21 any
```

This must be applied to the router interface, to which the internal network is connected, with the `out` keyword.

Administrators of enterprise-wide networks often prohibit the possibility of pinging internal hosts using the following condition:

```
access-list 101 deny ICMP any 192.78.46.8  0.0.0.0  eq 8
```

As can be seen from this condition, the access-list syntax for ICMP is different from the standard syntax used for extended access lists. The 8 parameter means that it is prohibited to pass ICMP messages of type 8, which corresponds to echo-request messages used by the `ping` utility.

The filter language of the *Gated* software router used in many UNIX versions is even more flexible. This language uses a syntax close to that of the C language, which allows the building of rather sophisticated logical constructs using the `if`, `then`, and `else` logical operators.

It is necessary to mention, that filtering of the user traffic can significantly slow the operation of the router, since processing of each packet requires checking of auxiliary conditions.

To avoid significant overhead on the router, thus "distracting" it from carrying out its main tasks, router filters do not use information on session prehistory. However complicated the filter condition might be, it contains only the parameters of the *current* packet and cannot use the parameters of the packets already processed by the router. This limitation is the main difference between routers and firewalls, special software systems that use information on the session prehistory to carry out better filtering.

20.2.2 Routing Announcements Filtering

For controlling the possibility of reaching specific hosts and networks, it is possible to limit the propagation of routing announcements along with user traffic filtering.

Such a measure prevents the records on certain networks from automatically appearing in the routing tables. This method requires the router to be significantly less powerful, since routing advertisements arrive at the router more rarely than user packets.

Cisco routers provide the possibility of limiting the propagation of routing advertisements on a specific network by specifying its description using a standard access list and then applying it to the interface using the `distribute-list` keyword (instead of the `access-group` keyword, as was the case with filtering user traffic).

For example, if a network administrator wants to prevent information on the company's internal networks 194.12.34.0/24 and 132.7.0.0/16 from propagating to external networks, it is sufficient to write the following standard access list:

```
access-list 2 deny 194.12.34.0 0.0.0.255
access-list 2 deny 132.7.0.0 0.0.255.255
access-list 2 permit any
```

Then, the administrator applies it to the interface using the following command:

```
distribute-list 2 out serial 1
```

20.3 IP QOS

KEY WORDS: Integrated Services, Differentiated Services, traffic classes, RSVP, QoS, ISP, microflow, aggregate flow, MPLS, token bucket algorithm, Random Early Detection algorithm (RED), Weighted RED (WRED), traffic profile, reference flow, token, smoothing, profiling, burst (RSVP), PATH-message, RESV-message, resource reservation, flow descriptor, filter specification, receiver request specification, source traffic specification, Expedited Forwarding (EF), Assured Forwarding (AF)

Technologies of the TCP/IP stack were created for elastic traffic, which is tolerant of packet delays and packet delay variations. Therefore, the attention of TCP/IP developers was concentrated on ensuring reliable traffic transmission using TCP. Nevertheless, to eliminate overloads and prevent congestion on slow links, many QoS mechanisms were gradually built into IP routers, including priority and weighted queuing, traffic policing, and feedback. However, each network administrator was free to use these mechanisms at his discretion without any systematic approach. Only in mid-1990s did research begin in the field of developing QoS standards for IP. Based on these standards, it became possible to create a QoS support system within the framework of internets and even within the Internet.

As a result of this research, two systems of IP QoS were developed:

■ *Integrated services* (*IntServ*) was oriented toward providing QoS guarantees for end-user data flows. Therefore, IntServ is mainly used at the network periphery.

■ *Differentiated Services* (*DiffServ*) was designed to do the same thing for traffic classes. Therefore it is mainly used at the backbones.

Both systems use all basic elements of the QoS system based on resource reservation — that is, both systems provide the following mechanisms:

■ Traffic conditioning
■ Signaling for router coordination
■ Reservation of the interface and router bandwidth for flows or traffic classes
■ Priority and weighted queuing

Neither of these technologies solves the traffic engineering problems, since packets are still forwarded along the path with the best metric, which is chosen using the standard routing protocol without taking into account the real load on communications links.

20.3.1 QoS Models of IntServ and DiffServ

IntServ technology development was started by IETF in the early 1990s. It was the first development and research area in which the problem of ensuring QoS for TCP/IP network was solved using a systematic approach. The basg IntServ model assumes integrated communication of network routers to ensure the required QoS along the **entire route of the microflow** between network end nodes.

Router resources (e.g., interface bandwidth and buffer sizes) are distributed according to the QoS requirements of various applications within the limits allowed by the QoS policy for the given network. QoS application requests are propagated across the network using the RSVP signaling protocol, which allows reservations both for flows between two end nodes (e.g., unicast destination addresses) and for flows received by several end nodes (e.g., multicast destination addresses).

However, this harmonious system of ensuring QoS has numerous opponents, mainly among ISPs. This is because implementation of IntServ requires the backbone routers of ISPs to operate with the status information of tens of thousands of microflows passing through ISP networks. Such nontraditional loads on routers require redesigning of their architecture, which sharply increases the cost of IP networks and their services.

Therefore, by the end of the 1990s, another IP QoS technology was developed, which became known as **DiffServ**. Initially, this technology was oriented toward use within the limits of the ISP network. It excluded end nodes that generate microflows out of consideration. For DiffServ technology, QoS support starts at the edge router of the ISP network to which a large number of microflows from user network arrives. Each DiffServ boundary router classifies and tags the incoming traffic, dividing it into small number of classes, which usually does not exceed 3–4 (maximum = 8). Then, each network router serves traffic classes on the basis of this differentiation, according to the carried out tagging, by allocating a certain amount of resources to each class. Resources on routers are reserved statically. Most frequently, this task is carried out manually by a network administrator. The role of the signaling protocol is played by the tags specifying that a specific packet belongs to specific class.

> Responsibility for coordinated serving of the traffic by all network routers is delegated to the administrator, since it is the administrator that decides the bandwidth and the amount of buffer space allocated to each traffic class on each interface of each router.

The DiffServ model significantly reduces the load on ISP routers, since it requires status information to be stored only for a small number of traffic classes. Furthermore, this model is convenient for ISPs because it allows them to organize QoS support autonomously within the limits of networks owned by those ISPs. However, these advantages must be paid for. In this case, the advantages are achieved at the expense of end-to-end QoS support. Even if every ISP implements DiffServ in its network, the entire pattern is fragmented, since individual administrators are responsible for each fragment. Coordination of reservation parameters remains an exclusively subjective procedure, which is not supported by any protocols.

Despite the significant attention drawn lately to DiffServ as a simple tool that can be used to ensure increased Internet QoS without significant expenses, there are alternative points of view. For example, Dr. Lawrence G. Roberts, one of the Internet founders, has expressed an extremely negative opinion about attempts at solving Internet QoS problems in a simplified form. The research of the combined use of the IntServ and DiffServ technologies also is in progress. In these models, each technology operates in its area of application: IntServ in access networks, where the number of microflows is relatively small, and DiffServ in backbone networks. Another component supplementing DiffServ is the multiprotocol label switching (MPLS) technology that allows the traffic engineering problem to be solved in IP networks. This technology will be covered in more detail in *Part V*, which concentrates on WAN technologies, since it appeared by combining IP with such popular WAN technology as ATM. Consequently, it is much easier to study it after learning about ATM.

IntServ and DiffServ (RFC 3290) rely on the same basic QoS mechanisms. Particularly, in IP routers, the Token Bucket algorithm is applied for traffic policing and shaping. Besides this, for congestion avoidance when using TCP, routers traditionally use a specific feedback mechanism, called random early detection (RED).

20.3.2 Token Bucket Algorithm

The *Token Bucket algorithm is based on a comparison of the packet flow to some reference flow that has a predefined average rate.* This reference flow is represented by tokens supplied to one of the server inputs, which decides when to forward packets arriving at the second input (Figure 20.1).

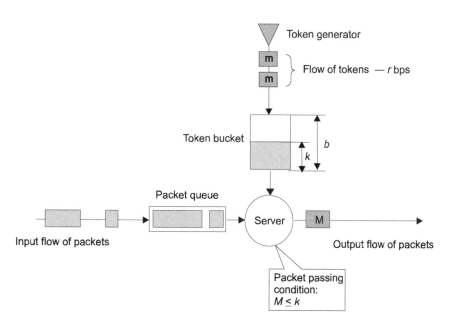

Figure 20.1 Token Bucket algorithm

In this case, the "token" is interpreted as some abstract object that is the carrier of some "portion" of information used for building the model of traffic servicing. The token generator periodically directs the next token into the "bucket" that has a limited volume of b bytes. All tokens have the same size, equal to m bytes, and are generated so that the bucket is filled at the rate of r bytes per second. Obviously, this rate is equal to $r = 8m/w$. The rate r is the maximum average rate for the traffic being shaped. The bucket size corresponds to the maximum burst size of the flow of packets. If the bucket is filled with tokens (i.e., the total amount of tokens in the bucket equals b), the token supply is temporarily stopped. Actually, the token bucket represents the counter that is incremented by m every w seconds.

When using the token bucket algorithm? The traffic profile is defined by the **rate** r and **burst size** b.

The comparison of the reference and real flows is carried out by the server, which represents an abstract device having two inputs. Input 1 is connected to the packet queue, and input 2 — to the token bucket. The server also has an output, to which it passes the packets from the input queue. Input 1 of the server models the input interface of the router, and output simulates the router's output interface.

> The packet from the queue is forwarded by the server only if at its arrival to the server the bucket is filled with tokens to a level no lower than M bytes, where M is the packet size.

If this condition has been satisfied, the packet is forwarded to the server output, and the tokens of the full amount of M bytes (with the precision m bytes) are removed from the bucket. If the bucket has not been filled to the sufficient level, the packet is processed using one of the following two nonstandard methods depending on the goal of the algorithm use.

■ If the Token Bucket algorithm is used for shaping the traffic, the packet is simply deferred in the queue for some additional time, during which it waits for the sufficient number of tokens to arrive in the bucket. Thus, it is possible to achieve traffic smoothing: Even when a large pack of packets has arrived in the system as a result of a burst, the packets leave the queue more uniformly at the rate specified by the token generator.

■ If the Token Bucket algorithm is used for traffic profiling, then the packet is discarded as the one that does not correspond to the profile. Another, more relaxed solution is re-marking the packet in such a way as to lower its status in the course of further servicing. For example, the packet can be marked by a special delete-eligible attribute. In this case, routers will discard such packets first if congestion arises. When using DiffServ, the packet can be moved to another traffic class that has lower priority and is provided a lower QoS.

NOTE   *The algorithm tolerates traffic bursts within certain limits. Suppose that the bandwidth of the interface, the rate of which is limited by the Token Bucket algorithm, is equal to R. Then it is possible to show that for any time interval t, the average rate of the flow from the server is equal to the minimum of the two values: R and r + b/t. If values of t are large, the rate of the output flow tends to r, which serves as the evidence that the algorithm ensures the desired average rate. At the same time, during a small* t *interval (when* r + bt > R)*, the packet can leave the server at the maximum rate possible for the interface, thus creating a burst. This situation takes place when the packets did not arrive at the server for some time, so the bucket was filled with tokens (i.e., during the time longer than* b/r*). If a large back-to-back sequence of packets arrives at the server, these packets will be passed to the output at the rate of the output interface* R*, also one by one without intervals.*

The maximum time of such burst is b/(R − r) *seconds, after which a pause is required to fill the empty bucket. The burst size is* Rb/(R − r) *bytes. Based on the provided formula, it can be seen that the Token Bucket algorithm starts to operate inadequately if the average rate* r *is chosen close to the bandwidth of the output interface. In this case, the burst may continue for a long time, which depreciates the operation of this algorithm.*

20.3.3 Random Early Detection

> The RED technique is the mechanism of profiling the TCP traffic developed by the Internet community for preventing congestion of the Internet backbones.

The main goal of RED is the avoidance of serious network congestion. RED operates with the reliable TCP transport protocol and uses the algorithm of the TCP reaction on packet losses. This reaction consists in that the traffic source slows transmission of packets into the network. RED uses this property as an implicit feedback for notifying the source that it generates data too intensely.

The RED algorithm uses two configurable thresholds of the congestion level (Figure 20.2). When the congestion level is below the first threshold, `LowThreshold`, packets are not discarded. When the level of congestion falls between two threshold values, packets

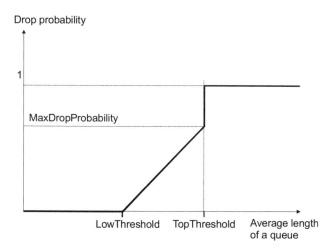

Figure 20.2 Probability of discarding packets using the RED algorithm

are discarded with the probability growing linearly within the range from 0 to the config-urable value MaxDropProbability. The latter value is reached exactly when the second threshold, TopThreshold, is reached (Figure 20.2). When the congestion exceeds the sec-ond threshold, the packets are discarded with the probability of 100%.

The average length of the queue of packets belonging to a specific TCP session is used as the congestion measure.

When it is necessary to ensure various feedback parameters for different traffic classes, the *weighted RED (WRED)* algorithm is used. This variant of RED allows separate values of LowThreshold, TopThreshold, and DropProbability to be specified for each traffic class. Usually, the WRED mechanism is used with WFQ, ensuring reliable delivery of the TCP traffic with a guaranteed rate.

20.3.4 Integrated Services Framework and RSVP

IntServ is based on the reservation of router resources along the path of the data flow from end node to end node. To be more precise, end systems, reserved in this case, are not computers. Rather, these are applications running on the end nodes (Figure 20.3). The application must use the appropriate API for passing the request for reserving re-sources for a specific flow. This reservation is unidirectional. Therefore, if it is necessary to guarantee QoS for bidirectional data exchange, it is necessary to carry out two reserva-tion operations.

Reservation in the IntServ model is carried out using the **reservation protocol** (RSVP). RSVP is a signaling protocol, which in many respects is similar to the signaling protocols used in **telephone networks**.

However, specific features of the datagram packet-switched networks naturally affect its operation. Thus, switching parameters in IP networks do not represent the reservation attribute, because routers will pass IP packets on the basis of the routing table with or without reservation.

Reservation of the required network resources using RSVP is carried out as described below, and all types of the messages mentioned in this description are outlined in Table 20.1:

1. Data source (computer C1 in Figure 20.3) sends the special PATH message to the unique or group address (Figure 20.3 illustrates the latter case), where it specifies the recom-mended parameters for high-quality reception of its traffic: upper and lower thresh-olds of the bandwidth, delay, and delay variation. These traffic parameters are con-tained in the *traffic specification* (TSpec). The PATH message is passed by the network routers toward the destination (or destinations) according to routing tables obtained

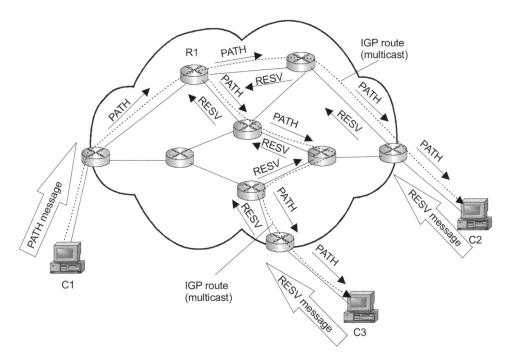

Figure 20.3 Resource reservation using RSVP

using any routing protocol (e.g., OSPF). For specifying traffic parameters, parameters of the Token Bucket algorithm are used (e.g., average rate and bucket depth). Besides this, the maximum allowed speed and the limits of the sizes of the packets of this flow can be specified additionally.

2. Each router supporting RSVP, having received the PATH messages, registers the "path state," which includes the previous address of the source of the PATH message — the next step in the backward direction (i.e., leading to the source). This is necessary to ensure that the response from the receiver follows the same path as the PATH message.

3. After receiving the PATH message, the receiver (an application running on the destination node) sends the RESV message resource reservation request to the router from which it has received this message. The RESV message is a request for resource reservation. Figure 20.3 shows two receivers, computers C2 and C3. In addition to the TSpec information, the RESV message includes the *request specification* (RSpec), in which the QoS parameters required for the receiver are specified, and *filtering specification* (filterspec), which defines to which packets of the session this reservation should be applied (e.g., by the type of the transport protocol and the port number). The combination of RSpec and filterspec is the *flow descriptor*, which the router uses for identifying each resource reservation. Requested QoS parameters in the RSpec specification can differ from the ones specified in TSpec. For example, if the receiver has decided not

to receive all the packets sent by the source but to selectively receive only part of them (which can be specified using the filter specification), then it will need less bandwidth.

4. When any router supporting RSVP along the route receives the RESV message, transferring in an upstream direction, it uses two processes to determine the acceptability of the reservation parameters specified in this request. Using the admission control mechanism, it checks whether the router has the resources required for supporting the requested QoS level. The policy control process is used to check whether the user has the right for resource reservation. If the request cannot be satisfied because of a lack of resources or because of an authorization error, the router returns an error message to the sender. If the request is accepted, then the router sends the RESV along the route to the next router, and data about the required QoS level are passed to the router mechanisms responsible for traffic control.

5. Reception of the reservation request by the router also means that QoS parameters are sent for processing into appropriate units of the router. The specific method of QoS parameter processing is not described in RSVP. However, usually it consists in that the router checks for the availability of the free bandwidth and memory required for

Table 20.1 RSVP messages

Message types	Contents
PATH message from source to destination	Traffic specification of the source
Traffic specification of the source	Recommended parameters for quality traffic reception: upper and lower bandwidth limits, delays and delay variations, parameters of the token bucket algorithm — average rate and bucket depth. Additionally, it is possible to specify the maximum allowed rate and threshold sizes of the flow packets.
Filter specification	Specifies, to which packets of the session this reservation must be applied (for instance, according to the transport protocol type and port number).
Receiver request specification	QoS parameters required for the receiver.
Flow descriptor	Filter specification + receiver request specification.
RESV message — request for resource reservation	Source traffic specification + flow descriptor.

the new reservation. If this check produces the positive result, the router stores new reservation parameters and subtracts them from the counter values corresponding to appropriate resources.

6. When the last router along the upstream route receives the RESV message and accepts the request, it sends a confirming message to the source node. Having carried out group reservation, the points of branching of the delivery tree that have several reserved flows are joined into one are taken into account. For instance, in the example under consideration, the RESV messages of the C1 and C2 receivers are joined in the R1 router. If the same bandwidth is requested for all reserved flows, then it is also requested for the joined flow. If different values of the bandwidth are requested, then for the common flow, the maximum value is chosen.

7. After establishing a reservation state, the source starts transmission of the data; along the entire route to the receiver or receivers, data are served with the specified QoS.

It is necessary to emphasize that the above-described scheme carries out reservation only in one direction. To ensure the required QoS parameters of the data transmission also in the reverse direction within the user session framework, it is necessary to ensure that the sender and receiver exchange the roles and carry out RSVP reservation once again.

To apply reservation parameters to the data traffic, it is necessary to ensure that RSVP messages and data packets move through the network along the same route. This can be ensured if RSVP messages are transmitted on the basis of the same records of the routing table used for the user traffic.

NOTE   *If RSVP messages are transmitted using the traditional method of choosing appropriate records from the routing table, the possibility of a full-value solution of traffic engineering is lost, since all possible routes will not be used for reservation. On the contrary, only the shortest route chosen according to some routing metric of the routing protocol will be used for this purpose.*

A reservation can be cancelled either directly or indirectly. Direct cancellation is carried out by the sender or receiver using appropriate messages of RSVP. Indirect cancellation takes place by timeout: The reservation state has a specific TTL, just like dynamic records in routing tables. According to RSVP, the receiver must periodically confirm the reservation. If confirmation messages cease to arrive, then the reservation is cancelled as its TTL expires. Such a cancellation is called a soft cancellation.

Many extensions have been developed for RSVP. These extensions make this protocol suitable for more than operation within the RSVP architecture. Among the most important solutions are traffic engineering extensions, which are used in the MPLS and generalized MPLS technologies that will be covered in *Part V*.

20.3.5 Differentiated Services Framework

DiffServ services are based on the same generalized QoS model as IntServ services. However, DiffServ consider traffic classes as service objects instead of individual flows.

> Recall that **traffic class** is a set of packets supplied for processing, which have the common parameters — for example, these might be all packets of voice applications or all packets having MTU that falls into the predefined limits.

In contrast to data flows, traffic classes do not differentiate packets by their routes.

Figure 20.4 illustrates this difference. Thus, router R1 relates all flows that require priority service and that come into its i1 interface to the same traffic class, no matter what their later route may be. Router R2 operates with another priority class, since it will not contain all flows of the i1 interface of the R1 router.

Usually DiffServ network supports differentiated servicing of a small number of traffic classes — for example, two (delay-sensitive and elastic) or three (when in addition to delay-sensitive and elastic traffic another traffic class is supported, which requires guaranteed delivery of packets with the predefined minimum of the traffic rate). Small number of traffic classes ensures the scalability of this model, since routers do not need to

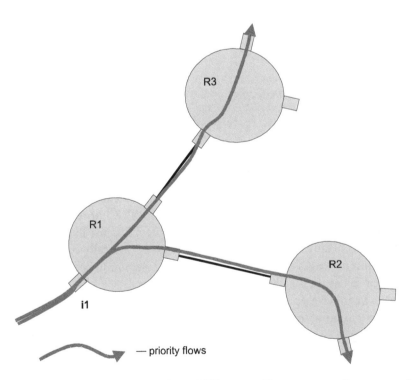

Figure 20.4 In contrast to IntServ, DiffServ considers aggregate flows as service objects instead of individual flows

store the states of each individual user flow. Furthermore, high scalability of DiffServ is ensured thanks to the fact that every router makes its own decision related to the service provided to a specific aggregate flow. This decision is made independently and need not be coordinated with other routers. Such an approach is called *per hop behavior* (PHB).

Accordingly, since DiffServ architecture does not trace packet routes, it does not use the resource reservation signaling protocol, similar to RSVP in the IntServ architecture. Instead, network routers carry out static resource reservation for each of the traffic classes supported by the network.

In DiffServ, a label carried by the *IP Precedence* field or by its successor, the *DiffServ byte* field, is used as an attribute specifying that the IP packet belongs to a specific traffic class.

As shown in Figure 20.5, although the *DS* field uses the *TOS* field, it redefines the bit values of this field as defined earlier in appropriate RFCs (791, 1122, and 1349). Currently, only the most significant six bits of the *DS-byte* field are used, and only the three most significant bits are used for defining the traffic class (which provides the possibility of having no more than 8 different classes). The least significant bit (out of the 6 used bits) of the *DS-byte* field usually carries the *IN* attribute, indicating that the packet has "dropped out" of the traffic profile (similar to the *DE* attributes of the frame relay technology or the *CPL* of the ATM technology). The intermediate two bits describe different variants of packet servicing within the same traffic class.

The router supporting DiffServ must support the processes of traffic classification, marking, measuring, and conditioning, as well as its smoothing and servicing in the priority or weighted priority queue.

Although every network router can mark packets, the DiffServ model considers packet marking at the network entry point as the main variant. This network entry point must support the DiffServ protocol and be under administrative control of a single organization. Such a network is called a DiffServ domain. As packets leave the DiffServ domain, marking is removed so that another domain may reapply it. DiffServ boundary routers play the role of the domain checkpoints. They check the incoming traffic and determine if it has the right for differentiated services.

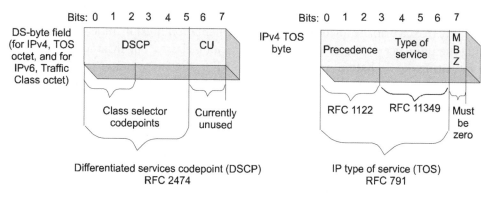

Figure 20.5 Correspondence of the fields of the DS byte to the fields of the TOS bytes

The DiffServ protocol assumes the existence of a service license agreement (SLA) between domains having a common boundary. The SLA specifies policy criteria and defines the traffic profile. It is expected that the traffic will be formed and shaped in the domain output points according to the SLA and that at the entry point of the domain the traffic will be shaped according to the policy rules. Any traffic that is out of profile (e.g., the traffic that exceeds the upper limits of the bandwidth specified in the SLA) will not get service guarantees (or simply will pay the high rates according to the SLA). Policy criteria might include the time of the day, the source and destination addresses, the transport protocol, and the port numbers. When the policy rules are observed and traffic satisfies the predefined profile, DiffServ domain must ensure servicing of this traffic with the QoS parameters defined in SLA.

For the moment, IETF has developed two standards for step-by-step packet forwarding (PHB), which represent two different services:

■ *Expedited forwarding (EF)*. This type of service is characterized by a single code value (10111). It provides the highest QoS level, minimizing delays and delay variations. Any traffic whose intensity exceeds the intensity specified by the traffic profile is discarded.

■ *Assured forwarding (AF)*. In this type of service, there are four traffic classes and three levels of packet discarding in each class, which adds up to 12 types of traffic. Each traffic class is allocated a predefined minimum bandwidth and buffer size for storing its queue. The traffic that exceeds the profile is delivered with a lower level of probability than the traffic that satisfies the profile condition. This means that the traffic that is out of profile might be served with lower quality but will not necessarily be discarded.

Based on these step-by-step specifications and appropriate SLAs, it is possible to provide end-users with end-to-end services — EF service and AF service, respectively.

The main goal of the EF service is providing QoS comparable to that of the dedicated lines. Because of this, this service is also known as the "virtual dedicated line service." It is also known under the name Premium Service, which emphasizes the highest QoS in DiffServ IP networks. Later, this specification was made obsolete by RFC 3246, which gives a more accurate definition of EF service.

If the EF service is implemented by the mechanism that allows unlimited discarding of other traffic (e.g., a priority queue), then its implementation must include some tools for limiting the influence of the EF traffic on other traffic classes. For instance, this can be done by setting the limitation on the rate of the EF traffic at the router input using the Token Bucket algorithm. The maximum rate of the EF traffic and, possibly, the burst size must be set by the network administrator.

Four groups of AF services are oriented toward guaranteed delivery, however, without minimization of the packet delay level as stipulated for the EF service. Delivery is guaranteed only when the rate of incoming traffic does not exceed the minimum bandwidth delivery allocated for this class. Implementation of the AH services is well combined with the EF service, since EF traffic can be used according to the priority method, but with limited intensity of the input flow. The remaining bandwidth is distributed among

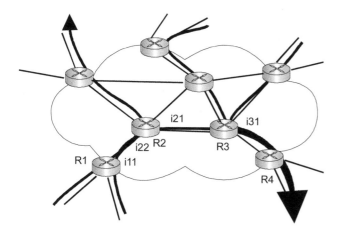

Figure 20.6 Uncertainty of the DiffServ services

the traffic classes of the AF service according to the weighted queue processing algorithm. This will ensure the required bandwidth; however, the delays will not be minimized. Implementation of the AF service suggests (but does not require) the use of weighted queue processing for each class with reserved bandwidth as well as the use of the RED feedback.

The relative simplicity of traffic servicing using DiffServ determines its drawbacks. The main drawback is the difficulty of providing qualitative guarantees to the service subscribers. Consider this drawback in the example of the network shown in Figure 20.6.

Servicing traffic classes assumes that the boundary routers police traffic without taking into account the packet destination addresses. This approach can be called destination unaware. Usually, for the input interfaces of the boundary routers, some predefined limit of the allowed workload is specified for each traffic class. For instance, suppose that the network services the traffic of two classes, *Premium* and *Best Effort*. The threshold for Premium traffic is set at 20% for all input interface of each boundary router. Besides this, suppose, for simplicity, that all interfaces of all network routers have the same bandwidth.

Obviously, despite this rather stringent limitation, the interfaces of the network routers will have different loads. For simplicity, Figure 20.6 shows only the flows that require Premium service. Thus, the i11 output interface of the R1 router serves two Premium service flows and has a load of 40%, and the i21 output interface of the R2 router serves only one such flow, since the second flow goes through another output interface. As for the i31 output interface of the R3 router, it is overloaded, since it serves three Premium service flows; consequently, its utilization coefficient is 60%. On the basis of the factors that influence queue generation (see *Chapter 7*), you know that utilization coefficient is the most significant factor, and its critical values are about 50%. Therefore, long queues of Premium service packets will be generated in the i31 interface. These queues will lower the QoS, because they result in considerable delays and even lead to packet losses. The traffic of the Best Effort class also will be affected, since it will have only 40% of the interface bandwidth.

Naturally, we have simplified the pattern, since the interfaces of the backbone routers usually are faster than those of the boundary routers; therefore, their utilization coefficients will be lower than the sum of the utilization coefficients of the input interfaces, as was the case for this example. To reduce the probability of overloading the internal interfaces of the backbone routers and the output interfaces of the boundary routers, it is also possible to decrease the allowed threshold for the Premium traffic load on the input interface, for instance, to 5%.

However, all these measures do not provide any guarantee that all interfaces of all network routers operate in the required range of the utilization coefficient and, consequently, ensure the required QoS. To provide such guarantees, it is necessary to use traffic engineering methods — for example, to control traffic flows instead of classes or, in this case, aggregate flows. An **aggregate flow** is the flow comprising packets of the same class and having a common part of the route across the network. This common part need not include the full path from the input interface of one boundary router to the output interface of another boundary router. For the packets, it is sufficient to pass at least two common interfaces to be considered as an aggregate flow. For instance, this is the case with the flow passing interfaces i11 and i22 in Figure 20.6.

Then, knowing the route along which each aggregate flow passes across the network, it is possible to check whether there are sufficient resources along the route for each flow. For example, it is necessary to check whether the interface utilization coefficients exceed the predefined threshold value. To achieve this, it is necessary to use policing with the account of the destination address of the packets — for example, use *destination-aware policing*. However, the implementation of such an approach in IP networks encounters several difficulties. First, the DiffServ technology does not use the signaling protocol such as RSVP of the IntServ technology. This means that all checks of the resource availability on routers for each aggregate flow must be carried out in the offline mode, manually or using some special software. Second, to carry out such computations, it is necessary to know the paths of flows across the network. Such routes are determined by routing tables built using some routing protocol, such as RIP or OSPF; using a combination if several routing protocols of the IGP class are used in the network; or manually. Therefore, for manual or automated computations, it is necessary to know the routing tables of all network routers and trace their changes. This is not a trivial task, taking into account that failures of network links or routers rebuild such tables. Furthermore, it is necessary to keep in mind that routers can apply load-balancing methods, dividing aggregate flow into several flows, which also complicates the computations.

A destination-aware version of DiffServ increases the QoS provided by the communications carrier. However, it also complicates the idea of the method, which is based on the independent servicing of traffic classes by each network router.

20.4 NETWORK ADDRESS TRANSLATION

KEY WORDS: security, address shortage, Network Address Translation (NAT), private addresses, traditional NAT, NAT device, Basic NAT, Network Address and Port Translation (NAPT), routing advertisements, incoming and outgoing sessions

Routing in the internet is carried out on the basis of destination addresses placed into the packet headers. As a rule, these addresses remain unchanged from the moment they are formed by the sender until the moment they arrive at the destination node. However, this rule has some exceptions. For example, in the widely used **network address translation** (**NAT**) technology, it is supposed that the packet is forwarded in the external Internet on the basis of addresses used for packet routing in the internal network of the company.

20.4.1 Reasons for Address Translation

One of the most popular reasons for using the NAT technology is the shortage of IP addresses. If for some reason a company that needs to connect the Internet cannot receive the required number of global IP addresses from the provider, it can use the NAT technology. In this case, **reserved (private) addresses** are used for addressing internal hosts. We described them in *Chapter 17*.

To enable hosts with private addresses to communicate using the Internet or connect to the hosts that have global addresses, it is necessary to use the NAT technology.

The NAT technology proves useful when a company needs to hide the addresses of hosts within its internal networks for security considerations. This prevents intruders from learning the network structure and scale as well as the intensity of the incoming and outgoing traffic.

20.4.2 Traditional NAT

The technology of NAT has several variants, the most popular being **traditional NAT**, which allows the hosts from the private network to access hosts located in external networks in a way transparent to users. It is necessary to emphasize that this variant of NAT solves the problem of organizing only **outgoing** connection sessions. Session direction in this case is determined by the location of its initiator. If data exchange is initiated by the application running on some host located in the internal network, this session is called outgoing even though the data from outside can be delivered into the internal network during this session.[2]

---

[2] Traditional NAT allows sessions of inverse direction only as an exception. For this purpose, it uses static address mapping for some limited set of hosts for which unique and unambiguous mapping between internal and external addresses is specified.

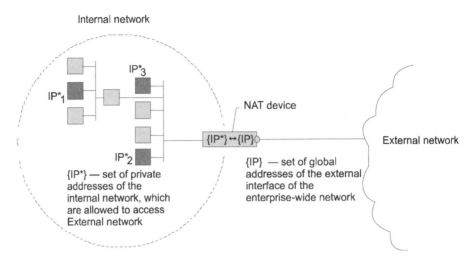

Figure 20.7 Method of traditional NAT

The idea of NAT is based on the following approach (Figure 20.7): Assume that a company network forms a stub domain, the hosts of which are assigned private addresses. NAT software is installed on the router connecting the company network to the external network. NAT dynamically maps the set of private IP addresses {IP*} to the set of global IP addresses {IP}, obtained by the company from the ISP and assigned to the external interface of the company router.

An important property of the NAT operation is the rule according to which route advertisements are propagated across the boundaries of private networks. Advertisements of routing protocols about external networks are passed by boundary routers into internal networks and are processed by internal routers. However, the inverse statement is not true. The routers of external networks do not receive advertisements about internal networks, since such advertisements are filtered out when passing information to external interfaces. Therefore, internal routers "know" the routes to all external networks, and external routers have no information about the existence of private networks.

Traditional NAT is subdivided into **basic network address translation** (basic NAT), the method using only IP addresses for mapping, and **network address port translation** (NAPT), the method for address mapping and transport identifiers are used. Most frequently, TCP/UDP ports are used as transport identifiers.

20.4.3 Basic NAT

If the number of local hosts for which it is necessary to ensure access to the external network does not exceed the number of available global addresses, then it is possible to guarantee unique mapping between a private and a global addresses. At any moment, the number of internal hosts that have the possibility of interacting with the external network is limited by the number of available global addresses. In this situation, the use of NAT is aimed mainly at ensuring security rather than solving the problem of address shortage.

Private addresses of some hosts can be *statically* mapped to global addresses. Such hosts can be accessed from the outside using the global address assigned to them. The mapping

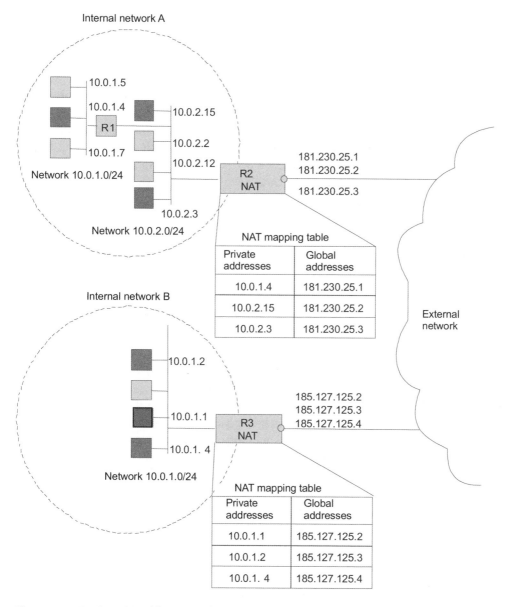

Figure 20.8 Basic NAT: Address translation for outgoing sessions

of internal and external addresses is specified by the table supported by the network router or any other device (a firewall, for instance) on which NAT software is installed.

Dead-end domains can use matching private addresses. For example, networks A and B (Figure 20.8) use the same block of addresses for internal addressing: 10.0.1.0/24. At the same time, addresses of external interfaces of both networks (181.230.25.1/24, 181.230.25.2/24, and 181.230.25.3/24 in network A and 185.127.125.2/24, 185.127.125.3/24, and 185.127.125.4/24 in network B) are globally unique. No other hosts on the internet use them. In this example, only three hosts in each of the networks can go "outside" the limits of the company network. Static correspondence of the private addresses of these hosts to global addresses is specified in the routing table of the boundary devices of both networks.

When host 10.0.1.4 of network A sends a packet to host 30.0.1.2 of network B, it places global address 185.127.125.3/24 into the destination address field of the packet header. The source node sends a packet to its default router, R1, which knows the route to the network 185.127.125.0/24. The router passes the packet to the boundary router R2, which also knows the route to the network 185.127.125.0/24. Before sending a packet, the NAT protocol running on this boundary router uses the mapping table to replace the private address 10.0.1.4 specified in the source address field with its corresponding global address: 181.230.25.1/24. When the packet, after it travels across the internet, arrives at the external interface of the NAT device of network B, global destination address 185.127.125.3/24 is transformed into private address 10.0.1.2. Packets sent in the inverse direction undergo the same procedure of address translation.

Note that in the previously described operation participation of the sender and receiver nodes is not required, which means that this procedure is transparent for users.

20.4.4 Address and Port Translation

Suppose that some organization has a private IP network connected to the ISP network by a WAN link. The external interface of the boundary router R2 has been assigned a global address, and all other hosts of the enterprise network have been assigned private addresses. NAPT allows *all* hosts of internal network to simultaneously communicate with external networks using a single registered IP address. A natural question can be asked: How can external packets arriving *in response* to the requests going from this private network find the sender host? After all, the source address fields of all packets sent to the external network contain the same address, namely, the address of the external interface of the boundary router.

For unique identification of the sender host, additional information is used. If an IP packet encapsulates the data of UDP or TCP, then UDP or TCP port numbers are used as such additional information. However, even this does not fully clarify the matter, since several requests might originate from the internal network that have matching sender port numbers. Consequently, the question again arises about ensuring unique and unambiguous matching of a single global address to the set of internal private addresses. The solution lies in that when the packet passes from the internal network to the external

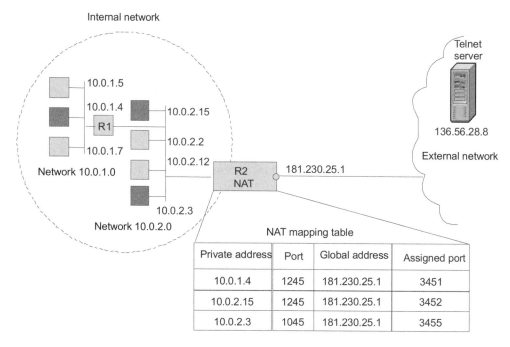

Figure 20.9 NAPT: Address and port number translation for outgoing TCP/UDP sessions

one, each pair *{internal private address; sender TCP/UDP port number}* is mapped to the pair *{global IP address of the external interface; assigned TCP/UDP port number}*. The assigned port number is chosen arbitrarily; however, it must be unique among all hosts that have access to the external network. This mapping is registered in the table.

This model satisfies the requirements of most medium-sized networks for accessing external networks using a single registered IP address obtained from a provider.

Figure 20.9 shows an example in which the dead-end network A uses internal addresses from the address block 10.0.0.0. The external interface of the router of this network has the address 181.230.25.1, assigned by the ISP.

When host 10.0.1.4 of the internal network sends a packet to the telnet server located in the external network, it uses its global address 136.56.28.8 as the destination address. The packet arrives at the R1 router, which knows that the route to the 136.56.0.0/16 network goes through the R2 boundary router. NAPT of the R2 router translates the 10.0.1.4 address and TCP port 1245 of the source to the globally unique address 181.230.25.1 and uniquely assigned TCP port (3451, in this example). In this form, the packet is sent to the external network and reaches the telnet server. When the receiver generates a response message, it specifies the only registered global address of the internal network as the destination address. This is the address of the external interface of the NAPT device. As the receiver port number, the server specifies the assigned TCP port number taken from the sender port number field of the packet that it has received. When the reply packet arrives at the NAPT device of the internal network, the port number is used for choosing the required row from the translation table. By that row, the internal IP address of the appropriate host and its actual port number are defined. This translation procedure is fully transparent for end nodes.

NOTE   *Note that the translation table contains another record with port number 1245. This situation is possible, since operating systems running on different computers assign port numbers to client programs independently. It is this ambiguity for the elimination of which unique assigned port number is used.*

The NAPT variant allows only TCP/UDP sessions going from the private network. However, situations are possible in which it is necessary to ensure access to some node of the internal network from the outside. In the simplest case, when the service is the registered one — that is, the service has assigned to it a well-known port number (e.g., Web or DNS) — and this service is represented within an internal network in a single instance, this problem is solved relatively easily. The service and host on which it operates are uniquely defined by a registered well-known port number of that service.

To conclude consideration of the NAT technology, notice that besides traditional NAT there are other variants of NAT. An example of such a variant is double NAT, when the source and destination addresses are modified, in contrast to traditional NAT, when only one address is modified. Double NAT is necessary when private and external address spaces have collisions. Most frequently, this happens when an internal domain has incorrectly assigned public addresses that belong to another organization. This situation can also arise because an organization network was initially isolated from the outside world, and addresses — the ones taken from a global address space — were assigned arbitrarily. Sometimes such a collision might arise because of a change of the ISP when the organization wants to preserve old addresses for the hosts of internal network.

20.5 ROUTERS

KEY WORDS: router, routing table, router interface, media access, forming bit signals, frame reception, CRC computation, ARP, backbone routers, edge routers, carrier routers, software routers, LAN and remote office routers multiprocessor organization, router OS

20.5.1 Router Functions

The main function of the router is reading the headers of the network packets received and buffered on each port (e.g., IPX, IP, AppleTalk, or DECnet). After that, based on the packet's network address, the router decides its route. As a rule, this address includes the network number and the host number.

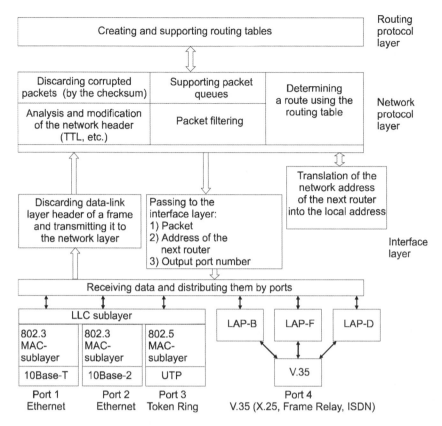

Figure 20.10 Functional model of a router

Router functions can be divided into three groups according to the layers of the OSI model (Figure 20.10).

Interface Level

At the lower layer, the router, like any device connected to the network, ensures physical interface to the transmission medium, including coordination of the electric signal levels, line and logical encoding, and equipping the router with a specific type of connector. In different models of routers, different sets of physical interfaces are usually provided that are combinations of ports for connecting LANs and WANs. The specific data-link layer protocol is inseparably linked with each interface — for instance, this might be Ethernet, Token Ring, or FDDI. Interfaces for connecting to WANs most frequently determine only some physical-layer standard. Over this standard, several data-link layer protocols can operate within a router. For example, a WAN port can support the V.35 interface over which several data-link layer protocols can operate: PPP (transmits the traffic of IP and other network-layer protocols), LAP-B (used in X.25 networks), LAP-F (used in frame relay network), LAP-D (used in ISDN networks), and ATM. The difference between LAN and WAN interfaces is explained by the LAN technologies, which determine both physical and data-link layer standards that can be used only in combination.

Router interfaces carry out a complete set of physical and data-link layer functions related to frame transmission, including accessing the medium (if necessary), forming bit signals, receiving frames, calculating checksums, and passing the frame data field to the upper-layer protocol if the checksum has the correct value.

NOTE   *Like any normal end node, each router port has its own hardware address (in LANs, this is a MAC address) by which all other nodes send frames that require routing.*

The list of physical-layer interfaces supported by a specific router model is the most important characteristic for the consumer. The router must support all data-link and physical layer protocols used in each of the networks to which it will be connected directly. Figure 20.10 shows a functional model of a router that has four ports implementing the following physical interfaces: 10Base-T and 10Base-2 for two Ethernet ports, UTP for Token Ring, and V.35 over which LAP-B, LAP-D, or LAP-F protocols can operate, ensuring the possibility of connection for X.25, ISDN, or frame relay networks.

Frames supplied to the router ports, after processing by appropriate physical and data-link layer protocols, are stripped from the data-link layer headers. The data retrieved from the data field of the frame are passed to the network-layer protocol entity.

Network Layer Protocol

The network protocol, in turn, retrieves from the packet the network-layer header and **analyzes and corrects the contents of its fields**. First, it is necessary to test the checksum; if the packet is corrupted, it must be discarded. Then a check determines whether the time that the packet has spent in the network exceeds the allowed threshold (known as TTL). If this time exceeds the TTL, the packet also is discarded. At this stage, all required corrections are entered into the contents of some fields — for instance, if necessary, the packet TTL is increased or its checksum is recalculated.

The most important router function, **filtering**, also is carried out by the network layer of the router. The network-layer packet encapsulated in the frame data field for bridges or routers is represented as an unstructured binary sequence. On the other hand, router software contains the network-layer protocol entity and therefore is capable of parsing frames and **analyzing individual fields**. This software is equipped with advanced GUI tools that allow administrators to specify sophisticated filtering rules without serious problems. As a rule, routers also can analyze the structure of transport-layer messages. Consequently, filters can prevent messages of certain application services, such as telnet service, from passing into the network. This kind of filtering is carried out by analyzing the protocol type field in the transport message.

The main router function of the router, namely, determining routes, also relates to the network layer. The network-layer protocol entity uses the network number retrieved from the packet header to find the row of the routing table that contains the network address of the next router and the port number to which it is necessary to pass this packet to ensure that it travels in the right direction.

Before the network address of the next router is passed to the data-link layer, it must be converted to the local address according to the network technology used in the network that contains the next router. For this purpose, the network protocol requests the *address resolution protocol* (ARP).

From the network layer, the local address of the next router and the port number of the router are passed to the data-link layer. Based on the specified port number, the packet is switched to one of the router interfaces, where the packet is then encapsulated in the frame of the appropriate format. the local address of the next router is placed into the destination address field of the frame header. After that, the frame is sent to the network.

Layer of Routing Protocols

Network protocols actively use the routing table in the course of their operation. However, they are not involved in its creation or in maintaining its contents. These functions are delegated to routing protocols. Based on these protocols, routers exchange information on the network topology and then analyze the received data to determine the best routes according to specific criteria. The results of this analysis make up the contents of routing tables.

Besides the previously listed functions, other functions can be delegated to routers — for instance, operations related to fragmentation.

20.5.2 Classification of Routers by Areas of Application

By their areas of application, routers are divided into several classes (Figure 20.11).

> *Backbone routers* are intended for building the core network of a communications carrier or large corporation. Backbone routers operate over aggregate information flows that carry the data of many user connections.

The main intention of the backbone router is the creation of a high-performance and reliable switching core of the network. To carry out this task, backbone routers are equipped with high-performance interfaces, such as ATM 155/622 Mbps, Gigabit Ethernet, and 10 Gigabit Ethernet, as well as SONET/SDH interfaces ensuring rates from 155 Mbps to 10 Gbps. For creating a fault-tolerant core topology, backbone routers must support several such interfaces.

Naturally, to avoid creating bottlenecks in the network core, the backbone router must provide very high performance. For example, if the router is equipped with eight 10 Gbps interfaces (Ethernet or SDH), then its total performance must make 80 Gbps. To achieve such performance, backbone routers have distributed internal architecture similar to the architecture of the LAN switches, which was covered in *Chapter 15*. Each port or group

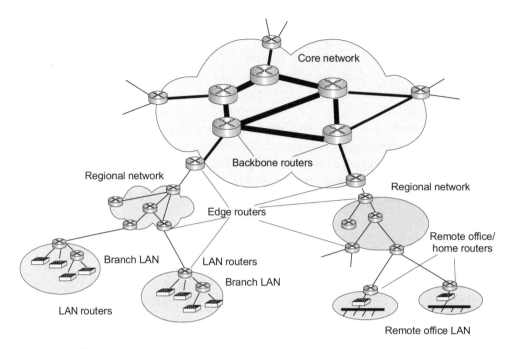

Figure 20.11 Types of routers

of ports is equipped with its own processor that forwards IP packets on its own, based on the local copy of the routing table. For passing packets between ports, the switching fabric based on shared memory, common bus, or circuit switching is used. Similar to LAN switches, high-performance routers have a central processing unit that carries out general tasks: builds the routing table, stores configuration parameters, supports remote administration of the router, and so on. Since functions related to the forwarding of IP packets are significantly more complicated than frame forwarding in LAN technologies such as Ethernet, the task of developing a high-performance port for the router is considerably more complicated than the similar task for switches. To make the port processor simpler and cheaper, the developers usually do not load it with additional router functions, such as traffic filtering or NAT. Even QoS support is not always fully implemented by such a processor. As a rule, only queuing mechanisms are implemented; traffic profiling is not. This is because the backbone router that operates only within the network and does not interact with the outside world, which means that it does not carry out boundary functions that require profiling and filtering. The main task of such a router is passing packets between its interfaces at maximum speed.

A large number of interfaces allows the construction redundant topologies close to the fully connected design and thus ensures network fault tolerance. However, the boundary router itself must provide high reliability. Reliability and fault tolerance of the router are achieved at the expense of using redundant modules such as central processing units, port processors, and power supply units.

Edge routers connect the backbone to the peripheral networks. These routers form a special layer that carries out the functions of accepting traffic from networks external in relation to the backbone. Edge routers are also called *access routers*. The peripheral network often is a network administered autonomously. This may be the network of the client of communications carrier directly connected to its backbone or the network of a regional department of a large corporation that has its own backbone.

In any case, the traffic arrives at all interfaces of the boundary router from the network that the backbone administrator cannot control. Therefore, this traffic must be filtered and is subject to policing. As a result, the requirements for the edge router are different from those for the backbone router. Router capabilities of ensuring maximum flexibility by implementing additional traffic filtering and policing functions come to the foreground. Furthermore, it is important to ensure that the performance of the boundary router is not sacrificed to these additional functions. Interfaces of the boundary router are not as fast as those of the backbone router. However, the boundary router is more versatile, since it has to connect to the backbone networks based on different technologies.

Dividing routers into backbone and edge is not strict and determined. Such a division simply reflects the area of application in which the router is preferred for use and where its advantages are the most evident. Any router can be applied outside its main application area. For example, the backbone router equipped with high-performance ports can simultaneously play the role of the edge router. A router that carries out the tasks of the boundary router of a large network and plays this role well can serve as a backbone router for a smaller network, where its interfaces will cope with the load on the backbone on such a network.

The division of routers into backbone and edge routers reflects only one aspect of their application, namely, their position in relation the local and external networks. Naturally, there are other aspects. For example, routers can be divided into routers intended for communications carriers and routers intended for use in corporate networks.

The main differences of **carrier routers** from other types of routers are high reliability and support of the complete set of functions required for commercial operation as part of the Internet, from BGP to the systems controlling user data flows, which are required for billing systems. High requirements for reliability are explained by the high cost of router downtime when providing commercial services. The requirements for the reliability of data transmission services are constantly growing; Internet and VPN users want these services be as reliable as telephone communications. Therefore, when we state that the availability of some routers has reached the boundary of 0.999 and tends to the similar parameter of telephone equipment, which is 0.99999, this mainly relates to carrier routers, both backbone and edge.

Corporate routers are intended for use within the limits of a corporate network; therefore, the requirements for reliability are lower than those of the carrier routers. Furthermore, corporate routers do not need the complete set of functionality required for operation as a standalone, autonomous system that is part of the Internet.

Naturally, the characteristics of carrier and corporate routers significantly depend on the scale of the communications carrier or corporation as well as on their specific features. Nowadays, an international communications carrier that relates to Tier 1 in the ISP hierarchy requires backbone routers equipped with 10 Gbps interfaces. Such routers are expected to be replaced soon by routers equipped with DWDM ports that operate with 40 waves and ensure the overall communications rate of the 400 Gbps port. The edge routers of such a carrier also will be qualified as top-end models. Routers of this class will have ports ensuring access rates of 622 Mbps – 2.5 Gbps.

Smaller communications carriers, such as regional and local ones, do not need routers with this performance level since the total amount of their traffic is significantly lower. Therefore, the backbone router of such a carrier can be limited by supporting 2 Mbps — 155 Mbps interfaces, and the edge router must ensure dial-up access of subscribers using telephone lines. In small networks, there may be no backbone routers since such networks usually comprise one or more edge routers.

A similar situation exists for corporate networks, where routers of different reliability and performance levels can be found. For example, large corporations can use backbone and edge routers with characteristics close to those of the routers owned by Tier 1 communications carriers. However, corporate networks are usually based on equipment with characteristics that are one level lower. This means that large corporations use equipment similar to that used by regional communications carriers, and so on.

> **Department routers** connect regional departments to one another and to the core network. The network of a regional department, similar to the core network, can comprise several LANs. Such a router is usually some similar version of a corporate backbone router.

If a department router is built on the basis of a chassis, then the number of slots in its chassis is four to five. Also possible is a design with a fixed number of ports. Supported LAN and WAN interfaces have lower speeds than those of corporate routers. This class of released routers is the largest. Their characteristics can range from the ones close to backbone routers down to the ones of the remote office routers.

> **Remote office routers** connect the only LAN of a remote office to the core network or to the network of a regional department using a WAN link.

As a rule, a LAN interface is Ethernet 10/100 Mbps, and a WAN interface is the leased line ensuring speeds of 64 Kbps, 1,544 Mbps, or 2 Mbps. A remote office router can support operation using a dial-up telephone line as a reserve link for the leased line. There are many types of remote office routers. This is because potential customers are numerous and there is a large variety of applications for such devices. This can be explained both by a mass character of potential customers and by specialization of this type of devices, some of which are oriented toward supporting a specific type of long-distance communications. For example, there are routers that operate only in ISDN networks. There are also models intended only for analog leased lines, and so on.

The lower the requirements for the router performance, the higher the probability that it is designed according to the classical design of the first routers (and bridges) of LANs — that is, on the basis of a single central processing unit and ports that have no dedicated processors. This design is considerably cheaper. However, its performance fully depends on the performance of the processor and cannot be scaled with an increase of the number of ports.

> **Software router** is a special software module of some general-purpose operating system of either the UNIX or the Windows family.

Only the advent of such high-speed technologies as ATM, SONET/SDH, and DWDM considerably increased the performance requirements for the routers. As a result, the representatives of the top-end class of routers have migrated to multiprocessor designs with switching fabric, which were successfully tested on LAN switches.

> **LAN routers** (Layer 3 switches) are intended for dividing large LANs into subnets. This is a special class of routers that usually have no WAN interfaces.

Many routers of this class originate from LAN switches, which gave them their name — Layer 3 switches. Layer 3 switches carry out all router functions, but in addition to this they can operate as normal LAN switches (i.e., Layer 2 switches). The operating mode (switch or router) depends on the configuration parameters.

Such devices can also operate in the combined mode in which several ports of the Layer 2 switch have the same IP address (Figure 20.12). In this case, the transmission of packets among a group of ports belonging to the same network is carried out in the switching mode at the data-link layer (e.g., based on MAC addresses). If the ports belong to

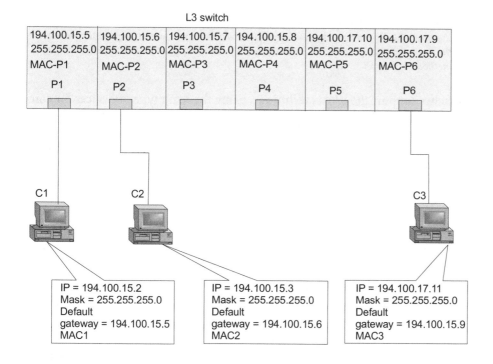

Figure 20.12 Combined operating mode of the Layer 3 switch

different IP networks, then the switch carries out routing between networks. The choice of the packet transmission mode is determined by the configuration of the IP addresses of the ports and, consequently, by the configuration of the computers.

EXAMPLE *For example, if two computers (C1 and C2 in Figure 20.12) have addresses belonging to the same network, then when exchanging information they will not pass packets to the default router. Instead, they will use ARP to detect the MAC address of the destination computer. Assume that computer C1 needs to pass the packet to computer C2. The Layer 3 switch passes the ARP request frame with the broadcast MAC address from computer C1 to all ports belonging to the same IP network (e.g., to ports P1, P2, P3, and P4). Computer C2 recognizes its IP address (194.100.15.3) in this request and responds by sending the frame to the destination MAC address of computer C1 (MAC1), carrying information on its own MAC address (MAC2). After that, computer C1 sends the IP packet to computer C2, encapsulating it in the frame with the MAC2 destination address. The Layer 3 switch passes this frame from port P1 to port P2 according to the bridge algorithm, based on the Layer 2 forwarding table. The Layer 3 switch will operate in a similar way.*

When computers belong to different IP networks, the behavior of the sender computer dictates the method of packet forwarding to the Layer 3 switch. For example, if computer C1 sends a packet to computer C3, which is located in a different subnet, it must pass the packet to the default router instead of trying to find the MAC address of the destination computer using ARP. Therefore, computer C1 sends the ARP request to get the MAC address of the known default router. In this case, this is port P1, which has IP address IP-R1. Having received the MAC address of port P1 (MAC-P1), computer C1 sends the IP packet intended for computer C3 (i.e., with the destination address 194.100.17.11) to that port. This IP packet is encapsulated into the Ethernet frame with the MAC-P1 destination address. Having received the frame with its own MAC address, the Layer 3 switch processes it according to the routing method instead of the switching method.

Layer 3 switches support the VLAN technique, being the main type of devices for connecting separate VLANs into an IP internetwork. Usually, each VLAN is assigned an IP network number so that packet transmission inside the VLAN is based on MAC addresses and data transmission between VLANs is based on IP addresses. In the example shown in Figure 20.12, ports P1–P4 can belong to VLAN1, and ports P5 and P6 belong to VLAN2.

SUMMARY

▶ IP routers allow filtering of user traffic on the basis of attributes that include the source and destination addresses, the protocol type carried in IP packets, and the UPD/TCP port numbers. This property of routers is widely used for the protection of networks against attacks and for limiting the access of legal users.

▶ Filtering of route advertisements ensures control of network connectivity as a whole, preventing records about specific links from appearing in routing tables.

▶ IP routers have long supported various QoS mechanisms, including priority and weighted queues, traffic policing, and feedback for TCP traffic. However, only in the mid-1990s did research in the field of developing the system of IP QoS standards start, when it became necessary to transmit delay-sensitive traffic over the Internet.

▶ Currently, there are two systems of IP QoS standards, IntServ and DiffServ. The first system ensures guaranteed quality for microflows using the RSVP signaling protocol for reserving router resources from end to end. The drawback of the IntServ approach is the significant load on the backbone routers, which have to store information on the state of thousands of user flows.

▶ The DiffServ technology uses an aggregated approach in which QoS is ensured for a small number of traffic classes. This significantly reduces the load on routers. Furthermore, DiffServ is based on the per hop behavior model in which each router decides which resources it must dedicate to each class. This also simplifies the operation of routers, provides the possibility for each router to decide which resources it must allocate to each traffic class, and provides the possibility of implementing Diff-Serv in a provider network. However, the simplified DiffServ approach reduces the guaranteed level of QoS — that is, increases the probability of situations in which QoS exceeds the limits required by the client.

▶ A typical router is a programmable computing device that operates under the control of a specialized OS optimized for carrying out the operations of building routing tables and forwarding packets on their basis.

▶ A router is often built on the multiprocessor design. Most often, symmetric multiprocessing, asymmetric multiprocessing or their combination are used. Most routine operations related to packet processing are carried out programmatically using specialized processors or implemented at the hardware level (LIC/ASIC). Actions of a higher level are carried out programmatically by universal processors.

▶ Routers can be classified using different methods: They can be divided into backbone and edge routers (by their position related to the network boundary) and into carrier and corporate routers (depending on the type of company that owns the network). Routers that operate in enterprise-wide networks are usually divided into corporate routers (the ones that operate in the core network of the company), regional department routers, and remote office routers. Also, there is a specialized class of routers intended for LANs. They do not support WAN interfaces and are usually called Layer 3 switches.

▶ The network address translation (NAT) technology enables a company to solve a shortage of IP addresses and improve network security by hiding host addresses. This is achieved using private addresses in the internal network. When the packet leaves the limits of the internal network, private addresses are translated into global IP addresses.

▶ Traditional NAT is further subdivided into the basic NAT technology that uses only IP addresses for mapping and into network address port translation (NAPT) technology in which so-called transport identifiers are also used for translation. Most frequently, TCP/UDP port numbers are used for this purpose.

REVIEW QUESTIONS

1. Which packet parameters can be used when traffic filtering on the router:
   A. Source IP address
   B. Protocol carried in the IP packet
   C. UDP/TCP port number
   D. Source IP address of the previous packet
2. What is the difference between the routing advertisements and the results of filtering user traffic?
3. What is the meaning of the word "integrated" in the name of the IntServ technology?
4. What parameter makes it possible to limit the burst of the input packet flow profiled using the Token Bucket algorithm?
5. Why does the probability of discarding packets in the random early detection (RED) method depend on the averaged queue length rather than on the current queue length?
6. Why the RED mechanism is not applicable for the UDP traffic?
7. Explain the main stages of router resource reservation using RSVP.
8. What is the principal limitation of the IntServ technology:
   A. It cannot be applied to multicast addressing
   B. The router must store information on the state of each link
   C. End nodes must periodically update the reservation
9. Why does the DiffServ technology not use a signaling protocol?
10. What is the difference between EF and AF services?
11. What specific features of the DiffServ technology made it popular among communications carriers:
    A. It can be implemented within the limits of the communications carrier network independently of the networks of other communications carriers
    B. Routers operate with traffic classes, which does not create a significant load on routers
    C. It ensures automation of QoS computations
12. What is the main goal of NAT?
    A. To thwart DoS attacks
    B. To solve the problem of IP address shortage in IPv4
    C. To protect the internal address space of the company
13. Which additional packet attributes are used in NAT for mapping the set of internal addresses to a single global address?

14. Fill in the "Designated port" column of the NAT table.

Private address	Sender port	Global address	Designated port
10.0.25.1	1035	193.55.13.79	
10.0.25.2	1035	193.55.13.79	
10.0.25.3	1035	193.55.13.79	
10.0.25.2	1047	193.55.13.79	
10.0.25.1	1047	193.55.13.79	

15. List the main variants of router architecture.

16. What are criteria used for classifying routers?

17. What are the specific features of Layer 3 switches?

PROBLEMS

1. Compose an access list or lists for a Cisco router connecting the company to the Internet (Figure 20.13). The access list must ensure the following:

   A. Communications of users of network 194.100.12.0/24, except for the user 194.100.12.25, with only the nodes of networks 132.22.0.0/16 and 201.17.200.0/24. These users must not exchange information with the Internet.

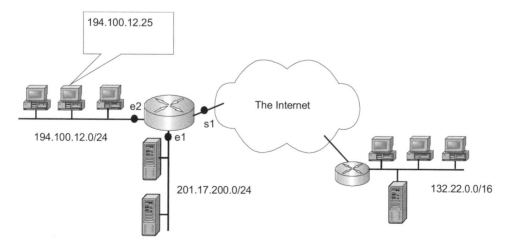

Figure 20.13 Traffic filtering using a router

    B. User 194.100.12.25 must be provided with the possibility of unlimited data exchange.

    C. Servers of network 201.17.200.0/24 must be accessible from the Internet only using ftp and http. Access to these servers using ICMP must be denied.

2. When describing the NAT technology, we simplified the pattern. In particular, we did not consider the problems that might arise when ICMP error messages arrive in the internal network. Suggest your own variant of the algorithm that should be used by the NAT protocol when an ICMP message arrives at its external interface.

TIP   *Before passing the ICMP message, ICMP must introduce corrections not only into the IP header but also into the ICMP data field.*

PART V

WIDE AREA NETWORKS

The IP technology considered in the previous part of the book allows the building of various types of internets, both LANs and WANs. Besides IP, there are other technologies specially designed for building WANs. These are X.25 networks, interesting only from a historical point of view, as well as Frame Relay and ATM networks, widely used today. These technologies have one common feature — they are based on the virtual circuit technique. As mentioned in *Part I*, this technique is an alternative to the datagram method of packet forwarding upon which both Ethernet and IP networks are based. The competition between these two principles of data transmission has existed since the advent of the first packet-switched networks.

Starting from the Internet revolution, commercial WANs have given preference to the virtual circuit technique. The main justification for this approach is that in comparison to the datagram method of packet forwarding, this technique ensures considerably higher level of control over the connections between network users and over the routes along which information flows travel between network nodes. As a result, the communications carrier has the possibility of rationally controlling the resource distribution among the services to which the users have subscribed. The problem of ensuring QoS also can be solved more easily when using virtual circuits. Naturally, this approach is not free from drawbacks, mainly significant overhead (both in time and money) for establishing each virtual connection. The datagram method of communication between network nodes, on the contrary, is distinguished by the simplicity of connecting any network node to any other network node. However, it limits the capabilities of the operator to control resource distribution among users. In contemporary networks, it is possible to find a compromise by combining both methods. In internets comprising WANs, most constituent networks operate on the basis of the virtual circuit technique, which means that these are Frame Relay or ATM networks. These networks are interconnected on the basis of the IP datagram protocol. Such a multilayer approach to building WANs produces the desired result; however, WAN organization becomes too complicated. Furthermore, some of its functions are partially duplicated. For example, routing protocols operate in ATM networks and at the IP layer.

Attempts to achieve closer integration between the datagram method and the virtual circuit method have led to development of the multiprotocol label switching (MPLS) technology. MPLS uses routing the protocols of the TCP/IP stack for investigating the network topology and finding rational routes. However, it forwards packets on the basis of the virtual circuit technique.

Ensuring high-speed access to the network backbone is an urgent problem. It is necessary to increase the access rate on billions of access links connecting user premises to the nearest central office of the communications carrier. Therefore, the traditional backbone solutions, mainly based on optical fiber and requiring the installation of new cables, often are economically inefficient for providing access for most home users. Technologies using the existing cable infrastructure — such as asymmetric digital subscriber line (ADSL), operating on the basis of local loops of the existing telephone network, or cable modems that use cable TV networks — are more efficient. Fixed or mobile wireless access is an alternative solution.

All these technologies and approaches are covered in the chapters that make up *Part V*, which considers different types of network services: information services, security services, and network management services.

Part V includes the following chapters:

- Chapter 21: Virtual Circuit WAN
- Chapter 22: IP WANs
- Chapter 23: Remote Access
- Chapter 24: Secure Transport Services

21

VIRTUAL CIRCUIT WAN

CHAPTER OUTLINE

21.1 INTRODUCTION

WAN technologies such as X.25, Frame Relay, and ATM differ considerably in their functional characteristics. At the same time, they all use a virtual circuit technique that is a variant of connection-oriented communication. In *Chapter 3* we covered general features of this mechanism. Now we consider details of its implementation and specific features typical for each of the previously listed technologies.

Virtual circuit technologies will be considered chronologically. The X.25 technology appeared at the dawn of the era of computer networks, practically simultaneously with the ARPANET project that became the origin of the Internet and IP datagram protocol. X.25 networks use virtual circuits for reliable data transmission, which was of primary importance in the 1970s and 1980s when this technology was exceedingly popular. This is because many links of that time were analog communications links that could not automatically ensure reliable transmission of digital data. Therefore, the capabilities of X.25 networks for restoring damaged or lost packets were so valuable at that time.

As a result of advent of fast and reliable digital links in the mid-1980s, X.25 functions related to ensuring reliable data transmission became redundant. This technological revolution led to development of principally new WAN technology — Frame Relay. This technology plays the same role in WANs as Ethernet plays in LANs: It carries out only the minimal set of functions required for delivering frames to the destination node. Getting rid of many functions unnecessary in the contemporary telecommunications world is not the only difference of Frame Relay from X.25. The newer technology also added one important feature, namely, QoS support for elastic traffic. Initially, developers of the Frame Relay standards did not plan to include support for delay-sensitive traffic. Therefore, delay level and jitter are not included in the list of parameters guaranteed to users. Nevertheless, high-quality voice transmission in Frame Relay networks is possible, provided that network switches support traffic prioritization.

The ATM technology provides a versatile and integrated set of transport services to its users. In contrast to X.25 and Frame Relay, ATM was initially designed as the technology oriented toward the transmission of all existing types of traffic: computer data, voice, video, object control, etc. The fixed and small size of the frame, which in this technology is called a cell, minimizes the delays of real-time traffic. ATM also can aggregate separate virtual circuits into virtual paths, which improves its scalability. However, the high quality of provided services also requires a high price, because ATM networks are technically sophisticated and expensive. Another reason that prevents ATM from becoming a universal transport is the difficulty of processing cells at ultrahigh transmission rates, such as 2.5 and 10 Gbps. Nevertheless, ATM is popular, and no other existing technology has reached comparable QoS and traffic engineering characteristics.

21.2 VIRTUAL CIRCUITS TECHNIQUE

KEY WORDS: Switched/permanent virtual circuit, switched/permanent virtual channel, switched/permanent virtual connection, signaling protocol, switch table, routing table, call setup, virtual channel identifier, short-term data flow, long-term data flow, aggregate traffic flow

There are two types of virtual circuits:

- **Switched virtual circuits** (SVCs). SVCs are created by the initiative of the network's end node, using an automatic procedure.
- **Permanent virtual circuits** (PVCs). PVCs are created beforehand by manually configuring network switches. This procedure is carried out by the network administrator, possibly using the centralized network management system and some control protocol (most frequently, this protocol is a proprietary one).

Abbreviations such as SVC/PVC are often also interpreted as *switched/permanent virtual channel* or *switched/permanent virtual connection*.

To begin with, consider the process of creating an SVC.

21.2.1 Switched Virtual Circuits

SVCs are created using a procedure similar to the one used for establishing a connection in telephone networks, which was briefly covered in *Chapter 3*. In telephone networks, the protocol implementing such a procedure is known as the **signaling protocol**. Therefore, protocols used for establishing a virtual circuit in packet-switched networks are often referred to by the same name.

The creation of a virtual circuit requires routing tables similar to the routing tables used in datagram networks, such as IP networks, to be present in network switches. The method used for creating such tables — either manual or automatic — is not important. An example of such a table is in Figure 21.1.

Figure 21.1 illustrates the process of creating a virtual circuit connecting nodes N1, A1 and N2, A2 through the network, which in this case is represented by two switches — S1 and S2. The routing table specifies the address of the destination network. This procedure takes place in three stages, which are numbered accordingly both on the illustration and in the description provided below.

1. The procedure of creating a virtual circuit starts when the initiating node (N1, A1) generates a special packet — a request for establishing a logical connection to node N2, A2. In this generalized example, this request is named **call setup** (the same term is used in some specific signaling protocols, such as the Q.933 protocol used with Frame Relay

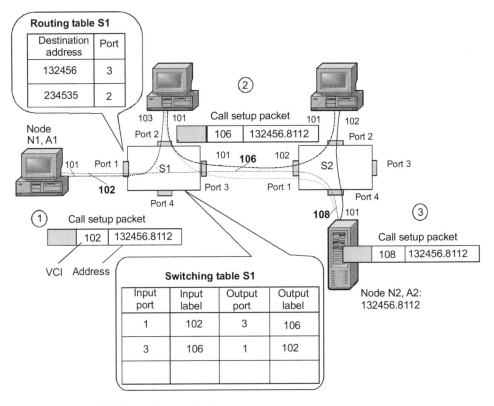

Figure 21.1 Establishing a virtual circuit

and the Q.2931 protocol used with ATM). This request contains a couple of values — the destination node address and the initial value of the **virtual channel identifier** (VCI). In this example, the initial Call Setup request has the following form:

$$(102, 132456.8112)$$

Here 102 is the initial value of VCI, and 132456.8112 is the destination address, where the most significant part is the subnet number and the least significant part is the node number[1].

The number 102, which was assigned to the virtual circuit, has the local value for the computer port through which the connection is being established. Since there is already a virtual circuit passing through this port (circuit number 101), the signaling protocol software running on the end node has chosen the first available number (i.e., the number that is not in use) from the allowed range. *This approach guarantees unique identification of the virtual circuits within each port.*

---

[1] This example uses 3-byte subnet addresses and 2-byte end-node addresses. In practice, WANs based on virtual circuits often use longer addresses.

The initiator must choose the network switch to which it is appropriate to pass the request for establishing a virtual circuit. This choice can be based on the routing table of the sender node; however, if the node is connected to the network by a single port, like in Figure 21.1, there is no need to have a routing table on the end node. After the call setup packet arrives at the buffer of port 1 on switch S1, it is processed according to its destination address and to the values found in the **routing table**. The record that carries the destination network address 132456 specifies that the packet must be passed to port 3.

NOTE   *Note that in contrast to the routing tables of IP networks, the routing table provided in Figure 21.1 does not contain information about the address of the next switch. This is because WAN switches are always connected by physical "point-to-point" links, which do not support multiple connections. Therefore, the number of the output port unambiguously identifies the next switch.*

2. After determining the output port number for the Call Setup packet, the S1 switch generates the next VCI number — 106. This number was chosen because it happened to be the first available number, and within the limits of this local section of the network it uniquely identifies the virtual circuit being established. This circumstance was taken into account when we stated earlier that VCI numbers are *local* by nature. After changing the value of the VCI, the Call Setup packet takes the form (106, 132456.8112) and is passed via output port 3 of switch S1 to input port 1 of switch S2.

Simultaneous with packet forwarding, the switch creates the **switching table** (do not confuse it with the above-mentioned *routing table*). This table will be required later, when virtual circuit will be implemented, and user data will be transmitted through it, this time without specifying the destination address.

Each record of the switching table contains four main fields:

- Number of the input port
- Input label (VCI) in packets arriving to the input port
- Number of the output port
- Output label (VCI) in packets transmitted via the output port

The "1-102-3-106" record in the switching table means that all packets arriving to port 1 and carrying VCI 102 will be forwarded to port 3 and that the *VCI* field will be changed to a new value — 106.

Virtual circuits can be unidirectional and bidirectional. In the previously considered example, the circuit is bidirectional; therefore, the switch creates another record in the switching table — for packet forwarding in the inverse direction from node N2, A2 to node N1, A1. This record mirrors the first one, so the packet that with label VCI 106 and arriving to port 3 of switch S1 will have the initial value of the VCI, 102, when leaving port 1. As a result, node N1, A1 will correctly recognize the virtual circuit to which the arriving packet belongs, despite constant changes of numbers in the course of packet transmission through the network.

3. Switch S2 continues the procedure of establishing a virtual circuit. To achieve this, it uses the destination address specified in the request. Using its routing table (not shown in Figure 21.1), the switch determines the output port to which it is necessary to pass the packet. Simultaneous with this operation, it updates the *VCI* field. In this case, the switch has assigned VCI 108 value to the Call Setup packet. As a result, the Call Setup request arrives at the destination node in the following form: (108, 132456.8112). Having received the request, the end node can either accept or decline it. In case of positive decision, it informs the initiator about its decision by sending the *connect* service packet, which travels through the network using "mirrored" records in the switching table. The connect packet confirms the establishment of a virtual circuit to all switches and to the initiator.

After the initiator receives the connect acknowledgment, end nodes can start using this virtual circuit to send user data. The cells sent by end node N1, A1 are forwarded on the basis of the VCI, which usually has a small length. For example, in the X.25 technology, its length is 1.5 bytes only. Compare this to the destination node address length, which in X.26 networks can reach 16 bytes.

In principle, the SVC technique uses two network operating modes:

■ When establishing SVCs, requests for establishing a connection are passed through the network using a standard routing mode. This mode uses destination addresses, which are global for the entire network, and it requires complete information about the network topology. This means that protocols for establishing virtual circuits (signaling protocols) operate at the network level of the OSI model.

■ After establishing a connection, the network starts operating on the basis of local addresses and local forwarding tables, which allows this mode to be classified as the data link layer of the OSI model. Communications devices are classified as switches (this is a standard name for devices of this level).

21.2.2 Permanent Virtual Circuits

The PVC mode does not allow end nodes to dynamically create virtual circuits. Instead, the network administrator manually creates switching tables beforehand. The administrator can carry out this task locally — for example, by connecting to the switch using the RS-232 interface and by using a notebook computer as a virtual terminal. Naturally, this method of configuring routing tables is not the most convenient one, especially for distributed systems such as WANs. Therefore, as a rule, administrators rely on network management systems. Such network management systems communicate with network switches using one of the management protocols covered in *Chapter 22*: simple network management protocol or common management information protocol. The administrator supplies the network management system with configuration data specifying through which

21.3 X.25 NETWORKS

> **KEY WORDS**: user-to-network interface (UNI), network-to-network interface (NNI), packet assembler–disassembler (PAD), international data numbers (IDNs), data network identification codes (DNICs), national terminal number, link access procedure–balanced (LAP-B) interfaces X.21 and X.21bis

21.3.1 Structure and Goals of X.25 Networks

The X.25 recommendation "Interface between data terminal equipment (DTE) and data circuit-terminating equipment (DCE) for terminals operating in the packet mode and connected to public data networks by dedicated circuit" was developed by the CCITT (now the ITU-T) in 1974. Since then, it has been revised several times.

According to its title, this standard does not describe the internal structure of X.25 networks. On the contrary, it only defines the user interface with the network typical for WANs. This interface is called the **user-to-network interface** (UNI). The internal structure of the network can be arbitrary and is chosen at the discretion of communications carriers. In practice, WAN switches communicate using protocols similar to UNI. To organize communications among networks owned by different communications carriers, it is usually necessary to develop a **network-to-network interface** (NNI), which often is a modified version of UNI.

The X.25 network technology has several important features that make it significantly different from other technologies:

- X.25 is the most suitable for transmitting low-intensity traffic typical for terminals that were widely popular in 1970s–1980s, and less suitable for higher requirements of LAN traffic.

- The presence of a special device, **the packet assembler–disassembler** (PAD), intended for assembling several low-speed start–stop byte flows from character terminals to computers for processing. The presence of PADs dates the X.25 technology, since in the early 1970s character terminals were dumb devices capable of carrying out only primitive operations. All other operations related to the functions of data link- and network-layer functions were carried out by PADs.

- The presence of a three-layer X.25 protocol stack using connection-oriented protocols at data link and network layers for controlling data flows and correcting errors. Such a redundancy of functions ensuring reliable data transmission is caused by the orientation of this technology toward unreliable communications links, which had a BER characteristic of 10^{-3}–10^{-4}.

- Orientation toward uniform stacks of transport protocols on all network nodes, because the network layer is intended for working with only the data link-layer protocol. In contrast to IP, it cannot interconnect heterogeneous networks.

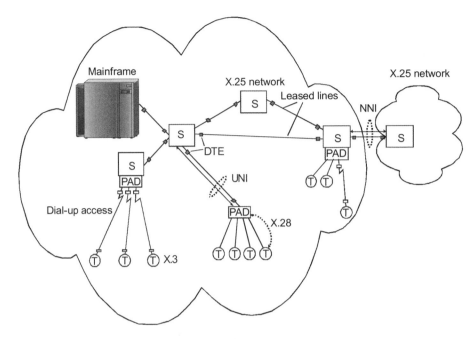

Figure 21.2 Structure of the X.25 network

An X.25 network consists of switches distributed geographically and connected by high-speed leased links (Figure 21.2). Leased lines can be both digital and analog.

PADs can be either remote or built-in. As a rule, a built-in PAD is mounted on the switch rack. Terminals access the built-in PAD through telephone lines using modems. Remote PAD is a small, standalone device connected to the switch by a dedicated X.25 link. Terminals are connected to the remote PAD by an asynchronous interface. As a rule, the RS-232C interface is used for this purpose. A single PAD usually provides access for 8, 16, or 24 asynchronous terminals. Terminals are not assigned end-node addresses of the X.25 network. Addresses are assigned to PAD ports, which are connected to the X.25 packet switch using a leased link.

Computers and LANs are usually connected to the X.25 network directly using an X.25 adapter or the router supporting X.25 protocols on its interfaces.

21.3.2 Addressing in X.25 Networks

If the X.25 network has no connection to the outside world, it can use addresses of any length (within the limits implied by the format of the address field) and assign any values to the addresses. The maximum length of the address field in the X.25 packet makes 16 bytes.

The X.121 CCITT Recommendation defines an international system for address numbering in public data networks. If an X.25 network needs to exchange data with other X.25 networks, it must comply with the X.121 addressing standard.

X.121 addresses, also called **international data numbers** (IDNs), have different lengths that can reach 14 decimal digits.

■ The first four numbers of the IDN are the **data network identification codes** (DNICs). The DNIC is divided into two parts:

  ● The first part (three decimal digits) defines the country in which the network is located

  ● The second part (one decimal digit) is the number of the X.25 network within that country

  Thus, only ten X.25 networks can be organized within each country. When it is necessary to have more, several codes must be assigned to that country.

■ All the other digits stand for the **national terminal number**. They allow a specific DTE device to be identified within the X.25 network.

21.3.3 Protocol Stack of X.25 Networks

The standards of X.25 networks describe three layers of protocols (Figure 21.3).

■ At the *physical layer*, there are two **synchronous interfaces**, **X.21** and **X.21bis**, to data transmission equipment — either to DSU/CSU, if the leased link is digital, or to a synchronous modem, if it is an analog link. The physical-layer protocol of the communications link is not predefined, which provides the possibility of using links corresponding to different standards.

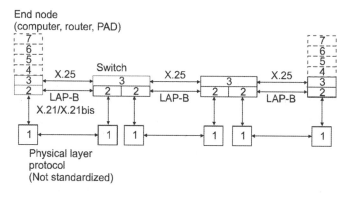

Figure 21.3 Protocol stack of an X.25 network

■ At the *data link layer,* **link access procedure–balanced (LAP-B)** is used, which ensures the possibility of automatic retransmission in case of errors in the line. This protocol ensures a balanced mode of operation, which means that both nodes participating in the connection are peers. According to LAP-B, the connection is established between the DTE (computer, IP router, or IPX router) and the network switch. Although the standard does not explicitly state it, LAP-B is also frequently used for establishing connections at the data link layer between directly connected network switches. LAP-B is a connection-oriented protocol that uses the sliding window algorithm for ensuring reliable frame transmission between two directly connected devices. In contrast to TCP, LAP-B uses a simpler implementation of this algorithm. In this case, transmitted frames are numbered instead of set as bytes. The window cannot be changed dynamically and has a fixed size of 8 or 128 frames. LAP-B belongs to the high-level data link control (HDLC) protocol family, which will be covered in more detail in *Chapter 22.*

■ At the *network layer* (the standard used the *packet layer* term instead of the term *network layer*), the standard defines the X.25/3 protocol of packet exchange between the terminal equipment and the data transmission network. LAP-B connections ensure reliable communications between a pair of NEIGHBOR nodes but do not enable the END nodes to exchange information. To establish a virtual end-to-end connection, the X.25/3 protocol is used.

Consider the operation of the X.25/3 protocol in more details. Its main functions are listed below:

■ Packet routing

■ Establishing and terminating virtual circuits between network subscribers

■ Controlling flows of packets

According to this protocol, the end node sends the *call request* packet encapsulated into the LAP-B frame.

NOTE   *In contrast to other networks based on the virtual circuit technique, X.25 networks do not use a separate signaling protocol. When necessary, the X.25/3 protocol carries out this function by switching into special operating mode.*

The *call request* packet specifies the source and destination addresses in the X.121 format. The *call request* packet is received by the network switch and routed according to the routing table, thus creating a virtual circuit. The routing protocol is not defined for X.25 networks; therefore, the routing tables here are always created manually.

As the Call Request packet travels along the route from switch to switch, it makes them generate new records in switching tables and assign it new label values. Thus, a new virtual circuit is created. The initial value of the virtual circuit number is specified by the user in the *logical channel number* (LCN) field of this packet. This field is the analogue of the *VCI* field mentioned when we described the principle of establishing virtual circuits.

> After establishing a virtual circuit, the end nodes exchange with packets of another format — *data* packets. In *data* packets, the source and destination addresses are not specified, and only the *LCN* label remains of all address information.

The difference of the X.25 technology from Frame Relay and ATM, which will be covered later in this chapter, lies in that it is the network-layer technology. Actually, after a virtual circuit is established, data transmission is carried out by a network-layer protocol instead of a data link-layer protocol.

21.4 FRAME RELAY NETWORKS

> **KEY WORDS:** ISDN technology, Frame Relay and Frame Switching, LAP-F (Q.922), LAP-F core, LAP-F control, LAP-D (Q.921) and Q.933, data link connection identifier (DLCI), C/R, DE, FECN и BECN, discard eligibility (DE), Committed information rate (CIR), Committed burst size (BC), Excess burst size (B_e), QoS

Frame Relay is a relatively new technology far better suited for the transmission of the bursty traffic typical for computer networks in comparison to X.25 networks. This advantage becomes obvious only when the quality of communications links becomes comparable to that of LAN communications links. As relates to WAN links, such quality usually can be achieved only if fiber-optic cables are used.

At first, the Frame Relay technology was standardized by CCITT as one of the integrated services digital network (ISDN) services (RFC 2955). The ISDN technology was first designed for implementing a worldwide, universal network providing all kinds of telephony and data transmission services. Unfortunately, this ambitious project did not reach its initial goal. A next generation network is being created on the basis of other technologies, such as IP. Nevertheless, several no-less-important goals were achieved in the course of the implementation of this project. The list of such achievements includes the development of the Frame Relay technology, which has become a standalone technology independent of ISDN[2].

In the I.122 recommendations released in 1988, this service was listed as an add-on ISDN packet-mode services. However, in 1992 or 1993, when these recommendations were revised, two new services were defined in the standards — **Frame Relay** and **Frame Switching**. The difference between these two services lies in that Frame Switching ensures guaranteed frame delivery and Frame Relay, as mentioned before, provides only best-effort service.

Simple but efficient for fiber-optic communications links, the Frame Relay technology immediately attracted the attention of most telecommunications carriers and organiza-

---

[2] ISDN technology will be briefly covered in *Chapter 22*.

tions involved in the standardization process. Besides the CCITT (ITU-T), there are other organizations that actively take part in the standardization of this technology. The list of such organizations includes the Frame Relay Forum (FRF) and the T1S1 ANSI Committee. As relates to the Frame Switching technology, it remained a standard that did not find a wide area of application.

Frame Relay standards developed by ITU-T/ANSI and FRF, define two types of virtual circuits — persistent (PVC) and switched (SVC). This corresponds to the user needs, since persistent circuits are better suited for connections that constantly transmit traffic. On the other hand, for connections that are practically used several hours per month, SVCs are more suitable.

However, manufacturers of Frame Relay equipment and providers of Frame Relay network services started by supporting only PVCs. Naturally, this is a considerable simplification of this technology. Equipment supporting SVCs appeared on the market with significant delay; therefore, Frame Relay is often associated only with PVCs.

21.4.1 Frame Relay Protocol Stack

Frame Relay protocol stack is organized considerably simpler than the X.25 technology stack. Frame Relay developers have taken into account high quality of fiber-optical communication links, which appeared in late 1980s. Therefore, they considered it possible not to include the reliability functions into the protocols of the stack. Errors are unlikely when using such communication links. If, despite low error probability, such a situation still arises, Frame Relay ignores it, leaving all the functions related to recovery of the lost or corrupted packets to higher-layer protocols, such as TCP.

> Because of the low protocol redundancy, Frame Relay is capable of ensuring broad bandwidth and low frame delays.

NOTE   *Simultaneously with Frame Relay, the Frame Switching technology was developed, which, similar to X.25, ensures reliable frame transmission at the data-link layer. This technology can be used in cases when communication links are not characterized by satisfactory quality, or when data link layer is required to ensure reliable frame transmission because of some reasons. In practice, however, the Frame Switching technology did not find wide application. Nevertheless, it is briefly mentioned here, because Frame Relay protocol stack was created with the account of the existence of this technology.*

Figure 21.4 shows the Frame Relay and Frame Switching protocol stack as they are described in the ITU-T recommendations. The control plane protocols carry out all operations related to establishing a virtual connection, and the data plane protocols transmit frames using the established virtual circuit.

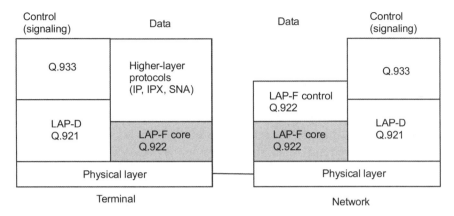

Figure 21.4 Frame Relay protocol stack

The *link access procedure for frame mode bearer services* (**LAP-F**) protocol, which in ITU-T Recommendations is called **Q.922** operates at the data-link layer of Frame Relay networks. There are two versions of this protocol:

■ The **LAP-F core** is a workhorse that works in all Frame Relay networks. The LAP-F core, which is in gray in Figure 21.4, provides the minimum set of tools on the basis of which it is possible to build a Frame Relay network. However, in this case, such a network will provide only PVC services.

■ The **LAP-F control** protocol, which must operate in the network if it also provides Frame Switching services.

Both LAP-F core and LAP-F control are data link-layer protocols that ensure frame transmission between neighboring switches.

At the *physical layer*, a Frame Relay network can use PDH/SDH links or ISDN links.

Now consider the control layer that is responsible for establishing dynamical SVCs. For ensuring the SVC mode, network switches must support two control plane protocols — **link access procedure D** (LAP-D or **Q.921**) at the data link layer and **Q.933** at the network layer. LAP-D in Frame Relay ensures reliable frame transmission between neighboring switches.

The Q.933 protocol uses addresses of the end node between which a virtual circuit is being established. Usually these addresses are specified in the telephone number format according to the E.164 standard. An address comprises 15 decimal digits, which, similar to normal telephone numbers, are divided into a *Country code* field (1–3 digits), a *City code* field, and a *Subscriber number* field. The ISDN address includes the number plus **subaddress** that can include up to 40 digits. The *subaddress* is used for numbering terminal devices after DTE, if subscriber has several devices of this type.

The protocol for the automatic creation of routing tables is not defined for the Frame Relay technology; therefore, a proprietary protocol from the equipment manufacturer can be used. As an alternative, it is possible to manually create the routing table.

The main advantage of the Frame Relay technology over X.25 is that, after establishing a virtual connection, frames are transmitted using only the data link-layer protocol. In X.25 networks, user data are transmitted by data link- and network-layer protocols after establishing a connection. Using this approach allows Frame Relay technology to reduce the overhead for transmitting LAN packets, since they are encapsulated into the data link-layer frames instead of network-layer packets, as was the case for X.25 networks.

The Frame Relay technology most frequently is classified as data link-layer technology, where the primary attention is paid to the procedures of transmitting user data. Procedures of establishing a virtual circuit are carried out using the network-layer protocol.

Frame Relay virtual circuits can be used for transmitting data of different protocols. The RFC 1490 specification determines the methods of encapsulating the packets of network protocols such as IP and IPX as well as SNA data into the Frame Relay frames.

The structure of LAP-F is shown in Figure 21.5.

The field of the **data link connection identifier** (DLCI) takes 10 bits. This allows the use of up to 1,024 virtual connections. The *DLCI* field might be longer; the length is controlled by the EA0 and EA1 attributes (here, EA stands for extended address). If the bit in this attribute is set to zero, the flag is known as EA0 and specifies that the next byte contains the continuation of the address field. If this flag is set to 1, the field is called EA1 and indicates the termination of the address field.

The 10-bit format of the *DLCI* field is generally used. However, when using 3 bytes for addressing, the *DLCI* field is 16 bits long, and when using 4 bytes, its length becomes 23 bits.

Frame Relay standards distribute DLCI addresses among users and the network in the following way:

- 0 — used for the LMI virtual circuit
- 1 — 15 — reserved for future use
- 16 — 991 — used by subscribers for numbering PVCs and SVCs
- 992 — 1007 — used by network transport services for internal network connections
- 1008 — 1022 — reserved for future use
- 1023 — used for controlling the data link layer

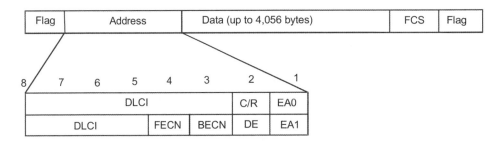

Figure 21.5 Format of the LAP-F frame

Thus, in any Frame Relay interface, 976 DLCI addresses are allocated for user terminal devices.

The data field can have a size of up to 4,056 bytes.

The C/R field has the normal meaning for this protocol of the HDLC family — this is the "command — response" attribute.

The DE, FECN, and BECN fields are used by the protocol for controlling the traffic and supporting the specified QoS for a virtual circuit.

21.4.2 QoS Support

For each virtual connection, several parameters are defined. Each parameter relates to the data transmission rate and influences QoS.

- **Committed information rate (CIR)** — confirmed information rate at which the network will transmit user data
- **Committed burst size (Bc)** — confirmed size of the burst (i.e., the maximum number of bytes from this user) that the network will transmit per confirmed time interval T, which is called **burst time**
- **Excess burst size (Be)** — excess size of the burst that the network will try to transmit in addition to the agreed B_c value during the predefined T

These parameters are unidirectional, so a virtual circuit can ensure different values of $CIR/ B_c/B_e$ for each direction.

If the previously provided values are agreed, then T is defined by the following formula:

$$T = B_c / CIR \qquad (21.1)$$

It is also possible to specify the values of CIR and T; then, the traffic burst value B_c will become the derived parameter. As a rule, for controlling traffic bursts, the T interval is chosen to be 1–2 seconds when transmitting data, and within the range of several tens or hundreds milliseconds when transmitting voice.

Figure 21.6 illustrates the relationship among CIR, B_c, B_e, and T (R is the rate of the access link; f_1–f_5 are the frames).

The main parameter on the basis of which the subscriber and network service provider make an agreement when establishing a virtual connection is the CIR. For PVCs, this agreement is part of the contract for providing network services. When establishing SVCs, the agreement is made automatically using the Q.933 protocol, and required connection parameters — CIR, B_c and B_e — are transmitted in the connection request packet.

Since the data rate is measured during a specific interval, T serves as a measurement interval during which the conditions of the agreement are checked. In general, during this interval, the user must not transmit data to the network at the average rate that

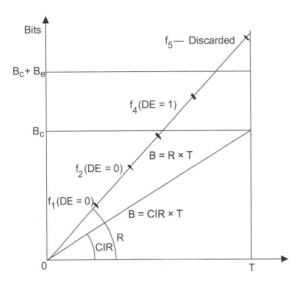

Figure 21.6 Network reaction to the behavior of the user

exceeds CIR. If the user violates this agreement, the network does not guarantee the delivery of such frames and marks them with the **discard eligibility** (**DE**) attribute set to 1. This means that such frames are the first candidates for discarding. Frames having this attribute set will be delayed from the network only if the network switches are overloaded. If the network is not congested, the frames with the DE = 1 attribute are delivered to the destination.

Such tolerant behavior of the network corresponds to the case in which the total volume of the data transmitted by the user during the entire period T does not exceed $B_c + B_e$. If this threshold has been exceeded, the frame is discarded immediately without setting the DE attribute.

Figure 21.6 illustrates a case in which five frames were transmitted to the network during T. The average data rate at this interval was R bps, and it exceeded the *CIR* value. Frames f_1, f_2, and f_3 delivered into the network so that the amount of data does not exceed the B_c threshold; therefore, they were transmitted further with the DE = 0 attribute. The data of f_4, added to that of f_1, f_2, and f_3, exceeded the B_c value but still did not exceed the $B_c + B_e$ threshold. Therefore, f_4 also was transmitted further; however, the DE = 1 attribute was set. The data of f_5, being added to the data of the frames transmitted earlier, exceeded the $B_c + B_e$ threshold; because of this, f_5 was discarded.

To control the agreement parameters, all Frame Relay switches support the leaky bucket algorithm. This algorithm belongs to the same class of algorithms as the token bucket algorithm that we considered in *Chapter 20*. It also allows control of the average rate and traffic bursts; however, it does this in a slightly different way.

The leaky bucket algorithm uses the counter C for counting bytes received from the user. Every T seconds, this counter is decremented by the value B_c (or is reset to 0 if the counter value is less than B_c). All frames whose data did not increase the counter value so that it would exceed the B_c threshold are passed to the network with the DE = 0 attribute. Frames whose data increased the counter value over B_c but did not cause it to exceed the $B_c + B_e$ threshold are also passed to the network; however, this time, the DE attribute is set to 1. Finally, the frames whose data pushed the counter value over $B_c + B_e$ are discarded by the switch.

The user can also make an agreement with the service provider according to which not all but only part of the QoS parameters are taken into account at a specific virtual circuit.

For example, it is possible to use only CIR and B_c parameters. This variant ensures higher quality of service, since user frames are never discarded immediately by the switch. The switch only marks the frames exceeding the B_c threshold during T by the DE = 1 attribute. If the network is not congested, frames of such a virtual circuit are always delivered to the destination node, even if the user constantly violates his agreement with the network.

There is another popular request for QoS, the one when only the B_e threshold is subject to the agreement and CIR is considered to equal zero. All frames of such a circuit are immediately marked by the DE = 1 attribute. However, they are sent to the network and are discarded only if the B_e threshold is exceeded. The check period T in this case is calculated as B_e / R, where R is the access rate of the link.

As can be seen from this description, the leaky bucket algorithm controls traffic bursts more strictly than token bucket. The token bucket algorithm allows traffic to accumulate the burst size during periods of low network activity and then use the accumulated reserve during burst periods. The leaky bucket algorithm does not provide this possibility, since C is forcibly reset to zero as every T expires, independent of the number of bytes received from the user during this period.

Figure 21.7 shows the example of the Frame Relay network with five remote departments. Usually, access to the network is ensured by the links with the bandwidth that

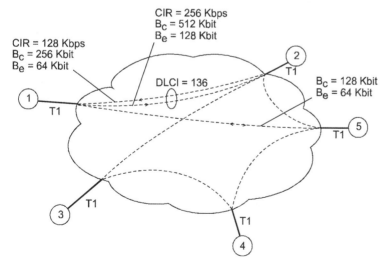

Figure 21.7 Using a Frame Relay network

exceeds the *CIR* value. However, in this case, the user pays for the requested values of *CIR*, B_2 and B_2 not for the link bandwidth. For example, if a T1 line is used as an access link, and the user has requested service at *CIR* = 128 Kbps, he will pay only for the 128 Kbps data rate. The data rate of the T1 link, which is 1,544 Mbps, will influence only the upper limit of the possible burst — $B_c + B_e$.

QoS parameters can be different for different directions of the virtual circuit. For example, in Figure 21.7, subscriber 1 is connected to subscriber 2 by the virtual circuit DLCI = 136. In the direction from subscriber 1 to subscriber 2, the circuit has an average data rate of 128 Kbps with B_c = 256 kb (the interval *T* was measured in seconds) and B_e = 64 kb. When transmitting data in the inverse direction, the average data rate can reach the value of 256 Kbps, with B_c = 512 kb and B_e = 128 kb.

> The mechanism of the reserving average bandwidth and maximum burst is the main mechanism of ensuring QoS in Frame Relay networks.

Agreements must be concluded in such a way as to ensure that the sum of the average data rates of the virtual circuits does not exceed the capabilities of the network switch ports. When requesting permanent circuits, the administrator holds the main responsibility for doing this; in the course of establishing switched circuits, this responsibility is delegated to switch software. When mutual obligations are specified correctly, the network does its best to eliminate congestion by discarding frames that have the DE = 1 attribute and frames that have exceeded the $B_c + B_e$ threshold.

Frame Relay technology defines one optional flow control algorithm. This is a mechanism of informing end users about congestion in network switches (overflowing with unprocessed frames). The forward explicit congestion notification (FECN) bit informs the receiver about this condition. Based on the value of this bit, the receiver must inform the transmitter (using higher-layer protocols such as TCP/IP, SPX, etc.) that it must reduce the intensity of frame transmission into the network.

The backward explicit congestion notification (BECN) bit informs the transmitter about network congestion. It requires the transmitter to immediately reduce the transmission rate. Usually, the BECN bit is processed at the level of Frame Relay network access devices — routers, multiplexers, and CSU/DSU devices. The Frame Relay protocol does not require devices that receive frames with FECN and BECN bits set to immediately stop frame transmission, as was the case with X.25 networks. These bits serve as indications for higher-layer protocols (TCP, SPX, FTP, etc.) to reduce the packet transmission rate. Since flow control by the receiver and the transmitter is carried out differently in different protocols, Frame Relay developers have taken into account both directions of transmission of control information about network congestion.

21.5 ATM TECHNOLOGY

KEY WORDS: ATM, broadband-ISDN (B-ISDN), PDH, SDH/SONET, IP, SNA, Ethernet, PNNI, QoS support, five classes of traffic: A, B, C, D, and X, constant bit rate (CBR), variable bit rate (VBR), packetizing delay, Peak cell rate (PCR), Sustained cell rate (SCR), Minimum cell rate (MCR), Maximum burst size (MBS), Cell loss ratio (CLR), Cell transfer delay (CTD), Cell delay variation (CDV), unspecified bit rate (UBR), special resource management (RM), cells forward resource management (FRM) cells, backward resource management (BRM) cells, feedback loops

The ATM technology was developed as a universal transport for a new generation of network with integrated services known as **broadband-ISDN** (B-ISDN). Principally, ATM was the second attempt at building a converged network after ISDN failed to achieve this goal. In contrast to Frame Relay, which initially was intended only for transmitting elastic computer traffic, the aims of ATM developers were considerably broader and more ambitious.

According to the plans of the developers, ATM had to be capable of ensuring several of the following capabilities:

- The single transport system for simultaneously transmitting computer and multimedia (voice and video) traffic, which is highly sensitive to delays; QoS for each kind of traffic must correspond to its requirements
- Hierarchy of transmission rates ranging from tens of megabits per second to several gigabits per second, with guaranteed bandwidth for critical applications
- The possibility of using the existing infrastructure of physical links or physical protocols: PDH, SDH, or high-speed LAN
- Interaction with existing LAN and WAN protocols, such as IP, SNA, Ethernet, and ISDN

It is necessary to point out that most of these goals were achieved successfully. Starting from mid-1990s, ATM has been a working technology that ensures the most complete, consistent support of QoS parameters for network users. Furthermore, ATM, like any other virtual circuit technology, provides broad capabilities in the field of solving traffic engineering problems.

Development of the ATM standards (RFC 2514, RFC 2515, RFC 2761, RFC 3116, etc.) is carried out by many telecommunications equipment manufacturers and communications carriers participating in the ATM Forum. Special ITU-T and ANSI committees also take part in this work.

Despite the obvious success of the ATM technology, which operates on the backbones of the largest communications carriers, it has shown limitations. Thus, ATM has not moved all other technologies out of use and did not become the only transport technology of telecommunications networks, even though this seemed inevitable in the mid-1990s because of the obvious technological advantages of ATM. In theory, ATM can be used directly by the application-layer protocols so that the network can operate without IP and TCP/UDP. ATM provides many features required to achieve this goal, including support for all kinds of traffic, scalability, and a native, sophisticated routing protocol. However, this will become possible only if the network is technologically homogeneous. For this purpose, all networks of all service providers must support ATM. As can be easily seen, such an approach contradicts the main principle of internetworking, according to which each network can support its own transport technology and the network layer combines these constituent networks into the unified internet.

Therefore, IP took the dominant position at the network layer by the mid-1990s and continues to be used for internetworking. As for ATM, it became one of the technologies on the basis of which many constituent networks operate. The problems related to interaction between ATM and IP will be covered in *Chapter 22*.

21.5.1 Main Principles of ATM Operation

The ATM network has the classical structure of a large-scale WAN. Workstations (end nodes) are connected to the low-layer switches using individual links. These switches, in turn, are connected to higher-layer switches. ATM switches use 20-byte end-node addresses for traffic routing on the basis of the virtual circuit technique. For private ATM networks, the private NNI (PNNI) routing protocol is defined, using which routers can build routing tables automatically and, moreover, with the account of traffic engineering requirements. As a rule, addresses according to the E.164 standard are used in public ATM networks, which simplifies the interconnection of these networks to telephone networks. ATM addresses have a hierarchical structure similar to telephone numbers or IP addresses. This ensures ATM scalability to any required level, even to the worldwide network.

To speed up switching in large-scale networks, the concept of a *virtual path* is used. A virtual path connects virtual circuits that have a common route in the ATM network connecting the source node and end node, or some common part of the route between two network switches. This property also improves ATM scalability, since it allows considerable reduction of virtual connections supported by the backbone router, thus improving the efficiency of its operation.

The ATM standard does not introduce individual specifications for physical-layer implementation. In this respect, it is based on the SDH/SONET technology and adopts its speed hierarchy. According to this, the starting access rate provided to network users is the STM-1 access rate, which makes 155 Mbps. ATM backbone equipment operates at higher speeds — STM-4 622 Mbps and STM-16 2.5 Gbps. There is also ATM equipment supporting PDH speeds, such as 34 Mbps and 45 Mbps.

All previously listed characteristics of the ATM technology do not serve as evidence of that it is a "specific" technology. Rather, it is a typical WAN technology based on the virtual circuit technique. Specific features of the ATM technology lie in the quality servicing of various kinds of traffic.

> The main property of ATM that separates it from other technologies is *integrated QoS support for all kinds of traffic.*

To ensure this property, ATM developers carefully analyzed all types of traffic and carried out its classification. You became acquainted with this classification in *Chapter 7* when considering QoS requirements of different applications. Recall that ATM classification divides all traffic into five classes: A, B, C, D, and X. The first four classes represent the traffic of typical applications. These applications have a stable set of requirements for packet delays and losses. Another distinguishing feature of such applications is that they generate traffic characterized by a constant bit rate (CBR) or a variable bit rate (VBR). Class X is reserved for unique applications for which the set of characteristics and QoS requirements cannot be classified as belonging to one of the first four classes.

However, the number of traffic classes in any classification does not introduce any principal changes into the solution to this problem — namely, finding a way of successfully supporting elastic and delay-sensitive kinds of traffic within the same channel. Requirements of these classes are nearly always mutually contradictory. One such contradiction is the requirement for the frame size.

Elastic traffic benefits from increasing the frame size, since this reduces the overhead for control information. On the example of the Ethernet frame, you saw that the effective data rate can change more than twice when changing the size of the data field from its minimal value of 46 bytes to the maximum value of 1,500 bytes. Naturally, the frame size cannot be increased infinitely since in this case the idea of packet switching would lose its sense. Nevertheless, for elastic traffic at a contemporary level of rates, a frame size of thousands of bytes is acceptable.

Delay-sensitive traffic, on the contrary, is served better when small frames of tens of bytes are used. When using large frames, two undesirable effects start to become noticeable:

■ Long delays of low-priority frames in queues
■ Packetizing delay

Consider these effects on the example of voice traffic.

We know that the *waiting time in queues* can be reduced if frames of delay-sensitive traffic are served in the priority queue. However, if the packet size can vary in a wide range (e.g., from 29 to 4,500 bytes, like in the FDDI technology), then, even though voice packets are assigned the highest priority for servicing in switches, the waiting time for computer packets may become too high to be acceptable. For example, a 4,500-byte packet will be transmitted to the output port at the rate of 2 Mbps (the typical rate of the operation of the Frame Relay access port) is 18 msec. When combining traffic, it is necessary to transmit 144 voice samples through the same port during the same time. It is undesirable to interrupt packet transmission, since in a distributed network the overhead for informing the neighboring switch about this interruption and on subsequent resuming of its transmission prove to be too high.

Packetizing delay is the time during which the first voice sample waits for the packet to be fully formed and sent into the network. The mechanism of this delay is shown in Figure 21.8.

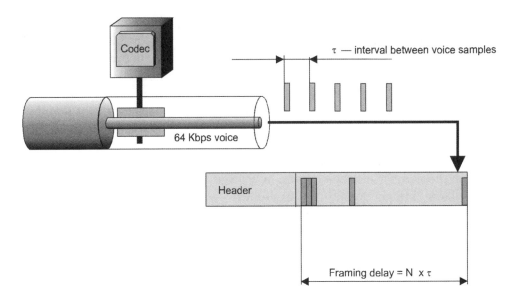

Figure 21.8 Packetizing delay

The codec produces voice samples periodically at the same interval. For instance, the PCM codec shown in the illustration does this at a frequency of 8 kHz — that is, every 125 μsec. If you use Ethernet frames of the maximum size for voice transmission, then every frame will carry 1,500 voice samples, since every sample is encoded by 1 byte of data. As a result, the first sample placed into the Ethernet frame will have to wait for the frame to be sent into the network for $(1,500 - 1) \times 125 = 187,375$ μsec, or about 187 msec. This delay is quite significant for the voice traffic. For example, according to the ITU-T recommendations, this delay must not exceed 150 msec. It is important to notice that the framing delay does not depend on the bit rate of the protocol. On the contrary, it depends only on the codec operating frequency and on the size of the frame data field. This separates it from the queuing delay, which is reduced with the increase of the bit rate.

The size of the ATM frame with the data field size of 48 bytes is a compromise between the requirements of elastic and delay-sensitive traffic. In other words, it is possible to state that this compromise was achieved by telephony and computer specialists — the first insisted on a data field size of 32 bytes, and the latter wanted 64 bytes. Because of this small and fixed size of the ATM frame, it became known as a **cell**.

Having a data field length of 48 bytes, a single ATM cell usually carries 48 voice samples taken with an interval of 125 μsec. Therefore, the first sample must wait approximately 6 msec before the cell will be sent into the network. This is the main reason telephony specialists insisted on a reduction of the cell size. The 6 msec is close to the threshold after which the voice transmission quality becomes degraded. If the cell size is chosen to be 32 bytes, the packetizing delay would be 4 msec, which would guarantee voice transmission of higher quality. The reason computer specialists are striving to increase the data field to 64 bytes is also justified, since if this condition is satisfied, the effective data rate would be increased. The redundancy of the service data when using a 48-byte data field is 10%; when using a 32-byte data field, it is increased to 16%.

For the packet that comprises 53 bytes, at the rate of 155 Mbps the time of frame transmission to the output port is less than 3 μsec. Thus, this delay is not too significant for traffic whose packets must be transmitted every 125 μsec.

To ensure that packets contain the address of the destination node and guarantee that the percentage of the control information does not exceed the size of the packet data field, ATM technology implements a technique that is standard for WANs, namely, cell transmission according to the virtual circuit technique. The total length of the virtual circuit number is 24 bits, which is enough for serving a large number of virtual connections by each port of the switch of the large-scale (possibly, worldwide) WAN based on ATM.

It is necessary to point out that using small cells in ATM provides excellent conditions for high-quality service for delay-sensitive traffic. The payment for this perfection is the high load on ATM switches when operating at high rates. Recall that the amount of work carried out by the router based on any technology is directly proportional to the number of packets or frames processed per time unit. Obviously, using cells with a data field size of 48 bytes produces a very high load on the ATM switch in comparison to, say, an Ethernet switch operating with 1,500-byte frames. Because of this, ATM switches could not exceed the interface rate limit of 622 Mbps for a long time. They began to support rates of 2.5 Gbps only recently.

The choice of a small data cell of a fixed size does not in itself solve the problem of combining different kinds of traffic in the same network. Rather, it simply ensures the prerequisites for finding a solution to it. *To fully solve this task, ATM technology implements and develops the ideas of providing the bandwidth and QoS on demand, an idea implemented in the Frame Relay technology.*

In the ATM technology, for each traffic class there is a set of quantitative parameters that must be specified by the application. For the class A traffic, it is necessary to specify a constant rate at which the application will send its data into the network, and for the Class B traffic, it is necessary to specify the maximum possible rate, average rate, and maximum possible burst. For voice traffic, it is possible not only to specify the importance of synchronization between the transmitter and the receiver but also to provide quantitative characteristics by specifying upper thresholds for delay and delay variation.

ATM supports the following set of main quantitative parameters for virtual circuit traffic:

■ **Peak cell rate (PCR)** — peak rate of data transmission
■ **Sustained cell rate (SCR)** — average rate of data transmission
■ **Minimum cell rate (MCR)** — minimum rate of data transmission
■ **Maximum burst size (MBS)** — maximum size of the data burst
■ **Cell loss ratio (CLR)** — share of the lost cells

■ **Cell transfer delay (CTD)** — cell transmission delay

■ **Cell delay variation (CDV)** — cell transmission delay variation

Rate parameters are measured in cells per seconds, MBS is measured in cells, and time parameters are measured in seconds. MBS specifies the number of cells that the application can transmit at the PCR, provided that the average rate is specified. The share of lost cells is the ratio of the number of lost cells to the total number of cells sent through this virtual connection. Since virtual connections are duplex, it is possible to specify individual values for each direction of data transmission.

ATM technology uses a nontraditional approach to the interpretation of the QoS term. Usually, QoS is characterized by bandwidth parameters (in this case, these are RCR, SCR, MCR, and MBS), packet delay parameters (CTD and CDV), and packet transmission reliability parameters (CLR). In ATM, information rate characteristics are called traffic parameters. They are not included into the number of QoS parameters although principally they are such parameters. In ATM, QoS parameters include only CTD, CDV, and CLR. The network tries to ensure a level of service that supports the required values for traffic parameters, for cell delays, and for the percentage of lost cells.

The agreement between the application and the ATM network is called the traffic contract. Its main difference from agreements used in Frame Relay networks is the choice of one of several traffic classes for which, besides bandwidth parameters, it is possible to specify cell delay parameters and the cell delivery reliability parameter. In Frame Relay, there is only one traffic class, and it is characterized only by bandwidth parameters.

If the support of bandwidth parameters and QoS parameters is not critical for the application, it can omit them by specifying the "best effort" attribute in the request for establishing a connection. This type of traffic is known as **unspecified bit rate (UBR) traffic**.

After concluding the traffic contract that relates to the specific virtual connection, the ATM network provides several protocols and services needed for ensuring the requested QoS. For UBR traffic, the network allocates resources as possible (i.e., the resources currently available for allocation) because they are not used by virtual connections that have requested specific QoS parameters.

21.5.2 ATM Protocol Stack

The ATM protocol stack is shown in Figure 21.9, and protocol distribution over end nodes and ATM switches is in Figure 21.10.

The ATM protocol stack corresponds to the lower layers of the ISO/OSI model. It includes the ATM adaptation layer (AAL), the ATM layer, and the physical layer. There is no direct correspondence between ATM and OSI protocol layers.

	Higher layers of the network		
ATM adaptation layers ATM (AAL1-5)	Convergence sublayer (CS)	Common part of the convergence sublayer	
		Service-specific part of the convergence sublayer	
	Segmentation and Reassembly sublayer (SAR)		
	ATM layer (packet routing, multiplexing, flow control, priority handling)		
Physical layer	Transmission reconciliation sublayer		
	Medium-dependent sublayer		

Figure 21.9 Structure of the ATM protocol stack

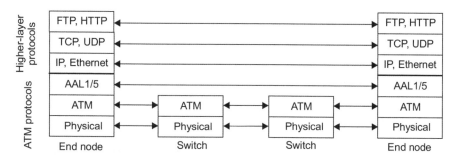

Figure 21.10 Distribution of ATM protocols over switches and end nodes

21.5.3 ATM Adaptation Layer

The AAL is the set of AAL1–AAL5 protocols that convert the messages of higher-layer protocols of the ATM network into ATM cells of the required format. The functions of these layers correspond conventionally to the OSI transport layer (such as TCP and UDP). AAL protocols operate only on network end nodes, like the transport protocols of most networking technologies.

Each protocol of the AAL layer processes user traffic of a specific class. At the initial stages of standardization, each traffic class had its own corresponding AAL protocol, which received the packets from the higher-layer protocol at the end node and used the appropriate protocol to request the traffic and QoS parameters for the specific virtual connection required by the application. In the course of the ATM standards evolution, this unambiguous correspondence between traffic classes and AAL protocols has disappeared. Now it is possible to use different AAL protocols for the same traffic class.

The AAL comprises two sublayers.

■ The lower sublayer is **the segmentation and reassembly (SAR) layer**. This part does not depend on the AAL protocol type (or, consequently, on the class of the traffic being transmitted). It segments the message received by AAL from the higher-layer protocol. After creating ATM cells, SAR supplies them with appropriate headers and passes them to the ATM layer for transmitting into the network.

■ The higher sublayer of AAL is the **convergence sublayer (CS)**. This sublayer depends on the class of traffic being transmitted. The CS protocol solves such problems as ensuring synchronization between transmitting and receiving nodes (for traffic that requires such synchronization), control and recovery of bit errors in user data, and integrity control of the packet of the computer protocol being transmitted (X.25 or Frame Relay).

To carry out their tasks, AAL protocols use control information located in AAL headers. Having received the cells that arrived through virtual circuit, SAR assembles the source message (generally split into several ATM cells) using AAL headers. AAL headers are invisible to ATM switches because they reside in the 48-bit data field of the cell, which is normal for a higher-layer protocol. Having assembled the source message, AAL checks the control fields of the AAL frame header and trailer and, based on this check, decides whether the received information is correct.

> When transmitting user data, neither AAL protocol recovers lost or corrupted data. The most that the AAL protocol can do is inform the end node about such an event. This was done to speed up the operation of ATM switches in hope that data loss and corruption are rare events. Recovering lost data (or ignoring such an event) is a task delegated to higher-layer protocols that are not included into the ATM protocol stack.

The **AAL1** protocol usually serves Class A traffic with CBR, which is typical, for example, for digital video or voice and is sensitive to delays. ATM networks transmit such traffic in such a way as to emulate normal leased digital links. The AAL1 header takes 1 or 2 bytes in the data field of the ATM cell, leaving 47 or 46 bytes for user data, respectively. One byte of the header is allocated for cell numbering so that the receiving node can decide whether or not it has received all cells sent to it. When sending voice traffic, the time stamp of each sample is known, since they follow each other at intervals of 125 μsec. Thus, if the cell is lost, it is possible to correct the timing of the bytes of the next cell by simply shifting it 125×46 μsec. The loss of several bytes of a voice sample is not critical, since at the receiving node the equipment smoothes the signal. The tasks of the AAL1 protocol include smoothing the unevenness of the arrival of cells at the destination node.

The **AAL2** protocol was developed for transmitting Class B traffic. Later, it was excluded from the ATM protocol stack. Nowadays, Class B traffic is transmitted using the AAL1, AAL3/4, or AAL5 protocol.

The **AAL3/4** protocol processes bursty traffic typical for LANs. This is a VBR, and traffic is processed in such a way as to prevent cell losses. However, cells can be delayed by the switch. The AAL3/4 protocol carries out a complicated procedure of error control when transmitting cells. To achieve this, it numbers each part of the source message and supplies each cell with the checksum. However, if cells get lost or corrupted, this layer does not attempt to recover them. Instead, it discards the entire message — that is, all remaining cells. This is because for computer traffic or compressed voice the loss of even a single cell is a fatal error. The AAL3/4 protocol is the result of merging the AAL3 and AAL4 protocols, which ensured support for computer traffic using connection-oriented and connectionless protocols, respectively. However, because they used close header formats and a similar logic of operation, the AAL3 and AAL4 protocols were combined.

The **AAL5** protocol is a simplified version of the AAL4 protocol. It operates faster because it does not compute the checksum for each cell of the message. On the contrary, it computes the checksum for the entire source message and places it into the last cell of the message. Initially, the AAL5 protocol was developed for transmitting the frames of Frame Relay networks. Nowadays, however, it is used for transmitting any computer traffic (RFC 2684). AAL5 can support different parameters of QoS except the ones that relate to synchronization between the transmitter and the receiver. Therefore, it is normally used for supporting all classes of traffic related to computer data transmission (i.e., traffic of Classes C and D). Some equipment manufacturers use AAL5 to serve CBR traffic; they delegate the synchronization task to the higher-layer protocols. AAL5 operates not only on end nodes but also on ATM switches. However, on the switches it carries out control functions that are not related to user data transmission. In switches, AAL5 supports higher-layer service protocols involved in establishing virtual connections.

There is a special interface between the AAL layer and the application that needs to transmit traffic using the ATM network. Using this interface, the application (e.g., a computer network protocol or a voice sampling module) requests the needed service by determining the traffic type and its QoS parameters. The ATM technology allows two variants of defining QoS parameters: directly by each application and using the default values depending on the traffic type. The latter method simplifies the task of the application developer, since the choice of maximum delay and delay variation for cell delivery are delegated to the network administrator.

AAL protocols are unable to ensure the required traffic and QoS parameters on their own. To observe the conditions of the traffic contract, it is necessary to ensure the coordinated operation of all network switches along the entire virtual circuit. This task is carried out by the ATM protocol that ensures the transmission of cells of different virtual connections with the required QoS level.

21.5.4 ATM Protocol

The ATM protocol takes approximately the same position in the ATM protocol stack as IP holds in the TCP/IP stack or LAP-F has in the Frame Relay protocol stack. The ATM protocol transmits cells using switches when the virtual circuit is established and configured, which means that this task is based on the port switching tables.

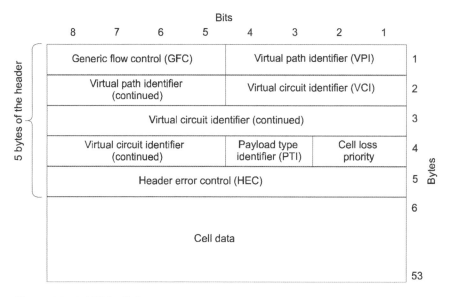

Figure 21.11 ATM cell format

The ATM protocol carries out switching using the **number of the virtual circuit**, which in the ATM technology is split into two parts:

■ The **virtual path identifier** (VPI)
■ The **virtual channel identifier** (VCI)

Besides this main task, the ATM protocol also carries out some functions related to allowing the network user to observe the traffic contract, marking the violating cells, discarding the violating cells in case of network congestion, and controlling the flow of cells to improve the network performance (naturally, provided that the traffic contract conditions are observed for all virtual circuits).

The ATM cell format is shown in Figure 21.11.

The *generic flow control* field is used in more than the course of interaction between the end node and the first network switch. Its exact functions are not defined yet.

The *VPI* and *VCI* fields take 1 and 2 bytes, accordingly. These fields specify the number of virtual connections divided into the most significant (VPI) and least significant (VCI) parts.

The *payload type identifier* field comprises 3 bits. It specifies the type of data carried by the cell — user data or control data (for instance, when establishing a virtual connection). Furthermore, 1 bit of this field is used to indicate network congestion. This bit is called the explicit congestion forward identifier (EFCI) and plays the same role as the FECN bit in the Frame Relay technology. It passes information on the network congestion in the direction of the data flow.

The *cell loss priority (CLP)* in this technology plays the same role as the *DE* field in the Frame Relay technology. ATM switches use this field to mark the cells that violate the agreement of the QoS parameters of the connection. Such cells will be discarded if network congestion occurs. Thus, the cell with CLP = 0 is a high priority to the network, and cells with CLP = 1 have a low priority.

The *header error control* (HEC) field contains the checksum computed for the cell header. The checksum is computed using the Hamming error-correction code. Therefore, it not only allows error detection but also is capable of correcting all isolated errors (and, under favorable conditions, even some duplicate errors). The *HEC* field not only ensures error detection and correction in the header but also allows the discovery of the boundary of the frame in the SDH byte flow, which is the preferred physical layer for the ATM technology, or in the bit flow of the physical layer based on cells. In ATM, there are no pointers that would detect the boundaries of ATM cells in the data field of the STS-n/STM-n frame of the SONET/SDH technology (similar to the pointers used for determining the boundaries of the virtual containers of the T1/E1 channels). Therefore, the ATM switch computes the checksum for the 5-byte sequence located in the data field of the STM-n frame and, if the checksum shows that the ATM cell header is correct, the first byte becomes the cell boundary. If this is not so, a 1-byte shift takes place, and the operation continues. Thus, the ATM technology detects the asynchronous flow of ATM cells in the synchronous SDH frames or in the physical-layer bit flow based on cells.

ATM switches can operate using two modes:

■ **Virtual path switching**. In this mode, the switch forwards the cell only on the basis of the *VPI* field and ignores the VCI value. Usually, the backbone switches of large-scale regional networks operate in this way. They deliver cells from network to network only on the basis of the most significant part of the virtual circuit number, which corresponds to the idea of address aggregation. As a result, one virtual path corresponds to the set of virtual circuits aggregated into the single whole.

■ **Virtual circuit switching**. After delivering the cell to the local ATM network, the switches of that network start switching cells, taking into account both VPI and VCI. However, for switching they need only the least significant part of the virtual connection number; therefore, they work only with VCI, leaving VPI without changes.

To create an SVC, ATM uses protocols that are not shown in Figure 21.11. In this case, the approach is similar to the ISDN approach. To establish a connection, a separate protocol has been developed, **Q.2931**, which can be conditionally classified as a network-layer protocol. This protocol has much in common with the Q.931 and Q.933 protocols (including the number). Naturally, however, some modifications were introduced into it related to the support of several traffic classes and additional QoS parameters. The Q.2931 protocol relies on a rather sophisticated data link-layer protocol named SSCOP, which ensures reliable transmission of Q.2931 in its frames. SSCOP, in turn, operates over the AAL5 protocol required for splitting SSCOP frames into ATM cells and assembling these cells into frames when delivering the SSCOP frame to the destination switch.

NOTE   *Q.2931 appeared in the ATM protocol stack after the adoption of the UNI 3.1 interface. In UNI 3.0, the Q.93B protocol was used instead. Because of the incompatibility between Q.2931 and Q.93B, the UNI 3.0 and UNI 3.1 interface versions are also incompatible. The UNI 4.0 version provides backward compatibility with UNI 3.1 because it is based on the same control protocols as UNI 3.1.*

Virtual connections created using Q.2931 can be simplex (unidirectional) or duplex (bidirectional).

The Q.2931 protocol also allows point-to-point and point-to-multipoint virtual connections to be established. The first case is supported in all technologies based on virtual circuits. The second case is typical only for ATM and is the analogue of multicasting except with a single multicasting node. When establishing a point-to-multipoint connection, the leading node is the initiator of this connection. First, this node establishes a virtual connection with one node; then, using a special call, it adds new members to this connection. The initiator becomes the root of the connection tree, and all the other participating nodes play the roles of "leaves." Messages sent by the leading node are received by all connection leaves; however, the messages sent by a specific leave (in a duplex connection) are received only by the leading node.

Packets of the Q.2931 protocol intended for establishing an SVC have the same names and the same purposes as the packets of the Q.933 protocol, which were covered earlier in this chapter with the description of the Frame Relay technology. However, the structure of their fields is different.

The end node address in ATM switches is the 20-byte address.

When operating in public networks, the address corresponding to the E.164 standard is used. This address has a flexible format and can be divided into parts to ensure hierarchical routing between networks and subnets. It supports more hierarchical levels than IPv4 and, in this respect, is similar to the IPv6 address.

The last 6 bytes of the address are allocated for the field of the **end system identifier** (ESI). This field plays the same role as MAC address of the ATM node. Its format also corresponds to the MAC address format.

The ESI address is assigned to the end node by the equipment manufacturer according to IEEE rules. This means that the first 3 bytes contain the manufacturer code, and the remaining 3 bytes are the serial number, the uniqueness of which must be ensured by the manufacturer.

When working in a private ATM network, the address format usually corresponds to the E.164 format with minor modifications.

When the end node is connected to the ATM switch, it carries out the so-called registration procedure. The end node reports its ESI address to the switch, and the switch reports the most significant part of the address to the end node — that is, the number of the network to which that node is connected.

Besides the address part, the end node uses the call setup packet of the Q.2931 protocol to request that a virtual connection be established and to include the parts that describe traffic parameters and QoS requirements. When such a packet arrives at the switch, the switch must analyze these parameters and decide if it has sufficient performance resources for serving a new virtual connection. If so, then a new virtual connection is accepted and the switch passes the call setup packet according to the destination address and routing table. If available resources are insufficient, the request is denied.

21.5.5 Categories of ATM Protocol Services and Traffic Control

To support the required QoS for various virtual connections and to ensure rational use of network resources, the ATM network implements several ATM-layer services related to serving user traffic. These are internal services of the ATM network. They are intended for supporting user traffic of different classes with AAL protocols. However, in contrast to AAL protocols that operate on end nodes, these services are distributed over all network switches. Their services are classified into categories, which generally correspond to the classes of traffic that arrives at the input of the AAL layer of the end node. ATM-layer services are requested by the end node through UNI using the Q.2931 protocol when establishing a virtual connection. As in the case with a request to the AAL, when requesting the service, it is necessary to specify its category, traffic, and QoS parameters. These parameters are taken from the similar parameters of the AAL layer or defined as default values depending on the service category.

> There are five service categories of the ATM protocol layer; they are supported by services with the same names:
> - **CBR** (Constant Bit Rate) — services for CBR traffic
> - **rtVBR** (real-time Variable Bit Rate) — services for VBR traffic, which requires constant average data rate and synchronization between the transmitter and the receiver
> - **nrtVBR** (non real-time Variable Bit Rate) — services for VBR traffic, which requires observance of the average data rate but does not require synchronization of the transmitter and the receiver
> - **ABR** (Available Bit Rate) — services for the VBR traffic, which requires some minimum data rate and does not require synchronization of the transmitter and the receiver
> - **UBR** (Unspecified Bit Rate) — services for the traffic, which does not provide any requirements of the data transmission rate and does not synchronize the transmitter and the receiver

The names of most service categories coincide with the names of the user traffic types for which they were developed. However, it is necessary to understand that ATM-layer services are internal mechanisms of the ATM network hidden from applications by the AAL layer.

CBR services are intended for supporting the traffic of synchronous applications — voice, emulation of digital leased lines, and so on. When an application establishes the connection of the CBR category, it requests the peak rate of the cells (PCR), which is the maximum rate that can be supported by the connection without the risk of cell loss. The application also requests the following QoS parameters: CTD, CDV, and CLR.

Then, the data are transmitted through this connection at the requested rate, which is not larger and, in most cases, no smaller than the requested one, although speed reduction is possible — for example, when transmitting compressed voice using the CBR service category. Any cells transmitted by the station at a higher rate are controlled by the first network switched and marked with the CLP = 1 attribute. When network congestion occurs, such cells can be discarded by the network. The cells that are delayed and do not fit within the interval agreed upon by the CDV parameter are also considered low priority and are marked with the CLP = 1 attribute.

For CBR connections, there are no limitations for a certain discontinuity of the requested PCR unlike, for example, in T1/E1 links, where the rate must be a multiple of 64 Kbps.

In comparison to CBR services, *VBR services* require more complicated procedures of requesting the connection between the network and the application. In addition to the PCR, the VBR application requests two other parameters — SCR, which is an average rate of data transmission allowed for the application, and MBS. MBS is measured by the number of ATM cells. The user must exceed the rate of the PCR threshold, however, only for short periods, during which the data volume not exceeding MBS is transmitted. This period is called **burst tolerance** (BT). The network computes this period as a derived value depending on the three specified parameters: PCR, SCR, and MBS.

If the PCR is monitored during a period longer than the BT, then cells are marked as violators of the service agreement — the CLP attribute is set to 1.

For *rtVBR services*, the same QoS parameters are set as for the CBR services, and nrtVBR services are limited only by support of the traffic parameters. For both VBR traffic categories, the network supports a certain level of the CLR, which is specified either explicitly when establishing a connection or is chosen as a default value for a specific class of traffic.

For controlling traffic and QoS parameters, ATM uses the so-called *generic cell rate algorithm*, which can check whether the user observes the agreement in respect to such parameters as PCR, CDV, SCR, BT, CTD, and CDV. It operates according to the modified leaky bucket algorithm used in the Frame Relay technology.

For many applications that are extremely bursty in relation to the traffic they generate, it is impossible to predict traffic parameters, which are agreed upon when establishing a connection. For example, transaction processing and traffic between two communicating LANs are unpredictable. The traffic intensity variations are so large that it is impossible to conclude any reasonable agreement with the network.

In contrast to CBR and both VBR services, *the UBR service* does not support traffic parameters or QoS parameters. UBR offers only best effort delivery without any guarantees. Being developed especially for when the bandwidth limits are exceeded, the UBR service provides a partial solution for unpredictable bursty applications that are not ready to conclude any agreements related to traffic parameters.

The main drawbacks of the UBR service are the lack of flow control mechanisms and the inability to take into account other types of traffic. UBR connections will continue data transmission even in cases of network congestion. Network switches can buffer some cells of the incoming traffic. However, a time will come when buffer overflow will occur and the cells will be lost. Since no traffic or QoS parameters are agreed for UBR connections, their cells are the first to be discarded.

The *ABR service*, similar to UBR, provides the possibility of exceeding the bandwidth. However, because of traffic control techniques, it ensures reliable transport and provides some guarantees of cell delivery.

> ABR is the first type of ATM-layer service that ensures reliable transport for bursty traffic because of its capability of finding unused time slots in the common network traffic and filling them with its cells, provided that they are not needed by other service categories.

Similar to CBR and VBR services, when establishing an ABR category connection, it is necessary to agree on the PCR parameter. However, no agreements are concluded in respect to cell transmission parameters or burst parameters. Instead, the network and the end node conclude the agreement on the required minimum transmission rate, the MCR. For the application running on the end node, this guarantees a small bandwidth, usually the required minimum for normal operation of that application. When concluding such an agreement, the end node agrees not to transmit data at rates that exceed the PCR, and the network agrees to always ensure the MCR.

If the values of the maximum and the minimum rates are not specified when concluding an ABR connection, then, by default, it is considered that the link PCR matches the rate of access line that provides end station access to the network and the default MCR value is equal to zero.

The traffic of the ABR connection gets guaranteed QoS in relation to the share of lost cells and the available bandwidth. As relates to the cell transmission delays, they are not guaranteed, although the network makes its best effort to reduce them to a minimum. Consequently, the ABR service is not suitable for real-time applications whose data flow is highly sensitive to transmission delays.

When transmitting CBR, VBR, and UBR traffic, explicit control over network congestion is missing. Instead, the mechanism based on discarding the violating cells is used. At the same time, the nodes using CBR and VBR services do their best to avoid violation of the traffic contract. If they do, they risk losing cells. Because of this, they usually do not use additional bandwidth even if it is available.

The ABR service allows the use of bandwidth reserves since it uses the feedback mechanism to inform the end node that the bandwidth reserve is available. The same mechanism can help the ABR service to reduce the transmission rate of the end node data into the network to the MCR in case of network congestion.

The node that uses the ABR service must periodically send **special resource management** (RM) **cells** with data cells. The RM cells that the node sends along the data flow are **forward resource management** (FRM) cells, and the cells that travel in the inverse direction are **backward resource management** (BRM) cells.

There are several **feedback loops**. The simplest one exists between two end stations. When it is present, the network switch informs end station about the congestion using a special flag in the field of direct congestion control (the EFCI flag) of the data cell carried by the ATM protocol. Then, the end station sends a special message through the network. This message is contained in a special BRM cell, informing the source station that it needs to reduce the rate at which it sends cells into the network.

When using this method, the end station holds the main responsibility for flow control, and switches play the passive role in feedback, just informing the sender station about congestion.

Such a simple method has several obvious drawbacks. The end station gets no information from the BRM message related to the value by which it is necessary to reduce the rate at which it sends data into the network. Therefore, it will reduce the rate to the minimum value, the MCR, although it might be possible that such a significant reduction is not needed. Furthermore, in a long network, switches must continue data buffering during the entire interval until notification about congestion travels along the network. Note that for WANs, this period can be long. Thus, buffer overflow may occur, so the desired effect will not be reached.

There are other, more sophisticated methods of flow control. In these methods, switches play a more active role, and the sender node is provided with more detailed information about the data rate that can be supported.

In the first method, the source node sends an FRM cell specifying the value of the data rate that it is capable of supporting. Every switch, passed by this message as it travels along the virtual circuit, can reduce the requested rate to the specific value that it can support according to the amount of available resources. It can also leave the requested rate without changes. The destination node, having received the FRM cell, converts it into the BRM cell and sends it in the inverse direction. Note that it also can reduce the requested rate. Having received an answer in the BRM cell, the source node knows exactly which data rate is available to it.

In the second method, each network switch can operate both as the source node and as the destination node. As the source node, it can generate FRM cells and send them over existing virtual circuits. As the destination node, it can send BRM cells in the inverse direction based on the contents of received FRM cells. This method is faster and is more suitable for long-distance networks.

As can be seen from the description, the ABR service is intended for more than directly supporting QoS requirements for a specific virtual connection. It is also suitable for more rational resource distribution among network subscribers, which, in the long run, improves the quality of services provided to all network subscribers.

ATM switches use various mechanisms for supporting the required QoS. Besides the mechanisms described in the ITU-T and ATM Forum standards, according to which the agreements on the traffic and QoS parameters are concluded and the cells violating these agreements are discarded, practically all ATM equipment manufacturers implement several cell queues served with different priorities.

The priority-based strategy for serving the traffic is in turn based on the service categories for each virtual connection. Before adoption of the ABR specification, most ATM switches implemented a simple single-layer service design, which gave the highest priority to the CBR traffic, the second priority to VBR, and the third to UBR. According to such a design, the CBR and VBR combination can potentially freeze the traffic served by another class of services. Such a design would not work correctly with the ABR traffic, because it would not ensure its requirement for the minimum rate of cell transmission. To ensure that this requirement has been met, it is necessary to allocate some guaranteed bandwidth.

To support the ABR service, ATM switches must implement a two-layer design of servicing that satisfies the requirements of CBR, VBR, and ABR. According to this design, the switch provides some portion of its bandwidth to each service class. The CBR traffic gets some portion of the bandwidth required for supporting the PCR, the VBR traffic gets some portion of the bandwidth required for supporting the SCR, and the ABR traffic gets the portion of the bandwidth sufficient for ensuring the MCR. This guarantees that every connection can operate without cell losses and will not deliver ABR cells at the expense of CBR or VBR traffic. At the second layer of this algorithm, the CBR and VBR traffic can take all the remaining bandwidth, if necessary, because ABR connections already have the minimum bandwidth guaranteed to them.

A separate task that needs to be solved for supporting correct operation of the previously described services and ensuring the specified QoS level for all traffic classes is optimization of the ATM network operation using traffic engineering methods. Using the virtual circuit technique in ATM (as well as in Frame Relay) networks provides good prerequisites for solving the traffic engineering problem. However, for the moment, there are no automated procedures for the dynamic choice of routes for virtual circuits to ensure a balanced network load. All work related to the optimization of the routes must be carried out beforehand, using some third-party network optimization or simulation software. After that, the result must be manually configured by establishing PVCs according to the chosen routes.

In ATM networks, the selection of the route for virtual circuits and virtual paths can be carried out using the PNNI routing protocol that takes into account not only the nominal bandwidth of the links but also the bandwidth available for establishing new virtual circuits.

SUMMARY

▶ The virtual circuit technique consists of separating the operations of routing and packet switching. The first packet of such networks contains the address of the called subscriber and creates a virtual path in the network by configuring transit switches. All the other packets go along the virtual circuit in the switching mode based on the virtual circuit number.

▶ Advantages of the virtual circuit technique are fast packet switching on the basis of the virtual circuit number as well as reduction of the address field of the packet and, consequently, reduction of the header redundancy. Drawbacks include the impossibility of parallel data flow between two subscribers by two alternative routes and the inefficiency of establishing a virtual path for short-time data flows.

▶ X.25 networks are the oldest and best-tested WAN technologies. The three-layer protocol stack of X.25 operates well on unreliable noisy communications links by correcting errors and controlling data flow at the data link and packet layers.

▶ Most of the first Frame Relay networks supported only permanent virtual circuits (PVCs). Switched virtual circuits (SVCs) were implemented and became used in practice only recently.

▶ Frame Relay networks were created to transmit bursty computer traffic. Therefore, in the course of bandwidth reservation, it is necessary to specify the traffic average rate, CIR, and coordinated burst size, B_c.

▶ The ATM technology is a further development of the ideas of reserving the virtual circuit bandwidth beforehand, which was first implemented in the Frame Relay technology.

▶ ATM supports the main types of traffic typical for different types of subscribers, including CBR traffic, typical for telephone networks and video broadcasting networks, and VBR traffic, typical for computer networks and used when transmitting compressed voice or video.

▶ For each type of traffic, the user can request from the network several QoS parameters, including the maximum bit rate (PCR), the average bit rate (SCR), the maximum burst (MBS), and several parameters controlling time relations between the transmitter and the receiver, which are important for delay-sensitive traffic.

▶ The ATM technology itself does not define new physical-layer standards. On the contrary, it uses the existing ones. The main standard for the ATM technology is the physical layer of SONET/SDH and PDH.

REVIEW QUESTIONS

1. Which parameters can be used to describe a virtual circuit?
2. What should be done in case of failure of the physical link through which the virtual circuit passes?
3. List all main stages of establishing a virtual circuit.
4. Can an X.25 network operate without PADs?
5. What can happen to the best effort traffic if priority traffic coming into the input Frame Relay interface is not limited by average intensity?
6. How can the user connect to the built-in PAD using the telephone network, provided that he works at a terminal that does not support automatic calls through the telephone network?
7. If your company needs to connect multiple remote office networks to the central network and to one another but you have only leased analog links with installed

synchronous 19.2 Kbps modems, which technology would you choose: X.25, Frame Relay, or ATM? Justify your solution and explain the factors that influenced it.

8. Which function of the token bucket algorithm is not supported by the leaky bucket algorithm?

9. What category of services is it expedient to choose for transmitting voice using the ATM network?

10. How many virtual circuits is it necessary to establish in each direction between each pair of ATM switches, provided that you need to transmit three traffic classes with different QoS levels?

11. For which service category does the ATM network explicitly control the data flow? Why does it not use flow control for other types of services?

12. Assume that you need to manually establish a PVC in two enterprise-wide ATM networks connected by a public ATM network. You do not need your VCI numbers to depend on the VCI numbers used by the administrator of the public ATM network. What kind of switching would you request from the public ATM service provider?

13. Suppose that you have connected two LANs by a remote bridge operating using a PVC in the Frame Relay network. NetBEUI sessions between computers belonging to different networks often are broken. When computers belong to the same LAN, there are no such problems. What reasons can cause such a situation?

PROBLEMS

1. Compare the number of frames generated by exchanging two TCP messages (sending the data and receiving an acknowledgment) between two end hosts connected by one switch when this switch is an X.25 switch and when it is a Frame Relay switch.

2. In which case will the percentage of frames delivered to the destination node using the Frame Relay network be higher: when the service is requested based on CIR, B, and B_e parameters or when the service is requested only on the basis of CIR and B_c (it is assumed that CIR and B_c values for both cases are the same)? Assume that the Frame Relay network is underloaded, and the sender node sends the data at a rate that often significantly exceeds the CIR value.

3. Suppose that the Frame Relay switch and the IP switch are based on the same architecture and processors with the same clock rate. Will the Frame Relay switch provide better performance than the IP router? Justify your opinion.

4. Solve the traffic engineering task for the ATM network shown in Figure 21.12. You must ensure the most uniform load for all network resources for the offered load provided in Figure 21.13.

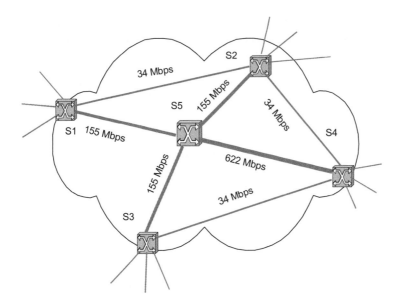

Figure 21.12 ATM network

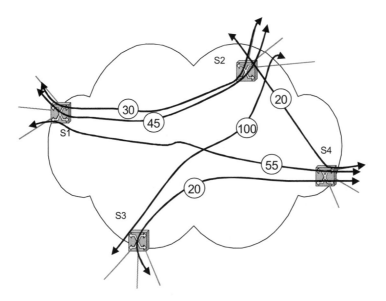

Figure 21.13 Offered load

22

IP WANS

22.1 INTRODUCTION

Because of the revolutionary growth of the Internet's popularity, practically every WAN must be capable of transmitting IP traffic. This means that nearly all contemporary WANs are IP internets, and all differences among them consist of the technologies below the IP layer.

IP WANs in which IP routers are directly connected by physical point-to-point links have the simplest structure. In this case, IP routers connect degenerate constituent networks. According to the common interpretation of the term "network," these constituent networks are not networks at all because they include only two nodes — the interfaces of the neighboring routers. In this book, such networks are called "pure" IP networks because there is no layer of packet switches below the layer formed by IP routers. This means that IP routers carry out all tasks related to packet forwarding on their own.

In the mid-1990s, the multilayer structure of the IP WAN became the most popular. In such WANs, ATM and Frame Relay networks are used as constituent networks. Using packet-switched networks based on different principles (datagram and virtual circuits) at both layers makes IP WANs complicated and expensive. However, these drawbacks are compensated for by the possibilities of transmitting multimedia information and using QoS and traffic engineering methods to balance loads and optimize network resource use.

The multiprotocol label switching (MPLS) technology is another innovation in the field of integrating IP with virtual circuit technology. MPLS takes an intermediate position between the IP layer and the layers of ATM, Frame Relay, or Ethernet, thus integrating them into the unified, more efficient structure.

This chapter concludes with a description of the network management systems based on the simple network management protocol (SNMP), which is widely used for controlling not only IP routers (the goal for which it was developed) but also telecommunications devices of any type, from SDH or DWDM multiplexers to telephone switches.

22.2 PURE IP WANS

KEY WORDS: pure IP WAN, transmission network, overlay network unnumbered interface, permanent virtual circuit (PVC), packet over SONET (POS), High-Level Data Link Control (HDLC), LAP-B , LAP-D, LAP-M, LAP-F, Asynchronous Balance Mode (ABM), sliding window, Point-to-Point Protocol (PPP), Link control protocol (LCP), Network control protocol (NCP), Multi Link PPP (MLPPP), Password Authentication Protocol (PAP), Challenge handshake authentication protocol (CHAP)

22.2.1 IP WAN Structure

To provide a range of high-quality services, most large WANs, especially those owned by commercial communications carriers, are built according to a four-layer design (Figure 22.1).

The two lower layers do not relate to packet-switched networks. At the lower layer of the *transmission network*, the DWDM technology is employed, which nowadays is the fastest. It creates spectral channels ensuring transmission speeds of 10 Gbps or greater. SDH technology (with the PDH access network) operates at the next layer. Using this technology, the bandwidth of these spectral channels is divided into TDM subchannels connecting the interfaces of the switches of the packet-switched networks (or telephone switches).

On the basis of a transmission network every communications carrier can quickly organize a permanent digital link between the connection points of the equipment of the *overlay network*, either telephone or packet switched.

The higher layer in the WAN model shown in Figure 22.1 is formed by an IP network.

NOTE   *Since both of these layers carry out the tasks of the OSI physical layer, the layers of the OSI reference model must not be directly compared to the layers shown in Figure 22.1.*

Figure 22.1 shows the most scalable variant used for building a transmission network today. This configuration includes both the DWDM and the SDH layer. For now, such a structure is typical only for the largest regional networks spanning countries or entire continents. In many smaller backbones, the DWDM layer is missing, and even the SDH technology may not be employed. Instead of DWDM or SDH, communications carriers may use the PDH technology, which is slower and less fault tolerant but more economical.

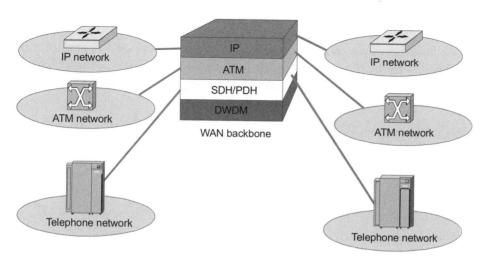

Figure 22.1 Four-layer design of contemporary WANs

In simpler cases, there is no transmission network at all, and below the IP layer there might be underlying ATM or Frame Relay network. The switches of this network are connected directly using either cables or wireless links. Although the latter solution requires fewer investments, it is less flexible because it is necessary to create a new physical link for connecting a new device. On the other hand, the availability of a branched transmission network allows a new channel to be created within the existing network by configuring the switching matrices of multiplexers or DWDM/SDH cross-connects.

The ATM network, whose main goal is *the creation of a permanent virtual circuit (PVC) infrastructure with guaranteed QoS*, forms the third layer of the design shown in Figure 22.1. The PVCs created by the ATM network connect the interfaces of IP routers. For each class of IP traffic, the ATM network forms a separate virtual circuit, which ensures the QoS parameters required for serving this traffic class — average rate, burst, delay level, and loss level. Using ATM as the underlying technology for IP only ensures the required QoS for user traffic but also solves the internal problems of communications carriers on the basis of traffic engineering. The solution to this problem ensures a balanced load for all physical links of the transmission network.

The IP layer, relieved from needing to ensure QoS parameters, carries out its classical functions — namely, it builds an internet and provides IP services to end users. End users might transmit their transit IP traffic through this WAN or connect to the Internet using this network.

Despite the complications of the multilayer structure, such networks have become widespread; for large communications carriers and service providers, they are the de facto standard. Using this standard, they can provide complex services such as IP services, ATM services, classical telephony services, and digital link leases. The users of services other than IP communicate directly to the required layer of the communications carrier network (i.e., ATM, telephone, SDH, or DWDM).

However, for a long time IP networks did not have such a complicated multilayered structure. A classical IP network consisted from routers directly connected by communication links. Such networks did not provide QoS support, because the applications of 1980s generated traffic that was not sensitive to delays. After arrival of multilayered IP WANs, it became necessary to distinguish these two types of networks; therefore, classical IP networks were called "pure" IP networks.

> Pure IP networks also find application. Their name emphasizes that there is no other packet-switched network below the IP layer (such as ATM or Frame Relay), and IP routers are connected directly by leased lines (physical or PDH/SDH/DWDM connections).

The structure of a pure IP network is shown in Figure 22.2.

In such networks, digital links are built by the infrastructure of the two previous layers as before. These links are directly used by the interfaces of the IP routers without employing any intermediate layer. If the IP router uses channels created within an SDH/SONET network, this variant is called **packet over SONET (POS)**.

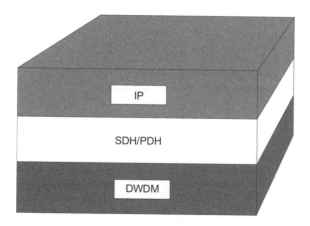

Figure 22.2 Structure of a pure IP network

Pure IP networks can be successfully used for transmitting delay-sensitive traffic of contemporary applications in the following cases:

- The IP network operates in the underloaded mode; therefore, services of all types are oversubscribed and need not wait in queues. The network, consequently, does not require QoS support.
- The IP layer ensures QoS support on its own by using IntServ or DiffServ mechanisms.

For IP routers in the pure IP WAN model to use digital links, some data link-layer protocol must operate on these links.

Several data link-layer protocols have been developed for point-to-point WAN connections. These protocols have built-in procedures for operation in WANs, including:

- *Data flow management.*
- *Mutual authentication for remote devices.* This feature is often required for protecting the network against a "false" router that sniffs and redirects the traffic for eavesdropping.
- *Coordination of the data exchange parameters* at the data link and physical layers. Before starting data exchange for remote communication, when two devices are located in different cities, it is useful to coordinate several parameters, such as the maximum size of the data field (MTU).

Nowadays, IP uses two of the existing point-to-point protocols: the high-level data link control (HDLC) protocol and the point-to-point protocol (PPP). There also exists an obsolete protocol, the serial line Internet protocol (SLIP), which for a long time was the main protocol used by individual clients for accessing IP networks through telephone lines. It has been replaced by PPP, which successfully operates both on backbones and on access channels.

Besides the protocols developed for point-to-point WAN connections, WAN IP routers use one of the high-speed Ethernet variants on leased lines. These may be Fast Ethernet, Gigabit Ethernet, or 10G Ethernet. These Ethernet protocols do not support the procedures listed previously. Naturally, these procedures are useful for WANs; however, the popularity of Ethernet in LANs is a factor that tips the scale in their favor.

22.2.2 Protocols of the HDLC Family

The High-Level Data Link Control (HDLC) is the family of protocols that create data link layers for the following networks:
- LAP-B — the protocol that creates the data link layer of X.25 networks
- LAP-D — for ISDN networks
- LAP-M — for asynchronous and synchronous modems
- LAP-F — for Frame Relay networks

The thing that should be noticed about HDLC is its complexity. It can operate in several modes different from one another, and supports both point-to-point and point-to-multipoint connections. HDLC also provides several different functional roles for communicating workstations. Readers interested in detailed description of the operation of this protocol can find it in popular and widely known books. Here we cover only the basic HDLC functions supported by all members of this protocol family.

HDLC supports three modes of logical connection, differing by the roles of communicating devices. We cover only one of them — *Asynchronous Balance Mode* (*ABM*),

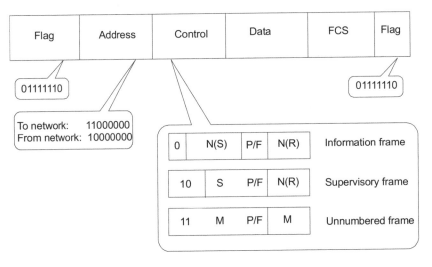

Figure 22.3 HDLC frame

because this mode is the one used by IP routers. In the ABM mode both devices have equal rights. They exchange the frames classified as command frames and response frames.

The format of the HDLC frame is shown in Figure 22.3.

HDLC frame contains the following fields:

- *Flags.* The HDLC frame is enclosed between opening and closing flags with the code 01111110. Using this flag, the receiver determines the starting and ending points of the frame. This technique eliminates the use of the frame length field in the HDLC frame. However, another problem arises when this technique is used — how to distinguish data bytes having the value 01111110, from the flag byte. Here is where the **bit-stuffing** technique becomes very helpful. Bit stuffing operates only during transmission of the frame's data field. If the transmitter discovers that five binary ones have been transmitted sequentially, it automatically inserts a zero into the sequence of bits being transmitted (even when this sequence of five ones is followed by a zero). Thus, the sequence 01111110 can never appear in the frame's data field. A similar design is implemented on the receiver; however, it carries out an inverse function. When a zero is detected after five sequential ones, it is automatically removed from the frame's data field.

- *Data field.* The HDLC frame's data field is intended for transmitting packets of higher-layer protocols over the network. These might be IP, IPX, AppleTalk, DECnet, or, on rare occasions, application-layer protocols when they encapsulate their messages directly into the data link-layer frames. In supervisory frames and some unnumbered frames, the data field can be missing.

- *Address.* These 1 or 2 bytes carry out the normal function of choosing the required device out of several possible ones (only in point-to-multipoint configurations). In the point-to-point configuration, the HDLC address is used for designating the frame transmission direction — from network to user device or vice versa. Obviously, this address function makes sense only when transmitting frames through UNI.

- *Control field.* This field has a length of 1 or 2 bytes, and its structure depends on the type of frame being transmitted. Frame type is defined by the first bits of the control field: 0 — *information frame*, 01 — *supervisory frame*, and 11 — *unnumbered frame*. The P/F bit is included into the structure of the control field of all types of frames. This bit (P/F stands for Poll/Final) is differently used in command frames and response frames. For example, if the receiver receives from the transmitter a command frame with the P bit set to 1, it must immediately answer with the response frame by setting the F bit to 1.

Now consider the structure and goals of different types of frames in more details.

- *Unnumbered frames* are intended for establishing and terminating logical connections as well as delivering information about errors. Unnumbered frames are used at the stage of establishing a connection between devices. The *M* field of unnumbered frames defines several types of commands used by these devices when establishing a connection. Here are some example commands:

- *SABME (Set asynchronous balanced mode extended)* — This command is the request for establishing a connection. Extended mode means using 2-byte fields for controlling frames of other types.
- *UA (Unnumbered acknowledgment)* — This command establishes or terminates a connection.
- *REST (Resetting connection)* — This command requests connection termination.

■ *Supervisory frames* are intended for passing commands and responses in the context of the established logical connection, including sending requests for the retransmission of corrupted information blocks. The list of supervisory frames includes the following:

- *Reject (REJ)* — this command is used as a negative acknowledgment of the receiver.
- *Receiver not ready (RNR)* — this command is used to slow the frame flow arriving to the receiver.
- *Receiver ready (RR)* — this command is often used as a positive acknowledgment when there is no data flow from receiver to transmitter.

■ *Information frames* are intended for transmitting user information. In the course of the transmission of the information blocks, they are numbered according to the sliding window algorithm.

After establishing the connection, data and positive acknowledgments are passed in the information frames. The logical HDLC channel is *duplex,* which means that information frames and positive acknowledgments can be transmitted in both directions. If there is no data flow in the inverse direction, or if it is necessary to pass a negative acknowledgment, then supervisory frames are used.

To ensure reliability, HDLC uses a *sliding window* of 7 frames (if the control field size is 2 bytes) or 127 frames (if the data field is equal to 2 bytes), and numbers from 0 to 127 are used cyclically for their numbering. To support the sliding window algorithm, information frames outgoing from the sender station provide two fields:

■ $N(S)$ field for specifying the number of the sent frame

■ $N(R)$ field for specifying the number of the frame that the station expects to receive next from its partner

Assume for distinctness that station A has sent an information frame with some values $N_A(S)$ and $N_A(R)$ to station B. If, in response to this frame, a frame from station B arrives, where the number of the frame sent by this station $N_B(S)$ matches with the number of frame expected by station A — $N_A(R)$, then the transmission is considered correct. If station A receives the response frame, where the number of the sent frame $N_B(S)$ does not match the number of expected frame $N_A(R)$, then station A discards this frame and sends the REJ negative acknowledgment with the number $N_A(R)$. Having received this negative acknowledgment, station B must retransmit the frame with the number $N_A(R)$, and *all* the frames with larger numbers, which it has sent already, using the sliding window algorithm.

When there is no data flow from receiver to transmitter, the *RR* supervisory command with the set *N(R)* field is used as positive acknowledgment. If the sliding window mechanism is unable to control the flow of frames, the *RNR* command is used, which requires the transmitter to suspend transmission until it receives the *RR* command.

22.2.3 Point-to-Point Protocol

Point-to-Point Protocol (PPP) is the Internet standard. Similar to HDLC, it also represents the entire family of protocol, which includes, in particular:
- **Link control protocol** (LCP).
- **Network control protocol** (NCP)
- **Multi Link PPP** *(MLPPP)*
- **Password Authentication Protocol** (PAP)
- **Challenge handshake authentication protocol** (CHAP)

NOTE   *When PPP was developed, the HDLC frame format was taken as the prototype and complemented with several new fields. The fields of PPP are encapsulated in the HDLC frame data field. Later, other standards appeared that encapsulate the PPP frame into the frames of Frame Relay and other WAN protocols. Although PPP can work with HDLC frames, in contrast to HDLC, it does not not support procedures for ensuring reliability of frame transmission and frame flow control.*

The main difference between PPP and other data link-layer protocols is that it achieves coordinated operation of different devices by using a special **negotiation procedure**. During this procedure, the devices exchange various parameters, such as line quality, an authentication protocol, and encapsulated network-layer protocols.

In a corporate network, end systems often differ in the sizes of buffers for the temporary storage of packets, the limitations on packet size, and the list of supported network-layer protocols. The physical link connecting end nodes might range from a low-speed analog line to a high-speed digital line with various QoS levels.

The protocol according to which connection parameters are accepted is the *link control protocol* (LCP). To handle all possible situations, PPP provides the set of default parameters that take into account all standard configurations. When establishing a connection, two communicating devices first try to use these default settings. Each end node specifies its capabilities and requirements. Then, based on this information, connection parameters are adopted that are satisfactory for both parties.

Negotiations between protocols may or may not result in an agreement on a specific parameter. For example, one node may suggest 1,000 bytes as MTU. The other node may reject this proposal and, in turn, suggest 1,500 bytes. The 1,500 bytes may be rejected by the first node. Thus, the negotiation procedure will fail after the timeout expires.

One of the most important parameters of the PPP connection is the *authentication mode*. For authentication, PPP provides either the *password authentication protocol*, which is used by default, or the *challenge handshake authentication protocol*, which does not transmit the password through a communications link, thus ensuring stronger network security. Users can add other authentication algorithms, and choose header and data compression algorithms.

Multiprotocol support is the capability of PPP to support several network-layer protocols has justified the wide use of PPP as a de facto standard. In contrast to SLIP, which is capable of carrying only IP packets, or LAP-B, which can carry only X.25 packets, PPP works with many network-layer protocols — including IP, Novell IPX, AppleTalk, DECnet, Xerox Network System, Banyan VINES, and OSI — as well as with data link-layer LAN protocols.

Every network-layer protocol is configured individually using the appropriate *NCP*. The configuration procedure first ascertains that this protocol will be used in the current PPP session then negotiates certain parameters of this protocol. The largest number of parameters is set for IP. The list of these parameters includes the IP addresses of the communicating nodes, the IP addresses of DNS servers, and the compression of IP header. For each protocol for the configuration of parameters of a specific higher-layer protocol, additionally to the general name NCP, other names are used. Such protocols are named using the name of the appropriate protocol supplemented by the control protocol (CP) abbreviation: IPCP, IPXCP, etc.

Protocol extensibility. Extensibility is interpreted as the possibility of including new protocols into the PPP stack as well as the possibility of using custom user protocols instead of the default ones. This allows an optimal PPP configuration to be created for each specific situation.

One of the most attractive PPP capabilities is the use of several physical links to create one logical channel, also known as channel trunking. This capability is implemented by an additional protocol known as *multilink PPP*.

22.2.4 Leased Lines Used by IP Routers

The method through which a leased line is used by an IP router is presented in Figure 22.4. To connect the router port to the leased line, it is necessary to use the appropriate type of DCE device. This device is required for transforming a router's physical interface to the physical-layer protocol used by a leased line, for instance, V.35 to T1.

If the leased line is an analog line, then it is necessary to use a modem as DCE device. When dealing with a digital line, then the data service unit/channel service unit (DSU/CSU) device must be used.

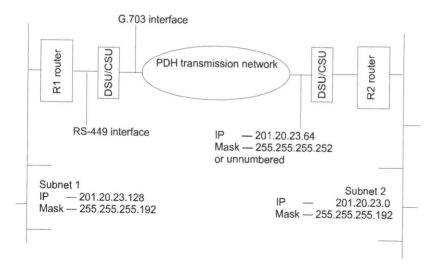

G.703 interface

R1 router

DSU/CSU

PDH transmission network

DSU/CSU

R2 router

RS-449 interface

IP   — 201.20.23.64
Mask — 255.255.255.252
or unnumbered

Subnet 1
IP   — 201.20.23.128
Mask — 255.255.255.192

Subnet 2
IP   —   201.20.23.0
Mask — 255.255.255.192

Figure 22.4 Connecting IP networks using a leased line

The router's port may include a built-in DCE device. For example, when the router uses an SDH channel, it usually has a built-in port with an SDH interface for a specific STM-N rate.

Built-in PDH/SDH ports may or may not support the internal frame structure of these technologies. When the port can distinguish subframes that make up the frame — for example, individual time slots of the E1 frame or individual VC-12 virtual containers (2 Mbps) that form the STM-1 frame — and can use them as separate physical subchannels, then such port is called a *channelized port*. Each such channel is assigned an individual IP address. If this is not the case, the entire port is considered one physical link with one IP address.

In the example illustrated by Figure 22.4, the connection between two routers is established using a digital E1 channel created in the PDH transmission network. To connect to the channel, the router uses a DSU/CSU device with an internal RS-449 interface and an external G.703 interface, which is defined as an access interface to PDH channels.

After routers are connected to the leased line and to the LAN, they must be configured. A leased line is a separate IP subnet like the Network 1 and Network 2 LANs connected by it. This subnet also needs an IP address from the address range managed by the administrator of this internet. In Figure 22.4, the leased line is assigned the 201.20.23.64 subnet address. This subnet includes two nodes according to the mask 255.255.255.252.

Interfaces of routers connected by a leased line must not necessarily be assigned IP addresses to the leased line. Such a router interface is called **unnumbered**. Actually, the routers will get them by sending packets of a routing protocol (RIP or OSPF) through the leased line. ARP is not used on the leased line because hardware addresses have no practical meaning on the leased line.

22.3 IP OVER ATM OR FRAME RELAY

KEY WORDS: IP over ATM/FR, topology of virtual circuits, overlay network, logical interface (subinterface), QoS, configuring the Router Interface, traffic of different classes Q.2931

22.3.1 Communication between IP and ATM Layers

When building an IP network over ATM or Frame Relay, an ATM or Frame Relay network operates between the data link layer and the IP layer. Because the rates at which a Frame Relay network operates usually do not exceed 2 Mbps,[1] and because delay and delay vari-

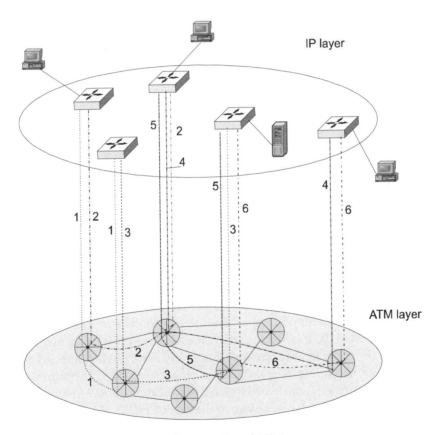

Figure 22.5 Communication between IP and ATM

---

[1] The latest versions of Frame Relay standards have raised the rate limit to 622 Mbps.

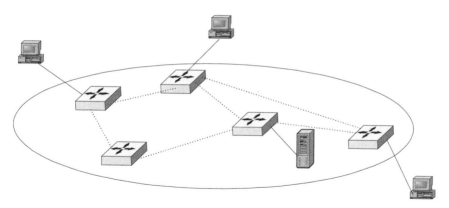

Figure 22.6 Topology of links between routers

ation levels are not included into the list of QoS parameters supported by this technology, ATM is most frequently used as the intermediate backbone layer.

Communication between the IP layer and the ATM layer is shown in Figure 22.5.

In an ATM network, there are six virtual circuits connecting router ports. Each router port must support ATM technology as an end node. After the virtual circuits are established, the routers can use them as physical links to send data to the port of the next router (in relation to the virtual circuit).

Virtual circuits form a network with its own topology inside the ATM network. The topology of virtual circuits corresponding to the network shown in Figure 22.5 is presented in Figure 22.6. The ATM network is transparent for IP routers because they do not need to know anything about the physical connections between the ports of the ATM switches. The IP network is an overlay network in relation to ATM.

22.3.2 Configuring the Router Interface

For IP to work correctly, it must know the mapping between the IP addresses of neighbors and ATM virtual circuit numbers, which can be used to reach the required IP address. In other words, it must know the ARP table. In this case, such a table is not created automatically by sending ARP broadcast requests. On the contrary, such a table must be created manually. The administrator of the IP network must configure each interface of the router by specifying the mapping table for all virtual circuit numbers coming to and going from this interface. At the same time, each physical interface is represented as a set of logical interfaces (or subinterfaces), which have individual IP addresses.

For example, in Cisco Systems routers, the configuration of the logical interface corresponding to the virtual circuit with the VPI/VCI address 0/36 appears as follows:

```
pvc 0/36
protocol ip 10.2.1.1
```

After accomplishing this command, the router will know that when it needs to send the packet to the 10.2.1.1 `NextHop` address, it will have to split the packet into the sequence of ATM cells (using the SAR function of the ATM interface) and send them all using the 0/36 PVC.

If a multilayer ATM/IP network must transmit the traffic of different classes and observe the QoS parameters for each class, then neighboring routers must be connected by several virtual circuits, one circuit for each class. A packet classification policy must be specified for each router that shows each transmitted packet belongs to a specific class. Packets of a specific class are sent to the appropriate virtual circuit, which ensures the required QoS parameters for the traffic. To guarantee that these parameters are observed, it is necessary to first carry out traffic engineering for the ATM network. To solve this problem, it is necessary to choose the routes for each virtual circuit so that they observe the average rates of the flows being transmitted through the virtual circuits. The load of each interface of each ATM switch must not exceed the predefined threshold value that guarantees for each traffic class an acceptable delay level.

An overlay IP network can also use the switched virtual circuit mode to transmit IP traffic. This mode is suitable for unstable flows that exist during short periods. Creating a PVC infrastructure for such flows is inefficient because they will remain idle most of the time. To enable routers to use a switched virtual circuit mode, it is necessary to specify the mapping of the IP addresses to the ATM addresses of router interfaces (e.g., the ATM addresses of the network's end points).

Similar to the previous case, this address resolution function is manually carried out by an administrator. One possible variant of such a mapping for Cisco routers appears as follows:

```
Map-list a
ip 10.1.0.3 atm-nsap
33.3333.33.333333.3333.3333.3333.3333.3333.3333.3333.33
```

If such a mapping has been specified, the router, to send a packet to the `NextHop` address 10.1.0.3, must have previously used the Q.2931 protocol to establish a switched virtual circuit with the address 33.3333.33.333333.3333.3333.3333.3333.3333.3333.3333.33. Then, having automatically received from this protocol a VPI/VCI address, the router sends there the cells into which the source packet was split. The next router's interface, having received all cells, combines them into the source packet and passes this packet to IP.

If a switched virtual circuit must pass the traffic with certain required QoS parameters, these parameters are passed according to the Q.2931 protocol, which takes them into account when choosing the route for the virtual circuit.

The IP-over-ATM structure is popular among communications carriers, which provide their services according to the service level agreement (SLA).

22.4 MULTIPROTOCOL LABEL SWITCHING

KEY WORDS: MultiProtocol Label Switching (MPLS), Label Switch Router (LSR), IP switching, tag switching, label forwarding unit, forwarding table, Label Distribution Protocol (LDP), Label Switching Path (LSP), Label Switch Edge Router (LER), penultimate device, MPLS VPN, MPLS IGP, Traffic Engineering, Forwarding Equivalence Class (FEC)

Most network specialists consider **MultiProtocol Label Switching** (MPLS) one of the most promising transport technologies.

> This technology combines the virtual circuit technique with the TCP/IP stack functionality.
> This combination is achieved because the same network device, the **label switch router (LSR)**, simultaneously plays the role of a classical IP router and a virtual circuit switch. However, this is not a mechanical combination of two devices. On the contrary, this is a close integration in which the functions of both devices are used together and mutually complement each other.

Multiprotocol support in MPLS consists in that it can use not only TCP/IP routing protocols but also routing protocols of any other stack, such as IPX/SPX. In this case, instead of routing protocols such as RIP IP, OSPF, and IS-IS, MPLS would use RIP IPX or NLSP; the general architecture of the LSR would remain the same.

22.4.1 Combining Switching and Routing within the Same Device

Such an idea as combining switching and routing within the same device was first implemented in the mid-1990s by *Ipsilon*, which started to manufacture combined IP/ATM devices. These devices implemented the new **IP switching** technology, which solved the problem of inefficient transmission of data flows with short durations using the previously described switched virtual circuit technology. To transmit the packets of short-term flows through the network of ATM switches without the time-consuming procedure of previously establishing a virtual circuit, Ipsilon suggested building IP routing units into all ATM switches. These units built routing tables using standard TCP/IP routing protocols such as RIP, OSPF, or IS-IS.

Transmission of packets belonging to short-term flows in Ipsilon networks was carried out as follows. The packet from the sender node arrived to the combined IP/ATM device, where it was split into ATM cells. After that, every cell, according to the IP switching technology, was passed between IP/ATM devices, from device to device, and then to the receiver along the route defined by normal IP routing tables stored in these devices.

> The standard virtual connection typical of the ATM technology is not established in this case; therefore, short-term IP flows are transmitted significantly faster. IP/ATM devices transmit long-term flows using the virtual circuit technique traditional for ATM.

> Because network topology is the same for both the IP and the ATM protocol, the same routing protocol can be used for both parts of the combined device.

To implement this technology, Ipsilon built proprietary protocols into IP/ATM devices. These protocols are responsible for recognizing data flow duration and establishing virtual circuits for long-term flows. These protocols were published in the form of Internet drafts, but they did not receive the status of Internet standards.

The IP switching technology was developed for use within a communications carrier's network, which receives IP traffic at the boundaries with other networks and transmits it using its own backbone at an accelerated rate. This is an important property because it allows this technology to be used *independently* of other ISPs and the carrier to remain part of an IP network from the outside world's point of view.

The IP switching technology was immediately noticed by communications carriers and quickly became popular. *Cisco Systems* further developed Ipsilon's initiative by creating the newer **tag switching** technology. Tag switching became a considerable advance in the field of merging IP with the virtual circuit technique. However, like IP switching, it did not gain the status of an open standard.

Based on these proprietary technologies, the IETF workgroup that included specialists from different companies developed the MPLS technology.

22.4.2 LSR and Data Forwarding Table

> The main principle of the predecessors of MPLS was preserved: MPLS uses routing protocols to discover network topology. It also uses the virtual circuit technique to forward data within the limits of the MPLS network of a single provider.

The principle of combining the protocols of different technologies is illustrated in Figures 22.7 and 22.8. The first illustration shows the simplified architecture of a standard IP router, and the second one shows the architecture of a combined LSR device supporting the MPLS technology.

Because the LSR carries out all functions of the IP router, it includes all its units. To support MPLS functions, the LSR also includes the range of auxiliary units related to control plane and data plane functions.

The **label forwarding unit** transmits IP packets on the basis of a label instead of the destination IP address. When making a decision about the next hop, the label forwarding unit uses the **forwarding table**, which is similar to the forwarding tables of other technologies based on the virtual circuit technique. An example of such forwarding table is outlined in Table 22.1.

You probably noticed that this table is slightly different from the generalized forwarding table covered in *Chapter 21*. Instead of the *Output interface*, this table contains the *NextHop* field, and instead of the *Output label* field, it contains the *Actions* field. In most cases of MPLS frame processing, these fields are used in the same way as the corresponding

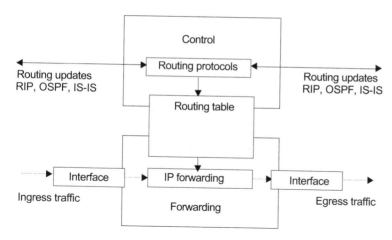

Figure 22.7 IP router architecture

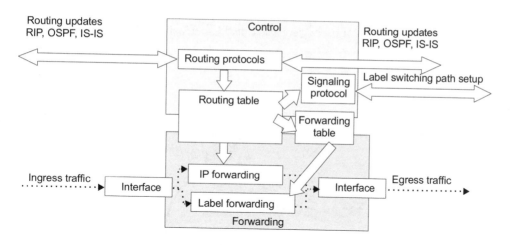

Figure 22.8 LSR architecture

Table 22.1 Example of an MPLS forwarding table

Input port	Input label	NextHop	Actions
S0	245	S1	256
S0	27	S2	45
...	...	...	...

fields of the generalized forwarding table. This means that *NextHop* fields are used as the interface number to which it is necessary to pass the frame, and the value contained in the *Actions* field is the new label value. The new names of these fields mean that MPLS has improved and generalized the operating principles of all preceding virtual circuit technologies. Therefore, the field values became more universal. Sometimes they are also used for other purposes, which will be covered later in this chapter.

MPLS forwarding tables for each LSR are formed using the *signaling protocol*, which in MPLS is known under the name of the **Label Distribution Protocol (LDP)**. This signaling protocol is functionally similar to the ATM and Frame Relay signaling protocols.

By creating forwarding tables on LSRs, LDP establishes virtual path, which in the MPLS technology has a special name: **Label Switching Path (LSP)**.

22.4.3 Label Switching Paths

Figure 22.9 shows an MPLS network communicating with several IP networks.

Edge LSRs in the MPLS technology are also called **Label Switch Edge Routers (LERs)**.

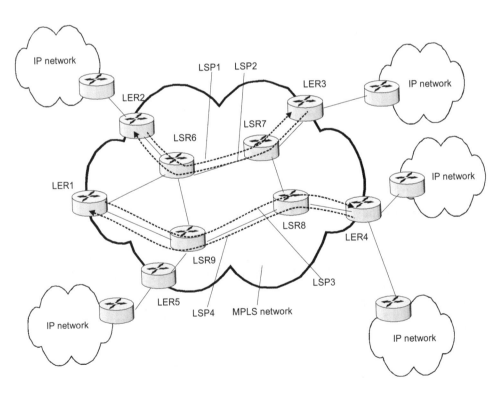

Figure 22.9 MPLS network

An LER accepts traffic from other networks in the form of standard IP packets, supplies this traffic with labels and sends it along the corresponding LSP to another LER. Every intermediate LSR forwards the packet on the basis of its label instead of the destination IP address. Like other technologies that use the virtual circuit technique, the label has a local value within the limits of each LSR. When the packet is passed from the input interface to the output interface, the label changes its value.

In MPLS, LSPs are established *beforehand*, according to the topology of existing internetwork connections, in contrast to the IP switching technology where they were established when creating a long-term data flow. An LSP is a *unidirectional* virtual circuit; therefore, to transmit traffic between two LERs, it is necessary to establish at least two LSPs, one in each direction. Figure 22.9 shows two pairs of LSPs, with one pair connecting LER2 to LER3 and the second pair connecting LER1 to LER4. Obviously, this is not sufficient for ensuring connectivity among all networks. For this purpose, it is necessary to have a fully connected topology of LSPs between LERs. This topology takes place in real-world MPLS networks and is not shown in Figure 22.9 only because it is too bulky for graphical representation.

The output (egress) LER removes the label from the IP packet and passes it to the next network in a standard form. Thus, the operation of the MPLS technology remains invisible to all other IP networks.

Usually MPLS networks implement an improved version of the above-described packet-processing algorithm. This improved version consists in that removal of a label is carried out by the next to last (*penultimate*) device, rather than by the egress LER. Actually, after the penultimate device determines the next hop on the basis of the label value, the label in the MPLS frame is no longer needed. The last device, e.g., egress LER, will forward the packet on the basis of the IP address. This small modification to the frame-forwarding algorithm allows the elimination of one operation over MPLS frame. Without it, egress LER must first remove the label, and only after that carry out lookup of the IP routing table.

22.4.4 MPLS Header and Data Link Technologies

An MPLS header consists of several fields (Figure 22.10):

- *Label* — 20 bits. The *Label* field is used for choosing the corresponding LSP.
- *Time To Live* (TTL) — 8 bits that duplicate the similar field of the IP packet. It is necessary to enable LSRs to discard misforwarded packets only on the basis of information in the MPLS header without requiring them to access the IP header.
- *CoS* (or *Experimental*) — 3 bits. Initially, this field was reserved for future use. More recently, it has been used mainly for specifying the class of traffic that requires a specific level of QoS.
- *S* — 1 bit. This is the indicator of the bottom of the label stack.

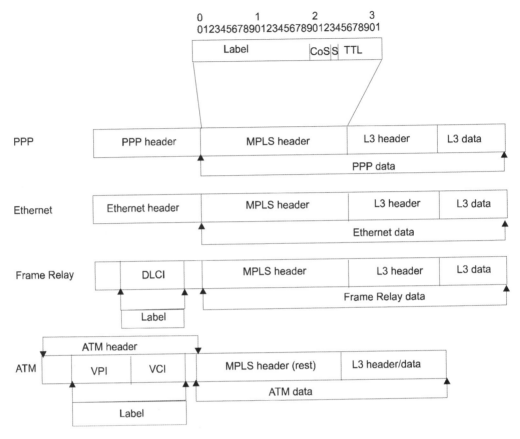

Figure 22.10 MPLS label formats

The concept of the label stack will be covered in more detail in the next section of this chapter. For the moment, to clarify the mechanism of communication between MPLS and data link-layer technologies, consider the situation in which the MPLS header contains only one label.

As shown in Figure 22.10, MPLS technology supports several types of the frames: PPP, Ethernet, Frame Relay, and ATM. This does not mean that any of these technologies operates below the MPLS layer. This only means that MPLS uses the frame formats of these technologies for encapsulating network-layer packets (today, these are practically always IP packets).

Frame forwarding in MPLS networks is carried out on the basis of the MPLS label and the LSP technique, not on the basis of the addressing information and the technique used by the technologies whose frame format is used by MPLS. For instance, if MPLS uses the Ethernet frame format, it does not use the destination and source MAC addresses for frame forwarding even though this information is in the appropriate fields of the Ethernet frame.[2]

For PPP, Ethernet, and Frame Relay frames, the MPLS header is placed between the original header and the header of the Layer 3 packet. ATM cells are processed differently. MPLS technology uses the existing *VPI/VCI* fields in the headers of these cells for virtual connection labels.

The *VPI/VCI* fields are used only for storing the *Label* field. The remaining part of the MPLS header, including the *CoS*, *S*, and *TTL* fields, is stored in the data field of the ATM cell. It is not used when transmitting cells by ATM switches supporting MPLS.

Later on, when considering for distinctness, it will be assumed that MPLS/PPP frame format is used.

22.4.5 Label Stack

The presence of the **label stack** is one of the features characteristic of MPLS. The concept of the label stack is a further development of the concept of two-layer addressing of virtual paths using the *VPI/VCI* labels adopted in ATM.

The label stack allows a system of aggregated LSPs to be created with any number of hierarchical levels. To support this function, the MPLS frame that travels along hierarchically organized paths must include such a number of MPLS headers that corresponds to the number of levels in the path hierarchy. Recall that MPLS header of each level must have its own set of fields, including *Label*, *CoS*, *TTL*, and *S*. This sequence is organized as a stack, so there is always one label located on the top of the stack and one label located on the bottom. The latter is indicated by the $S = 1$ attribute. The following operations can be carried out over labels, which are specified in the *Actions* field of the forwarding table:

■ *Push* — Push the label into the stack. If the stack is empty, this operation corresponds to simply assigning a label to the packet. If the stack already contains one or more labels, the new label shifts the existing labels down the stack, and takes the place at the stack top.

■ *Swap* — Replace the current label by another one.

■ *Pop* — Pop the top label from the stack. As a result of this operation, all the other labels of the stack move one level higher.

---

[2] The only exception is MPLS/Ethernet in a shared medium variant, in which ports are connected according to the "point-to-multipoint" design and the number of the output port does not provide information sufficient for determining the next hop. In this case, the destination MAC address is used with the label for packet forwarding. However, such a variant can be encountered very rarely nowadays with a domination of switched Ethernet, therefore, we will not cover this variant here. The use of MAC addresses with the output interface number explains why the *Output interface* field was renamed *Next Hop*.

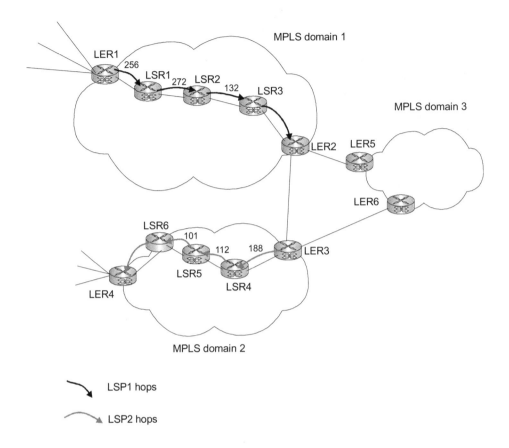

Figure 22.11 LSP1 and LSP2 paths built in MPLS domains 1 and 2

MPLS frame forwarding is always carried out on the basis of the label on the stack top. Consider the forwarding of an MPLS frame in the example of *one-level* LSP hierarchy shown in Figure 22.11.

The network comprises three MPLS domains. Figure 22.11 shows path LSP1 within MPLS domain 1, and another path, LSP2, for MPLS domain 2. LSP1 connects LER1 and LER2 and passes through LSR1, LSR2, and LSR3. Assume that 256 is the initial label of LSP1. This label was assigned to the packet by the ingress device LER1. Based on this label, the packet is supplied to LSR1, which defines the new value of the label — 272 — on the basis of its forwarding table, and then passes the packet to the input of LSR2. LSR2 acts in a similar way. It assigns the packet a new value of the label — 132 — and passes it to the input of LSR3. LSR3, being the penultimate device in LSP1, carries out the Pop operation and removes the label from the stack. LER2 forwards the packet further on the basis of IP address.

LSP2 connects LER3 and LER4, passing through LSR4, LSR5, and LSR6. This path is defined by the following sequence of labels: 188, 112, 101.

To transmit IP packets on the basis of the MPLS technique not only within each domain but also between domains (for example, between LER1 and LER4), two different solutions can be chosen.

- The first solution is to establish a *one-level* LSP between LER1 and LER4, connecting LSP1 and LSP2 (which in this case form a single path). This seemingly easy solution is inefficient when MPLS domains belong to different providers. Practical experience has shown that this solution lacks scalability, since it does not allow providers to act independently.

- The second solution is more promising. It consists in applying a multilevel approach to connecting two MPLS domains, possibly but not necessarily belonging to different providers.

In this example, a second-layer LSP, LSP3, was created to connect LER1 and LER4. This path defines the sequence of interdomain hops instead of hops between the internal LSRs of each domain. Thus, LSP3 comprises the hop sequence LER1–LER2–LER3–LER4 and does not define the exact path within *domains* 1 and 2. In this respect, the multilevel approach of MPLS is conceptually close to that of BGP, which defines the path between ASs.

Consider in more detail how MPLS operates when dealing with two levels of LSPs (Figure 22.12).

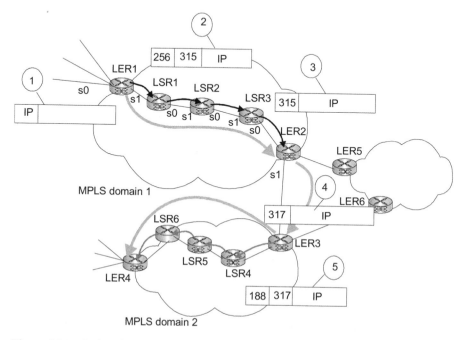

Figure 22.12 Using the label stack in the path hierarchy

LER1 is the starting point for two paths — LSP1 and LSP3. The following record in the forwarding table of LER1 ensures this (Table 22.2).

Table 22.2 Fragment of the LER1 forwarding table

Input interface	Label	NextHop	Actions
...	...	...	...
S0	–	S1	315 Push 256
...	...	...	...

IP packets arriving to the S0 input interface of LER1 are forwarded to the S1 output interface. At the output interface, an MPLS header is created that consists of one top-level label, 315 (LSP3), which is currently the label that resided on top of the stack. Then, this label is pushed to the stack bottom and another label, 256 (related to LSP1), becomes the top label. Finally, the MPLS frame with label 256 arrives to the S1 output interface of LER1 and goes to the input of LSR1.

LSR1 processes the frame on the basis of label 256 according to its forwarding table, which includes the following record (Table 22.3).

Table 22.3 Fragment of the LSR1 forwarding table

Input interface	Label	NextHop	Actions
...	...	...	...
S0	256	S1	272
...	...	...	...

Label 256, which resides on top of the stack, is replaced by label 272. Note that LSR1 ignores the presence of label 315, which is not on the stack top when an MPLS frame is forwarded. LSR2 proceeds the same way; it just swaps the label value to 132, and forwards the frame to the next device along the path, LSR3.

The operation of LSR3 is somewhat different from that of LSR1 and LSR2, because it is the *penultimate* LSR for LSP1. Its forwarding table looks as follows (Table 22.4).

Table 22.4 Fragment of the LSR3 forwarding table

Input interface	Label	NextHop	Actions
...	...	...	...
S0	256	S1	272
...	...	...	...

According to the record, LSR3 carries out the `Pop` operation on the label stack. It removes label 132, belonging to LSP1, so that label 315, belonging to LSP3, becomes the top label of the stack. Such behavior of the penultimate LSR on the path is typical for arrangements other than a multilayer path organization. The operation of label popping by the penultimate device is known as *Penultimate Hop Popping* (*PHP*).

LER2 forwards the frame that arrived to its S0 interface on the basis of the following record of its routing table (Table 22.5).

Table 22.5 Fragment of the LER2 forwarding table

Input interface	Label	NextHop	Actions
...	...	...	...
S0	315	S1	317
			Push
			188
...	...	...	...

LER2 first replaces the value 315 of the label of LSP3 with 317, then it pushes the label to the stack bottom and places label 188 on the top of the stack. Label 256 is the LSP2 label of the internal path within domain 2. Frame forwarding along LSP2 is carried out in the similar way.

This two-level model can easily be extended to any number of the paths of the level hierarchy.

22.4.6 MPLS Application Areas

Earlier in this chapter, you considered the main principles that form the foundation for MPLS technology. For the moment, MPLS technology has several areas of practical application in which these principles are complemented by specific mechanisms and protocols required for obtaining the necessary functionality. The following applications of MPLS are the most widespread:

- **MPLS IGP** — Here, MPLS is used only for *accelerated network-layer packet forwarding.* In this case, packets travel along the routes chosen by standard interior gateway protocols (IGPs), which gave their name to this area of MPLS application.
- **MPLS TE** — In this case, MPLS LSPs are chosen for *solving traffic engineering (TE) problems* on the basis of modified routing protocols. MPLS TE not only ensures a rational and balanced load on all resources of the provider's network but also creates a solid foundation for providing transport services with guaranteed QoS parameters.
- **MPLS VPN** — This area of MPLS application allows the provider to offer *VPN services* on the basis of traffic segregation without mandatory data encryption.

In this chapter, we consider additional mechanisms of the first two areas of MPLS application. MPLS VPNs will be covered in *Chapter 24* along with other types of VPNs.

Note that all three types of MPLS can be used within the same network, providing users with combined services.

22.4.7 MPLS Interior Gateway Protocol

The main goal of MPLS IGP is the accelerated forwarding of packets through the provider network by replacing routing by switching. Therefore, this area of MPLS application is also called **accelerated MPLS switching**.

When using MPLS IGP LSPs are created according to the existing topology of IP networks, and do not depend on the intensity of the traffic between these networks. This property is illustrated by Figure 22.13.

LSPs of MPLS IGP are created beforehand. Thus, the LSP required for transmitting a data flow must already exist when this data flow is generated. IGP LSPs are established automatically, and a network administrator does not need to interfere with this process. The source information for establishing an LSP is collected from the routing tables of all LSRs existing in an MPLS-enabled provider's network. For each destination network registered in any of the routing tables, an LSP is created. To reduce the number of such paths, each LSP can serve the traffic to several destination networks. This means that IGP LSPs serve aggregate traffic flows, and the aggregation attribute is the match (full or partial) of the routes along which traffic flows travel through the provider's network.

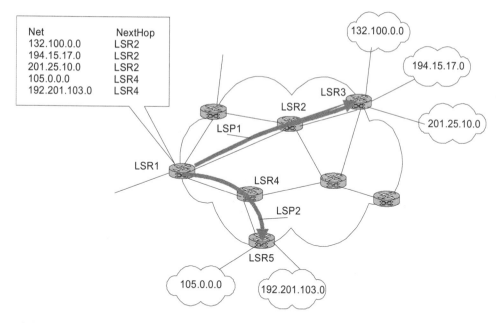

Figure 22.13 Establishing an LSP using LDP

All LSRs of the network support the **label distribution protocol** (LDP), which belongs to the class of *signaling protocols*. Each LSR also has to support one of the standard IGPs, such as RIP, IS-IS, or OSPF.

As a result of the operation of routing protocols, or after manual configuration of the routing tables by the network administrator, a new record about a new destination network can appear in the LSR routing table. An LSP is not yet established in the provider's network. In this case, this LSR automatically initiates the procedure of establishing a new LSP using LDP.

To create a new LSP, the initiating LSRs use standard packet forwarding algorithm based on routing tables. Assume, for example, that LSR1 detects that a new record has appeared in its routing table for the destination network 132.100.0.0 with LSR2 specified as the next hop. At the same time, there is no virtual path to this network, because forwarding table does not contain an appropriate record. In this case, LSR1 initiates virtual path creation. To achieve this, it sends the *Request LDP* message to the LSR2 device. In this message, it specifies the IP of the destination network to which it is necessary to establish a new LSP. LSR2 receives this message and processes it on the basis of information contained in its routing and forwarding tables. If LSR2 also detects that it has no LSP for network 132.100.0.0, it passes the LDP message to the next LSR, which is specified as the next hop to network 132.100.0.0 in its routing table. In the example shown in Figure 22.13, the role of this device is played by LSR3, where the LSP must terminate since the next hop is beyond the limits of the provider's network.

NOTE

A question might be asked: How does LSR3 know that it is the last LSR of the provider's network on the path to network 132.100.0.0? Note that LDP is a connection-oriented protocol. When establishing a logical connection, LDP can use automatic device authentication, so LDP sessions are established only between devices of the same provider that supplies all LSRs belonging to its network with information required for mutual authentication.

Having detected that on the path to network 132.100.0.0 it is an LER, the LSR3 device assigns a label unused on its S0 input interface for the LSP being created. It then informs LSR2 about this event by sending an *LDP Advertisement* message to it. LSR2, in its turn, assigns to this LSP a label that is not used on its S0 interface and sends an appropriate *LDP Advertisement* message to device LSR1. After that, the new LSP from LSR1 to network 132.100.0.0 is established, and packets start to be transmitted along this path on the basis of labels and forwarding tables instead of IP addresses and routing tables.

Establishing a separate LSP to each destination network for each router isn't rational. Therefore, LSRs try to establish aggregate LSPs along which the packets are transmitted to several destination networks. For example, LSR1 transmits through LSP1 the packets intended not only for network 132.100.0.0 but also for networks 194.15.17 and 201.25.10.0, because the paths to these networks are within the limits of the provider's MPLS network.

To transmit packets intended for the nodes of networks 105.0.0.0 and 192.201.103.0, LSR1 has another path, LSP2. Using LDP, it is also possible to aggregate not only the paths that coincide with the entire LSR sequence from the input LER to the output LER but also the paths that have only some of the common LSRs. All addresses of the destination networks that have the common next hop form the so-called **forwarding equivalence class (FEC)** for the current LSR.

MPLS IGP only *speeds* up packet forwarding by reducing the size of routing tables because, as a rule, routing tables contain more records than forwarding tables. This difference is especially noticeable for large backbones, where the routers may operate with routing tables containing tens of thousands of records.

Another factor that speeds up packet forwarding is the lack of the stage where data link-layer frames are replaced by each router, which is typical for the IP technology.

22.4.8 MPLS Traffic Engineering

MPLS TE carries out the functions of creating LSPs with guaranteed bandwidth according to the traffic engineering principles described in *Chapter 7*.

This is its main difference from MPLS IGP, which establishes LSPs on the basis of the known internetwork topology and ignores traffic flows.

Another distinguishing feature of MPLS TE is that it does not establish LSPs automatically, as was the case with MPLS IGP. The TE LSP, also called the **TE tunnel**, is established only on the initiative of the network administrator. In this respect, TE tunnels are similar to the PVCs of such technologies as ATM and Frame Relay.

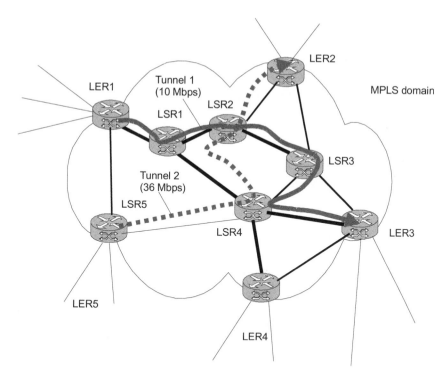

Figure 22.14 Two types of MPLS TE tunnels

MPLS TE supports tunnels of two types:

- **Strict** — Defines all transit nodes between two LERs.
- **Loose** — Specifies only part of the transit nodes from LER to LER. All the other transit nodes are chosen by the LSR.

Figure 22.14 shows both types of tunnels.

In this example, tunnel 1 is a strict tunnel. When creating such a tunnel, a network administrator has to specify not only the starting and ending nodes of the tunnel but also every transit node (i.e., the entire sequence of addresses: LER1, LSR1, LSR2, LSR3, LSR4, and LER3). Thus, the administrator solves the traffic engineering problem manually by choosing the path along which there always exists sufficient available bandwidth. When creating tunnel 1, the administrator specifies not only the required sequence of addresses but also the required bandwidth. Although the paths were chosen in the off-line mode, all devices along tunnel 1 actually check whether or not they are capable of providing the requested bandwidth, and the tunnel is established only if all devices give a positive answer.

Tunnel 2 is loose. When establishing this tunnel, the administrator specifies only the starting and ending nodes of the tunnel (i.e., only the LER5 and LER2 nodes). The starting node of tunnel 2 found transit nodes LSR4 and LSR2 automatically (i.e., by

LER5). LER5 then used the signaling protocol to inform these nodes and the end node about the necessity of establishing a tunnel.

Independent of the tunnel type, it always has such a parameter as reserved bandwidth. In Figure 22.14, tunnel 1 has reserved 10 Mbps for the traffic, and tunnel 2 has reserved 36 Mbps. These values were defined by the administrator, and MPLS TE technology has no influence on these values. It only carries out the requested reservation. Most frequently, the administrator evaluates the bandwidth being reserved for the tunnel on the basis of traffic measurements in the network, trends in its changes, and his own intuition. Some implementations of MPLS TE allow automatic correction of the reserved bandwidth on the basis of automatic measurements of actual traffic that passes through the tunnel.

However, establishing a TE tunnel in the MPLS-enabled network does not mean that traffic is transmitted through this tunnel. This only means that there is the possibility of transmitting the traffic through this tunnel in the network at an average rate that does not exceed the reserved value. To actually transmit the data through this tunnel, the administrator must carry out another manual procedure: specifying for the starting LER of the tunnel specific conditions defining which packets must be transmitted through it. There are lots of such conditions. All traditional attributes can be used as the attributes of the aggregate flow, including IP destination address, IP source address, protocol type, TCP/UDP port numbers, interface number for the incoming traffic, and DSCP or IP precedence values.

> Thus, the LER must first carry out **traffic classification**, and then **policing**, to make sure that the average flow rate does not exceed the reserved value. Then it has to **mark** the packets with the initial label of the TE tunnel to transmit the traffic across the network using the MPLS technique. In this case, the computations carried out at the stage of choosing the path for the tunnel will provide the desired result, namely, network resource balancing and observation of the guaranteed average rate for each flow.

We have not considered yet the specific set of protocols used by network LERs and LSRs for choosing loose tunnels, checking the possibility of organizing strict tunnels, or establishing a tunnel.

MPLS TE technology chooses and checks paths using special extensions of routing protocols that operate on the basis of the link state algorithm. For the moment, such extensions have been standardized for OSPF and IS-IS protocols.

To solve the traffic engineering problem, the OSPF and IS-IS protocols include new types of advertisements for distributing across the network all information about the nominal and unreserved bandwidth (available for traffic engineering flows) of each link. Thus, the edges of the resulting network graph, which is created in the topological database of each LER or LSR, will be labeled with these two additional parameters. Having such a graph at its disposal, as well as the parameters of the flows for which it is necessary to determine traffic engineering paths, an LER can find a rational solution that meets one of the requirements of network resource utilization, which were formulated in *Chapter 7*. Most often, such a decision is made on the basis of the simplest criterion, which consists of minimizing the maximum utilization along the chosen route. This means that the path optimization criterion is formulated as $\min \{K_{maxi}\}$ for all possible paths.

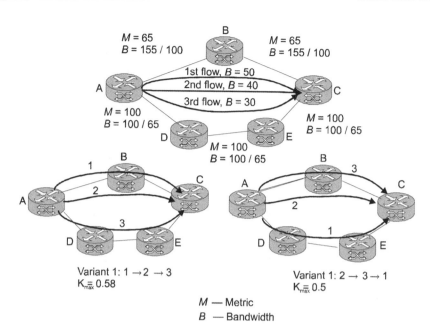

Figure 22.15 Dependence of the quality of the traffic engineering solution on the order in which the tunnels are chosen

In general, an administrator must establish several tunnels for different aggregate flows. To simplify the optimization task, the choice of paths for these tunnels is carried sequentially, one by one, and the administrator determines the order of steps in this process, relying only on her intuition. It is obvious that the sequential choice of traffic engineering paths reduces QoS because, if all flows are considered simultaneously, it is possible to find a more rational resource distribution.

EXAMPLE   In the example shown in Figure 22.15 for MPLS TE2, the limitation consists of a maximum allowed value of the network resource utilization of 0.65. In variant 1 the solution was found for the following order of flow consideration: $1 \to 2 \to 3$. For the first flow, the A–B–C path was chosen because it satisfies the limitation (use of all resources along the path, including links A–B and A–C; the appropriate router interface is 50 / 155 = 0.32). On the other hand, this path is characterized by the minimum metric (65 + 65 = 130). The same path, A–B–C, was also chosen for the second flow. In this case, the limitation also is satisfied because utilization is (50 + 40) / 155 = 0.58. The third flow is sent along route A–D–E–C and it uses resources of links A–D, D–E, and E–C (utilization is 0.3). Variant 1 can be considered satisfactory because use of any network resource does not exceed 0.58.

However, there is a better solution shown by variant 2. In this case, flows 2 and 3 were directed along path A–B–C, and flow 1 was directed along path A–D–E–C. Resources of path A–B–C are used by 0.45, and use of the lower path is 0.5, which means more uniform resource utilization. At the same time, maximum resource utilization over all network resources does not exceed 0.5. This variant can be obtained when simultaneously considering all three flows with the account of the min {Kmaxi} limitation or when considering flows one by one in the following order: $2 \to 3 \to 1$.

Nevertheless, today's MPLS TE equipment uses the variant in which flows are considered sequentially. This variant is easier to implement and closer to the standard procedures used in OSPF and IS-IS for finding the shortest path to one destination network (when there are no limitations, the solution for the set of the shortest paths does not depend on the sequence of considering networks for which the search is carried out). Besides this, when the situation changes (new flows appear or the rate of the existing flows changes), it is possible to find the path only for one flow.

In principle, it is possible to find an optimal solution for the set of flows by an autonomous system external to the network. This might be a sophisticated system that includes a simulation modeling subsystem capable of taking into account not only average flow rates but also their bursts. Such a simulator can evaluate not only resource utilization but also the resulting QoS parameters, such as delays and losses. After finding an optimal solution, it can be modified on the fly, when searching paths one by one.

In MPLS TE technology, the information about the discovered rational path is fully used, which means that the system "remembers" not only the first transit node, as was the case with IP routing, but also all transit nodes of the path, including the start and end nodes. Recall that this type of routing is known as *source routing*. Therefore, it is enough to delegate the task of searching paths to network LERs. The LSR can only supply them with information about the current state of the link bandwidth reservation.

After the path has been found, it must be established whether it was found by an LER or in the off-line mode. For this purpose, MPLS TE uses the extension of the resource reservation protocol (RSVP), which in this case is called **RSVP TE**. RSVP TE messages are transmitted from LSR to LSR according to the information about IP addresses of the route. When establishing a new path, the signaling message specifies the bandwidth being reserved along with the sequence of addresses along the path. Every LSR, having received such a message, subtracts the requested bandwidth from the pool of available bandwidth of appropriate interface and then declares the remainder in advertisements of the respective routing protocol, such as CSPF.

To conclude this section, consider the interrelations between MPLS TE and QoS technologies. As follows from the description, main goal of MPLS TE is to use MPLS functional capabilities to achieve the internal goals of the service provider, namely, a balanced load on all network resources. Furthermore, this creates a foundation for providing transport service with guaranteed QoS parameters because traffic transmission through TE tunnels takes place if some maximum level of network utilization has not been exceeded. As explained in *Chapter 7*, resource utilization has decisive importance for the queuing process. Thus, traffic flows transmitted through TE tunnels ensure some guaranteed QoS level.

To ensure various QoS parameters for each traffic class, the provider must create an individual system of tunnels for this traffic class. At the same time, reservation for delay-sensitive traffic must be carried out so that the maximum network utilization fits within the range of 0.2–0.3; otherwise, packet delays and their variations will exceed the allowed limits.

22.5 NETWORK MANAGEMENT

KEY WORDS: network management system, integrated network management system, Configuration Management, Fault management, Performance management, Security management, Accounting management, System Management System (SMS), Management Information Base (MIB), agent, manager, Simple Network Management Protocol (SNMP), community string, RMON

22.5.1 Goal of Network Management Systems

Any sophisticated telecommunications network requires specialized management tools besides those provided by standard network operating systems. This is because the correct operation of a vast amount of various communications equipment is vitally important for network operation. The distributed nature of a large-scale network makes its operation impossible without a centralized system that would automatically collect information on the state of each concentrator, switch, router, or multiplexer and pass this information to the network operator. One of the first network management systems that became widely used was SunNet Manager, released in 1989 by SunSoft. The SunNet Manager system was mainly oriented toward controlling communications equipment and network traffic. These are the functions that most network professionals mean when they mention **network management systems**.

As a rule, a network management system operates in the *automatic* mode and carries out the simplest tasks related to automatic network management. A human administrator must make the most complicated decisions on the basis of information collected and prepared by a network management system.

Network management systems are usually sophisticated combinations of hardware and software; therefore, there are certain limits within which their application is reasonable. In a small network, it is possible to apply individual, small programs for managing the most advanced devices, such as VLAN switches. As a rule, manufacturers supply an autonomous configuration, maintenance, and control utility with any device that requires a complicated configuration procedure. However, as the network grows, a problem might arise related to combining all standalone configuration and management utilities into the unified management system. To solve this problem, you will probably have to abandon these standalone tools and replace them with an **integrated network management system.**

22.5.2 Functional Groups of Network Management Problems

Whatever the managed object might be, it is desirable to have a management system capable of carrying out several functions defined by international standards, generalizing the experience of using management systems in various areas. ITU-T X.700 recommendations and the similar ISO 7498-4 divide the tasks of network management systems into the following five functional groups:

- *Configuration management* tasks consist of configuring network elements as well as the network as a whole. For network elements such as routers and multiplexers, these tasks include defining network addresses, identifiers (names), and geographical locations. For the entire network, configuration management usually starts from building a network map that displays actual links between network elements, such as building new physical or logical links and changing switching or routing tables.

- *Fault management* includes detecting, localizing, and eliminating network faults and their consequences.

- *Performance management* tasks relate to analyzing accumulated statistical information and using it as a basis for evaluating such parameters as system response time, bandwidth of a real or virtual channel connecting two network subscribers, traffic rate in individual network segments or links, probability of data corruption when transmitting information over the network, and availability of the entire network or its specific transport services. The results of performance and reliability analysis allow the SLA concluded between the network user and network administrators (or the service provider) to be observed and controlled. Without analysis of performance and reliability, a service provider offering public network services or an information technology department of a company would not be able to control or ensure the required QoS level for end users.

- *Security management* assumes that access to network resources (both equipment and data) is controlled and that data integrity is ensured in the course of their storage or transmission across the network. The basic elements of security control are authenticating users, assigning and checking access rights to the network resources, distributing and maintaining encryption keys, managing privileges, etc. Functions of this group are often implemented as specialized software products (such as Kerberos authentication and authorization systems, firewalls, and data encryption systems) or are built into operating systems and system applications.

- *Accounting management* includes billing for the use of various network resources, such as links, channels, devices, and transport services. Because different providers use different billing systems and different forms of SLAs, this group of functions is not usually included in commercial systems and network management platforms such as HP OpenView. Instead, it is frequently implemented in custom systems developed for individual clients.

NOTE   *Although the OSI model does not differ among the objects being controlled, including links, segments, switches, routers, modems, multiplexers, computer hardware, and software, in practice the division of management systems into types of controlled objects is widespread. Such classical network management systems as SunNet Manager, or HP OpenView, control only the communications objects of companywide networks, such as switches and routers. When it is necessary to manage computers, their hardware, and their software, the management system is often called a* **systems management system**. *Such a system usually collects information automatically about computers installed in a network and creates records on specific hardware and software, storing them in a specialized database. A systems management system can centrally install and administer applications that run on file servers and can remotely control the most important parameters of a computer, operating system, and DBMS (processor or RAM utilization, page fault intensity, etc.). A systems management system allows a network administrator to remotely control the computer in the GUI emulation mode. Examples of such systems are the Microsoft System Management Server, the CA Unicenter, and the HP Operations center. Practice has shown that over several years, network management systems tend to integrate with systems management systems into unified network management products, such as CA Unicenter.*

22.5.3 Architecture of Network Management Systems

The basic element of any network management system is the manager — agent — managed object method (Figure 22.16). Based on this method, it is possible to build systems of any complexity, comprising any number of managers, agents, and resources of various types.

For automating control over network objects, a special model of the managed objects is created, known as the *management information base* (MIB). MIB reflects only the charac-

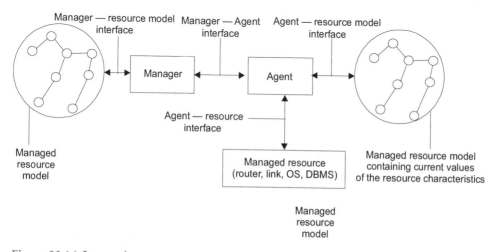

Figure 22.16 Interaction among an agent, a manager, and a controlled object

teristics of the objects needed for controlling it. For example, a router model usually includes such characteristics as the number of ports, their types, the routing table, the number of frames and packets of the data link, and the network and transport layers that have passed through these ports. The manager and the agent operate with the same model of controlled object. However, there are significant differences in the way they use this model.

The **agent** *fills* the MIB of the controlled object with the current values of its characteristics, and the **manager** *retrieves* data from the MIB. On the basis of this information, it learns which characteristics can be requested from the agent and which parameters of the object can be controlled. Thus, the agent serves as an interface between the object being controlled and the manager. It supplies the manager only with the data provided by the MIB.

The manager and the agent communicate through the network using the standard application-layer protocol. This protocol allows the manager to request parameters stored in the MIB and to supply the agent with information on the basis of which it must control the object. As a rule, the manager runs on a separate computer and interacts with several agents.

Agents can be built into the equipment being controlled or operate on separate computers connected to the controlled equipment. To obtain the required information about a specific object, and to send commands to that object, the agent must be capable of communicating with it. However, the variety of managed objects does not allow the method of interaction between agents and objects to be standardized. Developers solve this problem when building agents into communications equipment or operating systems. The agent might be supplied with special sensors for collecting information — for instance, relay contact sensors or temperature sensors. Agents also can differ in their level of intelligence. For example, they can provide only the minimum intelligence level required for counting the number of packets and frames passing through specific equipment. Some agents can provide an advanced level of intelligence sufficient for carrying out the sequences of controlling commands in emergencies, building time dependencies, filtering error messages, etc.

Control is classified into two categories: **in-band**, where control messages are transmitted through the same channel as user data, and **out-of-band**, where control messages are passed through a channel separate from the one used for transmitting user information. For example, if the messages about the protocol of communication between the manager and the agent built into the router are passed through the same network as user data, this is the in-band management. On the other hand, if the manager controls a transmission network switch operating on the basis of the FDM technology through a standalone X.25 network to which the agent is also connected, then it has out-of-band control. In-band control is more economical because it does not require a separate infrastructure to be created for transmitting control data. On the other hand, the out-of-band method is more reliable because it allows network equipment to be managed when some network elements fail and equipment becomes unavailable through the main communications links.

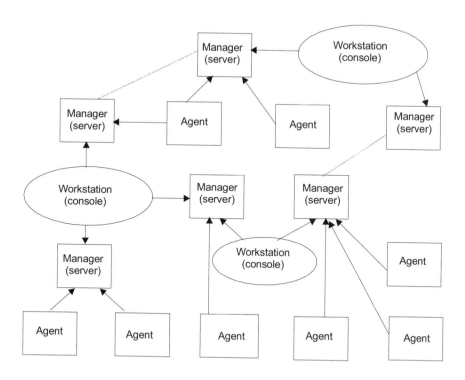

Figure 22.17 Distributed management system based on several managers and workstations

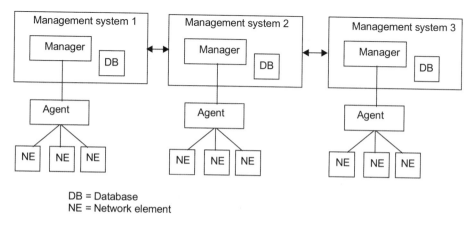

DB = Database
NE = Network element

Figure 22.18 Peer-to-peer connections between managers

The manager — agent — managed object method allows for distributed management systems to be built with sophisticated structure (Figure 22.17).

As shown in Figure 22.17, each agent controls a specific network element whose parameters are stored in the appropriate MIB. Managers retrieve the MIB data of their agents, process them, and store this information in special databases. Operators working at workstations can connect to any manager and, using GUI, view information about the managed network or send controlling commands to managers to manage the entire network or some of its elements.

The availability of several managers allows the load to be distributed among them, thus ensuring system scalability. As a rule, two types of links are used for connecting managers: peer-to-peer (Figure 22.18) and hierarchical (Figure 22.19).

In *peer-to-peer* connections, each manager controls its own network segment based on the information received from underlying agents. There is no central manager. Coordination of the manager's operation is achieved by information exchange between their databases. For the moment, the peer-to-peer method of network management systems is considered inefficient and obsolete.

The *hierarchical* method of connections between managers is considerably more powerful and flexible. Every lower-layer manager also plays the role of agent for its higher-level manager. Such an agent works with a generalized and larger MIB model for its network segment. This MIB accumulates information needed by the higher-level manager for controlling the entire network. As a rule, the development of network models for different

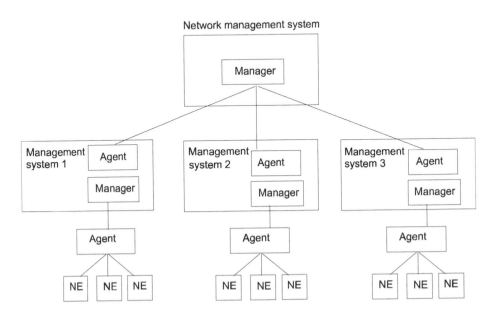

NE — Network element

Figure 22.19 Hierarchical connections between managers

hierarchical levels starts from top. At the top level, it is necessary to define the information needed from the underlying managers/agents. This top-down approach reduces the volume of information circulating among different levels of the network management system.

The manager — agent — controlled object model is the basis of such popular management standards as the Internet standards based on SNMP and the ISO/OSI standards based on the **common management information protocol** (CMIP).

22.5.4 Management System Standards based on SNMP

Temporary phenomena tend to become persistent. Simple Network Management Protocol (SNMP) can serve as another confirmation of this elementary truth. Being developed as a temporary and simple solution for IP networks, it became so popular with equipment developers and network administrators that it became the No 1 protocol in management systems and retained its position for a long time. This is despite the lengthy existence of a more powerful (and, consequently, more sophisticated) management protocol, CMIP, which has the status of an ITU-T international standard.

However, when the newer SNMP version appeared, SNMPv2, it was not supported by the manufacturers of network equipment and did not become widespread. Developers from IETF tried to improve this situation by offering the specification for a third version, SNMPv3. Significant improvements in the protocol, ensuring flexible agent administration of network management systems, protection of control information, and backward compatibility with systems based on SNMPv1, as well as an open architecture allow the authors of SNMPv3 to hope for success.

SNMP is an application-layer protocol developed for the TCP/IP stack, although there are implementations of it intended for other stacks, such as IPX/SPX. SNMP is used for obtaining from network devices information about their status, performance, and other characteristics stored in MIB. The simplicity of SNMP in many respects results from the simplicity of MIB SNMP databases, especially in their first versions, MIB-I and MIB-II.

In network management systems based on SNMP, the following elements are standardized:

■ The protocol of interaction between agents and managers, which is SNMP itself.

■ The description language of MIB models and SNMP messages. This is the ASN.1 abstract syntax notation language (ISO 8824:1987 standard, ITU-T X.208 recommendations).

■ Names of several MIB models (MIB-I, MIB-II, RMON, and RMON 2) registered in the tree of ISO standards. These standards define the MIB structure, including the set of database object types, their names, and the allowed operations over them (such as the read operation). The tree structure of MIB contains mandatory (standard) subtrees and private subtrees, allowing the manufacturers of intellectual devices to control specific device functions based on specific MIB objects.

All other functions are implemented by management system developers at their own discretion.

SNMP is the request — response protocol, which means that the agent must respond to every query received from a manager. The simplicity of this protocol is its distinguishing feature, because it includes only a small number of commands:

- `GetRequest` — This command is used by a manager to obtain a value from a specific object by its name.

- `GetNextRequest` — This command is used by a manager to retrieve the value of the next object (without specifying its name) when sequentially viewing the object table.

- `GetResponse` — The SNMP agent uses this command to pass to the manager replies to the GetRequest or GetNextRequest commands.

- `Set` — This command allows the manager to change values of a specific object. Actually, the Set command is the one that carries out device management. The agent must correctly interpret the object's values used for controlling the device. Based on these values, it must carry out the management operations, such as blocking a port or assigning a port to a specific VLAN. The Set command is also suitable for setting a condition under which the SNMP agent must send an appropriate message to the manager. It is also possible to specify the reactions to such events as agent initialization, agent restart, connection termination, connection restoration, incorrect authentication, or loss of the next router. If any of these events takes place, then the agent initiates an interruption.

- `Trap` — This command is used by the agent to inform the manager about exceptions.

22.5.5 SNMP MIB Structure

For the moment, there are several standards for the MIBs used by SNMP. The main standards are MIB-I and MIB-II, and the remote monitoring (RMON) MIB database version intended for remote management. Besides this, there are special standards for specific MIB devices (for example, MIB for concentrators or MIB for modems) as well as for proprietary MIBs from specific equipment manufacturers.

The initial specification, MIB-I, defined only the operations for reading object values. Operations such as setting or changing object values are part of the MIB-II specification.

MIB-I (RFC 1156) defines 114 objects divided into eight groups:

- *System* — General information about a specific device (such as the manufacturer's ID and time of the last system initialization)

- *Interfaces* — Parameters of the device's network interfaces (for instance, their number, types, exchange rates, and minimum packet size)
- *Address Translation Table* — Description of the mapping of network addresses to physical addresses (for instance, according to ARP)
- *Internet Protocol* — Data that relate to IP (such as the addresses of IP gateways, hosts, and statistics related to IP packets)
- *ICMP* — Data related to ICMP
- *TCP* — Data related to TCP (for example, information about TCP connections)
- *UDP* — Data related to UDP (such as the numbers of transmitted, received, and corrupted UDP datagrams).
- *EGP* — Data related to the EGP operation in the Internet (such as the number of messages received correctly and the number of messages received with errors)

From this list, it becomes obvious that the MIB-I standard was strictly oriented toward routers supporting protocols of the TCP/IP stack.

In the next version, MIB-II (RFC 1213) adopted in 1992, the list of supported objects was significantly extended (to 185 standard objects) and the number of groups was increased to ten.

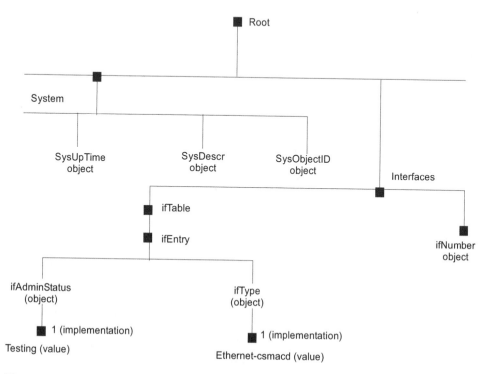

Figure 22.20 Fragment of the standard MIB-II tree

Figure 22.20 provides an example fragment of the MIB-II tree structure. It illustrates two (out of ten) possible object groups — *System* (object names starting with the `Sys` prefix) and *Interfaces* (names starting with the `if` prefix).

The `SysUpTime` object contains the time during which the system operated since the last reboot, and `SysObjectID` specifies the device ID (for example, that of a router).

The `ifNumber` object defines the number of network interfaces of the device, and the `ifEntry` object is the top of the subtree describing one of the specific device interfaces. The `ifType` and `ifAdminStatus` objects that are part of this subtree define the type and the status of the device, respectively (in this case, this is the Ethernet interface).

The list of objects describing each specific device interface includes the following.

■ `ifType` — Type of the protocol supported by this interface. This object takes the values of all standard data link-layer protocols, such as rfc877-x25, Ethernet-csmacd, iso88023-csmacd, iso88024-tokenBus, and iso88025-tokenRing.

■ `ifMtu` — Maximum size of the network-layer packet that can be sent through this interface.

■ `ifSpeed` — Bandwidth of the interface, in bits per second (100 Mbps for Fast Ethernet).

■ `ifPhysAddress` — Physical address of the port. For Fast Ethernet, this will be the MAC address.

■ `ifAdminStatus` — Desired port status:
  ● `up` — Port is ready to transmit packets.
  ● `down` — Port is not ready to transmit packets.
  ● `testing` — Port runs in the testing mode.

■ `ifOperStatus` — Current port status. The value is the same as for `ifAdminStatus`.

■ `ifInOctets` — Total number of bytes received by this port, including control bytes, since the last initialization of the SNMP agent.

■ `ifInUcastPkts` — Number of packets with individual interface addresses delivered to the higher-layer protocol.

■ `ifInNUcastPkts` — Number of packets with broadcast or multicast interface addresses delivered to the higher-layer protocol.

■ `ifInDiscards` — Number of packets received by the interface correctly but not delivered to the higher-layer protocol, probably because of buffer overflow.

■ `ifInErrors` — Number of delivered packets not passed to the higher-layer protocol because of errors detected in them.

Besides objects describing statistics about incoming packets, there are similar objects related to outgoing packets.

As can be seen from the description of MIB-II objects, this database does not provide detailed statistics about the typical errors of Ethernet frames. Furthermore, it does not provide any information related to how these characteristics change with time. Note that this information is of special interest to network administrators. Some time later, these limitations were eliminated by the newer MIB standard, RMON MIB, which is specially oriented toward collecting detailed statistics about the Ethernet protocol. RMON MIB capabilities include building time dependencies for parameter values.

For naming MIB variables and unambiguously defining their formats, an additional specification is used, known as **structure of management information** (SMI). For example, SMI includes the standard IpAddress name and defines its format as a 4-byte string. Another example is the Counter name, which is an integer number belonging to the range from 0 to $2^{32} - 1$.

The names of MIB variables can be written using both symbolic and numeric formats. Symbolic format is used for representing variables in text documents and displaying them on the screen. Numeric names are used in SNMP messages. For example, the symbolic name SysDescr corresponds to the numeric name 1.3.6.1.2.1.1.1.

The combined numeric number of the SNMP MIB object corresponds to the fully qualified name of this object in the ISO object registration tree. SNMP developers did not use the traditional approach of Internet standards consisting of registering numeric parameter values in a special RFC known as assigned numbers. Instead, they have registered the objects of the MIB SNMP databases in the ISO standards tree shown in Figure 22.21.

As in any complex system, the namespace of ISO objects has a tree-like hierarchical structure. The illustration shows only the root of this tree. Three branches go from the root

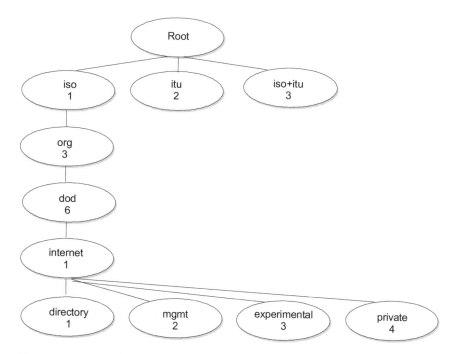

Figure 22.21 ISO objects namespace

corresponding to standards controlled by ISO, ITU, and both organizations. ISO, in turn, has created another branch for the standards created by national and international organizations (this is the org branch). Internet standards were developed under the control of the U.S. Department of Defense; therefore, MIB standards fit into the dod-internet subtree in the network management group of standards (mgmt). Objects of any standards created under ISO are uniquely identified by their complex symbolic names starting from the root of this tree. Protocol messages use numeric names unambiguously mapped to the corresponding symbolic names. Every branch of the name tree is numbered by integers from left to right, and these numbers replace symbolic names. Thus, the fully qualified symbolic name of the MIB object iso.org.dod.internet.mgmt.mib is mapped to the numeric name 1.3.6.1.2.1.

The private group (4) of objects is reserved for the standards created by commercial companies such as Cisco and Hewlett-Packard. The same registration tree is used for naming objects of CMIP and TMN classes.

Accordingly, each group of MIB-I and MIB-II objects, besides short symbolic names, has fully qualified symbolic names and appropriate numeric names.

22.5.6 SNMP Message Format

SNMP transmits data between agents and managers. SNMP uses the UDP datagram transport protocol, which does not ensure reliable message delivery. The protocol organizing reliable message delivery on the basis of TCP overloads the managed devices, which were not powerful enough at the time of SNMP development. Because of this, SNMP developers decided to abandon the use of TCP.

SNMP messages, in contrast to the messages of most other communications protocols, have no headers with predefined fields. Any SNMP message comprises an arbitrary number of fields, and each field is preceded by the descriptor specifying its type and size.

Every SNMP message consists of the following three main parts (Figure 22.22).

- Protocol version (version).
- Community identifier (community) used for grouping objects into management domains controlled by a specific manager. Community identifier is an analogue of a password. For devices to communicate using SNMP, they must have the matching values of this identifier (the `public` string is frequently used by default).
- Data area in which the previously described protocol commands, object names, and their values are contained. The data area contains one or more protocol data units (PDUs). Each PDU corresponds to one of the following SNMP commands: `GetRequest-PDU`, `GetNextRequest-PDU`, `GetResponse-PDU`, `SetRequest-PDU`, `Trap-PDU`.

The *PDU* field might contain one of the four previously listed commands. The command structure is illustrated by Figure 22.22, showing the SNMP frame in the example of the `GetRequest` command.

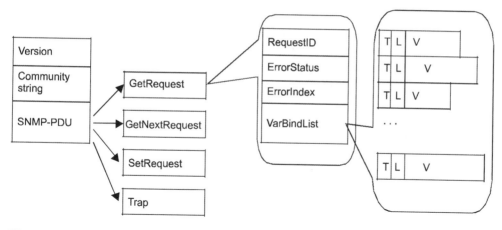

Figure 22.22 SNMP message format

The `RequestID` variable is the 4-byte integer value (used for mapping of replies to requests). `ErrorStatus` and `ErrorIndex` are 1-byte integers, which must be set to 0 in the request. `VarBindList` is the list of numeric object names whose values are requested by a manager. This list contains the triad of `Type`, `Length`, and `Value` (`T`, `L`, and `V`), which allows for flexible specification of any number of variables of any type. In the course of a request, the variable value must be set to `null`.

Here is an example of the SNMP message, which represents the request of the `SysDescr` object value (the numeric name of this object is 1.3.6.1.2.1.1.1).

30	29	02	01	00			
SEQUENCE	len = 41	INTEGER	len = 1	vers = 0			
04	06	70	75	62	6C	69	63
string	len = 6	p	u	B	l	i	c
A0	1C	02	04	05	AE	56	02
getreq	len = 28	INTEGER	len = 4	———— request ID ————			—–
02	01	00	02	01	00		
INTEGER	len = 1	status	INTEGER	len = 1	error	index	
30	0E	30	0C	06	08		
SEQUENCE	len = 14	SEQUENCE	len = 12	Objectid	len = 8		
2B	06	01	02	01	01	01	00
1.3	6	1	2	1	1	1	0
05	00						
null	len=0						

As follows from the previously provided description, the message starts from code 30 (all codes are in hex notation), which corresponds to the SEQUENCE keyword, one of the supported SNMP variable data types. This keyword defines the entire SNMP message as a sequence of variables. The length of this sequence is specified in the next byte (41 bytes), which corresponds to the total message length. This is followed by a 1-byte integer, which stands for the SNMP version (in this case, this value is set to 0, which corresponds to SNMPv1. The value 1 would correspond to SNMPv2). The *Community* field has the string type. This character string is 6 bytes long and has the value public. All agents support this value by default, provided that the administrator has not defined another value. The agent will reply to the manager's request only when the default values match.

Another part of the message is made up of the `GetRequest` command. The `GetRequest` operation is indicated by the code A0 (this value is defined in SNMP instead of in ASN.1 notation). The total length of the data block is 28 bytes. According to the structure of the `GetRequest` block, the data block is followed by the request identifier (it is defined as a 4-byte integer). Then there are two 1-byte integers of the status and error index, which in the request are set to 0. Finally, the message is terminated by the list of objects, which in this case includes a single object with the name 1.3.6.1.2.1.1.1.0 and the value set to `null`.

22.5.7 RMON MIB Specification

The RMON MIB specification, which improves the capabilities of remote communication with MIB, is an addition to the SNMP functional capabilities. The RMON MIB database contains aggregate information about the device, which does not require large volumes of information to be transmitted through the network. Because of this feature, it is convenient for remote control. RMON MIB objects include additional counters of errors in packets, more flexible tools for collecting statistics and analyzing trends, more powerful filtering tools for capturing and analyzing individual packets, and more sophisticated conditions for setting warning signals. The intellectual capabilities of RMON MIB agents are better than those of MIB-I or MIB-II agents, which allows them to carry out most jobs related to processing information about the device. Before the arrival of RMON MIB, these tasks were usually delegated to managers. These agents can be built into communications devices or implemented as standalone software modules running on universal PCs or notebooks.

A RMON object is assigned the number 16 in the set of MIB objects. The RMON object, in turn, comprises ten groups of objects (the tenth group, which is omitted from the list, is composed of special objects of the Token Ring protocol):

- *Statistics* (1) — Current accumulated statistics on packet characteristics, the number of collisions, etc.
- *History* (2) — Statistical data saved with the predefined periods for future trend analysis.

- *Alarms* (3) — Threshold values of statistical parameters. When these values are exceeded, the RMON agent sends a message to the manager.
- *Hosts* (4) — Data on network hosts, including their MAC addresses.
- *Host TopN* (5) — Table of the network hosts with the highest load.
- *Traffic Matrix* (6) — Statistics on the traffic intensity between each pair of hosts within the network, ordered in the form of a matrix.
- *Filter* (7) — Packet filtering conditions.
- *Packet Capture* (8) — Packet capturing conditions.
- *Event* (9) — Event generation and registration conditions.

These groups are numbered in the order in which they are listed; the Hosts group, for example, has the numeric name 1.3.6.1.2.1.16.4.

The total number of objects defined by the RMON MIB standard is about 200. They are divided into ten groups registered in two documents — RFC 1271 for Ethernet and RFC 1513 for Token Ring.

The distinguishing feature of the RMON MIB standard is its independence from the network-layer protocol (in contrast to the MIB-I and MIB-II standards oriented toward TCP/IP). Therefore, it is convenient for heterogeneous networks using various network-layer protocols.

Consider in more detail the Statistics group, which defines information about Ethernet frames (called packets in the standard) that the RMON agent can provide. The History group is based on the objects of the Statistics group, because its objects allow time dependencies to be built for the objects of the Statistics group.

The Statistics group, along with several other objects, includes the following.

- etherStatsDropEvents — Total number of events when packets were ignored by the agent because of a shortage of available resources. The packets as such need not be lost by the interface.
- etherStatsOctets — Total number of bytes (including erroneous packets) received from the network (excluding the preamble but including the checksum bytes).
- etherStatsPkts — Total number of received packets (including erroneous ones).
- etherStatsBroadcastPkts — Total number error-free packets sent to a broadcast address.
- etherStatsMulticastPkts — Total number of error-free packets received by a multicast address.
- etherStatsCRCAlignErrors — Total number of received packets that had a length (excluding the preamble) in a range from 64 to 1,518 bytes and that did not contain an integer number of bytes (alignment error) or had incorrect checksum (FCS error).
- etherStatsUndersizePkts — Total number of packets that had a length shorter than 64 bytes but were correctly formatted.

- `etherStatsOversizePkts` — Total number of packets that had a length longer than 1,518 bytes but were correctly formatted.

- `etherStatsFragments` — Total number of packets that did not contain an integer number of bytes or that had an incorrect checksum and were undersized (had a length shorter than 64 bytes).

- `etherStatsJabbers` — Total number of packets that did not contain an integer number of bytes or that had an incorrect checksum and a length longer than 1,518 bytes.

- `etherStatsCollisions` — Best evaluation of the number of collisions in the given Ethernet segment.

- `etherStatsPkts64Octets` — Total number of received packets (including the corrupted ones) with the size of bytes.

- `etherStatsPkts65to127Octets` — Total number of received packets (including the corrupted ones) that had a length from 65 to 127 bytes.

- `etherStatsPkts128to255Octets` — Total number of received packets (including the corrupted ones) that had a size from 128 to 255 bytes.

- `etherStatsPkts256to511Octets` — Total number of received packets (including the corrupted ones) that had a length from 256 to 511 bytes.

- `etherStatsPkts512to1023Octets` — total number of received packets (including the corrupted ones) that had a size from 512 to 1,023 bytes.

- `etherStatsPkts1024to1518Octets` — Total number of received packets (including the corrupted ones) that had a size from 1,024 to 1,518 bytes.

As can be seen from the descriptions of the objects, using a RMON agent built into a repeater or any other communications device, it is possible to carry out a detailed analysis of the operation of an Ethernet or Fast Ethernet segment. First, it is possible to obtain data about frame errors typical for this segment; then, it would be useful to build time dependencies for these errors using the History group (it is also possible to bind them to a specific time). Having obtained the results of the analysis of time dependencies, it is possible to draw preliminary conclusions about the possible source of erroneous frames. Based on this information, the administrator can refine the frame-capturing conditions with more specific attributes (by specifying them using objects of the Filter group), which correspond to the version of the error cause being investigated. After that, it is possible to carry out more detailed analysis by studying the captured frames, which are retrieved from the objects of the Packet Capture group.

Some time later, the RMON 2 standard was adopted. It extends the ideas of the intellectual RMON MIB database to the higher-layer protocols and carries out part of the protocol analyzer functions.

SUMMARY

▶ IP WANs can be divided into two classes: pure IP networks and overlay IP networks. Among the overlay networks, the most popular are IP over ATM, IP over Frame Relay, and IP over MPLS.

▶ In pure IP networks, there is no other layer operating on the basis of the packet switching technology. The problems of ensuring QoS and solving traffic engineering tasks in such networks are complicated by indefinite paths of traffic and the inefficiency of load distribution over routers because of the necessity of choosing the route characterized by the minimum metric.

▶ At the data link layer of pure IP networks, the point-to-point protocol is used, which ensures frame transmission between neighboring routers. Nowadays, the most popular and widely used protocols of this type are HDLC and PPP.

▶ HDLC is the oldest protocol, developed in 1970s, for reliable data transmission through noisy channels. It ensures control over frame transmission and recovery of lost or corrupted frames by using the sliding window algorithm.

▶ PPP was developed for contemporary, high-quality communications links. This protocol is not involved in solving problems related to reliable transmission, but it allows the parameters of neighboring devices to be coordinated at the expense of a flexible negotiations procedure that takes place when establishing a connection. Besides this, it ensures mutual device authentication.

▶ In overlay networks such as IP over ATM or Frame Relay, the routers are connected by virtual ATM or Frame Relay channels rather than by physical links. This provides the possibility of ensuring a rational network load using traffic engineering and makes use of the system of ATM services for ensuring a specific QoS level for each traffic class.

▶ The new MPLS technology is closely integrated with the protocols of the IP stack. The device combining functions of the IP router and the MPLS switch became known as the LSR.

▶ The LSR uses routing protocols of the TCP/IP stack for detecting the network topology and state as well as for choosing rational virtual paths called LSPs.

▶ MPLS can use frames of different data link-layer technologies, such as PPP, Ethernet, ATM, and Frame Relay.

▶ There are three areas of MPLS application and, accordingly, three variants of MPLS: MPLS IGP, MPLS TE, and MPLS VPN.

▶ MPLS IGP uses the LDP signaling protocol and automatically establishes paths to all destination networks known to the network routers. However, these paths are chosen by standard IGPs of the TCP/IP stack and, consequently, do not solve traffic engineering problems.

▶ MPLS TE operates on the basis of the modified IS-IS or OSPF routing protocols, which propagate routing advertisements that contain not only topological information but also data about the available link bandwidth. This allows the creation of TE LSPs, known as tunnels, reserving bandwidth for aggregate data flows.

▶ The functions of network management systems are standardized in the ITU-T X.700 recommendation and in the ISO 7498-4 document. There are five groups of functions: configuration management, fault management, performance management, security management, and accounting management.

▶ The basis for all network management systems is the manager–agent method. This method uses an abstract model of the managed resource called the MIB.

▶ The agent communicates with the managed resource using a custom interface. Communication between the agent and the manager is carried out through the network using a standard protocol. For IP networks, SNMP is used.

▶ The first MIB databases in the Internet standards were oriented toward managing routers: MIB-I for management only and MIB-II for management and control. A further development, RMON MIB, was aimed at the development of intellectual agents controlling the lower level Ethernet and Token Ring interfaces. The names of standard objects of MIB databases for the Internet are registered in the ISO standard names tree.

REVIEW QUESTIONS

1. What caused the development of several models of IP WANs (pure IP, IP over ATM, IP over Frame Relay, and IP over MPLS)?

2. Is it correct to state that an IP-over-ATM or IP-over-Frame Relay network consists of two levels of packet-switched networks and that an IP-over-MPLS network consists of only one layer? Justify your answer.

3. Compare the main properties of HDLC and PPP. Which of them are advantages, and which ones are drawbacks, under which conditions?

4. What is the purpose of the connection establishment procedure in the HDLC protocol and in PPP?

5. What is the mechanism used by HDLC for restoring lost or damaged packets?

6. What are PPP multiprotocol functions?

7. Why is the mutual authentication procedure provided by PPP needed?

8. List the main stages of the router configuration procedure for operation using a leased line.

9. What are the functions of the ATM layer in the IP-over-ATM model?

10. Which new ideas were implemented in the IP switching technology?

11. Which ideas of IP switching were preserved in MPLS, and which ones were modified?

12. List the main functional models of an IP router that are used in an LSR.

13. What new possibilities are ensured by the use of the MPLS label stack?

14. Suppose that an LSR uses the Ethernet frame format. Does this mean that this device forwards frames on the basis of the routing table obtained on the basis of the IEEE 802.1D standard?

15. How is it possible to establish an LSP passing through several MPLS domains?

16. What is the difference between MPLS IGP and MPLS TE?

17. Is it necessary to manually configure LSRs for operation in MPLS IGP?

18. What is the analogue of MPLS TE tunnels in the ATM and Frame Relay technologies?

19. Is it possible to pass part of the traffic using normal IP forwarding in an MPLS-enabled network?

20. List the groups of network management system functions according to the X.700 standard

21. Are there any differences between network management systems and systems management systems? If yes, what are those differences?

22. Which functions in a network management system are delegated to an agent and which functions are carried out by a manager?

23. List the standard MIBs.

24. Which types of names are used in SNMP for MIB objects — symbolic or numeric?

25. When is the `Trap` command?

PROBLEMS

1. Assume that you are an IP WAN network architect. What questions would you ask a customer that wants you to develop a large IP network so that you can choose the type of a multilayer model (non-overlay IP, IP over ATM, IP over Frame Relay, or IP over MPLS)?

2. Measurements have shown that the BER value of a communications link is 10^{24}. Which type of a protocol would you choose for this link — HDLC or PPP?

3. Compose a forwarding table for LSR1 shown in Figure 22.13.

4. What initial data have to be collected for the network shown in Figure 22.14 to enable a network administrator to solve a traffic engineering problem? Suggest your version of this data and solve the formulated problem.

23

REMOTE ACCESS

23.1 INTRODUCTION

The term "remote access" is often used when it is necessary to organize access from the computer of a home user to the Internet or to a private network of a company located outside the LAN coverage area. In this case, it is necessary to use WAN links. The concept of remote access has recently begun to include network access not only for standalone home computers but also for home networks connecting the computers of several home users. The offices of small businesses, where the total number of employees is two or three, also have such small networks.

The organization of remote access is one of the most urgent problems of computer networks. It also has become known as the "last mile problem." In this case, the "last mile" is the distance from the nearest communications carrier's point of presence (POP) to the customer's premises. The difficulty of finding a solution to this problem depends on several factors. Users require fast access ensuring high-quality transmission of all types of traffic, including data, voice, and video. For this purpose, it is necessary to support transmission rates of several megabits per second or at least hundreds of kilobits per second. However, the overwhelming majority of buildings in cities and especially in rural districts are still connected to communications carriers' POPs by local telephone loops, which limit the user to the rates of tens of kilobits per second.

Massive rebuilding of the cabling infrastructure is hardly possible in the near future because this task is too extensive. Consider the number of buildings and houses geographically distributed over the vast spaces. Although in some industrial countries communications carriers have started to install high-speed fiber-optic links in buildings and private houses, such countries are not numerous yet. Furthermore, for the moment, only large cities and large buildings, which have lots of potential subscribers, are involved in this process.

Dial-up access has long been the most popular technology for remote access. Using this method, users established dial-up connections to the Internet or to enterprise-wide networks through a modem. This method has one significant drawback: the access rate is limited to tens of kilobits per second. This limitation is implied because each subscriber of a telephone network is assigned a fixed bandwidth of approximately 3.4 KHz (recall the multiplexing technique used in telephone networks, which we covered in *Chapter 9*). Fewer users are satisfied with such access rates.

There are various new technologies for organizing high-speed remote access using the existing local loops of telephone or cable TV. After reaching the service provider's POP, computer data are not transmitted through a telephone or cable TV (CATV) network. Instead, they are passed to the data transmission network using special equipment. This increases the access rate and overcomes the limitation implied on the bandwidth allocated to each subscriber in a telephone or CATV network. The most popular technologies of this type are asymmetric digital subscriber line (ADSL), which uses telephone local loops, and cable modems, which operate over CATV networks. These technologies ensure a traffic rate from hundreds of kilobits per second to several megabits per second.

Besides this, various wireless access technologies are used that ensure both fixed and mobile access. The set of employed wireless technologies includes wireless Ethernet (802.11), various proprietary technologies, transmission through mobile telephone networks, as well as several fixed access technologies, such as those based on the new 802.16 standard.

In this chapter, we cover the most popular methods and technologies for remote access.

23.2 METHODS OF REMOTE ACCESS

KEY WORDS: remote access, unprotected connection, telephone access, TV access, Internet access, coaxial CATV cable, broadband wireless link splitter, dial-up modem, ADSL modem, cable modem, remote access server (RAS), remote access concentrator, access multiplexer, termination system, access to the public Internet domain, remote node mode, terminal access, remote control, telnet

Figure 23.1 illustrates the mixed and diverse world of remote access. Here you can see clients of various types, differing in the equipment being used and in their requirements for access parameters. Furthermore, there are various methods of connecting client premises to the nearest communications carrier's POP (or central office in telephone provider terminology). For example, this can be achieved using an analog or digital local loop, TV cable, or wireless link. Finally, the communications carrier might specialize in different types of services, which means that it can be a telephone provider, an ISP, a CATV provider, or a universal provider offering the entire range of services and owning networks of all types.

23.2.1 Types of Clients and Terminal Equipment

Consider in detail each element of the access method shown in Figure 23.1.

Clients 1 and *2* are the most typical users, because each has only one computer for which it is necessary to provide access to a remote computer network. Besides computers, these clients use telephone and TV; therefore, the terminal equipment of these devices can be used for organizing the remote access of this computer to the data transmission network.

Client 2 uses two cable local loops, the first similar to an analog telephone local loop based on a twisted pair and the second a CATV local loop using coaxial TV cable. These local loops have different characteristics. Thus, twisted pair, with a distance of 1–2 km between the client's premises and the provider's POP, usually has a bandwidth of several megahertz, and coaxial cable ensures a bandwidth of tens of megahertz.

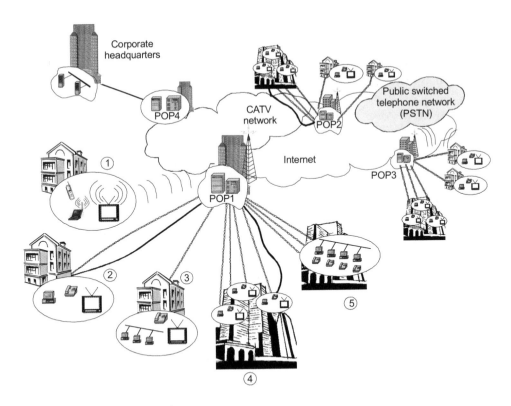

Figure 23.1 Remote access clients

Client 1 has no wired local loop because this client uses a mobile telephone. This client also does not use the cable TV service and receives a TV signal only by the wireless link.

Thus, to organize remote access for client 2, the provider can either use the existing TV cable or telephone local loop. For client 1, there is no such possibility; therefore, for this client, the provider must either ensure wireless communications or install a new cable connecting this client's premises to the nearest POP.

A distinctive feature of clients 1 and 2 is the asymmetric type of traffic, because home users typically download information from the Internet. Asymmetric technologies such as ADSL are the most suitable for satisfying such requirements.

Client 3 is different from clients 1 and 2 in that it has several computers connected into a LAN. Both individuals and small businesses can be this type of client. Ensuring remote access for a LAN is characterized by increased requirements for the bandwidth. Furthermore, the traffic of such a client can be symmetric if a home LAN contains a server that provides information to the Internet users or employees of other affiliations of the same company. Since client 3 has no CATV local loop, only the telephone local loop can be used for providing it with remote access. Client 3 can employ various methods of organizing its IP network. For example, it can request a pool of IP addresses from the provider so that every computer in its network would have a permanent public IP address. This is the most flexible variant for the client, because every computer of the client's network can be a full member of the Internet and play not only the role of the client machine but also that of a server with the registered domain name. In this case, the client LAN must have an edge router through which it would communicate with the provider's network. Another variant of the IP network can be based on the NAT technique described in *Chapter 20*.

Client 4 consists of residents of an apartment building connected to the provider's POP by multiple twisted pairs of telephone local loops (one local loop per apartment) as well as by CATV cable. Using a single CATV cable for a large number of clients creates additional problems, since the cable plays the role of a shared medium. Using telephone local loops for organizing remote access for residents of an apartment building is not different from connecting a single subscriber (such as client 2). Although most such subscribers use traditional analog local loops, there are several apartments in this apartment building whose lodgers are subscribers of the integrated services digital network (ISDN) service. This means that although their local loops are based on a twisted pair, similar to traditional analog ones, these are digital local loops. Although ISDN was initially designed as a universal network providing data transmission service with telephony service, in practice it is used as a normal telephone network.

Client 5 also consists of residents of an apartment building. However, in this case, the provider has installed a LAN in the building. All clients who decide to subscribe to the services offered by this provider connect to that LAN. This variant is efficient for the provider only when the number of potential clients is large enough. A LAN installed in an apartment building requires higher access rates than individual computers or home networks of individual clients. Therefore, the provider must ensure that a local loop used for organizing remote access has a broad bandwidth. For this purpose, it is possible to use the existing CATV cable, a specially installed Ethernet cable, or even a fiber-optic cable.

A remote access provider can either serve all types of clients or specialize in delivering a specific kind of service, such as offering services to owners of private houses or small businesses. A universal provider must support any variants of organizing the last mile, which inevitably complicates the required equipment and access technologies.

For any local loop, the provider must ensure bit transmission through this local loop and combine it with transmission of the information for which this local loop was initially designed, such as voice or CATV information. Then, based on this physical-layer equipment, the provider must deliver the requested type of access service to the client.

One of the problems that the access provider must solve is organizing access for the clients physically connected to local loops of *other* communications carriers. Use the configuration shown in Figure 23.1 as an example. Here, provider A owns POP1 and POP2, and provider B owns POP3. If provider A wants to offer network access services to clients connected to POP3, that provider must conclude an appropriate agreement with provider B. This agreement might regulate the various methods of interprovider communication, which were explained in *Chapter 5*. For example, provider A may lease from provider B those local loops used by its clients to forward the data received from there into its network and then forward this information according to the client's requirements. In another case, the local loops may remain at the disposal of provider B, which must separate computer data from telephone or TV information and forward them to the network of provider A. In both cases it is necessary to ensure communication among networks belonging to providers A and B.

The simplest variant of Internet access provides the client with **unprotected connection** with the servers of a corporate network, which is potentially dangerous. First, confidential data transmitted over the Internet might be eavesdropped or changed. Second, when using such a method, it is difficult for the administrator of the corporate network to limit unauthorized access. This is because IP addresses of legal users (employees of the corporation or enterprise) are not known beforehand. Therefore, most enterprises prefer secured access based on the virtual private network (VPN) technology. This technology will be covered in details in the next chapter.

23.2.2 Information Multiplexing at the Local Loop

As shown in Figure 23.1, most private buildings and apartment buildings are connected to POP by telephone or CATV local loops.

> Therefore, to provide the clients with the *three* types of access most common today (telephone access, TV access, and Internet access) it is necessary to ensure simultaneous transmission of various types of data through the same communications link. For instance, it might be necessary to combine voice and data transmission using the same telephone local loop or to combine data transmission with the transmission of the telephone signal through a coaxial cable.

It is desirable to use a single local loop capable of transmitting information of all three types. Unfortunately, twisted pair is not suitable for this role because its bandwidth at distances of several kilometers is only a few megahertz, with 1 MHz as a typical value. Clearly, this is not sufficient for simultaneous transmission of voice, video, and computer data at rates of several megabits per second.

Therefore, only coaxial CATV cable and broadband wireless links can be used as consolidating local loops. Naturally, we are referring to existing and widely used types of local loops. As relates to the installation of a new cable, typical mainly for large, new buildings, fiber-optic cable can be added to this list.

Practically all access technologies covered in the next few sections employ the multiplexing of two or sometimes all three types of information in the local loop. Thus, ADSL uses analog telephone local loops for multiplexing voice and computer data, and cable modems combine the transmission of TV signal and computer data through coaxial cable. Various wireless access technologies ensure the transmission of TV signal and computer data, sometimes with telephony, within the same local loop. The only exception is the oldest technology, dial-up access. In this case, use of the analog local loop alternates between a telephone and a dial-up modem connected to a computer.

The method of organizing access using a universal local loop is shown in Figure 23.2.

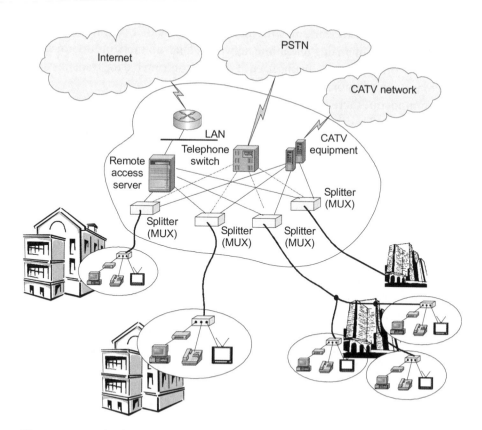

Figure 23.2 Multiplexing three types of information in local loops

Frequency division multiplexing (FDM) is used most often for information multiplexing in local loops. Specific bandwidth is allocated for every type of information according to subscriber requirements. For a telephone connection, bandwidth of 4 KHz is allocated, which corresponds to the standard bandwidth allocated for subscribers of analog telephone networks. For computer data, broader bandwidth is needed. In the case of asymmetric access, bandwidth of at least hundreds of kilohertz and preferably several megahertz must be allocated for prevailing downstream traffic. Less intensive upstream traffic requires bandwidth of tens of kilohertz. Cable TV traditionally uses bandwidth of 6 MHz for each subscriber; however, in this case, only downstream traffic is transmitted.

To implement the chosen FDM method, **splitters** are installed in the customer's premises and in the POP. Splitters carry out signal multiplexing and demultiplexing. Most frequently, a splitter is a passive filter that separates the required frequency ranges and transmits each range to a separate output. A subscriber's terminal devices, such as telephones, TV sets, or computers, are connected to the splitter output. Because a computer uses discrete signals for data exchange, it requires an additional device that transforms discrete signals to analog signals of the required frequency range.

Most users are accustomed to working with **dial-up modems** that operate within the standard 4 KHz bandwidth of analog telephone networks. Dial-up modems do not share this bandwidth with other devices, using it entirely for computer data transmission. In this case, there is no need to install a splitter.

Besides dial-up modems, there are **ADSL** and **cable modems**, which operate on telephone local loops and CATV cables, respectively. In this case, the splitter is required because with computer data these local loops transmit other information; telephone or TV signals are the main types of information for these local loops.

In a provider's POP, each local loop also is connected to a splitter that carries out similar multiplexing and demultiplexing operations at the other end of the connection. As a result, telephone information is supplied from the telephone outputs of the splitters to the provider's telephone switch, which transmits it into the telephone network. TV signals from the appropriate outputs of the splitters are sent to the CATV equipment connected to the CATV network of this provider.

Finally, computer data are supplied to the device that collects computer traffic and passes it to the provider's LAN. This device has several names. In Figure 23.2, it is designated by the most popular one, **remote access server (RAS)**. Sometimes other terms for the same device can be encountered, for example, **remote access concentrator**, and **access multiplexer**, or **termination system**. For clarity, we will use the most popular term, RAS. No matter what the device is called, all such devices have the same structure. They contain a large number of modems that carry out an operation inverse to users' modems; namely, they modulate downstream traffic and demodulate upstream traffic. In addition to modems, an RAS includes a router that collects traffic from modems and transmits it into the POP LAN. From this LAN, the traffic is transmitted to the Internet or to a specific enterprise-wide network in a normal way.

We have described a generalized access method, which, depending on the chosen type of local loop and modem, generates various access technologies. It is only necessary to emphasize that in terms of the OSI model, all these technologies are physical-layer technologies, because they create a stream of bits between the client's computer and the provider's LAN. For IP to operate over this physical layer, it is necessary to use one of the data link-layer protocols. For the moment, PPP is used most frequently for organizing remote access, because it supports such important functions as the assignment of IP addresses to client computers and the authentication of users.

23.2.3 Remote Node Mode

Nowadays, the most popular remote access service is **providing access to the public Internet domain**. This service assumes that the provider ensures the routing of IP traffic between users' computers and any Internet site with a public address (or a private address but using the NAT technique for public access).

As a rule, providers use the **remote node mode** for ensuring access for users of stand-alone computers. This mode allows the client's computer to participate in a remote LAN, and to access the entire range of services available to the users of the end node physically connected to that LAN.

For this purpose, the provider usually reserves a pool of IP addresses that can be assigned to its RAS clients in one of its subnets. For the clients that do not need permanent Internet access, this service is provided as a dial-up service and an IP address is assigned dynamically only for the connection time. The remote node mode is necessary for economizing subnet addresses because in a standard mode an IP router must assign a separate IP subnet address to each of its ports. Clearly, this is exceedingly redundant for the single node of most client networks. For the clients that need a permanent connection, IP addresses can be assigned both statically and dynamically.

For ensuring the remote node mode, the provider's RAS supports proxy-ARP, covered in *Chapter 17*. This feature, illustrated in Figure 23.3, differs RAS from a normal IP router.

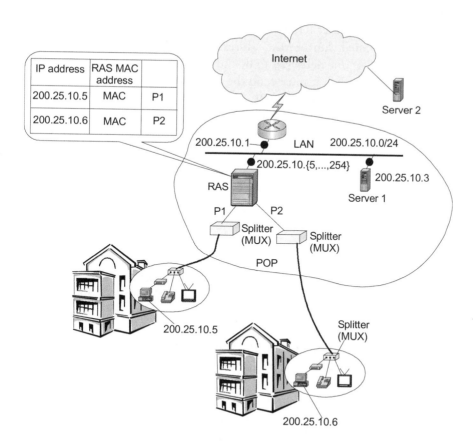

Figure 23.3 Using proxy-ARP when organizing remote access

For remote nodes belonging to the provider's LAN assigned address 200.25.10.0/24, a network administrator has allocated the address pool from 200.25.10.5 to 200.25.10.254. If the client uses a dial-up service to connect to the provider's network (for example, using PPP), it is *temporarily* assigned an address from this pool. Thus, the computer of client 1 was assigned address 200.25.10.5, and the computer of client 2 was assigned address 200.25.10.6. When these remote nodes are connected to the network, remote access server inserts the following records into a special table, which is an analogue of the ARP table:

200.25.10.5 — MAC —P1

200.25.10.6 — MAC —P2

Here MAC designates the address of the internal interface of the remote access server, and P1 and P2 are numbers of ports to which RAS clients are connected.

Thus, port numbers play the roles of MAC addresses in the ARP table. For example, if server 2 connected to one of the ISPs sends a packet to the computer of client 1, then router R1 of the ISP considers this packet to be directed to one of the nodes belonging to the directly connected subnet 200.25.10.0/24. Therefore, R1 sends an ARP request containing address 200.25.10.5. Instead of the client 1 computer, RAS replies to this request, supplying *its* MAC address to router R1. After this, R1 sends the IP packet encapsulated into the Ethernet frame supplied with the MAC address of the RAS. RAS then retrieves the IP packet from the Ethernet frame delivered to it, and, based on the IP address, finds in the table the port number to which it must send the packet. In this example, this is port P1. RAS then encapsulates the packet into the PPP frame used for operation over the local loop connecting RAS to the computer of client 1.

When a client has its own LAN whose hosts have registered public IP addresses, RAS operates as a normal router. In this case, the operating mode is not called remote node mode.

23.2.4 Remote Control Mode. Telnet

Terminal access, also called **remote control**, is a special access mode. This mode assumes that the user turns his or her computer into a remote terminal of another computer that he or she accesses remotely.

During the period of computer network formation (i.e., in 1970s), support of this mode was one of the main functions of a network. PADs of X.25 networks existed to ensure remote access to mainframes for users residing in other cities and working at the simplest character terminals.

Remote control mode is ensured by a special application-layer protocol operating over protocols that ensure the transport connection of a remote node to a computer network. There are lots of remote control protocols, both standard and proprietary. The oldest protocol used in IP networks for this purpose is telnet (RFC 854).

Telnet ensures the emulation of the character terminal, limiting the user by the command-line mode. Telnet operates according to the client–server architecture.

When the user presses a key on the keyboard, the telnet client intercepts its scan code, encapsulates it into the TCP message, and sends it over the network to the node that the user wants to control. When the packet arrives at the destination node, the telnet server retrieves the scan code of the pressed key from the TCP message and passes it to the operating system running on that node. The OS considers a telnet session to be one of the sessions opened by local users. If the user presses a key and the operating system reacts by outputting an appropriate character to the screen, then for the remote control session this character is encapsulated into a TCP message and returned to the remote node over the network. The telnet client retrieves the character and displays it in the terminal emulator window.

Telnet was implemented for the UNIX environment and, with e-mail and access to file archives through FTP, was one of the most popular Internet services. Nowadays, this protocol is rarely used in the public Internet domain because no one wants to allow third parties to control a computer. Although telnet uses passwords for protection against unauthorized access, these passwords are transmitted over the network as plain text. Consequently, they can be easily sniffed and used for unauthorized access. Therefore, telnet is mainly used within the limits of a single LAN, where there are considerably fewer possibilities for password sniffing. Currently, telnet is widely used for controlling communications devices, such as routers, switches, and hubs, and practically never used for controlling computers. Thus, it is not used as a user plane protocol. It became a management plane protocol, which serves as an alternative to SNMP.

The difference between telnet and SNMP is that telnet requires a human administrator to participate in the network management process. This is because the administrator, who configures or monitors a router or any other communications device, manually issues the required commands and telnet transmits these commands. In contrast to telnet, SNMP was designed for automatic monitoring and control, although it also does not exclude the possibility of the administrator's participation in this process. To eliminate potential danger caused by passing the passwords over the network as plain text, communications devices strengthen their protection level. Usually, a multilevel access method is used when a password transmitted over the network as plain text only provides the possibility of reading the basic characteristics of device configuration. Administrative access allowing changes to the device configuration requires using another password transmitted in encrypted form.

Remote control also can be carried out in GUI mode. For UNIX, the X Window system is a de facto standard, which was developed at the Massachusetts Institute of Technology. For Windows, there are several proprietary management protocols, such as virtual network computing, Microsoft terminal server, or protocols from WinFrame.

Remote control has specific advantages, but it is not free from drawbacks. For a user, it is often more convenient to use a more powerful computer installed in a corporate network than a home computer. Moreover, having gained terminal access, the user can run any application on the remote computer not just WWW or FTP services. Another advantage lies in that the user obtains the full rights of a user of the internal network of the company; in the remote node mode, his rights are usually strongly limited by the network administrator.

Remote control sparingly uses the network bandwidth, especially when a command-line mode is emulated. In this case, only the scan codes of the keys and screen characters are transmitted over the network rather than files or Web pages.

The drawback of remote control is the potential danger of unauthorized access to the enterprise-wide network. Furthermore, for an administrator, it is difficult to control resource use of a computer being controlled remotely.

23.3 DIAL-UP ANALOG ACCESS

KEY WORDS: Public Switched Telephone Network (PSTN), analog phone set, pulse method, tone dialing, signaling system 7 (SS7), analog-to-digital and digital-to-analog conversion, Point-To-Point Tunneling Protocol (PPTP), data encoding, data transmission rate, error correction, data compression, V.34, V.34+, V.90 and V.92, V.42, V.42bis, MNP-5

The main idea of dial-up access is using the ubiquitous public switched telephone network (PSTN) for organizing a switched connection between the computer of a home user and the RAS installed on the boundary between the telephone and the computer network. The computer of the home user connects to the telephone network using a dial-up modem that supports standard dialing procedures and simulates the operation of a telephone set for establishing a connection to the RAS. Dial-up access can be analog or digital, depending on the type of local loop provided by the network. In this section, we describe access through analog local loops; the next section covers digital local loops.

23.3.1 Principles of Telephone Network Operation

The first telephone networks were entirely analog because in such networks the terminal equipment (telephone set) transformed sound waves, which are analog signals, into electric oscillations, which are also analog signals. Telephone switches also transmitted user information in analog form by moving these signals into another area of the frequency range using the FDM method covered in *Chapter 9*.

In today's telephone networks, voice is often transmitted from switch to switch in a digital form through PDH/SDH links using time division multiplexing (TDM). However, analog local loops are still numerous, which allows continued use of relatively simple and inexpensive telephone sets.

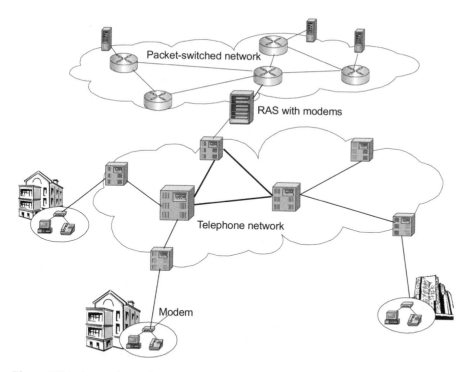

Figure 23.4 Access through a telephone network with analog local loops

Figure 23.4 shows the structure of a typical telephone network. The network is made up of a certain number of telephone switches connected to each other by digital or, rarely, analog links. In general, network topology is arbitrary, although multilevel hierarchy, where several lower-level switches connect to a higher-layer switch, is encountered frequently.

The telephone sets of network subscribers connect to low-level switches through copper pairs. Usually, a local loop length doesn't exceed 1 or 2 km. However, sometimes the communications carrier must use longer local loops of 5–6 km. This happens when there are several remote subscribers for which building a separate POP would be economically inefficient.

A telephone network, like any other circuit-switched network, requires a mandatory connection setup procedure. If this procedure is carried out successfully, a channel is established between the terminal devices of two subscribers through which they can communicate. This procedure is called a *signaling protocol*. We mentioned this term in *Chapter 21*, as WANs based on the virtual circuit technique borrowed a lot from telephone networks. Recall that in analog telephone networks every connection is allocated a bandwidth of 4 KHz. Out of this bandwidth, 3.1 KHz is used for voice transmission, and the remaining 900 Hz transmit signaling information between analog switches and as a guard band between channels allocated to individual users.

During telephone networks' long evolution, many signaling protocols have been developed. These protocols are divided into two classes: user–network interface (UNI), operating at the network section between the user's telephone set and the first network switch, and network–network interface, operating between network switches. Because a modem connects to a telephone network as a user's terminal equipment, it must support only the UNI protocol. You know these terms as X.25 network terms, but initially this division of protocols was introduced in older telephone networks.

An **analog phone set** is a primitive device; therefore, the signaling protocol that it supports must be simple. The subscriber calling procedure usually consists of nothing but sequentially closing and breaking an electric circuit formed by the wires of a local loop. In response to the first closing of this circuit, the telephone switch supplies a certain voltage to the subscriber's circuit, which is reproduced as a dial tone in the phone speaker. The user takes an active part in the calling procedure, dialing the required number in response to the dial tone.

There are two methods of sending the number into the network. When using the **pulse method**, each digit is represented by an appropriate number of sequential opening–closing pulses at a frequency of 10 Hz or 20 Hz.

When using **tone dialing** — Dual Tone Multi Frequency (DTMF), a combination of two audio tone frequencies is used for encoding digits and characters, one from a low-frequency group (697, 770, 852, and 941 Hz), and one from a high-frequency group (1,209, 1,336, 1,477, and 1,633 Hz).

This allows for 16 frequency combinations, thus providing the possibility of entering not only digits but also control characters such as * and #, as shown in Table 23.1.

Table 23.1 Encoding digits and characters when using tone dialing

1,209 Hz	1,336 Hz	1,477 Hz	1,633 Hz	
1	2	3	A	697 Hz
4	5	6	B	770 Hz
7	8	9	C	852 Hz
*	0	#	D	941 Hz

The frequency of 1,633 Hz is an extension of the DTMF standard, allowing for encoding additional characters — A, B, C, and D, which are missing from the standard telephone keyboard, but are used by modems and some applications.

Tones are dialed at a frequency of 10 Hz by 50 msec signals with pauses of equal duration.

When using pulse dialing, several pulses transmit a single digit. In contrast to this, tone dialing requires only one signal for the same purpose. Therefore, the rate of tone dialing is several times higher than that of pulse dialing.

Having received such a "message" from a subscriber's phone set, the telephone switch forwards it further. If the first switch, to which a terminal device is connected, is a digital switch, it converts the analog signal received from the user into the digital form.

To ensure advanced processing logic, contemporary telephone switches use **signaling system 7 (SS7)** protocols. These protocols use the packet-switching technique and are built according to the OSI models, covering layers from physical to application. Detailed descriptions of SS7 protocols go beyond the range of topics covered in this book. Descriptions of these protocols can be found in textbooks dedicated to telephony, for example.

It should be noted that telephone networks continue to transmit user data on the basis of the circuit-switching technique. The packet-switching technique is used only by signaling protocols for connection setup. With SS7 protocols, telephone networks use numerous older signaling protocols, including analog ones.

23.3.2 Remote Access through a Telephone Network

To access the Internet or a enterprise-wide network through a telephone network, the user's modem must dial one of the numbers assigned to the RAS modems. After establishing a connection, a channel with a bandwidth of 4 KHz is created between modems in the telephone network. The exact value of the bandwidth available to the modems depends on the type of telephone switches along the path from the user's modem to the RAS modem and on the type of supported signaling protocols. This bandwidth does not exceed 4 KHz, a principal limitation of the modem's exchange rate.

> The best rates for contemporary modems on a tone-dialing channel are 33.6 Kbps, provided that at least one *analog-to-digital conversion* must be carried out along the entire path, and 56 Kbps, provided that the information undergoes only *digital-to-analog conversions*. This asymmetry occurs because analog-to-digital conversion introduces considerably more deviations into the transmitted discrete data than digital-to-analog conversion.

Obviously, such rates are not satisfactory for most contemporary applications, which widely use GUI and various forms of multimedia data representation.

RAS modems are usually installed in the provider's POP. It need not be the provider that serves the specific remote user. In the 1980s and early 1990s, when the Internet was not as popular as today, many large companies ensured remote access for their employees on their own. In this case, RAS was installed in the POP nearest the LAN of the corporation's headquarters or even in the headquarters. Employees working at home or traveling on business could connect their modems to the POP of a local provider and then dial the modem number of a corporate RAS. Sometimes these could be international calls for employees abroad. Computer traffic traveled most of its path over the telephone network, and the cost of such access depended on a distance, which is typical for tariff options adopted in telephone networks.

Today, the Internet allows more economic use of telephone networks. Telephone networks are needed for connecting to RAS belonging to an ISP instead of a corporate RAS. If the user needs access to a enterprise network instead of the Internet, then the Internet is used as a transit network on the way to the required enterprise network, which also has a connection to the Internet. Since payment for Internet access does not depend on the destination host and the distance to it, remote access to corporate resources is considerably cheaper, including payment for a local call and Internet access. This two-stage access method, though, requires the user to authenticate twice — when accessing the RAS of an ISP and when accessing the servers of the company. Some of the existing protocols eliminate this need in double authentication. An example is the Point-To-Point Tunneling Protocol (PPTP), where the RAS of an ISP transmits the user's authentication request to a corporate server and, after a positive response, connects the user to the required enterprise-wide network using the Internet.

RAS can be connected to a telephone switch using either analog or digital local loops. Powerful RAS devices are equipped with tens of modems and usually are connected using digital local loops through T1/E1 physical links. In this case, analog-to-digital conversion is not needed for data transmission from network to user. Consequently, the downstream data rate can reach 56 Kbps. However, this rate can be achieved only provided that all telephone switches along the path are digital. If at least one of the switches is analog, the maximum downstream rate will be limited to 33.6 Kbps, like the upstream traffic rate.

23.3.3 Modems

Although dial-up modems provide physical-layer services to the computer, they are devices that implement the functions of the two lower layers of the OSI model — physical and data link. A data link layer is needed for the modem to detect and correct errors that occur because of bit errors during data transmission through a telephone network. In this case, the probability of bit errors is relatively high. Therefore, the error-correction function is important for the modem. For the protocol that operates over the modem connection between the remote computer and the RAS, the data-link modem protocol is transparent. Its operation has only one effect, namely, reduction of bit error rate probability to the acceptable level. Since PPP is the main data link-layer protocol used for connecting remote computers to RAS and this protocol does not recover lost or corrupted frames, the error-correcting capabilities of modems are extremely useful.

Protocols and standards for modems are defined in the series V ITU-T recommendations. They are classified into the following three groups:
- Standards defining data transmission rates and methods of data encoding
- Error correction standards
- Data compression standards

Standards for Data Encoding Methods and Data Transmission Rates

Modems are the oldest data transmission devices. They came a long way in their evolution before they were able to operate at 56 Kbps. The first modems operated at 300 bps and could not correct errors. These modems operated in the asynchronous mode, which means that every byte of the information transmitted by the computer was transmitted asynchronously in relation to the other bytes. For this purpose, it was accompanied by start and stop symbols different from data symbols. Asynchronous mode simplifies the device and improves the data transmission reliability. However, it considerably reduces the information rate, because every byte is complemented by one or two redundant start–stop symbols.

Contemporary modems can operate in both asynchronous and synchronous mode.

A crucial moment in the history of modems was the adoption of the **V.34 standard**, which has doubled the maximum rate of data transmission to 28 Kbps from the 14 Kbps rate of its predecessor, the V.32 standard. A feature of the V.34 standard is the presence of *procedures of dynamic adaptation* to the link characteristics in the course of the information exchange. V.34 defines ten procedures, according to which the modem chooses its main parameters after testing the line, including the carrier and bandwidth, the transmitter filter, and the optimal transmission level. Adaptation takes place in the course of the communications session without terminating the connection already established. The possibility of such adaptive behavior was the result of advances in microprocessor and integrated circuits technologies.

The initial connection between modems is established according to the V.21 standard at a minimum rate of 300 bps, which allows for operation over the worst communications lines. Modems continue the negotiation process until the maximum performance that is possible for the given conditions is achieved. The use of adaptive procedures immediately more than doubled the transmission rate in comparison to the previous standard, V.32bis.

The principles of adaptive tuning according to the line parameters were further developed in the **V.34+ standard**. The V.34+ standard increased the data transmission rate with the improved data encoding method. A single code symbol being transmitted carries 9.8 bits on average, in contrast to the 8.4 bits characteristic of the V.34 protocol. At the maximum rate of transmission of code symbols of 3,429 bauds (it is impossible to overcome this limitation, since it is implied by the bandwidth of the tone channel), the improved encoding method provides a data transmission rate of 33.6 Kbps ($3{,}429 \times 9.8 = 33{,}604$).

V.34 and V.34+ protocols allow a two-wire dedicated line to operate in duplex mode. The duplex mode of transmission in the V.34 and V.34+ standards is ensured by simultaneous data transmission in both directions instead of frequency multiplexing. The received signal is determined by subtracting the signal being transmitted from the total signal on the line using DSPs. For this procedure, echo suppression procedures are used because the transmitted signal, being reflected from the near and far ends of the channel, introduces noise into the total signal.

NOTE   *The method of data transmission described in the 802.3ab standard, defining the operation of the Gigabit Ethernet technology on the basis of category 5 twisted pair, has inherited many advanced features from the V.32–V.34+ standards.*

The **V.90 standard** describes the technology aimed at providing users with inexpensive and fast access to provider networks. This standard ensures asymmetric data exchange: up to 56 Kbps from the network and up to 33.6 Kbps to the network. This standard is compatible with the V.34+ standard. This standard was the one that we meant when describing the possibilities of ensuring the transmission of downstream traffic at a rate of 56 Kbps, provided that no analog-to-digital conversion takes place along the entire path.

The **V.92 standard** lets the modem accept another call during connection. In such cases, contemporary telephone stations transmit special dual tone signals to the telephone set so that the subscriber can recognize this situation and switch to the second connection (by pressing the Flash key on the telephone set), toggling the first connection to the hold mode. Modems of the earlier standards terminate a connection in such cases, which is not always convenient for a subscriber; she might be carrying out an important task, such as downloading information from the Internet (and all his or her work might be lost).

A typical structure of connection between two computers or LANs through a router using analog local loops is shown in Figure 23.5.

Error Correction

For modems operating with DTE through an asynchronous interface, the CCITT (now the ITU-T) has developed the **V.42 error correction protocol**. Before adoption of this protocol, modems operating using an asynchronous interface corrected errors according the protocols developed by Microcom. This company has implemented several error-correction procedures in its modems. These procedures became known as the Microcom networking protocol (MNP) of classes 2–4.

In the V.42 standard, another protocol is the main one: the Link Access Protocol For Modems (LAP-M). However, the V.42 standard also supports the MNP 2-4 procedures; therefore, modems corresponding to the V.42 recommendations can establish a reliable error-free connection to any modem supporting this standard as well as to any MNP-

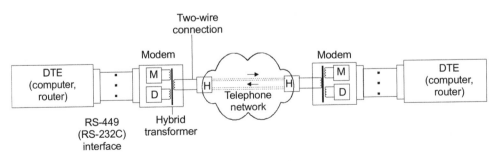

Figure 23.5 Connecting computers using dial-up modems

compatible modem. LAP-M belongs to the HDLC family described in *Chapter 22.* Generally, it operates the same way as other protocols of this family — using connection-oriented, data framing protocols with frame numbering, supporting the sliding window algorithm and frame recovery. The main difference from other protocols of the same family lies in more advanced negotiation procedures, for which LAP-M protocol provides additional types of frames — the *exchange identification* (XID) and *BREAK* frames.

Using XID frames when establishing a connection, modems can negotiate certain protocol parameters, such as the maximum size of the data field, the time-out value for acknowledgments, and the window size. This procedure is similar to the negotiation procedures of PPP. The BREAK command informs a partner modem about a temporary suspension of the data flow. Such situations can arise in an asynchronous interface to the DTE. The BREAK command is sent in unnumbered frames, and it does not influence the frame numbering in the session of data exchange. After resuming data delivery, the modem resumes data sending as if there were no pause in the operation.

Data Compression

Practically all of contemporary modems support the **CCITT V.42bis** and **MNP-5 data compression standards** (usually with a 1:4 compression ratio, although some models support compression ratios of up to 1:8) when operating through asynchronous interface. Data compression increases the link bandwidth. The transmitting modem automatically compresses the data, and the receiving modem automatically decompresses the received data. A modem supporting a compression protocol always tries to establish a connection with data compression. However, if another modem does not support this protocol, then the modem supporting data compression switches to normal communications without compression.

When modems operate through a synchronous interface, they most frequently use the **Synchronous Data Compression** (SDC) protocol developed by Motorola.

23.4 DIAL-UP ACCESS USING ISDN

KEY WORDS: Integrated Services Digital Network (ISDN), customer premises equipment, Terminal Equipment (TE), Network Termination (NT), B, D, and H links, Basic Rate Interface (BRI), Primary Rate Interface (PRI), Q.931 protocol, reference points, terminal adapter (TA)

23.4.1   Goals and Structure of ISDN

The main goal of the development of the ISDN technology was the creation of a world-wide network intended to replace traditional telephone network. Being as available and widespread as the latter one, ISDN was expected to provide millions of its subscribers with various services, both telephone and data transmission. The transmission of TV programs through ISDN was not planned initially; therefore, the developers decided to limit the bandwidth of the local loop to 128 Kbps.

If the goals of the ISDN developers were fully achieved, then the problems of organizing access for home users to the Internet and an enterprise-wide network were also fully solved. However, for many reasons, implementation was too slow. This process started in the 1980s and continued for more than ten years, so when the first home users appeared, most ISDN services had become obsolete. Thus, the access rate of 128 Kbps nowadays isn't an excellent solution suitable for all users. Another interface ensures access rates up to 2 Mbps; however, it is too expensive for most individual users and, as a rule, only companies use it to connect their LANs.

Although ISDN did not become a new public network in the role it initially pretended to play, its services are available and can be used if desired. Later, we describe the structure of this network and its capabilities for organizing remote access.

> ISDN architecture makes provisions for several kinds of services (Figure 23.6):
> - Leased digital links
> - General-purpose dial-up telephone network
> - Circuit-switched data transmission network
> - Packet-switched data transmission network
> - Data transmission network with frame translation (Frame Relay mode)
> - Network management tools

As can be clearly seen from the provided list, the transport services of ISDNs cover a range of services, including popular Frame Relay services. ISDN standards also describe a range of application-layer services: fax connections at a rate of 64 Kbps, telex communications at 9,600 bps, videotext at 9,600 bps, and several other services.

All services are based on the transmission of information in a digital form. The user interface also is digital; therefore, all terminal devices, including telephone sets, computers, and faxes, must transmit digital data into the network. The organization of DSL became one of the most serious impediments preventing ISDN from becoming widespread, because it required the modernization of millions of local loops.

In practice, however, not every ISDN supports all standard services. For example, although Frame Relay service was initially designed within the ISDN framework, as a rule it is implemented as a separate network formed by frame switches that do not intersect with the network of ISDN switches.

The basic rate of an ISDN is the rate of a DS-0 channel (i.e., 64 Kbps). This rate is oriented toward the simplest method of voice encoding, PCM, although differential encoding allows voice to be transmitted with the same quality at 32 Kbps or 16 Kbps.

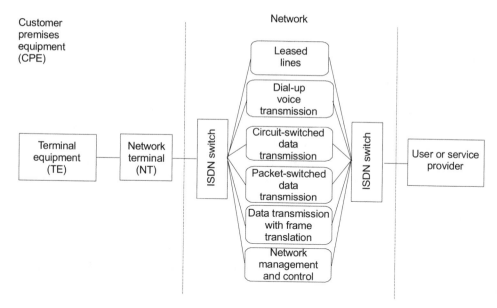

Figure 23.6 ISDN services

One of the original ideas that served as a foundation of ISDN was the combined use of circuit-switching and packet-switching principles. However, a packet-switched network operating as part of an ISDN carries out auxiliary functions. This network is used for transmitting messages of the signaling protocol. As relates to the main information, such as voice, it is still transmitted through a circuit-switched network. Such distribution of functions has obvious logic because call setup connections generate bursty traffic whose transmission is better suited for packet-switched networks than circuit-switched networks.

23.4.2 BRI and PRI Interfaces

One of the main ISDN principles is providing a standard interface clients can use to request various services from the network. This interface is established between two types of **customer premises equipment**:

■ The user's **Terminal Equipment** (**TE**), such as a computer with an appropriate adapter, router, or telephone set

■ The **Network Termination** (**NT**), which represents a device that terminates the communications link to the nearest ISDN switch

The user interface is based on three types of links — B, D, and H.

B links ensure the transmission of user data (digitized voice, computer data, or both) at rates lower than 64 Kbps. Data is split using the TDM technique. In this case, a B channel must be split into subchannels using user equipment, because an ISDN always switches only entire B channels. Channels of type B can use the circuit-switching technique to connect subscribers to each other as well as to organize so-called semipermanent connections equivalent to the leased lines of a normal telephone network. B channels can also be used for connecting subscribers to switches of an X.25 network.

A **D channel** is an access link to the auxiliary packet-switched network that transmits signaling information at rates of 16 or 64 Kbps. The transmission of address information used as the basis to switch B channels in network switches is the main function of a D channel. Another function of this type of channel is supporting services of a low-speed packet-switched network for the transmission of user data. Usually, the network provides this service when D channels are not carrying out their main function.

H channels provide users with the possibility of high-speed data transmission at rates of 384 Kbps (H0), 1,536 Kbps (H11) or 1,920 Kbps (H12). Services providing fast transmission of faxes, video, and high-quality sound can operate on the basis of these channels.

The ISDN user interface is a set of channels of a specific type with predefined transmission rates.

ISDNs support two types of user interfaces — **Basic Rate Interface** (**BRI**) and **Primary Rate Interface** (**PRI**).

BRI provides the user with two 64 Kbps channels for data transmission (B channels) and one 16 Kbps channel for the transmission of signaling information (a D channel). All these channels operate in full-duplex mode. As a result, the total rate of BRI is 144 Kbps in each direction; with the account of signaling information, it is 192 Kbps. Different channels of the user interface share the same physical two-wire cable using the TDM technology, which means that these are logical channels, not physical ones. Data is transmitted through BRI in frames, each frame comprising 48 bits. Each frame contains 2 bytes of each of the B channels and 4 bits of the D channel. Frame transmission lasts 250 msec, which ensures the data rate of 64 Kbps for the B channels and 16 Kbps for the D channel. Besides data bits, the frame contains auxiliary bits for frame synchronization and for ensuring the zero value of the DC component of the electric signal.

BRI can support not only the 2B+D design but also the B+D or simply the D design. The basic rate interface is standardized in the I.430 recommendation.

PRI is intended for users with high requirements for network bandwidth. PRI supports either the 30B+D or the 23B+D design. In both designs, the D channel ensures a rate of 64 Kbps. The first variant is intended for Europe, and the second is for North America and Japan. Because of the popularity of 2,048 Mbps digital channels in Europe and the adoption of the rate of 1,544 Mbps in all other regions, it was impossible to bring the standardized versions of PRI to the common variant.

It is also possible to organize variants of PRI with a smaller number of B channels; for instance, 20B+D. Channels of type B can be combined into a single logical, high-speed channel ensuring a total rate of up to 1,920 Kbps. When several PRIs are installed on the premises of the same user, they can have one common channel of type D, and the number of B channels in the interface that lack a D channel can be increased to 24 or 31.

PRI can be based on channels of type H. In this case, the total bandwidth of the interface still must not exceed 2,048 Mbps or 1,544 Mbps. For H0 channels, it is possible to use 3H0+D interfaces (North American variant) or 5H0+D interfaces (European variant). For H1 channels, it is possible to organize the interface comprising one H11 channel (1,536 Mbps) for the American variant or one H12 channel (1,920 Mbps) and one D channel for the European variant.

Frames of PRI have the structure of DS-1 frames for T1 or E1 channels.

PRI is standardized in the I.431 recommendation.

ATTENTION   *Both B and D channels are logical channels of a local loop. Physically, a local loop is a single twisted pair. D and B channels are organized using the TDM technique for the physical medium created by this twisted pair.*

23.4.3 ISDN Protocol Stack

In an ISDN, there are two protocol stacks: a stack of D channels and a stack of B channels (Figure 23.7).

The network formed by D channels within an ISDN serves as a transport packet-switched network used for transmission of signaling messages. The X.25 network technology served

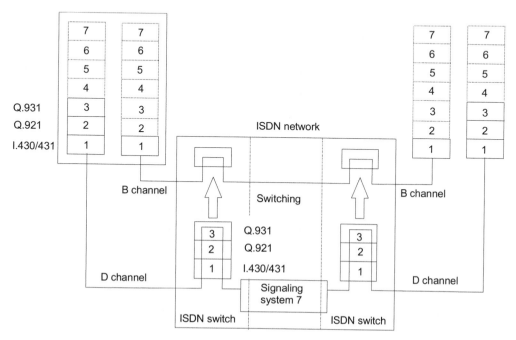

Figure 23.7 ISDN structure

as a prototype for this network. For the network formed by D channels, the following three protocol layers are defined:

- The physical-layer protocol is defined by the I.430/431 standard.
- The LAP on D channel (LAP-D) data link-layer protocol is defined by the Q.921 standard.
- At the network layer it is possible to use the Q.931 protocol (which carries out the calls of subscribers of the circuit-switched service).

Channels of type B form a network with the switching of digital circuits, which transmits subscriber data — namely, digitized voice. In terms of the OSI model, only the physical-layer protocol is defined on B channels in ISDN switches, namely, the I.430/431 protocol. For B channels, circuits are switched according to the commands received through a D channel. When frames of the Q.931 protocol are routed by a switch, the next part of the circuit from the caller to the subscriber being called is switched simultaneously.

LAP-D belongs to the HDLC family, which was already mentioned several times. LAP-D has all the generic characteristics of this family; it also has some specific features. The address of a LAP-D frame consists of 2 bytes, 1 byte defining the code of the service to which the packets encapsulated into frames are sent and 1 byte addressing one of the terminals (if several terminals are connected to the same local loop). Terminal devices can support various services, including a connection setup according to the Q.931 protocol, X.25 packet switching, and network monitoring. LAP-D ensures two modes of operation: connection oriented and connectionless. The latter mode is used, for example, for network monitoring and management.

The Q.931 protocol is the ISDN signaling protocol used on UNI sections. In its packets this protocol carries the ISDN address of the subscriber being called, based on which the switches are tuned for supporting an appropriate B-type circuit. Figure 23.8 illustrates the connection setup procedure according to the Q.931 protocol.

After the user lifts the handset and dials the number of subscriber to be called, ISDN phone set forms the Set up packet and sends it through the D channel to the ISDN switch, to which it has been connected. This switch replies to the subscriber's phone set by the Call processing packet. When this packet arrives, the telephone set of the subscriber starts generating long beeps. Simultaneously, the switch memorizes the fact of the connection setup request and passes the received message to the next switch, the address of which it finds in a table similar to routing tables found in routers of packet-switched networks. At the same time, the message of the Q.931 protocol is translated into the Initial Address Message (IAM) of the SS7 protocol (SS7 messages are not depicted in details in Figure 23.8). As SS7 messages travel across the network, they set the Connection Ready state in transit switches. Output switch of the network, to which the set of the called subscriber is connected, transforms the IAM message of the SS7 protocol into the Call message of the Q.931 protocol. Having received this message, the telephone of the called subscriber starts ringing. If the subscriber lifts the headset, the telephone generates the Connect message, which travels in the inverse direction through all transit switches (naturally, in the form of appropriate SS7 message). As the Connect message travels across the network, all transit switches establish the Connected state by switching B channels in an appropriate way.

Any ISDN terminal device must support Q.931; therefore, an ISDN telephone set is considerably more complicated than an analog telephone set. As can be clearly seen on the basis of Figure 23.8, an ISDN translates Q.931 messages into SS7 messages and then carries out an inverse procedure in local loops.

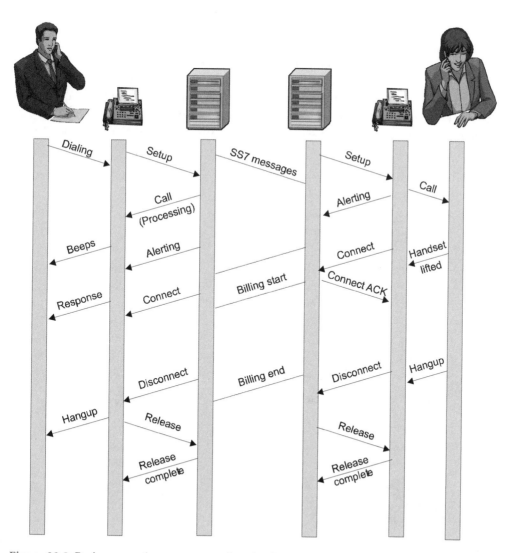

Figure 23.8 Basic connection setup procedure in ISDN according to the Q.931 protocol

23.4.4 Using ISDN for Data Transmission

Despite the considerable differences from analog telephone networks, ISDNs are used in a similar way — that is, as faster analog networks. For example, BRI establishes a duplex data-exchange mode at a rate of 128 Kbps (the logical combination of two B channels). PRI allows 2,048 Mbps. Furthermore, the quality of digital channels is considerably higher than that ensured by analog channels. This means that the percentage of corrupted frames will be considerably lower, and the useful rate of data exchange will be significantly higher.

As a rule, BRI is used in communications equipment for connecting individual computers or small home LANs. PRI is used for connecting medium-sized LANs through a router.

The method of remote access through ISDN is shown in Figure 23.9.

Figure 23.10 shows user equipment connected to an ISDN according to the method developed by ITU-T. All equipment is divided into functional groups; depending on the specific group, there are several **reference points** for interconnecting groups of equipment.

End user's Terminal Equipment (TE1) form the first functional group of equipment. This might be a digital telephone set or a fax. The *S reference point* corresponds to the

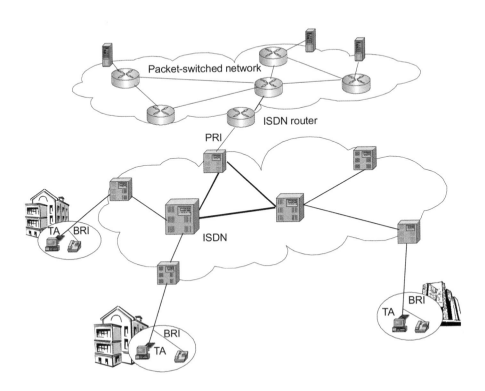

Figure 23.9 Remote access using ISDN

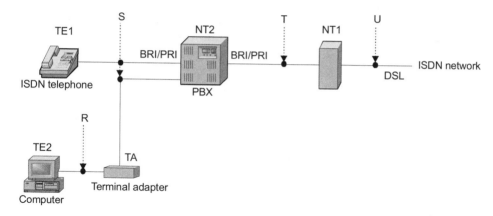

Figure 23.10 Connecting user equipment to an ISDN

point of connection of an individual terminal device — network termination (NT1 functional group) or concentrator of user interfaces (NT2 functional group). By definition, TE1 supports one of SDN user interfaces — BRI or PRI.

If the user's TE1 is connected through a BRI, then a digital local loop is implemented according to a two-wire design, similar to a normal local loop of an analog telephone network. In this case, the 2B1Q potential code is used for data encoding at the DSL section up to the connection point to the ISDN network (*reference point U*). The DSL duplex mode is organized by simultaneous signal transmission through the same twisted pair in both directions, with echo cancellation/suppression and the subtraction of the transmitted signal from the total signal. The maximum length of a local loop in this case is 5.5 km.

When PRI is used, DSL represents a T1 or E1 channel, which means that it represents a four-wire connection having a total length of about 1,800 m. Accordingly, for DSL, other PRI codes are used, HDB3 (in Europe) or B8ZS (in North America).

In contrast to TE1, devices of the **TE2** functional group do not support BRI or PRI. These might be computers or routers with serial interfaces other than ISDN, such as RS-232C, X.21, or V.35. To connect such devices to an ISDN, it is necessary to use a **terminal adapter (TA)**. TAs for computers are manufactured in the form of network adapters. The *R reference point* corresponds to the point of connection of a TE2 terminal device to the terminal adapter (TA). The type of local loop does not depend on whether terminal equipment operates through TA or communicates directly to the network.

Devices of the NT2 functional group are data link- or network-layer devices that concentrate and multiplex user interfaces. Examples of equipment of this type are office PBXs switching several BRIs, routers operating in the packet-switching mode (e.g., through D channels), and simple TDM multiplexers that multiplex several low-speed channels into one B channel. The point of connection of the NT2 equipment to an NT1 device is *reference point T*. In contrast to NT1 equipment, the presence of this type of equipment is not required. Because of this reason, the S and T reference points are connected and designated as *S/T reference point*. Physically, the interface in the S/T point is the four-wire line.

For BRI, the bipolar AMI encoding method was chosen, with binary one encoded by zero potential and binary zero encoded by a potential transition. For PRI, other codes are used, namely, the same as for T1 and E1 (i.e., B8ZS and HDB3, respectively).

Devices of the NT1 functional group are physical-layer devices that coordinate BPR or PRI interfaces with the digital local loop (DSL), connecting the user equipment to the ISDN network. Actually, NT1 is a CSU device that coordinates encoding methods, number of lines in use and parameters of electric signals. The *reference point U* corresponds to the point of connection of an NT1 device to the network.

NOTE   *An NT1 device can be owned by a communications carrier (although it is always installed in the user's premises); alternatively, it can be a user's property. As a rule, in Europe, NT1 devices are considered part of the network's equipment; therefore, user devices (such as routers equipped with an ISDN interface) are manufactured without built-in NT1 devices. In North America, NT1 devices are considered part of the user's equipment; therefore, user devices often are equipped with built-in NT1 devices.*

Thus, to organize remote access, it is necessary to equip user computers with TAs and to install a router equipped with one or more PRIs in the POP. In this case, the maximum access rate for the individual user will be equal to the rate of two B channels (i.e., 128 Kbps). Drivers of ISDN TAs can join two separate B channels into one logical channel. For this purpose, a special extension to PPP is used, known as multilink PPP (RFC 1990).

If a remote user is satisfied with the access rate of 64 Kbps, that user can use the second B channel of BRI for parallel operation of an ISDN telephone. Note that this was impossible when using an analog dial-up modem.

23.5 XDSL TECHNOLOGY

KEY WORDS: xDSL, ADSL modem, ADSL splitter, Asymmetric Digital Subscriber Line (ADSL), Symmetric DSL (SDSL), Rate Adaptive DSL (RADSL), Very high-speed DSL (VDSL), DSL access multiplexer (DSLAM), G.992.1 standard

In the mid-1990s, an alternative to digital ISDN local loops emerged. This family of technologies became known as **xDSL**. The xDSL family includes:

■ **Asymmetric Digital Subscriber Line (ADSL),** which in the advertisements of communications carriers is frequently called broadband access
■ **Symmetric DSL (SDSL)**
■ **Rate Adaptive DSL (RADSL)**
■ **Very high-speed DSL (VDSL)**

Consider the main principles of xDSL operation on the example of ADSL. This technology is the most popular because it was developed for the largest category of home users that needed either Internet access or access to their enterprise-wide networks through the Internet.

ADSL access, similar to analog dial-up access, uses telephone local loops and modems. However, the main difference between ADSL and dial-up access is that ADSL modems operate only on local loops and dial-up modems use the telephone network by establishing connections that pass through several transit switches.

In contrast to traditional dial-up modems (e.g., V.34 and V.90) that must ensure data transmission through channels with bandwidth of 3,100 Hz, ADSL modems have bandwidth of about 1 MHz. The actual bandwidth that an ADSL modem has at its disposal depends on the cable length from the user's premises to the POP and on the cross-section of the wires being used.

The method of ADSL access is shown in Figure 23.11. This method is close to the general method of using the universal local loop shown in Figure 23.2, except that ADSL access ignores TV sets and ensures access only to computers and telephones.

ADSL modems connected to both ends of a short line connecting the subscriber and the POP form three channels: the high-speed downstream channel for data transmission

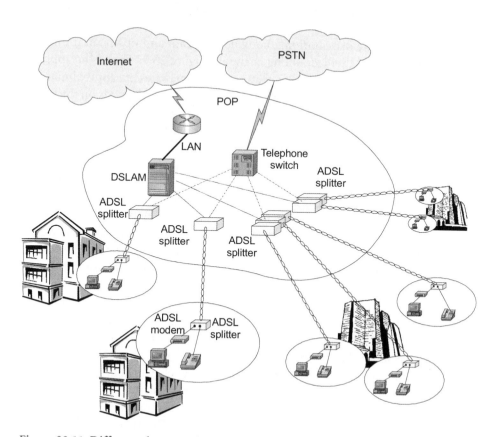

Figure 23.11 Difference between the operation of ADSL modems and of traditional modems

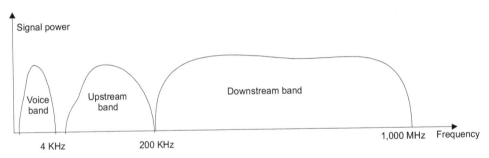

Figure 23.12 Distribution of the local loop bandwidth among ADSL channels

from the network to the computer, the lower-speed upstream channel for data transmission from the computer to the network, and a telephone channel for traditional telephone communications. Data transmission in the network–subscriber channel has a rate from 1.5 Mbps to 6 Mbps, the subscriber–network channel transmits data at rates from 16 Kbps to 1 Mbps, and the telephone channel has traditional bandwidth of 4 KHz (Figure 23.12).

To ensure asymmetric rate distribution among downstream and upstream traffic, the bandwidth is asymmetrically divided among channels. Figure 23.12 shows the approximate distribution of the bandwidth among channels. Channel rates are approximate because the exact value of the bandwidth is not known beforehand. It depends on the length of the local loops, the cross-section of the wires being used, and the twisted pair quality. Moreover, distribution of this bandwidth among channels depends not only on the technological possibilities and modem functionality but also on the provider's decisions. As a rule, ADSL modems allow tuning that can change the bandwidth distribution and the data transmission rate in each direction.

In the customer's premises, a splitter is installed, which distributes frequencies between the ADSL modem and the normal analog telephone, thus ensuring their coexistence.

In the POP, it is necessary to install a device known as a **DSL access multiplexer** (**DSLAM**). It receives computer data separated by splitters from voice data at the far end of the local loop. The number of ADSL modems in DSLAM must correspond to the number of remote users served by the provider using telephone local loops.

After the conversion of modulated signals into a discrete form, DSLAM sends the data to the IP router, which usually is also located in the POP premises. Furthermore, the data are supplied to the provider's backbone and are delivered according to their destination IP addresses — either to public Internet sites or to the user's private network. Voice signals separated by a splitter are transmitted to a telephone switch, which processes them as if the subscriber's local loops were directly connected to such a switch.

Wide deployment of xDSL technologies must be accompanied by a certain reorganization of the operation of ISPs and telephone network providers. This is because their equipment must operate in coordination. Another variant is possible in which a competitive communications carrier leases a large number of local loops from a traditional communications carrier or leases some DSLAM modems.

The G.992.1 standard describes the operation of ADSL modem transceivers. ADSL supports several variants of information encoding: DMT, CAP, and 2B1Q. The achievements of the xDSL technologies depend in many respects on the achievements of encoding techniques, which because of the use of DSP could increase the data transmission rate and simultaneously increase the distance between a modem and a DSLAM.

The rates of ADSL channels depend on the quality of the physical line and the distance between a modem and a DSLAM. The larger this distance, the lower the access rates. Usually, modems decrease the transmission rate; therefore, when installing a modem on a specific local loop, it is possible to choose an optimal operating mode, which would ensure the maximum transmission rate and satisfactory transmission quality.

High rates of ADSL modems create a new problem for the service provider, namely, the bandwidth shortage. If every ADSL subscriber would download the data from the Internet at the highest possible rate — for example, at 1 Mbps — then the provider serving 100 subscribers would require a 100 Mbps channel (Fast Ethernet). If users are allowed to operate at 6 Mbps, the provider will need a 622 Mbps ATM or Gigabit Ethernet channel. For ensuring the required rate, many DSLAMs have a built-in ATM or Gigabit Ethernet switch. The ATM technology attracts developers of DSLAMs because of both its high rate and its connection-oriented nature. When using ATM at the data link-layer, users' computers are required to establish connections to the provider's network prior to starting data transmission. This ensures the possibility of controlling user access and billing them for connection time and transmitted data, if the SLA takes these parameters into account.

The *SDSL technology* allows two symmetric data transmission channels to be organized on the same pair of subscriber's local loop. As a rule, the tone frequency channel is not provided in such a case, and upstream and downstream channel rates are 2 Mbps. However, similar to the ADSL technology, this rate depends on the line quality and on the distance to DSLAM. SDSL was designed for small offices whose LANs contain internal information sources, such as Web sites or database servers. Therefore, symmetric traffic is expected in this case, since SDSL access will be used not only for accessing external networks but also for ensuring access to such servers from outside.

Wide use of xDSL access creates strong competition to ISDN. When using this type of local loop, the subscriber also gets integrated services, this time through the combination of two networks: computer and telephone. However, the presence of two networks is transparent to users because the only thing that they perceive is the possibility of simultaneously using the standard telephone and the computer connected to the Internet. As relates to the rate of computer access, it considerably exceeds the possibilities of PRI ISDN. At the same time, its cost is significantly lower because of the low cost of IP network infrastructure.

23.6 ACCESS USING CABLE TV

KEY WORDS: CATV, cable modem termination station (CMTS), shared medium, time slot, arbitrator, subscriber, CATV local loop

Cable TV is one of the telecommunications services for which a specialized, distributed infrastructure of subscriber local loops was created. Although CATV networks are not as common as telephone networks, in some industrial countries the number of coaxial local loops connecting subscribers to provider's POPs already is comparable to the number of telephone local loops. Bearing in mind that coaxial cable has considerably broader bandwidth (at least 700 MHz), a CATV local loop is capable of handling simultaneous transmission of telephone, computer, and TV traffic.

You already considered the general method of using a CATV local loop as a universal local loop for accessing the Internet, a telephone network, and a CATV network. A CATV local loop was chosen as the example in Figure 23.2. Now, consider this kind of access in more detail.

The difference of the CATV local loop is that several subscribers are simultaneously connected to coaxial cable using the `wired OR` design (Figure 23.13). These might be several private houses or tens or even hundreds of apartments in an apartment building. Therefore, a CATV local loop is a classical shared medium, such as the one used in coaxial Ethernet.

If no cable modems are connected, CATV equipment is used for TV broadcasting from the information source located at the site of provider's POP to the TV sets of cable TV subscribers. For this purpose, a frequency range from 50 MHz to 868 MHz is used (the exact boundaries of this range depends on the national policy of frequency allocation). Each cable TV program is allocated a bandwidth of 6 MHz or 8 MHz from this range; the signal of this bandwidth is encrypted and can be decrypted by the TV sets of those customers that have subscribed to this program.

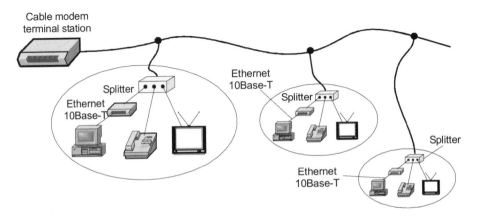

Figure 23.13 Connecting cable modems to a CATV local loop

To use these local loops, the premises of each subscriber are equipped with a splitter and a cable modem. At the POP site, the main modem is installed, called the **cable modem termination station** (**CMTS**).

For bidirectional data transmission, the user's cable modems and CMTS employ available frequencies unused by TV programs. Usually, this is a range of relatively low frequencies from 5 MHz to 50 MHz, below the TV range, and a high frequency range above 550 MHz.

The low frequency range is used for the slower upstream channel, and the high frequency range is used for the fast downstream channel. The data transmission rate in the upstream direction can reach 10 Mbps, and in the downstream channel it can be 30–40 Mbps. User modems can communicate only with CMTS.

Because the downstream and upstream channels use different frequencies, a CATV local loop forms two shared media.

For the downstream channel, CMTS is the only information transmitter; therefore, there is no competition for medium access. CMTS uses the downstream channel for transmitting frames intended for all subscribers, using Ethernet addressing and time division.

The upstream channel is used in multiple access modes by all cable modems connected to this local loop. In this shared medium, CMTS plays the role of an *arbitrator*. Each user's modem can transmit its data only after it gets permission to do so from CMTS. To prevent modems from using the channel for a long time, CMTS allocates each subscriber's modem a limited time slot. Time slots are distributed only among active modems, which allows the limited bandwidth to be used the most efficiently. For newly connected modems, special time slots are allocated. When a subscriber's modem gets connected, it uses one of such time slots to inform CMTS about its presence on the network. Later, it will use only the time slot assigned to it.

A subscriber's cable modem can have a connector for connecting a traditional telephone set, which is also allocated a 4 MHz bandwidth in the lower frequency range. In this case, the subscriber will get three kinds of access — telephone, computer, and TV — from the same provider.

23.7 WIRELESS ACCESS

KEY WORDS: wireless local loop (WLL), fixed wireless access, narrowband and broadband WLLs, multichannel multipoint distribution service (MMDS), local multipoint distribution service (LMDS), IEEE 802.16 standard, General Packet Radio Service (GPRS)

In previous chapters, we considered specific features of wireless access. In *Chapter 9* we covered the general principles of wireless communications, and in *Chapter 14* we described technologies of wireless LANs and PANs. Wireless data transmission is widely used for organizing remote access, especially when a provider cannot ensure its clients wired access. Most frequently this is the case with competitive providers that do not own the local loops connecting client's houses to their POPs. Another typical situation is the organization of temporary high-speed wireless access to a specific building for a conference (e.g., in hotel that is not equipped with wired access ensuring the required rate).

Wireless access can be either fixed or mobile.

Fixed wireless access is organized for subscribers whose computers are located within a limited area, most often within the same building. In this case, the provider can use a directed antenna and a transmitter of a predefined power to ensure stable reception of high-frequency signals within a limited coverage area, such as an individual building. If the provider has a large number of fixed wireless access subscribers, it uses several directed antennas to cover all sectors where its subscribers are located.

Fixed wireless access is also widely known as the **wireless local loop** (**WLL**). This term reflects that despite a lack of cables, subscribers are bound to a specific geographical location.

There are *narrowband* and *broadband* WLLs. WLLs of the first type do not ensure the transmission of a TV signal. They support only relatively low-speed computer access (64–128 Kbps) and the transmission of a telephone signal. WLLs of the second type are usually based on TV broadcasting signals; therefore, they operate in higher frequency ranges and ensure all three types of access. In this case, computer data are transmitted at a rate of hundreds of kilobits per second or several megabits per second.

The systems of the last type include **multichannel multipoint distribution service** (**MMDS**) and **local multipoint distribution service** (**LMDS**). MMDS operates around 2.1 GHz, and LMDS operates around 30 GHz in North America and 40 GHz in Europe. Both systems ensure bidirectional signal transmission for subscribers of TV, telephone, and computer services. Because MMDS operates at considerably lower frequencies than LMDS, it ensures a considerably wider coverage area. One pole with directional MMDS antennas usually can serve a territory with a radius of 50 km. The radius of LMDS transmitters usually does not exceed 5 km, and in the cities it is even smaller. On the other hand, LMDS can ensure for its subscribers considerably higher access rates, reaching 155 Mbps.

Narrowband and broadband WLLs use different methods of signal multiplexing for ensuring simultaneous operation of their subscribers in one sector of antenna direction and for separating TV, telephone, and computer traffic. Usually, a combination of FDM and TDM is used here. For example, for every kind of traffic, it is possible to allocate a specific range of frequencies according to FDM principles. Then, inside the frequency range allocated for computer traffic, it is possible to use asynchronous TDM with a predefined algorithm of access to the shared medium, for example, with a central arbitrator. For some subscribers that need a guaranteed bandwidth, synchronous TDM can be used, which forms wireless PDH/SDH channels.

Unfortunately, WLL technologies have been proprietary in many respects, which means that they are incompatible with access equipment and central stations. To eliminate this drawback, the IEEE 802.16 standard was developed, which defines some general principles of using the frequency range, multiplexing methods, and provided services. This standard allows various multiplexing methods based on FDM as well as on synchronous and asynchronous TDM. This takes into account the interests of different WLL equipment manufacturers and ensures maximum flexibility of such systems.

The 802.11 technology also can be used for organizing fixed wireless access. However, it is not frequently used for this purpose because it is oriented exclusively toward computer access and ignores specific features of telephone and TV traffic, namely, the possibilities of providing access at a constant bit rate. The CDMA/CA access method used in 802.11 cannot ensure the required QoS level for real-time traffic.

Nevertheless, some providers use the 802.11 technology for subscribers satisfied with Internet access without guaranteed bandwidth. This technology is also popular for nomadic access in zones where subscribers stay temporarily, for example, in airports or railway stations.

Wireless access to the Internet is nowadays provided by mobile telephone networks. 2G mobile telephony provides low-speed Internet access using the **General Packet Radio Service (GPRS)** protocol as the packet-switched transport. GPRS operates only in D-AMPS and GSM networks. The full rate of such access is low, 2,400–9,800 Kbps. In 3G mobile networks, which started to be deployed recently, this rate will grow considerably and reach 2 Mbps.

SUMMARY

▶ The term remote access is used when it is necessary to ensure access for home users and employees of small enterprises to the Internet or an enterprise-wide network.

▶ There are different categories of remote access clients, differing in the used local loop, the availability or lack of the home LAN, the requirements for the access rate, and the type of resources to which it is necessary to provide access — resources of the public domain of the Internet or resources of a private enterprise-wide network.

▶ Providers usually try to make local loops as universal as possible — that is, capable of transmitting the traffic of all three main types of terminal devices: telephone set, TV set, and computer.

▶ The base service of remote access is the remote node mode, where the user's computer becomes a node belonging to the provider's LAN or a private enterprise-wide network.

▶ Remote control is a special mode of remote access in which the user's computer emulates the terminal connected to another computer. Remote control allows the user to obtain full control over another computer and run any applications there. This is convenient for the user but presents a potential danger for corporate resources.

▶ The oldest type of remote access is dial-up access through PSTN analog local loops. Using a dial-up modem, the user's computer establishes a connection to RAS that connects to a packet-switched network.

▶ Fixed 4 KHz bandwidth allocated to the users of a telephone network limits the rate of dial-up modems. V.90 modems ensure an upstream rate of up to 33.6 Kbps and a downstream rate of up to 56 Kbps. However, a downstream rate of 56 Kbps can be ensured only when all transit telephone switches from the client to the RAS are digital.

▶ The ISDN technology was developed to create a universal network ensuring computer network services in addition to traditional services. However, nowadays its access rate of 128 Kbps is too low for most clients that require access to multimedia information.

▶ The ADSL technology fully used the bandwidth of the telephone local loop, dividing it into three channels — a duplex voice channel, an upstream channel ensuring a transmission rate of up to 1 Mbps, and a downstream channel ensuring a rate of up to 6 Mbps for computer data. The bandwidth limitation of 4 KHz for telephone subscribers does not influence the operation of ADSL modems because computer data are separated and directed to a packet-switched network at the nearest POP.

▶ Cable modems operate exclusively on a coaxial CATV local loop, a shared medium for several subscribers connecting to the same cable. A broad bandwidth of the coaxial cable ensures an upstream rate to 10 Mbps and a downstream rate to 40 Mbps.

▶ Fixed wireless access uses a large number of proprietary technologies for delivering telephone, TV, and computer information to users. To provide various services, such access uses a combination of FDM, TDM, packet-switching, and circuit-switching techniques.

▶ Mobile access exists as a popular additional service of low-speed data transmission through 2G cellular telephone networks. Standards for 3G mobile networks promise higher transmission rates, but they only are only starting to be deployed.

REVIEW QUESTIONS

1. What factors determine the complexity of organizing remote access?
2. How can a provider that does not own cabled local loops ensure network access services to its users?
3. Which characteristics of remote access clients must be taken into account when organizing remote access service for those clients?
4. What kind of a local loop can be considered universal?
5. In what network does the PC of the remote access user participate?
6. What is the difference between remote node mode and remote control mode?
7. What kind of access is used when configuring remote routers?
8. Why are the rates of dial-up modems considerably lower than the access rates of ADSL and cable modems?
9. What are the differences between modems and DSU/CSU devices?

10. Suppose that you have made sure that the operation of your modem is stable on a dedicated two-wire line in both synchronous and asynchronous mode. Which mode would you prefer and why?

11. To what layer of devices (according to the OSI model terms) is it possible to classify a dial-up modem?

12. What are DSLAM functions?

13. What are the differences between the requirements for the LAN of a dial-up service provider and those for the LAN of an ADSL service provider?

14. What method of access to the shared medium is used by cable modems?

15. Is it possible to use the same coaxial cable for ensuring access to the residents of one apartment building (more than 400 apartments)?

16. Why is the 802.11 technology rarely used for organizing fixed wireless access?

17. What is the difference between MMDS and LMDS technology?

18. Why will most home users not be satisfied with mobile wireless access?

PROBLEMS

1. Suppose that you have purchased a V.90 modem and are attempting to establish a connection, using a telephone network, to your colleague that also uses V.90 modem. You are sure that all telephone switches between you and your colleague operate in a digital mode. At what rate will you connect?

2. Which of the ISDN services is it expedient to use if two PCs are connected to this network using TAs, if they need to constantly exchange data at a rate of 2,400 bps with bursts reaching 9,600 bps, and if packet delays are not critical?

3. Which of the ISDN services is it expedient to use if two LANs are connected to this network through routers and internetwork traffic has rates from 100 Kbps to 512 Kbps during long periods?

4. In which cases is it more expedient to organize remote access through ISDN with a B+D interface? In which cases is it better to use a leased 64 Kbps digital line? When is it more profitable to use a persistent frame relay virtual circuit with a CIR equal to 64 Kbps?

5. What needs to be changed if an ADSL modem operates on a given local loops with an exceedingly high percentage of errors?

SECURE TRANSPORT SERVICES

24.1 INTRODUCTION

In this last chapter of the book, we cover some popular, secure transport services. These services allow traffic transmission using a public network such as Internet in a secure way, ensuring the authenticity, security, and confidentiality of the information being transmitted.

The easiest tool for providing such a service is the protected channel technology, which ensures the protection of traffic between two users of a public network according to the "point-to-point" topology. Such a protection applies the entire range of tools that use various methods of user authentication and traffic encryption. In IP networks, the following two technologies are widely used: secure socket layer (SSL) and Internet protocol security (IPSec). SSL operates at the presentation layer of the OSI model, which makes it nontransparent to applications, since they have to use explicit API calls for traffic protection. IPSec is a more universal tool because it operates at the network layer; consequently, it is absolutely transparent for applications. When using IPSec, applications do not need to be rewritten.

A more powerful tool of traffic protection is the virtual private network (VPN). VPNs are a kind of a "network within a network," which means that the VPN is a service that creates an illusion of a private network for the subscribers of a public network. One of the most important properties of a private network imitated by a VPN is the protection of traffic of VPN users against attacks from the users of a public network. Besides imitating this property of private networks, VPNs can provide their users with the possibility of using private address spaces (such as private addresses belonging to the 10.0.0.0 IP network). Furthermore, VPNs can provide QoS close to that provided by a leased line service.

VPNs are based on technologies that can be divided into two classes: technologies using data encryption and technologies ensuring security on the basis of traffic separation. The first class of technologies uses secure channel technologies, employing them for connecting any number of client networks, not only two network users. IPSec VPN is a typical representative of this class.

Another VPN class uses the technique of permanent virtual circuits, which ensures reliable separation of the client's traffic from the traffic of other network clients. VPNs based on traffic separation do not use encryption because the PVC principle eliminates external attacks from other clients connected to other PVCs. VPNs of this class are based on ATM, Frame Relay, and MPLS technologies. ATM VPN and Frame Relay VPN are nothing but other names for the PVC services of these technologies. These services were covered in *Chapter 21*. This chapter mainly draws your attention to the new type of VPN of this class, namely, to MPLS VPN, which significantly widens the range of VPN services.

24.2 IPSEC PROTECTED CHANNEL SERVICE

KEY WORDS: IPSec, Protected Channel, Secure Socket Layer (SSL) protocol, Transport Layer Security (TLS), Point-To-Point Tunneling Protocol (PPTP), Authentication header (AH), Encapsulating security payload (ESP), Internet Key Exchange (IKE) Data Encryption Standard (DES), Advanced Encryption Standard (AES), one-way function (OWF), hash or digest function, symmetric and asymmetric encryption methods, digital signature, security association transport and tunnel modes, security gateway Integrity Check Value (ICV), security databases

The main goal of the **IPSec** service is to ensure secure data transmission using IP networks. The application area of IPSec ensures data integrity, authenticity, and confidentiality. The base technology allowing these goals to be achieved is encryption.

For the protocols aiming at achieving this goal, the most common term is used — **secure channel**. The term *channel* emphasizes that data protection is ensured along the entire path connecting two network nodes (hosts or gateways)[1].

24.2.1 Hierarchy of the Protected Channel Services

IPSec is one of the most popular of the many available technologies of secure data transmission over a public network. Secure channel can be built using the built-in OS tools implemented at different layers of the OSI model (Figure 24.1).

Application layer	S/MIME	
Presentation layer	SSL, TLS	Non-transparent for applications, independent on the transport infrastructure
Session layer		
Transport layer		
Network layer	IPSec	Transparent for applications, dependent on the transport infrastructure
Data-link layer	PPTP	
Physical layer		

Figure 24.1 Protocols of different OSI model layers involved in creating a secure channel

---

[1] Properties of protected channels were briefly discussed in *Chapter 6.*

If data protection is carried out using higher layers of the OSI model (application, presentation, or session), this method of protection implementation is independent of the underlying technology (be it IP, IPX, Ethernet, or ATM) used for data transportation. This feature is an undisputable advantage of this approach. On the other hand, applications in this case become dependent on the specific security protocol because it is necessary that they have built-in explicit calls to secure channel protocol functions.

A secure channel implemented at the highest, application layer protects only a specific network service, such as file, HTTP, or mail service. Thus, the S/MIME protocol is exclusively intended for e-mail protection. When using this approach, it is necessary to develop an individual version of the protected protocol for each service.

The popular Secure Socket Layer **(SSL) protocol** and its open implementation, called **Transport Layer Security (TLS)**, protect the PDU of any application-layer protocol or individual application. Clearly, these protocols are more universal protection tools than the secure protocols of the application layer, because *any* application can use them. However, for this purpose, it is necessary to rewrite applications to include explicit calls to API functions of the secure channel protocol, which operates at the presentation layer.

The tools of the secure channel become invisible to applications when they protect frames of the network and data link-layer protocols. In this case, however, the developers must face another problem, namely, the dependence of the secure channel service on the underlying protocol. For example, the point-to-point tunneling protocol (PPTP), protects frames of point-to-point protocol (PPP) that operates at the data link layer by encapsulating them in IP packets. Note that at the same time PPTP itself does not belong to the data-link layer. On one hand, this makes the PPTP service universal because the client of the secure channel service can use any network protocol, such as IP, IPX, SNA, or NetBIOS. On the other hand, such a method implies stringent requirements for the use of the data link-layer protocol at the network section used for providing the client with access to the secure channel. When PPTP is used, *only PPP can be used at the data link layer*. Although PPP is widely used in access links, it has serious competitors, such as the Gigabit and Fast Ethernet protocols used not only in LANs but also in WANs.

IPSec operating at the network layer is a compromise variant. It is transparent for applications, but it can operate in practically all networks, since it is based on the widespread IP and uses any data link-layer technology, including PPP, Ethernet, and ATM.

24.2.2 Distribution of Functions among IPSec Protocols

In the Internet standards, IPSec is called the *system*. IPSec is a coordinated set of open standards. It has a well-formed core that can be easily complemented by newer functions and protocols.

The following three protocols form the IPSec core:

■ **Authentication header (AH)** — This protocol ensures data integrity and authenticity.

- **Encapsulating security payload (ESP)** — This protocol encrypts the data being transmitted, thus ensuring confidentiality. It also can support data authentication and integrity.

- **Internet Key Exchange (IKE)** — This protocol solves the auxiliary problem of providing the end nodes of the secure channel with the private keys required for the operation of data authentication and encryption protocols.

As can be seen from the brief descriptions of protocol functions, the functionalities of AH and ESP partially overlap. In contrast to AH, which is responsible only for ensuring data integrity and authenticity, ESP can encrypt data and carry out some functions of the AH protocol. However, as shown later, its functions related to ensuring data authentication and integrity are limited. ESP can support the functions of encryption and data authentication and integrity in any combination, which means that it can carry out both groups of functions or encryption only.

Table 24.1 Distribution of functions among IPSec protocols

Functions	Protocol	
Ensuring integrity	AH	ESP
Ensuring authenticity		
Ensuring confidentiality (encryption)		
Distribution of private keys	IKE	

The distribution of security functions between AH and ESP (Table 24.1) is justified by limiting export, import, or both to the encryption tools, a practice adopted by many countries. These protocols can be used independently or together. This practice is convenient when it is impossible to employ encryption because of existing limitations. In such cases, it is possible to supply the system only with the AH protocol. Naturally, data protection ensuring only AH will be insufficient in many cases. In these cases, the receiving party can only check whether the data was sent by the node from which it was expected and whether it was delivered in the same form as it was sent. The AH protocol cannot protect the information against unauthorized viewing when this information travels across the network. This happens because the AH protocol does not encrypt data. For data encryption, it is necessary to use the ESP protocol.

24.2.3 Encryption in IPSec

To encrypt the data, IPSec can employ any symmetric encryption algorithm. In **symmetric encryption methods**, confidentiality is based on both the sender and the receiver having only one parameter of the encryption function known only to them. This parameter is called the *private key*. The private key is used both for encryption and for decryption of the text.

Figure 24.2 illustrates the classical model of a symmetric cryptographic system. The theoretical foundation of this system was first published by Claude Shannon in 1949. In this model, there are three participants: sender, receiver, and intruder. The goal of the sender is to transmit a protected message using a public channel. For this purpose, the sender uses the key *k* to encrypt the plain text *X*. After that, the sender transmits cyphertext *Y*. The goal of the receiver is to decrypt *Y* to read the message *X*. It is assumed that the sender has his own key provider. The key, generated beforehand, is passed to the receiver through a reliably protected channel.

NOTE   *The* **Data Encryption Standard** *(DES) developed by IBM in 1976 was the most popular symmetric encryption algorithm for a long time. In 2001, DES was replaced by a newer and more advanced standard,* **Advanced Encryption Standard** *(AES), which provides a better combination of security and performance.*

The method of ensuring data integrity and authentication is based on a specific encryption technique using the **one-way function (OWF)**, also called the **hash** or **digest function**.

Such a function, being applied to the data that must be encrypted, provides the so-called digest value in the result. OWF must satisfy the condition according to which it is impossible to recover the source message on the basis of the digest computed using this function.

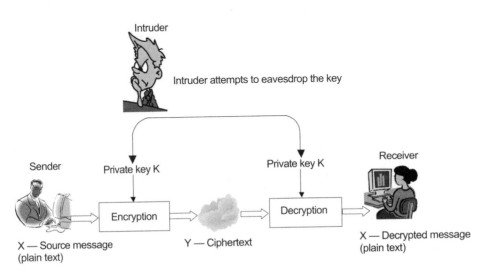

Figure 24.2 Method of symmetric encryption

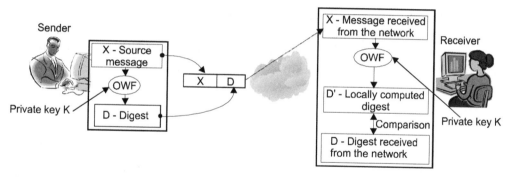

Figure 24.3 Using one-way encryption to ensure data integrity and authenticity

Before considering the example that illustrates the use of a digest functions, note that the digest value produced by such a function, consists of a small, fixed number of bytes, no matter what was the size of the source data.

Assume that it is necessary to guarantee data integrity when transmitting the information through unreliable network. To achieve this goal, the digest of the data to be transmitted is computed at the sender side.

The digest is then transmitted over the network *along with the source message* (Figure 24.3). The receiver, knowing the OWF used to produce the digest, recomputes it on the basis of the received message. If the digest value received over the network matches the value computed locally, the source message did not change during transmission.

NOTE   *The most popular and widely used digest functions in security systems are the MD2, MD4, and MD5 series. All these functions generate digests of a fixed length: 16 bytes. An American standard called SHA is an adopted version of MD4. In this standard, the digest length is 20 bytes. IBM supports the MDC2 and MDC4 digest functions.*

The digest is a kind of checksum for the source message. However, there is a significant difference between the digest and the checksum. Checksums are used for checking message integrity when transmitting messages through unreliable links. Its use *is not aimed at protection against malicious actions.* The presence of the checksum in the packet being transmitted will not prevent the intruder from spoofing the source message by adding a new checksum value. In contrast to checksums, digests are computed using a private key. If an OWF with a parameter (a role is played by the private key known only to the sender and receiver) was used for computing a digest, then any attempt to modify the source message will be immediately discovered.

Thus, a one-way digest function solves two problems simultaneously: It controls the message integrity, and it serves as proof of data authenticity. This method of data transmission, with other methods of proving the authenticity of the message author, is the **digital signature** in ISO terminology. The main area of application for the digital signature includes financial documents accompanying e-commerce and documents related to international agreements. Most frequently, the method of building a digital signature is based on the **RSA asymmetric algorithm**. This algorithm is based on the Diffie-Hellmann concept. This concept assumes that each network user has a private key required for building an encrypted digital signature; all other users check the signature using a public key corresponding to this private key.

24.2.4 Security Association

To ensure that the AH and ESP protocols are capable of protecting the data being transmitted, the IKE protocol establishes a logical connection between two end points; in the IPSec standards, this is called the **security association (SA)**.

IPSec standards allow end nodes of the protected channel to use one SA for the transmission of the traffic of all hosts communicating through this channel and to create for this purpose any number of SAs, for instance, one per TCP connection. This ensures the possibility of choosing the required level of security, from one common association for the traffic of many end nodes to protection of each application using a customized SA.

The SA is a unidirectional (simplex) logical connection; therefore, if it is necessary to ensure a secure bidirectional data exchange, you will need to establish two SAs. In general, these SAs can have different characteristics; for example, when transmitting database queries in one direction only, authentication is sufficient. On the other hand, for confidential data sent in response, it is necessary to ensure confidentiality as well.

The procedure of establishing an SA starts with the mutual authentication of both parties. This is because all security measures will be senseless if the data are transmitted or received by an unexpected person. The SA parameters that will be chosen later define

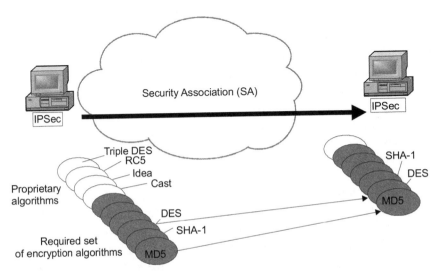

Figure 24.4 Coordination of parameters in the ESP protocol

which of the two protocols, AH or ESP, will be used for data protection and which functions will be carried out by the security protocol. For instance, it can check only authentication and integrity, or it can also ensure confidentiality. Other important parameters of an SA are the private keys used by the AH and ESP protocols.

The IPSec system provides the possibilities for using both automatic and manual methods of establishing an SA. When using the manual method, the network administrator configures end nodes to ensure that they support coordinated association parameters, including private keys. When using an automated procedure of establishing an SA, IKE protocols operating on different sides of the channel choose parameters in the course of the negotiation process. For each task carried out by the AH and ESP protocols, it is possible to choose from several authentication and encryption protocols (Figure 24.4). This capability makes IPSec a flexible tool. Note that the choice of the digest function for solving the problems of ensuring integrity and authenticity does not influence the choice of the encryption function for ensuring data confidentiality.

For guaranteeing compatibility, the standard version of IPSec defines a certain required "toolkit." For instance, data authentication always requires one of the standard one-way encryption functions, either MD5 or SHA-1, and the list of encryption algorithms must include DES. Manufacturers of products that include IPSec extend the protocol by including other authentication and encryption algorithms. For instance, many IPSec implementations support the popular Triple DES encryption algorithm and some relatively new ones, such as Blowfish, Cast, CDMF, Idea, and RC5.

24.2.5 Transport and Tunnel Modes

The AH and ESP algorithms can protect data in two modes: transport and tunnel. In the **transport mode,** the IP packet is transmitted through the network using the original header of this packet. In the **tunnel mode,** the source packet is encapsulated in the new IP packet and the data is transmitted over the network on the basis of the new IP packet header.

The use of a specific mode depends on the requirements to data protection and on the role that the node terminating the secure channel plays in the network. For example, this node may be a host (end node) or a gateway (transit node). Accordingly, there are three modes of IPSec application:

■ Host–host

■ Gateway–gateway

■ Host–gateway

In the first mode, the secure channel or the SA (which in this context are the same) is established between two end nodes of the network (Figure 24.5). IPSec in this case operates on the end nodes and protects data transmitted from host 1 to host 2. For the host–host mode, the transport protection mode is used most frequently.

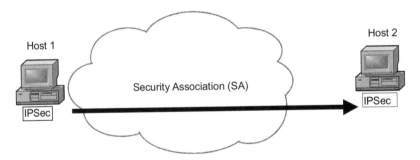

Figure 24.5 Establishing a secure channel according to the host–host mode

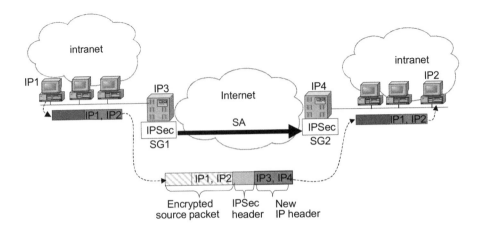

Figure 24.6 Operation of the secure channel in the tunnel mode
according to the gateway–gateway mode

According to the gateway–gateway mode, the protected channel is established between two transit nodes, called **security gateways (SGs)**, each running IPSec (Figure 24.6). The secure data exchange can take place between any two end nodes connected to the networks behind SGs. End nodes are not required to support IPSec. They transmit their traffic as plain text through the trusted intranets of their companies. The traffic sent to the public network goes through the SG, which ensures its protection using IPSec. Gateways can use only the tunnel mode of operation.

As shown in Figure 24.6, the user of the computer with the IP1 address sends a packet to the IP2 address using the tunnel mode of IPSec. The SG1 gateway encrypts the entire packet, including the IP header, and supplies the encrypted packet with a new IP header. In the new header, it specifies its address, IP3, as the source address and fills the destination address, IP4, with the address of SG2. All data is transmitted over IP on the basis of the data in the header of the external packet. The encapsulated packet serves as the data

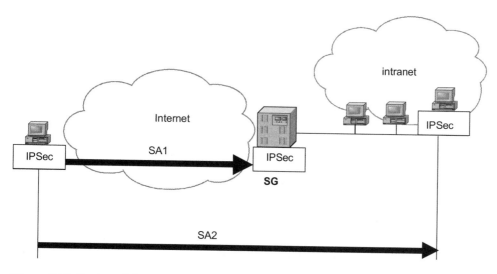

Figure 24.7 Design of the secured host–gateway channel

field for the external one. When the packet arrives at the SG2 gateway, IPSec retrieves the encapsulated packet and decrypts it, thus returning it to its initial form.

The host–gateway mode (Figure 24.7) is often used for remote access. In this case, a secure channel is organized between the remote host running IPSec and the gateway that protects the traffic of all hosts connected to the company intranet. This mode can become more complicated if you create another secure channel between the remote host and any other host belonging to the internal network protected by the gateway. Such combined use of two SAs will reliably protect the traffic within an internal network.

24.2.6 AH Protocol

The AH protocol allows the receiving party to ensure the following:

- The packet was sent by the party to which this association has been established.
- The packet content was not modified in the course of transmission across the network.
- This packet is not a duplicate of some other packet received earlier.

The first two functions are required for the AH protocol. The third function is optional and can be chosen when establishing an association. To carry out these functions, the AH protocol uses a special header. The format of this header is shown in Figure 24.8.

The *Next Header* field specifies the code of the higher-layer protocol — for example, the protocol whose message is encapsulated in the data field of the IP packet. This probably

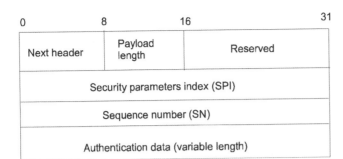

Figure 24.8 Structure of the AH protocol header

will be a transport-layer protocol (TCP or UDP) or ICMP. However, this might be the ESP protocol if it is used with AH.

The *Payload Length* field specifies the length of the AH header.

The next field, *Security Parameters Index* (SPI), is used for relating the packet to the SA corresponding to it.

The *Sequence Number* (SN) field specifies the sequential number of the packet. It is used for protecting the packet from being reproduced by a third party that may try to reuse the sniffed protected packets sent by the authenticated user. The sender sequentially increases the value of this field in each new packet transmitted within the framework of this association, so the arrival of a duplicate will be noticed by the receiving party — provided that the protection against false duplication was enabled within this association's framework. Regardless, the AH protocol does not restore lost packets and does not reorder the arriving ones. If it discovers that a similar packet has already been received, it discards the duplicate. To reduce the amount of buffer memory required for the protocol operation, the sliding window algorithm is used. Only those packets that have a number that falls within the window limits are checked for duplication. As a rule, the window size is set to either 32 or 64 packets.

The *Authentication Data* field is used for authenticating packets and checking the integrity. This field contains the **Integrity Check Value (ICV)**. This value, also known as the digest, is calculated using one of the OWF encryption functions that the AH protocol must support — MD5 or SAH-1. However, it is possible to use any other optional function about which the parties have come to an agreement when establishing an association. The symmetric private key is used as a parameter when computing the digest. The private key for an association can be specified manually or set automatically using the IKE protocol. Since the length of the digest depends on the selected function, this field generally has a variable length.

When calculating the digest, the AH protocol tries to take into account as many fields of the source IP packet as possible. However, some of these fields can change unpredictably in the course of packet transmission over the network. Therefore, such fields cannot

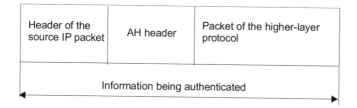

Figure 24.9 Structure of the IP packet processed by the AH protocol in the transport mode

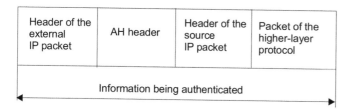

Figure 24.10 Structure of the IP packet processed by the AH protocol in the tunnel mode

be included into the authenticated part of the packet. For example, it is impossible to evaluate the integrity of the packet's *time to live* field in the receiving node because this field is decreased by one on any transit router and therefore will never be the same as the source value.

The location of the AH header within the packet depends on the mode of the secure channel configuration — either transport or tunnel. Figure 24.9 illustrates how the resulting packet will appear in the transport mode.

If the tunnel mode is used, when the IPSec gateway receives the transit packet and encapsulates it in the external IP packet, the AH protocol protects all fields of the source packet as well as unchanged fields of the header of the external packet (Figure 24.10).

24.2.7 ESP Protocol

The ESP protocol solves two groups of problems. The first group includes the functions similar to those of the AH protocol, namely, ensuring data integrity and authentication on the basis of the digest. The second group includes data protection against unauthorized viewing by encrypting the data being transmitted.

As shown in Figure 24.11, the header is divided by the *Payload Data* field into two parts. The first part, the *ESP header,* is made up of two fields, *SPI* and *SN,* similar to the

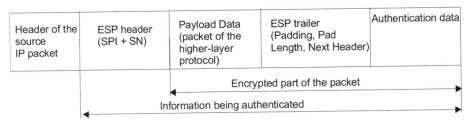

Figure 24.11 Structure of the IP packet processed by the ESP protocol in the transport mode

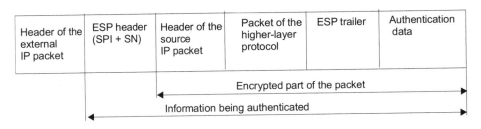

Figure 24.12 Structure of the IP packet processed by the ESP protocol in the tunnel mode

AH fields with the same names. The header is located before the data field. The remaining service fields of the ESP protocol, called the *ESP trailer*, are located at the end of the packet.

The two trailer fields are similar to fields of the AH header. These are the *Next Header* and *Authentication Data* fields. The *Authentication Data* field is missing if the ESP capabilities related to ensuring integrity are not used when establishing an SA. Besides these two fields, the trailer includes two auxiliary fields — *Padding* and *Pad Length*. The padding might be needed in three cases. First, normal operation of some encryption algorithms requires the text being encrypted to contain an even number of blocks of a predefined size. Second, the ESP header format requires that the data field terminates at the 4-byte boundary. Finally, the padding can be used to hide the packet size to ensure so-called partial confidentiality of the traffic. The hiding capabilities are limited by the relatively small padding size, 255 bytes. This is because a large amount of auxiliary data can reduce the effective bandwidth of the communications link.

Figure 24.11 shows the location of the ESP header fields in the transport mode. In this mode, ESP does not encrypt the IP packet header; if it did, the router would be unable to read the header fields and correctly forward the packet from network to network. The list of fields that must be encrypted does not include the *SPI* and *SN* fields, which must be transmitted as plain text to ensure that the arriving packet can be classified as belonging to a specific association. This protects the packet against unauthorized reproduction.

In the tunnel mode, the header of the source IP packet is placed after the ESP header and falls into the list of protected fields. The header of the external IP packet is not protected by the ESP protocol (Figure 24.12).

24.2.8 Security Databases

Thus, IPSec provides several methods of traffic protection. How does IPSec implementation operating on the host or gateway define the protection method it has to apply to traffic? The solution is based on two types of databases used on each node supporting IPSec:

■ Security association database (SAD)   ■ Security policy database (SPD)

When establishing an SA, as with any logical connection, both parties conclude several agreements regulating the flow transmission between them. Agreements are created in the form of a set of parameters. For an SA, such parameters are the type of security protocol (AH or ESP), the mode of protocol operation, the encryption methods, the private keys, the number of the current packet within the current association, and other information. The sets of parameters determining all active associations are stored on both end nodes of the protected channel in the form of a SAD. Each IPSec node supports two SADs, one for incoming associations and one for outgoing associations.

Another type of database is SPD, which specifies mapping between IP packets and processing the rules established for them. SPD records consist of two types of fields — the packet selector field and the security policy field for the packet with the current selector value (Figure 24.13).

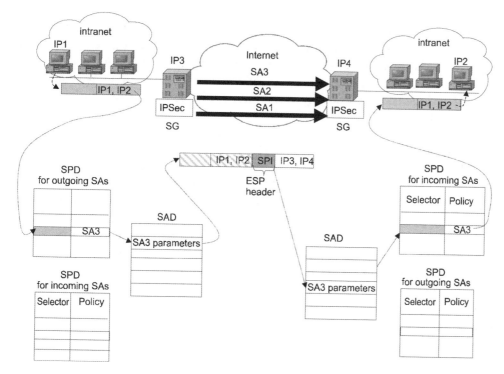

Figure 24.13 Using SPD and SAD

The selector in SPD includes the following set of attributes, which make it possible to detect the flow requiring protection:

■ Source and destination IP addresses that can be represented by a separate address of any type (individual, group, or broadcast) or by a range of addresses specified either by lower and upper limits or by using an address with a mask

■ Source and destination ports (e.g., TCP or UDP ports)

■ Types of transport-layer protocols (TCP, UDP)

■ User name in the DNS or X.500 format

■ System name (host, SG, etc.) in the DNS or X.500 format

For each new packet arriving at the secure channel, IPSec views all database records in the SPD and compares the selector values to the appropriate fields of the IP packet. If the field values match the specified selector, then operations defined in the security policy field of this record are carried out for the packet. The policy provides one of the following possibilities: passing the packet without changes, discarding the packet, or processing it using IPSec.

In the latter case, the security policy field must refer to the record contained in the SAD, which contains the set of SA parameters for this packet. (In the example shown in Figure 24.13, SA3 is defined for the outgoing packet.) Based on the parameters specified for SA3, a protocol is applied to the packet (ESP in Figure 24.13), encryption functions, and private keys.

If some security policy must be applied to the outgoing packet but the SPD record indicates that there is no active SA with the required policy, IPSec creates a new association using the IKE protocol. In this case, new records will be inserted into the SAD and the SPD.

SPDs are created and managed either manually by the user (a variant more suitable for a host) or the system administrator (a variant more suitable for gateways) or automatically by an application.

Earlier in this chapter, we explained how a relationship is established between the outgoing IP packet and the SA specified for it. However, there is another problem: how the *receiving* IPSec node determines how to process the arriving packet. After all, when using encryption, many key parameters that make up the selector will be unavailable; consequently, the parameters of the respective SA will be unavailable. To solve this problem, the AH and ESP headers provide the *SPI* field, which was mentioned earlier. This field contains the pointer to the SAD row that stores the parameters of the appropriate SA. The AH and ESP protocols fill this field when processing the packet at the beginning of a secure channel. When the packet arrives at the end node of the secure channel, the SPI pointer is retrieved from its ESP or AH header (in Figure 24.13, this is the ESP header). All further processing is carried out with the account of all parameters specified by this association pointer.

Thus, for the recognition of packets related to different SAs, the following means are used:

■ At the sender node — selector
■ At the receiver node — SPI

After decrypting the packet, the receiving IPSec node checks its attributes (which are now available) for matches with the SPD for the incoming traffic. This ensures that there were no errors and that packet processing corresponds to the security policy specified by the administrator.

Using SPDs and SADs for controlling the traffic protection gives the flexibility to combine the SA connection-oriented mechanism with the datagram nature of IP traffic.

24.3 VIRTUAL PRIVATE NETWORK SERVICE

KEY WORDS: private network, public network, Customer Provided VPN (CPVPN), Provider Provisioned VPN (PPVPN), Customer Premises Equipment based VPN (CPE-based VPN), or Customer Edge based VPN (CE-based VPN), intranet, extranet, QoS, Layer 2 VPN, (L2VPN), Layer 3 VPN (L3VPN), ATM VPN, Frame Relay VPN, MPLS VPN, IPSec VPN

24.3.1 VPN Definition

The term VPN means that such networks reproduce the properties of *truly private networks*. The network can be considered private only when the company owns it and has full control of all network infrastructure — cables, cross equipment, channel-building equipment, switches, routers, and other communications equipment.

The main feature of the private network from shared or public networks is its **isolation** from any other network.

The consequences of such isolation are as follows:

■ *Independent choice of network technologies* — The possibilities are limited only by the choice of a vendor or manufacturer.

■ *Independent addressing system* — In private networks, it is possible to choose any address.

■ *Predictable performance* — Owning communications links guarantees the predefined bandwidth between end nodes of the company (for WAN links) or communications devices (for local connections).

■ *Maximum security* — A lack of connections to the external world considerably reduces the possibility of attacking the network from the outside. It also reduces the probability of eavesdropping on the traffic along its path.

However, a private network is an extremely uneconomical solution. Only large and extensive corporations can afford such networks, especially on a national or international scale. The luxury of creating a private network is the privilege of those who have all the prerequisites for creating a private network infrastructure. For instance, large gas or petroleum companies are capable of installing private technological cabling systems along their pipelines. Private networks were popular until relatively recently before the infrastructure of public data networks reached the required level of evolution. Nowadays, nearly all such networks have been moved out of the market by VPNs, which provide a compromise between the QoS and the cost of the services that they provide.

> The VPN technology allows a medium shared by several companies to be used to implement services whose QoS characteristics are comparable to those of a private network (including security, availability, predictable bandwidth, and independent choice of the addressing system).

VPNs are classified into two types, depending on who implements them:

■ The name **customer-provided VPN (CPVPN)** reflects that all problems related to VPN support must be solved by the client. In this case, the ISP provides only the traditional services of accessing the public network to connect the client's end nodes. Network specialists employed by the company configure and manage the VPN tools.

■ The term **provider-provisioned VPN (PPVPN)** reflects the fact that the service provider uses its own network to build a private network for each client. "Private" client networks are isolated and protected from other networks. This method of VPN organization is relatively new. Therefore, it is not as widespread as the first method.

In recent years, PPVPN popularity has steadily grown because the job of creating and supporting VPN is difficult and specific. Consequently, most companies prefer to delegate this job to a reliable service provider. Implementation of VPN services allows the service provider to offer its clients a range of additional services: control over network operation, Web and e-mail service hosting, and specialized software hosting.

Besides dividing VPNs into CPVPNs and PPVPNs, there is another classification. According to it, VPNs are classified by the location of the devices that carry out VPN functions. VPNs can be built:

■ On the basis of equipment installed at the customer's premises: **customer premises' equipment-based (CPE-based)** or **customer edge-based (CE-based)** VPN

■ On the basis of the service provider's infrastructure: **network-based VPN** or **provider edge-based (PE-based) VPN**

The term *edge* in the names of the VPN types specifies that most (sometimes all) functions related to VPN support are carried out by edge network devices owned either by the client or by the service provider.

Provider-supported networks can belong either to PE-based or to CE-based types. The first variant is more obvious, because the provider maintains the equipment connected to its own network. In the second case, VPN equipment is located on the customer's territory, but the service provider controls this equipment remotely. This relieves the customer's employees from carrying out rather difficult tasks.

When a VPN is supported by the client (CPVPN), all equipment is always located in the client's network. This is the CE-based type VPN.

24.3.2 VPN Evaluation and Comparison Criteria

A VPN, like any *simulating system*[2], is characterized first by the property of the object being simulated, second by the level of approximation to the original, and third by the simulating tools being used.

Thus, consider the private network elements simulated in a VPN.

Practically all VPNs imitate *private, leased lines* in the infrastructure of the provider, intended for serving many clients.

NOTE *Here, some confusion with the terminology is possible. This happens because imitated private, dedicated links in the infrastructure of the communications carrier based on TDM (telephone, PDH, or SDH) traditionally are not considered a VPN. Networks built on the basis of network equipment owned by the client but using leased physical links are usually classified as private networks. This is because the synchronous TDM technology used in these networks guarantees that the information flows of different users are separated. This technology also ensures a fixed bandwidth for each flow and QoS parameters at the level of a shared medium. Because of this, such links are called dedicated — they are provided for individual clients for their exclusive use, and other clients cannot use them. This method is the one used by most private networks, which operate on the basis of leased lines instead of private ones.*

When simulating the infrastructure of links owned by the same company, VPN services are called **intranet** services. When such channels are complemented by links connecting the client to partner companies and data must be exchanged with them in a secure mode, the service is called **extranet**.

The term VPN is used only when "private" physical links are simulated by packet-switching technologies, such as ATM, Frame Relay, X.25, IP, or IP/MPLS. In this case, the difference between the communications quality provided by such VPNs and that ensured by **actually** private physical link becomes noticeable. In particular, the use of the word *virtual* becomes justified because the indeterminacy of the bandwidth and other characteristics start to manifest. When using packet-switched networks for building VPNs, clients are provided not only with physical links but also with a certain data link-layer technology (such as ATM or Frame Relay). When using IP, the clients are also provided with network-layer services.

A VPN can also simulate higher-layer network elements. For example, a VPN can operate at the network layer by supporting the client's IP traffic and simultaneously creating the effect of an isolated IP network. In this case, besides the simulation of physical links, the VPN carries out some additional operations over the client traffic, including accumu-

---

[2] In this case, VPN is considered as simulation of a private network of an enterprise.

lating various statistics and filtering and screening interactions among users and among affiliations of the same company. (This feature mustn't be confused with isolation from external users, which is the main VPN function.)

The simulation of application-layer services in VPNs is rare in comparison to the simulation of transport functions. Nevertheless, it is possible. For instance, the service provider can support the client's Web sites, e-mail system, or specialized resource planning applications.

Another criterion used when comparing VPNs compares the approximation level of VPN services to services provided by a truly private network.

Security is the most important property of private network services. VPN security includes the entire set of protected network attributes — information confidentiality, integrity, and reliability in the course of data transmission over a public network and protection of the internal resources of the client's and provider's networks against attacks from the outside. The VPN security level can vary broadly depending on the security tools being used — traffic encryption, user and device authentication, address space isolation (for example, on the basis of NAT), virtual channels and point-to-point tunnels, and complicated unauthorized user connections. However, because no single protection mechanism provides guarantees, security tools can be combined to create in-depth protection.

Second, it is desirable to ensure that VPN services approach the *QoS characteristics* of a truly private network. The quality of the transport service assumes, first of all, guaranteed bandwidth for the client's traffic. This might be complemented by other QoS parameters, such as maximum delays and an affordable percentage of data loss. In packet-switched networks, traffic bursts, variable delays, and packet loss are inevitable; therefore, the degree of approximation of virtual channels to TDM channels is always incomplete and has a probabilistic nature. On average, no guarantees are ensured for individual packets. Different packet-switching technologies differ by their ensured QoS levels. For example, in ATM, QoS mechanisms are the most ideal and well-tested; similar mechanisms in IP networks appeared only recently. Therefore, not every VPN simulates these specific features of a private network. Thus, security is a mandatory property of any VPN, and the quality of its transport service is only an optional, although highly desirable, feature.

Third, VPN becomes comparable to a truly private network if it ensures *independent address space* for its clients. This provides the client with the convenience of network configuration and the method of maintaining security. At the same time, it is desirable to ensure that clients have no information about the address spaces of other clients or the address space of the provider's backbone. In this case, the provider's backbone will be reliably protected against malicious actions or human errors. Consequently, the VPN will ensure a higher quality of provided services.

The technologies used for creating VPNs have considerable influence on the properties of VPNs. All VPN technologies can be divided into the following two classes depending on their method of ensuring data transmission security:

■ Traffic segregation technologies   ■ Encryption technologies

24.3.3 VPN on the Basis of Traffic Segregation

Traffic segregation technologies use the permanent virtual circuit technique to ensure reliable protection of each client's traffic from intentional or unintentional access by other clients of the public network. This type of technology includes:

- ATM VPN
- Frame Relay VPN
- MPLS VPN

Point-to-point virtual circuits simulate dedicated line service by passing from the CE device of one **client site** through provider's network to the CE of the other client site.

NOTE *In this case, the term* site *designates a standalone fragment of the client's network. For example, an enterprise-wide network connecting the headquarters and three remote affiliations comprises four sites.*

Data protection is achieved by ensuring that an unauthorized user cannot connect to the permanent virtual circuit without modifying the switching table on the provider's devices. This prevents unauthorized users from carrying out an attack or reading data. The traffic protection feature is a *native property* for the virtual circuit technique; therefore, ATM VPN and Frame Relay VPN services are nothing but normal PVC services of ATM or Frame Relay networks. Every user of an ATM or Frame Relay network using a PVC infrastructure for connecting LANs uses the VPN service. This is one of the generic advantages of the virtual circuit technique in comparison to the datagram technique, because the latter does not provide the user with any protection against attacks by other users if additional VPN tools are not used.

Since both ATM and Frame Relay use only two stack levels in the course of data transmission, VPN variants built on their basis are called **Layer 2 VPN** (**L2VPN**). The availability of QoS support mechanisms in ATM and Frame Relay allows for sufficiently good simulation of the dedicated line quality.

Layer 3 information in such networks is never analyzed or modified. This is both an advantage and a drawback of such networks. The advantage is that the client can use such virtual channels for transmitting the traffic of any protocol, not only IP. Furthermore, the IP addresses of the clients and the provider are isolated and independent. They can be chosen arbitrarily because they are not used for traffic transmission through the provider's backbone. The client does not need any information about provider's network except the virtual channel labels. The drawback of this approach is that the provider does not operate with the client's IP traffic and, consequently, cannot offer the client additional services related to IP. Note that nowadays such additional services are a rather promising business area attracting many providers.

The complexity of L2VPN is quite high, and the same is true for its cost. When organizing a fully connected client site topology, the dependence of configuration operations on the number of sites has a quadratic nature (Figure 24.14, *a*)

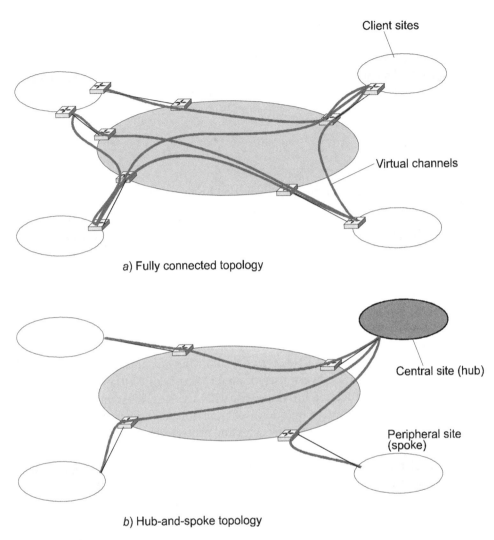

a) Fully connected topology

b) Hub-and-spoke topology

Figure 24.14 L2VPN scalability

To connect *N* sites, it is necessary to create $N \times (N-1)/2$ bidirectional virtual circuits (or $N \times (N-1)$ unidirectional ones). In particular, if $N = 100$, then 5,000 configuration operations will be required. Although these operations are carried out using an automated network management system, manual operations and error probability remain. When only intranet services are provided, the number of connections requiring configuration is directly proportional to the number of clients, which certainly is an advantage! The use of extranet services complicates the situation, because in this case it is necessary to ensure connectivity between sites of different clients. The scalability of ATM and Frame Relay

VPNs can be improved if the client abandons a fully connected topology and organizes star connections (hub and spoke) through one or more dedicated transit sites (Figure 24.14, *b*). Naturally, the performance of the client's network will decrease, since there will be more transit information transmissions. However, the economy of such a solution will be obvious, because providers, as a rule, bill their clients on per channel.

Clients of an ATM or Frame Relay VPN are unable to cause damage to one another. Furthermore, they are unable to attack the provider's network. Nowadays, any provider has an IP network, even if it provides only ATM or Frame Relay VPN services. Providers

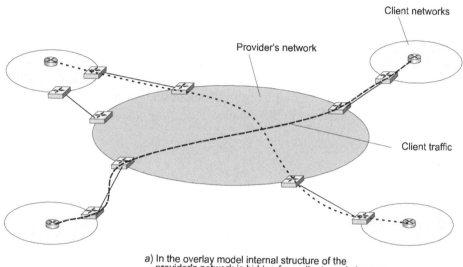

a) In the overlay model internal structure of the
provider's network is hidden from clients and vice versa

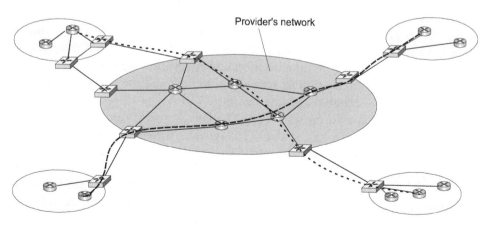

b) In the peer-to-peer model provider's network
and client networks "know" the structure of each other

Figure 24.15 Overlay and peer-to-peer VPN models

that limit themselves to ATM or Frame Relay VPN services are rare. After all, without an IP network the provider will be unable to manage and maintain its ATM or Frame Relay network. An IP network is an overlay network in relation to ATM or Frame Relay; therefore, ATM and Frame Relay have no information about its structure or even its presence.

MPLS VPNs are divided into **MPLS VPN 2L** (layer 2) and **MPLS VPN 3L** (layer 3). Both technologies use label switching paths (LSPs) for client traffic segregation within the MPLS-enabled provider's network.

MPLS VPN 3L communicates with client networks on the basis of IP addresses. MPLS VPN 2L uses layer 2 address information for the same purpose. For example, these may be MAC addresses or identifiers of Frame Relay virtual circuits.

Using an MPLS-enabled network significantly reduces the manual operations related to VPN configuration for service providers. The number of operations related to MPLS VPN configuration is directly proportional to the number of client sites. Note that with an ATM or Frame Relay VPN, this value is proportional to the square of the number of client sites. Another advantage of MPLS VPN is close integration of VPN with other MPLS applications, such as TE and QoS. Because of specific interest to the MPLS VPN this topic will be covered in more details later in this chapter.

24.3.4 IPSec VPN

Technologies based on **encryption** are another class of VPN technologies. They are used when a VPN is built on the basis of a datagram network, which cannot ensure traffic segregation. Classical IP networks belong to this class.

IPSec is the main VPN technology on the basis of encryption. It is used for creating an infrastructure of secure channels connecting the sites belonging to one company (intranet) or to several companies (extranet).

IPSec standards provide high flexibility, allowing companies to choose the required protection mode (with encryption or ensuring only data authenticity and integrity) as well as to choose among various authentication and encryption algorithms. The IPSec encapsulation mode isolates the address spaces of the client and the service provider by using two IP addresses — external and internal ones.

Most frequently, IPSec is used for supporting CPVPNs, in which case the client creates IPSec tunnels through the provider's network. The provider is required to supply only the standard internetworking service. Consequently, the client can access both the services available within the provider's network and Internet services. The procedure of IPSec VPN configuration is complicated, because IPSec tunnels are point-to-point tunnels. When fully connected topology is implemented, the number of such tunnels is proportional to $N \times (N-1)$. It is also necessary to take into account a difficult task of supporting the key infrastructure.

IPSec can also be used for creating provider-supported VPNs. In this case, the tunnels are again built on the basis of CE-based equipment; however, these devices are remotely configured and maintained by the provider.

> Of all the properties of a truly private network, IPSec VPNs simulate only security and isolation of the address space.

Link bandwidth and other QoS parameters are not supported by this technology. However, if the service provider ensures QoS services (for example, using DiffServ), these services can be used when creating an IPSec tunnel.

Encryption-based VPN technologies can be used with VPN technologies based on traffic segregation to improve their security level. VPN technologies based on traffic segregation often become a target for criticism because of insufficient security level. Sometimes clients think that the lack of traffic encryption allows the provider's personnel unauthorized data access. Such a possibility exists; therefore, the client receiving VPN services based on traffic segregation, such as MPLS VPN, can strengthen traffic security by using the IPSec virtual circuit technique, for example.

24.4 MPLS VPN

> **KEY WORDS:** MPLS L3VPN, MPLS L2VPN, multiprotocol BGP (MP-BGP), Provider Edge router (PE), Provider router (P), Global routing table, VPN Routing and Forwarding instance (VRF), VPN-IPv4, route distinguisher (RD), extended community attributes, Route Target (RT), virtual router

MPLS VPN today is attracting general attention. The range of services that leading providers offer to their clients is constantly growing. This makes MPLS VPN available to many users all over the world. In comparison to other methods of building VPN, including ATM, Frame Relay, and IPSec, MPLS VPN looks more advantageous because of its high scalability, the possibility of automatic configuration, and natural integration with other IP services offered by any successful provider: Internet access, Web and mail services, and hosting.

There are two types of MPLS VPN:

- **MPLS L3VPN**, where traffic delivery from client to the boundary device of the provider network is carried out using IP technology (layer 3)
- **MPLS L2VPN**, where client traffic is transmitted into the provider network using any of the layer 2 technologies, for example, Ethernet, Frame Relay or ATM

In both cases, transmission of the client traffic within the provider network is carried out using MPLS technology[3].

---

[3] For the moment, it is not easy to determine MPLS level, because terminology is this area has not been well defined yet. However, since packet forwarding on the basis of local labels corresponds to layer 2, in this book MPLS will be classified as layer 2 technology.

In this book, only MPLS L3VPN is covered in detail, because it is the most mature and reliable technology already employed in many provider networks. Although RFC 2547bis specification, which defines the main mechanisms of this technology, has only informational status, all implementations of MPLS L3VPN follow this document, thus making it de facto standard. In further discussion, the designation L3 will be omitted, and terms MPLS VPN will be used as synonymous to MPLS L3VPN.

24.4.1 Full Connectivity and Absolute Isolation

Every client wants a VPN service provider to connect her networks and ensure that the resulting internet is isolated from the networks of other clients.

Contemporary providers have to solve this problem under the domination of IP technology, which is used as a universal transport. One of the main principles of IP internet operation is the automatic interconnection of all networks into the unified internet. This is achieved by propagating routing information over the entire internet using various routing protocols such as BGP, OSPF, IS-IS, and RIP. This mechanism allows a routing table to be automatically created on each network router. Routing tables specify the paths along which packets are delivered to each constituent network. Although the paths to some networks can be aggregated, this does not change the essence of the problem.

How does the MPLS VPN technology solve the paradox of ensuring isolation while preserving the connectivity? The solution is quite elegant: by automatically filtering routing advertisements and using MPLS tunnels for transmitting client traffic through the internal network of the provider.

To isolate networks, it is sufficient to set a barrier that blocks the propagation of routing information. To exchange routing information within the limits of the network, nodes use one of the interior gateway protocols (IGPs), whose area of application is limited by the Autonomous System: RIP, OSPF, or IS-IS. If the routing table of node A does not contain a record on the route to node B and the record on the default route is missing, then node A "cannot see" node B.

In MPLS VPN, this is achieved because the routing advertisements from the client's network "jump over" the entire internal network of the service provider using the BGP. Because of a special configuration procedure, which is carried out using the extended version of BGP known as **multiprotocol BGP (MP-BGP)**, they are delivered only to the network of the same client. As a result, the routers of different clients have no routing information about each other. Therefore, they cannot exchange packets, which means that the desired isolation is achieved (Figure 24.16).

Another consequence of this approach is the isolation of the provider's internal network. This, in turn, improves its reliability and scalability, because in this case there is no need in supporting large routing tables storing information about the networks of numerous clients on the internal routers of the service provider network.

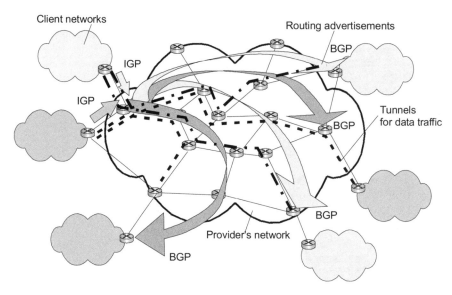

Figure 24.16 Isolating the client network using tunnels

However, there remains one problem that needs to be solved: How can geographically distributed client networks be joined into a unified VPN if the internetwork of the service provider has no information about them, at least at the level of standard routing tables? To achieve this goal, a traditional technique is used, namely, a tunnel is created between the edge routers of the internal network. The technology under consideration uses an MPLS tunnel. Alternative solutions might consist of creating IPSec tunnels or other kinds of "IP over IP" tunnels. The advantage of the MPLS VPN tunnel lies in its automatic creation and configuration. Additionally, an MPLS VPN tunnel has all generic properties of MPLS: it ensures accelerated forwarding (as compared to routing), and ensures traffic engineering and to implement the previously described principles of creating an MPLS VPN in a real-world network, several specialized mechanisms and network components were developed.

24.4.2 MPLS VPN Components

In any MPLS VPN, it is possible to detect two main areas (Figure 24.17):

■ IP networks belonging to clients
■ MPLS backbone belonging to the provider

In general, every client can have several geographically distributed IP networks (sites). Each site, in turn, may comprise several subnets connected by routers. Sites owned

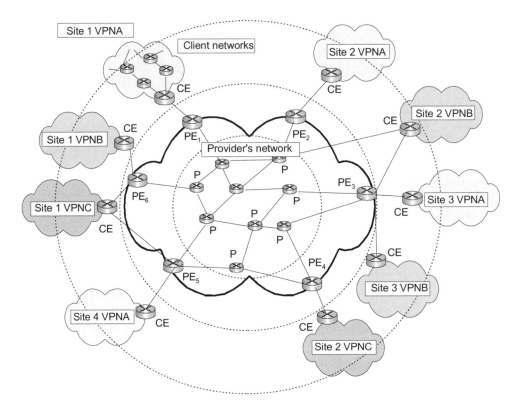

Figure 24.17 MPLS VPN Components

by the same client exchange IP packets over the provider's network and make up the VPN of that client.

The router through which the client's site connects to the provider's backbone is the CE router. For example, node C, being a component of the client's network, has no information about the existence of VPN. It can be connected to the provider's backbone by several links.

The provider's backbone is an MPLS network; IP packets are forwarded on the basis of local labels instead of IP addresses. The MPLS network consists of label switch routers (LSRs), which direct the traffic along previously created LSPs according to the label values.

In the provider's network, there are two classes of LSR devices, *provider edge routers* (*PE* routers), to which client sites are connected through their CE routers and *provider routers* (*P* routers) of provider backbone. CE and PE routers are usually connected directly by a physical link where some data link-layer protocol operates. For example, this may be PPP, Frame Relay, ATM, or Ethernet. All communication between CE and PE takes place on the basis of standard protocols of the TCP/IP stack. MPLS support is needed only for the internal interfaces of PEs (and for all P interfaces). Sometimes it is useful to separate traffic forwarding into **inbound PE** and **outbound** (remote) **PE**.

> In the provider's backbone, only PE routers must be configured for supporting VPNs, since they are the only ones that have information about the existing VPNs.

If you consider a network from the VPN position, then the provider routers do not directly communicate with the client's CE routers. Rather, they are located along the path between the input and output PE routers.

PE routers are functionally more complicated than P routers. These routers carry out the main tasks related to VPN support, namely, the segregation of the routes and data of different clients. PE routers are also end points of the LSPs between client sites. It is the PE that assigns the label to the IP packet for its transmission through the internal network of the P routers.

LSPs can be created using two methods: fast IGP routing on the basis of LDP or traffic engineering technology with RSVP or CR-LDP. The creation of LSP creates **label-switching tables** on all PE and P routers that make up the current LSP (examples of such tables are provided in *Chapter 22*). Together, these tables specify the set of paths for the traffic of different clients. VPNs implement various link topologies: fully connected, star (often called hub-and-spoke), or mesh.

24.4.3 Segregation of the Routing Information

For correct operation of a VPN, it is necessary to ensure that information about the routes using provider's backbone does not propagate beyond its limits. Furthermore, information about the routes within the client sites must not be known beyond the limits of the appropriate VPNs.

The barriers preventing the propagation of routing advertisements can be set by appropriately configuring the routers. The routing protocol must have information from the interfaces from which it has the right to receive advertisements and to which it has the right to propagate them.

The role of such barriers in MPLS VPN is delegated to PE routers. PE routers can serve as an invisible boundary between the zone of client sites and the zone of the provider's network core. On one side of this boundary there are interfaces through which PE routers communicate with P routers; on the other side there are interfaces to which client sites are connected. Advertisements about routes existing within the backbone arrive on one side of the PE; advertisements about the routes within the client networks arrive from the other side.

Figure 24.18 shows the method according to which routing information is delimited. Several IGP entities are installed on the PE router. One of them is configured for receiving and propagating routing advertisements only from internal interfaces that connect this PE router to P routers. Two other IGP entities process routing information from client sites.

Other PEs are configured in a similar way. P routers receive and process IGP routing information arriving from all interfaces. As a result, a routing table is created on every PE

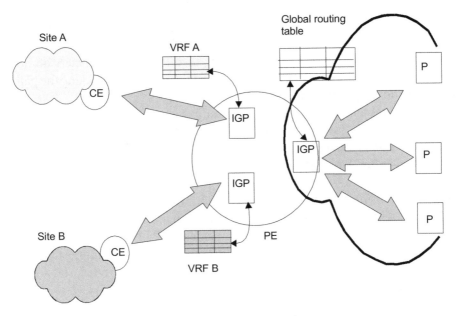

Figure 24.18 Method of routing information segregation

and P router. These routing tables contain information about all routes within the *provider's internal network*. It is necessary to point out that routing tables on P routers contain no information about the routes existing in *client networks*. Client networks have no information about the routes in the provider's network.

On every PE router routing tables of the following two types are created:
- **Global routing table,** created on the basis of advertisements from the backbone
- **VPN routing and forwarding (VRF) tables** — the tables that the PE forms on the basis of advertisements from the client sites

Client sites are normal IP networks from which routing information can be passed and processed using any routing protocol of the IGP class. Obviously, the service provider does not control this process. Routing advertisements are free to propagate within the limits of each site until they reach the PE routers serving as barriers for their further propagation.

The segregation of routes of different clients is ensured by installing a separate routing protocol on each interface of the PE router to which the client site is connected. This protocol receives and transmits client routing advertisements only from the interface defined for it without sending them to the interval interfaces through which the PE connects to the P routers. These advertisements are not sent to the sites of other clients. As the result, several VRF routing tables are created in the PE route.

Somewhat simplifying the situation, it is possible to consider that several VRF tables are created in each PE. The number of these tables corresponds to the number of sites connected to this PE. Actually, several **virtual routers** are organized on PE router, and each of them operates with its own VRF table.

Other relationships between the sites and the VRF tables are possible. For example, if several sites of the same VPN are connected to the same PE, it is possible to create a common VRF table for them. Figure 24.18 shows two VRF tables: One contains descriptions of routes to nodes of site A, and the other contains information about the routes to site B.

24.4.4 Using MP-BGP for Connecting Sites

To connect geographically distributed client sites into the united network, it is necessary to create for them the common space for propagating routing advertisements then to create within the internal network protected paths over which the nodes of the same VPN belonging to different sites would be able to securely exchange data.

The mechanism used by different sites of the same VPN to exchange routing information is MP-BGP. A detailed description of this protocol is provided in RFC 2858. Using this protocol, the PE routers exchange routing information stored in their VRF tables.

A feature of BGP and its extensions is that it receives its routing advertisements and passes them not to every directly connected router (as was the case with IGP) but only to the ones specified as neighbors in its configuration parameters. Note that it is possible to specify as neighbors routers that located at distances of many hops. PE routers are configured so that they send all routing advertisements received from client sites only to PE routers that are assigned as neighbors. They carry out this task using MP-BGP. Purposeful propagation of routes between PE routers is ensured by appropriate choice of the MP-BGP attributes[4].

The problem of detecting routers to which routing advertisements must be sent depends entirely on the VPN topology supported by this provider. For example, Figure 24.17 shows a network in which the PE_1 router passes routes from the VRF table of site 1 related to VPN A to the PE_2, PE_3, and PE_5 routers to which sites 2, 3, and 4 of VPN A are connected. The received routes are entered into the VRF tables of the appropriate sites.

Thus, besides the routes received from the sites directly connected to the PE, each VRF table is complemented by routes received from other sites of this VPN using MP-BGP.

24.4.5 Independence of Address Spaces

If a set of nodes never receives routing information from another set of nodes, then the nodes within each of these sets can be addressed independently.

---

[4] These attributes are described in the *"BGP Extended Communities Attribute"* document, which currently has the Internet Draft status.

Limiting the propagation area of routing information by the boundaries of specific VPNs isolates the address spaces of each VPN, allowing it to use within its limits both public Internet addresses and private addresses reserved according to RFC 1819.

In this case, why can you not choose addresses within a VPN arbitrary and limited only by the common addressing rules adopted for the TCP/IP stack? In most cases, clients do not want their VPNs to be entirely isolated. Most of them need at least Internet access. If addressing is not coordinated with the Internet authorities, it might match internal addresses to public addresses already in use on the Internet. Consequently, Internet access will become impossible. When using reserved private addresses, the problem of communication between VPN clients and the outside world is solved using the standard NAT technique. Regardless, the requirement of address uniqueness within the same VPN must be observed.

The use of the same address space in different VPNs creates a problem for PE routers. BGP was initially developed under the assumption that all addresses it manipulates relate to the IPv4 address family and are globally unique within the entire internet. Addresses are orientated to be globally unique because, having received the next routing advertisement, BGP analyzes it without paying attention to the VPN to which that route belongs. If descriptions of routes to the nodes of different VPNs arrive at the BGP input but contain matching IPv4 addresses, BGP considers them to lead to the same node. According to its operating algorithm, BGP places only the best route (selected according to the BGP rules of choice) into its VRF table.

This problem in MPLS VPN is solved by using extended addresses of a new type, **VPN-IPv4** instead of the ambiguous IPv4 addresses. These extended addresses are obtained by converting source IPv4 addresses. For the conversion, all IPv4 addresses are complemented by a **route distinguisher** (**RD**) prefix for the address space that uniquely defines the VPN. As a result, all addresses belonging to different VPNs will be different on the PE router, even if they have a matching part — the IPv4 address.

This is where the capability of MP-BGP to carry different types of addresses (including IPv6, IPX, and, most importantly, VPN-IPv4) proved especially useful. VPN-IPv4 addresses are used only for routes with which PE routers exchange using BGP. Before sending a specific route to its partner, the input PE router adds the RD prefix to its IPv4 destination address, thus converting it to the VPN-IPv4 route.

As mentioned before, RD must uniquely identify the VPN to avoid address duplication. To simplify the choice of RD without creating additional centralized procedures (such as the distribution of RDs by Internet authorities similar to the distribution of IPv4 addresses), it is supposed to use numbers guaranteed to be unique for RD use. These might be numbers of autonomous systems or global addresses of PE interfaces on the provider's backbone side.

The RD is 8 bytes long and consists of three fields.

■ *Type* — This 2-byte field defines the type and length of the second field.

■ *Administrator* — This field uniquely identifies the provider. If the *Type* field is set to 0, the *Administrator* field specifies the IP address of the PE router interface; the length of this field, consequently, is 4 bytes. If the *Type* value is 1, the number of the autonomous system is chosen as the provider identifier. If this is the case, the *Administrator* field is 2 bytes long.

■ *Assigned Number* — The goal of this field is to ensure the uniqueness of VPN addresses within the limits of the provider's network. The values of the *Assigned Number* field are chosen by the provider. These might be any numbers; the only requirement that must be observed is the existence of unambiguous mapping between these numbers and provider's VPN.

Figure 24.19 illustrates the process of exchanging routing advertisements in an MPLS VPN. This process includes address translation from IPv4 format into VPN-IPv4 format, filtering routing advertisements (import and export operations) and adding VPN labels to advertisements.

Figure 24.19 shows an example of translation of IPv4 addresses in order to ensure uniqueness of addresses within the framework of all VPNs of the same service provider. When creating an RD for every VPN, network administrator first selects global address of one of the external interfaces of the input router PE1 (in this example this is address 123.45.67.89). To obtain an RD value, administrator chooses the Assigned Number value,

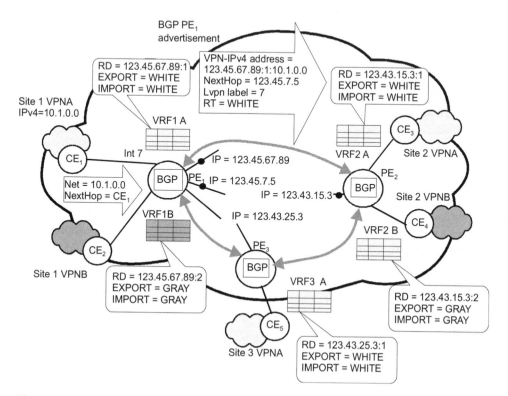

Figure 24.19 MP-BGP routing advertisements

which in this case is equal to 1, and adds it to the global address using a colon as a separator. Thus, the resulting RD value is equal to 123.45.67.89:1. Table 24.2 outlines the resulting RD format.

Table 24.2 RD format

Type field (2 bytes)	Administrator field (4 bytes)	Assigned number field (2 bytes)
0	123.45.67.89	1

This RD value is assigned to the VPN A network. When configuring PE routers, administrator specifies this RD value for all VRFs, which correspond to VPN A. In particular, it specifies this value when creating VRF 1A, so that for the MP-BGP protocol all addresses of the IPv4 format that were provided in the VRF1A table will have RD set to 123.45.67:1, including all addresses with prefix 10.1/16, which PE1 receives from router CE1 of the site 1 within network VPN A.

Similarly, for networks of VPN B administrator chooses the RD value 123.45.67.89:2, which is specified when configuring VRF 1B on the router PE1. This RD value will be added to all IPv4 addresses stored in VRF 1B, when they are processed by the MP-BGP protocol.

NOTE   *All routes in VRF tables contain addresses in IPv4 format.*

Router PE1 uses MP-BGP protocol to pass the routes translated into VPN-IPv4 format to router PE2, to which site 2 of the VPN B network is connected. Thanks to addition of RD, BGP protocols operating on remote PE routers can distinguish routes with matching IPv4 addresses that relate to different VPNs.

The RFC 2547bis document does not require all routes within the same VPN to be indexed by the same RD value. Furthermore, the same site connected to different interfaces of the same PE or to different PEs can have different RDs. Because of this, the path to the same node can be described by different routes, which provides possibilities for choosing a specific route for different types of packets. However, it is important to ensure that the RDs of different VPNs do not match.

24.4.6 Generation of MP-BGP Routing Advertisements

When receiving a new route from a client site using the IGP-class protocol (RIP, OSPF, or IS-IS), the PE router enters it into the appropriate VRF table and propagates it to other sites of this VPN. Routing information is exchanged between the sites of each individual

VPN under the control of MP-BGP. The MP-BGP routing advertisement has the follow-ing set of attributes, extended in comparison to BGP:

- **Address of the destination network in the VPN-IPv4 format.**
- **Address of the next router** (BGP Next Hop). BGP in this case specifies the address of one of the internal (connected to the P routers) interfaces of the PE where it operates.
- **The VPN label (LVPN)** uniquely identifies the external interface of the PE router and the connected client site to which the declared route leads. It is assigned to the route by the input PE it is assigned to a local route from the connected CE.
- **Extended community attributes**, one of which, **route-target (RT)**, is mandatory. This attribute identifies the set of sites (VRF) that are part of this VPN and to which PE must send routes.

The value of the RT attribute in the routing advertisement is defined by the *export target policy* specified when configuring the VRF table that contains the current route.

For instance, assume that the PE_1 router receives a routing advertisement in the IPv4 format according to the IGP-class protocol from site 1 in VPN A (see Figure 24.19):

Net = 10.1.0.0

Next-Hop = CE1

Based on this advertisement, an appropriate record is entered into the VRF 1A table. BGP periodically looks up VRF 1A and, having detected a new record, generates a new routing advertisement. To achieve this, it carries out the following operations:

- Adds an RD value (in this case, 123.45.67.89:1) to the destination network address.
- Overwrites the value of the *Next-Hop* field. To do so, it replaces the address of the external interface of CE_1 with the address of the PE_1 external interface through which the path to the destination address (123.45.7.5 in this example) passes.
- Assigns an L_{VPN} label pointing to VRF1A and the interface of the PE_1 router to the client site containing the destination node (in this case, the label value is 7, and the interface is designated as int 7).
- Specifies the RT attribute (in Figure 24.19, the RT attribute value is conventionally designated as WHITE, which identifies the set of sites that are part of VPN A).

The resulting routing advertisement appears as follows:

VPN-IPv4: 123.45.67.89:1:10.1.0.0

Next-Hop = 123.45.7.5

$L_{VPN} = 7$

RT = White

MP-BGP sends this advertisement to all its neighbors (in Figure 24.19, this is designat-ed by a broad arrow).

When the output PE receives the path to the VPN-IPv4 network, it carries out an inverse transformation, discards the RD prefix, and only then places it into the VRF table and declares this route to the CE router from this VPN. Thus, *all routes in the VRF tables contain addresses in the IPv4 format.*

As a result, the following new record will be inserted into the VRF2A table:

Net	Next-Hop	L_{VPN}
10.1/16	123.45.7.5 (BGP)	7

24.4.7 Packet Forwarding over the MPLS VPN

Now that we have described the method of propagation of the routing information over the MPLS VPN, consider how the *data* are forwarded between nodes of the same VPN.

For example, suppose that the node with the address 10.2.1.1/16, belonging to site 2 from VPN A, sends a packet to node 10.1.0.3/16 belonging to site 1 of the same VPN (Figure 24.20). Using standard transport, this IP packet is delivered to the CE_3 router. The routing table on that router specifies the PE_2 router as the next router for network 10.1.0.0. The packet is delivered to the PE_2 router from interface 2; therefore, to choose the path for packet forwarding, it is addressed to table VRF2A related to this interface.

Table VRF2A contains the record that maps address 10.1.0.0 to the BGP record according to which the PE_1 router is specified as the next router for this packet. The next field of the record contains $L_{VPN} = 7$, which determines the interface of the PE_1 router that must be assigned to the packet to deliver it into the required VPN. This record also specifies that it was inserted by BGP rather than by IGP. On the basis of this fact, PE_2 draws the conclusions that the next router is not a direct neighbor and that the path to it should be in the global routing table.

The global routing table specifies for the PE_1 address the initial value of the L label of the LSP path. In this example, this value is 3. We will not concentrate on the method of creating the path between PE_1 and PE_2 because this topic was covered in *Chapter 22.*

The MPLS VPN technology uses the hierarchical properties of MPLS paths using which the packet can be supplied with several labels placed into the stack. When entering the provider's internal network, made up of P routers, the packet will be supplied with two labels: the $L_{VPN} = 7$ internal label and the $L = 3$ external label. The L_{VPN} label is interpreted as the lower-layer label. It remains at the stack bottom and is not used when the packet travels through the PE_1–PE_2 tunnel. Packet forwarding is based on the higher-level label, the L label. Each time the packet passes through next P router along the tunnel, the L label is analyzed and replaced by a new value. The L_{VPN} label is retrieved from the stack only after the packet reaches the tunnel's endpoint on the PE_1 router. Depending on its value, the packet is forwarded to the required output interface *int 7* of the PE_1 router.

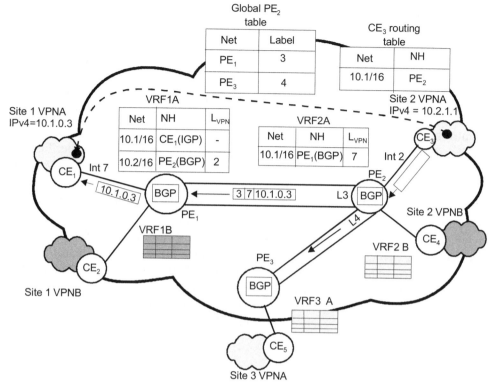

Figure 24.20 Packet forwarding over the MPLS VPN

Then the record on the route to the destination node specifying CE_1 as the next router is retrieved from the VRF1A table related to this interface and containing the VPN A routes. Note that this record was inserted into the VRF1A table by IGP. At the last section of the packet's travel from CE_1 to node 10.1.0.3, it is forwarded using traditional IP means.

24.4.8 Mechanism of Forming VPN Topology

The export/import policy is a powerful instrument for creating VPNs of different topologies.

When configuring every VRF table, two RT attributes are specified, one for defining export policy, and another — for defining the import policy.

MP-BGP routing advertisements always carry the RT attribute that specifies the route export policy. By means of comparing the RT attribute values in a routing advertisement and in VRF parameters it is possible to decide whether specific route must be accepted or declined. This mechanism is the one that forms the network topology. Consider it on a practical example.

Assume that router PE$_2$ (see Figure 24.19) has received an advertisement from PE$_1$. Before saving information about the route, it checks whether the RT attribute in the advertisement matches the import policy of any of its VRF tables (VRF2A and VRF2B, in this example). The value of the RT attribute is WHITE; therefore, the route, after conversion into the IPv4 format (by discarding RD), is inserted only into table VRF2A, because the WHITE import policy is defined only for this table. The VRF2B table remains unchanged, because its import policy specifies that only routes with GRAY RT attribute value must be entered into it.

Specifying the same values for export and import policies for all VRF of a specific VPN (as shown for VPN A in Figure 24.19) results in a fully connected topology. Each site sends its packets directly to the site to which the destination network belongs.

There are other variants of the VPN topology. For example, by configuring the export/import policy, it is possible to implement such popular topology as "star" (hub and spoke), where all sites (spokes) communicate through a dedicated central site (hub).

To achieve this effect, it is enough to define the policy for the VRF of the central site as import = spoke. The export policy must be defined as export = hub. As relates to VRF on peripheral sites, it is necessary to invert the policy by specifying import = hub and export = spoke (Figure 24.21). As a result, VRFs on peripheral sites will not receive routing advertisements from each other, since these advertisements are transmitted

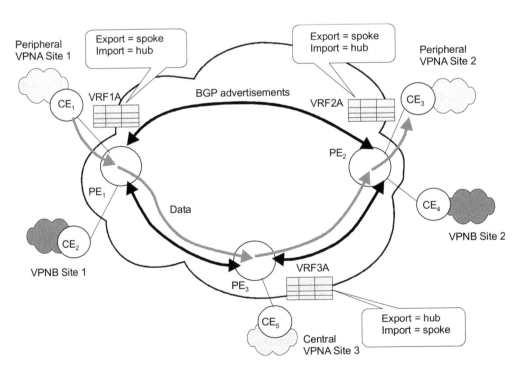

Figure 24.21 Configuring the hub-and-spoke topology for VPN A

through the network by MP-BGP with the route target attribute set to spoke and their import policy allows them to receive routing advertisements with `RT = hub`. On the other hand, VRF advertisements from peripheral sites are received by the VRF of the central site because they have the import policy set to spoke. This site generalizes all advertisements from peripheral sites and sends them back; however, this time, the RT attribute is set to hub, which matches the import policy of the peripheral sites. Thus, the VRF of every peripheral site will be supplemented by records on networks in other peripheral sites with the address of the PE interface connected to the central site specified as the next hop (because this interface was the one from which the advertisement was received). Therefore, packets between peripheral sites will pass through the PE_3 router connected to the central site.

On the basis of the description of the MPLS VPN mechanisms, it is possible to state that the process of configuring a new VPN or modifying the configuration of the existing one is rather sophisticated. However, this process can be formalized and automated. To eliminate possible configuration errors — such as assigning an erroneous import/export policy to the site, which can connect the site to a foreign VPN — certain manufacturers have developed automated software for configuring MPLS.

24.4.9 Security Level

The security level of MPLS VPN can be improved using traditional means — for instance, using authentication and encryption IPSec tools installed in client or provider networks. MPLS VPN service can be easily integrated with other IP services, such as providing the Internet access to VPN users and protecting them with the firewall installed in the provider's network. A provider can also offer to MPLS VPN users some services based on other MPLS capabilities — for instance, ensuring guaranteed QoS on the basis of MPLS traffic engineering methods. As relates to the difficulties of supporting user routing tables on provider's routers (emphasized by some professionals), they are somewhat exaggerated in our opinion. After all, routing tables are created automatically using standard routing protocols. Furthermore, they are created only on PE routers. The virtual router mechanism isolates these tables from the provider's global routing tables, which ensures the required MPLS VPN scalability and reliability. Still, the future will show the real quality of this technology — and this probably will happen soon.

MPLS VPN does not ensure security using encryption and authentication as is done in IPSec or PPTP. However, it allows these technologies to be used as additional protective measures when necessary.

MPLS VPN does not aim to ensure QoS support; however, when necessary, the provider can use DiffServ and MPLS traffic engineering methods.

SUMMARY

▶ Secure transport services allow clients to transmit traffic using a public network, such as the Internet, in a secure way, ensuring the authenticity, integrity, and confidentiality of the information being transmitted.

▶ Security services can be built on the basis of system tools implemented at different layers of the OSI model. The list of most popular secure transport services includes SSL, IPSec, PPTP, and VPN.

▶ IPSec is a coordinated set of open standards, which nowadays has strictly outlined core that includes three protocols: AH ensures data integrity and authenticity, ESP ensures data confidentiality using encryption as well as data integrity and authentication, and IKE establishes a logical connection and distributes private keys.

▶ When establishing a unidirectional logical connection, called IPSec security association (SA), the parties negotiate and agree on several parameters determining the process of data transmission: the type and operating mode of security protocols (AH or ESP), encryption methods, private keys, and so on. The sets of current parameters determining all active associations are stored on both end nodes of a secure channel in the form of SAD. Each party also supports another database, SPD, which specifies mapping between IP packet attributes and the processing rules established for them.

▶ The use of SPDs and SADs for traffic protection allows for the flexible combination of the SA mechanism establishing a logical connection with the datagram nature of IP traffic.

▶ The VPN technology allows the same network infrastructure to be shared among several companies to implement services close to those provided by a truly private network using ensured QoS (security, availability, predictable bandwidth, and independent addressing).

▶ A VPN can be implemented by a company (CPVPN) or by a service provider (PPVPN). It can be based on equipment installed on the customer's premises (customer premises' equipment-based VPN) or on equipment installed on the provider's territory.

▶ VPN technologies can be divided into two classes according to the method used for ensuring the security of data transmission: traffic segregation technologies (ATM VPN, Frame Relay VPN, and MPLS VPN) and traffic encryption technologies (IPSec VPN).

▶ The advantage of MPLS VPN over other VPNs, such as a VPN built on the basis of ATM, Frame Relay, or IPSec, is its high scalability, the possibility of automatic configuration, and natural integration with other IP services.

▶ The mechanism used by sites belonging to the same VPN for exchanging routing information is the multiprotocol BGP (MP-BGP) extension.

▶ The export/import policy for routing advertisements is a powerful instrument for creating MPLS VPNs of different topologies.

REVIEW QUESTIONS

1. Is it possible to use IPSec for secure data transmission of the traffic generated by a specific application without introducing any changes into that application?

2. The IPSec system provides the AH protocol for ensuring data integrity and authentication. For what purpose does it make a provision for the ESP protocol, which also carries out these functions?

3. To provide the receiver with the capability of checking data integrity, most protocols place the checksum into the packet. IPSec uses the digest for ensuring data integrity. Explain the difference between these two approaches.

4. Suppose that there are three applications running on your computer and you need to transmit data generated by these applications to your partner in the encrypted form using IPSec. How many SAs do you need to create to achieve this?

5. Compare the transport and tunnel modes of IPSec. Which one ensures a higher security level? Which one provides better scalability? Which one is more economical?

6. Provide several examples illustrating the methods that an intruder may implement to use information from the IP header.

7. Would the use of the AH protocol in the tunnel mode improve the security of the data being transmitted as compared to the use of the same protocol in the transport mode?

8. What mechanism of protection against duplicates by an intruder is used in IPSec?

9. Explain why padding is another means of ensuring confidentiality.

10. How does SG determine what type of processing is required for the packets arriving at it?

11. What properties of truly private networks can be supported by VPNs?

12. Suggest a VPN classification.

13. Which VPN technologies use traffic segregation for ensuring security?

14. List the advantages and drawbacks of L3VPN as compared to L2VPN.

15. What is the main drawback of IPSec VPN?

16. Describe the mechanism used in MPLS VPN for the segregation of the address spaces of networks belonging to different clients.

17. How is the VRF table created?

18. Assume that MP-BGP operating on the PE2 router sends a routing advertisement received as a result of translating the following routing advertisement arrived from the CE3 router (Figure 24.20):

   Net = 10.2/16

   Next-Hop = CE3

   How would this routing advertisement appear?

19. In the MPLS VPN network, the packet is supplied by two labels, the internal label (L_{VPN}) and the external label (L). Describe the roles of these labels in packet forwarding.

PROBLEMS

1. You have studied the operating principles of L3 MPLS VPN when all sites of all clients are connected to the backbone of the same provider. Try to advance these principles for when the backbone is supported by several providers. Assume that the sites of three clients, A, B, and C, are connected to networks belonging to the providers ISP2 and ISP3. The networks of these providers are, in turn, connected using the ISP1 provider network. Use a hierarchical approach for solving this problem by making ISP1 a top-layer provider. In this case, ISP2 and ISP3 will play the role of clients for ISP1 according to the MPLS VPN method described in this chapter. Suggest a possible implementation of the idea of the MPLS VPN provider hierarchy, taking BGP capabilities and the idea of the MPLS label stack as the basis.

2. Compare the number of required virtual circuits and the LSP that the VPN service provider must create for the following two cases:
   - The provider uses a Frame Relay network for providing VPN services
   - The provider uses the IP/MPLS network for providing VPN services

   The provider has 25 clients. The networks of each client comprise 10 sites connected to the provider's network. The clients need intranet services, which means that it is not necessary to provide connections between client sites.

3. In the section "Packet Forwarding over the MPLS VPN," there was an example illustrating packet transmission from node $10.2.1.1/16$ of site 2 in VPN A to end node $10.1.0.3/16$ of site 1 located in the same VPN (Figure 24.20). Using this illustration, describe packet transmission in the inverse direction from node $10.1.0.3/16$ to node $10.2.1.1/16$. Provide the possible contents of the CE_1 and PE_1 routing tables. Suggest your own values for the missing data and place the text into the illustration.

CONCLUSION: LOOKING INTO THE FUTURE

The further we look into the future, the less our chance of seeing computer networks in traditional sense of this term — in other words, networks that transmit only text and numbers. The trend for all types of networks, whether they are telephone, computer, or TV based, is convergence. Even now, computer networks transmit types of traffic that were not initially typical for them. This is sound in various forms: in the form of traditional interactive conversations between two subscribers of a telephone network, in the form of broadcasting by demand (either music or previously recorded speeches or interviews) over the Internet, and in the form of voice mail. The transmission of images requires considerably higher throughput and therefore is rarer. However, even at an access speed of about 64–128 Kbps, it is possible to view a telecast in a small rectangular window on the PC screen.

Thus, telecommunications networks of the future are networks equally capable of transmitting bursty data traffic and streaming sound or video. Networks of the future will inherit the best features of their predecessors — telephone and computer networks, as well as radio or TV broadcasting networks. However, they will use common transport technology that must ensure transmission of each type of traffic with the required QoS. Such a technology must, according to the common opinion of most specialists, be based on the packet-switching technique and widely use the winning protocol — IP. This makes networks of the future similar to contemporary computer networks; however, several significant technological innovations are expected.

The list of such technological innovations probably will include terminal devices of newer types, which would combine the functional power of a PC with the simplicity and ease of use typical of a telephone set. Smartphones and PDAs are prototypes of such devices. The arrival of such a device that would allow its users to access predefined Web pages by pressing several keys or buttons, organize a telephone conversation, send an e-mail message with multimedia applications, or request a video-on-demand demonstration (as well as access many more services that as yet exist only as projects) will serve as an incentive to the evolution of telecommunications.

The technology of controlled virtual paths on the basis of the DWDM and generalized MPLS (GMPLS) standards will become the response to the growth of the demand for super-high-speed and high-quality transport. The core of the new public telecommunications network will be based on multicore fiber-optic cables, which would ensure throughput among communicating nodes of several terabytes. This core also will create the basis for the transmission of amounts of information that seem an unattainable dream today. For economical purposes, the core must support switching of only super-high-speed data flows, such as data flow of only a specific wavelength (DWDM switching) and of even flow of only an individual core — without smaller switching units. As a result, the SDH technology will be moved out of the network core and play the role of an access network to DWDM switches. Another revolutionary achievement will be controllability of the network core on the basis of GMPLS technology, when the paths of member cores, wavelengths, and SDH containers would be created dynamically using the unified signaling protocol. The most important thing is that there also will be an end-user version of this protocol. This means that the core subscriber (for example, the service provider) would be able to flexibly use the throughput, depending on current needs.

For the moment, a low access rate, especially for the widest community of subscribers, is one of the main obstacles to broad use of new multimedia services. There are several solutions to this problem, including the use of existing copper local loops (the most suitable approach for most individual users), the adoption of wireless access (both fixed and mobile), and the installation of optical local loops using an economical passive optical network technology. ATM or IP/MPLS technologies will be used to share the channel bandwidth.

Despite a considerable increase in the throughput of both network core and access networks, traffic jams are still possible when traffic simultaneously exceeds the capacity of network connections. Therefore, for high-quality traffic transmission, the networks of the future will widely use QoS support methods. In the network core these will be methods that guarantee service to large aggregate data flows carrying data for a large number of subscribers, in other words, methods close to DiffServ, which is starting to find application in carrier networks. In access networks, methods similar to those used in ATM and IntServ technologies serve individual flows.

LANs are also changing. The passive cable connecting computers are being replaced by various communications equipment, such as switches, routers, and gateways. Because of such equipment, it has become possible to build large corporate networks connecting thousands of computers through a complicated structure. Interest in large supercomputers has been regenerated — mainly because, after the decline of the euphoria caused by the ease of working with PCs, systems made up of thousands of servers are more difficult to maintain than several large computers. Thus, on the new turn of the evolutionary spiral, mainframes are returning to enterprises. However, this time they have become full members of the network, supporting either Ethernet or Token Ring technology and the TCP/IP stack, which, because of the Internet, became the de facto standard.

These are only some lines of development for telecommunications networks, which are clearly visible even today.

REFERENCES AND RECOMMENDED READING

OUTLINE

RECOMMEMDED READING TO PART I

1. Armitage, G. *Quality of Service in IP Networks*. Pearson Education, 2000.

2. Black, U. *Internet Security Protocols: Protecting IP Traffic*, Ed.1. Prentice Hall, 2000.

3. Black, U. *Emerging Communications Technologies*, Ed. 2. Prentice Hall Professional, 1997.

4. Black, U. *Data Networks: Concepts, Theory and Practice*. Englewood Cliffs, New Jersey: Prentice Hall, 1989.

5. Comer, D.E. *Internetworking with TCP/IP*, Vol. 1: *Principles, Protocols, and Architecture*, Ed. 3. Prentice Hall, 2000.

6. Comer, D.E., Stevens, D. *Internetworking with TCP/IP*, Vol. 2: *Design Implementation, and Internals*. Prentice Hall, 1994.

7. Comer, D.E., Stevens, D. *Client-Server Programming and Applications*. Prentice Hall, 2001.

8. Dodd, A.Z. *The Essential Guide to Telecommunications 1*, Ed. 2. Prentice Hall, 1999.

9. Dorogovtsev, S.N., Ferreira Mendes, J.F. *Evolution of Networks: From Biological Nets to the Internet and WWW*. Oxford University Press, 2003.

10. Fitzgerald, J. *Business Data Communications*. John Wiley & Sons, 1993.

11. Ford, W. *Computer Communications Security*. Prentice Hall, 1994.

12. Freeman, R. *Telecommunications Transmission Handbook*. NY: Wiley, 1998.

13. Hamacher, C.V., Vranesic, Z.G., Zaky, S.G. *Computer Organization*. New York: McGraw Hill, 1984.

14. Halsall, F. *Data Communications, Computer Networks, and Open Systems*. Addison-Wesley, 1996.

15. Hardy, W.C. *QoS Measurement and Evaluation of Telecommunications Quality of Service*. John Wiley & Sons, 2001.

16. Hauben, M., Hauben, R., Truscott, T. *Netizens: On the History and Impact of Usenet and the Internet*, Ed. 1. Wiley–IEEE Computer Society Pr., 1997.

17. Ibe, O.C. *Converged Network Architectures: Delivering Voice and Data Over IP, ATM, and Frame Relay*. Wiley, 2001.

17. Keshav, S. *Efficient Implementation of Fair Queuing*. Proceedings of the ACM SIG-COMM, 1990.

18. Keshav, S. *An Engineering Approach to Computer Networking*. Addison Wesley, 1997.

19. Kleinrock, L. *Queuing Systems*, Vol. 1: *Theory*. Wiley-Interscience, 1975.

20. Kurose, J.F., Ross, K.W. *Computer Networking: A Top-Down Approach Featuring the Internet*, Ed. 3. Addison Wesley, 2004.

21. LaQuey, T. *The Internet Companion: A Beginner's Guide to Global Networking*. Reading, Massachusetts: Addison-Wesley, 1994.

22. Leiner, B.M., Cerf, V.G., et al. *A Brief History of the Internet.* Internet Society (ISOC), **www.isoc.org/internet/history/brief.shtml**.

23. Leon-Garcia A., Widjaja, I. *Communication Networks: Fundamental Concepts and Key Architectures*, Ed.1. McGraw Hill Science/Engineering/Math, 2001.

24. Le Boudec, J.-Y., Thiran, P. *Network Calculus. A Theory of Deterministic Queuing Systems for the Internet Series: Lecture Notes.* In: *Computer Science*, Vol. 2050, 2001.

25. Null, L., Lobur, J. *The Essentials of Computer Organization and Architecture Dimensions.* Jones & Bartlett Pub, 2003.

26. Osborne, E., Ajay, S. *Traffic Engineering with MPLS.* Cisco Press, 2002

27. Peterson, L.L., Davie, B.S. *Computer Networks: A Systems Approach*, Ed. 3. Morgan Kaufmann, 2003.

28. Rose, M.T. *The Open Book: A Practical Perspective on OSI.* Englewood Cliffs, New Jersey: Prentice Hall, 1990.

29. Rowe, S.H. *Telecommunications for Managers*, Ed. 3. Prentice Hall, 1995.

30. Stallings, W. *Data and Computer Communications*, Ed. 7. Prentice Hall, 2003.

31. Stallings, W. *Wireless Communications and Networks.* Prentice Hall, 2002.

32. Stallings, W. *Local and Metropolitan Area Networks.* Macmillian Publishing Company, 1993.

33. Standards. International Organization for Standardization. Information Processing System — *Open System Interconnection: Specification of Abstract Syntax Notation One (ASN.1).* International Standard 8824, 1987.

34. Stevens, R.W. *TCP/IP Illustrated, Vol. 1. The Protocols*, Ed. 1. Addison-Wesley Professional, 1993.

35. Young Moo Kang, Miller, B.R., Pick, R.A. *Comments on "Grosch's law re-revisited: CPU power and the cost of computation".* Communications of the ACM, Vol. 29, Issue 8, 1986.

36. Zheng Wang. *Internet QoS: Architectures and Mechanisms for Quality of Service*, Ed. 1. Morgan Kaufmann, 2001.

37. Zwcky, E.D., Cooper, S., Chapman, B.D. *Building Internet Firewalls.* O'Reilly, 2000.

RECOMMENDED READING TO PART II

1. Abbas, J. *The Wireless Mobile Internet.* John Wiley & Sons, 2003.

2. Ashwin, G. *DWDM Network Designs and Engineering Solutions.* Pearson Education, 2002.

3. Bertsekas D., Gallager, R. *Data Networks,* Ed. 2. Prentice Hall, 1992.

4. Black, U. *Physical Level Interfaces and Protocols.* Los Alamitos, California: IEEE Computer Society Press, 1988.

5. Couch, L.W. *Digital and Analog Communication Systems,* Ed. 6. Prentice Hall, 2001.

6. EIA232E p: *Interface Between Data Terminal Equipment and Data Circuit-Terminating Equipment Employing Serial Binary Data Interchange,* revised from EIA232D, July 1991.

7. Halsall, F. *Data Communications, Computer Networks, and Open Systems.* Addison Wesley, 1996.

8. Gibson, J.D. *Principles of Digital and Analog Communications,* Ed. 2. Prentice Hall, 1993.

9. Haykin, S. *Digital Communications.* Wiley, 1988.

10. Nicopolitidis, P., Obaidat, M.S., et al. *Wireless Network.* Wiley, 2003.

11. Proakis, J.G. *Digital Communications,* Ed. 4. McGraw Hill, 2001.

12. Rowe, S.H. *Telecommunications for Managers,* Ed. 3. Prentice Hall, 1995.

13. Sexton, M., Reid, A. *Broadband Networking: ATM, SDH, and SONET.* Artech House, 1997.

14. Shu Lin, Costello, D.J. *Error Control Coding,* Ed. 2. Prentice Hall, 2004.

15. Sklar, B. *Digital Communications: Fundamentals and Applications,* Ed. 2. Prentice Hall PTR, 2001.

16. Stallings, W. *Data and Computer Communications,* Ed. 6. Prentice Hall, 2004.

17. Stallings, W. *Wireless Communications and Networks.* Prentice Hall, 2002.

18. Sweeney, P. *Error Control Coding.* Wiley, 2002.

19. Wicker, S.B. *Error control systems for digital communication and storage.* Prentice Hall, 1995.

20. Wirth, N. *Digital Circuit Design for Computer Science Students. An Introductory textbook.* Springer Verlag, 1995.

21. Zeimer, R.E., Peterson, R.L. *Introduction to Digital Communication.* Prentice Hall, 2001.

RECOMMENDED READING TO PART III

1. Abbas, J. *The Wireless Mobile Internet.* John Wiley & Sons, 2003.

2. Bertsekas D., Gallager, R. *Data Networks,* Ed. 2. Prentice Hall, 1992.

3. Black, U. *Data Networks: Concepts, Theory and Practice.* Englewood Cliffs, New Jersey: Prentice Hall, 1989.

4. Bux, W. *Local-area subnetworks: a performance comparison.* IEEE Press Trans. Comm., vol. COM-29, Issue 10, 1981.

5. Cunningham,D., Lane, W.G., Lane, B. *Gigabit Ethernet Networking,* Ed. 1. Sams, 1999.

6. Gast M., Gast, M.S. *802.11 Wireless Networks: The Definitive Guide,* Ed. 1. O'Reilly, 2002.

7. Halsall, F. *Data Communications, Computer Networks, and Open Systems.* Addison Wesley, 1996.

8. Hillston, J.E., King, P.J.B., Pooley, R.J., editors. *Computer and Telecommunications Performance Engineering.* London: Springer Verlag, 1992.

9. Metcalfe, R.M., Boggs, D.R. *Ethernet: Distributed packet switching for local computer networks.* Comm. ACM 19, 7, 1976.

10. Miller, B.A., Bisdikian, C. *Bluetooth Revealed: The Insider's Guide to an Open Specification for Global Wireless Communications,* Ed. 2. Prentice Hall, 2001.

11. McNamara, J.E. *Local Area Networks.* Bedford, MA: Digital Press, Educational Services, 1985.

12. Norris, M. *Gigabit Ethernet Technology and Applications.* Artech House Publishers, 2002.

13. Perlman, R. *Interconnections: Bridges, Routers, Switches, and Internetworking Protocols,* Ed. 2. Addison-Wesley Professional, 1999.

14. Peterson, L.L, Davie, B.S. *Computer Networks: A Systems Approach,* Ed. 3. Morgan Kaufmann, 2003.

15. Riley, S., Breyer, R. *Switched, Fast, and Gigabit Ethernet,* Ed. 3. Sams, 1998.

16. Ross, F.E. *FDDI—A Tutorial.* IEEE Communications Magazine, Vol. 24, No. 5, 1986.

17. Schwartz, M. *Telecommunications Networks — Protocols, Modeling and Analysis,* Facsimile Ed. Addison Wesley, 1986.

18. Seifert, R. *Gigabit Ethernet: Technology and Applications for High-Speed LANs,* Ed.1. Addison-Wesley Professional, 1998.

19. Seifert, R. *The Switch Book: The Complete Guide to LAN Switching Technology,* Ed. 1. Wiley, 2000.

20. Spurgeon, C.E. *Ethernet: The Definitive Guide.* O'Reilly, 2000.

21. Stallings, W. *Data and Computer Communications,* Ed. 6. Prentice Hall, 2004.

22. Stallings, W. *Wireless Communications and Networks.* Prentice Hall, 2002.

REFERENCES TO PART IV

[RFC 751]　Lebling, P. *Survey of FTP mail and MLFL.* RFC 751, 1978.

[RFC 760]　Postel, J. *DoD standard Internet Protocol.* RFC 760, 1980.

[RFC 768]　Postel, J. *User Datagram Protocol.* 1980.

[RFC 791]　Postel, J. *Internet Protocol.* STD 5, RFC 791, 1981.

[RFC 792]　Postel, J. *Internet Control Message Protocol.* 1981.

[RFC 793]　Postel, J. *Transmission Control Protocol.* 1981.

[RFC 950]　Mogul, J., Postel, J. *Internet Standard Subnetting Procedure,* STD 5, RFC 950, 1985.

[RFC 1122]　Braden, E.R. *Requirements for Internet Hosts — Communication Layers.* 1989.

[RFC 1349]　Almquist, P. *Type of Service in the Internet Protocol Suite.* 1992.

[RFC 1517]　Internet Engineering Steering Group and Hinden, R. *Applicability Statement for the Implementation of Classless Inter-Domain Routing (CIDR).* RFC 1517, 1993.

[RFC 1518]　Rekhter, Y., Li, T. *An Architecture for IP Address Allocation with CIDR.* RFC 1518, 1993.

[RFC 1519]　Fuller, V., Li, T., Yu, J., Varadhan, K. *Classless Inter-Domain Routing (CIDR): an Address Assignment and Aggregation Strategy.* RFC 1519, 1993.

[RFC 1520]　Rekhter, Y. Topolcic, C. *Exchanging Routing Information Across Provider Boundaries in the CIDR Environment.* RFC 1520, 1993.

[RFC 1700]　Reynolds J., Postel, J. *Assigned Numbers.* 1994.

[RFC 1752]　Bradner, S., Mankin, A. *The Recommendation for the IP Next Generation Protocol.* RFC 1752, 1995.

[RFC 1878]　Pummill, T., Manning, B. *Variable Length Subnet Table For IPv4.* RFC 1878, 1995.

[RFC 2050]　Hubbard, K., Kosters, M., et al. *Internet Registry IP Allocation Guidelines.* BCP 12, RFC 2050, 1996.

[RFC 2131]　Droms, R. *Dynamic Host Configuration Protocol.* RFC 2131, 1997.

[RFC 2132]　Alexander, S., Droms, R. *DHCP Options and BOOTP Vendor Extensions.* RFC 2132, 1997.

[RFC 2373]　Hinden, R. *IP Version 6 Addressing Architecture.* RFC2373, 1998.

[RFC 2460]　Deering, S., Hinden, R. *Internet Protocol, Version 6 (IPv6) Specification.* RFC 2460, 1998.

[RFC 2998]　Bernet, Y., Ford, P., et al. *A Framework for Integrated Services Operation over Diffserv Networks.* 2000.

[RFC 3232]　Reynolds, J. *Assigned Numbers: RFC 1700 is Replaced by an On-line Database,* Ed. 2002.

[RFC 3246]   Davie, B., A. Charny, A., et al. *An Expedited Forwarding PHB (Per-Hop Behavior).* 2002.

[RFC 3290]   Bernet, Y., Blake, S., et al. *An Informal Management Model for Diffserv Routers.* 2002.

[RFC 3513]   Hinden, R., Deering, S. *Internet Protocol Version 6 (IPv6) Addressing Architecture.* RFC 3513, 2003.

RECOMMENDED READING TO PART IV

1.   Boney, J. *Cisco IOS in a Nutshell.* O'Reilly, 2001.

2.   Coltun, R. *OSPF: An Internet Routing Protocol.* ConneXions: The Interoperability Report, Vol. 3, No. 8, 1989.

3.   Comer, D.E. *Internetworking with TCP/IP.* Vol. 1: *Principles, Protocols, and Architecture,* Ed. 3. Prentice Hall, 2000.

4.   Davidson, J. *An Introduction to TCP/IP.* New York: Springer Verlag, 1992.

5.   Feit, S. *Architecture, Protocols, and Implementation with IPv6 and IP Security.* McGraw Hill, 1997.

6.   Hunt, C. *TCP/IP Network Administration,* Ed. 2. O'Reilly, 1998.

7.   Kleinrock, L. *Communication Nets: Stochastic Message Flow and Delay.* New York: McGraw Hill, 1964.

8.   Kleinrock, L. *Queueing Systems.* Vol. 2: *Computer Applications.* New York: John Wiley & Sons, 1976.

9.   Kleinrock, L. Queueing Systems, Vol. 1: *Theory.* Wiley-Interscience, 1975.

10.   Nogl, M. *Illustrated TCP/IP. A graphic Guide to the Protocol Suite.* John Wiley & Sons, 1999.

11.   Roberts, L.G. *Judgment Call.* Data Communications magazine, April 1999.

12.   Shenker, S., Partridge, C. *Specification of Guaranteed Quality of Service.* IETF draft, 1995.

13.   Snader, J. *EffectiveTCP/IP programming.* DMK Press, 2001.

14.   Specification: *NetWare Link Services Protocol (NLSP),* Revision 0.9. Part Number 100-001708-001. 1993.

15.   Stevens, W.R. *TCP/IP Illustrated.* Vol. 1: *The Protocols,* Ed. 1. Addison-Wesley Professional, 1993.

16.   Varghese, G. *Network Algorithmics: An Interdisciplinary Approach to Designing Fast Networked Devices.* Morgan Kaufmann, 2004.

REFERENCES TO PART V

[RFC 2514] Noto, M., Spiegel, E., Tesink, K. *Definitions of Textual Conventions and OBJECT-IDENTITIES for ATM Management.* **ftp://ftp.isi.edu/in-notes/rfc2514.txt**, 1999.

[RFC 2515] Tesink, K. *Definitions of Managed Objects for ATM Management.* **ftp://ftp.isi.edu/in-notes/rfc2515.txt**, 1999.

[RFC 2684] Grossman, D., Heinanen, J. *Multiprotocol Encapsulation over ATM Adaptation Layer 5.* **ftp://ftp.isi.edu/in-notes/rfc2684.txt**, 1999.

[RFC 2761] Dunn, J., Martin, C. *Terminology for ATM Benchmarking.* **ftp://ftp.isi.edu/in-notes/rfc2761.txt**, 2000.

[RFC 2955], Rehbehn, K., Nicklass, O., Mouradian, G. *Definitions of Managed Objects for Monitoring and Controlling the Frame Relay/ATM PVC Service Interworking Function.* **ftp://ftp.isi.edu/in-notes/rfc2955.txt**, 2000.

[RFC 3035] Davie, B., Lawrence, J., et al. *MPLS using LDP and ATM VC Switching.* **ftp://ftp.isi.edu/in-notes/rfc3035.txt**, 2001.

[RFC 3116] Dunn, J., Martin, C. *Methodology for ATM Benchmarking.* **ftp://ftp.isi.edu/in-notes/rfc3116.txt**, 2001.

[RFC 3134] Dunn, J., Martin, C. *Terminology for ATM ABR Benchmarking.* **ftp://ftp.isi.edu/in-notes/rfc3134.txt**, 2001.

RECOMMENDED READING TO PART V

1. Aboba, B. *NAT and IPSEC.* Internet Engineering Task Force, 2000.

2. *Advanced MPLS Design and Implementation.* Cisco Press, 2001.

3. Armitage, G. *Quality of Service in IP Networks.* Pearson Education, 2000.

4. Balaji, K. *Broadband Communications.* McGraw Hill, 1998.

5. Berkowitz, H. *Requirements Taxonomy for Virtual Private Networks.* Internet Engineering Task Force, 1999.

6. *Big Book of Multiprotocol Label Switching RFCs.* Morgan Kaufmann Publishers, 2000.

7. Black, U. *Internet Security Protocols: Protecting IP Traffic,* Ed.1. Prentice Hall, 2000.

8. Black, U. *Emerging Communications Technologies,* Ed. 2. Prentice Hall Professional, 1997.

9. *Building Switched Networks: Multilayer Switching, QoS, IP Multicast, Network Policy, and Service Level Agreements.* Ed. 1. Addison-Wesley, 1999.

10. Busschbach, P.B. *Toward QoS-Capable Virtual Private Networks.* Bell Labs Technical Journal, Vol. 3, No. 4, 1998.

11. Casey, L. *An extended IP VPN Architecture.* Internet Engineering Task Force, 1998.

12. Dobrowski, G., Grise, D. *ATM and Sonet Basics.* APDG Publishing, 2001.

13. Dutton, H., Lenhard, P. *Asynchronous Transfer Mode (ATM) Technical Overview,* Ed. 2. Prentice Hall, 1995.

14. Feit, S. *Architecture, Protocols, and Implementation with IPv6 and IP Security.* McGraw Hill, 1997.

15. Ford, W. *Computer Communications Security.* Prentice Hall, 1994.

16. Ginsburg, D. *ATM Solutions for Enterprise Internetworking,* Ed. 2. Addison-Wesley, 1998.

17. Gonsalves, M. *Voice Over IP Networks,* Bk & CD-Rom edition. McGraw Hill Osborne Media, 1998.

18. Hunt, C. *TCP/IP Network Administration,* Ed. 2. O'Reilly, 1998.

19. Ibe, O.C. *Converged Network Architectures: Delivering Voice and Data Over IP, ATM, and Frame Relay.* Wiley, 2001.

20. Ibe, O.C. *Essentials of ATM Networks and Services.* Addison-Wesley, 1997.

21. Jamieson, D., Jamoussi, B., et al. *MPLS VPN Architecture.* Internet Engineering Task Force, 1998.

22. Kompella, K., et al. *MPLS-based Layer 2 VPNs.* Internet Engineering Task Force, 2000.

23. Kurose, J. F., Ross, K.W. *Computer Networking: A Top-Down Approach Featuring the Internet,* Ed. 3. Addison Wesley, 2004.

24. Li, T. *CPE based VPNs using MPLS.* Internet Engineering Task Force, 1998.

25. McDysan, D.E, Spohn, D.L. *ATM Theory and Applications.* McGraw Hill, 1998.

26. McDysan, D.E, Spohn, D.L. *Hands-On ATM.* McGraw Hill, 1998.

27. Morris, S. *Network Management, MIBs and MPLS: Principles, Design and Implementation.* Prentice Hall, 2003.

28. *MPLS and VPN Architectures,* Vol. 1. Cisco Press, 2000.

29. *MPLS and VPN Architectures,* Vol. 2. Cisco Press, 2003.

30. Muthukrishnan, K., Malis, A. *Core MPLS IP VPN Architecture.* Internet Engineering Task Force, 2000.

31. Perros, H.G. *An Introduction to ATM Networks.* Wiley, January 2001.

32. Sackett, G.C., Metz, C. *ATM and Multiprotocol Networking.* McGraw Hill, 1997.

33. Siu, S., Jain, R. *A brief overview of ATM: Protocol Layers, LAN Emulation and Traffic Management.* Computer Communications Review (ACM SIGCOMM), 1995.

34. Stanford, H. *Telecommunications for Managers,* Ed. 3. Prentice Hall, 1995.

35. Stevens, R.W. *TCP/IP Illustrated*, Vols. 1, 2, 3, Ed. 1. Addison-Wesley Professional, 1993.

36. Sun, W., Bhaniramka, P., Jain, R. *Quality of Service Using Traffic Engineering over MPLS: An Analysis*. Proc. 25th Annual IEEE Conference on Local Computer Networks (LCN 2000), Tampa, Florida USA, November 8–10, 2000.

37. *The MPLS Primer: An Introduction to Multiprotocol Label Switching*. Prentice Hall, 2001.

38. Thompson, R.A. *Telephone Switching Systems*, Ed. 1. Artech House Publishers, 2000.

39. Zwcky, E.D., Cooper, S., Chapman, B.D. *Building Internet Firewalls*. O'Reilly, 2000.

40. Zorn, G., Pall, G., et al. *Point-to-Point Tunneling Protocol (PPTP)*. Internet Engineering Task Force, 1999.

INDEX